The Student Guide 2008

CHAMBERS
AND PARTNERS

Published by Chambers and Partners Publishing
(a division of Orbach & Chambers Ltd)
23 Long Lane, London EC1A 9HL
Tel: (020) 7606 1300 Fax: (020) 7600 3191
email: info@ChambersandPartners.co.uk
www.ChambersandPartners.com
Our thanks to the many students, trainees, pupils,
solicitors, barristers and graduate recruitment personnel
who assisted us in our research. Also to Chambers and
Partners' recruitment team for their knowledge and
assistance and to the researchers of *Chambers UK 2008*
from which all firm rankings are drawn.

Copyright © 2007 Michael Chambers and
Orbach & Chambers Ltd
ISBN: 978 0 85514 310 7

Publisher: Michael Chambers
Managing Editor: Fiona Boxall
Editor: Anna Williams
Deputy Editors: Michael Lovatt, Tom Wicker
Writers: Abigail Andersen, Alexis Hille, Alice Curtis
Rouse, Benjamin Derber, Christopher Nichols, Joanna
Mason, Josh Alexander, Jenna Course-Choi, Rav Casely
Gera, Russell Bramley, Samantha Rose, Viola Babakhan
Editorial assistant: Joanne Grote
Database: Andrew Taylor
A-Z Co-ordinator: Gemma Buckle
Production: John Osborne, Paul Cummings, Jasper
John, Pete Polanyk
Business Development Manager: Brad D. Sirott
Business Development Team: Neil Murphy,
Richard Ramsay, Bianca Maio, Michele Kirschstein
Proofreaders: Enrique Arias, Kristy Barker,
Jennifer Gallagher, Kathleen Grogan, Lindsay Jardine,
Sally McGonegal, John Quick, Charlotte Stretch,
Nicholas Widdows
Printed by: Butler & Tanner

so you want to be a lawyer...

We've written this book to give you the information, tools and confidence to help you make a sound career decision.

The Student Guide is the only publication to offer these three key ingredients:

- The True Picture: an insight into the training schemes at 150 law firms, based on in-depth interviews with hundreds of trainees. The trainees were selected by us, not by their law firms, and they to us spoke freely and frankly under the protection of anonymity.

- Chambers Reports: a look at life inside more than 50 barristers chambers in London and the regions. These reports were written after visits to each of the sets and interviews with pupils, barristers and clerks.

- Ranking Tables: covering law firms and chambers in all parts of England and Wales and a wide spectrum of practice areas. These are reproduced with the permission of *Chambers UK*, the well-known guide to the legal profession.

All the books we publish have one thing in common – they are independent. In a market flooded with publications for law students we take great pride in this fact. No one can buy an editorial feature and no one's money influences what we say about them.

This book could be the most useful thing you read this year and we wish you great success for your future career.

The Student Guide team
September 2007

CONTENTS

first steps

a-z unis & law schools 75

solicitors

the true picture

why do all law firm recruitment brochures say the same things? the true picture is the antidote. it is the product of six months spent interviewing hundreds of trainees and newly qualified solicitors at 150 firms in england and wales. we asked them to tell us about their training contracts in their own words... and they did!

a-z solicitors   705

the phone numbers, addresses and e-mails you need to make your applications. plus loads of really useful facts and figures on the top law firms. all in simple, easy-to-follow a-z format

barristers

chambers reports   893

impeneterable, incomprehensible and in another world... it's too easy to stereotype the bar. we banged on the doors of 56 chambers across the country to have a nose around and quiz the inhabitants

a-z barristers   1025

details of some of the leading pupillages

november 2007

1 law fair:
qmu, london

2 law fair:
university of east anglia

5 law fair:
university of leeds

6 law fair:
university of leeds

7 law fair:
university of hull   university of plymouth

8 law fair:
university of reading

9 vacation scheme deadline:
lovells (christmas)

10 law fair:
university of oxford

12 law fair:
lse

vacation scheme deadline:
herbert smith (christmas)

13 law fair:
university of essex   university of leicester
lse

14 law fair:
university of liverpool   university of bristol

15 law fair:
university of bristol

16 vacation scheme deadline:
cms cameron mckenna (christmas)

19 law fair:
university of newcastle

20 law fair:
university of warwick   cardiff university

21 law fair:
university of birmingham   university of exeter
queen's university, belfast

22 law fair:
university of sussex   university of manchester
university of southampton

23 vacation scheme deadline:
denton wilde sapte (christmas)

26 law fair:
ucl   university of durham

27 law fair:
ucl   university of durham

28 law fair:
university of sheffield

29 law fair:
university of cambridge (solicitors)

december 2007

31 vacation scheme deadline:
latham & watkins (easter)

training contract deadline:
lee & priestley (2009)

CALENDAR OF EVENTS

january 2008

4 — vacation scheme deadline:
skadden

15/16 — law fair:
king's college, london

17 — law fair:
university of cambridge (barristers)

18 — vacation scheme deadline:
freshfields   allen & overy
training contract deadline:
allen & overy (gdl)

25 — vacation scheme deadline:
pannone (easter)   slaughter and may

26 — vacation scheme deadline:
dundas & wilson

28 — vacation scheme deadline:
cleary gottlieb

31 — training contract deadline:
bristows (feb interviews)

vacation scheme deadline:

addleshaw goddard	latham & watkins
ashurst	lawrence graham
baker & mckenzie	leboeuf lamb
barlow lyde & gilbert	lewis silkin
berwin leighton paisner	manches
bird & bird	mcgrigors
clyde & co	mills & reeve
davenport lyons	norton rose
dickinson dees	olswang
dla piper	pinsent masons
dmh stallard	sj berwin
eversheds	taylor wessing
farrer & co	tlt solicitors
field fisher waterhouse	travers smith
hammonds	walker morris
herbert smith	white & case
jones day	withers
kirkland & ellis	

february 2008

1 — vacation scheme deadline:
lovells

8 — vacation scheme deadline:
denton wilde sapte   nabarro

11 — vacation scheme application deadline:
hbj gateley wareing

14 — vacation scheme deadline:
holman fenwick & willan   ince & co
weil, gotshal & manges

15 — vacation scheme deadline:
speechly bircham

17 — vacation scheme deadline:
stephenson harwood

18 — training contract deadline:
baker & mckenzie (non-law)

21 — vacation scheme deadline:
bates wells & braithwaite

24 — vacation scheme deadline:
watson farley & williams

28 — training contract deadline:
clarion solicitors

vacation scheme deadline:

bristows	kendall freeman
capsticks	michelmores
clarion solicitors	shadbolt & co
cms cameron mckenna	shoosmiths
covington & burling	ward hadaway

29 — vacation scheme deadline:

dechert	macfarlanes
halliwells	reynolds porter chamberlain
wedlake bell	

27	**training contract deadline:** maxwell winward	
28	**training contract deadline:** sidley austin	
30	**training contract deadline:** davenport lyons	taylor walton
31	**training contract deadline:**	

addleshaw goddard	hill dickinson
allen & overy (law)	holman fenwick & willan
asb law	howes percival
ashurst	hugh james
baker & mckenzie (law)	hunton & williams
barlow lyde & gilbert	ibb solicitors
berwin leighton paisner	ince & co
bevan brittan	irwin mitchell
bingham mccutchen	kendall freeman
bircham dyson bell	kirkland & ellis
bird & bird	k&l gates
brabners chaffe street	latham & watkins
bristows (aug interviews)	lawrence graham
browne jacobson	leboeuf lamb
burges salmon	lester aldridge
charles russell	lewis silkin
clarke willmott	lovells
cleary gottlieb	lupton fawcett
clyde & co	mace & jones
cms cameron mckenna	macfarlanes
coffin mew	manches
collyer bristow	martineau johnson
covington & burling	mayer brown
cripps harries hall	mcdermott, will & emery
dechert	mcgrigors
denton wilde sapte	memery crystal
dickinson dees	mills & reeve
dla piper	mishcon de reya
dmh stallard	morgan cole
dorsey & whitney	nabarro
dundas & wilson	norton rose
dwf	olswang
eversheds	o'melveny & myers
farrer & co	orrick herrington & sutcliffe
field fisher waterhouse	osborne clarke
fladgate fielder (2009/10)	paul hastings
foot anstey	penningtons
forbes	pinsent masons
ford & warren	prettys
freeth cartwright	pricewaterhousecoopers
freshfields	pritchard englefield
gov. legal service	reed smith richards butler
halliwells	salans
hammonds	shadbolt & co
harbottle & lewis	shearman & sterling
hbj gateley wareing	shoosmiths
henmans	simmons & simmons
herbert smith	sj berwin

skadden	warner goodman
speechly bircham	watson burton
stephenson harwood	watson farley & williams
taylor wessing	wedlake bell
teacher stern selby	weightmans
thomson snell & passmore	weil, gotshal & manges
thring townsend	white & case
tlt solicitors	wiggin
travers smith	wilsons solicitors
walker morris	withers
ward hadaway	wragge & co

august   2008

1	**training contract deadline:** beachcroft payne hicks beach	thomas eggar trowers & hamlins
8	**training contract deadline:** reynolds porter chamberlain	
18	**training contract deadline:** higgs & sons	
24	**training contract deadline:** hodge jones & allen (for 2009)	
31	**training contract deadline:** capsticks hewitsons jones day	laytons maclay murray & spens

september   2008

30	**training contract deadline:** stevens & bolton	

"The teaching was excellent at BPP and I owe my present training contract to the opportunities presented through the careers service."

Nigel Sharman,
Former LPC student

The Law Society
113 Chancery Lane,
London WC2A 1PL
Tel: 020 7242 1222
E-mail: info.services@lawsociety.org.uk
www.lawsociety.org.uk

Education and Training Department
Tel: 0870 606 2555
E-mail: legaled@lawsociety.org.uk
www.training.lawsociety.org.uk

Trainee Solicitors Group
The Law Society
113 Chancery Lane,
London WC2A 1PL
Helpline: 08000 856 131
E-mail: info@tsg.org
www.tsg.org

The Bar Council
289-293 High Holborn
London WC1V 7HZ
020 7242 0082
www.barcouncil.org.uk
For all other departments including the
Education and Training Department and the
Equality and Diversity Committee contact the
main switchboard.
Bar Standards Board 020 7611 1444
www.barstandardsboard.org.uk

Gray's Inn, Education Department
8 South Square, Gray's Inn,
London WC1R 5ET
Tel: 020 7458 7965
E-mail: quinn.clarke@graysinn.org.uk
www.graysinn.org.uk

Inner Temple, Education & Training Department
Treasury Building, Inner Temple,
London EC4Y 7HL
Tel: 020 7797 8250
www.innertemple.org.uk

Lincoln's Inn, Students' Department
Treasury Office, Lincoln's Inn,
London WC2A 3TL
Tel: 020 7405 0138
www.lincolnsinn.org.uk.

Middle Temple, Students' Department
Treasury Office, Middle Temple Lane,
London EC4Y 9AT
Tel: 0207 427 4800
E-mail: members@middletemple.co.uk
www.middletemple.org.uk

The Institute of Legal Executives
Kempston Manor, Kempston,
Bedfordshire MK42 7AB
Tel: 01234 841000
E-mail: info@ilex.org.uk
www.ilex.org.uk

Government Legal Service
Chancery House,
53-64 Chancery Lane,
London WC2A 1QS
Tel: 020 7649 6023
E-mail: glstrainees@tmp.com
www.gls.gov.uk

Crown Prosecution Service
50 Ludgate Hill,
London EC4M 7EX
Tel: 020 7796 8000
E-mail: recruitment@cps.gsi.gov.uk
www.cps.gov.uk

The Law Commission
Conquest House, 37-38 John Street,
Theobalds Road,
London WC1N 2BQ
Tel: 020 7453 1220
E-mail: communications@lawcommission.gsi.gov.uk
www.lawcom.gov.uk

Citizens Advice Bureaux
Head Office, Myddelton House,
115-123 Pentonville Road,
London N1 9LZ
Tel: 020 7833 2181
Volunteer Hotline: 08451 264264
www.citizensadvice.org.uk

Legal Services Commission
Head Office, 85 Gray's Inn Road,
London WC1X 8TX
Tel: 020 7759 0000
www.legalservices.gov.uk

Chartered Institute of Patent Agents
95 Chancery Lane,
London WC2A IDT
Tel: 020 7405 9450
E-mail: mail@cipa.org.uk
www.cipa.org.uk

Institute of Trade Mark Attorneys
Canterbury House, 2-6 Sydenham Road,
Croydon, Surrey CR0 9XE
Tel: 020 8686 2052
E-mail: tm@itma.org.uk
www.itma.org.uk

**Institute of Chartered Secretaries
and Administrators**
16 Park Crescent,
London W1B 1AH
Tel: 020 7580 4741
E-mail: info@icsa.org.uk
www.icsa.org.uk

The Law Centres Federation
293-299 Kentish Town Road,
London NW5 2TJ
Tel: 020 7428 4400
E-mail: info@lawcentres.org.uk
www.lawcentres.org.uk

Free Representation Unit
6th Floor 289-293 High Holborn
London WC1V 7HZ
Tel: 0207 611 9555
Email: admin@freerepresentationunit.org.uk
www.freerepresentationunit.org.uk

The Bar Lesbian & Gay Group
Email: info@blagg.org
(BLAGG) www.blagg.org
Lesbian & Gay Lawyers Association
www.lagla.org.uk

The Society of Asian Lawyers
c/o Saima Hanif
4-5 St Gray's Inn Square
Gray's Inn
London WC1R 5AH
Email: info@societyofasianlawyers.com
www.societyofasianlawyers.com

Society of Black Lawyers
11 Cranmer Road
Kennington Park
London SW9 6EJ
Tel: 020 7735 6592

The Association of Muslim Lawyers
PO Box 148, High Wycombe
Bucks HP13 5WJ
Email: aml@aml.org.uk
www.aml.org.uk

The Association of Women Barristers
1 Pump Court Temple
London EC4Y 7AB
Email: janehoyal@aol.com
www.womenbarristers.co.uk

Group for Solicitors with Disabilities
c/o Judith McDermott
The Law Society, 113 Chancery Lane
London WC2A 1PL
Tel: 020 7320 5793
Email: secretary@gsdnet.org.uk
www.gsdnet.org.uk

LPC Central Applications Board
PO Box 84, Guildford,
Surrey GU3 1YX
Tel: 01483 301282
www.lawcabs.ac.uk

CPE Central Applications Board
PO Box 84, Guildford,
Surrey GU3 1YX
Tel: 01483 451080
www.lawcabs.ac.uk

Online Pupillage Application System
Technical Assistance
E-mail: pupillages@gtios.com
www.pupillages.com

Career Development Loans
Tel: (freephone) 0800 585505
www.direct.gov.uk

what kind of lawyer do you want to be?

Let's start with one of the most basic questions – Do you want to be a barrister or a solicitor? Here we give a simple description of each so you know where next in this book to turn.

barrister

Ask a solicitor about the key difference between the two sides of the profession and they will probably tell you it's the size of your average barrister's ego. At first sight the role of a barrister certainly looks a lot cooler than that of a solicitor. Even if you've only ever seen fictitious ones in TV dramas, you know the deal – it's all about striding into courtrooms, robes flowing; tense moments waiting for missing witnesses and razor-sharp cross-examinations. Glamorous? It's downright sexy! The truth is there's a great deal more to the job than looking good in a wig and gown…

Essentially barristers do three things:

- appear in court to represent others
- give specialised legal advice in person or in writing
- draft court documents

How much of these a barrister does depends on the type of law they practise. Criminal barristers are in court most of the time, often with only an hour or two's notice of the details of their cases. By contrast, Chancery barristers spend most of their time in chambers writing tricky opinions and advising in conference on complicated legal points.

Barristers must display the skill and clarity to make complex or arcane legal arguments accessible to lay clients, juries and the judiciary. Their style of argument must be clear and persuasive, both in court and on paper. Of course, it has been some time since barristers have had exclusive rights of audience in the courts. Solicitors can, and some have, become accredited advocates in even the higher courts. This blurring of the distinction between the two halves of the profession hasn't been an utter disaster for the Bar, although solicitor-advocates are undertaking a lot more straightforward cases. With more complicated and lengthy matters barristers are still briefed to do the advocacy, not least because this is often the most cost-effective way of managing a case. As a point of interest, solicitor-advocates do not wear the wig and gown and are referred to as 'my friend' rather than 'my learned friend'.

Solicitors value barristers' detailed knowledge of the litigation process and, as a result, their ability to assess and advise on the merits and demerits of a case. A solicitor will pay good money for 'counsel's opinion'.

Certainly in the area of commercial law, a barrister must understand the client's perspective and use their legal knowledge to help construct a solution that makes business or common sense as well as legal sense. If you're hoping a career as a barrister will allow you to remain at the top of an ivory tower, you should consider life as an academic.

Most barristers are self-employed. This is why you hear the expression 'the independent Bar'. A minority are employed by companies, public bodies or law firms and they make up 'the employed Bar'. To prevent independence from turning into isolation, barristers work in groups called sets, sharing premises and professional managers, etc. Barristers do not work for their sets, just at them, and as 'tenants' they contribute to the upkeep of their chambers and give a percentage of their earnings to their clerks and administrators. Unlike employed barristers and solicitors, those at the independent Bar get no sickness pay, holiday pay, maternity leave or monthly salary. What they do get is a good accountant!

To enter practice, LLB grads need to complete the Bar Vocational Course (BVC) before starting a much sought-after year of 'pupillage'.

At the end of that it's a case of finding a set that wants you to join them as a member of their chambers – this is called 'tenancy'. Once you have that then the legal profession is your oyster.

Being a barrister is a great job, but the competition is fierce. If your appetite has been whetted you will find much more information in the final section of this book, where we have detailed the recruitment process and laid bare some of the more obscure practices and terminology. We have also tried to give a fair assessment of some of the difficulties that young hopefuls may encounter. The **Chambers Reports** give an invaluable insight into the lives of pupils and junior barristers at some of the best sets.

The Bar's professional body is the Bar Council, and it is regulated by the Bar Standards Board.

solicitor

Most budding lawyers qualify as solicitors rather than barristers. The role of a solicitor is to provide legal services directly to lay clients, who could be individuals, companies or public or other bodies. In short, clients come to solicitors for guidance on how to deal with their business or personal proposals and problems. These could be anything from drafting a will to defending a murder charge or buying a multibillion-pound business. The solicitor advises on the steps needed to proceed and then manages the case or the deal for the client until a conclusion has been reached. They will bring in a barrister if and when a second opinion or specialist advocacy is needed. The solicitor's role is much more like that of a project manager than the barrister's.

There are over 100,000 solicitors in England and Wales with practising certificates issued by the Law Society (these need to be renewed annually), the majority of them in 'private practice' in

- 'Sole practitioners' account for nearly half of the 9,000 or so private practice firms in England and Wales.
- Less than 2% of firms have 26 or more partners, but these big firms employ more than a third of all private practitioners.
- Almost half of all solicitors practise in London.
- Just over 20% of practising solicitors are employed by businesses outside the legal profession, public sector organisations or charities.

solicitors' firms. In the last 30 years the number of practising solicitors has risen by an average of roughly 4% per year.

If nothing else, these statistics should tell you that becoming a solicitor will not mean the same thing for everyone.

Most readers will be well aware that after the degree, law school awaits. Law grads need to take the Legal Practice Course (LPC). Non-law grads must first complete a law conversion course before being eligible for the LPC. After law school comes the training contract, which is presently two years in length and can be undertaken with firms of solicitors, law centres, in-house legal teams or public bodies. Proposals have been tabled that would allow the length of the training contract to be shortened to 16 months, but given that changes to the training framework are discussed more often than the average solicitor changes their socks, we suggest no one gets too excited for the moment. Upon satisfactory completion of their contract, a trainee is signed off and admitted to the Law Society's roll of those eligible to practice. In plain English that means they qualify. There is an enrolment ceremony at the Law Society for anyone who wants to give mum and dad a day to remember and a new photo for the mantelpiece.

- There are more than 14,000 new law graduates each year, over half of them with Firsts or 2:1s.
- Over 8,000 students sit the LPC exam each year. The pass rate is roughly 78%.
- The number of new traineeships in the year ending 31 July 2006 was 5,751, up from 5,732 the previous year.
- Over three-fifths of new trainees are women.
- Almost a fifth of new trainees are from ethnic minority groups.

Exactly when you should apply for a training contract depends on the kind of firm you hope to join. If you are studying for a law degree and you want to work in a commercial firm, the crucial time for research and applications is during your penultimate year at uni. If you are a non-law student intending to take a law conversion course before going to a commercial firm then you'll have to juggle exams and career considerations in your final year. Students wanting to enter high street practice usually don't need to worry about training contract applications quite so early. Unlike commercial firms, which generally offer contracts two years in advance of the start date, smaller firms do so closer to the start date.

Larger, commercial firms commonly offer their future trainees scholarships to cover law school fees and other basic expenses. Public sector organisations, eg the Government Legal Service, may also come up with some cash. Students hoping to practise in smaller firms soon learn that financial assistance is highly unlikely and this can make law school an uncertain and expensive endeavour. Reading our **Funding** section on page 72 may help.

Needless to say, your choice of training contract will determine the path (and perhaps also location) of your future career. A firm's clients,

its work and its reputation will determine not only the experience you gain, but probably also your future marketability as a lawyer. At Chambers and Partners, we've made it our business to know who does what, how well they do it and what it might be like working at a particular firm. In the **Practice Areas** section of this book, you'll find the core results of the research carried out for our parent publication *Chambers UK*. Our league tables show which firms command greatest respect from clients and other professionals in different areas of practice. In the **True Picture** section of this book we've profiled 150 firms in England and Wales. This section of the book should help you understand what kind of firm might suit you and the kind of work you can expect to undertake when you get there.

It will probably help you to envisage the scope of the legal market by grouping law firms into different categories.

magic circle

The magic circle is traditionally defined as Allen & Overy, Clifford Chance, Freshfields Bruckhaus Deringer, Linklaters and Slaughter and May. To those for whom bigger is better (bigger deals, bigger money, bigger staff numbers and bigger billing targets), these firms are the be-all and end-all. Corporate and finance work is central at these firms, as is international business. By organising their training on a massive scale, these firms can offer seemingly unlimited office facilities, great perks and excellent, formal training sessions. Although these five giants top many lists, not least for revenue and partner profits, consider carefully whether they'd top yours. Bigger is better for many people but not everyone. Training in a magic circle firm may be CV gold, but some students consciously sidestep these behemoths in favour of smaller firms with less corporate and finance focus, more personalised, hands-on training and greater client contact.

Another factor to consider is the requirement to work really long hours. Big profits and big international deals equate to one dreaded thing – a major intrusion into a trainee's personal life.

london: large commercial

The top-ten City of London firms (including the magic circle) offer around 1,000 traineeships between them each year, representing approximately a fifth of all new training contracts registered with the Law Society. There's not such a huge difference between the magic circle and such 'silver circle' firms as Herbert Smith, Ashurst, Lovells and a few others. Like the magic circle, training contracts at these chasing-pack firms are strongly flavoured with corporate and finance work. The salaries match those paid by the magic circle, which is only fair given that the lawyers work equally hard most of the time. As a trainee you can expect to assist on big, high-value deals and cases, although you certainly can't expect to be conducting particularly challenging duties all the time. If you are working against a deadline then you will be expected to stay until it is finished. This can mean working through the night and coming in at weekends from time to time.

london: american firms

Since the 1990s, there has been a steady stream of firms crossing the Atlantic to take their place in the UK market. Currently more than 40 of them offer training contracts to would-be UK solicitors. New training schemes are popping up all the time, so if you're an applicant with revolutionary leanings stay eagle-eyed if you want to be the first to jump on the bandwagon. At the risk of over-generalising, these firms are characterised by international work (usually corporate or finance-led), smaller offices and rather long hours. On the other hand they usually give trainees a good amount of responsibility and many of them pay phenomenally high salaries. Lawyers at the hotshot US firms frequently work opposite magic circle lawyers on deals; indeed many of them were magic circle and top-ten firm partners or associates before they joined a US firm. The arrival of the US firms has had a knock-on effect on City law, not least on City salaries, which have soared in the past decade.

london: mid-sized commercial

Just like their bigger cousins, these firms are almost entirely dedicated to business law and business clients. Generally, they don't require trainees to spend quite so many hours in the office; however, some of the most successful mid-sizers – eg Macfarlanes and Travers Smith – are giving the big boys a run for their money in terms of profitability, so trainees can expect their share of late nights. Ostensibly, the smaller deals and cases on which these firms work mean trainees can do more than just photocopying and bundling. The atmosphere in these firms is generally a bit more intimate than at the giants of the City and there is a greater likelihood of working for partners directly.

london: smaller commercial

For those who don't mind taking home a slightly more modest pay cheque in exchange for better hours, these firms are a great choice. After all, money isn't everything (note: if you don't agree with that statement, look above and read no further). Usually these firms will be full-service outfits, although some may have developed on the back of one or two particularly strong practice areas or via a reputation in certain industries. Real estate is commonly a big deal at these firms. Along with commercial work, these firms often offer services in areas such as private client or social housing. If you train at one of these firms, both partners and family members are more likely to recognise your face.

niche firms

London abounds with firms specialising in areas as diverse as aviation, media, insurance litigation, shipping, family, IP, sport... you name it, there's probably a firm for it. Niche firms have also sprouted in areas of the country with high demand for a particular service. How about equine law in Newmarket? If you are absolutely certain that you want to specialise in a particular field – especially if you have already worked in a relevant industry – a niche firm is an excellent choice. As well as making sure your heart is set on a niche area, you need to be able to back up your passion with hard evidence of your commitment. Some of these firms also dabble in other practice areas, but if any of these firms try to woo you by talking at length about their other areas of work, take it with a pinch of salt or at least ask some searching questions – they're called niche for a reason.

regional firms

Many of you will agree that there is more to life than an EC postcode. In the regions, there are some very fine firms acting for top-notch clients on cases and deals the City firms would snap up in a heartbeat. There is some international work going on outside the capital. The race for training contracts in the biggest of these firms is just as competitive as in the City, and some regional firms are even more discerning than their London counterparts in the sense that applicants may have to demonstrate a long-term commitment to living in the area, since these firms hardly want to shell out for training only to see their qualifiers flit off to the capital. Trainees at smaller regional firms tend to focus on the needs of regional clients and would therefore suit anyone who wanted to become an integral part of their local business community. Salaries are lower outside London, in some cases significantly so, but the cost of living is generally more reasonable. The perception of many is that working outside London means a chummier atmosphere and more time for the gym/pub/family of an evening; however, do bear in mind that some of the biggest and most ambitious regional players will expect you to work a bit longer than others.

national and multi-site firms

Multi-site firms are necessarily massive operations, some of them with offices spanning the length and breadth of the country. To give you just three examples, Eversheds has ten branches in England and Wales; DLA Piper has eight in England and Scotland; Shoosmiths mostly operates in smaller cities and towns from the South Coast up to Nottingham. These firms attract students who want to do big-ticket work outside London, but their national spread can sometimes mean that trainees in regional offices do London levels of work for a lower salary. Some of these firms allow trainees to be based in one office, whereas others expect them to move offices at the drop of a hat. Make sure you know the firm's policy or you could end up having a long-distance relationship with friends, family and significant other while you move to a new town for six months... or get up at 5am to sit in traffic on the M62. The work on offer is mostly commercial, although some private client experience may be available.

general practice/high street

These range from substantial, long-established firms in large town centres to sole practitioners working above shops in the suburbs. They act for legally aided clients, individuals funding themselves and local businesses. Staple work includes landlord and tenant problems, conveyancing, personal injury, employment, family, wills and probate, and crime. Given the changes to legal aid funding, these firms are having to take on more privately paying and commercial clients just to stay afloat. Be prepared to earn considerably less than your peers in commercial practice and don't expect there to be an abundance of amenities or resources in the office. Excessively long hours are unlikely unless you're on a rota for police station duty, in which case you'll be paid extra for that. If you want to grow up fast as a lawyer and see how the law actually affects individuals and the community in which you practice, then this is the kind of firm to go for. Larger firms may take on up to ten or so trainees a year; the smallest will recruit on an occasional basis.

Anyone thinking of entering this sector of the legal profession should be aware of that there are going to be dramatic changes to the public funding of legal services which will fundamentally affect the future of these firms. For a crash course on the major changes being introduced on the back of Lord Carters of Coles' review, have a glance at our special feature, overleaf, **Get Carter**.

Away from private practice there are many options for legal training.

law centres

From its roots in North Kensington in 1970, the network of UK Law Centres has grown to around 60 today, each set up as either a registered charity or a not-for-profit company and run by its own local management committee. Advice is given to the public without charge, with funding coming from local government grants (approx 60%) and the Legal Services Commission (LSC). The legal problems handled may vary from one Law Centre to another, but those who work in them can all be described as social welfare law specialists. A client with a consumer dispute is less likely to be taken on than someone who is affected by, say, a local authority's decision on rent arrears because of an alarming trend for social landlords to bring an ever increasing number of rent arrears cases. From here it's a case of using little matters to

change the big picture, perhaps by way of a test case that makes it to the House of Lords, the European Court of Justice and the broadsheets.

There are various routes to a career in this sector. Newly qualified solicitors with relevant experience in private practice are recruited, so too are people who have worked as paralegals for non-profit agencies and gained supervisor-level status. A career may also begin at a Law Centre. Every year the LSC funds a number of training contracts in 14 Law Centres. Mirroring a training contract in private practice, the trainee will experience different areas of law. At junior level salaries roughly match high street firms; at senior level the gap widens. Terms and conditions at work emulate those in local government. Flexible and part-time working is common. See www.lawcentres.org.uk

An extended version of this feature appears on our website.

working in-house for a company

A number of large companies offer training contracts and/or pupillages. In-house lawyers populate the banking, utilities, telecommunications and entertainment industries, to name but a few. There is no easily accessible comprehensive list of organisations which offer training contracts. For further information, aspiring solicitors should contact the Commerce & Industry Group (www.cigroup.org.uk) and aspiring barristers should contact the Bar Council. It's also worth keeping an eye out in the legal press and in *The Times* on Tuesdays to see who is recruiting.

We spoke to one recently qualified solicitor who trained in-house with an international bank. He had already built up experience of the financial sector through working as a transaction manager, and eventually asked the head of the legal department in the bank he worked at if they would be willing to fund him through part-time GDL and LPC courses. A training contract with the bank was the other vital piece of the jigsaw,

what kind of lawyer do you want to be? (continued)

Get Carter

In 2005 the government set out its strategy for the provision of legal aid. Lord Carter of Coles was then instructed by the Secretary of State and the Lord Chancellor, Lord Falconer, to review the present procedures and practices for the provision of legally aided services and to devise new, more efficient models.

Why?
- In the last nine years the cost of legal aid has risen 10% in real terms – from £1.5 to £2.1bn.
- The culprits are Crown Court defence costs and child care proceedings costs.

Carter's reforms are not just focused on these problem areas; the reforms aim to overhaul all legally aided services, civil and criminal.

What Carter didn't like about the old system
- 75% of criminal legal aid expenditure was spent on payments made on the basis of hours worked by lawyers. He saw this as a disincentive to efficient working practices.
- Currently there are around 2,500 suppliers of criminal defence services. Employing a diseconomy-of-scale argument, Carter presumed that this prevents them from structuring their work in a cost-effective way.
- The existing system involves high administrative costs for suppliers and the Legal Services Commission. Carter's answer is to issue fewer supplier contracts in a bid to force consolidation of suppliers. In other words fewer, but larger, firms.

The proposals in relation to crime
- Introduce fixed fees for police station visits.
- Defence services in Magistrates' Courts and Crown Courts to be paid for under revised systems of graduated fees.
- Defence services in very high cost cases to be paid for under individual case contracts with single defence teams working to strict cost and case management rules.
- Changes to be phased in from January 2008 alongside new criminal legal-aid contract.

The proposals in relation to civil and family
- Suppliers to concentrate on providing services to meet all civil legal aid needs of their communities.
- New supplier contracts to promote greater links between suppliers.
- New fixed-fee schemes for areas such as housing and debt advice.
- New graduated-fee scheme for private law family cases.
- New graduated-fee scheme to replace hourly rates in court in childcare cases.
- These changes to be implemented in stages from October 2007.

Why the profession criticises the proposals
- Bigger firms don't necessarily give better advice.
- Fixed-fee systems benefit larger firms that can handle a high volume of simple cases, but could endanger specialist firms and could discourage firms from taking on complex cases.
- The ultimate aim of competitive tendering is dependent on having sufficient numbers of firms to engender competition and there just aren't that many in certain areas like Wales and East Anglia.
- The new fees system might disproportionately affect black and minority ethnic firms.
- Legal aid practitioners are, to be frank, pissed off about the reforms and many feel disillusioned enough to consider leaving legal aid practice, which would mean less choice for clients.

In september 2007, the LSC announced it would appeal a High Court judgment that declared the Unified Contract for civil work breached European regulations. The full implications of the changes, and the manner and timing of their introduction, remain to be seen. To read more, check out www.legalservices.gov.uk and www.lawgazette.co.uk

and the bank agreed to this too. The proposal was feasible as the bank was already an accredited training provider and had a solicitor with sufficient experience (and interest) who was happy to take on the role of training supervisor. The only thing the bank couldn't provide was sufficient contentious training and so it arranged a secondment to one of the law firms on its legal panel.

Our source felt his training was as good as, if not better than, anything available in private practice. *"I was given my own work to manage and had a great deal more latitude than in a conventional training contract. I got responsibility earlier and a lot less grunt work to do."* In-house trainees certainly develop very marketable skills because almost everything they do has a practical application and their sector knowledge is immense. Cold-calling heads of legal at banks or companies you're interested is not recommended. Usually a trainee will be recruited after having already worked within the organisation in some other capacity, and even then *"you have to exercise discretion in trying to obtain a contract."* A softly-softly approach usually works best.

Most in-house lawyers started out in private practice, switching to the role some time after qualification. They do so because of a general perception that the rewards are good and the hours more manageable than in a law firm. In-house lawyers don't lose touch with private practice; indeed part of the job involves selecting and instructing law firms to provide specialist advice to the company. This part of the job ensures the in-house lawyer plenty of invites to parties, lunches and sporting events as the different law firms curry favour.

local government

Roughly 4,000 solicitors are employed in local authorities across the UK. Each authority acts as a separate employer; some offer training con-

tracts, but there's no central list of vacancies and no single recruitment office. Finding out about training contract opportunities is a challenge in itself, as is finding out which few councils offer sponsorship for the GDL and/or LPC. A good starting point for research is www.lgcareers.com. Click on 'career descriptions' and then head for 'supporting your community'. Also have a good rummage through the information at Solicitors in Local Government Limited www.slgov.org.uk, where you can find several testimonies from qualified solicitors and trainees of their day-to-day experiences. Most authorities advertise in the Law Society's *Gazette* and *The Lawyer*. You can also try the law and public service job ads in *The Times*, *The Guardian* and *The Independent*, or even approach local authorities directly.

Solicitors in local government advise elected council members and senior officers on a wide variety of topics, ranging from employment to land purchases and even the prosecution of rogue traders and suppliers. This breadth of practice is particularly true of solicitors in small authorities, while those in larger ones usually specialise in a particular area, such as housing, planning, highways, education or social services. Duties include keeping councils on the straight and narrow, making sure they don't spend their money unlawfully and advising councillors on the legal implications of their actions. The typical salary for a local authority solicitor is £29,700-£39,900.

Trainees usually follow the same seat system that prevails in private practice, but for local authority trainees there is the added bonus of having rights of audience in civil and criminal courts and tribunals that outstrip those of peers in private practice. Trainees shadow solicitors and gradually build up their own caseload, acting for officers from different departments of the local authority. If you want a sneak preview of what it's really like before you take the plunge then some authorities offer paid summer placements.

Others will arrange an informal unpaid attachment during vacations. Contact the head of legal services at a local authority to ask about these.

Be prepared to wade through the bureaucratic bog and at times be driven to distraction by the slow machinations of local government. However, the benefits of a great training contract, variety in your day-to-day work, flexible hours and a sense of serving the community often outweigh this. The best way to climb up the ladder is by hopping from one authority to another and many local authority chief executives trained as solicitors. Training in local government also opens doors to careers in private practice, the Crown Prosecution Service and the Government Legal Service.

government legal service

Lately, between 20 and 30 trainee solicitors and pupil barristers have been recruited each year by the Government Legal Service (GLS) to work within different government departments and offices. At one end of the scale there are full-time litigators, and at the other, people drafting new legislation or advising ministers. We'd recommend anyone applying to the GLS to have a long think about the role government lawyers take, particularly considering how law and politics interact and the impact that they can have on life and society in the UK, whether this is by bringing about the prosecution of drugs smugglers or human traffickers, or drafting new sexual offences or employment legislation. If the idea appeals, read our **True Picture** feature on GLS training contracts on page 400 and the pupillage feature on page 938 of the **Chambers Reports**. The GLS A-Z profile is on page 763.

crown prosecution service

If you have a passion for criminal law, and the idea of billable hours and contract drafting leaves you cold, the Crown Prosecution Service (CPS)

may appeal. The CPS is the government department responsible for bringing prosecutions against people who have been charged with a criminal offence in England and Wales. It handles all stages of the process, from advising the police on the possibility of prosecution right through to the delivery of advocacy in the courtroom.

The CPS employs over 2,700 lawyers in England and Wales to handle more than 1.2 million cases in the Magistrates' and Crown Courts. CPS prosecutors review and prosecute criminal cases following investigation by the police. They also advise the police on matters of criminal and evidence law, some working from Criminal Justice Units, which have been established within police stations to combat the problem of failed prosecutions. Lawyers here advise the police on the appropriate charge for the crime, spending one day in the office preparing cases and the next in the Magistrates' Court, dealing with administrative matters relating to each case. Lawyers in the Trial Unit handle Crown Court cases, including murder, rape and robbery.

CPS prosecutors can expect to come into contact with 30 or 40 cases each day in the Magistrates' Courts. Many Crown Court trials are conducted by self-employed barristers; however, there are increasing opportunities for CPS Higher Courts Advocates. The Director of Public Prosecutions, Sir Ken Macdonald QC, is keen to improve and modernise the service offered by the CPS, and an essential part of this is the development of in-house advocacy, such that the CPS will routinely conduct a large proportion of its own cases in all courts. Although prosecutors don't have the same intense client contact as defence lawyers, they do interact with everyone from magistrates, clerks, solicitors and probation and police officers, to civilian and expert witnesses. They also liaise with racial equality and victim support agencies as well as victims and witnesses themselves. For example, where a prosecution is abandoned, the prosecutor will inform the victim of the reasons.

Competition is fierce for training contracts with the CPS, but once you get in, unless something goes wrong, you are guaranteed employment at the end of two years. *"Strong communication and sound decision-making skills and advocacy potential"* are just some of the attributes you will need to apply, according to head of legal development Lesley Williams. The service is looking for those with *"commitment – not necessarily for a lifetime with the CPS, but those who at least see their next few years here."* Some lawyers give up lucrative careers in the private sector to join the CPS, taking pay cuts in return for a family-friendly working environment with good training opportunities.

Trainees liaise closely with supervisors to determine what they should be working on, sometimes on a daily, often on a weekly basis. All supervisors volunteer for the task, so you can be sure that they are willing participants in the relationship. Although they can state three preferences, trainees must be prepared to work anywhere within the region to which they apply. Expect to be shadowing prosecutors, observing pre-charge advice to those in custody or helping prepare pre-charge advice for those on bail, assisting colleagues who have *"files coming out of their ears"* and interacting with the police on a day-to-day basis.

As well as learning everything about criminal litigation within the CPS, there are opportunities in the form of three-to-four month secondments into private practice, the GLS or local government. There have even been opportunities to do placements at organisations such as the BBC. At around the 16th month, trainee solicitors begin a *"rather rigorous"* two-week course to become designated caseworkers, so that they have limited rights of audience in the magistrates court.

CPS trainee Sibylle Cheruvier recently created the Legal Trainee Network, which aims to connect the trainee solicitors and barristers scattered throughout in the service's different offices across the UK. Socials, a mentoring and buddy scheme and an on-line discussion board are just some of the benefits. It's *"a way to link trainees together to share knowledge, experience or good news,"* she told us.

Opportunities for training places in the CPS are advertised on the website www.cps.gov.uk. This is also the starting point for vacation placements and work experience. Vacancies may also appear in the legal, national and local press. The CPS will be advertising its 2008 campaign for legal trainees in October 2007 and places will be open to internal and external candidates. The CPS expects all trainees to have completed and passed the LPC or BVC before taking up a post. A trainee's salary starts at £18,425 nationally and £19,441 in London. Salaries for newly qualified lawyers start at £26,000 nationally and £28,662 in London.

The traditional LLB to LPC/BVC route is by no means the preferred route into the CPS. Many CPS trainees have juggled work and part-time study; some have entered the service sideways, having left school with few qualifications. CPS caseworkers are the beneficiaries of the service's eagerness to grow talent from within. This being so, perhaps becoming a caseworker is the way forward for future trainees. They assist prosecutors by researching cases and making recommendations on information required and charges to be brought. Beyond these duties, they liaise with advocates, witnesses, police and court staff; provide support to witnesses and victims; and additionally attend court to assist counsel on a regular basis. Impressive organisational skills and an ability to relate to people are essential. Remuneration runs between £18,425 nationally and £19,441 in London. Theoretically you could start anywhere within the CPS and end up as a prosecuting lawyer.

other career options

legal executive

If you haven't found a training contract or are thinking about moving sideways into a legal career, you could consider the Institute of Legal Executives (ILEX) course. Those who complete the course become legal executives – qualified lawyers who are sometimes known as the 'third branch' of the legal profession. There are over 24,000 legal executives and trainee legal executives across the country. No prior legal training is required to enrol on the course, which makes it suitable for school leavers, new graduates or those already engaged in a career and looking to branch out. It can be taken on a part-time basis, giving trainees an opportunity to combine study with practical experience.

Trainees initially study for a Professional Diploma in Law, which takes about two years part-time. The course includes an introduction to key legal concepts as well as legal practice and procedure and can be examined either by the mixed-assessment route (a portfolio, case studies and one end of course examination) or the examination route (four papers). Trainees then progress to the Professional Higher Diploma in Law, which allows specialisation in a particular area of practice, usually guided by the job the trainee is doing at the time. On completion, trainees become members of ILEX. To become a fully qualified ILEX fellow, it is necessary to gain five years of qualifying experience in a legal background (at least two after completing the exams) and be over the age of 25.

Law graduates are exempt from the academic part of the course and can take examinations solely in legal practice, enabling the qualification to be gained in a little over twelve months. For those without a law degree, the professional qualification will usually take three or four years to complete while in full-time employment. There is no set time to complete the examinations, so trainees can work at their own pace.

ILEX graduates end up in employment across the full spectrum of legal services from private practice to government departments and the in-house legal departments of major corporations.

Some ILEX fellows continue studying and eventually become fully qualified solicitors. As they will already have been examined in some of the core subjects required by the Common Professional Exam Board, and the others can be taken as single subjects over another one or two years of part-time study, most fellows can seek exemption from the GDL and move straight on to the LPC. ILEX fellows may also be exempted from the two-year training contract.

Although ILEX can provide a useful route to qualification as a solicitor, it is by no means the quickest. However, positions for trainee legal executives may be available when solicitors' training contracts are not and, crucially, the route does enable the student to earn whilst studying. A full list of colleges offering the course (including via distance learning) is available at www.ilex.org.uk.

paralegalling

If you have time to fill before starting your training contract or you are yet to be convinced you want to spend time and money on law school, paralegal work can provide a useful introduction to legal practice. Employers regard time spent paralegalling favourably as it demonstrates commitment to the profession and enables candidates to gain valuable experience and commercial or sector insight. Some firms and companies – though not all – offer traineeships to the most impressive of their own paralegals, but you should always keep in mind that the job is a valuable position in its own right. Guard against giving the impression that you will leave as soon as something better crops up. There is no single job description: some experienced paralegals may run their own cases; others with little to offer by way of experience may end up doing very dull document management tasks for months on end.

The paralegal market is competitive, so those with no legal qualifications or practical experience may find it harder to secure a position. Indeed, some top City firms require all paralegal applicants to have completed the LPC. The good news is that it is likely to be easier to find a paralegal position now than in the past couple of years, as the transaction market is busier.

When starting out, it may be necessary to work a number of short-term contracts until one firm decides it wants you on a long-term basis.

This can be a career in its own right, and experienced paralegals with specialist skills can make a very decent living. For information on current vacancies, check the legal press or register with a specialist recruitment agency. You should also find out if your law school's careers office has contacts and regularly check the websites of any firms in your area. Some firms employ paralegals from among those who write to them on spec.

her majesty's court service

On 1 April 2005 the old Court Service and the magistrates' courts were swept together into a single body aiming "to ensure that access [to justice] is provided as quickly as possible and at the lowest cost consistent with open justice and that citizens have greater confidence in, and respect for, the system of justice." After just two years as part of the Department for Constitutional Affairs, in May 2007 HM Court Service became an executive agency of the Ministry of Justice.

HMCS is responsible for the daily business of the civil, family and criminal courts in England and Wales – right up to the Court of Appeal. That involves the management of 725 properties and 591 court buildings, including the modernisation of their physical appearance. It deals with the timetabling of hearings and ensures that there are always ushers to manage the process. On a lighter note, the service is even responsible for making courts available as filming locations.

Most HMCS jobs are administrative in nature; however, the service recruits Judicial Assistants at various times throughout the year. JA appointments are temporary, with each successful applicant assigned to one of the Court's senior judges for a period of between three and 12 months. A former Judicial Assistant asserts that *"whether you're a barrister or a solicitor, just before or after qualification is probably the best time to do it."* There are usually ten positions available at any one time, and these are regularly filled by high-achieving types at the start of their careers, who are able to acquire a depth of understanding both of the law and of the appellate process. JAs assist the Lord Justices in the Civil Division of the Court of Appeal at the Royal Courts of Justice, where duties can include legal research, advice and providing assistance in drafting judgments. JAs may also help define the shape and nature of appeals in less well-presented cases.

Applicants for JA positions must be qualified lawyers who have completed pupillage or traineeship; possess word processing skills; are able to demonstrate intellectual ability (by way of a 2:1 or First); and have the ability to work under pressure as part of a team. It's worth pointing out that there is continued disappointment on the part of HMCS over the reluctance of the Bar to participate in the scheme. In terms of understanding the law and the appellate process, barristers have much to gain from time spent as a JA. As and when they become available, positions are advertised in *The Times* on Tuesday and the Law Society's *Gazette* as well as on the HM Court Service website: www.hmcourts-service.gov.uk.

Those looking for a long-term career might consider the roles of administrative officer, bailiff and county and Crown court ushers or clerks.

Court clerks do not have a legal advisory role and do not need legal qualifications. The 91 Crown Courts and 218 county courts in which they work are presided over by members of the judiciary. Magistrates' clerks do give legal advice to lay magistrates and managers of the court. Approximately 381 magistrates' courts operate in England and Wales, and between them they handle the majority of the country's criminal proceedings. In a busy metropolitan court, as well as the usual TV licence and traffic offences, the clerks will encounter drug trafficking cases and other serious crimes on a reasonably regular basis. A rural court is likely to be quieter and crimes of violence less common.

All court clerks need to be able to think on their feet and deal confidently with people.

Very occasionally they need to exercise the power to order individuals into custody for contempt of court, although the clerks we spoke to indicated that the vast majority of defendants treat them with respect. Magistrates' clerks must additionally provide magistrates with reliable advice on issues like self-defence, identification of suspects and inferences from the silence of defendants after arrest. A shift in recruitment policy has seen the traditional route (by which those without degrees could train while studying for the Diploma in Magisterial Law) overtaken by the recruitment of LPC and BVC graduates as trainee court clerks. As the individual progresses through a structured training programme, the number and complexity of their court duties will increase until ultimately they are advising lay magistrates on points of law and procedure. Most courts operate nine or ten sessions a week and most clerks will be in court for the majority of these. The remaining time will be spent exercising powers delegated to them by the magistrates, such as issuing summonses. For more information about careers with the magistrates' courts or any other part of HMCS, refer to its website.

the law commission

Many laws are the product of political expediency and are drawn up at the will of the government of the day. However, the government is not always best placed to see where reforms could best be made. The Law Commission, which is an advisory non-departmental public body now sponsored by the Ministry of Justice, was set up by Parliament 42 years ago to keep the laws of England and Wales under review and propose reform where necessary.

Its key purpose is to ensure that the law is as fair, modern, simple and cost-effective as possible, and to do so the commission employs about 15 research assistants to help with the task. At any one time, it will be engaged in about 20 projects of law reform. As a researcher you could be dealing with both common law and statutes going back many centuries. In the development of proposals for reforms you will analyse many different areas of law, identifying defects in the current system and examining foreign law models to see how they deal with similar problems. You may also help to draft consultation papers, instructions to Parliamentary Counsel and the final report. The commission additionally works on the consolidation of statutes and the repeal of obsolete statutory provisions. Recent papers were published on such diverse subjects as cohabitation and the financial consequences of relationship breakdown; a principled approach to criminal liability; and bringing the law of homicide into the 21st century.

The Law Commission recruits law graduates and postgraduates, those who have completed the LPC or BVC, and people who have spent some time in practice but are looking for a change. The job of research assistant involves some fascinating (and some less fascinating) subjects and is intellectually challenging. Candidates should have a First or high 2:1 at degree level plus a keen interest in current affairs and the workings of the law.

The job suits those with an analytical mind and a hatred of waffle; they must also love research because there's a lot of it. So far, more than two-thirds of the commission's recommendations have been implemented by the government – you can see what these are by looking at the commission's website – so you will get the satisfaction of seeing your work put into practice. Another plus point is that if you go on to train as a solicitor or barrister, you will be streets ahead of your peers in terms of your research skills and knowledge of how statutes work. For further information on short and long-term careers at the Law Commission, check out www.lawcom.gov.uk. The recruitment drive for positions as a research assistant commencing September 2008 starts in January 2008.

legal services commission

This government body was created by the Access to Justice Act 1999 and replaced the Legal Aid Board in 2000. It employs nearly 1,700 staff and operates from London and 12 towns and cities across England and Wales. It manages the distribution of public funds for both civil legal services and criminal defence services. The work of the LSC is essentially broken down into two departments covering these areas: the Community Legal Service and the Criminal Defence Service.

- The large Community Legal Service (CLS) handles civil cases. Caseworkers assess the merits of applications for legal funding and means-test applicants. They also assess and authorise claims for payment for legal services. The department helps ensure that people can get information and advice about their legal rights and help with enforcing them through bringing together legal aid solicitors, Citizens Advice Bureaux, Law Centres, local authority services and other organisations in over 200 regional CLS partnerships.
- The Criminal Defence Service (CDS) organ-

ises the supply of legal advice to those accused of crime through the use of local solicitors who are accredited by the service. It also performs an audit role, dealing with the authorised providers of criminal legal advice. There are no financial or other limits as to who is entitled to claim free legal advice on criminal cases, so it is merely the lawyer's financial claims and the quality of their services that are scrutinised. Part of the CDS' work is the Public Defender Service. Set up in 2001 with four offices, this has now increased to eight. The PDS offices are staffed by solicitors and accredited representatives who are directly employed by the LSC but provide independent advice. These offices employ their own lawyers to advise members of the public in what the LSC believes to be a more cost-effective and efficient way. A recent independent report said the PDS racked up substantially higher costs than other criminal defence providers during its formative years, but the PDS anticipates that as it grows it will become more cost-effective. The report also conducted a peer review of the PDS, which found that the quality of the PDS' work is roughly equivalent to or better than private practice criminal defence firms in most areas.

- The Contracting Sections of both departments audit claims for 'Legal Help', the funding used for preliminary and basic advice on how individuals might be represented.
- The Planning and Partnership Sections of both departments employ consultants and executives in order to better understand how the LSC should spend funds and place its resources, including initiatives such as electronic billing.

Jobs at the commission are advertised in local and/or national newspapers, as well as online. A first point of contact is www.legalservices.gov.uk. A few work-experience placements crop up, usually in the CLS, and these tend to last about six weeks.

patent attorney

The profession in the UK numbers some 1,700 attorneys, virtually all registered with the Chartered Institute of Patent Attorneys (CIPA). Patent attorneys can work in private firms, the patent departments of large companies or in government departments. It is their job to obtain, protect and enforce intellectual property rights for their owners. In short, a patent is a right conferred by the government to an inventor (either an individual or a company) which prevents others from exploiting the invention for a certain amount of time. In return, the inventor gives public disclosure of their invention.

The website www.cipa.org.uk has a useful careers section, but to summarise: it takes on average about four or five years to become a UK Chartered Patent Agent and/or a European Patent Attorney. All candidates must have a scientific or technical background (usually a relevant degree such as science or engineering) and the aptitude for learning the relevant law. Attention to detail, good drafting skills and a logical, analytical mind are essential and, increasingly, a knowledge of French or German is seen as key due to the increasingly international dimension to the work. The traditional route is to work and study for professional exams simultaneously. It is also an option to take the Certificate or Master's courses in intellectual property run by Queen Mary; University of London; Manchester University; Bournemouth University or Brunel University. By doing so, a candidate may gain exemption from certain of the professional examinations. Some employers may allow time off, and even funding, for these courses.

Once qualified as a Chartered Patent Agent, there is the opportunity to obtain a further qualification to become a Patent Attorney Litigator entitled to conduct litigation in the High Court, although all patent attorneys have the right to conduct litigation and to appear as advocate in the specialist Patents County Court. In order to become a European Patent Attorney, candidates must complete another set of examinations.

Tracking down a graduate trainee position is made all the easier by Inside Careers' useful guide to the patent attorney's profession: www.inside-information.com.

trade mark attorney

A trade mark is a form of intellectual property and is used to distinguish a manufacturer or trader's particular brand from its competitors, allowing consumers to identify certain goods or services. It can be anything from a logo, a picture, a name or even a sound or smell. There are about 530 fully qualified trade mark attorneys in the UK, all registered with the Institute of Trade Mark Attorneys (ITMA). Most work for large companies, or at firms of patent and trade mark attorneys.

The role of a trade mark attorney is to advise clients on all aspects of trade mark registration, protection and exploitation in the UK and Europe, liaising with counterparts in other parts of the world whenever necessary. They conduct searches in order to see if others are using a particular trade mark, advise clients on which classes of goods or services need to be covered with a registration and in which countries registrations need to be made, file applications in the UK and across the world, and advise when trade mark infringement occurs. The registration process is complicated due to the sheer number of registered trade marks, the tricky legislation and the added complexities of EU instruments, such as directives and regulations to which the UK is a party.

Good communication and drafting skills are required, but a degree is not a prerequisite to qualification. The minimum educational requirements are five GCSEs (grade A-C) and two A-Level passes in approved subjects. The road to qualification involves passing the exams set for ITMA – five foundation papers followed by three specialist papers. Candidates with certain degrees, such as law, may be exempt from some foundation papers. Again, it is most common for aspiring practitioners to study while learning on the job as a trainee trade mark agent. With no central admissions procedure, students need to approach firms or in-house trade mark departments directly. www.itma.org.uk has a helpful careers page.

compliance officer or analyst

Banks and other financial services companies are eager to recruit law and non-law graduates into their compliance units. These units take on the vital role of advising senior management on how to comply with the applicable laws, regulations and rules that govern the sector. They also ensure that the banks' own corporate procedures and policies are followed. Other functions relate to the handling of complex regulatory and internal investigations and examinations. Due to the proliferation of financial regulation in the past ten years the importance of compliance departments has grown enormously, so that in larger banks they are often equivalent in size to in-house legal teams and offer equally solid career prospects.

Through compliance risk management banks improve their ability to control the risks of emerging issues, thus helping to protect the organisation's reputation. The role of compliance officer or analyst requires astute advice, clear guidance, reliable professional judgement and the ability to work in a team. Attention to detail and a determination to see the consistent application of compliance policies and practices are essential. The extent of reliance on compliance teams means regular exposure to senior management occurs much earlier for trainees in this area than for trainee solicitors at law firms. A

minimum 2:1 degree is standard for successful applicants and salaries are typically comparable with other graduate trainees in the City. With some compliance teams numbering more than a hundred staff, in the longer term there is plenty of scope for career development.

The compliance unit at UBS bank, for example, is organised into the following teams that reflect the make-up of its business:

Product teams
- Equities
- Fixed Income, Rates, Currencies and Commodities
- Investment Banking, Research and Private Equity

Specialist teams
- Anti-Money Laundering Compliance
- Regulatory Management
- Chief Operating Officer

Jurisdictional teams
- Switzerland
- Continental Europe, Middle East & Africa

UBS, like other banks, offers a two-year compliance analyst training scheme, over the course of which a trainee will gain a broad base of business knowledge and technical experience. UBS' scheme starts with a six-week period of formal classroom training to develop core skills and knowledge; this is undertaken alongside new graduate recruits into other parts of the bank. After this, there are three six-month placements in the London office and a short placement in an international office. It is not usually necessary to have completed the GDL, LPC or even a law degree before undertaking a graduate scheme, although those with a mind to move across to an in-house legal role later in their career would need to find the time to qualify as a lawyer. Being legally qualified opens up the door to general counsel work and it is not uncommon for a bank's head of legal to also lead the compliance team.

hot or not?

In the race to secure a training contract or pupillage, you need to stand out from the crowd, by which we mean impress recruiters with a plethora of interesting talking points, not flail about in a clown suit. The road to success is smoother for some than others, but a few nips and tucks to your CV and a healthy dose of self-confidence can work wonders.

hitting a redbrick wall

So you've not got a law degree. So what? From the top sets at the Bar to the little-known solicitors firms on the high street, non-law graduates are just as able to secure training positions as their LLB peers. In the few cases where employers prefer law grads they will specify this, so unless you hear differently, conversion route applicants may proceed with confidence. Indeed, many recruiters tell us just how highly they regard staff with language skills and scientific or technical degrees, particularly where their clients' businesses will benefit. Believe it or not, being able to discuss literary criticism with your clients could come in handy, since clients, just like lawyers, are people, too.

It's a fact of life that many solicitors firms and barristers chambers subscribe to the idea of a pecking order of universities. It's not quite as widespread as it once was, but it's still there. Go to some firms in the City and around half the trainees will have attended Oxford or Cambridge University. A tour of the university law fairs – held over the autumn and spring terms – quickly shows which other universities are regarded as the richest pools for recruitment. Among the best attended by recruiters are Bristol, Nottingham and Durham. You can't change the identity of your university, so if you perceive it may put you at relative disadvantage, make sure you get the best degree possible and work on enriching your CV in other ways.

Your degree result is perhaps the single thing on your CV that has most impact. Net a First and you'll impress all and sundry (at least on paper); walk away with a 2:1 and your path to employment will be made smoother; end up with a 2:2 and you're going to have to perform some fancy footwork to get a training offer. In exceptional circumstances, the effect of a poor degree result can be softened by a letter from your tutor stipulating the reason why you underachieved. Alas, it's rarely relevant that you just missed a 2:1 by a percentage point or two; however, if you were a star student who suffered a serious accident or illness as finals loomed, confirmation of this (perhaps also by way of a doctor's letter) should assist. Having spoken to a number of trainees and a couple of pupil barristers who left university with 2:2s, we would never presume to discourage anyone from applying for a training position, but these people all had other impressive qualities and/or CV-enhancing experiences. If you find yourself at the back of the queue in the job market, think hard about what you can do to overcome that 2:2 – a year or more in a relevant job, a further degree, a commitment to voluntary work perhaps.

Possibly unaware that they could be applying for training contracts and vacation schemes in their second year, many new undergraduates are lulled into a false sense of security concerning their academic performance in the first year. If the only marks you have to show recruiters are amazing thirds, you'll struggle to make headway. As boring as it may sound, work for good results throughout your degree. At the very least, doing so will maximise your chances of a great final result.

get up, stand out

If you really want the lawyering gig, resist the urge to become an expert on daytime telly, rising only to pop down the students' union for a cheap pint. Instead, take advantage of your freedom and the practically unlimited opportunities on offer.

Almost every university will have a wide range of societies, meeting groups and sports clubs. At the vast majority, if your leisure pursuit of choice is not on offer, they'll give you the cash to set it up, providing you can rustle up a handful of like-minded individuals and it's not illegal. Pursuing your interests will give an extra dimension to both your university experience and, crucially, your CV.

Some kind of legal experience, whether it's involvement with the student law magazine or shadowing your aunt's neighbour's lawyer friend, is pretty crucial since you need to convince your prospective employers that you're serious about the profession, not just following an adolescent fantasy. You can also acquire this later on, through open days and vacation schemes, but it's never too early to start. Non-legal extra curriculars can be just as useful to show that you play well with others. It also gives you something to write about when an application form asks 'Discuss a time when you worked with a group to achieve a common goal.'

Sometimes the flood of info from university bodies such as the students' union and careers service can be so heavy that you feel you are drowning in e-mails, flyers and posters telling you of this job vacancy, that Amnesty meeting or another CV workshop. Resist the temptation to let it all wash over you. Relevant work experience is vital to almost every successful job application, so keep your eyes open for suitable positions and use them to test your own ideas of what you would like to do. Many universities run law-specific career seminars in association with solicitors firms or barristers chambers. Be savvy, go along and find out as much as you can by talking to trainee solicitors and recruiters. A bit of networking never ever goes amiss.

Do remember that only a minority of law firms and chambers throw drinks parties or sponsor libraries – the legal profession is not lim-ited to the folk who've actually bought you a drink. Build up a decent understanding of the structure of the profession before deciding what kind of lawyer you want to be and which firm you want to work for. Just because your friends seem to know what they want doesn't make their choices right for you. Similarly, your tutors and family can only help you so far. Research, research and research some more until you are confident of your preferences. Demonstrating your understanding of what the work will entail and being able to explain honestly and realistically why you want to do it will be one of the most important things to get across to recruiters.

worldly wisdom

If you want to become a commercial lawyer, you'll need this thing they call commercial awareness. We're not suggesting you become a mini-Murdoch, rather that you should gain a sense of what's going on in the commercial world: uncertainties in the global market because of US sub-prime mortgage fallout, interest rate fluctuations, the attraction of India as an international marketplace, the convergence of media technologies, big issues in the oil and gas sector. If you have zero interest in all this stuff, what makes you think commercial law will interest you? Why not read the *Financial Times* now and again or find an Internet site that will give you headline bulletins in bite-sized chunks. Keep up to date in a way that suits you and make sure you're not oblivious to the events going on around you at national and international level.

Don't think that just because you don't plan on going into commercial law that you don't need to do your homework. Students looking to go into criminal law should be aware of recent legislation, like the Violent Crime Reduction Act 2006. Future family lawyers should be able to discuss the major cases that have hit the headlines recently, including Miller, McFarlane and Charman. Needless to say, anyone interested in human rights issues will have a full-time job keeping up to date with all the cases and developments arising out of the war in Iraq and anti-terror measures here in the UK.

A candidate who has wanted to be a lawyer since the age of five and shot straight through university and the LPC without stopping to breathe may be dedicated, but is potentially less than attractive to recruiters. It's a cliché because it's true: taking time out to travel really does broaden the mind. As well as giving you more confidence to speak to people, navigating your way around a foreign country will develop your organisational and problem-solving skills. It also gives you another fertile ground of conversation at interview. If you've itchy feet and if you haven't already been out there for a look-see, then follow your heart – the career can wait. Recruiters do appreciate that not everyone has the desire or, more importantly, the money to swan off on a gap year to count fish or turtles or whatever. If travel is the last thing on your agenda, don't stress about it or feel you're going to be marked down for being a stay-at-home.

middle age spread

With the advent of new legislation, an employer discriminating against candidates on the grounds of age is officially a thing of the past. Nevertheless, some mature applicants still worry that their age will disadvantage them in the search for a training contract or pupillage. Remember (if you still can), with age comes experience and probably an impressive set of transferable skills. You already know how to work, your people/client-handling skills are doubtless better developed and you may even have relevant experience. We've chatted with successful barristers and solicitors who've done everything from secretarial work, pub management and film production to police work and a stint in the army. But when is old too old? If

you're still in your 20s, get over yourself – you're still a kid. If you're in your 30s, ask what it is you can offer a law firm that will make your application stand out. And if you're older still? Never say never. We have run into a small number of 40-something trainees, all of whom were glad to have made the career change. Given that each year after qualification a certain percentage of the UK's lawyers move firms or even drop out of the profession for good, the argument that employers expect 30 years of service from all new recruits simply doesn't hold water. Of greater relevance is the adage concerning old dogs and new tricks, so if your coat is greying, consider carefully how you'd cope with being asked to revert to puppyhood.

stranger in a strange land

London attracts young professionals from all over the world, so you can skip this bit if you're a Brit intending to work in the capital. If you hold an EU passport or have a pre-existing right to live and work in the UK and you are following the appropriate path to qualification, you should also proceed with optimism. Applicants who tick none of these boxes may find doors are easier to push open if they apply to firms with business interests in the country or region from which they come. This is because law firms have to show sound reasons why an overseas applicant is worth employing over someone who needs no work permit. Generally, the people we encountered who were neither EU nationals nor had a permanent right to live and work in the UK were training in City firms with international business. Additionally, a number of barristers chambers will take pupils who intend to return to practise in their home jurisdiction. In all cases, excellent written and spoken English is essential and you will need a convincing reason why you have chosen to commence your career in the UK.

Regional firms and sets are sometimes more comfortable recruiting candidates with a local connection, be this through family or education. Quite simply, they want to know that whoever they take on will be committed to a long-term career with them. They are wary of having their brightest and best skip off to higher-paying jobs in London on qualification. The picture across the UK is a variable one: some firms clearly state their preferences for local lads and lasses; others tell us that most of their applicants do have links with the region but that they are happy to consider anyone. Over the years we've found Irish trainees in Staffordshire, Londoners in Exeter and Scots in Birmingham.

inclusively yours

Despite the legal profession being more diverse than ever before, for students with mental or physical disabilities things are not straightforward. In the experience of the Group for Solicitors with Disabilities (GSD), many students with disabilities have great difficulty in securing work placements and training contracts. The good news is that there are sources of advice and assistance available and the GSD has been actively involved in approaching law firms to set up designated work placement schemes for disabled students. The group also provides a forum in which students and practitioners can meet in order to share experiences and provide one another with guidance and support. Would-be barristers should refer to the Equal Opportunities (Disability) Committee of the Bar Council.

sex talk

Gone are the days of firms and chambers populated exclusively by white men smoking fat cigars. Not only has the smoking ban put paid to the Cubans but women and ethnic minorities are now firmly ensconced in the profession. In

the course of our research around 150 firms provided us with lists identifying their trainees. In most firms the girls outnumber the boys, something we would expect to see given that more women have gone into the profession than men for well over a decade. The names on most of these lists also reflect a healthy spread of ethnic backgrounds. It is worth mentioning, however, that female and non-white trainees still have too few senior role models and there are always a small number of law firm sex or race discrimination claims going through the employment tribunals.

On the subject of sexual orientation, we know scores of gay and lesbian lawyers for whom their lifestyle choice is entirely a non-career matter. This subject sparked debate in mid-2006 when a Law Society report criticised law firms, and in particular those in the City, for having non gay-friendly working environments. It's fair to say that the report was widely viewed as way off the mark and the weeks following its publication saw many gay and lesbian City lawyers refute the claims and question the sampling methods used.

During the year from February 2005 to February 2006 a Law Society-commissioned study collected the following statistics on first-year trainees:
- 61.5% were women
- 17.6% were from minority ethnic groups
- 47.5% were located in London
- The average age of trainees was 27
- 22.3% were over 27
- 0.3% were over 50

A number of diversity-related organisations have sprung up and you may see evidence of them at your university. Without doubt anything that encourages genuine diversity in the workplace is to be commended, but before signing on the dotted line with any intermediary – especially if you are asked to hand over any money for their services – make sure you know you are dealing with a respected organisation. Ask if they are affiliated with particular law firms and if so how. Consider whether you actually need the services of these organisations at all. A cynic might argue that the big law firms are merely in competition with each other for the best students who just also happen to be non-white and that those students need no special help from third parties. If you know your university gets less attention from law firms than, say, Cambridge or Bristol, then a diversity-related organisation may well be just what you need to get your foot in the door. Remember too that the topic of diversity covers more than just ethnicity; if you think your accent or upbringing or a disability could stand in your way then find out if there is anything these organisations can do for you.

keep it in perspective

What with studying hard, reading the *FT*, helping out at the local CAB, captaining both the university rugby team and its netball team, debating, acting as student law society president, acting on stage and attending all the careers events that crop up throughout the year, you'll hardly have time for a pint, let alone the ten that students supposedly put away in between lectures. Your mum and dad may tell you your years at university are supposed to be a fun, carefree time, but frankly back in their day the job market was less competitive and no one built up a small mortgage in debt before the age of 21... well, only if they had a really wild time. Besides, what do the oldies know? They were too busy listening to Prog Rock and expanding their consciousness, man.

Of course you must have fun, and you absolutely must develop your interests and friendships because these, in many cases, last far longer and can be more rewarding than any career. Ultimately, it all comes down to finding the right balance.

pro bono and volunteering

Recruiters are always looking for candidates with practical experience in a legal environment. According to Kara Irwin, Director of the BPP Pro Bono Centre: *"As well as being something tangible that students can contribute to the community, pro bono gives them the opportunity to really develop important legal skills."* Volunteering can often be the best way to gain such skills, and there are plenty of available options for students who are willing to give up some of their spare time. Every little bit counts, whether it's a half-day a week helping out at a CAB or six months overseas as an intern on death row appeals. However, you should ask yourself – are you able to commit to the project you start? If you're just doing something to add gloss to your CV, it's going to look pretty obvious; *"we can always tell when students are doing it purely out of self-interest,"* Kara warns.

make the most of your law school

Most post-graduate law schools, and increasingly university law departments, now have pro bono initiatives in place. The College of Law in London, for example, operates a housing casework scheme that takes homelessness cases, tenants facing eviction, return of deposit and minor disrepair schemes. After receiving training, students can go on to represent members of the public before the Leasehold Valuation Tribunal and the Rent Assessment Committee. At some colleges pro bono is a compulsory element of the course. At the Student Law Office of Northumbria University, which has achieved Legal Services Commission Quality Marks for its housing and employment advice, all LPC and BVC students advise real clients from the initial interview through to advocacy before tribunals and the small claims courts.

Many law schools engage in outreach work in the local community. The College of Law's Streetlaw Plus programme for its London GDL students focuses on legal literacy, with students working directly with community groups, schools and prisons. BPP's Streetlaw activities have included presentations to schoolchildren and inmates of Pentonville Prison. In September 2007, the BPP centre further expanded its services by launching a telephone employment law helpline for those who have come into contact with the criminal justice system (either convicted or acquitted).

Pro bono is not necessarily just about providing advice to individuals. At BPP, for example, students in the centre's intellectual property group are engaged in an ongoing outreach project run in collaboration with a major IP charity. Its human rights unit, meanwhile, supports organisations across the world. Currently, BVC and LPC students are undertaking legal research for a defendant at the Special Court for Sierra Leone, which hears cases involving serious violations of international humanitarian and Sierra Leonean law.

For undergrads, it has often been more difficult to find a centrally organised pro bono initiative at university. In the past year, however, there have been some promising developments. LawWorks' 2006 report on pro bono activity revealed that only 53% of the universities and law schools surveyed offered students regular opportunities to undertake pro bono activities. About half of the remaining 47% were keen to do so, but felt they lacked the necessary support. As a result – and with funding from the Law Society – LawWorks has created the full-time position of The Law Society and LawWorks Law Schools and Student Pro Bono Project Manager. Solicitor Martin Curtis started the job on 1 October 2007. Although his title is a bit of a mouthful (and will probably be shortened to Student Officer), his job looks set to be invaluable. As well as advising universities and law schools on how best to establish pro bono initiatives, he will identify lawyers to supervise students and strengthening existing opportunities by facilitating new partnerships and contacts. LawWorks is also in the process of setting up an online forum for pro bono-related enquiries.

Another much-welcomed development is the move from June to November of the Law Society/Bar Council/ILEX-backed National Pro Bono Week (NPBW), which promotes the provision of free legal advice and puts attendees in touch with voluntary organisations. As Kara Irwin explains, this move is *"entirely to cater for law students. Until now, NPBW has always been in students' exam time, which prevented quite a few people from getting involved. Now that's no longer an issue we expect to see many more students involved in the week's events. To this end, letters have been sent to law schools and universities across the country detailing ways they can start up pro bono projects or hold events during NPBW itself."* For more information, check out the Law Society's website.

the free representation unit (fru)

Becoming a ratified member of the FRU is a really good idea if you're thinking of going to the Bar, but it's an equally good idea if you are intending to be a solicitor specialising in any contentious area of law, because chances are you'll be doing at least some of the advocacy yourself.

FRU representatives offer free advice and representation to clients who are not eligible for legal aid, appearing on their behalf before employment and social security tribunals. There is also a limited amount of work in criminal injuries compensation appeals and some immigration matters. Law students can train to become a social security representative in the final year of an LLB, while non-law graduates can do this in their GDL year. The employment option is only open to LPC and BVC students, and it should also be noted that FRU only operates in and around London, though several of the regional BVC and LPC providers have advice clinics that allow students to gain experience of tribunal advocacy.

To qualify, you'll must attend an induction day and complete a legal opinion exercise. You'll then be able to take on cases after discussing them with caseworkers. Once a case is yours, you must see it through to the end. A pupil barrister with a series of employment tribunal wins behind her told us: *"As a rep you'll get experience in using a whole bundle of practical legal skills. You'll conference with your client, conduct legal research, draft submissions, negotiate with your opponent, and if the case doesn't settle, you'll make oral submissions to the tribunal and get to examine and cross-examine witnesses."* From time to time, seasoned FRU reps have been known to take cases to the Employment Appeal Tribunal or the Social Security Commissioners and it's not unheard of for their names to appear in the reported decision.

If we haven't sold it to you already, be aware that most of the pupils and junior barristers who we interviewed for our *Chambers Reports* had worked for FRU or another similar organisation at some time during their training. It could well be the thing that saves your application from the shredder.

the possibilities are endless...

www.probonouk.net
This site will identify the organisations working in your area. It has a section devoted to students.

LawWorks
This is the operating name of the Solicitors Pro Bono Group. Its website www.lawworks.org.uk is a good source of advice and information, including details of student membership.

Amicus
This charity provides assistance to US attorneys working on death row cases. It gives training and arranges internships in the USA for UK postgraduate students. As internships are unpaid (though a limited number of scholarships do exist), interested applicants should have a plan for funding the placement. www.amicus-alj.org

The AIRE Centre

This organisation provides information and advice throughout Europe on international human rights law, including the rights of individuals under the provisions of European Community law. It also offers direct legal advice and assistance on a case-by-case basis to legal practitioners or advisers. Internships are available for students who have a good working knowledge of international human rights law and EU law. Students must be able to commit themselves to a minimum of one day per week. A second European language is an advantage. www.airecentre.org

Bar Pro Bono Unit

Established in 1996 by Attorney-General Lord Goldsmith QC, the unit matches individuals in need of legal representation with barristers in private practice willing to undertake work on a pro bono basis. Opportunities are available for students to provide administrative support to the unit on a part-time basis. This could mean anything from envelope stuffing to allocating cases to members of the panel. www.barprobono.org.uk

Citizens Advice Bureaux

The Citizens Advice service has over 22,000 volunteers in over 2,000 bureaux. Those with real commitment and enough time can train with the CAB on its Adviser Training Programme to gain a widely recognised qualification that may subsequently enable your law firm training contract to be reduced by up to six months. Not all volunteers have the time or the inclination to train as advisers, so if admin, IT or reception work is enough for you, why not request one of these roles or offer to help out with publicity and media activities. Debt, benefits, housing, employment, consumer issues, family matters and immigration are the most commonly raised problems, some six million of which are handled each year. www.citizensadvice.org.uk

Independent Custody Visiting

Independent custody visiting began in the wake of the Scarman Report following the Brixton riots of 1981. Independent custody visitors (ICVs) work in pairs, conducting regular unannounced checks on police stations in their area to monitor the welfare of the detainees. Anyone over the age of 18 can apply to become an ICV. The Independent Custody Visiting Association website contains full details. www.icva.org.uk

Law Centres

Law centres provide free and independent legal services to people who live or work in their catchment areas. Their work is typically in fields where legal aid is not available. Working at a law centre is very much a career in itself; however, some centres accept student volunteers to provide administrative support and casework assistance. The website www.lawcentres.org.uk provides links to individual law centres across the UK.

Liberty

This is a well-established human rights organisation providing advice and representation to groups and individuals in relation to domestic law cases involving the Human Rights Act. Liberty has opportunities for a small number of students to provide general office assistance and help with casework. Students should be able to commit at least one day a week. www.liberty-human-rights.org.uk

Victim Support

The Victim Support Witness Service operates in every Crown Court across England and Wales, providing guidance and support to witnesses, victims and their families before, during and after court proceedings. Volunteers need to be able to commit at least two full days a month. www.victimsupport.co.uk

Refugee Council

The Refugee Council is largest refugee agency in the UK with offices in the East of England, West Midlands, London and Yorkshire and Humberside. It provides advice to asylum seekers and refugees on the asylum procedure, support and entitlement. Volunteers can offer their assistance in three areas: direct services, office-based and community-based. www.refugeecouncil.org.uk

the graduate diploma in law (gdl)

If you opted to spend your time at university reading great books, perfecting your Ancient Greek or divining the inner workings of the human body, you can still come to the law via a one-year conversion course known as the Graduate Diploma in Law (GDL). You may also see the course referred to as the CPE (Common Professional Exam) or PgDL (Postgraduate Diploma in Law). The GDL will bring you up to a required standard in the seven core legal subjects that are typically taught in the first two years of an LLB. Because skills like textual analysis, research, logical argument, writing and presentation can be acquired in a whole range of disciplines from archaeology to zoology, legal employers tend not to make a distinction between applicants with an LLB and those with the GDL.

The standard requirement for admission is a degree from university in the UK or Republic of Ireland. It is possible for non-graduates to get on to a course if they've shown the requisite drive and determination and have exceptional ability in some other field. Such candidates – and those with a degree from an overseas university – must obtain a Certificate of Academic Standing from the Bar Council or Law Society before enrolling on the GDL.

The course is no day at the beach. Taken full-time it lasts a minimum of 36 weeks, during which you'll be expected to undertake 45 hours of lectures, tutorials and private study each week. It is possible to take the course part-time over two years. Assessment tends to be by written exams, with regular coursework and an extended essay thrown in. Depending on the institution you attend, there will be more or less emphasis on academic essays, written problem questions or practical preparation of debates for the classroom. Because the institutions that offer the GDL vary in perceived quality, their approach and the composition of their student bodies, it is well worth doing your research before you apply. City

University and Nottingham are renowned for offering more academic courses, often attracting a large number of students headed for the Bar. In London, BPP, for example, is packed with City types and there are reams of paper and manuals that need to be consigned to memory.

- There's a huge amount to take in so get into a good study routine early on.
- You're there to learn a set curriculum, not to think outside the box. Probably the best use of your creativity is to come up with amusing ways of remembering case names.
- Attend classes!

On the GDL you will be given a grounding in the core principles and statutes and be exposed to the key case law in each area. Legal reasoning is, for the most part, an exacting discipline – there is not much room for posturing, even if the opinions of some esteemed judges may defy any conventional standards of logic. Lord Denning's judgments, in particular, should be worth a chuckle or two, although some of his more convoluted legal inventions, like promissory estoppel, may make your head ache. English Common Law is an intriguing amalgam of cold logic and a concern for justice to be done – a combination of metaphysics, logic and ethics, with a good bit of policy (and arguably prejudice) thrown in.

- **Land Law:** The favourite subject at many a dinner party, the saleability of property is more crucial to the functioning of society than you might expect. Some academics even argue it's the reason the institution of marriage was created. Who owns what is a crucial question for all parties, from the biggest bank to the smallest squatter. Land law is dominated by checklists, which are used to determine everything from the existence of an easement to the identity of Equity's Darling, so you'll need to come up with plenty of creative mnemonic devices (we recommend Bald Priests Fight Like Winners). You can pick up several useful tips to apply to your own life, including how to ensure you're not screwed over if you decided to buy a house with a friend, how to claim a right of light when a new housing development blocks out the sun from your greenhouse and how to prevent the bank foreclosing on your mortgage. Finding the answers to these involves some mind-numbing jargon, and it's safe to say that at times the subject feels drier than the Sahara. But for the technically and metaphysically minded, it's like getting under the bonnet of an antique car with a box of medieval tools. Words to try and work into dinner party conversation: overreaching, chattel, fee simple, flying freehold, socage, bona vacantia.

- **EU:** The law of the European Union is massively important since the European Court of Justice (ECJ) is effectively the highest court of appeal for all its member states. This course studies the institutions, sources and underlying principles of the EU system and substantive European law. Big subjects include the establishment of a free market, the free movement of workers, competition policy and the freedom of establishment as well as the incorporation of the European Convention on Human Rights into our national law. For Europhiles it is a fascinating mix of politics, history, economics and comparative jurisprudence, but its case law contains some of the longest and most tongue-twisting names you're likely to see. Some of it can be quite dry, particularly when dealing with the free movement of goods, where every answer seems to be *"labelling"* or *"a certificate of safety."* Much more amusing is the case of Van Duyn, which established that the UK could

bar a Scientologist from entry into the country. Van Duyn is not likely to be followed today, although Germany's recent bans against Tom Cruise are an interesting exception. This is the stuff of competition law, an enduringly popular area of commercial practice, particularly for those with a love for Brussels.

- **Equity and Trusts:** The uninitiated (and fans of Dickens) would be forgiven for thinking that trusts are the preserve of tax-evading toffs. The truth of the matter is that the 'trust' (the legal arrangement whereby one person holds property for another) has a multiplicity of uses. It has applications in the worlds of high finance and charity as much as in providing a nest egg for a beloved grandchild. The trust is a key contribution made by 'equity' – a rather opaque term for a line of law that calls upon ideas of fairness to remedy any injustices brought about by the strict application of black letter law. Although some of it is tricky to get your head round, the subject is filled with plenty of gems of cases involving wealthy eccentrics. You'll learn how the courts decided the fate of little Penelope Pilkington and why a fat-cat should never use the words *"our yacht"* in front of his mistress. The course deals with how to set up a trust with its various formalities, quirks like how to set up trusts for illegitimate kids without your wife knowing, what happens in fiendishly complicated financial transactions when someone tries to set up a trust to avoid tax (the name Vandervell will haunt you for years) and how to establish a valid charity. You'll also look at the duties of trustees, remedies against them and how to recover money that has been misapplied. Equity is the bread and butter of Chancery practice, which preoccupies some of the biggest brain boxes at the Bar. The subject also crops up in solicitors' practice through anything from complex financial transactions to advice to individuals. For those destined to cater for the *Sunday Times'* Rich List, studying equity provides you with the basic tools which you'll later use to crack the taxman's safe.

- **Contract:** The law of contract governs when an agreement becomes legally binding and thus enforceable. The principles you learn here underpin any commercial agreement you'll have to draft, peruse or persuade someone to sign. You'll look at how to tell when a contract is formed, the required formalities, permissible terms and what happens if the seller has neglected to tell you the Jackson Pollock you've just bought is actually a product of his son's finger-painting. Interesting issues include how you can avoid paying a debt by giving the creditor *"a horse, a hawk or a robe"* instead, why a little notice saying *"see back"* is all-important on a ticket and why you might still be bound by a contract to sell your favourite guitar even if the buyer's letter of acceptance gets lost in the post. Armed with your knowledge of the Sale of Goods Act, you may find yourself bringing any number of small claims against the high street retailers whose products fall apart the minute you get them home.

- **Crime:** Some people think the law begins and ends at crime. Perhaps they watch too much CSI. In terms of human interest this subject reaches parts that the others don't even know exist. Whether your interest is in policy or in the gruesome things that people do to one another, the crime course should provide plenty to engage and surprise. The syllabus touches on all the usual suspects: sexual offences, theft, assault and homicide as well as more philosophical discussions, like what amounts to a 'reasonable man' in the eyes of the law. Also covered are the liability of sec-ondary parties, attempts, affirmative and capacity defences and the new offence of fraud, which is defined so broadly that almost any lie can be a crime (so watch your p's and q's). You'll find out just how much of your body you need to get through a window in order to count as a burglar and why epileptics are deemed insane. By the end of the course you'll also be in a better position to explain why it's okay for a wife to consent to her husband branding his initials on her backside, but not for grown men to allow each other to whip their genitals with stinging nettles.

- **Tort:** The law of civil wrong covers anything from tripping on a wonky paving stone to kicking a football into your neighbour's yard or publishing salacious celebrity gossip on your website. Fault is measured in terms of loss to the victim and damages payable by the 'tortfeasor'. To show that a tort has been committed you must show that the person suffering the loss was owed a 'duty of care', that there was a breach of that duty and that some kind of loss resulted from the breach. The big subject here is the tort of negligence, but also covered on a typical course are a veritable ragbag of wrongs ranging from defamation, occupier's liability, employer's liability and liability for defective products. The common thread is working out who is to blame for a chain of unfortunate incidents leading to some kind of injury – either physical or financial. The most famous case, Donoghue v Stevenson, involves a lady finding a snail in a bottle of ginger beer. Other intriguing problems are whether the fire brigade has a duty of care to answer an emergency call, what happens if you suffer some kind of psychiatric illness from witnessing a horrific accident and how much the law says your arm is worth. This is the field which fuels the so-called compensation culture and gives lawyers a bad name. You'll hear stories about people being impaled, trampled and crushed, so try to cultivate an iron stomach or a gruesome sense of humour.

- **Public:** Studying the nature of the UK constitution (hint: yes there is one, albeit unwritten and composed of several parts) and the process of judicial review is a far cry from learning about contractual terms or mortgages. The first part of the course features an accelerated study of the functioning and evolution of the Houses of Lords and Commons and the impact of the EU on UK law. Those with politics degrees will have a running start, and you're more likely to enjoy the constitutional bit of the subject if you're a history buff. When in doubt, questioning the strength of Parliamentary supremacy, the rule of law and the Royal Prerogative should suffice to convince the tutor you've done your reading. After the academic bit is over and done with, a large chunk of the rest of the course is devoted to judicial review, the process by which the courts can challenge the decisions of public bodies. The shift from constitutional to administrative topics is probably the most pronounced on the entire GDL, so those who don't enjoy thinking about how the Jackson case, concerning the fox hunting bill, highlighted the modern state of Parliamentary supremacy can instead focus on why a local authority can't compulsorily purchase your house just because you haven't paid your council tax. The last part of the course is arguably the easiest; you'll learn about the freedoms of speech and assembly, as well as the nitty-gritty of exactly how much force the police can use when they throw you in the back of their van.

All GDL applications are made through the Central Applications Board (www.lawcabs.ac.uk). It's worth getting your application in as early as possible if you have your heart set on a particular institution. Applications for first-round 2008/09 applications must be made by 1 February 2008. The institutions will consider these and make offers between 1 February and early April. Applications made from 1 February until early April will be considered in early April. Later applications will be considered as and when they are received. In short, the later you apply the more flexible you may have to be about where you study. It's also worth bearing in mind that if you intend to go on and do an LPC or BVC at a very popular institution you might stand a better chance if you choose it for your GDL. Many providers guarantee LPC places to their GDL graduates. The GDL is now offered at around 30 different universities and law schools in England and Wales. Our website has full details of course providers, fees and other useful information.

Most students find the LPC a year to get through rather than be enjoyed, but it's a crucial stepping-stone between the hallowed halls of academia to the gleaming corridors of practice. It can be taken full-time over one year or part-time over two years, and some part-timers combine it with a three-year training contract.

You should know from the start that the LPC is not an academic course. After you've been whisked about with basic legal ingredients and rolled out by the LLB or GDL, the LPC is like the cookie cutter forming you into the right shape for practice. Essays are replaced with letters of advice, mooting with advocacy and textbooks with manuals and precedents as students get to grips with the practical day-to-day of working as a solicitor. Students also delve into the technical knowledge with which every solicitor is supposed to be au fait, including tax, accounts, professional conduct and the low-down on money laundering.

Students straight from rigorous university degrees may feel like they've regressed back to junior school with all the rote learning of prosaic, spoon-fed information. It is an exercise in time management and organisation rather than creativity. You will start the year with literally a suitcase full of paper, so best clear a whole bookcase now.

The year begins with the subjects the Law Society deems compulsory, including company law, conveyancing and civil and criminal litigation. Students are also assessed on certain essential skills, like interviewing, advocacy, drafting, letter writing and legal research. After the compulsory subjects are examined in February, students spend the remainder of the course studying three elective subjects. City-bound types usually study debt finance, equity finance, private acquisitions or advanced commercial property. Those destined for non-commercial practice tend to choose family, private client, advanced criminal litigation, immigration or personal injury and clinical negli-gence. There are a plethora of electives to choose from. The range of available electives varies from one provider to another. For a full list of who offers what, refer to our website.

The LPC doesn't quite teach you BlackBerry etiquette or how to bundle, but it is chock full of handy tricks and tips for the budding solicitor, including:

- When to use 'Yours sincerely', how to conduct yourself in a meeting and the politest way to stop a chatty client mid-flow.
- What forms you need to submit to Companies House to register a new company or appoint a director.
- How much tax you need to pay on an old piece of equipment that you've had for five years and are selling on to your son.
- What procedure you need to follow when you're exchanging contracts to buy or sell a house over the telephone.
- When precisely you should post a claim form if it has to arrive on Tuesday and there's a Bank Holiday the day before.
- How to draft a witness statement.
- How many different bank accounts you'll need for your clients' money and why you can't switch funds between accounts willy-nilly.
- Who you can act for and who you can't.
- Your duties to the court.

Although the LPC is currently in stasis, big changes are afoot and it is widely anticipated that the LPC will be a radically different animal in a year or two, reportedly to be dubbed the LPC3. On the back of the Law Society's Training Framework Review, which aimed to widen access to the profession, the Solicitors Regulation Authority (SRA) held a consultation in the spring of 2007 which suggested reforming the LPC to minimise costs to students without sponsorship and provide greater flexibility. However, the sands are shifting constantly, so what may be the favoured framework now could well be quite different after another consultation. You should keep an eye open for further information, but the current plans are to change the LPC beginning September 2009 as follows:

electives

- Currently students complete their electives immediately after their compulsory subjects. This has the benefit of cohesion and enables students to use the skills they developed during the compulsory and skills part of the LPC in their electives.
- Students would be able to separate their electives from their compulsories. So the full-time LPC3 could be six months long and the electives could be taken during the training contract. Although it seems the SRA doesn't want to promote this as a rule, its proposal suggested some universities could create subjects for law students to take during the final year of their undergraduate course to fulfil the elective requirement. It also means students could study their electives with different providers.
- It would no longer be a requirement that students complete electives before their training contract is registered. Instead, the requirement would only be for the compulsory subjects to be completed before training contract registration.
- Firms could create tailored firm-specific electives to be taught to trainees in-house.
- Students would still have the option of doing the full-time LPC3 in one year, with electives immediately following compulsories.
- **Pros:** The course would be much more flexible and potentially students and firms could save time and money.
- **Cons:** It might cause some confusion as to which areas should be dealt with on the Professional Skills Course and which should be electives.

exemptions

- Currently no exemptions are permitted.
- The proposal is for students to be able to apply individually to the SRA (for a fee) to be exempted from certain parts of the course, presumably based on their previous experience (guidance to be published).
- The SRA thinks exemption might be possible for Business Law and Practice, Property Law and Practice, and Litigation and Advocacy, but not for skills like drafting, research, interviewing and advising.
- **Pros:** If course providers charged per subject rather than for the whole course, it could be cheaper for students and could save time.
- **Cons:** The LPC3 could become 'modularised' and incoherent.

SRA's regulatory role

- Currently the SRA closely monitors providers to broadly administer the LPC in a uniform way in order to ensure students have an equivalent experience.
- The proposal is for the SRA to loosen its grip.
- This would allow flexibility and freedom for providers to administer the LPC3 as they choose, subject to meeting certain standards.
- There would be no required length for the course, just a minimum number of study hours.
- **Pros:** The distinction between providers would be more obvious so students could make more informed choices.
- **Cons:** Less regulation could endanger quality. There would be no minimum contact hours, so e-learning could go berserk.

compulsory subjects

- There is a proposal that probate be a compulsory subject. The Law Society agrees, with the caveat that it should also include will drafting and the structure of wills.

There is a proposal that civil and criminal litigation should be able to be tailored to reflect whether the student plans to practise commercially or on the high street, so that providers could give more weight to civil litigation for commercial students and vice versa.

○ Overall LPC pass rate for 2006: 77.2% (8,262 students)

○ Pass with Distinction: 24.6%

○ Pass with Commendation: 32.7%

○ Pass: 19.9%

○ Refer/resit/defer/fail: 22%

○ Withdrawn: 1.3%

Figures published by the Law Society

The LPC table on our website will reveal that the cost of taking the course is substantial. This is of most concern to the many students who self-fund because there is no financial support from the type of law firm in which they intend to practise. Since the Access to Justice Act 1999, the government has promised to fill the massive gaps in the coverage of legal services in the UK, yet less than 0.5% of public spending currently goes on these services. The number of students training to provide advice to legally aided clients is shrinking and so the Legal Services Commission (LSC) has in the last few years set aside an annual figure of £3 million to help fund students who agree to go into legally aided practice for at least two years after qualification. With only around 100 students benefiting each year, the grants seem rather elusive. They are awarded via law firms so don't think about applying to the LSC direct. If you want to know which law firms will have available funds, this information is posted on the LSC website. To ensure good use of the funds, the LSC requires beneficiaries of the grant to take elective subjects that are pertinent to smaller and high street firms, law centres and local authority practice.

At the other end of the spectrum, those students signed up to train with the country's biggest and most profitable commercial law firms benefit from generous law school sponsorship packages. These rarely come without conditions; indeed with each passing year the conditions become more stringent. Ten years ago few firms cared which LPC provider you chose. Now, more and more firms are signing up to firm-specific LPCs or requiring their future trainees to attend a specific provider. This has been criticised as creating a two-tier LPC, limiting choice and stifling diversity (since students headed for corporate giants won't interact very much with other students headed for different kinds of practice). However, law firms like it because it means they get more for their money; future trainees get into the 'mindset' of the firm, learn the firm's internal day-to-day procedures and can start to specialise in the firm's areas of expertise sooner, making them more profitable. The two front runners in the rapidly changing race for LPC supremacy are BPP Law School and the College of Law. Each is busy signing deals with large law firms to provide either tailor-made electives or entire bespoke courses. For example, if you choose Linklaters for your training contract you must study a Linklaters LPC at the COL's Moorgate branch. The same goes for students heading to Allen & Overy and Clifford Chance. Choose Berwin Leighton Paisner, Barlow Lyde & Gilbert, Baker & McKenzie, Cobbetts or Halliwells and you must take the new LPC+ which contains elective subjects designed by the firms in collaboration with COL. Sign with Addleshaw Goddard, Simmons & Simmons, Macfarlanes, SJ Berwin or CMS Cameron McKenna and you must take a standard LPC course with commercial electives at one of BPP's three schools in Manchester, Leeds or London. Norton Rose, Slaughter and May, Freshfields, Herbert Smith and Lovells, collectively the City LPC consortium, also send their future trainees to BPP.

Students on firm-specific courses sometimes say it makes them feel hot-housed and worry that it will cause problems for them if they want to go to a different firm on qualification. However, as these marriages of convenience between law firms and LPC providers are gradually becoming the rule rather than the exception, it looks as though students with City training contracts will have to resign themselves to having a less diverse and more tailored LPC experience in future.

Another product of the increasingly competitive LPC market is the introduction of MBA-style modules onto the course. Behind this is the idea that young lawyers need a greater awareness of the business context in which their clients operate. If you think that as a crime or family lawyer such knowledge will be superfluous, think again. As a partner in a law firm, you too may one day be running a business of your own.

Yet another recent development in the fast-changing LPC arena is the use of e-learning. Instead of sitting in large lecture theatres with 200-odd other students being taught in real time by real people, students at some course providers now have to assimilate lecture information via online tutorials and CD-ROMs. Students still benefit from human contact by attending their small group tutorials. Some argue that e-learning is beneficial to students because it allows them to learn in their own time and at their own pace, rewinding bits that are unclear until understanding sinks in. However, others who have had a taste of e-learning see it as a money-making exercise in amateur dramatics and criticise the way in which it prevents students from asking questions and experiencing the dynamics of a live lecture. While the more cautious providers have introduced online lectures as an addition to live lectures, others have gone the whole hog and scrapped live lectures altogether. Only time will tell whether e-learning prevails over the old-fashioned combo of podium and PowerPoint.

the lpc providers

Anglia Ruskin University
Bournemouth University
BPP Law School, London
BPP Law School, Manchester
BPP Law School, Leeds
Bristol Institute of Legal Practice at UWE
Cardiff Law School
City Law School
College of Law at Birmingham
College of Law at Chester
College of Law at Guildford
College of Law at London
College of Law at York
De Montfort University
Kaplan Law School
Leeds Metropolitan University
Liverpool John Moores University
London Metropolitan University
Manchester Metropolitan University
Northumbria University
Nottingham Law School
Oxford Institute of Legal Practice
Staffordshire University
Swansea University
Thames Valley University
University of Central England in Birmingham
University of Central Lancashire
University of Glamorgan
University of Hertfordshire (p/t)
University of Huddersfield
University of Plymouth
University of Sheffield
University of Wales, Aberystwyth
University of Westminster
University of Wolverhampton

how to apply

The Central Applications Board administers all applications for full-time LPCs. Its website is www.lawcabs.ac.uk. Applications for the 2008/09 full-time course that are received by 1 December 2007 will be processed between 1 December and late March. Applications received before the end of March will be processed at the end of March. Applications received any later will be processed as and when they are received. Later applicants' chances of securing a place with popular providers are reduced, but be aware that, nationwide, there are more validated places than enrolled students on both full and part-time courses. Applications for part-time courses should be made directly to the providers.

There are plenty of things to consider when choosing a law school, so be sure to arm yourself with as much information as possible. Request prospectuses, attend open days, chat to representatives visiting your university, talk to current students and ascertain your priorities.

- **Career issues:** Your future employer (if you have one) may well specify where you go and at the very least they should be able to give you advice, based on the experiences of current trainees. If you don't yet have a training contract, look into the range of extra curricular activities, clubs and societies on offer that may help you improve your CV. Also think about the quality of careers advice available at each institution. Have they got a good record of getting students placements and training contracts?
- **Electives:** Find out if your future employer wants you to take any particular electives. Otherwise, find out which course providers offer the electives best suited to the type of practice you want to move into. If all else fails, pick the one offering the electives you fancy; although most offer a pretty standard package, some institutions also offer the odd media and entertainment or charity law elective. Some may have restrictions on elective combinations or run electives only when there is sufficient demand. For a full run-down on who offers what, see our website.
- **Assessment grades and pass rates:** Pass rates are published on the Law Society's website each autumn, but be aware that direct comparisons are impossible as each institution examines and marks independently of the others. The Law Society visits and inspects each institution and then publishes a report. Once based on a simple grading system from excellent to satisfactory, the picture has been muddied by the Law Society's decision to revise its assessment grading. As the new system will take another year to roll out to all LPC providers, direct comparisons between them will be difficult for a while.
- **Teaching and assessment methods:** Most institutions timetable around 14 hours of classes per week, but there uniformity ends. If you have travel plans, you may want to check term dates, as these can vary between institutions by a good couple of weeks. Similarly, if you are going to have a long commute to classes, or are hoping to fit in part-time work, check the timetabling of classes. Some places will fix you up with neat morning or afternoon timetables and a day off mid-week; others will expect you to hang around between classes that are spread throughout the day. Consider whether you are self-disciplined enough for e-learning or whether you feel better suited to attending lectures in person. Whereas some institutions only permit a modest statute book and practitioner text to be taken into the exam room, others hold entirely open-book exams leading to students precariously balancing files and books Jenga-style on tiny exam desks.
- **Facilities:** For every school where students must search plaintively for a quiet study corner,

there is another where they can spread out in blessed peace in their own 'office'. Take the LPC course at a university and you'll belong to a proper law faculty (complete with Klix coffee machine and last week's *Independent*); elsewhere, leather sofas and acres of plate glass may convince you you've strayed into the offices of a City firm. Given the importance of IT to the LPC course in general, it might be worth considering whether the institution offers endless vistas of the latest flat screens or a few dusty typewriters in a basement. A large institution may appeal to students keen to be streamlined through the system while maintaining desired anonymity. Conversely, the intimacy of smaller classes and easily accessible tutors may tip the scales in favour of a smaller institution.

- **Atmosphere and direction:** Some institutions are well known to attract Oxbridge types destined to be City high-flyers, while others cultivate the talents of those headed for regional practice. Still others purport to offer a mix of students so that the commercially minded can mingle with future high street solicitors. Consider which flavour of LPC you're after. Some providers offer LPCs with a noticeably corporate slant, both in the electives available and the manner in which the compulsories are taught; at other providers you can experience an LPC more suited to the high street. Elsewhere, students are offered several choices of direction all under one roof.

- **Tactics:** Some of the most popular institutions require you to put them as first choice on the LawCabs application form. We have included this type of information on the LPC providers table on our website. Check also whether your university, GDL provider or law firm has an agreement or relationship with a provider.

- **Money and fees:** Fees vary and so do the institutions' policies on the inclusion of the cost of textbooks and Law Society membership, etc. Even if you have sponsorship from a law firm, living expenses still need to be taken into account. The cost of living in London especially can be a nasty shock if you haven't lived there before.

- **Location:** Plenty of students find that tight finances restrict their choice of school. Living at home will save you a packet... if you can stand it. If you're lucky enough to be able to strike out on your own, it's worth considering what you like or don't like about your university or GDL provider and whether you want to prolong your undergraduate experience or escape it. Be aware that certain LPC providers are dominated by graduates of local universities. When weighing up providers in large cities, find out whether the campus is slap-bang in the city centre or out on the ring road. In London, consider whether you'd prefer to be near the bright lights of Soho or the distinguished fields of Gray's Inn.

- **Social mix and social life:** Studenty cities such as Nottingham and Bristol are always a lot of fun, but the bright lights of the capital may be irresistible. Experience tells us that compared to those in other cities, students in London tend to slink off the moment classes end.

the lowdown on the providers

In past editions we chose to write features on those LPC providers that were rated as 'Excellent' or 'Very Good' by the Law Society. The Society has now changed the way in which it grades providers and is no longer awarding a simple, single grade. Instead, providers are graded on six different elements, with marks ranging from 'commendable practice' through 'confidence in the provision' to 'failure to meet the required level of provision'.

The new grades will not be known for all providers for another year, effectively leaving students looking at two different grading systems.

We have decided not to use Law Society grades to identify the best providers for inclusion in the guide this year. Instead, we have included detailed features on the biggest providers, with 150 or more total LPC students, and shorter snapshots of smaller providers.

On our website you will find a table detailing all of the providers and allowing a comparison of their fees, student numbers, available option subjects and useful tips for applicants.

bpp overview

BPP's reputation as the Big Kahuna of City-oriented LPC providers is well founded. Students' first impressions are of a *"very professional," "slick operation,"* as evidenced by the wireless networking and laptop loan system. All this impressive kit must cost a bundle, and unsurprisingly, since BPP is the priciest of LPC providers, students were quick to note that the course is *"very expensive."* Its price tag clearly isn't a problem for the City firms which send their trainees exclusively to BPP's Holborn campus. These include Macfarlanes, Simmons & Simmons, Freshfields, Norton Rose, Slaughter and May, Herbert Smith and Lovells. In addition, BPP's high-flying atmosphere often attracts swathes of Oxbridge graduates and future corporate legal eagles. Teachers wear suits, and students in similar attire are a common sight. BPP in London does deserve its City reputation, but in Leeds and Manchester the student population is noticeably more diverse in career aspirations. BPP is very much in the business of getting students over the exam hurdle: *"They prepare students to pass exams. They don't stimulate people to think or analyse things too much."* In the midst of all this *"slick machinery,"* students are provided with *"everything they need,"* including copious handouts, textbooks, manuals and DVDs. The course is so slick that one of our sources said it is *"a bit too seamless; there's no character or fun about it at all."* Unfortunately, it is doubtful whether there is much fun to be had on any LPC course, given the *"formulaic"* nature of its procedural aspects, but students at BPP are generally happy to be *"spoon-fed"* by *"intelligent lecturers."*

From September 2007, BPP began trialling 'optional lectures' on the LPC. Students can still attend live lectures, but lectures are also available via MP3 download. BPP expects that most students will still choose to attend lectures in person, but will find the downloaded lectures a godsend for going over tricky bits and for revision crunch time. If all goes well, expect optional lectures to become a regular fixture on the course. Students have classes four days a week, timetabled between 9am and 5.30pm, with one day off for private study or, for the less diligent, watching daytime telly. Closed-book exams mean students *"very much have to understand and really get to grips with the issues." "It forces you to learn things."* BPP expects the learning to start straight away, before students even finish their pre-LPC holidays, with a whopping 100-plus pages of reading. However, for the majority of the year you won't be left to contemplate the impact of the Companies Act 2006 on your own; each student is allocated a personal tutor at the beginning of the year. In the spirit of its results-focused mentality, BPP offers mock tests and revision classes before exams *"which basically tell you what will be in the exam,"* so by the time the real thing rolls around, students feel well prepared.

Among those without City training contracts or deep pockets, a lucky few can profit from BPP's scholarships for disadvantaged students. If you don't have a training contract and don't manage to secure one of the sought-after scholarships, you can still benefit from BPP's dedicated careers service, which sounds to us to have developed rather an obsession with securing training contracts for students. According to our sources: *"They go out of their way completely to help stu-*

dents to find training contracts." BPP also offers an unusually broad range of pro bono activities, including a legal advice clinic, a human rights unit and IP projects which run out of all four centres. Apparently, if you have a particular yearning to engage in pro bono in an area not currently covered by BPP, the director of the programme will find you a project, even in something as out-there as space law. To further beef up your CV, BPP has now won degree-awarding powers. From 2008 the LPC can be topped up with an LLM, while those who complete their GDL and LPC at the school will be able to claim an LLB.

bpp law school, leeds

Number of places: 432 (full-time and part-time)

BPP's Leeds building seems to be covered with almost as much glass as its Holborn colleague. Students on the course say they're *"so impressed by the facilities,"* as well as the conveniently central location *"right next to the train station."* According to students, *"lots of tutors are ex-commercial practitioners"* and provide *"top-notch teaching."* BPP's Leeds centre boasts the north's only IP Centre of Excellence, in which students can assist local businesses and individuals to protect their IP rights. Socially, it is far from grim up north. The city of Leeds has plenty of after-hours fun to offer students, and the *"really tight social group"* of Leeds students clearly make the best use of their day off each week with a *"Big Wednesday"* ending in *"a hangover on Thursday."*

bpp law school, london

Number of places: 1080 full-time, 288 part-time (Holborn); 230 full-time, 76 part-time (Waterloo)

London is where BPP really merits its City reputation. From the leather orchids in reception to the massive expanses of glass, it clearly mimics the environment towards which most of its students are headed. As such, students say it lacks broad diversity, both in terms of teaching styles

and the range of firms at which students are hoping to train. One source advised: *"I'd recommend it if you're planning to work for a big City law firm in a corporate or commercial environment, but not for smaller firms or family/criminal/probate work. Those subjects are taught very briefly at BPP and they're not promoted at all."* Such specialisation isn't necessarily a bad thing, particularly if you know you want to be a cog in the wheel of a multimillion-pound deal rather than the main point of contact for a middle-income client seeking a divorce. With well over one thousand LPC students, it is understandable that the course feels *"fairly large"* and *"kind of impersonal."* The sheer numbers mean it can feel like a *"City churn-out machine."* Indeed, the course has grown so much over the past few years that now Waterloo houses the overspill of some 300 LPC students who came to the course a bit too late to secure coveted spots at Holborn. Students report that the quality of teaching is occasionally *"variable,"* but overall *"very good."* *"There are lots of young tutors who are on your level,"* most, if not all, of whom are *"ex-City."* As is often the case in institutions with so many students, resources are occasionally stretched. One student noted that Holborn *"maybe could do with a few more computers."* Overall, however, students praised the *"fantastic materials"* and *"loads of support"* on offer. For those students who don't rush off to catch a commuter train as soon as classes end, the social life at BPP seems quite respectable. Holborn's Red Lion Street location boasts a wealth of bars, the most popular among BPP students being the Square Pig. Students tend to stick to groups of friends from previous courses, from workshops or who have training contracts at the same firms, so cliques inevitably form. One student summed up the social scene as displaying *"a little bit of cliquishness from big-firm trainees,"* but *"it's also easy to find people who aren't part of that."* In addition to the pro bono projects offered at all of

BPP's centres, London has an environmental law clinic, a programme for students to shadow solicitors at local law centres and projects enabling students with foreign language skills to provide legal translation services.

bpp law school, manchester

Number of places: 360 full-time, 108 part-time

Manchester is the newest feather in BPP's cap, having opened in September 2005. Its foray onto the Mancunian legal stage caused a flurry among other northern LPC providers, some of the tutors and potential students of which defected to the newest gun in town. The law school is situated in a *"prime location"* in the centre of the city, handy for commuting students. Matching the young premises are *"tutors fresh out of practice."* Students also appreciate that *"everything is done in lots of detail"* using *"good supporting materials."* Like all of BPP's campuses, Manchester is kitted out with hi-tech equipment and modern decor. Any students who fancy a night out are well provided for by the profusion of bars, clubs, restaurants and music venues in Manchester.

bristol institute of legal practice at uwe

Number of places: 400 (full-time and part-time)

A proud holder of 'Excellent' and, more recently, 'commendable' ratings from the Law Society since 1995, UWE continues to provide *"absolutely top-class"* tuition. The tutors are all qualified solicitors or barristers, and students say they really make an effort to get to know those they teach. Both the course and its students are impressively diverse. At UWE, *"there is a mix of people with a broad age range and different career paths"* and *"not as many people are going to magic circle or City firms."* Instead, students tend to go on to train at almost every type of firm under the sun, from small South Coast operations to the big cheeses in Bristol to niche London firms to

national and international giants. Perhaps UWE attracts such diversity because its students have access to one of the widest ranges of LPC electives in the country. UWE is the only provider to offer a charity law elective, and students can also sample the delights of media and entertainment law, banking and capital markets and the aptly named family breakdown elective. The large law library is superior and there are *"plenty of books and resources"* to go around. Students can supplement their LPC qualification with an LLM. As the LPC course falls under the UWE umbrella, students do feel like they are *"back at university."* They can even live in the newly constructed student village, with free Internet access and freeview TV channels. However, there's no getting away from the fact that UWE is *"far away from the city centre, up by the M4."* As such, *"the social aspect is not as good."* Those who don't live in campus accommodation often tend to drive, so are more likely to head home when classes end rather than hang round to socialise on campus. For the students who do venture into the city centre of an evening, Bristol offers a legendary amount of establishments to suit almost every mood.

cardiff law school

Number of places: 180 full-time

Cardiff's LPC is firmly rooted in its Welsh landscape. It's also consistently rated highly by the Law Society. Home to many a Welsh student taking advantage of their parents' hospitality, the course also boasts *"a significant proportion of Cardiff grads."* It would be difficult not to notice the course's *"tie with the local community"* and *"strong focus on being in Wales."* There is even a short course available on advocacy in Welsh. Students often cite not being stuck in the big smoke as a major draw. Exchanging sardine-like Tube journeys and overpriced pints for the beauties of Cardiff Bay is a life choice that many Cardiff students are thrilled to make. Most of the teaching rooms, along with the library and computer facilities, are situated in a purpose-built extension of the Law School. The refurbished Graduate Building houses additional teaching rooms, mock courtrooms, a student common room and a cyber café. Classrooms are equipped with interactive smartboards, which save what is written on them and can link to websites to illustrate the discussion. With only 180 students, Cardiff is *"a small institution with a small intake, so you get more one-on-one time with tutors."* The course prides itself on offering *"a high level of interaction"* between tutors and students, which can translate to *"a lot of hand-holding."* As well as being able to chat to any of the tutors, each student is allocated a personal tutor. Such help is sometimes necessary, since students admit it is an *"intensive"* and *"tough course."* You needn't be anxious about asking for a bit of extra help, since the course's *"approachable staff"* are reportedly *"very understanding if you ever have any problems."* The administration seems to genuinely listen to students, not least via the medium of the staff/student panel, which meets three times a year and provides a forum for student concerns. Among such a small student population, soon *"everyone's face becomes familiar."* This familiarity certainly boosts Cardiff's social life. With balls, pub quizzes and frequent Friday nights out, students say the course is *"very good socially."* For those without training contracts, Cardiff's relationships with local law firms mean students are guaranteed one-week voluntary work placements at the beginning of the year. Around 50% of students take up the opportunity to work at firms ranging from large commercial players like Eversheds to one-partner high street firms. Local authorities, the Patent Office and the Welsh Assembly also participate in the scheme, so almost every taste is catered for. That should be enough to tip the scales in Cardiff's favour for any student with Welsh leanings, but be advised that Cardiff receives significantly more applications than it has places and favours students who list it as their first choice.

city law school
(formerly inns of court school of law)
Number of places: 176 full-time

Even under its new moniker as City Law School, this London institution continues to be a magnet for would-be barristers. However, it also caters for prospective solicitors seeking a relatively small intake. Since its inception seven years ago, City's LPC has consistently been ranked as 'Excellent' and, most recently, 'commendable' by the Law Society. City places a much greater emphasis than other providers on the use of primary sources rather than manuals tailored to LPC students, so arguably City LPC students are better prepared for practice, or at least know their way around Blackstone's. Even amidst the awe-inspiring surrounds of historic Gray's Inn, students admitted that the LPC sometimes seems like *"a colossal box-ticking waste of time."* Students who despair of the course's necessary tedium are somewhat mollified by City's *"very good"* tutors. Previously, students had said the course seemed *"too rigid"* because comparatively few electives were offered. However, City is now improving its elective offerings, with new private client and commercial dispute resolution options. Overall, students are *"very impressed"* by City's *"quite intimate"* LPC offering. During the period when the compulsory subjects are taught, students can choose between morning or afternoon sessions and have at least one day off per week. There are plenty of pro bono options for the altruistic student or for those whose CVs need a little boost. Students can choose from Streetlaw, the Blackfriars Settlement clinic, the Liberty letters clinic, general evening and employment advice clinics and a partnership programme with a range of legal advice centres and charities.

college of law overview

The College of Law seems to be driving the bandwagon that many other providers are keen to jump on. It casts the widest geographical net of all, with branches in Birmingham, Chester, York and Guildford, as well as two in London. As the longest-running provider of vocational education to prospective solicitors, it is well respected and has consistently garnered high rankings from the Law Society and the SRA. On the back of its prestigious reputation, COL was given degree-awarding powers in 2006. Students who complete both the GDL and LPC at COL now receive an LLB. From 2008, LPC students can receive an LLM by taking additional modules and completing a final assignment.

The College of Law is perceived as *"the best of the generalists"* because it caters for students of varying legal persuasions, offering corporate, commercial and private and public legal services study routes. Each route features the same law and procedure, but with case studies relevant to the particular route and with a variety of applicable electives. COL also runs the LPC+ programme, which offers firm-specific electives to future trainees of Baker & McKenzie, Barlow Lyde & Gilbert, Berwin Leighton Paisner, Cobbetts and Halliwells. Allen & Overy, Clifford Chance and Linklaters all send their trainees to complete a firm-specific course at COL's Moorgate centre.

Generally students find the course to be less of an intellectual challenge than a *"cramming exercise." "The work isn't difficult but the sheer quantity is a bit of a shock."* Students say they're *"spoon-fed"* through *"very good materials and handouts"* and *"very practical small group workshops."* Assessments take place throughout the year, and students appreciate that exams are open book, so *"you just need to know to flick to the right section of your notes and textbooks."* However, given the quantity of information students are expected to *"regurgitate"* in a relatively short amount of exam time, you still need to know your stuff. Befitting its status as a registered charity, the College of Law boasts a well-developed pro bono programme offering students a broad variety of rewarding and potentially CV-enhancing opportunities. Options vary by location, but usually include advice centres, not-for-profit placements and Streetlaw.

Students have ten hours of small-group tutorials each week to elaborate on material introduced in CD-ROM lectures, which are supposed to be viewed for four to six hours per week, depending on how often you pause the programme to jot down some notes or make a cup of tea. In addition to a large slice of preparatory reading, group assignments and research, students complete online multiple-choice exercises before each tutorial, which are *"a good way of making sure you have actually read what you think you've read."* Students are divided as to how the CD-ROM lectures, dubbed i-tutorials, compare to live lectures. Some note the benefit of being able to *"watch them again and again,"* which is particularly useful for getting to grips with *"the mathematical areas of accounting procedures."* They also prove handy when revision begins in earnest. However, others notice the lack of *"face-to-face contact." "It's so unengaging"* and *"you can't ask questions."* According to COL's research, students retain more information watching an i-tutorial than they do sitting in a lecture. The College maintains that its agenda is to prepare students for the daily realities of practice. So i-tutorials have replaced lectures because the lecture set-up bears no relation to practice. At the larger centres, students' ability to choose morning or afternoon sessions is now a distant memory, as the College now expects students to study on roughly a 9am-5pm timetable for four days a week, more in line with regular working hours. However, others still offer students some choice as to the days and times they are expected to attend. In addition to being in line with the realities of practice, COL's LPC also seems to be in sync with the way the entire LPC is heading, if the SRA has its way. Whenever the anticipated LPC reforms come into play, it is clear that the LPC will become much more modularised and more similar to the Australian system of legal training. With its new flat-pack-style teaching, COL will be well placed to implement the new LPC structure and may even be able to export its course to wannabe UK solicitors around the world.

college of law, birmingham
Number of places: 528 full-time, 200 part-time
No longer the newest COL centre on the block since Moorgate opened its doors in 2006, the Birmingham centre has clearly settled into its stride, scoring commendable practice ratings across the board on the Law Society's most recent visit. The relatively new premises are *"quite nice and modern with good IT facilities and classrooms."* Teaching is *"generally good and sometimes exceptional."* Students say the Jewellery Quarter location, *"on the edge of an industrial area,"* tends to deaden social life a bit and can even feel *"a bit scary if you're wandering round late at night."* Clearly the promised 'Kirstie and Phil effect' has yet to materialise in this particular neighbourhood. Organised social events abound, however. These include numerous sports, an annual quiz night for students and staff, student balls, student societies and Birmingham Trainee Solicitors Society events.

college of law, chester
Number of places: 600 full-time, 160 part-time
We heard more than one cry of *"I love it"* when asking students about the Chester campus. The most bucolic of the centres, Chester is also the most remote at almost two miles outside the city. Many students commute from Manchester, Liverpool and even Wales. With its walled orchard and *"very quiet, collegey feel,"* the Chester campus is about as far from the noisy traffic and distracting hubbub of London as an LPC student can get. However, this peaceful contentment comes at the price of students' social lives: *"Chester is beautiful but it's actually quite dull. The nightlife is rubbish."* Despite the lack of nearby drinking establishments, students do manage the odd *"sports day and drinking night."* Quite a few people who begin the LPC at Chester don't yet have training contracts, so the *"great," "helpful"* careers service is a very useful resource. *"They actually help you find what kind of firm you are suited to, as opposed to mailshotting everyone."*

college of law, guildford
Number of places: 720 full-time, 240 part-time
The leafy, *"picturesque"* environs of the Guildford campus provide students with a pleasant distraction from the *"relatively dry"* course. Students note how Guildford's *"campus feel"* and *"tranquil atmosphere"* help them tackle the LPC: *"Being away from the hustle and bustle of London is conducive to studying."* Indeed, there is many a grassy knoll on which students can while away the hours, either diligently memorising their notes or procrastinating with friends from workshops. It isn't just the location that makes students feel at home; there is also *"a big social side"* and, for a break from studying, *"tennis courts, hockey and other sports."* We also spotted a squash court and a croquet lawn, not to mention the Italian sunken garden. Lest you begin to think you've strayed into an E.M. Forster novel, we hasten to add that Guildford is only a short train ride away from London. However, students say there are enough *"nice shops and bars"* in the local area to keep them occupied without having to journey to the capital. We heard no complaints about the resources available, and students confirmed that *"there are loads of computers"* on which to watch

those all-important i-tutorials. Generally, *"tutors are very approachable"* and students praise the teaching as being *"very good on the whole."*

college of law, london
(bloomsbury and moorgate)
Number of places: 1200 full-time, 360 part-time (Bloomsbury); 1040 full-time, 100 part-time (Moorgate)

Students who choose the College of Law as their preferred LPC institution often do so because they think it offers a more *"laid-back atmosphere"* than the other major London provider. The behemoth of LPC providers, the sheer number of students passing through the College's London halls can promote a distinct whiff of the *"sausage factory."* The large student body means that at busy times Store Street seems to *"struggle for space."* According to students, it appears that *"they are clearly outgrowing the building"* after 15 years in Bloomsbury. *"In the library it is often a struggle to find a seat"* and *"IT resources are slightly stretched."* However, *"the classes are well run"* and *"there is a good support network of tutors."* The Bloomsbury campus is a *"very social location, right in the middle of central London."* Despite the proximity to all manner of pubs, clubs and bars, given the impression that *"there are thousands of people on the LPC,"* social circles are generally limited to workshop groups.

Whereas Store Street is home to students on the commercial and private and public legal services routes, the new Moorgate location is an exclusively corporate domain. Overlooking Bunhill Fields and handily close to Linklaters, one of its three magic circle patrons, Moorgate boasts 75,000 square feet of brand-spanking new facilities, including plasma screens, state-of-the-art teaching technology and even showers. Students have access to a Costa Coffee in the cafe, perhaps to acclimate them to the practice of taking their meals in-house during those future all-nighters.

college of law, york
Number of places: 504 full-time, 160 part-time

Unlike some of its more southerly colleagues, in York *"space is not an issue."* With a campus boasting 12 acres of private parkland, we can see why. York and Guildford seem to be running neck and neck in the competition for the prettiest campus and the happiest students. According to them, *"the support network is very good"* and *"it's small and very friendly, a bit like a school."* Even the most exemplary tutor can't always make the LPC a barrel of laughs, but in York students have additional, rather unusual means of counteracting boredom: *"If you get bored in a session there are always a few horses knocking past the window"* on the adjacent racetrack. Students *"all live around South Bank in York so everyone knows everyone."* Many participate in the *"really active social life,"* which involves taking advantage of the *"rugby pitches, tennis courts and netball teams"* as well as the many nearby pubs. Of those who have training contracts, there is a *"network of people at different firms,"* including several Leeds firms and a good mix of large regional and national firms. As a city, York is a beautiful, historic place still ringed by its original Roman walls. Beyond its cultural value, and much closer to the hearts of many students, is that the location means they can live at home, saving up their pennies for the many nights out. *"It's an affordable, studenty place to be."*

de montfort university
Number of places: 100 full-time, 130 part-time

For those who can't bear to leave Leicestershire or who simply want an inexpensive LPC near to home, De Montfort's course is a popular choice. On its last Law Society visit, De Montfort received grades of 'commendable practice' in all but one category, and they hope to improve their lagging learning resources mark by moving the LPC course to new city centre premises in September 2010. The £35m project to create Magazine

Square, complete with a massive new energy-efficient building, plans to house the entire Faculty of Business and Law and will include large lecture theatres, a mock courtroom, an integrated law library and new computing facilities. De Montfort already relies on Blackboard e-learning to provide students with extra practice questions for technical subjects like accounts, and plans are in the works to increase the amount of online multiple-choice questions available to students before workshops. De Montfort is particularly well known for its large cohort of part-time LPC students, who make up over half of the entire LPC student population. The part-time course is conducted via open learning, with students visiting the campus for one three-day weekend each month. The open learning LPC is run in conjunction with the Institute of Legal Executives Tutorial College, and many ILEX-qualified students study the LPC via this route. For those students without training contracts, there are several practitioner evenings each year, which enable students to network with practising solicitors and get the low-down from trainees who studied at De Montfort. This provider is keen to improve its pro bono opportunities, so in addition to a law clinic, where students can practise giving advice, there are also a few summer placements with the City Council and links with local charities.

leeds metropolitan university
Number of places: 105 full-time, 45 part-time
Former LPC students say that Leeds Met's LPC is *"very good"* and *"a brilliant course."* The Law Society largely agrees with that assessment, having bestowed 'commendable practice' grades in five of the six categories, with learning resources as the exception. Despite Leeds Met's recent move to modern new premises in the city's business district, the Law Society's assessment said that improvements could be made regarding the

number of computers, number of up-to-date library books, amount of study space and availability of an LPC common room at Cloth Hall Court. However, the location scores high marks with students, who say *"the new city centre location is fabulous."* Apart from a few practical issues, Leeds Met's course offers a good option for students who are wedded to the area or who want a solid LPC course without the rather intimidating fees of other providers. Befitting the ambitions of many of its students, Leeds Met offers several non-commercial electives, as well as some commercial electives, including private acquisitions. The housing and competition law electives only run if there is sufficient student demand. Some of the tutors are local practitioners, and students praise them as being *"so easy to approach."* Students can also benefit from Leeds Met's professional mentor scheme, which partners students with solicitors from firms and in-house legal teams in Leeds and West Yorkshire, including Pinsent Masons, Irwin Mitchell, Walker Morris, Lupton Fawcett, Addleshaw Goddard, Berwins and Clarion. The criminally minded can be paired up with a solicitor in the local Crown Prosecution Service. As an added CV bonus, students can top up their LPC with an LLM by completing a dissertation.

london metropolitan university
Number of places: 110 full-time, 100 part-time
As one of the largest universities in the UK after its 2002 merger, London Met is a big player in the London provider stakes for professional and vocational qualifications. Many students who want to be in London during their LPC but don't want to fork out quite so much money choose to study at London Met. The course is housed at the Goulston Street campus in Aldgate East, along with the rest of the law, governance and international relations department. Built in 2004, Goulston Street boasts the ubiquitous glass

frontage, concrete walls and vestibule atrium that seem to be prerequisites for any new London LPC premises. There are classrooms aplenty, a mock courtroom and a 175-seat lecture theatre, as well as wireless Internet access. The law library is located in nearby Calcutta House. London Met's part-time LPC is big business for the provider, and is offered on both day and evening bases. London Met clearly has designs to capitalise on the large market of part-timers looking for an inexpensive LPC course. In September 2007, it began a new part-time evening LPC at Canary Wharf, which reportedly aims to attract paralegals working at investment banks in the area. Both Aldgate East and Canary Wharf are home to a multitude of City law firms, but London Met's students often go on to other types of training contracts, at West End or high street firms or in local government. LPC diplomates can choose to top-up their qualification with an LLM by studying for an additional year on a part-time basis.

manchester metropolitan university
Number of places: 168 full-time, 64 part-time

Only *"200 yards down the road"* from BPP, on the other side of the Mancunian Way, Manchester Metropolitan University offers a much cheaper, university-affiliated LPC option on a course rated 'commendable' across the board. When the BPP giant stepped onto the Manchester scene in 2005, MMU felt the impact tremors, losing staff and potential students. Students at the time noticed the staffing and timetabling problems that followed, but we are happy to report that MMU seems to have weathered the BPP storm and is now trying to carve a new niche for itself as the Manchester LPC provider offering a cheap and cheerfully intimate course with enough frills on to make many a BPP hopeful think twice. Among the new bells and whistles to be introduced are a new pro bono initiative, online lectures for tricky subjects like accounts and revenue law and podcasts from potential employers offering interview hints and tips. The law school's facilities are pretty impressive and rather futuristic; sky-walk bridges stretch across the central 'sky well' area to reach double-height lecture theatres. In addition to the full-time LPC, MMU is keen to bulk up its part-time spaces as much as the SRA will allow in order to make best use of the sacks of applications they receive for their well-established part-time LPC. Classes are generally held for four full days a week, although MMU does offer a morning-only timetable to people with childcare issues or an especially long commute. The vast majority of MMU students have a connection to the North West, and about half completed their undergraduate degrees at MMU. Aside from their loyalty to the university, we're pretty sure that the £500 reduction in LPC course fees for MMU grads is effective persuasion. At the end of the LPC, about half of MMU's students go on to training contracts, and the majority of the rest find gainful employment in a legal-related job. MMU's aim is to service the legal study needs of the North West, so it's perhaps no surprise that MMUers often go on to training contracts in-house, at local niche firms, on the high street or in local government. Socially, MMU is *"integrated with the university,"* so there is no shortage of social opportunities. There is also a joint LPC/BVC social committee that organises charitable events as well as the odd drinks night. MMU has close links with the Black Solicitors' Network and the local Trainee Solicitors' Group, both of which sponsor social and professional events.

nottingham law school overview
The original Nottingham Law School has long been a favourite destination among LPC students for its lofty reputation and stellar social scene. In 2007, Nottingham joined up with US educational giant Kaplan to launch a new London LPC provider, dubbed Nottingham at Kaplan. The plan

is that Nottingham's excellent reputation combined with Kaplan's renown on the wider international stage will fuel the rise of Nottingham at Kaplan to rival the big players in the capital.

Nottingham's remit is to produce people who think commercially, so students are taught that even apparently non-commercial electives like family or social welfare law have a commercial aspect. One source observed: *"The teachers focused on business law and the skills we needed to know to be business-focused."* Given the course's commercial focus, it is appropriate that Nottingham's tutors have previously practised in major corporate and commercial firms. The theme that unifies all LPC courses is a dry procedural element, and Nottingham's is no different. One source described it as *"a document-heavy course with quite a lot to trawl through."* However, the dull bits are made easier to swallow by *"very lovely and clever tutors who give you real-life examples to relate to."* An added bonus is that each student is allocated a personal tutor at the start of the course, and the relationship isn't just a token gesture; students are actually required to keep in contact with their personal tutors, so even those who begrudge help will get a bit. Classes are timetabled for four full days of study each week. Although exams are nominally open-book, the only materials allowed into the exam room are primary sources, not notes. The method must work pretty well, since Nottingham's pass rates are usually about 95%. Outside the classroom, students can learn some useful non-law skills through subsidised language training. Students who complete both the GDL and LPC at Nottingham receive an LLB.

nottingham law school, nottingham
Number of places: 650 full-time, 90 part-time
When asked for his views on what's new in Nottingham this year, Bob White, the rather characterful course director, was quick to point out that *"there hasn't been a murder in Nottingham for a while, and there are fewer knives and guns than last year."* While Nottingham does have a somewhat rough reputation, its students are savvy enough to steer clear of *"dodgy areas."* Instead, students can spend their evenings in the pro bono clinic, interviewing and writing letters for *"real people."* Once students have enough experience under their belt, they can move forward to hearings. For students who prefer the FT to the Big Issue, Nottingham also offers a commercial pro bono clinic, in which student volunteers assist start-up businesses. Although Nottingham adamantly insists on students *"being taught by humans,"* it recently began videoing its lectures and posting them online immediately afterwards to give students the opportunity to watch lectures online either in lieu of attendance in person or for revision purposes, as *"you can go through the whole course in a couple of hours."* However, given Nottingham's preference for face-to-face tuition, it seems unlikely that online lectures will become anything more than secondary to the live delivery of lecture material. Bob White charmingly expressed Nottingham's stance on the e-learning issue: *"Around here it's not a ghost town because we're all out watching our computer screens at home. There's an indefinable but crucial feeling of community."* That sense of community extends to the *"wicked"* social scene. Nottingham's heady social brew seems to be based on the combination of *"a university feel"* and the fact that *"it's a reasonably compact city"* with *"a million places to go as a student."* Even though Nottingham is a relatively cheap city, the drinks budget goes even further because *"lots of people have already got training contracts with big firms in London, so they have a bit of money to spend."* Students readily acknowledge *"a high density of Oxbridge students"* on the course, as well as *"lots of like-minded people who work hard and play hard."* Perhaps it is the students them-

selves, as much as the course structure, that give Nottingham's LPC *"a good feel – it's professional but not too pressurised."*

nottingham at kaplan law school
Number of places: 300 full-time

At the time of writing, Nottingham at Kaplan was about to embark on its first year of LPC providership, so we can't give you any juicy comments from former students. However, we can reveal that in its freshman year it had already secured an exclusive deal with Mayer Brown and bagged a des res next to the Thames near London Bridge and Borough Market. Nottingham Law School is primarily responsible for providing the course structure, materials and tutors; Kaplan is the moneyman behind the project. Despite rumours to the contrary, we are told the two are contractually obligated to stick together for at least the next 15 years. Students of Nottingham at Kaplan receive exactly the same tuition as those on the established and respected Nottingham course. However, we did spot a few differences between the two campuses. For instance, while Nottingham is still fine-tuning its IT, Kaplan already has advanced online learning systems in place. The course has a 'bridge to practice' element, which aims to boost commercial awareness during the electives period. For the unsponsored student, Kaplan has a London-only scholarship programme. Offered only to the two most exemplary candidates who write the best 1,000-word essays on a current legal topic, these scholarships may seem rarer than hen's teeth, but they are up for grabs if you can go the distance to secure them. In addition to the regular course, future Mayer Brown trainees will receive extra training geared towards their firm's practice. For instance, they will learn a bit about US law to reflect Mayer Brown's cross-Atlantic origins. We also have it on good authority that a pro bono programme like the one at Nottingham should be up and running by 2008.

oxford institute of legal practice
Number of places: 303 full-time, 50 part-time

OXILP takes full advantage of its coveted Oxford location to attract students from the Thames Valley or those former Oxonians who still want to live among the city's dreaming spires. Since OXILP was divested of its links with City firms in 2006, its non-City bound students no longer need fear the embarrassment of admitting more regional ambitions, unlike a former student under the old City regime, who recalled: *"It was mostly magic circle students. They stared at me blankly when I said I wasn't going there."* Instead, the new incarnation of OXILP offers a broad commercial LPC taught by an even split of ex-City and ex-regional firm tutors and the institute is home to plenty of students headed to large regional firms. Despite the course's improved breadth, students say that only *"a restrictive number of electives"* are offered, two-thirds of which are commercial. Students have four days of classes, the exact days and times of which change week to week. Exams are open book. At OXILP, *"students are expected to be more autonomous"* than at other *"really spoon-fed"* providers. Students weren't sure whether this was because OXILP tries to build up their self-reliance or because the course itself is *"less well-organised."* Our overall impression from students' comments is that teaching standards vary. More than one student told us that they felt some tutors *"weren't knowledgeable enough. When you asked questions beyond what they'd prepared for the lesson they just didn't know."* Yet other tutors were praised as being *"fantastic."* Despite the institution's small size, students report that the majority of their friendships are formed within the boundaries of seminar groups. Within those circles, the social scene is *"generally quite good."* *"We all met up for drinks after seminars."* Additionally, there are quiz nights, summer boat trips and reasonably well-attended club nights. A handy tip for those who fancy OXILP: it gives priority to applicants who put it as their first choice on the application form.

university of central england, birmingham

Number of places: 120 full-time, 30 part-time

Although UCE is the oldest LPC provider in Birmingham, this is the first year we've included them, spurred on by their recent receipt of 'commendable' rankings from the Law Society. The biggest fish of Birmingham's LPC providers is clearly the College of Law, but UCE appeals to students because of its significantly lower fees. Any fan of TV property shows will tell you that to get a house on a smaller budget you have to sacrifice a bit on the location, and this mantra certainly rings true for students at UCE. In exchange for saving over £2,000, they have to trek out to UCE's Perry Barr campus three miles outside Birmingham city centre. There are local buses and half-hourly trains to Perry Barr from Birmingham New Street. Once on campus, students have access to a careers tutor as well as a personal tutor. For those without training contracts, there's also a mentoring scheme which pairs students with local solicitors. UCE acknowledges that most of its students will be headed to small or medium-sized commercial firms or high street firms rather than big City giants, and its broad spread of electives reflects this. Students can choose from commercial electives like mergers and acquisitions and commercial property, as well as non-commercial electives like welfare and immigration. There is also an EU law elective on offer. Some parts of the campus are hooked up for wireless Internet access, and students can access some course materials online through the charmingly named Moodle, UCE's e-learning platform.

university of northumbria

Number of places: 120 full-time, 50 part-time

Northumbria is one of only two institutions to offer a degree which exempts students from the LPC. Instead, students on Northumbria's four-year LLB (Hons) course cover the LPC subjects during their degree, so they are qualified to begin training contracts straight after graduation. Of those who choose to go down the traditional route, many students are initially attracted to Northumbria's LPC because it is one of the cheapest providers to have scored full commendable practice rankings from the Law Society. Even though the course fees are relatively easy on the wallet, the School of Law, buoyed by university backing, has invested serious money to bring the facilities bang up-to-date. In September 2007, the entire School of Law moved to impressive new premises in central Newcastle. Purpose-built at a cost of about £100m, we can't help but think the design looks rather pleasingly like an office building surrounded by a giant slinky. Clearly the school hasn't scrimped on providing *"a 21st century design for a 21st century university for those who wish to experience 21st century learning."* Apparently, 21st century learning includes wireless Internet access, high-spec mock courtrooms and a brand new cafeteria and library. A good choice for future commercial or high street solicitors, the course *"tries to cater for a wide variety of people."* This broad spectrum approach exposes students to several areas of law and a diverse mix of people, but it occasionally means *"you spend time doing things that aren't very relevant to you."* Students report that the quality of teaching is generally *"good across the board."* One of the most distinctive things about Northumbria is its rather unusual range of electives. In addition to a good range of commercial electives, including a planning and environmental law option, the course offers at least six options to aspiring high streeters, including mental health law, child care law, law and the elderly client and the student law office. Those who opt for the student law office, or SLO, spend time advising law centre clients, drafting court documents and briefing counsel in lieu of sitting in a lecture. Instead of an exam, students submit a portfolio of practical work. It sounds like an interesting option to us, and former students say the SLO *"looks attractive on your CV and gets you used to speaking to people."* Conscious of the need to help its students compete in the crowded legal job marketplace, Northumbria also enables LPC students to concurrently top up their qualification with an LLM in Legal Practice.

university of sheffield
Number of places: 180 full-time

Students on Sheffield's LPC still feel very much a part of the university. In fact, many of them went to university at Sheffield or Sheffield Hallam. Soon students will feel even closer to the university, literally, as the LPC course ups sticks and moves to *"nice historic"* premises closer to the central university facilities. Along with the new digs, students will have wider access to computers and a 24/7 library, just in case they feel a pressing need to consult old Times Law Reports at 3am. Classes are timetabled for four days a week, plus a dreaded 9am Monday lecture. Sheffield is one of the few providers to offer students the choice of morning or afternoon classes. Exams are fully open-book, with students allowed to take in a lever arch file crammed full of notes, study packs, manuals and core texts. On the whole, Sheffield's LPC is *"very well-organised"* and, because of its small size, students enjoy *"a lot of contact with personal tutors."* The course is geared towards allowing students to steer themselves in the direction best suited to their chosen area of practice. As such, Sheffield offers *"a good mix of electives."* The majority of students have some connection to the region, either having lived there or having secured a training contract at a local firm. Tutors tend to have previously practised in high street, regional or national firms. Ex-Irwin Mitchell solicitors are particularly well represented amongst the staff. Sheffield has long-standing links with national firms like Irwin Mitchell, Nabarro and DLA, as well as several Sheffield-only firms. *"There is a body of students that feed into those firms"* straight after finishing the LPC. For students who want to improve their soft skills, Sheffield operates the Freelaw scheme at a local legal advice centre, in which students give initial advice and draft letters for drop-in clients. In terms of culture, Sheffield has no shortage of music venues or trendy, dimly lit bars. It also boasts the largest theatre complex outside London. If students tire of the urban scene, the Peak District and the Pennines are right on their doorstep.

university of staffordshire
Number of places: 110 full-time, 40 part-time

Another well-established LPC provider that draws in students with the promise of a highly rated course and relatively low fees, Staffordshire offers a solid course with a good range of commercial and non-commercial electives. It is especially popular with alumni of the university and locals who want to capitalise on the opportunity to save a few bob by living at home. The *"really practical"* course is *"good at gearing you up for the profession."* There are mock courtrooms, IT facilities and simulated solicitors' offices aplenty, as well as a useful practitioner mentoring scheme which connects students with local solicitors and can even lead to work placements and potentially training contracts. Pro bono opportunities include Streetlaw, as well as other community-cased programmes. LPC students can also upgrade their diploma to an LLM. The campus is located in Stoke-on-Trent, birthplace of Robbie Williams and famous for its pottery industry. Although Stoke isn't the liveliest of places, the campus is near to the nightclubs, bars and restaurants of Hanley, and Alton Towers and the Peak District are only a short drive away.

university of westminster
Number of places: 120 full-time, 64 part-time

The University of Westminster has a distinctly special feel to it, and it isn't just the shopaholic-friendly location just above Oxford Circus. We don't know whether the Oxford Street sales have gone to the administrators' heads, but Westminster now offers £500 discounts on its already inexpensive course fees to all students who passed the LLB with a 2:1 or above, or the CPE with a Commendation or above. Students get a further 3% off if they pay their course fees in full by the end of September. Such deals are enough to entice many a would-be solicitor, but there is much more on offer at this little West End gem. First off, the course received top marks across the board on its latest Law Society visit. With a small intake by London standards, the course is *"smaller, with more of a university feel"* and students report that they really do get *"one-on-one"* time with *"excellent tutors"* who provide *"teaching of a very high standard."* The only negative point we could elicit from students is that *"the computers are a little dated,"* but given that Westminster has now rolled out Blackboard e-learning facilities, we anticipate that improved computers will necessarily follow. Classes are generally held from Monday to Thursday from 10am to 4pm, and exams are open-book. Subject to demand, Westminster offers a broad range of electives, including the rather unusual options of entertainment and media law and e-commerce. The majority of students don't have training contracts when they start, so they are grateful for Westminster's relationships with local law firms, some of whom offer positions exclusively to Westminster students. Students can also impress prospective

employers by gaining experience in the newly opened pro bono clinic, which is currently working on projects dealing with land registration, disability discrimination and IP. A unique selling point for hopeful high street solicitors is that students who take the immigration law elective can also study and sit for Level 1 of the Immigration Accreditation Scheme. Last but not least on the rather long list of Westminster's fringe benefits, LPC diplomates can also receive an LLM in Legal Practice upon completion of a dissertation.

lpc provider snapshots

CENTRAL AND EAST

anglia ruskin university
Number of places: 70 full-time, 30 part-time

Anglia Ruskin scored 'commendable' grades in five out of six areas on its last Law Society visit. The full-time course is run in Chelmsford, while part-timers study in Cambridge. Given the relatively small LPC intake, large group lectures can be delivered to all students at once, and small groups contain a maximum of 15 students. Each student also has a personal tutor. Ten percent of LPC places are initially reserved for disabled students, and the LPC provides credits that can be used towards the LLM qualification. An LPC team competes in the National Client Interviewing Competition every year, and the 2006-07 students managed to bag a trip to the Internationals in Australia.

university of hertfordshire
Number of places: 64 part-time

Hertfordshire only offers the LPC on a part-time basis, and this specialisation has enabled it to perfect its LPC, which received 'commendable' grades across the board from the Law Society. The six elective options are geared to students heading for high street or local commercial practice. Classes are held one full day per week for two years. The law school is located in the centre of charming and well-to-do St Albans in a much more enviable location than the majority of the university's courses. The university is investing heavily in improving electronic resources for all its courses. Students meet with their personal tutors at least twice a year. There are also various pro bono projects on offer, including live client work and Streetlaw community initiatives.

university of wolverhampton
Number of places: 60 full-time, 30 part-time
Students heading to law firms with office park locations can acclimate to park life early, since Wolverhampton's LPC is taught at the Wolverhampton Science Park, one mile outside the city proper. The purpose-built facilities include lots of high-spec technical equipment, including interactive whiteboards, DVD recorders and laser printers. Students use the 'WOLF' e-learning environment, which houses the virtual town of New Molton. Those with physical or learning disabilities receive dedicated support from the university. There is also an established mentoring scheme, a student law clinic and the LPC Plus programme, which invites speakers from legal backgrounds to describe what life as a solicitor is like in practice.

NORTH

liverpool john moores university
Number of places: 72 full-time, 72 part-time
The last Law Society grading visit was in 2004, at which time the course received a 'Good' rating, with the rather amusing caveat that the provider seriously considers *"clocks, additional whiteboards, sound proofing and appropriately sized furniture."* On the full-time course, classes are held for 12 to 15 hours each week, and small groups have a maximum of 18 people. Students are taught in three-hour blocks comprising a one-hour lecture followed by a two-hour workshop, with a fifteen-minute break in-between. The part-time student population is a mix of students who are working full-time, those doing a part-time training contract and legal executives and magistrates' clerks. Full and part-time students are offered a respectable eight elective options. The campus is located in the Liverpool's city centre near the Philharmonic Hall. There is also a solicitor mentor scheme in operation to assist students without training contracts.

university of central lancashire, preston
Number of places: 60 full-time, 48 part-time
UCLan's LPC is *"probably one of the cheapest in the north-west,"* but the smaller price tag doesn't come at the expense of quality teaching, a good range of electives and access to mock courtrooms and the latest IT facilities. One of its best features is its small class size of only 10 to 12 students per small group. UCLan also has an expanding pro bono clinic and a shadowing programme with local solicitors. Many students were undergraduates at UCLan and were probably keen to receive the 20% reduction in LPC fees offered to them as UCLan alumni. The rest of the student body tends to come from Manchester University or have ties to the area.

university of huddersfield
Number of places: 80 full-time, 35 part-time
In September 2007 Huddersfield expanded its postgraduate legal training by offering a new four-year Masters of Law and Practice degree, which exempts students from the LPC. For those who don't want to boldly go where no man has gone before, it still offers the standard LPC in full and part-time options. Elective choice is limited to

seven options which roughly balance general commercial subjects with non-commercial subjects. The course is taught on the Firth Street campus in central Huddersfield. Affordable fees, state-of-the-art IT facilities and a mock courtroom are all well and good, but we think the most impressive and pub-worthy Hud goss is that the Chancellor is none other than the erstwhile *Star Trek* captain and Shakespearean supremo Patrick Stewart.

SOUTH

bournemouth university
Number of places: 96 full-time

Bournemouth's small but beautiful LPC received five 'commendable' rankings from the Law Society, although some students remarked on the variable quality of the teaching. The course is taught on the Talbot Campus in Poole, two miles outside Bournemouth city centre. Many students go on to regional or high street firms, and the available electives reflect this. In addition to hardship grants and bursaries, several scholarships are available for any postgraduate course, including the LPC, and it's not only the brightest who can benefit. In addition to an academic scholarship, there are scholarships for citizenship, musical and sporting prowess, so some of those South Coast aspiring solicitors who also happen to be musical virtuosos or crack clay pigeon shots can get a little help with Bournemouth's already moderately priced LPC fees.

thames valley university
Number of places: 50 full-time

TVU is a huge London institution, so it isn't surprising that it has secured a piece of the LPC action. On its last Law Society visit, TVU received four 'commendable practice' grades. It recently shed its part-time LPC offering, presumably to concentrate on its full-time course. Electives are geared towards the high street and include immigration, housing, family and employment. TVU has a two-day work placement scheme for students to gain experience in firms or local courts. The student population is really diverse and the Ealing campus is within reach of central London, but easiest to get to for students who live in west London or Berkshire.

university of plymouth
Number of places: 120 full-time

In 2006, Plymouth took over Exeter University's LPC. The merged course received four grades of 'commendable practice' from the Law Society and offers a balanced choice of commercial and non-commercial electives. The LPC facilities are very much a part of the university, situated in the Cookworthy Building on campus. The Drake Centre Shopping Mall and Plymouth city centre are nearby. Exeter and Plymouth LLB or GDL graduates receive a 10% discount. In addition, three high achievers per year receive a £2,000 Saltram scholarship to assist with LPC fees. A 'top-up' LLM is available on a part-time basis.

WALES

university of glamorgan
Number of places: 108 full-time, 32 part-time

The law school is located across the River Taff from the main university campus in Treforest. Treforest is the birthplace of the legendary Tom Jones, and it's not unusual for the town's population to be significantly depleted every summer when a huge mass of students leaves for the holidays. The full-time course involves 18 hours of lectures and workshops each week. The number of electives is relatively small, but includes unusual options like planning and environmental law. An optional work-placement scheme operates in February and March.

university of wales, aberystwyth
Number of places: 100 full-time

The university's colloquial nickname, 'Aber', is widely used among the locals. The Welsh location is clearly dear to many students' hearts, and the Penglais campus, overlooking Aberystwyth and Cardigan Bay, reportedly boasts some of the best views of any British university. Although Aber has the oldest law department in Wales, it only began offering the LPC in 2006. Most of the tutors are qualified solicitors, although some members of the university's academic staff teach electives. For students aiming to practise in the Welsh courts, advanced criminal advocacy in Welsh is an unusual option.

swansea university
Number of places: 100 full-time

Swansea has strong links with the local community. One student, the only one of her class going to a City firm, noted how Swansea's LPC is more geared to non-commercial practice: *"There are no City electives on offer. Most people go on to high street practice."* However, the electives that are offered span a broad range of interesting options, including public governance, consumer credit and asset finance and advanced criminal advocacy in Welsh. There is also a good range of CV-boosting opportunities, including an established pro bono clinic and an Easter vacation scheme programme that provides placements at local firms. Swansea's LPC can be upgraded to an LLM in Legal Practice and Advanced Drafting.

the bar vocational course (bvc)

The BVC is the one-year vocational training course for barristers in England and Wales. It can also be taken part-time over two years. Eight law schools are permitted to teach the course at locations in London, Bristol, Cardiff, Leeds, Manchester, Newcastle and Nottingham. Applications are made online at www.bvconline.co.uk and the first application round opens on 5 November 2007. There is no cap on the number of schools you may apply to but during the first round only your top three choices will look at your application. These providers will be able to see where they have been ranked on your form. The first round ends on 9 January 2008 and offers are made from 3 March 2008. The acceptance period for these offers ends on 31 March 2008. Any unsuccessful applications then go into a clearing pool, along with late submissions. This opens on 4 April and closes to new applicants on 16 July. Offers can be made until 29 August 2008.

make a considered decision

Before firing off an application, ask yourself: have you really got what it takes to succeed at the Bar? As the table on page 866 shows, around one in three BVC students gain pupillage and even then there is no guarantee a tenancy will follow. Course fees of nearly £13,000 in London (and not much under £10,000 elsewhere) make the BVC prohibitively expensive for many potential applicants.

Bar Council committees have suggested various measures to address the problems and in a recent statement, Bar Council chairman Geoffrey Vos QC conceded: *"Doing nothing is not an option."* Suggestions include capping the overall number of places on the BVC, introducing an aptitude test to make it harder for ill-suited students to slip through the net or making a 2:1 degree the minimum requirement. However, the Bar Standards Board (BSB) and Bar Council have been unable to reach any agreement, meaning further action is stalled. A new review is proposed and it is anticipated that changes are likely to be implemented for the 2010 course. As and when more details emerge we'll update our website.

Currently, people are *"called"* to the Bar and may refer to themselves as barristers following completion of the BVC. Opposition to a proposal to delay 'call' until after 12 months of pupillage came especially from international students for whom the title 'barrister' confers great benefit due to its wide international recognition. It is believed that international students form about 30% of the total BVC intake each year, and at the Bristol Institute of Legal Practice, some 95% of these students have pupillage or the equivalent arranged in their home jurisdictions by the end of the course. This is compared with around a quarter of UK students. Following extensive consultation, the BSB confirmed in July 2007 that proposals to defer call had been rejected. Among the concerns stated was that deferral *"might be challenged on the grounds of indirect race discrimination."* For many students, keeping the right to the title of barrister after coughing up £25,000 to cover living costs and fees is small consolation. *"I'd much rather come out with a chance of getting a job at the end of it,"* said one typical student.

money matters

If you decide to go ahead you should do some serious number-crunching and work out exactly how you are going to raise the necessary cash. Be prepared to disclose just how many times you went over your student overdraft limit, how much debt you have racked up on store credit cards and how you intend to fund the next few years. The main funding options are BVC scholarships from the Inns of Court (see their websites for details), career development loans, bank loans and – if you're fortunate – the Bank of Mum & Dad. The Bar Council also has plans to provide a

the bar vocational course (bvc) (continued)

package of loans favouring candidates from poorer backgrounds and it's worth contacting your LEA in case they can help. For more information on funding see page 72.

securing a place

When it comes to getting a place on the BVC, don't underestimate the competition. While the Bar Council's criteria isn't onerous – you need to be a member of an Inn and have a 2:2 LLB or GDL pass – real entry standards are slightly higher and academic grades do matter. BPP, for one, has upped the ante by formally requiring a 2:1, although the *"save in exceptional circumstances"* get-out clause seems to stretch to a fair number of people. At all providers, the course directors emphasise that they want to see evidence of commitment to the Bar, be it through mini-pupillages, paralegalling or pro bono experience. Some experience in public speaking, mooting or debating helps an application, but don't panic: *"You don't need to be a high-powered debater at university to be assessed well under this heading."* Check out the individual application criteria on each course provider's website or send off for a prospectus so that your application is well targeted. Most providers focus on those who have listed them as their first choice: Cardiff Law School tells us: *"95% of our offers are taken up by candidates who have put us in first place."*

Although high demand results in competition for places, don't expect everyone on the course to be a future Star at the Bar. According to our research, academically, the standard of your classmates is likely to be *"patchy."* Increasing numbers of BVC places, combined with the lack of interviews during the application process, means institutions can and do take on students who are frankly not up to the course or have no real chance of a career at the Bar.

choosing a provider

Research thoroughly what each institution has to offer by reading prospectuses, attending open days and – if you can – chatting to past and current students. As a guide, we've covered some of the basic points on the following pages. Current Bar Council rules mean course content, class sizes and assessment vary little, but there are still considerable differences between schools that could make or break the year. Here are some things to think about:

- **Cost:** Some providers and locations are significantly cheaper than others. London is the priciest but even here there is variation. If you're an international student, look at the differential in price. Part-timers should note whether fees increase in the second year;
- **Success Rate:** Ask providers what percentage of their students pass the BVC, what percentage have to re-sit modules and what percentage of their students gain pupillage;
- **Location:** Out of London is a natural option for those looking for pupillage on the circuits, not least because of strong links and networking opportunities with the local Bar. However, it doesn't follow that London is necessarily the best place for a capital-bound pupil. Local practitioners do have input into the courses of the London providers, but this factor seems to count for more in the regions where the Bar is smaller and closer knit. London students do benefit from proximity to the Inns of Court, and for pupillage interviews it's a lot less hassle if you don't have to arrive carrying a suitcase on a delayed train. However, through compulsory dining and advocacy training courses in the Inns, regional students are able maintain their links with the capital – albeit with a little extra time taken up by travelling;
- **Size:** Smaller providers pride themselves on offering a more intimate and collegiate environment. Student feedback indicates that this

does make a difference and the friends you make on the BVC will be a source of support during the search for pupillage and beyond. There's definitely *"a different feel"* to the providers which are run as companies (the College of Law and BPP are both plcs), as opposed to those which are universities;

- **Facilities:** Students can tap into a far wider range of support services, sports and social activities by taking the BVC at a university. Library and IT resources vary from one institution to the next, as does the level of technology used in teaching – some places make it a key feature of the course;

- **Option subjects:** The available option subjects vary. For example, although judicial review and immigration are popular electives, they are not offered everywhere. The 'BVC Providers' table on our website sets out what's on offer at each place. This table also compares fees and offers provider-specific application tips;

- **Extra-curricular English lessons:** If you are an international student, you may wish to find out whether these are included within the course fees. At some providers, they are compulsory for anyone whose language ability does not meet a certain standard;

- **Pro bono:** Opportunities range from minimal to superb across the eight providers.

what can you expect from the course?

Academic study is not the focus of the BVC. Instead the spotlight is on developing the skills of advocacy, drafting, opinion writing, conferencing, negotiation, case analysis and legal research. In terms of substantive knowledge, students are required to familiarise themselves with study manuals outlining civil and criminal litigation procedure and the rules of evidence. Learning for the multiple-choice tests (MCTs) used to examine this component is *"a*

very time-consuming part of the course," but only counts for 15% of the final mark. It is only in the final term that students have some choice, picking two option subjects in areas of practice where they might see themselves specialising. These can provide a real confidence boost when encountering tricky research assignments during pupillage. Most teaching is delivered to groups of 12 students, with the rest tackled in classes of six or fewer for practical skills such as advocacy and conferencing. Methods vary slightly between providers, but learning is commonly by way of case studies that track the litigation process. Written-skills classes often involve interactive drafting exercises, which bring in the use of multimedia such as electronic whiteboards. Oral skills classes make increasing use of video-recording equipment in role plays. The skills acquired are then tested in over a dozen assessments in the second and third terms. Written skills are tested through a mix of unseen, seen and take-home tests (depending on where you study), while professional actors are drafted in to take part in oral assessments.

Course directors tell us *"it is a tough course, so students do have to work hard,"* yet student opinion on this differs. Some – but by no means all – report that the BVC experience is *"not a particularly testing year,"* although we suspect that a certain amount of bravado is attached to such claims. We think students tend to fall into three groups: those who struggle; those who rest on their laurels a bit because they already have a pupillage offer; and those who throw themselves into the course to achieve high marks and impress chambers' recruiters. As one course director conceded: *"There is a possibility that bright students with well-developed skills will find it frustrating"* and students of this nature commented that, after the demands of academic study and in anticipation of the ordeal of pupillage, the BVC year can *"feel like a strange interim period to be left hanging in."*

making the best of it

Whatever critics say, there's no doubt that the BVC provides a vital impetus to *"snap out of the academic mind-set and into a practical one"* – a transition every fledgling barrister must make. Try to extract as much worthwhile experience from the course as you can. The BVC is a great year for mooting and other advocacy competitions, while most providers also have their own pro bono units. On top of this, the Inns provide opportunities to socialise with barristers, judges and other students at compulsory dinners, lectures and advocacy training weekends, as well as running their own mooting and debating competitions. During holidays and reading weeks, grab the chance to squeeze in mini-pupillages or court marshalling, or try and get some hands-on experience in a Citizens Advice Bureau or through FRU. These experiences could be the difference between your name being added to a long list of mail-merged rejection letters or being invited to interview.

the lowdown on the bvc providers

bpp law school, london

Number of places: 264 full-time, 96 part-time

BPP is not just a professional education provider, it's a public company with a website providing as much information about corporate governance and share performance as careers guidance. If the school's motto – Serving the Client – isn't enough of a giveaway, its swanky glass and steel building should leave you in no doubt that this school *"takes itself very seriously."* With state-of-the-art facilities, including a series of mock courtrooms, nothing is spared to make the experience as realistic as possible. Students are even required to wear suits on certain days. Competition for places is intensified by the minimum requirement of a 2:1 which, except in *"exceptional circumstances,"* forms the school's admissions policy. Once there, students describe the BPP experience as *"a very time-intensive course... they keep you busy with exercises and a structured schedule."* Tuition is arguably geared towards those who may have difficulty passing the course – *"they are very professional about getting you to pass if you're struggling"* – and, on the downside, this can leave brighter sparks feeling uncatered for. Advocacy, negotiation and conference skills are the mostly highly praised parts of the course and these are taught by practising barristers in court dress. A total of nine electives are offered including Judicial Review, Company Law, Property and Chancery. Each student is required to complete five hours of pro bono activities over the year and there are also plenty of mooting competitions to get involved in. If you want to add an air of professionalism to your BVC year, BPP is where you'll find it.

bpp law school, leeds

Number of places: 48 full-time, 48 part-time

BPP jumped at the chance to exploit the northern market by opening a brand-new BVC programme in Leeds in September 2006. With the inaugural year nearing completion, we spoke to course director Nicki McLaren to find out if it had been a success. Following the London model, there is an almost identical course structure and equally modern facilities in Leeds, but the fact that the course is so much smaller means that *"each student knows everyone on the course"* and at meet-and-greet sessions with the local Bar *"the chances of being able to network and make those connections is much better."* A BPP London advocacy tutor spent time in Leeds in the first year to ensure continuity with the quality of teaching in the capital, while two practising barristers and a series of professional actors helped students perfect their skills in time for their final assessments. To assist with dining requirements and save the trip to London, a black-tie dinner organised in Leeds was a storming success. For mooting, while Leeds has its own competition, a team also entered the London-wide mooting competition, going up against BPP's London team. Pro bono opportunities are available. Heavy involvement from members of the Northern Circuit and fees significantly lower than in London have ensured high application numbers. Experience already shows that successful candidates invariably put BPP as their first choice.

bristol institute of legal practice

Number of places: 120 full-time, 48 part-time

If you're drawn to the South West, competitive prices and strong connections with the Western Circuit make this course well worth considering. Although stats show fewer high-calibre students are attracted to Bristol than some of its rivals, the institute responds by pointing out that a *"less traditional intake"* does not prevent the course from scoring highly in terms of added value. Course director Stephen Migdal believes *"passing the BVC at UWE is something that has to be earned, but thereby provides a real sense of achievement."* Students work in groups of 12 or fewer for 90% of the time and are given a base room, complete with their own set of keys, to which they have access seven days a week. These rooms are equipped with books and IT facilities and become like *"a second home"* to many students. The commitment and dedication of staff is *"constantly remarked upon by students,"* leaving us in no doubt that Bristol is working hard to achieve its goals. Students also commented on the *"strong sense of community."* Involving BVC students in the local community is one of the institute's core values, for example through mock trials in schools. Students can use pro bono work for FRU, alongside two weeks of compulsory work experience, to fulfil both of their optional modules. A new initiative also enables students to attend inquests, represent juveniles at police stations and carry out prison visits: vital preparation if you're thinking of going into criminal practice. Members of the local Bar assist in advocacy teaching, something students practise during three full trials, while the provision of digital cameras facilitates sometimes-excruciating self-scrutiny. The location of the university off the M4 is a downer. Said one: *"I didn't realise how far away from the city centre it was."* However, ample campus facilities mean students have full access to a range of sporting and social activities.

cardiff law school

Number of places: 72 full-time

Course leader Jetsun Lebasci sums up the BVC at Cardiff as *"an intense year where high standards are expected, but that is ultimately vastly rewarding."* If you're looking for a well-established, university-based law school you'd do well to give Cardiff some thought. But make sure you put it as your first choice – *"95% of our offers are taken up by candidates who have put us in first place."* Located on a campus that is *"green, pleasant and seconds away from the city centre,"* the law school is small enough for staff and students to know each

other by name, which *"gives us a chance to change, adapt and be flexible in a way that other providers can't."* While a number of students are from Wales, many come from other parts of the UK and around 25% are international students who benefit from compulsory two-hour TEFL sessions on a weekly basis if the school judges that it would be in their interest. The school prides itself on the *"quantity and quality"* of its skills teaching (advocacy, negotiation and conferencing) and goes beyond the mandatory syllabus, with tuition for these modules delivered to groups of four or six students. Coming in both written and oral form, feedback on students' complete performance over the two hours is extremely thorough. In turn, students are encouraged to complete anonymous online questionnaires to ensure any problems are quickly addressed. Jetsun explained that there is still a strong emphasis on the knowledge-based subjects during the first two terms as *"we feel that they need this to underpin the other skills."* Having said that, the course is now *"less front-loaded than in the past"* and a regular dialogue between the school and local practitioners ensures that the materials used are of an appropriate nature. Mini-pupillages and court marshalling are organised for students during two placement weeks. Other extra curricular activities include the recently launched Innocence Project, in which students investigate alleged wrongful convictions. This programme has received a lot of press attention over the last year.

the college of law, London

Number of places: 240 full-time, 48 part-time

Its London branch situated just off Tottenham Court Road, the College of Law is a thoroughly well-established supplier of legal education in the capital. It has recently gained new degree-awarding powers, meaning students who complete the GDL and BVC at the College will automatically gain an LLB. An LLM is also available if you're willing to put in extra time at the end of the year. The teaching on the course follows the litigation process, meaning the timetable *"is never the same from week to week"* and everything is done through classes (as opposed to lectures). These are based on groups of 12 students (or fewer for certain oral skills sessions) who work together until their optional subjects start in the final term. Judges and practitioners visit the college to give students feedback on advocacy and preside over mock trials. There are also after-hours speaker programmes on subjects such as commercial awareness and law and justice, which *"draw in high-profile lawyers and professionals from the business world, and provide plenty of opportunity for mingling afterwards."* Many students become involved in the Tribunal Representation Service, which provides opportunities to appear at the Leasehold Valuation Tribunal around the corner from the College. Students have also been able to handle small claims, social security and employment cases. Two teams enter the National Negotiation Competition each year; mooting is encouraged at all levels of proficiency, and for the last two years the College has organised prison visits. In short, *"our extensive extra curricular activities are one aspect of the course that we're immensely proud of,"* said course director Jacqueline Cheltenham.

college of law, birmingham

Number of places: 96 full-time plus part-time places

Starting in September 2007, the College of Law's Birmingham course will be identical in content and structure to that offered in the capital. A weekend part-time course will also be offered. Expect the college to capitalise on its strong links with local set St Philip's Chambers, one of the largest barristers chambers in the country, and to encourage plenty of networking with the local Bar. On both the London and Birmingham courses, a 2:2 is the minimum required degree grade, but don't let this mislead you as the grading system used by the college still gives more marks to a 2:1 applicant. The GDL and LPC have long been available in this city; now that the BVC has arrived too, this course will no doubt be inundated with applications.

city law school

(known as the inns of court school of law until july 2008)

Number of places: 575 full-time, 75 part-time

Once upon a time ICSL was the only BVC provider. The school developed the course and is still author of a series of manuals that are used by many students elsewhere and even those starting out in practice. Sited at the edge of Gray's Inn, the school has occupied a position in the heart of legal London for a very long time and, despite the undermining of its hegemony, ICSL still makes much of its longevity and traditional appeal. It educates more full-time BVC students than the other two London providers combined. Some question the school's ability to deliver the best course because of the sheer size of the student body, but City/ICSL points out that the majority of classes take place in groups of 12 (six for advocacy) and that students are split into four manageable cohorts, each with a course director. The course does include some larger group sessions, albeit that these make full use of some pretty smart facilities in the interactive lecture theatre. Pro bono opportunities are plentiful as the school enjoys links with numerous organisations across the capital, including FRU (with which students can complete one of their two option subjects). Relationships with practising barristers and judges are strong, and practitioners visit regularly for a variety of evening events. Keen students can choose to tack an LLM in Professional Legal Practice onto their BVC.

manchester metropolitan university

Number of places: 108 full-time, 48 part-time

Renowned for its close involvement with members of the Northern Circuit, MMU is a cracking choice for anyone wanting to break into the Bar in this part of the country. The strength of its professional links are impressive: at least seven two-hour advocacy master classes per year see local barristers coming in to give students feedback, and professionals also get involved in MMU's practitioner-mentor scheme, offering useful careers and study advice. Another way to rub shoulders with potential recruiters is attendance on the Additional Professional Programme. The BVC is taught at the university's five-year-old law faculty building and MMU adopts a 'syndicate group' approach, organising its students into groups of 12 with their own rooms with IT facilities and core texts. When they arrived, the 2007 students found brand new computers and audio-visual equipment in their rooms. MMU is massively oversubscribed: course director Alan Gibb informed us that for the 108 full-time places on the 2007/08 course there were 220 applicants who put MMU as their first choice. It allows the university to be picky, usually taking only those with a 2:1, sometimes offering places to candidates with a 2:2 but otherwise remarkable CVs. Those who pass muster on grades still have to produce an impressive application detailing *"clear, articulate reasons"* for wanting a career at the Bar. Alan advises that students *"approach the application form as if it were an application for pupillage, making sure it is word-perfect."* What will not count against you is a lack of northern credentials: *"We are happy to take people from anywhere as we know that students put us first because they want to practise on the Northern Circuit."* Around 15% of students intend to return to practise overseas, and typically around 30% of domestic students will have gained pupil-

lage by the time they finish the course. Recognising a lack of organised pro bono activities, the university appointed a pro bono director in 2007 and he hopes to put in place some programmes for BVC students during 2008. All in all, competitive fees, good facilities, and those all-important links to professionals make this provider stand out up north.

university of northumbria, newcastle

Number of places: 80 full-time, 48 part-time + 40 on exempting LLB

In addition to its conventional BVC, Northumbria offers an integrated LLB and BVC programme carried out over four years. Students apply for a place on this 'exempting degree' during the second year of their undergraduate LLB and, if successful, spend the following two years combining undergraduate options with components of the BVC. A parallel LLB/LPC course is also run. There are some very practical benefits to combining the two courses, not least a saving in cost, and students are generally able to extend their student loan to cover all four years. For those who are too late to take advantage of this programme, there are still benefits in taking the conventional BVC at Northumbria, which as of September 2007 will also offer 48 part-time places. The well-respected course has just gained a new lease of life by moving into swish purpose-built premises complete with mock courtrooms and live video-link equipment. The nationally recognised Student Law Office has also benefited from the extra space, which allows even more students and members of the public to benefit from the free advice clinics on offer. Take a few extra months to complete a research project and you could bag yourself an LLM in Advanced Legal Practice or an MA in Legal Practice & Policy. Having five practising barristers teaching on the course is an undoubted asset, yet with only a handful of sets based in Newcastle, staff encourage students to be realistic about their prospects of gaining pupillage in the city. *"We never mislead people at law fairs… they need to look beyond Newcastle."* Networking opportunities arise at guest lectures, moots, mock trials and Wednesday evening 'practitioner sessions'. In terms of structure, the course is described as *"short and fat,"* with all the teaching squeezed into the first two terms. This allows the whole of the summer term to be spent on revision. The university provides a series of revision lectures and seminars and is relaxed about giving students free time to organise their own revision schedules, something which *"helps prepare them for their own practice."*

nottingham law school
Number of places: 125 full-time

Part of Nottingham Trent University, NLS offers a challenging BVC that competes well with its London rivals. Indeed, in the future the school would like to offer a BVC at its London operation with Kaplan. Twice as many first-round first-choice applications are made to NLS as there are places available and this allows the school to only take on those applicants with a fighting chance of pupillage. On average 50% of enrolling students will have secured one by the March following the end of the course. To stand a chance of getting onto this BVC, you'll need a 2:1, good A-levels or a good post-grad degree, evidence of interaction with the legal profession (usually a minimum of three weeks' pupillages or vac schemes), evidence of public speaking and initiative (eg through positions of responsibility). Students come from all over the UK and enter practice across England and Wales. In the city of Nottingham itself, there are only four or five pupillages a year on offer. NLS has a relatively low intake of international students – usually less than 10%. By keeping student numbers down and having a dedicated BVC building, staff and students can get to know each other well. The school's director James Wakefield reveals: *"Staff meet every month to decide which students need pressure put on them or taken off them… this is not a place to come to be anonymous."* The BVC year at NLS is judged by students to be a demanding one and they know they are expected to spend five full days a week on their studies. Skills and knowledge learning focus on the seven briefs that are followed throughout the year. Criminal advocacy sessions are held in courtrooms at Nottingham's old Guildhall. The appointment of a full-time pro bono co-ordinator and a public-access advice clinic at NLS have enhanced the range of real-life experiences open to students, and there is no shortage of links with professionals in London and the Midlands. Barristers and judges present guest lectures on a regular basis, and there are sponsored plea-in-mitigation and mooting competitions plus a marshalling scheme. A pupillage-interview training day assists those who've not yet secured training and, to help students keep contact with their Inns in London, there are coaches to the capital for qualifying sessions. NLS can also dangle the carrot of an LLB for all those who successfully complete the GLD and BVC, and students can also tap into the social, sporting and other facilities offered by the university.

funding

Training a lawyer is an expensive caper. Fortunately many of the students who secure training contracts or pupillages before commencing their studies will receive funding to cover course fees and some living expenses. Details of what solicitors are now offering their future trainees are given in the Salaries and Benefits table on page 94. Further information about the pupillage funding is given in the Bar section.

taken for granted

There's a super-slim chance your local education authority (LEA) may come to the rescue with a grant or allowance. We contacted a number of different LEAs and encountered everything from a flat "no, we do not offer assistance to LPC students" through to a much more positive "send in an application and see." It is definitely worth a quick phone call or e-mail to get the lay of the land. See www.studentsupportdirect.co.uk. If this doesn't bring much joy, try an organisation called the Educational Grants Advisory Service. It can carry out a charity and trust search on your behalf. Its really useful website is www.egas-online.org.uk. Also see www.support4learning.org.uk.

Additionally, the Law Society has various schemes and bursaries that are worth looking into. Read our website feature **Funding News from the Law Society** for further information.

bank loans

Already got a huge overdraft? No problem. You could still qualify for a special package from a high street bank. Interest rates are relatively low and the repayment terms usually favourable, but sniff around to see what different banks are offering. A number of banks have graduate loan schemes tailored to the needs of the legal profession and will, for example, regard pupillage as a formal part of the training when it comes to determining the time for repayment.

Scott Jago, manager of legal student services at the NatWest Legal Centre, advises students to arrange any required loan as soon as they have been accepted onto a course. He recommends that students stick to a budget, drawing down against their loan on a monthly basis. *"If you want a manageable student debt when you start work, then monthly budgeting during your studies is essential."*

surf for a scholarship

Surf the Internet for scholarships and bursaries. Here are some of the funds we found:

- BPP Law School offers seven scholarship awards, set by key members of staff; each one has its own criteria, eg the applicant must be the first lawyer in his/her family.
- The Law Society Bursary Scheme is open to GDL or LPC students.
- The Law Society Diversity Access Scheme supports talented people who face obstacles to qualification.
- Inderpal Rahal Memorial Trust supports women from an immigrant or refugee background.

- The Kalisher Scholarship works with each of the BVC providers to ensure that every year one talented but financially disadvantaged student has a free place on the course.
- The Leonard Sainer Foundation provides financial assistance in the form of interest-free loans to help fund either the LPC or BVC.
- The Student Disability Assistance Fund can award up to £500 for students who are studying on a full time or nearly full time basis. See www.bahshe.demon.co.uk.
- Universities and publicly funded colleges have discretionary college access funds available to assist especially hard-up students.

NatWest can **help** with the **cost** of your **legal studies**

If you are looking to finance the costs of your legal studies then look no further

The NatWest Professional Trainee Loan scheme allows you to borrow for the GDL, LPC and BVC.

For more information please contact your local NatWest Legal Student Services Manager,

Scott Jago on 020 7353 7671 or visit natwest.com/professions.

Textphone users please dial 01189 639 148

career development loans

Barclays Bank, The Co-operative Bank and RBS provide these on behalf of the DfES. Full details can be found at: www.direct.gov.uk/en/EducationAndLearning/AdultLearning/CareerDevelopmentLoans. These allow you to borrow up to £8,000 to fund up to two years of study.

the inns of court

Pupil barristers and GDL and/or BVC students can apply for a range of scholarships from the four Inns of Court. Indeed, 25% of students studying for the BVC have managed to secure some funding from the Inns and many base their choice of Inn on the likelihood of getting their hands on some of the £3m-plus that is paid out each year. Some awards are merit-based; others consider

benefits, benefactors, begging...

Living at home while you study may not sound that appealing but sometimes needs must. Forget ideas of declaring bankruptcy to evade student debt; consider other creative ways to ease the debt burden.

- A student card will get you low-cost travel and all sorts of discounts.
- Law books are pricey so don't go on a spending spree before term starts. College libraries will have the core texts and you'll find past students with books for sale. Check out noticeboards for second-hand tomes.
- A number of law schools, chambers and solicitors firms run competitions. Do a Google search to find them.
- Market research focus groups will pay decent money for an hour or two of your time.
- In terms of more clinical options, consider carefully any decision to participate in a medical trial. And gents, if you choose to make a 'special donation' remember that, come 2028, a stranger might knock on your door and call you dad.

financial hardship. All pupils must be paid no less than £833.33 per month plus reasonable travel expenses. Some sets pay far more and allow students to draw on these awards while on the BVC.

part-timing and the four-letter word

If a decade of loan repayments doesn't appeal then you must do as fools and horses do – work. Do bear in mind that full-time study and earning money are uncomfortable bedfellows, so should you be studying part-time instead? Engaging in part-time work while studying for a full-time course is increasingly frowned upon by the providers and the law firms. When asked about their decision to end the guarantee of morning or afternoon classes, the College of Law told us that if students can't commit a full working week to the course they should be opting to study part time.

Studying part time may allow you to work in a more rewarding job and perform better at college. For LLB grads or students who have completed the GDL, paralegalling may be an option. Indeed, there are many options on the periphery of the profession, from commercial contracts negotiation and transaction management to social policy or other research.

capital concerns

Newsflash: London streets aren't paved with gold – just concrete, pigeon droppings and chewing gum. Rent and living costs in cities like Sheffield, Nottingham and Cardiff are lower, but out of London won't automatically mean within your price range if you're thinking of Guildford, for example.

Sit down and add up what you think you'll need and then add some more. If you intend to study at the most expensive places, course fees could be £19,000 (GDL/BVC) or £17,000 (GDL/LPC). Do so at the least expensive schools and this could be reduced to around £10,000 and £12,000 respectively. It's worth thinking about if money is the main sticking point.

a-z universities and law schools

BPP Law School

68-70 Red Lion Street, London, WC1R 4NY
Tel: (0845) 070 2882
Email: admissions@bpp.com   Website: www.bpplawschool.com

college profile

BPP is a leading provider of professional legal education in the country with over 4,500 students based across four specially designed and highly equipped Law Schools.

As a leading provider, they have the skills and resources to offer you the individual support needed to prepare you for the realities of legal practice. This is achieved using a unique mix of academic and practitioner lecturers, first rate facilities, award-winning pro bono projects and a dedicated Careers Service.

BPP's Careers Service comprises not only specialist careers advisors, but also careers tutors, who have worked in practice and sat on recruitment selection panels. This distinctive blend of knowledge and experience ensures you are fully equipped with the knowledge and support needed to secure a training contract or pupillage.

graduate diploma in law (full-time, part-time, and distance learning)

BPP's GDL is taught with a practical, student-centred approach to not only familiarise you with the basic principles of law, but to also introduce you to legal practice. You will be taught using a combination of large and small group sessions, allowing you to develop your knowledge and skills fully by receiving maximum support and individual feedback. Although competition for places at BPP is intense, graduates from BPP's GDL are guaranteed a place on the school's LPC and intending barristers can apply to join their BVC.

BPP's 'Distinctive GDL' offers the chance for you to add a specialist subject to your GDL by participating in an optional short-course in an area of law that interests you.

If you are unsure whether a career in law is for you, BPP's popular taster course, the BPP Law Summer School, is available to give you an insight into the legal world.

legal practice course (full-time and part-time)

BPP's LPC is designed to prepare you for real life as a trainee solicitor, and the new MBA-style approach to the programme offers business and financial training whilst working with sophisticated client portfolios and case & transaction simulations. Taught by experienced solicitors from a variety of practice backgrounds, you will benefit from a programme designed in close collaboration with the leading legal firms in the country and a wide range of electives ensuring you can study the area of legal practice most important to you.

bar vocational course (full-time and part-time)

Offered in Leeds and London, BPP's BVC is highly regarded by the profession and is the only programme in London to be unconditionally validated by the Bar Council for the full six-year term. Studying the BVC at BPP will allow you to concentrate on developing your essential barristerial skills of drafting, legal research, opinion writing, advocacy, conference and negotiation. These skills will be refined using groups as small as six students alongside practising barristers, who will act as your opponents in mock trials and final assessments.

BPP Law School operates an exclusive scholarship programme for selected BPP students. Applications must be received by the 1st of August prior to you commencing your programme. Please visit the website www.bpplawschool.com/funding_and_scholarships for more information.

contact
Admissions

apply to:
full-time GDL and LPC
Central Applications Board
www.lawcabs.ac.uk

part-time GDL and LPC
Directly to BPP Law School
www.bpplawschool.com/
apply_now

full-time and part-time BVC
BVC online
www.bvconline.co.uk

summer school
Directly to BPP Law School
www.bpplawschool.com/
apply_now

locations
Leeds, London (Holborn & Waterloo), Manchester

BPP
LAW SCHOOL
Preparing you for practice

Cardiff Law School

Cardiff Law School, Cardiff University, Museum Avenue, Cardiff CF10 3AX
Tel: (029) 2087 4941/4964 Fax: (029) 2087 4984
Email: law-lpc@cf.ac.uk or law-bvc@cf.ac.uk
Website: www.law.cardiff.ac.uk/cpls

contact
LPC: Byron Jones
Tel: (029) 2087 4941/6660
Email: law-lpc@cf.ac.uk

BVC: Lucy Burns
Tel: (029) 2087 4964
Email: law-bvc@cf.ac.uk

other postgraduate law courses:
The Postgraduate Office
Tel: (029) 2087 4351/4353

university profile

Cardiff Law School is one of the most successful law schools in the UK and enjoys an international reputation for its teaching and research. In the most recent assessment of research quality conducted by the Higher Education Funding Council, Cardiff achieved a grade 5 rating, placing it in the top law schools in the country. Cardiff offers opportunities for students to pursue postgraduate study by research leading to the degrees of M.Phil and Ph.D. In addition, taught Masters degrees in the areas of canon, commercial, European legal studies and medical law are offered in full and part-time mode.

legal practice course and bar vocational course

A part of the Law School, the Centre for Professional Legal Studies is the leading provider of legal training in Wales and is validated to offer both the Legal Practice Course and the Bar Vocational Course. Students are taught by experienced solicitors and barristers who have been specifically recruited for this purpose. The Centre prides itself on its friendly and supportive teaching environment and its strong links with the legal profession. Placements with solicitors' firms or sets of Chambers are available to students pursuing the vocational courses, while students studying the Bar Vocational Course additionally enjoy placements with Circuit and District Judges. In 2005 Cardiff's Legal Practice Course once again achieved the highest rating following the Law Society's assessment visit. The course has consistently been rated "Excellent" by the Law Society; one of the few providers of this course to hold the top ranking. The Law Society praised the challenging learning environment and stimulating range of activities.

facilities

The Law School has dedicated accommodation for the vocational courses which houses a practitioner library, courtroom facilities, fixed and moveable audio visual equipment for recording practitioner skills, inter-active teaching equipment and extensive computer facilities. In addition, the main law library contains one of the largest collections of primary and secondary material within the UK. The Law School is housed in its own building at the heart of the campus, itself located in one of the finest civic centres in Britain and only a short walk from the main shopping area. The University has its own postgraduate centre, together with a full range of sports and social facilities. Cardiff is a vibrant capital city with excellent cultural, sporting and leisure activities.

CARDIFF UNIVERSITY
PRIFYSGOL CAERDYdd

City University London

The City Law School, City University London, Northampton Square, London, EC1V 0HB
Website: www.city.ac.uk/law

contact

LLB (Graduate Entry)
(020) 7040 8167
law@city.ac.uk

GDL/CPE
(020) 7040 8301
cpe@city.ac.uk

LLM (all bar criminal litigation)
(020) 7040 8167
llm-lawdept@city.ac.uk

LLM criminal litigation
(020) 7404 5787
llm-icsl@city.ac.uk

BVC/LPC
(020) 7404 5787
bvc@city.ac.uk

college profile
The City Law School is one of London's major law schools, offering an impressive range of academic and professional courses. The School is the first law school in London to educate students and practitioners at all stages of their legal education.

The School's GDL course is one of the largest and most respected in the UK, with a strong reputation with the Bar and amongst City law firms. In addition to postgraduate legal training for both solicitors and barristers, The City Law School offers a well-established CPD programme which includes the PSC for trainee solicitors and Higher Rights training.

The School's professional courses are delivered through the School's Professional Centre (formerly the Inns of Court School of Law), which has been the leading educator of barristers in the country for generations. The School also offers an excellent Legal Practice Course (for intending solicitors) which has been awarded the highest grade possible across all SRA assessment areas.

graduate entry LLB (two years full time)
This well established conversion course for non-law graduates provides students with the opportunity to gain the required basic law knowledge, whilst identifying and developing special interest subjects.

LLM programme (full or part-time)
The City Law School offers a range of five LLM courses, each created to fit the needs of both the profession and the students. LLM International Law (with opportunities to specialise in Human Rights or Environmental Law). LLM International Commercial Law (with option to specialise in International Competition Law or Maritime Law). LLM Housing and Environmental Law. LLM Media Law. LLM Criminal Litigation.

graduate diploma in law/CPE (full time)
Designed to enable non-law graduates to complete the first stage of professional training, this GDL is one of the largest and most respected GDL courses in the UK, and has a long-standing reputation with the Bar and a strong reputation amongst City law firms.

bar vocational course (full or part-time)
A forward looking IT based course focusing on the needs of the modern bar, particularly advocacy. There is also the opportunity to enrol on the school's LLM in Professional Legal Practice, awarded on successful completion of the BVC and a supervised dissertation.

legal practice course (full time)
The School's 'top rated' LPC has been devised to meet the needs of students in practice, with a heavy emphasis on the teaching of practitioner skills. Small group teaching is emphasised to give students the most effective environment for learning and a wide range of elective subjects is offered.

The College of Law

Admissions, Braboeuf Manor, Portsmouth Road, Guildford GU3 1HA
Freephone: (0800) 328 0153
Email: admissions@lawcol.co.uk
Website: www.college-of-law.co.uk/perfectforpractice

contact
Freephone:
(0800) 328 0153
If calling from overseas:
+44 (0)1483 216500
Email:
admissions@lawcol.co.uk
Website:
www.college-of-law.co.uk/
perfectforpractice

college profile

At The College of Law you'll get the best possible start to your legal career. With centres in Birmingham, Chester, Guildford, London (two) and York, The College of Law is the UK's leading provider of legal education. It's innovative courses are designed and taught by lawyers, with a clear focus on building the practical skills, commercial awareness and independent thinking you'll need to succeed. This is supported by an award-winning pro bono programme and the largest and best-resourced careers service in UK legal education. You'll benefit from excellent tutor support and access to unrivalled on-line and off-line learning methods and resources.

graduate diploma in law (GDL) full-time/part-time

Designed to build knowledge and skills that more than match a law degree – with a clear focus on preparing you for life in practice. Academic training is built around real-life examples and case studies, and you'll be given research assignments that directly reflect the way you'll work as a lawyer. Students who pass the College GDL are guaranteed a place on the College LPC (as long as they apply within two years), and you'll graduate with a Bachelor of Law degree if you go on to successfully complete your LPC or BVC at the College.

legal practice course (LPC) full-time/part-time

The College LPC is rigorous and practical – equipping you with the skills you need to succeed. You'll get plenty of opportunities to practice your skills through real cases in a context appropriate to your area of interest. The College has the widest selection of elective subjects available and uniquely offers three different LPC routes, allowing you to specialise in your chosen field: corporate, commercial & private and public legal services. The majority of teaching is in small, student-centred groups and the course features extensive use of multi-media learning resources, including interactive i-Tutorials. And from 2008 the College will award a Master of Law degree to those students who successfully study modules in addition to the College LPC.

bar vocational course (BVC) full-time/part-time

The College BVC has been designed to resemble practice as closely as possible. The course is litigation-based with a heavy emphasis on developing and honing skills. Study follows a logical, realistic process from initial instruction to final appeal, and learning is based around the seven core skills and three knowledge areas stipulated by the Bar Standards Board. Most of your learning will be in small groups, and you'll have plenty of opportunities to put your learning into action through: practitioner evenings, mock trials, court visits, mooting, negotiating and advocacy competitions, and the College's tailored pro bono programmes. And from 2008 the College will award a Master of Law degree to those students who successfully study modules in addition to the College BVC.

information days

Find out more about The College of Law and its courses by attending an information day or arranging a centre visit. For further details and to book a place, visit www.college-of-law.co.uk/comeandseeus

The College of Law
of England and Wales

Kaplan Law School

Nottingham Law at Kaplan Law School
Palace House, 3 Cathedral Street, London SE1 9DE
Tel: (020) 7367 6400
Email: admissions@kaplanlawschool.org.uk
Website: www.nottingham-kaplan.org.uk

college profile

Nottingham Law School's market-leading LPC is now being offered in London through a partnership with Kaplan, the international education provider and a subsidiary of The Washington Post. Kaplan's UK training business has 50 years of experience as a leading provider of accountancy, finance and business education. Kaplan is now bringing its reputation for high quality training and education into the legal market.

Kaplan Law School's campus is in one of London's most vibrant neighbourhoods on the South Bank. Not only is the area famous for its cafes and restaurants, pubs, shops and renowned Borough market, it is a few minutes' walk from one of London's best served transport hubs with excellent tube, train and bus links. Directly across London Bridge is the legal and financial centre for the City. The campus overlooks the River Thames and has been custom-built with state of the art facilities designed to optimize the student and teaching experience.

legal practice course

The only LPC to receive the SRA's highest rating every year, the Nottingham Law School LPC is now being offered at Kaplan Law School in London. The course will retain Nottingham Law School's same stimulating design for students and will continue to be responsive to the needs of firms. The course integrates transactions and skills so that each advances the other, while ensuring the transferability of skills between different subject areas. The professionally qualified teaching team retains substantial links with practice.

London students are able to take advantage of Nottingham Law School's innovative 'Bridge to Practice' which delivers high impact practical modules tailored to the needs of trainees in participating firms.

Through the Kaplan Law School careers team all students will also have access to Nottingham Law School's well-known dedicated careers and recruitment service which provides students with as much guidance and assistance as possible in their search for a training contract.

graduate diploma in law

Nottingham Law School's GDL is a one-year conversion course designed for any non-law graduate who intends to become a solicitor or barrister in the UK. With a pass rate of over 90%, the course has been adopted by the GDL's governing body as the framework for other conversion courses. Nottingham Law School's winning syllabus will be replicated at Kaplan Law School in London with the same seven core academic subjects of an undergraduate law degree. Students who successfully complete the GDL can progress to study on the LPC.

Through the Kaplan Law School careers team all students will also have access to Nottingham Law School's well-known dedicated careers and recruitment service which provides students with as much guidance and assistance as possible in their search for a training contract.

contact

GDL and LPC full time:

apply to: Central Applications Board

Contact: admissions@kaplanlawschool.org.uk

LPC part time:

apply to: Nottingham Law at Kaplan Law School

Contact: admissions@kaplanlawschool.org.uk

NOTTINGHAM LAW
KAPLAN
LAW SCHOOL

Manchester Metropolitan University

School of Law, Sandra Burslem Building, Lower Ormond Street, Manchester
M15 6HB
Tel: (0161) 247 3050 Fax: (0161) 247 6309 Email: law@mmu.ac.uk

contact
CPE/GDL: Harriet Roche/
Becky Curtis (pt)

LPC: Paul Duffy

BVC: Wanda Clarke

college profile
The School of Law is one of the largest providers of legal education in the UK, and enjoys an excellent reputation for the quality and range of its courses. It is one of only six providers that offer the full range of law courses LLB, GDipL, LPC and BVC. The School's courses are well designed and taught, combining rigorous academic standards with practical application. In September 2003, the School moved into a brand new, state of the art building, in the heart of Manchester.

bar vocational course (full-time or part-time: part-time = attendance one day per fortnight over two years)
This course provides the vocational stage of training for intending practising barristers. However, skills learnt on the course such as advocacy and drafting are transferable to other professions. The BVC is skills based and interactive with particular emphasis on advocacy which is taught in groups of six. The course adopts a syndicate (mini-chambers) approach. Students are allocated to a particular group which has its own base room which contains extensive practitioner legal resources both in hard copy and online form. Each room has the latest in IT and AV equipment. There is also a BVC court room and a separate BVC resource room. Excellent student support is provided including careers advice and an additional professional programme that is designed to bridge the gap between student and professional life. A particular feature of the course is the close links it enjoys with the Northern Circuit whose members are involved in Advocacy Master Classes, the teaching of professional conduct and in a student mentoring scheme.

legal practice course
(full-time or part-time: part-time = attendance on Thursdays over two years)
The legal practice course provides the vocational stage of training for those wishing to qualify as a solicitor. Offering a full range of private client and commercial electives, the school aims to cater to students who are looking to practice in specialised areas (eg entertainment law or advanced criminal litigation) as well as students who wish to develop a broad subject base. A mentor scheme operates to put students in touch with local practitioners. Consistently recommended for its state of the art resources, student support and careers guidance and staffed by approachable and knowledgeable teaching staff, the LPC at Manchester Metropolitan University will provide a sound foundation for your legal career.

graduate diploma in law/cpe
(full-time or part-time: part-time = attendance on Monday and Wednesday evening over two years)
An increasing number of graduates enter the legal profession this way, with employers attracted by the applicant's maturity and transferable skills. The course places emphasis on the acquisition of legal research and other relevant legal skills. On completion students normally join the School's LPC or BVC Course. This means that if the full-time mode is followed a non-law graduate can become professionally qualified in two years. There is a guaranteed place for successful GDipL students on the school's LPC course.

**Manchester
Metropolitan
University**

Nottingham Law School

Nottingham Law School, Belgrave Centre, Nottingham NG1 5LP
Tel: (0115) 848 4498
Email: nls.enquiries@ntu.ac.uk
Website: www.ntu.ac.uk/nls

contact
Nottingham Law School
Belgrave Centre
Nottingham NG1 5LP
Tel: (0115) 848 4498
Email: nls.enquiries@ntu.ac.uk
Website: www.ntu.ac.uk/nls

Nottingham Law School has partnered with Kaplan Law School to offer NLS's Legal Practice Course and Graduate Diploma in Law from a brand new central London campus as well as from Nottingham.

legal practice course
The LPC is offered by full-time and part-time block study. This course has been designed to be challenging and stimulating for students and responsive to the needs of firms, varying from large commercial to smaller high street practices, and it still carries the endorsement of a large cross section of firms from major corporate through to high street.
Nottingham Law School's LPC features: integration of the transactions and skills, so that each advances the other, whilst ensuring the transferability of skills between different subject areas; carefully structured interactive group work which develops an ability to handle skills and legal transactions effectively, and in an integrated way; a rigorous assessment process that nevertheless avoids 'assessment overload', to maintain a teaching and learning emphasis to the course; a professionally qualified team, retaining substantial links with practice; the highest possible rating from The Law Society's Assessment Panel in every year of its operation.

graduate diploma in law
The GDL is offered full-time or by distance learning. Nottingham Law School's GDL is designed for any non-law graduate who intends to become a solicitor or barrister in the UK. The intensive course effectively covers the seven core subjects of an undergraduate law degree. It is the stepping stone to the LPC or BVC, and a legal career thereafter. It is a Graduate Diploma (Dip Law) in its own right and operates on a similar basis to the LPC (see above), although inevitably it has a more academic basis.
GDL students who embark on Nottingham Law School's LPC or BVC will also be eligible for a full LLB on successful completion of that professional course.

bar vocational course
Nottingham Law School has designed its BVC to develop to a high standard a range of core practical skills, and to equip students to succeed in the fast-changing environment of practice at the Bar. Particular emphasis is placed on the skill of advocacy. Advocacy sessions are conducted in groups of six and the School uses the Guildhall courtrooms for most sessions. The BVC is taught entirely by qualified practitioners, and utilises the same integrated and interactive teaching methods as all of the School's other professional courses. Essentially, students learn by doing and Nottingham Law School provides an environment in which students are encouraged to realise, through practice and feedback, their full potential.

NOTTINGHAM
LAW SCHOOL
Nottingham Trent University

University of Wolverhampton

School of Legal Studies, Molineux Street, Wolverhampton WV1 1SB
Tel: (01902) 321633   Fax: (01902) 323569

contact
Admissions Assistant
Tel: (01902) 321633
Fax: (01902) 323569
Email:
sls-enquiries@wlv.ac.uk
website:
www.wlv.ac.uk/sls

university profile

Based in Wolverhampton, the School of Legal Studies offers courses for students intending to follow a variety of careers in the legal profession. The law school has been offering these courses for over 30 years. Its LPC programme has had consistently good ratings. The lecturers are drawn from experienced solicitors, barristers, academics and individuals from business and industry. There are excellent IT facilities, a well-stocked library, bookshop and a sports centre. The School also offers an LLM in International Corporate and Financial Law, which draws together a number of legal issues with an international dimension such as the regulation of financial services and financial crime. It also deals with matters such as international banking law and international corporate finance. Another postgraduate course offered by the School is the MA in Practice Management, developed in connection with the management section of the Law Society. It is taught on a flexible, part-time, block-delivery basis and is designed to provide an outlet to complex managerial and organisational issues facing practice managers.

legal practice course (full/part-time)

The University's LPC vocational training course for those intending to practice as solicitors offers a sound basis for a professional career. The core subjects of Business, Litigation and Conveyancing are taught, together with a range of commercial and private client options. Professional skills courses, practical workshops and seminars are all part of the training. Additional benefits include close links with local practitioners, mentoring, CV distribution and group social activities. The Legal Practice Course is housed in modern, purpose-built, dedicated accommodation which includes LPC Resources room and video suites. The course is taught by experienced professionally-qualified staff with close links with the local profession. It has active personal tutor support, in-house and guest practitioners, a Practitioner Liaison Committee and a careers tutor.

common professional examination (full/part-time)

The CPE provides the academic stage of training for non-law graduates wishing to become solicitors or barristers. A full programme of lectures and tutorials is offered on this demanding course. Students are taught by experienced practitioners. Places on the LPC are guaranteed for successful students. Teaching methods on the CPE are varied and include lectures, group-led discussion and debate, workshops, oral presentations and independent research. The course includes an intensive induction programme involving use of library, methodology and an introduction to IT. The course benefits from its own dedicated teaching space within the school and also involves study skills sessions including advocacy, interview skills and drafting. The course as a whole is designed to provide the essential skills necessary for a successful career in law.

UNIVERSITY OF
WOLVERHAMPTON

www.chambersstudent.co.uk

solicitors

solicitors timetable

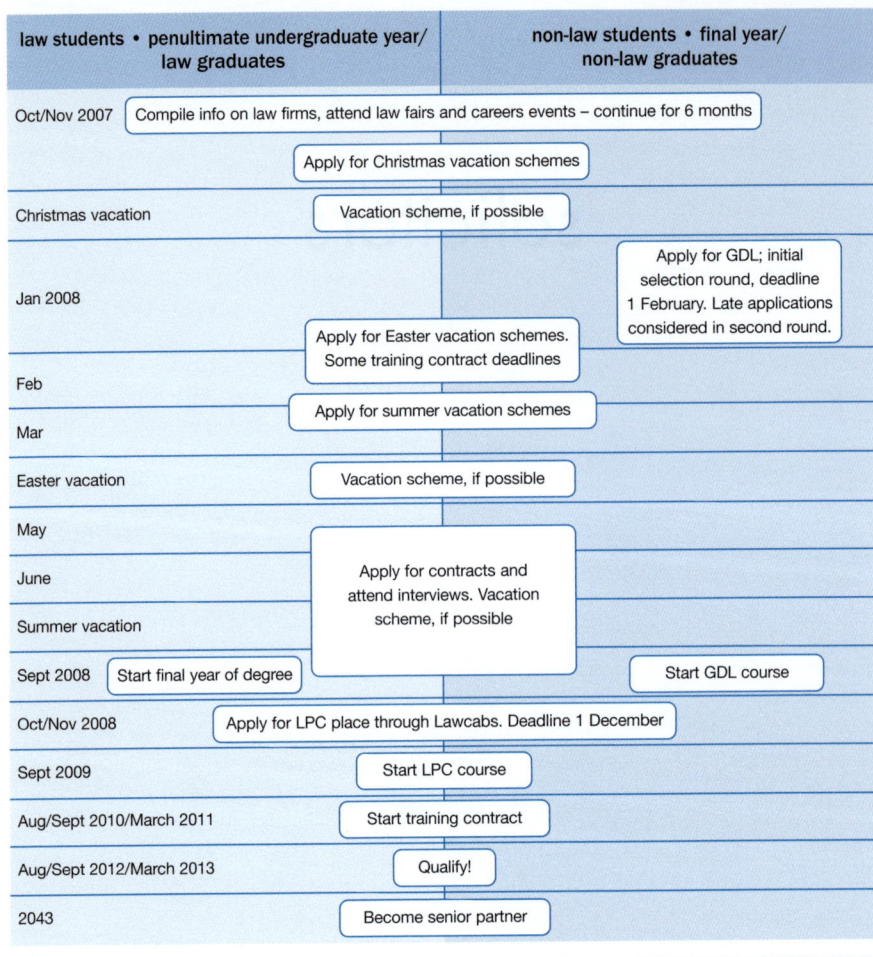

law students • penultimate undergraduate year/ law graduates	non-law students • final year/ non-law graduates
Oct/Nov 2007	Compile info on law firms, attend law fairs and careers events – continue for 6 months
	Apply for Christmas vacation schemes
Christmas vacation	Vacation scheme, if possible
Jan 2008	Apply for GDL; initial selection round, deadline 1 February. Late applications considered in second round.
	Apply for Easter vacation schemes. Some training contract deadlines
Feb	
	Apply for summer vacation schemes
Mar	
Easter vacation	Vacation scheme, if possible
May	
June	Apply for contracts and attend interviews. Vacation scheme, if possible
Summer vacation	
Sept 2008	Start final year of degree ··· Start GDL course
Oct/Nov 2008	Apply for LPC place through Lawcabs. Deadline 1 December
Sept 2009	Start LPC course
Aug/Sept 2010/March 2011	Start training contract
Aug/Sept 2012/March 2013	Qualify!
2043	Become senior partner

Notes

1 It is important to check application closing dates for each firm as these will vary.

2 Some firms will only accept applications for vacation schemes from penultimate-year students, whether law or non-law. See A-Z pages for further information.

3 Some firms require very early applications from non-law graduates. See A-Z pages for further information.

4 The timetable refers primarily to those firms that recruit two years in advance. Smaller firms often recruit just one year in advance or for immediate vacancies.

www.chambersstudent.co.uk

vacation schemes: i know what you did last summer

So you want to be a lawyer, but do you know why? Do you know how a solicitor spends their time and what goes on inside the offices of a law firm? If you are not too sure what's in store after law school then you may have problems convincing recruiters that you are committed to a career in law. And, deep down, even you may have doubts that you are on the right path. Vacation schemes are an ideal solution to several problems: lack of knowledge, lack of certainty and lack of CV material. Spending one, two or more weeks in a law firm gives you a taste of life as a solicitor and a chance to quiz trainees about their experiences. Even if you are not sold on a particular type of practice by the end of the experience, you'll know why and be able to look at firms of a different size or orientation.

welcome to the real world

Maybe you have already decided which type of training contract you want. Perhaps you even know exactly which firm you want to work for. If so, can you be sure your assumptions about it are correct? You wouldn't spend good money on clothes without trying them on, so why assume that you and an employer will be a good fit? You can pick up a lot about a firm at interview and on assessment days, but do remember that these are often conducted in stylish client suites that give little away about a firm's true character. Even the interviewers may be putting on an act, be it good cop, bad cop or yeah-I've-got-that-on-my-iPod-too cop. Spend an extended period of time in a place and you will see the reality of working there. All around you, deals will blow, people will stress, crises will be averted and people will bitch. Believe us, a lawyer is not going to postpone a rant or a resignation just because a student is in the office and might hear about it. Watching how lawyers interact with clients, with each other and with support staff, seeing how work is distributed and handled, even observing who makes the tea can be pretty enlightening.

playing your part

Reading about law firms' latest work on websites and perhaps even the national press makes it all sound rather exciting. How are these big deals and cases actually conducted? Attending a vacation scheme can be a useful way of understanding how court battles and M&A deals are broken down into component stages as you are likely to be given files to read through. Do your best to understand the key steps and any major problems within a file as you will probably be asked for your opinion and possibly asked to prepare a note on a particular aspect of the file. Another typical vac scheme exercise is to conduct research that will better inform the solicitors on a particular topic. Vac schemers are likely to be invited along to meetings, both internal and with clients, and court visits are also possible at some firms, either to watch an application on an actual case or for an arranged tour. In short, the tasks you will be given may contribute in some small way to live files, but you can't expect to do anything too significant.

bad manners

Aside from such exercises and other watch-and-learn type activities, the graduate recruitment team will commonly arrange talks about the firm's key departments and how its training contract is organised. There are also plenty of social events, partly to leave you with good memories of a fun working environment and partly to look at your social skills. While buying the rounds, recruiters and trainees will also be looking out for vaccies who revert to student union bar mode once the beer starts flowing. Best behaviour is advised at all times; bad-mouthing the firm, flirting with the HR assistant and throwing up on the pavement are not. And while we are on the subject of vac scheme etiquette, even if you are given your own Outlook account, we recommend you resist sending e-mail funnies across the intranet. We also recommend that you switch off your mobile phone when in the office.

under pressure

If a vac scheme confirms that you have found your ideal firm, you'll be happy to hear that your time there can act as a useful foot in the door. Just don't overestimate the size of your shoe. Even though many firms have a fast-track application process for those who have attended a vacation scheme, a training contract interview – never mind a job offer – is not guaranteed. Some firms do place their vacation schemes at the heart of the recruitment process, taking the lion's share of their trainees from the scheme. Does this make a placement a fortnight-long interview? Effectively, yes. It will serve you well to go in with the attitude that your actions will be scrutinised at all times and by anyone, including current trainees and secretaries. Don't get paranoid; just be yourself. The impression you want to leave people with is that you're polite, willing to put effort into whatever tasks you're asked to perform and confident enough to approach people in the office. Take your lead from how trainees interact with more-senior colleagues but don't get cocky. Any familiar behaviour you witness is likely to have developed after a period of assimilation into a team.

it's a numbers game

Having sold vacation schemes to you as a great idea, we should tell you it's not always easy to get your hands on one. The strongest candidates always manage to secure a clutch of vac scheme offers and a few become serial schemers, perhaps incentivised by the money on offer – as much as £250-£350 per week at City firms. Don't feel too disheartened if you don't manage to secure a place on an organised scheme; it doesn't mean you'll never get a training contract. After all, those serial schemers can only accept one training contract. Try to build up your CV in other ways. Firms look favourably on candidates who have gained other experience – perhaps in another legal or commercial environment or with a voluntary organisation.

Another thing to bear in mind is the timing of your application. Schemes are frequently targeted at penultimate-year law grads and final-year non-law grads, which can leave other students frustrated. The simple fact is that law firms most want to see those people who are ready to apply for training contracts. The law firms' literature should make it clear if applications are sought from particular groups of students.

Take care with application forms and prepare for interviews as thoroughly as for a training contract. For tips on how to prepare refer to **How to Make Applications and Get Selected** on page 93. The **Calendar** at the front of this book shows the application deadlines for major schemes.

The quality of vac schemes and how much of a 'real' trainee experience they offer can vary enormously. Here, one of our researchers in search of a training contract sums up two very different weeks spent at two similar-sized firms.

Firm One

- Only vac schemer that week.
- No set tasks, work included sitting in on meetings and admin jobs for paralegals.
- Brief contact with qualified solicitors.
- Structure of days left up to me.
- One arranged event, an informal lunch with three current trainees.

Firm Two

- Part of group of vac schemers.
- Tasks included research assignment, group activities and department-specific work. Given sample pieces of work to do for current trainees.
- Lots of contact with partners and associates.
- Informal meeting with grad recruitment team to talk through the process of getting a training contract with the firm.
- Three social events: two lunches and a night out with current trainees where I could ask questions in a neutral environment.

solicitors

vacation schemes

firm name	number of places	duration	remuneration	deadline
Addleshaw Goddard	75	1, 2 or 3 weeks	Not known	31 January 2008
Allen & Overy	120 – winter (grads & final year non-law); spring/summer (penult year law & non-law)	Not known	£250 p.w.	Winter: 31 Oct 07 Easter/summer: 18 Jan 08
Ashurst	Easter (grads & final year non-law); summer (penult year law)	Easter: 2 weeks summer: 3 weeks	£275 p.w.	31 January 2008
Baker & McKenzie	London: 30 international: 3-5	London: 3 weeks Lon/o'seas: 6-12 weeks	£270 p.w.	31 January 2008
Barlow Lyde & Gilbert	Yes, plus open days and drop-in days	Not known	Not known	31 January 2008
Bates Wells & Braithwaite	12	1 week	Not known	21 February 2008
Beachcroft	Summer	Not known	Paid	Not known
Berwin Leighton Paisner	Easter (final year law grads); summer (penult year & above)	Easter: 1 week summer: 2 weeks	Not known	31 January 2008
Bevan Brittan	50	Not known	Not known	31 March 2008
Bird & Bird	20	3 weeks	£275 p.w.	31 January 2008
Boodle Hatfield	10	2 weeks	Not known	Not known
Bristows	Yes	Easter: 1 week summer: 2 weeks	£200 p.w.	28 February 2008
Burges Salmon	40 plus open days	2 weeks	£250 p.w.	Not known
Capsticks	Yes	2 weeks	Not known	28 February 2008
Clarion Solicitors	30	1 week	Not known	28 February 2008
Cleary Gottlieb Steen & Hamilton	Christmas by arrangement 10 at Easter & 20 in summer	Not known	Not known	28 January 2008
Clifford Chance	Christmas, Easter and summer (some overseas)	Christmas: 2 days others: 2-4 weeks	Not known	Not known
Clyde & Co	20	2 weeks	Not known	31 January 2008
CMS Cameron McKenna	60, Christmas, Easter and summer	2 weeks	£250 p.w.	Christmas: 16 Nov 07 Easter/summer 28 Feb 08
Coffin Mew	Open week in July	Not known	Not known	31 March 2008
Covington & Burling	16	Not known	Not known	28 February 2008
Davenport Lyons	Yes	Not known	£200 p.w.	31 January 2008
Dechert	Easter and summer aimed at penult year law	Not known	Not known	29 February 2008
Denton Wilde Sapte	Open days in December and summer scheme	Not known	Not known	23 November 2007 8 February 2008

vacation schemes

firm name	number of places	duration	remuneration	deadline
Dickinson Dees	40	1 week	£200 p.w.	31 January 2008
DLA Piper	200	2 weeks	£250 p.w (Lon) £200 p.w (Ors)	31 January 2008
DMH Stallard	Yes	1 week	Unpaid	31 January 2008
Dundas & Wilson	Yes	4 weeks	Not known	26 January 2008
DWF	30	1 week	Paid	Not known
Eversheds	Summer: 150 Easter: in some offices	1 or 2 weeks	£240 p.w. London £175 p.w. regions	31 January 2008
Farrer & Co	30: Easter and summer	2 weeks	£250 p.w.	31 January 2008
Field Fisher Waterhouse	Yes	2 weeks	Not known	31 January 2008
Foot Anstey	Yes	Not known	Not known	31 March 2008
Forsters	10	Not known	£250 p.w.	15 March 2008
Freshfields Bruckhaus Deringer	100	2 weeks	£550 total	18 January 2008
Government Legal Service	60	2-3 weeks	£200-250 p.w.	31 March 2008
Halliwells	78	2 weeks	£210 p.w.	29 February 2008
Hammonds	64	2 weeks	£230 p.w. (Lon) £180 p.w. (Ors)	31 January 2008
HBJ Gateley Wareing	Yes	2 weeks	Not known	11 February 2008
Herbert Smith	130: some o/seas (winter: non-law)	Not known	Not known	Winter: 12 Nov 07 spring/summer: 31 Jan 08
Hewitsons	Yes	1 week	Not known	Not known
Hill Dickinson	12	2 weeks	Not known	31 March 2008
Holman Fenwick & Willan	Yes	2 weeks	£250 p.w.	14 February 2008
Howes Percival	Yes	Not known	Not known	30 April 2008
Hugh James	Yes	2 weeks	Not known	31 March 2008
Hunton & Williams	Yes	Not known	Not known	Not known
Ince & Co	15	2 weeks	£250 p.w.	14 February 2008
Irwin Mitchell	Yes	Not known	Not known	Not known
Jones Day	20 at Christmas: non-law 10 at Easter: non-law 40 in summer: law	2 weeks	£400 p.w.	Christmas: 31 Oct 07 Easter/summer: 31 Jan 08
Kendall Freeman	10	2 weeks	Not known	Not known
Kirkland & Ellis	25	2 weeks	£300 p.w.	31 January 2008

vacation schemes

firm name	number of places	duration	remuneration	deadline
K&L Gates	Yes	Not known	Not known	Not known
Latham & Watkins	Yes: Easter & summer	1 week	£300 p.w.	31 January 2008
Lawrence Graham	32: Easter and summer	1 week	£250 p.w.	31 January 2008
Laytons	6	1 week	Not known	31 March 2008
LeBoeuf Lamb	15	2 weeks	£300 p.w.	31 January 2008
Lester Aldridge	8	2 weeks	£75 p.w.	31 March 2008
Lewis Silkin	12 plus open days	2 weeks	Not known	31 January 2008
Linklaters	30: Christmas (non-law) 80: in summer (law) some o/seas	Christmas: 2 weeks summer: 2 or 4 weeks	Not known	Not known
Lovells	90: Christmas, Easter and summer	2 or 3 weeks	£300 p.w.	Christmas: 9 Nov 07 Easter/summer: 31 Jan 08
Macfarlanes	66	2 weeks	£250 p.w.	29 February 2008
Manches	24	1 week	Under review	31 January 2008
Mayer Brown	32: Easter and summer	3 weeks	Not known	Not known
Memery Crystal	4	2 weeks	Not known	Not known
Michelmores	Yes	1 week	Not known	28 February 2008
Mills & Reeve	Yes	2 weeks	Not known	31 January 2008
Mishcon de Reya	15	2 weeks	£250 p.w.	31 March 2008
Morgan Cole	Yes	Not known	Not known	30 April 2008
Morrison & Foerster	Yes	2 weeks	Travel + allowance	Not known
Nabarro	60	3 weeks	Not known	8 February 2008
Norton Rose	15 at Christmas 30 in summer plus open days	Christmas: 2 weeks summer: 4 weeks	£250 p.w.	31 October 2007/08 31 January 2008
Olswang	Yes	2 weeks	£275 p.w.	31 January 2008
O'Melveny & Myers	Yes	2 weeks	Not known	Not known
Osborne Clarke	20: Easter and summer	Not known	Not known	Not known
Pannone	120: Easter and summer	1 week	None	Easter: 25 Jan 08 summer: 13 July 08
Penningtons Solicitors	Yes plus information days	Not known	Not known	31 March 2008
Pinsent Masons	150	2 weeks	Not known	31 January 2008
Prettys	Yes	1 day	Not known	Not known

vacation schemes

firm name	number of places	duration	remuneration	deadline
PricewaterhouseCoopers Legal	Yes	2 weeks	Not known	Not known
Reed Smith Richards Butler	40	Not known	Not known	Not known
Reynolds Porter Chamberlain	24	2 weeks	£275 p.w.	29 February 2008
Shadbolt & Co	6	2 weeks	£200 p.w.	28 February 2008
Shoosmiths	Yes	2 weeks	Not known	28 February 2008
Simmons & Simmons	Yes	Not known	Not known	Not known
SJ Berwin	Yes	Not known	Not known.	31 January 2008
Skadden	Yes: Easter and summer	2 weeks	Paid	4 January 2008
Slaughter and May	60 (penult year of degree)	2 weeks	£275 p.w.	25 January 2008
Speechly Bircham	20	3 weeks	£250 p.w.	15 February 2008
Stephenson Harwood	18	2 weeks	£260 p.w.	17 February 2008
Stevens & Bolton	Yes	Not known	Not known	Not known
Taylor Walton	8	Up to 3 weeks	£195 p.w.	30 March 2008
Taylor Wessing	38	2 weeks	£250 p.w.	31 January 2008
Teacher Stern Selby	25	Not known	Not known	Not known
Thomas Eggar	Yes	1 week	Travel expenses	31 March 2008
TLT Solicitors	36	1 week	Paid	31 January 2008
Travers Smith	Christmas: 15 Summer: 45	2 weeks	£250	31 January 2008
Trowers & Hamlins	25-30 plus open days	2 weeks	£225 p.w.	1 March 2008
Walker Morris	48	1 week	£200 p.w.	31 January 2008
Ward Hadaway	Yes	1 week	Not known	28 February 2008
Watson, Farley & Williams	30	2 weeks	£250 p.w.	24 February 2008
Wedlake Bell	8	3 weeks	£200 p.w.	29 February 2008
Weil, Gotshal & Manges	20: Easter and summer 5: New York	Not known (NY: 3 weeks)	Not known	14 February 2008
White & Case	Easter: 20-25 Summer: 40-50	Easter: 1 week Summer: 2 weeks	£350 p.w.	31 January 2008
Wilsons Solicitors	Yes	1 week	Not known	Not known
Withers	Yes: Easter and summer	Not known	Not known	31 January 2008
Wragge & Co	Yes: Easter and summer	Not known	Not known	Not known

www.chambersstudent.co.uk

how to make applications and get selected

Firms can afford to be choosy so don't assume that a CV filled with any old guff and a half-hearted appraisal-day showing will secure you a training contract.

www.

Who? Why? What? Narrowing down the list of the firms you'd like to work for, assessing whether the firm's a good cultural match for you and making sure they do the kind of work you want are good starting points.

- The **Practice Areas** section of this book summarises the main types of work and ranks the best firms in those fields.
- Look at firm's own websites and those of the legal press – *The Lawyer* (www.thelawyer.com), *Legal Week* (www.legalweek.com) and *The Law Gazette* (www.lawgazette.co.uk).
- The **True Picture** will give you a sense of a firm's culture, the specifics of what work current trainees have experienced and how easy they found it to get the seats they wanted.
- Better still, take a vac scheme and sample the work yourself.

Once you've narrowed the field, remember to do a quick idiot check:

- Do your qualifications and experiences fit what the firm wants?
- When is the application deadline? Most commercial firms recruit two years in advance. A few of the big City firms have even earlier application deadlines. Smaller firms recruit one year in advance, sometimes even closer to the start of the contract. Some firms may offer a paralegal position for a trial period before a training contract is discussed.
- Are you applying at the right time? See the **Solicitors Timetable** on page 86.

mailshotshy

Word and mailmerge may enable you to fire off 100 applications in a day but it's not the best approach.

Targeted and carefully reasoned CVs, letters and application forms stand out. Here are a few tips:

- Don't put anything in your CV unless you can expand on it at interview.
- Avoid chronological gaps in your experience: if you've taken time off, put it down and be prepared to explain why.
- CVs are a chance to make your achievements shine: keep them to two, possibly three, pages max and make the most of your strengths by effective use of headings, bullets and bold text.
- Covering letter: Unless stated otherwise, always include one with your CV. It's a chance to expand on why you want to work for a firm and what experience/interests fit you for it, as well as giving the reader a more personal insight into your qualities. One page should do.
- No gimmicks: Avoid photos, bizarre fonts or lurid colours, bribes or jokey applications.
- Spellcheck: thers nothing moor distratcing ad unprofesional than mistakes.

good form

If firms don't ask for a CV they'll want you to complete a dreaded application form. Remember:

- Forms take time: start early and get them in on time. We've heard of online applications submitted just two minutes past a deadline being rejected. Construct a table of the firms you are applying to, their deadlines and where you are with your application to each.
- Practice makes perfect: photocopy any form that needs to be handwritten and prepare a rough draft. Tipp-ex and different colours of ink look shabby.
- Read the questions: make sure you're answering the question posed, not the question you want to answer. Plan each response carefully, making sure that however little you have to say, you fill much of the box available. Acres of white space look bad.

making applications (continued)

- On the other hand: make sure you use the questions to cover your whole range of skills and attributes.
- Include a covering letter: unless asked not to. Your letter should highlight the best aspects of your application and relevant experience is fine.
- Keep a copy: weeks later you may struggle to remember what you wrote.

show me what ya got

Qualifications, gap year conservation work, 17 A*s at A-level, endless vac schemes: applicants must show high levels of academic and personal achievement. The top applicants will always reap a sheaf of offers, but care and attention can go a long way.

- Applications should demonstrate teamwork and problem-solving skills as well as commercial outlook/commitment to practice.
- Get work experience or vac schemes and try to speak to lawyers wherever you can; it all helps you understand the reality of practice.

interphew!

Having secured an interview, make sure you prepare, prepare, prepare. After all, you wouldn't qualify for the Olympics, then laze around eating cheeseburgers until the day of the race. Remember:

- Detailed preparation helps boost confidence and gives weight to your answers. No one likes a bluffer.
- Be up to date with legal news and current affairs: the law doesn't exist in a vacuum. *The Lawyer*, *Legal Week*, *The Law Gazette* and Tuesday's law supplement in *The Times* are good ports of call.
- Study the firm's own literature just prior to interview. If you know which partner will be interviewing you, research him/her.
- Practise answering questions, even the most obvious ones. Can you actually justify why you want to be a lawyer? Don't find out that the answer is 'no' in your interview.

the big day

Here are some general tips:

- Arrive early: If you arrive late, in a rush or pouring with sweat, you're liable to flummox yourself, make a bad impression, keep partners waiting and undo all that hard prep. Arriving early to sit in a nearby cafe and review your application is a much better way to go. Keep the firm's number on you in case you are genuinely delayed.
- Dress appropriately: Casual dress won't convey the right message, nor will anything too racy or alternative. Even if you hate the idea, suits for men and something equally formal for women is the safest choice.
- Be polite to everyone you meet: don't take your nerves out on the receptionist and be careful what you say to those friendly trainees you meet. Bad impressions travel fast.
- Interviews are a two way process: remember the experience is also a chance to assess the firm, its people, atmosphere and whether you'd like to work there. You must avoid appearing arrogant, but you have every reason to be confident not awestruck.
- If more than one person interviews you: try to speak to everyone on the panel.
- Listen carefully and think clearly before answering questions.
- Body language: don't fidget; maintain eye contact as far as possible without scaring anyone.
- Expect to be tested: if your answers are challenged, don't get defensive or aggressive.
- Interviewers want you to shine, not trip you up: difficult questions are designed to test your reactions so try not to freeze.
- Any questions? Prepare a couple of sensible questions for the end of the interview.

testing times

Many firms put candidates to the test via written tests, negotiation exercises and group tasks. These sessions tend to be firm specific and can change year-on-year but your LPC or GDL provider may have a back catalogue of student feedback on different firms' assessment days.

- Reasoning tests can be hard to prepare for, because the companies who supply firms with papers guard their secrets carefully. Some law firms will post sample papers out in advance and your careers service may have a back catalogue.
- The Watson Glaser and HSL tests are the two most commonly used. These tend to feature multiple-choice, reasoning-based questions centred on snippets of commercial information. They test business awareness and intellectual rigour. Some tests need to be completed in a given time; others assess speed by having too many questions. Make sure you know which kind you're sitting.
- You may be asked to write a letter or summarise a piece of research. Such tasks should be equally accessible to law and non-law students.

- Group exercises determine how well you work in a team. Don't simply jockey for position: listen to others, pick up on what they're saying and make your own comments on their suggestions.
- Don't forget to ask around: a friend who attended the same assessment day can brief you on what to expect. Don't hang all your hopes on insider tips as firms may vary their assignments.
- Don't relax too much if there's a social event.

the hardest word to say…

No one likes being rejected but, if things don't work out and you just can't understand why, bite the bullet and phone up to ask.

- However hard it is to hear, finding out your strengths and weaknesses will help you.
- Should you reapply to a firm that has rejected you? It may work for some candidates, especially if they got through to a later stage of the process, however many firms will not want to revisit your application.

Case Study: A typical Linklaters' Assessment Day

8.45am: Arrive
- Current trainees are on hand to involve you and 2-3 other candidates in general chat and help calm nerves.

9.00am: One-hour critical reasoning test
- 10 mins to explain the process then 50 mins to answer 80 multiple-choice questions testing analytical and logic skills. Linklaters uses the Watson Glaser test, aiming *"not to catch people out but test their intellectual rigour and suitability to be commercial lawyers."*

10.00am: 45-minute first interview
- A lawyer (likely a managing associate) takes you off for an initial interview. This focuses on you, your abilities, experiences, leadership qualities, etc… essentially *"all the soft skills that would suit your work as a trainee lawyer."*

10.45am: 30-minute break
- A trainee escorts you on a tour of the building. HR assures us that *"trainees are not there to report back on candidates,"* but watch what you say.

11.15am: 30-minutes of case study preparation
- Time to prepare responses to a commercial case study. The exercise is presented as a brief in which the candidate is a trainee asked to review and analyse information about a client's position and report back to a partner. There will be several pages of information to read and process before deciding how to present your thoughts. No flip charts or PowerPoint presentations are involved.

11.45am: 45-minute second interview
- A partner takes you to the second interview. The first 15-20 minutes are spent presenting and discussing your thoughts on the case study. Discussion then moves on to broader commercial matters, including questions *"to test a candidate's ability to think speedily and dexterously on their feet."*

12.30pm: Leave
- The partner will escort you to the door. You stagger off down Silk Street to await a decision within days. Meanwhile, Linklaters' staff gather *"to discuss feedback and make a decision."*

applications and selection

firm name	method of application	selection process	degree class	number of contracts	number of applications
Addleshaw Goddard	See website	Interview + assessment centre	2:1	45-50	1,500
Allen & Overy	Online	Interview	2:1	120	2,500
asb law	Application form	Interviews + assessment centre	2:1	5	500
Ashurst	Online	2 interviews	2:1	55	2,500
Baker & McKenzie	Online	Oral presentation + interview	2:1	38	2,000
Barlow Lyde & Gilbert	Online	Interview day	Not known	18-20	2,000
Bates Wells & Braithwaite	Online	Interviews	2:1	5	600+
Beachcroft	Online	Interview + assessment centre	2:1 preferred	30	Not known
Berwin Leighton Paisner	Online	Assessment day + interview	2:1	40	1,500
Bevan Brittan	Online	Not known	Not known	Not known	Not known
Bingham McCutchen	Online	Interviews	High 2:1	2	Not known
Bircham Dyson Bell	See website	2 interviews	2:1 preferred	8	580
Bird & Bird	Online	Assessment day	2:1	18	900
Blake Lapthorn Tarlo Lyons	Online	Interviews & assessment day	2:1	17	300
Boodle Hatfield	Online	Interviews + assessment	2:1	6-8	Not known
BP Collins	Handwritten letter & CV	Interview + selection day	2:1	Not known	Not known
Brabners Chaffe Street	Online	Interview + assessment day	2:1 or postgrad	10	Not known
Bristows	Application form	2 interviews	2.1 preferred	Up to 10	3,500
Browne Jacobson	Online or CV & covering letter	Telephone interview + assessment centre or open day	2:1	12	700
Burges Salmon	Application form	Not known	2:1	20-25	1,500
Capsticks	Application form CV & letter	Interview	2:1 or above	4-5	200
Charles Russell	Online	Assessment day	2:1	20	1,500
Clarion Solicitors	Application form	Not known	2:1	4	230
Clarke Willmott	Application form	Interview	2:1 preferred	10	500
Cleary Gottlieb Steen & Hamilton	CV & covering letter	Usually via vac scheme	High 2:1	10	Not known
Clifford Chance	Online	Assessment day	2:1	130	2,000
Clyde & Co	Online	Interview + assessments	2:1	24	1,200+
CMS Cameron McKenna	Online	Interview + assessment centre	2:1	60	1,500
Cobbetts	Online	Assessment day	2:1	25	1,000

applications and selection

firm name	method of application	selection process	degree class	number of contracts	number of applications
Coffin Mew	See website	Interview	2:1 (usually)	5-6	400+
Collyer Bristow	Online	Interviews	2:1	Not known	Not known
Covington & Burling	Online	2 interviews	2:1	6	Not known
Cripps Harries Hall	Application form	Interview	2.1	8	Up to 750
Davenport Lyons	Online	Interviews	2:1	8	800
Davies Arnold Cooper	Application form	Not known	2:1 (usually)	5	Not known
Dechert	Online	Interviews + assessments	2:1	Up to 15	1,500
Denton Wilde Sapte	Application form	2 interviews + assessments.	2:1	35	1,500
Dickinson Dees	Online	Interview + assessments	2:1	Up to 21	800
DLA Piper	Online	2 interviews + assessments	2:1	95+	2,200
DMH Stallard	Online	Assessment days	2:1	10	525
Dorsey & Whitney	CV & Letter	Not known	2:1	4	Not known
Dundas & Wilson	Online	Assessment day	2:1 preferred	12 (London)	300
DWF	Online	2 interviews	2:1	16	800
Eversheds	Online	Assessment day	2:1	80	4,000
Farrer & Co	Online	Interviews	2:1	10	800
Field Fisher Waterhouse	Online	Interviews + written assessment	2:1	20	1,200
Finers Stephens Innocent	CV & covering letter	2 interviews	2:1	6	800
Fladgate Fielder	Application form	Assessment day + interview	2:1	4	Not known
Foot Anstey	Letter & CV or online	Assessment day	2:1 preferred	10	Not known
Forbes	Handwritten letter & CV	Interview	2:1	4	350+
Ford & Warren	CV & letter	Interviews + exercise	None	4	500
Forsters	Online	2 interviews	Not known	Not known	Not known
Freeth Cartwright	Online	Interview + selection day	Not known	Not known	Not known
Freshfields Bruckhaus Deringer	Online	2 interviews + written test	2:1	100	2,000
Government Legal Service	Online	Online test + assessment day	2:1	22-30	800
Halliwells	Online	Group exercise, presentation + interview	2:1	40	1,500
Hammonds	Online	Assessment + interview	2:1	40	1,300

applications and selection

firm name	method of application	selection process	degree class	number of contracts	number of applications
Harbottle & Lewis	CV & letter	Interview	2:1	5	800
HBJ Gateley Wareing	See website	Not known	2:1	11 (England)	Not known
Henmans	Application form	Assessment day	Not known	3	300
Herbert Smith	Online	Case study + interview	2:1	Up to 100	2,000
Hewitsons	Application form	Interview	2:1	10	850
Higgs & Sons	Online or letter & CV	Interview	2:1 usually preferred	4	250+
Hill Dickinson	Online	Assessment day	Not known	Not known	Not known
Hodge Jones & Allen	Application form	Interview	2:1	6-7	500
Holman Fenwick & Willan	Online	2 interviews + written exercise	2:1	8	1,000
Howes Percival	Online	Assessment centre	2:1	10	300
Hugh James	Online	Interview & presentation	2:1	7	500
Hunton Williams	CV & handwritten letter + app form	Interview + assessment day	2:1	2	300
IBB Solicitors	Online	Interview + assessment day	2:1	6	400
Ince & Co	Online	2 interviews + written test	2:1	12	1,000
Irwin Mitchell	Online	Assessment centre + interview	None	20-25	1,500
Jones Day	CV & letter online	2 interviews	2:1	15-20	1,500
Kendall Freeman	Online	Interview + assessement	2:1	8	Not known
Kirkland & Ellis	CV & letter	Interview	Not known	Not known	Not known
K&L Gates	Online	Assessment day	2:1	Up to 15	1,000
Latham & Watkins	Online	3 interviews	2:1	10-15	Not known
Lawrence Graham	Application form	Interview	2:1	20-25	800
Laytons	Application form	2 interviews	1 or 2:1	8	2,000
LeBoeuf Lamb	Application form	Not known	2:1	17	950
Lee & Priestley	Online	Group exercise + interview	Normally 2:1	2-3	Not known
Lester Aldridge	Letter, CV & application form	Interview	2:1	10	300
Lewis Silkin	Online	Assessment day	2:1	5	500
Linklaters	Application form	2 interviews + assessments	2:1	130	3,500
Lovells	Online	Assessment day	2:1	90	2,500
Lupton Fawcett	Online	Interview + assessment day	2:1 preferred	2-3	300

applications and selection

firm name	method of application	selection process	degree class	number of contracts	number of applications
Mace & Jones	Online	Interview	2:1	5-6	250
Macfarlanes	Online	Assessment day	2:1	30	900
Maclay Murray & Spens	Application form	2 interviews + assessments	2:1	30 London/Scotland	150 (London)
Manches	Online	2 interviews	2:1	10	900
Martineau Johnson	Online	Half-day assessment centre	2:1	10-12	500
Mayer Brown	Online	Interview + assessments	2:1	25-30	1,000+
Maxwell Winward	CV & covering letter	2 interviews	2:1	4	250
McDermott, Will & Emery	CV & covering letter	Interview + written exercise	Not known	Not known	Not known
McGrigors	Online	Half-day assessment centre	2:1	12-15 (London)	Not known
Memery Crystal	Online	Interview + assessment centre	2:1	5-6	150
Michelmores	Online	Interview + assessment	2:1	10	200
Mills & Reeve	Online	Assessment centre	2:1	22	650
Mishcon de Reya	Online	Not known	2:1	10-12	1,000+
Morgan Cole	Online	Assessment centre	2:1 preferred	Not known	Not known
Morrison & Foerster	See website	Interviews	2:1	3	500
Nabarro	Online	Assessment day	2:1	35	1,500
Norton Rose	Online	Interview + group exercise	2:1	55	2,500+
Olswang	Online	Interview + assessments	2:1	24	2,000
O'Melveny & Myers	Online	Interview	Not known	4-6	Not known
Orrick, Herrington & Sutcliffe	Online	2 interviews	2:1	Up to 8	Not known
Osborne Clarke	Online	Assessment day	2:1	20	1,000
Pannone	Online	2 interviews	2:1	14	1,000
Paul Hastings	Online	Interview	2:1	3-4	Not known
Payne Hicks Beach	Letter & CV	Interview	2:1	3	1,000
Penningtons Solicitors	Online	Not known	2:1	15	1,000
Pinsent Masons	Online	Assessment day	2:1	55	2,000+
Prettys	Letter & CV	Not known	2:1 preferred	5	Not known
PricewaterhouseCoopers Legal	Online	Not known	2:1	Not known	Not known
Pritchard Englefield	Application form	Interview	Generally 2:1	3	300-400

applications and selection

firm name	method of application	selection process	degree class	number of contracts	number of applications
Reed Smith Richards Butler	Online	Interview + assessment	2:1	32	1,500
Reynolds Porter Chamberlain	Online	Assessment day	2.1	15	900
Salans	Handwritten letter & CV	Interviews + workshop	2:1	3-4	500+
Shadbolt & Co	Online	Interview + assessment	Usually 2:1	4	100
Shearman & Sterling	Online	Interviews	2:1	15	Not known
Shoosmiths	Online	Full-day assessment centre	2:1	17	1,000
Sidley Austin	Application form	Interview(s)	2:1	15	500
Simmons & Simmons	Online	Assessment day	2:1	50	2,000
SJ Berwin	Online	2 interviews	2:1	45	2,000
Skadden	Online	Interview + exercise	2:1	10	700
Slaughter and May	Online or covering letter & CV	Interview	2:1	85-95	2,000+
Speechly Bircham	Application form	Interview	2:1	10	588
Stephenson Harwood	Online	Assessment centre	2:1	12	Not known
Stevens & Bolton	Online	2 interviews + assessments	2:1	4	200
Taylor Walton	CV & covering letter	2 interviews	2:1	Not known	Not known
Taylor Wessing	Online	Assessment centre	2:1	24	1,195
Teacher Stern Selby	Online	2 interviews	2:1 (not absolute)	3-4	500
Thomas Eggar	Online	Assessment centre + interview	2:1	Not known	Not known
Thomson Snell & Passmore	Letter & application form	Assessment interview	2:1	5	500
Thring Townsend Lee & Pemberton	Application form & CV	2 interviews	2:1 preferred	9	300+
TLT Solicitors	Online	Assessment centre	2:1 preferred	10	500+
Travers Smith	CV & covering letter	2 interviews	2:1	25	2,000
Trethowans	Letter & application form	Interview + assessment day	2:1	3-4	100+
Trowers & Hamlins	Online	Interviews + assessments	2:1	22	1,600
Walker Morris	Online	Interviews	2:1	20	Approx 800
Ward Hadaway	Application form	Assessment centre + interview	2:1	12	400+

applications and selection

firm name	method of application	selection process	degree class	number of contracts	number of applications
Warner Goodman	Online	Interview	Not known	3	Not known
Watson Burton	Application form & letter	Not known	2:1	6	1,000
Watson, Farley & Williams	Online	Assessment centre + interview	2:1	12	1,000
Wedlake Bell	Application form	2 interviews	2:1	7	Not known
Weightmans	Online	Not known	Not known	Up to 14	Not known
Weil, Gotshal & Manges	Online	Not known	2:1	12	Not known
White & Case	Online	Interview	2:1	30-35	1,600
Wiggin	Online	2-day selection	2:1	4	500
Wilsons Solicitors	Online or CV	Interview + assessment day	2:1	4	Not known
Withers	Application form	2 interviews + exercises	2:1	18	700
Wollastons	CV & online application form	3-stage interview	2:1	2	500
Wragge & Co	Online	Telephone discussion + assessment day	2:1	30	1,000

deal or no deal: the art of managing offers

After all the hard work involved in securing a training contract offer, you'll need to know what to do when you actually land one. The Law Society publishes its 'Voluntary Code to Good Practice in the Recruitment of Trainee Solicitors' at www.lawsociety.org.uk/becomingasolicitor/training.law#9 and we recommend you read through these guidelines if, at any stage, you are in doubt as to what you should do. The guidelines address the conduct of both recruiters and students.

On offers the guidelines say:

- If you're still an undergrad, an offer of a training contract can only be made on or after 1 September in your final undergraduate year. If you've impressed the firm during a vacation scheme or period of work experience, the firm must wait until this date before making you an offer.
- At an interview, you will be told if there is a further stage to the selection process. You should also be told within two weeks of reaching the end of the process whether or not you have been successful.
- Offers should be made in writing. If you receive an offer by phone you don't need to say yes or no: you can ask the firm to send a formal offer in writing for you to consider.

On deadlines, the guidelines say:

- No deadline should expire earlier than four weeks from the date of the offer. If you need more time to consider an offer, firms are supposed to consider your request 'sympathetically' provided you have a good reason. No definition of 'good reason' is given in the guidelines.
- If a firm is going to pay your law school fees, it should set out the terms and conditions of the arrangement in the training contract offer letter. The firm's willingness to provide financial assistance should not affect the time limit for accepting the contract.
- If you feel you need more time you will have to enter into diplomatic discussions with the law firm, telling them how much longer you need. Make sure you get written confirmation of any extension to the deadline as simply asking for it won't be enough.

You may want to hang on to an offer from one firm while you pursue applications with others. This is okay, but you must bear in mind the following:

- You should not hold more than two (as yet unaccepted or declined) offers at any one time.
- Students are supposed to respond promptly to a firm that's made an offer, either by accepting or rejecting it. The word 'promptly' is not defined in the code.
- Because offers can and will be made with time limits for acceptance, do guard against allowing a deadline to elapse. The stupidity tax you may otherwise pay doesn't bear thinking about.
- Once your preferred offer has been accepted in writing, you must then confirm to everyone else that you are withdrawing your application. This is only fair to busy recruiters and other applicants who may suffer if you clog up a shortlist.

The guidelines are silent on the issue of what happens if a student changes their mind after accepting an offer. It's a rare firm that will be particularly sympathetic to a post-acceptance withdrawal but, on occasions, these things do happen. We can give no general advice on this subject, as each individual case will have its own merits. What we can say is that the whole trainee recruitment market relies on all parties playing by the above 'rules'. So what if a law firm puts pressure on you to accept an offer earlier than the guidelines say they should? Again, there is no simple answer as the Law Society's code of conduct is voluntary. If this situation arises you will have to enter into delicate negotiations with the law firm. We also recommend that you report the problem to your university or college careers adviser and ask if they can recommend a course of action.

a quick look at the markets

The past two years have been a relatively good time to be looking for a training contract. Law firms have been really busy as the economy has been buoyant, so more training places were offered than ever before. For a segment of our readership, snagging a training contract in 2008 will still be easy business; however, if uncertainties in the financial markets lead to bigger problems in the economy then in the 2008 recruitment round firms could decide to take a slightly more cautious approach to the numbers of trainees they take on. The last time the deals market went quieter, quite a few commercial law firms deferred the arrival of some of their new trainees. This is a worst-case scenario and, in truth, it is impossible to make accurate predictions, either about the economy or the demand for new recruits. All we can say is that it is possible for law firm's requirements for trainees to go down as well as up.

If you're aiming for the City or a big regional firm you will certainly benefit from an increase in salaries this year. Just as last year, the *Student Guide* salary-o-meter went bananas over the summer of 2007 when law firms announced their latest pay and sponsorship rates. In 2007 City trainee and NQ salaries jumped dramatically across the board, certainly by a far higher margin than regional salary increases. Law school sponsorship has remained much the same as last year, following a large increase in 2006.

With commercial trainee salaries higher than they have ever been, it leaves us wondering how another segment of our readership will feel when they learn that the Law Society has been consulting over whether to do away with requirements for a minimum trainee salary. The last figures published by the society required that trainees receive no less than £17,110 pa in central London or £15,332 pa elsewhere. The idea behind removing the salary safety net is to encourage more firms to offer traineeships, albeit lower-paid ones. It's impossible to predict what effect such a change might have, or indeed whether the idea would be adopted, but if it were you can bet your parents' mortgage that any additional training contracts arising as a result would not be accompanied by law school funding. Though it would hardly be a return to the days when aspiring lawyers actually paid firms to train them, it would certainly leave us with a two-tier legal profession in which a generation of debt-ridden, extremely poorly paid lawyers co-exist with the fat cats. Arguably that's exactly what we have already.

Undeniably there are plenty of people who would welcome a training contract at any price, simply because the number of student hopefuls outstrips the number of training opportunities. While the factors affecting the number of training positions are many, all stem from the financial considerations which law firms face, be these general economic conditions or changes in legal aid rates and coverage.

Pay Cheques in the City

The most handsome law school sponsorship packages now approach £30,000 for those taking both the GDL and the LPC. New trainees in major City firms now typically start somewhere between £36,000 and £38,000 pa, with American firms paying as much as £40,000 to first-year trainees. When it comes to NQ salaries the news is even better, with the UK-firm benchmark now set around £65,000 and certain American firms paying astonishing rates. The firm still making the headlines on NQ salaries is Latham & Watkins: its 2007 NQ salary is a whopping £96,000. Not far behind is Cleary with a hefty £92,000. In between these two groups of firms are the US firms paying around £70,000-£75,000, among them Jones Day, LeBoeuf Lamb and Dechert.

salaries and benefits

firm name	1st year salary	2nd year salary	sponsorship/ awards	other benefits	qualification salary
Addleshaw Goddard	£24,750 (Manch/Leeds) £36,000 (London)	£27,600 (Manch/Leeds) £39,500 (London)	GDL & LPC: fees + £7,000 (London) or £4,500 (elsewhere)	Corporate gym m'ship, STL, subsd restaurant, pension, pte healthcare	£40,000 (Manch/Leeds) £64,000 (London)
Allen & Overy	£36,200	£40,300	LPC: fees + £7,000 GDL: fees + £6,000 (London), £5,000 (elsewhere)	Pte healthcare, PMI, STL, subsd restaurant, gym m'ship, in-house medical facilities	£65,000
asb law	£19,000	Not known	LPC: interest-free loan	Not known	Not known
Ashurst	£36,000	£40,000	GDL & LPC: fees + £7,500, £500 for first-class degree or LPC distinction, language bursaries	PHI, pension, life ass, STL, gym m'ship	£64,000
Baker & McKenzie	£36,500 + £3,000 'joining bonus'	£39,000	LPC: fees + £8,000 GDL: fees + £6,000	PHI, life ins, PMI, pension, subsd gym m'ship, STL, subsd restaurant	£63,500
Barlow Lyde & Gilbert	£32,000	£35,000	GDL & LPC: fees + maintenance	Not known	£58,000
Bates Wells & Braithwaite	£29,000	£31,000	LPC: fees + interest paid on student loans	STL, subsd gym, subsd restaurant, pension, 1 month unpaid leave on qual	£41,000
Beachcroft	£30,000 (London) £22,000 (regions)	£33,000 (London) £24,000 (regions)	GDL & LPC: fees + £5,000	Flexible scheme inc holiday, pension, pte healthcare, EAP	Not known
Berwin Leighton Paisner	£33,000 + £2,500 golden hello	£36,000	GDL & LPC: fees + £7,200	Not known	£62,000
Bevan Brittan	Not known	Not known	GDL & LPC: fees + bursary	Not known	Not known
Bingham McCutchen	£40,000	£45,000	GDL & LPC: fees + £8,000	PHI, travel ins, disability ins, STL, life ass, subsd gym	£91,429
Bircham Dyson Bell	£30,000	£31,000	GDL & LPC: fees	Pte healthcare, life ass, PHI, pension	£49,000
Bird & Bird	£31,000	£35,000	GDL & LPC: fees + £5,500	BUPA, STL, subsd sports club m'ship, life cover, PHI, pension, childcare and eyecare vouchers	£55,000
Blake Lapthorn Tarlo Lyons	£19,000	£20,500	LPC: fees + maintenance	Pte healthcare, life ass, pension, childcare vouchers	£33,500
Boodle Hatfield	£28,500	£30,500	GDL & LPC: fees + maintenance	Pte healthcare, life ass, STL, pension, PHI, PMI, conveyancing grant	£47,500

Notes: PHI = Permanent Health Insurance; STL = Season Travel Ticket Loan; PMI = Private Medical Insurance EAP = Employee Assistance Programme

www.chambersstudent.co.uk

salaries and benefits

firm name	1st year salary	2nd year salary	sponsorship/ awards	other benefits	qualification salary
BP Collins	£20,000	£21,000	Not known	Not known	Not known
Brabners Chaffe Street	£20,000	Not known	LPC: assistance available	Not known	Not known
Bristows	£33,000	£36,000	GDL & LPC: fees + £7,000	Pension, life ass & health ins	£50,000
Browne Jacobson	£24,000	£26,500	GDL & LPC: fees + £5,000	Not known	Market rate
Burges Salmon	£28,000	£29,000	GDL & LPC: fees + £6,000	Bonus, pension, pte healthcare, mobile phone, gym m'ship, Xmas gift	£41,000
Capsticks	£28,000	£29,000	GDL & LPC: financial assistance	Bonus, pension, PHI, PMI, death-in-service-cover, STL, childcare vouchers	£45,000
Charles Russell	£31,000	£35,000	GDL & LPC: fees + £6,000 (London) £4,500 (Guildford) £3,500 (Cheltenham)	BUPA, PHI, life ass, pension, STL	£53,000
Clarion Solicitors	Competitive	Competitive	Not known	Not known	Competitive
Clarke Willmott	£22,500	£24,000	LPC: fees	Life ass, pension, gym m'ship, bonus, STL, eyecare & childcare vouchers	£34,750-£36,000
Cleary Gottlieb Steen & Hamilton	£40,000	£45,000	GDL & LPC: fees + £8,000	Pension, PHI, disability ins, gym m'ship, BUPA, life ins, childcare vouchers, EAP subsd restaurant	£92,000
Clifford Chance	£37,500	£40,300	GDL & LPC: fees + maintenance	Subsd restaurant, fitness centre, pension, up to 6 weeks' leave on qual	£63,500
Clyde & Co	£31,000	£34,000	GDL & LPC: fees + £7,000 (Lon/Guild) £6,000 (elsewhere)	Interest-free loan on joining, pension, life ass, PMI, subsd gym m'ship, STL	£55,000
CMS Cameron McKenna	£36,000	£40,000	GDL & LPC: fees + up to £7,500	Bonus, gym m'ship, life ass, pension, pte healthcare, STL, care line, subs'd rest, buy-holiday scheme	£64,000
Cobbetts	£21,000	£22,000	GDL & LPC: fees + £4,000	BUPA, gym m'ship, pension, STL, death-in-service cover, counselling	£37,000
Coffin Mew	Competitive	Competitive	LPC: discussed with candidates	Not known	Competitive
Collyer Bristow	£25,500	£27,500	LPC: fees + £4,000	Pension, PMI, life ass, STL	Not known

Notes: PHI = Permanent Health Insurance; STL = Season Travel Ticket Loan; PMI = Private Medical Insurance EAP = Employee Assistance Programme

salaries and benefits

firm name	1st year salary	2nd year salary	sponsorship/ awards	other benefits	qualification salary
Covington & Burling	£36,500	£40,000	GDL & LPC: fees + £7,250	Pension, PHI, pte healthcare, life ass, STL	Not known
Cripps Harries Hall	£20,000	£22,000	LPC fees: 50% interest-free loan, 50% bursary	Not known	£33,000
Davenport Lyons	£32,000-£32,666	£33,332-£34,000	No	STL, client intro bonus, subsd gym m'ship, discretionary bonus, life ass	Not known
Davies Arnold Cooper	£29,000	Not known	GDL & LPC: fees + maintenance	PMI, STL	Not known
Dechert	£38,000	£43,000	LPC: fees + £10,000	Not known	£63,000-£72,500
Denton Wilde Sapte	£36,000	£40,000	GDL & LPC: fees + £6,000 (£7,000 in London)	Flexible benefit scheme, STL	£62,000
Dickinson Dees	£19,000	£20,000	GDL & LPC: fees + financial assistance	Not known	£36,000
DLA Piper	£36,000 (London) £25,000 (other English)	£39,000 (London) £28,000 (other English)	GDL & LPC: fees + up to £7,000	Pension, pte healthcare, life ass, PHI	£63,000 (London) competitive (other English)
DMH Stallard	£22,000 (Brighton & Gatwick) £27,000 (London)	£24,000 (Brighton & Gatwick) £29,000 (London)	LPC: 50% loan + 50% funded	Not known	Not known
Dorsey & Whitney	£35,000	£39,000	Not known	Pension, health ins, life ins	£65,000 + bonus
Dundas & Wilson	£30,000 (London)	£33,500 (London)	GDL & LPC: fees + maintenance	Life ass, PHI, pension, STL, holiday-purchase scheme	Not known
DWF	£23,000	Not known	LPC: fees	Flexible scheme inc life ass, pension	Not known
Eversheds	£35,000 (London)	£37,000 (London)	GDL & LPC: fees + maintenance	Regional variations	£62,000 (London)
Farrer & Co	£29,500	£32,000	GDL & LPC: fees + £5,000	Health & life ins, subsd gym m'ship, STL	£47,000
Field Fisher Waterhouse	£33,000	£36,500	GDL: fees + £5,500 LPC: fees + £6,000	STL, medical ins, life ass, pension, GP service	£60,000
Finers Stephens Innocent	£29,000	£31,000	GDL & LPC: fees	Pension, PMI, life ins, long-term disability ins, STL	£47,000
Fladgate Fielder	£27,500	up to £29,000	Not known	Pension, PHI, Life ass, STL, gym loan, bonus, PMI	£55,000
Foot Anstey	£19,500	£21,000	LPC: £9,600	Pension	£31,500

Notes: PHI = Permanent Health Insurance; STL = Season Travel Ticket Loan; PMI = Private Medical Insurance EAP = Employee Assistance Programme

www.chambersstudent.co.uk

salaries and benefits

firm name	1st year salary	2nd year salary	sponsorship/ awards	other benefits	qualification salary
Forbes	Not known	£18,322	Not known	Not known	Highly competitive
Forsters	£30,000	£32,000	GDL & LPC: fees + £5,000	STL, PHI, life ins, subsd gym m'ship, pension, EAP, pte healthcare	£51,000
Freeth Cartwright	£20,000	Not known	Not known	Not known	Not known
Freshfields Bruckhaus Deringer	£38,000	£43,000	GDL: fees + £6,250 LPC: fees + £7,250	Life ass, PHI, pension, interest-free loan, STL, PMI, subsd restaurant, gym	£65,000
Government Legal Service	£21,300 (London)	Not known	LPC: fees + £5,000-£7,000 GDL: possibly	Pension, subsd canteen	See website
Halliwells	£23,000 £29,500 (London)	£24,000 £30,500 (London)	GDL & LPC: fees + £6,500	STL, subsd gym m'ship, life ass	£39,000 £62,000 (London)
Hammonds	£35,000 (London) £25,000 (other)	£38,000 (London) £27,000 (other)	GDL: fees + £4,500 (£6,000 London) LPC: fees + £5,000 (£7,000 London)	Pension, life ass, subsd gym m'ship, STL + others	£60,000 (London) £40,000 (other)
Harbottle & Lewis	£28,000	£29,000	LPC: fees + interest-free loan	Lunch, STL	£47,000-£50,000
HBJ Gateley Wareing	£24,000	£25,000	LPC: fees + £4,500 GDL: fees	Not known	£38,000
Henmans	£20,000	£22,000	Not known	Not known	£32,000-£33,000
Herbert Smith	£36,000	£40,000	GDL & LPC: fees + up to £7,000	Bonus, PHI, PMI, STL, life ass, subsd gym m'ship accident ins, interest-free loan, pension	£64,000
Hewitsons	£23,500	£25,000	None	Not known	£35,000
Higgs & Sons	£20,000	£22,000	Not known	PMI, life ass, pension	£30,000
Hill Dickinson	£22,000 (north) £30,000 (London)	£24,000 (north) £32,000 (London)	Not known	Not known	Not known
Hodge Jones & Allen	£20,000	£22,000	Not known	Pension, life ass, disability ins	£30,000
Holman Fenwick & Willan	£31,000	£33,000	LPC: fees + £7,000 GDL: fees + £6,000	PMI, PHI, accident ins, subsd gym m'ship, STL	£55,000
Howes Percival	£23,500	£25,500	GDL & LPC: funding + maintenance grant	Pension, PHI	Not known
Hugh James	£17,999	£19,103	LPC: fees	Pension	£33,990

Notes: PHI = Permanent Health Insurance; STL = Season Travel Ticket Loan; PMI = Private Medical Insurance EAP = Employee Assistance Programme

salaries and benefits

firm name	1st year salary	2nd year salary	sponsorship/ awards	other benefits	qualification salary
Hunton & Williams	£33,000	£35,000	GDL & LPC: funded	PMI, life ass, PHI, pension, occupational health service	Not known
IBB Solicitors	£21,000	£23,000	Not known	Life ass, pension, PMI	Not known
Ince & Co	£31,000	£34,000	GDL & LPC: fees + £6,000 (London), £5,500 (elsewhere)	STL, corporate health cover, PHI, pension	£59,000
Irwin Mitchell	£19,000 (outside London)	£21,100 (outside London)	GDL & LPC: fees + £4,500	Healthcare, pension, subsd gym m'ship	Not known
Jones Day	£39,000	£45,000	GDL & LPC: fees + £8,000	Pte healthcare, sports club m'ship, group life cover, STL	£70,000
Kendall Freeman	£34,000	£36,000	GDL & LPC: fees + £6,500 (London) or £6,000 (elsewhere)	BUPA, STL, Sbsd gym m'ship, bonus, pension, life ass	£61,000
Kirkland & Ellis	£35,000	£40,000	GDL & LPC: fees + £7,500	PMI, travel ins, life ass, pension, EAP, gym m'ship	Not known
K&L Gates	£32,000	£35,000	GDL: fees + £5,000 LPC: fees + £7,000	Not known	£62,000
Latham & Watkins	£37,500-£38,000	£38,500-£39,000	GDL & LPC: fees + £8,000	Healthcare & dental scheme, pension, life ass	£96,000
Lawrence Graham	£30,000	£34,000	GDL & LPC: fees + £5,000 (London) £4,500 (elsewhere)	STL, life ass	£62,000
Laytons	Market rate	Market rate	GDL & LPC: funding considered	Not known	Market rate
LeBoeuf, Lamb, Greene & MacRae	£40,000	£45,000	GDL & LPC: fees + £8,500	Health, life & disability insurance contribs, STL, bonus	£75,000 + bonus
Lee & Priestley	Not Known	Not Known	Not Known	Pension, health scheme, flexible benefits	Not Known
Lester Aldridge	£17,250-£17,750	£18,250-£18,750	LPC: funding available	Life ass, pension, flexible benefits, STL	£31,000
Lewis Silkin	£31,000	£33,000	GDL: fees LPC: fees + £4,500	Life ass, critical illness cover, health ins, STL, pension, subsd gym m'ship, bonus	£48,000
Linklaters	£36,000	Not known	GDL & LPC: fees + maintenance	Bonus, life ass, PMI, PHI, pension, gym/health club m'ship, travel ins, STL, and others	£64,000 + bonus
Lovells	£36,000 + £1,000 joining bonus + £1,000 salary advance	£40,000	GDL & LPC: fees + £8,000 or £7,000 for GDL o/s London, £500 prize for first-class degree and £500 for top Lovells LPC, STL	PMI, life ass, PHI, STL, in-house gym, staff rest, in-house dentist, doctor & physio, local retail discounts	£63,500

Notes: PHI = Permanent Health Insurance; STL = Season Travel Ticket Loan; PMI = Private Medical Insurance EAP = Employee Assistance Programme

salaries and benefits

firm name	1st year salary	2nd year salary	sponsorship/ awards	other benefits	qualification salary
Lupton Fawcett	Competitive	Competitive	£10,000	Health ins, STL	Competitive
Mace & Jones	£17,000	£17,500	Not known	Not known	Negotiable
Macfarlanes	£36,000	£40,000	GDL & LPC: fees + £7,000, prizes for LPC distinction or commendation	Comprehensive package	£64,000
Maclay Murray & Spens	£30,000 (London)	Not known	LPC: £10,000	Pension, death-in-service benefit, conveyancing, medical & dental plans, income protection insurance	£54,000
Manches	£28,000 (London)	£31,000 (London)	GDL & LPC: fees + £5,000	STL, PHI, PMI, pension, life ass	£50,000 (London)
Martineau Johnson	£21,000	£22,500	Not known	Not known	£38,000
Mayer Brown	£36,000	£40,000	GDL & LPC: + £7,000 (Lon/Guild) £6,500 (elsewhere)	STL, sports club m'ship, pte healthcare	£64,000
Maxwell Winward	£29,000	£31,500	GDL & LPC: funding	STL, PHI	£48,000
McDermott, Will & Emery	£39,000	£43,000	GDL & LPC: fees + maintenance	PMI, dential ins, life ass, EAP, PHI, STL, subsd gym m'ship	£75,000
McGrigors	£32,000 (London)	£37,000 (London)	GDL & LPC: fees + £6,000	PMI, STL, life ass, pension, lunch allowance, income protection	£62,000 (London)
Memery Crystal	£27,500	£29,500	GDL & LPC: fees	Bonus, life ass, health cover, travel ins, STL, pension, subs'd gym	£54,000
Michelmores	£19,500	£20,500	LPC: fees + prizes for first-class degrees and LPC distinction	Pte healthcare, PHI, subs'd restaurant, subs'd gym, free pkg	£31,500
Mills & Reeve	£23,000	£24,000	GDL & LPC: fees + maintenance	Life ass, pension, bonus, subsd gym & restaurant, STL, PMI	Not known
Mishcon de Reya	£30,000	£32,000	GDL & LPC: fees + maintenance	PMI, travel ins, subsd gym m'ship, STL, life ass, pension, doctor, EAP, income protection	Not known
Morgan Cole	Competitive	Competitive	GDL & LPC: fees + maintenance	Not known	Not known
Morrison & Foerster	£32,500	£36,000	GDL & LPC: fees + £8,000	Life ass, health, dental & disability insurance, pension, STL	£68,000

Notes: PHI = Permanent Health Insurance; STL = Season Travel Ticket Loan; PMI = Private Medical Insurance EAP = Employee Assistance Programme

salaries and benefits

firm name	1st year salary	2nd year salary	sponsorship/ awards	other benefits	qualification salary
Nabarro	£36,000 (London) £25,000 (Sheffield)	£40,000 (London) £28,000 (Sheffield)	GDL: fees + £6,000 (London) or £5,000 (elsewhere) LPC: fees + £7,000 (London) or £6,000 (elsewhere)	PMI, pension, STL, subsd restaurant, subsd gym m'ship	£62,500 (London) £38,000 (Sheffield)
Norton Rose	£35,700	£40,200	GDL & LPC: funded	Life ass, pte health ins, STL, subsd gym m'ship	Not known
Olswang	£35,000	£39,000	GDL & LPC: fees + £7,000 (London) or £6,500 (elsewhere)	Pension, PMI, life cover, dental scheme, STL, subsd gym m'ship and staff restaurant, PHI	£62,000
O'Melveny & Myers	£37,500	£41,500	Not known	Not known	Not known
Orrick, Herrington & Sutcliffe	£32,000	£36,000	GDL: fees LPC: fees + maintenance	Pension, PHI, subsd gym m'ship, STL, PMI, dental care, childcare vouchers	Not known
Osborne Clarke	£30,000-£34,000	£31,000 £35,000	GDL & LPC: fees + maintenance	Pension PMI, STL, PHI, life ass, bonus, subs'd gym m'ship	£41,000-£63,000
Pannone	£22,000	£24,000	LPC: fees	Not known	£33,000
Paul Hastings	£40,000	£45,000	Funding available	Ptd healthcare, life ass, pension, STL	£90,000
Payne Hicks Beach	£28,500	£30,500	GDL & LPC: fees	STL, life ass, PHI, pension	Not known
Penningtons Solicitors	£28,000 (London)	£30,000 (London)	LPC: fees + £4,000	Pension, life ass, PMI, STL, critical illness cover	Not known
Pinsent Masons	£36,000 (London)	£39,000 (London)	GDL & LPC: fees + maintenance	Not known	£63,000 (London)
PricewaterhouseCoopers Legal	£30,000	£35,000	GDL & LPC: fees + maintenance	Not known	Not known
Pritchard Englefield	£22,250	Not known	LPC: fees	Subsd training, luncheon vouchers, PMI, STL	£42,000
Reed Smith Richards Butler	£30,000 (London)	£33,000 (London)	GDL: fees + £6,000 LPC: fees + £7,000	PMI, STL, life ass, pension, bonus, staff conveyancing, subs'd restaurant	£63,000 + bonus (London)
Reynolds Porter Chamberlain	£31,000	£35,000	GDL & LPC: fees + £6,500	Bonus, PMI, income protection, STL, subsd gym m'ship, pension, dealth-in-service cover, dental cover	£54,000
Salans	£30,000	£32,500	LPC: fees	Private healthcare, pension, STL, critical illness cover	Variable

Notes: PHI = Permanent Health Insurance; STL = Season Travel Ticket Loan; PMI = Private Medical Insurance EAP = Employee Assistance Programme

www.chambersstudent.co.uk

salaries and benefits

firm name	1st year salary	2nd year salary	sponsorship/ awards	other benefits	qualification salary
Shadbolt & Co	£29,000	£33,000	LPC: fee refund when TC starts	Private healthcare, PHI, life ass, paid study leave, STL, bonus, prof m'ships + subs	£52,000
Shearman & Sterling	£36,500	£39,500	GDL & LPC: fees + £7,000	Not known	£75,000
Shoosmiths	from £21,000	Not known	GDL & LPC: fees + maintenance	Life ass, pension, staff discounts, Christmas bonus, flexible holidays scheme	£36,000
Sidley Austin	£38,000	£42,000	GDL & LPC: fees + £7,000	PMI, life ass, subs'd gym m'ship, STL, income protection, pension, subsd restaurant	Not known
Simmons & Simmons	£36,000	£40,000	GDL & LPC: fees + up to £7,500	Not known	£63,500
SJ Berwin	£36,000	£40,000	GDL & LPC: funding	Pte healthcare, subsd gym m'ship, life ass, pension, STL, free lunch	£64,000
Skadden	£40,000	£43,000	GDL & LPC: fees + £8,000	Life ass, PMI, PHI, travel ins, subsd gym m'ship and resturant, technology allowance, EAP	Not known
Slaughter and May	£36,000	£40,000	GDL & LPC: fees + maintenance	BUPA, STL, pension, subsd health club m'ship, 24-hour accident cover	£63,500
Speechly Bircham	£31,000-£32,000	£33,000-£34,000	GDL & LPC: fees + maintenance	STL, PMI, life ass, pension	£56,000
Stephenson Harwood	£35,000	£40,000	GDL & LPC: fees + maintenance	Subsd health club m'ship, PHI, BUPA, STL	£62,000
Stevens & Bolton	£24,500	£26,500	GDL & LPC: fees + £4,000	PMI, life ass, pension, STL, PHI	£42,500
Taylor Walton	Not known	Not known	LPC: full sponsorship	Not known	Not known
Taylor Wessing	£35,000	£39,000	GDL & LPC: fees + £7,000	PMI, PHI, STL, subsd staff restaurant, pension	£62,500
Teacher Stern Selby	£31,000	Not known	Considered	Not known	£45,000
Thomas Eggar	Not known	Not known	LPC: 50% grant, 50% loan	Not known	Not known
Thomson Snell & Passmore	Competitive	Competitive	LPC: grant + interest-free loan	Not known	Not known
Thring Townsend	£17,750	£19,250	None	PMI, pte healthcare, subsd restaurant, prof m'ships & subs	£34,000
TLT Solicitors	£24,000	£25,000	GDL & LPC: fees + maintenance	Pension, PMI, subsd sports & health club m'ship, life ass	Market rate

Notes: PHI = Permanent Health Insurance; STL = Season Travel Ticket Loan; PMI = Private Medical Insurance EAP = Employee Assistance Programme

salaries and benefits

firm name	1st year salary	2nd year salary	sponsorship/ awards	other benefits	qualification salary
Travers Smith	£36,000	£40,000	GDL & LPC: fees + £7,000 (London) or £6,500 (elsewhere)	PHI, PMI, life ass, STL, subsd bistro, health club m'ship	£64,000
Trethowans	Not known	Not known	LPC: fees	Pension, death-in-service cover, PHI, bonus, car parking and others	Market rate
Trowers & Hamlins	£29,000	£31,000	GDL & LPC: fees + £6,000 (London) or £5,500 (elsewhere)	Bonus, pension, healthcare, life ass, STL, subsd staff restaurant	£57,500
Walker Morris	£22,000	£24,000	GDL & LPC: fees + £5,000	Not known	£38,000
Ward Hadaway	£19,500	£21,000	GDL & LPC: fees + maintenance	Death-in-service cover, pension, flexible holiday scheme	£35,000
Watson Burton	£18,000	up to £19,500	LPC: fees	Study leave, prof m'ship fees & subs	Not less than £35,000
Watson, Farley & Williams	£34,000	£38,000	GDL & LPC: fees + £6,500 (London) or £5,500 (elsewhere)	Life ass, PHI, BUPA, STL, pension, subsd gym m'ship	£62,500
Wedlake Bell	£28,000	£30,000	LPC: fees + £4,000	Pension, STL, subsd gym m'ship, life ass, PHI	Not known
Weightmans	Not known	Not known	GDL & LPC: fees	Pension, PHI, life ass	Not known
Weil, Gotshal & Manges	£41,000	Not known	Not known	Not known	Not known
White & Case	£41,000-£42,000	£43,000-£44,000	GDL & LPC: fees + £7,500 prize for LPC commendation or distinction	PMI, dental ins, life ass, pension, critical illness cover, travel ins, gym m'ship, retail vouchers, STL, green bikes	£76,000
Wiggin	£26,500	£31,500	GDL & LPC: fees + £3,500	Life ass, pte health cover, pension, PHI, subsd gym m'ship	£45,500
Wilsons Solicitors	Market rate	Market rate	LPC: interest-free loan up to £4,500	Pension, life ass, PMI	Not known
Withers	£31,000	£33,000	GDL & LPC: fees + £5,000	Not known	£55,000
Wollastons	£24,000	£25,000	LPC: fees	Not known	Not known
Wragge & Co	£25,000 (Birmingham)	£28,000 (Birmingham)	GDL & LPC: funding	Not known	£40,000 (Birmingham) £62,000 (London)

Notes: PHI = Permanent Health Insurance; STL = Season Travel Ticket Loan; PMI = Private Medical Insurance EAP = Employee Assistance Programme

want any help with your homework?

You can never be too informed about the law firms to which you are applying and you can never be over prepared for an interview. By doing your homework you can also save yourself time by eliminating from your shortlist the law firms that just don't suit you. What recruiters most dislike is applications from people who have no idea about the nature of their firm's business – the bullets, if you like, from a scattergun aimed indiscriminately at the profession at large. If you want to be a personal injury lawyer, why would you apply to Clifford Chance? If you want to be a capital markets lawyer why would you apply to Foot Anstey? You think people don't make these mistakes? Think again.

Of course, we know **you** would never make such a basic error; nonetheless we think we can help. The following **Solicitors Practice Areas** section of the book contains scores of ranking tables drawn from our parent publication *Chambers UK* and these will give you a good sense of how well each law firm is regarded in a particular area of practice. Take, for example, competition/European law in the Midlands where *Chambers UK* singles out Eversheds and Pinsent Masons as the two best firms in the business and also identifies the other lead players. You can use the *Student Guide* as your first port of call for information on law firms across England and Wales, in legal areas stretching from human rights and family law to derivatives deals and telecommunications law.

Having ascertained which law firms interest you, it is open to you to look more closely at the reasons why each firm is successful in its chosen fields. The editorial that accompanies the ranking tables in *Chambers UK* gives details of team composition, important clients and highlight work. This editorial is too long to be reprinted in the *Student Guide*, so you'll need to look at *Chambers UK* itself. This weighty tome is a bit pricey for students but you may find a reference copy in your law library or careers service. It is also available to read online – for free – on our website. There, you will also find other Chambers and Partners legal guides: *Chambers Global, Chambers USA, Chambers Europe,* and soon, *Chambers Asia.*

How does Chambers and Partners arrive at its findings? After a lot of hard graft, that's how. Every year our team of around 100 researchers and editors carries out thousands of in-depth interviews with lawyers and clients in order to assess the reputations and expertise of legal professionals in 175 countries across the world. The tally for interviews for our 2008 UK guide, for example, topped 14,800. This was made up of 5,300 solicitors, 1,235 barristers and 8,300 clients. We're delighted to say that Chambers' rankings and editorials are referred to extensively by general counsel and other purchasers of legal services who look to our recommendations when choosing their lawyers.

The only danger is information overload at a time when you are already stretched. If you feel that comprehensive use of our publications is becoming too onerous then stick to the *Student Guide* until you are prepping for an actual interview. At that stage, you may find that a partner with whom you are due to meet is not only one of the lawyers we rank but has also submitted a biography revealing an unusual weekend hobby. Forewarned is forearmed, we say.

DAVIES ARNOLD COOPER

Going up?

Next stop here

If your interest lies in commercial litigation, insurance, real estate or construction law, Davies Arnold Cooper could be your next stop. We're not the biggest law firm in the city, but if you want responsibility and the chance to make your own tracks in the snow, then you'll be working alongside like-minded people.

For more information visit **www.recruit.dac.co.uk** or call Charlotte Stanbridge on **020 7293 4110**

London Manchester Madrid Mexico City

DAVIES ARNOLD COOPER

solicitors
specialist practice areas

banking & finance

put simply

Banking and finance lawyers inhabit a world of their own and speak a language that can leave the layperson bamboozled. The following specialist areas all have one thing in common – they relate to borrowing money or managing a financial position. It is the lawyer's job to advise on the legality of the investment (or borrowing) proposition, to document the parties' contractual relationship, to negotiate with the other party and to discuss potential outcomes should problems arise. The lawyer is also sometimes involved in "due diligence" on behalf of the lender. This involves review or drafting of an information memorandum or prospectus that describes the borrower's business.

Straightforward bank lending – where a bank lends money to a borrower on documented repayment terms.

Acquisition finance – where a bank lends money to a corporate borrower or private equity sponsor in order to fund its acquisition of another company (refer to our corporate law section on page 107).

Property finance – where a loan is made to enable (usually) a property acquisition or development. It will commonly be backed by the security of a mortgage deed binding property assets but could also involve other types of security.

Project finance – the money required to allow a project (eg a road or a hospital) to be started, continued or completed. Could be backed by mortgages on property or other assets, by rights over company shares or other types of security.

Asset finance – allows the purchase or leasing of things such as ships, aeroplanes and machinery. The lender would normally take security over the assets in question.

Capital markets – the borrower issues bonds to investors. Bonds are listed, traded debt instruments. Unlike loans they are actively traded on a market, similar to the way shares are issued and traded.

Securitisation – essentially this is where a lender wants to sell its loans. It does so by selling them to a shell company which then issues bonds to the markets. Bond investors get paid from the interest and principal on the loans owned by the shell company.

Islamic finance – many borrowers, lenders and investors in Muslim countries only participate in transactions if they are Shari'a compliant. This usually involves specific structuring; for example, payment of interest is not permitted under Shari'a law. Usually a Shari'a scholar must confirm that the product is Shari'a complaint before it is sent to investors.

Derivatives – at its most basic, this product lets a company or bank deal with a mismatch between incomings and outgoings. For example, if a UK company sells most of its products to French customers, its income will be in euros but most of its expenditure will be in sterling. A derivative will allow it enter into a swap with a bank to fix the euro/sterling exchange rate for the year so that it does not lose out if the value of the euro goes down against the pound. Derivatives can be used to hedge against, or bet on, almost anything, from foreign exchange and interest rates to the weather.

who does what

The work of the banking and finance lawyer is mostly transactional. The following are the key functions.

- Meeting with clients to establish the commercial context of a deal and to understand the specific requirements of the client.
- Negotiating with other lawyers and their clients to agree the terms of the deal; ensuring that they are recorded accurately in the loan documentation and any documents giving security. Lenders' lawyers usually produce initial documents. In many cases deals follow a well-worn path, never veering far from standard-form documentation. Borrowers'

lawyers try to negotiate more favourable terms for their clients. Both types of lawyer must understand when they can compromise and when they must hold out on a point – they will be guided by their clients and by a good understanding of market standards.

- On complicated or ground-breaking financings, lawyers actually assist with the structuring of the deal, as well as ensuring compliance with all relevant laws.
- Carrying out due diligence – an investigation exercise to verify the accuracy of information passed from the borrower to the lender or from the company raising finance to all parties investing in the deal. If financial instruments, such as bonds, are being offered to investors, the report will take the form of a prospectus and must comply with the requirements of the EU prospectus directive and rules in other countries where the bonds are sold. This can involve on-site meetings for a few days with management of the company – you will learn how their businesses work.
- Gathering all parties for the completion of the transaction, ensuring all agreed terms are covered in the written documents and that all documents have been properly signed and sealed. Just as in corporate deals, many decisions need to be made at properly convened board meetings and recorded in written resolutions.
- Finalising all post-completion registrations and procedures.

the realities of the job

- City firms act for international banks whereas the work of regional firms is generally simpler and domestic in nature, usually for UK banks and building societies or the companies they lend to. If you want to be a hotshot in international finance then it's the City for you. And if you want international travel you're likely to be able to find a job that caters to your wanderlust, even if you'll have little time for exploration on short business trips.

- Lawyers need an understanding of where the client wants to be and the legal risks involved in getting there. This may involve the movement of money across borders and through different currencies and financial products. International deals have an additional layer of difficulty: political changes in a country can render a previously sound investment risky – just ask anyone involved in Russian deals or derivatives.
- Clients can be demanding and the hours can be long. On the plus side, your clients will be dynamic and just as smart as you. It is perfectly possible to build up long-term relationships with investment bank clients, even when you're still quite junior. Working on deals can also be exciting – the team (the lawyers, the client, and any other advisers) plus the other side are all working to a common goal, often under significant time and other pressures. It might sound geeky but there are adrenalin highs on deals and tremendous satisfaction – and occasionally champagne – when a successful deal is closed.
- Banking and finance requires hard work and teamwork. There are peaks and troughs as deal flow depends on the buoyancy of the economy.
- You need to become absorbed into the finance world. The best way to get a taster is to read the City pages in your daily newspaper.

current issues

- Until recently the buoyant economy meant plenty of liquidity in the market (ie assets could be turned into cash quite easily). Debt volume had reached record levels, deals were larger than ever and debt structures had never been so complex. The problems in the US subprime market have had adverse effects elsewhere in the world money markets and, at the time of going to press, a credit squeeze was reducing lending dramatically.

- The London banking market is more competitive than ever. Once-loyal relationships between clients and their lawyers can no longer be depended upon.
- Acquisition finance is really big right now and transactions often need to be completed quickly. Too much point-scoring by lawyers in the negotiation process can be a waste of precious time, so solicitors need to understand when it is time to stop talking and to get the deal done.
- In big City firms you'll become specialised

early on. This may or may not appeal to you, and if it doesn't then a smaller or regional firm may be a better choice.

- Secondments to banks are available, even for trainees. Subsequent moves in-house are common, especially for capital markets work or compliance roles to ensure that banks do not fall foul of financial services regulations. Banking law is also an ideal platform for a career in the financial markets; however, if you already know you want to become a banker, don't waste time training as a lawyer.

leading firms from Chambers UK 2008

Banking & Finance: High-end Acquisition Finance
London
Band 1
Allen & Overy LLP
Clifford Chance LLP
Band 2
Ashurst
Linklaters
Band 3
Freshfields Bruckhaus Deringer
Shearman & Sterling LLP
Simpson Thacher & Bartlett LLP
White & Case LLP
Band 4
Cleary Gottlieb Steen & Hamilton LLP
Herbert Smith LLP
Kirkland & Ellis International LLP
Latham & Watkins LLP
Lovells LLP
Band 5
Baker & McKenzie LLP
Berwin Leighton Paisner LLP
DLA Piper UK LLP
Macfarlanes
Simmons & Simmons
Skadden, Arps, Slate, Meagher & Flom
Slaughter and May
Travers Smith
Weil, Gotshal & Manges LLP

Banking & Finance: Mid-Market Best of the UK
Band 1
Berwin Leighton Paisner LLP *London*
CMS Cameron McKenna *London*
DLA Piper UK LLP *London*
Lovells LLP *London*
Band 2
Addleshaw Goddard LLP *London*
Bird & Bird *London*
Eversheds LLP *London*
Olswang *London*
Stephenson Harwood *London*
Band 3
Burges Salmon LLP *Bristol*
Nabarro *London*
Osborne Clarke *Bristol*
Taylor Wessing LLP *London*
Wragge & Co LLP *Birmingham*

Banking & Finance The South
Band 1
Bond Pearce LLP *Southampton*
Band 2
Blake Lapthorn Tarlo Lyons *Southampton*
Band 3
asb law *Crawley*
Shoosmiths *Fareham*
Stevens & Bolton LLP *Guildford*
Band 4
Clarke Willmott *Southampton*
DMH Stallard *Crawley*
Lester Aldridge LLP *Southampton*
Mundays LLP *Cobham*
Paris Smith & Randall LLP *Southampton*
Thomas Eggar LLP *Crawley*

Banking & Finance East Anglia
Band 1
Mills & Reeve LLP *Norwich*
Band 2
Birketts LLP *Ipswich*
Eversheds LLP *Cambridge*
Band 3
Kester Cunningham John *Bury St Edmunds*
Taylor Vinters *Cambridge*
Wollastons LLP *Chelmsford*

Banking & Finance: Islamic Finance

London

Band 1
Allen & Overy LLP
Clifford Chance LLP
Norton Rose

Band 2
Denton Wilde Sapte
Linklaters
White & Case LLP

Band 3
Baker & McKenzie LLP
Dechert LLP
King & Spalding International LLP
Stephenson Harwood
Taylor Wessing LLP
Trowers & Hamlins

Banking & Finance

Thames Valley

Band 1
Osborne Clarke *Reading*

Band 2
Boyes Turner *Reading*
EMW Law *Milton Keynes*
Pitmans *Reading*
Shoosmiths *Reading*

Band 3
Field Seymour Parkes *Reading*
Howes Percival LLP *Milton Keynes*
IBB Solicitors *Uxbridge*
Morgan Cole *Oxford*

Banking & Finance

North East

Band 1
Dickinson Dees LLP *Newcastle upon Tyne*

Band 2
Eversheds LLP *Newcastle upon Tyne*
Muckle LLP *Newcastle upon Tyne*
Ward Hadaway *Newcastle upon Tyne*

Band 3
Sintons *Newcastle upon Tyne*
Watson Burton LLP *Newcastle upon Tyne*

Banking & Finance

South West

Band 1
Burges Salmon LLP *Bristol*
Osborne Clarke *Bristol*

Band 2
Bond Pearce LLP *Bristol*

Band 3
Charles Russell LLP *Cheltenham*
Clarke Willmott *Bristol*
Rickerbys *Cheltenham*
TLT LLP *Bristol*
Veale Wasbrough Lawyers *Bristol*

Band 4
Ashfords *Bristol*
Bevan Brittan LLP *Bristol*
Foot Anstey *Plymouth*
Michelmores LLP *Exeter*
Stephens & Scown *Exeter*

Banking & Finance

North West

Band 1
Addleshaw Goddard LLP *Manchester*
DLA Piper UK LLP *Manchester*

Band 2
Eversheds LLP *Manchester*
Halliwells LLP *Manchester*
Hammonds *Manchester*

Band 3
Cobbetts LLP *Manchester*
DWF *Manchester*
Pannone LLP *Manchester*
Pinsent Masons *Manchester*

Band 4
Brabners Chaffe Street *Liverpool*
George Davies Solicitors *Manchester*
Hill Dickinson LLP *Liverpool*
Kuit Steinart Levy *Manchester*

Banking & Finance

Midlands

Band 1
DLA Piper UK LLP *Birmingham*
Eversheds LLP *Birmingham*
Pinsent Masons *Birmingham*
Wragge & Co LLP *Birmingham*

Band 2
HBJ Gateley Wareing *Birmingham*
Martineau Johnson *Birmingham*

Band 3
Browne Jacobson LLP *Nottingham*
Hammonds *Birmingham*

Band 4
Cobbetts LLP *Birmingham*
Freeth Cartwright LLP *Leicester*
Shoosmiths *Birmingham*

Banking & Finance

Wales

Band 1
Eversheds LLP *Cardiff*
Geldards LLP *Cardiff*
Morgan Cole *Cardiff*

Banking & Finance

Yorkshire

Band 1
Addleshaw Goddard LLP *Leeds*
DLA Piper UK LLP *Leeds*

Band 2
Eversheds LLP *Leeds*
Walker Morris *Leeds*

Band 3
Cobbetts LLP *Leeds*
Hammonds *Leeds*
Pinsent Masons *Leeds*

Band 4
Irwin Mitchell *Sheffield*
Nabarro *Sheffield*

banking & finance (continued)

Capital Markets: Debt
London
Band 1
Allen & Overy LLP
Linklaters

Band 2
Clifford Chance LLP

Band 3
Cleary Gottlieb Steen & Hamilton LLP
White & Case LLP

Band 4
Freshfields Bruckhaus Deringer
Gide Loyrette Nouel
Latham & Watkins LLP
Lovells LLP
Shearman & Sterling LLP
Sidley Austin (UK) LLP
Skadden, Arps, Slate, Meagher & Flom
Slaughter and May

Band 5
Ashurst
Baker & McKenzie LLP
CMS Cameron McKenna LLP
Davis Polk & Wardwell
Denton Wilde Sapte
Herbert Smith LLP
Simmons & Simmons
Sullivan & Cromwell LLP

Capital Markets: Derivatives
London
Band 1
Allen & Overy LLP

Band 2
Clifford Chance LLP
Linklaters

Band 3
Ashurst
Freshfields Bruckhaus Deringer
Sidley Austin (UK) LLP
Slaughter and May

Band 4
Baker & McKenzie LLP
Field Fisher Waterhouse LLP
Simmons & Simmons

Capital Markets: Equity
London
Band 1
Freshfields Bruckhaus Deringer
Linklaters

Band 2
Allen & Overy LLP
Cleary Gottlieb Steen & Hamilton LLP
Clifford Chance LLP
Herbert Smith LLP
Shearman & Sterling LLP
Skadden, Arps, Slate, Meagher & Flom
Sullivan & Cromwell LLP

Band 3
Ashurst
Davis Polk & Wardwell
Latham & Watkins LLP
Lovells LLP
Slaughter and May

Band 4
Baker & McKenzie LLP
Norton Rose
Simmons & Simmons
Weil, Gotshal & Manges LLP
White & Case LLP

Capital Markets: High-Yield Products
London
Band 1
Latham & Watkins LLP

Band 2
Cravath, Swaine & Moore LLP
Shearman & Sterling LLP
Simpson Thacher & Bartlett LLP

Band 3
Cahill Gordon & Reindel LLP
Milbank, Tweed, Hadley & McCloy LLP
White & Case LLP

Band 4
Cleary Gottlieb Steen & Hamilton LLP
Clifford Chance LLP
Freshfields Bruckhaus Deringer
Linklaters
Skadden, Arps, Slate, Meagher & Flom
Weil, Gotshal & Manges LLP

Capital Markets: Structured Finance
London
Band 1
Clifford Chance LLP
Linklaters

Band 2
Allen & Overy LLP
Ashurst
Freshfields Bruckhaus Deringer
Simmons & Simmons
White & Case LLP

Band 3
Cadwalader, Wickersham & Taft LLP
Herbert Smith LLP
Milbank, Tweed, Hadley & McCloy LLP
Sidley Austin (UK) LLP
Slaughter and May
Weil, Gotshal & Manges LLP

Band 4
Baker & McKenzie LLP
Gide Loyrette Nouel
Lovells LLP
Orrick, Herrington & Sutcliffe
Shearman & Sterling LLP

Capital Markets: Securitisation
London
Band 1
Allen & Overy LLP
Clifford Chance LLP

Band 2
Freshfields Bruckhaus Deringer
Linklaters
Sidley Austin (UK) LLP

Band 3
Baker & McKenzie LLP
Cadwalader, Wickersham & Taft LLP
Herbert Smith LLP
Mayer Brown
Slaughter and May
Weil, Gotshal & Manges LLP
White & Case LLP

Band 4
Berwin Leighton Paisner LLP
Gide Loyrette Nouel
Lovells LLP
Shearman & Sterling LLP
Simmons & Simmons

competition and antitrust law

put simply

It is the job of the UK and EU regulatory authorities to ensure that markets function effectively on the basis of fair and open competition. The competition rules in the UK and EU are substantially similar, but the UK bodies concentrate on those rules that have their greatest effect domestically, while the EU authorities deal with matters where the rules affect more than one member state. In the UK, the regulators are the Office of Fair Trade (OFT) or the Competition Commission; on matters also affecting other EU countries, it is the European Commission. Additionally, there are industry-specific regulatory bodies, such as Ofcom for the media and telecoms industry.

Competition authorities have extensive investigation powers – including the ability to carry out dawn raids – and can impose hefty fines. There were fines for the producers of herbicides when they were judged to have formed a Europe-wide cartel, and for companies involved in the price-fixing of football strips. In another example, the domestic authorities found a group of English public schools had formed a cartel for the purposes of setting fee levels. More recently, following a request from the Federation of Small Businesses, the OFT has persuaded the Competition Commission to investigate the activities of the UK's 'big four' supermarkets – Tesco, Asda, Sainsbury's and Morrisons.

who does what

The work of a competition lawyer can be divided into the following areas:

- Negotiating clearance for acquisitions, mergers and joint ventures
- Advising on the structure of commercial or co-operation agreements to ensure they withstand a competition challenge.
- Dealing with investigations by the regulators into the way a client conducts business.

- Bringing or defending claims in the Competition Appeals Tribunal
- Advising on cross-border trade or anti-dumping measures (preventing companies exporting a product at a lower price than it normally charges in its home market).

working for a regulator you would:

- Investigate companies and bring prosecutions.
- Advise on the application of new laws and regulations.

the realities of the job

- You won't get much independence; even junior lawyers work under the close supervision of experienced partners. In the early days the job involves a great deal of research into particular markets and how the authorities have approached different types of agreements in the past. You also need a genuine interest in economics and politics.
- The work demands serious academic thought, more so than in standard corporate transactional work. Even so, you can't just be a dry legal brain, you'll need to develop commercial acumen and really understand how clients run their businesses.
- This is a massively popular area of practice and hard to break into. You can enhance your prospects by knuckling down to some competition-specific studies; a master's degree will help.
- Advocacy is a relatively small part of the job, though in time you could end up appearing in the High Court or Competition Appeal Tribunal. Advocacy skills can also be honed on paper, and there will be ample opportunity to do this.
- In international law firms, you will get to travel abroad and may even work in an overseas office for a while. A great deal of business is done in Brussels. Unsurprisingly, fluency in another language can be a useful.

competition and antitrust law (continued)

current issues

- On 1 May 2004, when 10 new member states were admitted to the EU, antitrust enforcement ceased to be the monopoly of the EC Commission and European Court. An EC Modernization Regulation effectively handed more power back to member states with respect to the enforcement of Articles 81 and 82 of the Treaty of Rome. Domestic authorities are definitely upping their game.

- EU and UK competition lawyers are experiencing a high volume of merger control work, driven by an upsurge in M&A activity across Europe.

- The remit of the Competition Commission Appeal Tribunals has been widened to allow claims for damages brought by third parties. Private Enforcement can be a useful tool for competitor businesses and consumer groups, but thus far has not been extensively utilised, perhaps due to concerns over the cost of proceedings.

- Competition investigations by sector regulators are on the rise, with a substantial increase in appeals of OFT decisions and sector regulators in front of the CAT. The most prominent sector inquiries are in the energy, financial services, transport and insurance sectors.

- Regulators now have the power to impose criminal sanctions. This has forced solicitors firms to consider how they will advise clients on the 'white collar crime' element of competition law. A few have started to employ specialists; others have formed close ties with boutique white-collar crime firms.

- US-style class actions are appearing and US plaintiff firms such as Cohen Milstein Hausfeld & Toll are setting up in the UK. Law firms traditionally associated with white collar crime, such as Peters & Peters and Kingsley Napley are increasingly involved in criminal cartel defence work.

- There are increased opportunities to work for the regulatory authorities; the OFT, for example, employs many more investigators than before. There is also a trend for lawyers to switch between private practice and working for the regulators.

leading firms from Chambers UK 2008

Competition/European Law
London
Band 1
Freshfields Bruckhaus Deringer
Herbert Smith LLP
Linklaters
Slaughter and May

Band 2
Allen & Overy LLP
Ashurst
Baker & McKenzie LLP
Clifford Chance LLP
Lovells LLP
Simmons & Simmons
SJ Berwin LLP

Band 3
Addleshaw Goddard LLP
CMS Cameron McKenna LLP
Eversheds LLP
Latham & Watkins LLP
Macfarlanes
Mayer Brown
Norton Rose
Reed Smith Richards Butler LLP

Band 4
Berwin Leighton Paisner LLP
Bird & Bird
Bristows
Denton Wilde Sapte
DLA Piper UK LLP
Field Fisher Waterhouse LLP
McDermott Will & Emery UK LLP
Shearman & Sterling LLP

Band 5
Cleary Gottlieb Steen & Hamilton LLP
Clyde & Co LLP
Dechert LLP
Jones Day
Nabarro

Competition/European Law
The North
Band 1
Addleshaw Goddard LLP *Manchester*
Eversheds LLP *Leeds*

Band 2
Dickinson Dees LLP *Newcastle upon Tyne*

Band 3
Cobbetts LLP *Manchester*
Pinsent Masons *Leeds*

Competition/European Law
The South
Band 1
Burges Salmon LLP *Bristol*
Osborne Clarke *Bristol*
TLT LLP *Bristol*

Band 2
Beachcroft LLP *Bristol*
Bond Pearce LLP *Plymouth*

Competition/European Law
Midlands
Band 1
Eversheds LLP *Birmingham*
Pinsent Masons *Birmingham*

Band 2
Shoosmiths *Nottingham*
Wragge & Co LLP *Birmingham*

Competition/European Law
Wales
Band 1
Eversheds LLP *Cardiff*

Competition: White-Collar Crime: Cartel Defence
London
Band 1
BCL Burton Copeland
Corker Binning Solicitors
Kingsley Napley
Peters & Peters
Russell Jones & Walker

put simply

Construction law can broadly be divided into non-contentious and contentious work. The first involves lawyers helping clients at the procurement stage, pulling together all the contractual relationships prior to building work; the second sees them resolving disputes when things go wrong during or after the build. Because the amount of money at stake is relatively high, over the years many people have been tempted to take their disputes all the way to court in order to test a contractual or tortious point of law. Industry insiders also admit that it had become the norm for developers to recoup certain construction costs through litigation. As a result, construction cases litter English case law like chip wrappers on a high street on a windy Sunday morning.

About ten years ago a new trend began to take hold, and now people are increasingly working with each other when things go wrong. For example, most new contracts contain a mandatory arbitration procedure to be adopted in case of dispute and adjudication of disputes has become the industry norm. The process follows a 28-day timetable; far swifter than old-style litigation which frequently ran on for years. Since the Technology and Construction Court introduced its Pre-Action Protocol, many more disputes have been resolved through mediation and this, in turn, has changed the way lawyers must operate. All these developments have had a knock-on effect at the contract drafting stage. Some disputes are simply so complex, however, that the parties do still choose to slug it out in court.

projects

From an oil pipeline in Azerbaijan to a new prison in Bridgend in South Wales, specialist construction lawyers work hand in hand with finance and corporate lawyers to enable projects to come to fruition. A few City firms and the largest US practices dominate the biggest international projects,
but there's work for lawyers countrywide. In the UK, the Private Finance Initiative (PFI), a part of the Public Private Partnerships (PPP), is an important source of work. PFI introduces private funding and management into areas that were previously the domain of government. So, for example, the new prison in Bridgend is being built by Costain working with Securicor, and for the first 25 years of its life these private companies will have a contract to run the prison.

Some law firms consistently act for the project company, usually a 'special purpose vehicle' (SPV) established to build, own and operate the prison or power station or whatever it may be. Often the project company is a joint venture between several 'sponsors' who contribute equity to part-fund the project. Project sponsors could include the manufacturer of the gas turbines installed in a power station, the construction company that will erect the plant, and the power company that will buy the electricity. The company could also be partially owned by a government body or banks. Other firms consistently act for the project promoters, the organisations that commission projects – for example an NHS trust that wants a new hospital, or a foreign government that wants a privately financed motorway. Then there are the firms that act purely on the finance side for banks, guarantors, export credit agencies, governments and international funding agencies. Other categories of client include the contractors, operators and so on. Each party requires its own legal representation.

Projects run for years, and so can the legal work. After the initial tender process, in which bids are built up over a couple of years, the successful bidder is selected to manage the project. It then secures finance and all necessary planning permissions and agrees construction, service and employment contracts. Lawyers drafting these contracts must understand the big picture because changing one contractual term can have knock-on effects throughout the entire transaction. It's a real challenge putting together something so complicated, so the only thing to do is to put in deadlines for the different stages. Anyone considering projects work must enjoy the challenge of creating a complex scheme and figuring out all its possibilities and pitfalls. They also need the ability to work with a team of people including colleagues, clients, other lawyers and professionals, funders and subcontractors.

who does what

To describe the work of all the different breeds of projects lawyers would take forever, so here we'll simply say that the field has specialists with excellent drafting and organisational skills in the areas of funding, construction, real estate, planning, energy, telecoms and all aspects of the public sector, including health, education and housing.

construction lawyers working at the procurement stage:

- Lawyers negotiate and draft contracts – often based on standard-form JCT (Joint Contracts Tribunal) contracts – for programmes of building works, be these new builds or redevelopments. In any building programme there will be a multitude of parties; the contract stage is rather like creating a spider's web of relationships between landowners, main contractors, subcontractors, engineers, architects and others. A number of these relationships are documented by way of warranties.
- If the client has invested in the land as well as undertaking the building project, you will work in conjunction with property lawyers. Between you, you will have to seek and obtain all the necessary planning consents as well as local authority certifications. If your builder client is not the owner of the land, expect to liaise regularly with the owner's solicitors over things such as stage payments, architects' certificates and other measures of performance.

- Site visits will be likely at various stages of the development.

when a construction dispute arises:

- Assess the client's position and gather all related paperwork and evidence. There can be a huge volume of documentation, some of it very technical. You don't have to read it all, but you do have to identify what is important and home in on the detail of that. This evidence will be vital in proving the client's case, whether through mediation, arbitration or litigation.
- Follow the resolution methods set out in the contracts between the parties; the TCC Pre-Action Protocol leads to negotiations at an early stage.
- Where a settlement is not possible, issue, prepare for and attend proceedings with the client, usually having instructed a barrister to advocate on the client's behalf.

the realities of the job

- Good drafting skills require attention to detail and careful thought. Plus you need to keep up to date with industry trends and standards, and you really need to know contract law and tort.
- People skills are fundamental. On the one hand you'll encounter contractors and subcontractors who have been schooled at the University of Life; on the other you'll be dealing with structural engineers whose world is one of complicated technical reports. On top of this there will also be corporate types and in-house lawyers with whom you must speak on a sophisticated level.
- Is the construction world still a male-dominated environment? It's a point worth debating. Yes, some clients might see a visit to a lap dancing club as part and parcel of a good night out with business associates and advisers, but readers also need to know that there are many successful female construction

lawyers (and architects and engineers, etc) in the business and they don't have to get caught up in this kind of activity. It's probably safe to say that any residual imbalance in the culture of the construction sector is rarely down to the law firms. It's also worth noting that this kind of behaviour does appear in other business sectors too.

- Most lawyers have a natural bias for either contentious or non-contentious work, and some firms like their construction lawyers to handle both aspects, so pick your firm carefully if you want to concentrate on one rather than the other.
- If you're looking to break into this area of law, a background in construction or engineering is a major bonus because you'll already have industry contacts and chances are you'll be able to combine legal know-how with practical advice – you'll know how the client thinks.
- Anyone considering projects work must enjoy the challenge of creating a complex scheme and figuring out all its possibilities and pitfalls. They also need the ability to work with a team of people including colleagues, clients, other lawyers and professionals, funders and subcontractors.

current issues

- The health sector has seen investment on a massive scale in recent times. It is not unusual to find complex hospital projects running into hundreds of millions of pounds. Schools are no less magnetic in terms of the investment of public funds. Charged by central government with upgrading and rebuilding the education infrastructure, many local authorities are choosing to shop locally for their legal services. Urban regeneration is dominating the work of many firms up and down the country.
- Lawyers are beginning to see an influx of disputes from the PFI sector. With many projects

reaching tenth birthdays, cracks are beginning to show.
- With Wembley National Stadium now open, attention is being given over o Heathrow Terminal Five and Crossrail. And, of course, lawyers are already gearing up for the slew of work, both contentious and non-contentious, that will emanate from the construction of the 2012 Olympic Village, the modification of rail links and general infrastructure redevelopment. It will be interesting to see the effect of EU procurement directives on the tendering process, and the economic consequences of the anticipated migration of qualified professionals to London from the regions.
- A long list of other major projects – The Broadgate Tower, The Heron tower, the Shard of Glass and others – all point to the next few years being look like seeing the biggest rush in construction for decades
- Nearly all international construction and engineering projects are governed to some extent by English or New York law, so experience in this field is internationally marketable. American law firms, in particular, are recruiting experienced English lawyers, which has forced up salaries to make international projects one of the highest-paid specialisms around. Top-level arbitration lawyers can expect to be able to work in places such as Singapore and Hong Kong. There are also ample opportunities to work in-house for large construction companies.

leading firms from Chambers UK 2008

Construction: Supplier-led
Best of the UK

Band 1
Pinsent Masons *London*

Band 2
CMS Cameron McKenna LLP *London*
Fenwick Elliott LLP *London*
Mayer Brown *London*
Shadbolt & Co LLP *London*
Wragge & Co LLP *Birmingham*

Band 3
Campbell Hooper LLP *London*
Clifford Chance LLP *London*
Davies Arnold Cooper *London*
K&L Gates *London*
Kennedys *London*
Reynolds Porter Chamberlain *London*

Band 4
Beachcroft LLP *London*
Berwin Leighton Paisner LLP *London*
Bevan Brittan LLP *Bristol*
Corbett & Co *Teddington*
Glovers *London*
Lane & Partners LLP *London*
Nabarro *London*
Osborne Clarke *Bristol*
Speechly Bircham LLP *London*

Band 5
Addleshaw Goddard LLP *London*
Barlow Lyde & Gilbert LLP *London*
Beale and Company Solicitors *London*
Berrymans Lace Mawer *London*
Burges Salmon LLP *Bristol*
Freeth Cartwright LLP *Nottingham*
Maxwell Winward LLP *London*

Construction: Purchaser-led
Best of the UK

Band 1
Berwin Leighton Paisner LLP *London*
Clifford Chance LLP *London*
Freshfields Bruckhaus Deringer *London*
Linklaters *London*

Band 2
Allen & Overy LLP *London*
Ashurst *London*
Herbert Smith LLP *London*
Lovells LLP *London*
Pinsent Masons *London*
Trowers & Hamlins *London*

Band 3
Addleshaw Goddard LLP *London*
CMS Cameron McKenna LLP *London*
Denton Wilde Sapte *London*
DLA Piper UK LLP *London*
Eversheds LLP *London*
K&L Gates *London*
Macfarlanes *London*
Mayer Brown *London*
Nabarro *London*
Norton Rose *London*
Taylor Wessing LLP *London*

Band 4
Baker & McKenzie LLP *London*
Clyde & Co LLP *London*
Dundas & Wilson *London*
Simmons & Simmons *London*
Slaughter and May *London*
Wedlake Bell *London*
White & Case LLP *London*

Band 5
Field Fisher Waterhouse LLP *London*
Fladgate Fielder *London*
Forsters LLP *London*
Hammonds *London*
Lewis Silkin LLP *London*
LG *London*
SJ Berwin LLP *London*
Stephenson Harwood *London*

Construction
Thames Valley

Band 1
Blake Lapthorn Tarlo Lyons *Oxford*
Clarkslegal LLP *Reading*
Denton Wilde Sapte *Milton Keynes*
Morgan Cole *Reading*

Band 2
Boyes Turner *Reading*
Henmans LLP *Oxford*

Construction
The South

Band 1
Shadbolt & Co LLP *Reigate*

Band 2
Blake Lapthorn Tarlo Lyons *Southampton*
Charles Russell LLP *Guildford*
Cripps Harries Hall LLP *Tunbridge Wells*
Lester Aldridge LLP *Bournemouth*

Band 3
DMH Stallard *Brighton*
Thomas Eggar LLP *Crawley*

Construction
East Anglia

Band 1
Mills & Reeve LLP *Cambridge*

Band 2
Eversheds LLP *Cambridge, Ipswich*
Hewitsons *Cambridge*

Band 3
Greenwoods Solicitors LLP *Peterborough*
Prettys *Ipswich*
Taylor Vinters *Cambridge*

construction and projects (continued)

Construction
South West
Band 1
Bevan Brittan LLP *Bristol*
Osborne Clarke *Bristol*

Band 2
Beachcroft LLP *Bristol*
Burges Salmon LLP *Bristol*
Pinsent Masons *Bristol*

Band 3
Ashfords *Exeter*
Bond Pearce LLP *Plymouth*
Clarke Willmott *Bristol*
TLT LLP *Bristol*
Veale Wasbrough Lawyers *Bristol*

Band 4
Thring Townsend *Swindon, Bath*
Withy King *Bath*

Construction
Midlands
Band 1
Wragge & Co LLP *Birmingham*

Band 2
Eversheds LLP *Birmingham*
Freeth Cartwright LLP *Nottingham*
HBJ Gateley Wareing *Birmingham*
Pinsent Masons *Birmingham*

Band 3
Beachcroft LLP *Birmingham*
Cobbetts LLP *Birmingham*
DLA Piper UK LLP *Birmingham*
Hammonds *Birmingham*
Martineau Johnson *Birmingham*
Mills & Reeve LLP *Birmingham*

Band 4
Anthony Collins Solicitors *Birmingham*
Browne Jacobson LLP *Nottingham*
Geldards LLP *Derby*
Nelsons *Derby*
Shoosmiths *Birmingham*
Wright Hassall LLP *Leamington Spa*

Construction
North West
Band 1
Pinsent Masons *Manchester*

Band 2
Addleshaw Goddard LLP *Manchester*
DLA Piper UK LLP *Liverpool*
Eversheds LLP *Manchester*
Halliwells LLP *Manchester*
Pannone LLP *Manchester*

Band 3
Cobbetts LLP *Manchester*
DWF *Manchester*
Hammonds *Manchester*
Hill Dickinson LLP *Liverpool*
Mace & Jones *Manchester*

Band 4
Beachcroft LLP *Manchester*
Brabners Chaffe Street *Liverpool*
Trowers & Hamlins *Manchester*

Construction
Yorkshire
Band 1
Addleshaw Goddard LLP *Leeds*
Pinsent Masons *Leeds*

Band 2
Eversheds LLP *Leeds*
Walker Morris *Leeds*

Band 3
DLA Piper UK LLP *Sheffield*
Nabarro *Sheffield*
The Hawkswell Kilvington Partnership LLP *Wakefield*

Band 4
Beachcroft LLP *Leeds*
Cobbetts LLP *Leeds*
Denison Till *York*
Hammonds *Leeds*
Watson Burton LLP *Leeds*

Construction
North East
Band 1
Dickinson Dees LLP *Newcastle upon Tyne*
Watson Burton LLP *Newcastle upon Tyne*

Band 2
Ward Hadaway *Newcastle upon Tyne*

Band 3
Eversheds LLP *Newcastle upon Tyne*

Construction
Wales
Band 1
Eversheds LLP *Cardiff*

Band 2
Hugh James *Cardiff*
Morgan Cole *Cardiff*

www.chambersstudent.co.uk

Projects & Energy: PFI/PPP Best of the UK

Band 1
Allen & Overy LLP *London*
Ashurst *London*
Clifford Chance LLP *London*
Freshfields Bruckhaus Deringer *London*
Linklaters *London*

Band 2
Berwin Leighton Paisner LLP *London*
CMS Cameron McKenna LLP *London*
Denton Wilde Sapte *London*
Lovells LLP *London*
Norton Rose *London*

Band 3
Addleshaw Goddard LLP *London*
Bevan Brittan LLP *London*
Burges Salmon LLP *Bristol*
DLA Piper UK LLP *London*
Eversheds LLP *London*
Herbert Smith LLP *London*
Pinsent Masons *London*
Simmons & Simmons *London*
Wragge & Co LLP *London*

Band 4
Beachcroft LLP *Bristol*
Bird & Bird *London*
Dickinson Dees LLP *Newcastle upon Tyne*
Mills & Reeve LLP *Norwich*
Nabarro *London*
Trowers & Hamlins *London*

Projects & Energy: Energy Projects London

Band 1
Allen & Overy LLP
Clifford Chance LLP
Linklaters
Milbank, Tweed, Hadley & McCloy LLP
Shearman & Sterling LLP
White & Case LLP

Band 2
Latham & Watkins LLP
Norton Rose
Sullivan & Cromwell LLP

Band 3
Ashurst
Denton Wilde Sapte
Freshfields Bruckhaus Deringer
Slaughter and May
Trowers & Hamlins
Vinson & Elkins RLLP

Band 4
Baker & McKenzie LLP
Berwin Leighton Paisner LLP
Dewey Ballantine
Herbert Smith LLP
LeBoeuf, Lamb, Greene & MacRae
Simmons & Simmons

Projects & Energy: International Infrastructure London

Band 1
Allen & Overy LLP *London*
Clifford Chance LLP *London*
CMS Cameron McKenna LLP *London*
Freshfields Bruckhaus Deringer *London*
Linklaters *London*

Band 2
Ashurst *London*
Baker & McKenzie LLP *London*
Lovells LLP *London*
Norton Rose *London*

Band 3
Berwin Leighton Paisner LLP *London*
Debevoise & Plimpton LLP *London*
Dewey Ballantine *London*
Herbert Smith LLP *London*
Pinsent Masons *London*

corporate law

put simply

The life of the corporate lawyer is characterised by big money, big deals and long hours. Their work relates to the buying and selling of businesses, business assets and business equity. You'll often hear the umbrella term 'corporate finance'. Here are some of the other terms you'll encounter:

Mergers and acquisitions (M&A) are deals involving one company buying or joining with another. Depending on the relative sizes of the businesses it might be seen as a takeover (acquisition) or a fusion of the two businesses (merger).

Corporate restructuring involves changes to the composition of the businesses in a company's portfolio or the disposal of certain assets a company no longer requires. Perhaps it wants to concentrate on more profitable parts of its business; perhaps certain activities are no longer seen as acceptable to the general public or will fall foul of regulations.

Stock exchanges play an important role in corporate law. On the London Stock Exchange we have the Financial Times (FTSE) list, the Alternative Investment Market (AIM) and others. In New York they have the Dow Jones and NASDAQ lists among others, and there are many other exchanges and lists around the world. As a corporate lawyer, your work could involve exchanges anywhere in the world.

Rather than going straight to a bank for a loan, when businesses need money they are increasingly turning to private equity funds and venture capitalists. Familiar names in this sector include Blackstone Capital Partners, Apax Partners, 3i and Alchemy Partners. But what is private equity? Essentially it refers to the holding of stock in unlisted companies, ie those not listed on a stock exchange. The work of the PE lawyer takes in different forms of financing – eg when money is needed for a new business 'start-up', the expansion of operations, or when a company is bought.

It also covers management buyout (MBO) financing, say for a group of employees/managers who decide they want to buy, own and run the company they work for.

Private equity companies usually manage several different funds and have investment in numerous businesses at a time. Sometimes a number of private equity companies will compete to invest in the same business, as was the case with Canary Wharf Group, which eventually went to the highest PE bidder at nearly £5.3 billion. Other well-known businesses that have turned to private equity investment include DIY retailer Wickes, Legoland Parks, the AA and the shoe people Jimmy Choo. A surprising proportion of the UK workforce is employed by businesses that are under the control of private equity companies, sometimes without even knowing it!

On a smaller scale, venture capitalists are individuals or companies looking for a good return from an injection of money into a fledgling or growing business. If you've ever watched the BBC2 show *Dragon's Den*, you'll be familiar with the idea. As well as owning a stake in the business, it is common for the investors to have a big hand in its management.

who does what

The work of a corporate lawyer is mainly transactional, and whatever the type of deal, there are certain key phases:

- Negotiating and drafting the agreements – this will be done in conjunction with the client, the business that is being bought or sold, other advisers (eg accountants) and any financiers.
- Carrying out 'due diligence' – this is an investigation to verify the accuracy of information passed from the seller to the buyer, or from the company raising money to the funder. The ambit of the exercise is broad and will estab-

lish: the outright ownership of all assets; the status of employees; whether there are outstanding debts or other claims against the company; any environmental or other liabilities that could reduce the value of the business in the future, etc. If shares or bonds are being offered to the public, the report will take the form of a prospectus and must comply with statutory regulations.

- Arranging financing – this could come from banks or other types of investor; they will wish to have some kind of security for their investment, eg owning shares or bonds, taking out a mortgage over property or other assets.
- Gathering all parties for the completion of the transaction, ensuring all assets have been properly covered by the written documents and that all these have been properly signed and sealed. Company law requires that decisions are made at properly convened board meetings and recorded in written resolutions.
- Finalising all post-completion registrations and procedures.

the realities of the job

- Large companies listed on major stock exchanges tend to use the services of large City firms and the American firms in London. These firms will also take a large share of the international deals and compete with smaller City and regional firms for companies listed on AIM and privately owned companies.
- Your experiences will be affected by the type of client your firm acts for. Publicly listed companies, major private equity houses and the investment banks that underwrite deals have different demands and attitudes to risk than say rich entrepreneurs, owner-managed businesses and small to medium-sized enterprises (SMEs).

- Corporate lawyers need to be conversant in a variety of legal disciplines, and know when to refer matters to a specialist in, say, merger control, employment, property or tax.
- This is a very practical area of law, so commercial acumen is a must. Yet, the work is largely paper-based so you need to be well organised and have good drafting skills.
- Long hours arise through client demand, and their expectations have risen even further with instant communication via mobile phones, e-mail and BlackBerrys. Being surrounded by busy, intelligent, high-achieving people is half of the appeal.
- Corporate lawyers work in teams; indeed at times team spirit and adrenaline will be the only things that get you through yet another 20-hour day. It takes time to learn your craft, however, and in the beginning being the most junior member of a deal team can mean boring or unrewarding tasks. The banes of the corporate trainee's life are data room management (putting together and caretaking all the factual information on which a deal relies) and 'bibling' – the creation of files containing copies of all the agreed documents and information.
- A robust and confident manner is typical; stamina is a must. You have to keep pushing yourself because the deals wait for no one.
- The fortunes and schedules of corporate lawyers are tied to the general economy. Corporate lawyers are more likely to experience feast or famine than a steady flow of deals year after year; it is not unheard of for them to experience burnout after a few years.
- You need to become absorbed in the corporate world. The best way to get a taster while still a student is to read the City pages in your daily newspaper. If after six months you haven't developed a real interest then pick another area of practice.

current issues

- The M&A market is booming and corporate departments are recording cumulative deal values larger than ever before, keeping lawyers busy and hours long. The question is, for how long will it continue?

- Sarbanes-Oxley regulations in the US have made London an increasingly attractive financial centre. This is best illustrated in the success of the LSE's AIM market, on which companies from across the globe are floating.

- For firms playing at the high end of the market, the cosmopolitan nature of most of today's big-ticket M&A has made coordination between jurisdictions of paramount importance when executing deals; most firms are placing a large emphasis on international strategy. Right now the markets everyone is watching are China and India.

- Private equity is an active and dominant force in the market. Increasingly, private equity houses are clubbing together as consortia to bid for targets previously beyond their reach.

- A sound grounding in corporate finance makes an excellent springboard for working in industry. Lawyers move in-house to major companies, tempted by decent hours and salaries. Some go to banks, usually as in-house lawyers, occasionally as corporate finance execs or analysts. Company secretarial positions suit lawyers with a taste for internal management and compliance issues.

leading firms from Chambers UK 2008

Corporate Finance: High-end Capability	Corporate Finance The South: Kent & Sussex	Corporate Finance The South: Surrey, Hampshire & Dorset
London	**Band 1**	**Band 1**
Band 1	asb law *Crawley*	Shoosmiths *Fareham*
Freshfields Bruckhaus Deringer	Clarkson Wright & Jakes *Orpington*	Stevens & Bolton LLP *Guildford*
Linklaters	Thomas Eggar LLP *Worthing*	**Band 2**
Slaughter and May	Vertex Law LLP *West Malling*	Blake Lapthorn Tarlo Lyons *Portsmouth*
Band 2	**Band 2**	Clyde & Co LLP *Guildford*
Allen & Overy LLP	Brachers *Maidstone*	**Band 3**
Ashurst	DMH Stallard *Crawley*	Bond Pearce LLP *Southampton*
Clifford Chance LLP	Rawlison Butler *Crawley*	Lamport Bassitt *Southampton*
Herbert Smith LLP	Thomson Snell & Passmore *Tunbridge Wells*	Mundays LLP *Cobham*
Band 3		Paris Smith & Randall LLP *Southampton*
Lovells LLP	Corporate Finance South West: Devon & Cornwall	Penningtons Solicitors LLP *Basingstoke*
Macfarlanes	**Band 1**	Shadbolt & Co LLP *Reigate*
Travers Smith	Bond Pearce LLP *Exeter*	**Band 4**
Band 4	**Band 2**	Charles Russell LLP *Guildford*
Berwin Leighton Paisner LLP	Ashfords *Exeter*	Coffin Mew LLP *Southampton*
CMS Cameron McKenna LLP	Foot Anstey *Plymouth*	Moore Blatch *Southampton*
Jones Day	**Band 3**	
Mayer Brown	Michelmores LLP *Exeter*	
Norton Rose	Stephens & Scown *St Austell*	
Simmons & Simmons		
SJ Berwin LLP		

Corporate Finance: Mid-Market
Best of the UK
Band 1

Addleshaw Goddard LLP *London*
Ashurst *London*
Berwin Leighton Paisner LLP *London*
DLA Piper UK LLP *London*
Eversheds LLP *London*
Jones Day *London*
Macfarlanes *London*
SJ Berwin LLP *London*
Travers Smith *London*

Band 2

Baker & McKenzie LLP *London*
CMS Cameron McKenna LLP *London*
Dechert LLP *London*
Denton Wilde Sapte *London*
K&L Gates *London*
LG *London*
Nabarro *London*
Olswang *London*
Pinsent Masons *London*
Taylor Wessing LLP *London*
Wragge & Co LLP *Birmingham*

Band 3

Bird & Bird *London*
Charles Russell LLP *London*
Clyde & Co LLP *London*
Dickinson Dees LLP *Newcastle upon Tyne*
Hammonds *London*
Osborne Clarke *London*
Reed Smith Richards Butler LLP *London*
Stephenson Harwood *London*

Corporate Finance
Wales
Band 1

Eversheds LLP *Cardiff*
Geldards LLP *Cardiff*
M & A Solicitors LLP *Cardiff*

Band 2

Berry Smith Solicitors *Cardiff*
Capital Law LLP *Cardiff Bay*
Morgan Cole *Cardiff*

Corporate Finance: High-end
Global Coverage
London
Band 1

Clifford Chance LLP
Freshfields Bruckhaus Deringer
Linklaters

Band 2

Allen & Overy LLP
Skadden, Arps, Slate, Meagher & Flom
Slaughter and May *London*

Band 3

Cleary Gottlieb Steen & Hamilton LLP
Herbert Smith LLP
Sullivan & Cromwell LLP

Band 4

Ashurst
Baker & McKenzie LLP
CMS Cameron McKenna LLP
Jones Day
Lovells LLP
Mayer Brown
Norton Rose
Shearman & Sterling LLP
Simmons & Simmons
Weil, Gotshal & Manges LLP
White & Case LLP

Corporate Finance
West Midlands
Band 1

DLA Piper UK LLP *Birmingham*
Wragge & Co LLP *Birmingham*

Band 2

Eversheds LLP *Birmingham*
HBJ Gateley Wareing *Birmingham*
Pinsent Masons *Birmingham*

Band 3

Cobbetts LLP *Birmingham*
Hammonds *Birmingham*
Martineau Johnson *Birmingham*

Band 4

Browne Jacobson LLP *Birmingham*
George Green LLP *Cradley Heath*

Corporate Finance: AIM
Best of the UK
Band 1

Ashurst *London*
Berwin Leighton Paisner LLP *London*
DLA Piper UK LLP *London*
LG *London*
Nabarro *London*
Norton Rose *London*
Travers Smith *London*

Band 2

Addleshaw Goddard LLP *London*
Charles Russell LLP *London*
Eversheds LLP *London*
Field Fisher Waterhouse LLP *London*
Jones Day *London*
K&L Gates *London*
McDermott Will & Emery UK LLP *London*
Memery Crystal LLP *London*
Olswang *London*
Osborne Clarke *Bristol*
Pinsent Masons *London*
SJ Berwin LLP *London*
Stephenson Harwood *London*

Band 3

Clyde & Co LLP *London*
Denton Wilde Sapte *London*
Faegre & Benson LLP *London*
Finers Stephens Innocent *London*
Fladgate Fielder *London*
Halliwells LLP *Manchester*
Hammonds *London*
Howard Kennedy *London*
Hunton & Williams *London*
Marriott Harrison *London*
McGrigors LLP *Glasgow*
Mishcon de Reya *London*
Reed Smith Richards Butler LLP *London*
Rosenblatt *London*
Salans *London*
Shepherd and Wedderburn *Edinburgh*
Taylor Wessing LLP *London*
Trowers & Hamlins *London*

corporate law (continued)

Corporate Finance: Lower Mid-Market

London

Band 1
Field Fisher Waterhouse LLP
Lewis Silkin LLP

Band 2
Barlow Lyde & Gilbert LLP
Beachcroft LLP
Dundas & Wilson
Fladgate Fielder
Harbottle & Lewis LLP
Marriott Harrison
Mishcon de Reya
Morrison & Foerster MNP
Reynolds Porter Chamberlain LLP
Salans
Trowers & Hamlins

Band 3
Bates Wells & Braithwaite
Davenport Lyons
Davies Arnold Cooper
Farrer & Co
Finers Stephens Innocent
Fox Williams LLP
Holman Fenwick & Willan
Howard Kennedy
Kemp Little LLP
Kendall Freeman
Maclay Murray & Spens LLP
Manches LLP
Memery Crystal LLP
Watson, Farley & Williams
Withers LLP

Corporate Finance

East Midlands

Band 1
Browne Jacobson LLP *Nottingham*
Eversheds LLP *Nottingham*
Freeth Cartwright LLP *Nottingham*

Band 2
Geldards LLP *Derby*
HBJ Gateley Wareing *Nottingham*
Hewitsons *Northampton*
Howes Percival LLP *Leicester*
Shoosmiths *Nottingham*

Corporate Finance

Thames Valley

Band 1
Osborne Clarke *Reading*

Band 2
Blake Lapthorn Tarlo Lyons *Oxford*
Boyes Turner *Reading*
Pitmans *Reading*
Shoosmiths *Reading*

Band 3
Clarkslegal LLP *Reading*
EMW Law *Milton Keynes*
Field Seymour Parkes *Reading*
Howes Percival LLP *Milton Keynes*
Kimbells LLP *Milton Keynes*
Manches LLP *Oxford*
Matthew Arnold & Baldwin *Watford*

Band 4
Blandy & Blandy *Reading*
Darbys Solicitors LLP *Oxford*
Moorcrofts LLP *Marlow*
Morgan Cole *Reading*

Corporate Finance

North West

Band 1
Addleshaw Goddard LLP *Manchester*
DLA Piper UK LLP *Manchester*
Eversheds LLP *Manchester*

Band 2
Halliwells LLP *Manchester*
Hammonds *Manchester*

Band 3
Brabners Chaffe Street *Liverpool*
Cobbetts LLP *Manchester*
DWF *Liverpool*
Pannone LLP *Manchester*

Band 4
Beachcroft LLP *Manchester*
Kuit Steinart Levy *Manchester*
Pinsent Masons *Manchester*

Band 5
Baines Wilson *Carlisle*
Hill Dickinson LLP *Liverpool*
Mace & Jones *Liverpool*
Nexus Solicitors *Manchester*

Corporate Finance

South West: Bristol & Surround

Band 1
Burges Salmon LLP *Bristol*
Osborne Clarke *Bristol*

Band 2
TLT LLP *Bristol*

Band 3
Beachcroft LLP *Bristol*
Bond Pearce LLP *Bristol*
Charles Russell LLP *Cheltenham*
Clark Holt *Swindon*
Roxburgh Milkins LLP *Bristol*

Band 4
BPE Solicitors *Cheltenham*
Veale Wasbrough Lawyers *Bristol*

Band 5
Ashfords *Bristol*
Bevan Brittan LLP *Bristol*
Lyons Davidson *Bristol*
Rickerbys *Cheltenham*
Thring Townsend *Bath*
Wilsons *Salisbury*
Withy King *Bath*

Corporate Finance

East Anglia

Band 1
Mills & Reeve LLP *Norwich*

Band 2
Birketts LLP *Ipswich*

Band 3
Eversheds LLP *Cambridge*
Hewitsons *Cambridge*
Taylor Vinters *Cambridge*
Taylor Wessing LLP *Cambridge*

Band 4
Howes Percival LLP *Norwich*

Band 5
Greene & Greene *Bury St Edmunds*
Greenwoods Solicitors LLP *Peterborough*
Prettys *Ipswich*

Band 6
Ashton Graham *Ipswich*
Kester Cunningham John *Cambridge*
Leathes Prior *Norwich*

solicitors

Corporate Finance
Yorkshire
Band 1
Addleshaw Goddard LLP *Leeds*
DLA Piper UK LLP *Leeds*
Eversheds LLP *Leeds*

Band 2
Hammonds *Leeds*
Pinsent Masons *Leeds*
Walker Morris *Leeds*

Band 3
Cobbetts LLP *Leeds*
Gordons *Bradford*

Band 4
Irwin Mitchell *Leeds*
Keeble Hawson *Sheffield*
Lee & Priestley LLP *Leeds*
Lupton Fawcett LLP *Leeds*
Nabarro *Sheffield*

Band 5
Andrew Jackson *Hull*
Clarion Solicitors *Leeds*
Denison Till *York*
Gosschalks *Hull*
Langleys *York*
Rollits *Hull*
Schofield Sweeney *Bradford*
Schofield Sweeney *Leeds*
Shulmans *Leeds*

Corporate Finance
North East
Band 1
Dickinson Dees LLP *Newcastle upon Tyne*

Band 2
Ward Hadaway *Newcastle upon Tyne*

Band 3
Eversheds LLP *Newcastle upon Tyne*
Muckle LLP *Newcastle upon Tyne*

Band 4
Hay & Kilner *Newcastle upon Tyne*
Mincoffs *Newcastle upon Tyne*
Watson Burton LLP *Newcastle upon Tyne*

Private Equity: Buyouts
Best of the UK
Band 1
Clifford Chance LLP *London*

Band 2
Ashurst *London*
Freshfields Bruckhaus Deringer *London*
Macfarlanes *London*
Travers Smith *London*

Band 3
Allen & Overy LLP *London*
Dickson Minto WS *London*
Linklaters *London*
Weil, Gotshal & Manges LLP *London*

Band 4
CMS Cameron McKenna LLP *London*
DLA Piper UK LLP *London*
Jones Day *London*
Kirkland & Ellis International LLP *London*
Olswang *London*
SJ Berwin LLP *London*
Skadden, Arps, Slate, Meagher *London*
Slaughter and May *London*

Band 5
Addleshaw Goddard LLP *London*
Eversheds LLP *London*

Private Equity: Venture Capital Investment
Best of the UK
Band 1
Olswang *London*
Osborne Clarke *London*
Taylor Wessing LLP *London*

Band 2
SJ Berwin LLP *London*

Band 3
CMS Cameron McKenna LLP *London*
Jones Day *London*
Nabarro *London*

Private Equity: International Buyouts
Best of the UK
Band 1
Clifford Chance LLP *London*

Band 2
Ashurst *London*
Freshfields Bruckhaus Deringer *London*
Weil, Gotshal & Manges LLP *London*

Band 3
Allen & Overy LLP *London*
Debevoise & Plimpton LLP *London*
Kirkland & Ellis International LLP *London*
Linklaters *London*
Simpson Thacher & Bartlett LLP *London*

Band 4
Cleary Gottlieb Steen & Hamilton *London*
Dickson Minto WS *London*
Latham & Watkins LLP *London*
Skadden, Arps, Slate, Meagher *London*

crime

put simply

Criminal solicitors represent defendants in cases brought before the UK's criminal courts. Lesser offences are usually dealt with exclusively by solicitors in the magistrates' courts; more serious charges go to the Crown Courts, which are essentially still the domain of barristers, not least because most defendants still prefer this. In the year ending September 2005 there were 905,587 convictions in magistrates' courts and 71,099 in the Crown Court.

'Everyday crime' is the staple for most solicitors – theft, assault, drugs and driving offences. Fraud is the preserve of a more limited number of firms. Fraud cases aren't all as long-winded and complicated as the infamous Guinness fraud trial, but they do require a different approach from, say, crimes of violence.

A summary of the work of the Crown Prosecution Service is given on page 19. Details of the Public Defender Service are given on page 24.

who does what

Most days are busy; the others are frantic. A hectic schedule of visits to police stations, prisons and magistrates' courts, plenty of face-to-face client meetings and advocacy mean this is definitely not a desk job. The solicitor's work sees them:

- Attend police stations to interview and advise people in police custody.
- Visit prisons to see clients on remand.
- Prepare the client's defence, liaising with witnesses, medical and social workers' reports, probation officers, the CPS and others.
- Attend 'conferences with counsel', ie barristers
- Represent defendants at trial or brief barristers to do so.
- Represent clients at sentencing hearings, to explain any mitigating facts.

for fraud solicitors:

- There is a considerable volume of paperwork and financial analysis; a head for business is vital.
- For trainees, the early years will provide minimal advocacy and masses of trawling through warehouses full of documents. The caseload will be smaller but cases can run for years.

the realities of the job

- The hours are long and can disrupt your personal life. Lawyers who are accredited to work as Duty Solicitors will be on a rota and can be called to a police station at any time of the day or night while on duty.
- Confidence is essential. Without it you're doomed.
- In general crime you'll have a large caseload with a fast turnaround, but this means plenty of advocacy.
- The work is driven by the procedural rules and timetable of the court. Even so, recent figures show that almost a quarter of trials do not proceed on the appointed day, either because defendants or witnesses are absent, or at the request of the CPS.
- Your efforts can mean the difference between a person's liberty and their incarceration. You have to be detail-conscious and constantly vigilant.
- You'll encounter some pretty horrible situations and some difficult and distressed people. Murderers, rapists, drug dealers, conmen, football hooligans, paedophiles. If you have the ability to look beyond the labels and see these people as clients who are deserving of your best efforts then you've picked the right job. Some will have drug or alcohol problems, others will be mentally ill, others just children.
- It can be disheartening to see clients repeat the same poor choices, returning to court again and again.

the criminal courts of england and wales

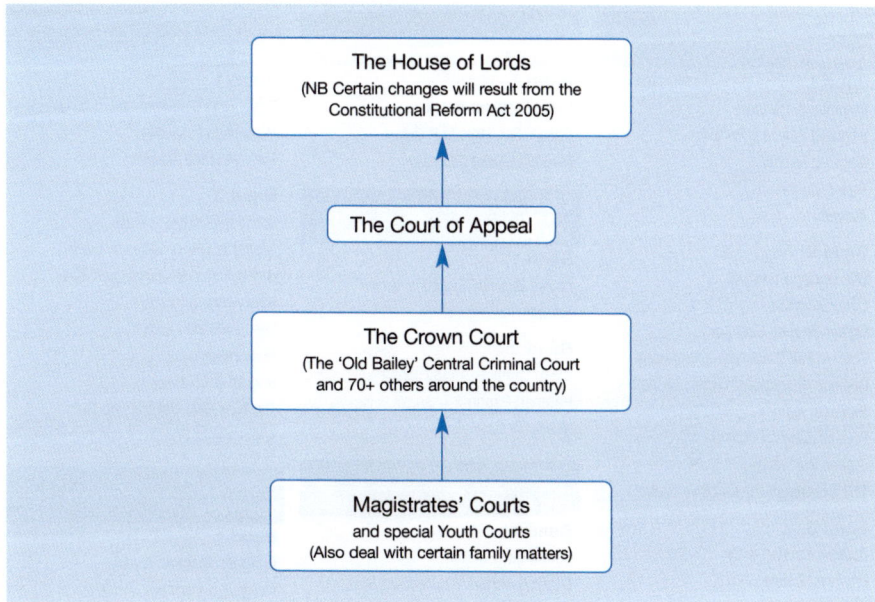

```
┌─────────────────────────────────────────┐
│          The House of Lords               │
│   (NB Certain changes will result from the│
│       Constitutional Reform Act 2005)     │
└─────────────────────────────────────────┘
                    ▲
            ┌──────────────────┐
            │ The Court of Appeal │
            └──────────────────┘
                    ▲
        ┌───────────────────────────────┐
        │        The Crown Court          │
        │ (The 'Old Bailey' Central Criminal Court│
        │    and 70+ others around the country)   │
        └───────────────────────────────┘
                    ▲
        ┌───────────────────────────────┐
        │       Magistrates' Courts        │
        │     and special Youth Courts     │
        │ (Also deal with certain family matters)│
        └───────────────────────────────┘
```

NB Certain military matters are dealt with by Courts-Martial

- Public funding of criminal defence means there's a good helping of bureaucracy. It also means you'll never be a millionaire.

current issues

- Vast changes in legal aid funding have caused cold shivers and clammy hands among lawyers. If you want to spook yourself, read Get Carter on page 17.
- Britain's FBI – the Serious Organised Crime Agency (SOCA) – has been operating for more than a year, its mission being to uncover and bring to justice the biggest and baddest crime bosses. Read its first annual report at www.soca.gov.uk
- In the past victims have been seen as merely witnesses. Not so since the introduction of the Victim's Personal Statement (VPS). A new 'victims' advocate' scheme has been piloted in the Old Bailey and Crown Courts in Birmingham, Cardiff, Manchester and Winchester.
- The Criminal Justice Act contains provisions concerning the possible abolition of juries for serious fraud cases. Not yet engaged, the proposal was forced onto the back burner as it was met with huge resistance from practitioners, though it will no doubt rear its head again.
- There has been a noticeable rise in the number of terrorism-related cases
- Check out www.clsa.co.uk for other news and discussion on major developments in criminal practice.

leading firms from Chambers UK 2008

Crime
London

Band 1
Bindman & Partners
Birnberg Peirce & Partners
Kingsley Napley
Taylor Nichol
Tuckers

Band 2
BCL Burton Copeland
Birds Solicitors
Corker Binning Solicitors
Edward Fail Bradshaw & Waterson
Hallinan, Blackburn, Gittings & Nott
Hickman & Rose
Russell Jones & Walker
Stokoe Partnership
TNT Solicitors (Thanki Novy Taube)

Band 3
Andrew Keenan & Co
Edwards Duthie
Fisher Meredith
Henry Milner & Co
Hodge Jones & Allen
IBB Solicitors
Meldrum Young
Powell Spencer & Partners
Russell-Cooke LLP
Saunders Solicitors LLP
Simons Muirhead & Burton
TV Edwards
Venters Solicitors
Victor Lissack, Roscoe & Coleman

Band 4
Christian Khan
Claude Hornby & Cox
Daniel Berman & Co
Galbraith Branley
Goldkorns
Hughmans
J D Spicer & Co
Kaim Todner
Lewis Nedas & Co
McCormacks
Reynolds Dawson

Crime
Thames Valley

Band 1
Blake Lapthorn Tarlo Lyons *Oxford*
Darbys Solicitors LLP *Oxford*
Macnab Clarke *Abingdon*

Crime
The South

Band 1
Clarke Kiernan *Tunbridge Wells*
Knights *Tunbridge Wells*

Band 2
Blake Lapthorn Tarlo Lyons *Portsmouth*
Hamnett Osborne Tisshaw *Haywards Heath*

Crime
East Anglia

Band 1
Belmores *Norwich*
BTMK Solicitors *Southend-on-Sea*
Hatch Brenner *Norwich*

Band 2
David Charnley & Co *Romford*
hc solicitors LLP *Peterborough*
Norton Peskett *Lowestoft*
TNT Solicitors (Thanki Novy Taube) *Harlow*

Band 3
Copleys *Huntingdon*
Fosters *Norwich*
Gepp & Sons *Chelmsford*
Hegarty LLP Solicitors *Peterborough*

Crime
West Midlands

Band 1
Glaisyers *Birmingham*
Jonas Roy Bloom *Birmingham*
Tuckers *Birmingham*

Band 2
Challinors *Birmingham*
Purcell Parker *Birmingham*

Crime
North East

Band 1
David Gray Solicitors *Newcastle upon Tyne*
Howells LLP *Sheffield*
Irwin Mitchell *Sheffield*

Band 2
Clarion Solicitors *Leeds*
Grahame Stowe Bateson *Leeds*
Hay & Kilner *Newcastle upon Tyne*
Henry Hyams *Leeds*
Lester Morrill *Leeds*
McCormicks *Harrogate*
Sugaré & Co *Leeds*
The Max Gold Partnership *Hull*
Williamsons Solicitors *Hull*

Crime
South West

Band 1
Bobbetts Mackan *Bristol*
Douglas & Partners *Bristol*
Kelcey & Hall *Bristol*
Sansbury Campbell *Bristol*

Band 2
Bay Advocates *Torquay*
Nunn Rickard Solicitor Advocates *Exeter*
Russell Jones & Walker *Bristol*
St James Solicitors *Exeter*
Stone King LLP *Bath*
Walker Lahive *Plymouth*

Band 3
Aidan Woods & Co *Bristol*
Dunn & Baker *Exeter*
Foot Anstey *Plymouth*
Stones Solicitors *Exeter*

Crime
East Midlands
Band 1
Cartwright King *Nottingham*
The Johnson Partnership *Nottingham*

Band 2
Fletchers *Nottingham*
Kieran Clarke Solicitors *Chesterfield*
The Smith Partnership *Derby*

Band 3
Banner Jones Middleton *Chesterfield*
Elliot Mather *Matlock*
Varley Hadley Siddall *Nottingham*

Crime
North West
Band 1
Brian Koffman & Co *Manchester*
Burton Copeland LLP *Manchester*
Draycott Browne *Manchester*
JMW Solicitors *Manchester*
Tuckers *Manchester*

Band 2
Cobleys LLP *Liverpool*
Cunninghams *Manchester*
Farleys *Blackburn*
Forbes *Blackburn*
Maidments *Manchester*
Pearson Fielding Polson *Liverpool*

Band 3
Olliers *Manchester*
Quinn Melville *Liverpool*
Rowlands *Manchester*

Crime
Wales
Band 1
Gamlins *Rhyl*
Huttons *Cardiff*
Martyn Prowel Solicitors *Cardiff*

Band 2
Clarke & Hartland *Cardiff*
Colin Jones *Barry*
Douglas-Jones Mercer (DJM) *Swansea*
Goldstones *Swansea*
Graham Evans & Partners *Swansea*
Harding Evans *Newport*
Howe & Spender *Port Talbot*
Hugh James *Blackwood*
Robertsons *Cardiff*
Savery Pennington *Cardiff*
Spiro Grech McSorley & Wilkins *Cardiff*
Wilson Devonald *Swansea*

Fraud: Criminal
Best of the UK
Band 1
BCL Burton Copeland *London*
Kingsley Napley *London*
Peters & Peters *London*

Band 2
Byrne and Partners *London*
Cooper Kenyon Burrows *Manchester*
Corker Binning Solicitors *London*
DLA Piper UK LLP *London*
Pannone LLP *Manchester*
Russell Jones & Walker *London*

Band 3
Bankside Law *London*
David Phillips & Partners *Bootle*
Eversheds LLP *London*
Irwin Mitchell *London*

Band 4
Bark & Co *London*
Bindman & Partners *London*
Cartwright King *Nottingham*
Clarion Solicitors *Leeds*
Farleys *Blackburn*
Garstangs *London*
Hanman Associates *Manchester*
Hugh James *Cardiff*
Simons Muirhead & Burton *London*
Tuckers *London*
Victor Lissack, Roscoe & Coleman *London*

employment law

put simply

Employment lawyers guide their clients through the ever-growing area of workplace-related legislation, and in so doing they become intimately involved in the relationship between employers and employees. The divide between employers' and employees' lawyers is usually clear-cut, although some firms do act for both types of client. A few firms are known for their union connections. Always remember that the nature of a firm's clientele determines on which side of the fence its lawyers end up. Usually the job includes both advisory work and litigation, but when choosing a training contract you may wish to check that this is the case, or if the two roles are split.

Disputes are almost always resolved at an Employment Tribunal, or before reaching one. Tribunals are far less formal than a court, so for example barristers do not wear wigs or robes and modify their performance. Oftentimes individuals will be unrepresented. In these situations the tribunal panel usually forgives their inexperience, and may expect the employers' representatives to do so too.

The grievances leading to litigation fall into the following broad categories: redundancy, unlawful dismissal, breach of contract, harassment and discrimination. This latter category can be brought on the grounds of race, religious or philosophical belief, gender, sexual orientation, disability and age. Newspapers regularly report the detail of high-profile cases, so it's easy to familiarise yourself with the area. Such reports also give you a flavour of the human drama involved in the job.

who does what

employees' solicitors

- Advise clients on whether they have suffered unlawful or unfair treatment at work and establish the amount to be claimed. This will either be capped, or in the case of discrimina-

tion, can include additional elements to cover loss of earnings, injury to feelings and aggravated damages.
- Gather evidence and witnesses to support the claim.
- Try to negotiate a payment from the employer or take the matter to tribunal. If there is a breach of contract element to the claim, it might be heard in a court rather than a tribunal.
- If the matter does reach tribunal, the solicitor may conduct the advocacy themselves.

employers' solicitors

As well as defending or settling the above claims, employers' lawyers give general advice on:
- Negotiating employment contracts or exit packages for senior staff.
- Negotiating with unions to avoid or resolve industrial disputes.
- Formulating HR policies, and providing training on how to avoid workplace problems.
- Helping out on corporate deals by investigating and summarising the employment law issues affecting the businesses concerned.

the realities of the job

- You quickly develop an understanding of human foibles. By their very nature employment cases are filled with high drama.
- Clients may assume your role is to provide emotional support as well as legal advice. You need to take care to define your role appropriately.
- If acting for employers, you won't always like what you hear, but you still need to protect the clients' interests. Soon enough you'll see the advantage of preventative counselling and training programmes.
- This is a job for solicitors who want to do their own advocacy, although barristers are commonly used for high-stakes or complicated hearings and trials.

- The work is driven by the procedural rules and timetable of the tribunals and courts.
- The law is extensive and changes frequently. You'll read more than your fair share of EU directives.

current issues

- In October 2006 the Employment Equality (Age) Regulations came into force and will undoubtedly prove significant, and not just for the 'stale, pale males' who will finally have a chance to bring a legitimate grievance. Thus far thee has been no avalanche of claims but businesses have been reviewing their employment policies to ensure compliance, especially in the areas of performance management, training, benefits, retirement and redundancy. One particular area of concern will be recruitment, where job descriptions should not indirectly discriminate. Looking for an 'energetic graduate' for a 'funky, young firm' implies that older candidates need not apply, while requiring a 'mature person with gravitas and ten years' experience' rules out younger applicants. Proving that ten years' experience is strictly necessary for the job may be difficult. Likewise, rejecting a candidate for being overqualified could be discriminatory. Some law firms are dropping the use of the term PQE (post-qualification experience) in favour of competency-based measures.

- The value of discrimination and harassment claims rises with no sign of abatement, particularly in relation to highly paid City executives at big banks. These cases carry substantial risk to the banks' reputations and illustrate the decision taken by a significant number of companies to fight claims. Investment banks are bulking up their in-house capabilities due to the rash of discrimination claims.
- The growth of in-house legal teams in large organisations means employer-led law firms need to specialise and offer added value to their clients. Many companies believe solicitors are too expensive and, privately, some solicitors acknowledge that they are indeed losing work to in-house teams.
- New disciplinary and grievance procedures have prompted employers and employees to seek legal advice sooner rather than later.
- Equal pay in the public sector (eg NHS and local government is a big thing.)
- There is consolidation in the trade union movement, in particular plans to merge GMB, Amicus and TGWU.
- There is huge competition amongst trainees for employment seats, and even more for NQ-level jobs. Consider applying to train at specialist or employment-heavy firms if this is your intended area for specialisation. In many mainstream firms, gaining exposure to employment work can be a lottery.

employment law (continued)

leading firms from Chambers UK 2008

Employment: Mainly Respondent
Best of the UK

Band 1

Allen & Overy LLP *London*	Baker & McKenzie LLP *London*
Herbert Smith LLP *London*	Lewis Silkin LLP *London*
Simmons & Simmons *London*	

Band 2

Eversheds LLP *London*	Freshfields Bruckhaus Deringer *London*
Linklaters *London*	Lovells LLP *London*
Mayer Brown *London*	

Band 3

Addleshaw Goddard LLP *London*	Beachcroft LLP *London*
Bird & Bird *London*	Charles Russell LLP *London*
Clifford Chance LLP *London*	Dechert LLP *London*
DLA Piper UK LLP *London*	Farrer & Co *London*
Fox Williams LLP *London*	Hammonds *London*
Macfarlanes *London*	McDermott Will & Emery UK LLP *London*
Nabarro *London*	Olswang *London*
Pinsent Masons *London*	Slaughter and May *London*
Travers Smith *London*	

Band 4

Berwin Leighton Paisner LLP *London*	CMS Cameron McKenna LLP *London*
Mishcon de Reya *London*	Norton Rose *London*
Osborne Clarke *London*	SJ Berwin LLP *London*
Stephenson Harwood *London*	Taylor Wessing LLP *London*
Withers LLP *London*	Wragge & Co LLP *Birmingham*

Band 5

Ashurst *London*	Barlow Lyde & Gilbert LLP *London*
Bevan Brittan LLP *London*	Burges Salmon LLP *Bristol*
Doyle Clayton Solicitors *London*	Reed Smith Richards Butler LLP *London*
Salans *London*	Speechly Bircham LLP *London*

Band 6

Archon *London*	Bates Wells & Braithwaite *London*
Bircham Dyson Bell *London*	Blake Lapthorn Tarlo Lyons *London*
Clarkslegal LLP *London*	Denton Wilde Sapte *London*
Dundas & Wilson *London*	Finers Stephens Innocent *London*
H2O Law LLP *London*	Harbottle & Lewis LLP *London*
Kemp Little LLP *London*	LG *London*
Manches LLP *London*	Reynolds Porter Chamberlain LLP *London*
Simons Muirhead & Burton *London*	Watson, Farley & Williams *London*
Wedlake Bell *London*	

Employment: International
Best of the UK

Band 1

Allen & Overy LLP *London*
Baker & McKenzie LLP *London*
Freshfields Bruckhaus Deringer *London*
Herbert Smith LLP *London*
Simmons & Simmons *London*

Band 2

Clifford Chance LLP *London*
DLA Piper UK LLP *London*
Eversheds LLP *London*
Hammonds *London*
Lewis Silkin LLP *London*
Linklaters *London*
Lovells LLP *London*
Mayer Brown *London*
McDermott Will & Emery UK LLP *London*
Norton Rose *London*
White & Case LLP *London*

Band 3

Ashurst *London*
Bird & Bird *London*
Dechert LLP *London*
Latham & Watkins LLP *London*
Slaughter and May *London*
Taylor Wessing LLP *London*
Travers Smith *London*
Wilmer Cutler Pickering Hale *London*

Employment
Wales

Band 1

Eversheds LLP *Cardiff*
Morgan Cole *Cardiff*

Band 2

Capital Law LLP *Cardiff Bay*
Geldards LLP *Cardiff*
Hugh James *Cardiff*

Band 3

Berry Smith Solicitors *Cardiff*
Clarkslegal LLP *Cardiff*
Dolmans *Cardiff*

Employment
Thames Valley

Band 1
Clarkslegal LLP *Reading*
Olswang Thames Valley *Reading*
Osborne Clarke *Reading*

Band 2
Boyes Turner *Reading*
Lewis Silkin LLP *Oxford*
Shoosmiths *Reading*

Band 3
Blake Lapthorn Tarlo Lyons *Oxford*
Cater Leydon Millard Limited *Abingdon*
Manches LLP *Oxford*
Matthew Arnold & Baldwin *Watford*
Pitmans *Reading*

Band 4
B P Collins *Gerrards Cross*
Doyle Clayton Solicitors *Reading*
Henmans LLP *Oxford*
IBB Solicitors *Uxbridge*
Penningtons Solicitors LLP *Newbury*

Employment
East Anglia

Band 1
Eversheds LLP *Cambridge*
Mills & Reeve LLP *Cambridge, Norwich*
Taylor Vinters *Cambridge*

Band 2
Birketts LLP *Ipswich, Norwich*
Greenwoods Solicitors LLP *Peterborough*

Band 3
Ashton Graham *Ipswich*
Hegarty LLP Solicitors *Peterborough*

Band 4
Charles Russell LLP *Cambridge*
Gotelee & Goldsmith *Ipswich*
Hatch Brenner *Norwich*
Hewitsons *Cambridge*
Howes Percival LLP *Norwich*
Leathes Prior *Norwich*
Prettys *Ipswich*
Quantrills *Ipswich*
Steeles (Law) LLP *Norwich*
Wollastons LLP *Chelmsford*

Employment
The South

Band 1
Blake Lapthorn Tarlo Lyons *Fareham*
Bond Pearce LLP *Southampton*
Clyde & Co LLP *Guildford*
DMH Stallard *Crawley*

Band 2
Charles Russell LLP *Guildford*
Cripps Harries Hall LLP *Tunbridge Wells*
Paris Smith & Randall LLP *Southampton*
Sherrards Employment Law and Human
Resources *Haywards Heath*
Stevens & Bolton LLP *Guildford*
Thomson Snell & Passmore *Tunbridge
Wells*

Band 3
asb law *Crawley*
Brachers *Maidstone*
Clarke Willmott *Southampton*
Clarkson Wright & Jakes *Orpington*
Rawlison Butler *Crawley*
Thomas Eggar LLP *Chichester*

Band 4
Coffin Mew LLP *Southampton*
Furley Page LLP *Canterbury*
Lamport Bassitt *Southampton*
Lester Aldridge LLP *Southampton*
Moore Blatch *Southampton*
Mundays LLP *Cobham*
Shoosmiths *Fareham*
Trethowans *Southampton*

Employment
South West

Band 1
Bevan Brittan LLP *Bristol*
Burges Salmon LLP *Bristol*
Osborne Clarke *Bristol*

Band 2
Ashfords *Exeter*
Beachcroft LLP *Bristol*
Bond Pearce LLP *Plymouth*
Clarke Willmott *Bristol*
Foot Anstey *Plymouth*
TLT LLP *Bristol*
Veale Wasbrough Lawyers *Bristol*

Band 3
Bevans *Bristol*
BPE Solicitors *Cheltenham*
Charles Russell LLP *Cheltenham*
Rickerbys *Cheltenham*
Stephens & Scown *Exeter*
Withy King *Bath*

Band 4
Lyons Davidson *Bristol*
Michelmores LLP *Exeter*
Thring Townsend *Bath*

Employment
North East

Band 1
Dickinson Dees LLP *Newcastle upon Tyne*
Eversheds LLP *Newcastle upon Tyne*
Ward Hadaway *Newcastle upon Tyne*

Band 2
Jacksons Commercial *Stockton on Tees*
Muckle LLP *Newcastle upon Tyne*
Samuel Phillips *Newcastle upon Tyne*
Watson Burton LLP *Newcastle upon Tyne*

Band 3
Archers Law *Stockton on Tees*
Crutes Law Firm *Newcastle upon Tyne*
Hay & Kilner *Newcastle upon Tyne*
Short Richardson *Newcastle upon Tyne*
Sintons *Newcastle upon Tyne*
The Endeavour Partnership *Teesdale*

employment law (continued)

Employment
Yorkshire

Band 1
DLA Piper UK LLP *Leeds, Sheffield*
Eversheds LLP *Leeds*
Pinsent Masons *Leeds*

Band 2
Addleshaw Goddard LLP *Leeds*
Hammonds *Leeds*
Walker Morris *Leeds*

Band 3
Beachcroft LLP *Leeds*
Cobbetts LLP *Leeds*
Ford & Warren *Leeds*
Gordons *Leeds*
Nabarro *Sheffield*
Watson Burton LLP *Leeds*

Band 4
Andrew Jackson *Hull*
Hempsons *Harrogate*
Irwin Mitchell *Sheffield*
Langleys *York*
Lupton Fawcett LLP *Leeds*
McCormicks *Harrogate*
Rollits *Hull*

Employment: Union/Applicant
Best of the UK

Band 1
Pattinson & Brewer *London*
Russell Jones & Walker *London*

Band 2
Bindman & Partners *London*
Ferguson Solicitors *London*
Palmer Wade *London*
Rowley Ashworth *London*
Thompsons *London*

Band 3
Irwin Mitchell *Sheffield*
Simpson Millar LLP *London*
Webster Dixon LLP *London*

Employment: Union/Applicant
Wales

Band 1
Russell Jones & Walker *Cardiff*

Employment
North West

Band 1
Addleshaw Goddard LLP *Manchester*
DLA Piper UK LLP *Manchester*
Eversheds LLP *Manchester*
Halliwells LLP *Manchester*

Band 2
Beachcroft LLP *Manchester*
Brabners Chaffe Street *Manchester*
Cobbetts LLP *Manchester*
DWF *Manchester*
Hammonds *Manchester*
Mace & Jones *Manchester*
Pannone LLP *Manchester*

Band 3
Hill Dickinson LLP *Liverpool*
Kuit Steinart Levy *Manchester*
Weightmans *Liverpool*

Band 4
Baines Wilson *Carlisle*
Berg Legal *Manchester*
Burnetts *Carlisle*
Keoghs LLP *Bolton*
Pinsent Masons *Manchester*

Employment: Union/Applicant
North East

Band 1
Stefan Cross Solicitors *Newcastle on Tyne*
Thompsons *Newcastle upon Tyne*

Band 2
Browell Smith *Newcastle upon Tyne*

Employment: Union/Applicant
North West

Band 1
Russell Jones & Walker *Manchester*
Thompsons *Manchester*

Band 2
EAD Solicitors *Liverpool*
Whittles *Manchester*

Employment: Union/Applicant
South West

Band 1
Burroughs Day *Bristol*

Band 2
Thompsons *Bristol*

Employment
Midlands

Band 1
Wragge & Co LLP *Birmingham*

Band 2
DLA Piper UK LLP *Birmingham*
Eversheds LLP *Birmingham*
Hammonds *Birmingham*
Martineau Johnson *Birmingham*
Pinsent Masons *Birmingham*

Band 3
Bevan Brittan LLP *Birmingham*
Browne Jacobson LLP *Nottingham*
Cobbetts LLP *Birmingham*
Freeth Cartwright LLP *Nottingham*
HBJ Gateley Wareing *Birmingham*
Howes Percival LLP *Leicester*
Mills & Reeve LLP *Birmingham*
Shakespeare Putsman LLP *Birmingham*

Band 4
Anthony Collins Solicitors *Birmingham*
Geldards LLP *Nottingham*
George Green *Halesowen*
Irwin Mitchell *Birmingham*

Band 5
BPE Solicitors *Birmingham*
Clarke Willmott *Birmingham*
Flint Bishop Solicitors *Derby*
Harvey Ingram LLP *Leicester*
Higgs & Sons *Brierley Hill*
KJD *Stoke-on-Trent*
Lanyon Bowdler Solicitors *Telford*
Reed Smith Richards Butler LLP *Solihull*
Shoosmiths *Birmingham*

Employment: Union/Applicant
Yorkshire

Band 1
Thompsons *Leeds*

Band 2
Morrish & Co *Leeds*
Rowley Ashworth *Leeds*

Employment: Union/Applicant
Midlands

Band 1
Averta Employment Lawyers *Solihull*

environmental law

put simply

Advice to corporate clients on damage limitation, pre-emptive advice and defence from prosecution is the stock-in-trade of the environmental lawyer. The majority of those in private practice are working for, rather than sticking it to, big business; roles on the saintly side of this area of law are scarce. Opportunities do exist to work in-house for organisations like Greenpeace and Friends of the Earth or for niche public interest firms but these jobs are highly sought after.

Local authorities, government departments such as the Department for Environment, Food and Rural Affairs (Defra) and regulatory bodies like the Environment Agency are all employers of lawyers working in the environmental field and worth looking into if commercial environmental law doesn't sound appealing.

Environment law overlaps with other disciplines such as property, criminal law, corporate or EU law. The small size of most law firm environmental teams, and the need for practitioners to keep extra strings to their bow, means there are relatively few pure environmental lawyers around. On the one hand this makes for a very competitive area, but on the other the breadth of the discipline ensures a diverse and stimulating career.

who does what

Generally speaking the work of private practitioners breaks down into three areas:
- Advice on the potential environmental consequences of corporate, property and projects transactions – due diligence, you might call it. Will your client's new housing development destroy a colony of rare newts? Does the manufacturing business your client is buying have a history of environmental problems? How much waste is it discharging into rivers? Environmental issues can be deal-breakers.
- Compliance and regulatory advice – helping clients avoid investigation or even prosecution by the Environment Agency by ensuring their businesses keep within the regulations controlling how they operate.
- Defending clients when they get into trouble over water or air pollution, waste disposal, emission levels or health and safety. Such cases can involve criminal or civil disputes, judicial reviews and even statutory appeals, and can be the subject of damaging media coverage. Remember the recent case of a firm prosecuted and fined £250,000 for transporting radioactive material while a missing safety plug allowed a beam of radiation 1,000 times above safe levels to be emitted along the 130-mile route?

work in local authority legal departments:
- Here lawyers have a massive variety of work covering regulatory and planning issues plus waste management and air pollution prosecutions. They must also advise the authority on its own potential liability.

work for defra:
- DEFRA employs over 80 lawyers including trainees on GLS-funded schemes. Broadly it aims to promote sustainable development without compromising the quality of life of future generations. Two examples of its varied mandates are access to and the protection of the countryside, and the maintenance of good water quality and water environments.
- The lawyers' duties include litigation, drafting of subordinate legislation, advisory work and contract drafting.

work for the Environment Agency (EA):
- The EA has lawyers in Bristol and eight regional bases and is responsible for protecting and enhancing the environment and the regulation of corporate activities that have the capacity to pollute. As such the scope of work

is vast: from waste management to flood defence, from air quality to environmental impact assessment, from contaminated land to climate change.

- As the prosecuting body for environmental crimes, there is plenty of prosecution work requiring the lawyers to gather evidence, prepare cases and brief barristers.
- Co-operation with government lawyers on the drafting and implementation of legislation.

the realities of the job

- The way in which environmental law spans disciplines means strong commercial nous and understanding of corporate structures are vital. All-round skills are best complemented by a genuine interest in a specific area (say renewable energy, conservation or water pollution) in this competitive and exacting field.
- Excellent academics are a must to help wade through, extrapolate from and present research and complex legislation; so too are sound judgement, pragmatism and a sense of improvisation in offering clients the most practical solutions.
- A basic grasp of science certainly helps.
- If you want to change environmental law, or crusade for a better planet, then nail your colours to the public mast; trying to get a company off the hook for having accidentally discharged three tonnes of mercury into a river may not be for you.
- Client contact is a big feature of this work and can endure over many years. Environmental risks can be inherently difficult to quantify and clients will rely on your gut instincts and powers of lateral thinking.
- What with visits to waste dumps or drying reservoirs, and a workload that can span health and safety matters, corporate transaction and regulatory advice all in one day, this

is neither a desk-bound nor a quiet discipline.

- Research constantly advances and legislation is always changing in this field, so you'll spend a lot of time keeping up to date.
- An interest in European law is increasingly useful as more and more EU directives prescribe the boundaries of environmental law in the UK.

current issues

- Changes in environmental law are coming thick and fast; keep on top of them via websites like www.endsreport.com. You should enhance your CV and prime yourself by joining organisations such as the Environmental Law Foundation (ELF) and the UK Environmental Law Association (www.ukela.org). Most environmental lawyers are members of UKELA and students are welcome to attend events across the country. Look out for UKELA's annual essay and mooting competitions. The charity ELF (www.elflaw.org) provides a referral service for members of the public with environmental problems, organises lectures in London and produces regular newsletters for its members.
- Swathes of new EU Directives are impacting the UK. The not-so-snappily titled Waste Electrical and Electronic Equipment (WEEE) Directive is keeping lawyers busy at the moment.
- The Contaminated Land Regime, introduced in England and Wales seven years ago, means clients acquiring sites can be liable for historic pollution. Now local authorities have woken up to the idea of taking action, the effects of the regime are starting to bite.
- Climate change isn't just for academics any more. Businesses need advice on how to navigate the EU Emissions Trading Scheme and the mechanisms for reducing emissions provided for under the Kyoto Protocol. Environmental lawyers in the top-flight firms are encountering this type of work more and more often. Inter-

national issues in general are coming to the fore with initiatives like the Equator Principles and Corporate Social Responsibility prominent.

● Finally, energy. We all need it and there isn't going to be enough of it. Scores of renewable

energy projects have led to environmental lawyers working alongside planning and project finance colleagues. Oil and gas schemes continue unabated and the prospect of new nuclear installations is also hot.

leading firms from Chambers UK 2008

Environment
Best of the UK

Band 1
Allen & Overy LLP *London* — Freshfields Bruckhaus Deringer *London*

Band 2
Ashurst *London* — Burges Salmon LLP *Bristol*
Clifford Chance LLP *London* — CMS Cameron McKenna LLP *London*
Linklaters *London*

Band 3
Berwin Leighton Paisner LLP *London* — Denton Wilde Sapte *London*
Eversheds LLP *London* — Herbert Smith LLP *London*
Macfarlanes *London* — Mayer Brown *London*
Nabarro *London* — Simmons & Simmons *London*
Slaughter and May *London*

Band 4
Addleshaw Goddard LLP *Manchester* — Baker & McKenzie LLP *London*
Barlow Lyde & Gilbert LLP *London* — Bond Pearce LLP *Bristol*
DLA Piper UK LLP *Sheffield* — LeBoeuf, Lamb, Greene & MacRae *London*
Lovells LLP *London* — SJ Berwin LLP *London*
Trowers & Hamlins *London*

Band 5
Dundas & Wilson *London* — Hammonds *London*
Jones Day *London* — K&L Gates *London*
Norton Rose *London* — Osborne Clarke *Bristol*
Pinsent Masons *London* — Semple Fraser LLP *Glasgow*
Stephenson Harwood *London* — Taylor Wessing LLP *London*
Travers Smith *London* — Wragge & Co LLP *Birmingham*

Environment: Claimant
Best of the UK

Band 1
Leigh Day & Co *London*
Richard Buxton *Cambridge*

Band 2
Hugh James *Cardiff*
Irwin Mitchell *Sheffield*
Public Interest Lawyers *Birmingham*

Environment
The South

Band 1
Bond Pearce LLP *Southampton*
DMH Stallard *Brighton*

Band 2
Blake Lapthorn Tarlo Lyons *Southampton*
Clarkslegal LLP *Reading*
Manches LLP *Oxford*
Stevens & Bolton LLP *Guildford*

Band 3
B P Collins *Gerrards Cross*
Brachers *Maidstone*

Environment
East Anglia

Band 1
Mills & Reeve LLP *Cambridge*

Band 2
Eversheds LLP *Norwich*
Hewitsons *Cambridge*

environmental law (continued)

Environment	
South West	
Band 1	
Burges Salmon LLP	*Bristol*
Band 2	
Bond Pearce LLP	*Plymouth*
Osborne Clarke	*Bristol*
Band 3	
Ashfords	*Exeter*
Bevan Brittan LLP	*Bristol*
Clarke Willmott	*Bristol*
Thring Townsend	*Bath*
Veale Wasbrough Lawyers	*Bristol*

Environment	
Midlands	
Band 1	
Eversheds LLP	*Nottingham*
Wragge & Co LLP	*Birmingham*
Band 2	
Pinsent Masons	*Birmingham*
Band 3	
Browne Jacobson LLP	*Nottingham*

Environment	
Wales	
Band 1	
Eversheds LLP	*Cardiff*
Band 2	
Clarkslegal LLP	*Cardiff*
Geldards LLP	*Cardiff*
Hugh James	*Cardiff*

Environment	
The North	
Band 1	
Eversheds LLP	*Manchester*
Nabarro	*Sheffield*
Band 2	
Addleshaw Goddard LLP	*Manchester*
DLA Piper UK LLP	*Sheffield*
Pinsent Masons	*Leeds*
Band 3	
Dickinson Dees LLP	*Newcastle upon Tyne*
Halliwells LLP	*Manchester*
Band 4	
Aaron & Partners LLP	*Chester*
Cobbetts LLP	*Manchester*
Hammonds	*Manchester*
Hill Dickinson LLP	*Manchester*
Walker Morris	*Leeds*

family law

put simply

Family lawyers deal with all the legal mechanics and complications relating to the process of marrying, having children, getting divorced, accessing children post-divorce, dividing shared assets, securing maintenance, and family disputes concerning passing on your assets after death. Pretty much the only part of family life they don't actually take part in is the moment of conception itself… except in the case of their own families of course.

Day-to-day matters include divorce, disputes between cohabitants, inheritance disputes between family members, prenuptial and cohabitation agreements, all matters relating to children and issues arising from registration of same-sex-marriages under Civil Partnership legislation. Whether working in the family department of a general high street practice with a high-volume caseload of legally aided work, or for a specialist practice dealing with high-value divorces and complex child or international matters, family solicitors are on their feet in court a good deal and fully occupied back in the office.

who does what

There is effectively a division within family practice between child law and matrimonial law, with some practitioners devoting themselves exclusively to one or other side of the fence and others planting a foot on either side.

matrimonial law tasks

- Interviewing and advising clients on prenuptial agreements, cohabitation arrangements, divorce and the financial implications of divorce. If this sounds narrow in scope don't be deceived – such cases can include issues over inheritance and wills, conveyancing, welfare benefits, company law, tax and trusts, pensions and even judicial review (particularly when it comes to public funding issues).

- Preparing the client's case for divorce and settlement hearings, including dealing with witnesses, and providing summaries of assets/finances. As such, accountants, financial and pensions advisers, and family lawyers from overseas jurisdictions are familiar faces.
- Attending 'conferences with counsel' – ie meetings with barristers.
- Representing clients in hearings or briefing barristers to do so.
- Negotiating settlements and associated financial terms.

child law tasks

- In private cases – interviewing and advising clients (husbands, wives or cohabitants) on the implications of divorce with regard to child contact and residence. In many instances this will result in court action. Dealing with disputes between parents or other family members over the residence of, and contact with, children.
- In public cases – representing local authorities, parents, children's guardians or children themselves on matters such as child care proceedings or abuse in care claims. Here social workers, probation officers, psychologists and medical professionals will also be involved in cases.

the realities of the job

- When it comes to relationships and families, no two sets of circumstances will ever be the same. You'll have a large and varied caseload with a fast turnaround, but this means huge scope for advocacy.
- You will encounter a real mix of clients, some at a joyful moment in their lives, many facing deeply traumatic and personal problems. A good family law practitioner combines the sensitivity, trustworthiness and capacity for empathy of a counsellor, with the clarity of

empathy of a counsellor, with the clarity of thought, commercial acumen and communication skills of a hard-nosed lawyer. Your client may treat you as a shoulder to cry on, but you need to retain the detachment to achieve the result they need.

- Tough negotiating skills and a strong nerve are must-haves because, like criminal practice, your work has immediate and practical consequences. How often your client gets to see their children, what happens to their home, their family or their livelihood are all in your hands. The prospect of telling a client that they've lost a custody battle does much to sharpen the mind.

- A pragmatic and real-world outlook is useful, but you'll also need to spend time keeping abreast of legal developments. The Human Rights Act opened up new legal ground, while action groups like Fathers4Justice have intensified the scrutiny on child residence and contact issues. Even matrimonial cases are continually push at the boundaries, such as the recent ruling that ex-Arsenal footballer Ray Parlour must pay his former wife a percentage of all future earnings because of her part in establishing his career.

- On publicly funded matters you'll face your share of bureaucracy and you'll never earn mega-bucks.

current issues

- London is arguably becoming the divorce capital of Europe. In the biggest cases the wealth and assets involved far outstrip the reasonable needs of the parties and lawyers are glad to now have precedents. The House of Lords' decisions in Miller, where the issue is how to deal with a short marriage, and McFarlane, where the wife had given up a career to raise a family have provided some clarity but left certain issues cloudy. In 2007 the High Court awarded a massive £48 million to the wife of insurance magnate John Charman when they divorced. The size of the awards was upheld by The Court of Appeal and everyone now waits to see if he will take the matter to the House of Lords.

- Cases such as these help explain increased interest in prenuptial agreements. Everyone's heard of a 'pre-nup', but since the arrival in 2005 of same-sex 'marriage' through the Civil Partnerships Act there is also the 'pre-cip'. Lawyers are interested to see how the courts will handle the division of assets following the breakdown of a civil partnership.

- Collaborative law is a new buzzword. For some lawyers it is the way forward for family disputes; others say they've seen it all before with mediation. In short it takes a round-table approach to resolving marital settlements. It doesn't suit every case, and if it doesn't work, the parties must change to new solicitors if they subsequently litigate. The take up of collaborative law is strong in some medium-sized cities (eg Cambridge and Bath), but negligible elsewhere.

- These are challenging times for the publicly funded lawyer not least because of the Carter Review. Many firms are feeling the squeeze and some are choosing to limit, or even stop, legally aided work altogether. This is the case with both matrimonial finance cases and child care proceedings, although some firm's have stuck with the latter as a result of idealistic committments.

leading firms from Chambers UK 2008

Family: Matrimonial Finance & Private Children Law
London
Band 1
Manches LLP *London*
Withers LLP *London*

Band 2
Alexiou Fisher Philipps *London*
Charles Russell LLP *London*
Farrer & Co *London*
Hughes Fowler Carruthers *London*
Levison Meltzer Pigott *London*
Miles Preston & Co *London*
Payne Hicks Beach *London*
Sears Tooth *London*

Band 3
Clintons *London*
Collyer Bristow LLP *London*
Dawson Cornwell *London*
Dawsons LLP *London*
Family Law In Partnership *London*
Kingsley Napley *London*
Mishcon de Reya *London*

Band 4
Anthony Gold *London*
Bross Bennett LLP *London*
CKFT *London*
Fisher Meredith *London*
Forsters LLP *London*
Gordon Dadds *London*
Harcus Sinclair *London*

Band 5
Boodle Hatfield *London*
Davenport Lyons *London*
Hunters *London*
International Family Law *London*
Irwin Mitchell *London*
Osbornes *London*
Rooks Rider *London*
Russell-Cooke LLP *London*
Speechly Bircham LLP *London*
Stewarts *London*

Family: Public Law Child
London
Band 1
Bindman & Partners *London*
Goodman Ray *London*

Band 2
Fisher Meredith *London*
Hodge Jones & Allen *London*
Russell-Cooke LLP *London*

Family
The South
Band 1
Charles Russell LLP *Guildford*
Lester Aldridge LLP *Bournemouth*
Paris Smith & Randall LLP *Southampton*

Band 2
Brachers *Maidstone*
Ellis Jones *Bournemouth*
Scott Bailey *Lymington*
Thomson Snell *Tunbridge Wells*

Band 3
Barlow Robbins LLP *Guildford*
Blake Lapthorn Tarlo Lyons *Fareham*
Coffin Mew LLP *Portsmouth*
Cripps Harries Hall LLP *Tunbridge Wells*
Max Barford & Co *Tunbridge Wells*
Mundays LLP *Cobham*
TWM Solicitors LLP *Guildford*
Warners *Sevenoaks*
Watson Nevill Solicitors *Maidstone*

Family
Thames Valley
Band 1
Blandy & Blandy *Reading*
Boodle Hatfield *Oxford*
Manches LLP *Oxford*

Band 2
Darbys Solicitors LLP *Oxford*
Henmans LLP *Oxford*
Horsey Lightly Fynn *Newbury*
Morgan Cole *Oxford*

Band 3
Blake Lapthorn Tarlo Lyons *Oxford*
Boyes Turner *Reading*
Field Seymour Parkes *Reading*
IBB Solicitors *Uxbridge*

Family
East Anglia
Band 1
Mills & Reeve LLP *Cambridge, Norwich*

Band 2
Buckles Solicitors LLP *Peterborough*
Cambridge Family Law Practice *Cambridge*
hc solicitors LLP *Peterborough*
Taylor Vinters *Cambridge*

Band 3
Birketts LLP *Ipswich*
Cozens-Hardy LLP *Norwich*
Hansells *Norwich*
Hatch Brenner *Norwich*
Leonard Gray *Chelmsford*
Overburys *Norwich*
Prettys *Ipswich*
Rudlings & Wakelam *Thetford*
Silver Fitzgerald *Cambridge*

family law (continued)

Family

South West

Band 1

Burges Salmon LLP *Bristol*

Clarke Willmott *Bristol*

Foot Anstey *Plymouth*

Stephens & Scown *Exeter*

TLT LLP *Bristol*

Tozers LLP *Exeter*

Band 2

Act Family Law Practice *Plymouth*

Hartnell Chanot & Partners Family Law Practice *Exeter*

Stone King LLP *Bath*

Wolferstans *Plymouth*

Band 3

Ashfords *Tiverton*

Gill Akaster *Plymouth*

Michelmores LLP *Exeter*

Withy King *Bath*

Family

Midlands

Band 1

Blair Allison *Birmingham*

Challinors *Birmingham, West Bromwich*

Band 2

Anthony Collins Solicitors *Birmingham*

Benussi & Co *Birmingham*

Divorce and Family Law *Birmingham*

Harrison Clark *Worcester*

Mills & Reeve LLP *Birmingham*

Rupert Bear Murray Davies *Nottingham*

Band 3

Freeth Cartwright LLP *Nottingham*

Harvey Ingram LLP *Leicester*

Higgs & Sons *Brierley Hill*

Irwin Mitchell *Birmingham*

John Hooper & Co *Nottingham*

Lanyon Bowdler Solicitors *Shrewsbury*

Nelsons *Nottingham*

Osborne & Co *Birmingham*

Rothera Dowson *Nottingham*

Tyndallwoods *Birmingham*

Wace Morgan *Shrewsbury*

Young & Lee *Birmingham*

Family

North West

Band 1

Pannone LLP *Manchester*

Band 2

Addleshaw Goddard LLP *Manchester*

DWF *Manchester*

Green & Co *Manchester*

Mace & Jones *Liverpool, Knutsford*

Morecrofts *Liverpool*

Band 3

Brabners Chaffe Street *Liverpool*

Halliwells LLP *Liverpool*

Hill Dickinson LLP *Liverpool*

JMW Solicitors *Manchester*

Laytons *Manchester*

SAS Daniels *Stockport*

Stephensons *Leigh, Manchester*

Family

North East

Band 1

Dickinson Dees LLP *Newcastle upon Tyne*

Band 2

Colette Stroud *Newcastle upon Tyne*

David Gray *Newcastle upon Tyne*

Hay & Kilner *Newcastle upon Tyne*

Mincoffs *Newcastle upon Tyne*

Samuel Phillips *Newcastle upon Tyne*

Sintons *Newcastle upon Tyne*

Ward Hadaway *Newcastle upon Tyne*

Watson Burton LLP *Newcastle upon Tyne*

Family

Yorkshire

Band 1

Addleshaw Goddard LLP *Leeds*

Band 2

Andrew Jackson *Hull*

Grahame Stowe Bateson *Harrogate*

Irwin Mitchell *Sheffield*

Jones Myers Partnership *Leeds*

Zermansky & Partners *Leeds*

Band 3

Clarion Solicitors *Leeds*

Gordons *Leeds*

Howells LLP *Sheffield*

Lupton Fawcett LLP *Leeds*

Rollits *Hull*

Switalski's *Wakefield*

Watson Burton LLP *Leeds*

Family

Wales

Band 1

Harding Evans *Newport*

Hugh James *Cardiff*

Larby Williams with Gwyn & Gwyn *Cardiff*

Nicol Denvir & Purnell *Cardiff*

Wendy Hopkins Family Law Practice *Cardiff*

Band 2

Avery Naylor *Swansea*

Howells *Cardiff*

Martyn Prowel Solicitors *Cardiff*

Robertsons *Cardiff*

intellectual property

put simply

Intellectual property can be protected in several ways. A patent provides the proprietor of a new, industrially applicable invention or process with the exclusive right to work it for a certain period. A trade mark provides its owner with a limited monopoly to use the mark on certain goods or services, and a registered design provides the exclusive right to use the design. Copyright is slightly different in the sense that it exists as soon as material is created, without the need for any registration. Things that are copyrightable include music, paintings and drawings, works of literature or reference, databases and web pages. So, for example, Chambers and Partners has copyright in this book and no part of it can be reproduced by anyone else without our permission.

Intellectual property can be extremely valuable; sometimes the most valuable asset a person or business owns. Admittedly, the average five-year-old's paintings will have no commercial value, but imagine the money that can be made by selling or exploiting a revolutionary idea for, say, a cyclone-effect vacuum cleaner. Think about the commercial value in the distinctive shape of the glass Coca-Cola bottle or Jif's plastic lemon.

Increasingly the work of IP lawyers is crossing over with other disciplines, not simply IT and life sciences but also areas such as competition law and employment law.

who does what

The IP lawyer's role can involve the following:

- Searching domestic, European and international registers of patents, trade marks and registered designs to establish ownership of existing rights or the potential to register new rights.
- Taking all steps to protect clients' interests by securing patents, trade marks and registered designs; appealing unfavourable decisions; attacking decisions that benefit others but harm the lawyer's own client.
- Writing letters to require that third parties desist from carrying out infringing activities or risk litigation for damages and an injunction.
- Issuing court proceedings and preparing cases for trial, including taking witness statements, examining scientific or technical reports and commissioning experiments and tests. In the world of brand protection, junior lawyers may find themselves conducting consumer surveys and going on covert shopping expeditions.
- Instructing and consulting with barristers. Solicitor advocates can appear in the Patents County Court, but usually recognise the advantages of having a specialist IP barrister for higher court hearings.
- Drafting commercial agreements between owners of IP rights and those who want to use the protected invention, design or artistic work. The most common documents will either transfer ownership of the right to another party or grant a licence for them to use it.
- Working as part of a multidisciplinary team on corporate transactions, verifying ownership of IP rights and drafting documents enabling their transfer.

the realities of the job

- Lawyers must be able to handle everyone from sophisticated or pushy company directors to mad inventors and quirky artistic types. Clients come from manufacturing, hi-tech, engineering, pharmaceuticals, agrochemicals, universities and scientific institutions, media organisations and the arts.
- A degree in a relevant subject is common among patent lawyers. Brand and trade mark lawyers need a curiosity for all things creative and must keep up with consumer trends. Both types of IP lawyer need to have a good sense for commercial strategy.
- Attention to detail, precision and accuracy:

words are important and you must be meticulous in their use, particularly when drafting.

- In patent and trade mark filing, everything has a time limit. You will live by deadlines.
- The volume of paperwork involved can be huge on patent matters, though on the upside you'll visit research labs or factories to learn about production processes, etc.
- You'll learn that the development of new drugs and inventions is motivated more often by profit than philanthropy. Success or failure in litigation can dramatically affect a company's share price.

current issues

- The systems for procuring international IP rights are becoming more harmonised. The Office for Harmonization in the Internal Market (OHIM), in Alicante, Spain, grants Community trade marks and designs. The European Patent Office in Munich grants European patents. Through the Patent Cooperation Treaty, which has been signed by most countries and is administered by the World Intellectual Property Organization (WIPO), patent applicants in one country can preserve their options for patent protection in others around the world. The number of patent filings continues to increase year on year.
- There has been a noticeable rise in the level of interest in IP from governments around the world, not least because of a need to get China to respect IP rights. Many law firms are getting involved in Chinese business.
- The Gower Review of the UK's IP framework has been published. While many questions have been left unanswered the Review does address the issues of counterfeit products and copyright.
- Manufacturing, pharmaceutical and research companies employ patent specialists and there are in-house legal teams at all the large pharmaceutical companies. In the media, major publishers and television companies have in-house IP lawyers.
- The name of the Patent Office has been changed to UK Intelllectual Property Office (UKIPO) to reflect its broader functions
- European patent attorneys and trade mark agents work as a parallel profession. You can find out more about what they do on page 26. There are early signs of convergence between the legal profession and these other professions. Some law firms provide in-house trade mark and patent-filing services, allowing clients to sidestep patent and trade mark attorneys. This is an increasing trend and one that many clients favour, even if patent and trade mark attorneys do not.

leading firms from Chambers UK 2008

Intellectual Property: General
London
Band 1

Bird & Bird

Band 2

Baker & McKenzie LLP	Bristows
Herbert Smith LLP	Rouse Legal
Taylor Wessing LLP	Wragge & Co LLP

Band 3

DLA Piper UK LLP	Field Fisher Waterhouse LLP
Freshfields Bruckhaus Deringer	Lovells LLP
Mayer Brown	Olswang
Redd	Simmons & Simmons
Slaughter and May	

Band 4

Addleshaw Goddard LLP	Allen & Overy LLP
Ashurst	Eversheds LLP
Harbottle & Lewis LLP	Howrey LLP
Jones Day	Lewis Silkin LLP
McDermott Will & Emery UK LLP	Reed Smith Richards Butler LLP
Roiter Zucker	SJ Berwin LLP

Band 5

Arnold & Porter (UK) LLP	Blake Lapthorn Tarlo Lyons
Clifford Chance LLP	Collyer Bristow LLP
Dechert LLP	Denton Wilde Sapte
Finers Stephens Innocent	Linklaters
Marks & Clerk Solicitors	Mishcon de Reya
Orchard Brayton Graham LLP	Wedlake Bell
White & Case LLP	Withers LLP

Intellectual Property: Patent Litigation
London
Band 1

Bird & Bird
Taylor Wessing LLP

Band 2

Bristows
Simmons & Simmons
Wragge & Co LLP

Band 3

Baker & McKenzie LLP
Herbert Smith LLP
Lovells LLP

Band 4

DLA Piper UK LLP
Freshfields Bruckhaus Deringer
Linklaters
Marks & Clerk Solicitors
McDermott Will & Emery UK LLP
Olswang
Powell Gilbert LLP
Redd
Roiter Zucker
SJ Berwin LLP

Band 5

Fasken Martineau Stringer Saul LLP
Field Fisher Waterhouse LLP
Howrey LLP
Milbank, Tweed, Hadley & McCloy LLP

Intellectual Property
The South
Band 1

Blake Lapthorn Tarlo Lyons *Portsmouth*
DMH Stallard *Crawley*

Band 2

Bond Pearce LLP *Southampton*
Shadbolt & Co LLP *Reigate*

Band 3

Clyde & Co LLP *Guildford*

Intellectual Property
Thames Valley
Band 1

Olswang Thames Valley *Reading*
Rouse Legal *Oxford*
Shoosmiths *Milton Keynes*

Band 2

Manches LLP *Oxford*
Osborne Clarke *Reading*

Band 3

Matthew Arnold & Baldwin *Watford*

Intellectual Property
East Anglia
Band 1

Mills & Reeve LLP *Cambridge, Norwich*
Taylor Vinters *Cambridge*

Band 2

Eversheds LLP *Cambridge*
Hewitsons *Cambridge*
Taylor Wessing LLP *Cambridge*

intellectual property (continued)

Intellectual Property
South West
Band 1
Burges Salmon LLP *Bristol*
Osborne Clarke *Bristol*

Band 2
Bond Pearce LLP *Bristol*

Band 3
Ashfords *Bristol*
Bevan Brittan LLP *Bristol*
TLT LLP *Bristol*

Intellectual Property
Yorkshire
Band 1
Addleshaw Goddard LLP *Leeds*

Band 2
DLA Piper UK LLP *Leeds*
Pinsent Masons *Leeds*
Walker Morris *Leeds*

Band 3
Hammonds *Leeds*
Lupton Fawcett LLP *Leeds*

Intellectual Property
Midlands
Band 1
Wragge & Co LLP *Birmingham*

Band 2
Browne Jacobson LLP *Nottingham*
Eversheds LLP *Nottingham*

Band 3
Cobbetts LLP *Birmingham*
DLA Piper UK LLP *Birmingham*
Freeth Cartwright LLP *Nottingham*
Martineau Johnson *Birmingham*

Intellectual Property
North West
Band 1
Addleshaw Goddard LLP *Manchester*
DLA Piper UK LLP *Manchester*

Band 2
Eversheds LLP *Manchester*
Halliwells LLP *Manchester*
Hill Dickinson LLP *Liverpool*

Band 3
Cobbetts LLP *Manchester*
Kuit Steinart Levy *Manchester*
Pannone LLP *Manchester*

Intellectual Property
North East
Band 1
Dickinson Dees LLP *Newcastle upon Tyne*

Band 2
Ward Hadaway *Newcastle upon Tyne*

Intellectual Property
Wales
Band 1
Geldards LLP *Cardiff*

Band 2
Eversheds LLP *Cardiff*
Morgan Cole *Cardiff*

litigation/dispute resolution

put simply

If you are an avid viewer of legal dramas on TV you could be forgiven for thinking that the average litigation solicitor is always in trial. Actually, this is far from accurate as the majority of disputes are resolved long before they reach the court steps. Less exciting maybe, but the law doesn't exist primarily to provide litigators with an adrenaline-charged career. Clients, especially commercial ones, usually want to finalise a settlement as quickly, cheaply and unobtrusively as possible.

Commercial disputes range from unpaid bills or unfulfilled contract terms to problems between landlords and tenants, infringement of IP rights, construction-related claims, the liabilities of insurers, shipping cases, defective products cases, media and entertainment industry wrangles – the list is long. To confuse matters a little, there are two divisions of the High Court – the Chancery Division and the Queen's Bench Division – and each hears different types of case. The following diagram shows the court system in England and Wales, and the Bar section of this guide summaries of the differences between the QBD and Chancery Divisions.

Unless settled by initial correspondence, disputes are concluded either by court litigation or some alternative form of dispute resolution. The most common of these other methods are arbitration and mediation, the former often being stipulated as the preferred method in commercial contracts, the latter commonly achieved through structured negotiations between the parties, overseen by an independent mediator. The increased use of such alternative methods is the reason why some law firms have renamed their litigation departments as dispute resolution departments. Even alternative methods of resolution have their problems: mediation is not necessarily adequate for complex matters, and there is a perception that it can be used by opponents as a means of 'bleeding' money or a covert form of interrogation.

As a trainee your workload will largely depend on the type of firm you go to and the type of clients it represents. The very biggest City firms are unlikely to give new recruits free rein on the latest international banking dispute, and it is quite possible that they may never go to court during their training contract, but they will be able to make a small contribution to major international cases that create newspaper headlines. Some of the biggest, longest-running disputes have been related to financial matters: the Equitable Life and BCCI litigations are good examples.

At firms handling much smaller claims trainees can usually deal with all aspects of a case, from drafting correspondence and interim court applications to meetings with clients and settlement negotiations. There are a number of litigation-led law firms that handle cases of all sizes and these represent the best opportunities for a litigation-heavy training.

who does what

claimants' solicitors

- Advise clients on whether they have a valid claim.
- Gather evidence and witnesses to support the claim.
- If correspondence with the prospective defendant does not produce a satisfactory result, issue court proceedings or embark on a process of alternative dispute resolution.
- Represent clients at pre-trial hearings and case management conferences.
- Attend 'conferences with counsel' (ie barristers) and brief barristers to conduct advocacy in hearings and trials.
- Attend trials with clients; provide assistance to barristers.

defendants' solicitors

- Advise on the validity of a claim brought against a client, making recommendations as to whether to settle or fight.
- Prepare defences, including gathering all evidence and witness statements.
- Represent clients at pre-trial hearings and case management conferences.
- Attend conferences with counsel and brief barristers to conduct advocacy in hearings, trials and arbitrations.
- Attend trials, arbitrations and mediations with clients; provide assistance to barristers when they are being used.

the realities of the job

- The work is driven by the procedural rules and timetable of the courts. This requires the solicitor to learn the rules and keep to deadlines. Good litigators understand how best to operate within the system, while also developing winning case strategies.
- A phenomenal amount of paperwork is generated and, certainly in the early years, litigators spend much of their time sifting through documents, scheduling and copying them in order to provide the court and all other parties with an agreed bundle of evidence.
- Litigators need to express themselves both concisely and precisely, especially when a high degree of legal analysis is involved.
- Unless the value of a claim is small, the solicitor's job is more about case preparation than court performance. Solicitor advocates are gaining ground, and once properly qualified they can appear in the higher courts; however, barristers still dominate court advocacy.
- Although there's a good deal of posturing required, only a bad lawyer will adopt a victory-at-all-costs approach. A good lawyer will understand the context in which the case is set and how the client's interests will be best served.

current issues

- The Law Society requires all trainee solicitors to gain some contentious experience, and they tend to discover early on whether they are suited to this kind of work. An increasing number of City firms find that they have more trainees than openings in their litigation departments and they get around this by sending some of them on a litigation crash course instead.
- The competition for litigation jobs at NQ level in big City firms is fierce. For most of them, it's simply not a mainstream activity in the way that corporate or finance is. Consider litigation-led firms if you are certain of your preference for this type of work.
- Herbert Smith made news in 2004 by opening an advocacy unit which now has more than 50 advocates. Denton Wilde Sapte also runs a unit, and many other firms have solicitor advocates within their ranks. While some people applaud this one-stop shop approach, sceptics point to the fact that for bet-the-company litigation, clients will invariably turn to barristers for their expertise and gravitas. In reality, solicitors rarely get enough exposure to become as good as the best QCs and junior barristers they encounter. Only time will tell if solicitor advocacy is the way forward or a passing phase in the development of commercial litigation. As a general rule, students who are passionate about becoming advocates in the area of commercial litigation should still consider their prospects at the Bar. If determined to become both a solicitor and an advocate, certain areas of practice have more scope for advocacy – ie family, crime and lower-value civil litigation to name three.
- It's worth knowing about the fallout from two gargantuan lawsuits that concluded in 2006 – BCCI and Equitable Life. We've summarised the story of each overleaf.

solicitors

- In general there is now less domestic litigation, but more international litigation and arbitration. Commentators speak of the rise of Eastern Europe, primarily Russia, as a locus for disputes involving investors with burnt fingers. The UK courts are respected for teir impartiality and our systems is seen to have teeth.

- Banking/finance and regulatory litigation is expected to increase as a consequence of an agreement between the Securities & Exchange Commission (SEC) and the Financial Services Authority (FSA). Also starting to bite are the corporate governance provisions contained in the Financial Services and Markets Act 2000, which acts in much the same way as the Sarbanes-Oxley legislation in the USA. Both of these pieces of legislation are designed to counteract corporate skulduggery of the likes that led to Enron.

- The concept of US-style class actions are gaining ground in the UK and American plaintiff firm Cohen Millstein Hausfeld & Toll has set up a London Office.

As the dust settles following the ignominious endings of the BCCI and Equitable Life disputes, the London legal market has engaged in a process of reflection and consolidation. Practitioners anticipate a dearth of major cases in the short term, as potential claims are channelled into mediation, arbitration and other forms of alternative dispute resolution. As well as a general reluctance to become embroiled in high-cost speculative litigation, this direction has been set by what clients and solicitors agree has been the escalating cost of disputes in general.

BCCI

After hearing evidence in this gargantuan case the judge, Mr Justice Tomlinson, turned to the then Lord Chief Justice, Lord Woolf, to express his reservations about the allegations of dishonesty and negligence brought against the Bank of England by the English liquidators of Bank of Credit and Commerce International SA (BCCI). The case, prosecuted by Lovells and defended by Freshfields Bruckhaus Deringer, collapsed spectacularly in 2005 after 12 years of litigation. Commentators immediately seized on the myriad contradictions, confusions and misdirections that dogged its progress, seeing them as endemic to a case unchecked by early intervention. There were also allegations that the courtroom conduct of the claimants' legal representatives was repellant and unnecessarily confrontational. It was as if the Civil Procedure Rules, aka the Woolf Reforms, designed to speed, smooth and minimise costs in litigation, had never happened...

Equitable Life

When Equitable Life, the world's oldest mutual insurer, dropped its long-running court action against Ernst & Young at the end of 2005, the auditors' barrister described it as "the biggest climbdown in English legal history." Barlow Lyde & Gilbert won praise for its representation of Ernst & Young and Allen & Overy attracted accolades for its performance on behalf of Equitable's six former non-executive directors, who were being personally sued by the Equitable. The case is viewed as the final nail in the coffin for multi million-pound speculative claims. While most commentators avoided the temptation of schadenfreude when discussing Herbert Smith's representation of Equitable – pointing out that, ultimately, a firm can only do as it is instructed – there was a general consensus that similar situations should be treated with greater circumspection in the future. The European Parliament subsequently made a recommendation in June 2007 that the British government compensate Equitable Life policyholders and put in place regulatory changes.

litigation/dispute resolution (continued)

leading firms from Chambers UK 2008

Dispute Resolution: High Value

London

Band 1
Clifford Chance LLP
Herbert Smith LLP

Band 2
Freshfields Bruckhaus Deringer
Lovells LLP
Slaughter and May

Band 3
Allen & Overy LLP
Ashurst
Linklaters

Band 4
Barlow Lyde & Gilbert LLP
Clyde & Co LLP
Norton Rose
Simmons & Simmons
SJ Berwin LLP

Band 5
Baker & McKenzie LLP
CMS Cameron McKenna LLP
Denton Wilde Sapte
Eversheds LLP
Mayer Brown
Reed Smith Richards Butler LLP

Band 6
Dechert LLP
DLA Piper UK LLP
Howrey LLP
Jones Day
Macfarlanes
White & Case LLP

Dispute Resolution

East Midlands

Band 1
Browne Jacobson LLP *Nottingham*
Eversheds LLP *Nottingham*

Band 2
Freeth Cartwright LLP *Nottingham*
Hewitsons *Northampton*
Shoosmiths *Northampton*

Dispute Resolution: Mid-Market

London

Band 1
Berwin Leighton Paisner LLP
Reynolds Porter Chamberlain LLP
Stephenson Harwood
Taylor Wessing LLP

Band 2
Addleshaw Goddard LLP
Bird & Bird
Holman Fenwick & Willan
Ince & Co
K&L Gates
Kendall Freeman
McDermott Will & Emery UK LLP
Nabarro
Olswang
Pinsent Masons
Travers Smith

Band 3
Charles Russell LLP
Davies Arnold Cooper
Hammonds
Lewis Silkin LLP
LG
Morgan, Lewis & Bockius
Salans
Watson, Farley & Williams

Band 4
Collyer Bristow LLP
Edwin Coe LLP
Finers Stephens Innocent
Fox Williams LLP
Halliwells LLP
Marriott Harrison
Memery Crystal LLP
Mishcon de Reya

Dispute Resolution

Wales

Band 1
Eversheds LLP *Cardiff*
Geldards LLP *Cardiff*

Band 2
Capital Law LLP *Cardiff Bay*
Hugh James *Cardiff*
Morgan Cole *Cardiff*

Dispute Resolution

East Anglia

Band 1
Birketts LLP *Ipswich*
Mills & Reeve LLP *Cambridge*

Band 2
Eversheds LLP *Cambridge*
Hewitsons *Cambridge*
Howes Percival LLP *Norwich*
Taylor Vinters *Cambridge*

Band 3
Ashton Graham *Ipswich*
Birkett Long *Colchester*
Greene & Greene *Bury St Edmunds*
Greenwoods Solicitors LLP *Peterborough*
Kester Cunningham John *Cambridge*
Prettys *Ipswich*
Steeles (Law) LLP *Norwich*
Wollastons LLP *Chelmsford*

Dispute Resolution

Thames Valley

Band 1
Clarkslegal LLP *Reading*
Pitmans *Reading*

Band 2
Boyes Turner *Reading*
Shoosmiths *Reading*

Band 3
B P Collins *Gerrards Cross*
IBB Solicitors *Uxbridge*
Manches LLP *Oxford*

Band 4
Blake Lapthorn Tarlo Lyons *Oxford*
Henmans LLP *Oxford*
Matthew Arnold & Baldwin *Watford*
Morgan Cole *Oxford*

Dispute Resolution
West Midlands
Band 1
Wragge & Co LLP *Birmingham*

Band 2
DLA Piper UK LLP *Birmingham*
Eversheds LLP *Birmingham*
Pinsent Masons *Birmingham*

Band 3
Hammonds *Birmingham*
HBJ Gateley Wareing *Birmingham*
Martineau Johnson *Birmingham*

Band 4
Anthony Collins Solicitors LLP *Birmingham*
Challinors *West Bromwich*
Cobbetts LLP *Birmingham*
George Green LLP *Cradley Heath*
Moran & Co *Tamworth*
Shakespeare Putsman LLP *Birmingham*

Band 5
Clarke Willmott *Birmingham*
KJD *Stoke-on-Trent*
Mills & Reeve LLP *Birmingham*

Dispute Resolution
South West: Bristol & Surround
Band 1
Bevan Brittan LLP *Bristol*
Burges Salmon LLP *Bristol*
Osborne Clarke *Bristol*

Band 2
Beachcroft LLP *Bristol*
Bond Pearce LLP *Bristol*
TLT LLP *Bristol*

Band 3
Charles Russell LLP *Cheltenham*
Clarke Willmott *Bristol*
Veale Wasbrough Lawyers *Bristol*

Band 4
Bevans *Bristol*
BPE Solicitors *Cheltenham*
Rickerbys *Cheltenham*
Withy King *Bath*

Dispute Resolution
The South: Surrey, Hampshire & Dorset
Band 1
Blake Lapthorn Tarlo Lyons *Portsmouth*
Clyde & Co LLP *Guildford*

Band 2
Bond Pearce LLP *Southampton*
Stevens & Bolton LLP *Guildford*

Band 3
Charles Russell LLP *Guildford*
Lester Aldridge LLP *Southampton*
Shadbolt & Co LLP *Reigate*
Shoosmiths *Fareham*

Band 4
Paris Smith & Randall LLP *Southampton*
Penningtons Solicitors LLP *Basingstoke*

Band 5
Barlow Robbins LLP *Guildford*
Clarke Willmott *Southampton*
Lamport Bassitt *Southampton*
Mundays LLP *Cobham*

Dispute Resolution
North West
Band 1
Addleshaw Goddard LLP *Manchester*
DLA Piper UK LLP *Manchester*
Eversheds LLP *Manchester*
Halliwells LLP *Manchester*
Pannone LLP *Manchester*

Band 2
Brabners Chaffe Street *Liverpool*
Cobbetts LLP *Manchester*
DWF *Manchester*
Hill Dickinson LLP *Liverpool*

Band 3
Beachcroft LLP *Manchester*
Hammonds *Manchester*

Band 4
Aaron & Partners LLP *Chester*
Forbes *Blackburn*
George Davies Solicitors *Manchester*
Kuit Steinart Levy *Manchester*
Mace & Jones *Manchester*
Weightmans *Liverpool*

Dispute Resolution
Yorkshire
Band 1
Addleshaw Goddard LLP *Leeds*
DLA Piper UK LLP *Leeds*
Eversheds LLP *Leeds*
Hammonds *Leeds*
Pinsent Masons *Leeds*
Walker Morris *Leeds*

Band 2
Andrew Jackson *Hull*
Cobbetts LLP *Leeds*
Gordons *Leeds*
Irwin Mitchell *Sheffield*
Nabarro *Sheffield*

Band 3
Beachcroft LLP *Leeds*
Brooke North LLP *Leeds*
Clarion Solicitors *Leeds*
Ford & Warren *Leeds*
Gosschalks *Hull*
Lupton Fawcett LLP *Leeds*
McCormicks *Harrogate*
Rollits *Hull*

Dispute Resolution
South West: Devon & Cornwall
Band 1
Ashfords *Exeter*
Bond Pearce LLP *Exeter*
Michelmores LLP *Exeter*
Stephens & Scown *Exeter*

Band 2
Foot Anstey *Exeter*

Dispute Resolution
The South: Kent & Sussex
Band 1
Cripps Harries Hall LLP *Tunbridge Wells*
DMH Stallard *Brighton*

Band 2
Brachers *Maidstone*
Rawlison Butler *Crawley*
Thomas Eggar LLP *Crawley*

Band 3
asb law *Crawley*
Thomson Snell *Tunbridge Wells*

litigation/dispute resolution (continued)

Insurance: Volume Claims

Best of the UK

Band 1

Beachcroft LLP *Bristol*

Berrymans Lace Mawer *Manchester*

Band 2

Davies Arnold Cooper *Manchester*

DWF *Preston*

Eversheds LLP *London*

Fox Hartley *Bristol*

Hill Dickinson LLP *Liverpool*

Keoghs LLP *Bolton*

Robin Simon LLP *Manchester*

Weightmans *Liverpool*

Wragge & Co LLP *Birmingham*

Band 3

Biggart Baillie *Edinburgh*

Brechin Tindal Oatts *Glasgow*

Davies Lavery *Maidstone*

Ford & Warren *Leeds*

Halliwells LLP *Sheffield*

Hugh James *Cardiff*

Morgan Cole *Cardiff*

Shoosmiths *Reading*

Simpson & Marwick *Edinburgh*

Insurance: General Claims

London

Band 1

Barlow Lyde & Gilbert LLP

Clyde & Co LLP

Band 2

Allen & Overy LLP

CMS Cameron McKenna LLP

Herbert Smith LLP

Ince & Co

Reynolds Porter Chamberlain LLP

Band 3

Holman Fenwick & Willan

Kennedys

Lovells LLP

Mayer Brown

Band 4

Chadbourne & Parke

Charles Russell LLP

Clifford Chance LLP

Davies Arnold Cooper

Freshfields Bruckhaus Deringer

Kendall Freeman

LeBoeuf, Lamb, Greene & MacRae

Norton Rose

Simmons & Simmons

Slaughter and May

Band 5

Beachcroft LLP

Clausen Miller LLP

Covington & Burling LLP

DLA Piper UK LLP

Eversheds LLP

Pinsent Masons

Reed Smith Richards Butler LLP

Steptoe & Johnson

the civil courts of england and wales

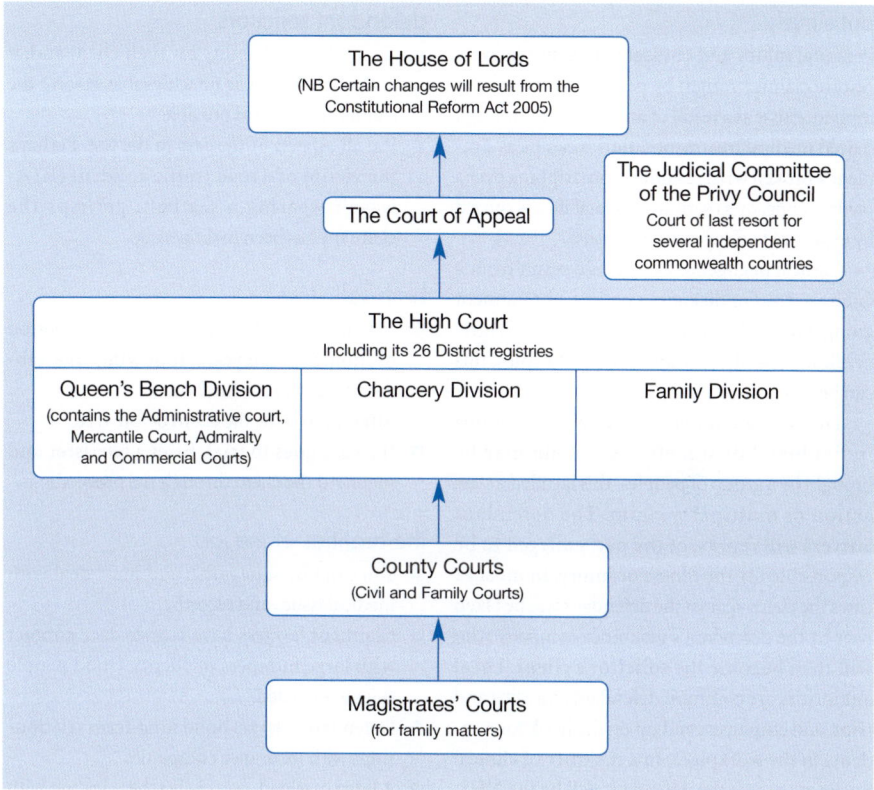

```
                    ┌─────────────────────────────────────┐
                    │      The House of Lords              │
                    │  (NB Certain changes will result     │
                    │   from the Constitutional Reform     │
                    │           Act 2005)                  │
                    └─────────────────────────────────────┘
                                   ▲
                                   │            ┌──────────────────────────┐
                    ┌──────────────────────┐    │  The Judicial Committee  │
                    │ The Court of Appeal  │    │   of the Privy Council   │
                    └──────────────────────┘    │  Court of last resort for│
                                   ▲             │  several independent     │
                                   │             │  commonwealth countries  │
                                                 └──────────────────────────┘
```

The House of Lords
(NB Certain changes will result from the Constitutional Reform Act 2005)

The Court of Appeal

The Judicial Committee of the Privy Council
Court of last resort for several independent commonwealth countries

The High Court
Including its 26 District registries

Queen's Bench Division	Chancery Division	Family Division
(contains the Administrative court, Mercantile Court, Admiralty and Commercial Courts)		

County Courts
(Civil and Family Courts)

Magistrates' Courts
(for family matters)

Other Specialist Courts

Employment Tribunals

Lands Tribunals

Leasehold Valuation Tribunals

VAT and Duties Tribunals

General and Special Commissioners (Tax)

Asylum & Immigration Tribunals

Europe

ECJ: Any UK court can refer a point of law for determination if it relates to EU law. The decision will be referred back to the court where the case originated.

European Court of Human Rights: Hears complaints regarding breaches of human rights.

personal injury and clinical negligence

put simply

Personal injury and clinical negligence lawyers resolve claims brought by people who have been injured, either as a result of an accident or through flawed medical treatment. Injuries can be as simple as a broken wrist resulting from tripping over a paving stone, or as serious as a fatal illness caused by exposure to dangerous materials.

Clinical negligence cases could result from a failure to treat or diagnose a patient, or treatment going wrong. From bad boob jobs to the heartbreaking tragedy of brain-damaged babies, this can be an emotive area.

The claimant lawyer will usually act for one individual, but sometimes a claim may be brought by a group of people – this is called a class action or multiparty claim. The defendant lawyers will represent the party alleged to be responsible for the illness or injury. In most PI cases the claim against the defendant will be taken over by the defendant's insurance company who will then become the solicitor's client. Local authorities are common defendants for slips and trips, and employers end up on the hook for accidents in the workplace. In a majority of clinical negligence cases the defendant will be the NHS, although private medical practitioners or healthcare organisations are also sued.

who does what

claimant solicitors

- Determine the veracity of their client's claim and establish what they have suffered, including how much income they have lost and any expenses incurred.
- Examine medical records and piece together all the facts. Commission further medical reports.
- If the defendant doesn't make an acceptable offer of compensation, issue court proceedings.

defendant solicitors

- Try and avoid liability for their client and, if and when this looks unachievable, resolve the claim for as little as possible.
- Put all aspects of the case to the test. Perhaps the victim of a road traffic accident (RTA) wasn't wearing a seatbelt; perhaps the claimant has been malingering.

both solicitors

- Manage the progress of the case over a period of months, even years, following an established set of procedural rules.
- Attempt to settle the claim before trial.
- If a case goes to trial, brief a barrister and shepherd the client through the proceedings.

the realities of the job

- You can't be squeamish and must deal with medical issues and records.
- Claimant lawyers have face-to-face contact with large numbers of clients. Good people skills are needed.
- Defendant lawyers build long-term relationships with insurance companies.
- A large caseload, especially when dealing with lower-value claims.
- There is some scope for advocacy, although barristers are used for high-stakes or complicated hearings and trials. Solicitors appear at preliminary hearings and case management conferences.
- The work is driven by the procedural rules and timetable of the court.
- There is a mountain of paperwork to manage and produce, including witness statements and bundles of evidentiary material.

current issues

- Conditional Fee Agreements (CFAs) – commonly known as no-win, no-fee agreements – continue to be hotly debated. There were some changes made to the law in 2005 in an effort to simplify CFAs and make them more transparent, but these changes seem to have had little or no impact on claimants. Many solicitors dislike working on a no-win, no-fee basis because of the risk of not getting paid for work done, and they can find it hard to elicit appropriate payment agreements from insurance companies.

- The Compensation Act 2006 contains new provisions relating to the law of negligence and breach of statutory duty.
- You may have seen claims management companies – sometimes derided as claims farmers – advertising on the TV. They cause concern to lawyers because they are unregulated and often adopt unscrupulous tactics to win clients and claims. There continues to be a push for the regulation of such businesses, as illustrated by certain provisions of the Compensation Act 2006. The practice of claims farmers selling cases on to solicitors is under intense scrutiny.

- A number of claimant law firms, including several of the most well-known in the field, have come under fire for their part in the distribution of a £7 billion government-backed compensation scheme to sick miners. At least 50 firms of solicitors have been referred to the Solicitors Regulations Authority and 17 firms to the Solicitors Disciplinary Tribunal.
- If, as envisaged by the Legal Services Bill, companies such as Tesco enter the market for legal services they are likely to have a big impact.
- Opinion is split as to whether there is a growing compensation culture in Britain. Those who recognise one say CFAs must shoulder much of the blame; those who don't say that increased difficulties in securing legal aid have led to a reduction in the number of claims brought.
- Clin neg lawyers are concerned about the likely effects of the NHS Redress Act 2006, which gives the power to introduce a scheme allowing lower-value claims to be handled by the NHS without going to court. Obviously this would cut away some of the lawyers' bread-and-butter work.

personal injury and clinical negligence (continued)

leading firms from Chambers UK 2008

Personal Injury: Mainly Claimant
London
Band 1
Field Fisher Waterhouse LLP
Irwin Mitchell
Leigh Day & Co
Stewarts

Band 2
Anthony Gold
Hodge Jones & Allen
Rowley Ashworth
Russell Jones & Walker
Thompsons

Band 3
O.H. Parsons & Partners
Pattinson & Brewer

Band 4
Bolt Burdon Kemp
Fentons
Levenes
Prince Evans
Russell-Cooke LLP

Personal Injury: Mainly Defendant
London
Band 1
Barlow Lyde & Gilbert LLP
Beachcroft LLP
Berrymans Lace Mawer
Greenwoods

Band 2
Davies Arnold Cooper
Davies Lavery
Hextalls LLP
Kennedys
Plexus Law
Vizards Wyeth
Watmores

Band 3
Badhams Law
Reynolds Porter Chamberlain
Weightmans

Personal Injury: Mainly Claimant
Thames Valley
Band 1
Boyes Turner *Reading*
Harris Cartier LLP *Slough*
IBB Solicitors *Uxbridge*
Thring Townsend *Swindon*

Band 2
Blake Lapthorn Tarlo Lyons *Oxford*
Field Seymour Parkes *Reading*
Henmans LLP *Oxford*
Osborne Morris *Leighton Buzzard*
Pictons Solicitors LLP *Luton*

Personal Injury: Mainly Defendant
Thames Valley
Band 1
Morgan Cole *Oxford*

Band 2
Henmans LLP *Oxford*
Pitmans *Reading*

Personal Injury: Mainly Claimant
The South
Band 1
Coffin Mew LLP *Southampton*
George Ide, Phillips *Chichester*
Lamport Bassitt *Southampton*
Shoosmiths *Basingstoke*
Thomson Snell *Tunbridge Wells*

Band 2
Blake Lapthorn Tarlo Lyons *Southampton*
Charles Russell LLP *Guildford*
Clarkson Wright & Jakes *Orpington*
Colemans-ctts *Kingston-upon-Thames*
Moore Blatch *Southampton*
Penningtons Solicitors LLP *Godalming*
Trethowans *Salisbury*

Personal Injury: Mainly Defendant
The South
Band 1
Beachcroft LLP *Winchester*
Berrymans Lace Mawer *Southampton*
Davies Lavery *Maidstone*
Vizards Wyeth *Dartford*

Band 2
Bond Pearce LLP *Southampton*
Lamport Bassitt *Southampton*

Band 3
Kingslegal *Fareham*

Personal Injury: Mainly Claimant
East Anglia
Band 1
Kester Cunningham John *Cambridge*
Taylor Vinters *Cambridge*

Band 2
Ashton Graham *Ipswich*
Edwards Duthie *Ilford*

Personal Injury: Mainly Defendant
East Anglia
Band 1
Eversheds LLP *Ipswich*
Kennedys *Chelmsford*
Mills & Reeve LLP *Norwich*

Band 2
Edwards Duthie *Ilford*

solicitors

Personal Injury: Mainly Claimant
South West
Band 1
Augustines Injury Law *Bristol*
BPE Solicitors *Cheltenham*
Lyons Davidson *Bristol*

Band 2
Bond Pearce LLP *Plymouth*
Burroughs Day *Bristol*
Clarke Willmott *Bristol*
David Gist Solicitors *Bristol*
Rowley Ashworth *Exeter*
Thompsons *Bristol*

Band 3
Ashfords *Exeter*
Pattinson & Brewer *Bristol*
Trethowans *Salisbury*
Veitch Penny *Exeter*
Withy King *Bath*

Personal Injury: Mainly Defendant
South West
Band 1
Beachcroft LLP *Bristol*
CIP Solicitors *Bristol*

Band 2
Bond Pearce LLP *Bristol*
Wansbroughs *Devizes*

Band 3
Bevan Brittan LLP *Bristol*
Lyons Davidson *Bristol*
Morris Orman & Hearle *Cheltenham*
Veitch Penny *Exeter*

Band 4
Stephens & Scown *Exeter*
Tayntons *Gloucester*

Personal Injury: Mainly Claimant
Midlands
Band 1
Irwin Mitchell *Birmingham*

Band 2
Barratt, Goff & Tomlinson *Nottingham*
Freeth Cartwright LLP *Nottingham*
Rowley Ashworth *Birmingham*
Russell Jones & Walker *Birmingham*
Thompsons *Birmingham*

Personal Injury: Mainly Defendant
Midlands
Band 1
Beachcroft LLP *Birmingham*
Berrymans Lace Mawer *Birmingham*
Browne Jacobson LLP *Nottingham*
Buller Jeffries *Birmingham*
Everatt & Co. *Evesham*

Band 2
Davies Lavery *Birmingham*
DLA Piper UK LLP *Birmingham*
Keoghs LLP *Coventry*
Weightmans *Birmingham*

Personal Injury: Mainly Claimant
North West
Band 1
Pannone LLP *Manchester*
Potter Rees, Serious Injury *Manchester*

Band 2
John Pickering & Partners *Oldham*
McCool Patterson Hemsi *Manchester*

Band 3
Colemans-ctts *Manchester*
Linder Myers *Manchester*
Mace & Jones *Liverpool*
Russell Jones & Walker *Manchester*
Silverbeck Rymer *Liverpool*
Stephensons *Manchester*
Thompsons *Liverpool*

Personal Injury: Mainly Defendant
North West
Band 1
Beachcroft LLP *Manchester*
Berrymans Lace Mawer *Manchester*
DWF *Liverpool*
Halliwells LLP *Manchester*
Keoghs LLP *Bolton*

Band 2
Hill Dickinson LLP *Liverpool*
Weightmans *Liverpool*

Personal Injury: Mainly Claimant
Yorkshire
Band 1
Irwin Mitchell *Sheffield, Leeds*

Band 2
Keeble Hawson *Sheffield*
Morrish & Co *Leeds*
Stewarts *Leeds*

Band 3
Bridge McFarland Solicitors *Grimsby*
Pattinson & Brewer *York*
Rowley Ashworth *Leeds*
Russell Jones & Walker *Sheffield*

Personal Injury: Mainly Defendant
Yorkshire
Band 1
Beachcroft LLP *Leeds*
Berrymans Lace Mawer *Leeds*
DLA Piper UK LLP *Sheffield*
Irwin Mitchell *Sheffield*
Langleys *York*
Nabarro *Sheffield*

Band 2
Ford & Warren *Leeds*
Halliwells LLP *Sheffield*
Praxis Partners *Leeds*

personal injury and clinical negligence (continued)

Personal Injury: Mainly Claimant
North East
Band 1

Thompsons *Newcastle upon Tyne*

Band 2

Browell Smith *Newcastle upon Tyne*
Irwin Mitchell *Newcastle upon Tyne*
Marrons *Newcastle upon Tyne*
Sintons *Newcastle upon Tyne*

Band 3

Hay & Kilner *Newcastle upon Tyne*
Russell Jones *Newcastle upon Tyne*

Personal Injury: Mainly Defendant
North East
Band 1

Berrymans Lace Mawer *Stockton on Tees*
Eversheds LLP *Newcastle upon Tyne*
Sintons *Newcastle upon Tyne*

Band 2

Crutes Law Firm *Newcastle upon Tyne*
Hay & Kilner *Newcastle upon Tyne*

Personal Injury: Mainly Claimant
Wales
Band 1

Hugh James *Cardiff*

Band 2

John Collins & Partners *Swansea*
Leo Abse & Cohen *Cardiff*
Russell Jones & Walker *Cardiff*
Thompsons *Cardiff*

Personal Injury: Mainly Defendant
Wales
Band 1

Dolmans *Cardiff*
Morgan Cole *Cardiff*

Band 2

Hugh James *Cardiff*

Band 3

Cartwright Black Solicitors *Cardiff*
Douglas-Jones Mercer (DJM) *Swansea*

Clinical Negligence: Mainly Defendant
Best of the UK
Band 1

Capsticks *London*
Hempsons *London*

Band 2

Barlow Lyde & Gilbert LLP *London*
Beachcroft LLP *Bristol*
Bevan Brittan LLP *London*
Browne Jacobson LLP *Birmingham*
Eversheds LLP *Newcastle upon Tyne*
Hill Dickinson LLP *Liverpool*
Kennedys *Cambridge*
Weightmans *London*

Band 3

Berrymans Lace Mawer *London*
Brachers *Maidstone*
RadcliffesLeBrasseur *London*
Ward Hadaway *Newcastle upon Tyne*

Band 4

DLA Piper UK LLP *Sheffield*
Mills & Reeve LLP *Norwich*
Reynolds Porter Chamberlain *London*

Clinical Negligence: Mainly Claimant
London
Band 1

Field Fisher Waterhouse LLP
Irwin Mitchell
Leigh Day & Co

Band 2

Charles Russell LLP
Kingsley Napley
Parlett Kent
Stewarts

Band 3

Anthony Gold
Bindman & Partners
Bolt Burdon Kemp
Hodge Jones & Allen
McMillan Williams
Pattinson & Brewer
Russell-Cooke LLP

Clinical Negligence: Mainly Claimant
Thames Valley
Band 1

Boyes Turner *Reading*
Osborne Morris *Leighton Buzzard*

Band 2

Darbys Solicitors LLP *Oxford*
Harris Cartier LLP *Slough*
Henmans LLP *Oxford*

Clinical Negligence: Mainly Claimant
The South
Band 1

Blake Lapthorn Tarlo Lyons *Fareham*
Mayo Wynne Baxter *Brighton*
Penningtons Solicitors LLP *Basingstoke, Godalming*
Thomson Snell *Tunbridge Wells*

Band 2

Moore Blatch *Southampton*

Clinical Negligence: Mainly Claimant
South West
Band 1

Barcan Woodward *Bristol*
Parlett Kent *Exeter*

Band 2

Clarke Willmott *Bristol*
Foot Anstey *Plymouth*
John Hodge Solicitors *Weston-super-Mare*
Michelmores LLP *Exeter*
Withy King *Bath*
Wolferstans *Plymouth*

Band 3

Bond Pearce LLP *Bristol*
Over Taylor Biggs *Exeter*
Tozers LLP *Exeter*

Clinical Negligence: Mainly Claimant

Midlands

Band 1

Anthony Collins Solicitors *Birmingham*

Challinors *Birmingham*

Freeth Cartwright LLP *Nottingham*

Irwin Mitchell *Birmingham*

Band 2

Barratt, Goff & Tomlinson *Nottingham*

Brindley Twist Tafft & James *Coventry*

Clinical Negligence: Mainly Claimant

East Anglia

Band 1

Gadsby Wicks *Chelmsford*

Kester Cunningham John *Cambridge*

Band 2

Attwater & Liell *Harlow*

Scrivenger Seabrook *St Neots*

Clinical Negligence: Mainly Claimant

North West

Band 1

Irwin Mitchell *Manchester*

Pannone LLP *Manchester*

Band 2

JMW Solicitors *Manchester*

Lees & Partners *Birkenhead*

McCool Patterson Hemsi *Manchester*

Walker Smith Way Solicitors *Chester*

Band 3

EAD Solicitors *Liverpool*

Linder Myers *Manchester*

Stephensons *Manchester*

Clinical Negligence: Mainly Claimant

Yorkshire

Band 1

Irwin Mitchell *Sheffield*

Band 2

Lester Morrill *Leeds*

Band 3

Heptonstalls LLP *Goole*

Langleys *York*

Clinical Negligence: Mainly Claimant

North East

Band 1

Ben Hoare Bell *Sunderland*

Hay & Kilner *Newcastle upon Tyne*

Irwin Mitchell *Newcastle upon Tyne*

Peter Maughan & Co *Gateshead*

Samuel Phillips *Newcastle upon Tyne*

Clinical Negligence: Mainly Claimant

Wales

Band 1

Geldards LLP *Cardiff*

Harding Evans *Newport*

Hugh James *Merthyr Tydfil*

Huttons *Cardiff*

John Collins & Partners *Swansea*

private client & charities

put simply

You have money. Perhaps a mountain of cash or maybe a carefully accumulated nest-egg, but either way you need to know how best to control it, store it and pass it on: enter the private client lawyer. Solicitors in this field advise individuals, families and trusts on wealth management; whilst some offer additional matrimonial and small-scale commercial capability, others focus exclusively on highly specialised tax and trusts, or wills and probate.

Whether it's for a multinational organisation such as the Red Cross, or for a slightly more local concern such as The Whitley Bay Fund for Disadvantaged Minors, specialised charities lawyers advise on all aspects of a not-for-profit organisation's activities.

who does what

private client lawyers

- Draft wills in consultation with clients and expedite the implementation of wills after death. Probate involves the appointment of an executor and the settling of an estate. Organising a house clearance or even a funeral is not beyond the scope of a lawyer's duties.
- Advise clients on the most tax-efficient and appropriate structure for holding money. If trusts are held in an offshore jurisdiction, lawyers must ensure their clients understand the foreign law implications.
- Advise overseas clients interested in investing in the UK, and banks whose overseas clients have UK interests.
- Assist clients with the very specific licensing, sales arrangement and tax planning issues related to ownership of heritage chattels (individual items or collections of cultural value or significance).

charities lawyers

- Advise charities on registration, reorganisation, regulatory compliance (such as Charities Commission investigations) and the implications of new legislation.
- Offer specialist trusts and investment expertise.
- Advise on quasi-corporate and mainstream commercial matters; negotiate and draft contracts for sponsorship and the development of trading subsidiaries; manage property issues and handle IP concerns.
- Charities law still conjures up images of sleepy local fundraising efforts or, alternatively, working on a trendy project for wealthy benefactors. In the wide middle ground you could be working with a local authority, a local library and four schools to establish an after-school homework programme, or you could rewrite the constitution of a 300-year-old church school to admit female pupils. Widespread international trust in British charity law means that you could also establish a study programme in Britain for a US university, or negotiate the formation of a zebra conservation charity in Tanzania.

the realities of the job

- An interest in other people's affairs is helpful. A capacity for empathy, coupled with impartiality and absolute discretion are the hallmarks of a good private client lawyer. Whether it's little old ladies with their savings in a stocking, well-heeled, excessively moneyed City gents, or fabulously flash celebrities, you'll need to be able to relate to and earn the trust of your clients.
- Despite not being as helter-skelter as some fields, the technical demands of private client work can be exacting and an academic streak certainly goes a long way, especially when it comes to tax and accounts matters.
- An eye for detail and a rigorous approach will

help you see through the mire of black letter law (and regular new legislation) so as to spot the loopholes and clever solutions that will save your clients most money.

- The 'green wellies, two smelly Labradors and a 1950s Land Rover' stereotype of the typical client is far from accurate: lottery wins, property portfolios, massive City salaries and successful businesses all feed the demand for legal advice.
- The combination of practical, technical and social skills means it is a testing discipline. If you are wavering between private clients and commercial clients, charities law might offer a nice balance.

current issues

The private client world is becoming increasingly internationalised. Wealthy people are selecting a wider geographical spread of assets and London has become a hub for the management of these assets. Many clients come from Russia, the Middle East, The USA, India and France.

- HMRC is clamping down on tax avoidance and the role trusts can play in inheritance tax planning. Ever-increasing property values mean that, on death, more and more little old ladies' assets are getting caught in a net really intended to catch bad guys.
- A Charities Bill is currently held up in the House of Commons, following its successful trip through the Lords in 2005. Charity lawyers are frustrated at the delay, but are for the most part anticipating a Bill that will clarify and simplify the registrations and incorporations of new charities.
- After an interminably long wait, the Charities Act 2006 was finalised. The Act addresses fundamental questions about what constitutes a charity and what 'public benefit' means. It also provides for greater regulation in some areas, and greater freedom for charities in others.
- Firms right across the country bemoan a dearth of young lawyers who can claim to be true private client specialists. It looks like a good time to put your hand up and be counted!

leading firms from Chambers UK 2008

Private Client
London
Band 1
Macfarlanes
Withers LLP

Band 2
Allen & Overy LLP
Baker & McKenzie LLP
Boodle Hatfield
Charles Russell LLP
Farrer & Co
LG
Speechly Bircham LLP
Taylor Wessing LLP

Band 3
Bircham Dyson Bell
Currey & Co
Forsters LLP
Payne Hicks Beach

Band 4
Berwin Leighton Paisner LLP
Collyer Bristow LLP
Harcus Sinclair
Hunters
May, May & Merrimans

Band 5
Harbottle & Lewis LLP
Penningtons Solicitors LLP

Private Client
Thames Valley
Band 1
B P Collins *Gerrards Cross*
Boodle Hatfield *Oxford*
Henmans LLP *Oxford*
Penningtons Solicitors LLP *Newbury*

Band 2
Blandy & Blandy *Reading*
Boyes Turner *Reading*

Band 3
Clarkslegal LLP *Reading*
Field Seymour Parkes *Reading*
IBB Solicitors *Chesham*
Matthew Arnold & Baldwin *Watford*

Private Client
The South
Band 1
Cripps Harries Hall LLP *Tunbridge Wells*
Thomas Eggar LLP *Chichester, Crawley*

Band 2
Adams & Remers *Lewes*
Blake Lapthorn Tarlo Lyons *Winchester*
Charles Russell LLP *Guildford*
Lester Aldridge LLP *Bournemouth*
Penningtons Solicitors LLP *Godalming*
Stevens & Bolton LLP *Guildford*
Thomson Snell & Passmore *Tunbridge Wells*

Band 3
Brachers *Maidstone*
DMH Stallard *Brighton*
Godwins *Winchester*
Lamport Bassitt *Southampton*
Moore Blatch *Lymington*
Mundays LLP *Cobham*
Paris Smith & Randall LLP *Southampton*
Rawlison Butler *Horsham*
Whitehead Monckton *Maidstone*

Private Client
Midlands
Band 1
Browne Jacobson LLP *Nottingham*
Hewitsons *Northampton*
Martineau Johnson *Birmingham*

Band 1
Mills & Reeve LLP *Birmingham*

Band 2
Higgs & Sons *Brierley Hill*
Lodders *Stratford-upon-Avon*

Band 3
Cobbetts LLP *Birmingham*
Freeth Cartwright LLP *Nottingham*

Band 4
Geldards LLP *Derby*
Hallmarks *Worcester*
HBJ Gateley Wareing *Birmingham*
Pinsent Masons *Birmingham*
Shakespeare Putsman LLP *Birmingham*

Private Client
South West
Band 1
Burges Salmon LLP *Bristol*
Wilsons *Salisbury*

Band 2
Charles Russell LLP *Cheltenham*
Clarke Willmott *Bristol*
Michelmores LLP *Exeter*
Osborne Clarke *Bristol*
Wiggin Osborne Fullerlove *Cheltenham*

Band 3
Ashfords *Exeter*
Coodes *St Austell*
Foot Anstey *Plymouth*
Hooper & Wollen *Torquay*
Rickerbys *Cheltenham*
Thring Townsend *Bristol*
Veale Wasbrough Lawyers *Bristol*

Band 4
TLT LLP *Bristol*

Private Client
East Anglia
Band 1
Hewitsons *Cambridge*
Mills & Reeve LLP *Norwich*
Taylor Vinters *Cambridge*

Band 2
Birketts LLP *Ipswich*
Greene & Greene *Bury St Edmunds*
Howes Percival LLP *Norwich*

Band 3
Barker Gotelee *Ipswich*
hc solicitors LLP *Peterborough*
Roythornes *Spalding*
Willcox & Lewis *Norwich*

Band 4
Ashton Graham *Ipswich*
Cozens-Hardy LLP *Norwich*
Hansells *Norwich*
Hood Vores & Allwood *Dereham*
Kester Cunningham John *Cambridge*
Prettys *Ipswich*
Stanley Tee LLP *Bishop's Stortford*
Wollastons LLP *Chelmsford*

Private Client
North East
Band 1
Dickinson Dees LLP *Newcastle upon Tyne*
Wrigleys Solicitors LLP *Leeds*

Band 2
Addleshaw Goddard LLP *Leeds*
Andrew Jackson *Hull*
Gordons *Leeds*
Rollits *Hull, York*

Band 3
Clarion Solicitors *Leeds*
Grays *York*
Irwin Mitchell *Sheffield*
Lupton Fawcett LLP *Leeds*
Ward Hadaway *Newcastle upon Tyne*
Watson Burton LLP *Newcastle upon Tyne*

Private Client: Contentious Trusts
London
Band 1
Allen & Overy LLP
Baker & McKenzie LLP
Withers LLP

Band 2
Boodle Hatfield
Charles Russell LLP
Clifford Chance LLP
Harcus Sinclair
Herbert Smith LLP

Band 3
Farrer & Co
Taylor Wessing LLP

Private Client
North West
Band 1
Addleshaw Goddard LLP *Manchester*

Band 2
Birch Cullimore *Chester*
Brabners Chaffe Street *Liverpool*
Cobbetts LLP *Manchester*
Hill Dickinson LLP *Liverpool*
Pannone LLP *Manchester*

Band 3
Halliwells LLP *Manchester*

Private Client
Wales
Band 1
Geldards LLP *Cardiff*
Hugh James *Cardiff*

Band 2
Margraves *Llandrindod Wells*

Charities
Best of the UK
Band 1

Bates Wells & Braithwaite *London*	Farrer & Co *London*
Stone King LLP *London*	

Band 2

Bircham Dyson Bell *London*	Withers LLP *London*

Band 3

Berwin Leighton Paisner LLP *London*	Blake Lapthorn Tarlo Lyons *Portsmouth*
Charles Russell LLP *London*	Russell-Cooke LLP *London*
Wilsons *Salisbury*	

Band 4

Addleshaw Goddard LLP *Manchester*	Allen & Overy LLP *London*
Anthony Collins Solicitors LLP *Birmingham*	Dickinson Dees LLP *Newcastle upon Tyne*
Harbottle & Lewis LLP *London*	Hempsons *London*
Henmans LLP *Oxford*	LG *London*
RadcliffesLeBrasseur *London*	Speechly Bircham LLP *London*
Trowers & Hamlins *London*	Wrigleys Solicitors LLP *Leeds*

Band 5

Campbell Hooper LLP *London*	Gordon Dadds *London*
Hewitsons *Cambridge*	Howard Kennedy *London*
Macfarlanes *London*	Mills & Reeve LLP *Cambridge*

Charities
Thames Valley
Band 1
Blake Lapthorn Tarlo Lyons *Oxford*
Henmans LLP *Oxford*

Band 2
B P Collins *Gerrards Cross*
IBB Solicitors *Ingatestone*
Winckworth Sherwood *Oxford*

Charities
The South
Band 1
Blake Lapthorn Tarlo Lyons *Fareham*

Band 2
Cripps Harries Hall LLP *Tunbridge Wells*
Lester Aldridge LLP *Bournemouth*
Thomas Eggar LLP *Chichester*
Thomson Snell & Passmore *Tunbridge Wells*

Band 3
Brachers *Maidstone*
DMH Stallard *Brighton*

private client & charities (continued)

Charities
Midlands

Band 1

Anthony Collins Solicitors LLP
Birmingham

Martineau Johnson *Birmingham*

Band 2

Cobbetts LLP *Birmingham*

Mills & Reeve LLP *Birmingham*

Band 3

Band Hatton *Coventry*

Charities
East Anglia

Band 1

Hewitsons *Cambridge*

Mills & Reeve LLP *Norwich*

Taylor Vinters *Cambridge*

Charities
North West

Band 1

Addleshaw Goddard LLP *Manchester*

Brabners Chaffe Street *Liverpool*

Lane-Smith & Shindler LLP *Manchester*

Band 2

Birch Cullimore *Chester*

Cobbetts LLP *Manchester*

Charities
South West

Band 1

Stone King LLP *Bath*

Wilsons *Salisbury*

Band 2

Burges Salmon LLP *Bristol*

Foot Anstey *Exeter*

Osborne Clarke *Bristol*

Veale Wasbrough Lawyers *Bristol*

Charities
North East

Band 1

Dickinson Dees LLP *Newcastle upon Tyne*

Wrigleys Solicitors LLP *Leeds*

Band 2

Addleshaw Goddard LLP *Leeds*

Muckle LLP *Newcastle upon Tyne*

Rollits *York*

Watson Burton LLP *Newcastle upon Tyne*

Band 3

Clarion Solicitors *Leeds*

McCormicks *Harrogate*

property/real estate

put simply

Students often tell us that land law lectures bore them, confuse them and provoke a deep-seated loathing for the subject. Many new trainees would rather stick pins in their eyes than take a seat in real estate, but thankfully it's a different story once they've experienced it in practice...

Property lawyers are essentially transactional lawyers whose jobs are fairly similar to those of their corporate law colleagues. The only real difference is that real estate deals require an extra layer of specialist legal and procedural knowledge. At university and law school you learn a lot about the law but little about what it's like to do a deal. That tangible nature of the subject matter is hard to envisage from the lecture theatre, but immediately evident from the first day in the office. The work centres on actual buildings and land – cinemas, supermarkets, churches, million-pound mansions, farms, factories – imagine Cribs meets Restoration with a load of paperwork. Even the most oblique legal concepts have a bricks-and-mortar or human basis to them; for example, you can physically see and touch a right of way or a flying freehold.

It is common for lawyers to develop a specialism – residential conveyancing, mortgage lending and property finance, development projects, retail or office leasing, social housing, agricultural land, and the leisure and hotels sector are some examples. Most firms have a property department, and the larger the department the more likely the lawyers are to specialise.

If you're wondering what the difference between 'property' and 'real estate' is, don't trouble yourself any further. Real estate is just a newer name that's migrated over here from the USA, and it doesn't matter which term a firm adopts.

who does what

The busy schedule of a property lawyer will include the following activities:

- Negotiating sales, purchases and leases of land and buildings, and advising on the structure of deals. Recording the terms of an agreement in legal documents.
- Gathering and analysing factual information about properties from the owners, surveyors, local authorities and the Land Registry.
- Preparing reports for buyers and anyone lending money.
- Managing the transfer of money and the handover of properties to new owners or occupiers.
- Taking the appropriate steps to register new owners and protect the interests of lenders or investors.
- Advising clients on their responsibilities in leasehold relationships, and how to take action if problems arise, eg non-payment of rent or disrepair.
- Helping developers get all the necessary permissions to build, alter or change the permitted use of properties.

the realities of the job

- Real estate lawyers have to multi-task. A single deal could involve many hundreds of properties; a filing cabinet could contain many hundreds of files, all of them at a different stage in the process.
- Because the work is so paper-based you must be well organised.
- Good drafting skills require attention to detail and careful thought. Plus you need to keep up to date with industry trends and standards, and you really need to know the law.
- Some clients get stressed and frustrated; you have to be able to explain legal problems in lay terms.
- There will be site visits, but this is a desk job with a lot of time spent on the phone to other solicitors, estate agents, civil servants and technical consultants.

- Most instances of solicitor negligence occur in this area of practice. There is so much that can go wrong.
- Your days will be busy, but generally the hours are predictable; you'll rarely be called into a meeting in the wee hours.
- If you want to write threatening letters – forget it! Property transactions require a collaborative approach from all concerned.

current issues

- The increasing sophistication of real estate in the UK means more deals involve complex funds or joint ventures. It is not uncommon for high-value deals to be structured as corporate transactions, so that a buyer can acquire a company that owns property rather than the property itself.
- A lack of UK property for investors (domestic and overseas) to target has encouraged the development of more sites for resale at a profit. While there is definitely more interest in investment and development, investors are getting bored of paying silly money for UK property when they could get a better deal elsewhere, say in Germany, France or the Eastern Bloc.
- With further growth in prime rents expected in Central London and elsewhere the UK development market is entering a new phase of activity.

- The domestic and European hotels and leisure sector has witnessed an increasing amount of consolidation, and there is a lot of money chasing the best-performing assets.
- London for sale! A number of trophy properties have been sold lately – The Gherkin for £600 million; CityPoint for £650 million and HSBC's HQ for a staggering £1.09 billion.
- Urban regeneration projects feature high on the agenda, as do Olympic preparations. The London Olympics and Paralympic Games Act 2006 created the Olympic Delivery Authority, responsible for building and delivering the 2012 games.
- New on the scene are Real Estate Investment Trusts (REITs), originally developed in the USA and useful as a means of channelling investment into real estate. Several of the UK's biggest property companies have taken advantage of the system and converted to REIT status.
- Law firms have experienced growth in income from real estate and many are undergoing recruitment drives as a result.
- Procedures are becoming increasingly streamlined and managed electronically.
- The London market has seen an influx of American and Scottish firms. Document-heavy and human resources-sapping projects are being divided up and farmed out to regional offices.

leading firms from Chambers UK 2008

Real Estate: Big-Ticket
London
Band 1
Berwin Leighton Paisner LLP
Clifford Chance LLP
Linklaters

Band 2
Ashurst
Herbert Smith LLP
Lovells LLP
Nabarro
SJ Berwin LLP

Band 3
Allen & Overy LLP
CMS Cameron McKenna LLP
Freshfields Bruckhaus Deringer
Macfarlanes
Slaughter and May

Band 4
LG
Mayer Brown
Olswang

Band 5
Addleshaw Goddard LLP
Dechert LLP
DLA Piper UK LLP
Eversheds LLP
Forsters LLP
Jones Day
Norton Rose
Simmons & Simmons

Band 6
Denton Wilde Sapte
Travers Smith

Real Estate: Mainly Mid-Market
London
Band 1
Forsters LLP

Band 2
Boodle Hatfield
Clyde & Co LLP
Davies Arnold Cooper
Field Fisher Waterhouse LLP
Howard Kennedy
Maxwell Winward LLP
Mishcon de Reya
Speechly Bircham LLP
Taylor Wessing LLP
Wragge & Co LLP

Band 3
Farrer & Co
Finers Stephens Innocent
Fladgate Fielder
K&L Gates
Lewis Silkin LLP
Manches LLP
Reed Smith Richards Butler LLP

Band 4
Beachcroft LLP
Hammonds
Harbottle & Lewis LLP
Osborne Clarke
Penningtons Solicitors LLP
Salans
Stephenson Harwood
Trowers & Hamlins
Wedlake Bell

Band 5
Bird & Bird
Dundas & Wilson
Halliwells LLP
McGrigors LLP
Shepherd and Wedderburn LLP
Wallace LLP

Band 6
Maclay Murray & Spens LLP
Maples Teesdale
Pinsent Masons
Russell-Cooke LLP

Real Estate: Hotels & Leisure
London
Band 1
Berwin Leighton Paisner LLP
Clifford Chance LLP

Band 2
CMS Cameron McKenna LLP
Freshfields Bruckhaus Deringer
SJ Berwin LLP

Band 3
Allen & Overy LLP
Davies Arnold Cooper
Denton Wilde Sapte
Field Fisher Waterhouse LLP
Fladgate Fielder
Linklaters
Lovells LLP
Reed Smith Richards Butler LLP

Band 4
Addleshaw Goddard LLP
Davenport Lyons
DLA Piper UK LLP
Douglas Wignall & Co
Gibson, Dunn & Crutcher LLP
Herbert Smith LLP
Stephenson Harwood
Taylor Wessing LLP
Wragge & Co LLP

Real Estate
East Midlands
Band 1
Browne Jacobson LLP *Nottingham*
Eversheds LLP *Nottingham*
Freeth Cartwright LLP *Nottingham*

Band 2
Geldards LLP *Derby*
Shoosmiths *Nottingham*

Band 3
Flint Bishop Solicitors *Derby*
Harvey Ingram LLP *Leicester*

property/real estate (continued)

Real Estate
Thames Valley
Band 1
Boyes Turner *Reading*
BrookStreet Des Roches LLP *Abingdon*
Pitmans *Reading*

Band 2
Blake Lapthorn Tarlo Lyons *Oxford*
Denton Wilde Sapte *Milton Keynes*
IBB Solicitors *Uxbridge*

Band 3
Field Seymour Parkes *Reading*
Harold Benjamin *Harrow*
Manches LLP *Oxford*
Matthew Arnold & Baldwin *Watford*
Olswang Thames Valley *Reading*
Penningtons Solicitors LLP *Newbury*
Shoosmiths *Reading*

Band 4
B P Collins *Gerrards Cross*
Blandy & Blandy *Reading*
Clarkslegal LLP *Reading*
EMW Law *Milton Keynes*
Kimbells LLP *Milton Keynes*
Owen White *Slough*
Pictons Solicitors LLP *Luton*

Real Estate
East Anglia
Band 1
Birketts LLP *Ipswich*
Eversheds LLP *Cambridge*
Hewitsons *Cambridge*
Mills & Reeve LLP *Cambridge*
Taylor Vinters *Cambridge*

Band 2
Ashton Graham *Bury St Edmunds*
Greene & Greene *Bury St Edmunds*
Greenwoods Solicitors LLP *Peterborough*
Kester Cunningham John *Cambridge*
Prettys *Ipswich*
Wollastons LLP *Chelmsford*

Band 3
Birkett Long *Colchester*
Leathes Prior *Norwich*
Thomson Webb & Corfield *Cambridge*
Tolhurst Fisher *Chelmsford*

Real Estate
The South
Band 1
Bond Pearce LLP *Southampton*
Clyde & Co LLP *Guildford*
Cripps Harries Hall LLP *Tunbridge Wells*
Stevens & Bolton LLP *Guildford*

Band 2
Blake Lapthorn Tarlo Lyons *Portsmouth*
DMH Stallard *Crawley*
Shoosmiths *Fareham*
Thomas Eggar LLP *Chichester*

Band 3
Charles Russell LLP *Guildford*
Clarke Willmott *Southampton*
Lester Aldridge LLP *Bournemouth*
Mundays LLP *Cobham*
Paris Smith & Randall LLP *Southampton*
Rawlison Butler *Crawley*
Thomson Snell & Passmore *Tunbridge Wells*

Band 4
asb law *Maidstone*
Brachers *Maidstone*
Coffin Mew LLP *Southampton*
GCL Solicitors *Guildford*
Lamport Bassitt *Southampton*
Laytons *Guildford*
Moore Blatch *Southampton*
Penningtons Solicitors LLP *Basingstoke*
Shadbolt & Co LLP *Reigate*
Steele Raymond LLP *Bournemouth*

Band 5
Barlow Robbins LLP *Guildford*
Clarkson Wright & Jakes *Orpington*
Warners *Tonbridge*

Real Estate
South West
Band 1
Burges Salmon LLP *Bristol*

Band 2
Beachcroft LLP *Bristol*
Bond Pearce LLP *Plymouth*
Clarke Willmott *Bristol*
Davitt Jones Bould *Taunton*
Michelmores LLP *Exeter*
Osborne Clarke *Bristol*
TLT LLP *Bristol*

Band 3
Ashfords *Exeter*
Bevan Brittan LLP *Bristol*
Charles Russell LLP *Cheltenham*
Foot Anstey *Plymouth*
Rickerbys *Cheltenham*
Stephens & Scown *Exeter*
Veale Wasbrough Lawyers *Bristol*

Band 4
BPE Solicitors *Cheltenham*
Davies and Partners *Gloucester*
Stone King LLP *Bath*
Thring Townsend *Swindon*
Withy King *Bath*

Real Estate
North East
Band 1
Dickinson Dees LLP *Newcastle upon Tyne*
Eversheds LLP *Newcastle upon Tyne*
Ward Hadaway *Newcastle upon Tyne*

Band 2
Muckle LLP *Newcastle upon Tyne*
Watson Burton LLP *Newcastle upon Tyne*

Band 3
Crutes Law Firm *Newcastle upon Tyne*
Hay & Kilner *Newcastle upon Tyne*
Sintons *Newcastle upon Tyne*

Real Estate
West Midlands
Band 1
Eversheds LLP *Birmingham*
Wragge & Co LLP *Birmingham*

Band 2
DLA Piper UK LLP *Birmingham*
Pinsent Masons *Birmingham*

Band 3
Cobbetts LLP *Birmingham*
Hammonds *Birmingham*
HBJ Gateley Wareing *Birmingham*
Shoosmiths *Birmingham*

Band 4
Clarke Willmott *Birmingham*
Higgs & Sons *Brierley Hill*
Knight & Sons *Newcastle-under-Lyme*
Martineau Johnson *Birmingham*
Reed Smith Richards Butler LLP *Solihull*
Wright Hassall LLP *Leamington Spa*

Band 5
Anthony Collins Solicitors LLP
Birmingham
KJD *Stoke-on-Trent*
Shakespeare Putsman LLP *Birmingham*

Real Estate
Wales
Band 1
Eversheds LLP *Cardiff*
Geldards LLP *Cardiff*

Band 2
Berry Smith Solicitors *Cardiff*
M & A Solicitors LLP *Cardiff*
Morgan Cole *Cardiff*

Band 3
Hugh James *Cardiff*
Morgan LaRoche Ltd *Swansea*

Band 4
Capital Law LLP *Cardiff Bay*
Dolmans *Cardiff*
Douglas-Jones Mercer (DJM) *Swansea*
Harding Evans *Newport*

Real Estate
North West
Band 1
Addleshaw Goddard LLP *Manchester*
DLA Piper UK LLP *Manchester, Liverpool*
Eversheds LLP *Manchester*

Band 2
Beachcroft LLP *Manchester*
Brabners Chaffe Street *Liverpool*
Cobbetts LLP *Manchester*
DWF *Manchester, Liverpool*
Halliwells LLP *Manchester, Liverpool*
Land Law LLP *Altrincham*

Band 3
Hammonds *Manchester*
Hill Dickinson LLP *Liverpool*
Mace & Jones *Manchester*
Pannone LLP *Manchester*

Band 4
JMW Solicitors *Manchester*
Kuit Steinart Levy *Manchester*
Pinsent Masons *Manchester*

Real Estate: Multi-site Firms
Best of the UK
Band 1
DLA Piper UK LLP *London*
Eversheds LLP *London*

Band 2
Addleshaw Goddard LLP *London*
Nabarro *London*
Pinsent Masons *London*
Wragge & Co LLP *Birmingham*

Band 3
Beachcroft LLP *London*
Halliwells LLP *Manchester*
Hammonds *London*

Real Estate
Yorkshire
Band 1
Addleshaw Goddard LLP *Leeds*
DLA Piper UK LLP *Sheffield, Leeds*
Walker Morris *Leeds*

Band 2
Eversheds LLP *Leeds*
Pinsent Masons *Leeds*

Band 3
Andrew Jackson *Hull*
Cobbetts LLP *Leeds*
Gordons *Leeds*
Nabarro *Sheffield*

Band 4
Beachcroft LLP *Leeds*
Hammonds *Leeds*
Lupton Fawcett LLP *Leeds*
Rollits *Hull*

Band 5
Gosschalks *Hull*
Irwin Mitchell *Sheffield*
Keeble Hawson *Sheffield*
Shulmans *Leeds*
Wake Smith *Sheffield*

Band 6
Denison Till *York*
Langleys *York*
Lee & Priestley LLP *Leeds*

human rights put simply

You know the kind of film where a crack team of secret operatives unites to save the world from government conspiracy or alien invasion, while average Joe Public carries on his everyday life blissfully unaware of any danger? Traditionally lawyers in this field are not dissimilar: they work long and unsociable hours to protest injustice enshrined in law and to fight for principle where most of us would offer little more than a pragmatic sigh, if we noticed a problem at all.

That said, events of the past few years have projected public interest issues to the forefront of national consciousness and brought concepts such as freedom of speech or movement to the top of the political agenda: the war in Iraq and its fallout; the War on Terror; extraordinary renditions; Guantánamo Bay; evidence gathered under torture; bombings in London; persecution of ethnic or religious minorities; ID cards; new arrest and detention laws; cartoons defaming religious figures and counter-protests inciting religious hatred. All these have put the relationship between the state and the individual under the magnifying glass, divided public opinion and had major implications in terms of legal challenges to new legislation and its impact on human rights.

Human rights cases invariably relate in some way to the UK's ratification of the European Convention on Human Rights through the Human Rights Act 1998 (HRA). Cases crop up in criminal and civil contexts, often through the medium of judicial review, a key tool by which decisions of public bodies can be questioned. Civil contexts could include claims regarding the right to education or community care under the Mental Health Act, cases of discrimination at work or, because the Act enshrines in law the right to family life, even family issues. Criminal contexts could relate to complaints against the police, prisoners' issues, public order convictions arising out of demonstrations, or perhaps extradition on terror charges. The raft of recent legislation spanning terrorism, security, religious tolerance and antisocial behaviour has intersected with the HRA and the Public Order Acts to create a whole new range of cases and issues. In one prominent case brought by Liberty in late 2005, the House of Lords ruled that evidence gained through torture in other jurisdictions is inadmissible in UK courts. Another instance saw the government and several police forces threatened with judicial review unless they investigated UK involvement in CIA extraordinary rendition flights via airports including Biggin Hill and Brize Norton.

immigration law put simply

This is an area that arouses considerable public and political interest. Lawyers deal with both business and personal immigration matters, the former having been embraced by the present government in its quest to manage economic migration. In this more lucrative area, lawyers assist highly skilled migrants obtain residency or leave to remain in the UK, and help non-nationals to secure visas for travel abroad. They also work with companies that need to bring in employees from overseas.

With issues of asylum and people seeking permission to stay in the UK on human rights grounds never out of the tabloid newspapers, this side of the immigration field is a hot potato. Lawyers represent individuals who have fled persecution in their country of origin, and for whom return could mean death or torture; they also take on cases for people whose right to stay in the UK is under threat or indeed entirely absent. Because changes in the public funding of such cases have left the area uneconomical to practise, there has been a reduction in the number of firms offering such services.

solicitors

who does what

human rights lawyers:

- Advise clients (predominantly individuals but sometimes groups in class actions) on how to appeal a decision made or action taken by a public body, whether an institution such as the police, a local authority, a court, or a branch of government.
- Collect evidence, take witness statements, prepare cases and instruct barristers.
- Pursue cases through the procedural stages necessary to achieve the desired result. The final port of call for some human rights cases is the European Court of Justice (ECJ) so lawyers need to be fully conversant with both UK law and European law.

business immigration lawyers:

- Advise and assist businesses or their employees on work permits and visas. They need to be fully conversant with all current schemes such as those for highly skilled migrants and investors.
- Prepare for, attend and advocate at tribunals or court hearings, where necessary instructing a barrister to do so.

personal immigration lawyers:

- Advise clients on their status and rights within the UK, ascertaining which is the most advantageous line of argument for their client to run.
- Secure evidence of a client's identity, medical reports and witness statements and prepare cases for court hearings or appeals. Represent clients at these hearings or instruct a barrister to do so.
- Handle an immense amount of unremunerated form filling and legal aid paperwork.

the realities of the job

- Vocation, vocation, vocation: a commitment to and belief in the values you're fighting for are essential because salaries in this field are considerably lower than in most other areas of law. Working in the voluntary sector for orgnisations such as the Refugee Council, or taking on important cases pro bono, can provide the greatest satisfaction.
- Sensitivity, empathy and sympathy are absolutely essential qualities because you'll often be dealing with highly emotional people, those with mental health issues or those who simply don't appreciate the full extent of their legal predicament. Whether it's an immigration case involving flight from an oppressive regime or an abuse in police custody matter, you'll need a keen eye for the truth, shrewd judgement and the facility for getting the right information from clients who may not be the most reliable or stable sources.
- Strong analytical skills are required to pick out the legal issues you can change from the socio-economic ones beyond your control. You need to be able to manage a client's expectations and your own idealism; pragmatic and sensible advice, even knowing when to quit, is important.
- In the battle against red tape, bureaucracy and institutional indifference, organisational skills and a vast store of patience are valuable assets.
- Opportunities for advocacy are abundant, which means that knowledge of court and tribunal procedure is a fundamental requirement. Often cases must pass through every possible stage of appeal before they can be referred to judicial review or the ECJ.
- The number of people looking for training contracts in the field far exceeds the number of available positions so you must evidence your commitment. A CV referencing voluntary work at a law centre or specialist

voluntary organisation (eg the Howard League for Penal Reform), or membership of Liberty or Justice will help. A healthy interest in current affairs and the latest cases in the news will also assist.

- Because much of the work is legally aided, the firms who specialise in these areas of work generally can't offer attractive trainee salaries or sponsorship through law school.

current issues

- Almost 40% of the cases in the Court of Appeal were public law cases, which is a remarkable statistic given that the modern form of judicial review was established as late as 1977. The bulk of these cases related to immigration, asylum and housing, and made full use of the Human Rights Act and European Convention of Human Rights. With the advent of Freedom of Information, and increased transparency in the public sector in line with Article 6 of the Convention, law firms have seen a greater willingness from the public to challenge the decisions of public authorities.

- The interface between terrorism and public law, and between public law and the Human Rights Act, has become even more acute. 2006 was dominated by control orders, with two cases going to the Court of Appeal, three appearing in the House of Lords and three appearing in the High Court. Secretary of State v MB was the first challenge to the control order regime under the Prevention of Terrorism Act 2005 and concerned Article 6 of the Convention. Secretary of State for the Home Department v JJ and others related to control orders and Article 5 of the Convention. Both went to the House of Lords on appeal to join cases examining the government's actions abroad, for instance in Iraq. R (Al-Skeini and others) v Secretary of State for Defence relates to the extra-territorial application of the Human Rights Act to UK troops in southern Iraq. Meanwhile R (Al Jedda) v Secretary of State for Defence concerns the use of indefinite detention of a dual UK/Iraqi national under UN Security Council resolution 1546.

- The European Convention of Human Rights continues to have a serious impact on coroners and the kinds of complaints that are being made about them. Many such claims based on Article 2 of the Convention (concerning an individual's right to life) have been rejected. The government has begun to consider coroner reform. The number of inquests continues to proliferate, with prison deaths and military deaths dominating the field.

- Because of the surplus of asylum and special educational needs cases in the Administrative Court, urgent healthcare cases are now taking weeks to get to permission stage. This is a significant problem for the NHS. One case that successfully raced through the system and ended up in the Court of Appeal was the Herceptin litigation. The case sparked a host of others relating to new drugs. Other major cases in the healthcare sector include GMC v Professor Sir Roy Meadow and R (Stone) v South East Coast Strategic Health Authority, in which Michael Stone, convicted of the murders of Lin and Megan Russell, tried to prevent the publication of the report into his care and treatment.

- The development of information rights continues to be a major feature. The past year has seen growing awareness of the Freedom of Information Act 2000 and the Environmental Information Regulations 2004, which are being increasingly used by businesses, most notably in the procurement and regulatory sectors. This growth may, however, be severely curtailed by recent proposals to strengthen the power of public authorities to refuse requests on the basis of cost, upon which a consultation was launched in December 2006. The issue of disclosure of documents in judicial review was highlighted in Tweed v Parades Commission for Northern Ireland, which went to the House of Lords in October 2006.

- One of the key events of 2006 was the enactment of the Legislative and Regulatory Reform Act 2006. After much controversy surrounding its impact on parliamentary democracy, its final form was somewhat different from that originally proposed, but still marks a step-change in the ability of government to make primary legislation without full parliamentary scrutiny. How it is used, and its implications for the legal and commercial sectors, remains to be seen, but its impact is likely to be substantial.

- Undoubtedly one of the biggest public law cases of 2007 was R (Greenpeace) v Secretary of State for Trade and Industry, in which Justice Sullivan struck down as unlawful the government's decision to support nuclear power because of inadequate consultation. Following this landmark case, law firms have witnessed an increase in challenges to governmental processes of instituting legislative change. As the government attempts to implement pledges made in relation to climate change, pollution control through Kyoto and emission reductions, solicitors predict that when the programme becomes more fleshed out, commercial entities could be less than happy with the effects on their businesses. Moreover, these controls may be seen as discriminatory in an EU environment, (where competitors are at an advantage). In this respect, EU regulation is having a growing impact on domestic commercial activity.

- In immigration law there have been many modifications of late, among them changes affecting the highly skilled migrant programme and people applying for leave to remain or settle in the UK. There is much criticism of the abolition of various appeal rights and the substitution of an administrative review procedure.

- In March 2006 the Home Office published a paper on proposals for the UK immigration system called 'Controlling our borders: Making migration work for Britain – Five Year Strategy for asylum and immigration'. It is part of a constant revolution in immigration rules and regulations. A new points-based immigration system is now being proposed.

- Lawyers dealing with business immigration increasingly need to help clients with more than just domestic inward-bound work permits. With large companies now shunting employees around various countries on placements, they are being asked to arrange multi-jurisdictional work permits.

public interest (continued)

leading firms from Chambers UK 2008

Immigration: Personal
London
Band 1
Bindman & Partners
Wesley Gryk Solicitors LLP
Wilson & Co

Band 2
Bates Wells & Braithwaite
Birnberg Peirce & Partners
Deighton Guedalla
Fisher Meredith

Band 3
DJ Webb & Co
Elder Rahimi
Glazer Delmar
Luqmani Thompson & Partners

Immigration
Thames Valley
Band 1
Darbys Solicitors LLP *Oxford*
Turpin & Miller *Oxford*

Immigration
South West
Band 1
South West Law *Bristol*

Education: Institutions (Universities)
Best of the UK
Band 1
Eversheds LLP *London*

Band 2
Beachcroft LLP *London*
Farrer & Co *London*
Martineau Johnson *Birmingham*
Mills & Reeve LLP *Cambridge*
Pinsent Masons *Birmingham*

Band 3
Berrymans Lace Mawer *London*
Blake Lapthorn Tarlo Lyons *Oxford*
Bond Pearce LLP *Plymouth*
Dickinson Dees LLP *Newcastle upon Tyne*
DLA Piper UK LLP *London*
Nabarro *London*

Immigration
East Anglia
Band 1
Fisher Jones Greenwood LLP *Colchester*
Gross & Co *Bury St Edmunds*
Wollastons LLP *Chelmsford*

Immigration
Midlands
Band 1
The Rights Partnership *Birmingham*
Tyndallwoods *Birmingham*

Band 2
Blakemores *Birmingham*
Paragon Law Limited *Nottingham*

Immigration
The North
Band 1
A S Law *Liverpool*
David Gray Solicitors *Newcastle upon Tyne*
Harrison Bundey *Leeds*
Parker Rhodes *Rotherham*

Band 2
Henry Hyams *Leeds*
Howells LLP *Sheffield*
Jackson & Canter *Liverpool*

Education: Individuals
Best of the UK
Band 1
Fisher Meredith *London*
Levenes *London*

Band 2
Douglas Silas Solicitors *London*
Langley Wellington *Gloucester*
Maxwell Gillott *Lancaster*
Teacher Stern Selby *London*

Band 3
Ormerods *Croydon*
Russell Jones & Walker *London*

Band 4
French & Co *Nottingham*
John Ford Solicitors *London*
Match Solicitors *London*

Immigration: Business
London
Band 1
Kingsley Napley
Laura Devine Solicitors
Magrath & Co

Band 2
Bates Wells & Braithwaite
CMS Cameron McKenna LLP
Penningtons Solicitors LLP
PricewaterhouseCoopers Legal

Band 3
Baker & McKenzie LLP
Gherson
H2O Law LLP
Reed Smith Richards Butler LLP

Band 4
DJ Webb & Co
Fox Williams LLP
Fragomen LLP
Harbottle & Lewis LLP
Lewis Silkin LLP
Mishcon de Reya
Sturtivant & Co
Taylor Wessing LLP

solicitors

Administrative & Public Law: Commercial & Regulated Industries
Best of the UK
Band 1
Clifford Chance LLP *London*
Herbert Smith LLP *London*

Band 2
Allen & Overy LLP *London*
Baker & McKenzie LLP *London*
Freshfields Bruckhaus Deringer *London*
Lovells LLP *London*

Band 3
Addleshaw Goddard LLP *London*
Bates Wells & Braithwaite *London*
Bird & Bird *London*
Field Fisher Waterhouse LLP *London*
Olswang *London*
Simmons & Simmons *London*
Wragge & Co LLP *Birmingham*

Administrative & Public Law: Public Sector Law & Governance
Best of the UK
Band 1
Beachcroft LLP *London*
Clifford Chance LLP *London*
Eversheds LLP *Leeds*
Field Fisher Waterhouse LLP *London*
Herbert Smith LLP *London*
Sharpe Pritchard *London*

Band 2
Allen & Overy LLP *London*
Baker & McKenzie LLP *London*
Bevan Brittan LLP *Bristol*
Capsticks *London*
Pinsent Masons *London*

Band 3
Bates Wells & Braithwaite *London*
Bircham Dyson Bell *London*
Trowers & Hamlins *London*
Wragge & Co LLP *London*

Administrative & Public Law: Traditional Claimant
Best of the UK
Band 1
Bhatt Murphy *London*
Bindman & Partners *London*
Leigh Day & Co *London*

Band 2
Christian Khan *London*
Hickman & Rose *London*
Howells LLP *Sheffield*
Irwin Mitchell *Sheffield*
Public Interest Lawyers *Birmingham*

Band 3
Birnberg Peirce & Partners *London*
Levenes *London*
Pierce Glynn Solicitors *London*
Public Law Solicitors *Birmingham*

Civil Liberties
Best of the UK
Band 1
Bindman & Partners *London*

Band 2
Bhatt Murphy *London*
Birnberg Peirce & Partners *London*
Leigh Day & Co *London*
Public Interest Lawyers *Birmingham*

Band 3
Christian Khan *London*
Deighton Guedalla *London*
Harrison Bundey *Leeds*
Hickman & Rose *London*
Irwin Mitchell *Sheffield*
Scott-Moncrieff, Harbour & Sinclair *London*
Simons Muirhead & Burton *London*

Band 4
Fisher Meredith *London*
Hodge Jones & Allen *London*
Howells LLP *Sheffield*
Mackintosh Duncan *London*
Pierce Glynn Solicitors *London*
Public Law Solicitors *Birmingham*

Police Law: Mainly Claimant
Best of the UK
Band 1
Bhatt Murphy *London*
Bindman & Partners *London*
Deighton Guedalla *London*
Fisher Meredith *London*
Hickman & Rose *London*

Band 2
Birnberg Peirce & Partners *London*
Harrison Bundey *Leeds*
Howells LLP *Sheffield*
Tuckers *London*

Band 3
Christian Khan *London*
Jackson & Canter *Liverpool*

Police Law: Mainly Defendant
Best of the UK
Band 1
Berrymans Lace Mawer *London*
Weightmans *London*

Band 2
Barlow Lyde & Gilbert LLP *London*
Bircham Dyson Bell *London*
Dolmans *Cardiff*

Band 3
Crutes Law Firm *Newcastle upon Tyne*

Civil Liberties: Prison Law
Best of the UK
Band 1
Bhatt Murphy *London*

Band 2
Hickman & Rose *London*
Irwin Mitchell *Sheffield*

Band 3
Bindman & Partners *London*
Birnberg Peirce & Partners *London*
Scott-Moncrieff, Harbour *London*

shipping

put simply

Essentially shipping law concerns the carriage of goods or people by sea, plus any and every matter related to the financing, construction, use, insurance and decommissioning of the ships that carry them (or sink carrying them, or are arrested carrying them or are salvaged carrying them). Despite being relatively self-contained and centred around specialist firms, or practices within firms, this is a varied discipline offering challenges for different breeds of lawyer.

who does what

Contentious lawyers' work is divided between:

- Wet or 'Admiralty' matters – broadly speaking tortious, concerning disputes arising from accidents or misadventure at sea anywhere in the world. Among other things it covers collision, salvage, total loss and modern day piracy, and requires swift, decisive action to protect a client's interests and minimise any loss.
- Dry matters – disputes and subsequent litigation relating to contracts made on dry land such as charter parties, bills of lading, ship construction or refitting, and sale of goods agreements. Like wet work it can require action in pretty much any jurisdiction in the world.
- Both wet and dry lawyers are involved in court and arbitration appearances, conferences with counsel, client meetings, taking witness statements and advising clients on the merits of and strategy for cases.

non-contentious lawyers:

- Are primarily engaged in contracts for ship finance and shipbuilding, crew employment contracts, sale and purchase agreements, affreightment contracts, and the registration and re-flagging of ships.
- May specialise in more niche areas such as yachts or fishing, an area in which regulatory issues feature prominently.

- Are less likely than their contentious colleagues to jet off around the world at the drop of a hat.

the realities of the job

- Wet work offers the excitement of international assignments and clients, reacting coolly to sudden emergencies and travelling to far-flung places to offer practical and pragmatic analysis and advice.
- Despite the perils and pleasures of dealing with clients and instructions on the other side of the world, back in the office shipping law has little of the all-night culture about it; hours are likely to be steady beyond those 'international rescue' moments.
- Non-contentious work touches on the intricacies of international trade, so it's as important to keep up with sector knowledge as legal developments.
- Dealing with a mixed clientele from all points on the social compass, you'll need to be just as comfortable extracting a comprehensible statement from a Norwegian merchant seaman as conducting negotiations with major financers. Shipowners, operators, traders and charterers, P&I clubs and hull underwriters will all come within your daily ken.
- Contentious cases are driven by the procedural rules and timetable of the court or arbitration forum to which the matter has been referred. A solid grasp of procedure is as important as a strong foundation in tort and contract law.
- Some shipping lawyers do come from a naval background or are ex-mariners, but you won't be becalmed if the closest comparable experience you've had is steering Tommy Tugboat in the bath, as long as you evince a credible interest in the discipline.
- Though not quite 'no place for a lady', parts of the shipping world are still male dominated. Women lawyers and clients are more commonly found on the dry side of business.

- If you decide to move away from shipping law, non-contentious experience should allow a transition into asset or more general finance. A few years of contentious shipping law should leave you with a solid grounding in commercial litigation.
- In the UK, shipping law is centred around London and a few other port cities. Major international centres include Pireaus in Greece, Hong Kong and Singapore. Some trainees even get to work in these locations.

current issues

- Increasingly there is a crossover between shipping, energy and international trade. Liquefied natural gas (LNG) is a big driver, with Floating Production, Storage and Offshore Loading (FPSO) taking much of the limelight. FPSO installations are big news in the Caspian Sea, the Middle East, West Africa and the Far East. One knock-on effect is the extent to which UK firms are now working with lawyers in these regions, and sending their own lawyers to work overseas.
- The rise of China as an economic power is impacting on the cargo market, on ship building and on financing. Most shipyards are fully booked for the rest of this decade.
- A boom in shipping has led to increased levels of resales of ships
- Increased lending from banks and even hedge funds has led to the involvement of law firms that were not previously associated with the sector. P & I clubs are beginning to employ more in-house lawyers.
- Super yachts! We've never been on one, but we'd not turn Mr Abramovitch down if he offered us a cruise on his 377ft gin palace. The yacht market is hot right now.

leading firms from Chambers UK 2008

Shipping: Finance
London

Band 1
Norton Rose
Watson, Farley & Williams

Band 2
Allen & Overy LLP
Clifford Chance LLP
Stephenson Harwood

Band 3
Berwin Leighton Paisner LLP
Clyde & Co LLP
Denton Wilde Sapte
Holman Fenwick & Willan
Ince & Co

Shipping
London

Band 1
Holman Fenwick & Willan
Ince & Co

Band 2
Clyde & Co LLP

Band 3
Hill Dickinson LLP
Reed Smith Richards Butler LLP

Band 4
Barlow Lyde & Gilbert LLP
Bentleys, Stokes & Lowless
Clifford Chance LLP
Jackson Parton
MFB
Norton Rose
Stephenson Harwood
Thomas Cooper
Waterson Hicks
Watson, Farley & Williams
Winter Scott

Band 5
Curtis Davis Garrard
Dale Stevens LLP
Fishers
HBJ Gateley Wareing
Holmes Hardingham
LG
Mays Brown, Solicitors
Middleton Potts
Waltons & Morse LLP

Shipping
The Regions & Scotland

Band 1
Eversheds LLP *Newcastle upon Tyne*
Mills & Co *Newcastle upon Tyne*

Band 2
Andrew Jackson *Hull*
Brodies LLP *Edinburgh*
Davies, Johnson & Co *Plymouth*
Hill Dickinson LLP *Liverpool*

Band 3
Ashfords *Exeter*
Bartons *Kingsbridge*
Birketts LLP *Ipswich*
HBJ Gateley Wareing *Edinburgh*
John Weston & Co *Felixstowe*
Mackinnons *Aberdeen*
Prettys *Ipswich*
Shoosmiths *Fareham*

sports, media and entertainment law

put simply

The bright lights, the red carpets, the reflected glory of stars of stage, screen and pitch… Is this a true reflection of legal practice in what we'll broadly call sports, media and entertainment law? So long as you know you'll always be a lawyer first and foremost, we are prepared to concede that this is one of the more exciting parts of the legal profession. In this area of the profession there's a niche for almost any kind of media tart or sports obsessive.

advertising and marketing law – put simply

Work encompasses pure advertising law advice – ensuring a client's products or advertisements are compliant with industry standards – plus general advice on anything from contracts between clients, media and suppliers, to employment law, corporate transactions and litigation.

the role involves:

- Copy clearance to ensure advertising campaigns comply with legislation such as the Consumer Protection Act (CPA) or regulatory codes controlled by the Advertising Standards Agency or Ofcom.
- Advice on comparative advertising, unauthorised references to living persons, potential trade mark or other intellectual property infringements.
- Defending clients against allegations that their work has infringed regulations or the rights of third parties, and bringing complaints against competitors' advertising.

the realities of the job

- Lawyers must have a good knowledge of advertising regulations, defamation and intellectual property law.
- The work is 'real world' and fast paced – a campaign that comes out today might need to be pulled tomorrow for legal reasons. Clients expect pragmatic advice that minimises the risks to which they are exposed.
- Clients are creative, lively and demanding. The issues thrown up can be fascinating and must be dealt with creatively.
- Many disputes will be settled via regulatory bodies but some, particularly IP infringements, end in litigation.

reputation management – put simply

These specialists advise clients on how best to protect their own 'brand'. Whether it's a footballer alleged to have been involved in rape, a newspaper that has made claims it can't back up, or a TV star snapped with a telephoto lens at a funeral, the client may require swift and decisive action be taken.

claimants' solicitors:

- Advise individuals – commonly celebrities, politicians or high-profile businessmen – on the nature of any potential libel action or breach of privacy claim, usually against broadcasters or publishers.
- A matter can be settled by way of an apology or retraction of published material, or it may go all the way to court. The lawyer must always consider whether allowing a case to reach trial is the best solution for the client, who may be averse to any further intrusion into their private affairs.

defendants' solicitors:

- Typically advise broadcasters and newspapers or other publishers on libel claims brought against them. With the burden of proof on the defendant, the lawyer's job is to help prove that what was published caused no loss to the claimant or was not in fact libellous. This requires an investigative approach and strategic thinking.

- Help clients stay out of trouble by giving pre-publication advice to authors, editors or production companies.

the realities of the job

- A comprehensive understanding of libel laws and a willingness to think laterally are essential.
- Individual claimants will be stressed and upset, so people skills, patience and resourcefulness are much needed.
- Solicitors prepare cases but barristers almost always get the glory attached to presenting cases in court.
- It's important to have a keen interest in current affairs, popular media and (whisper it quietly) keeping more than half an eye on the tabloids and gossip rags. If you combine that with ardent belief in freedom of speech and right to privacy, then so much the better.
- Tempting as it is, you just can't spill the beans on your latest case when you're out with friends... even if you do know more than popbitch.

entertainment law put simply

The film, broadcasting, music, theatre and publishing industries share a common need for commercial legal advice on contract, employment litigation and intellectual property law, among other things.

TV and film lawyers:

- Offer production companies advice on every stage of the creation of programmes and films, from research and development, to production and marketing, sponsorship and tie-ins.
- Film lawyers are closely involved with the complicated banking and secured lending transactions that ensure financing for a film. A trend for lending institutions to insure their loans to film production companies has led to a raft of related litigation.

- TV lawyers tend to be drafted in for specific purposes relating to the making of a programme: engaging performers; negotiating contracts; negotiating distribution and worldwide rights issues and defamation claims. As such, they need knowledge of compliance, defamation, privacy, confidence and finance law.

music lawyers

- Advise the three key components of the music industry: major recording companies, independent labels and talent (including record producers and songwriters as well as artists).
- Advise on contracts, such as those between labels and bands, or between labels and third parties, eg websites selling downloads and ringtones. The frequent breakdown of relationships, say when a band splits, together with the subsequent disputes over royalty payments and ownership of music copyright mean that litigation is not uncommon.
- Offer contentious and non-contentious copyright and trade mark advice relating to music, image rights and merchandising. Ensure correct crediting and royalty payments when other artists sample songs.
- Offer criminal advice when the things get truly rock n' roll. Imagine being Pete Doherty's lawyer...

theatre and publishing lawyers

- A small but select group of predominantly London lawyers advises theatre and opera companies, producers, agents and actors on contracts, funding and sponsorship/merchandising.
- Publishing companies and newspapers without an in-house legal team seek advice on contractual, licensing, copyright and libel matters.

the realities of the job

- Complete immersion in the chosen media allied to a good grasp of copyright and contract law are the basics, although a creative attitude to problem solving and a steady disposition help when faced with all those nervous artistic types.
- Fighting your way past the massive competition for a job in the entertainment sector may leave you feeling like the winner of Pop Idol, but it's important to remember that you're not. Keep your inner Simon Cowell on standby, to remind you that you are a lawyer and clients look to you for a rigour and discipline they may rarely exercise themselves.
- This is a sector where who you know makes a big difference, so expect to put in serious time getting your face known. And maybe dress more snappily than your colleagues in the tax department.

sports law put simply

Strictly speaking an industry sector rather than a specific legal discipline. Many firms boasting a sports law capability draw on the expertise of lawyers from several practice groups; relatively few have dedicated teams. But given the massive amounts of money floating around football, rugby, tennis, darts and most sports you care to mention, the desire to join the sports party is understandable. Whether representing a club, individual sportsperson, governing body, or company interested in offering sponsorship or funding, or working in-house at a sports broadcaster, a sports lawyer's workload encompasses regulatory matters, advice on media, advertising and image rights, plus general corporate and commercial advice.

sports lawyers' work involves:

- Contract negotiations, be they between clubs and sportspeople, agents and players, sporting institutions and sponsors, broadcasters and sports governing bodies.
- All manner of employment law issues. In the average football club, for example, there are contract renegotiations, transfers and player loans, player registration, work permits to be secured, internal disciplinary matters and defence of disciplinary matters at a governing body level, as well as all the employment issues associated with running a large institution with a large and varied workforce.
- Corporate and commercial work in the form of takeovers or public offerings (think Malcolm Glazer's aggressive and successful bid for Manchester United), debt restructuring and bankruptcy, and the securing and structuring of credit to finance stadium redevelopments.
- Intellectual property matters in a world in which official merchandise is a major part of sports teams' income. Litigation may be necessary to protect those income sources. Likewise, individual sportspeople's image rights have become increasingly valuable and require protection, often taking a central role in contractual negotiations.
- A variety of issues relating to the friction between sports regulations and EU or national law. In the field of competition law, the authorities ruled that Sky's football coverage in the UK constitutes an unfair monopoly and have forced wider broadcasting. Meanwhile, the UK government is considering returning cricket to the status of sporting national treasure, which would require coverage via domestic broadcasters. Then there's regulatory compliance within a sport, be it financial regulations or drugs policies, which can all easily lead to courtroom action or governing body hearings.

- Reputation management and criminal advice. The combination of young sportspeople, massive salaries and celebrity status is a heady one with sometimes unfortunate consequences. Whether it's combatting kiss and tell allegations, an invasion of privacy, or defending clients against more serious allegations of rape or affray, a sports lawyer can be kept very busy.

the realities of the job

- Sports lawyers need to be proactive, passionate and creative and have bags of commercial nous. It is sometimes said that a sports lawyer operates as a consultant, not a solicitor.
- Excellent interpersonal skills are essential, as is a capacity to see both sides of an argument. In transfers in any sport, lawyers can be dealing with several clubs, the clubs' lawyers, a player and multiple agents, all determined to secure the best deal possible.
- In multimillion-pound sporting industries, mistakes or loopholes will be ruthlessly exploited. Witness the current £150 million litigation by The Football League against Hammonds for allegedly failing to protect its interests during negotiations with ONdigital (now ITV Digital).
- You need to be able to deal with people involved at all levels of all sports, some of whom may be deeply conservative, structurally opaque and suspicious of outsiders.

current issues

- There have been developments in libel law. The 'qualified privilege' defence previously established in 2001 in Reynolds v Times Newspapers was re-examined when George Galloway MP sued The Daily Telegraph, and again in the case of Henry v BBC. The trend away from jury trials and towards trial by judge continues.

- The courts are now dealing with cases of ISPs being sued for publishing material sent by third parties through their servers or for hosting material on their websites.
- The courts have continued to develop the law of privacy.
- The popularity among claimants of no-win, no-fee Conditional Fee Agreements has led to an increase in the number of privacy and defamation claims brought.
- In the world of sport, the 2012 Olympics are keeping lawyers busy and football has filled the headlines. The sale of the Premier League's television and radio rights achieved a higher than ever figure and these were separated into a number of different packages and sold separately, both domestically and internationally. Several Premier League clubs have been the subject of corporate takeovers.
- On the regulatory side of football, there was an investigation by the English Football Association into agents and bungs following a BBC Panorama programme which indicated that illegal payments are rife in the sport.
- Although record companies' profits are on a downward spiral, consumer enthusiasm for new music and back catalogues has never been higher. Lawyers are busy working on rights issues as file shareing and illegal downloading cause headaches for those trying to turn a profit.
- Sale and leaseback schemes in the film industry are now a thing of the past. New tax credits for the financing of films have resulted in less collaboration between British film-makers but bigger budgets for projects.

solicitors

leading firms from Chambers UK 2008

Media & Entertainment: Broadcasting
Best of the UK

Band 1
DLA Piper UK LLP *London*
Olswang *London*

Band 2
Goodman Derrick LLP *London*
Reed Smith Richards Butler LLP *London*
Wiggin LLP *London*

Band 3
Field Fisher Waterhouse LLP *London*
Herbert Smith LLP *London*
Lovells LLP *London*
Taylor Wessing LLP *London*

Band 4
Baker & McKenzie LLP *London*
Berwin Leighton Paisner LLP *London*

Media & Entertainment: Music
Best of the UK

Band 1
Clintons *London*
Russells *London*
Sheridans *London*

Band 2
Bray & Krais Solicitors *London*
Forbes Anderson Free *London*
Lee & Thompson *London*

Band 3
Eversheds LLP *London*
Hamlins LLP *London*

Band 4
Michael Simkins LLP *London*
Olswang *London*
Swan Turton *London*
Wiggin LLP *London*

Band 5
Charles Russell LLP *London*
Collins Long *London*
Davenport Lyons *London*
Harbottle & Lewis LLP *London*

Media & Entertainment: Corporate
Best of the UK

Band 1
Berwin Leighton Paisner LLP *London*
Clifford Chance LLP *London*
DLA Piper UK LLP *London*
Field Fisher Waterhouse LLP *London*
Harbottle & Lewis LLP *London*
Herbert Smith LLP *London*
Linklaters *London*
Lovells LLP *London*
Mayer Brown *London*
Olswang *London*
Reed Smith Richards Butler LLP *London*
Travers Smith *London*
Wiggin LLP *London*

Media & Entertainment: Film & TV Finance and Production
Best of the UK

Band 1
Olswang *London*
Reed Smith Richards Butler LLP *London*
SJ Berwin LLP *London*

Band 2
Davenport Lyons *London*
Harbottle & Lewis LLP *London*
Lee & Thompson *London*
Wiggin LLP *London*

Band 3
DLA Piper UK LLP *London*
Howard Kennedy *London*
Michael Simkins LLP *London*
Sheridans *London*

Media & Entertainment: Computer Games
Best of the UK

Band 1
Bird & Bird *London*
Bristows *London*
DLA Piper UK LLP *London*
Harbottle & Lewis LLP *London*
LG *London*
Lovells LLP *London*

Defamation/Reputation Management
Best of the UK

Band 1
Carter-Ruck *London*
Davenport Lyons *London*
David Price Solicitors & Advocates *London*
Farrer & Co *London*
Reynolds Porter Chamberlain LLP *London*
Schillings *London*

Band 2
Olswang *London*
Wiggin LLP *London*

Band 3
Addleshaw Goddard LLP *London*
Charles Russell LLP *London*
Harbottle & Lewis LLP *London*
Simons Muirhead & Burton *London*

Band 4
Bindman & Partners *London*
Finers Stephens Innocent *London*
Foot Anstey *Exeter*
Russell Jones & Walker *London*
Taylor Wessing LLP *London*

Band 5
Clifford Chance LLP *London*
Dechert LLP *London*
Goodman Derrick LLP *London*
Lee & Thompson *London*
Lewis Silkin LLP *London*
Mishcon de Reya *London*
Reed Smith Richards Butler LLP *London*
Swan Turton *London*

Band 6
Atkins *London*
Best & Soames *London*
Brabners Chaffe Street *Liverpool*
Cobbetts LLP *Manchester*
Eversheds LLP *London*
Howard Kennedy *London*
M Law *London*
Pannone LLP *Manchester*
Taylor Macmillan LLP *London*
Teacher Stern Selby *London*

sports, media and entertainment law (continued)

Media & Entertainment: Publishing

Best of the UK

Band 1

DLA Piper UK LLP *London*

Band 2

Finers Stephens Innocent *London*

Taylor Wessing LLP *London*

Band 3

Arnold & Porter (UK) LLP *London*

Blake Lapthorn Tarlo Lyons *Oxford*

Davenport Lyons *London*

Farrer & Co *London*

Harbottle & Lewis LLP *London*

Manches LLP *London*

Olswang *London*

Reynolds Porter Chamberlain *London*

Swan Turton *London*

Band 4

Best & Soames *London*

Lewis Silkin LLP *London*

Pinsent Masons *London*

Media & Entertainment: Theatre

Best of the UK

Band 1

Clintons *London*

Harbottle & Lewis LLP *London*

Band 2

Bates Wells & Braithwaite *London*

Michael Simkins LLP *London*

Sheridans *London*

Sport: Horse Racing & Equestrian

The Regions

Band 1

Ashfords *Exeter*

Edmondson Hall *Newmarket*

Taylor Vinters *Cambridge*

Withy King *Marlborough*

Sport

London

Band 1

Bird & Bird

DLA Piper UK LLP

Band 2

Couchman Harrington Associates

Farrer & Co

Band 3

Charles Russell LLP

Olswang

Band 4

Addleshaw Goddard LLP

Collyer Bristow LLP

Denton Wilde Sapte

Field Fisher Waterhouse LLP

Freshfields Bruckhaus Deringer

Harbottle & Lewis LLP

Herbert Smith LLP

K&L Gates

Michael Simkins LLP

Teacher Stern Selby

Band 5

Bates Wells & Braithwaite

Clintons

Fladgate Fielder

Hammonds

Macfarlanes

McDermott Will & Emery UK LLP

Onside Law LLP

Slaughter and May

Wiggin LLP

Sport

Wales

Band 1

Hugh James *Cardiff*

Band 2

Loosemores *Cardiff*

Band 3

Dolmans *Cardiff*

Sport

The Regions

Band 1

Brabners Chaffe Street *Manchester*

Band 2

Addleshaw Goddard LLP *Leeds,*

Manchester

Clarke Willmott *Southampton, Bristol*

George Davies Solicitors *Manchester*

McCormicks *Harrogate*

Band 3

Halliwells LLP *Manchester*

Hill Dickinson LLP *Liverpool*

IPS Law LLP *Manchester*

Osborne Clarke *Bristol*

Walker Morris *Leeds*

Advertising & Marketing

Best of the UK

Band 1

Lewis Silkin LLP *London*

Osborne Clarke *London*

Band 2

Addleshaw Goddard LLP *London*

Hammonds *London*

Macfarlanes *London*

Swan Turton *London*

Taylor Wessing LLP *London*

Wragge & Co LLP *London*

Band 3

DLA Piper UK LLP *London*

LG *London*

Lovells LLP *London*

Mayer Brown *London*

Olswang *London*

Band 4

Baker & McKenzie LLP *London*

CMS Cameron McKenna LLP *London*

Field Fisher Waterhouse LLP *London*

Harbottle & Lewis LLP *London*

Kaye Scholer LLP *London*

Reynolds Porter Chamberlain *London*

tax law

put simply

Good tax advice saves money, and clients are happy to pay for it. The solicitor's job is to know the law inside out – no small task given that the Chancellor amends the tax regime every Budget day – and to ensure that clients structure their business deals or day-to-day operations such that they take advantage of breaks and loopholes while staying on the right side of the law.

On occasion matters veer into the territory of litigation. A case brought by Marks & Spencer against the Revenue in late 2005 earned the retailer's lawyers considerable kudos. The case found that UK tax legislation does not comply with European law, and that the Revenue could be liable for millions of pounds of repayments. Other companies swiftly cottoned on and are now seeking similar recompense in the form of copycat claims, spawning an influx of work for lawyers.

who does what

Private practitioners' work divides into four main headings:

- Tax planning – making sure that clients understand the tax ramifications of the purchase, ownership and disposal of their assets, including advice on structuring corporate portfolios in the most tax-efficient way.
- Transactional advice – working with corporate and other transactional lawyers on the structure of, say, an M&A deal, a joint venture or the acquisition of a large property portfolio. The tax lawyer's advice may determine not only how the deal moves forwards, but also whether it does at all.
- Ad hoc advice – colleagues from across the firm will ring up with quick queries on everything from VAT to their own income tax returns.
- Litigation and investigations – when a company is being investigated or prosecuted by HM Revenue & Customs for not paying enough tax. Perhaps the company believes it has been charged too much and wants to appeal. Litigation is always conducted against or brought by the government, so you could say that all private practice tax litigators have a common enemy.

working for HM Revenue & Customs:

- Investigating companies and bringing prosecutions.
- Advising on how new laws apply to different situations.
- Defending cases brought against the government.

the realities of the job

- This is an intellectually rigorous area of law and ideally suited to brainiacs, which is probably why tax lawyers have an anoraky image. Despite being (for the most part) inaccurate, it remains unlikely that announcing yourself as a tax lawyer will impress anyone at parties.
- Corporate tax lawyers are highly paid, treated well by their colleagues and find intellectual stimulation in their work.
- There can be an element of drama on the litigation side; elsewhere it is rarely cut and thrust. That said, clients are now demanding of their lawyers not only the ability to translate and implement complex tax legislation but also a savvy awareness of how to structure deals in a legitimate and tax-efficient way that bypasses trouble from the Revenue. To some extent this encroaches on what was traditionally accountancy firm territory, to the consternation of many an accountant. However, it is the combination of bean-countery know-how and legal expertise that clients are increasingly calling for.
- Frequent changes in the law mean you'll never stop learning. Put another way, your briefcase will always contain homework.
- If you don't already wear specs, you will after a

couple of years of poring over all that black letter law. The UK has more pages of tax legislation than almost every other country.

- Extra qualifications, such as the Chartered Tax Adviser exams, will be useful.
- It is not uncommon for lawyers to switch between government jobs and private practice. A number of tax barristers were once solicitors.

current issues

- The recent merger between the Inland Revenue and HM Customs & Excise (forming HMRC) has led to a more aggressive attitude to clamping down on tax avoidance. Other changes in the past three years, including rules relating to the disclosure of tax avoidance schemes, have also made HMRC more likely to clampdown on offenders. Law firms with tax practices that were once strictly transactional are building their litigation capabilities.

- Real Estate Investment Trusts (REITs), now allow property portfolios to be invested in trusts to, among other things, avoid capital gains tax. A popular mechanism already in the USA, it is estimated that the REIT market could be worth billions of pounds.

- London is becoming the nerve centre for the structuring of global tax transactions. A buoyant M&A market is generating big-ticket work, and corporate finance and capital markets transactions with a tax backbone are in plentiful supply. Tax structuring work in private equity and securitisation is similarly abundant and hedge funds are a major source of work.

- Law firms have come into their own in relation to tax advice. Before Enron it looked like accountancy firms were taking over. Aside from Sarbanes Oxley restrictions, clients prefer to take advice separately from their auditors. A number of non-lawyer tax consultants are moving to law firms, some with the idea of requalifying.

leading firms from Chambers UK 2008

Tax: Contentious
Best of the UK
Band 1
Dorsey & Whitney *London*
McGrigors LLP *London*

Band 2
Burges Salmon LLP *Bristol*
DLA Piper UK LLP *London*
Herbert Smith LLP *London*
Irwin Mitchell *Sheffield*
Reynolds Porter Chamberlain *London*

Tax
The South
Band 1
Osborne Clarke *Bristol*

Band 2
Burges Salmon LLP *Bristol*

Band 3
Blake Lapthorn Tarlo Lyons *Portsmouth*

Band 4
Ashfords *Exeter*

Tax
Midlands
Band 1
Pinsent Masons *Birmingham*
Wragge & Co LLP *Birmingham*

Band 2
DLA Piper UK LLP *Birmingham*
Eversheds LLP *Nottingham*
Hammonds *Birmingham*

Band 3
Bevan Brittan LLP *Birmingham*
Mills & Reeve LLP *Cambridge*

Tax
London
Band 1
Freshfields Bruckhaus Deringer
Linklaters
Slaughter and May

Band 2
Allen & Overy LLP
Clifford Chance LLP

Band 3
Ashurst
Herbert Smith LLP
Macfarlanes
SJ Berwin LLP

Band 4
Berwin Leighton Paisner LLP
Kirkland & Ellis International LLP
Lovells LLP
McDermott Will & Emery UK LLP
Norton Rose
Olswang
Shearman & Sterling LLP
Simmons & Simmons
Skadden, Arps, Slate, Meagher & Flom
Travers Smith

Band 5
Cleary Gottlieb Steen & Hamilton LLP
Debevoise & Plimpton LLP
Latham & Watkins LLP
Nabarro

Band 6
Denton Wilde Sapte
Fried, Frank, Harris, Shriver & Jacobson
Jones Day
Shepherd and Wedderburn LLP
Weil, Gotshal & Manges LLP

Tax
The North
Band 1
Addleshaw Goddard LLP *Leeds*
Eversheds LLP *Leeds*
Pinsent Masons *Leeds*

Band 2
Dickinson Dees LLP *Newcastle upon Tyne*
Hammonds *Leeds*

Band 3
Walker Morris *Leeds*
Ward Hadaway *Newcastle upon Tyne*

Tax: Structured Finance
London
Band 1
Allen & Overy LLP *London*
Clifford Chance LLP *London*
Debevoise & Plimpton LLP *London*
Denton Wilde Sapte *London*
Freshfields Bruckhaus Deringer *London*
Herbert Smith LLP *London*
Linklaters *London*
McDermott Will & Emery UK LLP *London*
Norton Rose *London*
Skadden, Arps, Slate, Meagher & Flom (UK) LLP *London*
Slaughter and May *London*
Weil, Gotshal & Manges LLP *London*

technology, telecoms & outsourcing

put simply

Technology lawyers differentiate themselves from more general commercial advisers by their specific industry know-how. They have to combine a keen understanding of the latest developments and advances in various technologies with a thorough knowledge of the ever-changing law that regulates, protects and licenses them. As forms of media and new technologies converge (think movies via cable, TV news to your mobile phone, record companies selling songs on the Internet), clients rely on Technology lawyers' skills of innovation and imagination in offering rigorous legal solutions to maximise and protect income and ideas.

As the dotcom crash fades in the memory, Technology law is once again a thriving and hectic sector. The majority of the top fifty firms possess dedicated groups of lawyers, there are specialists within the corporate/commercial groups of many more medium-sized firms, and there are numerous smaller specialist outfits. In short, there are plenty of job opportunities in this appetising and sexy area of law, in both the contentious and non-contentious spheres.

who does what

Technology lawyers:

- Advise on commercial transactions and draft the requisite documents to implement them. For example, a large public body or a multinational company might be outsourcing its IT functions or procuring a new system. There is a heavy emphasis on risk management advice, such as advising on the way in which a software agreement can prevent potential litigation in the future.
- Assist in the resolution of disputes. Clients in the technology sector (as in most others) tend to want to avoid the cost and effort involved with lengthy, protracted litigation. In addition, technology suppliers commonly have long-term working relationships with their customers, and realise that a heated punch-up in court would be detrimental to future business. Consequently, much of the litigator's work involves arbitration or other settlement procedures. Many disputes tend to be in relation to software or hardware that doesn't do exactly what it says on the tin, or simply doesn't work at all.
- Help clients police their IT and web-based reputation and assets. Cyber-squatting, ownership of database information and the Data Protection Act are common topics.
- Give clients mainstream commercial, corporate and finance advice.

the realities of the job

- You need to be familiar with the latest regulations and their potential impact on your client's business. How do you make the purchase of a ringtone by text a legally binding contract? Does a website need a disclaimer? What measures should your client take to protect data about individuals gathered from a website? Do sports highlights shown on mobile phones conflict with other broadcasting agreements or governing body regulations?
- You need a good grasp of the jargon of your chosen industry, firstly to write contracts, but also so you can understand your clients' instructions. You have to know your WLAN from LAN, your 3G from GPRS and your ISPs from your SMSs. Read trade journals or magazines like Media Lawyer and Wired, or magazines such as Computer Weekly or New Scientist.
- The ability to think laterally and creatively is a must, especially when the application of a client's technology or content throws up entirely new issues.
- Putting yourself about and being seen is important in a fast-changing industry with quick turnover, where law firms are forever merging or being founded.

In this 'frontier' world, gut instinct matters. The in-house lawyer who was laughed out of BT six years ago when he joined little-known Internet auction site eBbay is the one smiling now. He recently moved to head up the legal team of eBay's broadband-based phone service Skype, a perfect example of the convergence of Internet and telephone technology that is forcing traditional telecoms companies like BT to rethink their strategies.

current issues

- Investor confidence in the technology sector has returned after the damaging dot.comedy years, and IT budgets, particularly in the private sector, have increased. Companies find it necessary to invest in the latest technology to gain or maintain a competitive edge. All this means work for private practice lawyers although in-house advisers can handle many matters.

- Legislation and regulations, such as those upholding the freedom of information regime and the waste electronic and electrical equipment disposal regime, are also creating work. Crossborder issues relating to data protection are becoming more common.

- Now that every player in the top 100 offers some form of TMT, the onus is on law firms to ascertain what will make them most competitive in a crowded market. They are refining or reshaping their practices, and their long-term strategies.

- As early as the late 1980s companies began outsourcing their IT functions. Having tested the waters with 'ITO' agreements, many leading companies have now become sufficiently emboldened to pass more of their business process functions to third-party service providers in business process outsourcings (BPOs) covering functions such as human resources, finance and accounting. In recent times there has been a great deal of activity in

relation to UK public-sector procurement and the financial services sector. Multi-jurisdictional outsourcings are also on the rise.

- Outsourcing lawyers represent customers and suppliers in the negotiation and drafting of outsourcing agreements. Customer clients range from government departments and local authorities to owner-managed businesses and large corporates. On the supplier side, key outsourcing service providers include the likes of Accenture, EDS and Capgemini. A distinction needs to be drawn between the work done in the private sector and that done in the public sector. High-end private sector work involves complex, high-value, often groundbreaking and increasingly multi-jurisdictional outsourcings, deals most often done by magic circle firms or large US outfits with London offices. Outsourcings in the public sector involve representing UK government departments, local authorities or suppliers of services to those entities. This work can be more commoditised than private-sector work, with the value of the deals often much lower. National firms such as DLA Piper, Addleshaw Goddard and Eversheds have cornered the market in public sector outsourcings, partly due to the fact that they can offer more competitive rates. Having said that, the national firms also advise on a significant number of private-sector outsourcings, especially domestic deals.

- The long-term success of outsourcing agreements is aided by the involvement of experienced specialists, rather than general corporate or commercial lawyers. If outsourcing negotiations are approached in an adversarial, point-scoring way, this can cause rifts in the relationships between parties, which in turn increases the likelihood of an agreement needing to be renegotiated before the expiry of its initial term. In a worst-case scenario a breakdown can lead to actual dispute.

technology, telecoms & outsourcing (continued)

leading firms from Chambers UK 2008

Information Technology
London

Band 1
Baker & McKenzie LLP
Bird & Bird
DLA Piper UK LLP
Field Fisher Waterhouse LLP

Band 2
Allen & Overy LLP
Herbert Smith LLP
Kemp Little LLP
Linklaters
Lovells LLP
Milbank, Tweed, Hadley & McCloy LLP
Morrison & Foerster MNP
Olswang
Osborne Clarke
Pinsent Masons
Taylor Wessing LLP *London*

Band 3
Clifford Chance LLP
Freshfields Bruckhaus Deringer
Latham & Watkins LLP
Mayer Brown
Norton Rose
Simmons & Simmons
Slaughter and May

Band 4
Addleshaw Goddard LLP
Barlow Lyde & Gilbert LLP
Berwin Leighton Paisner LLP
Bristows
Denton Wilde Sapte
Eversheds LLP
K&L Gates
LG
Nabarro
Pillsbury Winthrop Shaw Pittman LLP
Reynolds Porter Chamberlain LLP

Band 5
Blake Lapthorn Tarlo Lyons
Harbottle & Lewis LLP
Technology Law Alliance

Information Technology
Thames Valley

Band 1
Boyes Turner *Reading*
Clark Holt *Swindon*
Manches LLP *Oxford*
NetworkLaw Limited *Bracknell*
Osborne Clarke *Reading*

Band 2
Moorcrofts LLP *Marlow*
Olswang Thames Valley *Reading*

Band 3
Rouse Legal *Oxford*

Information Technology
The South

Band 1
Blake Lapthorn Tarlo Lyons *Southampton*
Bond Pearce LLP *Southampton*
DMH Stallard *Crawley*

Band 2
Clyde & Co LLP *Guildford*
Shadbolt & Co LLP *Reigate*

Information Technology
The North

Band 1
Addleshaw Goddard LLP *Leeds*
DLA Piper UK LLP *Leeds*
Pinsent Masons *Leeds, Manchester*

Band 2
Eversheds LLP *Leeds*

Band 3
Halliwells LLP *Manchester*
Nabarro *Sheffield*

Information Technology
Midlands

Band 1
Wragge & Co LLP *Birmingham*

Band 2
Pinsent Masons *Birmingham*
Shoosmiths *Nottingham*

Band 3
Eversheds LLP *Nottingham*
Technology Law Alliance *Birmingham*

Band 4
Martineau Johnson *Birmingham*
Mills & Reeve LLP *Birmingham*

Information Technology
South West

Band 1
Beachcroft LLP *Bristol*
Burges Salmon LLP *Bristol*
Osborne Clarke *Bristol*

Band 2
Ashfords *Bristol*
Foot Anstey *Exeter, Plymouth*

Band 3
Bevan Brittan LLP *Bristol*
Rickerbys *Cheltenham*

Information Technology
Wales

Band 1
Eversheds LLP *Cardiff*
Geldards LLP *Cardiff*

Band 1
Hugh James *Cardiff*

Band 1
Morgan Cole *Cardiff*

solicitors

Outsourcing	Data Protection	Telecommunications
Best of the UK	**Best of the UK**	**Best of the UK**
Band 1	**Band 1**	**Band 1**
Baker & McKenzie LLP *London*	Bird & Bird *London*	Allen & Overy LLP *London*
Bird & Bird *London*	Field Fisher Waterhouse LLP *London*	Baker & McKenzie LLP *London*
DLA Piper UK LLP *London*	Linklaters *London*	Bird & Bird *London*
Latham & Watkins LLP *London*	Pinsent Masons *London*	Linklaters *London*
Milbank, Tweed, Hadley & McCloy *London*		
	Band 2	**Band 2**
Band 2	Allen & Overy LLP *London*	Clifford Chance LLP *London*
Addleshaw Goddard LLP *London*	Baker & McKenzie LLP *London*	Field Fisher Waterhouse LLP *London*
Allen & Overy LLP *London*	Bristows *London*	Freshfields Bruckhaus Deringer *London*
Clifford Chance LLP *London*	Clifford Chance LLP *London*	Herbert Smith LLP *London*
Field Fisher Waterhouse LLP *London*	DLA Piper UK LLP *London*	Kemp Little LLP *London*
Freshfields Bruckhaus Deringer *London*	Freshfields Bruckhaus Deringer *London*	Mayer Brown *London*
Linklaters *London*	Herbert Smith LLP *London*	Olswang *London*
Mayer Brown *London*	Hunton & Williams *London*	
Morrison & Foerster MNP *London*	Lovells LLP *London*	**Band 3**
Simmons & Simmons *London*	Olswang *London*	Addleshaw Goddard LLP *London*
Slaughter and May *London*	Slaughter and May *London*	Ashurst *London*
	White & Case LLP *London*	Charles Russell LLP *London*
Band 3		DLA Piper UK LLP *London*
Berwin Leighton Paisner LLP *London*		Eversheds LLP *London*
Lovells LLP *London*		Simmons & Simmons *London*
Morgan, Lewis & Bockius *London*		Taylor Wessing LLP *London*
Norton Rose *London*		White & Case LLP *London*
Pillsbury Winthrop Shaw Pittman *London*		
Pinsent Masons *Birmingham*		**Band 4**
Wragge & Co LLP *Birmingham*		Dechert LLP *London*
		Denton Wilde Sapte *London*
Band 4		K&L Gates *London*
Ashurst *London*		Lovells LLP *London*
Barlow Lyde & Gilbert LLP *London*		Osborne Clarke *London*
Beachcroft LLP *London*		Preiskel & Co LLP *London*
Blake Lapthorn Tarlo Lyons *London*		Towerhouse Consulting *London*
Browne Jacobson LLP *Nottingham*		Wragge & Co LLP *London*
Charles Russell LLP *London*		
CMS Cameron McKenna *London*		
Denton Wilde Sapte *London*		
Eversheds LLP *London*		
Herbert Smith LLP *London*		
Jones Day *London*		
Kemp Little LLP *London*		
Mills & Reeve LLP *Cambridge*		
Osborne Clarke *Bristol*		
Shoosmiths *Milton Keynes*		
SJ Berwin LLP *London*		
Stephenson Harwood *London*		
Taylor Wessing LLP *London*		

international opportunities

The idea of the international law firm is far from new: UK law firms have ventured overseas since the 19th century. What has changed in recent times is the number of firms with offices overseas and the desire on the part of the largest firms to plant flags all over the globe. The Brits weren't the first in the game but they've certainly made up for lost time. The largest firm worldwide is our very own Clifford Chance, though it still has some way to go to catch up with Baker & McKenzie for the prize for most offices in most countries.

There are so many UK and US firms with overseas networks that students are spoilt for choice and keeping track of which firms are opening or closing offices in different countries is almost a full-time occupation. Wherever possible, we have mentioned the main changes from the past year in our **True Picture** reports. What we can never predict is exactly who is going to merge with whom.

The last five years have been characterised by European mergers and alliances as well as transatlantic tie-ups. Among the firms that have completed US-UK tie-ups in the past decade are Clifford Chance, Mayer Brown, K&L Gates, Jones Day, Dechert, DLA Piper and Reed Smith Richards Butler. The spotlight is currently on two US firms that are about to merge – LeBoeuf Lamb and Dewey Ballantine.

The Americans have had a major influence on UK law firms in London since a wave of them came over to our capital in the mid-1990s. In response to this new competition, the UK firms have had to increase salaries, which in turn has led to a trend for raising lawyers' billing targets. At partner level, too, the UK firms have had to sharpen up. A drift of hotshot London partners from UK firms to American firms can, again, be explained by the higher remuneration on offer from the Americans.

The big UK and American firms are canny operators. They understand that to survive in a competitive legal market it is necessary to have a network of offices (or relationships with overseas law firms) in those parts of the world where the economies are active and/or growing. China and India are of real interest, as are the Middle East and the oil and gas-rich parts of Central Asia.

What all this means for trainees is simple: international work in London and overseas seat opportunities. The following table summarises where the seat opportunities lie and which firms send trainees to each location. As for international work back in London, the exact nature of a firm's clientele and worldwide office footprint will determine what trainees see from day to day. At White & Case, for example, there is a considerable amount of project finance work conducted in conjunction with Eastern European and Central Asian offices. CMS Cameron McKenna's superb energy practice brings similar work to London. At LeBoeuf Lamb African LNG deals have flowed from the firm's strong energy clientele. Trowers & Hamlins' dominance in the Middle East brings work back to London, as does Wiggin's relationship with the five major film studios in Los Angeles and Lawrence Graham's relationships with Indian businesses. These firms' international interests are certainly not limited to these sectors, but the above examples usefully illustrate the point.

If international work interests you then consider whether you would want to remain at home in the UK during your training or have the guarantee of an overseas seat. If it is the latter then pick a firm where you can be certain of securing a foreign posting. The competition at some firms is tough, while at others everyone who wants to go does. The **True Picture** reports should help you here. One other thing to bear in mind is your ability to speak another language. If you are fluent in Russian, for example, you may be collared for Moscow instead of the New York opening you've got your eye on. It also follows that, where language skills would be useful – say in Italy – those who possess them will prove to be more-attractive candidates.

Although time abroad gives you experience of working in another jurisdiction, you'll not normally practise foreign law. An overseas seat is without doubt a very rewarding and challenging experience. It will usually be taken in an office that is smaller than your firm's UK office, and you will normally have greater responsibility. The trick to securing the most popular overseas seats is to wage an effective campaign of self-promotion and to get the prerequisite experience in the UK office before you go. The exact nature of this experience will depend on the type of seat taken abroad.

On arrival in a new country you don't need to worry about feeling too isolated. The local lawyers and staff will invariably be very happy to see you and welcome you into their office and probably also their homes. In some cities with a large influx of UK trainees there is a ready-made social scene and it's likely that the first thing to pop into your inbox will be an invite to meet the others. In Singapore, trainees make the most of the region by jetting off for group weekends on Malaysian or Indonesian islands. In Brussels they hook into the social scene attached to the vast EU machine. Another big plus is the free accommodation provided by the law firms. Usually, trainees are housed in their own apartments in smart areas close to a city's centre. It may be some time before they can afford such plush digs – and domestic help – back home.

For more info on life as a trainee in an overseas seat check out the **Global Opportunities** section of our web site

overseas seats – who goes there?

location	firm
Abu Dhabi	Clyde & Co, Reed Smith Richards Butler, Shearman & Sterling, Simmons & Simmons, Trowers & Hamlins
Almaty	Denton Wilde Sapte, White & Case
Amsterdam	Allen & Overy, Clifford Chance, Freshfields Bruckhaus Deringer, Linklaters, Norton Rose, Simmons & Simmons, Slaughter and May
Athens	Norton Rose
Auckland	Slaughter and May
Bahrain	Norton Rose, Trowers & Hamlins
Bangkok	Allen & Overy, Herbert Smith, Watson Farley & Williams
Beijing	Allen & Overy, Baker & McKenzie, Bird & Bird, Clifford Chance, Freshfields Bruckhaus Deringer, Herbert Smith, Linklaters, Vinson & Elkins
Berlin	SJ Berwin, Slaughter and May
Bratislava (Slovakia)	Allen & Overy
Brussels	Allen & Overy, Ashurst, Baker & McKenzie, Berwin Leighton Paisner, Bird & Bird, Cleary Gottlieb Steen & Hamilton, Clifford Chance, Cobbetts, Dechert, Dickinson Dees, Freshfields Bruckhaus Deringer, Hammonds, Herbert Smith, Latham & Watkins, Linklaters, Lovells, Mayer Brown, McDermott, Will & Emery, McGrigors, Nabarro, Norton Rose, Olswang, Simmons & Simmons, SJ Berwin, Slaughter and May, White & Case
Bucharest	CMS Cameron McKenna, Linklaters
Budapest	Allen & Overy, CMS Cameron McKenna, Linklaters
California	Dechert, Weil Gotshal & Manges
Chicago	Baker & McKenzie, Mayer Brown
Cologne	Freshfields Bruckhaus Deringer, Osborne Clarke
Copenhagen	Slaughter and May

location	firm
Dubai	Allen & Overy, Clifford Chance, Clyde & Co, Denton Wilde Sapte, DLA Piper, Freshfields Bruckhaus Deringer, Holman Fenwick & Willan, Linklaters, Lovells, Norton Rose, Pinsent Masons, Reed Smith Richards Butler, Simmons, Simmons, Trowers & Hamlins, Vinson & Elkins
Düsseldorf	Bird & Bird, Simmons & Simmons, Slaughter and May
Falkland Islands	McGrigers
Frankfurt	Allen & Overy, Ashurst, Bird & Bird, Clifford Chance, Freshfields Bruckhaus Deringer, Linklaters, Lovells, Norton Rose, Simmons & Simmons, SJ Berwin, Slaughter and May, Weil Gotshal & Manges, White & Case
Geneva	Collyer Bristow, Withers
The Hague	Bird & Bird
Helsinki	Slaughter and May
Hong Kong	Addleshaw Goddard, Allen & Overy, Barlow Lyde & Gilbert, Baker & McKenzie, Bird & Bird, Cleary Gottlieb Steen & Hamilton, Clifford Chance, Clyde & Co, DLA Piper, Freshfields Bruckhaus Deringer, Hammonds, Herbert Smith, Holman Fenwick & Willan, LeBoeuf Lamb, Linklaters, Lovells, Norton Rose, Orrick, Herrington & Sutcliffe, Reed Smith Richards Butler, Simmons & Simmons, Skadden, Slaughter and May, Stephenson Harwood, White & Case
Istanbul	Denton Wilde Sapte
Kiev	CMS Cameron McKenna
Luxembourg	Allen & Overy, Linklaters, Slaughter and May
Madrid	Allen & Overy, Ashurst, Baker & McKenzie, Bird & Bird, Clifford Chance, Freshfields Bruckhaus Deringer, Hammonds, Linklaters, SJ Berwin, Slaughter and May

location	firm
Milan	Allen & Overy, Ashurst, Bird & Bird, Clifford Chance, Freshfields Bruckhaus Deringer, Linklaters, Norton Rose, Simmons & Simmons, Slaughter and May, White & Case, Withers
Moscow	Allen & Overy, Baker & McKenzie, Cleary Gottlieb Steen & Hamilton, Clifford Chance, CMS Cameron McKenna, Denton Wilde Sapte, DLA Piper, Freshfields Bruckhaus Deringer, Herbert Smith, LeBoeuf Lamb, Linklaters, Lovells, Norton Rose, Salans, Vinson & Elkins, White & Case
Munich	Bird & Bird, Clifford Chance, Linklaters, Norton Rose, Osborne Clarke, SJ Berwin
New York	Allen & Overy, Baker & McKenzie, Cleary Gottlieb Steen & Hamilton, Clifford Chance, Freshfields Bruckhaus Deringer, Linklaters, Shearman & Sterling, Slaughter and May
Oman	Denton Wilde Sapte, Trowers & Hamlins
Oslo	Slaughter and May
Paris	Allen & Overy, Ashurst, Bird & Bird, Cleary Gottlieb Steen & Hamilton, Clifford Chance, Denton Wilde Sapte, Eversheds, Freshfields Bruckhaus Deringer, Hammonds, Herbert Smith, Holman Fenwick & Willan, Latham & Watkins, LeBoeuf Lamb, Linklaters, Lovells, Norton Rose, Orrick Herrington & Sutcliffe, Reed Smith Richards Butler, Shadbolt & Co, Simmons & Simmons, Slaughter and May, SJ Berwin, Travers Smith, Watson Farley & Williams, Weil Gotshal & Manges, White & Case
Philadelphia	Dechert
Piraeus	Clyde & Co, Holman Fenwick & Willan, Hill Dickinson, Ince & Co, Reed Smith Richards Butler, Watson Farley & Williams

location	firm
Prague	Allen & Overy, Clifford Chance, CMS Cameron McKenna, Linklaters, Norton Rose, Slaughter and May, White & Case
Rome	Allen & Overy, Bird & Bird, Clifford Chance, Linklaters
São Paulo	Clifford Chance, Linklaters
Shanghai	Clifford Chance, Eversheds, Freshfields Bruckhaus Deringer, Herbert Smith, Linklaters
Singapore	Allen & Overy, Clifford Chance, Clyde & Co, DLA Piper, Herbert Smith, Latham & Watkins, Linklaters, Lovells, Norton Rose, Shearman & Sterling, Stephenson Harwood, Watson Farley & Williams, White & Case
Sofia	CMS Cameron McKenna
Stockholm	Bird & Bird, Slaughter and May, White & Case
Sydney	Baker & McKenzie
Toronto	Baker & McKenzie, Ford & Warren
Tokyo	Allen & Overy, Baker & McKenzie, Clifford Chance, Freshfields Bruckhaus Deringer, Herbert Smith, Latham & Watkins, Linklaters, Lovells, Simmons & Simmons, Slaughter and May, White & Case
Turin	Hammonds
Vienna	Freshfields Bruckhaus Deringer
Warsaw	Allen & Overy, Clifford Chance, CMS Cameron McKenna, Linklaters
Washington	Dechert, Freshfields Bruckhaus Deringer

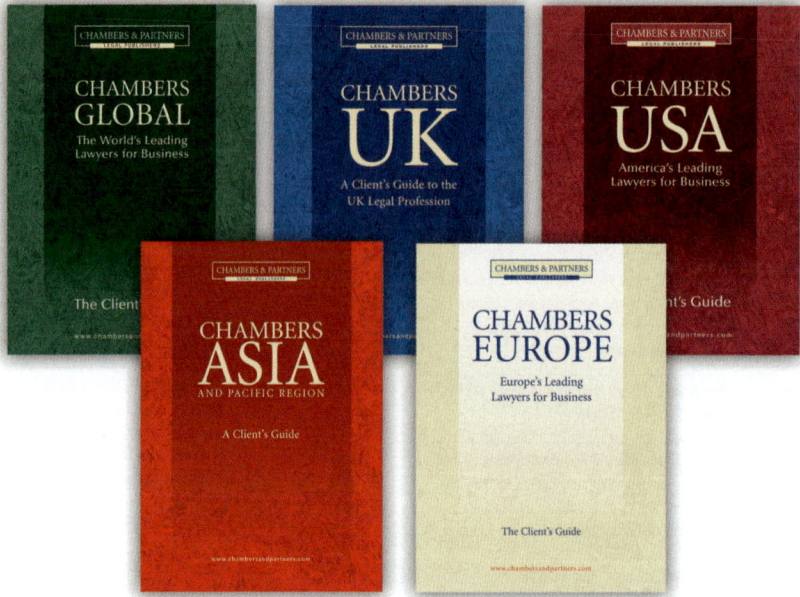

Chambers and Partners publishes a suite of legal guides that you should find helpful in your search for a training contract or pupillage.

- **Chambers UK** is the product of interviews with solicitors, barristers and their clients. It identifies the leading firms, sets and players across the full sweep of legal practice in the UK.

- **Chambers Global** sets out the results of our research into legal jurisdictions worldwide from Australia to Zambia. If you are considering a training contract with an international law firm, it's a must-read book.

- **Chambers USA** provides a more detailed analysis of the performance of the best firms across all US states.

- **Chambers Asia** covers 23 countries in one of the world's most dynamic legal markets.

- **Chambers Europe** looks at the leading law firms and individuals from Albania to Ukraine.

These guides can all be read at **www.chambersandpartners.com**.

the true picture

The True Picture reports on 150 firms in England and Wales, ranging from the international giants to small regional practices. Most handle commercial law, although many also offer private client experience. Others are general practice firms.

how we do our research

The 150 firms provide complete lists of their trainees. After checking the lists are complete, we randomly select a sample of individuals for telephone interviews. Our sources are guaranteed anonymity to give them the confidence to say exactly what they want. The True Picture is not shown to the law firms prior to publication; they see it for the first time when this book is published.

Trainees tell us why they chose their firm and why others might want to. We talk about seat allocation and the character and work of different departments. We ask about the hours and the after-hours fun, and we ascertain what happens to people on qualification. We look for the things trainees agree upon, and if they do not agree we present both sides of the argument.

We're bored by the tired lines used in many recruitment brochures. You know the ones that tell you Smashing, Great & Partners is a standout firm because of its friendly culture in which everybody is down to earth and where approachable partners operate an open-door policy. These traits are not the preserve of a few firms. What we try to focus on instead is the detail of what builds a firm's character.

our findings

This year, as last, a healthy job market has encouraged qualifiers to be pickier about the area of law in which they specialise after training and trainees to be more demanding about which seats they try. With the deals market buzzing, corporate departments have been run off their feet and the hours worked by corporate and finance lawyers are long. Several firms made corporate and/or finance seats compulsory for the first time and in 2007 the qualification market was characterised by a wealth of corporate and finance jobs. Unfortunately not everyone wanted to qualify into those areas and a good number of commercial firm's NQ's chose to jump ship rather than compromise on their goals.

If you intend to use retention rates as a determining factor in your choice of firm, do be wary of the statistics being bandied around. Law firms make their own rules on how to calculate retention rates – you may not be getting a full picture from them. For this reason we collect our own statistics and include them in each law firm feature. We have collated statistics since 2000 and publish them on our website. The results might surprise you.

We try not to concentrate too much on current market conditions when writing the True Picture, as we recognise that things may have changed by the time our readers start their training. Other things we just can't predict are law firm mergers or closures. Thankfully, the latter are rare, but mergers are a regular thing in the profession these days. When firms merge, trainees' contracts are honoured, though of course it does mean that new recruits find themselves in a different firm to the one they signed up with.

across the board:

- Some seats are more popular than others. The perfect example is employment law.
- Levels of responsibility vary between departments. In property you might have your own small files. In corporate you will generally work in a very junior capacity as part of a team.
- The experience in litigation depends entirely on the type of cases your firm handles; usually a trainee's responsibility is inversely proportionate to the value and complexity of a case. If your firm handles personal injury claims, you may have conduct of matters yourself. If your firm goes in for long-running financial services litigation or multi-jurisdictional matters, you

could be stuck for months on document management jobs. Your firm may even send you on a course rather than give you a litigation seat.

- In times of plenty, corporate and finance seats mean long hours, commonly climaxing in all-nighters. Again, the size and complexity of a deal will determine your role, but corporate and finance usually require the most teamwork.
- Most firms offer four six-month seats; some offer six four-month seats and others operate their own unique systems. Trainees switch departments and supervisors for each seat. Most share a room and work with a partner or senior assistant; others sit open plan, either with the rest of the team or with other trainees. Occasionally a trainee will even have their own room.
- All firms conduct appraisals, a minimum of one at the conclusion of each seat, and usually halfway through as well.
- Client secondments, where offered, are a great way to find out how to be a better lawyer by learning to understand a client's needs. They can be the highlight of a training contract.
- The Law Society requires all trainees to gain experience of both contentious and non-contentious work. Additionally, most firms have certain seats they require or prefer trainees to try. Some firms are very prescriptive, others flexible. Remember, a training contract is a time to explore legal practice to see what you're best at and most enjoy. You may surprise yourself.

jargonbusting

- agency work – making a court appearance for another firm that can't get to court
- all-nighter – working through the night
- cmc – a case management conference in court
- coco – company-commercial department/work
- dispute resolution – litigation, mediation, arbitration, etc
- grunt work – also known as donkey work, monkey work or even document jockeying. Administrative (and boring) yet essential tasks including photocopying, paginating, compiling court bundles and scheduling documents, bibling (putting together sets of all the relevant documents for a transaction), data room duty (supervising visitors to rooms full of important documents, helping them find things and making sure they don't steal them) and proof-reading or checking that documents are intact. Increasingly many of these tasks are being done electronically.
- high net worth individuals – rich people
- infant approvals – court authorisation for a settlement involving a minor
- mentor partner – a partner who will guide you and buy you lunch
- NQ – a newly-qualified solicitor
- PQE – post-qualification experience
- training partner – the partner who oversees the training scheme
- trainee partner – a trainee who acts like a partner

what kind of firm do I choose?

Your choice of firm will be based on location, size and the practice areas available... then it's a matter of chemistry. Some firms are stuffier; some are more industrious and some are very brand-aware and involve trainees heavily in marketing. Some work in modern open-plan offices; others occupy buildings long past their sell-by date. Some focus on international business; others are at the heart of their local business communities. Some concentrate on contentious work, others transactional. The combinations of these variables are endless.

and finally...

We hope the True Picture will help you decide on the firms you want to target. No matter how hard or how easy securing a training contract is for you, you'll want to end up with the right one.

the true picture firms

	Firms by size in UK**	City	Total English & Welsh trainees	Page
1	Government Legal Service	London	50	400
2	Eversheds LLP	London*	160	362
3	DLA Piper LLP	London*	164	349
4	Pinsent Masons	London*	125	567
5	Clifford Chance LLP	London	254	313
6	Linklaters	London	276	483
7	Allen & Overy LLP	London	240	219
8	CMS Cameron McKenna LLP	London*	120	323
9	Freshfields Bruckhaus Deringer	London	198	393
10	Addleshaw Goddard LLP	London*	88	215
11	Herbert Smith LLP	London	175	419
12	Berwin Leighton Paisner LLP	London	72	253
13	Beachcroft LLP	London*	76	250
14	Lovells	London	155	487
15	Slaughter and May	London	168	621
16	Norton Rose	London	101	541
17	Denton Wilde Sapte	London*	72	341
18	Ashurst	London	98	235
19	Hammonds	London*	80	407
20	Wragge & Co LLP	Brirmingham*	61	700
21	Mills & Reeve LLP	Cambridge*	45	524
22	Halliwells LLP	Manchester*	76	404
23	Nabarro	London*	52	537
24	SJ Berwin LLP	London	88	615
25	Blake Lapthorn Tarlo Lyons	Fareham*	31	271
26	Simmons & Simmons	London	100	609
27	Hill Dickinson	Liverpool*	32	427
28	Irwin Mitchell	Sheffield*	48	450
29	Shoosmiths	Northampton*	36	603
30	White & Case LLP	London	54	689
31	Osborne Clarke	Bristol*	42	550
32=	Burges Salmon LLP	Bristol	42	297
32=	Charles Russell LLP	London*	35	304
34	McGrigors LLP	London*	27	515
35	Dundas & Wilson	London*	9	356
36	Baker & McKenzie LLP	London	70	239
37	Mayer Brown	London	65	509
38	DWF	Liverpool*	27	359
39	Clyde & Co LLP	London*	48	317
40	Taylor Wessing LLP	London*	48	637
41	Reed Smith Richards Butler LLP	London*	57	575
42	Field Fisher Waterhouse LLP	London	36	369
43	Barlow Lyde & Gilbert LLP	London	39	243
44	Olswang	London*	48	545
45=	Reynolds Porter Chamberlain LLP	London*	32	579
45=	Bevan Brittan LLP	Bristol*	33	257
47	Trowers & Hamlins	London*	39	659
48=	Browne Jacobson LLP	Nottingham*	20	291
48=	Cobbetts LLP	Manchester*	50	327
48=	Macfarlanes	London	50	496
51	Dickinson Dees LLP	Newcastle*	32	345

**Firms are listed in order of size as measured by UK partner and solicitor figures provided to Chambers and Partners. *Head or primary UK office.

www.chambersstudent.co.uk

	Firms by size in UK**	City	Total English & Welsh trainees	Page
52	Travers Smith	London	36	653
53	Pannone LLP	Manchester*	35	556
54	Bird & Bird	London	31	267
55	HBJ Gateley Wareing LLP	Birmingham*	22	414
56	Lawrence Graham LLP	London	42	480
57	Watson Burton LLP	Newcastle*	18	675
58	Latham & Watkins	London	10	465
59	Farrer & Co	London	18	366
60	Stephenson Harwood	London	34	631
61	Withers LLP	London	32	697
62	Walker Morris	Leeds	34	667
63	TLT LLP	Bristol*	21	649
64	Morgan Cole	Cardiff*	22	532
65	Speechly Bircham LLP	London	14	627
66	Freeth Cartwright LLP	Nottingham*	13	389
67	Penningtons Solicitors LLP	London*	27	564
68	Ashfords	Exeter*	31	232
69=	Martineau Johnson	Birmingham*	20	503
69=	Mishcon de Reya	London	17	529
71	K&L Gates	London	18	546
72=	Ward Hadaway	Newcastle*	21	670
72=	Skadden, Arps, Slate, Meagher & Flom	London	7	618
74	Jones Day	London	33	453
75	Brabners Chaffe Street	Liverpool*	18	283
76	Holman Fenwick & Willan	London	22	435
77=	Manches LLP	London*	21	500
77=	LeBoeuf, Lamb, Greene & MacRae	London	17	468
79	Andrew Jackson	Hull	14	224
80	Russell-Cooke LLP	London	16	586
81	Bircham Dyson Bell	London	17	263
82=	Shearman & Sterling LLP	London	27	595
82=	Lewis Silkin LLP	London*	12	477
84	Hugh James	Cardiff*	17	441
85	Sidley Austin (UK) LLP	London	17	607
86	Dechert LLP	London	25	338
87=	Foot Anstey	Exeter*	13	378
87=	Wilsons Solicitors LLP	Salisbury	8	695
89	Weil, Gotshal & Manges	London	21	685
90	Watson, Farley & Williams LLP	London	23	679
91	DMH Stallard	Brighton*	19	353
92	Ince & Co	London	21	447
93=	Wedlake Bell	London	15	682
93=	Boodle Hatfield	London*	12	275
95	Michelmores LLP	Exeter*	11	522
96=	Cripps Harries Hall LLP	Tunbridge Wells	14	335
96=	Anthony Collins Solicitors LLP	Birmingham	15	226
98	Thomson Snell & Passmore	Tunbridge Wells*	9	643
99=	Forsters LLP	London	10	387
99=	Howes Percival LLP	Northampton*	12	438
101=	Forbes	Blackburn*	18	381

**Firms are listed in order of size as measured by UK partner and solicitor figures provided to Chambers and Partners. *Head or primary UK office.

Firms by size in UK**	City	Total English & Welsh trainees	Page
101= asb law	Crawley*	10	229
103 Veale Wasbrough Lawyers	Bristol	12	662
104 Thring Townsend	Swindon*	14	645
105 Mace & Jones	Liverpool*	11	494
106= Capsticks	London	8	301
106= McDermott Will & Emery (UK) LLP	London	6	512
108 BPE Solicitors	Cheltenham*	14	218
109 Stevens & Bolton LLP	Guildford	7	634
110= Lester Aldridge LLP	Bournemouth*	14	474
110= Bristows	London	14	287
110= Harbottle & Lewis LLP	London	7	411
113= IBB Solicitors	Uxbridge*	12	444
113= Finers Stephens Innocent	London	11	372
115 Coffin Mew LLP	Southampton*	15	330
116 Cleary Gottlieb Steen & Hamilton LLP	London	12	310
117 BP Collins	Gerrard's Cross	7	278
118= Lupton Fawcett LLP	Leeds	6	491
118= Higgs & Sons	Brierly Hill*	10	424
120= Bates Wells & Braithwaite	London	10	247
120= Memery Crystal LLP	London	10	519
122 Hodge Jones & Allen	London	13	431
123 Fisher Meredith	London	16	375
124 Salans	London	8	588
125= Henmans LLP	Oxford	6	417
125= Knight & Sons	Newcastle-Under-Lyme	5	463
127 Maxwell Winward LLP	London	7	506
128 Muckle LLP	Newcastle	10	535
129 Payne Hicks Beach	London	6	561
130= Ford & Warren	Leeds	7	384
130= Collyer Bristow LLP	London	6	333
132= Shadbolt & Co LLP	Reigate*	8	591
132= Warner Goodman LLP	Southampton*	7	672
134 BTMK Solicitors	Southend*	5	294
135 Rollits	Hull*	6	583
136= Teacher Stern Selby	London	7	640
136= Prettys	Ipswich*	11	572
138 Clarion Solicitors	Leeds	10	307
139 Trethowans	Salisbury*	7	656
140 Orrick, Herrington & Sutcliffe LLP	London	16	548
141 Bingham McCutchen (London) LLP	London	4	260
143 Wiggin LLP	Cheltenham*	7	692
144= Lee & Priestley LLP	Leeds	9	471
144= Sheridans	London	2	598
146 Paul, Hastings, Janofsky & Walker LLP	London	6	559
147 Palmers Solicitors	Basildon	5	553
148 Sherrards Solicitors	St Albans	7	600
149 Vinson & Elkins RLLP	London	7	664
150 George Green LLP	Cradley Heath*	4	398

*Firms are listed in order of size as measured by UK partner and solicitor figures provided to Chambers and Partners. *Head or primary UK office.

www.chambersstudent.co.uk

Addleshaw Goddard LLP

the facts

Location: Manchester, Leeds, London
Number of UK partners/solicitors: 182/555
Total number of trainees: 88
Seats: 4x6 months
Alternative seats: Hong Kong, secondments
Extras: Pro bono – Manchester Uni and Springfields Legal Advice Centres, Employment and IP advice lines (in conjunction with BPP Law School)

Since 2003, when it was formed through merger, Addleshaw Goddard has pursued a clear strategy to be one of the best – if not the best – UK firm outside the magic circle. In the words of one interviewee: *"We don't want to climb Everest, we want to climb K2, the world's second highest mountain."*

keeping things broad

Employing almost 1,400 people, this major national firm has been working hard to achieve consistency across its three UK offices. The latest financial results show average annual profits per equity partner have topped half a million pounds and income has increased to £176.7m, the big earners being real estate (£54.4m) and litigation (£50.8m), followed by corporate (£37m) and finance and projects (£34.5m). The firm is now ranked 7th in the UK according to the number of FTSE 100 Clients for whom it acts (Source: *Chambers UK, 2007*), and it is commended for its strong, balanced client roster of corporates, financial institutions and public sector organisations. AG's practice is enviably broad and this makes it a great choice for those looking for a broad commercial training contract, albeit one without much of an international dimension.

Recruits to the offices in Manchester, Leeds and London complete seats in at least three of the firm's four divisions – contentious and com-mercial; corporate; finance and projects; and real estate. Opinion was split over how well seat allocation works; some sources were entirely satisfied, while others indicated disappointment. The source of discontent seemed to be the notion that *"a small group of people get away without completing the compulsory requirements,"* while everyone else must comply with the rules and, occasionally *"due to business need,"* be asked to *"complete two transactional seats."* Trainees told us they were trying to encourage HR to be more explicit about the criteria used in decision-making.

what's the deal?

Corporate trainees know they work in an important area of the firm. In 2006, AG advised Atlas Capital Associates on its MBO of hedge fund manager Atlas Capital Group Holding. A few months later it assisted Kirk Newco, a company created by 3i, on its £500m MBO of cleaning and maintenance company Enterprise. These may not be the biggest deals going, but AG trainees don't seem to crave the *FT* headlines in the same way some others do. Private equity deals are especially relevant to the firm and it is now pushing to improve its private equity business in the capital, even relocating its top performers from the North to London. The trainees' role on deals may not always be that exciting (*"little client contact," "lots of reviewing documents from virtual data rooms, flagging due diligence and reviewing acquisition agreements"*), but they do at least feel valued. Compared to other seats, the pressure is on in corporate, as *"transactional work has much sharper deadlines and is very client-driven compared to the long drawn-out processes typical in litigation."* Needless to say, the hours can on occasion be rotten. We heard of someone staying until 5am in Manchester quite early on in their corporate seat, although London trainees probably stay late more often than those up north.

In the finance and projects department, trainees take on a surprising amount of responsibility and enjoy the full days *"moving from one task to another every hour."* Banking seats come in different varieties from property finance (*"a growing practice, gaining clients every minute, doing a good job"*) and social housing finance to acquisition finance, asset finance, insolvency, leveraged finance and securitisation. *"You're very much in charge of your own part of the transaction and you have a lot of responsibility early on. You're still heavily supervised and your work will get checked, especially your drafting, which is very heavily checked. You have to learn to manage your time and client expectations because you get quite a lot of contact with them."* The seat was described by one London trainee as *"really exciting, even though the hours were atrocious because the department was terribly understaffed... I was getting home by 9.30 or 10pm, having been in at 9am, and I worked every other weekend for a while too."* Among the top finance deals of the past year are HSBC's £151m bond and guarantee facility to the Gallagher Group to allow infrastructure works at a site in Bedfordshire where a new town with over 7,000 new homes will be built, plus the acquisition finance facilities for information company Datamonitor to fund its £40m purchase of Ovum.

Real estate seats allow substantial levels of autonomy too. In this *"really booming"* department, trainees get their own batch of up to 20 files and soon learn *"there is an awful lot of client contact."* This can lead to *"feeling quite under pressure at times,"* though we suspect more than one of our sources was *"addicted to the pace."* AG's real estate client list includes major names such as Sainsbury's, Travelodge and Admiral Taverns. The Leeds office handles a great deal of regeneration work, recent projects including the £300m Stockton on Tees Riverside Regeneration Project and the £100m Westgate regeneration scheme in Wakefield.

do you know who i am?

AG's litigators handle disputes covering everything from property to reinsurance. The firm recently won a freedom of information battle for *The Times* against HM Treasury, concerning details about the withdrawal of tax relief for pension funds in 1997. The top cases in the Leeds office have related to pensions, IT and projects; in Manchester the litigators have been working on finance disputes, product liability and health and safety problems; and in London there are numerous professional negligence cases and disputes in the media and sports sectors. A trainee's diet is *"document management-heavy,"* although some reported being allowed to *"draft witness statements from scratch"* and others talked about being steered away from the largest cases so they could try more interesting tasks than the dreaded bundling. Thus far, trainee seats have been specific to one type of work, but there is a drive to make the department more fluid and allow them to work with different teams. Similarly, NQs are now hired into the general litigation division, with a view to having them explore different areas before specialising. For trainees it means *"the onus is on you to get the work you want... If I didn't go out and get work, people wouldn't have known I was there."*

In theory it is possible to move offices for seats and were more Londoners to elect to head north, then more northerners would be able to satisfy their curiosity for the capital. A lucky few can wangle a seat in Hong Kong with one of AG's 'preferred firms' or complete a secondment with a client such as Barclays, Diageo, Harrods and AstraZeneca.

lost in translation

Supervisors encourage recruits to *"delegate as much as you can to secretaries"* and exploit the support network. *"The PSLs [professional support lawyers] are very good at steering you in the* right direction," confirmed one source. The Manchester corporate department is currently investigating whether staff can incorporate flexible and home working into their schedules. Everyone involved in the pilot project has been provided with a home office that is networked into the main IT system in the office. Watch this space for the results. For the most part, trainees were happy sitting with partners, although we did hear about a few personality clashes and tears in the toilets. We've always found AG trainees to be enthusiastic and proactive, and again this year our sources spoke about wanting to get the most out of seats and pushing supervisors for drafting opportunities and greater client contact. They were also quite willing to look critically at their experiences, telling us where the firm could do better, so it's a shame that this candour and enthusiasm is lost in translation in the podcasts on AG's website.

Once a year, all staff join colleagues from across the offices for a departmental away-day. These take place in locations like Dublin, Barcelona or, if you're really lucky, Reading. Training and workshops are followed by a social evening, during which cross-office networking is encouraged through treasure hunts and quizzes that are *"never taken too seriously."* We're reliably informed that these events end up *"drunken, basically."* There is also a two-day conference bringing trainees together (the senior partner is wheeled out to talk about AG's strategy and everyone gets stuck into training workshops) and a separate residential conference for future trainees. From 2007, new intakes will be able to take a pre-training contract trip to Romania to help build houses for a charity. And presumably most will already know each other from law school – the firm has signed a deal with BPP for all its future joiners to study a specially tailored course at its three branches.

above and beyond

Once again, in 2007 the firm earned itself a slot in the *Sunday Times'* 'Best Companies To Work For' survey. Our interviewees were acutely aware of the firm's defined cultural values, enshrined as they are in The AGWay. The values require people to be business-focused; team players; determined to succeed; open and honest; and dynamic, and it is apparently quite common to hear people utter things like: *"That's not very AGWay"* or (more supportively) *"come on, AGWay and all that"* or even *"ooh, very AGWay!"* Interestingly, trainees' views ranged from *"it's just corporate guff"* to *"it's very much a daily part of how we work."* We bet a cynic's attitude would change were they to win one of the monthly awards for those who show initiative in achieving any of the objectives. One award went to someone who patrolled the office turning off computer monitors and leaving a cartoon saying: 'The energy gorilla is angry with you.' Another went to someone who drove between Leeds and Manchester at 10pm to assist a colleague. In 2007, 35 of the 44 qualifiers walked the AGWay into permanent jobs at the firm.

hell bento on fun

In the North, AG resides in modern, airy buildings. Leeds has an outdoor seating area and a glass atrium with a giant chess board on the floor. When the canteen is shut, there are *"meals from M&S in vending machines."* Manchester has a glass elevator *"like the one in Charlie and the Chocolate Factory,"* except that it stops when it has reached the top floor. Both sound much nicer than the three London offices, the largest of which is pretty brown and pretty dated. Its interior has had a lick and a spit in the client areas, but everyone in the capital is crying out for a single big building. Luckily, there may be something on the horizon. The one area in which London seems to have the edge is its canteen food. Said one envious northerner: *"They have 'sausage of the week' and one time when*

I was there on a training session they had little boxes for sushi with different compartments..." The social scene in each office includes drinks on the first Friday of every month. In Leeds, lawyers often organise outings (a trip to the theatre to see *The Wizard of Oz*, bowling nights with staff from Yorkshire Bank) while the Mancunians can usually be found at the Pitcher & Piano or Rain Bar. London trainees frequent the nearby Lord Raglan pub on a Friday night. In each office, Christmas parties tend to be organised by department and range from considerable nights out to measly lunches, depending on the enthusiasm of whoever is in charge of festivities.

and finally...

If you're the sort who will happily buy into the AGWay (remember, that's 1,300+ people, in three cities, working with one set of values) and play a part in getting Addleshaw Goddard up the world's second highest mountain, then make sure you craft a good application. In the North it is fearsomely competitive to get a place here, and even in London, where applicants have a vast choice of firms, you'll need to shine brightly.

Allen & Overy LLP

the facts

Location: London
Number of UK partners/solicitors: 215/641
Total number of trainees: 240
Seats: 3 or 6 months long
Alternative seats: Overseas seats, secondments
Extras: Pro bono – Liberty, Battersea Legal Advice Centre, Caribbean death row appeals; language training

With offices in 19 countries, Allen & Overy is a fully paid-up member of London's magic circle of law firms and one of the top ten firms in the world, as measured by revenue. It is known in particular for its dominant position in practically every area of finance.

fuelled by finance

When Mr A and Mr O founded the firm in 1930, they had six rooms in Holborn, 12 staff and a taxi full of documents purloined from their former firm, Roney & Co. Oh, and the world was two months into an economic depression that would last 15 years. The new firm quickly developed a winning reputation, with George Allen famously advising King Edward VIII on the constitutional furore surrounding his romance with sassy American divorcee Wallis Simpson and his eventual abdication because of it. In the 1950s, it advised on what became Britain's first hostile takeover (British Aluminium by a US consortium), but by the 1960s it was clear that finance was going to be A&O's forte. Now, more than 40 years on, its capacity for working on the most complex financing is unrivalled. It put together a £2.37bn debt finance package for Goldman Sachs, Barclays, RBS and Dexia Credit Local to finance an investment consortium's takeover of Associated British Ports. It also advised BAA on financing issues arising out of its £10.3bn takeover by Ferrovial Group. And in project finance, the firm topped the global rankings in the first half of 2007, advising on 35 deals with a combined value of £13.4bn.

The capital markets group makes an equally impressive showing. It topped debt capital markets rankings in 2006 with 693 deals worth a total value of $371.6bn. In this area A&O advises the world's biggest banks on arranging note issues; for example, Citigroup and HSBC used it on a $1.5bn Euro Medium Term Note and Deposit Note Programme established by The Commercial Bank of Qatar. If such complex ideas don't make sense to you yet, don't worry. But if they sound like a complete snooze, you might want to think about turning the page.

The corporate division – around a quarter of the firm – hasn't achieved quite the same prestige as the finance or capital markets divisions, but it still has its fair share of mammoth deals. The firm advised Macquarie on the biggest UK buyout of 2006, its £8bn takeover of Thames Water; and Spanish energy group Iberdrola on its £11.6bn acquisition of ScottishPower. And this year, the department's improved turnover helped power A&O to an impressive 21% increase in earnings and a 36% profit increase, which seems to have shut up those pundits who were predicting doom and gloom during a less impressive 2005/06.

What about litigation, real estate, tax, etc? Well, we'd describe A&O as a stool with four legs: banking, capital markets, corporate, and everything else. That last category encompasses employment, pensions, private client, tax, and dispute resolution and accounts for only around a quarter of the firm's lawyers. The firm's international arbitration practice has been representing the Republic of Slovenia in a dispute with the national electricity company of Croatia concerning the ownership of a Yugoslavia-era nuclear reactor. The general litigation team boasts an impressive showing in regulatory and civil matters for the firm's core banking clients, for example, advising three of them on litigation arising from the sudden collapse of the Italian dairy giant Parmalat. And the employment team advised HSBC on a media-sensitive sexual orientation discrimination case brought by a former employee.

the right altitude

Of course, not everyone decides at age 20 that they're interested in derivatives (and wouldn't the world be a strange place it they did?) so for many the primary attraction of A&O was much simpler: "*The breadth of choice and the chance to work abroad.*" Some people noted the power of the A&O name on their CV: "*I thought I might as well start at the top and keep my options open,*" said one. As well as its reputation for technical prowess, the firm is also known for its well-mannered and almost low-key approach. "*It seemed more personal than the other large firms I visited,*" said one vac-scheme veteran. And at interview, "*you have two short talks with partners, not a whole assessment day with endless forms.*"

The firm draws its intake from around 40 universities worldwide. While the firm isn't quite as Oxbridge-heavy as some, it's still the case that the majority of trainees come from the best-regarded universities. The firm has joined forces with the College of Law to devise a bespoke LPC course. Once that's out of the way, around half of the trainees opt for a March start to their contracts, leaving them with several months in which to travel or (re)measure bits of coral reef. "*At the beginning, everyone in the March intake talks about where they've been – India, Nepal, Asia, even up Everest,*" reported one tanned recruit. Whether you opt for a September or March start, you'll join with 60 others, whom you'll know from law school. The first week is a general introduction to the firm, and the second a departmental induction. After all that, "*you settle in quite quickly.*"

mental gymnastics

Finance seats come in several flavours – banking, leveraged finance, asset finance, projects, restructuring, regulatory and global loans. In all areas, given the size and complexity of the deals, it's perhaps not surprising that trainees don't leap straight into drafting agreements and chatting to clients. "*For the first few weeks you're learning, reading endless documents, listening to your supervisor's phone conversations and so on, not talking to Barclays.*" The trainee's favourite – checklists of conditions precedent – also put in an appearance. Over time, though, the responsibility levels steadily increase: "*By the end of the seat I was drafting credit agreements… although they came back with huge amounts of red ink on them,*" said one source. Of leveraged finance, trainees told us: "*They aim for you to be running matters largely unsupervised by the end of the seat.*" However far you get during the seat, classic trainee tasks never cease completely, but as one stoical interviewee put it: "*Even partners and associates do proof-reading. It's not a skill you ever stop needing.*" Overall, the finance group is described as a "*bustling*" place. "*Companies always want the money yesterday,*" noted one trainee with a hint of exasperation.

The capital markets division is as diverse as the finance division and has seat options in general securities, derivatives and structured finance, debt, equity, securitisation and corporate trustee work. This "*cutting-edge*" work requires "*mental gymnastics,*" so trainees are introduced to this strange world slowly, with "*lots of lectures and intro sessions in the first few weeks.*" With deals taking longer, there is a risk of longer periods on boring tasks. "*I spent two months bibling,*" reported one veteran of the seat; "*but once you win the partners' trust, the responsibility level rises quickly.*" It's not uncommon for trainees to work closely with partners, negotiate simpler aspects of deals by phone and e-mail and draft ancillary documents. In addition, "*for the more commoditised matters there* [is software] *which helps you prepare the standard documents.*" "*The first one you do is really tricky, then you can churn them out in two weeks with minimal supervision.*"

Corporate trainees are inevitably landed with grunt work. "*You will spend time doing verification, due diligence, and the like,*" admitted one. "*They're important tasks but don't exactly set the heart on fire.*" At least extensive paralegal support means "*you'll never spend a day just photocopying.*" At the other extreme, "*you could be sitting in meetings where important decisions are being made, and you're putting forward suggestions.*" "*You have to build up trust and indicate that you're prepared to take on more responsibility,*" suggested one interviewee. Many trainees are happy to allow responsibility to build up gradually as "*they have no intention of qualifying into corporate and so the motivation isn't there.*" Maybe this is a good thing, given that "*the departments want to identify the most committed people.*"

livin' for the weekend

When it comes to non-core areas, the firm gets trainees to utilise the 'priority seat' system, effectively a golden ticket giveaway that leads to one seat in the trainee's department of choice. The niche departments offer a change of pace from the hectic transactional groups and quite often more intellectual stimulation. "*It's real law,*" one visitor to tax commented, "*and it changes every six months and you have to keep up.*" Employment, too, offers "*a lot of very technical research and discussions with partners. It's challenging stuff… I'm really enjoying it.*" The flipside is a considerable amount of transactional support work.

Experiences of dispute resolution vary widely. "*I was running to court the whole time with documents,*" said one trainee, while another recalled "*attending hearings, discussing strategy, and reviewing testimony.*" Others were left looking on enviously: "*I was mostly drafting my supervisor's e-mails,*" recalled one. "*We were in the early days of two big arbitrations. I spent a lot of time shuffling documents.*" Heavy document lifting is the price of working on the type of big-ticket disputes A&O takes on. In the past, there's been a distinct difference in experiences between those who had a three-month litigation seat and those who had a full six months there. Now A&O offers a two-week course at the College of Law as an alternative to the seat for those for whom litigation isn't a likely career option. "*I think it's good they're bringing it in,*" one source commented.

"The people in litigation have realised most of their trainees don't want to be there; now they can focus on those that do."

Some 70% of trainees go on either a foreign or client secondment. For the internationally minded, Hong Kong and New York are the most popular overseas seats, though other options include Paris, Tokyo and Warsaw. Hong Kong secondees reported a more independent style of working than in London. *"You do have a trainer but they're often travelling, so you could be responding to clients with minimal checks. There's more room to develop independence of style."* The small office enjoys a *"slightly frantic and dramatic atmosphere,"* and there can be antisocial hours. *"5pm is the earliest possible time for a conference call with London, and there's always follow-up work after,"* one source pointed out. Compensations come in the form of *"pretty much endless scope for weekend fun. You can go to Beijing, Shanghai or Hanoi; try water-skiing or wakeboarding, or just lounge about on the firm's boat."* New York offers *"responsibility more like that of an associate than a trainee."* Like some other large firms, A&O has faced something of an uphill struggle building its New York office and *"some departments are quite short staffed and quite dependent on UK secondees."* As a result – and thanks to the somewhat boot-camp-like work ethic of US law in general – *"the hours can be very, very long."* Fortunately *"excellent"* accommodation is just 15 minutes' walk from the office and well placed for trainees to unwind by *"worshipping Central Park."* The list of client secondment options is impressive, including Barclays Capital and the human rights organisation Liberty.

The qualification period is rendered less stressful by the fact that so many people are away in the fourth seat, either overseas or with a client. Realistically, those seeking a place in the smaller commercial and dispute departments should *"try to establish a relationship in advance with the part-*ner you'd like to work with."* In 2007, 101 of the 118 qualifiers took jobs at the firm. Banking took the largest number, but all areas of practice recruited NQs.

shooting the breeze

Allen & Overy conducted a values review a couple of years ago, generating a set of core principles that are deemed to be central to the way it operates. For the most part, it's bland stuff – our favourite for corporate meaninglessness is *"excellence in everyone and everything."* Some values, though, seem to stick. The ones about *"respecting and including everyone"* and *"working together as one firm"* make real sense. *"The people are the best thing about working here,"* said one source. Another told us: *"Even when the pressure's on, people remain human and polite."* The firm's supervisors seemed to ably meet trainees' rather modest expectations. *"They're nice, and helpful, for the most part,"* one interviewee reported – *"although you do get the occasional workaholic who expects you to be the same."* For higher-end queries, the partners were also deemed approachable. *"They're obviously really busy, so you don't expect to just walk in and ask questions all the time, but you feel confident approaching them generally, as long as you've taken the query as far as you can without checking. I mean, some of them are scarily intelligent."* Appraisals have recently been enhanced, as a result of feedback from the trainee liaison committee. The changes were seen as indicative of the firm's willingness to listen.

The firm moved to smart, Foster-designed offices in Spitalfields in late 2006. *"The old building had a lot of charm, and we were worried that the new one would be a bit sterile,"* said one trainee. *"But it works really well as it's designed for us – everything's exactly where you'd like it to be."* Particular praise went to the tenth-floor canteen, complete with roof garden. Having visited said terrace, we can confirm it is indeed an impressive, if windy, vantage point for a great view of the City. The new office is in a great location near Liverpool Street station and trendy Shoreditch isn't very far away. A trainee ball at Christmas and various social committee-organised events throughout the year keep each intake chatting as the work piles up, although participation in social activities is entirely optional. *"Quite a lot of people congregate in the bar* [in the office] *at the end of the week,"* reported one trainee, another adding that *"in the new building, the bar's about twice as expensive as before. Perhaps that's how they're paying for everything!"* For those more interested in sports: *"There's a good budget for sports and a gym in the basement."*

every little helps

It's just as well A&O's trainees seem to like their offices as they spend a fair bit of time there. *"It's not as bad as many think,"* one trainee maintained. *"I've done my fair share of late nights, but only a few weekends."* Most people we spoke to had experienced a couple of *"rough patches"* with *"a few weeks till 1am or later every day, weekends as well."* In securitisation *"they just work to a different clock."* If that leaves you palpitating, note that trainees for the most part said they didn't mind. *"There's team bonding that comes along with it. It's all hands on deck, and there is sympathy from trainers and associates."*

The *Student Guide* recalls its music teacher at school pointing out that learning music is *"10% inspiration and 90% perspiration."* Maybe this person had the same teacher: *"Training here you have to be intelligent, but it's 20% intelligence and 80% grit. I've been here till midnight reviewing a document and constantly keeping track of what's been done and who else needs to look at it. It's like learning an instrument: you've got to keep at it. You'll learn if you're willing to put in the time."* Naturally, the hours do get people down. *"There was one week where I and another trainee worked out that, per hour, we would have made more money working at Tesco,"* said one. *"That was depressing."*

So what sort of person is suited to A&O? *"Someone nerdy enough to appreciate the intellectual stimulation on offer, but also who enjoys the social side. Someone who's a bit ambitious, in terms of knowing what they want out of life. Introverts won't make the best of the experience."* *"Neither,"* our sagacious source continued, *"will people who are only here to please their dad. There are a couple of those, to be honest."* One told us: *"Consideration for others is very important... being prepared to throw your hat in the ring when needed."* Another emphasised that *"brains and skill are a given somewhere like this; what marks you out are team skills and client skills. You can see it in the younger partners."*

As at other large firms, we were struck by how few trainees saw themselves climbing the greasy pole to partnership. *"I'd rather have a family and some time in the evenings for a life,"* said one not untypical interviewee. *"I'd like to develop strong technical skills, to be really good at what I do, but I don't know if I'm driven enough for partnership,"* concluded another. A&O's new 'counsel' role (above associate but without the full benefits and obligations of partnership) seems tailor-made for such trainees, and was viewed positively by those we spoke to. *"You can have a much clearer idea of your career path now – you can make a decision which goal to aim for."*

and finally...

"They expect a lot of you here, but they really support you through it." That combination neatly sums up the Allen & Overy experience. The chance to train at a top firm – with the long hours and hard draft that goes with it – and get a top name on your CV from the start is something many students understandably find impossible to resist.

Andrew Jackson

the facts

Location: Hull
Number of UK partners/solicitors: 33/98
Total number of trainees: 14
Seats: 4x6 months
Alternative seats: None

Andrew Jackson has been around a long time in Hull and its mission is now to expand and compete with rivals in Leeds and Sheffield. In fact, it is quite literally growing out of Hull, as management struggles to find premises large enough to contain the expanding workforce. Like Popeye's shirt after he's downed a can of spinach, the present office is *"busting at the seams."*

liquid crystal in the rough

Hull occupies an unenviable spot in the national consciousness. It is the focal point for the country's anxieties over grim, urban post-industrialisation, and so strong is this aversion that Hull has become a witch's cauldron for brewing our national ills. It regularly tops Britain's worst lists for such crimes as being the most obese, the heaviest drinkers, the biggest smokers, having the highest rate of teenage pregnancies, and the highest inability to sing in tune on one leg whilst blindfold. Okay, that last one we made up but you get the point, if there's some human or social inadequacy causing a fuss in the press it's sure to be triply bad in Hull. Joking aside, although Hull immediately triggers a sense of death by concrete in most people, how many have actually sampled the city and have an accurate picture of it to draw on? Fair enough these conceptions did not spring out of nowhere and probably reflect a phase of cheerless modernisation in the eighties, but they should not overshadow the happier even admirable aspects of the town.

So what has Hull ever done for us then? More than you think actually. Historically, we have to thank its MP William Wilberforce for forwarding the first motion to abolish the slave trade. Its streets gave birth to Amy Johnson, the first female pilot to circumnavigate the globe, and its suspension bridge crossing the Humber is a genius feat of civil engineering. The ground-breaking playwright John Godber is artistic director at the highly acclaimed Hull Truck Theatre, a haven for new drama, and the town is also the home of liquid crystal technology, an invention utilized by NASA for its space shuttles. Are you beginning to glean a sense of innovation mixed in the mortar?

The word on everybody's lips at the moment is regeneration. Hull recently added Sir Terry Farrell's iconic submarium and the £45m Kingston Communications Stadium to its cityscape, and the Fruit Market, Quayside, station and St Stephen are all undergoing massive renovation. In the old town, cobbled streets and Georgian architecture are being slowly scrubbed of their grime to reveal the beauties underlying Hull's tarnished image. For sceptics, Leeds is the template which Hull can mimic. Against the odds, that Yorkshire city managed to transform itself into a cosmopolitan, trendy hotspot. If Leeds, why not Hull? Trainees agree, saying: *"It is quite an exciting place to be at the moment"* and, without embarrassment, state the postcode as a major reason for joining AJ.

Another obvious draw is the quality of AJ's training. The largest firm in Hull, AJ has traditionally been known for its buoyant maritime practice. With the decline of the fishing and shipping industries, the firm recognised the need to cast its nets into new areas of practice and has done especially well in real estate, employment, family law and private client. Most recently it has unveiled a corporate governance department that tackles white-collar crime. A raft of long-standing clients includes

Northern Foods, AXA Insurance, the Road Haulage Association and Seven Seas.

water's thicker than blood

The dynamo of the firm, the real estate department is rapidly expanding. Trainees say it is one of the most hierarchical of the departments, being led by a cast of *"strong characters."* Nevertheless, the partners make time to tutor trainees and in this respect act as *"a shining beacon for the rest of the firm."* The team attracts client instructions that run to millions of pounds and has lately been advising on American-style retirement villages. Indeed, the retirement sector is becoming something of a niche for AJ which, given the UK's aging population, sounds like a smart move. Other clients include Arla Foods, Associated British Ports, Carpetright plc and MFI. A seat in the residential conveyancing department means non-stop client contact over the phone. *"You have your own files from day one and you assist the partner who runs the team."* The only downside is that the commercial property department doesn't appreciate what the residential conveyancers do. *"There's some snobbery about residential work not being as highly thought of as the more profitable commercial work,"* but this merely serves to *"draw people together more"* in the team.

A corporate seat is somewhat different, not least because there is nowhere near as much client contact. Nevertheless, it is just about the most coveted seat of the lot and trainees felt they were *"making positive contributions"* on transactions. A record year saw the firm handling £388m worth of transactions in 2006, most of it for modest regional businesses, one deal worth £10m – a contract between the Port of Southampton and cruise line Royal Caribbean, relating to investment in a new terminal. The firm also advised UK rail infrastructure services company DMQA on the £8.5m sale of the entire issued share capital of its technical services and training divisions.

Happy to share its clients with the rest of the firm, the shipping and transportation department is a lively place. Perhaps this is unsurprising since the Humber Port still handles 15% of the UK's seaborne goods. The department is seen to offer a glamorous seat that takes trainees to *"sea ports up and down the country"* and some of its work is for international clients. As well as fishing matters (just imagine all the EC regulations covering this industry) there are contractual disputes and personal injury claims, commonly relating to slips and trips on board commercial and passenger vessels. On PI cases, new recruits are shown the ropes and then get straight into preparing witness statements and assessing settlement costs. Recently the team advised the owners of a cruise ship and their P&I Club in relation to an onboard Norovirus outbreak. The team also works on fisheries and Merchant Shipping Act prosecutions in courts around the UK.

A *"fantastic department,"* commercial litigation spawned talk of attendance at court and drafting. In this seat, as well as in employment and private client, the level of solo client contact is stimulating. Then again, private client can also veer on morbidity as trainees seek to impress on clients the urgency of writing a will. *"You don't choose family"* is a truth all too evident to some trainees. Apparently, the responsibility levels in this seat can be overwhelming, with newbies expected to hit the ground running and deal with more cases of family breakdown than Jerry Springer. One frank trainee readily admitted: *"It was difficult handling the emotional side."* Having reams of responsibility is fantastic, but we only recommend this seat if family law is a driving passion as it's no easy ride. Some of our sources were baffled that this department should offer two seats, when people were queuing up for the one seat in corporate; nevertheless, the team is embroiled in some whopping cases, with one pre-nup agreement weighing in at £77m.

your money or your life?

For those who run into problems, there are monthly meetings with their mentor partner *"to chat about how you're getting on."* In our interviews, aspects of the appraisals came under fire; in particular, the 1-5 grading system at the end of each seat caused widespread resentment among our sources. Part of the problem is the partners' varying conceptions of what the numbers indicated, with some refusing to accept that a trainee was capable of scoring higher than a '3'. Most trainees would like to see this element of the system scrapped. The mentor system was also said to be hit and miss, with some fighting harder than others to ensure that trainees win their seat of choice.

While they were at it the trainees also picked a few holes in the way the firm communicated with them. Some disliked hearing about top-level decisions on the grapevine and wished the partnership would be less secretive about things. In particular, there were requests for more transparency in terms of pay scales and pay reviews. The pay gap between Leeds firms and Hull is a big source of anxiety for trainees; on the other hand, working hours are very reasonable, leaving plenty of time for a life outside the office. A low-key social life at AJ is perhaps explained by the fact that many people have their own friends away from work. There are some sports played on the weekend, and once a month a partner puts money behind the local bar – The Jaz. There are also client marketing events, such as go-karting and golf, all of which trainees can participate in. Some who arrive new in town at the start of their contracts can find it a lonely experience at first, so unless you have a fondness for your own company, it's probably best to devise a robust plan for building a social network.

A suggestion panel composed of secretaries, trainees, solicitors and partners is slowly trying to make little changes to office life; however, after one trainee declared that the mandate of this body is *"to improve morale,"* we wondered why they didnt just go for the tried-and-tested option of regular cake and chocolate for all. The reformers meet for two hours once a month, and it sounds as if the firm is taking staff comments seriously. An outside specialist has been hired to canvass opinion and publish its findings. One of the initiatives on the table is the introduction of flexible benefits whereby staff can buy and sell holidays.

and finally...

Andrew Jackson inspires affection from trainees; however, it may be that the firm's training is too darn hot for its own good. Second-year trainees are perfect prey for firms outside Hull, who recognise the AJ credentials but realise they can offer a fancier NQ wage packet. In 2007 two of the five qualifiers stayed on at the firm, taking jobs in the real estate department. All those we spoke to who were leaving the firm maintained that, but for the salary, they wouldn't have hesitated to stay.

Anthony Collins Solicitors LLP

the facts

Location: Birmingham
Number of UK partners/solicitors: 21/70
Total number of trainees: 15
Seats: 4x6 months
Alternative seats: None
Extras: Pro bono – St Basil's Legal Advice Centre

Founded in 1973 by the recently retired Mr Anthony Collins, this Birmingham concern appears to have achieved that which satirists would claim impossible – an ethically aware law firm.

to good to be true?

Apparently not, according to our research. Recently ranked as the 60th largest UK firm by turnover, Anthony Collins has established itself as a serious contender in the Midlands, and following its move into new and, according to one of our sources, *"glamorous"* offices last year it certainly looks the part. The firm is grouped into three distinct practice areas: commercial services; private client and 'Transformation'. In the past, training contracts would focus on one of these strands; these days trainees are encouraged to try out seats across the board.

The seat possibilities in the commercial services department include business services (coco to you and us), dispute resolution, commercial property and employment. The division is also home to the firm's highly regarded licensing practice, which enjoys the patronage of a number of household-name clients, including The Restaurant Group Plc (which incorporates Frankie & Bennys, Chiquitos and Garfunkels) as well as leading local names such as the Birmingham Hippodrome, the NEC Group (NEC, NIA and ICC) and Birmingham City Council. The private client division consists of a family department, as well as wills and probate, estates and trusts and a well-known claimant PI/clin neg practice. The third division is not only the most distinctive but it is probably the one that best embodies the firm's community-minded ethos. The Transformation department focuses on the regeneration of down-at-heel communities and acts for local authorities and registered social landlords (housing associations, etc). The division combines the skills of property, projects and construction lawyers, as well as property litigators, charity lawyers and governance specialists.

well informed

Other than the first seat, which is generally allocated according to the business needs of the moment, the trainees were pleased with the degree to which their preferences were factored into the allocation process. They also spoke highly of the monthly trainee forum, at which they have a chance to discuss seats that they may be interested in, as well as listening to presentations by representatives of different departments.

The projects and procurement department, (previously known as the Best Value Projects department, which kind of made it sound like a budget supermarket) is a popular choice for many trainees. Its work includes EU procurement, local government projects and non-contentious construction work. Some of the things keeping the lawyers busy right now are the London Borough of Newham's Local Space Project for housing the homeless; Pendle Borough Council's strategic partnering contract to outsource various services, construct a business centre and create jobs within the borough; and advice to Adactus Housing Group, the repair, maintenance and tenancy management member of the preferred bidder consortium on Manchester City Council's Miles Platting HRA Housing PFI scheme, which is worth in the region of £30m. Our sources were pleased to experience large projects, but also noted that the size of the matters meant they necessarily had lower levels of responsibility. *"I didn't always get as much exposure to new work as I would have liked,"* stated one trainee. A typical week in this seat might include the odd client meeting and some drafting, as well as a slew of research assignments, some of which could last for several days. *"If you are the kind of person that wants a fresh challenge every day, then it might not be the best seat for you,"* concluded one interviewee.

By comparison, due to the nature of private client work, a seat in the family department offers trainees high levels of responsibility. To start with, they sit in on interviews between clients and other fee earners and then help to draft witness statements. After an initial period in the department, they are trusted to write letters of advice, interview clients and attend hearings alone. The family department's remit encompasses both ancillary relief and childcare work, covering adoption issues and some mental health matters.

Two options for contentious seats are commercial dispute resolution and housing litigation, both of which proved popular with the trainees we interviewed. Commercial dispute resolution is thought to provide *"a good introduction to litigation"* and the opportunity to have *"a lot of files to manage on your own."* Housing litigation brings all sorts of drama as it sometimes necessitates injunctions and measures to counter anti-social behaviour. Housing management on behalf of registered social landlords and retirement homes will certainly open your eyes to a side of life you might otherwise have been sheltered from. *"There is always an interesting story behind the work,"* commented one enthusiastic interviewee. For another, the real pleasure came from *"feeling like you are helping society, whilst at the same time being exposed to quite technical and satisfying work."* The firm appeared in Knowsley Housing Trust v McMullen, a leading case on the impact of the Disability Discrimination Act 1995 on anti-social behaviour and the extent to which a disabled tenant can be expected to control the behaviour of another member of their household.

Irrespective of their particular mix of seats, when our fourth-seat interviewees looked back over their two years with the firm, they were all thoroughly satisfied with the experience. *"The responsibility is really good throughout. They take the first couple of weeks to bed you into the departments, so that you don't feel out of your depth, but from then on they are really happy for you to take an active role."*

care and attention

In addition to the prestige that the new offices have brought the firm, they have also introduced a number of benefits for trainees, such as *"a chill-out point and a big terrace for sunbathing at lunchtimes."* (Sounds more like Ibiza than an office...) The open-plan layout of the new set-up helps facilitate a harmonious atmosphere. *"It doesn't matter who you are looking for to ask advice, as everyone is within shouting distance... although obviously we don't actually shout. And everybody is so nice that you can talk to anyone, even if your supervisor is unavailable."* Appraisals are scheduled to take place every three months: the mid-seat review is given by the seat supervisor and the end-of-seat-review is also attended by the trainee's individual appraiser, who may be an associate or a partner and who stays with the trainee throughout their training contract. These meetings are said to be quite informal as there isn't any grading. As one source put it: *"The appraisals are really just opportunities to feed back to your supervisor and visa versa."*

Some trainees are attracted to Anthony Collins for its expertise in a number of socially aware niche areas, namely charity law and social housing. *"I wanted to do charity law and the firm's focus on regeneration captured my imagination,"* stated one interviewee, adding: *"I particularly liked the idea of getting stuck in and helping to empower people to run their own communities."* The trainee group contains a genuine mix of ages and educational backgrounds. One thing they do seem to have in common is a desire to make a positive impact on the world around them. As one trainee commented: *"Someone who was completely ruthless wouldn't really fit in. While we are commercially focused, we are not here to earn a profit at any cost."* Only a small majority of trainees have firm links with the Midlands – Anthony Collins' reputation, it seems, has spread pretty wide. In 2007 five of the eight qualifiers stayed on with the firm, going into a variety of departments.

there's always one

One aspect that sets this firm apart from most is its faith base. A Christian ethos can be said to permeate the character of the firm; however, this does not make active participation in faith-inspired events, such as regular Monday prayer meetings, in any way compulsory. As one source explained: *"It is not shoved in your face, but it is there for the taking if you want it."* Whether religious themselves or not, trainees agreed that, if anything, the religious element makes the firm a rather nice place to work; *"everyone is really friendly and they go out of their way to catch up with you on a personal level. There is also a slightly wider appreciation that trainees have lives outside the firm because some partners themselves have commitments such as running church activities or youth groups in the evenings."*

With the average day lasting from 9am until 5.15pm, unless you've a scout meeting to rush off to, there is plenty of time for socialising. The trainees often take advantage of this on Friday nights by indulging in the free buffet offered in Bushwackers on Edmund Street. The firm's social co-ordinators also arrange day trips for everyone, such as a recent jaunt to Alton Towers. The big dates in the calendar are the Christmas ball in January and a summer fun day, which is a family-friendly event at which other halves and children are welcome. The firm has a relationship with a local brain-injury rehabilitation trust and, as a bonding exercise, the trainees have been helping to regenerate the trust's garden, through both fundraising and hard graft.

Our sources at Anthony Collins seemed incredibly contented; in fact, when asked if there was anything they would change, the only suggestion concerned the tea! As one shamefaced source admitted: *"We are a fair trade firm, which I really like, but the tea is not always that great and so I have to hide my PG tips."* Traitor!

and finally...

A training contract with Anthony Collins couples solid learning at a well-respected, commercial firm with the chance to make a real difference to communities through the group's specialist departments. Most definitely a unique choice, this one.

asb law

the facts

Location: Crawley, Maidstone, Brighton, Horsham, Croydon
Number of UK partners/solicitors: 36/38
Total number of trainees: 10
Seats: 4x6 months
Alternative seats: None

In 1999 a three-way merger between Maidstone's Argyle & Court, Stonehams of Croydon and Burstows (the three-office big-boy of the deal), created what we now know as asb law.

smile for the client

One of the South East's top dogs, asb has since 2005 had to deal with a number of job cuts and partner losses, plus some sluggish financial results. As recently as June 2006 it lost its high-flying head of corporate finance, Jonathan Grant, to its rampaging rivals DMH Stallard. Undeterred and now under new stewardship, asb is determined to charge full steam ahead and put the past behind it. *"There is a positive, hopeful air about the office,"* said one trainee. Or to put it another way: *"We are definitely moving in the right direction – as trainees we even have our own business cards now."* This is just one example of a number of internal incentives the firm has put in place to spark profitability. It has also hinted at an aggressive recruitment drive, which will be necessary if it is to achieve its goal of breaking into the country's top 100 firm; as measured by turnover. *"The new management are certainly on the ball and forward-thinking,"* declared one source. Proof of this can be seen in the firm's preparations for the post-Legal Services Bill era, with the launch of ASB Aspire, a standalone volume business that deals with simple residential conveyancing, personal injury and uninsured loss recovery. In a separate move, partners' chargeable hours targets have been cut to free up time for getting out to meet and greet old and new clients, because key to the firm's plan is an increase in instructions from the region's largest and most prestigious companies. Asb has already had some notable success in this respect; for example, one of its high-flying local clients is American helicopter manufacturer Bristow, whose Surrey arm turns to asb when facing any workforce-related issues. It also gives advice across the board to a number of local authorities, such as Wandsworth Borough Council, West Sussex County Council and Brighton & Hove City Council.

european mushroom mountain

A tailored, industry-sector approach has been asb's trade mark for a while. Technology, leisure and owner-managed and family businesses are the foundations of its corporate practice, and one of the department's largest transactions came from the media industry, where it represented Coltman Media on its sale to advertising and marketing agency Adventis. The firm's dispute resolution team also draws work from the firm's target sectors: it has recently been assisting on a £50m dispute relating to a services contract, advising a public authority in a £1m dispute relating to IT services, and advising a recruitment consultancy on a £3m fraud case. A strong list of

landlord and construction clients also delivers plenty of real estate disputes.

A sectoral approach to business has helped asb carve out some interesting niches. One salient example is aviation where it has been involved in some extremely complex matters, such as acting on behalf of TES Aviation Group on the purchase of four Rolls-Royce engines from Parkhead Leasing & Sales for $8.2m, with financing from DVB Bank. Another interesting example comes from the travel industry – through the representation of European industry leaders such as Virgin Holidays, Pure France and Unijet, asb's specialist travel law group can claim to be a countrywide leader in this discipline. Recently, it oversaw one of the firm's biggest ever instructions, when it advised First Choice Holidays on the £120m takeover of hotel booking website LateRooms.com. Another area in which asb consistently dominates the South Eastern market is insolvency. Over the past year, it acted in the administration and sale of Dutch supermarket supplier Haveco Mushrooms (one of many casualties in Europe's saturated mushroom market) and worked on a case relating to Newlands School, a 450-pupil independent school in East Sussex which was forced to close when its operating company went into administration. The case was picked up by the national press, because despite two of the parents (asb's clients) putting together a £2.5m rescue plan, the landlord opposed the arrangements in the High Court, reportedly because they were considering selling off the land to a developer. The challenge was successfully resisted.

diamond geezers

Two of the most impressive aspects of the asb training scheme are the vast array of practice groups in which seats can be taken and the fact that no seat is compulsory so long as Law Society requirements are met. Our interviewees had clearly made full use of their freedom, taking very different paths through their four-seat training contracts. Many were more attracted by the corporate, property, dispute resolution and employment groups; some had focused on areas such as personal injury (claimant representation is the firm's forte), environment, trusts and probate. The particulars of their work in these departments obviously differ massively, but across the seats trainees spoke favourably of *"getting stuck into proper work"* under the careful guidance of *"top-quality fee earners with great experience in their fields."* They talked about sitting in on client meetings or even acting as first port of call for smaller clients in more straightforward matters. All of this happens within *"hours that are nothing like the City."* Even in the busiest seats there is *"definitely time to do things outside work."* Our interviewees also cited occasions when they had voiced their opinions or stood up for themselves. Said one: *"I was in a department that hadn't taken a trainee before and there were a few times when they seemed to forget about me, but I wasn't bothered about speaking up to remind them I was there."*

Ideally located to capture business in the Gatwick Diamond (the region stretching from London down to Brighton and from Horsham over to East Grinstead), Crawley was traditionally the firm's commercial hub and the busiest office for trainees. However, a move into a new Kent stronghold in Maidstone in 2006 has marked a prominent shift in focus for the firm. By taking *"brand-spanking-new"* premises on a business park close to Junction 7 of the M20 it has consolidated business that was previously split between four separate high street buildings. Here, *"an archetypal open-plan office"* has ample space to accommodate an expected surge in staff numbers, something trainees fully expect. One told us: *"The Maidstone and Crawley offices are probably already on an equal footing, and Maidstone is an area the firm has made clear it wishes to push."* Trainees are now split roughly evenly between

these two main offices, with specific numbers fluctuating depending on business need. Each office offers the full spread of commercial and private client seats.

The Brighton office has lawyers in the areas of tax, property, insolvency, defendant litigation and family law, but only offers a trainee seat every now and then, which means the Brighton training experience is one often taken alone. Nonetheless, those people we spoke to who'd worked there had been happy enough, telling us: *"It is much more relaxed there than in Crawley and Maidstone, which have a more head office, corporate feel."* Similarly, the private client outpost in Horsham has a friendly and compact feel to it, although it rarely feature on a trainee's radar. The property litigation-led Croydon office is not visited by trainees.

wherever i lay my hat?
The location of a trainee's next seat can be hard to call and trainees have different ways of dealing with this. While some may prefer to up sticks and relocate when necessary, others settle for what can potentially be a lengthy commute. Usually they get six to eight weeks notice of their next posting and, where travel exceeds 25 miles per journey, the firm will pay them an extra £1,200 to cover expenses for the duration of that seat. With all this moving about, the most trusted ally of any asb trainee is their car. Unfortunately, this means post-work fun is often hampered by fear of the breathalyser. In Crawley this is not seen as any great loss, but in Maidstone more of an effort is made to plan the odd car-less outing, and on the last Thursday of most months you can find trainees at Young Professionals Network events *"drinking and socialising with accountants."* For a big night out most trainees head for the social Mecca of Brighton, where the office's location *"two minutes from the train station and ten minutes from the beach"* is a recipe for fun. In the summer especially, trainees from other offices

descend on the town in the knowledge that a beach volleyball match will likely be the catalyst for a West Street jolly.

Who does the firm like to take? *"I think they want people with a bit of initiative or character, not someone waiting to be moulded into the firm's pet dog."* It is no surprise then that the firm is known for being *"more flexible than lots of places in accepting people who have taken alternative routes to a training contract."* As for whether the firm tends to recruit those with a prior commitment to the South East, the answer is pretty much a yes. It recruits quite a few people from Sussex Uni and usually also attends law fairs in Reading and Southampton. Ideally the firm would like trainees to have a prior connection to the South East, but it stresses that this is not essential. In 2007, one of the four qualifiers took up an NQ position at the firm, going into the corporate finance department.

and finally...

For those who are prepared to be flexible about office location, asb offers high-quality regional work across a broad range of disciplines.

Ashfords

the facts

Location: Exeter, Plymouth, Bristol, Tiverton, Taunton
Number of UK partners/solicitors: 53/94
Total number of trainees: 31
Seats: 4x6 months
Alternative seats: Secondments
Extras: Pro bono – Tiverton Saturday Surgery

With established offices in Exeter, Plymouth, Tiverton and Taunton, as well as an ambitious new branch in Bristol, Ashfords is undoubtedly a key player in the increasingly competitive South West legal market.

racing forward

Since it split in 2004 from the firm that is now known as Bevan Brittan, Ashfords has been working hard to become dominant in the region. As one of our interviewees put it: *"In the next couple of years, we will have consolidated our position south of Bristol and we will be a major force in the city itself."* Fighting talk, from a firm that has some equally ambitious rivals in this neck of the woods. Certainly there seems to be a tangible sense of purpose in the air and an explicit drive towards building a stronger name and reputation. The newly established Bristol office is pushing its corporate and commercial practice, while the Plymouth office has also reinforced its business services offering. Exeter, the largest of all the offices, performs well across the board in commercial areas. Among the Exeter lawyers' recent highlights is advice to the South Western Fish Producers Organisation and the Secretary of State for Environment, Food & Rural Affairs on EU matters, following a submission to the ECJ. They have also been advising South West Water on potential contractual claims and picking up new blue-chip clients such as EDF Energy and National Grid Gas. The Exeter office harbours a sports law practice, too, and has recently advised champion flat jockey Jamie Spencer on the regulatory role of the Human Rights Act, the 2006 British Club Driver of the Year Sam Bird on sponsorship matters and professional cricketer Alan Searle in respect of a two-year worldwide ban. In contrast, the Tiverton and Taunton offices reflect a more traditional side of the firm, with many of the lawyers based in these satellites, working for private clients rather than commercial organisations.

ashfords' empire

Although trainees choose an office in which to base their training, due to the fact that *"you are not spoilt for choice in some of the offices outside Exeter,"* the firm does allow people to move in order to increase their seat options. Indeed, those trainees who are based in the Plymouth office are positively encouraged to try a seat in Exeter on the basis that it's good for them to sample a larger working environment. There is also the option for a few trainees to go on secondment to client Exeter University. The spread of trainees around the offices is as follows: Bristol (three); Plymouth (two); Exeter (around 20); Taunton (three) and Tiverton (three). And here's a list of the available seats: Bristol (employment, commercial property, coco, insolvency); Plymouth (marine, commercial property, commercial litigation); Exeter (everything except marine); Taunton (employment, commercial property, coco, private client); and Tiverton (property litigation, PI, private client and criminal).

All trainees need to take a contentious seat, and one of the main options is commercial litigation, where they can expect to handle all aspects of a claim from its issue onwards. A six-month seat in property litigation in Tiverton will include work for regular client Wandsworth Borough Council, which passes a good number of housing disputes to the firm. This seat will also bring trainees into contact with a number of the firm's oldest clients, some of them *"local landed gentry."* The trainees who'd experienced prop lit here told us: *"It's inevitable that there will be times when you feel out of your depth, because you are handling work that is completely new to you. But there is always somebody who is prepared to give you a hand and you never feel too intimidated to ask."* There are also a number of exciting niche litigation seats, such as marine and transport in Plymouth, which includes some (mainly claimant) personal injury work with a seafaring aspect.

A seat in the crime and matrimonial department in Tiverton was described by those who'd done it as *"fantastic"* and *"the most interesting and enjoyable seat in the training contract."* Typical

activities in this seat include sitting behind counsel in court, as well as handling simple family hearings and child protection matters alone. *"It's an incredible experience where you can glean invaluable client contact."* Part of the challenge comes from dealing with *"a lot of free half-hour appointments, which basically involve seeing people who come directly off of the street with a wide range of queries."* Although it's a complete contrast, the corporate seat in Bristol is also a popular choice. *"The attitude of the team is very ambitious – we are all very keen to put the firm on the map in Bristol, which makes for an exhilarating working environment if you do that seat."* Due to the nature of the work, there won't be as much client contact. Instead trainees are given *"tasks that are the building blocks of corporate deals."* According to the *Western Morning News*, Ashfords completed more South West-based M&A deals than any other firm in 2006. It racked up 36, just slightly ahead of Bond Pearce and Foot Anstey (at 33 each), with Stephens & Scown and Michelmores some way behind that.

who goes there?

Trainees are attracted to the firm's *"broad training contract"* and *"relaxed environment."* Exeter University supplies quite a lot of them, and although there are some individuals who originally come from outside the West Country, the firm clearly prefers people who have a demonstrable commitment to the area. As one of our interviewees commented: *"If they are going to invest in your training, then they need to know that you are not going to go anywhere afterwards."* Aside from this, Ashfords' recruiting criteria looks to be quite broad. The firm has *"people who are embarking on their second career training alongside those who have come straight through from university."*

In terms of matching people to the offices, *"it is mostly a case of where you want to go and if you are not happy, then you can move... or at least talk* to someone about it and see if they can do anything." The large Exeter office is thought to have most in common with the firm's ambitious new Bristol branch. Bristol is *"open plan and air conditioned and so it is a lot noisier and generally feels busier than the other smaller offices."* Tiverton and Taunton are both more traditional in their set-up and *"the partners all have their own offices and their own secretaries."* Quite possibly because of geography, the Plymouth office is still regarded as something of an outpost, although trainees suggest that it might be one of the ones that will expand most over coming years.

The cities in which the trainees are based obviously affect their social lives. *"The guys in Exeter go out informally quite regularly,"* and the Bristol trainees are keen to make the most of the city's social scene. Things are somewhat quieter outside these two locations, although we must mention Friday drinks in the boardroom in Taunton, which are a great way to get to know colleagues a little better. The entire trainee group manages to get together twice a year in Exeter, when they meet with the training partner to discuss how the scheme is running and then go out together afterwards for a meal and drinks. There is also a party to which future joiners are invited.

stripping down to the essentials

First-seat trainees have an appraisal after just one month *"to make sure they have settled in okay."* Thereafter appraisals are scheduled for the middle and end of each seat. The level of formality depends to a large extent on the supervisor, but on the whole trainees *"found them useful; a good chance to chat about where you are going."* Aside from the appraisals, the firm helps to support trainees by allocating them a mentor for the duration of their contract. Mentors are generally junior associates, on the basis that they are *"somebody who is closer to your own age, who can ease you in."*

Our sources certainly had positive things to say about the firm's culture. One told us: *"I think that the atmosphere in the office is really beneficial because everyone is approachable, you call everyone by their first name and there is no one that you worry about speaking to because they are too senior."* So how about the hours? A typical day runs from 9am to 6pm, although obviously there are some departments that require trainees to stay longer and others where the opposite is the case. *"When I was in Tiverton, if I was still there at 5.30pm I would be one of the only ones,"* reported a source. In this respect, you can't fault the firm's capacity to allow people to have genuinely good quality of life, something that is especially important to those who want to make the most of what the region has to offer. In terms of career choices, we used to feel that there were pretty limited options down in the South West; however, the region's largest law firms have definitely upped their game and are drawing in bigger, better instructions from clients, sometimes from outside the South West. And yet, if commercial law is not your bag, there is still oodles of choice on the private client front. All up, we reckon the West Country is hard to beat and that Ashfords is one of the best options in the region. Eleven of the 12 qualifiers clearly agreed and accepted jobs at the firm in 2007.

and finally…

Far from being a nondescript provincial outfit, Ashfords has entered an exciting phase in which its corporate and commercial divisions are getting a lot of attention. Recruits can easily take advantage of the new opportunities this presents by homing in on Bristol and Exeter; alternatively they may find the private client work of somewhere like Tiverton suits them better. Either way, the firm looks like a great place to start a legal career.

Ashurst

the facts
Location: London
Number of UK partners/solicitors: 130/311
Total number of trainees: 98
Seats: 4x6 months
Alternative seats: Overseas seats, secondments
Extras: Pro bono – Islington and Toynbee Hall legal advice centres; Disability Rights Commission, Business in the Community, death row appeals; language bursaries

Step this way if you fancy life in a City firm with a focus on corporate and finance but you're not all that interested in being one of the hundreds joining the magic circle. Ashurst has long offered a blue-chip clientele and top-quality experiences in an altogether more familial atmosphere than you might find at one of the biggest firms.

power rangers
A few changes in seat allocation mean that seats in corporate and finance are now on the cards for all trainees. This should come as little surprise to anyone familiar with the firm's business – it has long been the case that *"they are the biggest departments and it is in these two sectors that the firm makes most of its money."* Corporate deals have continued to come in thick and fast during the past couple of years and the firm's work frequently hit the business press. Ashurst lawyers advised RUSAL on its merger with SUAL/Glencore, a $30bn deal that created the world's largest aluminium producer. They also acted on behalf of Netcare Healthcare Holdings and Apax Partners Worldwide in the £2.3bn acquisition of General Healthcare Group, which called upon the collective resources of Ashurst's network of international offices. The mammoth £11.6bn acquisition of ScottishPower by Iberdrola fully utilised both the corporate and international finance arms of the firm in relation to advice to ABN AMRO, the arranger of the funding.

"Real estate is probably the next biggest department," sources tell us. This is interesting, given that many City firms have played down this practice in recent years. Here, however, it is flourishing. To illustrate, for client Westfield the firm has been helping on two mixed-use London developments, one in Stratford and the other in White City, valued at £4bn and £2bn respectively. It also advised Teighmore and Sellar Property Group on the pre-letting of office space in the soon-to-be-built Shard of Glass, which will be the tallest building in Europe. Another change to the London landscape will come in the form of the redevelopment of Battersea Power Station. Ashurst's client Real Estate Opportunities recently bought the property for £400m.

forget the photocopying
Trainees in the corporate department will sit in one of two groups – either mainstream corporate or private equity. Work in the former typically encompasses a lot of smaller tasks such as drafting board meetings and filing things with Companies House – *"the boring stuff that actually gives you a great understanding of what buying and selling is all about."* This seat provides *"a steep learning curve,"* but trainees were full of praise for the *"great support provided."* On the larger deals they can expect to become familiar with the joys of managing an entire data room but, even then, *"the hours tend to be better than in finance seats."* Trainees also found that in terms of the firm's culture, the corporate department is its true heart. *"Most of the partners have been here a long time, perhaps even trained here, so they have a great handle on what the place is all about."* This is in contrast to the finance department, which some sense *"has a higher turnover of lawyers."* Private equity, or 'funds' as it is known, will acclimatise you to *"working to short timetables."* It will also grant you time off in lieu for those

Forget the competition

At Ashurst we work as a team, which means less competition and more communication.

If you've got team spirit call Stephen Trowbridge, Graduate Recruitment & Development Manager, on 020 7638 1111, email gradrec@ashurst.com or visit www.ashurst.com

BRUSSELS DUBAI FRANKFURT LONDON MADRID MILAN MUNICH
NEW DELHI NEW YORK PARIS SINGAPORE STOCKHOLM TOKYO

ashurst

periods when you find yourself burning the midnight oil. Essentially, the purpose of this department is to help investors use their funds to acquire assets through corporate deals. *"In many ways the trainee's job is all about managing the process;"* instead of looking at the law, its more a case of managing the practicalities of a deal, things like *"organising draw-downs on funds and advising on the availability of information."* One thing is certain: *"You're not often called upon to do the photocopying. We have a brilliant reprographic department for all that."*

Having ticked off corporate there's the other must-do seat – finance. The international finance department is divided into three distinct branches: leveraged finance, real estate finance and securities and structured finance (SSF). Trainees enthused about the possibility of *"doing something truly fascinating"* in SSF, remarking on the *"high quality of work on offer here."* Explained one: *"Whereas in corporate there are lots of routine things to do, in SSF there is more scope for getting involved in the specifics, more opportunities to use your brain."* Leveraged finance also offers good work and provides the willing trainee with an array of challenges. The downside for one interviewee was that *"the hours there were horrendous. For three weeks I wasn't home before one o'clock in the morning and I was working every weekend."*

In addition to real estate, other seat options include IP, employment, incentives and pensions, competition, technology, commercial and tax. Many a trainee has also experienced life in energy, trade and infrastructure (ETI). Everyone we spoke to who'd sat here relished the variety of work on offer: *"Some of it was related to corporate, some of it was project-specific, while other elements were more financial."*

One of the biggest pieces of work was for Petrochemical Industries Company K.S.C, a subsidiary of Kuwait Petroleum Corporation. The firm advised on the $3bn Greater Equate Project in Kuwait, including joint venture arrangements with The Dow Chemical Company, drafting and negotiating a wide range of project agreements and the Shareholder Commitment Agreement with lenders. Some past occupants of the seat argued that *"the results are more tangible"* here than in corporate. Even if you find some of the PFI projects a little dull, *"you are given really good work, like analysing contracts."* Sitting in this department will expose you to plenty of research for oil companies, because *"if there are mergers and acquisitions involving oil companies then it is this department that will do the deal."* The tax seat is a love-it-or-hate-it experience. Those who love it do so because it is research heavy. Those who hate it cite precisely the same factor as its drawback. Some trainees are tempted by litigation seats, and why not when you consider some of the cases on which Ashurst has been instructed? In the past year lawyers have been working on things like Centrica's £80m claim against Premier Power in relation to disputed transportation costs under a long-term gas sales agreement, and the FSA's successful defence of judicial review proceedings brought by Yukos in relation to the listing of Rosneft securities in London and Moscow. Anyone not so inclined can opt for a two-week litigation course that leaves them free to enjoy an entirely transaction-based training contract.

Some trainees will be lucky enough to experience life in foreign parts. Ashurst's international network of offices includes Dubai, New York, Milan, Paris, Frankfurt, Madrid, Munich, Brussels, Stockholm, New Delhi, Tokyo and Singapore. Also on offer are client secondments, with possible placements at Abbey, IBM, Lehman Brothers and Reuters, among others. Each of these represents *"an opportunity to see how a client's business works, while working in a smaller team than you might be used to back at the firm."*

the good life

While end-of-seat reviews are quite formal, mid-seat reviews *"are relaxed affairs, nothing more than a chat with your supervisor really."* Relaxed was a word of which our interviewees were rather fond: despite working at one of the largest City firms, the trainees talked at length about its collegial atmosphere. *"No one is out to stab you in the back"* and being *"a team player really means something here,"* they assured us. How well you are likely to get on with everyone is thought to be a central tenet of the interview process. *"As much as it's about how well you can do the job, it's also about your personality. They make sure you have some common sense, but mainly it's about hiring people who will be pleasant to work with,"* said one recruit.

Each department has its differences, of course, but what they have in common is that *"there is no need to put in face time for the sake of it. You just do the work when it is there."* Corporate is *"perhaps the most informal department,"* while in the derivatives team *"you go for a cooked breakfast together every Monday at a place round the corner from the office."* Indeed, trainees characterise SSF as a place where *"everyone really gives a shit about each other; there's a real sense of community."* This sense of community is no doubt heightened by departmental away-days. In the past these have included whiling away an afternoon at a partner's country house and – much more exotic, we presume – taking a trip to Morocco. Generally, the hours here aren't too awful, with *"leaving around 7pm being the norm."* Even those who spoke of the horrors of life in international finance told us that if you stay late one evening *"no one will think ill of you if you leave at 5pm the next day."* Assuming the deal is concluded and there's no longer a rush in the office, of course. And throughout all of this, it's unlikely you will be wearing a tie *"unless you're meeting clients."*

Ashurst trainees take part in all manner of sports and activities, with football, netball, hockey and rugby matches all regular occurrences during evenings and at weekends. Less frequent but no less a feature of the firm's social life is dragon boat racing, which pits Ashurst crews against a litany of other law firms and professionals, before putting grudges aside to allow everyone to enjoy a barbecue. Shortly before our interviews at the firm, Ashurst had just come first at a charity regatta for the second year in a row. Elsewhere, trainees *"always look forward to the vacation placement week activities,"* which offer the chance to have a few laughs and a few drinks with prospective recruits. The summer party with its Ferris wheel and dodgems is generally held at the Honourable Artillery Company and has become something of a tradition. More off-the-cuff social gatherings occur in *"various bars in the Spitalfields and Hoxton areas."* The Paper Mill and the Coach & Horses are particular favourites with the younger set right now.

spread the word

Not so long ago this firm was called Ashurst Morris Crisp and it was known as a place where posh Oxbridge graduates came to practise. It has shortened its name, buffed and polished its two offices and pushed out the marketing boat to transform its profile from conservative and stable to fresher and more dynamic. While it continues to attract a sizeable portion of its recruits from Oxford and Cambridge, it has, like the networking website Facebook, opened its doors willingly to students from other institutions. Word of mouth seems to have played an important part in attracting the trainees we spoke to, with one recalling: *"Some people I knew from university said it was good."* Another told us Ashurst had been recommended by a friend of a sibling. The sense of community implied by such comments proliferated throughout our interviews. Though many were attracted to the firm because of its reputation in relation to corporate and finance deals, the majority were concerned about *"working with people I like as* much as *doing the right kind of work.*" This may well have been the thing that led to a very healthy 43 out of 47 of them staying on in NQ jobs in 2007.

and finally...

This firm attracts a very affable bunch of trainees. According to them: "*The relatively small intake and informal atmosphere here creates a genuinely communal spirit.*" Maybe your sister knows somebody at the firm; perhaps your friends have given it the thumbs-up; either way, this is one place in the City where "*you don't have to become a robot to do well.*"

Baker & McKenzie LLP

the facts

Location: London
Number of UK partners/solicitors: 88/195
Total number of trainees: 70
Seats: 4x6 months
Alternative seats: Overseas seats, secondments
Extras: Pro bono – Waterloo Legal Advice Centre, UN High Commission for Refugees, Trinidad and Tobago death row appeals, Prisoners Abroad; language training

With offices in 38 countries, Baker & McKenzie is the epitome of a truly global law firm. Established in Chicago in 1949 by hard-working fellow Russell Baker, it expanded rapidly, securing offices wherever it saw an opening in the market.

vip areas

Now, B&M has 3,400 lawyers on its books, but has always been keen to assert that, regardless of the vast international network it has created, each of its 70 offices enjoys autonomy. And yet its Visual Identity Programme (VIP) requires that the same "*logo, stationary and that sort of thing are found across the offices.*" One trainee summed it up perfectly, saying: "*It's a positive trait in all the offices around the world that each one operates on the premise of having a dual function – to be an international law firm with an international network, but also to be a strong domestic firm.*"

The allure of the international network is what gets B&M to the top of its applicants' shortlists. When faced with the question 'Why this firm?' each and every trainee gave variations of the same answer – "*Its international presence,*" "*so many offices with such a high profile,*" "*globally a huge firm,*" "*its ability to work closely with other branches.*" These comments are always followed by something along the lines of "*I wanted somewhere where the trainee intake wasn't too big.*" Sure enough, the firm delivers on its promises of global work and its twice-yearly trainee intake is kept trimmed to a reasonable size.

When a firm has so many offices, there is always a fear that some may lack depth or quality. The 46-year-old London office – the largest in the network – most definitely does not suffer from this problem. It boasts an impressive list of achievements and its heavyweight clientele includes the likes of Sony, Cisco Systems, Pfizer, PepsiCo and FedEx Corp. The firm has just secured a place on the BBC's legal panel. One example of the kind of deal the firm handles is the work it did for The Body Shop International following the £652m offer made by L'Oréal. Away from corporate, "*there are some strong standalone departments,*" including an employment team that is deemed one of the best in the UK. Its clients include major employers such as British Airways, Accenture, Prudential and Hewlett Packard. Another esteemed group is the IP/IT team, again benefiting from an impressive client roster of premium brands. And we mustn't forget the competition and pensions groups, which are also highly regarded. The growing London finance team is definitely one to watch and it is

London

BAKER & M^cKENZI

Baker & McKenzie in London offers unparalleled opportunities to become a first class lawyer in the world's largest global law firm.

Tel: +44 (0)20 7919 1000
Email: london.graduate.recruit@bakernet.com

Expand your horizons

WINNER *LC*ⁿ AWARDS 2007
BEST TRAINER
LARGE CITY FIRM

THE TIMES 2007
TOP 100
GRADUATE EMPLOYERS

www.ukgraduates.bakernet.com

Baker & McKenzie LLP is an English limited liability partnership and is a member of Baker & McKenzie International, a Swiss Verein.

currently the subject of much love and attention from management. It has closed several billions of pounds-worth of deals, particularly in the areas of structured finance and securitisation. As is typical with B&M, a significant number of the transactions were international.

privy to it all

The training scheme involves four six-month seats and recruits may state three preferences before the start of each seat. The firm is *"quite open about what you may do,"* and as a general rule the firm endeavours to give trainees *"one priority seat"* in an area of business that interests them. A corporate seat is compulsory, one insightful newbie noting how *"business demands have to be met."* Generally, trainees must either tick off their corporate seat or clock up their required contentious hours in their first year, *"so that in the second year it becomes easier to move people about."*

As well as corporate seats, mainstream options are available in banking, capital markets, property and disputes, and then more niche options are available in IT, IP, commercial, employment, pensions, tax, environment, private banking and EU competition and trade. In most seats trainees do a combination of *"tasks that are essential for the case, stuff that needs to be done"* and *"interesting work where you are being pushed and really using your brain."* Banking is said to be a good department to start off with, as it *"gives you exposure to a lot of the firm"* and gets you *"liaising with foreign counsel"* as well as ringing up clients to *"chase for documents."* Always popular, the competition team has *"a very, very broad practice"* and handles *"big cartel cases and trade work."* Trainees encounter *"household-name clients"* as they research, attend client meetings and help draft responses to investigations. The broad-ranging disputes department is one where trainees have *"a fair bit of client contact and do a lot of research and drafting witness statements."*

There are also trips to the High Court, Privy Council and House of Lords. The employment group offers a blend of advisory work and research. Again the seat involves trips out of the office in the form of attendance at tribunals to take notes and babysit clients.

Corporate seats instil fear but ensure thrills. *"The work is intense,"* said one trainee who had enjoyed the *"exciting, fast-paced, dynamic"* atmosphere. Although the department is divided into different areas, it isn't *"split into as many specialisms as some of the bigger firms, so you get a broader range of work,"* from M&A to capital markets. On the bigger deals, the trainee's role revolves around *"general transaction and project management, managing the flow of information and collating advice from different offices."* On smaller transactions, it's a different story; our interviewees reported much more autonomy, including *"heading off to meet with the other side alone."*

the jet set

Most often in their fourth seat, the majority of trainees make the most of the opportunity to go on secondment to another office in the B&M network or in-house with a client. This part of the training scheme is *"definitely not compulsory"* and *"very much your choice... some people simply don't want to go."* Wherever they went, trainees reported being well supervised and kept in the loop with issues back at home. The top destinations are Sydney, Beijing, Brussels, Chicago, Tokyo, New York, Toronto, Moscow, Madrid and Hong Kong, but it is also important to know that not all seats are available everywhere, and some locations will only offer experience in a limited range of practice areas. Anyone who misses out as a trainee, or whose appetite for a foreign secondment grows, can apply to go abroad after qualification.

Back in London, trainees praised the level of supervision and the review process. *"I can always knock on people's door to ask for work,"* said one, and supervisors are always careful to *"keep an eye on your workload and shield you from getting too much."* Many put their ability to get decent work down to the small trainee intake: *"It's not stressful because you're not trying to clamber over each other."* On the subject of hours there was a diversity of opinion on what was normal. Naturally some departments are busier than others, and certain times of the year are known to be more hectic. We heard stories about all-nighters and the odd 40-hour stint, although it sounds as if *"being taken out for breakfast the next morning"* is a nice postscript. As one trainee put it: *"You wouldn't last very long if people were working through the night and you said, 'I'm going home.' You are expected to put in the hours."* On a more normal day, it is possible to leave the office at about 6.30pm.

Can such a sizeable and successful firm maintain a hospitable atmosphere? One trainee insisted this was the case: *"In comparison to other large City law firms, there is a noticeably less hostile environment here... we don't have many lawyers that get off on being arseholes."* Which brings us to our next point. Although most come from the top universities around the world, recruits were clear about the kind of person who would fit in. *"If you're elitist, you won't fit in,"* suggested one, adding: *"If you exude too much self-importance, you won't get along here; the majority of people here don't accept that kind of attitude."* Trainees reckon this atmosphere permeates the entire network: *"You can ring anyone in any office really easily,"* which leads them to think *"it must be part of the criteria to be nice."* In 2007, 29 of the 37 qualifying trainees took jobs at the firm, settling themselves in a spread of departments, including corporate, banking, disputes and employment.

show me the way...

We quickly learned that implying B&M London is an American law firm was like touching a raw nerve. *"It is one in name, but it doesn't feel like one,"* considered a source, who then added: *"We operate as if it were an English firm in London."* Other trainees were more forthright: *"London is very much run by London, and if anyone says it's an American firm, we are quick to say we aren't."* So there you have it: the best advice is to use the term 'international firm'.

Every year the firm holds its very own European Cup football tournament, the 'Euro Baker Cup.' In 2007 it was Vienna's turn to host the event and the year before that it was Warsaw. *"We came fourth in Warsaw,"* explained one source, *"because the Moscow and Frankfurt offices took it far too seriously and didn't get involved in the evening activities."* We say, who needs a good night's sleep when there's partying and networking to be done? The trainees agree: *"It's great to actually meet people you chat to on the phone and through e-mail."* London hockey players also get some overseas action: at a recent tournament in Amsterdam, they trounced the Dutch. The other sports enjoyed by staff are netball and cricket, and the firm is an enthusiastic participant in the Manches Cup sailing regatta. Monthly Friday drinks tend to be a *"starting point"* for nights out at The Evangelist or one of the bars in Paternoster Square, next to St Paul's cathedral, and there are big parties at Christmas and in the summer. Budding thesps will be pleased to hear of the tradition for first-years to perform a revue at the Christmas ball. *"Quite often the partners come in for a bit of stick,"* but it's all good fun. The last one was *"loosely based on a Christmas Carol,"* and for some reason incorporated a movie of partners and associates singing Amarillo.

B&M recruits attend a tailored LPC course at the College of Law. Trainees give this their seal of approval, saying: *"The more overlap [between law school and the training contract] you can cut out the better."* The first intake to take the bespoke course start their training contracts in September

2008, so time will tell how beneficial they will find it. At the very least, the firm hopes it will *"foster stronger links between Baker & McKenzie and its future trainees."*

and finally...

If you're keen to get a training contract here then do yourself a favour and apply for the comprehensive vacation scheme, during which you can sample two different departments over three weeks. Said one source: *"A lot of people in my intake had done the scheme, and most of the people who were on it got a training contract interview."* If you've a whole summer to spare, why not apply for an international clerkship, which lasts 12 weeks – six in London and six in another office.

Barlow Lyde & Gilbert LLP

the facts
Location: London
Number of UK partners/solicitors: 74/181
Total number of trainees: 39
Seats: 4x6 months
Alternative seats: Hong Kong, secondments
Extras: Pro bono – Toynbee Hall, Caribbean death row appeals

A star in the insurance and professional indemnity spheres, Barlow Lyde & Gilbert is also positioning itself in the litigation firmament.

in contention

Although BLG's name might not be the first to spring to your lips when considering City training contracts, the firm is arguably the Kate Moss of the insurance industry. *Chambers UK*, our parent guide, consistently bestows top rankings on BLG's insurance repertoire, which covers everything from marine, aerospace, energy and transport, through to property and financial risk.

The firm busies itself with defending solicitors, accountants and other professionals against negligence claims, and has represented several leading firms in this regard. BLG's reputation attracts insurance clients by the score (eg the Society of Lloyd's, Zurich Global Corporate and Hiscox Group); it also represents insured companies in disputes (eg Rolls-Royce, BAE Systems and Cathay Pacific). BLG's PI and medical negligence department represents NHS trusts, local authorities and emergency services. Recently the department was involved in litigation surrounding a large food poisoning case in Wales and an explosion at a Sussex fireworks factory.

After a downturn for the insurance litigation market and several departures from BLG's partnership ranks, BLG has sought to revamp itself. The firm converted to LLP status, created a new associate director position for would-be partners and hired a PR firm to promote it as the go-to firm for all types of commercial litigation. It is one of the few firms willing to litigate against banks, a stance that has garnered new clients like British Energy, and it recently won a position on *Which?* magazine's legal panel. On a slightly more tabloid-worthy note, the firm represented The Ritz Hotel in Mohamed Al Fayed's battle to have a jury hear the inquests into the deaths of Princess Diana and Dodi Al Fayed. Other prominent clients include Tesco, Cable & Wireless, Abbey, the Ferrero Group and mobile phone company 3.

If you're a transactional junkie, look away now. BLG is a litigation firm through and through. It's not that it doesn't have non-contentious departments, but these are in no way a match for the firm's well-muscled litigation arm. As, one market-aware trainee explained: *"You always need a corporate department in a litigation firm to keep the firm buoyant."* However, another's view was that *"since the majority of partners are litigation partners, the corporate department lacks the support it needs. It feels like it's falling by the*

wayside." This can spell some *"horrendous hours"* for corporate trainees and could explain the swathe of recent departures from the team. BLG is currently trying to build the department up again, but we sensed that it has a hard job ahead of it in the current market. In addition to corporate, BLG's non-contentious expertise extends to banking and finance, employment and pensions, real estate and environmental, and commercial and technology.

fight or flight

The behemoth that was the professional liability and commercial litigation (PLCL) department, recently split under the weight of its massive size. Each half offers seats to several trainees at a time and, although strictly speaking there are no compulsory seats, it is *"generally accepted that you'll do one of your first two seats there."* It's a good introductory seat that's *"ideal for teaching you lawyers' skills. After seeing so many professional negligence claims against solicitors, you make sure you're properly organised and never miss deadlines,"* said one source. Others were quick to point out that even in the firm's largest departments, *"everyone's very conscious of getting you involved in things."* Trainees take attendance notes at client meetings, perform document management tasks, do *"lots of preparation for trial, including plenty of bundling"* and research civil procedure rules. The firm recently introduced a trainee pooling scheme which ensures work is better allocated between those who are working flat out and those who *"have capacity."* In addition, the department has several paralegals to assist with grunt work.

From PL and CL it's a *"natural progression"* to seats in smaller departments. Other insurance teams include reinsurance, aerospace, and marine, energy and trade. Aerospace is becoming popular as more and more trainees enthuse about the high levels of responsibility and *"quite glamorous"* work. The marine, energy and trade department has been renamed to reflect a growing emphasis on energy sector matters and its work ranges from *"wet and dry shipping"* to *"commodities trading in grain and sugar."* At the time of writing the department was occupied with *"a massive piece of international arbitration stretching across the Western world"* and worth upwards of $3bn. One trainee described it as *"a bit of a fight... It's fun and games!"*

Whereas most trainees sit with supervisors in an office, in casualty and commercial risk (CCR) they are grouped together in the middle of the open-plan office. On the casualty side they encounter PI and clinical negligence cases, areas in which tasks include drafting instructions to counsel and independent experts, speaking with clients over the phone and via e-mail, and even conducting advocacy. On the commercial risk side, insurance and reinsurance cases are the order of the day. Trainees receive *"an absolutely fantastic variety of work"* in this small team. They also enjoy high levels of responsibility, running their own cases, which range in value from *"a couple of thousand pounds to £100K."* Naturally there are some very big and complicated cases – often involving major disasters like the Buncefield oil depot explosion, hurricanes in the Gulf of Mexico and the 9/11 attacks – and on these, trainees take a tiny part.

hong kong queue-y

Most trainees only do one non-contentious seat; a few persistent (or lucky) ones wangle two. As well as corporate, non-contentious options are available in the employment, and commercial and technology departments. One seasoned trainee cautioned: *"They do have niche non-contentious departments, but don't come here thinking you'd like to specialise in corporate, employment or IP. BLG is certainly a contentious firm. It isn't for corporate diehards."* Another remarked: *"There are people who've always said* they wanted employment and never got a seat there." When we put this to the firm it told us it was shocked to hear this.

The number of trainees, combined with a shortage of the most popular seats, means that "sometimes [seat allocation] is done quite late... you might only be told a week before the change." Despite this, our sources acknowledged that, overall, "the process is quite fair." Secondments to clients are also offered, and at the time of writing the firm had two trainees in its Hong Kong office, working on "a beast of a case that has been going on for a while and will probably carry on for a long time." All we can divulge is that the beast in question is "the biggest litigation case in Hong Kong's history" and concerns a professional negligence claim against a firm of auditors. Securing the Hong Kong seat involves a bit of a tussle with other hopefuls via a formal application and interview process. Once there, the chosen trainees are pampered with "office views of Hong Kong harbour, fantastic parties and a fully serviced flat that's cleaned every day." The firm has a small and somewhat beleaguered Singapore office, though without a permanent resident partner we can't see it extending an invite to trainees any time soon. A third overseas office is located in Shanghai.

While the majority of supervisors are great, "there are some who trainees have problems with every single time." Since criticising someone to their face is "very difficult" to say the least, trainees suggested the firm rectify this recurring problem by introducing formal, confidential 360° appraisals. Aside from this issue, our sources generally praised the firm's training programme and the graduate recruitment team in particular. Said one: "Caroline is always there and happy to talk with you about seat allocation as much as you want." Another felt the firm had "a nurturing environment, so you feel cared for." Previously trainees had been rather disgruntled with their salaries, so it's good to hear that BLG has responded to market competition by upping trainee and NQ pay packets. The firm also introduced bonuses, for which trainees are eligible. In September 2007, a healthy 14 of the 17 qualifiers stayed on at the firm, 11 going into contentious departments.

slug it out

BLG's office is located at Aldgate East. One source bemoaned the fact that the location is "stuck out in the middle of nowhere" and "a bit of a struggle to commute to if you live in west or south London." Another described it as "not particularly pleasant as it's on the edge of the City." The firm is apparently "short on space," so it's a good thing that "there might be more room in the building for us to move into." At least the firm has "a roof garden that's perfect for eating lunch outside," although apparently this is also used by "Reed Smith Richards Butler people." In previous years we have often mentioned BLG's preference for a tipple at the Slug and Lettuce across the street. Trainees now seem to want to break new ground: "We try to go further afield because it seems so clichéd." Every time they think they're out, however, the Slug pulls them back in. "Invariably we end up there. It would be bizarre if you didn't find someone from BLG in the Slug on a Friday evening." Whatever the favoured pub, trainees at least have the time for a leisurely drink. As is common in litigation firms, office hours are generally 9am to 6pm or 7pm.

Actually, socialising is a big thing at BLG, not least because insurance clients "always expect to entertain or be entertained." Organised events range from golf days (trainees get to "guard the hole") through "firm-wide meet-and-greet drinks in the atrium" to "an 80s-themed fancy-dress karaoke party," at which we hear there was "all sorts of cross-dressing," including " partners dressed as ladies" and "Spandau Ballet outfits." Sports teams are mustered for football, netball, hockey, cricket and even Frisbee, all of it useful for networking. "Partners play too, so it's a good way to get your face seen around. They appreciate it if you participate."

Our interviewees were so chatty, we wondered if the firm values personality more than grades. They told us: "As long as you've got the minimum academics they require, the firm looks at whether you're the sort of person who if left alone in a lift with a client could make conversation. You have to be adaptable. Arrogance is also a big no-no." BLG makes a concerted effort to leave an impression on prospective trainees. It has long-standing links with the universities of Exeter, Southampton, Sheffield and Nottingham, and several trainees were sold on the firm through the university events it had sponsored. The BLG vacation scheme is now a critical part of its recruitment programme, accounting for around two-thirds of all recruits. As a side note: to the group of summer vacation students who answered our phone call by mistake and then nervously hung up – we have your names on file...

Given that most trainees' knowledge of the insurance sector before they start their contracts is limited to the Sheilas' Wheels jingle, BLG has chosen to remedy this by signing up to the College of Law's LPC+ programme on which all future joiners will take a specialised insurance law module.

and finally...

Litigation, litigation, litigation – we can't say it enough. If you're a born litigator or you already have insight into the insurance world, put on a winning smile and get yourself on Barlow Lyde & Gilbert's vacation scheme.

Bates Wells & Braithwaite

the facts

Location: London
Number of UK partners/solicitors: 20/43
Total number of trainees: 10
Seats: 2x6 + 3x4 months
Alternative seats: Overseas seats, secondments
Extras: Pro bono – Blackfriars Legal Advice Centre, St Bartholomew's free will service, LawWorks; language training

If you volunteer for Amnesty International, dabble in amateur dramatics and spend your summers braving the Great British seaside to lighten your carbon footprint, this commercial law firm might just be able to offer you a career that brings together all your passions...

busy bwbs

It's hard to categorise whether Bates Wells & Braithwaite is a City or a West End firm. Its "lush office" in the heart of the Square Mile overlooks St Paul's, but its outlook has more in common with smaller, "Holborn or Westminster-type firms." The areas in which it works range from the theatre to the environment, and it has a long-term commitment to the charity and social enterprise sectors. Without doubt, BWB is a firm with a conscience. Pro bono work is encouraged and more than 40 of the 63 fee earners act as unpaid charity trustees. Charity clients also benefit from a fee discount worth £1m a year, and not-for-profit organisations use the firm's conference facilities for free. In addition to having the number-one charity department in the UK, BWB has expertise in administrative, employment and immigration law and is keen to be recognised for this. Commercial and private client work is also handled alongside property, sports law, television, film and theatre. Various "client-facing groups" have been set up to focus on specific areas such as education and carbon trading. Bringing together lawyers from multiple departments, these groups capitalise on the fact that many fee earners are already *"embedded in their sector."*

In 2006 the firm shuffled the management pack and converted to an LLP. So far, with turnover at approximately £10m, it's been *"a spiralling success,"* but stepping into a more professional management structure has led some (more senior employees) to worry that *"the firm might become very impersonally driven."* Yet to trainees, the chances of BWB becoming *"just another corporate law firm"* seem pretty slim. In terms of appointments, things are *"moving quickly."* New partner Mike Townley was taken on in 2007 to head up the new sports law department, causing much excitement. Said a source: *"He works for the goodies in sport – the regulating bodies as opposed to the commercial interests,"* and is particularly experienced with regard to Olympic governing bodies. In the future, sports law is expected to join charities, theatre and immigration as one of the firm's best-known niches.

The past year has brought precedent-setting cases and some headline-grabbers. In February 2007, lawyers lodged an application for judicial review to challenge rule changes by the Home Office in relation to the Highly Skilled Migrant Programme. These changes mean individuals who have sold their homes abroad and moved their families here (as part of the original programme rules) now have no hope of extending their permission to remain in the UK. In employment law, partner Lucy McLynn is taking a landmark case to the European Court in Luxembourg, marking the first time a UK court has referred a Disability Discrimination Act case to Europe. If your reading material is more tabloid than law reports, then the case of a prominent Lib Dem MP at the centre of a sex scandal involving a male prostitute might ring more bells.

Speaking of politics, with all three main parties currently sharing the big idea of ramping up investment in the Third Sector, BWB's decision to place emphasis here is right on the money. While the interior design of the firm's offices is the work of the same consultants who revamped the Conservative Party's new HQ, political affiliations are firmly of the Lib Dem variety. Consultant Andrew Philips is a Liberal Democrat lord, and past trainees had the privilege of acting as his gopher on the Charity Bill, *"swanning round the House of Lords and becoming immersed in legislation."* There's definitely *"a sense of being involved politically."*

dodgy phone calls

Trainees follow an unusual system of two six-month seats followed by three four-month seats. A number of the non-contentious areas were described as *"really rewarding – people come to you with their visions and ideas and you are trusted to create something out of them."* In the charity seat this is certainly the case. Supervision is low key, while the atmosphere is *"buzzing;"* trainees spoke of the *"excitement of hearing partners talk about the things they're doing."* The hours can be long in what is now *"the engine room of the firm,"* especially if you get involved in a big case or a charity registration that needs to be done urgently. Case highlights include negotiating royalties for Jamie Oliver's Fifteen brand, as well as advising the Fifteen Foundation on financing and property acquisition for the restaurant leased to a chef in the TV series *Jamie's Chef*. Other *"huge institutional clients"* include Amnesty International, Christian Aid, the Eden Project and Save the Children.

To be a good charity lawyer, it helps to gain experience in corporate/commercial first. *"These days, charities want people who know about big contracts and commercial issues, including sponsorship, licensing, brands and setting up service agreements."* Proving this point, BWB handles corporate work for Friends of the Earth. The trainees who do best in the corporate seat are the ones who enjoy company law, and the firm is certainly hoping to find more recruits who think this way. Said one source: *"They'd lap up anyone who wanted to join the department." "The responsibility here is better than normal,"* enthused a trainee; *"I'm definitely going to come out with more experience than my friends in other firms."*

BWB's litigators take on public and administrative law, dispute resolution and property litigation, meaning cases range from boundary disputes to fall-outs between charity trustees, copyright claims and *"literally anything you could imagine."* The firm is the sole legal adviser to icstis, the telephone industry regulator, and this is its biggest client in terms of volume of work. Recent highlights include *Big Brother* rule changes concerning evictions, the *Blue Peter* 'fake' competition winner and the infamous *Richard & Judy* 'You Say, We Pay' debacle. This work also requires regular involvement with Ofcom and what was the DTI (now BERR). Since the team acquired two paralegals, trainees have found they spend less time bundling and photocopying. *"There are hardly any menial tasks... so when they do pop up, you don't mind,"* said one. The cost of litigation means charity clients *"can be reluctant to go to trial"* and *"quite a few cases end up settling,"* but *"the nice thing is, you usually agree with your clients."* Is there an opportunity to build up a rapport? *"My god yeah, you could be sitting in a mediation with them from 8am to 9pm."*

After the excitement of litigation where you are jumping from different areas of law and *"doing something different every day,"* property and employment can seem *"relatively sedate"* by comparison. Nevertheless, they're both growing departments with good future job prospects. In property, your work will *"basically consist of residential conveyancing,"* most of which will come through your supervisor. In employment,

trainees advise clients on policy and procedures and help to defend claims. The three-strong private client department has a focus on social entrepreneurs and *"people who have created their own wealth rather than inherited it."* With only five fee earners, immigration is another small department. The team no longer takes on legal aid clients since changes in the funding of such cases; privately paying asylum clients are still coming in *"fast and furious."* Given that the rules are *"constantly changing,"* it helps that the head of department contributes to the leading authority on immigration law. Said one source: *"Getting someone their indefinite leave to remain so they can stay with their family makes getting up in the morning worthwhile. There is no client more grateful than an immigration client."* From time to time, a tasty sports law or theatre and arts seat also crops up. Secondments are available to Tate Modern or icstis. What BWB lacks in overseas offices, it makes up for through its membership of the PARLEX Group of European Lawyers, which enables a few trainees to experience an overseas seat in any member firm's office.

you decide

First-year seats are allocated by means of *"a fairly opaque process"* which is *"slightly done behind closed doors,"* so the best approach is *"to make it known what you want to do."* Second-years decide on their seats by agreeing among themselves. The process is made to run more smoothly *"with the threat that if we don't sort it out, it will be done randomly by someone else."* For their final seat, trainees commonly choose to go back to the team they hope to qualify with. Although *"it's not a question of who shouts loudest,"* we sensed that there was scope for refining the system of second-year allocations. In 2007 three of the four qualifiers stayed on with the firm and it's worth pointing out that in the past three years NQ retention has improved dramatically. One thing that helps is the firm's ability to offer a sweetener to those who are not given jobs in their preferred team. For example, a trainee who'd been offered a post in the charity and social enterprise team was also asked to form the nucleus of the education focus group. Trainees summarised this approach to staffing as something *"you'll either be attracted to or hate"* – effectively solicitors are expected to take an active interest in the firm as a whole. Said one: *"If you want to be a proper lawyer offering genuine advice and having an impact, you'll love it."*

No matter how frantic work gets, *"you have to draw the line somewhere, particularly when you're not getting paid £40K like at a big City firm."* Trainees can regularly be found at The Wine Tun just below the office, or the Metropolis around the corner. During the summer, the firm organises a grand day out (last time to Leeds Castle in Maidstone), at which boat trips, football matches, races and archery are all part of the fun. It has an excellent record for Christmas parties: one trainee described last year's sit-down dinner and disco on a Thames river boat as *"one of the best parties I've ever been to... I remember looking up as we were going under Tower Bridge and absolutely everyone was dancing."* An abundance of theatre clients also has its benefits – as well as being invited to the annual Olivier Awards, some of our sources had received a seemingly endless supply of free tickets. *"I've been to the theatre five times in the last two months,"* enthused one.

and finally...

Bates Wells & Braithwaite is looking for committed, driven individuals who have done their research on the firm. If you want to find out more, apply for a summer placement or check out the wealth of material on the website.

Beachcroft LLP

the facts

Location: Birmingham, Bristol, Leeds, London, Manchester, Winchester
Number of UK partners/solicitors: 144/409
Total number of trainees: 76
Seats: 4x6 months
Alternative seats: None

Beachcroft is a national firm with 1,400 staff which, despite steady and deliberate steps to bulk up in transactional areas of practice for mainstream corporates, is still viewed as a particularly appropriate choice for applicants with an interest in the healthcare and insurance sectors.

geography lesson

Bristol is the firm's headquarters, and much of the impetus for a more commercial outlook comes from there. In size it is closely followed by the London offices, of which there are two, one in Holborn and the other on Eastcheap, close to the London insurance centre. North of the Watford Gap, the Manchester and Leeds offices are a little bit smaller, mostly fed on a robust diet of public sector work, insurance matters and litigation. Offices in Birmingham and Winchester do not take trainees.

The ongoing efforts to make Beachcroft into a more corporate outfit have been simmering away for a few years now. As to how far the firm has progressed in this mission depends on where you look. Our interviews with trainees up and down the network were remarkably similar to those of past years: they told us once again how the firm was *"on the cusp of bigger and better things,"* and that in relation to pushing the Beachcroft brand out to students, *"slowly but surely the word is getting around."* It was from Bristol in particular that trainees confirmed a trend towards more corporate work. Said one: *"That department is certainly* on the rise more than any other." However, up in Manchester the firm shows less inclination in this direction, and in 2007 two of the Manchester qualifiers moved on due to the relative paucity of the corporate offering. Even in London, where the corporate team has achieved some success with banks, our interviewees had to acknowledge: "*You shouldn't come to this firm for massive, hit-the-press deals.*" So, all this acknowledged, let's look at the many other reasons why you would choose to embrace a career here.

three little letters, one big client

Should you plump for the Bristol office, you'll find yourself with as wide a choice of seats as you could possibly wish for. There's everything from personal injury, clinical negligence, professional indemnity to projects, construction, insolvency, employment and commercial services. That's in addition to commercial property, corporate and seats in a healthcare team that is as good as any in the country.

The "*corporate department has been getting some of its work from London,*" so being a trainee in this seat will likely give you a national rather than local perspective. A place to "*get stuck in,*" the department may also require you to travel a little. One trainee spoke of "*flying down to Jersey and Guernsey to attend board meetings before popping back to Bristol.*" Our sources had been involved in all manner of transactions, "*including some AIM flotations,*" and there is every reason to believe the team has a bright future – it is built around a core of former Slaughter and May lawyers. One of the highlights of its first full year was the £122m share buy-back for Topps Tiles plc.

Healthcare seats expose trainees to some of the fascinating problems faced by core client the NHS; for example, "*whether or not hospitals can supply certain products to Jehovah's Witnesses while in a vegetative state.*" Even if you decide to sidestep the healthcare department, "*you will encounter

the NHS as a client in almost all the seats.*" The ever-popular employment law option brings plenty of court and tribunal visits, "*dealing with lots of unfair dismissal, harassment and discrimination cases.*" Again, this is mainly for the NHS, though if there is a suitable corporate deal on, "*you will also draft severance agreements.*" While there are officially no compulsory seats, commercial property seems to figure in most seat schedules in Bristol. Within that department there are three seat possibilities: development, health property (largely representing you know who) and asset management, the latter involving acting for a large owner of shopping centres, managing its various leases. This last seat has "*tons of small things for trainees to do.*"

plane speaking

In London the options are similarly wide. The smaller Eastcheap office is the place to go for insurance litigation, which is "*a well-rounded seat*" incorporating a spot of policy drafting on coverage issues as well as defending claims and "*chasing people that owe our clients money.*" Even trainees who were not initially inclined toward the idea of litigation found the variety of work and interaction with senior lawyers an inspiring element of this seat. "*I was meeting with counsel and interviewing witnesses, the whole shebang,*" purred one source. The larger office in Fetter Lane offers seats in employment, construction, projects, financial services, a litany of litigation departments and corporate. Corporate at this office was deemed "*brilliant*" by one interviewee who had enjoyed getting their hands on "*every type of deal under the sun.*" As well as "*nice M&A, MBOs, joint ventures and normal share purchases,*" trainees could encounter almost anything of a commercial nature. One noted how "*while I was there, we became defacto specialists in aircraft finance. All of a sudden, all sorts of wealthy individuals were using us to help buy their planes and helicopters. *It was fun work, but I was a little bitter as I was struggling to keep my Oyster card topped up at the time.*"

London trainees have an added seat option – a six-month secondment to Unilever, which can be the subject of much jostling for a place. Those who win out get to taste both contract drafting and *"managing bits and bobs of litigation."* *"You get more responsibility and control over your workload than you might back at the firm,"* and as such it is seen as *"the ideal transition from training to quali-fied lawyer."*

northern exposed

"The big money spinner for the Leeds office is per-sonal injury work," explained a helpful source up North. This particular department occupies its own office and those who take a seat there get as much insurance litigation, public sector and healthcare cases as they can handle. As in other offices, trainees *"certainly get to know the NHS back to front."* Indeed, the dedicated healthcare department offers *"a great seat"* and *"plenty of exposure to clients."* It basically involves solving all the client's legal problems, be these questions over whether or not a patient is capable of giving consent, the storage of tissues (human not Kleenex) and *"dealing with inquests when some-one dies in dodgy circumstances."* Here, as elsewhere, you will get plenty of litigation expe-rience, much of it sitting behind barristers while they make submissions, *"which teaches you to write notes really quickly!"* Life in the profes-sional indemnity seat is *"always busy"* and intellectually challenging on account of the con-stantly shifting sands. *"Just when you've got your head around architects, you move onto a case with surveyors. It is both varied and fascinating the whole time."*

The Manchester office, like each of its sisters, doesn't have any compulsory seats; however, *"it is highly likely you will sit in both property and insur-ance litigation."* Insurance lit is an ideal place to start your contract due to the perfectly pitched levels of responsibility and exposure – *"generally speaking, the water never gets too deep."* A broad sweep of work runs from larger cases through to small road traffic accidents. The other Manches-ter seat options broadly mirror what's on offer elsewhere, although be advised that *"no one really comes to Manchester for corporate work."*

not here, charlie

In all offices, there is an end-of-seat review where you sit down with your supervisor to talk through objectives achieved and what could have been done better. There is also a more informal mid-seat review where, depending on your supervisor, you may find yourself *"having a chat in Starbucks or the pub"* or sitting in a plain-old meeting room. The hours at Beachcroft are typically quite kind, and although across the firm we sensed the aver-age working day to be 9am to 6pm, there are so many permutations of seat, client, deadlines, start time and supervisor as to make averages relatively meaningless. The occasional midnight stay is per-fectly possible in transactional seats, for example, while in others *"few people would turn their heads if you left at 5pm."* For anyone on the Unilever sec-ondment, *"if you stayed until 6pm, you'd be the last person in the office."*

This is not a firm to attract the gutsiest, hungri-est Gordon Gekko types. Indeed we'd characterise Beachcrofters as people who want to see others' egos turned to the lowest setting. *"Big-time Char-lies will get short shrift here,"* said one, and from another: *"There is no hierarchy to speak of and superciliousness is at a minimum."* In terms of socialising, *"there is not a lot of mixing across the firm."* In fact, the whole firm is brought together only once every two years. The trainees fare better on this score as they all meet up for PSC training, and the very first day with the firm is spent in Lon-don regardless of which office trainees have joined.

The Bristol trainees are *"a pretty sociable bunch"* who can regularly be found after work in the trendy Toto Bar or having one of the excellent sandwich lunches at The Bridge Inn. There are plenty of sports on offer – football, netball, rounders, softball, touch rugby and the odd game of rugby sevens as well. We hear that one trainee helped organise a tug of war competition against property professionals and clients. Unfortunately the firm lost the competition: *"We need a little more muscle,"* a source chuckled. In 2008, the Bristol HQ is to move to a new office with *"a gym, restaurant and all sorts... it's all very ergonomically designed."*

London trainees can also get involved in football and cricket, though if like one of our interviewees you *"prefer to just delete those e-mails,"* there is always the alternative of *"popping to Meeting Room 12,"* the nickname given to the White Swan on account of its location in the same building in Fetter Lane. Around the office, staff enjoy a permanent smart-casual dress policy, *"though you can't wear jeans and you have to have a suit in the office for outings to court. It helps the office have a really chilled atmosphere."*

The Manchester contingent claims Mr Thomas's Chop House as its local, reserving an option over the more upbeat surroundings of Revolution. An active local TSG usually has a Beachcroft representative or two on its committee, helping to bring together the obligatory balls, barbecues and monthly drinks events. There are football and netball teams and the office is sited centrally in the city, *"dangerously close to the shops."*

The Leeds office, like Manchester, fronts onto a square that is ideal for sun worshipping (when the weather allows), although the old age of the building was an irritation for some who hankered after showers and other mod cons. For a post-work dousing of a different kind there is an All Bar One and Prohibition, which reels 'em in with half-price cocktails until 7.30pm. If you can drag yourself away, there are football and netball teams.

Across the network, Beachcroft has a very respectable record for keeping its qualifiers. In 2007, 26 of the 30 stayed on with the firm.

and finally...

When deciding to train at Beachcroft, it's important to choose the right location as each office has its own agenda and there is little, if any, possibility of moving between them. Despite the differences between locations, all our sources agreed on one fundamental thing – that Beachcroft was a really pleasant place to work.

Berwin Leighton Paisner LLP

the facts

Location: London
Number of UK partners/solicitors: 180/433
Total number of trainees: 72
Seats: 4x6 months
Alternative seats: Brussels, secondments

Berwin Leighton Paisner has long been known for its real estate prowess, but has worked hard to push a range of other practices to the fore. In doing so, an air of positivity has permeated throughout the whole firm, right down to its latest crop of trainees. Said one: *"The firm has been on an upward progression for a while and is showing no signs of slowing down."*

eye of the storm

The rest of the legal profession is well aware of BLP's determination to expand. Having become fully embroiled in the frenzy of lateral hires across the City, at times it has looked as if it's had a tit for tat thing going on with Clifford Chance. Critically, its core real estate practice has not been neglected as the firm pushes out elsewhere: top-level hires (from Clifford Chance and Herbert Smith) have added to what was already a market-leading practice. Following successive years of some personnel changes, the corporate department has had a pretty stable time in terms of staff turnover and this has aided its progress. Transactions such as the £659m sale of South East Water for Australian bank Macquarie and the AIM IPO of Playtech, whose market capital nearly reached £550m, have delivered some strong messages and cemented BLP's position at the top of middle-market league tables. Trainees also believed that tax law was *"set to become a pillar of strength"* following the hire of *"big shot"* Michael Wistow from Clifford Chance. The projects and investment management departments seem to be the exceptions, both of which fell foul of the City's latest hiring storm.

every building helps

There's no reason to deny it, the jewel in BLP's crown is its massive world-beating real estate group. Its influence on the City's skyline is huge, and with new projects such as the Shard of Glass in the pipeline, it looks set to remain at the forefront of the market. The firm's trophy client is Tesco, which was recently outed as Europe's largest property company with over £28bn in property assets. A client such as this demands serious manpower to manage its interests because, as well as vast quantities of day-to-day management, it always has a string of giant transactions on the go. It recently entered into a £650m joint venture with British Land for the sale and leaseback of around 3% of its UK property assets, and also embarked on a half-billion pound joint venture with BA Pensions. Other established clients include Hammerson and Canary Wharf Group.

Trainees all take a seat in the core real estate department, where they run a clutch of small files as well as providing support on headline transactions. The department is so big that it is split into three teams and, dependant on where you are placed, the dominance of Tesco will be more or less obvious. Working in such a big, high-flying

department can be a little *"daunting"* and the large workload means you need to *"hit the ground running,"* however, *"it is normally manageable and there is always someone to help if you get snowed under."* A popular new initiative encourages trainees to close as many files as possible, *"so that subsequent trainees don't get bogged down with old ones."* Client contact is part of the deal. Said one trainee: *"I am speaking to property execs most days."*

Because the real estate department offers the complete package for its clients, there are seats in a number of related areas. By far the most popular of these is planning, where *"you really have to fight to get a seat."* Hardly surprising considering the department is the biggest and best in the country. Its work covers all aspects of the market, including retail schemes, new settlements, urban regeneration, infrastructure and sports projects. The firm is currently acting for the Olympic Delivery Authority in relation to the London 2012 games. *"This seat is completely different from the other ones I have done,"* said one source; *"it has such strong political undertones."* There are also options in construction and real estate finance.

AIMing high

The effects of BLP's corporate drive are clear to trainees, who tell us: *"There has been a lot of recruitment on that side and it is making a much heavier contribution to the firm."* They even noted the increasingly corporate mindset of successive trainee intakes, which reflects the concerted effort by HR to push the area. We reckon BLP has much to offer corporate-minded candidates, having embedded itself at the upper end of the AIM market and leveraged its strong friendship network in foreign jurisdictions to operate more internationally. In particular it has attracted good real estate funds work (which is more corporate than the name implies) across Central and Eastern Europe.

There is now an expectation that trainees will spend time in one of a broad range of corporate-related teams. A mainstream corporate seat has lately meant *"IPO-based work and hotel acquisitions."* A number of our sources had been involved in *"huge deals,"* with one lucky enough to have *"liaised with directors on the board of a massive client."* More commonly they spend their time *"drafting, taking minutes, attending client meetings and running disclosure exercises,"* as well as *"some work that could be done by anyone."* On the subject of low-level grunt tasks, the firm has listened to its trainees and recently upped the paralegal presence to *"mop up some of the more repetitive work."* Making up the rest of the corporate offering, there are seats in corporate recovery, banking, business technology services and funds. Trainees were in little doubt that the firm would keep up the momentum and carry on building up its reputation as a corporate adviser.

speak to the hat

One area that seems to have avoided any major changes is the contentious side of the firm's business. BLP is a respected enough mid-market player in this respect, yet it is not what attracts trainees to the firm. Indeed, many of our sources were keen to use any opportunity available to avoid a straight commercial litigation seat. Popular ways of doing so include real estate litigation and a contentious employment seat. *"If you don't want to do proper litigation, it is quite easy to get away with it,"* suggested one interviewee. *"Seats like planning involve tribunals and satisfy the requirement for contentious experience."* Having said that, not all our sources had wriggled away from commercial litigation – we should say not all wanted to – and some of them were surprised by how much they enjoyed the *"intellectual demands"* of the seat.

Presuming most trainees take a property, corporate and contentious seat, this leaves one further seat to fill. An obvious choice for the more forward-thinking individual is tax, which trainees seem to have identified as a hot area. To date, the work of the department has largely been sourced from its corporate clientele but, going forward, trainees believe there will be an increase in *"tax-planning type work for our own* [standalone] *clients."* As in so many firms, the most popular seat options are *"the sexy niche areas like IP,"* and the competition seat is also expected to rocket in popularity due to the advent of a secondment to Brussels. This is the only overseas seat available at a firm that has *"made a conscious decision to build networks of work referrers rather than setting up or merging with overseas firms."* Other opportunities to get out of the main office are client secondments. With such a large trainee intake, the most popular seats are frequently oversubscribed and HR has a tough job on its hands to please everyone, leading one disgruntled trainee to speculate: *"I think they just put all your request forms in a hat and pick them out at random."* We asked HR if there was a hat. They said not and that they do manage to fit the vast majority of trainees into one of their three favoured departments at each seat rotation.

no hammer, no tongs

The odd gripe aside, our interviewees were all happy with their choice of firm, right down to the recently refurbished *"light and airy glass-fronted offices."* They were certainly all keen to remain at the firm after qualification, a fact reflected in the 2007 retention figures – 24 out of 27 qualifiers stayed on. *"Big but not monstrous,"* it is said to have *"a collegiate feel"* and trainees sensed they were respected and valued. They gave top marks to the training, telling us: *"They invest a lot of time and money in you and it really shows."* A good example of this is the fact that supervisors *"are handpicked for their strengths."*

The main downside is the lengthening hours. *"A deal can see you consistently in the office till 10pm and even till 1am or 2am when you've reached the signing stage."* The frequency with

We see a sunny day

What do you see?

Bevan Brittan is on a journey of growth and innovation. We are looking for the leaders of tomorrow.

You can expect to handle the highest quality work, including high profile and often ground breaking assignments, for a prestigious client base spanning the breadth of the private and public sector.

Our clients expect commercial solutions not just legal advice. In fact, we pride ourselves on our creative solution-driven approach to our client relationships - just one of the things, we think, makes us stand out from the crowd.

London Bristol Birmingham

"I enjoy working in an environment where I feel I have more control over my destiny and where I am given the support I need to do the job I want to do."

Bevan Brittan employee

**Please visit our website
www.bevanbrittan.com**

**or contact us on
t 0870 194 3050
e hr.training@bevanbrittan.com**

which this happens depends on the department, corporate being the main culprit – naturally. While trainees are expected to work hard, *"it is not a hammer and tongs approach; everyone helps to ease the burden and make it as relaxed as possible."* Little things like partners expressing gratitude were said to foster a good working environment, as well as the fact that *"there is little internal competitiveness or backstabbing."* Overall, trainees were of the opinion they were in a very privileged position in getting *"fantastic-quality work in a very supportive environment."*

bollywood-london-paris

Among the trainee group many a friendship has hatched. They can frequently be found sharing a bagel and a joke or two (*"there are some great senses of humour on display here"*) over lunch at the park, and are even known to take their much-talked-about BLP brand of humour overseas on shared holidays. Birthdays are big news and Fridays will nearly always see a band of BLPers with their ties thoroughly loosened migrating from local bars (usually The Fine Line or Monument) on to Fuegos for a dance. We struggled to hold back the tears when one trainee commented: *"I have made friends here that I hope to stay in contact with forever."* The fact that all future joiners will now study a BLP-tailored LPC together at the College of Law's Moorgate branch will presumably allow these strong bonds to develop even earlier.

The organised social scene pales almost into insignificance when compared to the instinctive trainee-organised knees-ups. Then again, it would be remiss of us not to mention the annual *"no expenses spared"* Christmas shindig, an event that in the past two years has included a masquerade ball in the Royal Courts of Justice and a Bollywood-themed bash at the Grosvenor Hotel. Each department has a budget for non-work related fun, and one trainee spoke highly of a ski day at the Snowdome in Milton Keynes. Client marketing events have included go-karting and drinks at the top of the Gherkin. Sport is also an option, and there are a range of teams, some quite serious, others less so. Take softball, for example – this basically involves *"going down to the park on a sunny day with loads of beer and food."* Surprisingly this still leaves space in the trainee calendar for charitable events. The most important dates are a quiz night and an annual bike ride from Paris to Riems over a bank holiday weekend. Cycling *"80-odd miles a day"* is not to everyone's taste, but *"it all seems worth it in the evening when you are out on the champers, drinking off a hard day's exercise."* Drawing all this together, it's easy to understand why trainees see working at BLP as *"a lifestyle not a job."* As one put it: *"Within very little time you feel like you are BLP."*

and finally...

Here at the *Student Guide* we have long talked about BLP being a firm that is going places. In May the benefits of this for trainees became all the more tangible, as NQ and salaries were raised to £62,000 and first-year salaries reached £33,000. There is also a £2,500 golden hello payment for new trainees. A cynic might say that extra cash would make any trainee as upbeat as the ones we interviewed, but we reckon there's a lot more to it.

Bevan Brittan LLP

the facts

Location: Bristol, Birmingham, London
Number of UK partners/solicitors: 63/173
Total number of trainees: 33
Seats: 4x6 months
Alternative seats: Secondments
Extras: Pro bono – ProHelp

Headquartered in Bristol but also working out of offices in London and Birmingham, Bevan Brittan is backing two horses. Its main strength lies in the healthcare sector, whether advising the NHS on clinical negligence or preparing major PFI projects for hospitals and trusts, but it is also working to positioning itself as a national firm with an eye on the corporate mid-market.

public vs private

Change can sometimes be a long time coming. For aeons this firm has been synonymous with the healthcare sector, advising various Primary Care Trusts (PCTs) and NHS Trusts on just about every matter you could think of. The employment, property, projects and even corporate departments work closely with these chief clients and the medical negligence division conducts a huge volume of work on behalf of the NHS Litigation Authority. Having said all that, there is 50-50 split between public and private sector clients and a noticeable *"push toward the private sector"* in each of BB's offices. The *"dress code has even changed from business casual to business formal,"* so everyone has a suit at the ready for an assault on corporate Britain. This isn't the first time we've heard this from BB trainees and the fact *"the corporate departments in all three offices are expanding"* probably bears some relation to a resurgent transactional market UK-wide that is generating work for all firms. Undoubtedly ambitions are fervent, but the real test will come in a quieter economy.

New trainees are allocated their first seat, but once ensconced at the firm they can influence the direction their contract takes. Of those people we interviewed, at least half had started their two years in MLPI (medical law and personal injury, otherwise known by the shorthand 'claims'). *"The seat sees you doing lots of NHS defendant work"* and is acknowledged as a great place to start off because the department *"eases you in quite gently."* The sweet start won't protect you from *"a medical record nightmare,"* warned one trainee, recalling time spent sifting through mountains of material. By the end of the six months, *"you're given a lot more responsibility – taking witness statements, visiting counsel and preparing the six-monthly reports on each case for the NHSLA."* The variety on offer in this seat is greater than you might imagine, and *"you never know what you are going to be doing next."* Attending a trial has to be the ultimate high, although be aware that you're expected to take detailed notes; for one trainee this task meant *"my hand almost dropped off trying to keep up."* Other trainees spoke of attending court *"at least once or twice a week"* and even *"conducting my own advocacy, presenting settlements to court."* Whether you have a burning desire to be a medical negligence lawyer or not, you are going to get a great introduction to the litigation process.

aiming for greatness

Projects has become an increasingly important area for BB and trainees frequently make a stop in this department. The projects handled by the firm are huge, so don't expect to be running your own files. Indeed one source suggests you should prepare for *"more than your fair share of photocopying and carrying boxes."* Much of the time is spent shadowing partners at meetings, while the highlight activity has to be working on the closing of a big deal, an experience that a couple of interviewees had sampled. One rather pertinently compared a seat in projects to an Olympic cycling race *"where they crawl around the track for lap after lap and then have a mad race right near the end. The seat was like that – four months of nothing followed by two weeks being absolutely manic."* Across the UK, the firm is doing a lot in relation to the NHS LIFT programme and the Building Schools for the Future programme. Other projects relate to leisure facilities, social housing and waste management.

The large property department plays host to

quite a few trainees. In contrast to projects, they can expect as much responsibility as they can handle. Some aspects struck one or two of our sources as *"almost Dickensian... the language was somewhat arcane,"* however, the chance to run their own files was a revelation. Dealing with leases and licenses, both large and small, trainees learn to draft all the basic documents required for transactions, safe in the knowledge that there are *"great supervisors who never roll their eyes no matter how basic your questions."* Commercial healthcare is a popular seat, perhaps unsurprisingly so given BB's market-leading reputation in this area. Our interviewees found this to be *"an excellent seat for learning as you can see files through from start to finish."* The work is *"extremely varied, as essentially you are advising PCTs on whatever problems they may encounter,"* be this a question about what is in the best interests of a patient to one about IVF research. Above all, this seat *"guarantees a lot of face-to-face client contact."*

Among the other potential seats are commercial litigation (*"from county court work through to big arbitrations and appeals to competition commission"*), construction (both contentious and non-contentious) and tax, a *"challenging"* seat that is only available in Birmingham right now. IP/IT is available only in London and Bristol, but thankfully employment and pensions seats are offered in all three offices.

In response to the firm's aforementioned ambition, the corporate department is growing and looking to hire new lawyers. A change of guard at the top end has also led the department to shift its focus to concentrate more on AIM listings and other private-sector offerings. Trainees spend a good deal of time on standard tasks such as preparing board minutes and drafting directors' letters of appointment and resignation, but they can sometimes also be put in charge of their own small transactions – perhaps a small purchase of shares or the setting up of an LLP. Hours-wise, this seat peaks and troughs according to the deal flow

and a trainee might leave at 6pm or 3am. Some trainees – mainly in London – suggest that an average time to leave in this seat is 8pm or 9pm. Generally speaking, however, this is not a firm that requires its recruits to be sat at their desks without good reason; *"there is no 'last man sitting' policy."* Elsewhere, average hours were deemed to be 9am to 6.30pm, and in some seats *"nobody will look at you strangely for leaving at 5.30pm."* In all seats trainees have formal reviews after six months and informal reviews every month.

always puzzling

Each of the branches has a relatively new building. Bristol trainees told us: *"It was great to leave the last shabby office; now we have somewhere you can be proud to bring clients."* The office plays host to a monthly drinks evening for all staff, and on Thursdays and Fridays people can always be found in The Bridge, a small old man's pub close by. Failing that, they are *"only about eight minutes' walk from the main watering holes of Bristol."* In Birmingham, a new social committee has recently been charged with responsibility for organising extra-curricular activities. So far it has managed a champagne reception in a dim sum restaurant, a night at the dogs and a French cookery evening. Of course, the trainees also have the option of the most active TSG in the country, the Birmingham Trainee Solicitors Society, which is responsible for all manner of distractions, from balls and drinks evenings to a formidable array of sports. The now-famous BTSS Ultimate Frisbee competition recently caused one trainee to break his hand, necessitating surgery, so take care.

London's new office is open plan, which *"produces an atmosphere where friends are easily made and moving a seat is never a problem."* The only hint of disgruntlement arises from the fact that many of the support services are largely based in Bristol. Said one trainee: *"If you are working on a deal until late in the evening or at the weekend then it is annoying to find that IT support in Bristol have gone home at 5.30pm or something."* There are plenty of opportunities to socialise here in the capital, though more often than not the choice of venue is The Puzzle, the pub underneath the office. *"The associates and partners rarely make it much further than there, so it's easy to know where everyone will be."*

's no joke

All three offices indulge in the usual Christmas party, though sometimes there is a twist. In London trainees are expected to take part in a short sketch show, the stated intention of which is the ribbing of a few partners. Apparently the most coveted role is the props manager, as this person has the least to do on the night. In Bristol, the last Christmas party had a sort of 'Pop Model' competition that involved partners in muscle suits. Thankfully, the summer event at all three offices tends to be a relaxed barbecue. Overall, trainees say BB has an atmosphere that *"isn't snotty or self-righteous,"* and maybe this comes from its background in public sector work.

Apparently, *"the training teaches you the idea that you talk to clients in a language they understand."* That may be the case, but there is also a new wave of management speak surging through the firm. Of all the buzz words going around, trainees spoke most frequently of their 'promises', 'promises in action', 'promised work' and 'promise champions', the latter being people who have proved particularly successful at delivering on their promises to clients. Everybody at the firm has been given a snow globe with the suggestion that they place a word inside it that will inspire them to great things and fulfil as yet unfulfilled promises. Having complied with the request, one of our interviewees admitted: *"It makes me giggle to myself everyday."*

Trainees reckon the firm *"favours people with a bit of experience."* That said, the group is a mix of people who have come straight from university, worked in a first career before the law or taken time to bring up kids. Every now and then, some recruits choose to take the LPC part-time while also completing a three-year training contract. In 2007, eight of the 13 qualifiers stayed with the firm, ending up in a variety of departments.

and finally...

Bevan Brittan continues to sit at a crossroads. The influx of American-style management speak and a shift in its corporate focus may be having some influence, but we reckon it will take a lot to shift the health sector away from the heart of the firm. The mix of private and public work, with a strong emphasis on the latter, is what characterises this place.

Bingham McCutchen (London) LLP

the facts

Location: London
Number of UK partners/solicitors: 12/28
Total number of trainees: 4
Seats: 4x6 months
Alternative seats: None
Extras: Pro bono – LawWorks

The London arm of America's Bingham McCutchen recently introduced a shiny new training programme. If you don't know anything about this 1,000 lawyer organisation, don't feel too bad – it's as if it has come out of nowhere in the last ten years.

merger fever

Boston-headquartered Bingham was founded in 1891. In the past decade it has transformed itself by merging with smaller firms no less than eight times. If you want to get more detail on this, Bingham's website will oblige, and there's a short web-cast from Jay Zimmerman, the firm's chairman and the mastermind of its development. In the USA, Bingham has ten offices on the East and West Coasts. Its other overseas offices are in Hong Kong and Tokyo. The firm is also known as a pop-ular place to work, having made it into *Fortune*'s top-100 survey of the best companies to work for in America. It is known to have an ethnically diverse workforce and a high proportion of female partners (around one quarter of the total).

Bingham McCutchen's London office opened way back in 1973, but since 2000, and particularly in the last seven years, the firm has taken a more expansive approach and grown to its current level of 40+ lawyers. All but a few of these are UK-qual-ified and the introduction of a training scheme reflects the independence and autonomy of an office which sources 90% of its work from the UK. Bingham in the United States is a full-service outfit that is highly regarded for its financial restructuring activities. A careful London strat-egy has centred on serving the needs of big financial institutions and funds in sizeable work-outs and restructurings across Europe. *Chambers UK*, our parent guide, particularly recognises the office's strength in insolvency and contentious financial regulatory matters. While the firm is not averse to further growth, there isn't any immedi-ate likelihood of it diverting from its current finance and insolvency/restructuring path in London. Financial restructuring has been a rela-tively quiet area in recent years, but there's no reason to think it will remain so in the long term.

distress finesse

In addition to financial restructuring, the Lon-don office's other primary teams are banking and finance, corporate, financial regulatory and liti-gation. The banking and finance department is currently trying to bounce back from the loss of a string of partners and associates. It is doing so through new lateral hires, including a well-known figure from Shearman & Sterling. The firm began taking on trainees in September 2006, and will continue to recruit two people each year to complete seats in financial restructuring, banking and finance, corporate and litigation, with a financial regulatory seat debuting shortly.

Bingham's star financial restructuring depart-ment boasts some big clients, including Gate Gourmet, Jarvis, Marconi, Queens Moat Houses and Concordia Bus Nordic, Sweden's largest bus company. A restructuring seat offers the opportu-nity to work on *"a lot of the main restructuring transactions,"* often those with an international angle. Trainees get involved in drafting and nego-tiating documents and conducting research.

Working in the 'distress' market involves com-pany securities, like bonds and bank debt, when the companies are in default or heading towards bankruptcy. No need to panic if you don't yet know the ins-and-outs of the sector or any of its jargon; Bingham trainees are inundated with training, including regular firm-wide lectures, departmental presentations and courses at BPP Law School.

re-structural survey

Other departments tend to play second fiddle to the restructuring practice, but the level of respon-sibility on offer still provides a steep learning curve. Bingham's banking and finance clients include Citibank, AIG Global Investments and Prudential Capital Group. A seat in banking involves drafting conditions precedent, legal opinions and security documents, as well as some research. Although trainees may have to stay late when working on a closing, they report that long hours only come when business needs dictate, not on the sadistic whim of a partner. *"When you're busy you're expected to get the work done, but people generally have a healthy attitude to work-life balance here."* Trainees sit with their supervisors, but are *"marketed to the department as a whole,"* so they are rarely short of work.

A seat in the small litigation team brings a good breadth of activities. Recently Bingham was instructed by a peer in the cash for honours investigation. In fact the lawyers must be developing a name among people accused of giving or taking bungs – they were also sought out by a company involved in the largest-ever series of investigations in the Irish Republic arising from allegations of illegal payments to politicians and offshore tax evasion by leading Irish citizens. On a range of different cases, when not conducting legal research, trainees draft confidentiality agreements and applications to court. One of our sources at the firm even managed his own landlord and tenant dispute with the help of a junior associate. Trainees in the corporate department spend their days setting up companies, preparing simple AIM and FTSE documentation and drafting small shareholder agreements. If trainees tire of acting for the likes of Management Network Group, KBC Peel Hunt and numerous hedge funds, they can salve their consciences with a little pro bono.

animal house

Bingham's London office is located at 41 Lothbury, in the old NatWest building near The Bank of England. The building's grand reception is kitted out with ionic columns, Italian marble walls and a checkerboard marble floor. All that Palladian splendour stands in marked contrast to Bingham's flashy website, which features arty pictures of a bear holding a baby, a zebra chasing a lion and a hang-gliding elephant. In yet another animal reference, one trainee described the London office as *"a small dog with a big bite."* How can a prospective applicant reconcile this cyberzoo

with the office's sedate façade? Would be prospective trainees would do well to remember that London remains a small part of a bigger worldwide picture with the USA in the foreground. That said, London *"isn't the outhouse"* of the firm. We wonder which office has that dubious honour.

Bingham wants trainees who are ambitious and savvy, yet sociable. It expects them to *"put in the hours"* and jump in at the deep end in terms of work before popping off to sophisticated City bars at Bond's or The Royal Exchange to socialise with the younger associates. Wallflowers are unlikely to bloom at Bingham, since even humble trainees are expected *"to be confident enough to be able to approach people at all levels and put yourself out there for work."* If trainees are sufficiently self-possessed, they can find themselves doing *"NQ-level work, which is a lot more than the admin tasks given to our peers at other firms."*

Bingham offers a huge salary, starting at £40,000 for the first seat, rising to £45,000 in the second year of training and hitting £91,429 on qualification. The rate is indexed to what associates earn in New York, so future trainees should benefit from any hikes in US salaries. Although there are currently no international seats on offer, there are rumours that the new Hong Kong office may offer a secondment in the future.

and finally...

If you think you know your derivative instruments from your commingled investment vehicles and are willing to take a leap of faith on a training programme that is still in its infancy, take a look at Bingham's revamped recruitment website to see if it's what you're after. This is definitely a firm on a mission.

Bircham Dyson Bell

the facts
Location: London, Cardiff, Edinburgh
Number of UK partners/solicitors: 52/75
Total number of trainees: 17
Seats: 4x6 months
Alternative seats: Secondments
Extras: Pro bono – Waterloo Law Centre, Migrants Resource Centre

Parliament, politics and legislative process. If you prefer watching Dimbleby and Paxman to Max and Paddy, and you understand that the transportation challenges facing the UK extend beyond the Road to Nowhere, then this could be your firm. Or maybe you have an appetite for private client work for Rich Listers. Whichever strand of Bircham Dyson Bell's practice appeals, you'll be sure of a vote-winning training at this Westminster old timer.

take your seat
BDB targets its services at four categories of client: businesses, charities, individuals and the public sector. We're talking about the likes of English Heritage, the London Development Agency, Marks & Spencer and the families of Jill Dando and Dr David Kelly. A trainee could, if they wished, sample work for all four client sectors via four six-month seats chosen from: company and commercial; employment; litigation; real estate; private client; charities; Parliamentary, public law and planning (PPP) and, presently, a secondment to client ESSO.

If you're wondering how a firm with such a broad practice became closely associated with the inner workings of Parliament, you need to understand that Parliamentary Agents Dyson Bell Martin had been operating in tandem with private client solicitors Bircham & Co for donkey's years. Some time later, there was a merger with

elements of the commercial law firm Bower Cotton and now the firm is on a growth trajectory that it hopes will allow it to *"crack the Top 50"* and achieve a £50m annual turnover by 2011. *"They don't want to become one of those massive firms, but they do want to move forward."* So far, the firm has grown to 52 partners (sadly just eight of them female) plus over 130 other solicitors, lawyers and paralegals. As one source put it: *"It's nice to be involved in something where there is a vision, not just plodding along."* As well as bringing in new partners from outside, in 2007 the firm made up seven of its own associates to partner – the first time it had made internal promotions for more than four years.

select few
The PPP department offers three trainees a range of experiences from planning and major projects to the very specialised work of Parliamentary Agents. All you really need to know is that these professionals are solicitors who are licensed to draft and promote – or oppose – Private Bills and that such Bills are most often put forward by organisations who need specific powers granted by Parliament. BDB is one of just six law firms employing so-called 'Roll A' Parliamentary Agents, and not only is it one of the biggest and best-regarded in this specialist field, it also has the distinction of being the only law firm to offer political consultancy services.

"PPP is a big driver of the firm," we learned. A huge proportion of the work is transport-related, for clients such as Network Rail, Docklands Light Railway and Transport for London (eg assisting on the enlargement of the congestion charging zone and on a new London-wide 'low emissions zone'). Despite the complexity, we spoke to trainees who loved the seat. *"There are various sub-specialities, for example procurement work, which deals with EU regulations about what public bodies can and can't do and involves complex con-*

Bircham Dyson Bell

CharitiesCompany Commercial • Employment • Litigation
Parliamentary, Public Law and Planning • Private Client • Real Estate

Bircham Dyson Who....?

One of the UK's most interesting and progressive law firms, built on its unique quality of insight, both individually and collectively. This means the firm understands the law and its application to its clients, knows what is important and not important, and will cut through to the critical issues.

What's in it for me?

Getting to work with some of the finest legal minds in the business, gaining hands on experience in meeting and dealing with clients right from the start of your career. Added to the training you will receive in four of our wide-ranging practice areas, why would you not want to play a part in our future?

Isn't that what they all say?

With us however it's not all hot air. Over the last five years the firm has doubled in size and turnover, winning numerous accolades along the way (Best Internal Communications – The Lawyer HR Awards 2007, Shortlisted Law Firm of the Year – The Lawyer Awards 2006, Charity Team of the Year – STEP Private Client Awards 2006). You can never have too much of a good thing, so whilst we have some of the brightest people in the profession, we're looking to recruit trainee solicitors with the potential and ambition to play a key role in our ambitious growth plans.

Bircham Dyson Bell LLP
50 Broadway
London SW1H 0BL
T: 020 7227 7000

Visit our careers section
W: www.bdb-law.co.uk

Bircham Dyson Bell

tract drafting. When you are working for a big public body you soon learn that there are so many acronyms." Even specialists would accept it can be mind-boggling, "but over time you do feel you are making progress. The longer you work for a client the more you know about their procedures. You end up absorbing a lot of information."

At the moment BDB represents over 25% of the petitioners against the proposed £13bn Crossrail scheme linking East and West London. "Your client could be anyone from a business with a lease of a building, to someone who lives in Islington and is concerned about a tunnel going under their house. They come to you having received a letter from Crossrail and you advise whether it is worthwhile them petitioning against it. If it is, you prepare a petition setting out objections on certain grounds," the ultimate goal being to make a deal between Crossrail and the petitioner. "During the petitioning stage you practise your analysis and drafting. Then comes the negotiation stage. I had assumed that commercial law wouldn't be my thing at all, but you are dealing with practical commercial issues all the time in this seat." Take, for example, negotiations on behalf of telecoms companies with mobile phone masts on buildings that will be demolished to make way for the 2012 Olympics. One of the most unusual assignments involved a consortium of theatres that petitioned for an exemption from the new smoking ban to allow actors to light up during performances. Another aspect of the seat concerns Parliamentary Select Committees, and trainees find it interesting to sit in on these meetings.

aiming high

Private client is another big department. Here, "a trainee will do a lot of wills and probate plus a bit of tax. Much of the job is estate planning for well-off business people and those with large landed estates." Really rich people may have complicated offshore trusts structures and sometimes "know more about that area of the law than you, which makes you wary when they phone up!" The dedicated charities team "can do whatever the clients need doing: setting up trusts; advising on trustee appointments and responsibilities; registering with the Charities Commission; drafting fundraising agreements and generally helping with the smooth running of an organisation. We act for everyone from big players to smaller ones, for sophisticated trustees who know what they are doing to inexperienced ones who don't." The charities team works closely with cocom where, "although your duties are primarily for your supervisor, you can track down the lawyers doing the work you are most interested in." Keep an eye on BDB's work for AIM companies (that's FTSE's baby brother, if you don't know) as a dedicated corporate transactions seat is likely to emerge. In 2006 the firm was engaged on approximately £600m worth of corporate transactions and achieved top-20 status in Hemscott's rankings of UK AIM legal advisers.

The real estate lawyers act for everyone from residents on the posh London estates, to companies signing office leases, to bodies such as the Metropolitan Police and The Law Society. The firm tried to build a social housing team, however this proved a largely unsuccessful venture. Indeed, the real estate practice has thrown up other problems of late, namely the resignation of five associates in quick succession. Apparently, "they felt swamped by their caseloads" and complained about lack of support. To address this issue a non-lawyer practice group manager was appointed. We also heard there were grumbles about salaries, yet this is not a new issue at BDB. People generally understand the trade-off between hours and salary at firms such as this. As one source pointed out: "Our salaries are not especially competitive, but we don't work the hours they do in the City so I'd much rather stay somewhere *like this."* For trainees, hours go up and down – especially in corporate – but they are never too painful. Usually trainees clock off by 6.30pm and *"there's none of that showing off about how many billable hours you can do."*

We should just mention that over in the litigation department the trainees' diverse caseload is likely to incorporate family, contentious probate and debt recovery. Whichever seats they'd taken, our sources agreed they'd benefited from *"a more intimate environment than in the big City firms and greater involvement from partners."*

mixed messages

With its beautiful Georgian-fronted offices in SW1, you'd be forgiven for thinking BDB is an old-school kind of place and many insiders are uncomfortable about the fact that this is how the firm is viewed. Arguably, elements of the firm are still traditional with a capital 'T' and conservative with a small 'c', yet *"the firm wants to get away from this image of being stuffy and old-fashioned and only acting for landed gentry. Yes, we have acted for old families for years and years and years, but we want to be seen as more modern."* The different departments play their part in the balancing act between established character and progress so, for example, while *"litigation is fiery and cocom is exciting, private client is much quieter. Everyone jokes that you have to whisper when you go there and there's a very civilised atmosphere."* Client meeting rooms reflect this dichotomy: some are modern; others have a traditional, antiquey look. The challenge for this *"not brash and pushy"* firm is *"to retain the charm of private client side,"* the *"nice manners and intimacy,"* as it grows and develops its commercial side.

BDB has always been willing to recruit older trainees; indeed, those with law degrees are commonly outnumbered by second careerers. As the firm and the trainee group expand, the training scheme has become increasingly systematised, a trend that unsettled some of our sources this year. *"The firm is trying to 'do the right thing' by getting proper procedures lined up, but as a trainee approaching qualification you feel you are looking down the barrel of a gun. I now have to update my CV and do two interviews like an external candidate. What sort of message are they are giving us?"* Although BDB's record on NQ retention is mixed, this is largely because of difficulties in matching vacancies to individuals' interests. It follows that jobs will be available in areas where the firm is performing best and where it hopes to grow. In 2007, five of the eight qualifiers took jobs with the firm.

With a quietish social life *"it's not the place to come if you want a big, boozy scene on a Friday."* There are drinks for the whole firm once a quarter and the odd Friday trip to The Old Star or The Feathers for a quick one, but it's hard to generalise: some trainee intakes are more sociable than others. The important dates are the Christmas party and a carol service at St Margaret's church next to Westminster Abbey, a rowing regatta on the Thames and a summer party. Sunny lunchtimes can be spent in nearby St James' Park, with its views of Buckingham Palace. Even in winter you'll find a few crazies jogging around the shrubbery when most sensible staff stick to the popular staff canteen.

and finally...

These days BDB is putting itself about more to capture student votes. It's got masses to offer anyone hoping to avoid a backbench experience in a big City firm or a corporate/finance-dominated training. If one of the firm's specialist departments appeals then it's a must-make application.

Bird & Bird

the facts

Location: London
Number of UK partners/solicitors: 62/146
Total number of trainees: 31
Seats: 4x6 months
Alternative seats: Overseas seats, secondments
Extras: Language training

Traditionally seen a top destination for science graduates, Bird & Bird has a great reputation for IP and technology and caters to a long list of multinational telecoms and pharmaceutical companies. So strong is it in these areas, the fact that the firm has considerable firepower on a range of other commercial fronts is sometimes overlooked.

two birds in the hand

Bird & Bird is spreading its wings. Breakneck international expansion has been achieved by overseas partners flocking in at the rate of one per month in recent times. In Spain, for example, lateral hires to the Madrid office have allowed Bird & Bird to establish a notable corporate finance practice. In Holland, a fledgling energy practice advised two gas network operators on a deal valued at around €400m – not exactly bird-feed – and from an outlying branch in Hong Kong the firm swooped the first licence to file trade mark applications directly with Chinese authorities. Big, star signings in the corporate and litigation divisions are making the firm's presence felt from Western Europe through to Asia and, by adding new offices, revenue and profits have soared. Significantly, performance has been optimised across a range of disciplines, dispelling the notion that the firm is no more than a one-trick pony.

Bird & Bird is an apt name for a firm that could almost be seen as two organisations in one in London. The powerhouse IP department occupies its own *"self-contained"* office, while everyone else is spread across another two buildings, effectively giving the firm a *"campus-style feel."* If this analogy holds true, then IP is the ivory tower overlooking the campus. Trainees say the IP partners take pride in *"doing things their own way"* and seem to work more closely with their counterparts across Europe than with other lawyers in the London office. This detachment – emphasised by a departmental retreat – is something of a sore point for those staff clamouring for greater togetherness with their European colleagues. As for trainee seats overseas, placements crop up on an ad hoc basis, most often to Madrid.

in the lab

There is no debate as to the sheer brilliance of the IP department: our colleagues at *Chambers UK* rank it as one of the very best in the country and its clients are *"as big as they come."* What is more uncertain is the level of involvement that is possible for a new recruit. IP generally divides itself into the hard and soft varieties. Soft IP refers to trade marks, copyright, design rights and database rights; hard IP to patents and industrial designs. The latter is more reliant on sophisticated, science-driven knowledge. Between their test tubes and their test cases, the firm's IP lawyers are seriously brainy people: of the two patent lawyers to be made up as partners in 2007, one had a PhD in chemistry and the other was an experienced software and electronics engineer. It goes without saying that it takes more than just legal knowledge to handle the complex issues raised in today's multimillion-pound IP disputes. When the rights to a new drug are at stake, for example, the clients spare nothing to get the right result.

Obviously with the stakes so high and cases so epic, there are few small discrete matters for new

A late night at Bird & Bird

join the celebration

BIRD & BIRD

www.twobirds.com/graduates

| Beijing | Brussels | Düsseldorf | Frankfurt | The Hague | Hong Kong | London |
| Lyon | Madrid | Milan | Munich | Paris | Rome | Stockholm |

birds to tuck their claws into. In fact, there were some mixed accounts of placements in the department. The objections raised by some against patent work centred on the excess of *"grunt duties,"* which effectively amounted to *"paralegal jobs."* By contrast, other sources felt they had had a significant amount of responsibility in a department that is heavily partner-dominated. So is it the case that the work is too complicated for every trainee to make an impact? Science backgrounds do apparently come in handy when reading witness statements and experts reports, but according to one source at least, even *"a GCSE grounding should carry you through."* While a few people were deterred, others were electrified by the energy levels in the department. One source attributed their enthusiasm for the seat to *"masochism"* and told us they *"loved running around like a blue-arsed fly."* Overall, there was recognition of the privilege of having a ringside seat on gigantic cases, and having the opportunity to watch the *"whole machine moving forwards in readiness for court."*

And what are the big cases getting trainees hot under the collar? In the run-up to the World Cup 2006, the firm advised the FA on trade mark enforcement and it had notable success in enforcing Nestlé's application to register its slogan *"Have A Break"* as a trade mark. In patent litigation, telecoms giant Sony Eriksson instructs the firm on protecting parts necessary to ensure its mobile phones comply with 2G and 3G technical standards. Trainee feedback suggests that the pharmaceuticals sector is the most rewarding strand of the department for applying scientific knowledge. Disputes in this sector have included Baxter International v Abbott Laboratories, a case concerning the patent on Sevoflurane, the best-selling inhalant anaesthetic world wide, and Pfizer's protection of its patent portfolio, including the cholesterol-lowering medication Lipitor.

crazy frog

The commercial team is the second powerhouse department in London, and from what we can tell it is even more popular than IP with trainees. The department scores in a number of sectors including media, sports and communications. The media and entertainment group, for example, boasts a caseload that charts the highs and lows of contemporary culture. The firm was responsible for licensing the Crazy Frog character to Mryiad Interactive Limited and, slightly less irritating by general consensus, has been working on Woody Allen's third outing into European cinema. It also manages a glut of computer games instructions, such as advising Sega on its right to use professional football players' names in its products.

Following the arrival of key players from Hammonds in January of 2007, the sports team is becoming a top striker at the firm. This year, it won numerous assignments including assisting tennis player Andy Murray on disputes with former agents, negotiating several large sponsorship deals for Chelsea FC, and helping international sports agency Sportfive on the sale of UEFA Euro 2008 television rights. Instructions get no bigger in the sporting world than the Olympic Games, and Bird & Bird's monumental mandate involves protecting the Olympic brand in the lead up to the to London 2012. Famously, the firm has also been advising Wembley Stadium on anti-ticket touting measures. Naturally competition for a spot in the commercial department is fierce, not least because trainees admire the team's willingness to *"draw a line under work"* whenever social events beckon.

Bird & Bird's IT crowd has been advising BT on its jaw-droppingly huge £2.6bn NHS Programme for IT contracts, the largest project of its kind in the world. Once installed, BT's system will connect 100,000 doctors, 380,000 nurses and 50,000 other healthcare professionals, leading to huge savings across the NHS. This team has numerous big clients and recently won its first instructions from Yahoo! Also new are three partners who have defected to the firm from Barlow Lyde & Gilbert. The firm is clearly on top of its game on large commercial and IT projects and, as such, allows trainees to experience what it is like to work on massive cutting-edge deals, while avoiding the draining hours culture of the City giants.

pecking order

Real estate trainees get their own files and quickly learn careful time management. The seat can leave you *"punching the air"* after successfully negotiating a deal or crawling through mundane post-completion tasks. Drawing on the firm's substantial portfolio of telecoms clients, the real estate lawyers recently represented Eriksson on a £3bn deal to establish service management centres throughout the UK. Employment seats bring contentious and non-contentious work and trainees enjoy *"never knowing what is coming next."* They draft letters of advice and assist with the preparation of defences to claims. The firm used its multinational employment expertise in France, Holland, Italy and the UK to orchestrate BT's sale of its Satellite Broadcast Services business.

Corporate trainees find the department has a more *"constrained, formal"* air, but still manages to be *"quite a good laugh."* For those who regard the prospect of a corporate seat as *"a nightmare,"* apparently *"it's not as bad you think."* Even so, we heard some moans about a lack of *"work of any substance."* Tasks include sorting through *"boxes and boxes of documents,"* in a workflow described as made up of of *"boring and exciting days."* There was however a conviction that the seat is useful. The firm exercises a cross-departmental approach to most client mandates and so trainees found it beneficial to learn *"how companies and directors think,"* even if their angle might, for example, have been the employment side of a deal.

1966 and all that

Much is made of the intellectual atmosphere of the firm. The words *"geeky"* and *"egghead"* suggest lab-coated scientists nit-picking over the finer points of the law. This caricature might find its adherents in the IP department, where the nature of the work involves *"lengthy technical debates that go into academic detail."* Generally speaking though, no one's trying to recreate Plato's Athens. The lawyers are mainly practical and commercial and prefer to give advice that is *"short and sweet."* Another equally inappropriate image arises from Bird & Bird's work in the technology sector. When we asked if the firm's culture bore any similarity to the leftfield work culture of a Silicon Valley dotcom company, trainees nipped this misconception in the bud. *"Table football is about as Google as it gets in our office – there are no space hoppers or anything…"* These days even dress-down Friday is a thing of the past.

Bird & Bird recently got its feathers in a ruffle when a burlesque club Volupte had the cheek to move into the basement of its Norwich Street premises. We hear that employees are banned from visiting it. At least they have a new *"canteen… Sorry, we're not meant to call it that – I meant restaurant."* Sounds like the perfect venue for one of the *Student Guide*'s romantic dates: a restaurant where you can get *"chicken and chips for £3.90."*

Sports and after-work drinks are important for *"getting your face seen."* The saturation of pubs in the vicinity of the offices makes drinks on Fridays easy to organise, and if you're a sports enthusiast there are several teams to join. Football gains the most attention as there is an annual Bird & Bird European cup. Predictably, the UK office has lost to Germany on penalties in the semi-finals and quarterfinals at the last two tournaments.

and finally...

A number of the current trainees are slightly more mature than the average new starter, having had experience in other fields. More important to note is that trainees are keen to stress that no one should be deterred by the firm's techie image. While science graduates are most welcome here, the majority of recruits don't have such qualifications. As one put it: *"There is life after IP."* Proving this point, in 2007, seven of the 11 qualifiers stayed on with the firm, going into the commercial, banking, real estate and dispute resolution teams as well as IP.

Blake Lapthorn Tarlo Lyons

the facts

Location: Fareham, Portsmouth, Southampton, London, Oxford, Winchester
Number of UK partners/solicitors: 105/256
Total number of trainees: 31
Seats: 4x6 months
Alternative seats: Secondments

Fresh from another merger, Blake Lapthorn Tarlo Lyons now has a string of offices from the South Coast to London via Oxford. Because each region is so different the firm as a whole is tricky to pin down. However, we think we've got a relatively secure handle on BLTL as an ambitious, commercially focused regional heavyweight with a good private client practice.

the urge to merge

Last year we correctly predicted that after its May 2006 merger with private client specialist White and Bowker, Blake Lapthorn Linnell would merge again. It did so in December 2006 with London firm Tarlo Lyons. This latest merger created an organisation with over 100 partners and 700 staff and a combined revenue of more than

£43m. One trainee plaintively told us: *"I hope they don't merge again. I've just got used to the new name, which is ridiculously long."* Although three mergers in four years seems a tad excessive, BLTL is trying to compete with a slew of other regional firms that have upped their game lately. It is hoped that a City office will attract new clients who, rightly or wrongly, prefer to have their business done in the capital rather than the regions. Another benefit of the new set-up is the ability to outsource London work to the regions, where it can be done more cheaply. Given the calibre of work on which BLTL has recently been instructed, it seems the plan is working. It was recently appointed to a government super-panel for property and IP matters. Not that BLTL couldn't already lay claim to an impressive clientele of banks, retail giants and other big names, including Allied Irish, HSBC, NatWest, Waitrose, John Lewis, First Choice and the BBC.

And where is the BLTL juggernaut now sheaded? *"The firm is still thinking in terms of expansion, but right now it needs a period of consolidation. It will still be a large regional firm, maybe even one day a large national firm, but it's never going to be a City firm."* One or two sources went so far as to say: *"We're regional now, so maybe the North is the next step. I think we're going for world domination!"*

all change please

Having spotted a few gripes about late notification of seat allocations last year, we were pleased to note that training partner Kevin Chard has answered the trainees' call for change. Now they are given two leisurely months to plan, instead of the previous *"last-minute allocation two weeks beforehand."* Prospective trainees can now apply for contracts in London, Oxford or Hampshire. Those who fancied the previous arrangement that sent trainees office-hopping as business needs required can still opt for a 'flexible' training contract

quality work and life...
in perfect balance

Blake Lapthorn Tarlo Lyons is one of the largest regional law firms in the UK. The firm has six offices at key locations on the south coast, Oxford and London. Our size and breadth of expertise allows us to offer a full range of legal services, including litigation, commercial, property and private client.

For further infomation, please visit our website
www.bllaw.co.uk
or email us at
graduateinfo@bllaw.co.uk

Offices in Southampton, Winchester, Oxford, Fareham, Portsmouth and London

the natural choice in law

Blake Lapthorn Tarlo Lyons

that does just that. The firm is keen for all trainees to be seconded to a client at some point, usually in their second seat. Among the possibilities are, National Air Traffic Systems (NATS), Capgemini and the Nursing and Midwifery Council (NMC). Trainees admit the nature of a secondment experience varies hugely according to which in-house legal team they go to. The NMC secondment, for example, offers a lot of responsibility on serious cases of unfitness to practice. Trainees can delve into investigatory roles as well as advocacy: *"I interviewed witnesses and reported to the council as to whether charges should be brought. I also did a lot of advocacy at interim hearings to suspend really serious offenders from practice."* Trainees state their top three seat preferences before their training contracts start. Usually the firm manages to give trainees their first-choice seat, but the other three seats tend to be dictated by business needs and pure luck. BLTL usually wants trainees to do seats in property, commercial and litigation, but we spoke to several trainees who had avoided the less popular property seat in favour of flashier things.

new kids on the block

In London the seats offered are employment, dispute resolution, property, insolvency and a commercial/corporate seat. Commercial property is a *"very paper intensive"* experience in a department which trainees say is *"a bit stuffy because it's full of older men."* By contrast, the *"young and vibrant"* commercial litigation department allows them to *"get involved in the more academic aspects of case formulation"* and experience a broad spread of work: *"I've dealt with tax, maritime and defamation issues... you name it."*

The London office is adapting to the merger, although one wonders if certain aspects of the two firms' fit have been misjudged. *"Blake Lapthorn Linnell just assumed that Tarlo Lyons had similar values, but in practice they were very different firms. They're gradually getting to know the London office better."* A few years back, Tarlo Lyons suffered because of the downturn in the technology market in which it had invested much. After a change in management, it became *"much more cautious and profit-orientated. It lost its work-life balance a little."* The merger was a lifeline to some junior lawyers who had been thinking of jumping the Tarlo Lyons ship. Post-merger, things are changing for the better, according to trainees, nonetheless one told us: *"They're conscious of not making sudden changes, and it's going too slowly for many of the junior lawyers."* It's not all doom and gloom: trainees were quick to note the merger's impact on the quality of their supervision: *"They're starting to sort out the supervision procedure. The existing supervisors were quite complacent."* Apparently, the quantity of training has *"increased unbelievably. They're certainly making the effort now."* New features of the London training programme include refresher courses at the beginning of seats, sessions to develop soft skills and external speakers to discuss recent changes to the law. The merger also precipitated a refurb of the London office to make it *"look like the others – nice and new."* All up, it sounds like a fresh start for the London training scheme too.

reel around the ring road

The Oxford office is a good choice for those who want a scoop of private client work with their commercial pie. The private client department recently expanded by recruiting a partner from a Newbury firm and a solicitor from City firm Macfarlanes. Clients tend to be local, middle-class folk who need probate and trusts advice, although *"there are a few multi-million-pound estates."* Even if they hadn't requested a private client seat, trainees said it offers a good level of responsibility and *"lots of smaller matters that you can get your head round reasonably easily. You can do your own case management."*

The commercial litigation department lets trainees loose on *"construction litigation, tax fraud and general commercial and property litigation."* Again, they run their own smaller caseloads, while helping out with *"pre-action work, drafting letters of claim and putting together pleadings"* on bigger cases. A seat in non-contentious construction, a department which is top-rated by our parent guide *Chambers UK*, offers trainees the chance to draft appointments and warranties for construction projects and review contracts. The nature of the work means *"client contact is relatively low and you don't get such a free rein as the matters you're working on are so big."* Oxford trainees can also do seats in corporate and commercial, residential conveyancing, commercial property, IP/IT, employment and family.

The Oxford office is a purpose-built affair in a business park on the Botley side of the ring road. The out-of-town location means *"you can't nip to the pub for a drink after work,"* but the oodles of parking space and *"a good canteen with a balcony for barbecues"* seems to compensate.

Trainees are given LPC fees as a £10,000 loan, to be paid back if they are offered a job on qualification but decline to take it. This combined with South Coast-level salaries – which Oxford trainees say are wholly inadequate – makes for some grumbles: *"We get the same salary as trainees on the South Coast, yet it's a lot more expensive here and higher up in the firm this difference is recognised with higher salaries. The management board has been less willing to listen to our views, because they know we're not going to go elsewhere, so there is a lot of discontent at junior levels."* Sounds like an issue to be addressed.

this scepter'd concrete isle

A Hampshire training contract involves a degree of moving between offices. Fareham, home to most of the firm's litigators, is *"where the brains are."* Southampton is home to insolvency, corporate, pensions, environment, banking, construction and franchising. Portsmouth offers a mix of private client and commercial seats, with commercial property, property litigation, corporate, private client, family and employment all present and accounted for. Winchester has got additional family and residential property teams. The Hampshire trainees were noticeably peppy and optimistic about their experiences at BLTL. This may be due to their proximity to the sea, since many of them are keen sailors, or it may be that training in the Blake Lapthorn 'legacy' locations offers a cohesive and settled atmosphere: *"It feels like a family. The partners still feel a responsibility towards us. There's a legendary incident where the firm talked about suspending its habit of giving us posh Waitrose hampers at Christmas. One partner bought them for everyone with his own money, then demanded reimbursement from the firm."*

Southampton is the undisputed *"social king"* because the office's city-centre location means that bars and restaurants are only a few paces away. Trainees frequent the Orange Rooms, despite its *"sticky carpets."* In Portsmouth, trainees struggled to name the most glamorous establishments near the office's business park: *"There's a Pizza Hut, a restaurant-pub and I think there's a KFC somewhere."* At the Fareham office (*"stuck out on the motorway on an industrial estate"*) if you make your way past the *"giant electricity pylon"* in the car park, there is a *"pretty cool little sandwich shop in the woods near the office."* Rumours abound that the Southampton, Portsmouth and Fareham offices will merge into *"one big super office"* in Chandler's Ford. Such a move would eliminate the last city-centre office BLTL has outside London, but trainees aren't packing their pencil cases just yet: *"The possibility gets closer and then moves away again. We're sitting waiting for it to happen, but we might be sitting here a long time."*

South Coasters have a civilised 75-minutes lunch break, and office hours tend to run from 8:45am to 6:00pm, in line with the claim on the website of "quality work and life in perfect balance." But even in paradise, the winds of change are blowing. One Hampshire trainee summed up the firm's ambitions: "*There will be a drive to increase profitability based on the firm's new larger size. We'll probably have to work a little harder.*" Actually, trainees are keen to be pushed a bit, but they don't want to work harder for free: "*I think the salaries will have to go up along with billing targets. I hope the firm realises it's now competing with different people in the legal market for its staff. Right now Shoosmiths seems to be an ever-open door for Blakes' talent...*"

and finally...

Outside London, all but one of the nine qualifying trainees took a job with the firm in 2007. In London neither qualifier stayed. Potentially, BLTL could become a massive firm with a wonderfully broad training programme, but it needs to match its commercial growth with a rise in salaries so it doesn't lose its carefully nurtured talent to higher-paying firms.

Boodle Hatfield

the facts

Location: London, Oxford
Number of UK partners/solicitors: 31/65
Total number of trainees: 12
Seats: 4x6 months
Alternative seats: None

Nestling in the heart of Mayfair, dangerously close to shopping opportunities that will leave your purse as light as a feather, Boodle Hatfield is an unassumingly modest firm with nearly three centuries of experience advising the wealthy folk of London on property, estate management, rural affairs and tax and financial planning.

boodle's about

It is impossible to understate the importance of property to Boodles – it accounts for over 50% of income. The firm's major client is Grosvenor (aka the Duke of Westminster's Estate), which sprawls decadently across all the dark blue and green bits of the Monopoly board, including Boodles' home in New Bond Street. "*We have a massive team dedicated to Grosvenor and we really put a lot of effort into it – they know that they're always getting the best from us,*" said a source. Departments other than property also draw a significant portion of their work from Grosvenor, but that's not to say this firm is a one-client band. Some of the other substantial names on the books are the Bedford Estates (in London), Marriott Hotels, Allied Irish Bank GB and RBS. Tax and financial planning for wealthy individuals is the firm's second strongest area – the private client team has seven partners to property's 15 – and the work of the family team is closely allied to this department. The picture is completed by a commercial litigation group and a small corporate team that focuses on private companies, entrepreneurs and wealthy investors.

Three property options are available to trainees – estates, construction and property development – and taking one of these is not only usual, but also essential to properly understand the firm. Property seats offer great responsibility, for example, managing a residential conveyance from start to finish "*gets you to look at all the key property principles,*" whereas property management for a large client brings lease negotiations, licences to assign and underlet and rent arrears problems. Juggling all these is excellent experience. Property finance and development can range from wax-jackets-and-wellies rural estates to helping with the co-ordination of multimillion-pound commercial deals. "*Property is fast, fast, fast; you see deal after deal,*" commented one trainee. Planning applications and negotiations to buy land for commercial development (shopping centres are a big one) also fall within the remit of this team, and trainees get the chance to run some fairly substantial files. "*You get to see absolutely everything. You're really at the coalface,*" enthused one interviewee.

Right now, construction seats concentrate on the massive Paradise Street redevelopment in Liverpool, all part of the preparation for Liverpool's status as European Capital of Culture in 2008. Valued at £920m, the project comprises over 200 sites with around ten sub-contractors per site. Each one needs an individually tailored collateral warranty to be drawn up, so if you do some simple multiplication, you'll quickly see that it's "*a big, big exercise.*"

house or home?

If you love academic law, you may know that leasehold enfranchisement (where householders have the right to buy their freehold or extend their lease) has given rise to some interesting cases, many of which now turn on the meaning of the word 'house'. Boodles has represented Grosvenor in a number of cases involving properties originally built as houses but which have for many years been used as offices or clubs. Having achieved a favourable decision from the Court of Appeal to prevent leaseholders making claims to acquire the freehold, one such case is pending appeal to the House of Lords and will set a precedent that resolves the current uncertainty.

Corporate trainees' bread and butter is company administration (filling in clients' annual returns, dealing with directors' appointments and resignations, liaising with Companies House on queries arising from clients' statutory books) and then, as and when they come in, helping out on deals. "*The transactions take up a large part of*

your time as they're very intense, and then, when they die down, it's a chance to catch up on the company admin work. That way you're always busy,*" explained one source. Going against stereotype, the team doesn't have a macho image at all; it's "*all very decent and civilised. We work hard during the day, but no one is expected to stay through the night.*" This reflects the nature of the work as much as anything else: the typical range of the firm's larger deals is £50m to £200m.

Litigation means employment, family, landlord and tenant and commercial disputes. Working on employment cases, trainees soon learn that employers are keen on preventative advice to keep them away from tribunals. They also get the chance to act as independent representatives to employees in disciplinary hearings, offering procedural advice on each step of the statutory grievance process. In commercial litigation "*it's all about what the other side are going to do,*" explained a trainee; "*it's about teasing out different bits of information from the other side and watching our case become stronger.*" When something needs to be issued or filed, trainees are responsible for the run to the Royal Courts of Justice and the Central London County Court. "*It can be quite intimidating the first time you go to the RCJ as it's quite a rabbit warren, but after the first few times you could do it blindfolded.*"

marriage counselling

The family team represents old-money clients and entrepreneurial City types going through high-stakes divorces. These sometimes throw up a whole host of issues including non-molestation orders, child proceedings, concurrent criminal proceedings, ancillary relief, maintenance and properties held in multiple jurisdictions. Thankfully, there are simpler matters that trainees can run themselves, such as "*a very short marriage without children settled by a* consent order." When clients feel the need to vent during a day at court, trainees can end up *"taking them out for lunch while the solicitor talks to counsel. Sometimes it's helpful to get away from the areas right outside the court room."* As a trainee, you'll become very familiar with the court room, and possibly even more so with the waiting areas, as so much time is spent there in last-minute negotiations. During these talks you'll be *"called on to remember names of people or numbers or facts, and you're an extra pair of hands to find things quickly."*

In private client *"protecting the wealth of future generations"* is the name of the game. For trainees this may mean reviewing wills and trusts following changes in legislation or *"disappearing into a cupboard a few times a day"* in order to look up information for colleagues. Trainees have a few small files of their own, although they can't always see them through to a conclusion as some matters have long life cycles. The tax side of the seat is *"really hard"* but *"satisfying. Though it makes your brain ache, you feel good when you get to grips with it."* Apparently some private clients view their lawyers as family assets, much like the old concept of the man of affairs. As a result, *"you have people coming in and asking all sorts of odd questions,"* so there's never a dull day.

As to how well seat allocation works, we hear that it requires a certain amount of proactivity from trainees. *"When we first got here we were told what our first seat was and after that it was sort of a process of negotiation,"* recalled one. We do wonder how long this informal approach will work, especially given the increase to seven recruits per year from September 2008. Doubtless the firm has a plan – it has after all doubled the intake in a short space of time. One more thing on seat choices: there is a second, smaller office in Oxford and any trainee can request to visit for a private client seat. In most seats, trainees share a room with their supervising partner.

boodles of enthusiasm

For the most part, clients stay loyal because of the service they receive when they send instructions. That said, it never hurts to keep up social contact. Grosvenor has scores of young surveyors and trainees for the Boodles trainees to meet for lunch and drinks. Additionally there are shared sporting and social events to which everyone is invited – things like dragon boat racing, a games night involving giant Jenga, darts, table football and snooker, a picnic and fun day, plus regular cricket, softball and football matches. Firm-only events include karaoke, quiz nights and trips to local pub Bond's. *"Everyone has a life outside work,"* added an interviewee. Indeed they do – everything from running the London Marathon to volunteering as a Girl Guide leader and raising money for the legal support centre in Fulham. And then there's the retail therapy... One side of Boodles' office overlooks Oxford Street, which is *"fantastic for the Christmas lights,"* but a disaster for the bank balance. *"It's so easy to pop out at lunchtime and then, 'Oh look, I've done some shopping,'"* lamented one trainee, before revealing how *"because it's quite a female-biased firm, you come in with shopping bags after lunch and everyone gets excited!"*

Trainees feel confident that the firm will continue to stick to its winning formula of property and private client work, while possibly supplementing the corporate team in line with current market trends. *"They're definitely doing things, like increasing the efficiency of the IT,"* explained one trainee; *"we've all got a BlackBerry now. I don't have to take it home at the weekend; it just means that if I'm in court and someone needs to get hold of me then they can. Or if I'm lost, I can ask for help."* In a busy department like property it's likely there will always be room for an extra pair of hands and the chances of staying on post-qualification are good. Of course not everyone wants to become a property lawyer and this can lead to disappointment. In 2007, two qualifiers hoping for family jobs discovered just that when they were told there was no room at the inn. Overall retention figures for 2007 showed one out of four people stayed on.

and finally...

What Boodle Hatfield does, it does extremely well, and that doesn't look set to change any time soon. So long as you're up for trying property law you might come to view this firm as the ideal combination of wellies and brogues. Just check out the website to see what we mean.

B P Collins

the facts

Location: Beaconsfield, Gerrards Cross
Number of UK partners/solicitors: 20/45
Total number of trainees: 7
Seats: 4x5 months followed by 1x4 months
Alternative seats: None

Twenty minutes on the train from London Marylebone, and with more than half its partners ex-City lawyers, BP Collins is a firm with its ear to the ground and its nose to the grindstone. Listen hard and you can almost hear the rumble of the capital. And if you really pay attention, you might also discern the faint whirr of London trainees turning in their machine-like firms. A satisfied sigh from inside the walls of BP Collins, accompanied by the moo of a nearby cow, says it all.

bun in the oven

Right now, BP Collins is a firm with babies on the brain. As associates take maternity leave right, left and centre, the baby boom allows trainees to benefit from added levels of responsibility. Thankfully the output of work wins hands down against the output of babies, so don't go thinking BP Collins is

a soft touch. Senior partner Ian Johnson may come across as more Easter Bunny than Darth Vader in his management style (he brought in hot cross buns for the entire office and has been known to distribute chocolate at Christmas), but he has an ambitious five-year plan to double turnover by 2010 and increase the number of fee earners by 25. Remember Ian, that's 25 more hot cross buns...

Trainees reckon the firm must be on track to meet its targets. *"All the partners seem really chirpy, so I guess it's going well,"* said one source. With strong departments in property, private client, litigation, charities and environmental law, BP Collins is certainly a leading Thames Valley player, and there are plans to go further still. *"We're trying to become a large, successful firm that can compete against the City,"* revealed one source. In the process, *"departments have developed a kind of professional rivalry; people are competing against each other to be the best."* For a trainee, loyalties to a department can develop quickly, even though *"you always have to move on so there's not much point getting too attached."* In all departments they are encouraged to show initiative from an early stage and *"everybody is welcome to pitch in, no matter what their level."*

share the love

BP Collins is split between a town centre office above a shop in Beaconsfield and three buildings in Gerrards Cross, where trainees are based. The firm runs an unusual seat system: four five-month seats followed by one of four months back in the area in which the trainee wants to qualify. The systems works well and *"even when people have been awkward and changed their minds, HR have still managed to accommodate them."* Perhaps this is because seat preferences are determined very early.

The largest of the departments, property works in a range of areas including the retail sector (Bonsoir, owner of the Lacoste label, is a client), the gravel and waste industries, secured lending (AIB and RBS) and commercial and residential development. Quite a few houses come in at £2m locally, so trainees get to see a few swish pads in the process. Trainees in this department have a pretty packed schedule and sometimes carry out *"obscure but interesting research into the restrictive covenants attached to buildings around Gerrards Cross."* The residential side of the department may clock off at 5.30pm but, as a trainee's work is generally more commercial in orientation, their hours are slightly longer. Even so, *"it never feels stressful. You might have lots to do and you might not be able to see your desk for all the work, but you still have a giggle and somehow the atmosphere is really bubbly."* Trainees described the department as the most *"inclusive,"* with the seven partners making it *"a great place to work."* On a Friday night, fee earners and secretaries regularly go out to the pub, and together with their peers in the family department, trainees have been known to challenge the partners to quizzes. *"There's a good bit of rivalry: we've told them we'll beat them one day,"* said a source, unwittingly identifying the stronger players.

A seat in the burgeoning employment department offers *"a really good blend of contentious and non-contentious work"* for both employers and employees. As well as enjoying the mix, trainees think that *"doing one side of things makes you better at the other."* Employment trainees also support the corporate department on M&A and other transactions. The corporate lawyers, meanwhile, regularly find themselves across the table from prominent City firms. As a trainee there's little opportunity to get out of the office on these deals and there are times when you could be in until 2am carrying out largely administrative tasks. One exasperated interviewee suggested law schools should teach bundling and bibling on the LPC: *"Introduce a three-week course on it and see how many people drop out!"* Another commented

that at times partners were too busy to provide much training: *"They'd just say fill in this form... I must have done 600 of them."* The team provides a broad range of services to clients ranging from start-ups to larger international companies with transactions in the millions and – increasingly – tens of millions of pounds. Could this be why *"partners are always so fearful that things will get posted to the wrong place,"* meaning that literally everything is checked and double-checked? On the plus side, it's a *"friendly, sociable team."*

By contrast, the litigation department *"gives responsibility early on because it's so fast-moving and there isn't time to check every little thing."* The department is bustling with energy and, along with employment, contains some strong characters. *"It doesn't make for the most chilled-out working environment, but then it's not supposed to be – it's a law firm."* The hours fluctuate. *"All the really late nights I've done were in litigation, either preparing for a freezing injunction or in the run-up to a five-day trial in Chancery. But to be honest, I eat better than normal when it gets busy!"* Having hungry lawyers across the road is a bonus for local restaurants, which perhaps explains their willingness to bend normal dining rules. *"Café Rouge lets you take the plate of food back to the office. It's a community thing: local businesses try and support each other,"* said a source. Canny as ever, BP Collins gets in on all this caring and sharing by hosting a monthly lunch club for local businesses.

waterworks

Private client mostly involves wills, trusts and probate, with tax a *"difficult and quite intellectual"* aspect of the seat. There's also work for charity clients, and if you express an interest supervisors will be more than happy *"to give you more of that type of work."* In family, like private client (where *"most clients are on their way to be buried or have been dead for some time"*), a certain amount of emotional detachment is required.

"You'll speak to clients every day and you will be the one helping them through: sometimes for as long as a year." The fact that trainees are only in the department for four or five months means it's harder for them to become the main contact, but client contact is still "one of the most important aspects of the seat." The department's work covers divorce, cohabitation and prenuptial agreements, the odd civil partnership and a smattering of children's cases. Don't expect a deluge of responsibility to start with but "bits of work start dripping in" and "by the end of the seat I was wading my way through quite complicated drafting and petitioning." Trainees spoke about the efforts of partners "not to impose their own style on you – they'll say, 'Here are a few precedents, see which one suits you best.'"

Of the social scene, said one trainee, "none of us are big drinkers, but we'll go out after work and have a coke." Knowing that they went to see The Rocky Horror Show together we asked if anyone dressed up. "No! We're not that out there!" Future plans include ice-skating and a trip to the dog races in Oxford. Neither in costume. In terms of the firm as a whole, trainees agreed "we should get together a bit more, there's only one big firm-wide event each year." Examples include a trip to the horse races at Windsor and, in celebration of the 40th anniversary in 2006, a sit-down dinner with founding partner Brian Collins. "We heard some hilarious stories," recounted one trainee, "like when all the partners had brand new cars and another lawyer managed to drive into all of them while trying to get out of a parking space." Oops!

the hole truth

Despite high-quality work and a great atmosphere, for some fee earners the pull of the capital is too strong and associate leakage can be a problem. "The firm is trying to expand but it keeps losing its associates, so there are vacancies across the board." "Either they've gone because they didn't believe there are partnership prospects or because they wanted to earn more money for the same work." Trainees seem to know exactly what kind of partners BP Collins likes: "They love people who used to work in the City and want to do the same kind of work, but also want a nice house in the country and time to spend with their kids..."

...or play a round of golf. Now golf lessons don't usually form part of the trainee curriculum, but BP Collins may just be the exception to the rule. With four courses within a five-mile radius, "a lot of the partners and senior associates play" and we suspect that a round of golf is probably the closest thing to a hard day's work for some Beaconsfield residents. Gary Lineker, who owns a house nearby, is apparently very good. All in all, teaching lawyers to improve their swing sounds like it makes good business sense, so we'll forgive the trainee who said the firm was "really driving forward with its marketing." Other initiatives have included bringing in a consultant to teach subjects such as "how to get someone to admit they're not entirely happy with the firm they currently use and agree to give us a try," "how to pin a name-badge on correctly" and "how not to stare at a woman's chest."

and finally....

This firm's combination of high-quality work coupled with rural serenity does sound rather attractive. Some trainees wish they'd known in advance "quite how boring Gerrards Cross is," but hey, there's a Marks and Sparks Simply Food on the way. And who can deny the appeal of "rounders games on the common in summer" and real ale round the open fire in the Ethorpe Hotel bar in the winter? The single trainee qualifying in 2007 was happy to stay on with a job in the family department.

BPE Solicitors

the facts
Location: Cheltenham, Birmingham
Number of UK partners/solicitors: 12/54
Total number of trainees: 10
Seats: 4x6 months
Alternative seats: None

This Cheltenham firm has an energetic approach that it has put to good effect by breaking into the Birmingham market.

flower power

Formed in 1989, BPE is the amalgamation of established Cheltenham firms Bretherton Price and Elgoods. It has achieved a great balance of old and new, building upon the strong commercial client base of each founding firm while presenting itself as a modern and progressive organisation. Size-wise, it is one of the largest commercial outfits in Gloucestershire and is especially well regarded in relation to property, which has long been the firm's busiest department. Last year it assisted long-standing client First Property Group in a number of sales and purchases with an aggregate value of £20m. It also benefited from a steady stream of instructions from key client Blooms of Bressingham, a Gloucester-based merchant of all things floral that sought the firm's advice on a £10.9m sale and leaseback of a freehold property in Bicester, a £1.3m freehold purchase of a garden centre in Stevenage and a £3m purchase and leaseback of a garden centre in Worcester. Involvement in the sale of the 20-acre Cheltenham Film Studios is further proof of how deeply rooted the team is in local matters. The addition of eight AIM-listed companies – of which the Jelf Group, Maxima Group and Mears Group stand out – has further expanded the firm's client roster in this area. Elsewhere, BPE has taken a leading position in local

claimant-based PI work, boasting particular expertise in relation to industrial disease. It is said to be attracting an average of 20 new clients each week.

Clearly, then, the firm is performing well in its traditional hunting ground, but it has also been bold enough to target lucrative areas further afield. Having decided against a move into what it perceives to be the relatively closed Bristol market, BPE set up a six-partner outpost in Birmingham in 2002. It may have entered the ring as an unknown contender, but it has done well to establish itself as a rival to some of the city's established middleweight combatants. "*A few years ago no one had heard of BPE outside Cheltenham, but that's not the case anymore,*" said one trainee. Our parent publication *Chambers UK* now recognises the firm as a serious player in Birmingham for employment and insolvency law, while extensive work for clients such as Hexagon Human Capital has raised the profile of its coco department. In the space of a year, Hexagon has acquired Euromedica, Roberts & Corr and BIE Interim Executive, as well as completing a £30m AIM listing. In response to rapid growth in its Birmingham business, the firm moved to new premises in late 2006 and its 35 lawyers now sit comfortably in a converted bank just off New Street.

all smiles

The training scheme is fairly Cheltenham-centric, with just two trainees joining the Birmingham office and only two seats on offer there. Despite the geographical divide there are strong links between the two offices, no doubt aided by most Cheltenham trainees' desire to undertake some work in both. No one is likely to be coerced into a move to Brum, because so many of them are keen to escape the serenity of the Cotswolds for six months of big-city living. Because Birmingham seats are limited to corporate and commercial property, Brum trainees must also spend time in Cheltenham.

Trainees are placed for all but the final seat, but tell us HR is *"very interested in finding out about you and what you want to get out of your contract."* As one source explained: *"It's a symbiotic relationship: they want you to be happy because this will be reflected in your work, which will keep your supervisors happy as well."* This helps when it comes to selecting the final seat, after experience of commercial property, coco and dispute resolution. Our interviewees all seemed keen to gain experience of the firm's core commercial departments, and none more so than the *"thriving"* commercial property group, where trainees are given *"a great level of responsibility"* and are on the front line of the firm's biggest transactions. *"I was sat down on my first day and asked to prepare a report on title, so it's proper work from day one,"* one told us. Others spoke of doing work for major client Pizza Hut, and there are always *"plenty of auction sales"* as well as *"completing Companies House forms, drafting contract clauses and general research duties."*

The *"dynamic and busy"* coco department was similarly high on our interviewees' wish lists. Here, trainees can expect to be *"relied on as part of the team"* and trusted to deal directly with clients. Frequently, this means liaising with the firm's banking clientele in relation to the funding of transactions. This is the only seat where the hours can be demanding, but *"time and resources are managed in such a way as to ensure that trainees are not dumped on to clean up at the end."* So, when trainees find themselves in the office past Simpsons o'clock they can rest assured they will be doing proper work alongside other members of the team, and that their efforts will be appreciated.

There is no better example of the trust the firm places in its trainees than in the litigation seat, which offers abundant opportunities to deal with clients in person and over the telephone. *"You don't just speak to them, you really get to know them,"* we were told. Trainees also get to flex their advocacy muscles in some instances. Said one: *"My supervisor is letting me handle a pre-hearing review. I've already done all the applications myself and will do the hearing on my own... with him behind me."* The firm is experienced in some niche areas of litigation: trainees gain exposure to IP disputes and there are numerous instructions from the construction industry, which provide *"interesting opportunities to go on-site and see the cause of a conflict first hand."*

After time in these three departments, six months are left to be filled by a seat in asset and credit finance, personal injury, private client or the ever-popular employment department. In all of these areas, interviewees report, the firm maintains its personalised approach to training. *"Your bosses always make time to sit down and talk you through the law. You are not pawned off with an assistant or associate."* As a consequence of this, there is no hiding behind the legs of others; trainees are expected to get involved and pull their weight. To help trainees keep up, regular appraisals identify *"strengths and weaknesses, so you can improve or capitalise on what you're good at."*

climb every mountain

Trainees who have been making efforts to improve BPE's social scene have found its presence in Birmingham very helpful in this respect. *"We had a great night out recently, where the firm threw money at us to help make sure it went well."* The firm's last Christmas party took full advantage of Birmingham's legendary curry scene, while, back in Cheltenham, the Number Seven wine bar and restaurant is viewed by trainees as their *"second office."* Huge efforts have been made to level the playing field between members of staff: *"Both offices are open plan, which means no physical divides. It creates a nice, team atmosphere,"* and a relaxed dress code also has an effect. Although there was some reluctance among trainees to ditch the suits, it seems that partners have no such inhibitions, certainly not when it came to getting down with the kids at the rodeo-themed summer party this year. *"It was quite amusing to see my training principal dressed up as a Red Indian,"* recalled one source.

Previously, we have noted the firm's tendency to recruit some trainees from its ranks of paralegals. Although this practice appears to have lessened somewhat, many of BPE's current trainees have significant paralegal experience either here or elsewhere in the UK or overseas. According to one, this makes perfect sense: the firm gives you *"such a high degree of responsibility that the skills and knowledge you gain as a paralegal really come in handy."* No amount of previous experience could prepare trainees for a (non-compulsory!) trek to the Atlas Mountains of Morocco, for which the BPE participants *"had two weeks off, on firm time, to raise £10,000 for charity."* We caught up with trainees just before five of them embarked on this adventure, so you'll have to wait until next year to find out how they fared. If their enthusiasm was anything to go by, they'll have been fine.

and finally...

If you only know Gloucestershire for its biblical floods and green-welly brigade, you might want to look a little closer. This training offers a good combination of Cotswold calm and Birmingham buzz, and the firm certainly seems to have it right when it comes to giving trainees decent responsibility. In 2007, the one qualifier took an NQ job at the firm.

Brabners Chaffe Street

the facts

Location: Liverpool, Manchester, Preston
Number of UK partners/solicitors: 57/83
Total number of trainees: 18
Seats: 4x6 months
Alternative seats: Secondments

In the increasingly competitive North West legal market, commercial and private client firm Brabners Chaffe Street is doing more than holding its own.

the contender

When, in 2001, 200-year-old Brabners of Liverpool and Preston joined forces with Manchester firm Chaffe Street to create a three-office North West contender, we admired its foresight. Revenue and profits rose and then, in 2006, well-known Manchester firm James Chapman & Co dissolved and delivered its commercial division to Brabners. And there's more to come. According to managing partner Michael Brabner (yes, there's still a Brabner at the helm), the firm is on a major recruitment drive to beef up all of its core areas of practice: corporate and commercial; property; litigation and employment. In addition, it is moving into new markets: sports law is a good example. Meanwhile the firm is making a renewed push in the private client realm and two Liverpool lawyers have relocated to build up a team in Manchester, contributing to *"plans to double the size of this office so that it equals Liverpool."* Both branches have already moved to bigger premises to accommodate the new arrivals.

do they know it's christmas?

Until now trainees have signed up to a single office, but this policy is under review. If cross-office training contracts do come into being, then

We Want You

Our Limited Liability Partnership

Leading North West (Top 100) Law firm, first established in 1815 with offices in Liverpool, Manchester and Preston.

Our Services

- Full range of commercial services built on core practice areas of:
    - Corporate & Commercial
    - Commercial Property
    - Employment
    - Commercial Litigation
    - Private Client
    - Banking
    - Sports Law

Recent Awards

- **The firm**
    - Ranked in 2007 for second year as Sunday Times 100 Best Companies to Work For
    - The Private Client Team ranked second in the Regional Private Client Team of the Year for the 2006 Society of Trust and Estate Practitioners (STEP) awards
    - Investors In People award for over 12 years
    - Ranked fourth in the UK for job satisfaction in the Lex 100, 2005. The Lex is an insider's guide to the UK's top law firms, the views and experiences of thousands of trainees and newly qualified solicitors have been analysed to help those looking for training contracts

- **Individuals**
    - Solicitor Anna Gregory was awarded Young Lawyer of the Year at the annual Insider Young Professionals Awards
    - Denise Walker and chairman Stephen Burrows were awarded Lawyer of the Year Award and the Lifetime Achievement Award, respectively, at the annual Insider Professionals Awards

Who we act for

- Owners and managers of private businesses
- Larger corporate clients and plc's
- Public sector and not for profit organisations
- Banks, pension funds and other institutions
- High net worth individuals

Clients include

- SITA UK Ltd
- TJ Hughes Ltd
- Adidas International
- Manchester United
- The Edinburgh Woollen Mill Ltd
- TM Retail Group plc
- NWF Group plc
- Typhoo Tea
- Urban Splash

The financial year to April 30 2007

- Fee income growth over 20%
- Turnover increased to over £25m

Our Trainees

We are now recruiting trainees for September 2009. Apply online to our Director of Training, Dr Tony Harvey at www.brabnerschaffestreet.com. The application deadline for 2009 is 31st July 2007 and, for 2010, 31st July 2008.

For further information about Trainee Recruitment email: trainees@brabnerscs.com or go to our website at: www.brabnerschaffestreet.com

WE WANT YOU . . .

. . . if you are intelligent, personable with a good sense of humour movement between offices will probably be on a voluntary basis. At present there are nine trainees in Liverpool, seven in Manchester and two in Preston. Liverpool has the most seat choices but Manchester is catching up, adding a new corporate/commercial seat this year.

In the past we've heard whispers of Masonic lot-drawing for seat allocation, and this year there were still one or two grumbles. *"In Liverpool trainees are asked for three preferences and then their seats are allocated. Here in Manchester we are not asked at all. If there is something you want, you have to push for it."* Others argue that a lack of formal structure in terms of how this is done means *"you can't put your case forward within the system because you don't really know how the system works."* What we do know is that everyone does litigation (or employment) to fulfil the Law Society's contentious requirement. Quite a few people also take a property seat. In Manchester, a seat with the corporate or commercial teams is highly likely. There are also banking and private client possibilities and the chance of a secondment to Mersey Docks and Harbour Company, one of the firm's major clients. The secondment is open to trainees in all offices.

Let's start with the property department, arguably the daddy in the firm. The North West is *"an exciting place to be and there is a lot of work for property lawyers,"* declared one trainee. This is due to the flow of European regeneration funding into Liverpool and Manchester's commercial renaissance. Brabners has grown off the back of projects such as Peel Holdings' construction of a new £25m canal connecting the Leeds-Liverpool canal to Liverpool's Albert Dock, and the development and sale of flats in places like Salford Quays and emerging neighbourhood Greengate.

Manchester trainees say their office is led by the corporate and commercial teams, but are candid about a basic issue: *"If you want the very biggest deals, we'll put our hands up and say that's not us."* Generally, the firm represents *"owner-managed businesses and small to medium-sized enterprises,"* not big plcs. *"We do some work for clients that are national, but the lawyers here have strong roots in the area and that's where their work comes from. Some people don't want to go to London to see a lawyer."* But what if you do hanker after the bright lights of the capital? *"That's where our training falls down,"* said one source. Even after taking a corporate seat here, *"you might not know the listing rules."* This doesn't mean that the work isn't good for the region: *"I was setting up companies and reviewing and amending terms and conditions,"* one Liverpool trainee told us. *"I saw quite a broad spectrum of clients, mainly North West companies but a couple of national ones too."* At least you won't be up all hours trying to meet deadlines. *"There's a strong work ethic here but people aren't wage slaves and they are not in every weekend."* One Manchester trainee had done *"two or three month-long stints until 9pm,"* and told us: *"this is as bad as it gets."* In fact, the experience you accrue during the tough times is *"rewarding and, ultimately, makes you a better lawyer. After a Christmas deal finished, all I thought was, 'Thank god, I can relax and go and eat turkey now.'"* At the top end of the firm's deals list last year was the £49m sale of Nationwide Autocentres to Phoenix Equity Partners, handled by the Liverpool office.

The arrival of the James Chapman commercial team has had a massive effect, not least because of its expertise in the sports industry. *"They have really good clients, like Manchester United* [senior partner Maurice Watkins is a non-executive director of the club] *and other Premiership teams and players."* One of our sources has this piece of advice for anyone hoping to become a part of the Manchester sports team: *"It's good as an incentive, but you should be prepared to give every seat a try. The firm likes people who are willing to be flexible."* Talking of the rejuvenating effect of the James Chapman merger, trainees told us: *"Before, Brabners was partner-heavy and full of older solicitors. Now there is a younger team, and they are bringing in really interesting work."* Overseeing the transfer of Javier Mascherano from West Ham United to Liverpool FC despite FIFA and Premier League rules barring the transfer is a case in point. Instructions such as these have *"raised the image of the firm loads."*

The trainees' litigation experience is broad, covering property and sports cases, as well as general commercial, employment, insolvency, shareholder and trusts disputes. *"I did no advocacy and had none of my own files because of the size of the matters the firm handles. That's fairly typical unless a partner takes on a small, lower value case for an old client,"* observed one. In the employment seat you need to learn to be organised, as you will be assisting several team members who will *"all ask you to do things for them."* The work is mainly for employers, with a few individual claims and a dose of corporate support jobs thrown in. *"I went to employment tribunals and assisted counsel,"* said one satisfied source. *"I also attended client meetings and prepared witness statements and responses."* Cases range from unfair dismissal claims to sex, race and disability discrimination suits. *"We thought there would be cases of age discrimination once the new legislation came into force, but there weren't any in my seat,"* said one trainee. Perhaps lawyers are doing too good a job of marketing their advisory services to clients: *"A lot of the work is preventative – drafting handbooks, policies and procedures."*

preston to service

In what is the UK's smallest city – Preston – Brabners is just about the best law firm around, undertaking commercial litigation, corporate, employment, property and agriculture and rural affairs work. Its mission is *"to get more and more*

quality staff. I'm not sure what it was like five years ago, but they want to keep raising the standard." Again, property is the biggest department. Trainees in this seat are supervised by two or three people and deal with business leases on behalf of landlords. The firm's longevity is key to its success in agriculture and private client matters. *"Old people who made their wills years ago come back to change them, and then there are high net worth individuals who need tax planning and estate planning advice."* Often, trainees will go out and see clients who can't travel easily, which is a *"good way of feeling connected to the local community."* Another way is to join the Preston Exchange Network, which organises lunches for bankers, solicitors and accountants. With Manchester and Liverpool more than half an hour away, *"you can sometimes feel a little out on a limb here,"* we were told. Luckily, the Preston social scene is pretty decent. There are regular social events (where partners pay for the drinks) and, every August, a summer barbecue.

part of the family

Of the seven firms that made it into the *Sunday Times'* 'Best 100 Companies to Work For' survey in 2007, Brabners was the highest climber, now occupying 67th place in the rankings. So how is it keeping its staff happy? One answer is chocolate – every Easter, the managing partner delivers eggs to everyone. More seriously, though, *"hard work is rewarded"* and the firm isn't *"a big, faceless commercial place. You get to know people and they get to know you."* There's always *"time for a proper laugh"* and a chat. *"Weightmans, Hill Dicks and DLA might be bigger, but their trainees seem to be quite small cogs in a large machine. Although we've expanded a lot in the last couple of years, we've retained a nice, family style."* And do all the members of this family come from the North West? *"Not necessarily,"* came the reply, *"but most do, yes."*

The partners play a big part in the trainees' daily lives. "*You always sit with one and you get a lot of support from them.*" Sometimes, though, "*everyone is so busy you have to go and find things out for yourself, off your own bat. Stuff gets checked, but it can feel like a leap of faith at times. You just have to add common sense to what you learned during your degree and at law school,*" said one source. Thankfully, grunt work is kept to a minimum: "*Most of the duller tasks like photocopying are done by the general office staff.*" It is only on the organisational side of the training scheme that some interviewees thought the firm could improve, arguing that "*mid-term appraisals need to be introduced.*" It sounds as though the director of training will be looking into this idea. The NQ recruitment process was also identified as a bit of a problem area. "*It's not transparent and you don't get the right info as soon as you could, so there are times when you feel like you are harassing people. They should set clear dates for the different steps.*" Nevertheless, seven of the ten qualifiers in 2007 stayed with the firm, going into a variety of departments.

Brabners holds an annual social event for future trainees, the most recent being in The Racquets Club in Liverpool. Rumour has it that the singing around the piano included a Beatles-Oasis face-off... Interviewees would like to see more of this kind of event. "*There aren't as many as there should be.*" Trainees spend the first week of their training contract together on a Liverpool-based induction course and don't meet again until the annual staff conference in June. One of the most recent challenges at this event was to build and race go-karts, a task best managed by the speed kings in the post room. The rest of the year, each office has monthly staff drinks. The Sports Bar is a favourite in Liverpool, while Sublime is popular in Manchester. Although the partners aren't always around on Friday nights "*they do make an effort for leaving or birthday drinks.*" Any big news will get into Brabners' own version of *Heat* – an online publication with plenty of pics and gossip called *Inside Story*. So be careful what you get up to!

and finally...
It is sink or swim for law firms in the North West, and Brabners Chaffe Street is demonstrating an excellent stroke.

Bristows

the facts
Location: London
Number of UK partners/solicitors: 21/53
Total number of trainees: 14
Seats: 4 to 6 seats of 3 to 6 months
Alternative seats: Secondments
Extras: Language training

Way back in 1837, one of this firm's first pieces of work was the patenting of the practical electrical telegraph; 170 years of finger-tapping IP practice later, Bristows remains a leader in trade mark, patent and copyright law, with a clientele to set the wires click-clacking. If you've dot what it takes, you'd be advised to make a dash for this perennially popular firm.

a break in the ranks
If you can name it, trade mark it, contest its copyright or infringe its patent, chances are Bristows has come into contact with it at some time. Some of the world's largest biotech, pharmaceutical, life sciences, telecommunications, media and software companies turn to the firm, entrusting it with the protection or commercial exploitation of their cutting-edge technologies and most famous brands. Diageo, Unilever, Freeview, Endemol, Dolby, BBC, French Connection, Sony Computer Entertainment Europe, Cadbury

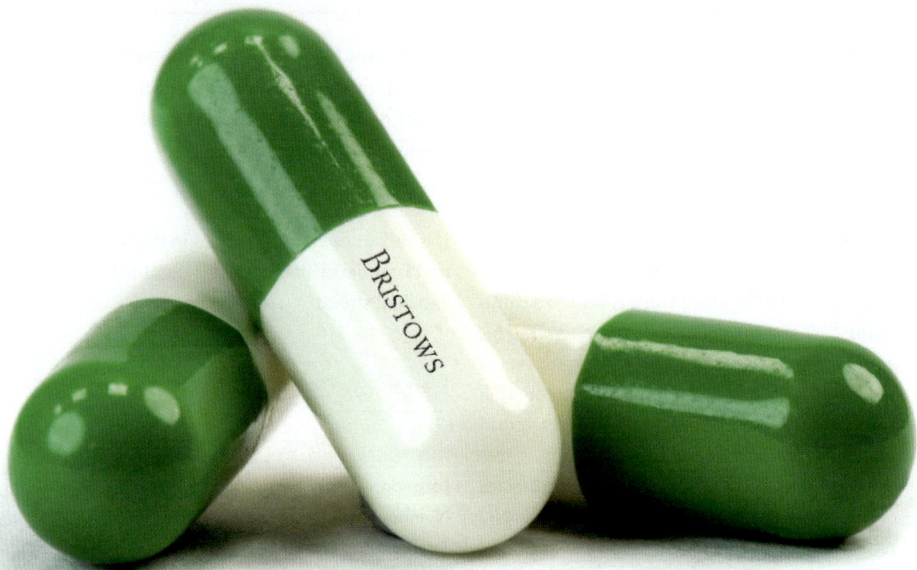

Schweppes, MTV, Bayer, sanofi-aventis, British Airways and Samsung Electronics are just a few of the mighty multinationals who have instructed the firm.

However, there is major news for us to report this year. In late 2006 five of the top IP litigation partners left the firm with five of their assistants to set up their own boutique Powell Gilbert. In truth it's a little early to pass judgment on the significance of this move, but here's what we'd found out by the time of going to press. On the positive side, our colleagues at *Chambers UK* report that the market seems to think Bristows will bounce back and that its prominent name and reputation will see it through. After all, most other firms could still only dream of having the IP litigation capability that remains at Bristows. Consequently the firm has only slipped a short distance to band two of the ranking tables. On the negative side, the five partners who left are all of a certain generation (late 30s/early40s) and this leaves a hole in the formerly balanced demographic of the department. The departees also took with them a big chunk of work, including matters for key clients such as Gillette/Procter & Gamble, Monsanto, Human Gene Sciences, Novartis and Medtronic.

A number of the firm's lawyers trained as scientists and of the 2006/07 trainee group all but two had a science, engineering or computer science background. So in this IP hothouse do you need several PhDs to make the grade? Even if *"it's easier sometimes for people who understand molecules,"* sources are adamant *"the work is accessible to non-scientists or non-engineers."* The official line is that those boffin statistics are *"more a reflection of the people applying than what the firm wants or needs."* Once out of the lab coat and into legal rags, ex-scientists told us: *"There are times when having chemistry or biology knowledge might help you understand a patent to do with a drug or therapy, but there are also times when an engineer-*ing background might help you understand an electronics patent and you're dealing with that kind of variety all the time."* In other words, you'll have to work substantially hard to get your head around the legal issues surrounding a complex area of the law, and one of the firm's main recruitment criteria is substantial intelligence.

Thankfully seat rotation is quite easy to grasp. As a rule there will be six months in IP litigation and six months in corporate or property, together with a likely spell in non-contentious IP. There is also the possibility of mixing things up a little by taking some three-month seats. This is much appreciated by trainees as it allows them to gain broader experience via Bristows' corporate, commercial property, competition/EU, trade marks, commercial litigation and employment departments, or to focus in on a particular area for a longer time. Toss in the prospect of a widely appreciated three-month stint in-house with a client and the breadth of a Bristows training contract is even more apparent.

frankie says...

As the slovenly younger sibling of *Chambers UK* we're always somewhat in awe of the meticulous research of our informed colleagues, but even they run short of superlatives when it comes to describing the calibre of lawyers in Bristows' IP teams. Small wonder that trainees aren't complaining about the compulsory period they spend in the practice group. Major tech-sector clients like Hitachi, Canon, Sony, Toshiba and Fujitsu have Bristows defend and enforce their valuable intellectual property rights, and the firm is currently assisting Korean electronics giant Samsung in relation to the UK aspect of its worldwide dispute with Ericsson and Sony-Ericsson over mobile handset and network equipment.

So much for the hard stuff; trainees also get to grips with all manner of so-called 'soft IP', including copyright, trade mark and design disputes across the fashion, software, consumer products and media sectors. Lawyers are currently awaiting the outcome of a contested Trade Marks Registry hearing in which they defended members of 1980s band Frankie Goes To Hollywood against the attempts of former lead singer Holly Johnson to scupper their plans to reform by filing UK and European trade mark applications for the band name. Whether hard or soft, *"acting for exciting clients"* on both *"defences and prosecutions"* is par for the course in a department that is *"very busy for trainees – people know you're available for work so they give it to you and you have to learn when to ask for a deadline extension."* It's true that on big cases *"you're the cheapest resource so if there's bundling or admin stuff to do, you'll do it,"* but sources had enjoyed *"meeting with experts, drafting expert witness statements and grasping the technology behind matters,"* pointing out that *"if you're keen and you put yourself out there, people will give you work. Even if it's just a first draft to be amended, it gives you exposure."*

On the non-contentious side, the commercial IP department is just as hot. Cadbury Schweppes, Tetley, MTV and Sony Computer Entertainment regularly instruct on everything from licensing and merchandising to brand strategy. Diageo (owners of Guinness, Smirnoff and Baileys) recently turned to the firm regarding its Johnnie Walker whiskey sponsorship of the McLaren Formula One Team. A *"very supportive"* department, it allows trainees to *"work closely with partners, negotiating draft advertising agreements for big clients"* or *"taking commercial considerations into account while drafting clauses or minor contracts."*

Beyond IP, seats in corporate or property *"really push you to think around the subject – you get interesting work."* In competition/EU or employment seats, involvement on transactions sits comfortably alongside *"being asked to draft advice to clients or review standalone agreements."* In general, both rotation and the experience of training left our sources satisfied, and if a few noted: *"People are so busy it's sometimes hard to get feedback,"* others suggested: *"I take it as my responsibility to seek a response on individual pieces of work, and anyway you'd know if something was wrong."* Training partners are apparently *"very aware of their duty to train you."* *"They'll point out why they've restructured your work and are keen to see you progress and develop your own personal style."* A *"supportive atmosphere"* means trainees rarely feel out of their depth, *"especially because of the overlap between seats, you're quickly up to speed in smaller departments, even in just three months."* And when trainees venture away on secondment for the delights of *"being the one with legal knowledge in meetings,"* there's always the safety net of *"a supportive contact partner for the client to turn to."*

breeze of change

We've long characterised Bristows as a genteel place, *"not stiff and standing on ceremony"* but *"a little old fashioned in atmosphere... in the best possible way."* Certainly, a strict dress code means *"everyone's in a suit."* Until now we've always drawn parallels between the culture and Bristows' historic and characterful Lincoln's Inn location. This year, change is in the air as Bristows plans its move to the newly revamped Unilever building on the Thames at Blackfriars Bridge. Soon to be spread *"over two levels with a big, central atrium"* and boasting *"all the mod cons, showers and bike-parking facilities, etc..."* our sources were understandably excited. *"There's going to be a similar layout of shared offices, definitely not open plan,"* they emphasised. *"The major difference will be bringing everyone under one roof; it's going to massively improve communication levels."* It's not that Bristows is suddenly about to undergo a personality change, but *"the move's created an atmosphere of positivity; everyone wants to evolve the firm for the better."* It will be interesting to see if the new home transfers any of its qualities to the firm's identity, but for the time being trainees still consider Bristows as *"one of the best options if you want a medium-sized firm with excellent niche work and an amazing client base."* Long regarded as a good place to come *"if you've no interest in working in a huge City firm,"* only time will tell if the *"quirky, everybody's-good-at-what-they-do-but-has-a-life-outside atmosphere"* will perpetuate.

lincoln's inn felled

Trainees are hoping that the *"great"* hours culture (*"9.15am to 6 or 6.30pm, maybe 'til 7.30 or 8pm in IP"*) won't change much when the firm moves. What they already feel sad about is moving away from picturesque Lincoln's Inn fields, where countless generations of Bristowians have picnicked, socialised, drunk and escaped the hurly burly of the office. Even we feel a bit sad, having vicariously enjoyed its delights over the years through our interviews with trainees. Hopefully they will regroup, discover new local haunts, and maybe venture to Temple Gardens for their habitual breath of fresh air. We hope too that the formidable social committee will continue to organise pub quizzes, comedy nights and Pimm's in the park. Department do's and *"lunches out together"* are also the stock in trade of a trainee population that *"tends to bond well,"* while the unquestioned highlight of the calendar is the annual *"black-tie dinner and dance."* There are also plenty of sports teams to help work out competitive urges, which is handy because when it comes to NQ jobs the process is pleasantly relaxed. Six of the seven stayed on in 2006, and in 2007 four out of five took up positions in the new surroundings of Unilever House, three of them going into IP jobs.

and finally...

With the split in the IP litigation team coming just before the move to Unilever House, you have

to ask what else might be going on at Bristows. The firm will want to grow into its new digs and it is very possible it might be planning to do so by expanding in areas beyond its traditional IP core. We've always said that this is a firm where you could qualify as either an IP lawyer or as something entirely different. Quite possibly this advice is sounder than ever.

Browne Jacobson LLP

the facts

Location: Nottingham, Birmingham, London
Number of UK partners/solicitors: 58/167
Total number of trainees: 20
Seats: 4x6 months
Alternative seats: Occasional secondmennts
Extras: Pro bono – CAB, ProHelp, Prince's Trust, Criminal Injuries and Compensation Scheme

Nottingham-headquartered Browne Jacobson has long outgrown its home market and added further offices in Birmingham and London to capture more business. The Birmingham operation has grown noticeably, but can Nottingham's favourite son prosper in this already-crowded legal market?

and in the east...

An established force in the East Midlands legal market, Browne Jacobson has always been an obvious choice for trainees who want to work in Nottingham, and with reason. Traditionally strong in insurance-related litigation but with a growing business services (read 'corporate-commercial') focus, it offers a near perfect blend of experience in training. However, our interviews this year highlighted a growing trend for Birmingham-focused applicants to target the firm. As you may be aware, the Brum legal market is a crowded one – there are big national firms such as

Eversheds and Pinsents and well-established, home-grown firms such as Wragge & Co and HBJ Gateley Wareing, and BJ is not the only firm to have tried to break into the city – also making a bid are the likes of Clarke Willmott, Bevan Brittan and BPE. So what is it about BJ that attracted West Midlands-oriented trainees? The thinking of one trainee was simple: *"I heard that they had an expanding Birmingham office and I thought that if I could develop my career with the firm I would have the opportunity to make a significant contribution to its growth in the area. There is still a long way to go to be up there with the bigger hitters, but the office is definitely a significant force within the firm right now."* Supporting this statement, from 2009 the firm will be offering a Birmingham-based training contract alongside its Nottingham-based option.

notts to be sniffed at

Aside from its ascent in the West Midlands, BJ has a lot to recommend it to potential trainees. The firm enjoys a reputation for being *"vibrant and progressive, not at all stuffy,"* and trainees were unanimous in their praise of a *"family feel"* pleasingly lacking in weighty hierarchy. *"Everyone is very approachable, regardless of their position,"* commented one source; *"I have sat in with partners and chatted away to them without feeling at all awkward."* The layout of the Nottingham office is currently *"a bit like Hogwarts,"* with a mix of small offices and larger communal spaces, but both Birmingham and London branches are open plan, meaning trainees generally sit near their supervisors. Nottingham is increasingly moving towards such an open-plan arrangement, much to the satisfaction of sources. *"The benefits are enormous: I can walk five paces and be in a different department, which has helped us to get to know each other better."*

As a full-service office, Nottingham has a broad selection of seats for trainees to sample.

Birmingham has a more limited menu of insurance and public risk, medical negligence, business and professional risk (including employment) and corporate. A property seat is in the process of being added. There is the option for trainees to try a seat in the firm's London office, although this isn't available all the time. When it does crop up, it is predominantly insurance litigation focused, but the office's small size means, *"if you make it known you want to experience something different, such as employment, you probably can."* The obvious downside to the seat is being the only young un' in the office, but the firm goes to some lengths to avoid lonely-trainee syndrome by covering travel expenses to and from trainee socials.

a coat of many colours

The firm's insurance division continues to account for a substantial part of its workload and revenue. Its structure is complicated so our hearts sank when a trainee told us: *"It has recently been through a revamp."* We understand the division is now subdivided into a department dealing with insurance and public risk and then teams for cases relating to social care and education; health (which mainly constitutes clinical negligence work and is kept busy due to the firm's coveted position as one of the firms on the NHS Litigation Authority panel); environment and advocacy; claims defence (which basically entails working for big insurers on motor claims) and technical claims (PI and stress at work matters). Somewhat confusingly, these team used to be known by different colours; for example, the environmental team was green and the health law team was purple. Officially the colour names are gone, but that doesn't stop some staff from using them: *"It always seems a bit of a muddle to people from the outside, but once you start you get used to it."*

The prominence of insurance work means trainees are unlikely to avoid a seat in this area, and it is quite likely that they will be posted there at the start of their training contract. This is no bad thing, as it can be *"a fun seat"* where *"you are always busy and allowed to get involved in important matters."* The market-leading position of BJ's personal injury teams was reinforced recently when the firm secured positions on both the NFU Mutual and Fortis legal panels. A stay in the insurance and public risk department also offers trainees the opportunity to handle their own caseload: *"I had about ten of my own files on the go and I was also assisting on larger files for other fee earners,"* said one trainee; *"because the cases were small, I never felt out of my depth and I left the seat feeling really confident about my own abilities."* Not every seat gives the same experience, however. The education and social services seat is *"quite document heavy"* and involves trainees in tasks that *"can get quite repetitive."* During the past year the firm has helped several insurers on education litigation matters, including Municipal Mutual, Norwich Union, Royal & SunAlliance, Ecclesiastical and Hiscox. The scope of claims ranges from failure to educate and bullying to issues relating to exclusions and breach of contract.

Another contentious seat option is commercial litigation and insolvency, a department that is getting some great work. This year, its lawyers negotiated the settlement of a significant dispute between the suppliers of components for the A400 Airbus. *"I really enjoyed the seat,"* said one enthusiastic source. *"It was very different to the litigation that I had experienced previously because I had always worked for insurance clients, whereas these people would be paying the costs from their own businesses."* Despite the difference, previous experience gained in the insurance teams really comes in handy, not least because confident, capable trainees get better work.

are you up for it?

BJ also has a lot on offer to trainees who are drawn to non-contentious practice. This year

the corporate lawyers acted for the management of Interflora Holdings on its $122m sale to the US-listed purchaser FTD Inc. Interflora's management had previously acquired its stake as part of a 3i-funded buyout. They also acted for William Sinclair Holdings on its move from the Official List of the London Stock exchange to AIM. A seat in the business services department in the Birmingham office offers trainees the chance *"to really get stuck into"* everything from banking and corporate to IP. Try the commercial contracts team in Nottingham and there will be plenty of opportunity to draft service agreements and liaise with clients on the registering of trade marks. Impressive levels of responsibility are certainly on offer to those who are up to the job. One source was proud to tell us: *"I did do a completion meeting on my own, although the partner knew about this and offered me help if I needed it."* The trainee recognised that this experience might seem daunting to some: *"There is always a chance you will flounder, but I have never felt like I couldn't ask for help."* Another *"loved the seat,"* telling us: *"I attended a lot of meetings and towards the end I was dealing with my own files and was much more confident as a result."*

any dream will do

Trainees were keen to emphasise the fact that BJ can fulfil all sorts of aspirations; one had decided the firm *"tends to pick trainees who are different, so that they can slot them into the different areas of work."* While there may be an element of truth in this, successful recruits do seem to share a number of characteristics. *"We are all quite opinionated, and I certainly wouldn't describe anyone as shy or quiet,"* said one. From another we heard that *"the people who shine on assessment days are the really friendly ones rather than those people who are massively intelligent but a bit snooty.*" In our experience, we'd certainly say BJ has a preference for people with a positive disposition. In 2007 eight of the 11 qualifiers stayed on with the firm, going into a variety of different departments and teams.

With working days that start at 9am and finish on average somewhere between 6pm and 7pm, trainees have a lot to be positive about. The time to socialise and to maintain that all-important work/life balance is central to this training experience. The social scene is definitely a lively one, in Nottingham especially. There are a number of sporting activities to get involved in, including a running club and boys' and girls' football teams, both of which play in a local league. *"We also spend almost every Friday in the local pub."* As they have done since time immemorial. Said pub – The Royal Children – is situated opposite the office. The trainee group has its own social budget which can be easily stretched to cover half a dozen proper get-togethers. Sometimes these will involve greyhound racing, go-karting or pitch and put; at other times a simple dinner and drinks suffices. For the firm-wide Christmas party (usually at the end of January) the firm thinks of everything, from a free bar and a buffet meal to a kebab van that you can take a token to at the end of the night to exchange for a snack.

and finally...

Browne Jacobson's breadth of contentious and transactional work and warmth of atmosphere make it a no-brainer choice for Nottingham-bound candidates. Yet there's increasingly sound reason to choose it for a wider Midlands-oriented training: sources predicted the next two years will see *"Birmingham just get bigger and bigger."*

BTMK Solicitors

the facts

Location: Southend-on-Sea, Chelmsford
Number of UK partners/solicitors: 13/35
Total number of trainees: 5
Seats: Varying in length
Alternative seats: None
Extras: Pro bono – Chelmsford and Southend CAB

On the northern tip of the Thames estuary, Southend-on-Sea has it all: miles of beautiful beaches, the longest pleasure pier in the world and star local legal performer BTMK.

pier we go...

Built in 1830 and destroyed by fire in 2005, the pier's recent repairs mean it is once again possible to tread the 1.33 miles of decking that take visitors to the end of the town's most historic landmark. But you don't need to go anywhere near that far in Southend to hear word of another, if slightly younger, institution. *"BTMK is by far the biggest firm in Southend and the broader area,"* trainees told us. *"If companies or buildings are being sold in town – basically anything of legal note going on – we're probably involved."* If this suggests BTMK's work is very much in and of its region, that's true, but it is decidedly *"not a sleepy high street practice."* Sources were quick to detect an *"ambition to go places,"* a drive that in recent years saw crime and family experts TMK merge with commercially focused local outfit Bates Travell to create the present-day BTMK. Strengthening the firm's grip on the Essex market, the merger has allowed it to offer company and commercial advice for local owner-managed businesses, a full conveyancing service and high-quality civil litigation, family, childcare, probate and criminal law advice. Indeed, the crime team draws particular respect from our colleagues on *Chambers UK*, who rank it as top in the region.

Helping it attain such credibility, in particular with cases involving an international aspect, was recent involvement on a Turkish heroin importation case and large white-collar fraud matters.

essexpress

BTMK's small Chelmsford office doesn't tend to feature in the training contract, so a trainee's two years is likely to be spent entirely in either County Chambers or Baryta House in Southend. Beyond this fact, there's little else that's compulsory about the scheme. The process of seat rotation involves continually *"being asked what you want to do... even before starting at the firm, the training principal is on the phone to check."* Indeed, BTMK is eager to tailor the training contract to individual preferences and offers a combination of six-month and three-month seats, the idea being to conclude with *"a six to nine-month seat in the department you want to qualify into."*

Another noteworthy feature is the excellent programme of in-house training and *"close day-to-day monitoring,"* particularly in the first year. The overall approach is one of *"learning by doing; you are given a lot of responsibility and trust from the start."* In part this results from the unceasingly fast pace of the firm's community law work, which puts trainees in contact with the public from day one, taking speculative calls from potential clients, assessing their needs and booking appointments with solicitors. *"They throw stuff at you, which is daunting, but it is simply the best way to learn,"* said our interviewees. One day you might accompany a solicitor to court, the next there's every likelihood you'll be *"standing there by yourself handling a charging order."* *"I like it,"* said one typically matter-of-fact source; *"there's variety and every day is a new challenge."* Throughout the training there will be plenty of advocacy opportunities on things like summary judgment applications, magistrates' court appearances and case management conferences.

If all this sounds rough and ready, be assured that there is strict supervision to help trainees avoid scrapes. *"Three-weekly supervision sessions"* are designed to monitor a trainee's workload and assess their experiences, such that *"you feel like you're being watched over."* Furthermore, *"most of the time you're immediately told what's wrong with your work and, more rarely, what's right."* The exact nature of the supervision sessions varies according to department and supervisor, but trainees wouldn't be drawn on whether they prefer *"the ones who are so hot on it they give you homework"* or *"the more laid-back people."*

not-so-smooth criminal

Experiences in the crime department are both absorbing and demanding. The team handles run-of-the-mill *"fights outside nightclubs,"* drugs, dodgy dealings and serious violence as well as *"meatier"* white-collar fraud. No two days are alike, either in hours or work. Especially taken as a first seat, the crime department could potentially be an overpowering experience, but our sources assured us otherwise. *"It's actually enjoyable: the clientele are demanding and the work fascinating,"* they enthused. One trainee couldn't help remembering the *"simple shock of a case involving a paedophile – from start to finish the circumstances were horrific and the images we had to consider were awful."* Gruesome moments aside, it's possible to learn a lot from the team members, especially those with higher rights of audience that allow them to advocate in the Crown Court. Second-years are also likely to sign up to the Police Station Accreditation Scheme, which gets them on the rota for police station duties – put simply, taking late-night calls from sozzled Southenders or petty thieves who've ended up in the clink.

In family *"you're expected to work quickly and accurately, which is difficult at the start."* The department handles everything – *"care proceed-*

ings, contact issues, divorce, ancillary relief and the fall-out from domestic violence." As in crime, a great many cases are publicly funded and the firm is confident that its all-round efficiency means the Carter reforms won't compromise its ability to offer legal aid services. Clients often come loaded down with emotional baggage. "You're dealing with upset people all the time; it's not stressful as such because you learn how to deal with it." Civil litigation seats are similarly varied, with trainees tackling "anything that turns up through the door that doesn't fit crime or family." We're talking landlord and tenant matters, neighbour disputes, commercial cases, debt issues and employment problems. Memorable moments for our sources included "an RCJ application for a bankruptcy registration," "getting an injunction about paving being taken up" and "a guy walking in off the street on a Friday with all his documents prepared for a trial on the Wednesday. We had to brief counsel, get witness statements, attend trial and celebrate the win in less than a week."

When it comes to BTMK's commercial practice, trainees say they work on deals for companies they actually know, whether it's "leases for local letting agents" or "assisting the local golf club." Taking familiarity with clients to the next level, one source recalled the slightly odd experience of "obtaining instructions from the director of the coach company that used to take me on my school trips."

and another thong...

... as that last anecdote illustrates, plenty of BTMK's trainees are locals, indeed several of the current crop worked as paralegals at the firm before getting their training contracts. But you'll need to show more than an Essex passport to gain admittance here. Traditionally, the firm has run a notoriously tough recruitment day that is as exhausting as it is thorough. Advocacy, spelling and maths tests feature, as do group dis-

cussions and interviews. The recruitment process is under review, but whatever form it takes in the future, the priority will be on face-to-face assessment rather than paper-based evaluation. Making the grade tends to mean being the kind of "confident," "self-starting" type that already populates the firm. Basically, if you could deal with the stresses and sometime excesses of the work and clients you've read about in this feature, all the while displaying calm equanimity, then BTMK will like you.

In case you don't know Southend, let us shed a little light. Baryta House, a "purpose-built office block," and County Chambers, a rather more atmospheric "converted Victorian house," are situated not too far from the seafront. There are plenty of bars and nightclubs within striking distance, with the nearby pub The Mews the top choice for a post-work beverage. Shortly before we spoke to trainees, there had been "a great turn out" at a "barbecue for graduating trainees" in the courtyard at County Chambers. Marking their ascent to the world of qualified practice, each qualifying trainee is ceremonially handed a parting gift, known in the firm as "the pen of doom." In 2007, one of the two qualifiers stayed on in an NQ position, a ratio that is typical of previous years.

Another annual event is the raffle of partners' skills at the Christmas party. One partner offered to take the winning bidder's place in a local fun run, wearing a costume of said bidder's choice. A potentially foolish move, we think he got off lightly in an Emu costume. Apparently "the Borat [mankini] costume was mentioned at one stage."

and finally...

BTMK is a great choice for anyone seeking a broad Essex-based training contract. No matter where you come from, you'll learn a lot by working here, not least how to cope in a demanding environment.

Burges Salmon LLP

the facts

Location: Bristol
Number of UK partners/solicitors: 68/230
Total number of trainees: 42
Seats: 6x4 months
Alternative seats: Secondments
Extras: Pro bono – CAB, Bristol University Law Clinic, Bristol & Avon Enterprise Agency, Bristol Area Community Enterprise Network

Every year we get a warm and fuzzy feeling from the Burges Salmon trainees as they coo about how everything is going swimmingly down in Bristol. The great lifestyle, coupled with first-hand experience of work traditionally reserved for City lawyers, makes training at Burges Salmon a very attractive prospect.

name dropping

This year was no exception, and within moments of talking to them we realised that the recruits share the same positive attitude that Burges Salmon exudes. We sat back and listened as the bright young things of Bristol spoke about the *"hard-working but friendly"* atmosphere of the firm and its *"promise of London work."* You have to ask: does this firm not have an Achiles heel?

It is easy to be impressed by Burges Salmon's long list of notable clients. *"When I saw it, I was really surprised to find out the firm was in Bristol,"* said one source. We'd say we don't like to name drop, but who are we kidding? Among the glossy names these lawyers act for are Coca-Cola, Orange, RBS, Reuters, EMI, First Group, Shell, Samsung, even the MoD, which admittedly probably struggles in the glossy stakes. Of course, no one is claiming BS stands alongside the magic circle on a continuous stream of ground-breaking, headline-grabbing deals, but they do rightly point to a consistent flow of

weighty instructions. *"I wouldn't want to be at a regional firm where I wasn't dealing with big clients,"* said one trainee. *"Here, I feel like there is nothing I can't achieve and I don't feel like I am missing out in any way."* All this, plus a riverside stroll to work, is tempting not only high-calibre trainees but also seasoned London lawyers exhausted by the rat race. *"We seem to be recruiting quite aggressively and there is a definite push to compete with the City,"* confirmed a source. It seems to be working: BS reported revenue of £60m for 2006/07, a tidy 10% increase on the previous year's figure.

from pole to pole

The firm is proud of its Bristol roots, and even though 75% of its work originates from outside the immediate area, there are no plans to stop being a single-site operation. It doesn't seem to be holding the business back; indeed, we heard about *"completions in New York"* and regular *"meetings in London,"* both at the premises BS rents as a meeting facility and in other lawyers' offices. By keeping all its eggs in one basket, the firm can afford to move to flash new digs in Bristol, scheduled to be ready in 2010. Until then the firm's objectives are clear: *"Expand into new and niche practice areas"* (such as Islamic finance) and *"go after bigger and bigger clients."* Evidence of the firm's widening horizons comes in the form of deals such as the sale of Quark Expeditions, the world's leading operator of expedition cruise voyages to the polar regions, which was bought by First Choice holidays, and ECI Partners' purchase of Clinisys, a leading pan-European supplier of Laboratory Information Management Systems, for £61m. The purchase target came with operations in Belgium, the Netherlands, France, Spain and Germany.

Traditionally the firm has acted for some big players in agriculture, including several of

the major dairy operators (eg Yeo Valley Farms and Milk Link), plus organisations like The National Trust and The Crown Estate. It has similarly strong links to other sectors, for example education (the real estate team worked on the relocation of Bath Spa University's city centre campus), financial services (corporate lawyers handled the flotation of stockbroker Hargreaves Lansdown, valued at £750m at the time of listing) and energy (the environment team has bagged itself a place on the projects panel of the Nuclear Decommissioning Authority, the public body which has been put in charge of the £70bn clean up and closure of all 20 UK civil nuclear sites). Arguably, the firm is all things to all clients; certainly this is the view held by our colleagues at *Chambers UK*, who rank BS and its lawyers highly across the board.

take your pick

In the six-seat training scheme, the first four are essentially compulsory. Time must be spent in: property; corporate and financial services or commercial; commercial disputes and construction (CDC) or agriculture, property litigation and environment (APLE); and then finally a group that contains employment, pension and incentives (EPI) and tax and trusts. Trainees have a free choice at the fifth rotation and use the sixth to return to their intended qualification department. Although this sounds fairly prescriptive, trainees point out that *"you do get a choice within* [the seat groups]." *"I can understand why they do it,"* said one trainee; *"they offer so many seats, so they want to make sure you get a breadth of experience around the firm."*

With so many options, it's impossible for us to delve into the details of them all, so we've selected a few of the core ones and one or two away from the mainstream. The property department, which is *"one of the big drivers"* at the firm, gets trainees to assist on matters ranging from *"massive Crown Estate transactions"* to *"standard commercial property deals."* Four months in coco might see you helping with pitches, collating information for deals and drafting small documents. One busy trainee told us *"you can dip in and out of quite a bit here – you're a department resource."* At times you may need to go to London for meetings: *"When I was there, the firm were involved in quite a big bid, so I was in London quite a lot,"* reported one source. Litigation experience can be clocked up by helping lawyers focusing on agriculture, property, construction, environment or general commercial disputes, meaning a trainee's work can be as varied as *"drafting witness statements in corporate manslaughter cases"* to *"advising on EU directives and their implications."*

In the *"fantastic"* construction seat, *"you're not just there to pour the coffee; you get a role and quite a lot of responsibility."* The role includes taking notes in meetings, liaising with agents and contractors, and gathering info via *"fact-finding missions."* Meanwhile trainees in the pensions and incentives group try their hand at legal research, drafting, advising trustees and attending client meetings. We were told this seat is *"good for client contact and you also get to deal with actuaries, accountants and consultants."* The *"small but busy"* employment department brings tribunals, plenty of contact with clients and witnesses, and research into legislation and case law, of which there is a considerable amount in this area of practice. Trainee secondments to top clients presently include Orange, Nationwide, Bank of Scotland, Nirex and Babcock.

old school?

In almost all seats trainees sit with their supervisor, but this doesn't mean they receive all of their work from this person. *"You get grabbed to do all sorts,"* said one interviewee, another explaining that *"your supervisor is there to make sure you have enough support and to protect you from having loads of work dumped on you."* The more we spoke with them, the more we got the impression that these trainees crave the pressure and challenges of hard work. *"You get a heck of a lot of responsibility, but that's the way I like it,"* said one trainee, before adding: *"If you don't get responsibility then what is there to motivate you?"*

So what of this work-life balance the firm likes to talk about? One of our interviewees said 9.30pm was the latest they had stayed in the office – *"Most people in London firms would laugh at the idea of that being late!"* The important thing to be aware of is that while the hours are reasonable compared to City of London jobs, they are generally longer than city of Bristol jobs. *"People should be careful if they think it's 9am to 5.15pm. That doesn't happen and coming here is not taking an easy route."* Delighted to carry on their journey with the firm, 14 of the 19 2007 qualifiers stayed with the firm.

Trainees were keen to dispel all sorts of myths about the firm and here are the top three. In third position: the firm's quirky pink notepaper *"has nothing to do with Salmon – it was from Burges."* The runner-up at number two: *"We didn't all go to boarding schools and Oxbridge; we're not the Farrers of the regions."* Topping the poll: *"People think it's really, really old school here, but it's not like that."* *"The old-fashioned, stuffy image isn't fair. Before I started I heard Osborne Clarke was meant to be the trendy firm and Burges Salmon was a bit square, but basically that's not true."* One trainee declared the conservative reputation to be *"a hangover from the past."* The message to readers from another was: *"Don't be put off – come find out for yourself. If you're on a placement or open day, they do involve you and you're told everything. There isn't much bullshitting."*

lounging around

Although many of the trainees *"have links to Bristol or the South West,"* we're told this is not a prerequisite. That said, there's no doubt that Bristol itself features large in the reason why people come to the firm and why it receives so many applications. As if the city doesn't have enough to keep people occupied, the firm organises plenty of activities. Its social club *"subsidises a whole lot of stuff, such as sports teams, films, gigs and the gym, and you only have to pay £2 a month to be a part of it."* Big parties are held in the summer and at Christmas, and there's a trainee party to welcome new arrivals. Last year, *"there was a free bar and food, which meant it was a really good, fun night!"* Other high spots in the calendar are dragon boat racing and regular charity fundraisers, which are often best enjoyed by the adrenalin junkies among the staff.

Informally, trainees get together for regular Friday nights out. *"We work in the centre of the city, so there is a lot of choice,"* but the favourites seem to be the Pitcher & Piano, the *"cheesy"* K2 and The Lizard Lounge, which we heard so much about. *"It's awful,"* whispered one shamefaced source, *"It's such a hole in the ground, but it's really funny!"*

and finally...

If bars on the waterfront, a leisurely commute or a stroll to work, a decent salary and affordable housing in a beautiful part of Britain sound enticing, then Burges Salmon could be the firm for you. You'll have to submit a seriously impressive application though – this is a winning firm that employs people who are more than used to success and hard work. Earlier on we asked if the firm had an Achilles heel. Having looked closely, we've yet to find one.

Capsticks

the facts
Location: London
Number of UK partners/solicitors: 32/48
Total number of trainees: 8
Seats: 6x4 months
Alternative seats: Secondments
Extras: Pro bono – Wandsworth Law Centre

Twenty-six years young, Capsticks is an energetic Putney-based firm that has evolved into a formidable force serving the manifold needs of the modern NHS and private healthcare providers.

medical ethics
Undoubtedly *"at the top of the field"* in matters medical, and working at *"the cutting edge of developments in areas like foundation trusts,"* it's hard to imagine where this firm could go except down. Clearly mindful of this, trainees had noticed *"all the departments have quite consciously started looking at business development in the last year. It's about ensuring we retain and enhance our reputation in what we do, continue to serve the needs of clients and take advantage of new areas."* In the quarter-century of its existence it has evolved from a small provider of specific clinical negligence advice to its current status as an eminent legal adviser to a vast NHS. As the needs of that organisation and the wider healthcare sector have proliferated, so too have Capsticks' capabilities. Alongside major clinical negligence claims and advisory work, it now handles employment matters, commercial advice on huge transactions, LIFT schemes and property issues, as well as general commercial litigation and professional misconduct prosecutions. As well as its work for trusts, strategic health authorities and for a major proportion of the primary care trusts in London and the South East, the firm also represents charities like the Healthcare Commission and the Terrence Higgins Trust. Its private sector roster includes Nuffield Hospitals and Nations Healthcare. Whether it's policy advice, help on the impact of EU legislation, next-generation public-private partnership funding, commercial contracts with suppliers, patients bringing negligence claims or public inquiries on hospital closures, Capsticks will, can and does do it.

Trainees are likely to sample at least four of the firm's five departments in their six four-month seats, meaning that dispute resolution, employment, clinical negligence, commercial and property are all possible. By doubling-up on a seat they can add weight to a push for qualification into that area. Across the board, the overriding influence of healthcare clients creates *"a collegiate atmosphere"* that is *"not quite as hierarchical as other firms seem to be – no one's swaggering down the corridors."* In fact, our sources diagnosed Capsticks' character via one distinctive symptom: *"Passion – people in every department are passionate about what they do. They are here because they care about the work."* Other symptoms of this condition include the fact that *"no one wants to work in the City,"* something which is definitely not to be confused with apathy. *"Everyone is ambitious enough to want a firm that is top in its specialisation."* Trainees additionally recognised a moral dimension to their work, telling us: *"The ethos is not so cut-throat as in the corporate world."* Even if they are representing hospitals, trusts or private companies against individuals in what can be difficult litigation cases, *"it's generally in the interest of a trust to settle to the satisfaction of all parties and rectify mistakes, so you rarely feel you're sticking it to the little man."*

a world of pain
What? Up where? were the questions we were left asking ourselves when one trainee told us: *"In clinical negligence I was involved with helping to get a psychiatric patient to consent to treatment*

to get... how can I say it?... *certain objects removed from certain orifices.*" Not everyone is guaranteed such a vivid experience, but as the largest department in the firm a stint in the clinical department (with the attendant possibility of a short secondment to an NHS client) is highly likely. Split over two floors of the office, the department's work breaks down into two distinct sections: the clinical negligence group and the advisory group. Time in the former involves working for the NHS Litigation Authority, primary care trusts, health authorities and private healthcare providers on matters as dramatic as wrongful birth claims or "*a case involving a child who had spilled hot coffee on himself and died from blood poisoning.*" Such issues bring "*tragedy, human interest and tears in court,*" but also "*highly complex legal aspects*" and "*at treatment inquests, the chance to see partners on their feet as advocates.*" While it is possible to run some smaller files yourself, in general there is "*more supervision in this department because we're working for trusts and insurers simultaneously, so supervisors need to keep a tight grip.*" Over in the advisory team, trainees are exposed to "*mental health and service reconfiguration work,*" the latter arising "*when hospitals decide to shut down or move staff and have a duty to consult the users of hospital.*" Variety is a constant feature of life here because "*one day you're doing a RCJ best-interest case and the next you are at a conference on brain damage.*" Secondments to an NHS client can be "*daunting at first*" because "*you can find yourself acting as a trust's legal manager.*" Close contact with the partner managing the client goes some way to calming the nerves.

Staying with the theme of orifices, this time oral, a spell in the dispute resolution department incorporates a strong strand of professional regulatory issues for two key clients – the General Dental Council and The General Chiropractic Council. This means a good deal of "*tracking*

down and prosecuting fraudsters and incompetents*" who have wrecked people's mouths as dental practitioners. At the same time, health bodies are continually engaged in a stream of commercial agreements, so that "*dipping into random contractual issues like on-site liability or whether care homes need TV licences*" is par for the course in what is a "*young, busy*" team.

The commercial department brings "*standard commercial work, bread and butter contractual type things*" for anything and everything a hospital might need. It also involves a lot of foundation trust work, which will quickly get you clued up on what has become a new governmental response to care provison. The policy has caused the decision making over facilities and planning to be devolved to local organisations and communities and, naturally, Capsticks is at the forefront of developments. The other side of the department's work concerns major joint-venture LIFT, PFI and PPP transactions surrounding NHS revitalisation and rebuilding programmes. These deals see lawyers "*come up against big City firms*" and are on a scale that means "*if you're given a task, a lot of people are relying on you to do it.*" The real estate elements of such transactions ensure that trainees in the property department become an integral part of the deal. At the same time, property trainees get plenty of bog-standard real estate experience as the NHS owns "*vast swathes of land*" and there is also a stream of work for private healthcare providers on "*things like purchasing residential houses for use as care homes.*"

The employment department is popular for "*loads of hands-on experience: you attend tribunals, run files of your own and get the most client contact of all the seats.*" Given that the NHS is one of Europe's largest employers, it shouldn't be surprising that "*you're dealing with everything from consultants to medical secretaries on matters from whistleblowing to discrimination and unfair dismissal." Advocacy opportunities pop up, but trainees were just as delighted with *"attending hearings with counsel and being the first port of call."* In fact, across the training our sources were satisfied with the quality of work they received. Generally working for teams rather than single supervisors, they had found informal mid-seat and more structured end-of-seat appraisals more than adequate.

to help the medicine go down

If you've read this far and like the sound of the firm but worry that you'll need a BM and evidence of a lifelong passion for the NHS to effect entry, fear not. We have come across doctors or nurses who changed careers for Capsticks in previous years, but it's no prerequisite. The common theme between trainees is simply that *"most people have some reason for coming across the firm, whether it's a Putney link or a connection via parents to the healthcare or public sector world."* Attending the firm's vac scheme is a first-class way of exploring the territory and showing concrete interest (successful applicants also return for a second stint *"just to keep in touch during academic training").* Intriguingly, those who arrive with a defined interest *"often find that once they're here in practice they gravitate to other areas."* It's also worth mentioning that as the NHS is in a state of perpetual flux this results in *"incredibly interesting and intellectually demanding work, often stuff that has no precedent."* Beyond a relish for this type of challenge (and some leaning towards the health sector), trainees found it hard to pick out shared qualities.

Capsticks' eight-storey *"60s/70s"* building in South West London may rank as *"crap"* or *"a monstrosity"* from the outside, but inside *"the décor's fine"* and *"tea ladies come round morning and afternoon"* to dispense beverages and a sweet spoonful of *"maternalness towards trainees."* With space at a premium and a lease expiring relatively soon, a move is likely in the near future, but we doubt very much whether Capsticks would desert its long-term turf in South West London. *"All the indications are that we'll stay close to here or Wimbledon,"* revealed a source. This is a good thing as far as trainees are concerned as *"most people live in South West London."* Local watering holes Putney Station and Red are regularly patronised, to the extent that *"because the firm isn't huge you mingle with most staff there at some point."* Average working hours of 9am to 6 or 6.30pm mean trainees can expect *"a lunch offer most days," "drinks on a Friday,"* a positive welter of sporting opportunities and frequent social outings organised by a dedicated committee.

When it comes to qualification, trainees sense that they are already at *"one of the preeminent firms in medical law and doing cutting-edge work."* For the majority this leads to one thought – *"if they'll have me, I'll stay."* Most also feel that *"you can make a career here; there are only so many other firms where you could do this sort of work... and few in London."* Unfortunately, the firm's size means jobs are not always available in qualifiers' preferred areas. In 2007, all four qualifiers were able to accept jobs, going into employment, clinical law, property and disputes.

and finally...

Capsticks offers a unique training experience just a few miles southwest of the City but a million miles away in terms of lifestyle and attitude. If you think you'd like your training with a dose or ten of medicine, then tailor your application carefully and make the vac scheme a priority.

Charles Russell LLP

the facts
Location: London, Guildford, Cheltenham, Oxford, Cambridge
Number of UK partners/solicitors: 93/205
Total number of trainees: 35
Seats: 4x6 months
Alternative seats: Secondments
Extras: Pro bono – Bethnal Green Law Centre, CAB, LawWorks, Surrey Law Centre; language training

A firm that goes back more than two centuries, Charles Russell is branching out from its established bases in London, Guildford and Cheltenham by opening new offices in Geneva, Oxford and Cambridge. No other City firm can boast a presence in both varsity cities, but then CR has been treading its own path for quite some time, adopting at the heart of its business plan the concept that private client and commercial expertise can indeed share the same bed.

from this day forth
Successive years of growth bear testimony to the success of this unusual marriage between tradition and ambition, and the powers that be at CR are keen to ensure its longevity. Private client has long accounted for between a quarter and a third of the firm's workload and the opening of the new offices, perfectly located to service yet more of the most heavily taxed amongst us, demonstrates its intent to maintain a degree of parity as it moves forward. This distinctive approach is of great benefit to those trainees who are keen to gain exposure to a spread of practice areas.

The majority of recruits are based in London, where – should they choose to – they can encounter four very different seats during their two years. Many seem keen to spend time in the firm's oldest areas – the prestigious private client and family departments. The former provides a popular mix of personal will administration (where trainees are trusted to run files and deal with clients directly) and more complex tax, probate and property matters (where trainees support more senior practitioners). A majority of the department's new clients bring work with an international dimension and the lawyers regularly advise non-UK nationals, especially people from the Middle East, Far East, former Soviet Union and Europe. According to wealth-obsessed US publisher Forbes, the firm's private clients have a combined net worth of well in excess of $25bn. The family department plays in the premier league of matrimonial finance practices and also represents clients with serious wealth at stake. Both private client and family seats include *"a great level of contact with clients."* And interestingly, this is also the area of the firm where you may get most exposure to the other offices, not least the one in Geneva. Recently there has been speculation about a new office in Bahrain, which as we all know, has its fair share of rich folk.

As popular as these seats proved to be, there was some sense of regret among our sources that the NQ jobs on offer were skewed in favour of other areas. However a little digging revealed that in fact jobs were offered across the board in 2007: three each in litigation and corporate, two in employment and one each in real estate, private client and family. This should come as little surprise considering the amount and quality of work that the firm is attracting in areas beyond private client. Sitting in the middle of the mid-market, the coco team has a cracking track record in relation to AIM deals and its achievements quite often make it to the pages of the *FT*. Among its proudest moments recently was the transfer of Canadian mining client Yamana Gold (UK) from AIM to the main FTSE list. While trainees cannot expect to play a pivotal role in such matters, they do support more senior colleagues with enthusiasm, telling us that drafting and menial admin tasks sit alongside regular attendance at client social events and meetings, where *"you are not treated as an underling, but very much as a member of the team."* At all times, trainees are encouraged to *"produce work as if it was going straight out the door."* Trainees say they typically work *"9am to 7pm... not often on weekends, maybe three times over the two years."* Although one of the busier departments, with slightly longer hours, putting in a little extra time in the evening in corporate must be set against the benefits of having the more relaxed atmosphere. As one aspiring young comedian observed: *"You can make jokes in corporate that you wouldn't dream of uttering in private client."* There is an expectation among trainees that they will all do a corporate seat and a popular option is a six-month secondment with a client such as Actis Capital. Arrangements also exist with a leading telecoms company and a global resourcing firm. These opportunities are always viewed as *"invaluable."*

sheikherbreaker

The most glamorous part of the firm these days is its litigation practice, which has taken the firm's name well beyond broadsheet fame. CR's high-profile telecoms, media and sports clients have a habit of becoming involved in well-publicised disagreements; for example, last year the defamation team was called in to help Sven Göran-Eriksson sheikh off a bit of *News of the World* bother, and this year the sports team made sure the FA was able to wrist-slap Wayne Rooney's agent for his contravention of Rule K in its conduct handbook. Less well-known perhaps but interesting because it was settled by way of a mediation, was a dispute between CR's client, one of the UK's largest print music publishers, and a rival music publisher and distributor. Other clients include ntl, Telewest, the Horseracing Regulatory Authority, consumer magazine *Which?* and the RSPB. Naturally the media and sports cases attract huge interest from prospective trainees, so be aware that you're not the only person who'll have their beady eye on a seat with one of these teams.

Contentious seats are extremely popular, but none can compete with employment, which is consistently the most over-subscribed department. This area of law is big business for CR and accounts for around 10% of its revenue. The lawyers recently advised on MFI's sale and restructuring and it acts for other major names such as Pfizer and EDF Energy. However, the really big news this year was a raid on the East of England firm Hewitsons. By swiping 80% of Hewistons' employment lawyers for its new Cambridge operation, CR is signalling that it means business in this area. Apparently the firm now has the Oxford market in its sights.

Throughout departments, supervisors received top marks for *"judging the right level of responsibility"* and enabling trainees to spread their wings *"without ever feeling out of their depth."* Moreover, even the top partners were praised for *"taking the time to thank or praise you for a job well done."* But sometimes thank you is just not quite enough – we did catch word of some sources being wined, dined and even rewarded with flowers for their hard work. Now there's a nice touch.

cr olympics

If all this talk of headlines and flowers has you firing up your computer to get that application off by the end of the day, you would be well advised to pause for thought because the CR application form is far from an exercise in data entry. The firm has previously enquired as to what animal your friends would most liken you and what film role you'd like to play. In 2007, recruiters looked for someone who knows a good superpower when they see one. Whatever the criteria for answering these questions, trainees were unanimous that something about the process was working, as everyone seemed to have a lot in common. *"We all get on so well and are always on the e-mail to each other,"* said one. The firm recruits a mixture of law and non-law graduates, and although it does not discriminate against those wishing to march straight into a contract, the current batch includes a significant gap year contingent with an impressive combined knowledge of the best spots to catch a ray in South East Asia.

Anyone worried about what you would do with a trainee's salary will be glad to hear that therapy was offered this year in the form of a trip to the dog track, while those immune to the lure of gambling will have a chance to shed some unwanted pounds on a new outfit for the Summer ball. Here the mixed-table policy means that there is no hiding from authority, although the relaxed atmosphere ensures that *"everyone always looks forward to it."* Post-work drinks on a Friday in Bertorelli's or the White Swan are very popular and can run on into the early hours on occasion.

Much of the organised social scene revolves around sporting events with clients; indeed the firm's calendar of fixtures would turn Lord Coe green with envy. Participants of all standards are welcome and there is something for everyone, so if softball, cricket, football, rugby, hockey and netball don't do it for you, there is always the annual sailing regatta or a dragon boat racing event to fall back on. The main event of the year is the legendary Charles Russell Sports Ball, when all the teams unite and compete in one big drinkathon. *"Anyone with any sense books the next day off work."*

best of both worlds

The firm is quick to emphasise a one-firm culture, and trainees in Guildford and Cheltenham certainly felt this to be the case. They expounded the benefits of living the regional lifestyle while receiving *"City-quality training and a competitive regional salary."* A two-week induction in London is when many trainees form bonds across offices,

and while regional trainees struggle to tempt Londoners away from the bright lights of the capital, they always receive a warm welcome at HQ.

It's all change in Guildford this year as it moves in line with the rest of the firm to a four-seat rotation. It is expected that everyone will still do a property and litigation seat, with other options including coco, private client and family. Again, the social scene is quite sporty, with the latest inter-office football match of sufficient importance to lure Guildford's managing partner to the terraces.

The two trainees selected each year for the Cheltenham office follow a four-seat rotation comprising property, litigation, coco and private client. The Cheltenham office was described as *"bright and spacious"* with *"large windows, ideal for day dreaming while overlooking the hills."* It is just a two-minute walk from the bars and eateries of trendy Montpellier. Both Cheltenham and Guildford offices are thriving, with Cheltenham being the firm's fastest growing in terms of turnover for the last financial year. All of this leads the regional trainees to claim they have *"the best of both worlds."* The only fly in the ointment for some readers will be the firm's desire for applicants to demonstrate some link or commitment to one or other locale.

In 2007 the firm kept on only ten of its 16 qualifiers, partly because dispute resolution was oversubscribed. It also welcomed one extra trainee to each office in its September intake, meaning two new Cheltenham starters, four in Guildford and 13 in London. It expects to build on this in the coming years.

and finally.....

As one source concluded: *"The breadth of departments at Charles Russell is really unique and the people are fantastic."* The firm's reluctance to abandon old, traditional strengths in its quest for new business and commercial clients is what has allowed it to stand apart from the crowd.

Clarion Solicitors

the facts
Location: Leeds
Number of UK partners/solicitors: 13/31
Total number of trainees: 10
Seats: 4x6 months
Alternative seats: Secondments

Clarion Solicitors is the new name for McCormicks' Leeds office, which was bought out back in February 2007 by six of the firm's partners. The eponymous founder, well-known lawyer Peter McCormick, moved over to McCormicks' smaller Harrogate office to continue business with its existing staff and two other partners.

out with the old...
Just weeks after the buyout, the plan for Clarion was made clear at the annual fee earners' conference in Skipton. *"It was explained that Peter had owned a massive amount of the firm and was effectively the one guy in charge. The buyout happened because the current six equity partners wanted to move forward in an equal way."* Dispensing with Peter's celebrity and a widely recognised emphasis on sports clients, Clarion is now focusing on the other areas that have helped make it a *"streamlined, mid-range, commercial Leeds outfit."* Sources agree: *"It will take a while to completely get the Clarion name out and about,"* but already *"the firm feels more modern, punchier and younger,"* they say.

It's worth us highlighting the sports law issue because McCormicks' sports practice was a major draw for students in previous years. If finding a sports law firm is your priority, you might want to investigate what's going on over in Harrogate because Clarion is not going to be able to offer as much in the way of exposure to this type of practice.

what's the plot?
So let's examine what is on offer. The six departments – coco (including IP and employment), property, corporate recovery, dispute resolution, business crime/regulatory and private client (including family) – each offer seats to trainees. These are usually for six months, but can be extended or shortened according to business needs and staffing issues. Corporate is an important growth area, say trainees, and they should know – the department takes two or three of them per rotation. The department has also taken on three new partners: two in corporate finance and one employment specialist from Addleshaw Goddard. If Clarion's official launch party for commercial clients is anything to go by, developing a reputation as a credible alternative to the national firms in Leeds shouldn't be an insurmountable task – we hear clients were in party mode until 2am. Examples of the firm's corporate work include advising the shareholders of MS Vehicle Management and facilitating the acquisition of The Syndicate Superclub in Blackpool. Winners Bingo, The Duke of Edinburgh's Award and ghd hair people, Jemella Group, are all regular clients too. According to one trainee, this is *"a good department because the work is hard and really knocks you into shape."* It offers *"some great opportunities for learning, some typical corporate idiots and some people who take the time to explain things to you."* Take a broad commercial seat and you'll get to work on IP matters as well as giving day-to-day operational advice to clients. On the property side, you'll be in regular contact with housebuilders such as Bellway Homes, Wild Bennett Homes and McInerney Group. In terms of contentious commercial experience, the seat options are corporate recovery (insolvency), employment and commercial disputes. Reports on the latter were mixed: while one person felt there was far too much bundling and document management, another talked at length about the

great work on offer. *"On the first day I went to a con with counsel, on the second a CMC and on the third a negotiation. I got real hands-on experience there, even taking part in tactical discussions. You aren't treated like a droid."*

A seat in business crime and regulatory sounds like a blast. The team is top-ranked in the region by our colleagues on *Chambers UK*, and trainees can be certain of seeing some juicy cases. Typical tasks include shadowing lawyers at police stations, visiting prisons, attending trials alone to take notes and participating in conferences with barristers and clients. There's also a fair amount of document scheduling and data inputting in preparation for fraud trials. Prison visits *"are not for everyone,"* a source tells us. *"People ask if it's like The Silence of the Lambs, but it's not as scary: you're watched all the time by prison guards."* Anyone considering qualifying into this department should definitely train for police station accreditation. Once attained, this gets them onto the list of lawyers able to advise those being held in custody. Given the nature of the work – anything from blood and guts to corporate crime – and the fact that there is *"so much responsibility... more than in other seats,"* we are surprised the seat isn't more popular. *"People tend to go for the more-corporate seats,"* was one answer.

The family team no longer accepts legal aid cases. *"It's high-value cases now, so you're dealing with people with quite a lot of assets to divvy up,"* some of which run into millions of pounds. About 30% of the work here is child-related, consisting of *"contact cases, CSA applications or husbands challenging CSA orders."* Shadowing the associate in the department, trainees will start with attending client meetings and simply taking notes. In time, however, they should progress to handling their own cases, which entails *"doing everything the associate does but having it checked first."* This includes drafting affidavits, first-appli-

cation documents and consent orders, as well as briefing counsel and, on occasion, meeting with clients alone. As far as photocopying and bundling duties are concerned, a source reassured us: *"I feel as though I have only had to do what was necessary to understand the process better."* An unusual part of the job is providing Yorkshire Television with script advice relating to matrimonial and children issues in *Emmerdale*. The same is true in the crime seat, where one trainee had to advise on courtroom layout and where cast members should sit during trial.

On the subject of appraisals, separate monthly meetings are set up with the managing partner and respective department heads. They might occasionally get rearranged, *"but you do have them. You can bring up what you need and talk about what you want to do next,"* we were told. When it comes to how much grunt work you are expected to do, mixed feedback leads us to wonder if a trainee's fortunes are made or lost depending on how well they fit in with the team in question. *"Each department feels very different, certainly,"* observed one source. *"It's down to the style of the partner in charge."*

go purple cobras!

And now the fun stuff for which this firm has become known. *"Every Monday, Tuesday and Wednesday you can take an hour and a half for classes in the Virgin gym. It's a bit like a PE lesson... When we're playing stick in the mud, the partners are often the last ones standing, wondering why no one will crawl between their legs to un-stick them."* Well, it certainly doesn't sound like an attractive prospect to us. Seeing as gymgoers also get to play dodgeball, we had to ask: is it like Average Joe's or GloboGym? Readers, dig out your Lycra and codpieces because our source suggested it was the latter. Back in the office, corridor cricket is the sport of choice. Upon arrival, one corporate trainee was handed a ball and *"told to bowl hard at a part-ner."* After hours, a social committee organises such activities as the monthly Last Friday Club drinks. *"Historically these were in Ha!Ha!, but Revolution is becoming popular,"* said one source. Themed events are all the rage at the firm and in the summer of 2007 it held a Wimbledon-style private client party complete with table tennis. When meeting clients on such occasions, *"trainees get in there like everyone else. You arrive, get your name badge and set off to talk to people."* If you're concerned you may not be a natural at this, don't worry. There is a formal networking group at the firm called ClarioNet, which organises events for younger clients and contacts and is a good way to polish up your act. Nevertheless, we were told, *"you have got to be quite fun and sociable to work here; there's a lot of going out for drinks and a big emphasis on sport."* By all accounts you don't have to have Northern roots to get in. What's most important is demonstrating a genuine interest in the firm as *"they quickly weed out those people who make 100 applications."*

When it comes to securing a training contract, our interviewees told us that *"loud or confident people"* do well on assessment days, while less ebullient types often fare better on a vac scheme. Interestingly, there seems to be an increasing emphasis on the latter, with the firm *"looking to recruit more trainees this way."* Said one source: *"Historically, the people appointed were all outgoing and had a lot of character. It isn't like that now. I think there's just as much room for someone quieter who works hard and produces quality work."* Leaving aside the ratio of personality types, we were left wondering where all the male trainees were –

in 2006/07 there was just one guy to nine girls, and a majority of females in the junior ranks. Apart from the negative impact on the men's footie team, this doesn't seem like an ideal demographic, especially when the firm is so male dominated at partner level.

air time

New for 2007 is a proposal to introduce *"a proper mentor scheme with trainees picking their mentors."* This doesn't mean the big bosses are unapproachable. Indeed, according to one trainee, *"you can talk to the partners more easily than some of the middle members of staff."* Overall, the firm was deemed to be *"very consultative."* Said one interviewee: *"I feel able to air my views to the partners. Even though they have a lot on their plate they listen to everyone."* The standard of training is deemed to be high, *"which makes for a great learning environment,"* and of those who qualified in 2007, four out of five were offered jobs and accepted them. Those who leave the firm for pastures new find that *"other places recognise the amount of experience, responsibility and client contact we have had."* Said one source: *"Having trained at a unique firm, I realise that I am a unique pick."*

and finally...

This is definitely a firm with a touch of the Ben Stillers about it. It's a lively and fun place to be but – make no mistake – coming here will mean pushing yourself for two years. The comments of one departing trainee were telling: *"The firm has a great image in Leeds. You can proudly hold your head up in front of DLA and Eversheds. I think our training is as good, if not better, than theirs."*

Cleary Gottlieb Steen & Hamilton LLP

the facts

Location: London
Number of UK partners/solicitors: 18/30 (plus 20 US-qualified lawyers)
Total number of trainees: 12
Seats: 4x6 months
Alternative seats: Overseas seats
Extras: Pro bono – various legal initiatives

Some Europeans view their American cousins with a mixture of mirth and suspicion, but it wasn't always so. After the Second World War the USA was Europe's saviour, sending millions of dollars and hundreds of brainy people over to help rebuild the shattered continent. Newly founded New York law firm Cleary Gottlieb came along for the ride and when many of the diplomats and technicians went home, Cleary stayed behind.

sans frontières

Cleary was founded in New York in 1946 and opened its Paris office in 1949. That should tell you something: this is a most internationally minded US firm. Admittedly, the London office wasn't opened until 1971, but that's still about 25 years before most other US firms now operating from our fair shores. Our subject firm now has 12 offices from Frankfurt to Beijing and only two of them are in the USA. Like many US firms, Cleary's London office is firmly focused on corporate and finance matters, and with a Brussels office since 1960 it also boasts a phenomenally good reputation in regulatory matters such as competition law. Bear this in mind if you're thinking of applying here. Also bear in mind that if you've got your eye set on property or employment law, for example, you should look elsewhere.

It's not just its international pedigree that marks Cleary out. The firm operates without departments, with even some of the most senior partners experienced in more than one area of law. Apologies for the length of the quote, but this rather useful snippet from the firm says much about its philosophy on this and other fundamental points: "Our firm's founding partners recognized that Cleary Gottlieb's success would depend on our commitment to work together to provide clients with the highest quality legal services. This philosophy is at the heart of our 'lock-step' seniority-based compensation system that is applied without exception to all lawyers (including partners), helping us develop a culture of collegiality in which we focus not on our individual advantage but on achieving the right results for our clients. Collaboration is a way of life at Cleary Gottlieb, and we regularly apply the firm's full resources across all practice areas in service of our clients. Each client is treated as a client of the firm, not of a single partner or group of partners." In practice, what you will find over the three floors of Cleary's office on London Wall is private equity lawyers sharing corridors with IP lawyers and competition lawyers, etc. As a result, the training contract is not overly compartmentalised, something that our sources valued highly. *"You still do four seats with four different partners, each working in a different area,"* explained one trainee, *"but you'll also take things from all over the firm."* How does this work? *"An e-mail goes round asking if anyone has some time to work on a particular task, or if something comes up which your supervisor or the training partner thinks would be good for you to work on, they might suggest you."* The system is a good way of getting to know the whole firm as *"you do, literally, work with everybody."* But if the whole office can throw work at you, isn't there a risk of becoming overloaded? *"There is the potential for that, I suppose, but in practice it doesn't happen,"* one trainee confirmed.

"They've introduced a new system so that when a new deal comes in they review the staffing and can properly decide which trainees get involved."

no logo

The main activities of the office are corporate, private equity, capital markets, banking and finance, tax, IP and competition law. Time in competition, tax and IP can provide enough contentious experience to satisfy those pesky Law Society requirements, but be aware that most of the work in these teams is likely to be in support of transactions. A notable exception on the competition side was the firm's representation of The Lawn Tennis Association and The All England Lawn Tennis and Croquet Club (which run Wimbledon) plus Tennis Australia (which runs the Australian Open) in two joined High Court actions brought by manufacturers of tennis clothing (including adidas, Nike and Puma) relating to alleged breaches of EU and UK competition law concerning a dress rule that regulates the size and placement of manufacturers' logos. There is also some scope for trainees to try arbitration in Paris or spend time in Brussels, New York, Hong Kong and Moscow.

Whatever your supervisor's line of work, you won't be spending your time at the photocopier. *"I had a telephone call with a client on my first day in my first seat!"* recalled one trainee. Tasks such as drafting agreements and commenting on contracts are the bread and butter of trainee work here. A little bibling and research is inevitable, of course, but *"there's a good print room and lots of paralegals, and I've never felt I was doing work just because there was no one else to do it."* Trainees are invited to contribute to meetings with clients and the other lawyers on deals, and it's not unheard of for them to conduct meetings unsupervised. *"I met some trainees from a magic circle firm who were collaborating on a deal,"* one first-year explained. *"They'd just proofread their documen-*

tation, I'd helped draft ours. They couldn't believe how much responsibility I had."

that'll do nicely

The responsibility level really ratchets up when it comes to foreign travel. *"Everyone in my intake has already been somewhere,"* confirmed one trainee who'd been with the firm just a few months. Common destinations include Russia and the Middle East; one trainee spent a week closing a deal in India. Often trainees travel with a partner but it's by no means rare to go alone. Isn't it nerve-racking jetting off alone to a meeting after mere months at the firm? *"I didn't really think about it,"* said a source. *"Round here, they like you to just get on with it."* Supervision is of the light-touch variety. *"They like you to take minimum instructions and just take a task and run with it." "They don't want to overload you, but if you show that you want responsibility, that you're ready for it, you'll get it."*

The workload is undeniably heavy. Trainees work until 8pm or 9pm frequently, and with all that travel, weekends aren't sacred. There are compensations however – a hefty salary, a laptop, a BlackBerry, a luxurious leather chair and your own corporate American Express card. When travelling, *"you stay in the best hotels, eat good food and get taxied everywhere."* It's indicative of the trust Cleary puts in its trainees.

It's about time we told you about some of the deals trainees will have assisted on in recent times. In one of the biggest capital markets transactions for the London lawyers in 2006 Cleary represented Banc of America, JPMorgan and Lehman Brothers in connection with a $2.6bn offering of several euro and dollar-denominated floating rate notes by the Vodafone Group. In the world of banking, lawyers advised Arcelor Mittal on the largest funded corporate purposes loan in the European syndicated loan markets. The transaction brought together terms from the existing Mittal Steel and Arcelor loan facilities and was structured to provide for future flexibility in light of the merger between the two companies to create the world's biggest steel producer. One very recent transaction was the London Stock Exchange listing of the Russian precious metals company Polymetal, in which Cleary advised the investment banks. In the area of private equity Cleary represented Texas Pacific Group in its acquisition of Mey Alcoholic Beverages, the leading spirits producer in Turkey. With all this hard work and jetsetting, it's a wonder Cleary's trainees have any time at all to relax. No one would claim there's much of a social scene going on after work – people are grafting too hard for that – but *"there have been a few social evenings,"* one source confirmed. The venue in question is normally the local Corney & Barrow. In short, you should choose this place for its career opportunities not its partying.

want to be a part of it?

The firm denies offering any guarantee, but we've been unable to find an example in recent years of a trainee not sticking around on qualification. What's more, associates are able to continue specialisation-free for a few years, so there's no painful choice to be made at the end of the contract. Associate salaries are pretty astronomical (a market-surfing £92,000 for NQs in 2007) and all newbies get their own office. *"It's actually really nice,"* admitted one young associate. *"You can put your phone on speaker and work as you talk."* We're not sure if it was the lure of the office or the salary that led all three 2007 qualifiers to stay with the firm.

Sold? OK, here's the bad news: you're not the only one. With over 2,000 applications each year for up to ten places, the firm is superchoosy. *"There are some extremely bright people here,"* admitted one trainee. *"They do like high achievers."* First-class degree, Oxbridge, a Master's degree (maybe

from somewhere such as Harvard) – you'll probably want at least two of these three. If you like the sound of Stateside study, and you're sporting a law degree, there is the option of time in the USA and qualifying for the New York Bar, though the firm prefers its recruits to complete their UK training before embarking on this. When a firm has quite as much applicant sifting to do, it looks at more than just grades. Cleary's long-leash approach to training requires the recruiters to be incredibly picky about who they think will gel with the firm, and even with the massive ratio of applications to places, it's not unheard of for the firm to leave openings unfilled if they don't feel they've found a proper match. So what are they looking for? *"They do like personalities,"* our source confirmed. *"Everyone here could take you out for dinner and be funny and entertaining."* In addition, *"although it's a cliché, they are looking for team people,"* another explained. Arrogance, brown-nosing and excessive nerves were all identified as no-nos but if this all sounds a bit restrictive, be reassured that the firm isn't looking for clones. *"Eccentricity they're quite happy with,"* admitted one. *"Someone in knowledge management painted a big picture of a guy with dreadlocks and Union Jack shades, and they put it up in the canteen."* Lastly we'll point out that the trainee intakes tend to be quite international, with recent joiners hailing from Portugal, Trinidad and Singapore as well as the UK.

The most important thing to know is that if you're interested you should apply for the vac scheme. *"They're definitely trying to recruit from it,"* trainees stressed. *"It's the best kind of interview, after all."*

and finally....

Trainee life at Cleary comes complete with all the trappings of a role as a fully active solicitor, including a heavy workload and major responsibilities. If you think you're up to the challenge, we reckon it's a superb bet. Just make sure you've a Plan B.

Clifford Chance LLP

the facts

Location: London
Number of UK partners/solicitors: 231/768
Total number of trainees: 254
Seats: 4x6 months
Alternative seats: Overseas seats, secondments
Extras: Pro bono – various law centres; death row appeals; language training

How do you feel when you see a skyscraper? Exhilarated at the thought of the big-money business that must go on inside? Envious of the beautiful fittings and epic views? Or slightly repelled by the materialism of it all? If you ticked one of the first two options then welcome to Clifford Chance, the world's most skyscraping law firm.

reaching for the skies

When the UK's biggest law firms set their sights on world domination in the late 1990s, Clifford Chance led the charge. Its 1999 merger with New York firm Rogers & Wells created the world's largest law firm by turnover. As CC adjusted to its new giant size, it naturally stumbled a little, with static profits, morale problems in New York, and an ill-fated West Coast expansion. But it was big enough to ride out these problems and after some cost-cuttings here and there it continued its quest for world domination. The firm now boasts 28 offices in 20 countries from the UK to the UEA and from Belgium to Brazil. *"I think the phase of geographical expansion has finished,"* one trainee concluded. *"The focus now is on developing our relationships with key clients."*

CC's original area of dominance was banking and finance. It has reached the enviable position where it is a natural choice for assisting the world's leading investment banks in supplying the readies for some of the world's largest transactions. The team recently advised Citigroup, RBS, HSBC, Calyon and Santander on financing Ferrovial's takeover of BAA, the UK airports operator, and Barclays Capital, Dresdner Kleinwort, HSBC and Royal Bank of Canada on Macquarie's £4.8bn takeover of Thames Water. It has an army of finance lawyers in its London office and even more worldwide. Over time, CC's corporate division has become an equally important part of the firm's success. Its lawyers crop up on all sorts of megadeals, among them Barclays' £80bn merger with Dutch bank ABN AMRO and Siemens' merger of its communications service provider business with Nokia. The firm has also established itself in the red-hot private equity world, advising KKR on its (albeit failed) £9.7bn bid for Alliance Boots, and the Macquarie-led consortium (which included 3i, Canada Pension Plan Investment Board and Canada Pension Management) on its £2.58bn bid for Associated British Ports.

down to business

Clifford Chance may be a full-service law firm, but make no mistake: it is heavily weighted towards its largest, most profitable departments. At the heart of the firm are the mammoth finance and capital markets divisions and all trainees will take at least one seat here. The options are: general banking; energy and infrastructure (ie project finance); insolvency finance; derivatives; asset finance and, of course, capital markets. In general banking you'll be *"manically busy"* helping out teams of more senior fee earners on their deals. A common trainee task involves the confirmation of conditions precedent, which are an essential part of any deal. The job won't require much in the way of legal analysis, but it will test your organisational skills. *"You have to keep on top of the transaction, wherever it is happening in the world,"* one source explained. *"You might also* need to travel in order to confirm some of the details with the clients in person." Finance seats do at least offer drafting experience, even some negotiation on smaller side-deals. "The more you impress on simpler tasks, the more responsibility you're given," one interviewee noted. "You start off with check-lists, but you could end up drafting agreements."

The corporate division comes next in size and prestige. It too breaks down into several departments – general corporate finance; private equity and investment banking; financial institutions; commercial business; private funds; communications, media and technology; and European competition and regulation. Like corporate departments anywhere, it is "sometimes horrifically busy and sometimes much quieter." With multibillion-pound/euro/dollar deals going on, there are no prizes for guessing that trainees see "a fair amount of grunt work: collating documents, proof-reading and so on." However, "if you've got a good supervisor, they'll see to it that you're copied in on all the e-mails and invited to conference calls, so you understand what's going on." On smaller deals you might work directly with a partner, meaning a leap up in responsibility, especially if your visit is during your second year.

The regulatory side of the division offers respite from deal making and more academic, research-heavy responsibilities. "Long discussions about capital adequacy requirements left me needing coffee to stay awake," one interviewee confessed, "but once you get a grip on it, it's quite interesting." At the opposite end of the scale, the capital markets group was generally considered the most frantic, particularly in the area of securitisation. "There is a lot of work," a survivor told us, "but it's good as you're integral to the team. You're left to deal with signings and draft support documents from early on, so you have to put your thinking cap on."

And what about litigation? First, let's put things in context: the number of commercial disputes going through the courts each year has plummeted, along with it the clout of litigators in many a City firm. "Litigation brings a huge amount of money, although I'm not sure everybody realises that," one contentiously minded trainee told us. "However, the London managing partner is a litigator, so that must be a good thing." Because the kind of major arbitrations and litigation that CC pursues can go on for years, seats often only show a small slice of a particular case, and the nature of the trainee's role will differ from one stage of a dispute to another. One trainee's experiences amounted to "a lot of case law research, helping out with disclosure, reviewing documents and bundling." If a hearing looms, they may get to "prepare memos for clients or background research that might be referred to in court." Among the cases CC litigators have been handling are Multiplex's High Court claims against its subcontractors, Cleveland Bridge, in relation to the construction of Wembley Stadium; litigation seeking to overturn the Hunting Act 2004; and claims for major investment banks in relation to the collapse of the Italian company Parmalat, Europe's largest corporate fraud in many years. Anyone dead set on a contentious seat is guaranteed one – but only one. Their choices are general litigation; international commercial arbitration; insurance litigation; insolvency litigation; intellectual property and public policy litigation. As for the others, they can sidestep this part of the training contract and opt for classroom tuition and pro bono activities instead. If you're considering a contentious career, there's no need to cross CC off your list entirely but do be aware that when NQ job time rolls around litigation tends to be oversubscribed. As a result, in 2007 it was the only group that interviewed applicants for NQ positions.

all over the place

Other London seats are available in the real estate division (general real estate; environment and planning; real estate litigation; real estate funds and investments and real estate finance) and the tax, pensions and employment group. In addition, there are secondments to UK clients plus a raft of overseas seats (see page 206 for the full run down). The chance to work abroad was a key factor in why most of our interviewees considered CC and the other magic circle firms, so it's a good job there are plenty of slots. There are in fact enough overseas places for all who want them, though this is not to say that everyone gets their preferred location. Allocations are based on business need and trainees' language skills. Be aware that your language skills can benefit or hinder your chances of getting a particular seat – speak fluent Russian or Portuguese and we don't fancy your chances of getting the New York slot.

As ever with overseas seats, your experience depends on both where you go and which department you work for. Generally, smaller foreign offices give increased responsibility. In the Frankfurt office's banking team, for example, *"there's only about eight English lawyers so you work directly with a partner on all of their deals, drafting and negotiating side documents. The client treats you like a full team member."* The flipside is hours: most of our sources had done their longest hours while abroad. One Hong Kong secondee told us: *"There were 30 or 40 British trainees out there in total and I was definitely doing some of the longest hours."*

It's not all work, of course. In Dubai, for example, trainees *"live the expat lifestyle: clubs, beaches, brunches, shopping."* Hong Kong visitors enjoy *"flying out to Shanghai, Vietnam and Australia"* at the weekend and the Dubai lot get to try *"dune bashing... You take a 4x4 out into the desert and just sort of tear it up."* Spare a thought for Frankfurt trainees: *"People say Frankfurt doesn't have much of a social scene. They're right, it's full of bankers who go home to Switzerland at the weekend."*

up all night

With 250 trainees at a time, we shudder to imagine the spreadsheet HR uses to keep track of them all. Nonetheless, the people we spoke to said their seat preferences had been met most of the time. Of course this may be because expectations are well managed and the right messages have gone out to students about the nature of CC's practice leanings. To help people pick through the long list of options, trainees produce a guide detailing their experiences of different seats.

The partners and senior associates who supervise trainees work on some of the biggest deals around and are among the highest earners in their profession. So what are they like? *"I've found people very down to earth,"* one trainee reported. *"There's no superstar partners swaggering around... well, not too many."* Actually, supervisors are just as varied as their trainees. *"I had one in asset finance who was into kickboxing, which was quite interesting,"* recalled an interviewee. It makes sense that trainees can request specific supervisors, not just departments.

Even in traditionally shorter-hours departments like litigation, between 7pm and 8pm seems to be a standard departure time. In transactional seats, when things get busy, well, let's just pass on one trainee's experience: *"I have done one double all-nighter. I came in Tuesday morning and left Thursday night. And I've done about ten single all-nighters, usually in the lead up to a signing."* We reckon this is close to the bad end of the spectrum, but the majority of our interviewees had done at least one 24-hour session. Apparently, *"the adrenalin keeps you going – that and the gallons of coffee."* Thank goodness for round-the-clock secretarial support (*"at least if you are in late it'll be to do real work, not photocopying"*) and free food and drinks in the dead of night, even if one rueful source noted: *"They don't do Red Bull."* Some trainees admitted that, occasionally, late hours stem from more than just heavy workloads. *"You do feel the presentee-ism thing a bit and stay late to make a good impression,"* admitted one.

keeping perspective

While CC trainees seem a confident bunch, it nevertheless must be daunting turning up on your first day at the firm's enormous building in Canary Wharf. The trick is to think small and *"just settle into the department you're sitting in."* This way it is *"no different to working in a small company with one or two floors of a big building – except, of course, that the people on the other floors are all your colleagues too."* And, while we're on the subject, let's not forget the hundreds of people grafting away in an outsourced service centre in Delhi. Many larger teams have up to nine or ten trainees at any one time, so you'll likely share your initial experiences with another newbie. In addition, *"we have three weeks of induction when you see the rest of your intake of 60,"* and anyway, with all CC trainees studying their LPC together at the College of Law, you'll probably recognise everyone's face.

We're betting the atmosphere at the start of the training contract is something akin to Freshers' Week. *"It does start off busy, but it quietens down quickly as the work piles up,"* trainees told us. *"Getting people together in the evenings is notoriously difficult, so I see people at lunchtimes and sometimes at weekends."* On Thursdays the coffee bar on the fourth floor transforms into a bar, though more formal events such as summer and winter trainee balls attract a better turn out. The trainee social committee organises half a dozen events each year and then there's a reasonable array of team outings in most departments, covering everything from horse racing to *"a departmental retreat to Amsterdam. We had a couple of talks to justify the trip and the five-star hotel, then we started drinking..."*

In 2003, CC pulled out of the City and relocated to Canary Wharf where some of its biggest banking clients reside. The move was a reminder of the firm's lack of tradition. Get yourself inside and you'll find staff breeze around tie-less and that the office is equipped with its own gym, swimming pool, restaurant and coffee bar, even a games room. You should also know that CC has a good record on diversity. *"It seemed cosmopolitan and varied,"* one trainee recalled from his first interview, and by our reckoning, in summer 2007 about a fifth of the trainee group was from an ethnic minority. *"There's no Clifford Chance stereotype,"* said one source categorically. Recent trainee intakes include plenty of straight-from-university types, but also a large number of trainees with previous career experience and someone who's rowed for England. *"I heard they interviewed someone last year just because he said something interesting on his CV, and they wanted to ask him about it,"* one trainee told us.

While Canary Wharf is few people's idea of a cultural paradise, *"there is a lot of parkland, which is nice in summer, and there's a good shopping centre and busy bars."* If you do find the area too artificial, *"it's possible to come in and leave direct via the tube station, without actually going outside."* Of course, it's not just the massive London office trainees need to try to get their heads around. Do they, we wondered, have anything in common with a CC lawyer in Singapore or Moscow? *"Not really,"* one source admitted. *"It's easy to feel isolated from the other offices, though it's nice to know they're there if you've got a query."* Trainees who had been abroad, however, naturally felt more plugged into the global network. The firm certainly tries to assist bonding, funding an annual global hockey and football tournament with teams from all over the world.

all the way to the top

At the end of the two years, an NQ job changes from a goal to a reality for most. The selection process received mixed reviews from our interviewees. HR announces vacancies a few weeks before decisions are due, but *"the jostling begins even before the end of the third seat."* The best way, trainees told us, is to approach partners in departments of interest. Alternatively, *"if they're interested in you, they'll probably approach you."* Such politicking can spoil the atmosphere a little but it's not overwhelming. *"It's rare for people to be particularly competitive or cloak and dagger; everyone's quite open about where they'd like to go."* The firm encourages single selections: *"You can choose more than one, but only if you're genuinely just as happy with either. I get the sense it's not recommended, though."* Indeed, we detected some confusion about how many applications is considered acceptable. The problem is that *"while departments can give you a signal, they can't promise anything."* With so many people to fit in, *"it's all a bit tortuous."* In 2007, 94 of the 119 qualifiers stayed on.

This doesn't mean they're wedded to CC forever. The partnership track takes an average of eight years, although the majority of NQs depart by the time they are three or four years qualified. *"I want to stay for a few years for the foreign opportunities,"* one trainee told us; *"but as for partnership, I don't know if the rewards justify the long slog."* Considering the rewards – some equity partners took home well over £1m last year – that's saying something.

and finally...

Whether you see the firm as a launch pad or see yourself as one of its future partners, training at Clifford Chance means starting at the very biggest firm in the profession. Whatever your background, if you're confident, smart and prepared to miss a few friends' birthdays, you can get off to a great start here.

Clyde & Co LLP

the facts

Location: London
Number of UK partners/solicitors: 104/170
Total number of trainees: 48
Seats: 4x6 months
Alternative seats: Overseas seats, secondments
Extras: Pro bono – RCJ CAB, Lambeth Law Centre, Guildford CAB

Clyde & Co is currently going through a phase of international expansion. It set up three new offices in 2006 – New York, Los Angeles and Shanghai – and added another in 2007 in Doha, Qatar. All up it now operates from 18 locations across the globe, including places as far flung as Caracas, Singapore and St Petersburg.

the full skinny

Clyde & Co's traditional strengths lie in shipping, international trade and insurance. These areas are still of huge importance to the firm, even though it has expanded the scope of its activities enormously. In marine, transport, aviation, commodities and energy work it would be no exaggeration to say that wherever and however goods are moved around the world Clydes' lawyers are involved in some way. Through its unshakeable relationship with the insurance sector, it has become a Trojan of the Commercial Court, acting in many of the biggest litigations of recent years.

As much as we'd like to go on ad infinitum about the firm's amazing feats of dispute resolution, it would be wrong to ignore all the other aspects of its business, especially as it has worked so hard to develop them. In the energy sector, the firm has worked on transactions that it deems both commercially and legally innovative, for example, public sector-sponsored district heating and waste-to-energy power schemes. Many of the transactions and projects are located overseas,

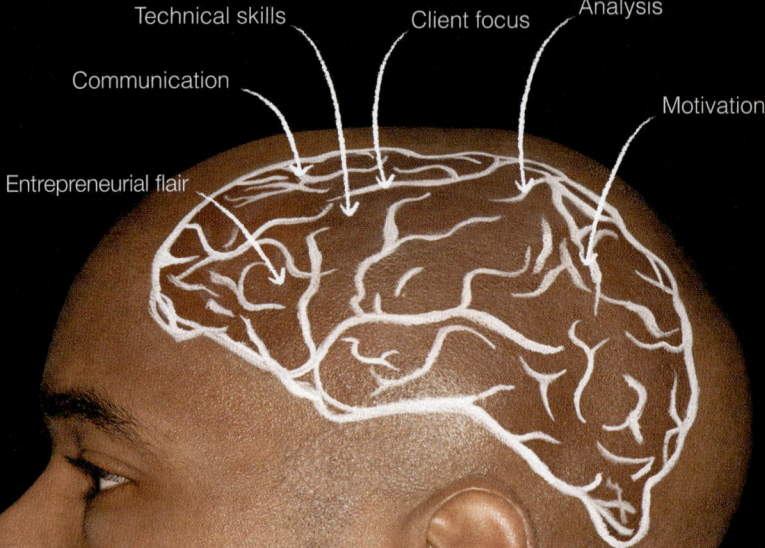

Technical skills

Client focus

Analysis

Communication

Motivation

Entrepreneurial flair

What makes a great lawyer?

At **Clyde & Co**, we believe that a variety of different qualities combine to make a really great lawyer. So if you've got what it takes, we'll provide the rest: first-class training and top-level exposure at an internationally renowned firm.

In terms of a career choice, we think it's a **no-brainer.**

Email us at: **theanswers@clydeco.com**

Apply at: **www.clydeco.com/graduate**

CLYDE&CO

among them a multibillion-dollar LNG project in Yemen, on which the firm is advising the state oil company and the Republic on all aspects of the project from gas field development to finance. Back in the UK, the employment team is adviser to worldwide logistics company DHL and helped BSkyB with its acquisition of Easynet.

The full seat menu for trainees is as follows: corporate, property, construction, banking, employment, corporate insurance, shipping finance, aviation finance, banking finance, commodities, EU/competition, trade litigation, general commercial litigation, insurance and reinsurance, marine transport, aviation litigation and trade and energy. Do not underestimate how important dispute resolution is to the firm, so if this side of the law is not to your taste you'll want to think twice about applying here. On the other hand, *"if you love litigation, you probably couldn't be at a better firm."* This point can't be understated: what Clydes can offer to aspiring litigators stands in stark contrast to the post-qualification opportunities at the biggest City firms, where a wannabe litigator's prospects can be slimmer than Amy Winehouse on a thin day. In most City firms transactional seats tend to dominate the training contract. The firm reckons that it can offer a 50/50 split between contentious and non-contentious seats.

dreamboats

Trainees are encouraged to do seats in the firm's core areas of shipping, corporate, insurance and trade and energy. By its own reckoning, Clydes has the world's largest shipping practice, with almost 150 specialist marine lawyers (including a team of six master mariners) based in 15 offices and located in 11 countries. In contentious shipping seats, trainees can sample wet and dry work. Put very simply, if everything goes well and cargo arrives after its voyage, it's a dry shipping matter, perhaps a problem has arisen over payment or

late delivery and so on. If the ship has a collision or sinks, then it's a wet shipping matter. Some dry shipping cases are small enough for trainees to run themselves under supervision. Wet matters – or Admiralty as they are sometimes known because of the division of the High court in which they are heard – are a different kettle of fish altogether, and it takes a good deal of experience to handle some of the trickier incidents. Clydes has advised on a multitude of important cases, but one recent matter relates to what is potentially the largest container ship casualty ever. After the Hyundai Fortune suffered a huge explosion below deck in March 2006, while sailing off the coast of Yemen, Clydes was instructed on $106m worth of instructions by 57 separate cargo underwriter clients from 19 countries. The Paris and Hong Kong offices were instrumental in gathering instructions and worked in tandem with the UK lawyers and external experts from Yemen, Djibouti, Saudi Arabia and Korea. Other marine work involves ship finance, sometimes dealing with *"interesting megayacht work for high net worth individuals."* Megayacht deals appear *"deceptively glamorous;"* the reality is that picking over contracts can feel rather like *"destroying a rich person's dreams."* Unsurprisingly, when dealing with cargo ships clients are rarely emotional.

In the insurance and reinsurance department, the range of issues dealt with is phenomenal. Whatever an insurance company might need, Clydes can help them with it. General claims, reinsurance disputes and corporate and regulatory advice is all covered. Working on general claims, if a case is small enough trainees are *"given quite a lot of responsibility,"* sometimes *"effectively administering the whole thing and working out what needs to be done and how to do it."* A word of advice from one of our sources: *"If you are a shrinking violet, you wouldn't necessarily get the same quality work as someone that expresses interest and keeps abreast of what's going on around them.*" Of course, one of the things Clydes is known for is its expertise in absolutely giant cases, and if you land up working on one of these you'll have to take your share of more administrative tasks with good grace. Among the topics covered by big cases recently are hurricanes, 9/11, oil spills, defective drugs, nuclear leaks, Enron and dodgy investments.

One of the insurance seat options – corporate insurance – is transactional and advisory in nature. The work is split between providing regulatory advice to insurance companies to ensure they are FSA compliant, and assisting them to buy and sell insurance businesses. The trainees' role sees them "*drafting due diligence reports, writing disclosure letters and responding to client queries*" in relation to deals such as the AIM listing of Heritage Underwriting Agency, which raised £15m through the placing.

We should stress that not all the litigation being conducted here at the firm is insurance related. One good example of this is the class action that consumer organisation Which? wishes to bring before the Competition Appeals Tribunal. Which? has instructed Clydes to take on JJB Sports on behalf of people who bought replica England and Manchester United football shirts between 2000 and 2001. This case led the firm to pursue a novel tactic – placing ads in Manchester newspapers asking people who were affected to come forward.

fly away!

In 2005 Clydes bolstered its aviation practice through a merger with Beaumont & Sons, a specialist aviation firm. Regular clients include India's budget airline SpiceJet, Siberia Airlines, Iran Air Tours, JAT Airways, China Eastern Airlines and a host of other carriers. Those trainees keen to gain corporate experience can spend time in a department that works on AIM and smaller mid-market transactions. Based mainly in Lon-

don, the lawyers take full advantage of the firm's good name in the natural resources, trade and energy and financial services sectors, and many of the deals have a cross-border aspect to them. Trainees reported working on "*quite boring things to start with, then sitting in on more meetings and doing more drafting later.*" Property seats go down well. Here, trainees are given a mixture of residential and commercial work, with the residential matters being ideal for learning how to manage a whole transaction. Trainees spoke of having up to 20 or 30 files of their own, while also helping to gather and process information and write lease reports on larger deals.

The most regular overseas secondment is to Dubai, but there are sometimes trainees out in Abu Dhabi, Hong Kong, Piraeus and Singapore. Dubai offers both litigation and corporate options and it sounds like it's a busy place to be. One trainee told us: "*It was a shock in terms of how much work there is out there.*" Trainee tasks are mostly "*good quality,*" with new arrivals "*pretty much thrown straight in*" and becoming "*more involved because of the smaller size of the team.*" No doubt the transition is made considerably easier by the perks – a car and petrol allowance (or taxi allowance for those who prefer) and an apartment in a complex with a gym and lagoon-style pool.

making the grade

Each new seat begins with an induction, which is especially useful for those seats focusing on industries with which recruits are unfamiliar. When it comes to end-of-seat appraisals, trainees are expected to rate themselves in various categories with the following options: "*Fully effective, highly effective, generally effective and so on…*" The partners then decide whether they agree. It sounds as if there is some inconsistency in the way different partners grade trainees and this led our sources to call for a more uniform process. The mid-seat appraisal isn't overly structured, and while the firm tells us that the vast majority of appraisal forms are completed, we sense that it can take a bit of pushing with some partners.

On seat allocation, some sources felt the most important thing was to *"stay in the good books with HR;"* others suggested it helps to *"approach a partner and say you are interested in doing a seat in their department."* Overall, trainees recommended the application process be made more formal because, at present, things were too *"vague"* and people *"don't really know what goes on."* Their views were much the same regarding the mysterious qualification process in which *"there is no job list circulated."* Whatever improvements might be made to the system, in 2007 a very healthy 17 of the 19 qualifiers accepted jobs with the firm, ten of them going into contentious areas.

One area where Clydes scores well is on hours. *"It's a big firm, but it's not like the magic circle… if you finish your work at 5.30pm or 6pm, it's fine, you can go home."* One trainee told us they usually left the office around 7pm and were slightly bemused by the concept of work-life balance: *"If you're enjoying it, surely it doesn't matter?"* Apparently you mustn't be fooled into thinking Guildford has shorter hours; *"it's on par with London."* In some respects you could say this is a *"what you see is what you get"* type of place. Among the partnership, for example: *"You can have somebody who's completely bonkers and someone who is completely boring."* In the opinion of most, *"there isn't a particularly competitive atmosphere, but it is ambitious."* There are clearly differences between London and Guildford, but these relate more to the practicalities of getting to work and the environment in which the office is located than the nature of the work conducted in each office. All trainees must expect to be moved between the two UK locations, and some others will, of course, also visit overseas seats. Usually there are ten trainees in Guildford, up to four in Dubai, occasionally a couple in other overseas seats and the rest in London. Client secondments crop up every now and then.

Occasionally trainees get their own offices, but it is more common for them to share with another trainee or an assistant solicitor. One of the two London offices is a relatively old building on Eastcheap. *"It's not the prettiest of buildings, but people think it has a better atmosphere than the one at the Corn Exchange."* The Corn Exchange office is a modern, glassy building in which Clydes' insurance team occupies a single floor. In Eastcheap, the mod cons include a subsidised Starbucks and an eighth-floor terrace with views over the City that staff can enjoy during summer drinks parties. The office in Guildford is big and buzzy enough that it is never going to feel like a backwater of the firm. If you're looking to have a drink with colleagues after work then in London you need to head for The Ship, and in Guildford it is the The Tup.

and finally...

If your interests and Clyde & Co's practice leanings are a good match, then we doubt you could find a more respected firm to train at. If you are already certain that non-contentious work is more to your taste, then we recommend you think carefully before applying as there are scores of firms that could offer you a more transactional training. Opportunities to go abroad are improving with the widening of the network of offices… but do remember that a stint in Guildford is on the cards for all.

CMS Cameron McKenna LLP

the facts

Location: London, Bristol, Aberdeen, Edinburgh
Number of UK partners/solicitors: 130/700
Total number of trainees: 120
Seats: 4x6 months
Alternative seats: Overseas seats, secondments
Extras: Pro bono – Islington Law Centre, Bristol ProHelp, LawWorks, Advocates for International Development; travel bursaries; cultural/language training

Hovering at the edge of the top ten largest firms in the UK, CMS Cameron McKenna is multiply attractive. As if its stellar energy practice, a network of European offices and allied firms – especially in Central and Eastern Europe – and breadth of practice at home in the UK weren't enough to attract recruits, it can also pull out the nice-place-to-work card.

the goldilocks of the city

Gaining a broad-based City training in a large but not giant-sized firm is the goal of many students. For them Camerons fits the bill perfectly. You could call it the Goldilocks of the City: not too corporate focused, not too finance focused, not too litigation focused. Just right. Reflecting this, the firm requires trainees to spend time in either a corporate or banking seat and then a contentious seat. They also all have a chance to identify the priority seat which they would like to try at some stage. The departmental structure rests on the following main practice areas: corporate; banking; property; energy, projects and construction (EPC); commercial; and insurance.

We'll look first at the corporate department because the firm has vowed to raise its profile. *"The next three-year strategic period is about us recruiting people to build up the corporate practice, and doing that will benefit other practices,"*

explained a source. Aspiring Cameronites should note that the firm will consequently be looking to recruit corporate-minded trainees, and this is significant because until now it's fair to say that although all trainees do a corporate seat (sometimes banking instead) *"a lot of people have shied away from the department,"* seemingly *"put off by menial tasks like photocopying and data rooms"* and the infamous long hours. Even those who loved their time in the department admitted *"the seat can be very intense – I did a week or two up to midnight every night."* The only consolation is that *"you are usually aware when you are going to be working late; it's not often that at 5.15pm someone asks if you can stay."* As to what they work on, one of last year's biggest deals was construction client John Laing plc's £1bn recommended cash takeover by Henderson Infrastructure Holdco Limited. The lawyers also played a part for RBS in a series of major hotel acquisitions totalling more than £2bn, and they worked on Pfizer's $16.6bn disposal of its consumer healthcare business to Johnson & Johnson. This last deal is indicative of the great importance of pharmaceuticals clients to Camerons' business.

burning issues

Everyone does a contentious seat, which can be taken in IP/IT, EU and competition, corporate recovery, insurance, commercial disputes, construction, SHEP (safety, health, environment and product liability) or even employment. The insurance group has opened a second office in Leadenhall, near to Lloyd's of London, in premises shared with client AIG. Clients include London market names such as Swiss Re and worldwide market players like GE, Chubb and Allianz. Reinsurance cases in particular can be complicated and are mostly dealt with by way of arbitration rather than litigation. *"I really enjoyed it, although it needs a little time to get into it properly,"* recalled a trainee. *"You do a lot* of research and have a liaison role as the contact person for counsel, clients and other lawyers." Among notable recent instructions are disputes in energy (Buncefield oil depot fire), construction (Singapore Tunnel collapse), banks and financial institutions (Enron issues) and professional negligence.

Other seats are chosen from an extensive list that ranges from tax and pensions to corporate and leveraged finance, project finance, real estate, non-contentious technology/IP/media, non-contentious corporate recovery and immigration. The most popular are employment and IP/IT (both contentious and non-contentious), and the pensions seat is increasingly favoured. The least popular seats tend to be the small handful presided over by more difficult partners.

power rangers

Readers with an interest in the energy sector or Eastern Europe may already be aware of Camerons' stature in these areas. There are four trainees in energy seats, plus three working in the firm's Aberdeen office on oil and gas matters. *"The energy team is divvied up into oil and gas, electricity – those are the main two areas – and then you have one partner who does renewable energy and another who is taking on the nuclear decommissioning of power stations"* (not personally we hope). The energy work is mainly for UK companies, although not necessarily concerning UK matters; for example, *"we worked for BP when it was auctioning its Dutch subsidiaries"* and *"wrote the entire legislation for the Saudi Arabian electricity industry privatisation."*

The projects team is aligned with the energy team, and London lawyers in both practices often work in conjunction with offices in the CMS network across Europe and beyond. They lately assisted on projects concerning Romanian refinery facilities, a biodiesel plant in Hungary and a gas-metering project in the UK. Spend time here

and there's a fair chance you'll develop a good knowledge of Europe's motorways and toll roads: the firm has worked on the construction and/or financing of the A1 motorway and A4 toll road in Poland, the Moscow Central Ring Road, the E18 Grimstad-Kristiansand road in Norway and the A5 motorway in Austria.

we're all going on a camerons' holiday

Almost everyone spends their second (or possibly third) seat out of the main London office. The options are many: seats can be taken in an overseas office chosen from Bulgaria, Czech Republic, Hungary, Poland, Romania and Russia; or elsewhere in the UK – Edinburgh (*"the firm recruits a few Scots trainees too"*), Aberdeen (*"more popular in summer"*) and Bristol. Interest in Bristol was noticeably higher this year, with commercial real estate, insurance litigation and banking seats all on offer and small groups of friends opting to go there and work together for six months. *"I was able to walk to work every day,"* recalled a source wistfully. Alas the *"very sought after"* Hong Kong seat is no longer going to be available as the office is closing in 2008, and the seats in Western European countries also seem to be off the menu now. Those who don't go to another Camerons or CMS alliance office spend six months on secondment with a client, where it's *"really good for your confidence not being bottom of the heap."* Client secondments include AIG, Wellcome Trust, National Australia Bank, Exxon, and Erste Bank in Vienna. Leaving the main London office for a seat is not optional, but the majority aren't complaining. *"You have your first seat to get used to the office and then it's nice to spread your wings a bit; you couldn't feel the international connections without it."* True, each rotation means *"forcing five or six people to go abroad,"* but *"they seem to be alright once they go",* trainees told us, explaining, *"the only way* round it is to have a child!" Hardly a quick fix to the problem...

Like any foreign holiday, a trip overseas can leave some disappointed: "Going to a non-English-speaking office can mean just doing proof-reading and translation checking." A trainee who visited Prague bemoaned how "it was boring – certain partners didn't delegate to trainees." By contrast, "a friend in Budapest got really good work drafting a facility agreement, something you'd never get in London," and "Moscow's been snowed under lately." A word of advice from our interviewees: "If you don't push for the place you want you might get somewhere you don't." Of course, with all these trainees living and working in different countries, there are ready-made excuses for group weekends away.

regime change

Arranging seat rotation at larger firms can require a PhD in maths and in the past some trainees have questioned Camerons' transparency on this score. The arrival of a new "switched-on" head of recruitment and the appointment of a grad recruitment partner is much applauded. This regime "is definitely improving things – there's been a lot of consultation about how to change." Even after the improvements, "there are a few seats consistently oversubscribed, but most people end up doing the ones they most want to do." The firm tries to give people their first choice in the third seat, but it's important to make your own luck, certainly in relation to NQ jobs. "The firm offers jobs to individuals – it's not done on a numbers basis. People will usually talk to partners around the time of qualifying to let them know they are interested in being taken on." Many NQ positions crop up in corporate and banking – "last time round they had half to two thirds of the jobs" – so be aware that the smaller departments won't always have jobs available. In 2007, 45 of the 56 qualifiers stayed with the firm, with a slight move towards EPC being a key recruiting department.

Formal training was praised. "They front-load the departmental training so you learn what you will need for the seat... When you go into techy seats like tax or pensions you do feel out of your depth so the weekly training early on helps." A thumbs up, too, for the policy that allows NQs time off before starting in their qualification job. Everyone who wants it will get "six weeks, part paid and part unpaid."

high wires and headlines

All new recruits are required to take their LPC at BPP in London, but what else will they have in common? The firm recruits from many universities worldwide, including Canada, the USA and various parts of Europe. Language ability clearly impresses the recruiters and the firm always has a handful of trainees who have made a career change. Beyond that we'd say that people are generally unpretentious and pretty sociable. Trainees have their own social budget and reps from each of the four intakes organise monthly trainee-only socials. The highlight is the annual trainee ball – "all the boys in DJs, all the girls in nice dresses." "Last year it made The Times' legal supplement... talking about drunken excesses... There was some talk about getting rid of it after that but we did have another one this February." Future joiners are invited to the event and trainees are flown back from overseas seats. There's also a firm-wide extravaganza, the last one being "a brilliant party at The Roundhouse in Chalk Farm with Cirque du Soleil performers."

Is the firm really the halfway house between the fiery magic circle and softer, smaller City outfits? This is definitely what trainees had in mind when they signed on the dotted line. Well, the claim of "exposure to a huge breadth of practice with magic circle pay" does hold up, even if securing preferred seats takes effort. Our sources insist that the perception that Camerons is "more fluffy

and forgiving than the magic circle" is "basically true; there is a certain amount of late-night working but trainees are less consistently beasted." In telling us that people "shouldn't be put off that this is not the magic circle" their logic was simple: "We get the same opportunities without the outrageous expectations." Yet, once tried, this vibe isn't for everyone. One individual felt "on one level I really like it here, it is very relaxed, but on another I am still aware that I am not at the magic circle and I sometimes think there's not enough oomph." Such hardcore tastes might be better suited elsewhere, and a number of extremely corporate-minded qualifiers have moved on to US firms lately. For the majority of those recruited, however, Camerons' mix maintains its potent appeal.

and finally...

If you hanker after somewhere with an Eastern European empire or a top energy practice then make a beeline for CMS Cameron McKenna. If your tastes are domestic and broadly commercial, it's also a good option, especially if you suspect the magic circle might be too impersonal and an American firm too hectic.

Cobbetts LLP

the facts

Location: Manchester, Birmingham, Leeds, London
Number of UK partners/solicitors: 108/117
Total number of trainees: 50
Seats: 4x6 months
Alternative seats: Brussels, secondments

At the turn of the century, property-led Manchester firm Cobbetts was determined to become the UK's biggest regional firm and embarked on a spree of mergers. Having grown at a frenzied pace, you'd think the firm would have had its fill of change and happily spent a few years getting comfortable with itself. But that wasn't the case: next on the agenda were partner cuts and new offices.

regional culling, london calling

Branching out from its Manchester roots was perhaps the most notable of the changes of the past five years. In Birmingham, a merger with Lee Crowder put the Cobbetts flag on Midlands soil. It became established in Leeds when Read Hind Stewart, Walker Charlesworth & Forsyer and Wilbraham & Co all became subsumed under the Cobbetts name. And the Manchester office didn't stand still: in 2003 niche mining law firm Fox Brooks Marshall was drawn into the equation.

Following these mergers, Cobbetts' management decided the organisation was top heavy and that many practice areas were over populated with partners. Around 20 partners were axed and some others left of their own accord. "It happened quite quickly, kind of like a dawn raid... but it didn't really affect morale," asserted one source. "It felt like we almost got stronger because of it. It was well planned and structured, and the whole point was to take us in the right direction." We listened intently as many recruits played down the consequences of the shake-up: "There was a bit of a tremor from it, but it was never going to affect trainees... it doesn't even get mentioned," they told us. And yet, just like pulling off a plaster, short and sharp might be the best way, but it's going to sting afterwards. It sounds as if the Birmingham trainees agree. Here, the effects of the restructuring were deemed to be "the most painful." "It was a bit shocking," one source mused; "there was such an altered mood and it was a bit like walking into the middle of an argument." From another, we heard that "the fact that it was so aggressive and large means it's not going to happen regularly. It was a one-off and the balance is now correct in terms of partners and fee earners."

Prior to the cuts the financials weren't looking too healthy – in 2005/06 Cobbetts announced average partner profits of just £190,000. This figure increased to £240,000 for 2006/07. The other big news circulating around the offices is the opening of a corporate practice in London spearheaded by a couple of partners swiped from mid-sized Holborn firm Wedlake Bell. *"It's not to compete with the London market; it's a base to advertise us and the work will be done in the regional offices,"* clarified one trainee. *"I don't think it takes away from the regional firm idea."*

auntie's new home

With all these big-picture changes, we wondered what was shifting down at trainee level. Reassuringly little it seems. The scheme still follows a classic four-seat model that is, in theory, free of compulsory elements. In practice, it is almost *"a given"* that recruits take one property seat and one corporate seat. To be more specific, *"in Manchester it's quite property driven, but in Birmingham it's corporate driven, so a few people there have avoided doing a property seat."* The property department is large – particularly so in Manchester – and generates around a third of the firm's income. Its client roster includes the likes of H3G, Orange and Matalan. It also acts for many public sector clients, with the Metropolitan Borough Councils of Bury, Oldham, Rochdale and Stockport all regular customers. Those trainees who don't spend a seat in commercial property might end up in one of the *"different manifestations of property,"* such as construction, property finance, property litigation or planning. Some trainees do two property seats, though this is not always through choice. *"Some people weren't too happy about it,"* revealed a source, although most understood that *"if you have done your research, you will know property is a big thing. If you didn't know, then you were not researching properly."*

The good news is that *"there is a genuine role for trainees in property, be it proof-reading, drafting leases and tenancies, or going to client meetings – it's a good opportunity to get heavily involved."* In the planning department, trainees prepare bundles for inquiries and draft appeal applications, meanwhile the property development seat involves site meetings where *"you get to meet the client, the surveyors – the whole team."* One of the big projects at the moment is Peel Holdings' Media City: UK development at Salford Quays, which will house the BBC's new HQ. Property litigation brings boundary disputes, landlord and tenant issues and housing authority matters.

see you in court

It's not all property at Cobbetts. A spell in the banking or corporate banking department allows trainees to *"get involved quite quickly."* Regular clients include RBS and Nationwide Building Society. For a dose of client contact, make your way to corporate where *"there is a heck of a lot of it."* *"I was involved in marketing events, such as away days with clients... they aren't just reserved for the senior fee earners."* And there are plenty of opportunities to learn the tricks of the trade within the office: *"In this department they focus on things that will develop your skills rather than just on the volume of work."* Trainees said they'd had a go at drafting share buy-back agreements, board minutes and various ancillary documents as well as a good run at due diligence exercises. The business recovery services seat is a *"bit of a mix between corporate and personal insolvency"* and the work on offer includes court applications, either for the possession and sale of property or for charging orders.

If you're partial to a bit of litigation, then there are plenty of seats that might tempt you. We've already mentioned property litigation, but there is also banking and commercial litigation, the latter being described as *"a brilliant seat."* If you're up for it, you might even get to try a spot of advocacy: *"You're not forced to do it, but the opportunity is there."* Our sources recommend giving it a go as *"it's nice to know how it works, the etiquette and so on – you're always learning."* Other available seats include IP, trusts and probate, employment and construction, as well as secondments, including one to a Brussels law firm.

when the chips are down

Should trainees wish to raise any issues regarding their training, they can do so in one of their many appraisals. The dedicated training officer takes monthly meetings with the trainees and there are also mid-seat appraisals with supervisors and then the training officer and training principal. The same process is repeated again at the end of every seat. This constant contact is indicative of a *"supportive"* atmosphere; *"it certainly isn't intimidating and you never feel like it's wrong to ask questions."* Trainees additionally plugged a fairly attractive work-life balance: we heard of *"the odd 10pm finish,"* but *"the pay-to-hours ratio is unbeatable – it's definitely an early-hours-culture firm, which is good."* Unless you're not a morning person...

Despite all the drama of the past year, trainees insist the atmosphere at the firm remains *"very positive."* Who knows, perhaps their hearts were warmed by newly re-introduced staff bonuses. And yet, this year our sources weren't so quick to paint a picture as rosy as the Cobbetts love-in their predecessors had described. *"There are really great people here, but you do have to go through some expectation adjustment when you start. It's friendly, but let's keep it a bit real – of course people can be rude and dismissive... by and large it's got a nice feel."* Some sources picked up on *"a nanny state-ish feel,"* which irritated them a little as *"we don't necessarily always have freedom to organise our own affairs."* On the whole, however, trainees said they felt *"valued and part of the team."* In 2007, 18 of the 24 qualifiers elected to stay a part of the team, taking jobs with the firm.

When offered a training contract, candidates are asked which office they would like to join. It is rare for someone to not get their preferred choice, although *"it has happened before."* The Manchester staff have recently moved into swish new offices, following in the footsteps of their Brummie and Yorkshire counterparts who had already moved to better addresses. Because of Cobbetts' 'one-virtual office' vision, *"all the offices have a similar corporate branding."* The Manchester lot were suitably impressed with their new surrounds: *"It's brilliant – all modern and gleaming!"* gushed one. The *"sociable"* open-plan set-up was welcomed, but it was the new canteen that got trainees' hearts racing: *"We used to rely on the vending machine, now we have gourmet snacks,"* they told us. The real highlight is 'Fish 'n' Chip Fridays', which *"the chef takes very seriously. We have square plates and the potatoes are chopped in a criss-cross form and there's even some shaping of the mushy peas."*

buddy up

Cobbetts has several sports teams, among them football, cricket and netball. There are regular tournaments played against clients and *"it's easy to get involved... you're not going to have to battle to break any cliques."* The Manchester, Birmingham and Leeds crowds do sometimes get together for a night on the town. As for which town, the trainees seem happy to take it in turns to visit each other. *"We all went to Birmingham a little while ago, and we know the Leeds lot quite well,"* said one Manchester-based recruit. One thing mentioned by trainees in all three offices was the Cobbetts Young Professionals group. It organises various events for younger business contacts and is excellent for developing nascent networking skills. *"It's really good,"* enthused one source; *"we do fun things like beer tasting."* Since the big move, the trainees in Manchester have been seeking a new after-work haunt. *"All Bar*

One was our regular, but now we have to find somewhere new because its no longer a few steps walk across the road... a five-minute walk is too far." The team in Birmingham remain All Bar One devotees, but also regularly go to Metro and Utopia, while the Leeds gang can be found soaking up the atmosphere in the many bars on Call Lane or in the trendy Oracle. If all this socialising sounds appealing, bear in mind that new recruits don't have to wait until their training contract begins to be invited to join in. Cobbetts' buddy scheme pairs current trainees with future recruits and this *"makes you feel part of the firm before you start."*

and finally...

If you want to get a real taste of life as a Cobbetteer then apply for the *"superb"* vacation scheme. To give you an idea of the importance of the placements, we were told that it is now *"a major part of the recruitment process,"* with at least 50% of trainees recruited from the scheme last year and the intention that up to 70% will come off the scheme in future years.

Coffin Mew LLP

the facts

Location: Southampton, Fareham, Gosport, Portsmouth
Number of UK partners/solicitors: 21/48
Total number of trainees: 15
Seats: 6x4 months
Alternative seats: Secondments

Contrary to the morbid connotations inferred, this South Coast firm is definitely not dead in the water. Quite the opposite: a recent rebranding has boosted the firm's profile, giving it a new lease of life as it juggles a well-balanced private client and commercial caseload.

turning over a mew leaf

It may have been established way back in the 1800s, but this regional player has certainly kept up with the times and now boasts the latest legal fashion accessory – LLP status. Having also trimmed the 'Clover' bit off its name this year, the new-look Coffin Mew LLP seems happy with its four-office network and eager to move forwards. This is an exciting time for Coffin Mew: keen to *"boost its image,"* the North Harbour office in Portsmouth is developing and growing, particularly in its corporate and commercial departments.

But what does the firm's relaunch mean for potential applicants? *"It should tell people that we are in line with current thinking and that we are modern and progressive,"* responded trainees. That said, we don't believe the firm is ditching its traditional side, and nor did our sources. *"We are still the same established firm,"* said one, keen to stress that Coffin Mew's private client side remains just as important as its business services. This is evident from the firm's newly jazzed-up website, which clearly shows the two different sides of the firm. Indeed, the general consensus among trainees was that *"one side feeds off the other"* and striking the right balance is one of the most important challenges for the firm. For a taste of both the private client and commercial world, trainees may get the opportunity to go in-house to the high-net-worth department of a major bank. Trainees say: *"There isn't really a divide: we are a regional firm operating a general practice, so you would expect a mix of work and clients."* And a mixed bag is exactly what trainees get... The seat selection process is far from arbitrary. The first seat is usually chosen for a trainee, and thereafter things are decided after a *"relatively comprehensive"* appraisal with the training partner, who is uncannily good at *"knowing the type of things you might enjoy, even if you think you won't."*

going for a dip

"Dipping your feet into many pools" via a six-seat training scheme is an ideal way to work out which area of law you are best suited to. Recruits are encouraged to try both commercial and private client seats *"to get a well-rounded training contract"* and with so many options there's always the possibility of *"discovering a niche little area which might attract you."*

The available seats are spread across three of the four offices, with Gosport being the only one which normally doesn't take trainees. One immediate consequence of the expansion of the North Harbour office is that there are now more opportunities for trainees to go into certain seats. For example, there is now space for two people to do commercial property at the same time. The full seat list is: commercial services, contentious commercial services, commercial property, corporate finance, employment, PI, private client, family and social housing (both contentious and non-contentious). One of the real benefits of a six-seat scheme is that trainees can spend an extra four months in their intended qualification area, and usually this will be their last seat. Beyond this, the only other obvious thing to say about seat allocation is that everyone works in commercial services for at least four months and quite typically will try out two commercial seats.

office space hoppers

The broad-ranging commercial services seat is available in the Southampton and Portsmouth branches. A *"challenging but interesting"* caseload touches on anything from competition to charities law. *"One day I was drafting an assignment of IP, the next day I was reviewing a charity's constitution,"* explained one past occupant. Among the firm's commercial clients are Oxfordshire's Direct Air, Kent's Premier Marine Fuels and local Portsmouth business Cornelia Care Homes. The

commercial property department is another common stop-off point and here trainees can expect to draft leases and other deeds. This department has been working for NatWest and Bank of Scotland on property lending, as well as the University of Portsmouth on various transactions. When working for larger clients such as these, trainees *"tend to assist rather than do things off your own back,"* but they at least get a flavour of the bigger deals.

Client contact is particularly evident in the private client arm of the firm, and on this side of things several trainees told us they'd had a chance to try out claimant personal injury. This seat also involves them in drafting witness statements and liaising with insurance companies. Clinical negligence cases are a big part of the work in the department and one of the best aspects of the seat is tagging along to court when major claims, such as brain injury cases, are settled. It was agreed that although days in court can turn out to be *"really long and taxing,"* the experience is most definitely worth it. Take a seat in the family department and you can expect to help out with everything from *"basic divorces right through to clients who have come to us via corporate work and people with international assets."* The seat can throw you into situations which are *"quite emotionally intense,"* but these are always *"a good test to see how you cope."*

Although Southampton edges ahead in the number of seats on offer in its *"really buzzing"* office, over the two years you will probably experience all three training locations. This is no bad thing, according to our interviewees: *"It's nice to move around and meet different members of the firm."* Whenever possible, the network of offices is viewed as a whole rather than each one working in isolation, and many trainees spoke of *"a desk-hopping culture."* Roughly speaking, the Southampton and Portsmouth offices both have commercial departments and the Fareham branch is home to the private client department. Seating arrangements differ from one office to another and from one department to another, but there looks to be a trend to become *"more open plan – it's more space-efficient and teams work better together."* Decisions like this are *"not imposed from above;"* rather there is a *"democratic"* culture where everyone gets to voice their view. Most trainees drive to work, and although the M27 can have a tendency to get busy, *"it isn't a nightmare commute by any means."* The train links between the cities are not bad and the hours are viewed as reasonable. At worst this means being in at 8.30am (to help out with the post in the Southampton office) and finishing around 6pm.

One recurring theme was the *"high level of interaction with clients."* Be it in probate, commercial litigation or personal injury seats, our sources enthused that they were treated as *"part of the team dealing with the case,"* and had a sense of involvement and importance which many feared they would have missed out on had they headed to a London firm. Said one: *"You're definitely not the forgotten trainee; you are included in pretty much everything, which is great."* Even first-years are expected to knuckle down and get involved in their department's work. *"You're given responsibility from day one,"* they told us, clearly thriving on this expectation. Although it may seem that on occasions *"you're thrown in at the deep end as a sort of test,"* the trainees assured us they never felt left to drown: *"Supervisors keep an eye on you to make sure you're coping OK."* The general feeling is that the level of work is *"spot on and enough to keep you busy,"* but you can always *"probe for more."* Likewise, if you're feeling snowed under you can *"knock on anyone's door anytime."*

c.o.f.f.i...

Coffin Mew declares that it is searching for people who are the perfect fit. But what does this mean? *"Someone who is prepared to get involved,"* said one trainee, perhaps thinking about the many ways in which Coffin Mew is connected with the community. *"Making sure we have a grass-roots connection is very important – it's not just done for PR, it's an integral part of the firm's culture,"* we learned. Trainees have pitched in with various events, such as sponsored quizzes and charity bike rides. And what else? *"You have to be quite open minded,"* a source explained; *"if you came here and said, 'I definitely want corporate and nothing else,' you wouldn't get very far."* *"It's not difficult to fit in, but you have to be prepared to want to,"* trainees said.

A look-a-like client party was held to celebrate the firm's LLP conversion earlier in 2007. The guest list included David Beckham, Marilyn Monroe and Pierce Brosnan, or at least people who looked very very similar: *"It was a lot of fun and helping out gave us a role which was a real ice-breaker,"* explained a source. A pirate-themed party, this one just for staff, was held at the Hampshire Rose Bowl. *"There wasn't one person who didn't dress up – it was such good fun."* The Christmas party (what, another one?) is always a time for people to let their hair down and clearly some manage this with a bit more pizzazz: *"One of the partners went as a cheerleader with a blonde wig and pink skirt."* No names mentioned, but let's just say he is a familiar figure with the trainees. More regularly, trainees meet up for *"hilarious"* curry and karaoke nights, not least to make sure they keep in contact. The current group makes an effort to sample the scenes in Portsmouth, Southampton and Fareham: *"We don't stick to one place and we try and find a mutually convenient venue."* When they want to make a night of it, Southampton is chosen as *"it is quality and it has a studenty atmosphere."* Favourite venues are Varsity, Mono and Orange Rooms.

and finally...

Trainees emphasise that Coffin Mew is a firm that tries to retain people on qualification. Previous retention figures confirm this, although in 2007 the numbers slipped slightly, with two out of five taking jobs at the firm. *"Go to an open day"* is advice to be heeded as *"many trainees are recruited from the scheme."*

Collyer Bristow LLP

the facts
Location: London
Number of UK partners/solicitors: 30/21
Total number of trainees: 6
Seats: 4x6 months
Alternative seats: None
Extras: Pro bono – CAB

An undoubtedly classy outfit, Collyer Bristow is well aware of its strengths and *"is constantly looking to improve and develop."* The firm is never going to rival the City giants in terms of the quality and size of its corporate work, but if you're looking for a smaller employer that's a dab hand at litigation and has the added bonus of some famous clients then you'll want to read on.

just do it

Established over 250 years ago, the outward appearances of this firm plays up its traditional side. Yet behind the façade of its Georgian townhouse in Bedford Row lies a firm with several fingers in the media pie and a whole host of other interesting clients. It has a strong con-

tentious leaning but is proud of its flourishing corporate practice, and in particular its developing AIM expertise.

Among the firm's recent work highlights are the negotiation and commissioning of song writing and soundtrack agreements for the Walt Disney film *The Prestige*, Paramount Pictures' film *Four Brothers* and Sony Pictures' most recent James Bond flick, *Casino Royale*. Sports law and clients are also high on the agenda. Knocking at the door – golfer Ernie Els, double Olympic gold-medallist Ben Ainslie, long-distance swimmer Lewis Pugh and a string of boxers, football players and motor sports folk. The lawyers have advised NIKE on several sponsorship agreements, among them the company's collaboration with Midnight Madness and Limelight in relation to the subsequently named NIKE Midnight Madness Basketball Event and Tour in 2006. Among the other matters that have kept the sports lawyers busy are the international broadcast rights agreement for the 2010 Delhi Commonwealth Games and the dispute between Leeds United FC and Brighton & Hove Albion FC relating to the payment of compensation for footballer Damien Harding. Having such glamorous clients and work is all well and good but the firm does worry that students might become so dazzled by the bright lights that they ignore the fact that sports and entertainment are merely strands of the firm's practice. Accordingly we must emphasise all the other areas in which it works.

CB is pushing its corporate team to bigger and better things. One of the deals of which it is most proud was AIM-listed Inspace plc's acquisition of two companies from Willmott Dixon for £64.5m. The team also advised the vendor in the management buyout of Rope & Marine Services Ltd, a leading agent and stockist for high-quality lifting equipment. Other corporate department clients include Brazil's TAM Airlines and brewer

Fuller Smith & Turner plc. Litigation is another expanding area for the firm. Lawyers in this department have been advising the defendant in a case that involves elements of civil conspiracy as well as the question of whether a foreign government has the ability to sue in this country. The firm, on behalf of its client, has obtained an order to strike out the claim, which has been upheld by the Court of Appeal. All pretty exciting stuff in our opinion!

Then there is the highly esteemed private client team, which benefits from the loyal relationships with the great and the good. Unfortunately we can't name names; suffice to say some of them are phenomenally wealthy. The team is known to specialise in family businesses, offshore trusts or other complex asset structures, high-value divorce cases that involve an international element, private Children's Act disputes and, increasingly, pre-nuptial agreements. The firm recently illustrated its commitment to this practice area by appointing John Saner, the head of the private client team, as senior partner. Furthermore, it has invested in a well-placed international office in Geneva to solicit the business of wealthy individuals resident there. The office is also useful for the sports lawyers as it gives them easy access to Swiss-based bodies such as FIFA. And as if two reasons weren't enough, the Geneva branch further supports the firm's link with one of its biggest clients, multinational tobacco company Philip Morris International.

a consensus democracy

Back at the Bedford Row office, after the first seat, allocation is left up to trainees. "*We talk amongst ourselves and after we have worked out what we want to do and a way of doing it, we check with the firm to see if they are happy with it. There are some departments that prefer to have a second-year trainee, but otherwise it is fairly open and very flexible.*" The choices are: family, private client, coco, dispute resolution (incorporating employment, insolvency and IP) and property.

By and large, our interviewees were thrilled with the quality of their training, telling us it achieved the correct balance between nurturing them and giving them responsibility. "*I have been to lots of client meetings and I always feel involved in the meeting and in the case. They make sure that they keep you in the loop,*" reported one. Trainees seem to be able to co-ordinate the process to their advantage, due to the way the supervision is structured. "*Rather than a single supervisor, we have an overall mentor, a department mentor and a room mentor, so we get work from all the partners in our current department.*" While "*there will always be a partner to whom you are just a photocopier, you soon learn which partners to ask for work.*" In the litigation seat, trainees also get the opportunity to do agency work on behalf of other firms of solicitors, an activity that enables them to develop advocacy skills at district judge appointments in the county courts.

remember me?

Among their work highlights, our sources had contributed to the inquest into the death of a soldier in Iraq and been before the Privy Council with the firm's pro bono consultant to handle death row appeals from the Caribbean. Trainees' average hours are incredibly decent – 9.30am to 5.30pm is not abnormal. The fact that the firm went on a drive to encourage employees to take their lunch break rather than work through it, makes us take more seriously assurances that "*it wouldn't be frowned upon if you stuck to the set hours as long as you do your work and do it well.*" Naturally there are times when late working is required, but it is certainly not standard practice. One area in which the firm does fall down is its appraisal system, which is... "*a good question,*" according to one source. *"We are supposed to have appraisals every three months – in the middle of the seat and again at the end – but this is a bit shaky. We are all trying to get on top of it at the moment."* The only other area trainees suggested could be improved was the level of communication between the firm and its future joiners. *"Two years is a long time not to hear anything... at one point I thought the training contract must have been withdrawn,"* cautioned one interviewee. On this point the firm vows to do better.

noblesse oblige

Trainees are usually drawn to Collyer Bristow because of a belief that they will *"thrive in a smaller and more personal environment, where people have different and varied interests and are seen as individuals rather than as an employee or a product."* Other than this, it's hard to pin down a type at this slightly quirky outfit. If we were to isolate a common factor then the strength of their various extracurricular interests would have to be it. In spite of the differences in the nature of the pursuits, *"everybody seems to have done interesting things in their past."* Indeed, a quick look at the trainee profiles on the firm's website confirms this statement, revealing someone who once appeared on *They Think Its All Over* in the 'Feel the Sportsman' round, a former TV producer and the founder of a motivational company in South Africa. Having hired such an interesting bunch of trainees, the firm is *"keen to encourage us to continue with our individual pursuits and interests and is open to new suggestions."* For example, a running club has just been set up to complement the existing netball and football teams. Meanwhile, the CB social committee is kept busy organising theatre trips, quizzes and, most recently, a Jack the Ripper tour. There are the requisite Christmas and summer parties, the former being a themed affair and the latter an informal barbecue at which trainees can kick back and get to know the other staff. Perhaps the most pointed evidence of the firm's continuing attitude of noblesse oblige is the fact that once a month the partners take turns to put their credit card behind the bar of a different pub for the rest of the staff to abuse.

Further evidence of the charming individuality of the firm can be found in the fact that it has turned the ground floor of its office into an art gallery which has regularly changing exhibitions, from contemporary Russian art to shows of wooden, Brazilian sculptures. The trainees are tasked with keeping charge of the sales desk at the openings of these exhibitions and, at Christmas, the proceeds are donated to charity.

and finally...

This old London outfit has a lot on offer for anyone looking to sidestep the factory firms in the EC postcodes. As with other employers of this size, the obvious downside is that opportunities for trainees to remain with the firm on qualification are not always abundant and entirely dependent on which departments are in need of fresh talent. Accordingly, we're pleased to announce that 2007 was a pretty good year and two of the three qualifiers stepped into NQ positions, going into property and dispute resolution/insolvency.

Cripps Harries Hall LLP

the facts
Location: Tunbridge Wells, London
Number of UK partners/solicitors: 41/50
Total number of trainees: 14
Seats: Commonly five of varying length
Alternative seats: None

The genteel little Kent town of Royal Tunbridge Wells is used to people searching for a remedy for their troubles. In the early 17th Century, suffering nobleman Lord North drank the water from the town's spring and was instantly cured of his maladies. Word spread quickly and the town became a Mecca for Georgian fashionistas as well as those with persistent indigestion and gouty feet. And then, in 1852, when Cripps Harries Hall set up in business, the prosperous folk of the South East had another good reason to come to town – the quest for legal remedies.

don't go changing

Some 250 years on and Cripps still has a flourishing private client practice. What's more it has also achieved success in many commercial areas of practice, particularly commercial property, which is dubbed the firm's *"biggest money-spinner."* Turnover for the whole firm in 2006/07 was a healthy £17.6m, up 12% on the previous year. The property group increased its income by nearly 50%. Now, don't go thinking property is taking over – at one of the regular 'Ten Year Vision' seminars held to ensure that staff understand what the partners want to achieve, trainees learned that one of the central aims is *"to maintain the balance between private client and commercial work."* Having gone through a strategic reorganisation in 2005, Cripps is now divided into eight groups, including 'services for individuals', 'public sector' and 'property developers and residential investors'. Aside from its real estate capabilities, the firm is a strong regional player in agriculture and rural affairs, charities law and construction, and possesses a skilled litigation department that is particularly hot in property-related disputes. Furthermore, its Kent location sees it handling inward investment deals from France. This all makes for an interesting training contract in which recruits can expect to take five or six seats.

With *"loads of departments to choose from"* the scheme is ideal for those who arrive with no clue about the area of law into which they might eventually want to qualify. *"I think it makes you more*

well-rounded," said one; *"the firm isn't too heavily swayed one way or the other."* And it sounds like the current bunch haven't been shy about letting the firm know their feelings on this matter. *"It's great,"* one told us; *"I said to HR, 'Don't ever change it!'"* The entire seat plan is decided for each person before their contract commences: *"We were asked to express preferences and then we got sent our programme of six seats."* It might sound rigid but apparently it's not. Trainees describe the system as *"flexible"* and stress that the firm *"tries to fit you in and allow your preferences."*

la ola

Property is a big deal at the firm and its client portfolio in this area is impressive. On the commercial side, the roster includes the likes of Land Securities and Wagamama plus government departments and agencies such as the CPS, HM Revenue and Customs and the Home Office. A unique feature of Cripps' work is its 'Mexican Wave' collaboration with City firm Lovells. To summarise, Lovells outsources some of its lower value work for its lucrative client Prudential Property Investment Managers. The arrangement has obviously been a rewarding one for all parties as it has spurred another big City player – Herbert Smith – to jump on the bandwagon. Other property seat options include residential conveyancing, estates and farms and property dispute resolution. Trainee tasks range from research into land law, drafting title reports and making site visits in the farms and estates seat, to drafting leases and dealing with agents in commercial property. In the property litigation seat in particular, trainees *"really get into the nitty gritty of land law."*

Although property may be Cripps' golden boy, trainees still shimmered with enthusiasm about the other seats available. The contentious seats on offer include specialist dispute resolution (personal injury claims and clinical negligence) and commercial litigation, where recruits assist with a lot of debt recovery claims. In the family seat, tasks include going to court to take notes and preparing bundles. Most importantly, there is a good amount of client contact in the family seat: *"I loved dealing with the clients, although I didn't enjoy the trek up to London to go to court,"* said one past occupant of the seat. If dealing with clients is your thing, then ask for a seat in private client. Here, responsibilities include drafting wills and making attendance notes at client meetings. *"They make good use of you,"* said one source who had thrived on the client contact, *"and it helps motivate you if you know the person you are working for."* In this seat *"you are given a lot of responsibility"* and the lawyers are *"sticklers for procedure and accuracy."* Trainees put this down to the fact that they are dealing with *"wealthy clients who expect a certain standard of service."* In an employment seat you may get *"chucked in at the deep end,"* but this doesn't put off trainees. They get to experience the thrill of attending tribunals, which makes up for some of the more administrative chores back in the office. Because the department receives instructions from *"a real range of clients – higher scale employees as well as big employers"* – they can see the practice area from both sides of the fence. Other available seats are corporate and construction. In most seats supervisors adhere to a system of monthly reviews. These are *"normally fairly quick"* as people commonly *"give you feedback as you go along."*

mo money mo problems

So what is it about Royal Tunbridge Wells, and indeed Cripps Harries Hall, that attracted the current intake? One trainee told us in no uncertain terms: *"It's a straightforward choice between lifestyle and money."* Most of the people we chatted to were from the local area, with many growing up either in Tunbridge Wells or relatively near it. Several of them told us they weren't interested in *"the kudos and money associated with London firms,"* but what if you are? Tunbridge Wells, as lovely as it might be, is not the right place for everyone. *"You don't have your gym or your Costa downstairs; we're not like a London firm,"* said one source. From the sound of it, Cripps trainees believe there's a clear choice to be made. Either head to the City, endure London Underground and spend your days toiling by the photocopier *"doing crazy hours,"* or enjoy a gentle stroll into work past lovely Georgian architecture, *"enjoy more responsibility than trainees at bigger firms"* and *"don't stay until a ridiculous time every night."* If you opt for the latter then be prepared to make do on a far lower wage. *"It's a lot less than I expected, and it is quite an expensive area to live in,"* they typically moaned. There has been a meaningful salary rise in 2007, which may make things slightly easier for trainees. To be clear: Cripps' small London outpost plays no part in the training scheme and is chiefly used as a meeting place for clients.

Although there is much about Cripps that is traditional, it is *"not so in the sense of being stuck in the past."* The atmosphere is described as being *"relaxed but professional"* and the hours are reasonable: *"You're expected to stay and work if you have to, but you're not expected to stay late every day, which is definitely one of the attractions."* Almost all our sources assessed their work-life balance to be *"spot on,"* telling us trainees can expect to be in between 8.30-9am and leave at around 6pm. On the subject of IT and office systems, they told us: *"We are quite advanced and have the same systems that London firms have."*

So there you have it: don't be deceived by Cripps' long and deep roots in Kent. Indeed, trainees were at pains to label this a *"forward-thinking"* firm, citing as evidence the recruitment of a former Barclays bigwig, William Arthur, as a non-executive director. One of his jobs is to attract and retain staff, so it is obvious that Cripps is keen to grow. The firm is also hoping to *"develop its pro bono work as part of its corporate social responsibility,"* so watch this space. One of the key items on the agenda at a recent Ten Year Vision meeting was the idea of relocating the firm. *"They spoke about how we are getting too big for our current offices and how they would like us to move."* This could be no bad thing as staff are currently dispersed across several buildings. *"Ideally they want to stay in Tunbridge Wells,"* our source continued. As did the trainees it seems, as all seven qualifiers in 2007 took jobs with the firm.

horseplay

What with saving on the commute and working sensible hours, trainees presumably have plenty of time to socialise: *"At the start we went out together a hell of a lot, though it has quietened down a bit now,"* confirmed one. Tunbridge Wells has *"a few bars and some really nice restaurants,"* but you're not going to get the *"buzz or the glamour of London."* Cripps' younger generation commonly head for Sankeys, which has *"a nice garden for when it's sunny,"* and then there's the legendary Davinchi's, now running with the name Beluga. *"It used to be absolutely awful"* and after a major refurbishment is still *"very cheesy,"* revealed sources who go there more often than they'd care to admit.

Second-year trainees are in charge of organising end-of-month drinks at different local venues. *"It's a good way to get to know people,"* especially considering the departments are split between several buildings. Other events at Christmas and the annual summer ball are said to be *"great fun."* Trainees play their part in the ball preparations, most recently organising 'A Night at the Races' at the nearby Lingfield racecourse. There is an annual softball match against the partners and if you've a taste for sports you can join in with football, touch rugby, cricket and netball.

and finally...

In the Cripps training scheme, variety combines well with flexibility as to how long trainees stay in each seat. Do heed this trainee's advice though: *"Don't apply just in case you don't get into a London firm; do it because you really want to work here. If you're looking for the fast pace of the City, Cripps isn't for you."*

Dechert LLP

the facts

Location: London
Number of UK partners/solicitors: *37/75*
Total number of trainees: 25
Seats: 6x4 months
Alternative seats: Overseas seats, secondments
Extras: Pro bono – North Kensington Law Centre, RCJ CAB, LawWorks

Back in the 1990s a respected mid-sized London firm called Titmuss Sainer & Webb entered into an alliance with Philadelphia-based Dechert Price & Rhodes. In 2000, the alliance between the two was cemented by a full merger into a single organisation – Dechert. This firm now has over 1,000 lawyers in 17 offices in the USA and five European jurisdictions.

sheikonomics

The English side of the operation has changed measurably. Its once-broad practice profile has shifted such that the office is now best known for its financial services and developing corporate practices. The once-dominant property team has been absorbed into the broader finance and real estate group (FRE), and various lawyers whose work was no longer central to the grand plan for London left the firm altogether. Effectively the London office set about mirroring the corporate and finance-driven model found in the US HQ in Philadelphia.

After having his jail sentence for perjury commuted by President Bush, things are looking up for Lewis 'Scooter' Libby, former managing partner of Dechert's DC office. After a period of falling staff numbers and uncertainty, Dechert's prospects have similarly improved in London and a new, more resolute firm is emerging, although without any sniff of a criminal record. Turnover in London rose by 13% in the last financial year, and the firm boosted its London FRE offering with a lateral hire from Lawrence Graham. The client roster and deal list are showing dramatic improvements. Dechert's hedge fund practice – top-ranked by our parent guide *Chambers UK* – has a list of clients longer than Bao Xishun's arm, including Artemis UK, Troika Russian Fund, Swiss Alpha Fund and the Sturgeon Fund. The firm is also making a name for itself in Islamic finance, recently advising on the first shari'a-compliant private equity vehicle and the LSE listing of a 'sukuk scheme' worth $1bn.

With financial services and corporate work central to business, seats in these departments are to be expected. Each department hosts up to five trainees at a time, whereas teams like IP or employment or tax can take just one at a time.

hedge hugs
The financial services group focuses on the creation and management of vehicles for collective investments by groups of people or companies who want to put their money in specific sectors or projects. *"It is the flagship department and there is a sense of pride in the work that's done there. It's nice being a part of something that has such a good reputation and where you are dealing with the magic circle."* Don't let that faze you; new trainees aren't expected to have any prior knowledge. *"Even though you are at a loss when you first start, you are brought into everything quickly,"* said an old hand reassuringly. Typical trainee tasks include drafting board minutes, co-ordinating

and *"getting the signatures"* for key documents and wading through the obligatory bibling. Deemed to be *"one of the friendlier teams in the firm,"* a typical source said of the department: *"When people are passionate about what they do, that is infectious... even if FS doesn't appeal to you."* Be aware that the days are consistently long but *"they don't drag. When you're in for 13 hours they should, but they don't!"*

The other key department is corporate and a seat here is compulsory. If that bothers you, then go elsewhere. One source hadn't expected to enjoy the seat but was pleasantly surprised: *"It was my best seat and my most approachable supervisor. I started off on AIM listings so I was drafting admission documents and working on verification and checklists for the stock exchange. As the seat went on I was involved in more acquisitions, so then I did due diligence and that sort of thing."* With a handful of trainees in corporate, there is *"good company and solidarity"* to keep them going when things get busy. And busy you will be too. The hours can certainly be tough: *"It was 9am till 8pm generally, and then there were three weeks when I was also in at weekends."* As one trainee put it: *"In FS people work late every night but not all night; in corporate it's reasonable hours until a deal reaches its climax and then it is killer hours."* Given how frequently trainees have to spend the evening in the office, it's no surprise they've become so familiar with the dinner menu of takeaway company Deliverance.

land of the FRE
In FRE, seats are available on both the finance side and the real estate side. A real estate seat feels *"relatively quiet and laid back because it's a relaxed friendly team that's not in the thick of things."* Someone who'd enjoyed real estate told us: *"I got really lucky as I had a residential sale and purchase to do. I did everything from drafting the contract*

and negotiating it until the deal was almost finished. I also helped others with business leases and
did a lot of post-completion matters." Though not
the same force it was a decade ago, the real estate
group acts for very decent clients including John
Lewis, Wagamama, BHS and Waitrose. Unfortunately, the department's fee earners are
reportedly "dropping like flies." In the finance half
of the department there are "the banking people"
who handle "corporate finance and other banking
work." The trainees are all in the same FRE e-mail
group so if one person is busy and needs help
they all get the distress signal. It's up to you
whether you volunteer assistance; some people
are keen to try new work, alternatively "you can
duck and dive the finance work if you want to
avoid it." Our interviews revealed that not everyone enjoyed the banking side of FRE. One
trainee "found it a macho, long-hours culture
where some people would brag about how long they
had worked. There was one associate who did 101
billable hours in a week and people were practically
worshipping him for it." There were also some
complaints about the trainee's role in banking: "I
did a lot of standing at the photocopier and proof-
reading," grumbled a source.

Everyone agreed that the litigation department had been quiet when they sat there. To be
honest, most had little interest in this side of legal
practice. "The team has contracted so much and it
is now a combined litigation/employment department with property litigation included there, too.
The work levels are very unpredictable... when I
was there it was as if some people hadn't done any
billable hours for months." With no documents
for trainees to bundle and paginate into the wee
hours, they are free to attend client meetings,
have a stab at drafting letters and carry out
research. The employment team is well regarded
and, when it has two trainees to share the proofing, copying, bundling and billing, the seat can
be excellent. When there is just one, these

"trainee jobs" must be fitted in around better
tasks such as drafting pleadings and instructions
to counsel, negotiating compromise agreements
between employers and departing employees
and attending tribunals. The clients benefiting
from all this include Saatchi & Saatchi and
Freeport Leisure.

The other seat options are EU/competition in
Brussels and secondments to the High Court and
the BBC.

greed is good

At the start of their contract, trainees are flown out
to Philadelphia for a "very organised" orientation
event with the 90-plus new associates from other
offices. The trip helps trainees realise they are "a
part of something quite huge," and while they're
away they agree seat allocation for the first of the
six four-month seats among themselves. "The second years had already picked their seats so we got the
remainder" – mostly corporate and FS last year. It
matters little whether they get a preferred seat so
early on as the six-seat system allows ample
opportunity to sample what Dechert has to offer.

Years ago it may have been a traditional kind
of place, but today this is no Little Britain: "You
will hear various accents – there are a lot of Americans here." Decisions are made in Philadelphia,
and as a daily reminder of where the seat of power
lies, "even the IT help desk is in Philadelphia." The
American influence has had a big impact on
salaries. "Recently people have started talking
about bonuses and target hours more – we are getting more American-style rewards and we are
becoming more commercial with it," a source concluded. This equates to higher than magic circle
rates of pay in some departments. We heard that
after a recent rise in trainee salaries, the firm
upped the numbers still further on the back of an
e-mail sent from a ballsy trainee who said the
salaries weren't high enough. We hope the others
bought that trainee a few drinks!

While Dechert may have become leaner, slicker and more profitable, not everyone we spoke to liked the new-look firm. *"There have been massive changes and it's a shame because largely it's a lot of the things I like that have gone or are going. The traditional English law firm culture is rapidly making way for an outpost of a hard-nosed American law firm."* Another source was less emotional about the changes, aware that they will mean little to future joiners: *"It is changing the way it recruits. At the stage I was recruited it was a more rounded firm, and that's why they lost so many qualifiers last year. Now that they are telling students this is a financial services and corporate firm, you are going to get people who are really interested in that work."* In 2007, six of the nine qualifiers chose to stay with the firm, taking jobs in corporate, financial services, tax and employment. Non-law graduates should be aware that although Dechert recently upped its LPC maintenance grants to a mouth-watering £10K, the firm doesn't pay anything towards the GDL.

Let's assume you're keen to try Dechert's brand of legal practice. Will Dechert be keen to give you a try? *"Academics clearly are important. I couldn't see them picking a new university; there's a leaning towards really top-end universities,"* concluded a current trainee. Another agreed: *"There are a lot of Oxbridge people here."* The firm occupies three floors of a building near Ludgate Hill overlooking the Thames... *"well, you can see the river from one side of the office if you squash your face against the window."* Cos Bar is a regular hangout for Friday drinks. An annual summer party has replaced the Christmas party, and the summer is also a time for a visit from about 70 interns from the USA. It's a week of dinners and theatre trips and last year there was a big party at Madam Tussauds. At Christmas the highlight is the 'associates party', which in actual fact is open to all at the firm except partners. A good job, too – it sounds like a lively event.

and finally...

Dechert's transformation into a US-style operation in London is only one part of the story. Of greater importance is the need to match your practice preferences to what it has to offer and make sure you can handle the hours. Get that part of the equation right and it's a great choice.

Denton Wilde Sapte

the facts

Location: London, Milton Keynes
Number of UK partners/solicitors: 134/324
Total number of trainees: 72
Seats: 4x6 months
Alternative seats: Overseas seats, secondments
Extras: Pro bono – incl. PopLaw, The Prince's Youth Business Trust; language training

City firm Denton Wilde Sapte has emerged from early noughties traumas, steadied itself and made important lifestyle changes. It is slimmer, more wary, uses its energies carefully and certainly isn't about to run the legal equivalent of a 100-metre sprint anytime soon. It is placing its trust in a newly streamlined international network, a sector-based approach to work and a reliable name for finance, energy, transport and real estate.

the road to recovery

For those who only know the modern DWS, the merger of Denton Hall with Wilde Sapte in 2000 is *"ancient history"* and they have *"a real sense that the firm is in a position to look forward to exciting times."* That said, we feel it is important to mention that there have been problems in the recent past, if only because it makes it easier to understand the make up and priorities of the firm today. In short, a couple of years after the union of energy, media and real estate firm Denton Hall with banking bods Wilde Sapte there was a period

aspirational focused international
high profile **supportive** challenging
friendly growing award winning

Interested?

Denton Wilde Sapte is a commercial law firm with over 700 lawyers and a network of offices in the UK, Europe, Middle East, Africa and the CIS. This gives us the scale and reach to secure some of the best instructions. With them come the best opportunities for our people. As a trainee, we'll give you as much responsibility as you can handle. You'll have direct access to partners and will work with the law – and with clients – in real business situations.

To find out more about our training contracts and vacation schemes, and how to apply, visit:
www.dentonwildesapte.com/graduates

DentonWildeSapte...

of significant lawyer and support staff redundancies and resignations and certain overseas offices were abandoned. The past two years have seen the firm regroup around sector specialisms and reshape its international presence such that its efforts are now centred around four key industry groups: financial institutions; real estate and retail; energy, transport and infrastructure; and technology, media and telecommunications (TMT). Under this approach, *"the focus is very much on generating new business though relationships across sectors."* Hard evidence for one trainee was *"the time in corporate when I was working on a transaction involving the purchase of a wind farm and we were able to bring in the expertise of some of the best energy lawyers in the City."* Indeed, the energy, transport and infrastructure group is performing excellently. Regaining its place on Royal Dutch Shell's international panel this year and acting for EDF Energy, RWE npower and British Energy, it is also admired in the areas of renewables, nuclear power and energy trading.

This sector strength has allowed the firm to gain a real foothold in developing economies and the Middle East. Close associations with firms in Botswana, Ghana, Tanzania, Uganda and Zambia have brought in *"lots of chocolate and coffee work,"* while *"following the scent of oil and gas"* has resulted in energy and infrastructure instructions in Dubai, Russia, Kazakhstan and Uzbekistan. In turn these forays have generated work for the financial institutions group, whose lawyers this year advised KazakhGold on its first high yield bond issue, worth £105m. TMT, interestingly, is generating income in the Dubai office: for example, the Dubai and London teams combined to work for Emirates Integrated Telecommunication Company, which is owned by the Dubai royal family. Back in the UK, Nokia, Virgin and the Office of the Deputy Prime Minister instruct the TMT team. Also in the UK, energy, transport and infrastructure lawyers have been acting for the Ministry of Defence this year, on discussions with Devonport Management regarding contracts for maritime facilities and related agreements with BAE Systems on fixed-wing aircraft. Stagecoach and Laing Rail are also DWS clients and the firm had cause to celebrate in 2007 when it was appointed as sole adviser to the UK's largest rail company, Northern Rail. Over in the real estate and retail division, lawyers perform well across planning, retail and development matters and have been instructed on the regeneration of Brent Cross-Cricklewood, a development valued at more than £3bn.

banking on finance

Having steadied the ship and allowed strengths to flourish, the sector approach is clearly working, but trainees were aware that recent progress is still somewhat uneven: *"There's a sense that we're being outperformed by contemporaries in some areas,"* one source admitted, *"and that leads to a determination to compete more consistently."* Despite generating nearly 40% of the revenue last year, financial institutions is the sector perceived to be punching below its weight. That said, DWS is impressive on insolvency matters, having advised on the Federal-Mogul restructuring and edged out rival Ashurst to gain the lead role advising lenders on the £180m restructuring of Focus DIY. DWS has also been ahead of the pack for Islamic finance, with partners advising Barclays, Credit Suisse and National Bank of Abu Dhabi on a landmark $2.5bn financing of Aldar Properties, involving the first Islamic Bond in 2007. Despite having lost a key Dubai lawyer to Linklaters, this capability should continue to serve the firm well. More broadly, with seven partner promotions into banking and finance in 2006 and a further four made up in banking and corporate in 2007, the firm is clearly determined to bump up profitability and performance in this area.

Overcoming adversity *"has bred a stronger sense of cohesion and identity,"* together with *"an urgency to improve and increase profits."* That last comment is particularly telling. DWS has now stabilised at the size of pre-merger Denton Hall, but with vastly higher partner profits. In other words, *"it seems we've got the fundamentals secure and now want to get as profitable as possible, get every department hitting budget and then do things on our own terms."* Consequently, the *"whispers of merger with a US firm"* that *"are only ever responded to in terms of denial"* seem likely to remain whispers, at least so far as trainees are concerned. *"Merger is the way to grow substantially in a mature legal market and the message we get is that the firm doesn't want to merge as a defensive measure."*

managing expectations

In terms of seats, *"it is an unusual person who doesn't do real estate and a finance seat, normally both in the first year."* Apparently, *"HR has to spend a lot of time persuading people to go into banking seats"* and one source even remarked how *"it amazes me why people choose a mainstream finance and real estate firm if they're not interested in those areas."* Under the broad finance banner there are seats in asset finance; trade and project finance; corporate lending and reconstruction; financial markets and regulation; and structured finance. The other seat options are energy and infrastructure, tax, competition, employment and pensions, dispute resolution, TMT, corporate and, of course, real estate. As securing *"a scarce seat like tax can be quite difficult,"* sources advise that *"a little compliance at a key moment can smooth the way later on."* Similarly, there is *"some stiff competition"* for regular overseas seats in Paris, Istanbul, Moscow, Dubai, Muscat or Almaty. A few opportunities also arise with allied firms, although none so far in Africa, and secondments to clients in the energy and banking sectors are readily available in the UK. Basically, arrive with the right expectations and don't expect to niche your way through training. You should also be aware that the number and type of seats available mirror the qualification jobs, and the firm's recent poor record for retention is not unconnected to this fact. *"This year and last year there were jobs available for everyone who wanted to stay, including overseas jobs, but not necessarily in the areas people wanted,"* explained a source. In 2007, a much healthier 26 of the 32 qualifiers accepted jobs, going into a variety of departments. Three of the qualifiers will actually be working in Dubai and Muscat for a year before returning to London.

Trainees are satisfied with the *"effort put into training"* and mid and end-of-seat feedback sessions do their job. Supervisors additionally *"appraise you as you go"* and are admired for being *"quick to let you know when you've ballsed up and quick to forgive you if you do."* Beyond these constants, trainee life is *"dependent on the seat,"* so that *"much more is expected of you in terms of accuracy and speed as a fourth seater, even though a first and fourth seater in banking, say, would do very similar work."* Consequently, a *"very intense"* seat in banking will involve *"large deals early on,"* *"a steep learning curve,"* *"document-heavy work"* and *"engaging with overseas clients."* Time in real estate will on the one hand involve *"assisting on major strategic issues for huge retail clients with vast portfolios"* and by contrast *"handling 30-40 licences to assign or permissions to make alterations."* The *"academic slant"* of pensions might be balanced by the *"need to understand the market when looking after the pensions account of a company in administration,"* just as a financial markets seat with its *"commercially focused clientele"* might also require a *"surprising amount of quite complex research."* And with *"criminal court hearings and bundling"* in insolvency litigation, *"drafting verification notes and essentially glorified* filing" in corporate, *"very precise research and tribunal attendance"* in employment and *"learning to entertain a variety of commercial perspectives"* in dispute resolution, each sector and team obviously has its specific charms and drawbacks.

puzzle me this...

Denton's Fleet Place office on the fringes of the City boasts *"all the features you'd expect"* plus *"a very good canteen."* Yet it's the people inside that really caught trainees' imaginations: *"There are a lot of independent thinkers"* and *"well-rounded individuals with a lot to say for themselves."* At trainee level this is reflected in the decent variety of good universities from which trainees come and the *"pronounced international flavour"* of the group. Sources also pointed to *"the number of people who've done different things or worked in a relevant sector first,"* telling us: *"They really try and develop individuals here;"* *"we work hard but there really is a recognition that people aren't robots."* True, the hours can be as long as anywhere in the City (*"in the core seats you can regularly be working very late"*) but at the same time there are endless after-work activities to get involved with. Teams are kitted out in the firm's trademark orange to take part in everything from dragon boat racing to cricket, sailing to pilates, tennis to football. There's also a music group, a choir, a Christian society and a theatre group that manages the impressive task of staging full-scale shows. And let's not forget all the organised events, parties and drinks evenings, including *"a first and last-week party for trainee leavers and new starters at which awards are given out in categories like 'most likely to make partner' or 'most likely to be late for work.'"* When not at an organised event or working late, many trainees go to some of the pubs around Smithfield... but only if they escape the *"inexplicable"* gravitational pull of *"the dreadful Puzzle pub which is right under our building; we always end up going there for some reason."* It's called laziness.

and finally...

Denton Wilde Sapte has steadfastly worked its way out of a tricky period and looks set for a much brighter future. It will give you breadth of training involving both international and domestic work, but don't forget that you'll have to give those core practices some serious face time.

Dickinson Dees LLP

the facts

Location: Newcastle, Stockton-on-Tees, York
Number of UK partners/solicitors: 78/143
Total number of trainees: 32
Seats: 4x6 months
Alternative seats: Brussels, secondments

So you want to work at a prestigious commercial law firm that gets big-ticket work from blue-chip clients. But you don't fancy an hour's commute into work, you'd like to be able to afford a house nearby, and you don't care much for pollution. Basically, you want a London firm that's nowhere near London. Fortunately for you, especially if you've northern leanings, Dickinson Dees can tick all the right boxes.

geordie giant

Dickinson Dees has had an imposing presence in the Newcastle market for over 200 years. It is the North East's largest independent firm by far, and most of the region's major corporations feature on its client roster. Its breadth of expertise covers pretty much any practice area you could think of, from charities, commercial litigation and construction to corporate finance, commercial property and corporate tax. And those are just the areas beginning with the letter C. If there's a big deal in the region, you can bank on Dickie Dees getting stuck in.

Having conquered the North East, the firm is

chasing work elsewhere – and getting it. Armed with a glowing reputation and the enticing offer of *"City-standard advice at regional fees,"* it is winning over national and international businesses and organisations. On the PFI and projects front, it scored big advising Partnerships for Schools on its national framework to deliver £1.6bn of new schools and academies throughout the UK. In the pharmaceutical sector, it represented Huntsman Petrochemicals in the $813m sale of its UK petrochemicals business to SABIC Petrochemicals. On the transport side, it acted for Thameslink Rail in relation to the transfer scheme made by the Secretary of State for Transport between Thameslink Rail and First Capital Connect. These are just a few examples, picked from a plethora of equally top-notch deals.

A combination of new business growth and existing client needs has led to the opening of a London facility. For now it has no permanent legal staff and is merely a base from which clients located in the South East can be more effectively serviced. Planting a flag in the capital met with approval of trainees, who told us: *"It's really the only way we can compete with the big London firms."* *"In my opinion,"* offered one source, *"we've always needed a London office; it's silly having the amount of work we do in London and not having a base there."* The other big news in 2007 was the opening of a small York branch through a merger with tiny corporate boutique Philip Ashworth & Co.

geordie soul

One consequence of the growing volume of prestigious national work is an increase in hours. Not so much for trainees, but for those a few rungs up the ladder leaving the office in the early evening cannot be taken for granted. Perhaps it's inevitable: you can't expect to take on the London firms without adopting a similar work ethic. A few years ago, the firm was selling itself on the idea that its lawyers could grab high-grade work

while keeping a firm grip on hours. The high-grade work is there, and growing, but *"the firm culture is changing a bit – they expect a higher level of dedication."* If this is giving you pause for thought then listen further to the trainee who said: *"It's still nowhere near City hours, but the working day is getting longer. If I'm going to be working hours that are comparable to London, I'd like the salary to be comparable too."*

Despite this perceived change in attitude, there's no danger of the firm morphing into a City wannabe and shedding its North East character. *"We've got two offices in Newcastle, one in Teesside and one in York. Clearly the North is still home to the firm.... we've still got a Geordie soul."*

As you'd expect from a large firm, there is immense variety when it comes to the seats on offer. Trainees are required to take three of their four postings in the coco, litigation and property groupings, but there is plenty of scope within each. Practice areas include agriculture and rural affairs, banking and finance, charities, urban regeneration, litigation, private client and transport, to name a few. Employment is a popular seat, *"possibly because it's a good mix of preparatory work and court experience."* Construction is another hit. *"I absolutely loved it,"* gushed one trainee; *"the team is really geared towards taking on trainees and giving them a broad range of work. I don't think anyone has disliked being here even if it's not ultimately for them."* Trainees surprised themselves by identifying private client work as a hot seat: *"I just love being immersed in drafting... and because the files are smaller than in other areas you can also see them through from start to finish. It's a lovely team and you get lots of client contact too."* The property seat is undoubtedly the least favoured; *"most people seem to be trying to put it off for as long as they can."* Once you're there though, it's really not so bad: *"Mostly you're working for large residential management companies and there's a lot of development work, purchases,* leases and licences." Even if you're not going to qualify into the department, a property seat doesn't have to be painful. *"It's not really my cup of tea but the team is nice and I'm enjoying myself,"* one source reassured us.

life vest under your seat

As far as responsibility and volume of work go, trainees say the firm gets it bang on. *"What you're given is relative to your level in every seat. To start with there's lots of supervision, and then gradually your leash is loosened, until your last seat where you just ask for help when you need it."* We're not saying you'll never be pushed out of your comfort zone – *"you do have to step up to the mark"* – but you're not left floundering in the deep end of the pool. Well, actually, *"you are a bit – but there's someone standing at the side with a life belt."*

"They put a lot of emphasis on trainee development and really go the whole hog. If you e-mail the training department and say you have a particular interest, or you need a bit of help in an area, they'll have a session on it." For example, when trainees said they were nervous of going up to *"important people"* at business development events, the firm organised a session on networking. Supervisors and partners seem to genuinely want to help; *"they're really good at talking me through any amendments they make to my work, even when I can see they're really busy,"* reported one interviewee. The strong network of support extends to secretaries who *"do all the adminy-type things."*

the proof is in the pudding

The main St Anne's office often gets a ribbing from trainees based in the newer Trinity Gardens building. Trinity houses the private client, financial planning and property lawyers, and *"although fairly similar in layout, it's a bit more spacious. There's a café and our staffroom has windows."* Since when have windows been something to crow about? Another key source of triumph seems to be the fact that Trinity has air conditioning. In our view, the deciding factor is the catering and, here, it seems that Trinity does indeed win. *"They've started this trolley service in the afternoon, with delicious tea and cakes that are impossible to resist."*

Away from Newcastle, trainees can do a family, commercial litigation, property or corporate seat in the Teesside office. The main drawback for most is the distance (*"we're just not used to commuting in the North East"*), but a petrol allowance or a lease car goes some way towards placating reluctant travellers. Trainees say: *"It's very much the same as the Newcastle offices."* And they really do mean the same: *"The same carpet, wallpaper, doors, desks... it's like you're in some parallel universe, it's a bit freaky really."* Teesside's smaller size means *"you get amazing partner exposure and everyone's your best friend within three days of your arrival."* From 2007, the office will recruit two of its own trainees, who will do one seat in Newcastle and three in Teesside. This will leave one seat open to Newcastle trainees.

When the Philip Ashworth merger was announced, there was excitement all round. *"We haven't been down there because we don't have the office space yet, but personally I think it's great. There is significant potential for us to expand there."* Apart from the administrative system, not a lot has changed in the Ashworth office, however it will soon move to new premises (doubtless with the same carpet and wallpaper). The firm will recruit specifically for this office, with trainees likely to do a stint in Newcastle.

For those who want to experience something entirely different, there are two six-week placements at a Brussels law firm. Previously three months long, the trip has been shortened to make it *"more of a possibility for people who couldn't be away for that long."* And it's working. *"We're literally in the process of applying at the moment and there's a lot of interest."*

Be different...

Be yourself...

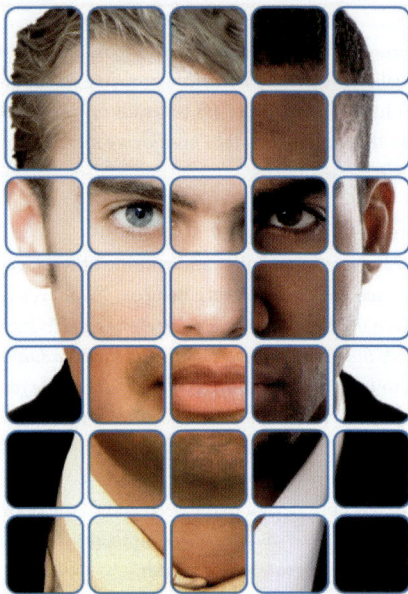

Be part of...

DLA Piper – one of the largest global legal services organisations in the world – and we're still growing! Our impressive client base, combined with the emphasis on high quality service and teamwork, provide a challenging fast paced working environment.

We have offices in Birmingham, Edinburgh, Glasgow, Leeds, Liverpool, London, Manchester and Sheffield as well as 55 international locations in a further 23 countries across Asia, Europe, the Middle East and the US. Our current vision is to be the leading global law firm.

To find out more about our summer vacation placement scheme or our training contracts, please visit our website **www.dlapiper.com**

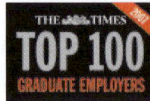

INVESTOR IN PEOPLE

DLA PIPER

out on the toon

The friendly reputation of Northerners is well founded. "*Most Fridays you can find Dickie Dees people in either the Pitcher & Piano or a bar called Stereo. You can never predict where we'll end up after that.*" There are no divides between year groups, departments or offices, "*it's just whoever's about.*" The firm makes serious effort with organised events: "*There's the trainee Christmas meal, your team Christmas meal, the department's Christmas party and then all the client parties.*" The firm-wide dinner dance, held at St James Park in either October or February, is "*a good laugh... it's pretty difficult not to have a good time.*" A Stars in Their Eyes talent contest was revived in 2007 after a couple of years off, and the annual pantomime is always popular. "*They did The Wizard of Oz last year. We were quite sad that they'd already cast it before we joined the firm,*" explained a first-year. Not all events are greeted with the same enthusiasm: "*There has been talk of having an American-style firm picnic, with people bringing their families. I'm hoping that was a joke as frankly I'd rather put pins in my eyes.*"

and finally...

You've got to be a hot candidate to be taken on here at Dickinson Dees. Once your foot is in the door, the chances of staying with the firm on qualification are excellent, although in 2007 only eight of the 12 qualifiers did so. Trainees add just one caveat: "*People will judge you, so from the beginning you should be very aware that you're under the microscope. It's not a constant rat race, but you are aware you're trying to get a job here.*" Their advice is to "*make sure you're on top of your game from the start.*" These are wise words for training contract applicants too.

DLA Piper UK LLP

the facts

Location: Birmingham, Leeds, Liverpool, London, Manchester, Sheffield, Scotland
Number of UK partners/solicitors: 346/793
Total number of trainees: 184 (164 in England)
Seats: 4x6 months
Alternative seats: Overseas seats, secondments
Extras: Pro bono – The Prince's Trust and other regional schemes; language training

DLA Piper is certainly living up to its reputation for being "*ambitious, driven and focused.*" This Anglo-American has 3,400 lawyers in 64 offices spanning 25 countries – a far cry from its humble origins as a Sheffield practice with big ideas.

fly me to the moon

After two decades of mergers – originally just in the UK – DLA entered into a tripartite liaison with US firms Piper Rudnick and Gray Cary Ware & Freidenrich. This tie-up seems to be maturing well. Expanding eastwards, the recent acquisition of 80 lawyers from the CIS network of Ernst & Young Law has enhanced the combined firm's Moscow presence and brought St Petersburg, Tbilisi and Kiev into the fold. In Western Europe, it recently poached a banking and finance team from German firm Luther Menold as part of a plan to swell its 20-strong department to 50 within three years. Meanwhile, in Italy a six-lawyer, Milan-based public law team joined from Orrick. Fledgling offices are sprouting up across continents, including those in Warsaw, Munich, Oman and Phoenix. Far from static in the UK, the firm raided Denton Wilde Sapte for 40 TMT lawyers and snagged the head of DWS' Africa department a couple of years ago. It is also extending its tentacles down under and, in November 2006, the antipodean Phillips Fox entered into an exclusive alliance with DLA Piper.

The firm's aggressive exponential growth is surprising even for those within, as one trainee exclaimed: *"DLA is planning to take over the world!"* Another *"wouldn't dare to guess"* how big the firm would be in a few years time, while some trainees predicted mere organic growth and expected the next few years to be a period of consolidation. It all equates to more opportunities for trainees to get involved in international work and, as the various mergers bed down, this is likely to filter out beyond London to the other UK regional offices. From September 2007, trainees from all UK offices have the opportunity to go on secondment to Hong Kong, Moscow, Singapore and Dubai, as advertised in the 2007 brochure: "Be local, go global." There is also the chance to socialise with counterparts worldwide on the induction course, as *"they bring over trainees from everywhere from Bosnia-Herzegovina to Hong Kong and we all get together somewhere exotic like Milton Keynes…"*

With exciting developments going on around the world, you'd be forgiven for wondering if the UK regional offices might be feeling a little neglected, or at least sidelined. True the firm is keen to pump up its London presence to compete with the big boys of the City, but in terms of work, it is not just London that gets the headline-grabbing deals. Liverpool and Manchester's corporate teams recently advised on the £160m buyout of fashion brand Good Hair Day. In the Leeds office the finance and projects, real estate and employment groups advised three Peterborough NHS trusts on a £446m PFI healthcare project, while the technology, media and communications (TMC) department was involved in the £2.3bn national NHS IT procurement project. Multi-departmental deal highlights for the Manchester office include acting for the Bank of Scotland-led consortium on the £1bn-plus acquisition of McCarthy & Stone and the £351m acquisition of the House of Fraser Group.

a whistle-stop tour

What you might gather from the following whistle-stop tour of the seats, departments and offices is that there is no uniform training experience for us to describe. What we can say is that overall our sources were pretty happy with their lot and keen to encourage others to look further at the firm.

While there are no compulsory seats, a corporate seat in any office will land you *"in at the deep end."* This seat elicits every type of reaction, from *"popular"* to *"horrible."* Expect to work *"relentless, gruelling, long hours,"* but also know that full all-nighters are *"few and far between"* and there is *"certainly no photocopying."* Meanwhile, in banking you may be involved in post-completion work and be taken out for celebratory lunches at fancy London restaurants, where *"the champagne is popped and everyone's smiling."* The offices in Yorkshire and the North West are renowned for their prowess in real estate. In the Sheffield office, it is almost inevitable that you will do a real estate seat in your first year, as this is one of the office's largest departments. Tasks might include assisting on complicated lease transactions and making site visits. Employment seats are *"incredibly popular"* and give trainees the opportunity to work on their own cases for employers, attend tribunals, prepare presentations and legal updates and generally experience plenty of client contact. A seat in the regulatory department will bring a wide range of work, including white-collar crime and tax investigations, as well some US-sourced issues. A TMC seat can include anything from IP and the occasional contact with a celebrity, to assisting on IT outsourcings and playing a small part in a large public sector project. In an insurance seat you might handle road traffic accidents and employers' liability claims and in a general commercial litigation seat you may also get to run your own small files.

Experiences of supervision range from being *"wrapped in cotton wool"* to being left to your own devices. All trainees agreed that taking a proactive approach was the way to go: "*If you want responsibility you ask for it – it's very much up to you what you make of your training contract. The more you put into your office, the more you get out of it.*" If you want to do interesting work then "*keep pestering them.*" Trainees are encouraged to let people know what their capacity is and to voice their interests. The only cause for concern seems to be the stressful qualification process, which was described by one trainee as "*extremely fraught*" and by another as "*a bit cloak and dagger.*" Competition to qualify into departments such as TMC, litigation and regulatory is intense, and some of our sources felt the process "*was not open enough.*" Seat changes can also feel a little stressful: "*They generally put you where you want, but on two weeks' notice.*" At least there isn't any office-hopping for seats. Indeed the way to get a change of scene is to get yourself onto a client secondment to the likes of RBS, Barclays, the London Stock Exchange, Carillion and ICI.

the blue squares

DLA Piper likes its slogans, as a quick look at the website demonstrates. Phrases such as "positively charged" pop up on a background of furiously whirling windmills, suffused with a luminous orange glow. Such images are accompanied by the firm's infamous blue-square logo and the ubiquitous catchphrase "everything matters." Among trainees, there are varying degrees of conversion to the DLA brand, from those that are "*true-blue DLA through and through*" to "*those that don't buy into the brainwashing… not brainwashing I mean…you know….*" Trainees are certainly aware of the power of the blue square, as one commented: "*The brand is very central; we're very much told to promote the DLA Way and Visions. I'm happy to do it and think it's important to do.*" Marketing speak is lapped up and regurgitated by many trainees, who talk of the firm "*forging rela-*

tionships and building bridges, not resting on its laurels or coming off the pedal…" Rather amusingly though, even one seeming ideologue admitted that it was pretty hard to keep on top of all the re-branding. At the time of writing there was a "*Mark Rothko type of branding going on – all in different colours and fuzzy edges.*" The benefits were evident: "*I like being able to do PowerPoint presentations in purple and orange, not just blue…*" not to mention the goodie bags of freebies and no longer having "*that long name that no one could remember.*"

earthbound

DLA has recently changed its partnership constitution to allow it to shed underperforming equity partners more easily. However, the firm has also promoted more partners than most UK firms in recent years, and far from people climbing over each other to get to the top, the atmosphere within the firm remains generally supportive and open. Trainees speak of a "*no-blame culture,*" particularly in the regional offices, where if you make a mistake, those in charge will say "*fine, it's gone pear-shaped, let's sort it.*" "*I've never felt out at sea and always been supported,*" said one trainee, echoing the sentiments of many.

Almost everyone we interviewed sang from the same hymn sheet, the constant refrain being that DLA Piper looks to recruit unpretentious people who are "*up for a laugh.*" They don't go for those who are "*too cocky, arrogant or full of themselves.*" Interestingly, not one of the trainees interviewed went to Oxbridge; most were from redbricks and other well-respected universities in the regions in which DLA has offices. To be successful in getting a training contract here, you "*don't have to win all the prizes at university, but you can't be a wallflower either.*" The people who get recruited are "*all-rounders,*" so if you are someone who tends to get involved in a variety of activities, then you're halfway there.

Despite being a global juggernaut, the firm still manages to retain its down-to-earth feel. It has *"a different atmosphere to magic circle firms"* and is described as *"unstuffy, outgoing and full of team spirit,"* a feat that is in no small part down to joint CEO Nigel Knowles. He is *"definitely a very powerful figure and yet is not overwhelming – you can talk with him in the lift as easily as with the people from recruitment or other trainees."* This *"non-hierarchical"* attitude spans the entire country, and trainees say they can *"pop in to partners' rooms and have a chat about the weekend."* Knowles does the rounds of offices throughout the UK, and regional trainees find it reassuring that *"the top brass come up from London to tell you what's going on."* Knowles' rise from a trainee in Sheffield to CEO typifies the firm ethos, and trainees in this office still describe themselves as *"common-sense, plain speaking and northern."* They are proud to be working in the city that spawned the DLA giant, as well as being in a flagship development area in the centre of Sheffield. Local ties are still extremely important to the firm and regular network nights are organised for those three years' qualified and under, giving them the chance to socialise with the young professionals that will grow up to be their clients.

work hard, play hard

A night out at Ha!Ha! followed by breakfast together in the canteen before work is just one of the ways in which Sheffield trainees like to relax. Meanwhile, the Liverpool outfit likes to think of itself as *"even more laid-back and friendly than other offices."* People congregate daily in the canteen, where a sizeable flat screen television is always good for watching the football. The social committee organises barbecues and trips to the races; raucous karaoke might take place at the summer party and people regularly run across the road to Newz. The Liverpool office often works and parties with the Manchester set. Here,

the Pitcher & Piano below the office is *"almost too handy..."* and with *"lovely big steps leading down to the bar,"* it is the perfect place to sit and eat lunch in the summer. New office managing partner Simon Woolley has introduced monthly drinks and dress down days, contributing to a more convivial atmosphere and allowing for further integration between teams. In Birmingham, favourite watering holes include Penny Blacks, Utopia and All Bar One. This year's Brum summer party had a Wild West theme, including a quick-draw game and a casino. It is here that the firm hosts new-starters drinks every summer for those about to join its UK offices. There is a real *"team spirit"* in the Birmingham office and although *"everyone works hard"* there is also an element of *"I'll take a bit longer for lunch if I'm working long hours."* By way of contrast, the Leeds office is *"more work hard, than work hard, play hard."* Our sources suggested that many people are less bothered about socialising and more concerned with getting home. Not to be outdone in the entertainment stakes, examples of outings in the London office include the likes of bowling and cocktails at All Star Lanes. Thursday and Friday nights are big in the City for the *"hardcore,"* with trainees sometimes frequenting the incense and suit-filled Bedouin Bar opposite Smithfield meat market.

mind the gap

If you are applying for a training contract in one of the firm's regional offices then bear in mind that the pay gap between London trainees and their regional counterparts is larger. In 2007, a 19% salary rise for City NQs was matched by a meagre 4% rise in the regions this year and just 3% in Scotland. Salaries are to be reviewed again in January 2008. Reflecting the mood at some other large national firms, some in the regions found what they described as *"the* obscene wages in London" to be "a bone of contention." As one trainee commented: "We're doing London hours for regional pay." Regional trainees also thought that the "friendly banter" between themselves and London was cooling along with the widening pay divide, commenting on some "snobby, snappy" elements in the City office. Meanwhile, London trainees registered a certain amount of "animosity towards London, with the slight feeling of 'them against us.'" Some thought that the movement of trainees down to London on qualification was a good way to remedy this, although bear in mind that the firm likes to keep those that train in the regions in the regions. When recruiting for the regional offices the firm does look for those with ties to the area, be it through going to university or having family nearby. In 2007, the firm did rather well in the retention stakes, keeping 72 of the 80 English-qualifying trainees.

and finally...

"What you see is what you get" with DLA Piper, and that may mean smiling faces, blue sky and Smarties if you are looking at the same brochure we had. The firm's interview process reflects the down-to-earth nature of the firm and "you don't feel so much on trial" as at some other national firms. Doing a vacation scheme is highly recommended if you really want to "get your foot in the door" and "seal the deal." Once you have your training contract, "throw yourself into it, as you don't get if you don't ask." For more information on how well each office performs in its region, and how well the firm performs in different jurisdictions across the world, take a look at our directories on www.chambersandpartners.com.

DMH Stallard

the facts
Location: Brighton, Crawley, London
Number of UK partners/solicitors: 50/51
Total number of trainees: 19
Seats: 4x6 months
Alternative seats: None

With over 360 people working in London, Crawley and Brighton, the DMH Stallard of today bears little resemblance to the high street Brighton firm of 30 years ago. Bursting with ambition, it has transformed itself into one of the largest firms in the South East, billing £23m in 2007.

once upon a time
DMH was a child of the seventies. Born out of the merger of three Sussex firms, it was christened Donne Mileham & Haddock and enjoyed a happy childhood by Brighton's seaside. Twenty years on and keen to expand its horizons, it opened an office in Crawley, near to Gatwick airport, changed its name to a more streetwise DMH and placed increasing emphasis on commercial practice. In 2005, it married (stay with us, here) Stallard Solicitors and boosted its London credentials. If this was a fairy tale we might be inclined to end it at this point with a happily-ever-after, but the DMH Stallard's story is far from over.

Since the 2005 merger, the firm has won some major instructions – and we really mean major. Recently, for example, it advised the management team of Lloyds TSB Registrars in connection with the sale of its businesses and assets to Advent International for a total cash consideration of a cool £550m. Already firmly ensconced in the top 100 UK law firms (as measured by turnover), it has set its sights higher still and aims to be in the top 50 within eight years. So what does DMH Stallard see when it looks in the mirror – a regional firm with a London office or a London firm with a presence in the South East? Trainees believe it's still the former. At least for the moment. *"They seem to be concentrating on the Gatwick hub,"* mused one. *"I think the firm wants to be a leader of this regional economy, with a strong presence in London as well." "Change is certainly afoot,"* added another. *"The London office may soon be comparable in size to the Crawley office and there will be more opportunities to work in London."* Pehaps referring to rumours of another London tie-up, trainees told us: *"It's exciting when we merge – there are new people, new clients and new opportunities."*

DMH Stallard's services can be broken down into five core areas: real estate; corporate; dispute resolution; employment; and residential conveyancing, PI and private client. Trainees are all expected to do one property-related seat, but apart from that *"the firm does its best to put you where you want to go."* With 19 trainees *"it can be a bit of a jigsaw puzzle, fitting people in where they can. But you do pretty much get the opportunity to map out your career."* Moving offices is part of the deal, so expect to do seats in at least two, if not three of the offices. Having nominated a base office, travel expenses are given for commutes elsewhere.

don't feed the animals

If your first seat is employment, consider yourself lucky. *"It's a gentle start because it's such a well-run department; everything is done by the book and you learn how to use all the systems. They invest a lot of time in their trainees."* The team is subdivided into three areas: public sector, City clients and corporate support. The work ranges from tribunal claims to training and policy/procedure updates. Recent cases have involved whistle blowing and claims of race discrimination and victimisation by staff at a nursing home. *"They use trainees for quite a lot of the research, possibly because we're more up-to-date."* By the end of the seat *"you're*

basically functioning as a junior solicitor, preparing witness statements and putting all the documents together." There's a fair bit of client contact, as well as dealing with solicitors on the other side. *"Sometimes the claimants represent themselves, so you're speaking to them as well."*

Commercial property is a common seat. *"You're given two or three files a week and suddenly you've got 40 files to juggle. It can be quite a shock."* It's just as well there's plenty of support. According to one trainee, *"everybody should do this seat; you learn so much and it crosses into a lot of other areas."* On a daily basis trainees might be helping a bank with property finance, dipping into residential conveyancing, or assisting on a landlord and tenant dispute. *"There is an element of filling out boring stamp duty forms, but there's also interesting research. You work with good clients and they don't give you the rubbish stuff."* Recent matters include the property aspects of the £50m stadium for Brighton & Hove Albion FC, advising the London Development Agency on property regeneration issues at Crystal Palace and the acquisition of a zoo.

The London dispute resolution department is big and it has meaty work. There's a fair amount of property litigation – dilapidations, boundary disputes and breaches of restrictive covenants – plus commercial contract and insolvency disputes. *"Speaking to trainees from other firms, I can tell you the experience you gain here is just amazing,"* declared one source. For starters, you get your own files to run, loads of client contact and a supervisor who *"takes you along to absolutely everything."* Somehow one trainee found themselves representing the firm at the directions stage of a multimillion-pound arbitration, when the lawyer on the other side was the Attorney-General of a large African country. 'Nuff said.

A specialist team within the commercial litigation department, the technology and media group proves extremely popular with trainees. If you're lucky enough to land here, you'll be *"advising people about the realities of litigation and whether they want to make an issue of something. You go to a lot of trade shows, which are good fun, looking at whether people are infringing IP rights."* The clients range from big companies to individual inventors, and the team handles defamation claims as well. There is a distinct scientific leaning to the practice and *"all sorts of exciting gadgets lying around that department."*

i can see the sea
There's a lot to like about the Brighton office. Currently in the process of shifting all its commercial capabilities to Crawley, the firm intends to use Brighton as a base for its private client practice. Seats here will therefore include residential conveyancing, PI and trusts, tax and probate. In a PI seat, *"you get given your own workload"* and an excellent supervisor ensures it all runs smoothly. *"You mainly do the low-value claims yourself and then assist your partner on fatalities and clinical negligence. I did go to a couple of court sessions, but it's quite rare for them to go to court."* Whatever seat you're in, it seems Brighton is a great place to be. *"It's about five minutes away from the beach and the client-facing areas are very distinctive – there is an in-house art gallery."* The lawyers' quarters aren't so swish… *"but if I crane my head I can see the sea from my window."*

We couldn't help but wonder if the increasing focus on London and the commercial parts of the firm might leave Brighton out in the cold. Trainees are confident this won't happen. *"We have important clients in Brighton and we still have a huge presence down there. In many ways it's still the head office – the AGM is held there every year. I wouldn't have thought it would feel like it's being forgotten."* In fact, some trainees pointed out a positive side to the new arrangement: *"It will probably have a stronger definition as a private client office, rather* than being a bit of everything. I think it will give it more of an identity in its own right."*

learning to love crawley
There's little doubt that the Crawley office will benefit from the restructuring. *"It's a fairly typical non-descript English town with a Woolworths and a Boots just like everywhere else. Brighton and London are much more exciting,"* one source pronounced. With most workers commuting, people tend to dash off to the station at the end of the day and the social life is best described as *"a work in progress."* But with the additional office space of a newly refurbished Gainsborough House, and the entire litigation team coming together under one roof, it looks like Crawley's on the up. *"Having more people here will improve the atmosphere – already I've noticed more people going out for a quick drink after work."* Some trainees were eager to jump to its defence: *"It's a financial hub, it's growing and it's going to be increasingly important for the firm. People moan about it, but no one really hates it."*

The London office is *"in the heart of the City and the atmosphere is buzzy."* Because it was originally Stallards prior to the merger, *"the look of the building is a bit different,"* and unlike the other offices it's not open plan. With quite a few youngsters, there's a good social scene. *"Anyone who wants to have a few drinks after work does so, from secretaries to partners."* Inter-office cohesion is reasonably good, a fact reflected in the similar hours worked in each office. *"When I joined, I expected to have to work really long hours in the City, but it's not like that at all."* As to what it's really like switching offices for seats, *"the commute can be a bit of a pain, but you know what you're signing up to when you join."*

Chances are the firm will continue to grow, especially if rumours of the appetite for another merger are true. However, trainees reckon some things will always stay the same: *"This firm has a very strong identity and a strong ethos of being business-led."* When it comes to business development, *"we're involved in meetings, we do research and prepare pitch packs. We're thoroughly involved in the background and it makes you aware of the process you have to go through to get new business."* Breakfast seminars, Law Society dinners – *"it's all there for the taking. The more you want to do, the more you can do."* Fancy beach volleyball with a team of bank managers? Look no further!

and finally…

Whatever your background, it sounds as if DMH Stallard is keen to hear from you. Second-careerers will certainly find *"different skills are encouraged and valued."* In the past couple of years, the firm had a lower NQ retention rates than it would have liked and has now *"made a concerted effort to keep everybody."* In 2007, there were more jobs advertised than qualifying trainees and all seven of them chose to stay with the firm.

Dundas & Wilson

the facts

Location: London, Edinburgh, Glasgow
Number of UK partners/solicitors: 82/208
Total number of trainees: 9 in London
Seats: 4x6 months
Alternative seats: Edingburgh, Glasgow, secondments

Up in bonny Scotland Dundas & Wilson has long been a force to be reckoned with. The firm operates in the upper echelons of almost all areas of commercial practice and frequently lands a part in the country's headline deals. For example, it is currently advising South Lanarkshire Council on a £320m PFI project, one of the largest of its kind. So far, so Scottish. But with its London branch gaining momentum, D&W is fast cementing its profile as a national firm.

a cinderella story

As the firm's work became ever more national in scope, the need for a London base became ever more apparent. The Scottish giant established a City presence in 2002 and hasn't looked back since. At just six years old, it's not yet the belle of the ball, but nor is it an ugly sister. Trainees were most indignant at the suggestion that their office was simply a tag on: *"It doesn't feel like it's a support leg for the Scottish offices at all. I'm rarely engaged on work coming out of Scotland. Certainly property and corporate – two of the largest departments – are free standing."* That's not to say there aren't benefits to being the younger sibling: *"The links to the Scottish offices are handy because of the name and the big clients they have up there, and it's great to have that foot in the door to get their English work."*

All our interviewees noted *"massive growth"* in the London office, and we're not surprised. Turnover has shot up and the London headcount has risen to around 150. For trainees, *"this can only be a good thing – there are new seats opening up all the time because departments are growing, and new departments themselves are being set up."* Seats exist in the staples of corporate, property and employment and also cover more specialised areas such as EU/competition and environment. Quite possibly the growth is a rare case of all silver lining and no cloud – because the expansion has been organic, it's not been accompanied by an identity crisis. *"They haven't sacrificed anything to achieve it,"* stressed one source. Another told us: *"I think it's got a much bigger buzz about it these days. Some new and enthusiastic partners have started and people seem more dynamic and the teams seem busier. There's just a sense that we're on the up."*

lawyers' lawyers

Property, corporate and employment seats are all likely destinations for trainees. If you land in commercial property, expect a hectic six months, as *"it's arguably the busiest department in the office."* The firm receives instructions from some heavyweight clients: it was, for example, recently involved in the transfer of about 1,900 operational gas properties on behalf of National Grid Gas, following the disposal of Southern Gas Distribution Network. Property finance is a major aspect of the work and, in one of the biggest deals of recent times for the office, the property lawyers acted for London & Regional Properties in connection with the £256m securitisation of an investment portfolio. Even if the pace is exhausting and the demands high, it does at least set you up for the rest of your seats. One of the best lessons is learning how to deal with working for several fee earners – *"if you can get the hang of balancing all the different demands on your time here, then you're sorted."* There are other advantages too: *"Because it's a big department, there's huge scope for learning and lots of people to answer your questions."* Trainees run smaller files on their own and provide support on the bigger deals when they come in. *"Often I was doing post-completion jobs, but there's also a fair amount of drafting and dealing with points on leases. I wasn't quite negotiating things myself, but I'd discuss points with my supervisor and then go talk it over with the opposing side."*

Experience in the corporate arena is forged in a similar way. The department saw five additional senior lawyers join in London in 2006 alone and clients such as Bank of Scotland, Scottish & Southern Energy plc and Aquila Developments provide a steady flow of transactional work, sometimes worth up to £100m. Trainees do the usual itty-bitty jobs such as drafting board minutes and Companies House forms. In time they also get to draft small ancillary transaction documents, as well as taking charge of data rooms. *"That entails talking to the client and to the other side too, passing information on and acting as the go-between,"* explained one source. Trainees report reasonable

working hours: *"In fact, compared to friends in other firms they've not been bad at all. Normally 7pm is considered quite late."* Of course, if there's a big transaction then the office may become your temporary home. *"But then everyone stays late, it's not just the trainee up all night photocopying."* One deal that might have felt more pressured than most was the instruction from global firm Squire Sanders & Dempsey in relation to the acquisition of the London and Frankfurt practices of now defunct law firm Haarman Hemmelrath. This transaction saw the London lawyers working in conjunction with a separate German firm. Hardly a case of being tied to Scotland's apron strings.

Somewhat smaller but offering no less valuable experience, an employment seat requires trainees to get stuck into anything from writing articles and producing notes for clients to attending tribunals. *"One day you're helping with an unfair dismissal case, the next you're looking something up for a fee earner."* Client time depends on the job in hand, so *"if you get a dispute, then you might be interviewing clients and taking notes for the case."* Unfortunately, disputes appear to be thin on the ground in this seat: *"I went to a tribunal a few times,"* recalled one trainee, *"but there wasn't a great deal of court time and I didn't have the opportunity to gain any experience of advocacy."*

predicting the future

In the past we've noted a general lack of major litigation in the London office. There are undoubtedly contentious experiences to be gained in the construction, employment and property litigation seats, but trainees tend to agree that thus far the office has maintained its strong leanings towards transactional and advisory work. As one candid source admitted: *"To be honest, I have not gained quite the level of contentious experience that I'd have liked."* As to how the contentious areas of the firm will develop in the future, we can't say, so it may be worth asking the firm at interview what it envisages will be the case by the time you start your training.

Our sources were in large part very complimentary about the training environment: *"You get excellent guidance and can ask any question, no matter how silly."* In each new seat, trainees are eased in, *"letting you become familiar with the subject matter before you take on meatier work."* If you do find yourself with too much work, it's not a problem – but it is up to you to say so. *"You just have to learn to manage your own workload. People will always be willing to give you more work and so you need to know what your threshold is."* Aside from supervisors, there are always other people to turn to. *"We have mentors assigned to us – usually fee earners who are a few years' qualified – they're there to discuss any worries and offer advice and it's nice to have them."* Not that we heard much in the way of trainee moans: our interviewees rarely spent the day by the photocopier (*"Well, occasionally you have to copy things, but you never get landed with a huge bulk because there are people to do that"*) and mid and end-of-seat appraisals allow trainees to raise any issues and get feedback before things start to fester.

We asked current trainees to lay out their tarot cards and tell us what the future holds for the firm. *"I think the departments will be quite developed by the time your readers start their training and there will be more interesting seats available,"* surmised one. Chances are the Scots and English offices will also be more integrated: *"You can tell there's an internal drive for the firm to be seen as a UK firm rather than a Scottish one,"* reported an observant source. To this end, differences between the Scottish and London offices are lessening: *"There used to be a slightly more laid back vibe in London, but you get the* impression it's becoming more ambitious. New arrivals have come in with high aims and their enthusiasm is infectious."* Recently a similar dress code has also been introduced for all the offices. *"It used to be ties in Edinburgh and then more casual in London, but now they've relaxed things north of the border too."*

one-way traffic
Scottish trainees frequently come down to London for a seat, but alas it's usually one-way traffic. *"We could easily head up there for six months if we wanted to,"* said one trainee, *"but none of the folk in my year have."* To ensure it's not a case of ne'er the twain shall meet, D&W organises events at which staff can all get together. The entire trainee intake completes an induction course in Edinburgh and Glasgow, by the end of which *"you know everyone quite well, so when you happen to be in another office there are people to go to lunch with."* The entire London office also gets flown up to Scotland and put up in a hotel for the annual Spring Ball. *"This year, the theme was James Bond. We had a vote: black tie or casual, and black tie was the clear winner. We all wanted to dress up!"* On a smaller scale, *"there are always lots of excuses for lunches with your team or drinks after work. It's all quite impromptu but always a laugh."*

and finally...
It may not be one of the biggest names in town, but Dundas & Wilson is clearly a firm keen to build on its reputation in Scotland. *"Things are moving here – you feel like you're going somewhere and that the firm is on the up."* And as it expands, *"the training is only going to continue to improve, with more opportunities and more variety of choice."* Both of the 2007 qualifiers stayed with the firm going into tax and planning/real estate jobs.

DWF

the facts

Location: Liverpool, Manchester
Number of UK partners/solicitors: 119/158
Total number of trainees: 27
Seats: 4x4 + 1x8 months
Alternative seats: Occasional secondments
Extras: Pro bono – eg Manchester Uni Legal Advice Centre

Late in 2006, Liverpool and Manchester firm DWF revealed that it was looking to double turnover by 2009. The northern rumour mill went into overdrive and soon after a merger was sealed with Leeds and Preston firm Ricksons. DWF has now created a four-city network of offices, turning over £50m annually and employing more than 800 people, many of them in its insurance division.

the big plan

Everything happened quite quickly: in December 2006 the plans of the merger went public and on New Year's Day the merger went live. How much did trainees know before the deal was announced? *"We had heard rumours from about October time, it was all a bit hush-hush, and by the time it was announced to us, we already knew."* The firm then put on *"a big conference with regards to what would happen next, what would change."* Although some trainees reported that, at times, *"the communication lines have been slightly blurred,"* they appreciated that management have had *"a lot on their plates."* The mood among trainees was good when we rang them in summer 2007: *"We all thought it was a positive thing, more opportunities, bigger firm."* They judged the cultures and ethos of Ricksons and DWF to be similar, each having *"a strong commitment to the North, our people, our clients and our community."* *"It was almost like DWF was a bigger version of Ricksons,"* thought one; although another sensed that *"DWF is probably more business-focused in terms of marketing, PR and tactical strategies for developing."*

The effects of the merger were felt more strongly in certain places. The Liverpool office, for example, doesn't really have any Ricksons people in it, whereas the Manchester office has been slowly welcoming the legacy Ricksons employees *"in dribs and drabs."* Preston is mostly Ricksons people with some DWF faces lurking around; meanwhile the small ex-Ricksons branch in Leeds has welcomed in one DWF partner to set up an employment team. Traditionally, trainees have been recruited to a single office with no requirement to switch locations for seats. This is still the case for now, although the firm has indicated that rotating between offices could be a possibility in the future. Liverpool and Manchester take the largest numbers of trainees. Preston has three, while Leeds presently has room for just two. More places will become available in Leeds *"as business grows,"* and further growth is exactly what the trainees expect, despite the fact that *"there is nothing specifically in the pipeline."* As for future mergers, *"I wouldn't rule it out,"* said one source. *"DWF hasn't made any secret about wanting to grow both organically and through merger."*

desperately seeking...

The firm has been putting on events so the trainees in different offices can get to know one another. With five different locations (there are two buildings in Liverpool), it was too complicated to *"get everyone in one place at one time,"* so things were done on a departmental basis. The commercial departments, for example, had a speed-networking event (think speed dating, but with lawyers): *"You talked to everyone for about two minutes each... it's a quick way to get to the point where you recognise each other."* The seat rotations used by the two firms were quite different, so a harmonisation process has had to be implemented and now all trainees follow the old DWF system of four four-month seats followed by a final seat of eight months in the trainee's intended qualification department. As an alternative, some trainees opt for six four-month seats, using the last seat to gain extra experience in the area they hope to work in after qualifying. Our sources praised the system, especially the aspect that allows them up to a year of experience in their preferred practice area. The Liverpool and Manchester offices offer the same seats (except there is no family seat in Liverpool), and the range of options in each is good. The only gripe we heard on the subject was that sometimes trainees *were only told a week beforehand* as to what their next allocation would be. At least this is an improvement on some previous years, *when it was sometimes just a couple of days before.*

DWF is now a formidable player in several practice areas but, staying true to its roots, trainees reported that *you will almost inevitably have to do an insurance seat.* The department is one of the largest in the country and is divided into over 20 sub-departments, including personal injury (defendant and claimant), catastrophic injury, health & safety, fraud, product liability and liability for animals. Its client portfolio includes the likes of Royal & SunAlliance, Norwich Union and Capita, and the team has been working on some very interesting cases, such as defending claims for stress and harassment, asbestos exposure, deafness and pollution caused by oil spillages. Given that there are so many different teams, we can only give an overview of the kind of tasks a trainee could be expected to do. These amount to taking witness statements, attending inquests and trials, drafting case materials, dealing with medical chronologies and reports and having plenty of contact with clients, other solicitors, experts and barristers. Going to court is said to be a *weird adrenaline rush,* partly because there's always the fear of *saying something stupid.* When pressed further, our sources assured us *it's never that bad actually.* Not everyone loves their time in their insurance seat, but with so many other seats available this doesn't seem to dampen their enthusiasm for the training contract as a whole.

in the loop-the-loop

The corporate department has worked on some sweet deals, and the jammie dodgers who happened to take a seat at the right time may have assisted on Burton's Foods on the disposal of its confectionary business or the refinancing of Iceland, a deal worth £160m. The corporate department's clients are a mixed bag and include food company Princes, Preston North End FC, Manchester School of Flying and NatWest. Trainees reported getting their hands on some *great work* in the property department, such as drafting leases, being involved in construction deals, liaising with contractors, and conducting plenty of research. Banking and asset finance is one where you will get to *help out on big deals,* while also wading through numerous mortgage registrations. Although there may be a couple of late nights, the hours are generally okay. The employment department is popular *because you eventually get to do varied jobs.* Our sources might have started off making tribunal and court bundles and doing research, but they progressed to a role as the main assistant on some files. Commercial litigation will see you working on an array of matters: boundary disputes, holiday complaints and sale of goods disputes were just some of the issues our interviewees had encountered. It is a department where *you get more experience and far more responsibility than some others.*

When we asked about the atmosphere in the firm, we heard those all-too-familiar words... "*It sounds corny; it is really friendly.*" Trainees emphasised the ability of people at all levels to get on together and that there was "*no snobbishness.*" They told us they'd been able to sense this attitude from the moment they'd been interviewed as students: "*I felt comfortable,*" said one; "[whereas] *at some of the other firms it was like the Krypton Factor in the things they made you do.*" And as for who wouldn't fit in at the DWF happy camp, recruits said "*prima donnas would annoy everyone*" and that, although there can be "*rivalry for seats,*" everyone "*generally gets on well.*" Those who are "*outgoing and willing to make an effort*" are likely to get on splendidly; "*quiet and reserved people may struggle.*" In short, trainees felt the best thing was to "*not take yourself too seriously outside of work, but take yourself very seriously at work.*"

Our sources were happy that they were kept in the loop on the firm's comings and goings via a monthly missive from the managing partner Andrew Leaitherland who, at just 38 years old, cuts quite a youthful figure. His e-mails are said to "*go into quite a lot of detail,*" so trainees are now aware of "*how much the firm is making, updates on our values and updates about new people joining.*" We hear Leaitherland has taken a "*more businesslike approach*" and that it is down to "*individuals like him that DWF is going places.*" Speaking of going places, we hear that in late 2008 the firm is set to wave goodbye to its "*old listed building*" in Liverpool and say hello to "*a brand-new building, which is in the process of being constructed.*" Naturally people are excited at the prospect: "*We are impatient to get out of here; it's a very old building and everyone is looking forward to leaving it.*"

licence t' thrill

This is a large firm and so it's no great surprise that nights out tend to be organised departmentally. Some have regular monthly drinks events; others get together "*more on an ad hoc basis.*" Trainees in each office regularly attend events hosted by the firm's own Young Professionals groups, which are designed to get them schmoozing with contacts and clients of a similar level of seniority. A James Bond night at Prohibition in Manchester was the one several of our interviewees recalled best. "*There was James Bond music and a quiz,*" but luckily "*no villains!*" Of course, no 007 night would be complete without "*lethal cocktails.*" Other social highlights include being treated by the firm to the Trainee Solicitors Group Ball and the Alder Hey Children's Hospital White Ball. After a bit of digging, we discovered where you can find the DWFers on a Friday night. Regular hotspots in Preston tend to be the Forum Bar, Revolution or "*one of a few nice Italian restaurants.*" Liverpool trainees said that although the popularity of Friday drinks in the office has "*waned,*" they more than make up for it by heading to The Living Room, Rigbys and the First Friday Club in the Slug and Lettuce, where they "*mingle and network.*" The Manchester trainees also frequent their local Slug and Lettuce, although one trainee declared they were "*sick of it*" and some people were trying their hardest to convince the group to explore the rest of the city. Such a healthy social scene can lead one to feeling a little unhealthy, so it's a good job the firm has just introduced discounted gym membership for staff.

We found that most of the people we spoke to had some kind of connection to the city or area in which they worked. Certainly, "*a large majority of people who apply are from the North,*" however, trainees emphasised that this does not rule anyone out. Said one: "*If you can show a genuine interest in working in the North, then I couldn't see them having a problem with that.*" In 2007, as usual, the NQ retention stats looked great with eight of the nine qualifiers opting to stay with the firm.

and finally...

If you fancy working at one of the heavy hitters of the North, then consider DWF. This phase of its 22-year history is defined by rapid growth, so we'd agree with the trainee who said: *"Be prepared for an interesting ride and see where it takes you."* One other piece of advice from us – check out the staff pics on the website.

Eversheds LLP

the facts

Location: Leeds, Manchester, Newcastle, Cardiff-Birmingham, Nottingham, London, Cambridge, Ipswich, Norwich
Number of UK partners/solicitors: 333/1056
Total number of trainees: 160
Seats: 4x6 months
Alternative seats: Overseas, secondments
Extras: Pro bono – various projects, eg Mary Ward Centre; language training

Giant firm Eversheds is the UK's largest private practice employer. Already powerful in the regions, it is on a mission to beef up its City profile. In 2006 the firm unveiled a three-year strategy document detailing plans to boost its annual London turnover from £70 million to £110 million by 2009, while expanding its transactional reputation in the global marketplace. For those who believe that bigger equals better, Eversheds holds obvious attractions.

a capital idea

Boasting a name that split the magic circle in a recent survey of top brands, Eversheds grew in the 1980s, franchise style, from Midlands firm Evershed & Tomkinson into a formidable ten-office UK network with outposts overseas. While Birmingham has traditionally been the firm's spiritual home, nowadays the Eversheds persona is all about adapting to change and right now this means resetting sails in the direction of the capital and outsourcing its IT function to Computacenter. Chief Executive David Gray's management philosophy is "To provide clear direction and clear understanding for everyone of what they need to do to align themselves with that direction."

We spoke to Eversheds trainees across the country and learned that most were drawn to the firm by its reputation, client base and extensive network, which these days is spreading its tentacles to more foreign parts. Last year the firm gained a licence to do business in Shanghai and it is currently in the process of setting up in Qatar. A few lucky trainees can do seats in Eversheds offices in Paris and Shanghai and, if sitting in the right department, they also find international work is available back home in the UK.

centres of excellence

A strong reputation for client service and value for money has helped secure some high-profile work. Recent landmark deals include the £1.46bn sale of telecoms giant The Caudwell Group to private equity buyers Providence and Doughty Hanson. Regeneration schemes are an increasing feature of the work of the construction and planning departments, with the Manchester teams especially gaining some great instructions. Eversheds is advising Citibas Investments on a £1bn redevelopment to the East of the city, which is expected to bring in work for the next ten years. The firm has also drawn in names such as Samsung UK, insurance provider AXA, giant US chemicals company DuPont and US conglomerate Tyco, from which it recently won a £10m mandate to cover all its legal needs across Europe, the Middle East and Africa.

The ten UK offices are organised into three main areas: the Central region (Cardiff, Birmingham, Nottingham); the North (Leeds, Manchester, Newcastle); and London and the

South East (which joins Ipswich, Cambridge and Norwich with the capital). From a trainee's perspective, each office operates as a self-contained entity; however, there is a fair amount of communication between teams when the work calls for it. At a senior level, movement between different offices is quite common and *"if you want to ring someone elsewhere it's as if they're sitting in the same office."* The firm operates a 'centres of excellence' approach, whereby work drawn in through one office is often fielded out to another with greater expertise in the required field. Trainees rarely move between offices for seats unless they reside in East Anglia, where it becomes highly likely. Along with a compulsory seat in something contentious, assignments to property and corporate (or commercial) are virtually guaranteed. Those who choose carefully can combine these required elements with their own interests; for example, a trainee with an interest in the environment could ask to work with the environmental team within corporate criminal defence.

first-class, five-star

In the Central region, trainees say: *"We tend to take it as a given that whatever team we're in will be one of the best in the country."* Birmingham is dominant in the Midlands, while Welsh trainees are certain that they work for *"the best firm in Cardiff, if not in the country."* This leaves Nottingham, which has long been the subject of *"rumours by competitors"* as to its subordination to Birmingham and viability as a standalone office. Although interviewees admitted *"there were always those fears,"* they happily dismissed them and referred to strong local client relationships. In Birmingham, as in many other offices, real estate forms *"the backbone of the business"* and is also the connective tissue between Nottingham and Cardiff. The work involves both national and international clients, *"but generally there is some kind of regional connection... a client that is based in the Midlands but may have massive operations all over the world."* According to some sources, client contact could be better, but with many transactions lasting way longer than the length of a seat *"it's difficult to integrate a new trainee every time we change seats."* Efforts are made to counter this problem where possible and *"trainees run residential purchases for some clients."*

Another leading department is employment. This popular seat has scope for getting trainees out of the office and into tribunals, even stepping into an associate's shoes in one source's case. *"Getting a first-class ticket and a five-star hotel was a good perk,"* they chuckled. Responsibility grows incrementally and *"by the second half of my seat I was sent over to get instructions, compile witness statements and conduct meetings by myself."* Corporate criminal defence (or white-collar crime as it's sometimes known) has thus far been a well-kept secret. *"I'd have done four seats there if I could,"* said one satisfied source. The team works for clients being investigated or prosecuted by the Serious Fraud Office, the CPS, the Office of Fair Trading and a whole host of other regulatory bodies. With opportunities to travel (*"I've been to almost every Eversheds in the country"*) and varied work (*"I went out with every member of the team at least once to meet clients, attend interviews under caution, go to court, anything that was interesting"*) it is certainly an exciting posting.

brand positivity

Up north, strong departments include environment, health and safety (*"a niche area but it doesn't matter if you haven't studied it at uni"*), personal injury defence (clients include Co-operative Insurance and Hertz), commercial litigation (*"great opportunities for advocacy: I've gone to court and done my own applications. You literally just go into a room with a judge for half an hour"*) and the recurring trio of corporate, real estate and employment. Newcastle boasts one of the country's leading shipping teams, carrying out work on the case of the Tasman Spirit oil tanker that ran aground off Pakistan and spilt over 12,000 tons of oil into the Arabian Sea. Eversheds represented the ship-owner and insurers in one of the largest commercial arbitrations of last year.

"A massive and tangible change" in Leeds is the opening of a brand new office building. *"It's a huge step forward for the firm in terms of its appearance to clients. As the tallest building in Leeds it has already changed the landscape,"* trainees reported proudly. The office has taken Leeds open plan and, more slowly, the same process is taking place in Manchester where *"walls are being knocked down. It's all part of the Eversheds philosophy,"* sources explained, adding that the philosophy also requires *"a lot of team-work"* and for people to be *"hard-working, willing to learn and positive about the brand."* While the hours can be long – very long at times – trainees say that if you stick your head above the parapet then recognition is readily gained.

musical seats

In East Anglia, smaller offices mean a narrower choice of departments, but if a seat isn't available in one office, there is the possibility of getting it in another. Although everyone is allowed to specify a base office close to their home, there's no guarantee their training contract will be spent there and some trainees can find themselves with a long commute. One told us: *"Yesterday I left the house at 5.30am and I got home at about 11.30pm."* To make matters worse, when assistance is needed, HR can sometimes be hard to get hold of. *"I was struggling to get an answer for a couple of weeks on one point,"* a source reflected. Another told us: *"I think it was a bad idea to make someone who's in London responsible for us because obviously we are rather out in the sticks. Most of the time we don't seem to get our first-choice seats."*

In the east of England, Cambridge has *"a very*

different atmosphere" to Ipswich and Norwich. *"My impression is that Cambridge works longer hours,"* mused a source. *"Maybe it's because in the open-plan office everyone can see who's in, or maybe we just have more work..."* In Ipswich the atmosphere is *"even more relaxed than Norwich... until there's a big deal on, which I think I'm about to experience – I've just discovered that I'm going to be working this weekend,"* revealed a Suffolk source. Activities in Ipswich are limited to projects and construction with a fair amount of overlap between the two: *"It's all basically Private Finance Initiatives, where a private company is created to finance a project like building a school or a hospital."* In Norwich, seats are available in real estate, planning and employment; Cambridge meanwhile offers by far the widest choice, including employment, education, corporate, banking, commercial litigation and real estate. Unsurprisingly, trainees based in Cambridge did the least moving around and were able to establish the best social life: *"We play pool a couple of lunchtimes a week in Mickey Flynn's on Mill Road, and sometimes the partners will come out for drinks... which we encourage as they buy them!"* In corporate and commercial litigation, work is frequently co-ordinated from the capital and overall we got the impression that Cambridge trainees had the most contact with London trainees, some of them even going on secondment to the capital. *"The newly qualifieds are being encouraged to work between different offices and we are supposed to be getting even more work from London."*

The focus in the capital is now squarely on corporate and financial services. For a trainee in a corporate seat typical tasks include company searches and compiling reports that *"put everything into a logical order and summarise the key facts – a snapshot of the company."* Trainees quickly become familiar with accounts and annual returns and tell us: *"Once you've had training it makes sense, but before that it's quite alien."*

The seat involves a fair few late nights: *"It's a case of churning work out constantly... there are large sums of money being thrown around and you never know what could come in tomorrow."* Due in 2008, a shiny new office, some 50% larger than the previous one, is expected to do wonders for the firm's City profile which trainees say currently *"lacks credibility"* given the size of the firm nationally. We're told that management is determined to fill the new premises and, spurred on by these growth plans, London trainees feel confident of their future prospects.

a question of identity

A new strategy, described within the firm as Networked Law, revolves around the idea of drawing high-profile clients into the firm using the flashy new London office and then subsequently fielding it out to regional offices where it can be dealt with at lower cost to the firm and the client. It's an approach very much in keeping with the Eversheds vision of becoming *"the most client-centred international law firm."* However, a few trainees from the regional offices suggest that fee earners are less than happy at the idea of being used as a cost-effective alternative to London, with the disparity between salaries proving to be a particular bone of contention. One source commented: *"I do think it's a bit of an anomaly for Eversheds, as it marks itself out as an international law firm... but though working hours and practices are in line with other international law firms, the pay is very much regional. People work hard and generally there is more pressure here than in local firms. If we are supposed to be the best and the strongest firm in the region, surely we should be getting paid more for working those hours."* The only figures publicised relate to the headline London salaries. After promising not to publish them, we did manage to get the regional salaries and this allowed us to make a comparison with other leading firms in each region. Undoubtedly the firm is paying at the top end of regional rates, but given the huge jumps in London salaries of late, knowing this doesn't necessarily make people feel any better about the gap.

However the plans for London develop, arguably much of Eversheds' rainmaking power will remain concentrated in the regions. The massive Caudwell deal, for example, was brought in by Manchester partner Danny Hall. Said one trainee: *"I think it's crucial that we have a strong footing in the local commercial community because otherwise our competitors could point out to local clients that we don't actually need to be here."* We don't sense that Eversheds is interested in nurturing local connections. The regional offices recently lost some of their individual identities as the role of managing partner in each office was scrapped in favour of three head partners for the Northern, Central and Eastern/London regions. Eversheds may have a big footprint outside the capital, but its gaze seems firmly fixed on London and international growth.

visionaries

In terms of after-hours fun and games, Eversheds varies from place to place, with Birmingham coming out on top for office-wide socialising. Several of Brum's big firms are situated on the same street so there's a strong legal presence in local bars and restaurants. The Birmingham Trainee Solicitors Society is also particularly lively. In Cardiff, the lack of an office-wide Christmas party is keenly felt: *"For the last two or three years there have only been department socials and a lot of people have said they'd rather there was a big party or ball that we could all go to."* It sounds as if an effort is being made to counter this, with a recent quiz night in the Hard Rock Cafe held for all who wanted to participate. In Newcastle, office drinks are held on the first Friday of every month, with themed nibbles (*"gorgeous food but bad for the waistline"*) provided by in-house chef

Richard. In Cambridge, on a weekly basis, *"they provide wine, beer and soft drinks, and all the department groups are encouraged to go along."*

If you're keen to get your face known there's plenty of opportunity to participate in graduate recruitment activities such as The Big Deal, an event to help first-year university students raise their commercial awareness, as well as fundraising and pro bono work. Trainees in Birmingham organised a screening of *Breakfast at Tiffany's* for the Prince's Trust and managed to get their hands on some Tiffany jewellery to raffle. They are now discussing an Eversheds version of *Strictly Come Dancing*. A highlight of the training contract is definitely the residential PSC in Warwick, where trainees get to meet their peers from other offices. *"It's all pretty good fun: they put on a massive meal and a dance, then on other nights we went out to local clubs and student nights. By Friday I definitely noticed a lot more people making trips to the watercoolers."* The week gives a great opportunity to check out all the trainees. According to one source: *"It seems very strange but everyone is really similar, you can almost see that there's an Eversheds persona."* This comes down to being *"self-confident but not cocky,"* with many people *"coming from a background where we've done quite well academically but where it's not necessarily come easily – we've had to work for it."*

We mentioned the firm's 'Visions and Values' earlier. You can read them in full on its website and we recommend that when you do, you bear in mind that any organisation as big as Eversheds requires a degree of conformity from staff in order to achieve its common goals. We can't help wondering whether, in its efforts to grow and change as a business, the part of the visions and values about Eversheds being a great place to work will have to become subordinate to other goals. One trainee commented: *"I have heard remarks along the lines of, you're working for Eversheds and that should be something you're proud of,*

what more do you want?" For some people in some locations adapting to change and fitting in with the firm's goals has evidently required sacrifices they would rather not have made. For others, fitting in is what the whole Eversheds experience is all about.

and finally...

In 2007, 64 of the 86 qualifiers chose to continue their Eversheds experience and stay with the firm, many taking jobs in the flagship corporate and real estate departments. Eversheds recruitment machine is very much looking for people to subscribe to its big picture plans so, if like us, you are interested in finding out about the small details – what life is really like in an individual office – we suggest you track down a kindly trainee to chat to.

Farrer & Co

the facts
Location: London
Number of UK partners/solicitors: 62/120
Total number of trainees: 18
Seats: 6x4 months
Alternative seats: Secondments
Extras: Language training

With a reputation stretching back over three centuries, Farrer & Co must seem like a dear family friend to its oldest clients. Carefully planned strategic growth has, however, successfully kept at bay any hint of the musty or the superannuated while seamlessly preserving the firm's distinguished reputation.

filthy rich and fabulous

While the landed gentry may feel comforted by the old-school aesthetic and physical remnants of antiquity within this firm (it still stands on the spot it has occupied since 1790), it is perhaps these clients who teeter most dangerously on the edge of anachronism. With the buoyancy of various markets translating into serious amounts of money sloshing around, a new breed of high net worth individual is making its debut in the Farrers' client book: the ultra high net worth individual. Is this evolution, or capitalism gone mad? Who knows, but with Russian oligarchs, Swiss bankers and media moguls flocking to take advantage of the UK's favourable tax regimes, this is a clientele the firm has been quick to respond to. Avoiding the need to jump on bandwagons, Farrers has guaranteed a steady flow of such clients through its doors by providing the kind of discreet, expert advice that any discerning individual with loads of money looks for. Of course, the firm has also remained faithful to its more traditional brand of clientele, with waxed jackets and wellies continuing to receive a warm welcome at 66 Lincoln's Inn Fields. The Chancellor of the Exchequer's recent budgets have done their bit to keep tax lawyers on their toes, and with inheritance tax representing a continual threat to the proverbial silver spoon, Farrers looks set to continue its work for those sharing *"the common objective of protecting their wealth and handing it on"* well into the future.

Having established that clients come from many walks of life, including business, agriculture, sport, art and the media, and bring work spanning a range of disciplines, it's little wonder that a trainee's role in the private client department stretches from *"sorting out visas for clients to come and work in UK"* to attending meetings with *"one of Italy's most wealthy families"* and, as *"a worst case scenario, getting a director's resolution to pay a gas bill."* The work involves a lot of research for senior partners, and although this can feel like a test (*"you sometimes wonder if they actually know the answer"*), trainees agreed it was also when they felt the most valuable.

education, education, education...

Yet we mustn't fall into the trap of pigeonholing Farrers as just a private client thoroughbred; this fine filly has more than one trick to perform. Trainees may well have chosen it because of its private client pedigree but they soon learn there is much more on offer through the six-seat scheme. One seat must be taken in each of the following four groupings: charities or private client; commercial (including banking, IP and employment); property (commercial and private/estates options); and litigation (family, media or general disputes). Then follows a 'wildcard' seat of the trainee's choice before the final four months is spent in the department into which they hope to qualify.

Illustrating the degree of multidisciplinary working at Farrers, a long list of institutional clients use the firm's strong employment team and its *"untouchable"* charity and education practices, both of which are top ranked by our parent publication *Chambers UK*. Major educational clients include Eton, Marlborough College, Trinity College of Music and the London Business School. As well as bringing in a varied portfolio of instructions, enabling trainees in these seats to gain experience of other departments, some of these clients' cases can be high profile. A good example is the defence of the independent schools at the centre of the OFT investigation into alleged price-fixing in relation to school fees. Some clients also offer secondments, among them the Lawn Tennis Association in Roehampton, and a pair of well-known London museums. Along with the obvious opportunities for client exposure, these opportunities enable trainees to *"grow in confidence"* and take on extra responsibility. One trainee ended up *"negotiating a contract which was in the national press,"* while another was asked to *"rewrite the client's document retention advice in line with new data protection legislation."*

...reputation, reputation, reputation

The defamation and reputation management team is considered to be one of the best in the land, bringing in many celebrity clients as well as newspapers. The firm represented Sharon Stone in a successful libel claim against Associated Newspapers, which printed a story alleging she had left her young son in a car while she dined at The Ivy. The team also represented News Group Newspapers in defence of a claim brought by one of the alleged gang members plotting the kidnap of Victoria Beckham. However, a brief word of warning: don't expect the work to be all glamour and glitz. There's still plenty of *"very low-level, basic work"* which falls to trainees, and while it's easy to see how media or even private client work *"could be a lot of fun further down the line,"* the nature of many matters means that trainees will inevitably take *"an ancillary role."* As one told us: *"Doing administrative work for other people... is a bit depressing."*

In all departments, responsibility comes in due course, and trainees spoke glowingly of the moments when they were *"invited to attend a celebratory lunch with the client"* or *"found out that a client had taken on the recommendations I'd made."* One trainee described the moment when a supervisor gives positive feedback as being *"just the best feeling in the world,"* explaining that *"at some firms it's not cool, but here if you've done something well they'll say, 'Wow, that was great.'"*

know thyself

Undoubtedly aware of the firm's *"distinctive public profile,"* Farrers' trainees exude the quiet confidence traditionally associated with having been educated at a frightfully good school. Smug isn't the word – they're far too nice for that – but put it this way, none of them ended up here by fluke. Whether it's securing that cherished seat with the arts and heritage team, or getting a Farrers training contract in the first place, these individuals have thought long and hard about their future careers. As one person put it, Farrers *"don't go marching into law schools and uni's enticing people with sweets and biros... so the people who end up coming here have actually done their homework."*

Advanced apologies if this makes you feel slightly nauseous, but in addition to being intelligent, self-aware individuals, the trainees we spoke to were also extremely modest. The repeated refrain of *"I don't want to beat my own drum"* from one interviewee summed it up well, as did another's conviction that *"if I had to apply here now, I wouldn't get in."* Does the firm provide lunchtime briefings in humility or are they born like this? One source remarked: *"It's strange; it's not diffidence because that would suggest that people aren't confident, but there's a certain amount of bashfulness from people about their own achievements... and then it turns out they won the Nobel Peace Prize."* A cynic might scoff, but the *"defining"* characteristic of this firm really does seem to be its good manners, and *"that's something you can have no matter what your upbringing or background."*

And yet Farrers people are equally capable of doing hard business. If your greatest aspiration is to become a faceless, corporate lawyer, sending your kids a goodnight message via your BlackBerry, look away now. But if you're hoping for something a little more personal with the possibility of a few free evenings thrown in, Farrers' corporate team might just be for you. Focusing largely on AIM deals the opportunity is there for *"very good client contact,"* often working closely with *"wealthy entrepreneurial types"* from *"the very first moment they walk through the door."* Hours vary and *"obviously there will be times when you do have to work a little bit harder,"* but we rarely heard of a trainee staying beyond 8pm or 9pm. Having doubled its partner numbers in just the last twelve months, now is quite a good time to visit the department. Most commercially minded trainees felt confident about their chances of staying on post-qualification.

As well as *"very reasonable"* hours, trainees stressed a positive attitude towards having a life outside work, telling us partners believe *"people are a lot more interesting to have around if they don't live in the office."* Socialising is important, but remains an optional activity. *"If there is one place where you can pursue your interests and have free time in the evenings it's here,"* enthused one trainee who, like most others, came to the firm with *"an armful of extra curricular activities."* These range from having *"walked and cycled across Europe with tents strapped to their bikes,"* to *"performing in a Village People tribute band"* and taking on the challenge of *"attending every single 80s night across London."* Farrers also boasts a number of *"really brilliant musicians"* who showcase their talents at an annual Christmas concert, an event which has proved so successful that a bigger venue is now being sought.

For the philanthropically minded, the private client department does a lot of charity work for some *"big names"* including the Cancer Care Foundation, the London Bombings Relief Charitable Fund and the Laureus Sport for Good Foundation. *"A lot of people want to develop the pro bono side of the firm's offering"* and, as proof of the firm's willingness to listen to staff, the corporate social responsibility policy is now being discussed with this very development in mind. As one source explained: *"That's indicative of the way Farrers is. When you start speaking to colleagues you realise there are a lot of people in the firm who already do a lot, and always have done, it's just never been branded as such."*

and finally...

Trainees feel confident that this is their firm. In 2007 seven out of nine qualifying trainees stayed within the Farrers fold, taking jobs across the firm's departments. *"The grapevine is very*

lively and everyone jokes that the trainees are always the first people to know things," said one jovial source. On a more serious level, trainees are invited to twice-yearly breakfast sessions *"where we get to have a go at the management board and see what's happening."* So what would a trainee say is the answer to this question? Here's a telling answer: *"Farrers just grows at its own pace. Any institution – a museum or a political party – has to grow and change, and Farrers is just the same."* This source hit the nail on the head: Farrer & Co is as much of a British institution as any museum or political party.

Field Fisher Waterhouse LLP

the facts
Location: London
Number of UK partners/solicitors: 92/165
Total number of trainees: 36
Seats: 6x4 months
Alternative seats: Secondments

Mid-sized London firm Field Fisher Waterhouse is on a roll. When we rang trainees in the summer of 2007 there was much excitement about the firm's decision to open its doors to European expansion. Offices had been unveiled in Hamburg and Brussels, and managing partner Moira Gilmour was busy keeping everyone in the loop via lunchtime seminars and regular e-mails.

great expectations
Trainees spoke in a modest, almost guarded, way about *"prudent development"* and *"incremental steps,"* implying that the invasion of continental Europe had more to do with evolution than revolution. So far, it has only opened in two countries, preferring for now to settle for tie-ups with old friends in Spain and Italy, but a merger with its former alliance partner in Paris is a possibility.

Things are changing back at home, too. The London partnership has grown in recent years and now hovers just below 100. There is a clear appetite among the partners to further raise the firm's game and it hopes to bill more than £75m annually by 2008. This year it bolstered its relationship with the UK government by successfully tendering for a mandate to advise the Foreign & Commonwealth Office on plans to develop its website. There has also been noticeable interest from Chinese corporates and banks, leading some to conclude that FFW may try to set up in business over there.

apple of your iPod

FFW's training programme is based on six four-month seats. On the plus side this means trainees have exposure to both mainstream and niche areas and are not condemned to the long haul if a department is not to their liking. Then again, a whistle-stop tour only gives a passing acquaintance with a department, something that can only be rectified once over the two years by repeating a seat. A tour of duty coco and something contentious is mandatory. Viewed by some with trepidation, corporate promises tougher hours and more grunt work than most seats. The enforced visit caused frustration among some trainees; others, however, confirmed that with determination and a cunning choice of supervisor, it was possible to nab interesting pieces of work. Love it or loathe it, corporate is the bread and butter of the firm's business and, along with IP, looks set to carry the burden of its fortunes. Among the deal highlights from the past year are the £61m flotation on AIM of Australian company Ceramic Fuel Cells Limited, and the £71m AIM flotation of Sun TV Shop Plc. The firm is a dynamo in the AIM market and advises a good number of companies on that and other lists.

The full-service IP department represents some of the juiciest brands around. It does a lot of work for Apple, Inc (the computer people), including recently buying the Apple portfolio from Apple Corps (The Beatles' company). Other work has concerned the iPod and iPhone, and the lawyers have advised on what they call "*a blizzard*" of iPod infringement and counterfeiting matters. Away from disputes, the lawyers helped MTV Networks Europe secure a major licensing deal in the Middle East. The IP team has grown by five new partners and 15 solicitors over the past year, suggesting preparations for a large campaign ahead. New clients include Elvis Presley Enterprises, H&M, Liberty plc, Marvel Comics, Monsoon, Nissan Motor Co, Pearson plc and the Trustees of the Muhammad Ali Family Trust. This lot join a client roster that already includes Laura Ashley, Xerox Corporation, Crocs, Reiss, Coca-Cola, Hamleys, Dell Computers and Marylebone Cricket Club. The work scores a thumbs-up from trainees for being varied and interesting, and providing interaction with so many blue-chip clients. The telecoms and technology group has placed quite a lot of emphasis in the past on large public sector outsourcing projects and regulatory and competition matters, but under the leadership of a new head of department, it will now chase more work from technology start-ups and sell its expertise in relation to the distribution of media content.

Often perceived as an unsexy area to work in, real estate has brought surprising satisfaction to trainees. What they particularly relished was the chance to handle their own files and co-operate on larger transactions being run by partners. One of the perks of the department is "*the good, regular hours,*" another is being recognised for your contribution. The department has teams specialising in hotel and leisure clients, developments, property litigation and investments. Between them they have worked on high-profile matters such as a £100m mixed-use scheme at

King's Cross, the £25m sale of Erith Shopping Centre, the acquisition of Donington racing circuit (for development), various projects for BP and National Grid and major litigation for Southwark Council.

heroes and villains

Professional regulation is a popular, if daunting, seat option. The team represents the General Medical Council in various High Court hearings including one arising from Channel's 4 allegations regarding Andrew Wakefield, the doctor at the centre of the MMR debate. Trainees take great pleasure in the fact that the cases they work on are splashed over the front pages of the national press, even if their role initially involves fairly low-level tasks such as bundling documents for court. Fortunately they do also get to prepare witness statements and frequently attend hearings to take notes and assist barristers. This is a *"hands-on"* department that releases its lawyers from the shackles of deskbound duties and there is also a good deal of human drama.

Another emotive area is medical negligence/personal injury. In this seat you can expect *"to be thrown in at the deep end"* and, once you've *"earned it,"* there is the chance to draft witness statements as well as instructions to counsel. Much of the work involves doing research to gauge the appropriate level of damages. To give you an idea of the gravity of cases, the team recently won a big payout for the Singaporean presenter Tan Yieu, the most seriously injured victim of the Potters Bar rail crash. Acting mainly for claimants, this department can justifiably be seen as the knight in shining armour of the firm.

Other seat options include financial services, aviation, employment, construction, competition and commercial litigation. FFW also has a veritable treasure trove of client secondments to media companies, public bodies and government offices.

i am the law

One tip from those in the know relates to the need to be vocal about your seat desires. *"Don't be afraid to ask"* may sound a trite message, but it is important to remember that there is scope to cut your own path through this training programme. We heard plenty of touching examples to show the firm was happy to cater to individual preferences rather than assume one size fits all. For now, working hours are perfectly civilised. This is not a firm where you're likely to be moaning down the phone to your mum or burning with suppressed indignation. A 'big brother' scheme between first and second-years ensures that new starters have a shoulder to cry on if they feel so inclined. There is more support available from HR and supervisors who *"always keep an eye on you."* There are also forums through which people can offer feedback, and trainees assure us that staff comments are taken seriously.

With so many different departments, teams and types of lawyers at the firm it is perhaps misleading to speak of an overall FFW personality. Indeed, the firm can appear like a cluster of departments rather than a Transformer-esque unity of parts. Trainees tell us the departments tend to stick to their own floors and are largely left to their own operational devices, as is reflected in the varying dress codes up and down the office. There have been initiatives to stamp a corporate identity through mergers of departments and pooling of talents, but trainees report that insularity is still rife with the medical negligence and regulatory practices in particular known for doing things their own way. In terms of recruitment, this tolerance of individuality has not taken the firm beyond a leaning towards Oxbridge candidates, and trainees estimate that these two universities have supplied a third of the intake over the past two years.

Whether you regard it as very sad or very cool, FFW has sniffed a business opportunity and become the first law firm to set up shop in virtual world Second Life. With heaps of the latest must-have virtual accessories becoming available every day online (star-studded rocket boosters anybody?), the firm reckons it's struck gold with this particular cyberventure. One definite upside is that if you ever get frustrated with the constraints of office life you can always log on, arm yourself to the teeth like Judge Dredd and go berserk, screaming in upper case *"I AM THE LAW!"*

squashed in

For many, FFW's key attraction was its medium size and sacred work-life balance, so they worry that in its mission to up the ante, the firm could tarnish its image as an escape route from the big firms. Trainees revealed that bonuses were being introduced for assistants on the back of a tougher work ethic that might see the working day rub shoulders more regularly with its dreaded counterpart – the working night.

Based in the heart of London, it is hardly surprising that the firm does not take an active hand in the employees' social life. Nevertheless, there were a few grumblings that no social evenings were arranged for trainees in their first couple of weeks, especially when so many were new to the Big Smoke. As it is, first-years tend to flock together on Friday nights in the pub adjoining the office. Indeed, it is so adjoining that it even has a connecting door. The firm does stage an annual Christmas dinner and a summer barbecue, and one bonus of FFW's patchwork culture is that in the run-up to Christmas every Tom, Dick and Harry feels entitled to throw a party making December a wheeling succession of Champagne soirées. Testament to the easy airs of the partners, they have been known to be seen *"cutting sharp moves on the dance floor"* at the big festive bash.

Back in the office there's a bona fide piece of history in the basement 'bolt hole' – a fragment of the London Wall. Typically, it was hard to tell whether the trainees took more satisfaction from this archaeological gem or the plasma screen with which it shares a room. Another feature of this Tardis-like area of the firm is a squash court. Although the offices were recently revamped, it was notable that the improvements were not drastic. As one trainee put it: *"It's smart but not flashy – there are no waterfalls or anything."* Once again, the firm's tendency to shun excess comes through.

In 2007, only 11 of the 16 qualifiers stayed on with the firm, a lower number than in previous years. Those who stayed spread themselves across the different departments.

and finally...

Field Fisher Waterhouse was always a good pick for students looking for a smörgåsbörd of niche areas. Whether they qualify into something offbeat or standard, or they use the firm as *"a jumping-off point into other City firms,"* trainees understand that it is a refuge from the excessive demands found elsewhere. Naturally, the push to grow mainstream corporate work and promote pan-European business will have an impact; however, this side of the firm's character is unlikely to be lost entirely. For a taster of this novel firm, why not try the two-week vacation scheme.

Finers Stephens Innocent

the facts

Location: London
Number of UK partners/solicitors: 36/37
Total number of trainees: 11
Seats: 4x6 months
Alternative seats: None

When property firm Finers hooked up with IP and media specialists Stephens Innocent in 1999, a full-service, mid-tier West End outfit was born.

looking mighty fine-r

With so many makeover programmes on TV attempting to transform people into younger, more beautiful, trendier versions of themselves, it's no wonder law firms are starting to do the same. Finers... sorry, FSI (*"You're supposed to call it FSI,"* our sources corrected us) is fresh from a rebranding exercise which has included a revamp of its website and marketing literature. The firm is now billing itself as a *"vibrant and ambitious"* firm, and to reflect this it has chosen bright orange as its signature colour. *"There has been both positive and negative feedback,"* a source revealed; *"but it's a colour you don't forget – it stands out."* FSI's website now boldly displays the eight key attributes the firm believes best describes it: unstuffy, businesslike, forward-thinking and entrepreneurial are among them. And trainees readily concur with the firm's definition of itself: *"There is a shift in attitude about how we sell ourselves, these are key differentiators, key selling points."* As old hands at this game, we're not convinced these descriptions will set the firm apart from all the others that have plumped for exactly the same concepts, nevertheless it's always nice to see a firm deciding to formally adopt them. Trainees also noted an accompanying shift in management style too: *"There is now a greater emphasis on billing targets – they have cracked the whip a bit more."*

The best way to distinguish the firm is to outline the areas of practice at which it is most adept. FSI offers a service in eight core areas: property; corporate; commercial dispute resolution; family; employment; IP & media; private client and personal injury. If you're after a bit of retail therapy, this is definitely the firm for you because within its client portfolio you'll find the likes of Monsoon Accessorize, Kookai, Boxfresh, LK Bennett and Littlewoods. If shopping doesn't float your boat, there are always clients like Pizza Hut and quirky transactions such as assisting The Tetris Company in the infringement of IP rights relating to the much-loved retro game. Cricket fans will be interested to learn that FSI was the firm of choice for Darrell Hair in his employment tribunal case against the ICC and Pakistani Cricket Board.

dead cert

The training scheme incorporates four six-month seats and, like most other firms, the first seat is chosen for the new arrivals. Typically it will be *"a property seat of some description,"* given that this is FSI's biggest department and it accounts for 35% of annual turnover. Property is the only compulsory element to the training contract, and if you don't do it in your first seat, you will end up spending six months there at some point, *"whether you like it or not."* The seat *"might not be straight property; it could be property litigation or planning."* Once in the property department, your six month stay could be divided between two teams, something trainees generally welcomed as *"it gives you varied work."* There is one disadvantage: *"Three months is the point at which you start to feel settled"* and when you begin to *"get to grips"* with the work. Interviewees described the property department as *"fast-paced"* and seemed to thrive on the level of responsibility given to them. The reality of this is *"running an awful lot of files,"* which in turn is no bad thing as *"it gets your file-management skills honed."* The kind of tasks you can expect are drafting leases, lease summaries, land searches, assignment or alteration licences and lots of conversations, messages and meetings with clients. The property department has been involved in some tasty pieces of work guaranteed to keep trainees busy, among them assisting Tragus Holdings with the sale of the Café Rouge, Bella Italia and Ortega chains, as well as assisting the UK's largest leisure fund, X-Leisure, in its disposal and purchase of several cinemas.

feeling lucky?

Following your first seat, you will be asked where you would like to go, but *"you won't always get your first choice."* It would be unlikely for anyone to get a seat in the *"hugely oversubscribed"* media/IP department in their first year, and it can be relatively difficult to secure a spot there in the second. *"Only in unusual circumstances will there be a seat in this department. I had to argue my case,"* explained one of the lucky trainees. Anyone who takes an interest in how legal matters are reported on TV and radio will undoubtedly have heard the name Mark Stephens, who is a partner in the *"flamboyant media arm"* of the firm and is known as *"one of the faces of Finers."* (Oops!) He regularly *"appears prominently in the news,"* and his commentary on high-profile media cases is said to *"bring in a hell of a lot of work."* The department also scoops up any unusual pieces of work that land on FSI's doorstep, as the team is *"really good at thinking around problems."* Those who do manage to persuade the powers that be to let them into the department for six months will work on *"IP mortgages, copyright and passing off matters, and obviously some corporate support."* At times they might also be *"sent on the most random missions."* One of the sexiest matters the team has handled in recent times is Lionsgate's IP rights to the film and musical *Dirty Dancing*.

Several of the trainees we chatted to had earned their corporate stripes, and although one noted how *"it wasn't the friendliest [department] to begin with,"* they did then tell us: *"As it got busy, it sort of defrosted and you got really good work."* Due diligence, board minutes, running minor client meetings and assisting on AIM flotations are all on the agenda. Interestingly, one trainee made a point of the fact that corporate is *"partner heavy,"* stating that there were *"too many chiefs and not enough Indians."* This manifested itself in a shortage of mid-level fee earners to whom trainees could turn with relatively simple queries.

For contentious experience, most trainees are dropped into either the commercial litigation or property litigation departments. Some go into both. In the former, trainees recalled a lot of construction disputes and said they were kept busy drafting chronologies and summaries of claims, attending hearings and assisting with instructions to counsel. The latter involved landlord and tenant matters and was *"very interactive with clients."* All our interviewees agreed that those who prove themselves get more responsibility. *"I'd rather feel under pressure than sit twiddling my thumbs unengaged,"* said one. No one is let loose on clients unsupervised, but if you *"show willing and you are enthusiastic then you can really succeed here."*

get me out of here

Unlike those firms that besiege potential candidates with a never-ending barrage of questions on an application form which often turns out to be demoralising and massively time-consuming, until now FSI has simply asked applicants to send in a CV and covering letter, detailing as much information about themselves as they like. This was a definite attraction to the current batch: *"A lot of firms go over the top with psychometric tests, at Finers* [Oops again!] *it's all very personable, and the firm is interested in individuals rather than certain criteria;" "they are keen to ascertain your personality rather than whether you fit into a certain category."* We hear that changes to the procedure are currently being discussed and *"they have asked the current trainees to go through anonymous psychometric testing to decide whether they want to use it for future trainees."*

Trainees insist there is no particular type of person who would fit in best at FSI, although they claim *"an interesting background is definitely of use"* and add that clients would probably find trainees with *"extra life experience"* to be *"more reassuring."* We did manage to spot one thing trainees had in common – the desire to train at a mid-sized London firm where they could avoid the pressures of the City. *"I didn't want to go to the City and be a small fish in a big pond,"* explained one. A West End location in Great Portland Street is a big plus for trainees, who describe it as *"a fantastic location, close to Oxford Circus and Soho and a stone's throw from Camden."* As we reported last year, in the offices staff are *"pretty crammed in"* and trainees suggested something needs to be done. A move was on the cards, but as nowhere suitable was found, it was decided the firm would stay put, and take out secondary offices close by. Given that it already occupies two separate buildings, placing staff into a third *"poses problems and is a major bugbear."*

The Friday dress-down policy also runs for the entire month of August: *"It's smart casual, but no jeans or flip-flops and nothing indecent."* Dates to mark in the social calendar are the monthly beer, wine and nibbles evenings in the basement of the main office, karaoke nights, an annual quiz and various softball matches. For nights out in bars, staff are *"spoilt for choice."* If they are feeling flush, they head to Villandry. The last summer party was held at London Zoo and involved a bush tucker trial. When trainees recounted tales of testicle consumption, we didn't dare ask about the previous owner's identity. If you enjoy watching that kind of thing, FSI has added a video of the event to its website, complete with warning for viewers of a sensitive disposition.

and finally...

If you're looking for a creative yet hard-working London outfit, away from the stresses of the City, then look no further. Finers Stephens Innocent embraces individuality and offers a good grounding in a selection of commercial and private client disciplines. In 2007, two of its five qualifiers stayed with the firm, going into corporate and commercial litigation positions.

Fisher Meredith

the facts

Location: London
Number of UK partners/solicitors: 13/47
Total number of trainees: 16
Seats: 4x6 months
Alternative seats: None

Based in Kennington in South London, Fisher Meredith has long been regarded as one of the key players in the UK's legal aid fraternity. As the firm negotiates the choppy waters created by the Carter reforms, our sources were not only confident that it will adapt and flourish in the new *"sink or swim environment"* but felt certain that it would do so without abandoning its core principles.

uncharted waters

The firm still holds true to its original values, notably a belief in the right to legal advice, no matter what a person's circumstances or behaviour. Since the firm was founded in the idealistic 70s, these core principles have led it to represent clients who have been vilified, persecuted, prejudiced or just plain old down on their luck. Over the years, the firm has advised various clients in cases of considerable public interest, for example, Sonia Sutcliffe, the former wife of the Yorkshire Ripper and the families of the teenage victims of the Deptford Fire in 1981.

No doubt about it, *"it has been a difficult time with the Carter reforms in the offing and there is definitely a nervousness amongst the trainees that we are training into areas that won't exist in the legal market in the future."* Fisher Meredith was one of the last firms to sign the Legal Services Commission's Unified Contract earlier in 2007, and only did so after it had put up a fight. The fact that in the end the partners and staff felt compelled to sign was obviously a massive blow: *"We* thought that lots of firms would be [boycotting the contract] *and we were excited to be part of something, so to find out that everyone else had signed – that was disheartening."*

When the crunch time came, the partners canvassed staff opinions on what they wanted the firm to do. *"We all voted to decide upon the action we were going to take, trainees and qualifieds, paralegals and the partners."* As a result – and in spite of the inevitable uncertainty in the sector – morale at Fisher Meredith remains high. As one source told us: *"People here are quite good at taking a fighting stance; if anyone can survive Carter then we will."* Another explained: *"They definitely have a strategy worked out to make sure they increase the private side of the business without losing the firm's identity. Although certain departments will always be legal aid – like housing and crime – there are others that can adapt quite easily... for example, most of the ancillary relief work in family is private now. We have a lot of young partners and a dynamic attitude. We are definitely going the right way about it."* In truth, FM has been going the right way about it for a while: there's nothing new in its bid to increase the proportion of its revenue that comes from privately paying clients and in 2007 this stood at 35%.

crimes and passion

It used to be the case that it was compulsory for trainees to do a seat in crime and family, but this seems to have drifted into an informal understanding that most trainees will do one or other seats... or maybe neither. It's not that these seats are unpopular; indeed, both are highly rated by trainees. For example, *"crime is a good department to start off in because the fast pace makes it possible to see cases from start to finish during your six-month seat."* Trainees are also impressed by the quality of work that Fisher Meredith wins. *"A lot of the work attracts signifi-*

cant media interest," such as the case of the so-called fifth bomber in the 21/7 terrorist attacks in London.

A seat in crime will entail taking responsibility for clients when they turn up at the door or phone in. Apparently this is *"particularly good for helping to get your knowledge up to scratch because the queries could refer to almost anything."* With the high level of client contact and also the *"high-impact nature of the seat – where a client may come in one day and the trial will be the next day"* – there is a chance that trainees may feel a little overwhelmed. If so, *"there is always someone senior to consult if you get stuck and most people seem to swim rather than sink because of that support."* The firm tells us that it encourages trainees to complete police station accreditation training to allow them to go on the rota for police station advice. What it does not do is insist that trainees follow this course.

A seat in family is also demanding, not least because *"there are some clients that they expect you to deal with on your own."* The seat is seen as a perfect place to *"develop your own caseload, especially with domestic violence injunction cases where you do the advocacy yourself, even from the beginning of your first week."* There is inevitably a degree of crossover between a family seat and a seat in the children's department, which is considered to be *"a really enjoyable, nice department, where everyone works together as a team."* The issues trainees encounter are frequently incredibly sensitive. *"There are often multiple parties involved and everything has to be copied to each of them, so you have to be very careful what you put in the statements because you don't want to harm any of the other parties."* As a result, the experience is document heavy.

making a difference

After the first seat, trainees are given the opportunity to express a choice as to which departments they visit. They meet with the business manager in order to discuss their ideas and she allocates people to teams accordingly. As with many firms, the closer a trainee is to qualification, the higher priority their case is. That said, *"trainees are good at meeting to discuss it amongst ourselves, so everyone can say what they want to do and no one is left doing a seat that they really don't like."*

The other seat options include public services law, police and prison law, housing, immigration, property and private client. *"Public service law is extremely popular. It is quite a unique area and includes a lot of human rights work, which people like."* The department takes on cases involving mental health, community care and education, and trainees normally have access to a good mix of work from across each of these areas. Our interviewees spent most of their time *"seeing clients, drafting witness statements and preparing bundles, as well as there being a good amount of hearings to go along to."* Over the past year the team worked on K v London Borough of Newham, which was one of the first successful human rights challenges in the education sector and concerned the breach of Article 9 in the local authority's admissions procedures. The team has also been active in the area of continuing care and has successfully litigated and mediated a number of cases, through which it has been able to obtain fully funded care provision for clients who were previously being charged by social services departments.

Immigration law also appeals to many trainees *"because you can make such a fundamental difference in the lives of your clients... the stakes are really high and so it is incredibly satisfying when you win."* And presumably it can be heartbreaking when you don't. Trainees find the attitude of others in the department to be inspiring: *"The immigration team here is quite innovative in how it approaches the law and so it will take on cases that others have abandoned."*

shiver me timbers

The firm was praised for the attention it gives to future joiners before they commence their training contracts. Said one source: *"The firm gives us the opportunity to do work experience with them before starting, which is really worth doing,"* not least because it familiarises you with the reality of this kind of practice. Said one wise source: *"You have to be prepared to deal with the type of clients that the firm has, many of whom have quite deep-seated, non-legal problems."* Learning this before you start your training contract is by far the best way, as *"you will be expected to deal with clients yourself from quite early on."*

In order to fit in at Fisher Meredith *"you will need a pretty strong social conscience and motivation to help people."* The majority of trainees are slightly older than the average, with most of the current batch between 26 and mid-30s. Since leaving university, many had gained experience working at similarly focused legal aid firms or working for NGOs, either here in the UK or abroad (eg in Bolivia and Cambodia). There is also a sprinkling of postgraduate qualifications among the current trainee group, with one person sporting a Master's degree in Human Rights. The applicants that seem to do best are certainly not *"your typical Oxbridge type;"* they are *"slightly older, perhaps slightly wiser, and completely committed to working for the underdog."* Needless to say, if you are in it for the money, then you should definitely consider other options. As one trainee pointed out: *"I hate the fact that there is such a misconception that because we are lawyers we must be making a fortune, when actually I am eligible for legal aid myself with my salary and my rent."* Like all our sources, you ought to be attracted to this firm because of its continuing commitment to the legal aid sector. Indeed in this part of the profession, Fisher Meredith has to be one of the top firms to go for, not least because of its good track record in management and its size. As one typical source told us: *"I didn't want to be the only trainee at the firm, I wanted a group of people around me."*

Their decision paid off: the trainees are supportive of each other and spend a lot of social time together too. They make a beeline for the pubs in Kennington a couple of Fridays every month, and all look forward to the annual Fisher Meredith day out. *"This year we had a day trip to Richmond on a boat. We were lucky as it was hot and sunny, and we spent the afternoon eating and drinking. It was good fun – we got a pirate's outfit for the managing partner to wear, with an eye patch and everything. He declined unfortunately."* Despite said spoilsportery, *"it was really good to see everyone when they were relaxed."* Back in the office, there is *"a friendly and supportive environment... it's not at all starchy and there is no need to wear an expensive suit to work or anything like that."*

and finally...

If you aren't intimidated by the prospect of early responsibility or contact with potentially difficult clients, then Fisher Meredith is a top, top choice. Said one trainee: *"I feel I am really making a difference and getting on with proper work, whilst a lot of the people that I did the LPC with are stuck doing photocopying."* In 2007, five of the six qualifiers stayed on with the firm.

Foot Anstey

the facts

Location: Plymouth, Exeter, Taunton
Number of UK partners/solicitors: 30/82
Total number of trainees: 13
Seats: 4x6 months
Alternative seats: None

Down in the West Country, Foot Anstey displays real strength in a good spread of practices. Currently enjoying new offices in Taunton and Exeter, with a brand new building in Plymouth on the way, this upwardly mobile firm provides services to businesses, privately paying individuals and those in receipt of legal aid.

bedding down

The trainees we spoke to at Foot Anstey knew they were onto a winner: *"It seemed like a growing firm and there was a good choice of different areas to do seats in... plus it's well known and right up there with the big guns,"* said one locally bred source. Another added: *"I was told that they were looking to nurture new lawyers and grow organically."* These are apt words. Having grown too big for Exeter and Plymouth alone, the firm hopped over to the traditional market town of Taunton, where it has been spreading with the speed and vigour of a tomato plant on Baby Bio. In 2005, it gained a foothold in Somerset through a merger with Taunton's Alms & Young. Clarke Willmott was the next firm to be Foot Ansteyed, when its family law, new homes and bulk conveyancing teams were swiped. Foot Anstey then struck again, expanding its clinical negligence team via the recruitment of further lawyers from Clarke Willmott. It now boasts a second, brand new office on the Blackbrook business park to hold everybody. Trainees have been actively involved in helping these new teams to settle in, carrying out seats in both Taunton offices as well as the firm's more traditional Devon heartland.

Just as Devon (recently declared the number-one organic county by Defra) aims to become the UK's greenest region, Foot Anstey seeks to become the premier firm in the South West and grow revenue to £22m by 2010. It is proud of its big ambitions and looks for trainees who are equally gung ho. Our sources say an expansion into Cornwall would come as no surprise, yet questions were raised as to whether the new Somerset teams have yet been fully grafted onto the firm: *"I think they're waiting for the dust to settle before they move further West,"* said one source. In August 2007, Foot Anstey kicked up the Devon dust again by merging with ten-lawyer Plymouth firm Serpell Eaton Solicitors, which specialised in commercial property, private client and charity law. We also heard rumours of other strategic mergers in the works to beef up the firm's Devon and Somerset offices still further. Clearly Foot Anstey hasn't played all its aces just yet.

transplants

The firm prides itself on representing some major national clients, including NatWest, Wrigley and the Royal Shakespeare Company. Highlights include acting for British entrepreneur Peter de Savary on the £26m sale of Bovey Castle, advising Odeon Cinemas on its 6,000 employees and working on the deal between Virgin Health Bank and Plymouth company Biovault regarding Virgin's storage of stem cells harvested from newborn babies' umbilical cords. Biovault will process and cryogenically store the cells until they are needed to treat illnesses such as leukaemia and Parkinson's disease. A strong media and publishing practice is one of the firm's best assets. Associated Newspapers is a client and the team provides defamation advice to over 400 regional newspapers.

The South West clientele is broad and varied. Recently chosen to participate in a pioneering partnership with the public sector, Foot Anstey is now part of a panel of nine firms supporting the in-house legal teams of 18 local authorities on issues including employment, planning, commercial, litigation, property, housing, highways and specialist governance issues. The firm's leisure and licensing practice advises local public houses, off-licences, clubs, restaurants, hotels and leisure facilities, so when an enterprising farmer sets up a caravan park in the field opposite your rural retreat, you might want to get on the phone to a Foot Anstey lawyer. Other local clients include the University of Plymouth, Arts Council England (South West), Cornwall Farmers Co-operative and the Plymouth Marine Laboratory.

Seats can be taken in insolvency, charities, contentious private client, family, crime, planning, property litigation, commercial property, coco, media, employment, private client, IP, marine litigation, personal injury and clinical negligence (although crime is only available in Plymouth, while IP, property litigation, insolvency, charities, contentious private client and media are only available in Exeter). *"We have to negotiate our own seats,"* said one trainee; *"the training principal puts us into our first seat but it's then our responsibility to go to the person we'd like to sit with next and say, 'Have you got room for me?'"* Moving around offices is encouraged, but for those who choose not to, interaction with other offices is minimal. *"There are trainees in Exeter who don't know anyone in Taunton, and there are people in Plymouth I wouldn't know without looking up to see what department they're in,"* explained one interviewee. For those who do move, the firm is good about reimbursing travel expenses (*"I'm being paid about £16.50 a day towards petrol"*) and many of those travelling cross-county car-share, making for a more enjoyable and more environmentally friendly commute.

breeding new varieties

In terms of popularity, up to now private client, family and clinical negligence are the areas most people have hoped to qualify into. *"Those aren't commercial areas so there may be a need to redress that balance: a firm can't survive by having 20 newly qualified private client lawyers,"* concluded one source. Commercial property and family offer more responsibility than most seats, as each allows trainees to run their own caseload. Corporate, commercial and litigation are the seats in which trainees most commonly take a back seat role: *"You just have to accept that your role is going to be an ancillary or supporting one, but then you can't just expect to come in on day one and be a corporate lawyer."* Some of the coco team's work involves charities, which can be really rewarding: *"When you're working with individuals or charities, where it's just one or two people who've come up with an idea, they're always so impressed with everything we do. It may just be a small family or just one or two friends or individuals within a local community."* Crime seats commonly leave trainees with a sense of having made a difference to people's lives: *"I've been allowed to be a part of everything from assault and affray right up to complex fraud and sexual assault,"* enthused one trainee.

The only compulsory is litigation. The seat involves *"a lot of to-ing and fro-ing with barristers and clients, making sure witness statements are right before trial,"* in some cases even *"negotiating the final witness statement and having it served on the other side."* The highlight for one source was attending High Court proceedings to sit behind counsel and take notes: *"I was conscious my handwriting had to be legible!"* Simple advocacy duties are also on the cards, most frequently in the family seat. Indeed, family team trainees can expect to be in court a couple of times a week in places such as Truro, Torquay, Exeter, Taunton and Plymouth. Said one: *"I loved the advocacy. Just being in court is a great experience – it suits certain types of people better, but we all get to do it."*

In areas where there might not be enough work to keep a trainee busy it's not uncommon to work for two teams. This has been the case with insolvency, banking and debt collection recently. The firm is accommodating towards those who wish to repeat a seat in their preferred qualification practice; in fact, for fourth-seaters this is fairly normal. Trainees usually find out about qualification jobs halfway through their third seat, and while not everyone gets offered

their ideal position, the firm can usually offer a range of alternatives if the department of choice has no room.

The Plymouth staff eagerly await their new office. It is to be built close to the city centre so as to remain accessible to its significant proportion of legal aid clients. For the time being, the firm occupies an old television studio, which although outdated is not without character. The Exeter staff occupy a smart open-plan office which means *"you never have to go and knock on someone's door and creep in to ask a question."* Another advantage is that *"you can see and hear your supervisor without having to get off your chair, which is good if you're lazy."* Of the two Taunton offices, Wellington House is the smaller but it's close to the town's shops and amenities; Blackbrook is about a 20-minute walk from Tesco and Sainsbury's and *"it's a nightmare to get into town and back in an hour, so we're asking if we can have a two-hour lunch break and be allowed to make up the time. They're usually good about things like that so we'll probably get it."* Again, watch this space.

weeding them out

In past editions we have revelled in describing Foot Anstey's *X-Factor* style interview day, which saw the also-rans sent home at lunchtime. New training partner Louise Widley is keen to *"take the mental scarring away"* while preserving the rigour of the process. Future interviewees will still undergo a psychometric test, presumably still conducted by *"a guy from Wales who has his own methods."* However, the written test will be replaced by a group exercise, and the morning and afternoon interviews will be condensed into one panel interview. Don't let the softer approach lull you into complacency; Foot Anstey is a stickler for *"quality"* applicants. Their methods clearly pay off, as this year nine out of ten qualifying trainees are staying on at the firm.

The current trainees are *"sociable, hard-*

working and active." Their weekend pastimes are exactly as you'd hope of people who live in the West Country and they also enjoy impromptu social events. On a more professional note, *"we asked if the firm would fund us to go to a TSG conference in Northampton and they gave us a budget of £1,000 for four people to go and hired us a car."* Memorable firm-wide social events include the Christmas party at the Grand Hotel in Torquay: *"There's a band and a disco and people make fools of themselves. I think one girl flashed her knickers falling over on the dance floor! The firm gets a cheap rate on hotel rooms and most people stay over."* On the last Friday of the month, the firm pays for a free bar in each of the office locations. *"I'll go to the Taunton one this month, but we might go to the Exeter one next month,"* said one trainee.

and finally...

With a five-year expansion plan and a buzzing, stimulating environment, Foot Anstey is a firm with plenty to offer a new recruit. If the roar of the Atlantic calls you and you won't be left baffled by Jannerisms, this could be your ticket to a prosperous career in one of the most beautiful areas of Britain.

Forbes

the facts

Location: Blackburn, Preston, Accrington, Chorley, Manchester, Leeds
Number of UK partners/solicitors: 29/58
Total number of trainees: 18
Seats: 4x6 months
Alternative seats: Secondments
Extras: Pro bono – Saturday drop-in clinic

One of the larger firms in the North West, Forbes continues to grow at a steady pace. The recent opening of a Manchester branch brings the total number of offices to an impressive nine. Its broad practice incorporates both commercial and private client services, offering trainees a wealth of experience. For those unsure of the area of law in which they want to specialise, Forbes offers the opportunity to find it.

forging ahead

With over 350 people, most of them in Accrington, Blackburn, Chorley and Preston, it's no surprise that Forbes is a major presence in this neck of the woods. *"As soon as you say Forbes to anyone, they nod in recognition."* The firm is known for its insurance and public sector work, and boasts excellent family and claimant PI departments. The jewel in its crown, however, is undoubtedly its criminal practice. The crime team takes on everything from motoring offences to murder trials and acts for both legal aid and privately paying clients. In the area of business crime, a recent highlight was the defence of a company director accused of conspiring to launder over £10m. With its mix of high street and commercial work, the firm has figured out a sound recipe for success in the region and is reaping the rewards. Its revenue increased from £13.4m to £16m in 2006, a growth of almost 20%.

Never one to rest on its laurels, Forbes is upping the ante on the commercial side of its business. *"Commercial litigation, defendant insurer and company commercial seem to be the hot areas at the moment."* The firm is also looking to beef up its presence in Manchester and Leeds: *"At the moment Manchester focuses on defendant insurer work, but I think it will soon be bumped up with more departments."* Aside from a small merger 15 years ago, however, the firm prefers organic growth, so don't expect any dramatic takeovers. *"We prefer the slow and steady approach."*

being jack bauer

A training contract at the firm will see the trainee taking seats in any four of the following areas: crime, civil litigation, family, probate, employment, PI, defendant insurer, property and company/commercial. One seat must be non-contentious, but otherwise there are no compulsories or typical seat patterns, although you could say that crime, family and PI are common. There's obviously a lot of variety, but all seats have certain common themes: interesting work and a delicate balance of autonomy and support. In property, for instance, a seat in residential conveyancing offers an enviable degree of independence. *"To begin with you assist other fee earners, but after you're familiar with the process, you're given your own files."* A good seat to start in, *"it's very procedural, but it's not boring. Things always crop up on different files, which prevents the work from becoming repetitive."* Trainees see matters from initial instructions, through the contract drafting and checking title stage to completion. Client contact is constant and *"you're speaking to other solicitors quite a bit too, especially when you're in a property chain."* Offering a different angle, a seat in commercial property involves a lot of leasehold deals.

In the defendant insurance seat, trainees deal with PI and other types of claim. *"It gives you a good grounding in the subject and experience working with commercial clients."* The team acts for major insurance companies and a lot of the Greater Manchester local authorities, and on any given day a trainee might be preparing witness statements and instructions to counsel or researching issues that crop up in relation to particular claims. *"You're always out and about, either sitting with counsel at trials or representing the firm at conferences. My supervisor is anxious to make sure I get experience of all stages of the litigation process."* In this area of practice there is also the opportunity to go on a client secondment to the Co-operative Group or an insurance company, usually two days a week for six weeks. *"You become familiar with the clients and spend time evaluating medical reports, sorting out claimants' solicitors' costs, and reading liability reports. It was incredibly valuable experience for me to work in-house."*

In the crime department *"trainees work very closely with their partner."* At the moment there are four trainees in crime seats, spread across the offices. They quickly get up to speed preparing cases for trial – seeing clients to get their instructions, taking witness statements, explaining the CPS documents to clients and even making the occasional field trip. *"You might go check out undercover surveillance for a case, for example."* It's not exactly Jack Bauer, but let's face it, it's probably as close as you'll get as a solicitor. Attending court with your supervisor is another highlight of the seat: *"It's a brilliant learning tool, watching how to interact with the CPS people and the magistrates. I've picked up so many helpful tips about how to carry myself in court."* When not busy in court or out in the field, perhaps visiting a client in prison, chances are your diary will be packed out with client appointments in the office. *"People come in off the street needing advice. You never know what's coming through the door next; it keeps you on your toes."* Trainees who attain their police station accreditation can add their names to the duty rota and be on call for advice to those who have been arrested. It sounds hectic, *"but it's all overtime, so there's the opportunity to make a bit of extra dough."* Overall, trainees were extremely positive about the experience: Said one: *"I never dreamed I'd be involved in high-profile cases at such an early stage in my career. The opportunities are fantastic, if you're confident enough to grab them."*

tour of duty

Seating arrangements vary between the departments and all have their pros and cons. Some trainees sit with their supervisor ("*great, as they're right there to answer any question*") others are in their own office ("*which I like because it makes you feel a bit more senior and you're really left to get on with it*"). Work often comes to the trainee from around the team and our sources suggested it was easy enough to speak up when they had too much on. In fact, in most cases any work that is given to a trainee goes through the supervisor first. "*If they think you've got a lot on then they say you're too busy – it's like having a personal bodyguard.*" As well as a seat supervisor, trainees are assigned a mentor. "*It's reassuring to know someone is there. Personally I find you can talk to anybody, but the mentor scheme gives you a guarantee that there's someone who'll listen.*"

It's unusual for trainees to do all four seats in one location, not least because certain seats are only available in certain branches. At any one time, most of the trainees will be based in Blackburn or Preston, but chances are they will move around a fair bit over the two years. For the majority, this isn't a problem. "*People don't mind it at all; the offices are quite close together anyway.*" Granted, Leeds is considerably further – so how does the one trainee working there cope? "*One person moved to Leeds for six months; another commuted there and was given a travel allowance.*" If it's really going to be a problem then "*they do their best to accommodate you,*" but in most cases trainees view moving around the offices as the best way to meet colleagues and get to know the firm from all angles. With so many different locations, creating a cohesive, firm-wide culture has presented a challenge. "*They are trying very hard to promote Forbes' values and bring everyone together,*" said one source. And it seems to be working. "*You'll always know some of the people in the different offices and they do feel connected. There's the Intranet, the e-mail updates, monthly department meetings and events organised between the various offices.*"

in or out?

Admittedly firm-wide social events are limited to the annual Christmas party, where "*everyone descends upon Ewood Park to enjoy a hot buffet, a free bar and a disco.*" Each office also has its own Christmas gathering, and there are other regular informal get-togethers. "*My office goes for dinner and a few drinks every so often,*" said one trainee, while another told us: "*My department is always going out for lunch.*" The firm also puts on trainee socials throughout the year. Shortly before seat moves in September and March, HR organises "*drinks and canapés for the trainees, the supervisors and the mentors.*" It gives everyone the opportunity to suss out who they're going to be working with in their next seat, and the following intake of trainees is also invited along to the March session. With working hours "*pretty much nine to five,*" there's plenty of time to get involved in extra-curricular activities. The Saturday drop-in clinic in Blackburn offers the chance to get stuck into some voluntary work. "*Anyone can come in for legal advice,*" so you never know what you're going to get. Trainees are proud of this contribution: "*It shows the firm wants to help people.*" On the sporting front, there's the Forbes football team, which is "*open to anyone, even the senior partners. We played and beat the police the other night.*" Got to show them who's the boss, eh?

Forbes has trainees from all manner of backgrounds, from redbrick graduates straight out of law school (we'll call them the externals) to those who have paralegalled at the firm first (the internals). Perhaps the one common thread we picked up on was a strong link to the North West. "*I think that remains an important feature,*" said one source; "*they look for people who want to stay here long term. From our point of view, I think it's often useful as your background helps you to understand the mentality of the clients here.*" Both full-time and part-time training contracts are offered, with part-time trainees taking four seats over three years. With regard to the application process, trainees couldn't agree on whether internal candidates have an easier time of things. *"External trainees have two interviews, whereas I think internal candidates only have one,"* said one source. This sparked a robust response from the internal candidates' corner: *"You still have to go through the interview process – in fact it's worse when you apply internally because you have to do presentations and things."* Regardless of which route you take, the overall consensus is that *"the firm makes it fair"* and once you're in *"you're all in the same boat – it doesn't matter what your background is."* In 2007, two of the three qualifiers stayed on with the firm, and in September 2007 eight of the 18-strong trainee group were internal applicants and ten were externals.

and finally...

With such a wide range of seats, this firm is great for those who have not yet understood the precise nature of their calling. We were asked to issue one warning however: *"Big egos need not apply. It's just not how we are here."*

Ford & Warren

the facts

Location: Leeds
Number of UK partners/solicitors: 21/30
Total number of trainees: 7
Seats: 4x6 months
Alternative seats: Occasionally Canada

Flashy. Showy. Slick. If these are adjectives you'd like to be able to apply to your law firm, there's really no point you reading any further. This single-office Leeds firm is staunchly resisting the trend towards über-sophisticated marketing techniques. Its website does not feature pictures of seedling plants that symbolise its organic growth or smiling lawyers perched on desks in an informal yet professional manner. At Ford & Warren, it's all about substance over style...

drink and drive

We're not in the habit of making ill-advised suggestions; it's just that drink and drive seems to perfectly sum up the two client sectors that are most important to the firm. Its road and rail transportation department enjoys a national reputation for regulatory advice and dispute resolution. For example, when Bath & North East Somerset Council got fed up with the noise and air pollution caused by open-topped tour buses in Bath, it was F&W to the rescue. An application to the Traffic Commissioner was filed for a restriction to the operation of the buses and, despite objections from the operators, granted in exactly the terms the council wanted. Peace returned to the city of Bath and F&W notched up another victory. Its impressive client roster also features major goods and passenger transport and rail organisations including the Road Haulage Association, National Express and the Balfour Beatty group. Before trainees put the pedal to the metal, however, it would be wise to keep in mind that *"it's difficult to get a whole seat in this practice area because the work is very complex."* But there's no need to stall completely. Because transport clients are so intrinsic to the firm, you'll most likely touch on the sector in corporate, litigation and employment. *"It's more probable that you'll get to dabble in it for a couple of weeks as part of commercial litigation."*

The second important client sector is the licensed and leisure industry, where the work seems to revolve largely around pubs. No, not in pubs. Around pubs. Put that beer down and pay attention. Established in 2005, it's still a relatively small department, but one that is growing year on year. *"It's a real mix of local authority work and court work. There's quite a lot of advocacy experience to be gained – it's very hands-on."* Trainees run cases alongside the partner, and because files have a relatively short life span of three to four months *"you can see things through from beginning to end."* Daily tasks might include negotiating with the council or the police, liaising with clients, researching and taking instructions. *"I did quite a lot of licensing sub-committee hearings myself and it was an excellent experience. Two-hour hearings to yourself: you don't often get that chance!"*

The property litigation seat also predominantly features licensed premises. The team handles the majority of litigation for Punch Taverns and also acts for major players such as Greene King, Admiral Taverns and Scottish & Newcastle Breweries. *"You start off with basic claims for possession, rent arrears, that sort of thing, and there's lots of precedents and standardisation in the department, so that's not too taxing. Then there are the High Court injunctions for breach of leases or writs of possession."* As in some other areas of the firm, *"there's a bedrock of high-volume work, which helps you get up to speed with the basics, and then there's the bigger work which stretches the grey matter a bit more."* An example of the latter is a boundary dispute where an adjoining neighbour of a pub is claiming rights of way over the car park on the grounds of 20 years' continuous use. A variety of work, from high-volume, fixed-fee files to High Court cases, means *"there is a pronounced learning curve as you progress through the seat."* Client contact is also excellent. *"I've sat down and discussed things with the heads of plcs,"* beamed one source.

a job well done

Employment is *"a fantastic opportunity to work alongside some very experienced people – it's always a popular seat."* The team is skilled in industrial relations, advising employers on union recognition and strike action. It acts on behalf of rail companies and bus operators, providing strategic advice in relation to pension or pay disputes.

Work has also reached fever pitch in the healthcare sector, with the team acting for Primary Care Trusts and NHS hospital trusts. F&W advocates appear across the country in employment and appeal tribunals, and counsel is rarely used except in High Court proceedings, so it's a great chance to see how it all works. Trainees regularly attend meetings with witnesses, and there's a fair bit of drafting and research. *"People often want to qualify in this seat because they know the firm has such a good reputation in employment."*

Although none of the seats are compulsory, commercial property will more likely than not feature somewhere on the agenda. Our interviewees were in two minds about its popularity. *"People don't tend to enjoy it at law school, so they don't look forward to it."* Then again, *"because it's such a major department, there's a lot of big work going on there."* Because the files are large, you're more likely to be doing bits of work for several fee earners, rather than running your own files. *"I was completing forms, drafting leases and purchase agreements. There's quite a lot of due diligence because we specialise in licence and leisure, and that's quite exciting and different."* Strict deadlines can lead to extra hours: *"We've just been told we have to come in this weekend to finish something off,"* a source revealed. At least *"you're really valued as one of the team."*

If you find yourself in the insurance litigation seat you'll be dealing with *"small claims and road traffic accidents, mostly from the defendant's side."* Every now and then a big catastrophic injury claim will crop up. Said one source: *"I went to quite a few court appearances and settlement meetings. I wasn't advocating myself – they only had very big trials on so it wouldn't have been appropriate – but you can learn a lot by observing the process."* The practice has also expanded to include product and public liability claims, sports injuries and fraud. In fact, the dedicated fraud team has stood up to numerous fraudulent accident claims, including staged motor accidents, and last year litigated in a trial involving an alleged motor accident fraud ring. *"It's a good beginner seat because there's a nice balance of forms and procedures. You also get to grips with high volume work."*

on the factory floor

"Many of the trainees here are that little bit older and have some experience under their belt, so the firm does expect you to be able to take a lot on and get on with things." Several of the trainees of 2007 had previously worked as F&W paralegals, *"one used to be in the police and another was a tennis coach in a former life."* Despite the *"fairly hefty workload, you're never left to flounder."* Within the open-plan office, *"you can wander into anyone's space and pick their brains. We're all on the factory floor together and there's a heavy emphasis on being part of the team."* You can also rely on your fellow trainees to steer you through: *"We don't sit with our supervisors, we have trainee banks where we sit together. You can ask each other things you don't want to ask your partner."*

At first glance, this seems a very traditional firm. Everyone still has his or her own secretary and the dress code is rigidly formal. External e-mails are automatically forwarded to supervisors, so personal e-mail is limited to lunchtimes and a dedicated terminal. Trainees were remarkably upbeat about all of this. *"You feel a bit disconnected at first, but then you're busy anyway. It removes the temptation."* Online, this practical, no-nonsense image is more than evident. *"Our website is not an award winner,"* confessed one interviewee; *"it's been like that for years and it was hardly state of the art to begin with!"* Maybe so, but it illustrates and important aspect of the firm's philosophy. *"We're not really into fuss. Our approach to external marketing has always been low key; you won't see advertisements on TV or on the radio. Our work speaks for itself."*

f&w's got talent

Dig deeper and there is evidence to suggest that the firm is not as old-fashioned as you might think. *"Internally, our intranet system is really quite advanced. You have online up-to-the-minute information on your billing and time recording, and all these fancy graph formats. Documents are all hyperlinked and you can get information at the click of a mouse."* Flexibility with working hours is another surprise: *"They aren't too authoritative about time keeping, as long as you get the work done."* After work, trainees sometimes go to the bars around Millennium Square, and at the last Christmas party they got together with the NQs to perform an alternative nativity play. *"It was funny in the end, but we had to get quite drunk before we had the guts to do it in front of everybody."* The party also showcased the talents of the F&W band.

In truth, this firm is not averse to change; in fact it is open to suggestions and willing to try new ideas. In 2007, second-years voiced their desire for a four-month rotation instead of six-months. *"A proposal was put forward; we had meetings with the managing partner and they decided to try it."* Unfortunately when the four months were up, nobody felt they'd had sufficient time in their seats and partners weren't ready to let go of their trainees. The experiment was not a success because *"it took quite a long time to finalise the decision to switch back and I think people were stressing. But then it was our own doing..."*

and finally...

F&W has a strong identity and it's important to make sure you're a good fit. One trainee summed it up well: *"This is a firm for people who want to be lawyers, not people who want to be candidates on The Apprentice or are interested in making money pure and simple. It's a down-to-earth place, and the focus is on doing the job at hand."* In 2007, all three qualifiers took jobs with the firm.

Forsters LLP

the facts

Location: London
Number of UK partners/solicitors: 29/60
Total number of trainees: 10
Seats: 6x4 months
Alternative seats: None

Formed as recently as 1998, Forsters is a young West End property and private client-led practice. Nudging its way towards the top 100, the firm is more than a match for other Mayfair outfits over ten times its age.

breakaway faction

Forsters' relatively recent inception came as a direct consequence of the creation of the Eversheds juggernaut. When established firm Frere Cholmeley Bischoff decided to become Eversheds' London branch in the late nineties, a key group of real estate lawyers decided they just didn't fancy the gig. Quitting their old firm for a very des West End res, and taking the name of Frere's founder for good measure, this crack team of experts has since built up an excellent reputation in all things property-related. It has also gradually diversified into private client, family, employment and commercial practice. The firm now has 29 partners and around 160 staff.

The real estate practice is the big cheese at Forsters, with instructions pouring in from the retail sector, public bodies, private developers and big-hitting property investors. Emphasising its transaction abilities, the firm last year won business from US fund Westbrook on the property aspects of the £190m acquisition of Dolphin Square, a 1930s Pimlico landmark building comprising over 1,000 flats. It also advised long-time client Knight Frank on the lease of a new global HQ building at 55 Baker Street and acted for BA Pension Fund on a sale and leaseback transaction involving a £500m joint venture with Tesco Stores. There was also the small matter of assisting private investors in letting 25 Hanover Square, the world's most expensive office space at £100 per square foot. The addition of a property finance lawyer from Macfarlanes, as well as construction, planning and property litigation hires from Eversheds and DLA, have served to further broaden Forsters' capabilities, and notable client gains include The Crown Estate which appointed the firm to handle its City, Midtown, Westminster and Kensington portfolios.

Forsters' noted private client team represents moneyed clients, including over 30 traditional landed estates, foreign nationals and those in the field of arts and entertainment. Lawyers recently worked on a Privy Council appeal regarding allegedly sham Guernsey trusts, on a Claims Resolution Tribunal in the Holocaust Victim Assets Litigation concerning a family's loss of assets, having fled Austria after the Anschluss with Nazi Germany, and on the sale of the contents of a stately home to the National Trust. Moving with the times, the matrimonial department has added a dedicated civil partnerships practice, while the recently formed employment team has continued to represent wealthy individuals and businesses on the employment aspects of transactional work.

Forsters has made its home in a beautiful eighteenth-century townhouse on Hill Street close to Berkeley Square. It's a location rich with literary and cultural associations, not to mention being a popular spot for well-established property outfits. *"I often feel like I'm walking through a Jane Austen novel,"* chuckled one source. That said, trainees delight in the *"quirky"* and *"distinctive character"* of a firm they describe as being *"very comfortable with what it is"* – a *"young, fresh and forward-looking firm."* They like *"the idea that staff are cared for; you're not just a number."* Unsurprisingly, given this ethos and the firm's age, our sources described *"a relatively relaxed hierarchy"* in which *"there's little divide between you and people with 20 years' experience."* Trainees additionally pointed out that *"our client base has a lot to do with the atmosphere. Even in commercial or commercial property, where you're dealing with the largest clients, there's a personal, even quirky edge to dealings. There is no over-the-top corporate persona."*

round the houses

A six by four-month seat rotation allows trainees to sample the full range of Forsters' work while also specialising in something. Certain of our interviewees, for example, had arrived with *"a desire to focus on private client and family work."* Seats are available in employment, commercial litigation, corporate/commercial, family and private client, as well as commercial property, residential property, construction and property litigation. Most trainees return to a preferred area for the final seat, which means that *"second-years tend to get priority at rotation time."* If this leads to the occasional compromise for first-years, the majority are happy to accept the trade-off for the benefit of *"eight months in the area you want to qualify into... it's useful whether you stay here or look elsewhere for a job."*

It is unheard of not to sample at least one property-flavoured seat, but given the quality of the work in those departments few are complaining. The teams' work spans the public, investor/developer and retail sectors, meaning that in commercial property trainees end up assisting on sizeable transactions as well as taking on portfolio management activities. *"I talk to contractors and project managers, deal with clients over the phone and set out changes to documents,"* explained one source. By contrast, time spent in construction offers *"one of the most bookish experiences – it really is almost pure contract law."* Lest this sound too dry, be assured *"there's lots of*

appointments, liaising with clients and the other side." Residential property is *"a totally different pace; it's very busy."* Trainees *"handle sale and purchase files alone"* and fit in myriad other tasks such as *"sorting out registrations for big estates."* Similarly, property litigation seats also offer exposure to residential as well as commercial disputes. There's *"inevitably a fair bit of mundane paperwork as well as drafting and research,"* but more often than not the chance to do *"telephone hearing applications."* We did hear of one 'lucky' trainee who had been *"sent to court to do a squatters hearing case. I was told that squatters never turn up but they did... very nerve-wracking."*

practice makes perfect

Although supervised in each seat, sitting in *"small open-plan groups of six or so"* means trainees generally exist as *"more of a resource for the department under the aegis of a supervisor."* A common thread in our interviews was *"the fantastic quality of practical training."* *"Partners really take the time to teach you and whenever you feel like you're entering a comfort zone, you're given work at the next level of sophistication."* A mentoring system adds an extra level of support: *"It won't be your work supervisor, it'll be someone you can go out with and ask stupid questions of, or raise issues casually."* In a *"hectic in a good way"* department such as family, it's good to have the cushion. Here, *"wealthy people going through divorce"* is the stock in trade (along with *"some bits of children's stuff"*) and for trainees this means *"lots of meetings, client contact"* and an endless stream of ancillary relief, unmarried couple and civil registration issues. Private client also offers plentiful contact with clients, and although the work focuses on wills, trusts, probate and coco/employment support, our sources traced a common thread between the popularity of these two areas. *"You're seeing the real-life impact of law on people, which is more immediately satisfying."* Seats in commercial litigation, employment and corporate apparently offer a similarly pleasing amount of *"face-to-face contact"* and *"a good degree of responsibility."* Corporate is fully developed *"in the context of a West End property practice"* (ie small deals/AIM) and litigation seats provide opportunities to assist on cases involving clients such as international banks and foreign retailers.

westenders

Forsters' Hill Street location is ideal for nipping to Bond Street, Oxford Street or pretty much anywhere in the West End. The Red Lion is a popular post-work haunt, although on a summer's day it must compete with the period charms of the office itself as *"a fantastic roof terrace"* is routinely called into action. *"We had barbecues and watched World Cup matches out there last summer,"* recalled one source. Drinks parties, wine-tasting evenings, it manages the lot... *"and sometimes the book club will meet out there."* Ah yes, the book club. Basically staff meet to chew over the merits of a literary tome and chow down on a meal. Apparently *"the food is always wonderful, so it's worth going for the lunch even if you've only glanced at the book."*

Regular softball, cricket and football fixtures against neighbouring property firms complete the social picture. Trainees are also likely to bump into their peers when attending shared PSC sessions with Boodle Hatfield and Bircham Dyson Bell. Such a context gives Forsters types the opportunity to compare themselves with trainees at these other firms. *"It sounds a bit sappy, but we are a fairly quirky bunch,"* concluded one. Equally divided between northern and southern, public and private school, Oxbridge and redbrick backgrounds, trainees here share the common desire *"to avoid the City, work in a smaller-firm environment but still get good work."* Working days generally lasting *"to 6pm or 7pm, with the odd later spell,"* helped our sources feel they'd come up

trumps in their choice of firm. Of course there's always another side to the coin, and in Forsters' case it relates to the availability of NQ jobs. Even though the process has been *"made much clearer and the decision moved to as early as Easter,"* there won't necessarily be jobs for all in people's preferred areas. In 2006 one qualifier out of four accepted a job in commercial property, but in 2007 the figure was much better, with all four qualifiers staying on. They took up jobs in commercial property, residential property, construction and family.

and finally...

Entirely comfortable in its Mayfair skin, Forsters represents a lively option for property and private client-minded applicants.

Freeth Cartwright LLP

the facts

Location: Nottingham, Derby, Leicester, Manchester
Number of UK partners/solicitors: 68/84
Total number of trainees: 13
Seats: 4x6 months
Alternative seats: None
Extras: Pro bono – Nottingham Law Centre

Once best known for civil litigation, especially multiparty claims over products such as infant MMR vaccine and the Trilucent and 3M breast implants, Freeth Cartwright has emerged as a leading commercial firm in the East Midlands.

wragged road to riches

The *"massive class action stuff"* that had made the firm so well known may have dried up, but this is no disaster as its eyes are now fixed elsewhere. In particular, *"property has thrived, as have commercial and corporate,"* so much so that one trainee enthused: *"The growth I have seen at the firm has been stunning."* A 13% rise in turnover to £31m for the year 2006/07 is credited to a *"chair and CEO* [who] *have brought in driving ambition"* and a clear aim *"to be regarded as the Wragges of the East Midlands."*

The rise of the property department is definitely the biggest story. With over 100 fee earners, Freeths has the largest commercial property offering in the region and it racked up deals worth a combined value of £1bn in 2006. Being on regeneration agency Blueprint Limited Partnership's legal panel ensured involvement for the firm in Blueprint's first major project – the extension to the existing Nottingham Science and Technology Park, the initial phase alone being worth more than £25m. Freeth lawyers have also been busy assisting on the redevelopment of the 240-acre former RAF Newton, just east of Nottingham, and on the £12m sale of a site for residential development down in Kent.

While this department is unquestionably strong, *"it's not true to say we're just a property firm, as we have a lot of other good commercial clients too."* More specifically, *"a lot of the firm's core clients were and still are East Midlands-based, but over the last five or six years we've won clients with big national profiles."* Those wins include credit services company Experian, energy company E.ON, sports agency SFX, the HMV Group, a swathe of big banks and a selection of local and other public authorities. It all gives credence to trainees' assertion that Freeths is *"an East Midlands firm with a national profile."*

sitting comfortably

Freeths' new priorities mean trainees are highly likely to visit commercial property (which includes construction and planning) and corporate finance. Thankfully those who'd never imagined they'd enjoy property found *"it is a really good seat because it's a sociable department with good networking events."* Our sources had

worked on sales and purchases, landlord and tenant matters and corporate support exercises, and explained that the lawyers are *"particularly keen on supervision. Other departments are a bit more old school in the way they use the trainees; property uses them more intelligently and everything is explained thoroughly and appraised."* There is also the benefit of steady hours: *"I left at 6.30pm at the latest,"* claimed one interviewee.

A planning seat meshes well with property. The department employs qualified planners as well as lawyers, so trainees see the whole discipline from two very different angles. When working with the lawyers they learn how to draft Section 106 'planning gain' agreements for developers, and when working with the planners they are exposed to appeals and the full application process. Freeths' employment law team is well established and represents *"major employers and some famous names."* In IP/IT trainees experience everything from patent litigation, trade mark infringement and registrations, to copyright and defamation for *"high-value UK companies and individuals protecting ideas, music industry and public sector clients."* There is additionally a private client seat *"if there is space and if someone is eager."* Here trainees work both for wealthy clients and little old ladies who live locally, running their own files *"including the billing and client contact."* A tax seat may or may not be available, depending on how the small team is staffed at the time.

golddiggas

Litigation experience can be gained in comlit in Leicester or 'business services 1' in Nottingham, where the group deals with insolvency and sport plus general litigation. *"It's mainly motor sport work: sponsorship, licensing and a few driver disputes. For me it was identifying claims and doing research before drafting a letter of claim."* 'Business services 2' is a commercial/corporate seat in Nottingham with a fair bit of company secretarial work and some exposure to drafting terms and conditions. *"It's nuts and bolts stuff, but it gives you a good background."* The clients of this department are mostly local (*"family businesses mainly, a little plc work"*) and, within the department, the PFI team represents local authorities and primary care trusts (PCTs). Be aware that the public sector is an area the firm is targeting for further growth. It is already a part of the EM Law Share legal group, the UK's largest public/private legal partnership.

One source particularly enjoyed the straight corporate seat they'd taken: *"I progressed so much,"* they told us. *"I did board minutes and resolutions, and as deal-wise there was lots going on, I drafted smaller things."* In 2006, Freeth handled some 77 corporate finance deals totalling over £1bn in its three Midlands offices. These included the £18.5m sale of Designdock Limited (aka clothing designer Golddigga) to a management team backed by venture capitalists. And what of the hours? Because *"partners do value their quality of life,"* trainees aren't driven like slaves. That said, *"you have to be prepared to work quite hard: in corporate you'd leave at 8pm on average, some days well beyond that."* Trainees are appraised at the end of each six-month seat, and can ask for a mid-seat review if they wish. At Freeths the practice is for trainees to work directly for partners: *"It's one of the things I like about the firm,"* said a source; *"they always comment on work you do."*

seeing the big picture

The biggest office by far is Cumberland Court in Nottingham, which unsurprisingly has the most seats. The firm does like trainees to circulate around its East Midlands locations, not least because the two smaller Derby and Leicester offices *"always need trainees."* Leicester possesses *"a clinical negligence team, commercial litigation/employment, a handful of people in cor-*

porate finance, commercial property and private client. Oh, and a guy who does licensing."* Trainees who pitch up here are either resident in the Leicester area or live in Nottingham and are willing to give the office a try. As one put it: *"It's only when you work in another office of Freeths that you see the whole picture of the firm."* Derby offers seats in commercial, property and litigation and is described as a miniature version of the Nottingham HQ, with a comparable trainee experience. FYI, Derby is about 30 minutes from Nottingham by train *"perhaps slightly longer by car"* and the journey to Leicester is much the same. Apparently, Freeths' attachment to three East Midlands offices is *"historical."* According to one source: *"Derby is fairly sizeable and serious. Leicester, I am less sure what we are doing there. I'd say the office needs to be updated to take it away from the big-high-street-practice feel."*

And then there is Manchester. Last year a surprise opening of an office in the North West got us scratching our heads, so we asked trainees what it was all about. *"We had one or two extremely good contacts there and so it made sense,"* said one. Having started out with two lawyers working only on insolvency and construction matters, there are now five and the plan is to keep growing. As yet there are no trainee seats, but that could change in the future.

having a ball

"We're are all very personable, there's no starch," trainees told us, likening themselves to their peers over at Browne Jacobson but refusing any connection to Eversheds. *"We stand slightly above them on the hill,"* a cheeky source laughed, *"which is where we should be I think!"* The most important quality for a young Freether is *"enterprise: we need to be on the ground with the clients. Freeths wants you to be able to go out there in the market."* Nights at the dogs, comedy shows, go-karting with Grant Thornton and the region's Dealmak-

Shahab, trainee

RELENTLESS.

THE TRAINING, NOT THE WORKLOAD.

We won't deny that joining us is a tough challenge. This is one of the world's biggest and most successful law firms and our clients have expectations to match.

But that doesn't mean we leave our new graduates to sink or swim – quite the opposite. Our training and support is as varied and wide-ranging as our business. And it doesn't just stop at qualifying, but continues virtually non-stop throughout your career.

To find out more about our trainee opportunities go to:

www.freshfields.com/uktrainees

FRESHFIELDS BRUCKHAUS DERINGER

ers Ball all help. A slight grumble concerns *"salaries – they have been going up a grand per seat and we are now at about market level,"* but not, others pointed out, at the same level as Browne Jacobson or Eversheds.

Socially, *"you wouldn't be able to tell who the partners were, except for the fact that they are obviously older."* This is apparently truer still in Leicester, *"where half of the building goes out for a beer on a Friday night."* In Nottingham, they told us: *"We always go out as friends to The Castle on a Friday night"* and a few years ago two trainees went so far as to marry each other. Alas, there were no peals of bells in 2007, but one tradition that did continue was the trainee stage performance at the Christmas party. A Grease v Saturday Night Fever dance competition was *"terribly embarrassing,"* recalled one participant; *"nevertheless, we stepped up."* By all accounts *"having a lot of wine helped."*

As for the future, trainees feel Freeths is *"just the right size"* to offer quality of work, a *"good compromise on work-life balance"* and the excitement of a firm that *"still wants to go places and get larger."* The goal is to *"break through the £30-mill turnover mark"* and sources were confident *"there is still room to grow in Nottingham."* Connections have been made with two other firms: Anthony Collins in Birmingham and Fenwick Elliot in London. *"Fenwick Freeth is not as formal as a partnership,"* we were told, *"but we have had some good referrals through them on the construction side."* In 2007 six of the seven qualifiers signed up for NQ positions.

and finally...

Many of Freeth Cartwright's trainees end up at the firm having enjoyed life as a Nottingham student, so a connection to the region definitely looks like it helps. There is no vac scheme at the moment, so an open day is a good way to sample this excellent firm.

Freshfields Bruckhaus Deringer

the facts
Location: London
Number of UK partners/solicitors: 167/620
Total number of trainees: 198
Seats: 3 or 6 months long
Alternative seats: Overseas seats, secondments
Extras: Pro bono – RCJ CAB, Tower Hamlets Law Centre, Liberty, US death row appeals; language training

Freshfields was an indispensable adviser to leading City institutions for more than 200 years until WWII, after which the very English gents decided to become men of the world. The firm then grew like topsy in London and established offices in Asia, the USA and mainland Europe. In 2000, it cemented its global status by merging with two German firms to become Freshfields Bruckhaus Deringer.

flexible friends
While Freshfields (and, yes, they do say the full name when they answer the phone) can be found in 27 cities and has over 2,500 lawyers, there's still something of the English gent about it. From its low-key recruitment material to a rather medieval website, the firm eschews brash, modern marketing and keeps things simple under the watchful eye of an angel logo that harks back to the Freshfield family crest. Something else hasn't changed since the old days: the firm still has an uncanny knack of getting in on the biggest deals around. It advised Indian mobile operator Hutchison Essar on Vodafone's £5.7bn purchase of its shares, and it helped Dutch utility company Essent on its £16bn merger with rival Nuon, the biggest ever M&A deal in the Netherlands. Also active in private equity, Freshfields advised Cinven and CVC on the £870m IPO of packaging company Smurfitt Kappa. Not to be outdone,

Freshfields' real estate team advised HSBC on the sale and leaseback of its Canary Wharf headquarters for a whopping £1.09bn.

With so much top-flight transactional work on offer, you'd assume that trainees would simply be dropped into the corporate department on day one and left there for two years. Not so. A distinctive training scheme replaces the standard four by six-month model with something more flexible. After an initial six-month seat, all others last three months, with an option for a three-month extension. The exceptions are certain niche seats like competition, insolvency and IP, which only ever last three months. Trainees say the system *"encourages you to be adventurous. If there's something you suspect you won't like, you can give it a go knowing you'd only lose three months if you hated it."* Of course, short placements can be risky: *"There's always an element of luck with these things,"* one source noted. *"If a department's busy you can make a real impression; if it's quiet and you don't do much with partners, there's less of a chance."* It's a fair point; nonetheless, we did speak to people who'd secured positions in areas where they'd only spent three months.

uk for sale

Seats in the finance and corporate departments are compulsory. With over 650 corporate lawyers around the world, the corporate department is Freshfields' powerhouse, last year generating over a third of worldwide revenue. The London corporate division alone brought in over £100m, and recently advised German engineering giant Linde on the £8.9bn takeover of British rival BOC, and Gruppo Ferrovial on its £15.6bn takeover of airports operator BAA. Lest you think the firm exists purely to sell off the cream of British business to Johnny Foreigner, its lawyers also helped the London Stock Exchange fend off the attentions of New York rival NASDAQ.

The division comprises four separate departments, together occupying four floors of Freshfields' mammoth building just off Fleet Street. Seats can be taken in a range of areas and all give a slightly different experience. For example, private equity clients *"are known as particularly demanding, so that seat tends to be one of the busiest."* For the most part, the actual work is similar across the seats: *"Basically it's a lot of due diligence, verification and bibling, with little bits of drafting here and there."* There is undoubtedly *"an element of tedium,"* but we did notice that those trainees who hit the division in their second year, or returned for another seat, found greater responsibility, including *"plenty of phone and face time with clients."* The corporate division exhibits *"a really urgent atmosphere, where everything has to be done today,"* and yet those expecting Patrick Bateman types will be pleasantly surprised (or disappointed) as *"it's very much a team; people are collaborative."*

"A shelter from the deals rollercoaster" can be found in the funds and regulatory team, which offers such delights as research into the Financial Services Authority (FSA) handbook and the Markets in Financial Instruments Directive. Supporting transactional teams can still be a real chore for academic types: *"I had hoped for analytical work,"* said one, *"but I ended up working on an IPO for several weeks, mostly liaising with the London Stock Exchange and the FSA. It was like filling out one very long tax return."*

giving it a whirl

Finance seats bring the same rapid-fire deadlines. The options are: structured and asset finance, banking, energy and infrastructure, and insolvency. *"[Dealing with] conditions precedent is the absolute classic trainee task, so you have to be super-organised and keep on top of the transaction."* Dreaded bibling duties are also common, but *"at least you have a lot of help from paralegals, so it's* really more a case of overseeing things." There are more opportunities than in corporate to work independently on smaller matters. The asset finance team, for example, handles "a lot of repeat work on orders for three to four aircraft, and because little changes from one deal to the other you can take care of them."

Dispute resolution seats are no longer compulsory since Freshfields signed up to a litigation crash course at the College of Law. Thanks to the option of three-month seats, plenty of born deal makers do give it a whirl though: "I just thought, why not?" said one. "If I didn't try it, perhaps I'd always wonder." Freshfields' Paris office has a world-beating reputation for international arbitration, and the London team is not far behind, so naturally this aspect is popular. Wherever you sit in dispute resolution, you're likely to work on long-running cases and this can mean trainee experiences vary wildly depending on when they arrive in the department. One unlucky source "spent weeks until 3am each morning putting together bundles and formatting documents. The whole time I was in the seat I didn't even see a claim form or witness statement, let alone write one." Others reported much happier times: "It was too early for bundling on the big case when I was there, so it was mostly research, which was really interesting." The highlight for some was the chance to "liaise with counsel and attend hearings." The division offers a change of pace: "It's a little more academic, and although it's not as fast-paced, it's quite intense." The downside, for sociable types at least, is that "there's not as much team working." Freshfields doesn't claim to offer the most comprehensive litigation training out there, but by the standards of big City firms, it's pretty good. The problem comes at qualification: "There's usually 20 applications for five jobs, and in the likely event you don't make it, because you have so little hands-on experience in three months, it's a crap training for going somewhere else." When we put

this point to the firm, they thought it had been made too strongly and that it is possible to do six months in litigation.

fresh pastures

Other seat options include competition, IP, employment, environment, real estate and tax. These teams were lauded for being more relaxed and offering varied and interesting tasks. However, it's important to understand that such departments are subordinate to the corporate department, and its needs come first. "I really enjoyed competition – I was carrying out research on an EU commission enquiry," said one source; "but there were also a lot of surveys for corporate, checking the competition implications of a transaction. Once you've done one, it just becomes a case of seeing how quickly you can get them out of the way."

In an organisation like this it would be virtually careless to spend your entire training contract cooped up in the London HQ. Freshfields offers a bewildering range of secondments, the majority of which are for fourth-seaters. The list stretches from the Paris office's famous arbitration team to Tesco's HQ in Hertfordshire via clients such as UBS, Morgan-Stanley and IBM, and Freshfields' vast network of overseas offices. See page 206 for the definitive list of foreign seats. Usually the smaller overseas offices have a more intimate atmosphere in which "you know everyone's name and say hello in the lift, which is very different to London." A visitor to Moscow described the team there as "super nice: a mixture of Russian, British, German, American and French... all very friendly." In general, trainees reported having greater responsibility when abroad, and naturally details like accommodation are taken care of. We did hear some complaints about instances of poor organisation. "I was a bit annoyed that, once I arrived, I never heard from London," one trainee recalled. "A quick 'How's it going?' call would have been nice." Secondments are amongst the most coveted seats, particularly the Asian options. Most people we spoke to had got their second or third choice and therefore recommended picking your back-ups carefully. On this point the firm estimates that two out of three people get their first choice.

when reality bites

Any big firm has its aggressive partners and associates; however we heard little but good things about the supervisors on the training scheme. *"Helpful"* and *"approachable"* were the most common descriptions, one source noting: *"I've been surprised how well everyone treats me. It's all open doors – you pop in, ask a question, get an answer."* One trainee's supervisor was *"so friendly, efficient and organised"* that they told us: *"That's exactly what I want to be like in 20 years."* Of course, there are a few awkward characters, *"but it's known who they are and they're not given trainees."* The group ethic at Freshfields tends to deflate any overblown egos, and it is illustrated well in the story of the trainee who *"did work for one partner who was really disorganised and he'd blame me for things that weren't my fault. Once, he really shouted at me, but everyone could see it wasn't my fault and he apologised the next day."*

This group approach means you're more likely to work for a range of partners and associates; indeed, we heard of some trainees who hadn't seen much of their supervisor at all. While this has the advantage of *"getting you to experience different ways of working,"* *"there's an immersion you get from sitting with someone and hearing their phone calls, which you can miss out on if you're working with several different people."* Serving many masters requires trainees to learn how to manage their own workload: *"You simply have to explain to people that you're doing a lot for others and you have to be fair to everyone."* Most of our sources had developed this knack.

We wonder if this fondness for sharing trainees around has contributed to Freshfields'

reputation as one of the tougher firms hours-wise. This aspect came under scrutiny following the death of a young associate in 2007. A rash of newspaper reports about the long hours and stress suffered by young lawyers ensued and these certainly didn't help the young man's team mates come to terms with the tragedy. Later, an inquest ruled a verdict of accidental death. Our trainee sources were generally philosophical about the hours they'd worked: *"It's been much as I expected, but maybe with a few more lairy patches,"* one observed. 'Lairy patches' could be *"a few weeks leaving at 11pm each day"* or *"a few nights with only a couple of hours' sleep."* *"I worked till 4am on my first day,"* recalled one source. *"That didn't exactly fill me with hope."* Real, sleep-free all-nighters aren't unheard of, but our sources pointed out that *"there's overnight secretarial support, so you won't be in late photocopying – it'll be real work."* Once things quieten down, time in lieu or early departures might be offered by some supervisors to make up for any horrors. Overall, *"it never seems to be a case of staying late for the sake of it,"* although *"leaving before six is like spitting on the cross."*

hands off our bananas

Why pick Freshfields over any other magic circle firm? For most of our sources the firm's low-key, old-school approach to recruitment was part of the appeal. *"At interview, partners were so straightforward; they didn't try to wow me, they just laid it out – this is the work, it's hard but it's rewarding."* You may be aware that Freshfields has long had a reputation for hiring a certain type of trainee: *"Mainly Oxbridge, posh, quite sporty, confident and a little bit glamorous."* We subjected the firm to our highly scientific Facebook Test and we suggest you do the same. And what do the official stats say? Some 50% of trainees come from Oxbridge, even if this figure is declining as recruiters step up their involvement with other universities. In early summer 2007, the firm's website confirmed that 12.5% of trainees were from ethnic minorities (this will rise to 20% in 2008) and 56% were women.

Whether or not you bounced from university straight into law school, you're unlikely to be prepared for an office of over 1,000 people. Cue a three-week induction which *"really eases you in and allows you to meet the other 50 or so new trainees."* Mostly dedicated to introducing the firm's structure, IT systems and so on, the induction makes time for an infamous style lesson. *"It's more of a laugh than anything,"* one immaculately groomed source explained. *"The woman who does it is a real character, especially with the boys."* *"It's mostly stuff you should know anyway, like how long your sleeves should be... how to dress professionally."* To those of us who know exactly how long our sleeves should be, it all sounds a bit OTT, but our interviewees had mixed views. *"I really liked it, actually,"* one confessed; *"there's a lot of psychology to it."* In contrast, one (female) source *"did object to being told off for not wearing lipstick."*

With over 100 trainees starting each year, you'd think it would be easy to find drinking buddies. Not so midweek, though *"on Fridays you can usually get people down to the Witness Box"* or the Cheshire Cheese. Alternative entertainments are numerous, and if you're more interested in stretching your body than your mind or your wallet there are *"dance classes, football, cricket, walking, boxercise, a sailing team – you name it, we have it."* There's even a gym on site. The healthy outlook extends to free fruit in the office. *"They did try to take away the free bananas, but there was such uproar they had to bring them back."*

annus horibilis

A sweeping restructuring in 2007 (over 50 partners were shed) followed the exit of 30 older partners as a result of changes to the firm's pen-

sion scheme. The finance department seems to have borne the brunt of the losses, leading many to conclude that Freshfields has given up on any ambition to develop a top-band finance practice and is contenting itself with being a king in corporate. As well as those partners the firm chose to shed, others made the leap voluntarily. We wondered what tantrums and almighty rows our sources had witnessed. *"It's something we've all been aware of,"* admitted one. *"I mean, we were front cover of the legal press every week for a couple of months."* And in the finance department? *"I think some of the more recently qualified lawyers have been a bit nervous, wondering what's going to happen. But the tension hasn't really filtered down to our level."* Ultimately, the difficult restructuring *"seems to have boosted what it was meant to boost – billable hours and profits and so on."* Is Freshfields' renewed focus on the bottom line related to its stated interest in a US merger? We could speculate till the cows come home...

Whatever the partners are up to, what concerns trainees most is qualification. The process itself looks to be a model of organisation. *"They actively discourage cloak-and-dagger networking with partners, especially as so many people are away in their fourth seat."* Instead, *"you fill in a form listing all the places you'd consider working and they send each department the names of those who are interested."* *"Then the departments draw up their own list and they cross-reference them. If there's no match, you get the chance to try some other departments."* The process seems to work: in 2007, 90 of the 94 qualifiers were offered jobs and 84 accepted them. All departments recruited and 41% of NQs went into corporate and finance positions. Further down the track, the signs aren't so auspicious. Freshfields made up a measly five partners in London in 2007, suggesting that a person's chances of making it to the top are *"vanishingly small."* This is not dissimilar to other top City firms, and neither was the step of introducing an 'of counsel' role to placate associates who see their partnership prospects retreating. Another initiative in the quest to better understand the concerns of its lawyers has been the introduction of an associate away-day to give participants a chance to discuss partnership, training, working patterns and various other issues.

and finally...

Freshfields has been through some major changes, but its vital assets and gentle(wo)manly conduct remain sound. If you know you want the big time – with all that entails – it's a perennially great choice.

George Green LLP

the facts

Location: Cradley Heath, Halesowen, Birmingham
Number of UK partners/solicitors: 10/12
Total number of trainees: 4
Seats: 4x6 months
Alternative seats: None

This little Black Country stalwart has stayed true to the values upon which it was founded back in 1897. If you can point to Cradley Heath on the map, read on and see if George Green can tempt you its way.

green & black country

One hundred and twenty years old, George Green is very much the grand old man of Black Country commerce and there are few small businesses in and around Cradley Heath and Halesowen that won't have knocked on its door at some point. George Green has remained keyed in to the needs of the community in which it grew up, and over the years it has grown only modestly, sticking to the tried-and-tested formula of offering a high-

quality, partner-led service at a competitive price. One astute trainee explained the firm's approach nicely: "*Our offices are not plush with sparkly marble floors like the city centre law firms – they are basic. Our clients have traditionally been Black Country-based, and they don't want to pay higher fees for fancier offices – they just want good service.*"

The no-frills, customer-first approach certainly works well with Greorge Green's clientele. The firm draws around 90% of its instructions from the West Midlands, the majority of it from owner-managed Black Country businesses. This translates into regular instructions on transactions worth between £1m and £10m, and occasionally deals worth in excess of £25m. Two recent deals came from the vendors of Hadley Industries, a Smethwick-based company specialising in cold-rolled steel and allied products, and Paddock Fabrications, a Walsall-based hardware manufacturer. As these examples suggest, the client base is studded with manufacturing and engineering companies and, as a result, the firm also represents the interests of several related business associations, among them the British Healthcare Trades Association, which looks after manufacturers of medical devices.

The corporate department is definitely the "*jewel in* [George Green's] *crown,*" with the three-partner, four-solicitor team achieving impressive results. In 2006, it advised on 60-plus transactions with an aggregate value in excess of £150m, and through several large transactions in early 2007 it looks set to improve massively on this. Included in the 2006 figure was a good deal of business for acquisition-happy, Oldbury-headquartered Caparo Industries.

In relation to finance, the George Green lawyers also receive instructions from mainstream banks, recently assisting in relation to deal funding from HBOS. In the area of insolvency, PricewaterhouseCoopers turned to the firm for the administration of Cuppa Vending. Across its core areas of work, the firm sees itself as *"doing something a little unique,"* and we can't disagree. Our parent publication *Chambers UK* ranks it alongside some heavy-hitting Birmingham firms as a good choice for corporate and litigation advice in the West Midlands. It has achieved this accolade by concentrating on keeping its faithful band of regional businesses happy and providing a realistic alternative to Birmingham's top-brass firms, fully aware that some smaller Brum businesses are unwilling to fork out the fees demanded by the big firms. Aiming to better service those clients and hoping to generate new business in the city, October 2007 saw the firm open a small office in Birmingham. Initially a hot-desking, stop-off point for lawyers meeting clients, if all goes swimmingly the firm's presence could become more concrete, which would be a bold new chapter in its history.

close encounters

The firm runs a standard four-seat training contract, with recruits most likely to be based in the Cradley Heath HQ. Corporate is without doubt the most popular department with trainees. Here, they encounter *"a huge variety of work, from research into consumer credit or competition issues to drafting board minutes, or even drafting sale and purchase agreements."* What really sets the seat apart from the others, however, is the quantity and quality of client contact. Said one trainee: *"You are often building long-term relationships with clients who will come back, and will know you when they do."* Another added: *"What I liked about the work was that you are dealing, hands-on, with owner-managed businesses. The people you deal with are enthusiastic and incredibly grateful, as what you do directly affects their livelihood."*

In stark contrast, the dispute resolution seat can lead to contact with some clients who are *"never happy whatever you do, and they never want to even pay their legal fees."* It's the difference between clients hiring a lawyer who will do something to enhance their business or their bank balance, as opposed to paying for a lawyer to dig them out of a hole they never wanted to be in. Difficult clients aside, litigation seats allow trainees to sink their teeth into some juicy disputes. Recently, the department has been embroiled in the pre-action stages of a bust-up over an alleged breach of a commercial supply agreement involving potential damages of over £1m. The litigation department is also the gateway to the esteemed employment team (a separate seat), which has recently been defending a group of employees who left their employer to establish a competing business in proceedings seeking springboard injunctions (to prevent the use of confidential information) and damages.

Beyond corporate (which can also take the form of a non-contentious commercial seat) and dispute resolution, trainees usually spend time in commercial property then either employment, family or private client. Whatever the department, great efforts are made to ensure trainees feel welcome and appreciated, and this is particularly evident on the rare occasions when they find themselves in the office beyond 6pm. *"People will always ask if you want help and thank you for staying."* The firm's small size leads to a personalised approach to training and our interviewees indicated they quickly became accustomed to the sight of training partner Paul Bennett's head *"popping round the door to see if we have any problems and how we are."*

hot gossip

The reasonable hours leave plenty of out-of-office time; however, a combination of a small trainee intake, the dire entertainment offering in Cradley Heath and the fact that most people drive to work means that George Green is never going to top the charts for fun and games. That said, thanks largely to the efforts of trainees, a rejuvenated social committee has made an impact and a number of activities have begun to find their way onto the George Green social calendar. One of the most memorable was a day trip to Windsor, during which everyone's tastes were catered for. There were options to take family members to Legoland, watch a spot of polo or just hit the shops. On the last Thursday of every month there is an intriguingly named event called 'Hot Gossip'. Alas, no one squeezes into gold Lycra hot pants for a dance session led by the senior partner; it's drinks and chit-chat in a meeting room from 4.30pm onwards. As many of the firm's employees live in Birmingham itself, it is also not unheard of to find some of them drinking in bars around the Mailbox at the end of the week.

Only two people a year get a chance to join George Green as trainees, and there is at least one big barrier they need to overcome before getting a foot in the door. Unsurprisingly, the firm is attracted to recruits who have some previous experience in a legal or other commercial environment, and it also likes applicants who have a link to the region. Given the importance of local clients to the firm's character and work, is this any wonder? Otherwise, the recruiters sound like they are pretty open minded, although one trainee did offer the following opinion on what they were looking for: *"They want people who are going to be enthusiastic, even if they are not doing the most exciting work all the time."* Those people deemed to fit the bill will be invited to join what trainees describe as *"a genuine meritocracy."* As one saw it: *"You get the big fish in a small pond opportunity. High-fliers can really make their mark."* Indeed they can; in the not too distant past, one such over-achiever even made partner only two years after qualification. This is by no means the norm, but one thing's for sure – it just wouldn't happen at a larger firm. Overall, our sources seemed genuinely happy with their lot: *"I look forward to coming into work most days,"* declared one. In

2007, the one qualifier didn't stay on, but this contrasted markedly with the three of three who took GG NQ jobs the previous year. It's worth adding that those who don't accept the offer of a job come qualification may be asked to repay the LPC contributions the firm made on their behalf.

and finally...

At George Green it's not about working on deals that make it into the national press, and at the end of the working week you won't find yourself comparing battle scars with a legion of fellow trainees. Nor will you be on the sort of salary that contemporaries at commercial Brum firms will enjoy. Instead it's a case of getting stuck into the local business community and working with company directors who are often passionate about what they do. All that, plus very decent hours... not a bad deal at all, we reckon.

Government Legal Service

the facts

Location: London, Manchester
Number of lawyers: 1,950
Total number of trainees: 50
Seats: 4x6 months
Alternative seats: Occasionally Brussels
Extras: Award-winning GLS Pro Bono Network; language training.

Private practice law firms expend so much energy bombarding students with novelty key rings and biros at careers fairs, it's little wonder the Government Legal Service – the UK's largest employer of lawyers – is somewhat overshadowed. No doubt some of you are already thinking about skipping this feature, fearful that if you read just a line further, you'll end up a grey-suited civil servant trudging along on a bureaucratic treadmill until the day you retire. Relax, put your preconceptions to one side and give this career option some thought. We're convinced; you just might be too.

movers & shakers (and policy makers)

The GLS has only one client – Her Majesty's Government – however, as you adapt to its esoteric language you soon realise that when government lawyers refer to 'clients' they generally mean the policy makers and managers within various governmental departments. The role of a typical GLS lawyer is at the centre of policy making, as they are charged with finding practical, effective and, most crucially, legal ways of putting policy into practice. In addition there is advisory work and plenty of contentious matters.

So, how do you recognise your inner civil servant? Maybe you have a fascination for the functions of government, or perhaps the subjects you most enjoyed on your degree were public law topics. One trainee told us: *"I've always been interested in current affairs, so the idea of working in the heart of government was quite appealing."* For others, the GLS represented a refreshing alternative to private practice and a chance to truly engage with the law without going the whole hog and becoming an academic. *"The standard thing at uni was that everyone would go into a law firm, but after carrying out a vacation scheme at one I felt completely disillusioned,"* explained one interviewee. *"I was thinking at one point about giving up law altogether and going into teaching. Then someone from the GLS came to our uni and gave a talk."* And the rest, as they say, is history...

the big seven

Variety is standard for government lawyers; in all areas of the training scheme recruits end up coming into contact with a wide range of people, from prisoners to parole officers, asylum seekers to cabinet ministers. Take HMRC (that's Her Majesty's Revenue & Customs), for example, which deals with every business in the UK (or so

it hopes) as well as most adult citizens. The variety doesn't stop with the end of the training contract: GLS lawyers are encouraged to switch departments every three or four years. It's not a case of clicking your heels and finding yourself in Oz – or the Department for Health – *"You have to go through an application process just like any other job."* Some people do opt to stick with a department for many years, although in reality *"it's probably harder to get promotion if you do."*

The GLS has lawyers in a multitude of departments and offices, most in London, in Whitehall, The Strand and Holborn. The seven main departments trainees work in are: the Treasury Solicitors department (TSol), the Department for Transport (DfT), HMRC, the Department for Community and Local Government (DCLG), the Department for Business, Enterprise and Regulatory Reform (BERR – formerly known as the DTI), the Department for Work & Pensions/Health (DWP/H) and the new, Orwellian-sounding Ministry of Justice (which replaced the Department for Constitutional Affairs in May 2007). However, every year presents a different picture and options are also often available in the Home Office and the Department for Environment, Food and Rural Affairs (Defra). If you want to read more about the work of each individual department – and we strongly recommend you do – it's explained at www.gls.gov.uk

yes minister

TSol, the largest GLS department, is split into divisions catering for three key clients: the Prison Service, the Border and Immigration Agency (previously the part of the Home office called the Immigration and Nationality Directorate) and the Ministry of Defence (MoD). On the contentious side, work includes personal injury, judicial review, inquests, planning, charities matters and all manner of other unexpected issues. Work for the MoD and you'll deal with questions that become news headlines. One source had encountered *"the families of soldiers sent to Iraq wanting to make a claim against the government regarding the legality of the war"* and a case in which WWI soldiers shot for cowardice were retrospectively pardoned. Elsewhere, trainees represented the DfT and the Highways Agency in situations where people have been injured on roads. These can be *"very technical and challenging... it all comes down to how the road was designed and so you have to get on well with the experts."*

Working for the Border and Immigration Agency, you soon learn just how many judicial reviews involve asylum seekers who have exhausted all appeal rights. Of course, immigration is a hot potato and for trainee lawyers the pressure *"mounts up at times."* In terms of the statistics, *"everyone wants to see an improvement; this government has very tough targets as regards failed asylum seekers."* It's a good example of how the government of the day influences the GLS's work, as do changes in government or policies. It's worth mentioning here that, if you're an overly political type who spends the weekends canvassing for a particular party, *"the GLS might not be a good career choice..."* It's not that you have to be apolitical, more that *"lawyers generally keep their private views separate from their day-to-day work."* And what if you have strong views on other issues? Again, staff are perfectly entitled to act on these in their private time: *"We have people here whose religious views disagree with government policy and who go on marches,"* commented one trainee. Presumably, it's just a question of balance.

Advisory seats are usually less pressured. Trainees run their own files and carry out bits of research for other members of the team. Said one HMRC source: *"Looking into points of equity is really interesting. It's not run-of-the-mill research; it's long, involved and challenging. I'll often head downstairs to the library and disappear for several days."* Thankfully, working in a department that deals with finances does not require a good head for figures: *"It's more about the economy in general and seeing the bigger picture."* The Home Office is very popular and offers a challenging body of work for those with an interest in constitutional and public law issues, criminal justice and the development of human rights law. Here trainees work closely with ministers and officials on politically sensitive areas of policy. And with cases appearing before the European Court of Human Rights, there's also a fair chance of getting a trip to Strasbourg or Brussels. Over in DWP/H trainees have dealt with queries about what advice NHS Direct can legally provide over the phone, how the CEO of an NHS Trust should go about getting rid of a senior employee and the practicalities of allowing staff to offer private advice in a building that's publicly funded, such as a hospital. There's also a lot of *"liaising with Whitehall"* and meeting clients face-to-face.

In relation to policy work, proposals are put together by government departments and passed on to the GLS for lawyers to draft detailed instructions to the Parliamentary Counsel (a specialised team of Whitehall lawyers) about what should go into the Bill. *"If you've been involved in drafting a Bill, you're encouraged to go along to the debates. You'll be sitting in the boxes in the House of Commons or the House of Lords passing bits of paper back and forth, and you're expected to respond to ministers' questions pretty quickly."* Sounds exciting. *"The first time you go it's a bit of a buzz; being in the hub of parliament and meeting ministers you've seen on TV,"* confirmed an enthusiastic source.

money isn't everything

In addition to a supervisor, trainees have a line manager and a training principal, who will attend their mid and end-of-seat reviews. Supervisors go through a file on a weekly basis, examining all the work that has gone out, so *"if you've got something wrong, you'll hear about it pretty quickly."* High levels of responsibility are a major attraction of the GLS: you're trusted to send out letters in your own name, carry out advocacy before a master in the RCJ and deal directly with clients almost from day one. Of course the pay isn't anywhere near comparable with the best in private practice, so what are the other benefits? The main one is definitely the opportunity to engage directly with the law and see it being shaped. Then there's the attraction of a state pension, healthy working hours and a plethora of flexible alternatives to the standard nine to five (or nine to nine, as those in big City firms would remind us). One popular benefit is 'compressed hours', where staying for an extra hour at the end of each day wins you every other Friday off. Other alternatives include working from home, working flexi-time and job shares.

Maybe you see the civil service as a rabbit warren and worry about falling into a deep hole of bureaucracy. No one claims the GLS doesn't suffer from an element of this, but at least *"there are no piles of paper anywhere – everything is electronic."* Which takes us on to the subject of IT resources. According to our sources, *"they're slow and difficult to use; not what you'd get in a City firm."* (Hmm – they should visit one or two of the firms we've heard about.)

GLS departments are increasingly going open plan and as you look around different offices there is typically a lack of hierarchy: *"All the senior civil servants and team leaders sit in the open-plan bit, and the desks go round in a big circle."* TSol's offices are described as *"architecturally interesting,"* which we think is a euphemism for lots of concrete and glass. It spans 15 floors and the views are magnificent: *"I can see St Paul's, the Thames and the London Eye,"* remarked a trainee as Big Ben bonged in the background. A Bond-themed Christmas party held on the 15th floor was a great success, and with London all lit up below the effect was *"spectacular."* Other after-hours activities have included quiz nights, trips to The Comedy Store and *"general social events down the pub."* These are actively encouraged by a series of social committees. A particular favourite was *"a whisky-tasting event, appropriately held in the Scotland office."*

a foot in the door

Applications for GLS training should be submitted two years in advance. Make it through an online reasoning test and you may be invited to a day-long assessment centre for a written exercise, group exercise and individual interview, during which a previously prepared topic is argued out with a panel of GLS lawyers and independent consultants. The topic for discussion in the group exercise is *"always a ridiculous thing that would never happen,"* such as *"extending human rights to animals."* Between 21 and 25 places are offered, the majority for trainee solicitors, a few for pupil barristers. Those who've been successful in the past include law and non-law graduates, second-careerers and people with young families. Said one mature trainee: *"A lot of private practice firms that I thought would value my experience turned me down. The GLS has a totally objective recruitment process; they're not just looking to take people straight from uni and mould them into what they want them to be."* Sponsorship is provided for the LPC and, in exceptional circumstances, for the GDL. If you're interested in reading more about the GLS, why not also read our pupillage feature on page 938.

and finally...

Like teachers who prefer to work within the state sector, or doctors who are loyal to the NHS, those who choose a legal career in government are commonly committed to the cause and couldn't see themselves doing anything else. *"No one ends up here by mistake,"* said one trainee. Fantastic responsibility, a diverse workload, 30 days' annual leave, a pension and decent work-life balance... could you ask for more? An all-but-guaranteed job at the end of it all, you say? Sure, you get that too.

Halliwells LLP

the facts

Location: Manchester, Liverpool, London, Sheffield
Number of UK partners/solicitors: 164/242
Total number of trainees: 76
Seats: 5x21 weeks
Alternative seats: Secondments
Extras: Pro bono – Manchester Law Centre

Like Pinky and The Brain, Halliwells is up to its usual tricks. What's it doing this year? The same thing it does every year, Pinky. Trying to take over the world...

halliswells

...well maybe not the world, but definitely the UK. You want proof? In the last five years Manchester-headquartered Halliwells has been growing at an astonishing rate via a potent blend of takeovers, lateral hires and raw ambition. Renowned for its highly profitable corporate expertise, possession of branches in Sheffield and London wasn't enough, so in 2004 the firm annexed Liverpudlian property boutique Cuff Roberts, quickly building up its transactional abilities with lightning quick raids on heavyweight rivals like DLA Piper and launching an IP/technology practice there in 2006. Then came last year's swiping of Mancunian insurance experts from James Chapman & Co – scores of them – and on all sides and at all sites lawyers have arrived by the bucketload to reinforce existing strengths and create new ones: corporate

recovery in Sheffield; private client refocused to Liverpool; a tax disputes team arriving in London and corporate hires in Manchester.

Hang on, did we say only the UK? Early 2007 saw the launch of a Far East team operating out of Manchester and London that will focus on AIM work from China, Hong Kong and Singapore. The team has already advised West China Cement on a £66.8m AIM listing. Naturally there has been a positive effect on the firm's financials: Halliwells recorded a 37.5% rise in turnover to £86.2m. Behind the big money are some big deals. Corporate lawyers advised on the £1.5bn sale of telecoms giant Caudwell Group and on the £300m disposal of First Industrial to Deutsche Bank. They also helped new company Ensus with the £250m launch of one of the UK's largest ever renewable fuels production plants, and won a place on the AA's first commercial and corporate panel.

Naturally, after a period of rapid expansion and diversification, it's time for R&R, consolidation and collective catching of breath, right? Wrong. Deeply wrong. Halliwells' slogan claims it is a 'solution-driven firm', but we reckon it's just plain old driven and responds to success by seeking even more success. In 2007, managing partner Ian Austin outlined a plan for the next five years to take an ever-swelling Halliwells into the top 25 in the UK – and to do it as soon as possible. This aim centres on the goals of achieving turnover in excess of £125m and growth to more than 2,000 staff by 2011. Mind boggling! Trainees, whose numbers have *"ballooned"* from around 30 to around 80 in recent times, are as aware as anyone of *"the dynamic, fluid, fast-growing outlook"* currently characterising the firm. *"It's extraordinary to be somewhere that keeps growing and growing,"* they said, telling us of *"a go-get-'em attitude towards bringing in new business and clients."* With so many new faces each week, trainees quickly feel like old timers and *"the steady stream of e-mails from management about changes"* keeps them in the loop. *"It will be harder to maintain cohesion in the long term as we grow,"* thought one, *"but at the moment it's fine."*

a five-start training

A somewhat unusual five-seat training contract gives plenty of scope for variety. Essentially, despite a lack of strict compulsories, trainees are likely to experience dispute resolution, corporate and real estate, and will tend to return to a preferred department in their fifth and final seat. More niche seats are available in private client (which includes family and trusts), business services (including employment and IP options) and corporate recovery. There are also secondments to clients such as Cable & Wireless and brewer InBev.

As the largest office, Manchester offers the widest variety and greatest number of seats, but trainees across the UK may take a seat at an alternative office in order to sample a desired area (for example, *"family is only on offer in Liverpool and it's popular"*) or as part of the *"push for offices to get more involved with each other."* Almost all our sources had spent time away from their home office. *"It really helped give a sense of our national identity,"* said one who'd switched from Manchester to London for a seat.

The average Halliwells trainee turns up *"confident, knowing what they want,"* and can safely be described as *"not overly aggressive but definitely ambitious."* The firm has an established habit of offering training contracts to the best of its paralegals and we also spotted a recurring tendency to favour some local connection to each office. True, *"as more trainees have arrived there's less of a defined type"* but we reckon the firm is still recruiting in its own ambitious, direct image. Being *"confident and self-starting"* are important attributes in a system of training in which *"in every seat you can get the good work, not just the*

menial work." Corporate seats with *"long hours"* can be *"a baptism of fire"* but they allow trainees to *"take the lead on smaller transactions under supervision"* and *"get work that associates might be doing elsewhere."* Seats in the insurance department, with their focus on personal injury, public liability and professional negligence cases for clients like AXA and Zurich, mean *"handling a number of slip-and-trip, subsidence, fire and damage claims,"* *"drafting witness statements"* and *"going to county court hearings."* Property seats require trainees to *"go to auctions by yourself,"* *"manage sales and leases"* and *"have regular contact with property surveyors."* Best of all, the seat allows *"drafting and negotiating on mid-sized commercial deals by yourself."* Elsewhere in the miscellany of seats on offer, IP and employment are perennially popular, the latter offering *"close involvement in cases going to mediation"* and *"a lot of advisory work."* The corporate recovery department is also popular for its *"smaller teams,"* *"client contact on personal insolvencies"* and *"the great opportunity to do court hearings yourself, despite the nerves."* No one denies the exacting expectations of the training contract: *"You've got to understand you'll work hard."* Most departments see 9am to 7pm as standard; in corporate *"8pm or much later is normal and it's frowned on if you leave before 6pm."*

prize fighters

Self-sufficiency is a must for trainees in this entrepreneurial, outward-looking firm. In the past we've heard that a small minority of supervisors don't cut the mustard, despite the fact that the majority are *"great and help you as much as they can."* And therein perhaps lies the rub: although trainees had nothing but praise for supervisors this year, they did admit that *"exactly how much day-to-day feedback and help you get depends to an extent on how busy supervisors are."* Their advice is to *"tailor yourself a bit to the person you're working* for and ask questions at the right time; that way everyone is happy to sit down and go through work."

Trainee impetus improves the formal feedback sessions too. These amount to objective-setting at the start of seats and "lengthy, telling you where to improve" mid-seat appraisals. Both "tend to happen because HR are involved." End-of-seat appraisals are completed less commonly; indeed, one source declared: "We might as well not actually have formal end-of-seat reviews." Delayed mid-seat reviews can be blamed for occasional hold-ups in the process of seat allocation, although for the most part the five-seat rotation works well enough and allows "extra experience in a further area without really losing anything."

If knowing what they want and possessing the nous to work out how to get it is a characteristic of Halliwells trainees, it's unsurprising that they are attracted to "the opportunity at the firm to progress quickly and push on for associate and even partner." It certainly puts the relatively minor step of gaining an NQ job in context. Technically there is a formal application procedure for jobs; in practice we sensed that most of our interviewees had an eye on a definite prize and a clear sense of their chances of getting it. However, 2007 saw the biggest cohort of qualifiers the firm has ever had and the poorest retention rate since our records began. Just 23 of the 31 qualifiers stayed on at the firm, many taking jobs in dispute resolution. Of course, one year's figures alone do not make a trend, so it will be interesting to see how things go next year.

magnetic north

There are four points on Halliwells' compass: north, north, north and south. There's no doubting where the needle comes to rest: "Manchester is the hub," trainees told us, some whispering: "It's becoming more City-like as it grows" and "maybe a little more competitive and impersonal." Not everyone agrees with this analysis: "It's easy to speak to people here," countered one. In autumn 2007 the office relocated to new premises in Spinningfields, "the new 'City' part of town where all the banks are moving." Some sources preferred to describe the area as "the Bond Street of the north – there are 80 new bars and shops and the designs look amazing." The move won't take the firm far from the centre of town, so regular departmental drinks and trainee outings will continue unabated. Halliwells still manages to get the whole firm together a couple of times a year in celebratory mood; "last year we all squeezed into The Palace Hotel in Manchester for a sit-down meal." Whether this will continue to be possible in the future is not clear, but "departmental cross-office days are certain to figure for new arrivals." Thankfully, each of the other offices has a well-developed sense of self. In Liverpool, the "smaller, more intimate atmosphere" means "it's more relaxed" and here "a great social culture" fits in comfortably around fairly regular hours of 9am to 5.30pm. Ensconced in the rapidly regenerating business district, the office is moving in March 2008, but only to another floor within its current building. Trainees are willing participants in Liverpool TSG events and can also regularly be found out with associates at local drinking holes.

Across the Pennines and down the M1, the Sheffield office is also an "easygoing" place. Now spread over three floors of its building, the sprawl is a result of an expansion of activities in the office. Originally focused on insurance litigation, the office now handles real estate, construction, employment and, more latterly, corporate recovery. Hours here are a seemly 9.15am to 5.15pm, with the daily commute just a "short hop" for many. Consequently an "active social calendar" involves "drinks, pub quizzes, sporting fixtures" and all the usuals. Veering off the M1 and following the A1 right to its roots in the heart of the City of London, Halliwells' southern office is situated in a "buzzing location near Bank tube station and The Bank of England." Despite "a slightly more formidable atmosphere" and Manchester-like hours, staff still make time for drinks in the local Corney & Barrow or *"on the office's beautiful roof terrace."*

and finally...

"The appeal of Halliwells is that it's an exciting and rewarding firm that is going places." In Manchester, Liverpool or Sheffield it's a stand-out choice for an ambitious trainee willing to work their butt off and keen to hold their head high with the biggest and best in the north. In London, it is a choice for the applicant who wants their firm northern-flavoured and expansive of mind.

Hammonds

the facts

Location: Birmingham, Leeds, London, Manchester
Number of UK partners/solicitors: 136/302
Total number of trainees: 80
Seats: 6x4 months
Alternative seats: Overseas seats, secondments
Extras: Pro bono – various legal advice schemes; language training

On Hammonds' website you can read the story about how a lad from Bradford started what became a legal empire with approaching 1,000 staff in four UK offices and over 350 others across mainland Europe and Asia.

from nineties to noughties

It's an impressive record of achievements and yet far too often Hammonds' successes have been overshadowed by a deluge of bad press. All law firms get bad press at some point or another, but Hammonds seems to have had more than its fair share in the past five years. Given that, at times, it looked from the outside as if the firm was in meltdown, it's worthwhile understanding what went on. It all began in the 90s, that ab fab decade of New Labour, Britpop, *Gladiators* and an expanding Hammonds. The huge costs attached to international and domestic expansion were mounting and then profits plummeted in 2004. And again in 2005. What followed was a turbulent time at the firm: an £8m hole in the accounts, an extensive multimillion-pound overdraft, a plethora of partner departures and an embittered partnership dispute would all be worrying singly, but together they caused a huge amount of speculation. Hammonds desperately needed to do something. The past two years have seen the firm make a slow but steady recovery, achieved by a management overhaul, cost-cutting redundancies, a 14-month equity partner lock-in agreement and a new remuneration structure. The firm also bolstered its management by placing Crawford Gillies (MD of Europe at Bain & Co) as non-executive chairman as well as hiring the CEO of Capgemini as a non-executive director.

The lock-in period meant that equity partners could not resign, and this period lasted until June 2006. The current policy is that there are only two days a year in which equity partners can hand in their resignation. This hasn't prevented Hammonds from losing some key figures this year and trainees were frank with us about the departures. *"In terms of moving forward, we have lost a few people, but we have also recruited too,"* one summed up. *"All businesses go through periods of people coming and going; it's part and parcel of business life."* This forthright attitude was shared by others: *"When people left, it didn't go unnoticed, but it's a business at the end of the day and everyone now is committed to working hard and doing their bit to make the firm profitable."* One trainee focused on the positive attitude shared by those who remain at the firm, saying: *"The negative people have already left."* Last year Hammonds saw a small increase in turnover, and in 2007 this was boosted by a 23% jump in partner profits and further growth in turnover.

Be involved

'Premier League football, international cricket, sports worldwide.
From trainee to partner, a real opportunity to turn my passion into a career. Where else?'

STEPHEN SAMPSON | PARTNER – HEAD OF THE SPORTS LAW GROUP | LONDON

0800 163 498
hammonds.com/trainees

Hammonds

Trainees see these figures as proof that the firm has hauled itself back from the edge and put itself back on more of an *"even keel."*

pressgang

Trainees told us how it felt to know their firm was *"always the butt of other people's jokes... 'How can they afford to pay you?'"* was a common jibe. *"But we all felt that it was quite an exciting time to be a trainee."* *"We're not demoralised by* [the negative press reports], *we just wonder why they still continue."* One person got straight to the point: *"Everyone is getting sick of the constant press, most of it is inaccurate – the whole firm is on a real up and people are motivated and excited. The media ignore the good news stories and they keep dragging us down."* What Hammonds really needs now is attention for all the right reasons. Actually you don't need to look too far to see it's been doing some pretty good work for a great roster of clients. Here's just a few we picked out: Tesco, Honda, Bradford & Bingley, RBS and Royal Mail. Its sports team, for example, acts for the likes of UEFA, FIFA and the International Tennis Federation, and has recently advised on the Aston Villa FC takeover, helped the former Thai prime minister net Manchester City FC and assisted Chelsea FC to score a victory against disgraced former striker Adrian Mutu.

Trainees praised a firm-wide strategy review undertaken by a team of consultants in 2006. *"It seems to be paying dividends,"* beamed one recruit. The strategy is centred on one fundamental thing – clients. *"We are going to be winning more clients, building up our existing relationships and showing the market we are doing a good job."* *"Our big focus is making sure our clients are happy and providing an excellent service."* Each and every trainee we spoke to proudly delivered the firm's new motto: *"We'll move mountains for you"* and it seems *"whatever mountain that is, that's our line."*

fix up, look sharp

Hammonds used to do this thing called 'location-rotation' training, which shunted recruits around at least three offices during their contracts. A limited number of fixed seats were then introduced, but following *"a massive discussion"* with trainees, it was decided that location rotation would be binned and trainees would be recruited to a single office. Trainees talked about some of the reasons why it was out with the old and in with the new, among them the greater likelihood of *"getting to know your colleagues in the office you qualify into"* and building up a reputation there, and also the fear that the old system was putting people off joining the firm. Location rotation will be a distant Hammonds memory by the time readers start at the firm in 2010.

The six-seat scheme requires that everyone does a corporate seat (which includes tax, banking and insolvency), a property seat (which includes construction and planning) and a contentious seat. *"Being made to do core subjects is good because it gives you general knowledge,"* concluded one trainee. Our interviewees praised the six-seat system, with one commenting: *"It is great because you can test yourself in various environments and not become specialised from a very early stage."* As Hammonds has an international network, trainees can request an overseas seat. Choices include Madrid, Paris, and Hong Kong, and the department they work with depends on which office they go to. The Brussels office, for example, focuses on competition and trade work. Still on the subject of office moves, Leeds, Birmingham and Manchester trainees can also request a seat in London.

corporate co-operation

In Manchester *"corporate drives all the other departments,"* while in Birmingham it has *"expanded a lot in recent years."* The transactions on which the corporate lawyers have worked include Co-operative Group's £50m acquisition of the Gordon Davies chemist chain and the £130m sale of Metal & Waste Recycling to Barclays Private Equity. There is no shortage of international transactions either, one example being ProLogis' £72m acquisition of Severn Trent's property portfolio. Trainees' thoughts on corporate seats were mixed, with *"some people desperate to do it"* and others keen not to. One trainee felt it was *"a good seat, but massively dramatic and [blighted by] hideous hours."* Another said work came in *"peaks and troughs"* and the experience was *"not as bad as everyone makes out."* The work ranges from drafting documents such as option agreements and powers of attorney to liaising with clients and *"organisational and people-management"* tasks. The hours depend entirely on the *"cycles"* of work that pass through the department, with trainees reporting that some days they *"struggled to fill nine to five,"* while other days kept them in the office *"till 2am or 3am."*

A seat in the property department results in *"really good client exposure."* The work is extremely varied as the group is divided into several sub-departments. Recruits told us they did title investigations, negotiated and drafted leases and prepared documents for disposals, as well as the *"mundane form-filling"* exercises. Trainees enjoyed the level of responsibility they got in this seat, noting that once they settled into the department they were *"let loose on more complex things"* and took a useful role in *"big deals for big clients."* Hammonds' property clients include HBOS, English Partnerships, Yorkshire Bank and Leeds City Council.

The pensions team was highlighted for its *"really good reputation"* and *"work for blue-chip clients"* such as Land Rover, Cadbury Schweppes and Royal & SunAlliance. The *"very demanding and technical"* tax seat is one where trainees *"learn an awful lot,"* but in more reasonable hours than corporate. *"I don't think it would be possible to use your brain so much doing silly hours,"* chuckled one past occupant of the seat. Also offering *"complex"* work, the commercial/IP team was described as *"amazing in terms of people's intellect and experience."* The seat is said to be *"brilliant for developing your drafting skills."* The employment department is described as *"very popular,"* so expect a fight to park your bum on that particular seat. In the commercial dispute resolution seat, trainees felt they *"worked closely with members of the team"* and gained excellent experience. One recruit excitedly told us that on some smaller cases they were given *"the freedom to run with the file."*

Across the seats and the offices, a *"two-tier"* supervision structure gives trainees the advantage of having a daily supervisor as well as a partner supervisor. *"The system works really well, it's something the graduate recruitment team has worked loads on."*

one for sorrow, two for joy

When an interviewee precedes a sentence with *"it sounds a bit corny but its true…"* we always prepare ourselves for a cliché, so when the line that followed was *"everyone makes the effort to be a team,"* we thought we'd take it with a pinch of salt. However, each and every interviewee made this point in some way or other. *"It's very team-orientated, rather than being out for yourself;" "it's a welcoming attitude, we're a tightly knit bunch;" "you have to be willing to dig in and do things for different people;" "everyone is down-to-earth and willing to help each other out."* This attitude extends to the more senior figures: *"I would happily wander in and ask the managing partner the same stupid questions I would ask anyone else,"* said one confident newbie.

The *"corporate-driven"* London office was inevitably described as being slightly more *"pressurised,"* but *"very nice and modern."* One trainee *"expected the people in London to be grumpier, but* they aren't." The slightly more *"relaxed"* Birmingham office is having a £9m *"total refit inside and out."* Trainees enthusiastically told us that the new offices will have *"everything updated"* and will boast *"new furniture and new IT systems."* Leeds is described as having *"a strong traditional atmosphere,"* and we hear there is a *"bit of a buzz"* at the Manchester branch, which apparently *"doesn't have many old faces – it's very young"* and is also undergoing a refurb.

Hammonds is reintroducing a three-week induction programme for new arrivals, which gets everyone together from across the network and puts them up in an Oxford College. *"I'm gutted we missed out on that,"* said one source. It's a fantastic way of *"getting to know each other,"* although there are ongoing opportunities to do so too. Trainee Solicitors Groups in each region *"bombard you with e-mails about entering things like Ultimate Frisbee competitions and football tournaments,"* not to mention *"the most random and ridiculous things like speed dating."* As for office nights out, the hot favourite location in the capital is The Magpie (*"We joke about it being the only pub in London"*), in Birmingham it is Oceana (for a *"cheesy night"*) and Greek Street or Call Lane beckon in Leeds. The Manchester trainees opt for the *"quite posh"* Restaurant Bar & Grill, and typically follow it with a trip to the local greasy spoon the next morning. We understand that Effy's is *"a very important place for Hammonds' trainees."*

and finally...

"Don't believe everything you read – try out the vac scheme instead" is the message from trainees. For all of the troubles they've witnessed, Hammonds' trainees have remained positive. As the firm steadies itself, a reassuring number of them choose to stay put on qualification. In 2007, 33 of the 39 did so.

Harbottle & Lewis LLP

the facts

Location: London
Number of UK partners/solicitors: 23/51
Total number of trainees: 7
Seats: 4x6 months
Alternative seats: Secondments

In the good old days when someone wrote a book or a play that was basically it. Now, the possibilities are endless. Marketing execs rub their hands together and think about a musical or a movie and how it should come with a soundtrack album and some ring tones, and better still a video game and, of course, a whole bunch of merchandise. Each of these elements involves a multitude of funding and contractual issues, so it's just as well Harbottles is on hand to help.

reach for the stars

Harbottles' expertise spans all aspects of the entertainment industry – and more. On the music front, the firm represents record and management companies such as Mercury and Polydor. On the big screen, it recently helped out with production work for feature film *Starter For Ten*, while on the small screen there were production, finance and distribution issues for *The Hogfather*. It has carved a niche in advising talent show contestants and acts for finalists of both the BBC's *Any Dream Will Do* and *How Do You Solve A Problem Like Maria*? Originally set up by a theatre aficionado, Harbottles still has a group of theatre lawyers who are no strangers to centre stage, advising on *Dirty Dancing*, *We Will Rock You*, *Wicked* and *Spamalot*. In the gaming world, the firm assisted on aspects of best-selling game *Guitar Hero* and represented an advertising company on the in-game advertising agreements for the Pro Evolution Soccer franchise. On the football field itself, lawyers scored in the libel match for Liverpool player Steven Gerrard after the London *Sport* magazine claimed he was considering a move to Real Madrid. And let's not forget the catwalk: here the firm helped Kate Moss in relation to her venture with Topshop.

Harbottles' corporate, employment, property and litigation teams are also on hand to assist clients, and each department benefits from the firm's media focus, whether it's drawing up employment contracts for the cast of a play or helping that A-list celeb purchase yet another mansion. The corporate team, for example, advised Ministry of Sound in relation to its acquisition of the dance music label Hed Kandi, and the firm also works on general branding and contractual issues for major companies including Sony Ericsson, Philip Morris and Virgin Group.

all mapped out

Choosing which seats you fancy is never a problem, mostly because Harbottles decides for you. Upon arrival, trainees are told which four seats they will do and it's a pretty standard template. Litigation and corporate are a dead cert, employment or property will come up, and then either film, television and theatre (FTT) or the music and IP seat. "*The firm does ask you if you're okay with your schedule and they are quite flexible.*" For planners, it can work out well: "*I really like the way they do it... It's nice to have it all mapped out.*" The only caveat is that "*you're unlikely to be able to do both FTT and IP/music, because those are the popular ones.*"

A seat in FTT will see you involved in all three areas. "*They aren't really separate departments, but they each have their own partners.*" "*You might be drafting agreements for writers or a creative team, or helping with a finance deal for a film.*" The other entertainment team (known as MIPIES, "*an absolutely ridiculous name*") used to just deal with IP and music but now also incorporates interactive entertainment and sports. Its rechristening can be seen as a response to the trend for convergence in the industry at large. "*Everything crosses over these days, so it makes sense,*" mused a source. Trainees spend most of their time handling IP matters. "*I did a lot of infringement work and a lot of work for Virgin... protecting the brand and handling third-party infringers. It was mostly the early stages of the contentious side of IP.*" Supervisors constantly check trainees' workloads, which is a good job because this seat "*definitely offers a lot of autonomy. There just aren't enough people here for them not to use you to your full potential.*" The music team has gone through a few personnel changes lately, leading one trainee to lament: "*You may not get the chance to do as much music as you wanted.*" With just the one IE partner, work in this area is scarce too: "*You don't get much of it, but when you do it's great and the partner is brilliant.*"

Employment is ideal for first-years as there's less pressure than in, say, litigation. "*It's formulaic and quite procedural, which is good for getting you settled in.*" The seat involves quite a bit of research and writing memos, or making preliminary reviews of employment contracts. You might land some immigration cases too. Similarly, property offers a gentle introduction: the relatively small department handles residential and commercial deals, and here you might be sorting out planning applications, drafting leases or doing straightforward conveyancing. "*There's a fair bit of client contact as people are always asking if you want to go along to a meeting with them.*" "*The work isn't hugely entertainment-related; in fact, it's the least media-oriented department here.*" On the upside, "*it's probably the nicest department to work in people-wise – everyone's lovely.*"

There was praise for the litigation department on account of its "*high-profile work – the celebrity names are all here and it makes it that bit more interesting when you see things that you've been working on in the papers.*" Perhaps it's not surprising that "*it's more intense than the other seats and* more is expected of you." Appearances before High Court masters are definitely a possibility, and *"because we don't have a clerk, the two litigation trainees and the paralegal take it in turns to do all the filing and running to court."* The seat covers commercial disputes, such as copyright infringement and debt claims, and libel. In the recent Whiter Shade of Pale case Harbottles defended sixties prog-rock one-hit wonder Procol Harum against a guy from Croydon who claimed to have come up with the song's distinctive organ melody.

chicken or fish?

The corporate seat involves the usual board minutes and due diligence, but at least the subject matter is engaging. *"I worked on the sale of some recording studios,"* said one source. *"The odd late night meant staying through until midnight, but they were few and far between. You're usually out by half-six."* Some lucky trainees replace this seat with a secondment to Virgin Atlantic Airways. *"I was nervous to begin with because you are completely thrown in the deep end and you aren't monitored as much. But it's great to have the contrast of working in-house."* The Virgin team is said to be super friendly, possibly because *"half of them came from Harbottles, having done the secondment and decided to return."* If the posting appeals (bear in mind it is located in Crawley), make sure to show interest early on.

Trainees noted two opposing elements at play in the firm's culture. *"It has its eye on being cutting edge and moving forward, but there is still a bit of an olde-worlde feel to it."* The latter presents itself chiefly at lunchtime when everyone, partners to post boys, assembles for a free meal. *"There is a sense of tradition to it. I had imagined this Harry Potter-style great hall; it's not quite like that, but they have seven big tables and there's always a starter, a main course, a cheese platter and a big bowl of fruit. You can sit next to anyone. It's a great way for everyone to get to know each other and there's a real family feel to it."* In contrast, the dress code implies a more modern outlook. According to one trainee: *"It's rather relaxed; in fact, I think I always look a bit of a mess. There was a phase where people didn't even bother changing their shoes after coming to work in trainers... they had to put a stop to that."* The partnership apparently reflects this dichotomy, but the two sides don't seem to conflict. *"They each add something to the firm and it's what makes us different,"* concluded one interviewee. Perhaps going forward, the firm will opt for the slicker modern persona: *"I think the plan is to be the City's foremost entertainment law firm. We're looking for bigger clients – the Channel 4s, the record labels. In music, for example, while they still do private client stuff, it's becoming more about licensing mobile phone ring tones."*

A recent office refurbishment should go some way towards helping the firm achieve its goal. *"The meeting rooms are now super slick and swanky, with built-in speakers and drop-down projector screens. It's very media trendy,"* noted one trainee. The offices themselves got a fresh lick of paint, and trainees like the layout. *"You normally share an office with your partner. It's conducive to working and I prefer it to open plan. When you're new and not used to talking to clients over the phone, you can feel a bit exposed. I feel safer being tucked away in my room."* Outside the office *"there isn't a great deal of organised socialising. We probably have one trainee night out per seat, which the firm pays for, but mostly it's off the cuff."* When Harbottles puts on a big event, it does so in style, and the good news is future trainees are always invited. The second the music comes on, *"everyone rushes to the dance floor – we're a pretty wacky lot!"* Pressed further, one trainee mumbled something about *"break dancing partners... quite hysterical."*

As this image suggests, Harbottles tends to attract *"bubbly, gregarious"* folk. And experience in the entertainment industry will also stand you in good stead: *"I think at least a quarter of us have worked in the media industry before,"* reported one source. With quite an informal approach to appraisals and the like, it also pays to be assertive. Qualification jobs are allocated in *"quite an informal way. There's no formal request or interview process and it's not all that transparent."* This works well in most cases, but largely because trainees make it known that they'd like a job when they hit their favourite department. A bit of gentle politicking is advised: *"Go and sit with the partner at lunch,"* suggested one trainee. In 2007, three of the four qualifiers stayed on, one going into FTT and two into IP.

and finally...

With a glittering client roster, it's easy to picture yourself schmoozing with celebs, so be warned: *"You shouldn't kid yourself that your role as a solicitor here will be any different than if you were working for any other industry."* As one trainee put it: *"Although it might seem like a glamorous firm, we aren't in glass offices wearing power suits."* Thank goodness for that.

HBJ Gateley Wareing

the facts

Location: Birmingham, Leicester, Nottingham, London, Edinburgh, Glasgow
Number of UK partners/solicitors: 75/127
Total number of trainees: 22 in England
Seats: 4x6 months
Alternative seats: None

The increasingly crowded commercial legal market in Birmingham can be divided into the following groups: the independent firms, the national firms that have been in the city for ages, and the newcomers. HBJ Gateley Wareing is a proud member of the first group.

brum and beyond

Gateley Wareing *"started out as a tiny high street firm"* in central Birmingham and apparently four of the top partners *"were trainees here about 20 years ago."* Over the years the firm has changed quite a bit. Phase one was characterised by slow and steady growth in the Midlands. The firm established itself as a great little performer and ended up attracting several experienced partners from bigger firms such as Eversheds, Wragges and Hammonds. The main office in Birmingham and two smaller Nottingham and Leicester branches grew extensively and the firm's name became synonymous with strong client relationships and Midlands deals. Then in January 2006 came phase two, when GW merged with Scots lawyers Henderson Boyd Jackson and the union pushed the new firm into the top 60 (by revenue) in the UK. Post-merger, HBJ Gateley Wareing set itself the task of winning more work from national clients and cross-referring clients between the English and Scottish offices. In May 2007 the firm had exactly those aims in mind when it entered phase three, by completing another merger with London shipping and transport boutique Shaw & Croft. This tie-up provides a foothold in London that should help the banking and corporate practices flourish.

Trainees agree that the core of the firm in England is its corporate department, where *"all trainees have to do a seat... our deals are why we get in the press so much."* As usual, the past year has brought an impressive number of transactions, some for well-known names, most for Midlands-based, small to medium-sized companies. Indeed, the client roster is still stuffed with owner-managed businesses, albeit that some have grown pretty big. *"The fact that we do a lot of work for OMBs is due to the relationships the partners have built over the years,"* explained a source. *"There's still the same spirit today and I don't think we will ever move away from that – not while those partners are still here."*

it's a shirty job...

While you probably won't recognise the names of the majority of clients, you'll certainly have heard of the likes of BT, Pertemps, Allianz, Tamworth Snowdome and Lloyds TSB. One trainee was pretty chuffed that following the firm's involvement in the management buyout of fancy shirt makers TM Lewin, *"we all get discounts."* On another deal, lawyers acted for AIM-listed client Titan Europe on its €270m acquisition of the whole issued share capital of industrial vehicle manufacturing giant Italtractor. Someone who'd spent time assisting on this deal explained their role: *"It was a big Italian reverse takeover. For me it involved a lot of verification, which I actually found interesting, as well as attending the completion meetings, which meant going down to London with the partners. I was the only trainee at the meetings – there were none from the magic circle firm on the other side – and it was great to see how a completion meeting works and how a boardroom works. I had a lot of contact with the other solicitors on the deal; they were a couple of years PQE and I really felt like I got a lot of responsibility."* A third trainee had also found the biggest challenges in corporate, describing what had felt like some *"deep-end moments."* It goes without saying that corporate seats can bring the longest days.

Real estate is another important department. It offers four or five seats in both commercial and residential development work, each presenting the trainee with plenty to get their teeth into and direct contact with clients. While the hours in property are largely predictable, one posting that is *"deadly busy all the way through"* is corporate recovery. Regarded by some as *"a tough seat,"* it is nonetheless popular. *"The work is largely insolvency litigation and that's an area of law that can be quite technical,"* explained a past occupant. Another added: *"You are given training beforehand – there's a lot scheduled for the start of the seat. In terms of work, it will vary from repossession*

hearings to restoring companies to the register and various applications on the emergency list at court. These can be character building, but at least you get a lot of advocacy." The non-contentious aspects of the seat revolve around *"selling companies in insolvency and taking responsibility for negotiating deeds of release with the banks."* Bear in mind, too, that *"you'll do a lot of marketing and meeting clients, and that's great early on in your career."*

the swing of things

Among the other seats are banking, construction, employment, tax and commercial, this last one being *"a really wide-ranging seat covering practically any area of law. There was a lot of analysing contracts and drafting terms and conditions. And then we had a dispute about a swingers' club!"* For the most part trainees thought seat allocation worked well. A corporate seat is understood to be central to the two years and *"the occasions when business needs kick in and you get to do something you are not so keen on"* aren't too painful because most people get to tailor their experience. A word of caution from one source: *"As we take on more trainees there's going to be a scramble for seats; even our seat allocation was a bit cloak and dagger this year and we were not told until the last minute."* At least *"it seemed to work out in the end, and last year all the trainees got taken on in areas they wanted to go to."* It wasn't quite so perfect in 2007, when four of the six qualifiers stayed on in the firm's English offices.

That old chestnut of work hard, play hard is certainly mentioned a lot. *"We're all high achievers,"* concluded one trainee. Any other similarities? *"I probably shouldn't say it, but we're all middle class – though from a mix of private and comprehensive schools – and we've all been to good universities."* While almost everyone has above-average levels of confidence, *"no one is really bolshy."* The classic Gateley disposition is best described as *"upbeat and positive."* The firm as a whole is said to be *"aspirational but still down to earth... a people place where getting to know clients is important, and it's really easy to get to know partners because there's such a flat structure."*

Each summer English senior partner Mike Ward delivers his State of The Firm address to assembled Midlands staff. *"It's a précis of what has happened during the year and the plan for the rest of the year."* So what's on the agenda? Well, we spoke to trainees before the latest London merger, but even then they were openly debating another join-up and ongoing expansion. The merger agreement with Shaw & Croft underlines their view that *"we're looking for more panel work and more cross-border work, more national clients."*

all work and no play...

A staff council meets monthly with management to raise requests and voice any concerns. On the trainees' wish list in spring 2007 was *"a study day during each seat, more recycling and energy saving, and discounted gym membership."* How effective is the council? *"While the firm would always listen to you, you won't always get the solution you want but it's nice to have the chance to raise things."*

One very important trainee duty is providing input into a social committee that organises events every two months. With a budget of around £1,000 per event, it's no small responsibility. *"First-year trainees do the bulk of the organising and it's a great way for them to get to know staff,"* even if *"people don't mind moaning to trainees if an event was rubbish."* *"We've done a casino night, pub games, a quiz..."* recounted one interviewee. Some of the events are held in Bushwackers, a well-frequented bar in the basement of the next-door building. It's also a venue of choice for the Birmingham Trainee Solicitors' Society (BTSS), and when we rang, the netball and football teams were doing rather well in the BTSS league.

Sports and social events are a good way to keep Nottingham and Leicester trainees in the loop. The Scots trainees on the other hand are rarely sighted: after the huge post-merger haggisfest of January 2006, it was the turn of the English to host the firm-wide extravaganza in September 2007. New recruits don't miss out on the fun and games, and all are invited to the summer party before starting. Shortly after they join, they must face 'Welcome Night', one of the biggest events on the social calendar. *"About 90% of the staff turn up"* to meet each new intake and enjoy a variety of entertainment centred on the recruits. In past years there have been blindfolded human sheepdog trials and a blind date-style game, but apparently HR put its foot down and *"now the firm is much nicer to the new trainees... last time they just had a Q&A session on their new supervisors."*

Gateleys used to be renowned for its party-hard nature, which *"originally came from some of the senior figures, and then generations have come through and taken on the mantle."* Rather than partying just for the sake of it, there's frequently a sound business reason for the jollies: *"Everyone is encouraged to get out there and socialise and we're linked up with organisations like Birmingham Future* [a young professionals' group]. *We get plenty of soft-skills training on things like working a room and networking."*

and finally...

"Quality work for good clients, but not so vast and soulless that you are just A.N. Other off the treadmill," was one trainee's summing up of HBJ Gateley Wareing's appeal. If you want to be a big fish in what can probably still be described as a smallish pond, and are prepared to help rustle up business, then this is a great option. We'll be keeping an eye on that new London office to see how it allows the firm to develop.

Henmans LLP

the facts

Location: Oxford
Number of UK partners/solicitors: 22/36
Total number of trainees: 6
Seats: 4x6 months
Alternative seats: None
Extras: Pro bono – Oxford CAB

Oxford outfit Henmans has traditionally been known for its charities and litigation expertise; however, having doubled in size over the last nine years and moved to shiny new premises in 2007, there's now even more to catch the eye of the discerning trainee.

aspiring to bigger things

Henmans has been around for nearly three decades and this year a dramatic makeover marks *"a sea-change"* for the firm. Shedding *"quirky old offices"* in picturesque Woodstock and Oxford High Street for a one-site, *"very modern, open-plan"* address at 5000 Oxford Business Park South, just inside the ring road near to Cowley, reads to trainees as *"a statement of commercial intent."* They say the place is *"going through a transition"* and *"we want to project ourselves as a larger, more corporate firm."* Trainees insist: *"We're still very strong in the areas of personal injury, professional indemnity and general litigation,"* but they also understand that now the firm has a new home that is *"much more what you'd expect of a commercial law firm,"* it intends to capitalise on the change. The aim is *"to focus on building up all our areas of practice from family to corporate to charities"* and, as such, the firm is *"upping the game"* and *"marketing all areas equally."*

Just an hour away from central London, you'd think the firm might be overshadowed by the goings on in the capital; not so, it seems – our sources were convinced of the relative merits of training in the Shires. *"You get the best aspects of a regional firm here,"* we were told by one; *"that's what I applied for and that's what I've got."* Another explained how *"you can get the London experience if you work in the right departments."* Apparently, some areas are *"more locally or regionally focused: for example property is more laid-back in a way you'd expect of a local firm,"* but *"litigation has a different atmosphere – and aggression – lots of the lawyers have trained in the City."* *"Clients continually tell us they get just as good a service as from the London firms they use, but of course we're able to charge cheaper rates."* Then there's the fact *"you can be in London literally every week, meeting with the top barristers and going to court."* All that and the benefits of *"a nice quality of life"* and *"the vague possibility of being able to afford somewhere to live"* by staying in Oxford. Certainly, *"you're not out in the sticks coming here."*

boardroom brawl

A trainee's first seat is chosen for them and thereafter they rotate through up to three more of the six available practice areas. Just how is up for negotiation and the firm is deemed *"very accommodating"* on this score. *"They'll ask you what you want and encourage you to be open-minded, but will let you follow an interest."* It is often possible to bag two seats in a hoped-for qualification department, so long as this doesn't cause problems for others. The full menu includes family, personal injury (incorporating clinical negligence), professional negligence and commercial litigation, private client (incorporating charities) and property. Despite growing corporate finance abilities, Henmans currently has no seat for trainees in the area, although this may well change in the future.

Time spent in prof neg/comlit brings exposure to some of the firm's most complex activities. *Chambers UK* ranks the team very highly, and with good reason. In 2007 it successfully defended an Internet service provider at the Court of Appeal in a claim that turned on the question of whether an Internet domain name can be regarded as property. It also assisted a large insurer facing serious allegations of copyright/database infringement, breach of confidence and conspiracy to damage a company's business in relation to a boardroom split. The team represents a large number of professional indemnity insurers, and in 2007 its reputation for prof neg litigation led it to defend a firm of solicitors from a £100m claim relating to after-the-event insurance, following the collapse of a major legal expenses insurer. The breadth and scale of experience within the department makes it sensible for trainees to *"work for many different people,"* doing everything from *"research and discrete bits of drafting"* to *"taking on work in local courts as agents for other law firms, so trainees get the chance to do advocacy."*

In contrast, a PI seat *"allows you to run lower value cases under supervision."* In doing so, trainees get vital experience of *"talking about case plans and strategies, and how to move a case forward. You need that experience because you can't always be waiting for partners to advise you on what to do."* On the claimant side the firm has represented individuals who suffered breathing difficulties brought about by exposure to toxic plastic resin at work, and a truly unlucky cyclist who was knocked off their bike and then run over by a lorry. On the defendant side the team represents several large motor insurers and specialises in high-value fatal and catastrophic injuries, including accidents abroad. Cases often involve HGVs or buses and multiple claimants. In the clinical negligence team, lawyers work on cases of medical misdiagnoses, botched operations and birth injuries. Of late the team has achieved a settlement for a victim of Erb's palsy and worked on a high-value cerebral palsy case. Aware that the clin neg work handled is of a high calibre, some of our sources indicated that it was this team that had attracted them to the firm in the first place. The point to be aware of is that the complexity of the issues dealt with in major cases can mean trainees have to take a back seat role, effectively handling a PI caseload while tagging along to conferences and meetings on the big clin neg claims.

fighting over the family silver

In the private client team, will drafting, tax and trusts for the well-off are the stock trainee experience. To spice it up this seat gives access to Henmans' renowned charity law practice, allowing trainees a taste of constitutional, trusts and contentious advice to a plethora of charities such as Save the Children, RSPCA, Oxfam, British Red Cross, Cancer Research UK, Great Ormond Street Hospital Children's Charity and Macmillan Cancer Relief. Last year the team was shortlisted for the Society of Trust and Estate Practitioners' Charity Team of the Year award, and it also managed to entice the former head of trusts and estate planning at Manches out of retirement. He is now giving the firm the benefit of his expertise on the formation/administration of charities and the law relating to universities, particularly Oxford Colleges. Trainees *"love"* this side of the work, telling us how matters can be extremely complicated, especially when it comes to legacy administration. In 2007 the lawyers wrapped up the complex disposal of a £1m estate on behalf of three charities, and went to the Court of Appeal for a large national charity over a will that was being contested by the children of the deceased.

It is almost inevitable that the *"busy"* property seat is a less glamorous experience involving *"a lot of research and work for quite a few different people,"* but it also has a *"broad clientele that you get good exposure to."* When trainees work on commercial and residential matters, these *"tend to be more local."* The agricultural and estates matters, meanwhile, offer *"more geographically widespread* work." Finally, the three-person family team sees trainees assume assistant-like levels of responsibility. The clients here tend to be well heeled or at least comfortably off. There are no legal aid cases.

In 2007 the three qualifying trainees found *"there was one job available, in property,"* so only one stayed on. Well aware that mismatches and shortfalls in NQ positions are common problems in smaller firms, our sources nevertheless were full of praise for the way in which they had been trained. *"Typical hours around 8.30am to 5.30pm"* and a *"smart-casual"* dress code seem to hit the right note too, though on the clothing issue a careful balance needs to be struck: *"You need to be smart enough to impress but not so sharp that you scare off local clients."* On the subject of things local, we noticed the firm seems less concerned with applicants having a connection to Oxford than it has in the past. Trainees agreed, telling us: *"They're looking more for what the individual can offer."* A demanding assessment day involving an interview with presentation, verbal reasoning test and written skills and group exercises gives plenty of opportunity to show what you're made of. Should you want proof that the firm offers an inclusive and supportive working atmosphere – nearly half of all partners are women.

everyone for tennis

Uniting the firm under one roof brought immediate benefits: *"Now you can use other departments' libraries or pop over to someone to ask a question; it's great for cohesion."* The new office has *"great facilities"* including *"showers"* and trainees *"meet up a lot more regularly because it's easy to head to the canteen at lunch."* *"There's plenty of parking, so most people drive to work,"* and should it prove necessary *"the firm has offered to lay on a minibus into the city."* On the social side, not only are there Pilates classes, *"we've now got a forum where people put up details of the pubs they've visited with clients or after work."* When we

rang, staff had yet to find a regular pub for office outings, though we suspect establishments *"within walking distance"* may triumph over *"cute pubs in villages a drive away."* Every year there are summer and Christmas celebrations and a tennis tournament hosted at the house of the eponymous Mr Henman (ex-head of firm and father of Tim). Because *"a lot of people have families, our events aren't the wildest, but they are enjoyable,"* reported a source. *"Younger fee earners tend to go on to central Oxford after events."* We should also mention that the firm was helpful in assisting a trainee set up the Oxford TSG and *"has indicated it will sponsor an event, although we haven't got that far yet."*

and finally...

If you want your training to have a contentious slant and to be delivered by a regionally rooted yet nationally minded firm then Henmans would be a good bet. It is a convincing alternative to other Thames Valley firms, or even smaller London firms, especially as it intends to move up a gear in terms of its commercial work.

Herbert Smith LLP

the facts

Location: London
Number of UK partners/solicitors: 175/491
Total number of trainees: 175
Seats: 4x6 months
Alternative seats: Overseas seats, secondments
Extras: Pro bono – RCJ CAB, death row cases, FRU and others; language training

This top-ten City player has positioned itself just outside the magic circle, and that's a pretty comfortable place to be. A training contract here has for years opened doors to some of the best and biggest litigation in Europe, but you mustn't be

Ringing the right numbers.

When Phones4U, one of the UK's biggest mobile phone chains, went on sale, the private equity firm buying it needed to ensure its bankers got the very best legal advice. And fast. So they turned to Herbert Smith LLP. Trainee Elliot Beard was part of the team and the non-stop action that followed...

To find out more about Elliot's story and for more information on our training programme and vacation schemes, request a brochure from our graduate recruitment team on 020 7374 8000 or via graduate.recruitment@herbertsmith.com, or visit our website at www.herbertsmith.com

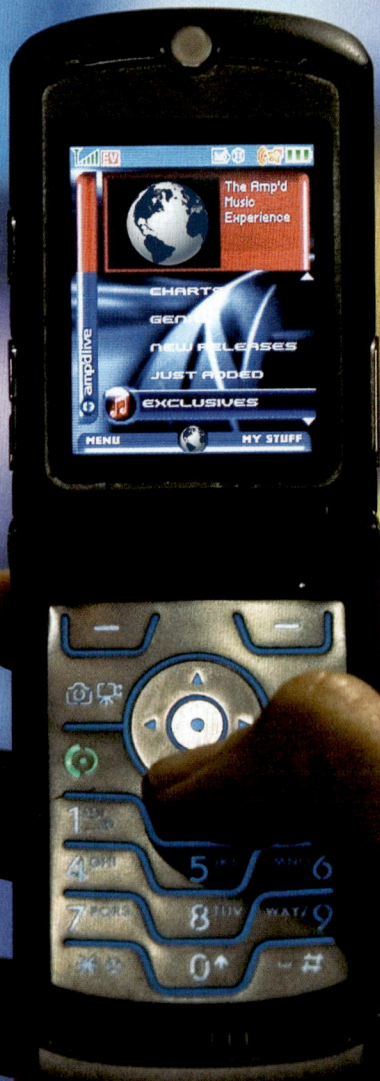

Herbert Smith

blinded by this aspect of Herbert Smith's brilliance. There's a very simple message for anyone looking at Herbies these days: don't overlook its corporate expertise and rapidly developing prowess in the finance sector.

smokin' aces

If Herbert Smith was a politician, its mantra 20 years ago might well have been *"litigation, litigation, litigation."* A quick look at the firm's recent achievements, however, shows that times have changed. That's not to say that it doesn't still have a winning hand when it comes to top-notch dispute work. It's just that these days it's coming up trumps in more than one suit. The Lawyer Awards provide a fitting illustration: in 2007 Herbies picked up both Litigation and Corporate Teams of the Year.

For the unbelievers among you who wish to see hard evidence of the firm's performance, here are some examples we prepared earlier. The corporate group advised BAA on its recommended £15.6bn acquisition by the Grupo Ferrovial-led consortium in one of the biggest headline-grabbing deals of 2006. It also acted for Tata Steel, the listed Indian Steel manufacturer, on its successful £6.2bn takeover of Anglo-Dutch steelmaker Corus. The acquisition resulted in the creation of the world's fifth-largest steel group, and the firm is now advising Tata on its long-term financing of the takeover. The firm also recently scored a part in The Blackstone Group's £12.8bn acquisition of Hilton Hotels Corporation, boosting Blackstone's portfolio of hotels, which includes Conrad Hotels and the Waldorf Astoria collection. And Sir Alan Sugar said "you're hired" for a change, when he got the firm to advise Amstrad on BSkyB's proposed £125m acquisition of the company.

In the courtroom, Herbies continues to get stuck into the tastiest of cases. In some instances, we mean this almost literally: the firm acted in a long-running dispute concerning the ownership of the Patak's Pickles business. The family business supplies over 75% of Britain's Indian restaurants, as well as being a familiar household brand. Representing Patak's holding company, the chairman and CEO Kirit Pathak and Kirit's mother, Herbies reached a settlement leaving Kirit Pathak with full ownership and control of the company. Elsewhere, the firm successfully defended Goldman Sachs International against a claim for damages in excess of €100 million for negligent misrepresentation and misstatement, and it is currently advising Chevron on the investigations following the 2005 explosion at the Buncefield oil depot. Last, but certainly not least, it scored a historic victory for Eurotunnel in the first large international arbitration ruling against Western governments. The panel ruled that the British and French governments were liable for the disruption and financial losses incurred by Eurotunnel in the 2000 security fiasco that saw thousands of asylum seekers invade the Channel tunnel. It also marked the first such case where solicitors undertook the advocacy rather than barristers.

Clearly, then, guns are blazing in the litigation department. But these days it's just not the only attraction for applicants. *"Everyone always goes, 'Oh, Herbies is such a litigation firm,'"* sighed one trainee; *"but people come here for all sorts of reasons now."* Indeed they do. Our sources ranged from those who simply applied *"to all the big firms,"* to those who specifically aimed for Herbies because of its *"wider scope of work. I think there are more angles to this firm and it's nice to know you've got stellar practices in quite a few areas."* This latter group of interviewees also pointed out the pros of choosing a firm that's on the up rather than one that has already reached the top. *"Because we're smaller in finance at the moment, trainees probably get much more responsibility than those who have gone to firms with larger departments. And I'd say there are excellent chances of a job in finance because it's growing."* In fact, *"there's quite an emphasis on growing all round,"* one trainee intimated. *"Talking to partners, there also seems to be an increased focus on the international aspects of the practice areas, so I think we'll see more co-ordination with our other offices and partner firms."* This certainly looks likely if the heavy overseas investment is anything to go by. The firm has recently shelled out for new premises in Brussels, Paris, Moscow and Tokyo, in addition to expanding in Beijing and Shanghai and launching in Dubai. However, don't expect the firm to turn into a global one-stop shop. *"I think it would like to go into certain markets and excel there, rather than being average everywhere."*

in the corus line

Seat allocations have recently changed slightly. As well as doing the standard litigation and corporate seats, trainees must now do either finance or real estate. Allegedly. *"I'm not doing a finance or real estate seat,"* whispered one trainee. Luckily, secondments and overseas seats can count as one of the compulsories, if taken in the right practice area, and the already impressive choice of destinations has recently expanded. *"Hong Kong, Tokyo and Singapore tend to be perennially popular,"* observed one source, while a six-month swap with a Kiwi trainee *"caused quite a bit of excitement."* Remarkably, all the second-year trainees we spoke to had done at least three of their four top seats. *"If you're dying to do a certain seat, chances are you'll get it."* When it comes to overseas and client secondments the water gets a little murkier. *"I wonder if the process is quite as transparent as it could be,"* mused one. *"You get the feeling some placements are allocated to people before they've even filled out the forms."* Such allegations only affect a minority of postings, and it sounds as if the firm has just changed the process *"to make sure the committee knows what exactly everyone's preferences are."*

The corporate department is a common starting point for trainees, some of whom described it as *"a baptism of fire."* The learning curve is guaranteed to be steep, but one source explained: *"I requested it as my first seat as I thought it would involve liaising with other departments and thus give me a good overview of the firm."* They were right: *"My group handled a lot of corporate stuff for the real estate department so I liaised with them quite a bit."* The focus of a seat could be M&A, insurance/regulatory work or a specialist area such as energy or telecoms, media and technology. Trainees might be put onto two or three huge transactions, with smaller matters bubbling away in the background. *"It really does depend on who you sit with and what work is on at that minute though,"* pointed out one interviewee. *"For instance, I didn't get stuck into any big deals – it was all company reorganisations and private equity stuff."* Not that this is a problem. *"The smaller the matter, the smaller the team, which means more responsibility for the trainee."* At the other end of the scale, working on a giant deal like Corus, trainees must resign themselves to proof-reading and data management. *"On the Corus deal I had no responsibility whatsoever,"* recalled one source. *"I drafted some board minutes and did random bits of research that sometimes turned into notes for a client. Weeks later I'd spot a paragraph halfway through page ten of a client memo that was mine. Yess! But you can't complain. It is perfectly understandable when it's a billion-dollar deal."* The variety of work also lends itself to unpredictable work hours. *"I was quite lucky hours wise,"* recounted one trainee. *"I was done by 7.30pm on most nights."* Not so with another: *"There were weeks of finishing at around midnight at the start of my seat."* Raising the bar still further, one trainee reported leaving the office at 6am on one occasion and coming straight back into work hours later.

Apart from *"occasional spikes of mad activity,"* litigation offers a much more reliable timetable.

"Because you have court schedules, you can plan around them, and it's unlikely things will need doing overnight unless a trial is looming." Again, the seat can take many forms, with the umbrella title of commercial litigation covering specialisms in banking, insurance, IT, energy and public law, among others. And, like corporate, it's a case of potluck when it comes to the size of the matters on which trainees work. Said one: "I helped on two big cases, where I just did research, but my supervisor tried hard to let me see about half a dozen smaller cases as well." Smaller matters, which can range from breaches of directors' duties or contracts, to nuisance or negligence claims, may involve a bit of bundling, as "they don't have the devoted paralegals that the big cases do." They also offer more responsibility – "drafting instructions to counsel or letters to the other side and attending meetings." If you're lucky enough to be there during a trial, trips to court will be frequent and you'll be busy "sorting documents and dealing with points as they arise during the trial." As for the atmosphere in the department, while "there are still a few old-school types who can be pretty damn ruthless and hardnosed," trainees praised their supervisors to the skies. "My partner took his training role very seriously; I learnt a hell of a lot from him. It's great when they realise that they're your teacher, rather than treating you as their proof-reading bunny."

Trainees anxious to clock up as much litigation time as possible should bear in mind that Herbies doesn't guarantee any more than six months in a contentious seat, and it is unlikely for anyone to get two general litigation seats. However, "that's not to say you can't also do a contentious client secondment or a specialist contentious seat like IP or trusts." A stint in the firm's in-house advocacy unit counts as a secondment and offers great experience for those who are lucky enough to get it. As competition for the specialist seats tends to be fierce, "make early noises if you've got your sights set on one."

The real estate department is said to be "the perfect last seat. It's a completely different style from the other areas of the firm; most matters are small, which is great because experienced trainees can really take control of things. I was liaising with clients and authorities on a daily basis, and when my supervisor went on holiday she trusted me to handle things in her absence." If it is your final seat, it's also a relatively relaxed way to end to a training contract: "I think the latest I stayed was 10pm, but that was a complete one off. You're normally out the door by 6pm."

roll out the barrel...

Our interviewees agreed that Herbert Smith has got its training and supervision down to a tee. "In my entire training contract I have done hardly any proof-reading and the data room didn't engulf me. At any big firm, you know you're going to have to do certain boring jobs, but we've got a photocopying department, a document centre and secretaries working the nightshift at times, so there's really a high level of support." Should you need someone to talk to apart from your supervisor, there's a mentor system in place. True, "some partners are more active about it than others, but they're always there if you need them." As far as training programmes go, it seems like there's always something on. "They have both academic and practical courses, some of which are compulsory and some optional." Back-to-basics lectures on the law get a mixed reception: "They aren't that helpful because it's just going over law school stuff," said one trainee, although others found them invaluable. There are workshops to help you to manage your priorities and cope with stress, and in the second seat "you go away for a few days to do teamwork exercises in a nice country hotel – climbing on barrels, etc."

If the barrel-climbing whets your appetite for sport, back in London you can join in with football, cricket, netball and a more unusual annual tug of war against other firms and banks. "A group of trainees got here and said, 'Where's the sailing group?' So now there's a sailing group." Socially, there's also plenty to choose from – subsidised theatre trips, departmental drinks and trainee evenings, but nothing is enforced. Most trainees are more than happy to join in, particularly around Christmas time when they're spoilt for choice with firm, department and group parties. The big, firm-wide bash is *"similar to a wedding reception, with drinks and canapés. You only realise how huge the firm is when you get everyone together."* There's always a good turnout for the biannual trainee ball, usually held at Kensington Roof Gardens. *"There's a sit-down meal, a free bar and then partying into the night. The recruitment partners come, but they're all so laid back, so you don't feel like you have to behave. There were certainly a few interesting dance moves going on..."*

When asked about a Herbert Smith personality, the only overriding feature identified was that *"people get on with people."* Apart from that, trainees were clueless – in a good way. *"I don't really know about people's backgrounds so I couldn't point out any trends. It's just not important once you're here."* Some had, however, observed that Oxbridge numbers were fairly high, with one commenting: *"There is still a bit of that stereotype. Partners' eyes light up when they hear someone went to Cambridge."* But others noticed that the recruiters have been *"going to places you might not expect... so things are changing and they're definitely trying to draw in a variety of people."*

and finally...

Trainees were keen to stress the breadth of activity covered by this training scheme. The message is simple: *"Don't pigeonhole us as a litigation firm."* Oh, and be open-minded about where you want to qualify, as you're quite likely to plump for something you'd not planned on. In 2007, 67 of the 74 qualifiers stayed on at the firm, distributing themselves across a range of departments.

Higgs & Sons

the facts

Location: Brierly Hill, Kingswinford, Stourbridge
Number of UK partners/solicitors: 28/36
Total number of trainees: 10
Seats: 4x4 + 1x8months
Alternative seats: None

Black Country stalwart Higgs & Sons has a two-pronged action plan that it hopes will allow it to challenge larger Birmingham rivals in a range of commercial practice areas, while also maintaining a dominant position in its home territory. Consecutive years of growth have translated into an expanding training scheme that is luring some good candidates away from the Bullring.

anchored down

Higgs & Sons was born in 1875, back in the days when coal and iron ore were plentiful and the Black Country was home to some of the countries most renowned metal bashers; even the Titanic was sporting an anchor mined and crafted in the region when it went down. And during this period of prosperity its founding father, David Higgs, was there to guide the region's manufacturers through any legal strife, thus rooting the firm deeply into the fabric of its home territory.

Times have obviously changed radically since the firm's foundation, but Higgs has managed to keep a foot in the past as it looks forward. Just look at the blurb on its website: "One might expect a law firm founded in 1875 to pride itself on its history and experience. Slightly more surprising to discover that same practice boasting an equally strong reputation for being at the cutting edge of the modern legal profession." So, as Higgs has passed from hand to hand, it has retained a Higgs within its walls to this very day. This is symbolic of the lingering family feel of a firm, which has earned a reputation for looking after its staff. *"A lot of fee earners and support staff have been here a long time and as a result you feel like you are part of something."* Perhaps most remarkably, 12 of its 15 equity partners trained with the firm. This personal touch has allowed it to retain its local owner-managed business clientele, who have themselves passed from generation to generation and remained faithful to Higgs.

Local families and businesses are the bedrock of Higgs' practice, but it has also made an impact beyond its traditional hunting ground. In particular, it has made some inroads into the Birmingham market, attracting entrepreneurs and small businesses away from the second-city's mid-tier firms. A good example is Edgbaston-based nursing and care services provider Claimar Care, which recently sought the firm's advice on three multimillion-pound acquisitions. The firm is also attacking Brum's mid-tier through lateral hires, with recruits from Cobbets, Martineau Johnson and Thames Valley firm Pitmans. This extra firepower has aided its appeal to clients even further afield and it is now involved in work up to £15m in value for some large national clients. Among the lenders it acts for are RBS and NatWest. The firm has no intention of losing contact with its roots: the powers that be have ruled out a move into Birmingham or dramatic shift in focus away from its homeland. Trainees seem equally keen to keep the firm anchored down where it all began: *"We are proud to be a Black Country firm and are not looking to become a massive national."* Drawing all of its local and national work together, trainees believe the firm offers a *"middle way"* between high street and big city commercial practice.

(4x4) + 8...

The training scheme consists of four seats of four months followed by eight months in the trainee's preferred department. The first four are assigned, which would appear to slightly detract from the benefits of an otherwise incredibly wide choice of practices. However, *"nothing is set in stone"* and three out of the four current first-year trainees had successfully tinkered with their allocation. Overall trainees appreciated this approach. *"Within four months you know if you like a seat and can decide where you would like to specialise. Then you amass 12 months of experience and feel ready for action when you qualify."*

One seat option that features for most trainees is private client, the firm's largest department. In Bob Leek, this highly regarded team has one of the pre-eminent individuals in the field, and he has steered the team to some impressive financial results, which see the department chipping in a quarter of the firm's fee income. Trainees can expect *"a great level of client contact"* as well as *"lots of will drafting, tax planning and drafting of powers of attorney."* Clients may come from round the corner on their way to the post office or from the other side of the country on referral from a financial institution.

Another large department is property, where 11 fee earners have also had a great year in terms of turnover. Trainees' experiences centre on leases, both *"drafting them and handling the registration process."* The flagship client here is London and Cambridge Properties, one of the country's largest private owners of industrial and retail property. Elsewhere, the coco team peaked this year in the representation of Prosper Engineering, assisting it through a joint venture with Midsteel Pipeline, to create a group with companies in Scotland, China, Hong Kong, the USA and, of course, central England.

The litigation seat is the most varied and was extremely popular with our sources. It includes a range of commercial disputes and also *"private individual stuff like boundary disputes and breach of contract."* Add to this a healthy crop of low-cost, high-volume debt recovery work, which affords trainees a great degree of autonomy and bolsters greatly the number of files they have access to. *"I am currently running between 40 and 50 files. A lot is debt recovery, although I also have commercial disputes, injunctions and some defamation files,"* gasped one busy source. The employment seat provides further contentious exposure; and who could complain about involvement in juicy tribunals, such as the sex and disability discrimination claims brought against Higgs' client Wolverhampton and Dudley Breweries? The group also reached out to local employers with the creation of a subscription-based HR service, with Warwickshire County Cricket Club the first to sign on the dotted line.

Further options include family and personal injury, while the possibility of some work with the firm's single private criminal practitioner adds further flavour to the Higgs melting pot. In all seats a common theme emerged: *"The firm is small enough to get your own files to work on but large enough to attract good clients and bigger deals."* Even on the bigger deals trainees felt they were doing *"proper work"* and not just running errands. *"You get a good balance of quality work without having to be in the office until 10pm every night."* The firm was also praised for inspiring confidence in its trainees. *"There are so many equity partners trained here that it is clear they want you to stay."* As such, *"everyone takes a real interest in what you are doing and from early on you feel settled and valued."* In 2007, all three qualifiers took jobs at the firm, going into dispute resolution, family and corporate.

our survey says

Of the firm's three offices, the Brierly Hill HQ is the busiest. Although the office itself is nothing to write home about, it does at least have a convenient location near the Merry Hill Centre. The Stourbridge office is home to around half the private client team plus the personal injury and family law groups. Kingswinford, meanwhile, is the base for residential conveyancing and is largely off-limits to trainees. In social terms, both Brierly Hill and Stourbridge are seen as decent options for post-work refreshments, although active membership of the Birmingham Trainee Solicitor Society leads to not infrequent trips to the city to hang out with trainees from other firms. But don't start thinking membership of the BTSS is all about sharing a pint and a few tales from the office. It's actually all about fighting for the honour of your firm in various grudge matches on the sports fields of Birmingham. Once they'd started we could barely stop the Higgs trainees bragging about their recent victories over Hammonds and Martineau Johnson on their route to the final of the BTSS netball competition. As if this achievement weren't enough, they followed it with another Goliath-slaying exercise in Ultimate Frisbee.

We noted that charity fundraising events were often the catalyst for socialising at Higgs. At the more dignified end of the scale there is an annual partners v staff cricket match; significantly further along the cheesey scale was a *Family Fortunes* style quiz, organised and hosted by trainees. As to where the Tom Jones tribute night fell, we wouldn't like to say. It's worth knowing about this side of the firm because trainees recalled that involvement in charity and social events had been a focus in their interviews.

and finally...

Higgs is a Black Country institution and its prominence in the local press attracts many applicants every year. Closer inspection reveals *"it is a different sort of firm to what people expect... it combines the commercial and the high street, and balances work well with life."*

Hill Dickinson LLP

the facts
Location: Liverpool, Manchester, Chester, London
Number of UK partners/solicitors: 152/179
Total number of trainees: 32
Seats: 4x6 months
Alternative seats: Piraeus, occasional secondments

Double-centenarian Hill Dickinson is busy broadening its practice and raising its profile. Oh, and it is also proud to be the official lawyers to the European Capital of Culture 2008.

back together
Hill Dicks' long history is inextricably interwoven with the shipping industry. Since its foundation in Liverpool in 1811, the firm has assisted on many major nautical matters. In 1911, for example, its then senior partner played a prominent role in the inquiry and legal repercussions that followed the sinking of the Titanic, having fortunately turned down a freebie voyage on the ill-fated vessel. Then, in the late 1980s, a developing interest in insurance litigation and general commercial practice led the firm's smaller, shipping-dominated London practice to sail off under its own steam to become a separate firm called Hill Taylor Dickinson, so causing frequent confusion in the profession. The larger of the two firms kept the Hill Dickinson name and operated from four locations – two smaller ones in London and Chester, and two larger ones in Liverpool and Manchester.

The past five years has been a time of much consolidation in the North West market, and Hill Dicks has been involved as much as any other firm. In that time it has merged with smaller Manchester practice Gorna & Co and Liverpool property boutique Bullivant Jones. It has also broadened its business by hiring partners in construction, professional indemnity, fraud, environment and clinical negligence. Meanwhile,

down at Hill Taylor Dickinson in London it was business as usual, with the firm servicing its shipping clients from the capital and a small office in the Greek port of Piraeus.

Then, in November 2006, more than 20 years after going their separate ways, the two firms reunited. But why? Trainees from the old Hill Taylor Dickinson side explained: *"It was presented to us that we needed to achieve critical mass for big international litigation"* and that *"we lacked the wider services and greater resources that clients need. We now have a huge employment team, a huge property team and good insurance capability after the merger."* For Hill Dickinson trainees, *"combining the shipping strengths of the two firms"* – not least HTD's specialist abilities in cargo freight commodities work – made total sense. What's more, an increased footprint in London was perfect for Hill Dicks' *"increasingly national aspirations."*

In terms of size, the re-merger instantly created a top-40 firm with 152 partners and a turnover of £68.4 million. The plan was not simply to be bigger though, and one North West source kindly joined the dots together for us. *"Post-merger, the firm views building up Manchester in commercial work as the future for the firm... the commercial litigation team has moved there, employment's bulked up and there's an emphasis on realigning departments into practice groups."* Giving some weight to this assessment, in 2007 the newly conjoined firm made two major hires into Manchester – a former head of pensions at Hammonds and Beachcroft's corporate head. It also scooped an employment partner in London to help the department stand alongside others (professional risk, insurance and shipping) as national groups.

what the dickinsons?
Six months on, our sources were still enthusiastic about the *"vibrant"* feel of the firm and saw *"no*

downsides" to the merger. Even in London, where two offices combined at HTD's Aldgate premises, beyond a few *"silly, that's-my-mug issues that you always get when you start sharing a new kitchen,"* things have gone smoothly. *"Getting-to-know-you presentations,"* explaining what different groups do, aided integration and the northern trainees have been doing their bit with video-conferenced training sessions and department meetings. For the most part the former HTD trainees have welcomed increased opportunities more than they miss a firm that *"did things in its own, often informal, way."*

At this stage in the new firm's development trainees are being recruited for either northern or London contracts. Up North, they spend the greater part of their time in Liverpool, with *"one or two seats in Manchester or Chester."* No seats are compulsory in these offices. Those applying to the capital spend the entirety of their two years in London, unless opting for a shipping seat in Piraeus. Across offices *"you don't have input for the first seat,"* but thereafter the firm does its best, especially to help *"get what you want in the second year."* The seat list includes general shipping litigation, yacht finance, yacht litigation, coco, property, private client, employment, insurance, insurance litigation, PI, cargo freight commodities, professional risk, IP/IT and construction.

risky business

In this litigation-heavy firm, trainees have significant exposure to contentious matters across a dizzying array of fields. The insurance services group is made up of teams specialising in the public sector, retail, transport, and regulatory and environmental areas, plus a well-developed healthcare division that continues to sign up NHS trusts and hospitals across the North West. Clients like Vauxhall Motors, National Grid and Merseytravel all use the firm for litigation in Liverpool; Manchester meanwhile has won personal injury business from clients like Liberty Mutual First Choice and Bolton Metropolitan Borough Council. Then there's the fraud and policy team – one of the largest in the country – which represents CIS, Zurich, AXA Coproate Solutions and Hertz, not to mention a dedicated claims management service, One Liability Services, which handles bulk matters for Littlewoods and South Yorkshire Police, recently gaining Tesco, Marks & Sparks and Britvic as clients. Trainees say the insurance services group has *"very good seats,"* where they can *"run small-value insurance liability baggage claim cases for an airline carrier"* or enjoy *"lots of responsibility, going to court, helping investigate industrial disease claims."* The pace is hectic, *"the pressure is on and good time management is vital."* Interestingly, they sense a desire to shift business *"more towards commercial matters."*

The professional risk department handles a massive number of cases, many of them *"delegated authority matters from Norwich Union."* In this part of the firm, trainees are engaged in *"drafting letters and investigating claims"* and *"have the authority to settle professional negligence cases worth up to £5,000."* Some people get to work with the interventions team, which helps the Law Society when good solicitors go bad; others find themselves enlisted onto *"highly technical construction matters,"* and even *"a few medical or veterinary"* cases. In commercial litigation some trainees have worked for retailers such as Iceland and Somerfield, and in the *"growing"* employment team they have assisted with *"a massive class action on a Department of Health pension case"* as well as *"smaller issues for the NHS and various commercial clients."*

take a load off

Of course, you can't discuss Hill Dicks and ignore its marine expertise. In relation to dry shipping (see page 186 for an explanation of wet and dry shipping), the firm has experienced an increase in marine PI and regulatory work in the North West. It has been involved in four major regional port infrastructure projects and receives instructions from the main marine insurers in the region. Shipping seats offer both contentious and non-contentious experiences, everything from contractual issues like berthing agreements, regulatory matters such as the disciplining of a ship's captain, or the more unusual cases of deaths at sea. And let's not forget the glitz and glamour of the yacht finance team in London, where trainees can gawp at *"people buying yachts for absurd amounts of money."*

Generally, shipping seats are popular because they combine responsibility on smaller matters with *"close involvement in huge disputes."* Wet shipping can be dramatic: the London team recently acted for the US salvors of large, loaded container ship Al Panama, which was grounded off the coast of Mexico and refloated after an operation taking three months. The combined ship and cargo value of $150m made it the largest Lloyd's Form salvage to date. Lawyers also acted for the owners and underwriters in the sinking of Al Salam Boccaccio 98 in the Red Sea, which resulted in the loss of over 1,000 lives. Those trainees who get to try out the Piraeus seat experience life *"at the front line"* of shipping law and *"meet ship owners face to face on every kind of matter from salvage to PI."* Away from shipping clients, Hill Dicks' aspirations in the commercial sphere have led to an increase in the number of non-contentious seats available. The regular options are property, construction, IP/IT and coco.

what's that flipper?

Across the network, mid and end-of-seat appraisals with supervisor and members of the trainee committee *"help you through: they're not overly formal, but formal enough to know the support is there."* In the past we have heard about a few more difficult supervisors, but this year trainees seemed generally satisfied and more inclined to take a philosophical view. *"Yes, sometimes it would be good to have a little more communication and more feedback as you are going along, but you also have to be realistic, people have to get on with their own work."* In Liverpool the prevailing atmosphere is of *"relaxed efficiency,"* with the firm currently comfortably spread over four offices. *"If there's a specific project on you're expected to work slightly longer hours, but not on a daily basis."* The upcoming move to one building on a new city centre development is viewed as a positive step, even if it *"may bring changes"* that make Liverpool more akin to the *"slightly less friendly, taking itself more seriously, more corporate-style"* Manchester branch. There, allowances are made for trainees commuting from Liverpool, but as the hub of the firm's commercial expansion, hours of *"8am to 8pm"* are not uncommon. Completing the North West triumvirate is a 50-person office in historic Chester.

The traditional *"detachment"* between north and south seems likely to continue, although trainees do meet up and *"form good friendships"* at shared PSC sessions. London trainees say working in departments like shipping, yacht finance or commercial property can involve *"longer hours, because you're dealing with people all around the world,"* but stress that occasional nights *"finishing at 8pm or 9pm"* don't equate to *"a face-time culture."*

Hill Dicks' trainee recruitment material features a grinning dolphin. Thankfully this doesn't mean trainees must communicate through whistles and squeaks; indeed, we found our interviewees to be an articulate and straightforward bunch who seemed to fit well with the firm's *"ambition... but without the excesses found in some other places."* They certainly get on well with each other: *"We socialise a lot, and recently one trainee was a bridesmaid at another's wedding."* Those who had been recruited by Hill Taylor Dickinson in London did observe: *"We seem to be a little bit older and many of us speak foreign languages and were specifically interested in shipping law."* This may or may not continue, as the London office embraces its broader identity. What trainees do suggest is that, whether applicants target the North or the South, showing an awareness of the firm's shipping history and some degree of interest in its dynamic marine practice is sensible for those who make it to an assessment day. In 2007, seven of the 11 qualifiers stayed on with the firm.

and finally...

Hill Dickinson is playing to its existing strengths while also creating an environment in which new skills can flourish. With mergers designed to promote a more national outlook and develop commercial possibilities away from core insurance and marine business, it looks as if the firm should appeal to an even greater number of students.

Hodge Jones & Allen

the facts

Location: London
Number of UK partners/solicitors: 20/41
Total number of trainees: 13
Seats: 4x6 months
Alternative seats: None

Hodge Jones & Allen has come a long way since it was conjured up over a couple of pints in Covent Garden's Freemasons Pub in 1977. Three friends – Henry Hodge, Peter Jones and Patrick Allen – began their enterprise by renting a tiny office above the Archway Loan Company on Camden High Street, seeking to "promote fundamental human rights and dignity and to fight against injustice, discrimination and intolerance." Over the next three decades the firm blossomed into one of the best-known legal aid firms around.

However, for the first time since its inception one partner admits: *"We can't really say that we're a [solely] legal aid firm anymore – the truth is, we're now a mix with the percentage split in favour of private clients."*

the metamorphosis

In April 2007 the firm moved from the urban grit of Camden Road to the slightly more salubrious surrounds of North Gower Street in Euston. Many trainees were impressed with the smart new office and its convenient location, closer to courts and chambers and within spitting distance of six Tube stations and three railway stations. Cafes and restaurants abound, and a short walk will take you to the trees of Regent's Park, the hoards of shoppers on Tottenham Court Road or a contemporary dance performance at The Place theatre. Far from missing the *"distinctive, trendy, alternative vibe"* of Camden Town, many were happy to be operating in a more *"up-market"* environment, *"working in a business area closer to the City."*

The move seems to mirror the direction of the firm as it inches away from a scruffy, leftie Camden towards the more commercial centre of London. One trainee thought that the move towards a larger private client base was *"inevitable given our location – some view it as a natural progression."* There is *"ultimately a metamorphosis going on here,"* said another. In a post-Carter world, cases for privately paying clients now form the bulk of the practice, with recent expansion in the following areas: private family, wills and probate, property, personal injury and clinical negligence. The creation of a dedicated civil litigation team is another indicator of the change in focus.

There were some trainees less happy with the move, as one lamented: *"I miss Camden – it had more soul."* Likewise, not all trainees were feeling great about the change of direction, and those that had come to the firm specifically for its legal aid reputation were somewhat demoralised: *"It's not quite been the firm they were expecting – it has the reputation of being a social justice firm with politically active fee earners, but this is a reputation born of previous generations of work and is not entirely true now."* *"Passionate and vociferous"* partners such as Judith Cass from the housing department and Greg Foxsmith from crime left recently and will be sorely missed. To some trainees, the current ethos feels *"extremely profit-driven"* and they get the sense that *"departments are put in competition with each other in terms of billing – even legal aid departments are still expected to make a profit."* One trainee said: *"There is a lot of pressure to take on cases that are better remunerated rather than looking at need, for example litigation and disrepair rather than homelessness in the housing department,"* where trainees described morale as *"very low."* The Carter reforms are a cause of *"frustration,"* said several trainees, and the *"family, housing and crime departments are feeling squeezed."* Interestingly, the typical response from trainees when asked if they were kept informed of the firm's long-term game plan was a quiet but definite snort of derision.

This was not a particularly easy set of trainee interviews, as there were a couple of incidents this year involving *"problems and the breakdown of relationships"* between supervisor and trainee. The firm feels that it addressed these clashes to the satisfaction of all parties, but some trainees were still perturbed. They believed these incidents were *"brushed under the carpet"* and suggested that this had *"created a climate where problems are more likely to happen."* The behaviour of certain supervisors was thought to *"carry on with impunity."* This is not something we've come across before when researching this firm, so we have no reason to presume it is a chronic problem. When given the right to reply on these issues HJA commented: *"We recruit people who*

are feisty characters." Perhaps it is a fair assumption that this holds true throughout the firm, not just at the junior end. Trainees called for a more *"proactive"* stance from the firm when it came to problems such as these and suggested formal management training for supervisors. One trainee described supervision here as *"rather informal, so it depends how approachable your supervisor is – there are some very unapproachable ones and, with billing pressures, there are some that have no time."*

On a brighter note, trainees also told us about constructive monthly meetings and formal end-of-seat appraisals, adding that there is genuinely positive support available from mentors, who are usually one or two years' qualified and veterans of the HJA training programme. The firm pays for and is keen that trainees lunch with their mentor a couple of times per seat to encourage them to chat confidentially and ask for off-the-record advice.

fun-lovin' criminals

Trainees have been *"very, very happy"* in the crime department, describing a hard-working, fun and supportive team that *"gels well."* *"Certainly if you fancy a quick 'cup of coffee' at the pub after work, people are always happy to do that."* If you relish the idea of a *"baptism by fire,"* then a crime seat may be just the thing to excite you. Trainees have no choice but to learn fast, and they get to know their colleagues in the department extremely quickly because it's all about *"running around discussing matters urgently, rather than being stuck behind a desk."* The seat provides a fantastic grounding, as trainees get to meet clients from day one and are given their own caseload straight away. The department handles work ranging from murder cases and gun-crime investigations to small driving offences. Recent matters include representing UK hip hop artist Skinnyman on drugs charges. HJA encourages its crime trainees to gain accreditation as a police station adviser. Continuing with *"a bit of crime on the side"* when in other seats not only adds variety, but is also a great way of bolstering your salary with overtime (although the Carter reforms will affect this to some extent).

On the whole, the firm is *"quite good at accommodating what you want in terms of seats."* The family seat is described as *"a nice balance"* between the *"hectic"* nature of crime and the more measured pace of personal injury. The department is taking on an increasing number of privately paying clients, particularly for divorce and ancillary relief. Children in care and child abduction are also areas of specialty. Experiences of trainees in this seat ranged from *"being given photocopying"* to *"handling your own caseload, including Children's Act and divorce cases."* In the housing department trainees can also see cases from start to finish, from being the first point of contact with clients as they walk through the door to instructing barristers. This is *"not mundane stuff"* and trainees are given a good deal of responsibility, as they are in wills and probate.

The civil liberties seat is extremely popular and highly recommended by trainees. The work is *"really newsworthy and topical, including actions against the police and inquests into deaths in custody, prison and active service in Iraq and Afghanistan."* Headline-grabbers over the years include the Bridgewater Four case, investigations into Gulf War illness and representing families at the New Cross fire inquest. The team acts for clients in criminal cases involving freedom of expression and association, such as anti-war demonstrations, actions against the international arms trade and the stop and search of protestors under the Terrorism Act 2000. Trainees find the whole team *"very committed to civil liberties and interested in the plight of clients."*

Personal injury trainees are given their own caseload and can expect to handle everything from road traffic accidents to employer's liability claims. Property is another seat on offer. Although clinical negligence is not offered as a seat, there may be scope for someone to gain experience of this work, especially if they first spend time in the department as a paralegal. Like many high street and general practice firms, HJA allows the best of its paralegals to become trainees. Others are recruited a year in advance via a standard application and interview process. Trainees applauded the firm's down-to-earth and straightforward approach to recruitment. Said one: *"In the interview you don't get asked silly questions about what you would do if a Martian landed in your city."*

bridging the gap

"Trainees, paralegals and clerks are pretty tight knit across the firm" and will go out for meals or organise the odd poker night. Each department has its own social network, usually based around Friday drinks, birthdays and leaving-do's. Trainees predict that the bar in the basement of the firm's new building may help change the social dynamic of the firm and allow for more interaction between teams at all levels. Although it was skipped this year, the annual summer outing is usually well attended, and recent excursions include a Regent's Park picnic and a dose of sunburn in Brighton. Charity events and raffles are not uncommon, with the most popular raffle prize being an extra day's holiday. No surprise there then...

and finally...

HJA *"has a lot to offer in the variety of work and seats"* and a *"pool of knowledge and experience to tap into."* If you are looking for something to get your teeth into, the firm *"goes out of its way to make sure you're not bored."* There have been dramatic changes over the past year and it's certainly

HOLMAN FENWICK & WILLAN

We expect our trainees to become partners.

That's why we expect to offer only ten training contracts.

We are one of the world's leading specialists in Shipping & Transport, Trade & Energy, Insurance & Reinsurance and Commercial Law. The firm is a leader in the field of commercial litigation and arbitration and offers comprehensive commercial advice.

With offices worldwide, our client base is truly international, with a reputation for excellence and innovation. You'll work in a friendly, professional and interesting environment.

Please apply online via our website.

www.hfw.com

The closing dates are 14 February for our summer vacation placements or 31 July for our training contracts.

Marlow House, Lloyds Avenue, London EC3N 3AL
Telephone +44 (0)20 7488 2300 Fax +44 (0)20 7481 0316

HOLMAN FENWICK & WILLAN

LONDON · PARIS · ROUEN · PIRAEUS · DUBAI · HONG KONG · SHANGHAI · SINGAPORE · MELBOURNE not the firm we've described in the past. It is going through a transformation and edging closer to the heart of the capital, both geographically and in its outlook. It remains to be seen whether the new creature that emerges will still be attractive to those *"people that give a damn"* about legal aid. In 2007, four of the seven qualifiers stayed with the firm.

Holman Fenwick & Willan

the facts
Location: London
Number of UK partners/solicitors: 69/69
Total number of trainees: 22
Seats: 4x6 months
Alternative seats: overseas seats, secondments

Holman Fenwick & Willan has been delivering shipping advice around the world since 1883. The merchant adventurers who built the practice bequeathed it an entrepreneurial spirit that lives on today.

learning the ropes
For those of you who thought shipping meant galleons in bottles or the odd swinging boat ride then think again. Ships are responsible for shifting 90% of the world's traded goods and that's unlikely to change any time soon. With so much chopping of water, a multitude of accidents can occur from ships capsizing to enormous oil spills and modern-day piracy. This is when the firm's well-respected Admiralty department steps in. Whether by helicopter or desk computer, the team is ready at a moment's notice to assess the damage and advise insurers and owners on salvage action and compensation issues. This year it handled the legalities following an explosion on a container ship off the coast of Yemen and the sinking of a vessel in the Red Sea with the loss of over 1,000 lives.

In reality, the bulk of shipping claims are completely unrelated to collisions and sinkings. Dry shipping law concerns cargo shipments, ship building and chartering and other contractual matters, all of which is largely based on the principles of tort and contract law. Have you ever cheerfully bought an enormous carton of cigarettes from a dodgy-looking street vendor and then, to your horror, come home to find it mostly stuffed with newspaper? Well, take this situation and times it by several million pounds and you have a classic carriage of goods dispute. One scam involves sprinkling a top layer of wheat over a vast consignment of chaff, passing it all off as the real deal. The firm's caseload has also recently required it to wrestle with the Iraqi grain authority for refusing a shipment of rice. Shipping disputes might all sound exciting, especially the wet ones, but in reality trainees suggest that the nearest you're likely to come to an environmental catastrophe yourself is the vast amount of photocopying some cases require. Nevertheless, for the glory-mongers among you, there is the thrill of seeing cases hit the front page of the newspaper over breakfast. And if you do boast to your friends about conducting a multimillion-pound investigation into a capsized oil tanker, who is going to know better? Unless their bedside reading includes the *Student Guide*, nobody will be the wiser that your role mainly involves babysitting counsel at hearings and keeping track of documentation. In a market-leading department, standards are high and trainees say the seat can be both *"daunting and exciting."* Apparently, there's an unspoken assumption that it's *"better to move back deadlines than produce work half-baked."*

For anyone who yearns for adventure on the high seas, but doesn't know their stern from their bow, never fear. One source confessed that they *"get seasick in the bath,"* but was soon able to pick up the lingo. The firm is really pushing the transactional side of shipping practice, with trainees being drummed into the shipping finance department at a steady rate. The explanation is twofold: advances in safety technology have meant fewer big accidents, and also the rise in the appetite for ships around the world (and especially from China) has led to an increase in the number of ship purchases, re-sales and loans. Future joiners can expect more of the same, as various lateral hires and a raid on the team at Stephen Harwood have given the department a powerful boost. *"The firm used to just work for shipowners, but the area has really boomed and we are now acting for major banks. One of the big attractions of this seat is the chance to work with some of the best names in the field,"* said one source. Indeed, there is a growing excitement in the department as the firm teeters on *"the brink of competing with big boys."* Another point to note is that *"we are moving into aviation finance too – it's going to be big."* Trainees who liked ship finance also tended to opt for the commercial property department, which although *"very small"* is an excellent place for fine-tuning transactional and drafting skills. *"It's been good,"* said one veteran of the seat, *"and a lot more law-intensive than I realised previously."*

landlubbers ahoy!

For the landlubbers among you, it's worth noting that HFW is widening its repertoire. Indeed, it is said that you could complete a training contract here without doing a shipping seat. Then again, why you would want to is beyond us. HFW's Singapore office has learned a thing or two about diversification: it also deploys a robust projects finance team that has its eyes firmly set on the wider region. Evidence that the strategy is paying off comes with instructions from Indonesian mining giant Bumap on its $3.2bn sale of two mining operations. Sometimes the boundaries between shipping practice and international trade and energy work are indistinguishable, and so it is that the London trade and energy team is made up of lawyers of all dispositions, between them tackling issues ranging from the transportation of commodities to oil disputes.

The commercial litigators steer clear of shipping matters too, instead setting their compass towards international asset recovery. This seat epitomises the highs and lows of the traineeship, as it involves both routine work and interesting cases. Those who hanker after the limelight of advocacy should make a beeline for this department, as there is scope for making small applications at court. Among the firm's recent work was a politically fraught case concerning a claim brought by a Greek Cypriot against an English couple for misappropriating property following the Turkish invasion of the island. The fact that Cheri Booth stood as opposing counsel added a bit of zest to the proceedings. The team is said to breathe an *"old-school air"* and have a taste for *"deep academic discussions on points of law."*

jetting off

The reinsurance seat struck some as *"very hands-on,"* although others complained of too much standing in front of the photocopier. Indeed, admin work was a source of frustration across the programme. Yet even within the same seats, trainees seem to have had different experiences, leaving one to wonder if some were more adept at gaining the trust of supervisors and fee earners. Trainees are encouraged to take the initiative and *"get work from other people in areas that interest you."* And from what we could tell, some of the savviest recruits had done well in this regard.

Lately, HFW has been extending its tentacles around the globe, with new offices launched in Melbourne and Dubai. Part of the appeal of the firm is the scope of its international work, and this is especially alluring to trainees with a taste for travel. Play your cards right and you could find yourself in Paris, Singapore, Dubai, Melbourne or the Greek port of Piraeus. On overseas seats, we are told: *"If you make enough fuss, you'll get one,"* and apparently *"the new office in Dubai is crying out for somebody."* This year, one trainee even elected to qualify into the Singapore office. As well as overseas seats, there may also be short business trips to get documentation signed by clients overseas.

underwater jazz

The appraisal system, although constructive when it works, can be somewhat erratic depending on the whim of the supervisor. Some trainees, for example, felt they really missed out on regular mid-seat reviews. Although most supervision was described as first-rate, many interviewees could relate one awkward encounter with a partner. The advice given in these situations was to keep quiet and give the person time *"to cool off."* In this high-pressure environment tempers can understandably flare, or, in the case of one partner who notoriously spends most of the day *"screaming and shouting at his computer,"* remain a perpetual fireball. Our sources didn't want to overstress this aspect of the firm and maintained that the supervisors and partners were, for the most part, friendly and affable. Nevertheless, they advised diplomacy when speaking with partners suggesting *"always remember who's the boss."*

There is no doubt that the senior end of the partnership does tend to have a fair number of *"white, male, public-school types,"* including some for whom it is important to ask which Oxbridge college you attended. This did irk some of our interviewees, especially as the hierarchy at the firm is hard to ignore. For example, apparently everyone knows *"who the equity partners are and who the high earners are."* The danger, however, is that the extremes of an environment become confused with the general feel of a place. Here the extremes come in the form of *"typical, old-school English lawyers."* Look at the new blood though and you'll find a mix of backgrounds, attitudes and personalities – *"loud, quiet, aggressive, passive..."* In an effort to promote its accessibility, the firm recently set an essay competition for school students in Tower Hamlets, the prize being work experience. Not exactly a lottery win, but maybe a first step to a legal career for someone. In reality, the firm has people from various walks of life: as well as a couple of salty-sea-dog types, there is one partner who used to be a journalist and another who moonlighted as a musician. The firm looks to us to be interested in applicants with a strong academic background and enthusiasms beyond the law. So if your CV is currently looking as interesting as the fields in Holland, it might be high time you switched off the telly and developed a passion for origami or progressive underwater jazz.

The hours are generally pretty good as the working day normally ends between 6pm and 7pm. People shoot off to other things on Friday evenings and some sources noted a general dislike of *"group bonding sessions."* Not completely averse to sentiment, however, the firm looks like a good place to get hitched. This year at least: three final-seaters were married within the space of a few months (none to each other) and there were whispered reports of romance among the first-years. Perhaps it develops over shared lunches at Wagamama or Thai Square, restaurants that appeal to the trainees' cosmopolitan tastes. A dislike of forced fun aside, departmental drinks are *"jolly affairs,"* where trainees and partners can mingle freely. The office, although a little crowded and chaotic, is situated in a Georgian building in Lloyd's Avenue in the heart of the City. Fittingly, its nautical décor includes model ships.

and finally...

This distinctive firm is said to run a pretty good vacation scheme that gives real insight into the way it works, so if you're curious about what Holman Fenwick & Willan has to offer, we'd suggest you get that application filled in. In 2007, seven of the ten qualifiers took jobs with the firm.

Howes Percival LLP

the facts

Location: Northampton, Leicester, Milton Keynes, Norwich
Number of UK partners/solicitors: 31/58
Total number of trainees: 12
Seats: 4x6 seats
Alternative seats: Secondments

This top-100 firm offers a broad commercial training. Mainly drawing its trainee intake from the areas surrounding its four offices, Howes Percival has acquired a substantial foothold in the East Midlands through its three offices near the M1, and in East Anglia, where it operates out of Norwich.

motoring ahead

Some of our sources had come to the firm expecting a relaxed and even *"chilled-out atmosphere,"* and we can see why as we recall an old recruitment brochure that featured a picture of two well-fed, cuddly cows with a caption promising that the grass would be greener at the firm. So has it been a tranquil escape from the City? Not exactly. The buzz phrase of the moment for trainees is *"organic growth,"* although this might sell the firm a little short. Last year it grew revenue and staff numbers by 20% and seems determined to reach a point where it can take on rivals such as Mills & Reeve and Eversheds. Most of the branches are outgrowing their premises, requiring staff to move into additional floor space or nearby buildings. It sounds as if corporate and commercial work is the main driver at the moment – this area of practice generates 30% of revenue, and along with the commercial litigation and property departments, has the seats trainees most want. That's no surprise with the firm's client portfolio including such names as insurance company St Paul's, National Geographic Channel, Lloyds TSB, Kia Motors, ATS Euromaster, Renault, HR Owen and Bentley Motors.

There are no compulsory seats, however the firm does like trainees to visit the core areas of corporate, commercial litigation and property. The nature of the work differs between departments and the vibe between offices, but the general rule is that coco can be a slog in any office and the nearer the office is to London the more full-on it feels. As such, Milton Keynes metes out the longest hours of the four, while Northampton has a more *"laid back"* feel and Leicester is a happy medium. East Midlands trainees get the chance to find out which office best suits them, as they are encouraged to move around for their seats. Journeys up and down the M1 aren't mandatory, but some trainees are willing to give them a go.

star in the east

By contrast, Norwich normally keeps its trainees parked for the full two years. Commercial property is an important area of practice for this office, as is corporate. A busy past year saw the lawyers act on the successful buyout of electrical retailer Bennetts and the sale of Galaxy Travel to Australian operator Harvey World Travel. An impressive insolvency litigation department has clinched a three-year contract with what was previously called the Department of Trade and Industry (now the Department for Business, Enterprise and Regulatory Reform) and it recently took a case to the High Court concerning the disqualification of directors, successfully obtaining a 15-year ban for two directors of an alcoholic beverage business guilty of promising unrealistic returns to investors. Trainees say you mustn't bank on a pressure-free training contract here: one even admitted to occasionally *"lying in bed nervous about work"* and advised applicants to be sure they were comfortable with a significant responsibility. One team that's performed well in the last year is licensing. When the new licensing regime came into force in late 2005, it spawned in excess of 400 applications on behalf of clients. The team has some not insignificant clients in the sector, among them Enterprise Inns, Number Ten (bowling alleys) and the Orgasmic bars in York, Lincoln and Norwich.

The AGM (which last time involved bungee jumping, quad bikes, volley ball and a fancy dress party – definitely our kind of AGM) sounds like a heck of a lot of fun and is the main opportunity for Norwich recruits to get to know staff in the other branches. They also socialise with trainees from other Norwich firms, the tenor of these relationships being camaraderie rather than competition. An aptly named pub, The Lawyer, by the river, is the usual venue for their get-togethers.

cool runnings

Across the firm, HP has thrived in the current buoyant economy, its corporate division in particular reaping some larger instructions as a result. In Milton Keynes, lawyers won instruction to act on the takeover of Oxford United FC. For its hard work, the team is regularly rewarded and recently took an overnight trip to Paris on the Eurostar. The price of a ticket, though, is heavy toil that can mean staying until after 8pm for stretches of up to a month. After sampling other offices, one trainee declared the working culture at MK *"came as a jolt to the system."* Litigation – another thriving department – is

headed by *"three fantastic partners"* in MK. These bods recently handled a £540m Commercial Court case in London centering on a Russian shipping company. A veteran of the property seat recalled: *"It was shocking when I realised how much I had tried my hand at in six months."* Overall, supervising partners in MK were applauded for *"taking the time to train you."* Indeed, our sources described the relationship as a *"teacher-student"* set-up, one remembering a time in corporate when they had been given a crack at the first draft of a share purchase agreement worth £13m.

Legend has it that Milton Keynes derives its name from an amalgamation of the 20th century Economist Maynard Keynes with 17th century poet John *"Paradise Lost"* Milton. The collocation, so the story goes, was meant to reflect the city's status as a socio-economic paradise. If your eyes are popping out right now, don't worry the anecdote isn't true. Nevertheless, the strength of your indignation may indicate your suitability to live here. Employees accepted that MK was *"a bit soulless"* and so, yes, if you're romantically inclined, the town is going to grate. Yet they were keen to extol its superb shopping, entertainment and sports facilities. Fair enough, not every town can claim a snowdome with indoor skydiving capabilities. And if you're a music lover, The Bowl is a conveyor belt of headline acts.

rol up

As HP's original office, the Northampton branch is rich with history and it was only in 2005 that the last descendant of the original Mr Percival retired. The office is felt to be less thrusting than those in Leicester and MK, and the atmosphere more easygoing. The substantial Northampton property team works for a variety of investors, developers, house builders and Welwyn Hatfield Council. Its top deal last year was the purchase of a substantial development site in Oxfordshire for a sum in excess of £21m. Major matters mean *"hardly any face-to-face client contact or human element"* for trainees but it is good to see the partners in action. The corporate lawyers, meanwhile, assisted Saxby Brothers, a traditional family run pastry company, on its multimillion-pound deal with leading frozen pastry maker Jus-Rol. A typical local deal was the BIMBO of Arnold (Hose) Limited from its existing family owners.

Northampton is somewhere between a large market town and a city. Its compact size makes it easy for trainees and juniors to organise nights out, as so many of them live within walking distance of the centre of town. The trainees get on famously and often invite each other over to house parties, even taking holidays together. A hectic round of office social events at this branch has included white water rafting and watching international cricket.

howes-at?

Like MK, coco at Leicester has a reputation as a busy seat, although not everyone appreciated the volume of admin tasks passed their way. The litigators, by contrast, entrust trainees with some of their own files and allow plenty of exposure to clients via the phone and correspondence. Again, trainees were complimentary about the social aspects of working at this office. The youthful partners organise cricket matches at weekends, a pursuit which benefits from the firm's relationship with cricket equipment manufacturer Kookaburra. At one office party, two partners turned up dressed as Starsky and Hutch driving their trade mark 1976 Ford Gran Torino. Mid-life crises came as standard.

Unlike huge firms, where *"nobody knows your name after four months,"* HP embraces new recruits into the fold. Even though one forthright source dismissed this as a soppy reason to choose the firm (theirs was *"the money"),* for most the

working environment was a crucial consideration. One trainee-philosopher told us: *"What you put in, you get out."* There is certainly wisdom in this, as confirmed by another interviewee who identified their lowest point as *"bundling documents at one o' clock in the morning,"* closely followed by her highest point *"the next morning when the judge commented how well the documents were bundled."* Overall, trainees only had a few minor quibbles – the IT system is a little creaking and there should be more consultation down the chain on *"how to push the firm forward."* Client secondments are not unheard of, but their existence failed to interest trainees one way or another, so perhaps this is an area for further improvement or at least better PR. Speaking of which, trainees revealed that business development was a part of their duties, either through research or after-work mingling with clients. *"It helps break you in for the experience once you're qualified,"* explained one. And speaking of qualification, in 2007 four out of seven people took up NQ jobs after finishing their training contracts.

A quick run around the firm's website and it's clear that HP invests a good deal of time in its local communities and is an enthusiastic dispenser of pro bono advice to a range of groups. A champion of local business, too, we are also aware of its fight for the Melton Mowbray Pork Pie in its David and Goliath battle with Northern Foods over the right to use the Melton Mowbray name. For this we'd like to extend a big thanks from all the staff at Chambers and Partners and pork pie lovers around the world.

and finally...

Ambitious commercial firm WLTM gregarious type with love for all things East Midlands... or East Anglian. If you're minded to answer this ad, be prepared for a busy two years.

Hugh James

the facts

Location: Cardiff, Merthyr, Blackwood, London
Number of UK partners/solicitors: 48/70
Total number of trainees: 17
Seats: Notionally 4x6 months
Alternative seats: None

As one of the biggest and best-known law firms in Wales, Hugh James is a popular choice for trainees seeking diverse experience. Its clientele runs from local residents in the Welsh Valleys to large organisations such as Glamorgan County Cricket, the Millennium Stadium and Mencap in Wales

on the road

Hugh James is making good progress in its drive for growth and modernisation. In the past year the firm has streamlined its business outlook on more than one front. Its four divisions of claimant PI; publicly funded law; business litigation and business services have been restructured into just three: corporate/banking; property; and claimant. Trainees see this as part of the firm's evolving image: *"Obviously two of the three new key business areas are quite commercial, which picks up on the firm's focus on business over the individual."* However, some suggest the realignment is more a change in style than of substance. *"The nature of our work hasn't changed, it's just the way the firm runs on a business level." "I think it was to encourage departments to work together and pass more work between practice areas."*

The partners have also decided to concentrate on the Cardiff and Merthyr offices by closing Blackwood to the public and using the location for certain back office functions. Some 135 new jobs are being created as part of an expansion in Cardiff, and the firm is taking on extra office space to accommodate the growth. Also hot off the press is news of the firm's first office in London. Based at Canary Wharf, its strategy is to start off in the niche field of business process outsourcing, with a view to developing a full corporate/commercial legal service over time. While it is unlikely that any trainees will be posted here straight away, this development is certainly indicative of the firm's ambition and drive.

All these changes have met with approval from trainees. As one wise sort explained: *"Law is like any business – you have strong competition. In terms of keeping abreast of that and keeping ahead of the game, the firm is evolving with the times. It's an exciting time, and I don't think trainees should be put off by the fact that it's a transition period. Sometimes change is a good thing."*

bigsmall

Property litigation in Cardiff is one of the more intense seats. *"The firm gives you a high level of responsibility at an early stage and you handle cases from start to finish."* The work ranges from gathering witness statements to attending hearings and instructing barristers at trial. However, *"you have to prove you can give good advice before you're unleashed on a client... it's a sensible approach."* Commercial property is another *"highly pressured environment and things often need to be done yesterday. You have to manage your clients' expectations as far as timescales go and keep abreast of their commercial interests. It's really quite exciting."* In some instances it will involve working with commercial lawyers, perhaps on the sale of a business. In one instance, *"we sold a business from start to finish in five working days... it was very rewarding though. The client had suffered an injury and needed out asap, so we really helped them."* The firm has an enviable client base, even in the branch office. *"Client retention is impressive and you notice the same people popping up again because they're happy with the firm."* Regular customers include Barratt Homes, the Welsh Rugby

Union, the Environment Agency and the Welsh Pony and Cob Society.

A seat has recently been introduced in the construction, energy and projects department. The team now comprises two partners, two solicitors, a paralegal and a trainee. *"It's an awesome seat,"* said one source; *"it was a bit frightening at first because they hadn't had a trainee there for ages and it's a partner-heavy department. I think it was a learning experience for everyone."* There's a lot of liaising with experts and going over documents, and trainees can expect to work on big, long-running projects. *"I spent most of my seat working on a huge PFI deal for Grwp Gwalia Housing Association,"* said one source. *"It was a six-month slog on a huge project for Bangor University Student Accommodation, and a stark contrast to handling small files that you pick up and put down in a week."*

big bangs

The reputation of the defendant fast-track litigation seat seems to be a little unfair. *"It gets bad PR with the trainees, but it turned out to be a valuable experience,"* a veteran told us. Using a rigid case management system may not be for everyone as *"you're prompted to do things, letters are already structured and you're not utilising those skills as much as in other seats. But you do get to know the cases and the clients really well and it gives you a great basis for your later seats because you understand how cases proceed through the courts."* It sounds as if the firm has responded to the heavy caseload in this seat: *"When I started I had about 60 files…that was hard. During the seat they decreased it to about 40 files, which is so much more manageable."* Best of all, it's a relatively young department and therefore one of the more sociable. The mammoth claimant PI division represents in excess of 100,000 clients nationally and internationally, covering all sorts of cases from pavement slips and trips to serious head and spinal injuries, such as those sustained by a client

who dived into a shallow swimming pool while on holiday in Greece.

If variety really is the spice of life, then commercial litigation is one spicy dish – a vindaloo, perhaps. *"You can deal with anything from Joe Blogs walking in with a £3,000 dispute with his neighbour, to massive cases that run into the hundreds of thousands of pounds."* One of the major cases of recent times relates to the Buncefield oil depot which exploded so dramatically December 2005 and has led to claims which may exceed £600m. Litigation is one of the firm's most important departments and a great seat to have as your first because *"it lends itself so well to picking up basic skills: how to write letters and speak in business terms, etc. It might sound silly but you learn that clients don't want to hear about complex legal issues. They just want to know what they have to do."* The debt recovery unit is part of the department and its two major clients include Welsh Water and Royal Mail. *"You get a fairly continuous stream of work and then ad hoc jobs on top of that. I was sent to court to do mortgage repo hearings and I did all the advocacy at a chambers hearing. I was quite chuffed with that."*

A family seat in the small department in Cardiff can be a rewarding challenge. Both private and public work is handled and tasks include drafting instructions to counsel, witness statements and divorce documentation. Then there are the client meetings and court visits. *"You frequently accompany counsel to court,"* said one trainee. *"I've been to Swansea, Newport and Cardiff courts."* Those with a hankering for large amounts of client contact will be happy: *"You see clients all the time and get to know them."* Of course, *"there is the odd bit of photocopying, but you're treated as a valuable member of the team, particularly because it's one of the smaller departments."* Trainees tend not to get their own caseload, instead working as a team with other fee earners. *"The subject matter is often emotional;*

you end up being a bit of a counsellor as well as a legal adviser so it helps to be a people person." When you get a good result, *"there's a great feeling of accomplishment, like you've really made a difference. Some clients still ask after me, which is lovely."*

expect the unexpected

It helps if trainees are flexible with seat allocation. In theory, trainees have four six-month seats, but in practice *"there's no hard and fast rule and some people do the bare minimum of two seats."* At times, trainees are whisked away to other departments, depending on the needs of the firm. *"Recently they took on a lot of remortgage work from one of the lenders, so they called in more trainees who had experience to help with that."* This approach to staffing can bring mixed results. On the one hand, those who know where they want to qualify from early on can stay in one seat for a year or more, gaining a real depth of experience. For them *"it can certainly work in your favour."* On the other hand, trainees can find themselves switched into a different department sooner than they'd like. It sounds as if you should expect the unexpected. A few people had issues with seat allocation itself, telling us: *"In your full seat appraisal they ask you where you'd like to go next, and say it's taken into account...but it's not really a discussion so much as a question they just tag on at the end of the meeting. I'd like it if they discussed it with you more."* Others disagreed, telling us those who speak out will be heard. *"Everyone I know has been happy with where they were put, even if they wouldn't have chosen it,"* said one.

"Friendly, open, informal" – whichever way you put it, it's clear that HJ genuinely offers an enjoyable work environment. *"There are some real characters here, they're good fun,"* was the common consensus. *"We work hard but it's not competitive and you feel at ease in the office."* Nevertheless, trainees are expected to grab the bull by the horns: *"You have to show you're up for it and prove yourself; people aren't going to mollycoddle you."* Overall, trainees report a balanced experience: *"I've had a good rapport with all my supervisors, you could always say if you had too much on. Their motto seems to be 'dedication' – as long as you try, no one has a problem."*

As for defining a typical trainee, there are a few sweeping generalisations that can be made. Whether Welsh or English, most trainees have Cardiff University in common. And *"people who keep to themselves wouldn't really fit in – we're big on the socialising."* Across the firm there are organised events such as bowling, rounders and inter-firm rugby. In Cardiff on a Friday you're guaranteed to see HJ people having a drink in Copa, the pub across the road. In Merthyr it's a bit different: *"We don't do as much on a weekly basis because most people are commuting, but for Christmas craziness I think we beat Cardiff! It's a smaller office and people tend to have worked here for longer, so people know each other better."* They're not wrong – the Merthyr Christmas parties are legendary! Firm-wide summer and winter balls are a good opportunity to get all the offices together, and *"they're always held on a Friday night, which is great because you have the weekend to think up ways to explain your behaviour."*

and finally...

"It's not until you see new trainees arriving that you realise how much you've learnt over the two years," remarked one of our Hugh James interviewees, making an important point succinctly. This training scheme does exactly what it promises – it gets people ready for life after qualification, whatever that might entail. In 2007, seven of the ten qualifiers stayed with the firm.

IBB Solicitors

the facts

Location: Uxbridge, Chesham, Ingatestone
Number of UK partners/solicitors: 32/41
Total number of trainees: 12
Seats: 4x6 months
Alternative seats: None

Leaving the chaos of central London behind, you decide to strike out to the fringes of the city on the Metropolitan line. Once you arrive at Harrow-on the Hill, you can go one of two ways. Both lines terminate at IBB.

capital gains

IBB's main offices are located at the frayed western end of the Tube's maroon line in Chesham and Uxbridge. Such places might seem the sort only snoozing commuters wake up in, but trainees were unanimous in *"singing the praises"* of an IBB training. Making the most of the locale, the firm caters for commercial activity stimulated by the nearby airports at Luton and Heathrow and has an impressive client portfolio that reveals aspirations above and beyond its location. On the list are Bellway Group, Credit Suisse, Hertz, Norwich Union, Meridian Hotels and Frontier Estates.

IBB promotes itself as one of the leading law firms in West London. It's a claim at which some more central outfits might take umbrage, but one that speaks of ambition. IBB is aiming to compete with mid-tier London firms, recently signing up partners from Berwin Leighton Paisner and Taylor Wessing into a humming real estate division that spearheads the firm's fortunes. Nearly half the firm's partners are concentrated in this department, with recent advice to Dolce & Gabbana on the leasing of premises at 18 Hanover Square, London W1, a triumph to sit alongside instructions from fashionista clients Patek Philippe and Max Mara. There's also the small

matter of a tidy 29% rise in the department's revenue in 2006. The *"oft-stated aim of breaking into the top 100"* also means the firm is bent on bolstering its corporate capabilities, although the loss of a banking partner last year hurt a little. As one trainee pointed out, considering that as recently as the 1980s this was a high street firm, IBB's rise to the cusp of the top 100 deserves no small praise. Our sources were enthused by the idea of *"getting caught up in the flow"* of a business in expansion mode.

While commercial services form the basis of new ambition, the private client and criminal work that has long been IBB's bedrock is unlikely to disappear anytime soon, and as such the firm advises a wide cross-section of clients across its offices and practice areas. There is financial help for city slickers in Capital Court, magistrates' courts appearances for delinquents in Lovell House and private client trusts and wills assistance in Chesham for elderly, wealthy, retired folk. A smaller fourth branch at Ingatestone in Essex does not host trainees, so for the purposes of this feature we'll leave it in the sidings.

IBB is a dream for those who are uncertain of what type of law they want to practise, as the training covers everything from legal aid to six-figure corporate deals. Without any compulsory seats, trainees are encouraged to follow their interests. Moving between all three western offices they can sample seats as diverse as serious crime, IP, employment, personal injury, childcare and commercial property, to name but a few.

simply capital

It doesn't take Sherlock Holmes to deduce that the Capital Court office in Uxbridge is well suited to its *"really hard-working"* commercial team. Plasma screens on the wall, air conditioning and up-to-the-minute conference rooms tell a strictly corporate story. Chesham by contrast is an old manor house situated in three acres of rolling parkland, including a lake and a couple of ghosts: the perfect setting for a detective whodunit. We even heard a rumour from one trainee that Sir Arthur Conan Doyle was a one-time customer of the firm in its Edwardian past, but sadly at time of going to press there was no evidence to support the claim. Where's Holmes when you need him, eh? A business-oriented, *"quieter and more heads-down"* style pervades at Uxbridge, with property litigation helping to *"get you used to talking to clients,"* even if partners can sometimes be *"reluctant to relinquish responsibility."* The size of the cases for property titans such as Bellway Homes requires trainees to get stuck into a fair amount of admin. Employment law proves enjoyable, as trainees write assessments on the merits of cases, *"build relationships and attend tribunal hearings,"* often on good-quality, union-fed instructions. It's not all about acting for the little guy though – Coca-Cola and Hasbro are clients. The *"serious and focused"* commercial litigation metes out a few bits of advocacy to trainees and it does a far bit of work for big-name clients itself. Notable on the client roster is Renault.

Described as the *"golden department"* in the firm's future plans is banking. The loss of a key banking partner has stepped up the pressure on everyone else, trainees too, and they tell us the seat is characterised by *"much responsibility and lots to do."* New lawyers are expected to arrive in autumn 2007 to help out with the full caseload. Among the most important clients is RBS, for which the firm advises on debt restructuring solutions and acted on the acquisition of ITV's outside broadcast facilities business and the setting up of a Bulgarian-owned TV playout system. Occasionally, hours *"as late as 9pm"* can be on the cards in this seat. This isn't typical, so trainees can generally sidestep the microwave meals aisle in the supermarket and take time preparing a leisurely dinner.

bust ups and bling

Lovell House is a *"bit run-down"* but nevertheless buzzing. Lawyers here represent every category of criminal from big-time gangsters to small-time hustlers and it can't be unrelated that, in stark contrast to hushed Capital Court, staff are free to *"scream across the office."* Such work almost invariably springs trainees from the manacles of deskwork. Wednesdays, for example, are spent in Uxbridge magistrates' court, probably *"interviewing somebody who beat someone on a Saturday and will be appearing in court on a Monday."* Other matters might include dealing with the fallout from allegations of sexual misconduct to a bite by an uncontrolled dog. Serious white-collar crimes fall under the auspices of the business investigations and governance team, aka BIG. Work here and, if you ever luck out on a legal career, you'll have garnered enough material to pen a blockbuster. The team recently worked on an investigation by the SFO into drug-pricing fraud by individuals and companies supplying the NHS, and is defending seven clients on charges of intent to rob Swissport Heathrow of gold bullion, foreign currency and diamonds.

chesham revisited

The Chesham branch is exclusively dedicated to private client practice. A little sleepier than the other offices, it offers an overwhelmingly friendly environment with work that is not so high pressured even though it offers decent portions of responsibility. Here, trainees can look on as wealthy clients with kids in tow attend meetings to discuss the ways in which they can ensure their multimillion-pound fortunes pass on smoothly to the next generation. The *"so-lovely"* surroundings are a suitable backdrop to these cases. Here, tax is said to be one of the most intellectually challenging areas for a trainee. Although family law can initially seem to novices as understandable as *"Egyptian hieroglyphics,"* the *"fantastic"* supervision ensures a quick learning process. In childcare, trainees are introduced to the ins and outs of the litigation process, normally handling their own advocacy within three months. Instructions, ranging from child adoptions to non-molestation orders, expose them to highly fraught emotional situations. Even so, interviewees declared the seat to be *"fun and interesting,"* and owing to the extensive client contact, *"a good morale booster."* The personal injury team meanwhile deals with every scale of incident from slips and trips to catastrophic injuries. One complex case involved a client who suffered memory loss when he fell from a height.

Lately, second years have been gunning for the commercial seats on offer at the firm, spurred on perhaps by the prospect of higher salaries in these departments. Ever flexible, HR is working on improving the method of seat allocation and is even considering offering first-years their preferences too. A *"good support structure"* means it is easier to handle the vagaries of a training programme in which experiences can differ dramatically between departments – *"more administrative"* in one seat, *"very hands on"* and *"exhilarating"* in another. Reassuringly, seniors seem to be approachable *"if you mess up"* and there are quarterly trainee meetings to keep everyone talking.

gladiators… ready?!

Applicants to IBB can expect an assessment day demanding Crowe-like levels of psychological and physical endurance. Victorious survivors advise to *"keep confident and enjoy yourself,"* adding that the firm's preference for team players means it's worthwhile making *"other people feel comfortable and welcome as well."* Designed to be *"creative and light hearted,"* the day involves such tasks as devising a radio snippet on what it takes to be a lawyer. Distinctly less jolly is the moment

when applicants are called out one by one to discover publicly whether they have the thumbs up or down from IBB's august recruiters. Intimidating it's true, but at least there are no tiger-filled pits to avoid.

As you've likely gathered, IBB's social character changes significantly across offices. Chesham's medium size means a friendly face in every department, with ample camaraderie in a *"work is not the be all and end all"* atmosphere. Beware, though, the potential diplomatic minefield of… cake. There's a regular supply of home-baked goodies from various staff members, so don't profess to having favourites and remember to *"say thank you at least three times."* Over in Uxbridge, the more corporate atmosphere gives way to *"an early finish for Friday drinks"* and there are not infrequent social events that can sometimes lead to *"some scandal."* Across the firm, activities include cricket and netball, and some trainees have recently set up a book group, fomenting regular literary chit-chat in a local pizzeria. Chesham is also a fertile reading ground, with some employees whiling away their lunch hour in a state of semi-undress by the lake. Sunbathing, of course. The grounds hosted a local theatre company's production of *The Importance of Being Earnest* in 2007 and there are croquet and badminton events in the pipeline.

Trainees admitted they'd enjoy a slightly more switched-on social scene, but few felt they'd compromised on ambition in choosing the firm. Hailing from a range of *"not-the-top-five"* but certainly decent universities, this *"hungry and hard-working"* bunch predict a bright future for the firm. In 2007, six of the seven qualifiers bought into that future by accepting permanent positions. On a related note, while many staff find digs in Uxbridge, the 45-minute overland journey from central London is far more pleasant than the average commute.

and finally...

Thar's gold in them thar hills... the location might not make it an obvious choice, but for the pioneering graduate IBB offers a rich vein of responsibility, broad experience and good future prospects. As the IBB trainee might say, 'Why not go west?'

Ince & Co

the facts

Location: London
Number of UK partners/solicitors: 52/48
Total number of trainees: 21
Seats: 4x6 months
Alternative seats: Overseas seats
Extras: Language training

In business since 1870, Ince & Co is renowned for its shipping and insurance litigation practices. A network of five offices in Europe, and another four in Hong Kong, China, Singapore and Dubai, evidences the international nature of its business and outlook.

altogether different?

On its website Ince describes itself as 'altogether different' and, if its training scheme is anything to go by, this is a fair description. Unlike the vast majority of commercial law firms, Ince does not put its trainees through seats. Yes, they move offices every six months to sit with a different partner, but that does not mean they change their workload every six months. The differences go even further – Ince does not get hung up on lawyers having to belong to departments in the way most commercial firms do. As a result, its lawyers are able to develop and maintain broad practices. Sitting with a partner who is best known for shipping litigation, for example, won't mean a trainee sees six months of shipping cases.

The partner might also be a whiz at other types of disputes, and besides, the trainee might only spend part of his or her time working on that partner's cases.

Soliciting work from around the office can be quite a daunting process in the first few weeks; after all, there are no law school sessions on how to market yourself to partners. So how exactly is it done? *"You go and meet people, introduce yourself and tell them what you are interested in or why you are interested in their work,"* explained a source. *"You get used to it,"* apparently, *"and everyone is interested in meeting you."* After a couple of months trainees build up a rapport with a group of partners and the stage is set for the rest of their training contract. Of course every system needs checks and balances and this is where the room switching comes into play. Monitoring everyone's workload is a 'Resource Committee', which essentially makes sure that some people are not twiddling their thumbs while others flog themselves to death. When it comes to the specific pieces of work trainees take on, the committee is not overly intrusive and trainees say: *"It is your responsibility to cover the areas you need to, and everyone realises they should try a bit of almost everything."*

Before we tell you about the types of work available to trainees, we should stress just a couple more points. Within the Ince training system, you build your own reputation, be this good or bad. Fail to impress a partner and the work could dry up from that particular source. The moral here is simple: tread carefully to begin with and be clear about what you have taken on. Another reason why you need to know exactly what you have taken on is because you're unable to fob it off on some other unsuspecting trainee after six months. If you're considering this firm you'll doubtless see the requirement to take cases with you whenever you move as a real benefit: *"You don't have to worry about handing over the meat of* your case after six months," said one typical source. Asked for their view on how well the system worked, our interviewees believed that the flexibility and freedom enshrined in the approach allowed them to home in on a certain practice area quite early and to develop their skills in that area further than a rotational system would allow.

port and starboard

The two sectors that generate most work for Ince are shipping and trade, and insurance. But what if you don't know your port from your starboard and your only encounter with an insurance company was when you pranged your mum's Panda? Fear not, for a two-week introductory course at the beginning of your training contract will give you enough basic law and terminology to set you on your way.

Never underestimate the importance of shipping in international trade, say trainees. "Without ships, there would be no bananas in the supermarkets," added one solemnly. There are two types of shipping law: 'wet' and 'dry'. The former deals with incidents at sea – collisions, spills, sinkings, mutinies, piracy, etc; the latter concerns contractual disputes relating to anything from charter parties, bills of lading, ship mortgages and building contracts. Trainees can get involved in both types of work, although wet cases are harder to get hold of without experience. They also sound considerably more exciting: Ince trainees have jetted off to places such as Venezuela, Turkey and Egypt in recent times. If you want a hint as to how exciting it all gets, just check out the International Emergency Response button on the firm's website. Please don't press it – we don't know what happens if you do. The idea, of course, is that 24 hours a day, 365 days a year, Ince lawyers are poised, ready to leap into action at the first hint of a maritime disaster, be it a flaming oil rig, a listing cargo ship or Captain Jack Sparrow swinging, cutlass in hand, through your rigging. We can't

help wondering if the button was ever pressed by Ince's shipowner client whose vessel got caught up in an Israeli attack on Hezzbolah and Lebanon as it was about to discharge cargo by the Zouk oil terminal in Beirut. Of course, Ince has some very respectable transactional work too: in the summer of 2007 it advised Seaway Heavy Lifting on a ship building deal worth $460m.

If matters maritime don't float your boat, there are other options. The most notable of these is insurance and reinsurance law, where the work ranges from advising shipyard underwriters following delayed construction after hurricane Katrina to advising the owner of a South East Asian power station after a major fire and disputes with its underwriters/reinsurers. Trainees told us they had a great deal of independence and could take on their own smaller cases: "I analyse all the documents myself and then offer an opinion to the partner, basically starting from scratch," explained one interviewee. As any litigator will tell you, this work is very procedural and "experience suggests the smaller jobs like document management are vital elements." However, trainees do get out of the office to take witness statements and "support counsel in arguing applications in court." Trainees can also experience commercial disputes.

flight risks

The firm's developing expertise in the aviation and energy sectors has opened up more opportunities for trainees, as has growth in its business and finance practice. Among other things, specialist aviation lawyers have advised in connection with the crash of an ADC Boeing 737 passenger jet in Nigeria in 2006 and on various helicopter crashes. On the regulatory and commercial side they represent airlines such as Emirates Group, Etihad and Royal Jet. Ince's energy sector work, meanwhile, takes in matters as unusual as advice to oil and gas contractors in relation to loss of life claims, kidnapping and ransom issues arising from the campaign of violence in the Niger Delta. At the height of the trouble, Ince & Co had personnel on the ground in Port Harcourt assisting various contractors. The business and finance team is *"fast expanding"* off the back of matters such as the sale of American pipeline contractor Willbros Group's Nigerian interests for $155m and the reverse takeover of asbestos specialists Silverdell into an AIM cash shell. Interestingly, there was disagreement between our sources as to whether a student primarily interested on non-contentious work should put Ince on their shortlist.

The absence of a billable hours target is rather unusual in the City, but the reason for not having one is, put simply: *"Being a good litigator has nothing to do with the number of hours you work."* It's not that the lawyers don't record how many hours they work, it's just that there is no official minimum that they need to reach. Instead of working practices being dictated by targets, it is client work that determines how long and when lawyers must stay in the office. Even for trainees, the hours can be harsh at times, but usually it's a 9.30am to 7pm regime. Decent support from secretaries and the *"repro"* and *"word pro"* departments means arduous photocopying and typing jobs can be delegated much of the time. But not always. We were reminded that as trainees sit at the *"very bottom of the pile"* they do get their fair share of mundane tasks. *"Until I am blue in the face, I will say the only way to learn to paginate properly is by making mistakes,"* said one.

The months running up to qualification can be an intense time. *"In firms where there are four seats in set departments, you can get a nod from one so the others don't matter so much. Here you have to work hard the whole time."* And because those who do stay on – and the figure fluctuates a good deal – are able to maintain a broad practice post-qualification, trainees are not pinpointed for specific NQ roles. The qualification process sounds like it couldn't be simpler: *"If you have performed well during your training contract you will be offered a job."* Clearly the 2007 qualifiers were a bumper crop, since all nine stayed on.

pane sailing

Ince's new offices at St Katherine's Dock on the north bank of the Thames reflect its desire to modernise a firm that was beginning to feel a little too traditional for comfort. The old office used to have pictures of ships and oilrigs hung along the corridors. Initially these were banned from the new building but old habits die hard and certain pictures have appeared in partners' rooms. Astonishingly, smoking was also allowed in the old building – particularly unpleasant if you shared a room with a pal of Nick O'Teen. Indeed, horror stories abound concerning the old office, such as a partner who when showing a client something through a window had the window fall off when he opened it.

Socially, the firm is tighter than most. As well as the usual sports – football, rugby, squash, etc – staff can sail together and even sing together. And we don't mean karaoke. The Ince & Co choir has practice sessions twice a week from around September to prepare for carol performances in the office and at St Olave's Church, where Samuel Pepys is buried. Its most formal event of the year is a May ball (the table plan deliberately mixes partners with trainees and support staff) and every second Thursday of the month there are free drinks, either in the office or in a local pub, The Vineyard being the nearest one. Bearing in mind that *"if you are shy this isn't the place for you,"* trainees recommend going along to get to know the partners and senior lawyers in a social setting.

and finally...

Ince & Co should definitely be high up on the list for anyone set on litigation or shipping law. Its non-contentious workload is growing, but that still doesn't make it a number-one choice for transactional experiences. Those who are confident, bright and outgoing could do very well here, especially if international trade or insurance issues are of interest.

Irwin Mitchell

the facts
Location: Altringham, Birmingham, Glasgow, Leeds, London, Manchester, Newcastle, Sheffield
Number of UK partners/solicitors: 100/228
Total number of trainees: 48
Seats: 4x6 months
Alternative seats: None
Extras: Pro bono – RCJ CAB

From its humble beginnings representing gang-members in pre-WWII Sheffield, Irwin Mitchell has grown steadily to become a vast operation that is defined by its breadth of practice and volume business.

at the dawn of a new age
Of the multiple pies in which IM has its fingers, it is its world-beating claimant-based clinical negligence and personal injury practices that really carry the flag for the firm. This year saw the successful conclusion of damages claims for over 80 workers and local residents affected by the Immingham oil refinery explosion in Lincolnshire in 2001. Staying with group litigation, this time in the employment law arena, the firm has recently initiated a class action on behalf of Heyday – Age Concern's membership organisation for those in or near retirement – challenging the government's implementation of the European directive on equal treatment in employment. These are just a couple of examples of the more pioneering cases from a vast caseload,

which at the lower end also includes bountiful low-value PI and conveyancing work processed by an army of part or non-qualified case handlers. Add to this a healthy batch of commercial clients and the firm's vastness begins to make sense. If you're looking at the partner, solicitor and trainee numbers above and thinking they're not as big as you've seen for other firms, then bear in mind that IM has a total staff of 2,300 across eight offices, making it one of the largest domestic employers among law firms.

It is hard to ignore the irony of a firm renowned for fighting for the little man turning into such a large organisation. What has happened is that the firm has chosen to harness its size and power in preparation for battle in the new open arena proposed by the Legal Services Act, which creates an environment in which alternative business structures are permitted to compete with traditional law firms. It is expected that commercial giants such as the Co-op and the AA will enter the market and threaten the established players in areas such as conveyancing and PI. It should come as no surprise then that IM has been at the vanguard of preparations for this new 'Tesco law' era. Having added firepower in 2006 through a merger with Midlands PI-boutique Alexander Harris, it recently kicked off a new repositioning strategy by merging with Scottish firm Golds. The stated aim of this is to strengthen the firm's footprint prior to the entrance of high street super brands into the market. While our interviewees seemed largely indifferent to these goings on, we feel it is a good example of the proactive nature of the firm.

on the hop
The majority of the firm's large troupe of trainees did not go straight from uni to law school to a training contract. *"They let you have a life in advance of training and regard experience gained from other places as positive,"* said one source. As a

result there were many gap-year veterans in the group, as well as a surprising number of candidates with paralegal experience. The threshold for getting in is undoubtedly high, but trainees felt that the recruiters were more open-minded than at many firms. *"They let you come in through the back door more commonly than some traditional firms might."*

One very important characteristic for a prospective trainee is a willingness to move around the country. The firm offers training in six of its offices, and while seat request forms allow for preferences to be stated for both department and location, first-years cannot bank on having either of these requests met. Indeed, we did encounter people who had very little luck at all in getting the seats they wanted. Although they had all signed up knowing the policy about moving around, many of our sources found the reality quite hard to deal with. One told us: *"It is very unsettling to live with a potential move over your head, which could see you off to the other end of the country within six weeks."* While this short notice period was widely disliked, some people did enjoy the actual city-hopping. Moreover, the firm does what it can – within limits – to make things easier, offering removal cost allowances, loans to cover deposits and travel expenses for scouting trips.

IM's Sheffield homeland is still very much its hub. It hosts roughly twice as many trainees as any other office and it is also where many trainees form lasting bonds through attending the PSC lecture days during their first year at the firm. *"We all go out in town on these days and catch up, which is always nice as many of the people you know well are working in other offices."* Leeds, Birmingham and the rapidly growing Manchester office each take around eight trainees at any one time, with London slightly fewer and Newcastle limited to two. These smaller offices have a quieter social side and post-work tipples are usually more department-based than trainee-centric. Each office has a social committee with a budget and there are also abundant opportunities to represent the firm through sport.

king of torts

IM has been behind some of the most important common law developments for claimants over the past few decades, so if the quirks of tortious case law were what made you tick at university, there is simply no better place to train. Massive cases such as Lockerbie, the King's Cross fire, CJD/BSE litigation and a whole host of miners' disease claims all have the IM signature to them. Unsurprisingly therefore, the majority of trainees take at least one seat in a claimant department.

Personal injury seats are available in each of the firm's six main offices. The department is a powerhouse with numerous partners and an army of fee earners, nonetheless, trainees bore testimony to the cohesion between offices. Center Parcs would no doubt agree, having recently hosted a mob of 500 personal injury fee earners on a department weekend break. In 2006, in Yorkshire alone, the department achieved 21 settlements worth more than £1m. A highlight was the Byrne lung cancer case, where it reached a settlement after proving a link between asbestos exposure and lung cancer without the development of asbestosis. Current trainee experiences of major cases largely revolved around neurotrauma, on which they are charged with a variety of tasks for the lead partner or associate on each case. This necessarily involves some menial work, but also regular court visits to observe counsel and *"direct client contact every other day."* Other areas of activity include child abuse and industrial disease, where some trainees found themselves running smaller files. Such small matters are extremely popular as they allow trainees to follow an entire case cycle. *"Naturally it is quite sad at times, but very rewarding when you get to help people."*

The IM clinical negligence department is highly respected. It offers trainees in all offices a popular mix of personal responsibility for small cases and work on multimillion-pound cases for senior fee earners. The latter includes *"attending conferences, instructing counsel, looking into quantum and drafting letters of claim and witness statements."* In the line of duty, trainees even found themselves in the Court of Appeal. The department handles a large amount of birth injury cases and so the job can be *"heart-wrenching at times."* This must be set against the feel-good factor of *"helping someone who's in a terrible situation."* Closely allied to this group is the product liability team, which dominates the claimant landscape nationwide and continues to act on newsworthy group actions such as those surrounding anti-inflammatory drug Vioxx and foetal anti-convulsant drugs. In the Vioxx case, UK claimants were recently denied forum in New Jersey and have sought counsel from IM in relation to possible domestic claims.

These monster departments also feed some interesting niche groups that are popular among trainees. Perhaps the best example is the Birmingham-based international travel team, which works in conjunction with outposts in Madrid and Marbella. It has a good reputation for bringing package holiday providers to book. Meanwhile the Court of Protection team, which is there to *"manage the finances of individuals not able to do so themselves,"* benefits from many referrals from the PI and clinical negligence teams after clients have been successful with their claims. *"This work is incredibly interesting and something you just wouldn't get elsewhere."*

change of plan

In addition to its flagship claimant work, the firm has *"a rapidly expanding business side."* The main centres for commercial work are Sheffield, Leeds and London, although trainees felt that in practice the three teams operate as fairly distinct entities. Commercial seats include litigation, corporate and employment. Of this last option, one source told us: *"We work for a lot of big organisations, so we draft policies and handle disciplinary proceedings. I play a support role and therefore do a lot of research tasks and draft tribunal documents."* Across the seats in what is termed 'IM Business' it is not unheard of to find yourself in the office until midnight, but such occasions are rare and usually the hours are deemed to be *"fairly sociable."*

Many trainees saw the option of gaining exposure to claimant and commercial client work as invaluable. In some cases it served to confirm a long-held view on which part of the profession they wanted to go into. One told us: *"I wanted to try something different and I am glad I did, but it really wasn't my cup of tea. I prefer working with individuals who I have more sympathy for."* Other people, who had previously defined themselves as future champions of the little guy, found themselves attracted to the pace and glamour of commercial law.

The huge growth at IM has created many opportunities for those wishing to train at the firm. Several sources felt they were *"part and parcel of the firm"* as it moves forward; others, however, felt the machinery had grown so large that it made it difficult to feel anything other than a small moving part. One enduring *"bone of contention"* relates to pay scales. *"We now compete as a top-ten firm in the UK, but we don't pay like one,"* came the complaint. Those placed in London were the most vocal, feeling that insufficient allowance is made for the higher living costs of the capital. We asked for details of the salaries and learned that first-years are paid £19,000 in the regions and £23,250 in London. In the second year this rises to £21,000 and £24,870. Some sources also felt that effective communication was a casualty of the firm's rapid expansion. *"At times, life is made a lot harder than it has to be* here," said one cryptic source. In particular, some interviewees were left feeling out of the loop regarding the qualification process and stressed that the firm could do better in this regard. In 2007, 19 of the 25 second-year trainees qualified into the firm.

and finally...

Irwin Mitchell is *"a rapidly expanding, ambitious national law firm covering a huge range of services."* If you subscribe to the school of thought that says variety is the spice of life, and you are not overly attached to a particular locale, this firm offers *"good prospects for a great career."*

Jones Day

the facts

Location: London
Number of UK partners/solicitors: 43/98
Total number of trainees: 33
Seats: Non-rotational
Alternative seats: None
Extras: Pro bono – Waterloo Legal Advice Centre, Jamaican death row appeals

Your own office. No switching department every six months. Having your say about what work you do and when. Perhaps Jones Day is the way forward for you.

perfect partners

Our subject is the product of the 2003 merger of Jones Day, a Cleveland-headquartered giant with a vast international network and a polished reputation for litigation, and London-based corporate firm Gouldens, with its maverick style and ability to punch well above its weight class. Five years on and post-merger turbulence is all but a distant memory. The original plan – a) extend the international reach of the London lawyers and allow

them to take on more multi-jurisdictional work and b) nab a bigger chunk of the London market for Jones Day – has come to fruition. Last year Jones Day lawyers squared up to Herbert Smith and Linklaters on the £1.62bn purchase of Irish energy business Viridian by ElectricInvest Acquisitions, a company that is owned by an international investment firm based in Bahrain with offices in London and Atlanta. Jones Day acted for the lenders Dresdner Kleinwort and Dresdner Bank. Another international deal was for client Pamplona, which spent €226m buying the ceramics division of Johnson Matthey plc, including operations and assets located in Europe, Brazil, India, China, Malaysia, Vietnam, Australia and Indonesia. As active as ever in London, the capital markets team advised on a total of 15 IPOs in 2006, 13 of which were on AIM. Overall, our sources believed *"the firm is getting work from bigger and better clients and is achieving a newfound status as a result."*

One constant through everything has been the training system, an almost unique set-up that sees trainees managing their own workload and choosing who they wish to work with. There are huge advantages to this method of training, but it isn't for everyone. Carry on reading only if you have heaps of confidence...

On your first day at the firm you'll be shown to your own office and on the desk will be your first piece of work. Your caseload then grows in the way you direct: it's up to you to go knocking on doors, meeting people, asking for jobs and building up relationships. Even though you can approach anyone in the office, location tends to determine where the majority of your work comes from, simply because *"you don't have to walk so far."* This being so, trainees are encouraged to move offices every now and then to ensure they at least see a range of practice areas. Speaking to people you quickly learn that most love the system: *"We're not pigeon-holed"* and have the *"flexibility and freedom to do what we want,"* said one source. *"I would hate to share an office or be stuck in a department,"* said another. Just imagine: *"What if you didn't get on with a person in your office or if you are in a mood?"* The system also gets people talking to each other, so *"you get to know virtually everyone,"* and it's pretty darned obvious that the partners and associates have to place a lot of trust in trainees in order for the system to function. For their part, the trainees need *"real motivation"* and nerves of steel not to be *"daunted"* by low levels of supervision and a sense of being *"out there on your own"* and *"sending out stuff without it being checked."* To be clear, Jones Day is *"not for those who want to be spoon-fed,"* have their hand held or be able to return something when they realise they don't enjoy it. Take on a piece of work and it is yours until the bitter – or glorious – end.

great expectations

With corporate a key strength of the office, trainees see some interesting capital markets, M&A, private equity and all manner of other corporate finance transactions. They can expect to draft ancillary documents, assist on placings, review sale and purchase agreements, and one source told us how they *"acted for individual vendors who were selling their company... I really felt I was guiding them through the sale."* There is also a great deal of *"verification, due diligence and dealings with Companies House"* to wade through, but at least our sources had been *"left to run meetings on our own, taking lead on drafting documents and running parts of the deal."* All up there is no shortage of responsibility and the firm encourages trainees to develop relationships with clients. To illustrate this point, one source told us: *"One company I've worked for that buys others left, right and centre now expects me to be on all their deals."* Similarly, there is *"always property work going around"* and in this area especially trainees really do take control of transactions. One source had developed a taste for *"negotiating amendments with the other side: it's quite enjoyable to say, 'No, you're wrong' and when they say 'OK' you celebrate a little victory!"* Trainees see a lot of the usual licences and leases and have plenty of opportunity to assist on larger deals for major clients such as Arlington and Ashtenne.

In litigation, trainees can edge their way into some big trials. The firm is representing Goldshield in multimillion-pound Warfarin pharmaceuticals litigation, which commenced after the SFO accused the company of conspiring to defraud the NHS through cartel conduct. The firm has advised in relation to both criminal and civil proceedings. Other clients include Motorola, Occidental Petroleum, Dell, Dole Food Company, BOC Group, Intercontinental Hotels, IBM, JPMorgan, Chevron and Morgan Stanley Real Estate Funds – a fantastic client roster by any standards. Working with the litigators, trainees learn how to liaise with counsel and clients, engage expert witnesses, draft witness statements and, of course, *"prepare documents and bundles for trial."* If they are lucky, trainees can also *"effectively run smaller cases,"* taking control of negotiations or mediations in the process. Working with lawyers in this department is very popular and so it can prove difficult to secure involvement on cases. The department's work can effectively be split into general commercial litigation and international arbitration. Despite the popularity of disputes work, transactional matters dominate in the office and so it is necessary for many trainees to skip practical learning in the office for a *"pretty tedious"* two-week litigation course run by the College of Law. A fair few of the trainees we spoke to had completed this course, which involves tutorials, role-play and a couple of pro bono cases.

Other areas worth mentioning are a not inconsiderable finance practice and more niche areas such as employment (*"really kicking off now"*), tax (*"very technical"*), IP (*"one trainee found it best to move down there to really immerse themselves in the department"*) and competition (*"they've done some great cases"*). As the firm is busy across the board, most trainees should be able to at least sample most of the things they set their hearts on. With this style of training JD takes the attitude that it needs to keep its trainees in the office, so don't expect any international or client secondments. Sometimes people go on secondments post-qualification, but these are not structured and only happen as and when the need arises.

reward and punishment

With all this independence, how does the firm keep an eye on trainees and keep them on the right track? The answer is twofold. On each piece of work the trainee will be answerable to the lawyer from whom they got it. With regard to the big picture, at the end of each week trainees must submit a work diary to the powers that be so that he or she can be guided away from doing too much of one type of practice... or too much full stop. Technically, within this system, *"if you wanted to do no work for a week you could get away with it, but ultimately that's not going to benefit you."* We doubt it ever happens! Checklist reviews are scheduled every three months and there are appraisals every six months with two partners. In terms of formal training sessions, there are lunchtime seminars twice a week in the first year and weekly thereafter. The in-house caterers usually put on a decent spread for these. Once a week on Friday a newsletter is e-mailed to everyone in the firm, detailing *"what deals are happening and what pitches are being made."* However, in terms of the future game plan, things are more hush-hush and partnership decisions do not immediately filter down through the ranks.

No one denies that the hours can become pretty horrendous at times. Most interviewees reported that their average day ran from 9.30am to 7pm, but enough of them admitted to *"plenty of nights until 3am or 4am."* Having taken work from several departments, it may not always be possible to take time off after a few late nights on a deal; others will still expect you to fulfil commitments to them. It is possible to log on to the firm's computer network at home and this at least means it's not always necessary to hike in at the weekend if there is stuff to be done that doesn't require physical paper shuffling. If the regime is beginning to sound rather too demanding for your liking, then maybe the salary will be too rich for your taste as well. At the time of going to press, NQ salaries were £70,0000 and trainee salaries started at £39,000 for first-seaters, rising to £50,000 for fourth-seaters. In 2007, the firm achieved almost perfect retention with 20 of the 21 taking jobs.

behind you

Jones Day's office is located on Tudor Street, just behind Fleet Street with its selection of great cafés to pop out to for lunch. The relatively modern building has a plush reception with a bird's eye view down into the library (no reading the Beano unnoticed), and at Christmas a huge decorated tree towers up from among the books right into the main reception. Staying on the theme of Christmas, the partners at Jones Day must like it as they put their hands in their pockets for a huge party. The main attraction at the bash is a pantomime that was described as an *"immense,"* *"proper production."* Trainees devote hours to preparation and rehearsals, and everyone in the firm turns out to watch. Usually it is a traditional story *"written in an amusing way"* in order to ridicule certain characters, usually partners. It's all taken light-heartedly and everyone thoroughly enjoys the night, including the fearful vac schemers who are roped in to play minor parts.

Last year's production of Robin Hood was performed in the Blue Mermaid Theatre by Blackfriars Bridge. This was the first year the firm had hired a professional stage, which just shows how seriously it takes the event. Anyone thinking of that work hard, play hard cliché?

Another infamous event is the weeklong Washington DC trip for trainees. It is designed to bring together all new associates from across the international network and trainees saw it as a great bonding experience. After seminars during the day to learn about Jones Day's history, plans and practice areas, there are nights out, summed up by one source as *"a week of very heavy boozing!"* Hmm... maybe that's just the Brits because our American cousins are generally known for their relative temperance. As for socialising back in Ol' Blighty, the majority of Friday-night pub-goers choose The Harrow, two seconds' walk from the office. The partners frequently pick up the tab.

and finally...
If you plan to train at Jones Day, your contract will be unlike those of your friends. Its almost unique non-rotational system is not for everyone, but for the confident, independent types, it suits them very well.

K&L Gates

the facts
Location: London
Number of UK partners/solicitors: 54/72
Total number of trainees: 18
Seats: 4x6 months
Alternative seats: Secondments
Extras: Pro bono – Battersea Law Centre; language training

A lot has happened since sleepy London mid-sizer Nicholson Graham & Jones hopped into bed with ambitious US firm Kilpatrick & Lockhart in 2005.

merge! merge! merge!
NGJ's beau, the ten-office Kirkpatrick & Lockhart, was founded by seven young Pittsburgh lawyers after WWII. It went on to collect a string of offices in Washington, DC, Boston, LA, Dallas and all manner of other US cities. After the English merger, there were talks in 2006 with law firm Salans, owner of a swathe of Central and Eastern European offices. These foundered but the appetite for expansion wasn't blunted. In 2007 the firm went on to join forces with Seattle-born Preston Gates & Ellis, which had its own string of offices in the USA and Asia. Without pausing for breath it then scooped most of Taylor Wessing's Berlin office following a partnership squabble at the Anglo-German firm. A Paris office is on the cards, a licence has been procured to allow a Shanghai opening and there are even intimations of a Moscow office. The sky's the limit, it seems, for this 1,400-lawyer, 22-office giant with an annual worldwide revenue approaching £400m.

K&L Gates' chairman, Peter Kalis (pronounced kay-liss), is clearly a man with a plan of mammoth proportions. But how sound is it? Well, the Preston Gates & Ellis merger seems sensible: PGE had West Coast US coverage and a foothold in Asia, while K&L had East Coast coverage and a foothold in Europe, meaning the only duplication was in San Francisco and Washington. Oh, and Preston Gates had some juicy clients in the form of Microsoft, Starbucks and Amazon and the Gates bit of the name belongs to Bill's dad.

all white by us
So what do the London trainees make of it all, particularly as they were recruited by snoozy NGJ before any of these huge changes. Generally, they approve: *"NGJ was falling into the doldrums and the mergers gave it direction and drive. The London office has more energy now, although it's not a mad corporate hothouse yet."* Some had needed con-

vincing: *"The reason I'd decided to join the firm appeared to be sliding away and I wondered if it would just become a big American firm."* Reassurances to trainees that *"the merger would not change the firm or the hours"* seem to have soothed such worries. Nevertheless, trainees are *"regularly told that the firm is looking to merge and expand elsewhere."* And why complain? The mergers have been a real tonic for the London office, with a ready-made portfolio of American clients shifting them into a higher gear and bringing in noticeably larger deals.

The London office is already the joint second largest in the network and, as the first step in K&L's plan to enter Europe, is looking to double in size, particularly in the areas of IP/media, investment funds, insurance and construction litigation. The firm has moved into the whole of the Cannon Street building it used to part occupy and has spent millions on a great refurbishment. The snow-white, minimalist client suite on the tenth floor is a dream. To be precise it is the dream of the same designer behind every K&L office.

a piece of the american pie

Trainees take four six-month seats, almost always sitting with and *"working directly for a partner,"* with the result *"you get entrusted with a big enough part of the case for it to be interesting."* They are allocated a mentor in each department too – *"a senior associate who is there for work and non-work-related matters."*

You'll almost certainly do a property seat in the first year. NGJ always drew a substantial income from its property practice and things are still much the same. In 2006 lawyers advised on the property aspect of a £553m PFI deal for two new hospitals in Birmingham and on the £325m sale of The Adelphi office building next to Shell-Mex House on The Strand in London overlooking the Thames. At present there are six trainees in the department, one with a mixed residential/commercial caseload involving *"expensive houses and leasehold enfranchisement,"* one doing planning and environment, two tackling purely commercial work and two specialising in property finance. As well as *"all the menial stuff,"* they are involved in bigger deals, *"see the whole thing and are told about all the discussions."* The department is known for *"really good hours,"* usually 9.30am to 6.30pm, *"and by no means are you made to feel guilty for leaving at 5.30pm."* The seat can be a shock to a new trainee: *"I felt thrown in at the deep end as I had 30 concurrent matters to deal with,"* recalled one source. *"It was really busy but I felt supported."*

Expect a seat in the corporate department too. Again, there are choices as to the type of seat: *"There is a seat with a private equity partner, three seats with M&A lawyers and one seat which is AIM. The financial services seat is predominantly advisory."* The *"feast or famine"* nature of corporate transactions does have an effect on the hours trainees work. A general downturn in AIM deals meant one source *"wasn't hit as much as other trainees"* and only needed to do *"a couple of nights in the office until 11pm or midnight."* Another source had it much harder and *"was in until midnight for three weeks."* The department is now proud to be working for clients like Halliburton, T-Mobile and Viacom, with *"many bigger deals coming through for American companies."* As the size of matters grows, *"less responsibility than in other seats"* becomes a fact of life for trainees.

panda to their every need

Financial services *"is the main area which the London arm of the firm is keen to develop and it is a main practice in the States."* The seat is currently a mystery to most trainees, but will probably *"become more popular as the department reaches its desired size."* One trainee in the know explained the drill: *"At the upper end the work involves fund formation, so a trainee helps with the preparation of* documents to form a fund and the prospectuses used to raise money." At the same time, a proliferation of Financial Services Authority material "relating to MiFID [Markets in Financial Instruments Directive]" means plenty of research, and trainees also help "with promotional materials and talks for up to 200 people."

The litigation department is a guaranteed stop for all trainees. The biggest case of the past year has been the heavyweight battle between WWF (Worldwide Fund for Nature) and K&L's client WWE (World Wrestling Federation Entertainment). The case concerned a disputed agreement over the use of the initials WWF. Round one went to the pandas, who are now tussling with the wrestlers over the level of damages to be paid. Other litigation clients include AOL, The British Film Institute, Sanyo, PGA European Tour, Ryder Cup and CD WOW!, which is up to its neck in litigation with the British Phonographic Industry over selling cheap CD imports from Asia. "Our charging rates are increasingly aligned with the top City firms so we don't get too many low-value instructions. Naturally a trainee is not going to run a litigation by themselves, but you might have two or three smaller cases where you can take a lead role – personal cases for partners, debt recoveries, statutory demands, etc."

Specialist dispute resolution teams work in niche areas such as travel and leisure, music/IP, insolvency and construction. Other possible seats include employment, tax ("very academic, no staple trainee tasks, no form filling") and banking ("a very informal team with a lot of banter"). In short, this is a firm at which you'll get a broad training in commercial areas of practice, but be aware that certain niche areas are tricky to get into. "The training partner, Gail, really looks out for us and she tries to accommodate everyone, but it's the nature of the beast that not everyone gets the seats they want." Twenty trainees and just one employment seat and two IP seats per rotation can make tricky math.

gobble, gobble

All new trainees are flown to the USA to a 'first-year academy' or induction week for new associates across the network. The 2006 event was run in Washington, DC and the 2007 event in Boston. The real benefit lies in helping trainees understand the relationship between home and the US. "Without it," said one source, "London might feel like a satellite that doesn't know where its home is." Back in London there are good training sessions at the start of each new seat and "as a trainee you are encouraged to attend every department's training." As a hidden benefit, "there's always a free breakfast or lunch."

Reflecting on just how American the London office has become, trainees suggested "the atmosphere is still that of a mid-sized City firm – it feels English primarily because everyone in the office is English." Cultural imperialism thus far extends no further than "turkey and pumpkin pie in the lunchroom" for Thanksgiving. In fact, despite the many mergers, trainees felt that the logic of choosing the firm for "medium-size, good work, a small number of trainees and a whole range of different departments" is still potent. There has been no attempt to reposition the firm in the London salary market. Remuneration remains at second-tier UK levels and trainees know that if salaries go up so will expectations. Last year we were told there were no plans to up the 1,400 billable hours target for associates. This year "they are planning to up the billable hours, not to top American firm levels, but they will be pushing people harder to keep us in line with other UK City firms." In short: "If you want to get more money you need to work harder."

At a much-anticipated biannual weekend away, shoptalk and team building are followed by fancy dress revelries into the wee hours. "The associates recount stories from past years and there is always gossip." More regularly there are after-work drinks on a Friday in the Vintry pub near to the office, and the various departments aren't averse to the odd social event – bowling for property, a pool night for corporate. The firm's girls' and boys' football teams are apparently worth joining for the post-match socialising alone. As for the trainees, they go out together reasonably often and act as *"a good support network for each other; there is no sense of competition."* Trainees are recruited from good universities and are almost all in their 20s. *"The firm doesn't like people who are too cocky,"* cautioned one. In 2007 seven out of ten confidently accepted their NQ spurs.

and finally...

K&L Gates became the 25th biggest firm in the world overnight, so who knows what will happen between now and 2010. London's mission is clear – to win bigger clients and bigger deals. Inevitably this will mean a more demanding regime so don't pick this firm for its cuddly reputation of yore, pick it if you have an appetite for success and if you want to try a breadth of practice areas.

Kendall Freeman

the facts

Location: London
Number of UK partners/solicitors: 19/20
Total number of trainees: 15
Seats: 4x6 months
Alternative seats: Secondments
Extras: Pro bono – RCJ CAB, LawWorks; language training

London's legal scene is thick with corporate and banking law firms, but what if you just can't get excited by them? Luckily there's another species prowling in the City – the insurance firm. More litigation-focused than their fellow City-dwelling creatures, they occupy a crowded and fiercely competitive part of the market. Kendall Freeman is one of the smaller, younger members of this species, but it's holding its own.

from dj to k

Once upon a time, there was a well-regarded commercial firm called DJ Freeman. It was well known for media work, property, public international law and insurance. In 2003, the firm stunned pretty much everybody by deciding to split itself in two. Its property department and some of the media teams joined Olswang; its litigators and insurance lawyers reinvented themselves as a more niche outfit. Four years on and Kendall Freeman still has just a handful of practice areas: insurance litigation, commercial litigation, corporate, public international law, employment and insolvency. Initially the decision to go it alone seemed to have paid off. The firm acted for insurance giant AXA in mammoth litigation stemming from several failed film projects, the corporate team developed a strong reputation in the insurance industry for complex finance and policy work, and the commercial litigation team developed a name for libel cases, recently scoring a notable victory for a Saudi businessman falsely accused of ties to Osama bin Laden. The sheikh and the book's publisher reached a mutual settlement. The deal? Every single copy of the book was pulped.

Yet the young firm now finds its habitat becoming less friendly. Last year saw its staple diet of major insurance disputes (until now half the firm's income) hit by a serious drought. The result was a 9% slump in profits. The market has begun to pick up again, and the firm is nowhere near the endangered species list, but it's expected to seek out a more balanced diet in the future, building its non-insurance practices to guard against future downturns. It is safe to say, however, that Kendall Freeman will remain, for the foreseeable future, a small firm focused on a defined set of practice areas.

What this means for trainees is that *"pretty much everyone"* visits insurance litigation, corporate and either commercial litigation or public international law. The one remaining slot is filled by insolvency, employment or a client secondment, most recently to Shell or Harrods.

border control

Most trainees' first seat, insurance litigation, seems quite a challenge: *"It's quite technical, so not as accessible as some other areas,"* noted one; another called it *"rather dry."* At least they can be reassured that *"because no one's done it at law school, everybody asks the same questions"* and the team is both patient and adept at helping trainees settle in, providing glossaries and extra training to get them up to speed. Fortunately, *"once you can understand the law involved, the disputes can be enthralling."*

The meat and potatoes of the department's work is reinsurance arbitration. Reinsurance is basically just insurance for insurers, and disputes tend to be big and complex, often going on for years. If you're lucky enough to catch one at the arbitration stage, you could be in on some *"exciting and adversarial"* proceedings. Catch a major matter in its earlier phases though and you'll have *"much more of a support role,"* carrying out research or preparing costs estimates. Solid photocopier time seems unlikely at any stage, thankfully.

A second contentious seat can be taken in either commercial litigation or public international law. Seats in PIL are hotly contested so if you're one of the lucky few, you really need to understand just how lucky you are. There are only a few firms that conduct this type of work and we were entirely unsurprised to hear one trainee call the seat *"one of the best things I've ever done."* Trainees see boundary disputes, and we're not talking common or garden boundary disputes, we're talking major spats between countries. Surely on matters of such importance, trainees

don't do anything significant? *"I got much more responsibility than I expected,"* said one former occupant of the seat. Tasks include poring over maps, consulting experts and even meeting government officials. As to whether these matters of state are nerve-wracking, *"you just get on with it and you make sure the arguments are right."*

Commercial litigation shares a floor with PIL and works on its own fair share of governmental matters. The firm has been advising foreign governments, such as that of Nigeria, in recovering assets stolen by former officials or elected leaders. *"It's fascinating,"* confirmed a source. *"It's changing all the time, so you've got to use your initiative to stay ahead, checking press sources for new evidence and so on. And there's an academic element: you've got to learn a lot about the systems and laws of other countries."* Exposure to this kind of work is not guaranteed, of course, and some trainees in commercial litigation work exclusively on business matters. Even if you're working on a large commercial arbitration, *"you really do everything the supervisor does,"* including consulting with clients and counsel, interviewing witnesses and drafting statements. *"I prepared the first draft of pretty much everything,"* one source said proudly.

want my catastrophe?

In case you're thinking Kendall Freeman trainees do nothing but litigation, rest assured that a trip to the corporate department is all but inevitable. By concentrating on its core insurance clients, the firm has developed a presence in the medium-sized deals market that belies its size. The insurance world is complicated and insular, and leading London insurers, particularly in the strange world of Lloyd's, rely on Kendall Freeman for its specialist expertise. Last year the firm advised insurer Catlin on the structuring and purchase of a $200m catastrophe swap agreement. Don't worry, we asked our insurance expert what that means and he didn't know either!

www.chambersstudent.co.uk

461

Your corporate seat will expose you to some brain-stretching matters. *"My supervisor was a real whiz and working on a ground-breaking new product. And there I was, suddenly in the middle of it!"* recalled a source. As with many corporate seats, the bigger the deal, the smaller the trainee's role. As a result, experiences vary. One trainee might work on smaller matters, maybe running the disclosure exercise or helping to draft the deal documents; another, working on a larger matter could spend their time *"reviewing policies, proofreading, drafting boilerplate clauses and organising schedules."* Greater responsibility seems to come to every trainee in time, and no one we spoke to had missed out on client contact.

Other seat possibilities include employment and insolvency. Whatever your seat, you'll share an office with your supervisor, either a partner or senior associate, and have mid-seat and end-of-seat appraisals. It does sound like supervisors vary from department to department: one source described their insurance litigation supervisor as *"one of the strictest people I've ever met."* This seems the exception. *"Generally, they give you a fairly long leash."* You'll also have a pastoral partner who you'll meet with occasionally, and managing partner Laurence Harris was praised for taking an interest in trainees' development. *"I had a 15-minute chat scheduled with him to discuss job options and it wound up going on for about an hour,"* revealed one source.

on the shop floor

Overall, the firm's small size means *"everyone knows your name"* and *"with the secretaries all together in the middle of the floor, there is a chance for a bit of office banter."* If you're eager to escape the office, however, there are secondment options. London's most famous shopkeeper is a core client of the firm, both in an individual capacity and through Harrods and his other enterprise, Fulham FC. Spend time in the legal office at Harrods and you should get to handle *"some really good litigation."* If you're after a less unusual experience of the in-house world, there's energy giant Shell which works from offices on the South Bank of the Thames next to the London Eye. *"It's mostly contractual review; everything from fuel supply deals to the fitting of cabinets in a power station,"* our source told us. Compared to the small London office, the massive multinational does feel *"a bit anonymous."* The flipside is independence. *"You're part of a team, but it doesn't really feel like that,"* our source explained. *"You handle your own workload. You are supervised, but you're supposed to meet deadlines and know when to say no to extra work."*

The firm's small size has an upside, of course. Trainees say that, from the interview on, KF is unusually friendly and personal. *"They'd read my CV really well, and they seemed really interested in me and what I wanted to achieve,"* one recalled of their interview. *"There were a couple of jokes and so on. I was probably slouching a bit too much in my chair by the end!"* For those offered one of the firm's eight training places per year, there'll be several events and get-togethers before training actually begins. KF throws firm-wide summer and Christmas parties plus a separate trainee party and there are also plenty of trainee outings to the dogs, ice-skating and the like. New starters get three full weeks of PSC, induction and further training before they touch down in their first seat. *"We'd really got to know each other and the firm by the time we started properly,"* one trainee told us. *"I felt very settled."* And after two years? Well KF's record on NQ retention is up and down to say the least, but in 2007 five of the eight qualifiers took jobs with the firm.

and finally...

If you're looking for high-quality work in an intimate environment, and litigation is a big interest, you shouldn't ignore this gem. However, if you suspect you're headed in a non-contentious direction, it's worth noting that KF's corporate, insolvency and employment work remains heavily focused on insurance clients.

Knight & Sons

the facts
Location: Newcastle-under-Lyme
Number of UK partners/solicitors: 14/44
Total number of trainees: 5
Seats: 4x6 seats
Alternative seats: None

If you harbour more than a passing fancy for Staffordshire, then chances are Knight & Sons is looming large on your radar.

white knights
The photo of Knight & Sons on its website shows a solid, white, palatial mansion, accessed by a sweeping driveway lined with silver birch trees. The unmistakeable impression is that this is no high street outfit. Staffordshire's wannabe solicitors might send out feelers to other firms, but this is the one they're really angling for. Situated halfway between Manchester and Birmingham in Newcastle-under-Lyme, it has the largest commercial property team in between these two cities and crack teams with expertise in the mining and agriculture sectors.

Knight & Sons traces its origins to 1767, when it was set up to cater for local bigwigs and landowners. Not a whole lot has changed since then – it continues to advise the ancient families of the area and a quarter of its clients are involved in the running of large agricultural estates. Long-standing connections with the agricultural community have earned it the accolade of membership of the National Farmers Union (NFU) legal panel.

In the past decade the firm has grown a lot: it now has 150 staff, some 60 of them lawyers. News of their abilities has spread and the firm now services clients from around the UK and beyond. Following a move of premises in 1995, it has been keen to adopt a modern edge, and this in turn has helped it attract some impressive clients. How about The Tussauds Group (which incorporates Alton Towers, Thorpe Park and the London Eye), Phones 4U, Stoke City FC and nearby Keele University, which also happens to supply many of the apprentice Knights. And what sort of thing do the lawyers do for these clients? Well, the commercial litigators recently acted on a massive dispute for the London Eye against its former solicitors for negligence in renewing a lease.

sons and lovells
Each year the firm normally welcomes two or three recruits and a limited number of departments means they make a near-complete tour of the firm during their contract. There are basically four main areas: commercial property; litigation (employment or comlit options); tax, trusts and private client; and corporate/commercial. The property team won a major vote of confidence when City law firm Lovells solicited its skills to subcontract work for key client Prudential Property investment Managers (PruPIM) under its 'Mexican Wave' banner. Such a supreme endorsement from a highly respected player in the legal profession has worked wonders. Property is now the standard bearer of the firm and the department management hopes will command allegiance from top-calibre graduates, who in the past may have absconded to larger firms. Due to its trailblazing status in the firm, all trainees are obliged to do a seat in real estate and it certainly manages to keep them busy by landing them with up to 40 of their own files. Other departments, notably including litigation, have captured a rising tide

of work from the Lovells referral, so it sounds as if everyone is happy with the fruitful relationship between the two firms.

Our sources felt *"well looked after in the employment department,"* which is just as well considering the catalogue of sexual discrimination cases and unfair dismissals it plays witness to every day. Elsewhere, the specialist mining team has dug deep into the region, carefully looking after its long-standing links with local pottery, coal and aggregates businesses. These folk are accustomed to advising on issues involving hard rock, coal, clay, gravel and silica sand. In litigation, trainees have a busy time of it assisting partners on the big cases, while running their own show on smaller debt recovery claims. Across the departments, our sources agreed the firm lived up to its *"strong reputation."* The only quibble was that owing to the small trainee group the firm had a tendency to err on the side of caution and we sensed that at times our sources would have welcomed a longer leash. However, they did call their employer *"a London firm outside of the City"* and further enthused over how much *"it punches above its weight."* It was also extolled for a continuing education programme that features university-style lectures to update staff on new legislation.

arthurian knights

There is a general rule that firms expand in inverse proportion to the rate at which their names contract. Knight & Sons is currently undergoing a rebranding exercise, so we presume it's only matter of time before it adopts the letter 'K'... or maybe just a squiggle. Actually we think it would be a shame to drop the filial associations from its name, not least because it helps us distinguish it from the huntin' and fishin' folk at Knights Solicitors down in Tunbridge Wells. Another reason for keeping the

sons on board is that the idea of old-fashioned family values sits comfortably with the ethos of the firm. An unusually large number of the junior staff are married or betrothed, which tends to mean Friday nights aren't usually spent painting the town red. Instead, think long weekend walks in the countryside accompanied by *"dogs and family."* Moreover, with days finishing frequently at 5pm and no *"guilt about not staying later,"* this firm adapts itself well to a *"female view of family life."* The employees are also given extra days off over Christmas to spend with their nearest and dearest.

These Arthurian knights operate a modern-day round table approach, epitomised by the frequency with which the managing partner eats breakfast with the trainees. Said one: *"They treat staff extremely well and there is no massive pressure on billing."* It sounds as if the only thing that would complete the circle of happiness for trainees is a pension scheme. The *"fundamentally friendly atmosphere"* is no fluke. There are actually two breaks scheduled into the day – one for breakfast at ten and one for lunch – allowing the different departments to mingle. Arguably, the flip side of this stability is Scandinavia Syndrome – it's all very stable and prosperous, but there's *"very little by way of pizzazz or excitement."*

Graduates who want to join the *"biggest and broadest practice"* in this particular corner of the country shouldn't be disappointed. The firm tries to recruit from the surrounding area, but stresses that it is happy to look at other candidates too, so long as they can show a reason why they would want to commit to Staffordshire. The county means a good deal to the firm and it has lately renewed its sponsorship of the Citizen of the Year award run by the local newspaper and donated money to a local hospital. Our top tip is not to confuse its address in Newcastle-under-Lyme with its upon-Tyne namesake. The point of finding out who is committed to the area is simple. The firm wants people who are more likely to stay on qualification. In 2007 both of the qualifying trainees wanted to qualify into the employment department, but there was room for only one.

may i have this dance?
The Christmas party has been scrapped this past two years and funds have been redirected into paying for departmental drinks and a meal once or twice a year. The central atrium of the office, with its skylight and expansive wooden floor, has been the venue for a number of events. Most recently, it was transformed into a space for employees to learn ballroom dancing, and the wooden planks have also been pounded to the rhythm of aerobics classes. There are always plenty of marketing events to get involved with, including trips to international rugby matches. If a night out does get organised, expect the guest list to include local surveyors and accountants. The venue normally picked on is the Hand and Trumpet. Trainees are also fond of Nantwich, an old market town of daub and timber houses 20 minutes' drive away, which is the setting for an annual re-enactment of English Civil War battles.

and finally...
This is by common consent the Camelot of firms between Birmingham and Manchester. The keen applicant would be well advised to arrange a vacation scheme to improve their chances of acceptance. But a word of caution, don't let your guard down too far in front of trainees – their feedback has a lot of bearing on who is awarded a contract.

Latham & Watkins LLP

the facts
Location: London
Number of UK partners/solicitors: 38/150
Total number of trainees: 10
Seats: 4x6 months
Alternative seats: Overseas seats
Extras: Language classes

Employing nearly 2,000 lawyers across 24 offices, this US giant is one of the world's most successful law firms. And London is probably the most important of its 14 offices outside the USA. So why haven't you heard of it?

below the radar
Those in the know trace Latham & Watkins' London legacy back to 1996, when a small team of its attorneys landed on UK shores to set up a project finance boutique. The UK arm of the firm has since grown steadily into a wide-ranging practice with more than 180 lawyers. However, despite carving a strong niche in the finance realm and posting healthy financial results of its own, its footprint on the UK legal landscape has been light. *"We are a very discreet presence here. We have been growing a lot but no one really knows of us,"* said one trainee. Undoubtedly this is due to Latham's modest progress in securing the largest City-born mandates. In contrast, the office has been at the heart of some very meaty international work. It even led on one of the year's largest IPO's, when it acted for Russian bank VTB on its £4.4bn London listing, and also advised Italy's largest power company, Enel, on the acquisition finance aspects of its £23.8bn joint offer (with Acciona) for a 26% stake in Spanish power giant Endesa.

To its benefit, Latham has discovered a number of perks associated with a low-key existence. Under a cloak of near invisibility it has poached some excellent lawyers from rivals and massively expanded its range of services. In this vein, it has developed a growing contentious practice and also started up a few smaller niche teams, eg tax. Of course, invisibility can only last so long and a number of high-profile strikes in its favoured realms of corporate and finance have started to destroy the illusion. Hires such as ex-Maclay Murray & Spens private equity guru Graeme Sloan – bringing with him Bank of Scotland and clients of similar ilk – and structured finance big-shot Mark Nicolaides (ex-Mayer Brown) are perfect examples of Latham raising its head above the parapet. And the firm looks set to further distance itself from its silent assassin persona as it launches more offensives on the recruitment market, seeking to bulk up its London arm to match the strength it has in the key financial centres across the pond. It is also said to be in the market for a high-profile real estate partner, having already lured a small associate team away from the magic circle. In April 2007, outsourcing partner Andrew Moyle was appointed managing partner in London and he looks set to be the man charged with belatedly announcing Latham's arrival in the big smoke.

busy bees

For a firm of its size, Latham has been relatively slow in setting up a training scheme, with 2006 starters the first formal intake. Having begun, it is now taking things seriously and the number of trainees will increase rapidly. Eight new recruits arrived in 2007 and ten more have been recruited for 2008.

Readers should bear in mind that the structure of the scheme may change significantly but, for now, we know that trainees follow a standard four-seat rotation, during which they sit in finance (incorporating project, structured and banking), corporate (including capital markets and outsourcing) and litigation (covering competition, public international law and employment). For their fourth seat they can return to their favoured department, spend time in a niche department such as tax, or apply for secondment to the Brussels, Paris, Tokyo or Singapore offices.

Understandably, finance is the most important seat for most trainees – the London office's roots lie in project finance, and this variant is a popular option for satisfying the finance component of the training contract. Another option is banking, where trainees can expect to see a lot of work on the lender side and instructions from the wider firm's sterling high-yield practice. This dominance in high-yield also forms the backbone of its capital markets offering and is the source of numerous cross-border instructions. In 2006, a multi-office group oversaw the first high-yield issuance to come out of Pakistan, advising underwriter ABN Amro on Pakistan Mobile Communication's €250m offering of senior notes.

Whether you understand the nuances of each financial sub-division or not, one thing you need to know (and may well have guessed) is that they are all fairly complex and intellectually demanding. *"You need a certain amount of self-confidence, otherwise you could be overwhelmed by being asked to do things you have not done before. You can't be scared to ask for help or advice."* This applies to the often-daunting workload as well. *"Some days you just can't cope with the amount of e-mails flooding into your inbox and you need to rely on support from other members of your team."* Transactions are large, but as they often span jurisdictions, the deal teams in the London office are quite small, meaning high levels of responsibility for trainees. *"On one deal, we essentially had three closings and I was managing a lot of documents to ensure they all ran smoothly."* Contact with attorneys in New York and Washington is frequent and we also heard stories of trainees jetting around the globe on deal closings.

The big news in finance is undoubtedly the hours. *"You can't really plan your life during the finance seat and your body clock gets completely messed up. I ended up learning the menu for Deliverance take away off by heart."* However, the flipside of this is that *"no other seat can compare with the buzz you get here. You live off the energy of your last closing."*

barrister chasing

Corporate is an area the firm has singled out for expansion in London. Currently stronger in private equity than M&A, the group has had a hand in various monster transactions, perhaps the most notable being the £19.19bn Banca Intesa merger with Sanpaolo IMI. While these deals make for good reading in marketing brochures, the UK lawyers have thus far been restricted to fairly minor roles. The same cannot be said of the US attorneys and the firm is now keen to close the gap between the two nations. In the meantime, the extent of London's involvement did not bother trainees, who were simply happy to be *"working on matters that get loads of coverage in the financial press."* In six months, one source was involved in work for Indian, Russian and Ukranian clients and even found some time to work for domestic ones. The corporate seat can also involve the trainee in the work of the firm's market-leading outsourcing group.

Litigation is a comparative breath of fresh air, offering much more regular hours and routine than the transactional seats. Trainees can expect a steady diet of *"bundling, bibling and pagination,"* as well as *"a lot of running around after and liaising with barristers."* In addition to domestic disputes, trainees are exposed to some large international arbitrations and the office is home to one of the UK's premier public international law teams. One of this team's recent highlights was representing the state of Barbados in its maritime boundary and fisheries arbitration against Trinidad and Tobago under the UN Law of the Sea Convention. While you wouldn't currently go to Latham purely for its litigation practice, trainees believe its growth *"from a small commercial litigation practice to a more rounded offering including public international and antitrust"* is a sign of things to come.

californication

Training at Latham means working for an international law firm which, to borrow the words of The Boss, was born in the USA – Los Angeles to be specific. Considering that ten of its offices are in the USA and still generate the majority of its work, we were keen to find out just how Americanised life in the London office is. In spite of the fact that around a third of the London lawyers are US-qualified, we found trainees quite dismissive of the idea that this was a US enclave. Unperturbed, we continued to search for Latham London's inner Yankee and did indeed find a number of telltale signs. For starters, it has inherited the American appetite for big salaries. In fact, any trainee lucky enough to qualify with the firm will be rewarded with the largest NQ pay packet in the City, currently £96,000. Alas, this comes at the cost of only 20 days annual holiday, in line with the American holiday-is-cheating mentality. In 2007 both of the qualifiers stayed with the firm going into corporate teams.

One influence that has travelled well across the Atlantic is a commitment to pro bono projects. In 2006 the London office contributed more than 4,000 hours in free representation, an average of 33 hours per lawyer. This figure includes advice in relation to the recently renovated Roundhouse Theatre in Camden Town and sending lawyers to the European Court of Human Rights to fight for various aggrieved Eastern Europeans. The lawyers recently won a preliminary verdict in a case for two Romanian journalists who were prosecuted for writing articles on corruption in the police force and judiciary in their home country. Trainees contribute lower than the average – *"probably 12-14 hours a year"* – although anyone qualifying will be encouraged to up this commitment greatly.

Something else that defines the office is the idea that *"there is no real hierarchy like you may get in more traditional English firms."* Trainees are actively encouraged to express their views and believe *"the openness and ability to make a difference is indicative of the consultative management style."* Collaboration is clear in the process for selecting new lateral hires, all of whom are subjected to at least five separate interviews with a panel of partners and associates before they are accepted at the firm. Trainees have a similar screening process, although they only need to please six individual lawyers. This backs up the suggestion of one trainee that the firm is interested above all else in personality (although a simple glance at the trainees' resumes suggests that a winning smile will not be enough without the academics and experience to back it up).

The final proof of the firm's legacy is in its various US-based conventions. Last year UK trainees were invited to the summer academy for associates, held in Phoenix, Arizona. *"It was fun meeting the US associates and learning a little more about Latham."* The firm also has a biannual business meeting for all of its lawyers worldwide. *"This year 2,000 of us descended on Orlando for all sorts of training from senior experts in different fields. It's a good opportunity to socialise with colleagues from different cities."* There are also ample opportunities to socialise with London colleagues through the usual complement of Christmas and summer parties, as well as office-wide *"quarterly quaffs."*

and finally...
Latham London offers *"challenging, exciting work"* with lashings of the international and a hint of the American. You will be worked really hard but rewarded phenomenally well. This scheme may be small and relatively unheard of right now, but it won't stay that way.

LeBoeuf, Lamb, Greene & MacRae

the facts
Location: London
Number of UK partners/solicitors: 28/63 (plus 7/17 Overseas-qualified)
Total number of trainees: 17
Seats: 4x6 months
Alternative seats: Overseas seats
Extras: Pro bono – Liberty Advice Line, FRU, East London Small Business Centre, The Medical Foundation, LawWorks; language training

As we went to press in Autumn 2007 all eyes were on two true-blue New Yorkers – LeBoeuf Lamb, Greene & MacRae and Dewey Ballantine. They were due to join forces to create Dewey & Leboeuf, a mighty behemoth with 1,300 lawyers located in 13 US and 13 international offices and a projected revenue approaching $1bn.

fast friends
In late September the merger deal was still subject to a partner vote, which is why in this feature we've predominantly focused on the experiences of LeBoeuf (say it 'LeBuff') trainees. Dewey Ballantine's London office hadn't run a training scheme, so even assuming the union is achieved, it seems likely a trainee's experience in London will remain heavily LeBoeuf-flavoured. Nevertheless, we were keen to find out the reasons for the merger.

Increased clout in New York is the primary rationale – the combined Dewey & Leboeuf would boast a 550-strong Big Apple office. The deal makes sense here in the UK: some 170 lawyers in the London branch would make it one of the largest City practices of a US-headquartered outfit, something LeBoeuf has been aiming at for a while. Then there's the fact that the firms' European networks are fairly compatible: Dewey would offer LeBoeuf a presence in Germany, Poland and Italy for the first time, while LeBoeuf would return the favour with its Paris, Brussels and Moscow branches. Further afield, two Beijing offices would combine, while LeBoeuf would also contribute outposts in South Africa, Kazakhstan and Hong Kong, plus an affiliated office in Saudi Arabia. A similar degree of profitability also helps the pairing – both firms achieved a profit per partner figure of around $1.4m in 2006 – but it's the good match between practice areas that really makes the two a comfy fit. Looking just at the contentious side, Dewey, for example, has strong litigation capacity focused on financial institutions, while LeBoeuf's highly regarded litigators assist clients in the insurance, telecoms, energy and utilities sectors. In fact, when a list was drawn up there was no overlap whatsoever in the combined outfit's top 50 clients and an almost 50-50 split between the firms. On paper, the tie-up seems to make rather good sense, so we'll look forward to reporting on progress in a year's time. However, sounding a note of caution, we will observe that Dewey has been here before: as recently as January 2007 it abruptly exited advanced merger talks with Orrick, Herrington & Sutcliffe.

energy boost

In London, the perception is that Dewey's smaller office with its M&A capacity could add something to LeBoeuf's excellent energy and insurance abilities. LeBoeuf has been in London since the mid 1990s and its non-US office locations give a clue as to the strength of focus on particular industry sectors. *"Most of my seats have been dominated by insurance and energy work,"* one trainee explained, *"and I don't see that there will be any*

massive shift away from that." In this vein, hotspots such as Africa, Russia and (increasingly) China are of particular interest to the London office, and the firm's long list of energy clients includes Chinese and African state-owned enterprises. One of the highlights of 2006 was advising a subsidiary of China National Petroleum Corporation on its joint acquisition with Indian state-owned company Oil and Natural Gas Corporation (ONGC) of Petro-Canada's assets in Syria. Worth €484m, this was the first joint purchase of oil and gas reserves by two fast-growing economies you might expect to be competing for resources. Elsewhere, lawyers have been helping Finnish company Fortum to invest in the Russian electricity industry and providing The Volta River Authority with advice relating to the development and financing of Ghana's Takoradi Thermal Power Project. The legal teams working on such deals are generally made up of lawyers in different offices, and it is perhaps because they spend so much time working with colleagues across the globe that the London team is said to be *"socially and professionally self-contained."* None of our sources were fazed by the specialist nature of the work (which also contains a significant public law element): *"We have special training sessions and as you go on, you realise that there are a lot of precedents for the documents you encounter."*

The mainstream corporate group has been handling far more US and UK capital markets instructions following the arrival in January 2007 of two new partners with emerging markets expertise from Dewey. Some say these hires were the trigger for discussions leading to the merger. Trainees get involved in both M&A and capital markets work. Said one interviewee: *"This means you get a feel for what you like, and what you like less, at an earlier stage."* *"Learning to deal with pressure"* is important here, because, *"there is often a lot to do and it gets intense."* You can find yourself assisting a single associate or an entire team, depending on the size of the deal. The firm's origins mean it's likely that some of your work will have a US element, even more so if the merger goes through. *"On one deal it was just me and an American associate and I was able to do everything from beginning to end,"* reported a source. *"There wasn't any mollycoddling and I was communicating with clients directly."* Although you'll be *"picking things up as you go along,"* the firm doesn't skimp on formal training. The corporate team runs group sessions *"every month or so"* and holds regular departmental breakfast meetings.

to russia with love

We've talked about the energy sector, but it's arguable that clients from the insurance industry have an even greater impact on the London office. *"We represent a lot, and we advise them in a variety if areas,"* said one source. *"Recently, we've even done some capital markets work for insurance companies."* Alongside familiar names like Aegis, Lloyd's and Royal & SunAlliance, the firm is acting for NFU Mutual in connection with issues arising from outbreaks of foot and mouth, botulism and other nasty diseases. This busy caseload also covers issues relating to Hurricane Katrina and claims brought by miners against a number of law firms in the North. Our favourite dispute is the London Fire Brigade's scrap with the contractors responsible for building a fire fighting training establishment in Southwark in 2004 – it caught fire in January 2005 and is now unusable. There is *"never a dull moment"* in the international arbitration seat. *"It was a terrific experience. I was intimately involved with cases,"* reported a source. *"I even interviewed a witness myself."* Cases often relate to construction disputes or public international law. It is unusual for a US firm in London to have such a major disputes practice, and taking two contentious seats out of four isn't uncommon.

Of course, the merger could affect this and other aspects of the training, but what we can say is that currently, seats separate into two categories: corporate and litigation. On the corporate side, the options are M&A; capital markets; energy; insurance regulatory; employment; tax, real estate and competition. Where contentious work is concerned, trainees can choose commercial/insurance litigation or international arbitration. Overseas seats are an option for some. For Paris you need French; for Moscow there is no language requirement. Because *"there aren't many English lawyers"* in Moscow *"you have an insane amount of responsibility,"* we were told. The work is largely M&A and capital markets-related, with a smattering of IP cases. Said one source: *"I can't emphasis the importance of the relationship between the Moscow and London offices; partners are constantly going back and forth, and Russian companies are investing abroad non-stop."* What further prospects of international travel the merger might bring we can't say, but the trainees we spoke to even before it loomed were optimistic about their prospects of staying at the firm post-training. In 2007 four of the five qualifiers took up positions at the end of their contracts.

no messin'

How American is LeBoeuf in London? Well, it depends on who you're talking to. Some argue that because of its size, *"London carries its own weight,"* while others are adamant that *"direction still comes from New York."* What happens to that power balance post-merger remains to be seen in what would be a meeting of equals rather than a takeover, even if LeBoeuf London definitely makes bigger waves here. LeBoeuf's current chairman, Steve Davies, would head up the merged firm, with his Dewey counterpart returning to practice, but no decision has yet been taken on who would lead the London office. Dewey staff would almost certainly take up the extra space currently available in LeBoeuf's Mincing Lane premises. Being joined by 40-odd Dewey lawyers would undoubtedly heighten the sense of *"institutionalisation"* that steady growth over recent years has generated at LeBoeuf. *"It used to be that if you wanted to do something you just had to make a case for it; now, there are more procedures to go through."*

Where salaries are concerned, the firm pays its first and second-year trainees £40,000 and £45,000 respectively. It has resisted the trend evident at some US firms to pay super-salaries to its NQs, opting instead for £75,000 – a figure somewhere between the top whack and the magic circle wages. *"People assume that because this is an American firm they'll demand their pound of flesh,"* one trainee told us, *"but we're not like that. In the corporate group, the hours are the same as in the magic circle."* For some self-motivated interviewees, though, this isn't necessarily enough: *"Leaving at 6pm is great, but if you want to appear keen... I think certain corporate associates would rather be in the office at midnight than anywhere else.* The message here is: *"If you intend to work in the City, you have to accept that you are going to need to put in a lot of hours to make a name for yourself."* What does this mean in practice? *"It depends. People in corporate usually arrive 9.30-10am and work quite late; in the litigation department, most will have gone home by 6.30pm."* Several sources noted this difference in working patterns. *"You don't have the same deadlines in litigation so the hours are usually more stable."*

With so much to do, *"there's not a lot of messing around."* However, heads-down doesn't have to mean stony faces. Although it's sometimes hard to gauge the partners, *"most people here have a sense of humour. You need one if you find yourself proofing all night!"* In terms of who the firm wants to recruit, great academics are a must, and a second language – especially French, Russian, Arabic

or Chinese – is also useful. If any of this sounds intimidating, current trainees are keen to stress that the atmosphere in the office isn't. *"People expect me to do my work well, and on time, but I'm not worried about anyone."* Trainees have group meetings with HR and there are trainee representatives on the associates' committee. For one-on-one advice, new joiners can turn to their 'LeBuddy.' Reports on the social life at the firm were somewhat mixed. *"There's not a lot of organised stuff,"* one source told us. *"People will just say, 'We deserve a drink.'"* The two big office jollies are the summer party (last year's was in a bowling alley) and a lavish black-tie event at Christmas.

and finally...

With the merger in prospect, we can't say exactly what kind of firm those starting their contracts in 2010 will be joining. However, we can be fairly sure those who do sign up here will be part of a trainee population topping 30. If you're after international work, you'll definitely get it here, particularly for energy or insurance clients, and in all likelihood other specialisms will develop. One thing that definitely won't change is the need to meet some seriously exacting standards.

Lee & Priestley LLP

the facts
Location: Leeds
Number of UK partners/solicitors: 15/21
Total number of trainees: 9
Seats: 4x6 months (or 2x 6 + 1x12)
Alternative seats: None

Historically a firm with a high street feel, Lee & Priestley is now keen to get a bigger bite of the Leeds market. With this goal in mind it is steadfastly evolving into a lean, mean, corporate machine. Well, not quite – it's actually not very mean at all. In fact, if you're looking for a firm that's ambitious and commercially focused, while retaining its warm, familial atmosphere, this might be just the ticket.

game on

Previously operating out of Bradford and several satellite offices, in 2004 Lee & Priestley decided it wanted more from life. It suddenly developed *"a vision of becoming a leading commercial firm with a Leeds-wide reputation."* It embraced this self-imposed challenge wholeheartedly, shed its personal injury arm and residential conveyancing operation and moved into new offices in the centre of Leeds. Commercial instructions now account for the majority of the firm's workload, although its successful private client and family departments have been retained. It's a happy balance, enabling L&P to offer a broad learning experience.

What do trainees make of all the changes? *"There's a lot of recruitment going on; departments are expanding around us."* Quite literally: in 2007 the firm had to take over a third floor in its office building. *"The people they're recruiting are from big firms. They are bringing that big-firm mentality with them, which is affecting the mindset of everyone else."* Is this a good thing? *"I think it is. I feel like the firm is becoming much more of a name in the Leeds market."* Whatever their view, anyone with opinions about the firm's direction is given the opportunity to voice them: *"Just last week we had a big meeting to discuss the direction of the firm. Everyone was there, including the support staff. It's great that you feel so involved and that your opinion matters."*

Any attempt to become better known must be accompanied by a marketing drive, so it's only right that trainees are encouraged to get out there and be part of it. Among the many conferences and networking events is *"a ladies cocktail evening and an annual rugby match."* Trainees are expected to play their part, so *"you have to want to represent* the firm... but it's such a good opportunity to make contacts, I don't see why you wouldn't want to go."*

you dim sum, you lose sum

Although none of the seats are compulsory, it's quite likely you'll experience a dose of commercial property or family during your training contract. Property is a key practice area for the firm. Its client roster features familiar names such as O'Brien's Sandwich Bars and The Yorkshire Linen Co, and among recent highlight transactions was the £10m sale of a portfolio of five chemists. Despite being one of the firm's largest departments, it's also one of the friendliest: *"I was never afraid of asking a question and they really ease you into it,"* one trainee assured us. Having said that, *"the department has been incredibly busy lately, so you get a fair number of files to yourself – it's quite a workload."* *"As well as drafting commercial leases and dealing with freehold sales, you do a fair bit of marketing too – I went to the opening of a Chinese restaurant, which was great fun."* Overall, *"It's given me a great understanding of the area and I love the amount of autonomy I've been given."*

A seat in family shares many of the same positive aspects. *"You have the chance to run your own files from start to finish because there are simple matters you can get stuck into without lots of experience."* A trainee might work on a simple change of name deed, help with ancillary financial work for a divorce, or assist on a care case. They can expect to get involved at all stages of a case; *"from applications and interviewing clients, to attending court."* In fact there is an immense amount of court experience to be gained here: *"I've seen a great variety of hearings. Partners are always asking if you want to go to court and they'll give you an hour to read the file beforehand."* The subject matter is far from dry: *"There's always a story behind every file."* The team handles a great deal of children's issues, ranging from custody and abuse to international child abduction. Said one source: *"You get to do* everything, it's almost scary! I've done loads of applications in court, and because there's legal aid work you can get into the nitty gritty."

In addition to these two staples, corporate, insolvency, commercial litigation, employment and private client are all regular seats. And with the growth of the firm comes new opportunities, such as a seat in the IP/IT team. *"Officially, this department has only been going for a couple of years, so it's quite small, but since I've been here we've taken on another body and it's definitely an area of growth,"* reported a source. The seat includes a lot of commercial drafting (terms and conditions, supply agreements, etc) plus trade mark registrations and licences. *"We've been doing some IP infringements too and I was able to handle a couple of litigation files. It's interesting work."* When you add a decent amount of client contact into the mix, it's unsurprising *"there's a lot of interest in this seat."*

up, up and away

With all this talk of growth and change, you may well wonder what the firm will be like in a couple of years. *"Well, we'll still be in Leeds, that's for sure,"* said one source. No plans for global domination then, at least not just yet: the crystal ball gazers at L&P confidently announce that *"in two or three years, we're still going to be the same firm, we'll just have a more prominent reputation."* The firm took on five new trainees in 2007, which reflects growth at all levels of the organisation. But can you expand and still retain a family feel? Apparently it's perfectly possible. *"I don't think it is less personal,"* said one trainee; *"it's just a bigger family."* Whatever happens in the future, the influx of (relatively) young people means the atmosphere is now positively buzzing. Astute trainees point out that *"partners here have a young and vibrant mentality anyway, as is evidenced by their visionary expansion."*

Some change is, of course, inevitable. The firm has had to introduce a more stringent hiring policy, with a revamped application process. *"When I applied a few years ago I just sent in my CV,"* recalled one trainee wistfully. The firm still tries to make the process as engaging as possible but apparently it's *"a bizarre interview process... a bit like speed dating."* Intrigued, we asked the firm for more info and they told us that rather than picking a smaller number of interviewees from the pile of CV's, they now invite 30 or so people to a 'speed interview' at which they are asked to introduce themselves, answer four simple questions and give a short presentation. Among the topics they have chosen are *Coronation Street* and female drivers. It is also worth noting that the firm is increasingly taking on paralegals to see how they perform, with a view to offering those they rate a training contract further down the line. There is also some concern that with more trainees will come more competition for seats, and in particular qualification jobs. For now, *"the firm is good at letting you know what positions are available, and because the firm is growing there is more than enough room for everyone to be accommodated."* In 2007 all three of the qualifiers took NQ jobs at the firm, two going into insolvency and one onto IP. Those people who know where they want to qualify early enough in their contract can often do 12 months in a single area.

When you get down to it, it's clear that this is still an incredibly approachable firm. *"You're expected to pull your own weight, but the workload is more than manageable."* It's not frowned upon to leave at half five, and the partners are *"more than happy to set time aside to go over things with you."* The social life is varied. *"It's common for us to go out, but we don't venture very far – All Bar One and Prohibition are just down the road."* If you're lucky, the partners will whip out the credit cards on a Friday. There are trips to the races or to the theatre every so often, and then the big annual events: a Christmas party (very big, very messy, lots of embarrassing dancing with partners) and a summer BBQ (family focused, fun and informal, it rains every year.) Even with its rapid recruiting, the firm continues to attract the same sort of people: *"We're friendly people – ambitious, but willing to have a balance between life and work."*

and finally...

It's an exciting time to be at Lee & Priestley. *"This firm is going places, and it's great to know you're part of something that has such direction."* It's never going to be a national behemoth, but then it doesn't want to be. If you want an idealistic, commercial firm where you'll be exposed to high-quality work but get to have a life outside too, then this might just be the place.

Lester Aldridge LLP

the facts

Location: Bournemouth, Southampton, Milton Keynes, London
Number of UK partners/solicitors: 31/43
Total number of trainees: 14
Seats: 4x6 months
Alternative seats: Occasional secondments

Lester Aldridge has branched out from its flagship Bournemouth location in several directions. Initially it sailed into Southampton's legal waters, it then anchored in Milton Keynes and finally navigated its way to a London merger with niche property practice Park Nelson.

hit the road

In 2006 it was reported in the legal press – and by us – that the firm had plans to expand still further, particularly in its Southampton location. *"I do recall reading that,"* mused one trainee, *"but no one at Lester Aldridge actually said it."* Hmmm... Well, since then a new managing partner has taken the helm and the good ship LA is plotting a different course. New skipper Matthew Giddins presides over an organisation that has taken a step back to look at where it should be going. It has done this with the help of consultants from Hildebrandt, whose advice was to consolidate and restructure. This in turn involved making a dozen or so redundancies. Trainees explained that the purpose of the excision was to *"start afresh by cutting a bit of dead weight and bringing the firm into the 21st century."* When we quizzed the firm about it all, we were told of the need to *"galvanise the progress"* made so far and *"change the dynamics"* of the firm. Whatever that means.

LA has always been billed as a positive place to work, so we wondered how the cuts affected morale. *"It did affect it a bit, but it has recovered now that things seemed to have calmed down,"* one source confided. *"I think it was the best thing to do, it made business sense,"* said another. Just in case anyone at LA was in any doubt about the future of the firm, the managing partner embarked on a series of roadshows to explain all and reassure staff there were no further plans for staff cuts in the near future.

Having attended one of Cap'n Giddins' presentations, trainees relayed the message that LA was looking to *"focus on what we are good at"* and develop in certain areas. First and foremost they were talking about expanding in the capital. *"I know they are trying to expand the corporate team in London,"* whispered one interviewee, before adding: *"Real estate is also a successful department and the London office has really great relationships with quite major clients."* For fear of being asked to eat our words in 2008, we checked in with the official LA machinery. *"London is a growth area,"* they confirmed. So there you have it. Southampton is not the big focus after all. Indeed, after the cuts the corporate team in

Southampton merged with the Bournemouth team, such that *"the department is now predominantly in Bournemouth, with a couple of people hopping offices."*

driving force

That the firm offers *"every kind of area of law, bar criminal"* is a particularly persuasive selling point for someone who is *"fresh out of uni, doesn't know what they are doing and wants to experience different areas of law."* They have the chance to get stuck into private client work as well as sampling the commercial world, and *"the combination of the two is key."* Our sources judged the split between the two types of training to be *"fairly balanced,"* although if anything *"it's a bit more commercial than private client."*

The firm may have an assortment of departments, but it is particularly well known for its finance practice, which in turn has a good deal of experience in asset finance and debt recovery. The Hurn office (LA's second site in Bournemouth), situated near the airport, is devoted to these areas. The banking and finance practice acts for a plethora of prominent names in the motor industry, including Toyota, Ford Motor Credit and Volkswagen. LA is also pretty hot on the commercial property side, with one trainee stating that it was *"the biggest thing for the firm."* Most of LA's biggest property clients have come via its London office: its roster includes the PC World-Dixons-Currys family of companies and mobile media company H3G.

Away from commercial matters, on the private client side LA has a well-respected family team that occupies a tier-one spot for the South of England in our parent publication *Chambers UK*. Trainees also saluted the tax, trusts and wills department, which *"takes up a whole floor in the Bournemouth office"* and is split up into several sub-departments including a very interesting overseas probate team.

luck of the draw

Recruits shift seats four times over the two years of the training contract. So how much of a say do they have over where they get to unpack their pencil cases? *"It's up to you,"* said one; *"obviously we all have our own ideas of what we want to try out."* The impression we get is that the first seat is one where *"you're pretty much told where you're going to go"* and for the following three they have a fair degree of input. *"You have one-on-one meetings with the training principal and you tell them what you want and what you don't want."* No single seat is compulsory and the firm *"doesn't push you to try out both private client and commercial."*

Many people do stints in commercial property and corporate. The property seat is good for learning the day-to-day business of lawyering (*"dealing with information updates, writing letters, phoning clients"*) as well as *"drafting and amending leases."* It is a good opportunity to *"learn how to deal with people as well as learning stuff on the legal side."* Trainees also like *"seeing transactions through to the end, which is really satisfying,"* in contrast to corporate where *"you're just a cog in the whole scheme of things."* Speaking of corporate, we also quizzed trainees on what this seat held in store for them. *"A lot of due diligence,"* came one blunt answer. It can depend on what work is passing through the department at the time, but things like *"preparing terms and conditions for clients, helping to draft share purchase agreements and going to completion meetings"* are all on the corporate menu. In the disputes seat, there's a decent prospect of getting a portfolio of your own smaller cases. *"I was always encouraged to think about the next step for myself, but also reminded of what things needed to be done,"* recalled a source.

Aspiring socialites should head to the tax, trusts and wills team because it has *"a lot of wealthy clients."* On the non-contentious side, they *"draft wills and other documents,"* while the disputes side has them *"putting together bundles* and instructions to counsel." The employment seat is great for striking a *"good balance between private client and commercial work, as well as contentious and non-contentious."*

law's a beach

For the first six months *"you could be placed in either Bournemouth or Southampton,"* which have the lion's share of seats. This was a bit of a bugbear for one trainee: *"It would be better if incoming trainees were given plenty of notice of where they would be working... I think that issue has come up quite a few times."* On this point, the firm told us it is now liaising more closely with trainees to remedy the problem. After the first seat, people have more say in where they go and with regard to London, *"you won't be placed there if you don't want to be."* Away from the Bournemouth-Southampton nucleus, there is an option of fast-track debt recovery in Hurn, or commercial property in London. Milton Keynes focuses on finance and rarely takes trainees, although there is an option for one person to go there.

We listened with envy to descriptions of the view from the Bournemouth office: *"I can see the sea, a couple of speed boats, clear blue skies..."* Let's just say we weren't too sympathetic when the same trainee added: *"...and I'm stuck here at work."* The office is located *"smack bang in the middle of town"* and is *"a two-minute walk to all the pubs and bars."* Downes wine bar is where you're likely to find trainees on a Friday night *"and several other evenings too!"* The Southampton office is located in the city centre, while the *"cosy"* London office is described as *"busy but relaxed because everyone knows each other."*

The managing partner, finance director and marketing team are good at keeping everyone informed of developments. Often you'll see them *"going round different floors and having a chat"* and speaking to any staff who want to raise issues. The HR department follows suit and *"sends someone around the different offices monthly,"* and there are also quarterly meetings between the trainees and the managing partner, who is *"quite receptive to what we say."* A good example of this is the re-introduction of the happy hour drinks on the last Friday of every month. *"Everyone loves it,"* enthused one trainee: *"Free drinks, hot food, something to nibble on – good times!"* For out-of-hours fun, the firm holds a Christmas party and a summer ball, and to work off all those happy hour drinks and nibbles you can always sign up to play football, netball, cricket or touch rugby.

When you hear something enough times, you start to believe it, and one thing all of the trainees emphasised was the good work-life balance at LA. *"Work hard, play hard is the cheesy motto,"* said one source. We're told trainees can generally expect to be out of the door by 5.30pm. We also listened attentively as trainee after trainee told us that the firm is *"not at all hierarchal,"* a point best illustrated by the fact that *"everyone goes out together – trainees, associates, support staff, finance..."* When asked to describe the kind of person who wouldn't fit in at LA, it didn't take long for trainees to conjure up their answers. *"Someone who is very very serious – we do take our work seriously, but we know how to chill out and have a good time too."* If *"barbecues on the beach"* sound like your idea of chilling out, then LA could be the firm to pick.

and finally...

When a firm is able to offer such a healthy work-life balance, it is often the case that a compromise is going to be made elsewhere. In LA's case trainees got straight to the point in telling: *"There could be a more competitive salary."* Although it had recently been increased, recruits still said: *"I'd put the wages up a bit more."* And yet such concerns didn't prevent a good number of them staying on qualification in 2007 – six out of seven people took NQ jobs.

Lewis Silkin LLP

the facts

Location: London, Oxford
Number of UK partners/solicitors: 45/76
Total number of trainees: 12
Seats: 4x6 months
Alternative seats: Secondments
Extras: Language training

Mid-sized London firm Lewis Silkin is defined by its interesting clients, its focus on certain areas of practice and the warm orange glow emanating from its Chancery Lane office.

mtv generation

The origins of the firm lie with the Silkin family, which spawned a number of Labour MPs. Lewis Silkin himself was the man responsible for creating the UK's town and country planning legislation and the first new towns after WWII. The last Labour MP to lead the firm was John Fraser in the 1990s. He was responsible for much of the UK's consumer protection legislation. *"It's always good to know where you come from, even though there's not too much of an association with all that now,"* said one trainee. With the emergence of the advertising industry, the firm found a new direction. Roger Alexander, *"who is still around in the chairman role and is still influential,"* became known as a sort of legal godfather to the industry. From this, Lewis Silkin developed a broader media-sector profile, while also being one of the first firms to wade into the area of employment law. *"We are not the largest of firms, but we are relatively well known... for certain specialisms above all else – employment, media work and advertising clients."* We would also flag up here the firm's well-established social housing practice.

A veritable giant in employment law, Lewis Silkin represents employees as well as employers. It is much admired across the country, and is spreading its wings internationally. Could there be better recommendation than a string of law firm clients? In 2007, the firm represented Freshfields in the age discrimination claim brought by former partner Peter Bloxham. In brief, Bloxham claimed that the firm's controversial pension reform programme forced him to retire early and therefore take a smaller pension. Needless to say, the case received considerable coverage in the legal press. The employment lawyers also have some great media clients, among them MTV, which chose the firm because of its membership of international employment law network ius laboris. All MTV's employment issues outside the USA are now either dealt with by Lewis Silkin or referred to another ius laboris member firm, and Lewis Silkin even sends lawyers to work in MTV's New York HQ. Also on the client roster are: Saatchi & Saatchi; Procter & Gamble; International Cricket Council; BAA; Ford Motor Co; Fiat Auto; Grosvenor Estates; the House of Lords; Levi Strauss; Viacom; Warner Brothers; Blackwells and Simon & Schuster. Despite these weighty names, trainees do get to run some of their own files. *"I was drafting documents and interviewing witnesses and there was a lot of tribunal attendance. It's great to be the client's contact at the firm,"* said one.

Occasionally, clients also need immigration advice, for example, Abercrombie & Fitch, which sought help in obtaining work permits for its first operations outside North America. Others who have called on the firm for such advice include Oxford University Press, PizzaExpress and Cardiff Rugby Club.

It's easy to understand why media, business and technology (MBT) seats are so sought after. Lewis Silkin has been representing mobile phone company 3 in its long-running dispute with O_2 over its use of bubble imagery, the latest twist in the tale being the Court of Appeal's decision to refer the matter to the ECJ. The MBT lawyers have also lately advised Rayat TV on the launch of two digital channels targeted at British Asians, and in relation to sports there has been plenty of call for sponsorship advice. Clients include global sports communication network Havas Sports and EDF, which turned to the firm in relation to its bid to sponsor London 2012. For sheer novelty value you can't beat advertising agency clients. *"I did clearance work for advertisements,"* said one trainee. *"There was a lot of research and I also managed an Advertising Standards Authority complaint. That was fantastic – the partner was keeping an eye on me and it was the highlight of my seat. Daunting, but the ultimate satisfaction was huge."* Working with another of the partners, the MBT trainees encounter IP issues, such as domain names and trade marks.

the princess and the peabody

Other seats are offered in corporate, litigation, property, housing and construction, and client secondments also crop up. No seat is compulsory, however there are obvious favourites. *"Media and employment are the two strongest areas and people come here thinking that's where they want to qualify. This year, the media department was what everyone was fighting for and, in particular, to go there in the second or third seat when they can show themselves at their best. If it is known you want to qualify into a department, they will get you in there at some point. The only real problem comes with the politics and games as to when to go in."* Trainees issue a health warning: if you're aiming at both employment and MBT, you might not be able to also guarantee time in your third-choice department, so think carefully about which other mainstream areas you should be building into your training programme.

Lewis Silkin's litigators are handling one of the most talked about cases of the moment – the inquest into the deaths of Princess Diana and Dodi Al Fayed. Trainees have had contact with client Mohamed Al Fayed and spoke about how inspirational eminent QC Michael Mansfield is. Said one source: *"I have spent time at every hearing, assisting counsel, and helped to draft submissions. I have been involved in creating the court bundles and attended pre-hearing meetings. I have been heavily involved in the disclosure and managing that side of things. It's been quite a lot of responsibility and it's so good to see your work product used by counsel."*

"In corporate," said one trainee, *"compared with my friends at magic circle firms who work almost every hour god sends and often have to cancel social engagements, I work fewer hours."* The department gets some sweet deals at the lower end of the mid-market, for example the management buyout of Conran Restaurants for £25m and the £12.2m sale of the Fitness Exchange chain to Fitness First. The commercial property lawyers have well-known clients too: they regularly advise Hewlett-Packard and Rio Tinto, which made a major London office move in 2007. One area for which Lewis Silkin is extremely well respected is social housing. It represents many of the great and the good in the sector – Notting Hill Housing Group, Peabody Trust, Salvation Army Housing, Shaftesbury Housing and a constellation of smaller associations and local authorities. Among its top deals is the regeneration of Elephant & Castle, a project in which several of its clients are involved. Property supervisors were especially praised: *"It was a great seat and I totally thrived on it,"* recalled one trainee, who'd taken on a stack of files. *"My supervisor would say, 'Let's go through your workload and prioritise things.'"* The construction seat got people less excited: *"The trouble was that the department is so small that the level of work is not up to the same standard."*

talent war?

While there have been some great years (in 2002, for example, all qualifiers stayed), Lewis Silkin's long-term NQ-retention stats are at best mediocre, partly because all too often too many people to want to qualify into the sexiest departments. In 2007 there were more than enough positions available for the six qualifiers, though in the end only two stayed on, one going into corporate and the other into litigation. With interviews and written tests to pass, some trainees wondered if *"there is too much focus on the few hours of assessment and not on how you've performed over the course of the training contract."* On this point, the firm was clear in telling us that a person would not stand or fall on such assessments alone. Have certain departments become so successful that they are trading up when they fill NQ jobs, we wondered? And it sounds like we weren't the only ones. Said one trainee: *"Employment is a top-tier department and they can take on people coming out of the magic circle – top people. This means if you want a job, you have to come up with the goods or it will go to an outsider."* Again, when we put this to the firm, it wanted to make it clear there was no such policy of trading up. Fair enough, but perhaps this point needs making: when there are plenty of refugees from the big firms who are more than happy to make the trade-off between top-level City salaries and Lewis Silkin's target hours that are *"hundreds of hours below,"* no one approaching qualification should consider themselves a shoo-in for a job.

tails of the city

In 2006 Lewis Silkin moved to a new office *"right next to the RCJ"* at the bottom of Chancery Lane. For the first time in many moons, staff are together in one place with acres of space to run around in. *"It feels more cohesive now we are all in the same building. There have been events and parties organised by different departments for the whole firm. The* [support staff] *organised a sports day outside the back of the office... sack races, egg and spoon races, all on fake grass with lanes marked out."* MBT put on a Strictly Come Dancing night – *"incredibly amusing – a couple of people put on bad accents and compered as Bruce and Tess, and a guy from accounts was brilliant at the tango."* At such occasions – and generally – young managing partner Ian Jeffrey leads from the front. *"He has a really nice, hands-on management style and is keen to get involved. At Strictly Come Dancing, he wore a sequined satiny number."* Easy to find in the canteen at breakfast time, *"there is such a drive about him – at every quarterly staff briefing he is focused on the wellbeing of the workforce."* And speaking of the canteen, staff are currently enjoying free lunches every Thursday. *"The firm didn't quite make certain targets so a bonus wasn't due, but the partners wanted to give staff something to say thanks anyway."*

At a firm-wide forum, *"the partners are keen for everyone to have a say."* Any examples? *"Our basement isn't put to much use and we've been asked if we have ideas on how to use it. There has also been a discussion on the maternity and paternity policy and whether anyone wants to see any changes."* Trainees have their own forum: *"We set the agenda and we might have a partner or the finance director in to discuss their role. One time, Ian came in to tell us what the management board actually does."* Said one trainee: *"It's easy to join a firm and not know how everything else operates. We recently had a discussion about rainmaking; it's not important for fulfilling a training contract, but for the future it's good to know these things."*

The firm is said to suit *"people who want to be an individual at work,"* and this can be especially heart-warming for gay and lesbian recruits, who perhaps hadn't imagined they'd find as many role models at the firm. The fact that *"they don't like to put people in a box or categorise people"* doesn't seem to weaken the *"community ethos."* Indeed, the atmosphere is so conducive to building relationships that one trainee told us: *"People say our firm is a bit like a dating agency!"* Clients are treated in a similarly individualistic way: *"On small things like the dress code for meetings, you tailor it to the client. The way we speak to the clients, it's as if to say, 'We are on your level, we're not stuffy lawyers speaking in jargon you don't understand.'"*

and finally...

For one source the deciding factor in choosing the firm was its website: *"The informal, personal style reflects the fact that it's a very nice place to work, regardless of the pressure to achieve certain standards. It takes into account that people don't want to be here all night. You can't see the firm's driving ethos from just one webpage, but all the profiles of the people make it clear."*

Lawrence Graham LLP (LG)

the facts

Location: London
Number of UK partners/solicitors: 79/112
Total number of trainees: 42
Seats: 4x6 months
Alternative seats: Occasional secondments

Having resided comfortably in the London mid-market for what seems like several millennia, Lawrence Graham has suddenly got all upwardly mobile with a trendy new name, big corporate ambitions and a futuristic new office.

big game pursuit

Whoever said a leopard can't change its spots may well have had Lawrence Graham in mind, but today the firm seems determined to sweep away the perceptions of yesteryear. *"We've always been seen as a firm of gentlemen who conduct themselves as gentlemen and that implied an atmosphere lagging behind others firms,"* explained one source. A rebranding replete with that most ubiquitous of modern legal trends, the abbreviated name, has allowed the newly self-christened LG to project *"a more cutting-edge image, with the general feel of clean lines being cut..."* even if a certain electrical manufacturing giant does share the moniker. *"We're still Lawrence Graham technically, but on the website and notepaper it's LG."* Apparently, *"the new look is a key part of putting ourselves out there to a wider audience; we're trying to rise above the cosy mid-level."* Trainees are on-message with the initials, but generally agreed the firm's new slogan 'Lawyers. Just Different' is *"only marginally on the bearable side of a cliché – there were a few sniggers about it."*

At least no one's laughing about the *"beautiful"* new building at the More London development on the south bank of the Thames. Trainees see the office as *"an embodiment of the new approach,"* telling us: *"It gives everyone added incentive."* Indeed, trainees were very clear about their part in the firm's aim to *"push the corporate work, up our profile and compete with the likes of SJ Berwin."*

LG has always been best known for its real estate practice, yet it knows the SJ Berwins of this world subsist on hearty transactional fayre and so it has been working hard to build up its corporate and finance abilities. It is worth knowing that 2005 was a watershed year: powered on by the 2004 merger with small London firm Tite & Lewis, LG's corporate department made more money than property for the first time.

lassie's true value

In the corporate department, around half of the lawyers focus on capital raising, roughly 30% on traditional M&A, with the rest working on specialist tax advice. They believe there is real progress to be made by targeting AIM floats from the Asia-Pacific region and so, getting right on with the job, lawyers this year advised Indian power project developer KSK Power Ventur on its

£136.18m AIM listing, stockbrokers JM Finn on a £5.3m placing for Kiotech International and Pacific Alliance Group on a £146m AIM admission. Of course the M&A lot weren't twiddling their thumbs while all this was going in: they assisted Entertainment Right on its $305m acquisition of Classic Media, owners of rights in *Lassie* and *The Lone Ranger*, and advised *X-Factor*'s voting services provider Harvest Media Group on a £4.1m investment by FF&P Private Equity.

Working in one of the corporate teams means being subject to *"the longest hours in the firm – you could stay until 11pm or all night."* The chance to *"accompany a partner overseas for a completion or have a meal and drinks to celebrate"* does help soften the blow; nonetheless, *"the novelty soon wears off!"* The corporate team is just one part of the broader business and finance division; the other areas here are banking, competition/EU law and the local government sector, as well as IT and outsourcing. All these teams offer seats, and trainees must experience at least one seat in this division. Banking seats can be as demanding as corporate ones in terms of hours and the trainee's role is pretty similar. *"You gain exposure to a lot of different deals, managing data rooms and collecting documentation,"* explained one past occupant. Some find the experience *"too much like paper shuffling,"* but others tell a different story: *"It's absolutely brilliant; you're straight in on the deal and left to your own devices to project manage, liaise with solicitors on the other side, make sure documents are in the right place at the right time and draft smaller documents while partners and senior solicitors are engaged with the bigger ones."* Working with the partner in the LPA (*"councils, local authorities and charities"*) team means *"going all over the country with him to pitch to councils,"* so you'd better enjoy train journeys. Despite losing important people from the IT and outsourcing team, the firm is still working in this area for the likes of Lloyds TSB and Skandia.

more hotels than monopoly

Property *"doesn't have the same intensity"* and yet its *"9am to 6pm culture"* doesn't exactly make it backwater. An impressive clientele includes Sainsbury's, O2 and the London Development Agency, and then there is new client Lasalle UK Ventures, a £1bn private equity fund. Lawyers recently advised Blenheim Property Group on its £1.1bn acquisition of 47 Marriott Hotels from RBS, and through their place on Hermes' real estate panel became involved on a £267m shopping centre sale in Scotland. Seats here, whether in construction, planning, environment or straight real estate, are *"good for your confidence levels. You inherit individual files from the previous trainee and just get on with them. You have all your work checked, but can work on your own on things."* Expect to be *"phoning clients a lot."* When assisting on larger deals, longer hours and more repetitive tasks do crop up, but overall property seats mean *"actually doing things – there's minimal research and grunt work."*

Trainees also like the commercial litigation department because *"you run your own files but also get involved in the work that partners and senior associates handle,"* although, admittedly, on the larger cases *"you're not so much making a mark as getting on with discrete matters."* Lawyers recently represented long-term client Grant Thornton on a major insolvency matter – a simultaneous administration application for over 800 companies involved in an HM Revenue & Customs search. It was an innovative tactic that certainly pleased the presiding judge, who had to peruse only four lever-arch files, rather than the 3,000 that separate applications would have required. If it's understandable why *"support tasks"* constitute a trainee's role on such matters, *"debt collecting on behalf of a client"* allows them to get close to the litigation process. Court visits are a mixed bag. One might involve *"waiting three nervous hours alone to make an extension of stay* application, then going before a judge and saying just two words;" another could require the trainee to "accompany clients and counsel on a big fraud or general contract dispute trial."

Seats are also on offer in tax, private capital, the growing private client group, shipping and reinsurance, and there are very occasional short secondments to clients such as Merrill Lynch. As you'll have gathered from all this, breadth is what defines this training scheme. As to how well the seats are divvied up, opinion is mixed: some trainees report satisfaction, others believe the process "could be clearer," especially because "they tend to announce seats at the last minute." The system definitely benefits those who make their preferences known.

tough love

We also learned that "when you ask for specific feedback it is given, but people don't tend to offer it unless you ask." This last point is important, not least because trainees are expected to be fairly autonomous here at LG. It's not that support isn't there (every one has "a buddy in the year above to turn to for help and advice)," it's just that the firm believes responsibility for solving problems encountered during training lies first and foremost with the individual. A source explained: "I had a problem with poor supervision during one seat; basically I saw little of my partner and got all my work through assistants. But when I raised the issue at appraisal I was told by HR that it was my fault and I should be proactive and make myself more available." This experience resonates sufficiently with other such "isolated incidents" we've been told about in previous years to confirm a pattern. The issue this interviewee raised was "fully addressed for the better by HR for the next trainee coming in," but in the short term the problem had to be faced head on. On this topic, there does seem to have been a shift this year: "They've been looking beyond the classic trainee-partner-HR structure by appointing additional partners in each team who have responsibility for trainee matters."

"Self-starting and confident" types perform most successfully here; certainly when it comes to NQ jobs, the process privileges those with intiative. "You give your choices, but you don't know which departments will have jobs. Both HR and the trainee partner spelled out how important it is not just to go through the official process, but to speak to different partners." While some people believe "the process should be more transparent," others seemed quite at ease with the idea of having to rely on their networking skills. In September 2007, 12 of the 17 qualifiers manoeuvred themselves into NQ positions.

pee for positive change

LG's new premises wins unanimous praise from trainees and, having had a peek inside ourselves, we can confirm that the "glass, white and light" riverside abode lives up to its billing. Up on the eighth and ninth-floor client rooms, views of the City Hall, Tower Bridge and the Tower of London mean "you could stand all day looking at the river and the tourists going by." One thing you don't have to watch any more is people making the loo-walk: "In the old office you had to walk past everyone to get to the toilets, now they are discreetly hidden away." Sources also see the fact that "all trainees now share an office with their supervisor" as a "positive change," but have been left slightly nonplussed by a rubbish policy that means "we don't have bins in our rooms, we're supposed to take waste to a central recycling point." Sounds like a designer's idea soon to be widely ignored...

A "basement Garden Cafe with an outdoor terrace at ground level" has quickly become a lunchtime meeting point for trainees. Possibly they discuss the loss of the firm's old local watering hole, Daly's on The Strand. "To be honest, we're still on the search for a new pub; we're trying all the opportunities," slurred a source. Horniman on the riverfront and More Champagne ("*though only on pay days*") are early front runners. The firm's tradition of hosting winter and summer staff parties has survived the move. We liked the sound of the 50s-themed event which saw everyone from partners to support staff strutting their stuff to the sounds of a proper rock 'n' roll band. Whatever else might change at LG, we'd put money on it hanging on to its love of a good party.

and finally...

Exactly where Lawrence Graham's new ambition will take it remains to be seen, but the most likely destination is up the rankings and right along Corporate Street. Then again, that's exactly where a lot of other mid-sizers are headed...

Linklaters

the facts

Location: London
Number of UK partners/solicitors: 210/625
Total number of trainees: 276
Seats: 4x6 months
Alternative seats: Overseas seats, secondments
Extras: Pro bono – Hackney Law Centre, Mary Ward Legal Advice Centre, FRU, RCJ CAB, Legal Connections Centre; language training

Among London's elite magic circle no firm has performed as impressively in recent times as Linklaters. Market leading in the areas of corporate and finance, it saw its worldwide turnover shoot through the £1bn mark this year.

mammoth moments

Like several of its rivals, Linklaters is a global beast: it operates from 30 offices in 23 countries from Hong Kong to Hungary. Traditionally a corporate-led firm, it's been involved on some of the most mammoth deals of the last year, including advising energy group ScottishPower on its £11.6bn takeover by Spanish group Iberdrola. Equally happy acting for buyers as it is for the bought, the firm has been advising RBS Group on its approach for Dutch bank ABN AMRO, potentially the largest banking takeover in history. As for mergers, the firm represented aluminium giants Sual and Glencore on their £15.1bn three-way international tie up with Rusal to create the world's biggest aluminium company.

But there's more. Taking it a step further than rivals Freshfields and Slaughter and May, Linklaters has also cracked the world of finance. It recently worked on a £1.5bn revolving multicurrency facility for BT and a $1.2bn deposit facility for Bahraini bank Ahli United Bank – the largest syndicated bank loan in the Middle East. Tellingly, in a rare magic circle-to-magic circle transfer, the firm this year snatched Freshfields' star finance partners David Ereira and Brian Gray. On the capital markets front, lawyers showcased their effective penetration of the Russian market recently, completing not one but three IPOs in a week. These involved advice to underwriters – five of the world's largest investment banks – on floats totalling over £9bn, including the Sberbank IPO, the second-largest in Russian history. The firm takes pride integrating key clients across departments; to wit, the property team recently worked for banking client Merrill Lynch on the £480m sale and leaseback of its London HQ.

angelic behaviour

The bottom line of all this activity is profit, and boy, does Links deliver – an eye-watering, market-leading profit per equity partner of £1.2m was recorded in 2007. In nine years as managing partner, Tony Angel has overseen a programme of international expansion and a difficult restructuring process focusing the firm aggressively on its leading clients.

This robust plan put Links ahead of the curve and now other major firms are following. Linklaters has become one of the most integrated of the global firms and trainees marvel at *"how well run it all is."* Yet, with Angel stepping down this year, Linklaters' challenge will be to maintain its edge.

Linklaters' 2007 trainee recruitment brochure states that *"ultimately, this is all about ambition,"* so we'd venture a guess the plan is to carry on in the best Angelic tradition. Trainees agree, telling us the firm is *"constantly striving"* and that, *"not happy to be just another of the magic circle, it wants to be the best."* In fact, many chose the firm for precisely this quality: *"I thought, if I'm going to go into law, I'll go into it big, the top people, the best deals..."* However, according to the same sources, the firm's undoubted ambition is tempered by team focus and a human touch. Even at the application stage *"nothing was automated, they'd actually phone you up,"* and throughout training *"they have seemed really interested in my potential, not just ticking boxes."* It was this combination that meant our interviewees weren't intimidated by the prospect or reality of working in an office filled with more than 1,000 staff. *"I'd tried smaller firms,"* said one, *"but I just thought a larger firm would have more support, so you'd get a higher quality of work and less admin."*

As you may have gathered, our sources were ambitious, yet they were definitely not all of a type. Links has a deserved reputation for the diversity of its trainee group: even a cursory scan of a list of trainees' names suggests around a quarter are minority ethnic. While there is still a heavy leaning to Oxbridge and top redbricks, you do get a sense that the recruiters are open minded about where they find future trainees. In a bid to grab the best students, the firm is now making forays into India and Australia to track down talent. *"It's a mixed bunch,"* said one source, *"although you do have to be hard-working, intelligent and well rounded."* Almost all are *"team players"* because the firm employs a group approach from the off. It was the first to launch a bespoke LPC at the College of Law, and even before that future trainees were brought together for a course of *"team exercises and business games – trying to develop a commercial mentality."* Once the training contract proper starts, each intake of 60 arrives week by week in cohorts of 20 and is shuffled straight into three weeks of team-oriented hypno-suggestion, sorry... induction.

to those who wait...

A four-seat system sees trainees take three seats in the areas of banking, projects, corporate, capital markets, real estate and litigation. The fourth seat is taken in a commercial team. Given Links' strengths, it is no surprise that *"corporate definitely directs things"* and, with almost 70 partners in the division, *"it really feels like the firm's hub."* Because of the size and breadth of the department, trainees can work on anything from private equity transactions and investment funds to mind-boggling cross-border M&A. And even in a given specialist area, experiences can vary wildly, simply because of the feast or famine nature of deal flow. *"I did a little proof-reading, but mostly I was drafting, managing aspects of the deal and working with clients,"* recalled one source, happy that their experiences had not been like those of their friends who *"just ran data rooms the whole time. It's the risk you take with corporate,"* they concluded. Here's where the patience comes in: a higher quality of work comes to most trainees eventually: *"You build up trust with your supervisor and win more demanding tasks."* Apparently, *"the mid-seat appraisal is a good chance to flag up things you'd like to do."* Prove your worth and you could be *"advising a client whether they can sell their product in Oman"* or *"becoming the go-to expert on what could go into a particular prospectus."* One of the best rewards of working in this part of the firm is *"picking up the FT and seeing your deal.*" Some say that along the way you might have to deal with the odd big ego. In truth, opinion on this point was split: while some sources believed *"the partners really only want to talk to other partners,"* others were quick to tell us the department was *"friendly and non-hierarchical."* Apparently, busting a gut to *"gain partners' confidence"* is the prescribed approach.

Befitting its recent successes, the finance division feels *"noisier and hungrier"* right now than corporate. It has some *"flamboyant characters"* and life feels, well, more hectic. In the equity and debt capital markets seats, for example, *"deals can go from inception to completion in six weeks or less;"* in structured finance it's *"more like four days."* The result is a *"high-pressure, fast-paced"* atmosphere with trainees in the thick of things from day one. *"I had a nine-hour meeting with clients in my first week,"* one recalled; *"it was quite a change from the LPC."* Others found their first few weeks filled with *"bibling and working on conditions precedent,"* but thankfully *"progressed to drafting within a few weeks."* While business needs will be a factor to some extent, the level of responsibility a trainee takes on is proportional to *"how capable you portray yourself to be."* To help join the dots in what can be a complex field, the division offers a lot of training, with initial department inductions followed by a series of lunchtime sessions.

no schmucking about

As well as the mainstream finance and corporate practices, a host of other seats are available including tax, employment, IP, environment and planning, trusts, TMT and real estate. Such areas apparently attract the type of lawyer who wants *"the challenge of the complex law but without the pressure of the transactional departments,"* and are consequently regarded as more cerebral. *"You don't feel so much of a schmuck if you ask a partner a question,"* a source noted. Generally speaking, there's also more likelihood of gaining responsibility. Real

estate offers *"repeat work on leases and the like which you can do yourself,"* while employment brings *"smaller claims run by junior associates, where you can have a really important role."* One downside is time spent on corporate support duties, and trainees seem far less impressed with what they describe as *"so-so due diligence."*

Contentious needs can be catered for by a brief litigation course at the College of Law or a full seat in a dispute resolution department where lawyers work on mammoth litigations, arbitrations and regulatory investigations. They recently advised several investment banks on disputes arising out of the collapse of the Italian food giant Parmalat and Southern Water on investigations by Ofwat and the Serious Fraud Office. Such large-scale cases mean a *"heavily administrative"* role for trainees. *"I expected to be going to court, but all I got was document management,"* said one disappointed source. Another agreed: *"All the drafting was held at partner level – I got tasks the paralegals could have done."* Regulatory matters in particular involve *"a lot of document review"* and research *"which some people really enjoy."* In essence, born litigators might find Linklaters – like any magic circle firm – a somewhat frustrating place to train. On the plus side, the firm does take on some highly complex arbitration work which, if you get yourself in the right place, can be great to observe.

work hard, sleep pod

For the most part trainees were pretty upbeat about the standard of the work allotted to them. *"They're careful with billing and bundling jobs and really apologetic when they occasionally have to give you it."* Some spoke of several weeks of mundane tasks at the start of seats, only for responsibility levels to improve after the mid-seat review. Said one: *"Sometimes you hate doing something, but it's actually good for your training. I loathed two months of proof-reading, but it developed my attention to detail."* The opposite problem is an excess of responsibility. *"When you're starting out, it's immensely challenging just handling the sheer volume of it all,"* recalled one second-year. *"You have to quickly learn to prioritise and organise your time."* Close attention from supervisors stops trainees becoming seriously overloaded. *"Mine said to tell him if I found several associates pushing work on me, and he's stepped in a few times to keep things under control."*

It's a statement of the obvious that training here is about as far from an easy ride as the firm's Chinese office is from its Czech branch. In a year when concern about young lawyers' hours hit the mainstream press, trainees were more than ready to paint us an accurate picture of their working lives. *"I was nervous about* [the hours] *when I started,"* admitted one; *"it's not a myth that you work hard, but it's not as bad as the newspapers made out."* During relatively calm periods, *"if you're there after 8pm your supervisor will be asking you why – there's no face-time culture."* At other times – generally as a deal completion nears – *"you could well be there all night."* In general most trainees had found late-night sessions exhilarating rather than a drag. *"It's a laugh; it reminded me of cramming for exams,"* one recalled. *"It's you and the team, all hands on deck."* Nevertheless, *"it can be depressing having to cancel plans for the evening"* and the novelty wears off as soon as you realise that this is the reality of normal life for the rest of your career. Banking stood out as the department most likely to lead to prolonged periods late nights. Trainees spoke of several weeks of leaving at 10pm rather than 8pm, although to ease the pain the firm does pay for taxis home at that hour. And if there's ever a time when the journey home just isn't worth it, there are the legendary basement sleeping pods – *"like miniature hotel rooms with en suite showers."*

the 'when-i' club

All trainees can complete either a foreign or client secondment, meaning that practically everyone gets to bore everyone with tales of 'When I was overseas...' or 'When I was at the bank...' Client opportunities include six months spent in Citigroup's mammoth HQ in Canary Wharf, while popular foreign destinations including Dubai, Hong Kong and Prague. A full list is available on page 206. One Hong Kong veteran told us the office there had *"a completely different atmosphere – smaller with an incredibly hard-working approach."* Returnees from elsewhere agreed: in Paris, for example, despite the supposed French enthusiasm for a 35-hour week, *"they work incredibly long hours."* Small offices allow trainees to occupy a more central position on deals; however, *"there isn't the same level of administrative support, so out of hours you do your own photocopying."* Of course nobody goes on a foreign secondment with their mind just on work. Locations like Hong Kong and Dubai host several UK firms' trainees, meaning there's something of an *"expat culture."* In Hong Kong, this takes the form of *"getting together with other trainees, hiring a junk and going off to drink and water ski for a day."* Sounds strenuous! Even more so is the ultra-competitive sport of dragon boat racing – the firm's head of Asia is reportedly the team's lynchpin. In Dubai, Islamic law forbids the sale of alcohol outside hotels, so *"there are little enclaves of British around each hotel bar."*

A population of more than 270 trainees means HR has quite a job getting everyone into their seats and secondments of preference. Halfway through their first-seat, trainees chat with HR and a plan is mapped out for their remaining three seats. The idea of planning the second year just a quarter of the way through the first might not sound very appealing, but don't worry. *"In practice, it all changes down the line; you can apply for a swap if you change your mind, and when you apply for secondments, it replaces the scheduled seat anyway."*

The firm retained 114 of its 132 London qualifiers in 2007. Of those trainees we spoke to who didn't plan on staying around, for some it was the law itself rather than Linklaters they were uncertain about. Said one: *"I do look at the stress partners are under and think, 'Is it worth it?'"* Others were lured by American firms paying jaw-dropping salaries or were headed for smaller firms where the hours are kinder and the focus less 'City'.

rock da mic, right?

Linklaters' social scene offers a smörgåsbord of activities. *"It's like being back at uni,"* one source chuckled. Formal events include a trainee Christmas party, and trainees *"dominate"* the firm's many sports teams. Beyond the usual football and hockey teams, there are also groups dedicated to yoga and sailing. We also hear that departmental socialising is all the rage, with *"summer parties, barbecues at partners' houses and frequent karaoke nights."* Apparently capital markets seats are particularly microphone-prone. Do those guys know how to freestyle? Perhaps not, but *"everyone comes along, from secretaries to senior partners."*

The job of managing the balance between trainees' daily grind and their downtime tends to fall to departments rather than HR. The responsibility is taken seriously and in each division a partner is charged with looking out for trainees' welfare. There's also a trainee forum with elected representatives from each cohort of 20. This group meets regularly with management and recently negotiated changes to the bonus structure. It hasn't yet been able to convince the firm to guarantee unpaid leave for NQs before starting, something which the firm used to push hard just a few years back during slower economic conditions. *"They do listen to us, but they can't always take action because of business needs,"* explained one trainee.

Size, reputation and spectacular profits mean Linklaters looks down from on high on the rest of the legal market. As do some trainees. What sort of person, we wondered, really thrives in such an environment? *"You have to be very motivated,"* we heard, *"you're not here to do a nine-to-five – you're here to work hard."* In this hot house environment, *"there are people who are driven to the point of being competitive, trying to outstay each other at night and so on,"* admitted one source. *"But once they mature into it they calm down." "If you're arrogant it won't do you any favours,"* another noted. *"But equally, if you're the kind of person who doesn't seize opportunities when they're presented to you, you won't make the best of your time."*

and finally...

Mammoth deals, foreign adventures, decent responsibility enough of the time and a human edge to its mighty machinations: if you want a top-level training at one of the best firms going, Linklaters is going to be an obvious choice. But remember, like anything really worth having, getting in and staying in takes seriously hard work.

Lovells LLP

the facts

Location: London
Number of UK partners/solicitors: 162/366
Total number of trainees: 155
Seats: 4x6 months
Alternative seats: Overseas seats, secondments
Extras: Pro bono – Disability Living Allowance hearings, Criminal Injuries Compensation Appeal Tribunals, Bow County Court Advisory Service, National Centre for Domestic violence, CAB and many other schemes; language training

Lovells rubs shoulders with the big boys of the City while avoiding many of the stereotypes associated with it. As a result, it is extremely popular with prospective trainees. Having endured some testing years, the firm is in a period of rapid change, something that always provides an interesting backdrop to a training.

orchestrating change

Well established as a top-ten UK firm, Lovells has long been characterised as a kind of apprentice to the magic circle, snapping at the heels of its larger competitors while never quite breaking into the Premier League fully. Indeed, it seems impossible to mention Lovells without some reference to the magic circle. *"I applied to Lovells because, for me, it was as close as I wanted to get to the magic circle,"* said one interviewee, adding: *"I think it offers the best balance between quality work and a training contract that doesn't completely beast you."* Despite these apparent benefits, Lovells has never seemed happy playing second fiddle to the magic circle. However, lacklustre financial results since 2004, and some costly partner defections, have necessitated a shift in focus to protect its standing at second fiddle.

Traditionally talked about as one of the friendliest faces in the City, Lovells has had to show a much tougher side to get things back in tune. This has involved one of the biggest ever top-level redundancy programmes and tighter regulation of partner remuneration to link it closer to performance. Even trainees noted the effects: *"There is a drive to maximise profitability and work the workforce as hard as possible."* This has undoubtedly steadied the ship, but its financial recovery still falls short of its ambitions. To address this, it concluded a major strategic review in November 2006 by issuing a statement vowing to reposition itself as a serious contender to the magic circle. (Haven't we been here before?) The methods of achieving this are not set in stone, but it has made it clear that its thriving international network will be instrumental to the plan. Perhaps the most debated aspect among trainees is the fact that Lovells has vouched to prioritise investment in the powerhouse areas of corporate, finance and litigation.

millions and billions

Lovells is first and foremost a corporate and finance firm, with almost half of its work coming into these practices. This bastion was rocked by the loss of some key private equity partners, but has rallied well and is now looking forward once more across the whole spectrum of transactions. At the heart of its sterling client list are some of the world's leading investment banks, including Merrill Lynch, Lehman Brothers and JPMorgan Cazenove. Its client roster is further beefed up by names such as Barclays Capital and HSBC, for whom it acts on a range of securitisations. In this realm, one highlight was advice to Terra Firma and Deutsche Annington on a €5.4bn commercial mortgage-backed security of a German residential housing portfolio. In structured finance it has been behind 24 collateralised debt obligations with an aggregate value of €4.6bn. Its trophy client here is BNP Paribas, for whom it acted on the €265m Fairway CDO. Another corporate highlight was Insurance Australia Group's £570m acquisition of Equity Insurance Group. Whether or not you understand the nature of these deals, you can take note of two things – they are worth shed loads and they prove that the Lovells name carries weight well beyond the UK. Almost half its transactions transcend jurisdictions. No wonder it attracts so many top-notch candidates to its training scheme every year.

With working at the highest level comes the *"small cog on a massive deal"* syndrome, an ailment that results from grafting on isolated aspects of a big deal and precious little client contact. In terms of their day-to-day duties, trainees' reviews were incredibly mixed. Some sources had enjoyed interesting research assignments, while others were confined mainly to administrative tasks such as photocopying and document administration. Anyone tired just from reading the transaction highlights should know that trainees are pushed hard in the corporate and finance departments, and in this respect our sources seemed to take a little comfort from the notion that they were not the worst off in the City. Admittedly, this conviction offers less solace *"when you are falling asleep at your desk as the sun rises outside the office window."* Hard slog is rewarded in quieter periods with time in lieu, and the work-hard, play-hard ethos means plenty of opportunities to kick back with colleagues and clients when a deal is done. Looking at the bigger picture – the firm's recent commitments and the fact that this side of its business dominates NQ vacancies every year – Lovells offers good career prospects for aspiring corporate and finance lawyers.

Lovells' transactional strength is *"well balanced"* by its contentious muscle. Just like its corporate counterweight, the litigation department has also weathered some storms of late, one of which was the controversial collapse of the BCCI litigation in 2005, following 12 years at the forefront of its agenda. Even so, the department remains dominant across a range of contentious areas, and for trainees this means a good number of seats in banking and finance litigation, general commercial disputes, pensions litigation, real estate litigation, product liability, professional negligence, insurance and reinsurance, contentious insolvency and international arbitration. From this list it is the defendant-based product liability team that provides the most interesting contemporary showcase of the firm's ability. Here it has been at the heart of such hot topics as MMR, Vioxx and tobacco claims, the latter on behalf of its prized client British American Tobacco. Trainees coming to litigation from corporate appreciated the more sociable hours and greater inclusion in the matter in hand. *"A highlight for me was being involved in client meetings. I was at one with barristers that lasted all day and the tactics were being discussed. It was really interesting and I felt like it was something I really wanted to do."* The popularity of these seats comes at a cost though: *"A lot of people come to Lovells due to the firm's name in litigation, but there are not enough jobs here. They retain their litigators well and need new bodies elsewhere."*

out and a boat

One of the most appealing features of the firm for trainees is that it has not sacrificed too many of its niche departments to the altars of corporate and finance. Having satisfied the firm's expectations of taking a seat in its two strongest streams, trainees are free to swim free in a veritable ocean of choice. With so many people to try and please, HR has a tough job and a new system has been implemented to try to streamline the seat allocation process. Essentially, a few months into their first seat trainees will have an interview with HR concerning their wishes for the rest of the contract.

A department with many a seat to offer is real estate, and with *"less of a killer culture"* and high-calibre work, what's not to like? Its lawyers are involved in the regeneration of Kings Cross Central and recently worked on the £524m acquisition of a 50% share in the Merry Hill Shopping Centre in Dudley by an Australian client. The firm promotes this seat as the one that allows trainees the most responsibility: as well as working on the largest transactions, they also look after small files and *"liaise directly with the client."* Trainees say the closely linked planning department is *"extremely busy and doing some important, innovative stuff."* There, duties are likely to involve research and drafting agreements between developers and local councils.

Away from the big departments, there are a number of *"sexy"* niche areas, the most popular of which are technology, media and telecoms, competition, IP and employment. These hot seats can be hard to secure and there are limited opportunities to qualify into any of these departments. In light of the firm's strategy to reposition itself, some trainees feared that the scope for getting into these departments was likely to reduce rather than increase in the future. On the other hand, the programme of client secondments is going from strength to strength. In addition to placements with UK companies and banks (BAA, Equitable Life, John Lewis and Lloyds TSB to name but a few), there are myriad seats in Lovells' extensive international network of offices. The firm recently added Dubai to a list of seats that already included Brussels, Paris, Moscow, Singapore, Frankfurt, Tokyo and Hong Kong. The overseas offices are all smaller than the London HQ, so trainees get more hands-on responsibility when visiting. Hong Kong is consistently the most oversubscribed option and the reasons why were kindly explained by one interviewee who was lucky enough to go there. "*It is a great all-round package. You get loads of good work fired your way, an apartment, bills and travel paid for, a salary uplift and even the use of a private boat if you fancy.*"

training the heart

Lovells takes formal training very seriously and this is certainly appreciated by trainees. "*They provide tonnes of general training for the PSC, as well as loads of department-led training. You get presentations from every sub-division of an area, so you really get a sense of the big picture.*" Our sources were also happy with the concern the firm shows for their opinions. A liaison committee exists to feed trainees' views up to management and it can claim various successes. One of these is the ability to take an overseas seat in the final six months of the training. On a less positive note, we did pick up on issues that may well be keeping the committee busy in the future. Top of everyone's list of complaints were long hours and the "*inability to make any plans for the weekend.*" Indeed, in some cases people had difficulty in making any forward plans at all and we felt most sorry for the trainee who had to cancel a Valentine's Day dinner. Also worth noting is that many of our sources hankered after more responsibility: "*I think they could give us less admin work and let us get more involved in the substance of cases,*" said one trainee. "*Often big discussions take place while I am photocopying.*" There was also some dissatisfaction expressed at the qualification process, although the objective and considered approach employed by the firm is probably preferable to the certainty provided to the odd candidate by a golden nod system. In 2007, 48 of the 66 qualifiers stayed with the firm, but not for lack of overall vacancies – the firm actually had double the number of vacancies to qualifiers.

whoddunit

So who is Lovells looking to get into its trenches as it prepares to launch another offensive on the magic circle? A simple question on the face of it, but our interviewees seemed intent on making a game of it. Indeed their love for the negative created a scenario reminiscent of Cluedo. Drawing their clues together, why not see if you can figure out who they mean: "*We are certainly not wallflowers,*" "*we are not an identikit bunch,*" "*we are not as blue-blooded as people think...*" We reckon we know who fits the bill – someone with a strong academic record and a degree from Oxbridge or a redbrick uni, something on the CV to mark them out from the crowd (a sports captaincy or presidency of some or other society), and finally a confident, easy manner with people. Okay, we cheated a little on this last bit, as we were given this hint from a source who wasn't in on the game. "*They want someone who can sit on a ten-hour flight with a client without feeling awkward.*"

The large trainee intake fuels a lively social scene and this in turn results in trainee friendships, flatshares and foreign holidays. We heard many a tale along these lines: *"Never a Friday goes by when I don't go to the pub for at least one drink with somebody."* And on many a Friday far more than one drink is quaffed by Lovells trainees, who share their wages between several of Farringdon's finer drinking establishments. A generous social budget also plays its part in the social scene. *"At the last party we managed to find out quite late that there was still two grand left on the tab, so we all started ordering the fanciest drinks we could imagine."* If Slippery Nipple Screwdriver Slings are not your bag, your morale may be better boosted as a member of one of the firm's sports teams. All sorts of games are played, but it was cricket that provided the highlights in 2007. A Cricket Legends corporate event enabled aspiring Lovells spinners to test their arms against the batting might of Mike Gatting and co. *"It's by far the best day I have ever had at work,"* one source laughed heartily. There are also ample opportunities to share a drink or two with more senior members of staff. The main event is the Christmas bash, which last year employed a James Bond theme and came with *"a high-budget, pretty nifty little video"* made by the senior partner. Departmental events are of varying interest, with the pensions team top of the pops this year. Its karaoke night was a hit due to the relaxed atmosphere, helped in no small part by a senior partner with a taste for The King.

and finally...

A training contract at Lovells offers extensive formal training, an impressive salary and some pretty pleasant people to work with. Will the experience be any different from the magic circle? To an extent, but not fundamentally.

Lupton Fawcett LLP

the facts
Location: Leeds
Number of UK partners/solicitors: 33/31
Total number of trainees: 6
Seats: 4x6 months
Alternative seats: Secondments

Leeds-based Lupton Fawcett is a fast-growing Yorkshire firm determined to raise its profile in the North. Choose this firm if you're after a well-rounded commercial training contract in an environment where a healthy work-life balance takes on an entirely new meaning.

law of advantage
Leeds outfit Lupton Fawcett regards itself as a strong mid-sized player in the Leeds market. Referring to the existence of the established Big Six law firms in the city, a trainee announced categorically: *"We aren't looking to be the Big Seventh."* Yorkshire through and through, the firm has no plans to branch out of the region, preferring instead to continue its *"definite focus on Leeds and regional clients,"* more specifically *"larger owner-managed businesses and smaller plcs."* Although the firm's focus is on commercial advice, it doesn't ignore the fact that the owners and directors of its corporate clients also need the services of private client lawyers, so *"if we have done a corporate deal, the director might then use the trusts group for his will."* Lupton Fawcett's client roster includes many big-name lenders – NatWest, Bank of Scotland, Yorkshire Bank, RBS, Citigroup – and major companies such as RAC, Northern Energy, British American Tobacco plc and Serco. The firm has a good reputation for IP, where it takes on work for clients such as Textron and Jacuzzi, and it also has a strong insolvency practice, acting for the likes of PwC and KPMG. Of course

these are the big names and there are a multitude of smaller clients of whom you've probably never heard.

Take a look at the Lupton Fawcett website, and if you can see past the cheesy pics of the staff and partners, you'll notice the firm talks about "the law of advantage." We weren't quite sure what this meant, so who better to ask than the trainees? They told us how the firm has adopted a group of mottos, all of which combine to explain *"why Lupton Fawcett is great and why we are better value and... just better than everyone else."* The mottos have been placed on billboards around Leeds: *"They're in the city centre, the train station – it's quite good,"* reported a source. This streak of creativity seems to be in the firm's nature and over the years there have been *"quite a few"* exercises to position the Lupton Fawcett brand.

Proving it's not all style over substance, the firm has a clear strategy to grow from within and without. Several sources remarked how *"we are expanding quite rapidly"* and *"we have taken on a fair few people and are looking to recruit more."* It's no secret that the firm has recruited two partners from Gordons, one from Pinsent Masons and one from Cobbetts recently. Trainees assured us the firm has plenty of room to put all these new bodies: *"We recently refurbished the first floor and we are in the process of negotiating the refurbishment of the second."*

it's good to talk

Until this year trainees have spent six months in four prescribed departments: insolvency, commercial litigation, corporate finance and commercial property. Now the firm has increased its trainee intake to three people per year, seats have been added in IP and employment. Each trainee now takes four of these six seats, with no required combinations or compulsory elements. At the moment, new arrivals are placed into their

first seat without consultation and subsequent allocations are made after consultation between the trainees and HR. Our sources had found it best to *"discuss seat allocation with each other"* and, *"luckily, so far it has worked out that there have been no clashes."* The private client, family and charities/social enterprise teams are still out of the reach of trainees.

Property is split into two sections: commercial lending and commercial property. In this department a trainee will get *"loads of client contact,"* *"a lot of responsibility and some of their own files."* While there are process-driven tasks for lender clients like Citibank, trainees also have the chance to gain *"lots of drafting experience."* Commercial litigation has them handling a variety of work, such as drafting claims, instructing barristers and preparing trial bundles. The department is pushing its Chancery Division and Mercantile Courts expertise and places a great deal of emphasis on cases relating to the Companies Act (typically shareholders' and directors' disputes), professional partnerships and property disputes. Much of the team's work fits in nicely with the activities of the insolvency department, where lawyers normally act for insolvency practitioners but also advise banks and asset-based lenders. Trainees rated both the work and supervision in this seat. Attending client meetings, drafting applications and letters of advice and dealing with title documentation are just some of the tasks that come their way. Those trainees who go into the corporate finance department quickly become a team resource. Acquisitions and disposals plus MBOs are all common fare in this core department and one trainee gained a great deal of satisfaction from the fact that on a particular deal they were *"involved in every stage of the process, from start to finish"* and that the partner *"always took the time to explain things."* For them, the training contract had delivered precisely what they had been looking for – direct exposure to clients and partners.

This source was not unusual; indeed all those we spoke to had chosen the firm because it could offer them exposure to a good commercial clientele coupled with high levels of attention from supervisors. They attribute the success of the training scheme to the firm's moderate size and modest trainee intake and claim the decision to choose Lupton Fawcett couldn't be easier. Said one: *"I just wanted a Leeds firm that wasn't too huge... I didn't want to be anonymous."* As for what the firm wants, the typical recruit has some sort of connection to Leeds or the wider Yorkshire area. On qualification, one of the two second-years stayed with the firm in 2007.

mind, body and soul

All staff sit together in an open-plan environment and trainees say this means it is *"never that stressful really."* The hours are very reasonable: things *"kick off around 9am"* and, according to one typical trainee: *"Most of the time you get to leave before 6pm. They actively encourage you to go home and the building is locked at 7pm anyway."*

We often hear about firms advocating a healthy work-life balance, but at Lupton Fawcett it is really taken to the next level: *"They love it! They absolutely love it,"* said one trainee speaking of the firm's initiatives to encourage staff to live a healthy lifestyle. When we asked what spurred the firm on in this area, one trainee answered: *"I don't know! It's all about wellbeing – your job is really important, but if you're not healthy..."* Intrigued, we probed further. Every month all staff receive a leaflet *"detailing all the things going on that week."* Every Monday morning *"each department gets a bowl of fruit"* and training rooms are filled

with dried apricots. The firm is keen to help smokers quit so there is *"loads of anti-smoking stuff around"* and it also hands out leaflets on *"how to make soup and the benefits of eating bananas."* In a competition to see which department can lose the most weight, *"personal legal services and admin are the two contenders."* And it doesn't stop there: for the Mount Everest challenge *"each department submits a team, everyone counts how many times they climb the stairs and whoever reaches the height of Everest first wins."* Other healthy delights include Tai-Chi classes and lunchtime walks around the city.

For those of you who can't imagine anything worse than being weighed in front of colleagues while clocking up how many steps you take, rest assured the firm is aware that this might not be everyone's cup of tea. *"You get involved as much as you want to,"* explained one trainee. You can't say fairer than that, but we can't imagine anyone turning their nose up at our favourite Lupton Fawcett spa treatment – lunchtime massages. *"It's really bizarre,"* said a source; *"you just go upstairs, have your massage, then go back to your desk refreshed and revived."*

For refreshment of an entirely different sort, the trainees are spoilt for choice as they are *"right in the centre of Leeds on a street full of bars."* They can often be found not too far from the office in Quid Pro Quo. *"All you have to do is trundle downstairs on a Friday and the majority of the firm will be there,"* one of them admitted. Other favourites include All Bar One, Henry's and The Slug and Lettuce.

and finally...

A decidedly commercial training, an innovative working environment and all the fresh fruit you can eat. What more could you want?

Mace & Jones

the facts

Location: Liverpool, Manchester, Knutsford
Number of UK partners/solicitors: 36/45
Total number of trainees: 11
Seats: 4x6 months
Alternative seats: Secondments

Right now we reckon you're wondering how Mace & Jones differs from the likes of DWF, Brabners, Hill Dickinson or any other firm with offices in both Manchester and Liverpool. Read on and we'll tell you how.

keeping up with the mace & joneses

Most people are rather hazy on the early chapters of the Mace & Jones story, which goes back a couple of centuries. The current firm is the result of a merger between Grundy Kershaw, an old Manchester firm, and Liverpool stalwart Mace & Jones. According to one amateur sleuth, *"they must have been the lawyers for the Manchester Ship Canal because there are a lot of old Manchester Ship Canal pictures in the boardroom with labels like 'Meeting With Grundy Kershaw Solicitors.'"* For most trainees, however, the firm's past is of less interest than its immediate future. *"They seem to have a three or four-year plan,"* confides one. *"They had a radical overhaul not long before I joined the firm when they stopped doing legal aid and got rid of the Huyton office. They're moving away from being a firm that deals with everything to being one with a much more commercial focus."* As to what is driving this change, you need only look at what is going on in the North West legal market. Lawyers in both of the major cities are busier than ever as money flows into the region. *"The Manchester office in particular is very market driven because of all the private sector investment at the moment."* Interviewees tell us that the Liverpool team tends to act more for public authorities and

development agencies than its Mancunian counterpart. This is useful for prospective applicants to know, because according to the conditions of M&J's training scheme they will be expected to work in both Manchester and Liverpool.

The firm, which covers the full range of disciplines, stands out in hot areas like employment, litigation, insolvency and family law (a particular strength of the small 'neighbourhood' office in Knutsford). Its client list includes big names such as the North West Regional Development Agency; West Lancashire District Council; Liverpool City Council; Ask Property Developments; University of Wales and Shell UK.

just love that m62

Imagine a contract in which you don't know where you will be working from one six-month block to the next, add some uncertainty as to the department you'll be placed in and there you have it – that's the way things work here. The first seat is chosen for each person; after that they indicate their preferences to a trainee representative who compiles a list and submits it to the training principal. Everyone gets to see what everyone else is going for and there's no skulduggery. The seats on offer are: coco (Man/Liv); commercial property (Man/Liv); employment (Man/Liv); dispute resolution (Man/Liv); construction (Man); family (Liv) and a mixed private client/family option in the tiny Knutsford office for anyone who wants to give it a whirl. The fact that any given time there is only one trainee per department per office is a major advantage, sources tell us. It means *"you aren't competing with each other for the best work."*

A cracking employment team works for major clients like Littlewoods Pools, the Highways Agency, Merseyside Police and the National Probation Service as well as a string of high-earning executives. It's a flagship department for the firm and, as such, *"there are enough seats for everyone who wants to try it."* Whether it's because of the size of the clients and cases or the fact that the lawyers have a reputation to uphold, it's hard to say, but trainees find that *"sitting in employment is quite a formal, observational experience. Although there's some drafting to do, and you get taken out to tribunals, there's also a lot of research and working in the background. It's less to do with getting stuck in."* Not having much hands-on experience doesn't, however, make this a bad seat. *"You see a lot – there weren't many things I didn't cover – and they don't throw you in at the deep end."* In contrast, the property seat offers a reasonable amount of involvement in transactions, even if what was described to us sounded a touch heavy on post-completion tasks. *"They start you off on the easy stuff and then try and vary what you are doing. I worked for a whole load of people – all nine fee earners in the Manchester office in fact."* In 2007 the firm was named Property Law Firm of the Year at the North West Insider Property Awards.

along came a spider

Progress well in your dispute resolution seat and you might get to look after a couple of cases or go to court to make small applications. On the property litigation side *"we act for a number of large and well-known companies."* Contractual dispute work is *"mainly for local businesses, people whom the corporate and property departments have acted for in the past."* It can also be for *"the odd high net worth individual with a boundary dispute who has instructed us in a business capacity."* Additionally, the firm undertakes judicial review work for the Legal Services Ombudsman. *"We do about 30 cases a year, one or two of which raise interesting points of law."* The litigators sometimes work with the employment lawyers and last year took an employment case to the House of Lords. Trainees are less proud of the claimant PI cases that come to the Liverpool office through InjuryLawyers4U. *"If I were in charge, I would get rid of the PI department. You either do PI as the sole activity of your firm or*

you don't do it at all – it doesn't look good in a commercial context," asserts one. Unsurprisingly, there is much delight at the removal from the menu of the Liverpool PI seat, which saves trainees from *"petty claims that don't stand up."* One woman brought a claim alleging she had crashed her car because a spider crawled in through the window...

how to shine

So what kind of person comes here? *"It's helpful to have North West roots in terms of understanding the regional scene,"* reports one source. Beyond this, though, the firm *"tends to be less narrow than others in its recruitment and has a much shorter lead-in period* [one year not two]. *And it doesn't simply sign up second-year university students."* M&J *"likes to take people who have done other things before becoming a trainee – been in industry for a few years or completed another degree, for example."* The trainees sound like hard-working types: *"We're willing to put 100% into our jobs; there are no slackers here,"* we were told. One area of responsibility trainees enjoy is playing their part in marketing events and client seminars, where *"you can go off on your own accord and meet people."* One source had made inroads through sports, playing cricket and football matches against clients and other lawyers. *"It's a really good way of getting your name known. The firm doesn't want quiet, shy, sit-behind-a-desk types as trainees."* After speaking to a few of them, we don't think that's what they've got. Without exception, we found our interviewees to be lively, prompt, informative and great at analysing the firm. Is M&J an especially clever recruiter or is it something about the training contract that polishes people up so well? It might, in the words of one trainee, be because *"the firm is large enough and has sufficient clout to get the good work, but small enough to care about the individual as more than just another number on the payroll."*

crime stories

Although Liverpool houses the firm's official HQ, Manchester is regarded as the office that is *"going places."* This seems to be reflected in the length of the working day, which rarely extends beyond 5.30pm in Liverpool but can go on until 7pm in Manchester. The hours may not be that bad, but for some the early start and length of commute between the two can be a right pain. *"It was a real low point for me, made worse by not knowing where I would be moving for my next seat,"* recalls one trainee. *"In winter you have to make a conscious effort to go out at lunchtime, just to see daylight."* The extra expense involved in shuttling between cities is around £40 per week in petrol – even more if you use the train. Bear this in mind, because M&J trainee salaries lag behind those of the main commercial firms in the region. Having signed up to the deal, however, they accept the split-site training with good grace and appreciate the long-term benefits. *"Looking back,"* said one, *"it was a good way to get to know people and how the different offices operate."*

A great partner-assistant ratio means that trainees have the opportunity for *"close involvement"* with lawyers at the highest level. Socially, it's no drama spending time with them. *"Mr Downey the managing partner came across quite scary at first but he introduced himself to us early on and sometimes buys us drinks and stops for a chat at 'First Friday' drinks."* Generally *"if a partner doesn't know you, they will always introduce themselves."* The trainee social scene is cordial enough, although the moving around does make a difference. *"Trainees come and go from each office and it's a shame we don't all have more contact,"* regrets one. Nevertheless, they have still found time to go out for a meal in Manchester and go bowling in Liverpool. The trainees get to demonstrate their sense of fun at the Christmas party when they perform a sketch in front of the assembled staff. *"We had a 'comedy characters v the Spice Girls' Family Fortunes face off this year,"* recalled one. *"Someone dressed up as Vicky Pollard in a fat suit and wig, someone else was Catherine Tate and the boys were the Spice Girls. A couple of the partners joined in too. One played the hostess of the show."* It's not just drag that the partners are into: one of them is a crime novelist with 11 titles to his name. *"Oh, and he's also writing The Equal Opportunities Handbook."*

Every six months three qualifiers complete the training scheme at M&J, but despite there being jobs for all in 2007 only three of the six stayed on. You could argue that this is a telling figure – that the ultimate test of satisfaction and fit is how many trainees remain after qualification. Our interviewees told us that this isn't the case here. *"When people leave it tends to be because the position they'd like to fill isn't available. The firm won't create a position just so someone can stay."* With smaller firms there's always the issue of the right job cropping up at the right time.

and finally...

Try and get onto one of Mace & Jones' work-experience placements if you want to sample the firm for yourself. It looks to us to be an increasingly attractive option in the North West.

Macfarlanes

the facts

Location: London
Number of UK partners/solicitors: 72/153
Total number of trainees: 50
Seats: 4x6 months
Alternative seats: Secondments
Extras: Pro Bono – Cambridge House Advice Centre, death row appeals; language training

Compact of size and clear of thought, Macfarlanes is a perfectly formed outfit that stays true to itself while competing on even terms with bigger City players. Renowned for mainstream corporate expertise, the firm is also rather handy at private client, real estate and commercial litigation and offers training that is, *"put simply, quality."*

respect mah qualitah!

Ah, that word. Quality. *"It's drummed in from day one,"* so trainees are as aware as anyone of *"focusing on providing a quality product... it's the watchword across the board."* Elsewhere we might consider such statements a touch self-indulgent or over optimistic but, knowing this firm of old, we suspend our cynicism without hesitation. Unconcerned with the faddish vagaries of the legal profession, quality has been Macfarlanes' consistent focus and the thing that has made it one of the most profitable firms in the UK. That's no mean feat considering there is no overseas network, no culture of growth through lateral hires and *"a conservative with a small 'c' approach"* to management and change. Quibbling with that particular 'c' word our sources proffered alternatives. *"It's classic rather than conservative, civilised maybe... it doesn't see the point of changing things for the hell of it."*

Macfarlanes' long-term success rests on its historical focus on corporate work and it's a strategy that continues to bear fruit. In 2007 lawyers advised the executive chairman of Alliance Boots on his £9.7bn takeover bid for the group. Corporate makes up *"over 50% of our workload"* and has been prominent in generating an increasing number of international instructions despite a traditional leaning toward domestic transactions. Advising Brazilian steelmaker Companhia Siderurgica Nacional on a £4.3bn approach for Anglo-Dutch rival Corus was one recent highlight, with a lead role advising private equity client Oaktree on the rare acquisition of a Polish vodka company another. The gradual shift into

major international deals was evidence for our interviewees that *"this is a place continuing to ask questions of itself."* Revolution no, evolution yes. For example, *"the IP side of litigation is getting more work, and some of the more one-man-bandy areas like debt finance and pensions are growing."* At a firm renowned for promoting internal candidates, recent partner-level lateral hires into the pensions and real estate teams show it isn't unthinkingly stuck in its ways.

Trainees seem entirely comfortable in Macfarlanes' skin, enjoying *"the work of a larger practice with all the stresses and rewards that come with that, but at the same time the intimacy of a smaller firm."* The value of this *"smallish community by City standards"* was a key factor for those who drew away from the magic circle. So too was the opportunity to explore a range of practices without compromising on quality. In the words of one interviewee: *"There are consistently excellent standards of work across the board; the firm might be centred on corporate, but private client, property and litigation are all highly regarded, standalone departments."* A straightforward rotation system means *"it's easy to get what you want, the caveat being that you have to be clear with HR from the start."* Trainees all experience mainstream corporate, something contentious (either litigation or employment) and property, with a fourth seat taken in a more specialised corporate area or in private client. Pensions, competition, tax or debt are options within corporate, and those particularly keen to focus on transactional matters now have the option of taking a short litigation course instead of a full seat. Overseas seats are not available, though there are regular secondments to client 3i.

not so vaguely speaking

Macfarlanes' size means *"you always have access to whoever brain you want to pick."* It also means *"you can't escape people."* In fact the two combine so *"as trainees we aren't encouraged to seek out work, but only because you don't need to. Generally speaking there's a culture that means the most sophisticated work, and as much of it as you can handle, drifts down to you."* Trainees agree: *"You certainly have a lot on your plate early"* and *"what has consistently impressed us is that people take time to say why and how* [things need to be done] *and are glad for you to come back with questions."* One stressed how *"we get almost none of the classic vague instructions that leave you scratching your head and guessing, condemned to the office for four days while an assistant goes out to lunch."* What the firm does share in common with much of the City is long working days. While *"9am to 7.30pm is the average"* across the firm, corporate seats in particular require *"regularly staying to 11.30pm, midnight or even later."*

A stint in the busy mainstream corporate team brings a range of private and public transactional matters. *"It was amazing,"* blushed one source; *"within a month I was involved in two FT front-page, multibillion-pound deals."* Another spoke enthusiastically of working on *"a portfolio of disposals in private equity."* True, the size of matters means *"none of the headline documents will be in your name,"* but *"a trainee's work is 80% drafting and very engaging."* The opportunity to take *"direct responsibility on something like the documentation and management of a start-up"* is commonplace. Here, as elsewhere in the firm, trainees enjoy *"an absence of internal competition"* and assured us that *"people are all pulling in the same direction."* As for other seats, employment brings *"defendant tribunal work,"* the chance to *"draft almost all the documents"* for employment incentive contracts, corporate support tasks and a fair amount of research. Tax possesses a *"distinctively cerebral, less client-facing atmosphere"* that is *"heavily technical."* Likewise, pensions brings *"an enormous amount of work,"* but *"a strict dividing line between what you can*

and can't do. Often you'd leave at 7pm with the partner staying later, just because there'd be nothing you could actually help with."*

courtroom bandits

The private client team is among the best in the UK and begs a second glance from trainees. *"I was surprised by how fast-paced it was,"* admitted one interviewee. *"There are lots of new corporate-style clients with very exacting expectations about speed of turnaround."* Trainees can expect the challenge of *"taking an instruction over the phone for a will and drafting it yourself,"* not to mention a good dose of black letter law. Remember though, even if it is possible to *"handle small things yourself,"* *"partners' relationships with clients take first priority on larger matters."* Sometimes small problems arise, for example *"a client's removal company caused damage to their belongings,"* and these are then sent over to the litigation department where a grateful trainee will gobble up the instruction. For the most part a seat in lit *"means less responsibility as a lot of it can't be done without partner involvement."* The other drawback to the seat is that there can be *"an enormous number of documents in an ongoing case that you never get your head around."* The seat has its fans though. Said one: *"I went to Downing Street to deliver documents for an afternoon hearing at the Privy Council – I was so close to the Law Lords I could have flicked them with a rubber band."* Meanwhile, the *"very businesslike, document-heavy"* construction litigation team handles matters both *"huge and surprisingly small."* This means a trainee can end up *"handling a £5,000 claim alone."* The real estate department's work covers commercial property, environmental and agriculture/estates/private client matters. Again, corporate support is a feature of life and trainees worked closely with colleagues in corporate on client Dunedin's £664m refinancing of three commercial property portfolios. The *"transactional nature of property work means it is paper-heavy,"* a source explained, adding that *"they're good at letting you handle correspondence and so you're liaising directly with clients."*

reddy...

Throughout the two years, training seminars and updates keep the grey matter fuelled and there's ample one-on-one tuition to be gained from supervisors. *"If a piece of work comes back with a little red pen on it and you discuss how you got to that point then things are fine, but if there are a series of red pen points, chances are you haven't done it so well."* Daily interactions like this are supplemented with *"mid and end-of-seat reviews, which some people do in more detail than others."* Should any really tricky issues arise, there's always the opportunity to speak to a neutral partner who will act as mentor. *"Some are better than others, mainly according to their personality and match with a trainee, but it's a good system."*

...steady, flow

"This is not a place to be cut-throat," said trainees; *"people give each other respect."* The *"spirit of co-operation"* is paramount in this *"thoroughly decent"* workplace. These are not the only constants though. *"It's true that trainees here tend to be middle class and well adjusted,"* we were told. *"We're all very clever and noticeably disinclined to be competitive with each other."* Take a glance at the online profiles of every trainee and you'll notice a majority come from Oxbridge and top redbrick universities, although the firm has been proactively seeking talent further afield in recent years. In another development, Macfarlanes has signed up to a bespoke LPC run by BPP, in which tailored electives will prepare students for seats in the firm's range of practice areas. Having increased the number of recruits and having long followed a path of growing from within, the firm gives trainees every reason to commit long term. Their affection for the place is very apparent, both in what they say (*"I wouldn't want to work for another London firm"*) and in the choices they make on qualification. Macfarlanes' admirable record for retaining NQs continued in 2007 when 19 of the 22 qualifiers stayed on, all having been offered jobs.

wilkommen, bienvenue, welcome...

Trainees admitted: *"It's no secret our offices are a little bit shabby, but it's almost like a badge of value for money for our clients."* At least the arrival of a swish new building just round the corner from the three existing offices on Norwich Street will provide a plusher welcome to clients. Socially, things are warm and *"there's a good culture of going out."* There are cricket, football and hockey teams to join if you're sporty, and a local pub, The Castle, is regularly filled on a Friday. The social committee keeps things ticking over with new joiners' drinks, trips to the dogs, *"maybe a cruise on the Thames,"* and a legendary ball is held once every four years. Future joiners are invited, so chances are all trainees will experience one by the time they qualify. In 2007 a *"charity cabaret"* was held *"in aid of our charity of the year, Mango Tree,"* which supports orphans in Tanzania. *"There was an abridged version of Me and My Girl, as well as various partner and trainee turns."* Liza Minelli eat your heart out.

and finally...

What you get here is a full-on training contract hitting the main bases of corporate, property, litigation and, for those that want it, private client at a self-assured firm. That, and being stamped with the Quality hallmark. Most Macfarlanes trainees couldn't bear the idea of working anywhere else.

Manches LLP

the facts

Location: London, Oxford
Number of UK partners/solicitors: 57/78
Total number of trainees: 21
Seats: 4x6 months
Alternative seats: Occasional secondments

London and Oxford-based Manches was founded in the 1930s by Sydney Manches and is still home to a few prominent members of the family. Its chairman and the London managing partner are, respectively, daughter Jane Simpson and son Louis Manches. There is even a third-generation Manches among the ranks of assistants.

an ever-changing gene pool

Now before you start imagining a small family firm, you need to be aware that over the past seven decades Manches has expanded into a much-respected mid-sized commercial-private client hybrid. And the evolution of the firm continues: most recently it has completed a small merger (with Marshall Ross & Prevezer in November 2005) and made a string of lateral hires at all levels from newly qualifieds to partners. It has also lost a few people along the way, most recently some property lawyers, almost the entire construction department and charismatic IP and defamation specialist Alex Carter-Silk.

If you know one thing only about Manches, it is probably that the firm is a giant in family law. To give you an idea of how giant, it is ranked number one by *Chambers UK*. Needless to say, its reputation in this field attracts many prospective trainees, and yet people seem to be equally attracted to the idea of mixing commercial and family/private client seats to produce a well-rounded training.

London trainees are generally allotted family and property seats in their first year, although *"if you have a burning desire to do something else, they'll try their best to change things."* Family and property take on several trainees at any one time, which is indicative of their importance to the firm's business. Second-year seats can be chosen from construction, commercial litigation, corporate, employment, property litigation and IP/tech/media.

queens of the lone age

Let's look first at the mighty family law practice. When Beverley Charman, ex-wife of insurance magnate John Charman, secured the largest divorce settlement in UK history – a cool £48m – she did so with the help of Manches. High-profile cases are a common feature of this stellar department's work, as are cross-jurisdictional cases for globally wealthy clients who are attracted by London's reputation as the divorce capital of the world. It's no surprise that trainees are consistently busy: *"You don't stop until you leave for the day,"* said one breathlessly. Despite calling the experience *"a baptism of fire,"* trainees aren't actually given as much responsibility as in other departments. Their work more often involves taking attendance notes and bundling papers for court, with the odd client meeting and ring-side seat at hearings. The team has a clear hierarchy and is somewhat less likely to engage in spur-of-the-moment drinks evenings than other departments. Nevertheless, trainees generally feel involved, albeit they may remain a little awestruck by the key figures. Jane Simpson, or Mrs Simpson as she's known around the office, is *"a big noise in family law generally."* She is also a trained marriage counsellor, which must come in handy given the emotional nature of the work. *"As much as you get upset by certain situations, the fact you can do something to help gives you a lot of satisfaction,"* said one source on this point. Interestingly, some trainees implied that the emotional nature of family law and Manches' female-dominated family department make it a less attractive choice for male trainees.

house of plenty

The property department is central to the firm's success and boasts clients like WHSmith, Pizza Hut, British American Tobacco, Swarovski, Gap and Jigsaw, as well as several banks and property development companies. Trainees say property is *"a complete change in atmosphere, work and tempo"* from the family department, which isn't a great surprise considering the emphasis trainees place on the difference between the departments' personalities. Doing a seat in property involves *"a fair amount of drafting of leases, licences to assign and letters to clients,"* but offers little chance for face-to-face client contact. Trainees can find themselves working late on occasion, and if really unlucky this might involve *"sitting amongst a huge pile of thousands of deeds to schedule."* However, Manches largely lives up to the expectation of a firm where trainees *"aren't guaranteed to do long hours every week."* Apparently, *"people would have less respect for you if you were hanging around the office at 8pm or 9pm without a big deal on."*

This firm has big characters in each department, and property is no exception. Louis Manches is *"very much the face of the department,"* and despite being rarely seen around the corridors *"when you do see him he's really welcoming."* One of the dominant personalities in the firm, he isn't averse to donning a pirate's costume. We should explain that his moment of fancy-dress madness took place at the annual Manches Cup sailing regatta, in which trainees are encouraged to participate. Such antics show trainees that outside the office, even the big names at the firm *"are just normal people underneath."*

In the small litigation department, Clive Zietman is a sought-after supervisor because he's *"particularly good"* at getting trainees involved in interesting work. A seat here is likely to include a visit or two to the Royal Courts of Justice, conveniently located just round the corner, and back in the office trainees are *"allowed to run with quite a large caseload"* of small claims.

Over in the technology, media and IP department, lawyers continue to pull in clients that are prominent players on the pop culture stage. We're talking about the likes of Damien Hirst, Channel Five, Endemol and Darryn Lyons' photographic agency Big Pictures, which featured in the TV show *Paparazzi*. The *"ambitious, young and dynamic"* IP team really pulls its weight in the firm and does not seem to be bemoaning the loss of Alex Carter-Silk, especially since the arrival of former Lovells lawyer Richard Dickinson. In addition to sexy clients like Universal Pictures and *"very good-quality work,"* a seat here throws up the occasional perk, such as free tickets to premieres. The London team works in tandem with an established group of IP lawyers in the Oxford office, where long-standing clients include Oxford Gene Technology and the JRR Tolkien Estate.

for better or worse

Although its commercial practice is both established and well-respected, and the number of people from the Manches clan is minimal, the firm still has *"a family-led feel, for better or worse."* This contributes to *"a feeling that everybody knows everybody,"* which in turn can lead to a somewhat frustrating qualification process. *"Before it starts you don't know how many jobs there are and then it involves a little bit of reading between the lines. Often departments may well have made up their minds pretty early on, possibly even before you put yourself forward."* Trainees also felt frustrated at how long the process took, given the relatively small numbers of qualifiers involved. According to the firm, there is a calculated method to their madness: *"We want trainees* to take charge of their own future, so they need to network and climb to the top of that greasy pole, which may mean knocking off their peers. Life isn't easy and they need to get to grips with that now." In 2007, six of the 11 qualifiers took jobs at the firm. Our sense is that some of those who left would have been better suited to *"corporate work at a top-ten firm"* all along.

As well as a substantial *"Oxbridge contingent,"* there is a good mix of trainees from top redbrick universities. We noted a certain lack of ethnic diversity in the ranks, although one trainee supposed this was *"probably normal for what Manches do and in the marketplace in which they do it."* The newest intake is an ambitious and social bunch. Their preference for tech/IP and employment seats has led to some healthy competition between them and their competitiveness extends to a fondness for sport, which is well provided for by Manches' football and mixed softball teams.

As well as the Manches Cup regatta, the firm hosts several social events including a big Christmas party, last year held in a funky London nightclub with a free bar and a casino. A *"more refined"* summer party gets the London and Oxford staff mingling over a barbecue on the hallowed grounds of Lincoln's Inn Fields. Manches additionally invites future trainees to drinks evenings three times a year, so they can meet the rest of the firm before they join. Whether people go out for casual drinks depends very much on the department. The usual group consists of trainees and junior assistants, and it isn't unheard of for someone more senior to tag along. The Aldwych location allows the London set to choose from an array of bars around Covent Garden and Fleet Street. Indeed, the location scores high marks all round: *"It's brilliant,"* said one trainee; *"you're right on the edge of the West End and the City. It's very nice to be able to walk down to the courts and feel very much in the middle of it all."*

two houses, both alike in dignity

Manches' Oxford office normally takes on two trainees each year and offers seats in corporate, litigation, family, property, employment and tech/IP/life sciences. The popular IP department is especially known for its work with biotech start-ups that have spun out of Oxford and London Universities. As befits a small office, trainees are generally given a high level of responsibility and they tell us they are very satisfied with the quality of training they receive. In litigation *"you get your own little cases to handle,"* while the property department offers a mix of commercial and social housing deals and has *"consistently long hours."* As with their colleagues in London, Oxford trainees in the family department are exposed to international cases. All in all, it is clear that choosing to train in the smaller regional office does not mean abandoning the goal of experiencing high-calibre work.

The Oxford trainees tend to be *"more mature and work-focused,"* most being older or married with children. The office is located on the Oxford Business Park, just south of the city, and the rather dull location does unfortunately stifle the social life a bit. That said, it is *"ideal for parking and convenient for stopping off at Tesco and Mothercare."* The relatively small size of the office fosters a genuinely friendly atmosphere in which *"there's no face you don't know."* Interaction between London and Oxford trainees is not extensive, being pretty much limited to the big firm-wide parties and the induction week for new starters.

and finally...

With its *"quite formal, jacket-and-tie"* atmosphere, Manches maintains an element of the old school in some departments while representing cutting-edge clients in others. Perhaps because of this, it has what trainees describe as *"a real character in the marketplace and within its walls."* Those recruits who are happiest and find a permanent place here are the ones who fit with Manches' distinctive personality and have made *"the conscious decision"* to sidestep the big City giants.

Martineau Johnson

the facts
Location: Birmingham, London
Number of UK partners/solicitors: 46/100
Total number of trainees: 20
Seats: 6x4 months
Alternative seats: None
Extras: Pro bono – various projects

Martineau Johnson has been a feature of the Birmingham legal landscape for 150 years. A move in 2005 to large modern premises signalled the start of a new era for this mild-mannered Midlander.

which flavour?
Just another commercial law firm? Hardly! MJ competes well on its home turf with other commercial players, but also stands out for its top-grade private client and education practices and considerable expertise in the energy sector. In the private client sphere, its growing team (including a recently-added family law unit) represents an array of Midlands Rich Listers and landed estates. The firm's truly impressive grip on the education sector, meanwhile, sees it acting for 80 further and higher education institutions throughout the UK. Among these are The College of Law and every single university in the West Midlands. The list of clients for the energy practice is full of recognisable names – National Grid; British Energy, Severn Trent, Thames Water and the Environment Agency for starters.

Arriving to start your training contract at MJ is like deciding to buy an ice cream, opening the freezer cabinet and discovering that there are all the regular flavours plus a load you've never tasted before. To help trainees with their choices MJ has put some rules in place. Everyone is required to do a property seat and *"we are also expected to do a corporate seat – M&A, banking or funds. Then we have to do a commercial seat, which can be employment, IP, energy or projects."* Quite a few people will also take education or private client seats. A total of six seats enables trainees to explore a number of areas and then return in the last four months to the department in which they hope to qualify. Our interviewees agreed that this is a good system.

The property department is a big one. Working on leases and disposals of individual properties grants trainees a good degree of autonomy. *"I was running ten to 15 of my own files and taking things all the way to completion,"* said one. *"I gained a lot of confidence from doing good things so early on."* Their role in property finance deals is to assist more senior fee earners. *"I worked on large shopping centres in Liverpool and did a lot of work for Lloyds Bank. Some days I couldn't see my desk for all the papers covering it. This seat really teaches you about time management."* Property is also good for client contact *"because you're picking up the phone to them all the time."*

Not everyone looks forward to the corporate seat, but *"I enjoyed it more than I thought I would,"* reported one trainee. *"I had to co-ordinate a lot of things and had daily conferences with the client to update them on everything."* Especially pleasing for another was that *"the senior associate I dealt with on the other side didn't treat me as a trainee."* Work includes the usual board resolutions and shareholder consents to draft, offer letters to check and mountains of post-completion matters – such as share certificates – to climb. *"You're trusted to get on with things,"* a source explained. The seat also brings with it a mix of M&A and funds work. Because *"the funds side is more com-*

plex, and the tax and legislative requirements are so strict, you never get anything to deal with on your own," said one trainee. In the past year the firm has worked on the £18.5m management buyout of the Golddigga fashion business and a string of venture capital-funded matters. FTSE 100 food-services company Compass Group and NYSE-listed human resources supplier CTI Group are among its biggest clients.

MJ is targeting the banking sector, and not just in relation to property finance. In 2006 it advised lenders on deals valued at £793m, while undertaking a range of disputes and recovery work on their behalf. In addition to key client Lloyds TSB, the firm also serves RBS, HSBC, Harrods Bank and Bank of Ireland. There is a banking litigation seat in the smaller London office. "We've recently moved to new, larger premises and are looking to recruit to fill them," sources told us, confirming that the firm has its eye on growth in the capital. Those who visit get four months in a free flat in Docklands and a salary uplift. "I had a lot of my own files and one of the best supervisors in the firm," says one source, summing up this seat's appeal. "As long as you don't mind there being no other trainees, it's great." Unsurprisingly, it also offers great advocacy opportunities. "I did a lot of court work on my own, things like charging order hearings. Going with other people, you also get to see how they deal with it," reveals one trainee. "There were a variety of cases, but the bulk of it was small claims – a lot of them. It's a matter of keeping on top of things through good file management." Given that the London seat is "quite fought over," it's good news that a second will now be offered, split between property and energy, projects and commerce (EPC).

al gore and me

There is always one trainee in the education team, and work in this area often feeds into other departments. "Even though I haven't done an edu-cation seat, I have come across education sector clients." The range of issues tackled in this field is quite remarkable. A sample of the firm's work includes advising on the provision of education by British universities in India, Italy, Egypt and China; assisting with a PFI-backed university development of an offshore wind farm; handling an unprecedented number of student discrimination claims (many of which relate to dyslexia and mental illness); and advising on a unique project that will enable a university to conduct a number of its hospitality courses at a purpose-built, four-star hotel.

The energy seat has much to offer. Said one past occupant: "I did a broad range of work for clients ranging from large Plcs to start-ups in the renewables sector. I even helped some private clients with large estates that were looking into the turbine and wind farm markets." Renewable energy is fairly high on the agenda at the firm; "as I speak the senior partner is in Brussels at a climate change conference with Al Gore." Trainees may not get to meet the ex-next President of the United States, but they are exposed to different types of commercial agreements and learn how to draft simple terms and conditions for supply and service contracts.

Despite being a growth area the private client work didn't seem to be as popular with interviewees as we'd anticipated. You need to get your thinking cap on for this one as much of the work has a tax element to it and there is a lot of drafting to be done. During their time here trainees will encounter clients ranging from the super wealthy to "little old ladies." An excellent agriculture and rural affairs department provides advice on anything from tax and inheritance planning to leases of land and sales of farms. Some of this requires collaboration with the planning team, while in matters such as the repossession of land from tenant farmers the MJ litigators will help out.

Trainees had some minor concerns over seat

allocation. "*It isn't always as well thought out as it could be,*" said one, "*and we are sometimes told where we are going only a couple of weeks before rotation.*" The prioritisation of second-years can also cause problems. "*When I was a first-year, the year above were all keen on corporate so none of us could do it until we were in the second year too.*" Not everyone had issues with the process; one interviewee praised the HR folk for inviting them to "*come and have a chat if we wanted to explain the thinking behind our choices.*" There was also a reasonable match between NQ desires and NQ jobs in 2007, with sources confirming a "*good spread of interests this year.*" Upon qualifying, eight out of nine trainees stayed with the firm.

reiki-ing up the past

So why MJ and not, say, one of the big nationals that operate in Birmingham? Because "*there is a sense of warmth and togetherness here,*" explained one source, summing up the views of others. "*You can really tell that the firm has its roots in the Midlands.*" According to some, its reputation for "*being a bit staid*" is still valid, "*but it is doing what it can to change this.*" On the subject of internal communication we were told: "*The firm doesn't want to be seen to be keeping things hush-hush, so they are making an effort to improve things.*" One trainee was invited to a workshop run by the managing partner and head of marketing, focused on "*ways to develop the Martineau Johnson brand.*" The senior partner even has his own blog in which he writes about "*taking all the opportunities we can.*"

The touchy-feelies don't stop there. Fancy a spot of yoga or Reiki? "*During lunch and in some evenings you can make a 15 or 30-minute appointment with one of the secretaries in commercial disputes. She's been doing this for about*" eight months now and is still fully booked up." And that's not all – there's also free fruit. As well as "*the usual apples, oranges and bananas we sometimes get something exotic. Last summer we had pineapple...*" During a recent Wellbeing Week held by the firm, trainees could take advantage of "*massages, blood pressure and cholesterol testing*" and knock back smoothies "*in the break-out areas.*" Law firm? Sounds more like a health spa...

Trainees here don't seem to be too stressed. "*I've not been yelled at or been given horrendous jobs, all of which I was expecting to be par for the course.*" They like the hours, the atmosphere and an open-plan environment where supervisors are less likely to "*let rip and speak without thinking.*"

Socially, MJ's Colmore Square office is in the centre of the legal quarter, so when visiting local bars after work "*you can't move for the suits.*" Membership of the Birmingham Trainee Solicitors Society ensures that young lawyers in the second city know each other well. Three of the ten 2006/07 committee members came from MJ, reflecting the firm's desire to play a prominent role in the organisation. An annual BTSS inter-firm sports competition involves a dozen events ranging from football and netball matches to pub games and Ultimate Frisbee. MJ is not too bad at the footie and netball, "*but we didn't even put in a team for water polo this year.*" You can lead a horse to water...

and finally...

If like some of our interviewees your choice of where to train will be "*mainly a Birmingham decision,*" Martineau Johnson is a good bet. Not only is it one of the oldest firms in the city, it is a good size. Any bigger and you're looking at Wragges or the nationals; any smaller and the name doesn't carry the same weight.

Maxwell Winward LLP

the facts
Location: London
Number of UK partners/solicitors: 21/35
Total number of trainees: 7
Seats: 4x6 months
Alternative seats: Potentially secondments

The product of a 2007 merger between Maxwell Batley and Winward Fearon, this year has been one of many changes for the staff of this newly combined London firm. A change of address, new colleagues, new computers and a wealth of opportunities all lie ahead. We spoke to the firm's trainees, all of whom had come from the Winward side of the equation. For them the most significant change was the wider range of work being conducted.

looking good
Winward Fearon had been plying its trade as a West End construction specialist for over 20 years, servicing major contractors and insurers with such success that, despite its relatively small size, it managed to compete convincingly with the profession's biggest names. City-based Maxwell Batley was formed in 1896 and had developed a strong reputation for real estate (around half its workload) as well as a notable presence in banking, corporate and litigation. It also had some private client lawyers. Over the years, both firms were the subjects of merger and takeover rumours, with any number of other firms mentioned as possible bedfellows. Finally, they found each other and the portents look good for the star-crossed lovers.

To be clear, Maxwell Winward essentially covers five distinct practice areas: real estate, construction, corporate/commercial, litigation and projects. Real estate is by far the largest department and it lays claim to significant clients such as The British Land Company, Coutts, Hermes Real Estate, the Duchy of Lancaster and Stadium Capital Group. Construction law played more of a supportive role at Maxwell Batley, but the Winward Fearon team's array of major clients from Barratt Homes to Hochtief UK and UBS puts it centre stage. With the powers of both firms now combined, there is every indication that the name of Maxwell Winward will rise ever higher in the consciousness of the real estate and construction sectors in particular.

laying foundations
When we interviewed trainees they were still in the final months of the old Winward Fearon training regime, but about to see the system change to one in which four set seats would be offered in construction, real estate, coco/projects and commercial litigation.

Before the merger each firm had a slightly different focus when it came to construction: Maxwell Batley's work was primarily non-contentious, whereas Winward Fearon concentrated more on settling the many disputes that emerge from construction sites. Trainees in the construction seat are now encouraged to try out both types of work before deciding which one to spend most time on. Those who plump for contentious matters may find themselves *"in adjudications almost immediately"* and becoming familiar with the ins and outs of the Technology and Construction Court (TCC), working closely with barristers. Back in the office, a policy that puts all trainees to sit with partners allows them to get their hands on some tasty work, including *"taking witness statements and constantly communicating with adjudicators."* Those more inclined to the non-contentious side of the practice will see *"drafting and contract skills come to the fore."* A trainee might well get a small transaction to lead on, however, *"most of the work is team-based and you'll take a part in large PFI deals, doing proof-reading and that sort of thing."*

Company/commercial and projects are combined as a seat, though in fact the work involved in each aspect is quite different. On the coco side the trainee's role includes a fair amount of company secretarial duties plus a selection of other commercial work, including some employment law. Furthermore, since the firms came together trainees *"now have access to banking and tax partners as well,"* adding variety to the experience in this seat. Another change in this department has been the altered focus of the corporate team – greater emphasis is now placed on AIM and PLUS clients. The projects aspects of the seat entail drawing up performance bonds for PFI/PPP deals. Some trainees got quite excited about the idea of working on international energy projects and helping with *"power stations for the likes of Nigeria and Greece."*

Trainees told us that prior to the merger the property seat essentially amounted to real estate litigation, much of it dealing with *"leasehold enfranchisement on high-end flats in Belgravia,"* frequently acting for the tenants and aiding them in their efforts to collectively buy shares in their buildings. With the solid real estate practice brought to the merger by Maxwell Batley, things are set to change in this seat and trainees will have a much more standard experience... not that we should necessarily call the team's excellent work standard. Its clientele includes leading pension funds, institutional investors, banks, blue-chip property companies, developers, private investors and corporate occupiers. The team also has overseas investment clients, particularly from Scandinavia and South Africa. Among the deals completed by the lawyers lately are the creation of a massive £500m property fund for Hermes Real Estate Investment Management and the regeneration of the area around the former Arsenal stadium for new client Stadium Capital Group.

The commercial litigation seat is the new one for trainees, and while none had completed this assignment by the time we interviewed them, in order to gain some sense of what might be expected we can look at their contentious property experiences. On this aspect of their training, one told us of *"sitting in on a two-week trial at the Lands Tribunal behind a QC, which was fantastic."* By all accounts the work was *"pretty full-on,"* not least because of the *"court deadlines looming on your own files."* Naturally the subject matter covered in the commercial litigation seat will be much wider, and it looks as if there should be plenty to see. There have been some fascinating cases keeping the former Maxwell Batley litigators busy lately. How about a league football club's £12m dispute over its ground and the defence of a Royal Society against allegations of conspiracy.

eastward bound

It's too early for us to pass judgment on the culture of the new firm; what we do know is that the hours sound pretty reasonable and our interviewees were rarely in the office later than 7pm. One commented: *"I have stayed as late as 9pm perhaps a dozen times over two years, though I have never worked at the weekend."* This looks likely to remain the case as *"despite the firm being ambitious, everyone is insisting that the work-life balance remain the way it is."* We did note our interviewees' sadness at the prospect of leaving the West End for a new office at Ludgate Hill. At the same time the idea of a swanky new office is the cause of great excitement and gathering the whole firm together is seen as a vital step in ensuring that the two halves integrate. Our interviewees expected the firm *"to step up a gear when it moves closer to the City,"* though nobody

You want the best
And so do we

Making the right choice for your future career may take time. You'll need to weigh up the options, and get the real flavour of the firm you want to join.

Mayer, Brown, Rowe & Maw is one of the largest international legal practices in the world and given our ambitious growth plans there's plenty of opportunity for the best to share in our success.

For more information on the opportunities available and to apply on-line, please visit our website: www.mayerbrownrowe.com/london/careers/gradrecruit

Further enquiries should be made to: Maxine Goodlet, Graduate Recruitment Manager. Tel: 020 7248 4282 Email: graduaterecruitment@mayerbrownrowe.com

MAYER
BROWN
ROWE
& MAW

www.mayerbrownrowe.com

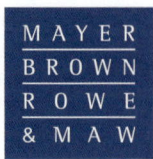

BERLIN • BRUSSELS • CHARLOTTE • CHICAGO • COLOGNE • FRANKFURT • HONG KONG • HOUSTON • LONDON • LOS ANGELES • NEW YORK • PALO ALTO • PARIS • WASHINGTON DC

Mayer, Brown, Rowe & Maw is a combination of two limited liability partnerships, each named Mayer, Brown, Rowe and Maw LLP, one incorporated in England and one established in Illinois, USA.

wanted to lose *"the relaxed atmosphere and close relationships with clients"* that have developed so successfully up to this point. One thing seems clear: *"The increased size means the firm can now take on bigger work that we might have had to turn down before."* As one trainee succinctly put it: *"It is an exciting time for the firm, I wouldn't want to be anywhere else."* In 2007, both qualifiers stayed, one going into construction, the other into coco.

It sounds as if the social committee is up to the job of finding a new local bar after the office move. It has plenty of experience at organising karaoke and darts, bowling, rounders in the park and skating at Somerset House, which means that staff are rarely at a loose end. *"There is usually someone to go for a drink with on a Friday,"* confirmed a trainee. Of course, office Christmas parties can be a real eye-opener and we find it amusing that neither of the old firms quite know what to expect of the other. Winward Fearon's Christmas parties always used to be themed. One party had a Cluedo theme; staff dressed up as characters and even got the chance to 'murder' one of the partners.

and finally...

Maxwell Winward likes its trainees to be *"commercially minded"* and ideally have experience of the office environment. It is going to increase its intake to four people a year and hopes that whoever it recruits will be the sort who is quickly *"up and running, answering calls from clients rather than spending three days in a basement researching something."* If that sounds like you, and you've a hunch that you'd be interested in the very practical areas of law on which Maxwell Winward focuses, then the firm is one to consider seriously.

Mayer Brown

the facts

Location: London
Number of UK partners/solicitors: 106/176
Total number of trainees: 64
Seats: 4x6 months
Alternative seats: Overseas seats, secondments
Extras: Pro bono – RCJ CAB, Toynbee Hall Legal Advice Centre, Liberty, LawWorks; language training

In 2007 Mayer Brown Rowe & Maw announced that it was abbreviating its name to Mayer Brown. It also announced that annual turnover had smashed through the $1bn mark. So, it's just another US giant that's overcharging, overpaid, overworking and over here, right? Not quite...

trousers yes, pants no

With more than 1,500 lawyers in 16 offices in six countries (including a newly opened Hong Kong branch), various international alliances and that calculator-defying turnover figure, it might seem logical to conclude that MB has got its maths perfectly figured. However, a new management team of three – including Londoner Paul Maher – reckons the sum of the firm's parts doesn't add up profitably enough and they've got a plan. In essence it hinges on doubling the size and revenue of the New York office, ambitious targets for improving worldwide revenue even further and the introduction of a UK-originated remuneration model linked to overall profitability rather than rewarding individual performance. Make no mistake: the team is not being overly dainty with its proposals. It announced an almost unprecedented cull of 45 equity partners in 2007, mainly from the firm's traditional core of litigation and with the largest number departing from MB's Chicago homeland.

Given that many UK arms of US firms are the

weedy sibling of a Stateside big brother pulling all the strings, the leverage of MB London might seem unusual. It dates back to the 2002 merger of UK all-rounder Rowe & Maw and Chicago playa Mayer Brown & Platt (which had a small finance law team here in Blighty). *"America categorically doesn't wear the trousers – London is a strong base,"* asserted one source. The evidence for this is all around: *"Although we're always copied into e-mails from the States," "our HR and admin functions are here onsite"* and culturally speaking *"we feel like a big City firm."* London's strength is also explained by impressive financial performance – turnover up by 22% to £96m in the past year.

what's the big deal?

Long associated with broad commercial practice, MB London performs well across multiple disciplines and represents household-name clients like AstraZeneca, BP, Reuters, The Football League, Motorola, EMI, Selfridges, Bank of America and Cable & Wireless. Most recently, our interviewees have been talking about *"big targets in terms of us growing and improving,"* which in turn translates into *"focus on the corporate and finance practices,"* with the office aiming to double turnover and boost average equity partner profits from £650,000 to £800,000 or even £1m within three years. Finance lawyers already advise Citibank, Lehman Brothers and JPMorgan, as well as being on the European panels for ABN AMRO, ING Group and Nationwide, so *"plans to grow enormously and move into hedge funds work"* seem feasible. A *"recruitment drive"* has already seen the hire of a structured securities specialist from French firm Gide Loyrette Nouel. Meanwhile the corporate team is *"aiming to increase turnover"* on the back of high-profile deals like Cambridge Antibody Technology's £702m disposal to AstraZeneca and ICI's £410m competitive auction sale of Uniqema. Lawyers have also won new mandates from clients such as

Macquarie Bank and Starwood Capital. Giving yet more credence to the idea of there being a *"change in focus,"* the well-regarded (and always popular with trainees) public law team has been dispatched to Beachcroft.

So, where will these grand plans leave future trainees? Well, the growing emphasis on corporate and finance means seats in these areas are likely to become more central to the training scheme, so we'll begin our tour of the London office with the transactional seats. Corporate is currently the only compulsory element in the four-seat scheme, and here trainees experience *"M&A, private equity, AIM listings and IPOs,"* usually assisting on *"large-scale transactions."* The size of larger deals can be problematic, because *"even if you're working on something interesting like a big ICI deal, in general it's difficult to get to grips with what's going on beyond your discrete bits of research and drafting."* One realistic source observed how *"seeing large deals for three months or more is interesting, and vital, but you couldn't pretend the work was challenging."* Trainees' hours are long at times, so *"leaving at 3am is not uncommon"* and there is a definite expectation that *"you search for work if you haven't already got it... I left at 6pm for a few weeks and was spoken to about it."* That said, *"people are good about you being flexible with hours if you've slogged your guts out one week,"* and working with a *"great group"* makes late nights *"more bearable,"* as do free meals and taxis home.

Finance seats offer the same perks and troughs, but having *"previously had a similar reputation for not delegating interesting enough work to trainees,"* the team has *"turned it right around."* Finance transactions are made more accessible because *"if, say, you're managing the conditions precedent they'll let you take charge of it and run it yourself."* Similarly, *"if a partner's drafted the final documentation, you'll be able to take responsibility for it going forward."* Sources relished this kind of exposure, as well as the atmosphere in what is described as a *"very young, aggressive and expanding"* team.

a bite of the apple?

Time spent in another of MB's mainstays – commercial dispute resolution – can sometimes bring an equally *"small degree of responsibility."* This is perhaps unsurprising given that the firm handles disputes worth billions of pounds, including the defence of EMI against the Beatles' record label Apple in a claim regarding allegedly underpaid worldwide royalties, advising in relation to the Sudan 1 food dye scare (one the largest ever product recalls) and multimillion-pound claims for the likes of GE, Persimmon Homes and BASF. At least the perils of *"mindless bundling"* can at times be relieved by *"drafting and liaising with counsel."* More popular are stints in other contentious seats like insurance and reinsurance litigation or construction litigation. Working from a smaller office at Lloyd's, right in the heart of London's insurance market, the former allows trainees *"close involvement in matters like a big negligence case involving a City law firm"* and *"a good mix of tasks, with a marked degree of responsibility."* Here, as in construction lit, the hours are shorter (*"9am to 7-7.30pm"*), but with *"the expectation you work incredibly hard while you're there, so it can be a baptism of fire as a first seat."* Assisting on *"massive arbitrations for Jordanian construction companies or Saudi oil companies"* in construction lit finds a counterbalance in *"running your own smaller, bog-standard subcontractor disputes."*

Other seats rating highly with trainees include pensions (*"quite varied and academic as a subject area; I've done drafting and research for corporate-type work"*), employment (*"almost like working in a different firm," "the biggest client is the corporate department so there's a lot of admin work, but I did get to draft smaller agreements"*) and real estate, (*"you're given small matters to run with, manage and be the primary contact point for the client"*). Crossover with the finance team on real estate finance deals means grunt work isn't out of the question in this last seat, but supervisors were praised for *"having gone on courses to learn how to train us properly."* The remaining options are international arbitration, IP, tax, EU/competition and environmental law, but there is also the ready possibility of taking one of several client secondments. Usually taken only after a corporate seat has been completed, client destinations include Unilever, Reuters, AstraZeneca, EMI, Cargill, ICI, Lehman Brothers and Brussels-based client Cerestar. The experience was universally praised: *"It was great to see what they think of lawyers and get to understand that they'd maybe prefer a good draft late than a sketchy draft on time,"* concluded one source. That said, beware the less popular National Starch seat in Slough, which – probably because of its location – almost always ends up receiving *"someone chosen forcibly by HR."*

Currently overseas seats are restricted to Brussels for competition law and one or two finance seats in Chicago. Other options might arise in time given that the firm is increasing its emphasis on international secondments for qualified lawyers. Until now, apart from a group trip to Chicago for new qualifiers, MB associates have tended to stay in one office. A new, more internationalist philosophy will encourage lawyers to move around more, so the prospects for NQ travel look better than ever.

not so easy riders

Our sources say MB is now *"a fairly aggressive-thinking firm rather than the mid-sized lifestyle firm many of us applied to."* To their minds the appealing equation of *"great City work with magic circle pay, but without the magic circle hours"* is *"just not there anymore."* And for all that *"you get half days off if you've worked a hard stint,"* the norm is *"to be seriously busy with long hours all the* time." Yet they were just as quick to point out the advantages of an *"exciting"* evolution and *"big future plans,"* telling us these have created *"good morale within departments"* and brought *"a lot of opportunities and better work."* We're particularly indebted to the interviewee who summed up the likely appeal of the firm at the moment as this: *"If a candidate wants corporate or finance work, they're going to find an atmosphere like or aspiring to be like a cross between the magic circle and a well-developed US boutique in those teams. But they'll still get the medium-sized, generalist atmosphere in smaller teams like real estate, pensions or employment, because the work there is standalone and the departments are well established."*

The sense of there being two aspects to the firm's personality also cropped up when we tried to identify an MB type. *"I would have said it was defined by people being different and down to earth, but our culture is definitely changing,"* we heard; *"it's almost as if the firm has decided to compete with magic circle firms for more corporate-style personalities."* Whether or not they are right, the 2007 retention figures showed that 18 of the 28 qualifiers took NQ positions with the firm, going into corporate, finance, real estate, construction, environment and employment.

MB's offices are a touch cramped, so plans are afoot for a move into a new home at 201 Bishopsgate in early 2009. In the meantime, the lack of a canteen is made up for by *"trolleys that do the rounds"* and life is generally made happier by dress down Fridays and a more-relaxed dress code in the summer months. It sounds as if the firm abounds with *"motivated, outgoing individuals who communicate clearly and who you're happy to share a drink with at the end of the week in The Evangelist."* Departments tend to arrange events and quarterly firm-wide socials are well attended. *"One month they might hire out the Corney & Barrow,"* another it might be *"the annual corporate department against the rest of*

firm football match with drinks afterwards." There are enthusiastic football, squash, tennis and netball teams, and trainees have been known to arrange group trips to foreign parts, most recently Brussels and Dublin.

and finally...
Think carefully about Mayer Brown's aspirations to ramp up its corporate and finance offerings. It still offers a breadth of well-defined seat options, and in its smaller departments there are echoes of the old mid-sized firm it once was in London, but effectively this is now a hybrid firm that will best suit applicants who can adapt easily to any environment.

McDermott Will & Emery UK LLP

the facts
Location: London
Number of UK partners/solicitors: 29/51
Total number of trainees: 6
Seats: 4x6 months
Alternative seats: Brussels, secondments
Extras: Pro bono – eg Amnesty International

Chicago, home of Al Capone and Oprah Winfrey, is a metropolis of over three million people. But it's also the capital of the rural Midwest and takes a more low-key approach to things than its coastal sisters, New York and Los Angeles. It's a city at ease with itself. Not unlike one of its favourite legal sons, McDermott Will & Emery.

you win some, you lose some
Not that the firm lacks ambition. One of the USA's top-20 firms by turnover, MWE has come a long way since its foundation in 1934. It now boasts over 1,000 lawyers across the States and in Germany, Italy, Belgium, China and, of course, London. The UK office opened in 1998, at a time

when many American firms crossed over the pond. Since then it's grown slowly but steadily. Typical of its peers, it offers *"the chance to work on major matters but in a smaller, more personal environment than at a magic circle firm,"* and this was the central attraction for the trainees to whom we spoke.

But what exactly sets MWE apart from its US brethren in London? While most have sought to develop London business by focusing on corporate and finance transactions, MWE London has, at times, been led by its employment and IP teams and can even at this stage of its development be viewed as a small all-rounder. The firm is no slouch in the transactional arena – its flagship corporate achievement last year was advising on all aspects of the start-up of Paternoster, the first life insurer to be launched in the UK for 30 years. This start-up secured £500m of equity financing from a consortium of investors led by Deutsche Bank and Eton Park International. The capital markets group advises issuers and underwriters/brokers/nominated advisers in respect of debt and equity fundraisings. On the equity side, the focus is on the higher end of the AIM market (£50m market capitalisation and above) and on mid-market Official List transactions. On the debt side, MWE has been involved in a number of capital market transactions for US investment banks. The point to make is that it is just as good at litigation, competition law, projects, tax, employment and IP.

In the past year the firm has been buffeted somewhat by partner departures: employment star Fraser Younson jumped ship to Berwin Leighton Paisner and litigation head John Reynolds headed for American rival White & Case. Then, in January 2007, the office's entire three-partner pensions team jumped ship to K&L Gates. The firm has come back with some impressive hires, including finance partner Georgia Quenby from Nabarro and project finance lawyer Cam Brockie from Simmons & Simmons. Turbulent times, but our trainees didn't exactly seem like rats preparing to leave a sinking ship. *"People have left, but more have arrived,"* noted one. *"There's a whole new securitisation department, for example. It feels like we're still growing fast and doing phenomenally well."* True enough, even after the departures, the office is around the same size as it was, and more hires are planned.

more chelsea than chicago

Trainees are normally supervised by a senior associate and *"take work from all over the department, sometimes even other departments."* Usually working as part of a tight team with an associate and a partner, they have a good deal of attention lavished on them. *"I was eased into my first seat with proof-reading and the like,"* one told us; *"but as it progressed I got more and more interesting opportunities. Attending client meetings and helping write articles, which is where a lot of the actual law comes in."* Not that trainees only see the technical side: we heard of one who'd attended a deal completion alone. *"They wouldn't send you into a situation you weren't ready for,"* they assured us. Another key role is co-ordinating conditions precedent on transactions. It's *"a good way to track a deal from start to finish,"* and *"because you're working on that deal, lots of other miscellaneous tasks can come up and add some variety."* Grunt work seemed limited: although one trainee admitted: *"I have no problem with being given responsibility one minute and photocopying the next."* Heavy loads can be dumped on support staff: *"I have a good relationship with the document centre,"* one trainee observed.

Spend time in the dispute resolution litigation group and you could be helping defend financial institutions against investigation by the Financial Services Authority or assisting Chelsea FC with a copyright dispute. *"We get the chance to work on both litigation and arbitration, which not all firms* give you," said one. Working directly for a partner is common – "*I essentially took on an associate role,*" said one source. "*I've been with clients to see the FSA, drafted letters and so on... they'll give you as much responsibility as you can take, and with smaller matters, such as pro bono cases for example, they just let you run with things.*" Pro bono is taken seriously: "*Everyone does it and it counts towards your billable hours, so you can give it as much priority as the rest of your work.*"

A contentious seat is compulsory for all, and those who don't try commercial dispute resolution can sample IP or employment. Apart from that, things are pretty flexible and we even heard of two final-seat trainees swapping with each other half way through to produce two three-month seats. The fact there are so few trainees means most people's preferences can be accommodated. Until now we would have said that overseas postings were conspicuous by their absence. A new seat has now opened up in Brussels, and those who miss out can at least look forward to the fact that "*there are plenty of chances to go abroad after qualification when you're more valuable.*" Client secondments to the likes of Barclays Capital are there for anyone with a burning desire to see life beyond MWE London.

mountaineering

Working for several different people can be good, but it can also be a ticket to overwork. Our interviewees seemed unfazed, perhaps because standard trainee hours tend to be around 9.30am to 7pm. At busy times, of course, standards go out the window – all-nighters aren't unheard of, but they won't necessarily be as unpleasant as they might seem: "*I came home the next morning,*" said one source of her first all-nighter, "*and everyone asked me if I was OK. But I felt like I'd climbed a mountain! You feel like you're really achieving something to finish the deal.*" Nevertheless, working for several people does put the onus on

trainees to manage their own workload. "*It helps to be entrepreneurial,*" one suggested. "*Because the contract isn't that structured, you have to grasp the opportunities when they present themselves. But equally you have to know when to say no – and they do take no for an answer. Partners appreciate you learning to juggle priorities.*" In general, our sources had found their supervisors "*proactive*" and even "*lovely.*" Those who'd been allocated partners as supervisors had found them a little harder to get hold of for feedback, but "*if you can pin somebody down they'll always find five minutes to talk.*" Formal appraisals at the middle and end of seats – "*both over lunch*" – were described as "*detailed and really helpful.*"

Despite the lack of overseas seats, trainees "*do feel very much part of a larger, international firm.*" "*There's an induction week in Chicago when you first start, which really gives you a perspective on what you're joining.*" Once back home, the Londoners link up with Chicago for live video training and "*you notice in the early afternoon when America wakes up because the e-mails come pouring in.*" Should you acquire a taste for American accents, "*there are always US lawyers about the office and senior partners from Chicago visit often.*" If that sounds like Big Brother watching, we're assured that London has its independence and "*it doesn't feel like every decision needs to go to Chicago.*"

jerk-free zone

Those trainees seeking an intimate and rewarding atmosphere are unlikely to be disappointed with MWE London. "*I think we must have some sort of no-jerk HR policy,*" one source remarked. "*Even when you work really hard, it's noted and appreciated. You never feel like you're just a hamster in a wheel.*" There naturally isn't the thriving trainee social scene you get at larger firms, and mostly socialising takes place with other colleagues. "*There is an event once a month; for example, there's a barbecue coming up which should be good.*"

And everybody goes, from the secretaries up to the top partners." Best of all are the quiz nights, "sometimes held in a nearby pub, sometimes in the office."

So what sort of person makes MWE their home? "They try to recruit people who show initiative, often people who've done more than just the LPC since college," one trainee commented. It's certainly not an easy process getting in: the firm wants to see your CV before even sending you an application form and those who do get short listed then face a partner interview and a two-hour exercise. "The fact that the process was so rigorous made me want to get in more. I could tell the firm was serious about its training scheme," said one source. Indeed it must be: MWE has a track record of retaining all of its qualifiers, and did so again in 2007 when all three took jobs.

and finally...

McDermott Will & Emery treats its trainees like full team members from day one. If that sounds like your cup of coffee, you might want to give this Chicago institution a whirl, but keep a watch on the legal press over the next year, just in case the partner shuffling continues.

McGrigors LLP

the facts

Location: London, Edinburgh, Glasgow, Aberdeen, Belfast
Number of UK partners/solicitors: 78/218
Total number of trainees: 27 in London
Seats: 4x6 months
Alternative seats: Glasgow, Edinburgh, Falklands, secondments
Extras: Pro bono – legal advice clinic in Hackney

Major Scottish firm McGrigors dates back over 200 years and north of the border it is in the premier league of law firms. Its English practice is a relatively recent development and came alive when it embarked on what we might call its KLegal Adventure.

kwho?

It's worth rewinding the tape six years or so. Back then, McGrigors, along with its major rivals, wanted in on the London market. In 2002 the firm saw an opportunity it couldn't ignore. The dramatic collapse of Enron led to a change in attitudes towards allowing accountancy firms to work in conjunction with legal firms to provide joint services to clients. KLegal, the legal arm of global accountancy practice KPMG, needed a lifeline as its parent lost its appetite for the law. McGrigors stepped in to adopt it. It was an astute move giving the Scottish firm access to an established legal practice in a vital international business hub.

The merger meant KLegal trainees got a different deal from the one they'd bargained for, and in the immediate aftermath we did hear moans about this. These days the KLegal Adventure is ancient history for recruits: "It didn't even cross my mind, particularly when I arrived. It's almost as if people are tired of talking about it." So why bring it up, you ask. Because the legacy of the merger – a strong link to KMPG – is still very much alive and kicking. "Our history explains why KPMG is such a massive client for McGrigors; there isn't one department where we don't do work for them." McGrigors benefits enormously from this relationship, most notably through valuable instructions and client referrals, particularly in tax litigation, corporate and employment.

Although important, KPMG is by no means the only blue-chip client on the firm's roster. BP, RBS, O$_2$, Ministry of Defence, Royal Mail and Lloyds TSB are just some of the other major names. In its core areas of corporate, banking and real estate, the London office has made a few headlines. For example, it recently beat Lovells to

an eye-catching M&A mandate from retail entrepreneur Michael Cannon on the £155m sale of West Country pub chain Eldridge Pope to rival Marstons. The real estate team is working exclusively with O_2 on the roll-out of the infrastructure of its mobile network in London and the South East, while the corporate team acted on 15 AIM listings in 2006, raising an aggregate £365m. The tax litigators have been busy working alongside other City firms to represent a number of clients in a successful group litigation seeking to recover money wrongly paid to HMRC through advanced corporation tax.

Leaving aside speculation in the legal press about another merger (stemming from the fact that McGrigors had some work referred to it by Eversheds), trainees divulged how *"it's safe to say the London office will carry on expanding."* There have certainly been changes in the past year. *"New people have joined and old people have left – it feels like it has been quite fluid."* While this had been *"unsettling"* for some, most trainees had taken it in their stride, confident that McGrigors is dedicated to getting its London office on the map. *"The office is a priority in terms of the future and the growth of the firm,"* concluded one source. Another already saw results: *"It is making a name for itself and it doesn't just feel like a tag on."* Those who had been up to Scotland for a seat, however, could see the London branch still has some way to go. *"When you're in a Scottish office, you really feel like you are part of a firm that is seen as one of the best. It's only once you go up there that you realise how important the firm is, and in London you don't always feel like you're part of that."* Another agreed: *"It's been difficult for the London office; we really have to sell ourselves down here. But we are making progress. I did a careers fair in my first year and then again this year, and far more people recognise the name now."*

peaks and troughs

One of your four seats will be corporate(ish) and one will be contentious. Within these guidelines, however, there is scope for variation, so banking could count as corporate, for example, and contentious seats exist in construction, tax litigation and employment, as well as mainstream dispute resolution. Before trainees start at the firm they attend an early induction in May, at which *"they give you a form to fill in and you put three* [seat] *preferences down."* Do most people get what they asked for? *"Actually I think they do. No one has been screaming at any rate. Inevitably not everyone gets their first choice, but the firm is good at making sure you'll get the next seat that you want."*

Corporate trainees draft minor documentation, sit in on conference calls, attend client meetings, project manage and liaise with lawyers in other jurisdictions. *"Dull admin work is kept to a minimum – I had hardly any photocopying or due diligence,"* reported one satisfied source. The longest hours are found here, *"but people make sure you don't have to stay unless you're really busy. I usually finished at 7pm."* Typically there are peaks and troughs: *"When I was there the department was incredibly busy and it was quite daunting,"* said one trainee. *"Looking back though, I realise it means I can now cope with absolutely anything that gets thrown at me."* Unfortunately when the department is relatively quiet, trainees may not get to do any public company work. *"But then my working hours were brilliant – you can't have it all."*

The substantial real estate team comprises *"about 40 people,"* many of whom are devoted to client O_2. Trainees run their own files and assist on bigger matters. *"We happened to have a huge project on when I joined the team, so it was manically busy. I had to compile a lot of information from various fee earners, chase up the different parties and monitor searches from the Land Registry."* Trainees draft certificates of title, assist with due diligence and complete quite a lot of Land Registry forms. Quite boring work then. *"No, sometimes I almost wish there had been a bit more photocopying to do."*

Employment is *"probably the department that has grown the most"* and, here, trainees *"get more responsibility than they would elsewhere."* Attending client meetings on a weekly basis ensures a steady flow of files comes your way, not to mention the instructions flowing in from KPMG. *"There's a lot of tribunal work and letters of advice to clients."* In quieter moments trainees compile client bulletins: *"We had to monitor lots of articles and draft punchy bulletin notices on a weekly basis. It meant that we were always bang up to date, but it did get a bit tiring."* Our sources didn't have a bad word to say about the dispute resolution experience. Once settled in, trainees might even get a file of their own. *"Granted it will just be a county court matter, but you get decent autonomy which is brilliant."* In the projects seat, *"the team tries to get you involved, but with the department getting such major work it's difficult for trainees to play a big part."* Keep in mind that on the PFI side of things it's quite document heavy and *"pulling together tenders for new work is a traditional trainee job."* Seeing a project in its final stages can be extremely satisfying, despite the last week involving *"ridiculously long hours."*

city break

London trainees are encouraged to spend a seat in Edinburgh or Glasgow. The firm pays for flights, a baggage courier service and rent, and it continues to pay a London wage for the duration. *"The fact that you can save a lot of money is a big incentive,"* explained a source. *"If you're married, for instance, or you have a mortgage, then the firm is perfectly fine with that. Nobody is forced to go."* Those who do have good cause to stay in London should make this clear at the outset because several trainees were *"completely shocked"* to discover they were due in Scotland for their first seat. *"I hadn't realised that was a possibility,"* admitted one. All our sources thought their Scottish seats were *"brilliant – when I look back, it was so good to get to know the other offices and to live in a different city."* Not to mention the shorter hours. *"It's definitely more relaxed up there,"* they told us. It sounds as if the Scottish trainees are into sport in a big way: *"Tonight I'm playing hockey and tomorrow it's rugby. There's something on about four times a week and we usually get involved."* Pack appropriately, warned one interviewee: *"It rained pretty much every day I was there."*

Having recently acquired the oil and gas team from Aberdeen firm Ledingham Chalmers, McGrigors also landed a couple of satellite offices abroad. Last year we scoffed that it seemed unlikely McGrigors would offer a seat in its little Falklands office anytime soon. Boy, were we wrong. *"There were quite a few applicants for it and one of us is out there now. She's having a wonderful time."* Clients include the Falkland Islands Tourist Board and various fishing and shipping companies, which give a strong international element to the work as the shipping clients often have interests in South America. Some trainees saw the attraction: *"You get to do a whole range of work that you wouldn't be able to in any other office."* Others didn't: *"Personally I can't see myself working alongside penguins."* As yet, there is no seat on offer in the Azerbaijan satellite office, and we'll make no predictions on that one! If you don't fancy leaving London, there are secondments on offer to clients such as O_2 in Slough, KPMG and BP.

With offices right above All Bar One, we weren't surprised to learn *"you can walk in on any day and find someone there."* The trainee group describes itself as *"highly social"* – possibly related to the fact that *"partners are pretty good at buying the drinks."* There are themed socials every now and then – *"for St. George's*

Day, St. Patrick's Day, a big Burns Night supper and, of course, the Christmas party." Ah yes, the Christmas party... "I would tell you about it, but I'm afraid I was far too drunk to remember anything," confessed one trainee. Although full firm-wide events are rare, the various departments organise away-days for staff in every office. "One team went to Southampton for a day of sailing, and they flew everyone in the Scottish team down. Another department had a day in Edinburgh, which included a tour of the parliament." Sadly, "the Falklands guys never get invited." Fitness freaks can rest assured that "there's always stuff going on" and can take their pick of football, cricket, swimming, mountain biking and even decathlon competitions.

and finally...
McGrigors seems partial to people who have taken a few years off to travel or work in industry. "I'd say the firm sees extra experience as an asset. They like people with confidence, people who are perhaps a little more mature and who don't mind being thrown in at the deep end." This is not to say youngsters should be put off and there are trainees who have come straight through uni and law school. In 2007 eight of the 11 London qualifiers took jobs with the firm.

Memery Crystal LLP

the facts
Location: London
Number of UK partners/solicitors: 21/42
Total number of trainees: 10
Seats: 4x6 months
Alternative seats: None

One year shy of its 30th birthday, Memery Crystal, formed in 1978, was the brainchild of John Memery and Peter Crystal (who recently stepped down as senior partner). Placing corporate at its nucleus, it has more latterly become a specialist in AIM and is consistently cited as one of the market leaders in that area.

AIMing to be the best
One trainee had some words of advice for potential applicants: "I wasn't aware how centred it is on AIM work; it is something you do need to be aware of." Memery Crystal boasts a client portfolio which includes Accuma Group, City of London Investment Group and Ashcourt Holdings, and it handles many deals for investment bank and broker Seymour Pierce. In M&A the firm is upping the ante, and although many of the deals it works on stem from its AIM practice, it has advised on deals such as RAK Petroleum's £208m acquisition of Gulf Keystone Petroleum. Our sources were adamant that this is no place for anyone who wouldn't enjoy corporate, as it accounts for 35% of the turnover. "The firm is corporate-focused, there is no getting away from it. If you do any research, you'll be aware of its main strengths."

Occasionally there may be a chance to split a seat between two teams, but usually trainees will shift seats four times, spending six months in a department or team. They are placed in their first two seats, have "slightly more choice for the third" and then the fourth seat is very much within their control. "Everyone has got their top choice," confirmed one source. The fact that trainees' views on the process of seat allocation is mixed seems to have filtered back to the powers that be, and we're told: "It is an area the firm is trying to improve; it's trying to address the fact that historically you weren't given much choice."

Of course, corporate is a dead cert. Here trainees are given "responsibility right from the start – it's a good challenge and you feel lucky to be doing what you are doing." So what exactly were they doing? Drafting board minutes and due diligence reports seemed to feature in most of the trainees' schedules, as well as putting together data rooms and helping co-ordinate completions. Inevitably AIM listings involve verification exercises: *"This can be a bit tedious, but someone has to do it and it is usually the trainees."* Typically the hours are *"quite long"* and by that our sources meant *"9am till about 7ish, sometimes a lot later depending on how far the deal was progressing."* In its favour, *"it's a department where everyone gets on well and you can have a laugh."* Some trainees found the experience exhilarating but also perplexing at the same time. *"Corporate is such a massive group – you get involved in one transaction and you come out at the end of it and then you get involved in something else you have no idea about, so you feel you are back at the beginning again."* Seeing the process through to the end makes all the difference. Said one source: *"I was lucky enough to be there from the moment the client met the partner to the day it went to the stock exchange."*

easy does it

Apart from corporate, what does an MC training contract offer? Property is the firm's second-largest department. Described as *"a lot more relaxed,"* the group has *"a few fairly big clients which keep everyone busy most of the year round."* We guess our sources were referring to the likes of ASDA Wal-mart, Homebase, Argos, Carpetright and the Department for Education and Skills. Trainees busy themselves with a variety of tasks, including drafting leases and title reports and attending client meetings. On the property litigation side the work involves preparing instructions to counsel and witness statements. Some very satisfied trainees told us how they were allowed to run their own files for smaller cases. To clarify, there are small MC offices in Belfast and Dublin and these work closely with the property department in Lon-

don. Although no seats are offered there, trainees do sometimes fly over for meetings.

A spell in the mainstream commercial dispute resolution department might also involve IP matters, not least the defence of companies embroiled in trade mark disputes with easyGroup. Recently the firm has taken on the orange giant in relation to easynet (owned by BSkyB), easyart and easypizza. Recruits described their time as *"enjoyable"* and recounted that it is a seat where there is *"lots of exposure to clients."* Trainees sitting with the non-contentious IP lawyers will often divide their time between this group and the corporate department. As you might expect, the employment team is popular, and there the lawyers work for both employers and employees. They have some good clients too, among them Universal Pictures, Dorsey & Whitney, Norddeutschelandesbank and Sage Print.

value added

Trainees did seem a bit put out with the short notice they got prior to seat changes; however, the firm is trying to make changes to the system and give trainees advance warning of where they'll be sat next. On the subject of supervision, trainees were very positive. They always share an office with their supervisor, but their work can come from several fee earners. *"You get work from lots of people, especially when it's all hands to the pump"* but you *"take on what you are able to cope with and then after that the partners do their best to protect you,"* said one contented trainee. Moreover, *"everyone is incredibly open; if you have any questions you don't feel intimidated asking."*

The appraisal system comprises a mid-seat review and another at the end of each seat. The three-month review was a bit of a bugbear for some people: *"The system isn't particularly well-adhered to; it is quite relaxed and you don't always get the feedback you should be given. It is better to know halfway through a seat if there's any area in* which you're not performing." One trainee felt they had been "wondering for quite a while whether I was doing a good job or not." Another suggested that supervisors were "good at overseeing you, but they don't have time for feedback." Not everyone had a problem though, and some thought the system worked fine "as long as you're given feedback while you're doing your work." Again trainees were quick to tell us that this matter has been brought to the attention of partners, who are "working on it... they have noted that some of them have been lax."

We asked trainees where they think Memery Crystal is headed. They told us of a push to "make us more modern, with a view to becoming a bigger firm." A new executive board has replaced the former position of senior partner and, spurred on by this, the firm has embarked on a mission to discover the values underlying its business. This culminated in a conference for all staff, held at the Café Royale. The values that emerged centre on MC lawyers being "trusted business advisers" who deal with clients in such a way as to "achieve their commercial goal" while getting people to maintain "individuality and personal responsibility and a friendly, supportive approach." At the same time, the firm wants to grow and a "reshuffle" at its Holborn office has been completed to allow this. The process of change has also involved bringing in consultants to look at things like "improving communication between various departments." Sometimes the changes have been easy to effect: trainees now have access to their time recording reports, something which our sources thoroughly approved of. "We used to operate in a vacuum, now we are going to get a certain level of access [to this information]." Overall, our interviewees felt they were kept in the loop regarding the new developments: "An internal bulletin called The Memo keeps everyone updated and brings a community feel to the office."

grease is the word

One of the points which emerged from the values conference was a "need to do a bit more on the social front." In light of this the previously disbanded social committee has been resurrected and is now looking to organise a variety of events. The Christmas party, normally held at a posh venue in Knightsbridge, sounds like a lively event. Staff are given an extra day off for Christmas shopping, and although it can be taken at any time in December, "if you're sensible, you take it the day after the party." Throughout the year there are monthly drinks in the boardroom and "literally every Friday a group goes to the pub." Favourite haunts include The Cittie of Yorke, The Seven Stars and The Blue Anchor. Trainees also talked about "Friday lunchtime fry-ups to celebrate the end of the week."

Every one of the MC trainees we spoke to was keen to emphasise the firm's warmth of character. "You couldn't really ask for a friendlier firm, it struck me as soon as I walked through the door," said one. "People look out for one another," we heard from someone else. As such, anyone who is "quite stiff and can't mix within a group" wouldn't get on so well here. Typical of firms of this size, MC looks for "outgoing and personable" candidates who will be totally at home "mixing with clients."

and finally...

A love of all things corporate will stand you in good stead at this ambitious firm. If you can handle the pressures and deadlines that inevitably accompany this kind of work, then Memery Crystal is a great option if you also want to train at a smaller mid-sized City firm. Four of the five qualifiers stayed on in 2007.

Michelmores LLP

the facts
Location: Exeter, Sidmouth, London
Number of UK partners/solicitors: 31/62
Total number of trainees: 11
Seats: 4x6 months
Alternative seats: None

Having already paddled in the London legal pond, South West stalwart Michelmores has gamely shed its parochial trunks and aims to make a big splash in the increasingly interesting Devon, Somerset and Cornwall markets. A commercial firm with a well-established private client practice, Michelmores can offer a broad training and very scenic surrounds.

michelmoreish
Senior partner Will Michelmore's great-grandfather established the firm in 1887. After 120 years in pretty much the same building in Exeter city centre, in 2005 the firm moved out from under the shadow of the Cathedral to a business park just outside the city. The same year saw the launch of the firm's London office. Michelmores is going great guns, with turnover up almost 20% in 2007 and a steady stream of partners recruited from City and large national firms. One of the most notable recent hires was TLT's former head of financial services regulation Philip Ryley, who joined in late 2006 to head up the firm's new financial services and markets team. This team also includes lawyers formerly at Freshfields and McDermott Will & Emery. Despite acting as a magnet for City refugees, Michelmores insists on growing organically and we have it on good authority that no tongue-twisting mergers or new locations are on the horizon. Instead, the firm wants to keep things simple and expand its Exeter and London offerings, which sound as if they are working well together. London attracts new clients and farms out the work to Exeter, while Exeter finds great advantage in having a Mayfair address on the letterhead.

The commercial litigation team – top-ranked by our parent guide *Chambers UK* – acts for an impressive range of companies, from locally based owner-managed businesses to companies in Europe and the Cayman Islands. In a slightly different area of litigation, the claimant-led clinical negligence team recently brought claims against a privatised provider of healthcare services outsourced by the NHS. Over in the commercial property department, Michelmores acts for loads of hush-hush government departments, including the Ministry of Justice and HM Prison Service (ssshhh). Also on the books are numerous local authorities. On the back of its existing public sector expertise, the firm recently won a position on the government's new Catalist scheme for buying legal services. Other big-ticket commercial property clients include The Bank of England, NatWest and the National Trust. Judicial review work, as well as a range of general property disputes work for clients like HM Courts Service, is common in the property litigation department. The private client team, recently boosted by partner recruits from Foot Anstey and Macfarlanes, dispenses high-value domestic and overseas tax planning advice, as well as working in charity law and on the administration of estates.

All trainees must do seats in property, litigation, corporate/commercial and private client, but within these departments a broad spread of choices awaits. The property seat could be taken in property litigation, projects, private work for developers and public sector work. The litigation options include medical negligence, family, construction, commercial disputes and IP. The corporate/commercial requirement may be satisfied with a seat in employment, and private client encompasses probate, residential conveyancing and tax and trusts. Trainees can also spend six months in the London office, though the *"very olde-worlde"* Sidmouth office, which exclusively deals with private client work, doesn't take trainees at all.

devon knows what they're up to

Commercial property is the biggest department, so it's no surprise that trainees had a lot to say about it. For many, a seat in the public sector side of commercial property proved to be the best option. The team *"deals with government property all over the country"* and trainees extolled the virtues of *"really feeling like a part of a big project."* Our interviewees were quick to praise the *"excellent"* levels of feedback from supervisors in this seat, recognising that positive interaction always encouraged them to work that bit harder. In other departments, supervision has occasionally been less structured, but the firm has acknowledged the problem and is actively trying to improve the entire training programme, not least by introducing grants to cover LPC fees. Also in the works are lunchtime training sessions on soft skills to complement the current programme of in-house legal training.

A seat in the powerhouse private client department exposes trainees to everything from probate through to residential conveyancing and *"exciting"* tax and trusts work, when trainees *"get to use a bit of imagination to figure out how high net worth clients can avoid capital gains tax and inheritance tax."* The family department also has a spread of work, from high-value divorce cases to *"quite traumatic"* publicly funded child cases. In this *"lovely team"* trainees *"learn a lot, both as a solicitor and as a person."*

The top-flight commercial litigation department handles *"lots of proceedings in strange jurisdictions,"* meanwhile the business of the *"young"* property litigation team also incorporates planning and environmental law. One trainee spoke of *"working with some big Devon estates whose tenants were being a bit naughty."* Sounds intriguing! A typical day's work involves *"drafting instructions to counsel and long letters of advice to clients,"* as well as *"conducting research into technical points of law."* The supervisor in property litigation sounds like a real gem – *"She's very, very supportive and protective of her trainees."*

from mayfair with love

When it comes to a good view, none of Michelmores' offices disappoint. The Exeter HQ has views of the Exe estuary towards Haldon Hill. The Sidmouth office is tantalisingly close to the beach and the firm's appreciation for the good life even permeates its two-year-old London office, which sits in the heart of well-heeled Mayfair, close enough for trainees to take tea at the Ritz. Actually, a pack of sarnies in Green Park or a cheap pint at the Samuel Pepys across the road is far more likely. The London office is growing at such a pace that it may soon have to up sticks and move. The busy office has space for a single, busy trainee, ideally someone who doesn't mind mucking in with the other 20 or so staff. The compact size of the office equates to high levels of responsibility in either a corporate or a property seat. *"On a lot of the deals it was just the partner and me,"* enthused a source. *"He was really good at letting me have a first go at things and always took time to explain stuff to me."* Indeed the trainee-partner relationship can be so close in London that you might often spy such a pair having a morning chat in Starbucks. Since the London office is in the ascendant, involvement in business development and marketing is also on the cards for the trainee.

London trainees sometimes find themselves assisting on deals for the Ministry of Defence, so if you've always secretly fancied working as a secret agent it could be the seat to bid for. The office is located in among London's many gentlemen's clubs (some of which now accept ladies), so you can pop down after work to try out your best 007 impression. Although it isn't quite a pad worthy of James Bond, the firm does keep a flat in Clapham for those doing a London seat. Oh, and trainees also get a London allowance on top of their regular salary. Since the firm covers rent and bills, we presume this is for club membership fees and vodka martinis.

the exe-factor

Where to begin? Michelmores' social calendar is bursting at the seams. On the sporting front, there's the Michelmores corporate yacht race, firm-sponsored charity runs, departmental golf days, cricket, football, surfing and blokarting, to name but a few activities. Perhaps in search of another sport to add to its roster, Michelmores has even had staff involved in the daft-sounding game of human table football, which involves the lucky participants *"getting strapped to a bar and trying to kick a ball with their feet."* This year, the annual quiz night had an Oscar winners theme, which saw trainees and partners dressed as famous film characters. One source mischievously recounted: *"There was one round on current affairs which the partners thought they'd do really well in – it turned out to be all about news from celebrity magazines so the young ones won it."* Other opportunities for mirth include the Christmas party, barbecues and family fun days. On any given Friday, trainees, staff and partners can be found in local haunts like The Blue Bell.

Although in the past Michelmores has tended to recruit largely from certain universities in the South West, it is keen to emphasise that even if you have no connection to the area other than a desire to live by the sea (or a passion for blokarting), the firm wants to hear from you. Our interviewees displayed a well-developed sense of humour and an air of quiet self-assurance. They were *"chatty, not cocky"* and *"very loyal to Michelmores."* Such loyalty isn't just empty talk; in 2007,

all four qualifiers stayed with the firm, taking up jobs in private client and property litigation in Exeter and corporate finance in London.

and finally...

It's easy to fall for the charms of this regional dynamo, and its current trainees clearly have done. One besotted source told us: *"I can see myself working here my whole life."* The firm is definitely going places, so if you fancy hopping on for the ride, get that vacation scheme application in gear.

Mills & Reeve LLP

the facts

Location: Birmingham, Cambridge, Norwich, London
Number of UK partners/solicitors: 79/330
Total number of trainees: 45
Seats: 6x4 months
Alternative seats: Occasional secondments
Extras: Pro bono – Free Legal Advice Group, ProHelp, Business in the Community

Now employing some 750 staff across four UK offices, the firm that could claim to be the dominant player in East Anglia is now providing stiff competition in the West Midlands. Excelling in a wide range of practice areas, many of them unusual, Mills & Reeve is a top choice for anyone seeking breadth in their commercial training but keen to avoid the capital.

mills & boom

Mills & Reeve began in 1880 with one office in Norwich. More than a century later, in 1987 it opened an outpost in Cambridge, which quickly became a hub for the firm. Two decades on, its relatively young Birmingham office is stealing the limelight, while its small London office remains focused on insurance clients. The firm recruits into all offices save London and is more than happy to cater to trainees' desires to sample other offices, covering any extra travel and accommodation expenses. This pan-firm approach sometimes results in trainees choosing to qualify in a different office to where they began and lends extra weight to the firm's claim to have burst out of its home region.

In all offices the training contract consists of six seats of four months which allows recruits to try out diverse areas and then have the option of a second seat in their preferred qualification area. The numerous seats available are: corporate, banking/finance, corporate tax, education, public law, technology, real estate, planning and environment, projects, construction, insurance, commercial disputes, probate and trust administration, agriculture and estates, private tax, employment, family and matrimonial, real estate disputes and regulatory defence. By any standards that's some list. Sometimes trainees are offered split seats when departments cannot justify taking on a full-time trainee which, depending on how you look at it, can be viewed as an opportunity to experience yet another area of practice. Cambridge, Norwich and Birmingham all offer near enough the full range of seats.

brum, here we come!
Since it began life as a specialist healthcare branch back in 2000 the Birmingham office has expanded rapidly. To give you a sense of by how much, we can tell you that M&R's turnover rose 79% between 2001 and 2006, and in Birmingham alone it quadrupled. Perhaps reflecting a shift in the focus from East Anglia to the West Midlands, in October 2006 the head of the Birmingham office, Guy Hinchley, was appointed as the new managing partner of the firm as a whole. M&R's Birmingham strategy has been to exploit its niche practice areas such

as healthcare – and then private client work following the hire of a team from Wragge & Co – before gradually building up its commercial strength. Healthcare clients include Nottingham Healthcare Trust, Sandwell and West Birmingham Hospitals Trust, Portsmouth Hospitals Trust, Shropshire County Primary Care Trust and the NHS Blood and Transplant Authority. The commercial clients using the Brum office include mid-sized regional businesses plus some from further afield, for example Manchester-based Intempo Digital which manufactures DAB radios, iPod docking stations and GPS equipment. The higher education sector is hugely important to the office and has led to major instructions coming from existing client Imperial College London and new client the University of Birmingham. In the area of construction law (contentious and non-contentious) lawyers have undertaken a lot of work for education sector clients. One such project was the £200m Aston University student project in the heart of Birmingham city centre.

dreaming spires
The Cambridge office takes on the greatest number of trainees and is still the largest office in the network. It leans more towards corporate and commercial work than the others and this could explain why trainees think the people who work there seem busier and more stretched. A trainee reported how in the projects department, for example, "*I always had so many tasks on my desk.*" Given that Mills & Reeve is a firm that some senior lawyers escape to when they've had enough of slogging it out in the City, one wonders just how much of a "*more relaxed approach to work*" they can actually achieve in Cambridge. Another trainee added that supervisors "*sometimes didn't have time to stop and explain things.*"

The Cambridge office has a sterling reputation for its IP and technology work. At the heart of the team's success are relationships with leading universities' research and technology transfer departments (eg Cambridge, Imperial, Nottingham, Leicester and Aston), and another major client of the department is University of Cambridge Local Examinations Syndicate (UCLES), which provides a great deal of trade mark instructions. The range of national/London work has grown and lawyers have been lured from City firms such as Linklaters, Bird & Bird and Lovells. One interesting development has been the creation of the Mills & Reeve China Group, which services an increasing number of clients doing business in that country.

M&R's expertise in healthcare is again in evidence, and in April 2007 the Cambridge team was strengthened with the addition of three new lawyers from rival firm Kennedys. Last year M&R was appointed primary adviser to West Suffolk NHS Trust and the mandate will bring employment, planning, governance, finance leasing, PFI, procurement, judicial review and real estate instructions. Over in the commercial property department trainees get the chance to work with Cambridge colleges, sometimes *"being given the first crack at drafting things,"* and can also take control of smaller files.

booming bootiful business

Having moved to a plush new building in Whitefriars a few years ago, in 2005 the Norwich office pulled in the corporate team from the local branch of Eversheds, a coup that underlined its status as the top-dog commercial law firm in town. Billing this office as a commercial powerhouse may not be what you'd expect given the traditional prominence of agricultural and private clients, but there's no denying its credentials in the Norfolk business community. However, we rather like writing about farmers and the landed gentry so it's a good job the office

has a sterling client list in this respect, including such fine names as The Holkham Estate and the Norfolk Historic Buildings Trust. Trainees who take a private client seat learn about *"will drafting and tax planning,"* sometimes meeting clients on their own. Supervision is given where necessary, but trainees are given responsibility for their work relatively quickly. An emphasis is placed on getting to know all the private client teams in the network and cross-office, lunchtime videoconferences are held twice a month. A seat in real estate disputes also allows trainees to take a lead role. The work includes lease renewals, boundary disputes and the tricky task of evicting squatters from clients' land. Recruits reported *"feeling more than just a trainee"* in this seat, telling us about *"a great deal of court work," "taking witness statements," "shadowing counsel alone"* and *"spending a whole day at a mediation."* Overall, our interviewees' assessment of the two years was that their experiences went from *"just challenging enough to take you out of your comfort zone"* in a first seat to *"thrown in at the deep end in a controlled way"* by the final seat.

One major draw of the Norwich office is standard hours of 8.30am to 5.30pm and *"no brownie points for staying late."* M&R's senior partner, Mark Jeffries, is based in this office and trainees described him as *"a very nice chap who happily joins people at lunch, knows everyone's names and is probably the nicest person you could wish to have as senior partner."* Clearly he sets a good example: most of those we spoke to across the offices felt they were well looked after and not merely well trained. Little wonder the firm secured a place in the *Sunday Times*' 2007 'Best Companies To Work For' list, its second appearance in the annual survey. Niceness aside, if being *"near the countryside"* and having *"easy access to the coast"* is a priority then Norwich is definitely the office for you. It maintains close ties with the local community and last year held a school sports day, cricket match and cake sale for a local drugs and alcohol awareness project. The office also has a box at Norwich City football ground for entertaining clients and trainees are sometimes included in marketing events.

variety is the spice of life
The London office, located halfway between the Bank of England and the Tower of London, is essentially an office for insurance and re-insurance law. Trainees can elect to take a seat there if they wish, but for now the office does not recruit on its own account. Of all of the offices this is the one that is most distinct, not least because of its much smaller size. You get the impression that the differences matter less than the similarities at M&R, however, and certainly many departments do *"a great deal of cross-office work,"* especially when particular expertise is required in a location that does not possess it.

Across the offices trainees talked of being attracted to M&R's desire to *"produce confident, competent lawyers"* and the fact that *"it values its trainees and wants to nurture them."* Our sources had on occasion liaised with magic circle firms on the opposite side of deals and noted that their counterparts were often more experienced, qualified lawyers. One thing's for sure: trainees don't come out overspecialised here. They may find that certain niche areas they've trained in are not available in that many firms, but they are certainly not bred to be one-trick ponies. The only negative concerning the seat system relates to the timing of seat announcements. Often trainees don't find out about their next posting until quite late, sometimes just two weeks before the changeover date. If a move to another office is involved this can be awkward. When we raised this issue with the firm it was like the proverbial shooting of the messenger.

reeve-erdance
The PSC is spread throughout the training contract, but one component is given right at the beginning and this brings all the trainees together from across the firm. The firm as a whole gets together once every two years for a summer party, which was last held at Knebworth House in Hertfordshire and partly organised by trainees. Individual offices celebrate Christmas with parties and all first year trainees attend the Cambridge bash to meet the future joiners. The brave bunch from Norwich dressed up as elves and performed some Irish dancing.

The Birmingham office sounds like the *"most sociable."* Here, lawyers head down to the Old Joint Stock on a Friday evening and the youngsters usually end up at a club, occasionally accompanied by the odd partner with a late pass. Speaking of passes, Cambridge staff have free entry to the nearby University Botanic Gardens and some 15 of them even went so far as to help transform an overgrown part of the site into a new 'schools garden'. Another charity event was Bring a Bra to Work Day, raising money for the breast cancer unit at Addenbrookes Hospital. When the Cambridge lawyers let their hair down, the usual haunts are trendy bar Sauce and the more traditional Flying Pig pub. Norwich lawyers can often be found in the Wig & Pen and spoke of a healthy inter-firm social scene in town. At lunchtime the trainees sometimes frequent the oldest alehouse in Norwich, The Adam & Eve. In each city there are Young Professionals Groups and Trainee Solicitors Groups with which the trainees are involved. In 2007, 15 of the 19 qualifying trainees decided to stay on at the firm, taking jobs across a wide range of practice areas.

and finally...
You're unlikely to run out of options at this firm, be it location, practice area or client type. From private individuals to public bodies and plcs,

Mishcon de Reya Solicitors

Rise to the challenge
Realise your potential

Mishcon de Reya is a mid-sized law firm based in central London providing a diverse range of legal services for businesses and individuals.

Why us? We offer an innovative and friendly environment, which provides great prospects for commercially minded people. Is this you?

To learn about career opportunities with Mishcon de Reya, please visit www.mishcon.com/trainees

Mills & Reeve can provide exposure to them all. Your only difficulty might be narrowing down which type of career you want at the end of the two years.

Mishcon de Reya

the facts
Location: London
Number of UK partners/solicitors: 54/92
Total number of trainees: 17
Seats: 4x6 months
Alternative seats: Secondments
Extras: Pro bono – various projects, eg LawWorks

Mishcon de Reya is a commercial firm with a twist that can normally be relied upon to create a buzz in the press. Its litigation practice serves a galaxy of red-carpet clients as well as snapping up a host of intriguing cases, ranging from holocaust denial to football bungs.

cross star lovers
Mishcon has crafted a glittering reputation for dispute resolution and this powerhouse department generates a huge chunk of its income. There are in fact four main divisions in the firm: dispute resolution, 'business', 'personal' and real estate. Within these groupings, sub-categories are wedged in, the most glamorous of which is undoubtedly the media and public advocacy group, whose remit covers defamation and privacy advice to both private and corporate clients. Other niche areas include art law and immigration.

If you're a consumer of gossip magazines then you'll be pleased to hear that Mishcon handles the sort of cases that will make your weekly *Heat* fix seem rather dull indeed. Its family lawyers have represented a procession of people from every walk of public life – Princess Diana, Heather Mills and, most recently, Arsenal striker

Thierry Henri. Heather Mills' divorce from Sir Paul McCartney set the scene for a rematch between legendary advocate Anthony Julius and Fiona Shackleton, who previously pitted their wiles in the break-up of Diana and Prince Charles. Best not to reveal your love of celebrity gossip and scandal though: the firm landed in hot water last year when papers outlining Heather Mills' reasons for divorce were leaked to the press.

mish' mash
Trainee seats can, in theory, be taken in the following teams: real estate; corporate; banking; general commercial; insolvency; media; employment; family; and contentious and non-contentious private client. How these seats are allocated is less clear. Although all are potentially available, there is no formal list of options complete with convenient boxes to tick. One source remembers requesting a seat, uncertain whether it actually existed. The process is apparently *"shrouded in mystery"* and can require recruits to schmooze the relevant partner to get in with the department. No seat is mandatory, but chances are you'll do a stint in both corporate and litigation, and the firm definitely encourages real estate seats. The good news is that training programme provides trainees with heaps of responsibility in all seats and a minimum of grunt work.

In litigation there are all manner of cases from straightforward commercial spats to disputes centring on real rights and wrongs. In the media and public advocacy group, don't be surprised to bump into Anthony Julius padding the corridors or even help on some of the cases under his care. Among the past years' highlights was a case for a group of miners from Mansfield, all of whom had contracted industrial diseases and been awarded compensation by the Department of Trade and Industry. The miners started a group action against the Union of Democratic Mineworkers and its claims handling company, Vendside, but their action failed and they ended up with costs liability to the union, plus the fees of their own lawyers. Many risked losing their homes. At this point, Mishcon stepped in and negotiated a favourable settlement on behalf of the miners.

Those entertaining a fancy for family will certainly want to home in on this firm. The department, with its mostly female detail, has acquired a reputation for Amazonian fierceness. This perception is, according to those in the know, somewhat different from the reality, as the team members are *"all perfectly nice."* Still, the seat is a challenging one for a number of reasons. The hectic atmosphere where everything is *"rush, rush, rush"* leaves supervisors little time to take trainees by the hand, thus trainees have to learn quickly in what is sometimes a stressful environment. Secondly, the cases can be quite distressing, dealing as they do with tricky divorces and child abductions. Veterans revealed that the thrill of the job came when they informed a parent that they could keep custody of their child. *"You're happy you delivered a real service and made a difference to people's lives,"* said one.

bunged up

Much like a SWAT team, the fraud lawyers are known for their hard-headed, no-nonsense approach. Famously representing Microsoft in relation to software infringements, they espouse a method dubbed Tulip (Turning Losses into Profits). This amounts to hitting counterfeiters hard and quickly, extracting the maximum and then evacuating the area. In defence of the tactic, one trainee said: *"We're paid to be aggressive."* Trainees can expect to be present on raids, kicking the bad guys out of business. Clearly aware of the firm's reputation in this area, Lord Stephens appointed the fraud team in relation to his football bungs inquiry.

The firm is pushing to grow its corporate and property departments, and the partner-heavy corporate team has expanded rapidly on the back of some choice lateral hires, picking up a clutch of multimillion-pound deals in the process. There are no subdivisions in this department, so expect six months in which you will *"learn about everything."* The department's highlights include acting on London Town's acquisition of a portfolio of 167 pubs in the capital and advising on the sale of £220m worth of shares in online gambling business partygaming. Not to be outdone, the property lawyers scored big when they acted on a £25m deal to develop the stadium of Luton FC. Obviously enjoying the appeal of large crowds, they also acted on the sale of a 50% stake in Earls Court and Olympia. Michcon can rightly claim to have both shaken and stirred the City when it advised on the £72m sale of the property that adjoins The Bank of England and featured heavily in the 1964 James Bond film *Goldfinger.*

The sterling employment team won £800, 000 for a former company secretary of Deutsche Bank after serial bullying from fellow employees led her to suffer a nervous breakdown. With such juicy work in the department, it would take a pretty enticing client secondment to lure trainees away. That's exactly what's on offer though – trainees have previously been seconded to assist on a House of Commons inquiry into anti-semitism in the UK.

Although there is an Aladdin's Cave of dream instructions available, unless you badger partners, explained one trainee, *"you might not get a sniff at the interesting stuff."* In most seats the hours are friendly, with one recruit declaring it would be *"scandalous"* if he wasn't home for dinner. Bear in mind that corporate seats can be much more demanding in terms of hours. If the work does wear you down, there's a weekly yoga session in the office. Or if you fancy a break from the office entirely, there are usually a couple of commercial client secondments to investigate.

many are called, few are chosen

These lawyers are renowned for their cultured outlook, which even extends as far as seeing the point of an English degree. It's not for nothing that the firm resides in Bloomsbury, London's intellectual heartland and the stomping ground of such Bluestockings as Virginia Woolf and Edith Sitwell. The office building is a brightly coloured art-deco affair that resists the stereotype of the legal profession as stuffy and unimaginative. The recruiters pick trainees with an interesting edge who, in one interviewee's memorable words have done *"crazy stuff,"* which for one trainee meant doubling as a lawyer-cum-licensed football agent. Apparently, there exists a particular *"Michcon person"* that is almost instantaneously recognisable. Old hands watch vac schemers with practised eyes and immediately sense who will fit into the organisation. And yet, even when we applied the thumbscrews, our interviewees' responses were vague, even bordering on mystic. *"It's just intuitive,"* one insisted. Enthusiasm is definitely a common trait, as is the ability to thrive in a sometimes quirky atmosphere. We're not suggesting that the firm is looking for wacky characters, indeed there are quite enough big personalities in the firm already and arguably it takes a certain calmness of character to be a trainee here. Staying with the subject of who the firm takes on, trainees were adamant that the firm does not deserve its *"high-falutin"* reputation and that, in fact, there were also some *"London geezer types"* at Mishcon.

An easygoing social life centres on the delectably named Bountiful Cow pub, the take-it-or-leave-it approach suiting those people who have a lot going on in their personal lives. Some of the partners are keen photographers, and one is, amazingly, also a stand-up comedian in his spare time. The fact that the 2007 summer party included an M-Factor contest highlights the wealth of talent in the ranks. Could it be that the training contract interview is merely an early audition for the party? Each applicant is asked to give a five-minute presentation and one successful raconteur amused the panel with a vindication of *"the wolf's actions against the three little pigs."* Obviously one of the devil's advocates...

talk to him

The best advice trainees gave us for making the best of your contract is to keep lines of communication open and never be afraid to ask questions. This shouldn't be difficult since trainees believed they *"could knock on any partner's door and not feel nervous talking to anybody."* Good communication is facilitated by a general hotline straight to the head honcho himself. Anybody with an issue is encouraged to e-mail the managing partner directly. In 2007 the trainees were clearly content with the Mishcon Way, with seven of the eight qualifiers applying to stay on at the firm. Unfortunately, because of the shortage of places in the *"jazzier"* departments, only five of them were retained.

and finally...

Mishcon de Reya's little black book would be worth an absolute fortune, and its work is so interesting that it must be nigh impossible to get bored here. If you fancy applying to the firm, do so on the basis that it will recognise whether you're its type, and be prepared to defend a much-loathed storybook character.

Morgan Cole

the facts

Location: Cardiff, Swansea, Reading, Oxford, Croydon, Bristol
Number of UK partners/solicitors: 51/113
Total number of trainees: 22
Seats: 4x6 months
Alternative seats: None

In the last few editions of the *Student Guide* we have introduced Morgan Cole by detailing some of the financial and partnership struggles it endured following its inception in 1998, when Welsh firm Morgan Bruce merged with Thames Valley outfit Cole & Cole. This year, however, there's very much a sense that the firm has overcome past problems.

on the up

Morgan Cole's decision to open a new office in Bristol, a city that nestles between its strongholds in Wales and the Thames Valley, is indicative of the fact that almost a decade after the original merger the two branches of this regional firm have at last been able to find common ground. As one trainee commented: *"Lots of good things are happening here at the moment. The firm has been on the up since I arrived at the end of the bad years and now we have consolidated our base and started to expand with the opening of the Bristol office."* Now that the firm looks to be back on track, it is no surprise that our sources were uniformly up beat about the prospect of completing their training contracts at a firm *"that feels as if it is really expanding."* The opening of the new corporate-focused office in Bristol in April 2007 is not the only evidence that the firm is back in calmer waters – its financial results are moving in the right direction too. Although MC is by no means the most profitable firm around, the 2006/07 figures show that average partner profits have risen by 15% to £195,000. And in terms of client wins, the firm was one of only five to land a coveted place on the Government's legal panel for construction work.

The training scheme is still defined by the original pre-merger firms, so trainees choose between either a Welsh or a Thames Valley contract. Once that decision has been made, individuals are unlikely to move between the two regions during their training. Likewise, it is rare for trainees to move from one region to the other on qualification, although if the job you want is located in the other region, the firm is happy for you to go ahead and apply for it. By all accounts, the firm does *"give those candidates a fair go."*

Understandably, geography limits social interaction between the Welsh and Thames Valley trainees. At the beginning of their two years, they gather in Oxford for a fortnight to study the PSC together. *"We all make great friends before being sent off to our different areas of the country, after which we don't see each other so much,"* lamented one source. While the lives of the two intakes of trainees is relatively separate, we were assured that when it comes to work the firm acts as a single unit, thereby utilising strengths from across the offices. This certainly seems to be the case in the corporate department in particular, one TV trainee telling us: *"I dealt with the teams in both the Oxford and Reading offices regularly, but if we are busy we know that there is a large team in Wales and they can just as easily do the work... likewise with the new Bristol office. I might not recognise everyone across the firm, but I am pretty confident that I would know most people's voices."*

a tale of two cities

The majority of the TV trainees are located at one or other of the firm's two Reading offices; the remainder work in the Oxford office. Each city has its own distinctive character, with the Oxford office often being described as *"quiet and family orientated..." "as a rule people live near to the office and drive into work and then they go home to their families at the end of the day."* The seats available in Oxford are commercial property, commercial/IP, comlit and private client. If you want to do property or private client/family in the Thames valley then this is your office.

By contrast, trainees were thrilled with the active social life in the Reading offices. There are regular drinks on a Friday and football matches involving the full range of staff, from vacation scheme students and trainees to partners. As with the football, MC's social scene is generally organised on an office or department-wide basis, rather than being centred on the trainees.

A TV trainee would be unlikely to spend their entire training contract in the same office, and while there aren't any compulsory seats, the volume of insurance work handled by the firm makes it likely that they will take at least one seat in this department. It normally comes in their first year, which is no bad thing, according to most of our interviewees. *"This is the firm's big thing and so the work is full-on and keeps you busy,"* explained one source. Indeed, it is: the firm handles a broad spectrum of defence work, including personal injury, industrial disease and professional indemnity, for household names such as AXA Insurance, Brit Insurance, Hertz Claims Management and Norwich Union Insurance. Trainees talked enthusiastically about the level of responsibility they were given. *"By the end of the six months I had one file, a noise-induced hearing loss claim that I handled on my own from scratch, and I even attended a couple of client meetings on my own with counsel."* Other Reading seat options include commercial IT, employment and corporate. The firm's branch in Croydon does not offer trainee seats.

the mc eisteddfod

MC is one of the small handful of elite firms in Wales, which means the trainees who are based here are guaranteed a steady stream of quality work. Much of it is for a portfolio of regional public companies, among them Pure Wafer plc, Tinopolis plc, Jelf Group plc and fully listed Admiral Group plc and Medicx Fund. Then there's the National Assembly for Wales, Milford Haven Port Authority, The University of Wales, the Welsh Development Agency and a whole bunch of other public and local authorities. As in England, there are no compulsory seats, although here the insurance department seems to have a less weighty influence on the training. Our interviewees had experienced a good mix of corporate, commercial property and litigation, with the litigation seat affording one trainee the highlight of their training contract when, in their third seat they attended the High Court in London. Here the firm mounted a successful appeal of an adverse possession case that they had prepared for the deputy adjudicator for the Land Registry in their first seat. *"I was the only person who had been at the original hearing, which was really exciting."* However, wannabe litigators should beware: *"The litigation department makes new starters sing in front of the rest of the department at the Christmas night out, so I had to sing by myself."* It seems that standards are slipping: *"The trainees got away with doing a duet last year."*

Just as Reading dominates the seat list in the Thames Valley, so the larger Cardiff office dominates over Swansea, where our sources admitted to feeling *"a little bit cut off – you are 40 miles away from the rest of your trainee group, so it is harder to go for after-work drinks."* At least Swansea does *"have the flip side of being really friendly and in a great location by the marina."* The seats available in Swansea are commercial litigation, corporate and commercial property. Over in Cardiff there are the same choices plus also employment, pensions and benefits, IP and health professional indemnity.

tea and sympathy

With seats in the corporate and employment departments hotly contested in both regions, it's good to hear that the system of allocation is deemed a fair one. As is common in most firms, second-years are given priority, but all trainee get to list their preferences. *"We fill out a form with our first three choices and why we want to do them; there is also a box to put down anything that we really don't want to do."* This won't always guarantee satisfaction, as we found out from one tolerant soul – *"HR did speak to me afterwards, and I think that I will probably get what I want next time. I am just trying to approach this seat with an open mind."*

MC has always had a well-earned reputation for providing its trainees with a solid, down-to-earth training. This year's interviewees were full of praise for the supportive environment, one telling us: *"I have yet to come across someone who isn't approachable, and that includes the managing partner."* Another commented on the fact that *"there isn't any snobbery and I never hear snide comments."* Extra support is available from mentors who are assigned to the trainees at the beginning of their contract. Part of their role is to sit in on the trainee's mid and end-of-seat appraisals and sources found it comforting *"to know that there is somebody who you can go to and tell if, for example, you had a problem with your supervisor."* Get yourself in the right department and *"even the partners make you cups of tea!"*

The only moans we heard concerned pay. *"I didn't know my salary until our first day when we signed the contract and it was significantly less than I was expecting,"* grumbled one trainee. The firm was surprised to hear this news and so we suspect it's not something future joiners will have to worry about. While MC trainees may salivate over magic circle-sized pay packets, their hours must be an equally tempting mirage for those working in the City. The average day runs from 9am to 6pm, and although the corporate department is recognised to have a longer-hours culture, *"if you haven't got anything to do then you're not expected to stay."*

According to one source, *"there definitely is a Morgan Cole type, although I find it difficult to put my finger on what that is."* What you won't find are any *"wannabe City types;"* the firm wants people who are *"happy with a mid-sized regional firm that handles work for local businesses."* We found that a significant number of recruits had experienced the world of work or further academic study before they commenced their training. Whether it was time spent as a paralegal, completing a PhD or working in IT, the recruiters seem to appreciate the qualities that experienced candidates can bring. Beyond this, we'd say that a majority of the trainees have a connection to the area in which they work. Bear in mind that it is not necessarily going to be possible to name your qualification office, especially if you are hoping to move from one valley to the other. This was an issue for one of the Welsh qualifiers in 2007, who had hoped to qualify into an English office. In the end, nine of the 14 qualifiers stayed on with the firm, all going into commercial departments.

and finally...

Having steadied itself, Morgan Cole has confirmed its status as a leading location for trainees in Wales and a solid option for students' in the south of England. It will be very interesting to see how the new Bristol venture develops and whether it acts as a bridge between the two halves of the firm.

Muckle LLP

the facts

Location: Newcastle-upon-Tyne
Number of UK partners/solicitors: 19/36
Total number of trainees: 10
Seats: 4x6 months
Alternative seats: None

This 17-partner Newcastle firm offers a very personal training for commercially minded trainees.

weighing in at...

Renowned for *"punching above its weight,"* pound-for-pound Muckle is one of the hottest competitors in the Newcastle legal market. Its core strengths lie in coco and commercial property, and it has recently supplemented its strong entrepreneurial client base with some big plc names. A good example is UK Land, which it has advised on the development of Newcastle International Airport. Its position on the panel of the One NorthEast development agency continues to feed the property division with valuable instructions, one of the most notable being the Science City Project. Moreover, the hire of senior public sector guru Alan Grisedale from local rival Dickinson Dees demonstrates that it is more than capable of keeping larger Geordie sparring partners on their toes.

The Muckle approach is *"tailored to the way the North East does business."* Trainees were very impressed with this and shared the firm's motivation. Said one: *"I think that given half a chance some local firms would like to wave a magic wand and find themselves part of the magic circle. But I like the North East and here we are focused on what is going on locally, growing as our clients do."* And as the cranes continue to appear across the city, Muckle is indeed growing with its home town. It increased turnover by 19% in the last financial year and exceeded its targets in every area, heralding a sense of *"euphoria"* across the firm. A recent rebranding (until July 2007 it was known as Robert Muckle, but this was deemed to make the firm sound too small) and an imminent move to new premises near St James' Park add to the sense that it is an exciting place to be at the moment.

down to the biscuits

Muckle prides itself on being entrepreneurial and is a sterling example of a law firm operating on very businesslike principles. *"You are encouraged not to take an overly legal outlook on things, but more of a business advisory role."* To help new trainees fit into this fold, business development plays a prominent role in training. *"They encourage you to network and equip you with the skills to do so,"* confirmed a source. In true Muckle fashion, this training is very hands-on and, in addition to lessons on how to work a room, trainees are expected to assist in hosting corporate events. Beyond this, training is offered in such basics as grammar and IT, leading sources to claim that *"the quality and variety of training is what really sets Muckle apart from its competitors."*

Key to the firm's business plan has been the adoption of ideas from other industries. The most obvious example of this is its insistence on *"service excellence,"* a concept borrowed from the USA. The importation of this fundamental set of principles is relatively new, but has taken root in the firm. To aid its implementation everybody has regular meetings with a 'service excellence group' and is consulted as to the best ways to improve service delivery, both internally and externally. This is indicative of a wider focus on encouraging all staff to express an opinion on everything... even down to the choice of biscuits in conference rooms. While various trainees accepted that *"some people may see this as Americanish nonsense,"* there are few firms that trust staff with such weighty decisions. What's more, empowerment of the little people is paying dividends. Our parent publication *Chambers UK* is bombarded with praise from satisfied clients who have sampled the meeting room snacks.

Other examples of people power include the Green Initiative, which invites the opinions of all and sundry on how to reduce the firm's carbon footprint. The hotly anticipated move to a newly built office near St James' Park was also the product of extensive meetings with staff to decipher what makes the perfect working environment.

if you can't stand the heat...

Anyone tempted by front row seats at the country's premier biscuit boutique would do well to heed the warnings of its trainees before sending off their application. *"I was given genuinely challenging work even on my vacation placement and that has continued through my training contract. Don't apply here if you want to spend the day reading Heat and e-mailing your friends."* For those up for the challenge, Muckle provides an immensely rewarding training, which entails three seats in each of the firm's flagship departments. Within property there are options in construction and development, the commercial component offers corporate finance, banking and IP work, while contentious options include employment and commercial dispute resolution. Most trainees return to their favoured department for their fourth seat, but there is also a possibility of sampling the new private client and wealth protection group.

Property was the most popular department among our interviewees, both on the construction and the development side. The work also touches on planning, landlord and tenant matters and corporate support, and the seat gives *"responsibility from day one."* Trainees manage small files *"in which you can negotiate your own leases"* while also helping out on larger transactions. A notable example of the large-scale work is City & Northern's development and sale of 24 office units at Phases IV and V at The Watermark in Gateshead.

There is a certain amount of crossover between the property and litigation departments, although the latter is mainly involved in more traditional commercial dispute resolution. A seat here offers ample opportunity for advocacy, with our sources speaking of appearances at charging order and bankruptcy hearings. *"I wasn't expecting anywhere near the level of advocacy that I have undertaken,"* said one trainee, clearly incapable of supressing a smile. Get involved in contentious employment matters and you'll see how unusual some cases can be. The lawyers recently represented Sterling Scaffolding in a complex claim concerning Nigeria's offshore oil industry.

Epitomising the hands-on training at the firm is the popular corporate finance seat. *"If you are expecting it to be like university then it could be very intimidating. But for those ready to take on a high level of responsibility it is incredibly rewarding."* In terms of workload, *"there is no messing about ghost-writing letters for partners. You are present at meetings and used as the first port of call for many clients."* The department has tempting career prospects and even newly qualified lawyers get close to the group's headline transactions, which have lately included VTL Holdings' acquisition of precision engineers Taylor & Whiteley, and the AIM flotation and listing of the newly formed Vertu Motors.

heal the world

Speaking about the emphasis on support and training, one trainee told us: *"They make a massive investment in trainees, which is why they take so few. They aim to retain and are very successful in doing so."* Perhaps as a result of the focus on business skills, Muckle trainees rarely seem to come fresh from university. *"It is not just black letter law that we're involved in, so office experience and previous client exposure will undoubtedly help an application.*" Indeed, there is an air of maturity about the firm that shows through in all sorts of ways including its social events. *"The summer party is a family affair and people bring their children along during the day for various activities. During the evening there is entertainment."* Similarly, the firm's Christmas party is to be opened up to spouses for the first time in 2007. Post-work drinks attract trainees, associates and partners alike and are clearly not a ten-pints-and-fall-over affair. *"There is no pressure to drink and you won't get called a stick in the mud if you don't want to go out."* However, for those who do, generally decent office hours mean that tie-loose-with-the-boss moments are regularly available. *"Everyone knows each other and is on first name terms. There is no real feeling of hierarchy."*

Such humility extends to the sports field, where the Muckle football team *"supports the weight of the league on its shoulders, but troops out to face the music every week regardless."* The cricket team goes some way towards saving face for the firm, but *"it would be wrong to label us as a sporty place."* Unsurprising, considering the time its staff devote to making the world a better place for us all: its strong commitment to charity work in the community is matched by an equally good record for pro bono legal advice. A register of voluntary work undertaken by staff allows for the sharing of experience and encouragement of others to take part, while a centrally administered trust fund also provides for charitable donations. *"Recently, people have been going down at weekends to a piece of reclaimed parkland to clean things up and chop down trees."* Overall, trainees felt that the firm is making *"a genuine contribution to the local community,"* extending its service excellence ethic to yet another realm. Keen to remain a part of it all, three of the four 2007 qualifiers stayed with the firm, going into the property, banking and corporate teams. The fourth decided to pursue a non-legal career.

and finally.....

If you are a mature-minded applicant who is committed to a commercial post in the North East and you want a training that will push you, we think Muckle is a very worthwhile option. The more we hear about the place the more we like it.

Nabarro

the facts

Location: London, Sheffield
Number of UK partners/solicitors: 126/248
Total number of trainees: 52
Seats: 6x4 months
Alternative seats: Brussels, secondments
Extras: Language training

Nabarro's 200-odd real estate lawyers are its core, but bricks and mortar are only a part of the story at this much-loved London and Sheffield firm.

varied properties

"In terms of property we compete with the magic circle, we're a big firm and higher up the rankings than people realise," a trainee advised. Land Securities, Slough Estates, Frogmore, Grosvenor, British Land and English Partnerships are just some of the property industry big hitters serviced by the firm, but *"it is now trying to grow its corporate side by building on its strengths."* Accordingly, *"corporate is being pushed,"* particularly via *"financial services and corporate real estate,"* and *"the projects team is developing too."*

This is all good for trainees who want a brand-name training that offers *"an alternative emphasis to corporate."* Joining either in September or January, they follow a six-seat programme in which property, corporate and litigation are compulsory. After fitting in a couple of other choices, the aim is to finish off with a seat in their hoped-for qualification department. In each seat supervi-

Before you can follow your lawyer's advice, you have to be able to follow it.

Do you sometimes feel you need an interpreter when you meet with your lawyers?

Someone to decipher the mumbo-jumbo of legal jargon into language you can understand?

You're not alone.

At Nabarro, many of our clients tell us that not all lawyers are as clear and unequivocal in their advice as we are. To quote:

"All too often when you take advice from lawyers, it's couched in any number of "get out of jail" cards. Nabarro's lack of conditionality is extremely refreshing."

"What sets Nabarro apart is a willingness to delve beneath the surface of legalities and truly understand the commercial result required."

"We don't want a learned dissertation. Nabarro are very good at telling you how it is."

Such compliments are testimony to our passion for clarity. Clarity in the way we understand your objectives. And clarity in the way we deliver our advice.

We call it user-friendly law. And it's our way of helping you move your business forward quickly and painlessly.

www.nabarro.com/graduates

NABARRO
CLARITY MATTERS

sors – predominantly assistant solicitors – allocate day-to-day work, with a supervising partner in the same department on hand, though not necessarily hands-on. Sources reflected: *"A partner can be quite intimidating to sit with and they shouldn't really be spending their time going through and amending trainees' letters. I think our system works well…"*

scaling the heights

The giant property division takes around ten trainees every four months and is *"made up of five teams classified by client groups, a couple of which are more popular as the teams are really friendly."* Recent mandates include Paddington Development Corporation's 1.8m sq ft residential and office scheme at Merchant Square, Paddington Basin; Hammerson's £110m development of the former site of the London Stock Exchange; and Land Securities' proposed redevelopment of 20 Fenchurch Street to provide a 37-storey tower block. In all teams *"trainees get their own small files, which is good,"* but beware, *"there is unfortunately a lot of admin – scheduling of documents and post-completion tasks."* When required to chip in on more complex deals the usual hours of 9.30am to 6.30pm can stretch as late as 8pm.

"Tons of responsibility" is on offer in the *"busy"* top-ranked property litigation department, which works closely with the transactional property groups. A former occupant of the property lit seat spoke of *"serving notices, preparing witness statements, instructions to counsel, statements of claim and attending court. I did a possession claim from start to finish, including the hearing."* With plenty of training on *"how to do our own applications at court"* the seat is known as a good place to learn but also as *"tough, no two ways about it."* The hours can be long (*"9am until 8pm or later"*) and the department is *"a law unto itself – not so friendly as others, nor as social because it is so hard-working."* Although many trainees' least favourite

posting, other really enjoy the seat because of *"the excitement of litigation."*

the sky+ is the limit

For mainstream M&A experience across a swathe of industry sectors, *"Nabarro is not going to be your number-one choice to be a corporate lawyer."* However, for corporate real estate deals it is up with the best. Here deals are structured towards *"property investors, plus pension funds and major landowners,"* commonly involving complicated, tax-led, offshore elements. Trainees explained that this is *"a complex area… I was helping to set up indirect property investment opportunities – trusts and REITs* [Real Estate Investment Trusts]." Typical matters involve a partner, two or three associates and a trainee, so *"there is a degree of normal corporate trainee work – board minutes and all the dull things"* – but there were also opportunities to *"help work up the structures and explain them to the client."* Hours can be long: even if *"you sometimes get away at 6pm,"* *"if there is a big deal on Sky+ is a good investment!"* The value of such deals totalled over £6bn in 2006, with the list including the formation of the UNITE UK Student Accommodation Fund, which has an expected capitalisation of £1bn.

On the contentious side of things, construction litigation is also *"developing on the back of the property department and drawing in big clients itself."* Nabarro helped out Wembley Stadium builders Multiplex on one of the most significant claims relating to the stadium, while further away from home lawyers were instructed on a dredging dispute in Thailand and a major PPP dispute in Dublin. *"That seat blew my mind,"* said one trainee. *"In terms of responsibility, if you step up you will get the good work."* Other seat options include financial services and regulatory law, mainstream corporate (M&A, private equity, AIM), general commercial litigation, planning, projects, IP, pensions, employment (usually offered, devilishly hard to get), an employment law secondment to Oxford University, various other secondments as they crop up, plus a competition law seat in the firm's Brussels office. *"If you are interested in a popular seat you have to keep saying it at every appraisal,"* our sources recommended, adding that *"employment, IP and comlit are competitive."* It's important to remember that the need for trainees or NQs in smaller departments reflects the firm's *"property and corporate focus."* In other words, *"some people will always miss out,"* even if the six-seat system does increase the chance of getting a particular seat.

sheff's choice

Nabarro's smaller Sheffield office was once the in-house legal department of British Coal, the state-owned enterprise that ran the UK's coal industry. Trainees here all take property, litigation and a seat in the health claims team, which is a legacy of the office's sooty past. Of the two health claims seats, one deals with high-level policy issues and compensation schemes for miners with chronic obstructive pulmonary disease; the other sees the trainee defending the DTI on a caseload of miners' claims for noise-induced deafness, vibration white finger and respiratory diseases. Trainees in the latter go to court, often alone, and may even attend trial as the firm's sole representative. *"There is a lot to do in both the seats,"* including weeklong trips to London in the policy seat. Meanwhile, the environment team involves *"waste management matters, some due diligence on property deals and some contentious health and safety matters."* Trainees are constantly researching, as most things are new to them. Over in the projects/construction team *"we do public and private sector work, so on a PFI, such as a Building Schools for the Future project, we could be acting for a council or the private company."* Rounding off the seat list are comlit, construction lit and

corporate. *"Some supervisors are better than others, obviously. Some go out of their way to sit you down in a meeting room and talk you through everything; others give you work to see if you cope."* Overall the hours are good – often 9am to 5pm, at times as late as 7.30pm.

So why choose this Sheffield firm? *"The free parking!"* our sources chuckled. If they're honest, the most important factors are the weight Nabarro's name carries and the warm atmosphere within the office. Socially, there is a Winter Ball, a summer barbecue, monthly wind-down drinks in the office and a lot of trainee lunching.

is that clear?

Nabarro recently shed its old surname – Nathanson – after brand consultants advised that doing so would be symbolic of broader clarity. The firm's 'Clarity Matters' relaunch involved presentations to staff, newspaper ads and a revamp of the web site. *"Overnight, all the old stationery, pencils and notepads, everything, was removed from the office." "The consultants talked to us about being more concise and making less use of legalese, being more informal and addressing people by their first names,"* trainees recalled. Scepticism was rife, according to one interviewee. *"In particular, I became suspicious of how much they cost as their presentation was so slick... but they were clearly effective because I now ask myself, 'Is this advice clear enough?' and I rewrite e-mails and draft things much better. I didn't want to buy into it, but I had to because it works. I was converted in about a week!"*

Trainees did flag up concern about lack of evening secretarial support in London and a perceived reluctance by the partners to flash the cash *"on the little extras, things like departmental do's having bigger budgets."* That said, for the most part our sources were *"bowled over"* that they had chosen Nabarro. Said one: *"I get a good deal here: I get paid well and get good experience, and I will* qualify into a department I enjoy and that wants me." Of course, not everyone enjoys such luck. A proliferation of would-be employment lawyers in 2006 when there was a lack of employment NQ vacancies was a timely reminder that "the emphasis here is on property and even the other seats will commonly have a property flavour, if only through the clients. People need to realise that this emphasis can lead to hassle for the niche seats." In 2007, 25 of the 27 qualifiers proved to be a good match and stayed on in NQ roles.

Trainees are adamant "there's definitely a Nabarro type of trainee... hard-working, but someone who appreciates the work-life balance. There are one or two corporate types but generally trainees are not massively competitive. Everyone is very nice... and the girls are all quite girly." They see Nabarro as "less aggressive" than other big London firms and for many "the culture and hours make it stand out. I wouldn't have survived anywhere with ridiculous hours."

Nabarro has always helped trainees develop their networking skills. A trainee-run group called Clear Contacts lays on three events a year – presentations, wine tastings, etc – with a view to trainees meeting their peers at client companies and other professional organisations. The same thing goes on in Sheffield. "We sit down every three months and say, 'We have X amount of money in the pot, what do you want to do with it?' It's basically about meeting up with contemporaries and establishing a friendship. It's good for us because at the huge networking events put on by the firm only senior people attend and you can sometimes think 'I am a junior – why do you want to talk to me?'"

Trainees have no issues getting to know each other. At the start of the training contract they attend "a really good two-week induction" and are then reunited in Sheffield for further PSC sessions in their second year. Last time the trip up north included "a lot of drinking and extremely cheesy music in a club called Hotpants." Back in

London, the trainees organise karaoke and bowling nights, and a trip to a roller disco near King's Cross was "disturbingly well attended." On Friday nights people hang out in The Enterprise nearby. "You can just turn up for one drink or you can be out until 4am." Remember, this is not the Square Mile: "We are in a really nice location close to Covent Garden and with a bit of personality."

and finally...

"If you want to get a job at Nabarro, do a vac scheme." Around 90% of the firm's trainees are selected this way and our sources agreed the scheme gave them an accurate picture of the firm's character and its property-centric business.

Norton Rose

the facts

Location: London
Number of UK partners/solicitors: 142/324
Total number of trainees: 101
Seats: 6x4 months
Alternative seats: Overseas, secondments
Extras: Pro bono – Tower Hamlets, Tooting and Battersea Law Centres, RCJ CAB, FRU; language training

Are you attracted by big-firm training and a high salary but can't see yourself working for a magic circle or US firm? Several of our Norton Rose interviewees indicated they wanted to "go somewhere with a strong international component and the quality of deals featured in the FT." If that strikes a chord, read on...

high-speed training

Norton Rose is one of the best known of the bigger firms in the City. It has a pedigree stretching back into the mists of time and a network of 21 offices around the world employing 1,000 lawyers from

Brussels to Beijing. The area for which the firm is best regarded is finance, more specifically asset finance, project finance and Islamic finance. The firm's asset finance lawyers worked on a £2bn credit facility for the world's largest cruise line Carnival, advised easyJet on its first Japanese operating lease and helped AerCap BV on the $4bn purchase of 70 Airbus A320 aircraft. The Islamic finance team meanwhile has been busy putting together an Abu Dhabi Islamic Bank EMTN programme 'sukuk' worth $5.2bn. And while we're talking big numbers, what about the work for Dubai Islamic Bank and Dubai World on the launch of its $5bn family of private equity funds?

Its projects work is much admired, particularly in relation to the rail and energy sectors. The NR lawyers in London have been advising Equinox Minerals on the $600m project financing on the Lumwana copper mine in Zambia, the largest mining project finance transaction to have ever taken place in sub-Saharan Africa. Staying on the right side of the tracks, they advised HSBC Rail and Lloyds TSB on the £87m financing of two rail maintenance depots at Ashford and Ramsgate. Next time you are whizzing past on the Eurostar, perhaps you can spare a thought for the lawyers on the deal. Not wishing to be left in the shadows, the corporate lawyers at NR have been active too, last year advising Aer Lingus Group on its admission to the Irish Stock Exchange and the London Stock Exchange. When Ryanair then made a hostile takeover bid for the company, it again turned to NR to help fend off its rival's advances.

champagne breakfasts

If corporate and finance leaves you cold, forget about NR, but if you've a hunch you'll enjoy them then rejoice in the fact there are many varieties to choose from. As well as teams focusing on things such as asset finance, Islamic finance and project finance, the corporate department contains groups dedicated to assisting M&A, AIM and private equity clients. Many trainees opt to spend time in more than one transactional team. It is possible, for example, to follow a straight banking seat with a stint in the aviation finance team, which has made quite an impression in the aviation sector and this in turn has helped other teams to win work from airlines. The transactional departments can get extremely busy and workflow is unpredictable, so arriving in a new seat can be *"a real baptism of fire."* *"My supervisor remembers me sitting open-mouthed in meetings, like a fish gaping for air,"* one trainee recalled. It's no wonder some trainees admit to feeling daunted at first, although *"once you get into it the deals are interesting and challenging."* Be warned; it will take more than a tidy desk and being *"super organised"* to get you through a training contract at NR – sheer stamina is often a requirement. *"There was a month when I stayed until midnight every evening... although I never came in at weekends,"* said one not-atypical source. Several people spoke about *"3am finishes,"* and one recalled a completion that didn't wrap up until 7am. On that occasion the trainee was sent home *"in a taxi with what was left of a bottle of Champagne,"* so it's not all bad. Generally, trainees say they work late nights only if *"something major is going on,"* adding that *"it's important to get as involved as possible on a deal so that you understand what's happening."*

Away from corporate and finance options, there are seats in real estate (including property litigation, environment and planning), dispute resolution, competition and regulatory, employment incentives and pensions, tax and IP.

second bite of the cherry

With so much emphasis placed on corporate and banking, it comes as no surprise that trainees must do a seat in each of these departments as well as one in dispute resolution. Considering too that most trainees do a second stint in their favourite team and a secondment either at home or abroad, this generally leaves one totally free seat to play around with. Our interviewees were universally enthusiastic about the firm's six-seat training contract. It makes a client secondment or an overseas seat even more appealing as you *"are not gone for so long"* so there's no concern about missing out on crucial time in the London HQ. The firm currently offers placements in-house with companies including Nestle, ExxonMobil and AIG. Trainees tend to come away from the in-house experience with a *"jack-of-all-trades"* knowledge of company law. In general, the six-seat rotation is good for *"all-round exposure to a lot of departments, which helps you identify your favourite seat, so you can go back again."* This second bite at the cherry is a big deal: the team you return to *"knows what you can be trusted with,"* which can *"ease the transition between trainee and NQ."* The firm's handling of qualification and retention was complimented by our interviewees, who told us: *"HR lets you know where you stand as soon as they can."* It was also nice to hear that the firm offers CV-building assistance to those trainees not being offered a job in order to help them find one elsewhere.

one world, one firm

Never underestimate *"the strong international aspect"* to the work on offer at NR. As a result the firm *"really emphasises its overseas seats."* In fact *"it's stressed from such an early stage that if you don't want to go on an international secondment, people might ask why you applied to this firm in the first place."* Here's what trainees say about the experience of living and working abroad for four months: *"It makes good business sense for us to be on the ground in other countries, and it means we get to meet the people we will be dealing with in future."* One trainee who had done their homework also observed: *"Financially, the international offices are more self-sufficient than they have been in the past, so it's not all about London anymore, anyway."*

Assuming you're going to go abroad, where might you end up? If *"flash, modern offices"* and *"panoramic views"* float your boat, Hong Kong, Singapore and Dubai are recommended as the most *"glamorous"* of the options. Reflecting the firm's impressive reputation for Islamic finance, Bahrain is another hot destination. Trainees also report having *"a blast"* in Athens, Amsterdam, Paris, Milan and other European destinations. Don't imagine that an international secondment is a holiday, even if you will get to enjoy an authentic croissant or cappuccino on your way to the office. *"You get chucked in the deep end, and because you are part of a smaller team you tend to do mid-level associate work and often go to client meetings alone,"* is a typical story. In short: *"You work really hard."* That said, *"if the office is quiet you have the joy of exploring a new country at the weekends."* And because *"everything stays open well into the night, you can work late and still go out."* If the hours on the Tube are wearing you down, there is also the appeal of a well-located flat from which *"everywhere important is within walking distance."*

more london

Then again, with a brand new building by the Thames, turning up to work in London is pretty exciting at the moment. Said one interviewee: *"The office is palatial in comparison to the old one. I feel like I'm walking through an architect's sketchbook!"* And not just any old architect. The design is by Norman Foster – he of the Gherkin and Millennium Bridge fame. While the building itself wins plaudits, it has, more importantly, *"brought the whole firm together."* For many years NR was split across several shabby offices. In practice this meant *"you hardly knew what some people looked like. It was just easier to pick up the phone."* Now, "there are a lot more meetings" and it's not uncommon to "bump into your friends in the lift." Kempson House may have had "cutesy charm," but none of the trainees we spoke to were sorry to leave it – or the "minging canteen" – behind. Nowadays, riverside seating and "flash new dining facilities" where meals are "freshly cooked to order" make lunchtime a far more pleasurable experience. Trainees also enjoy drinks on the roof terrace, "overlooking Ken" in the Greater London Council offices situated nearby. Right below the office is the Scoop, a new outdoor entertainment venue that frequently hosts free concerts on a summer evening.

Those who want to venture further afield have several opportunities each year to enjoy trainee parties. "These are usually held on a Thursday in an attempt to encourage us to drink less because we have to come in the next day... it doesn't usually work," declared one conspiracy theorist. Other potential distractions include football, rugby and cricket. The popularity of these sports doesn't surprise us given NR's well-documented emphasis on teamwork. Indeed fun and friendship seem to be pretty high on the agenda. "The trainees get on really well – it's not competitive at all and we all stick together. There's real camaraderie here." This goes as far as group photos of each trainee intake (rather like an Oxbridge college freshers' photo minus the gowns and mortar boards), allowing you to "have a photo of your mates to keep." So who is the firm recruiting, we wondered. According to trainees, it is "not overly-ambitious, ultra-high-flying" types. "Basically, we're the down-to-earth people you'd have liked at university, not the oddballs nor the super-competitive, in-your-face ones," argued one trainee. "There aren't lots of plummy-voiced, posh people. We're outgoing, chatty and easy to get along with," another added. In 2007, 57 of the 60 qualifiers were offered jobs and 53 stayed on with the firm.

nice work if you can get it

NR's workplace reputation seems to have been the clincher for a large percentage of our interviewees. It came as no surprise to learn that many had visited the firm in advance or taken part in its vacation scheme. "A surprisingly friendly feel to the place" and "nicer, more enthusiastic people than I had met at other firms" were typical first impressions. Trainees agree that there seems to be "less of a hierarchy" here than at other firms. "I wouldn't be scared about asking a partner something," declared one. "At some point you're bound to ask a silly question, but you're actively encouraged to make sure that you understand everything, so everyone is very patient." Apparently, it is not unusual for trainees to accompany senior lawyers, "who never snub you," to business development socials. "Being able to talk to all kinds of people is a skill the firm is keen on." This attitude makes the less favourable aspects of City training far more palatable. For instance, "working long hours is so much easier when everyone is nice."

This talk of niceness is all well and good, but does it mean that training at NR leaves you more docile Dalmatian than hungry hound? Trainees were quick to assure us that "we may not be nasty, but this doesn't mean we don't have a go-get-'em attitude." Interestingly one insightful source noted a shift in priorities at the firm. "Norton Rose's strategy seems to have changed. When we signed up it was trying to compete with the very top, the magic circle. When that didn't happen, the firm decided to adapt itself and it seems more comfortable now."

and finally...

At time of going to press, NR's website and graduate recruitment material was full of photographs of trainees fooling around on motorcycles. We couldn't help noticing that among bikes picked for the shoot there were no growling, attention-seeking Harley Davisons – vintage scooters were the order of the day. This sums up the firm rather well. If you are looking for something to make as much noise as possible, Norton Rose probably isn't the best choice, but if you'd rather have fun with your mates riding a classic, internationally known model, then it could be well worth a look.

Olswang

the facts
Location: London, Reading
Number of UK partners/solicitors: 80/174
Total number of trainees: 48
Seats: 4x6 months
Alternative seats: Brussels, secondments
Extras: Pro bono – Toynbee Hall and Tower Hamlets Law Centres

Born in 1981, Olswang was the darling of the dot-com boom. Things got hairy after the post-millennial crash, but undeterred by mere market forces the plucky folk over at The Swang transformed themselves into a more diverse operation which has blossomed into a top-30 law firm.

holborn's answer to logan's run
Olswang's success has often been attributable to wunderkind ex-chief executive Jonathan Goldstein, an Olswang lawyer who was appointed to the post at just 31 and who resigned when he hit 40 earlier in 2007. Trainees considered that *"Johnny epitomised Olswang"* and *"he was definitely the entrepreneurial driving force. It was a surprise when he resigned but there's no real panic. He'll pass the mantle on and the top boys here are good at what they do."*

You can still see the skeleton of a one-time media firm in Olswang, but this side of the business is only part of the story today. Sure, the client list is laden with technology and media clients, from eBay, FilmFour, BSkyB and ITV to MTV, Working Title Films, M&C Saatchi and Guardian Newspapers, and yes, some of the most notable recent hires have been connected to the IP and technology sector (eg top Slaughter and May IT partner Nigel Swycher, an IP team from US firm Kilpatrick Stockton); however, Olswang hasn't become stuck in an old business model. In 2003 it acquired a legion of property lawyers from disbanded firm DJ Freeman, and then more followed with the absorption of property boutiques Julian Holy and Kanter Jules. The real estate sector has become Olswang's second major success story in its quarter of a century of practice.

With the corporate and property departments now the twin engines of the firm, trainees can expect ample exposure to both these areas. No one's saying that in sport, entertainment, defamation and other areas of media law the firm isn't still at the top of its game, it's just that *"the whole media thing can easily be oversold."* As one trainee warned: *"Media is only a small part of what we do now. If you want to come here you need to know that a lot of the work is corporate-based."*

partner-poking
Everyone does a corporate seat, either private equity/mainstream corporate or tax. In the former, trainees are *"spread around the department and are fair game for various members of the department."* One source told us how their supervisor was *"flat out on an all-consuming deal, so I had a great corporate experiences but also many sleepless nights."* Facing a challenging workload of *"AIM acquisitions and floats, especially matters referred from media clients,"* trainees admit *"the responsibility was daunting at times."* Sure, *"you get caught up in drafting board minutes a lot,"* but *"you are also invited to sit in on conference calls so you understand their purpose"* and *"there's lots of interesting research."* Naturally the hours *"depend on the deals,"* but are generally *"hard – you've got to accept that."* Prospective applicants are encour-

aged to be realistic about the corporate-centricity of modern Olswang: *"Some people sign up for something they assume isn't as corporate as the bigger firms, so often they're taken aback."* Around 8pm is a common time to leave the office but when things are frantic clocking-off time is a moveable feast. At least you get a free dinner, a taxi home and the occasional day off after your diary has taken a pounding. In 2006 Olswang advised on over £11bn worth of M&A deals and its AIM practice became increasing international. On the cards were the £250m AIM IPO of an Indian property fund and PartyGaming Plc's acquisition of the online operations of Empire Online/Intercontinental Online Gaming.

The banking and insolvency department has its fans, not least because it boasts an inspirational head of department and is *"full of young people who really want to be there."* The team acts for both borrowers and an increasing number of lenders. Said one source: *"Quite a lot of the deals are property finance and we work for big investors."* By way of example, the Dawnay Day group of companies has been active in the European real estate market, which led to Olswang advising it on over £1bn worth of syndicated financing arrangements plus funding for the purchase of a shopping mall in Lithuania. In banking, a trainee's life is filled with *"conditions precedent"* and preparation of *"all the junior legal documents – that's board resolutions and directors' certificates, etc, as well as the post-completion paperwork."* Our sources enthused about the challenges involved: *"Acting for the borrower, you end up chasing documents from them and have to poke more senior fee earners to make sure they are doing what they need to. You have to be able to take ownership of the job and do whatever you can to progress things."* Like corporate, hours can be long: *"Quite often I'd be in at 9am and leave at 10pm or 11pm,"* but without a face-time culture *"when you do stay late, there's a sense of camaraderie; I never felt shafted."*

bring out the gimp

"Drafting and responsibility" sums up the appeal of property seats, which grant trainees relative autonomy on a portfolio of *"something like 25"* smaller files. One interviewee had *"assisted on sales of shopping centres by preparing reports and sales packs,"* *"dealt with the owners' managing agents,"* *"negotiated over lease terms and dealt with e-mails and phone calls."* Here the hours are *"a pretty civilised 9am to 6.30 or 7pm – the latest I worked was 9pm,"* and solid support means no one gets overloaded. *"We had training from the day we started in the department for three months – hour-long talks on leases and other essential topics,"* confirmed a satisfied source.

Sadly, commercial litigation *"doesn't have a great reputation,"* largely because it is *"heavy on document management and your involvement is gimp-like at a junior level."* Smart trainees persuade someone to give them a small case that's not cost-effective for anyone else to handle, thus giving them a shot at proper drafting. Even in the media litigation seat people can end up disappointed: *"I often spent time doing menial tasks and I'm not sure that's right for someone who is expected to be an assistant solicitor in a few months' time,"* moaned one trainee. *"If I were to qualify into litigation, I wouldn't know where to start in terms of witness statements and applications."*

The commercial group is comprised of an IP team, a media, communications and telecoms (MCT) team and a competition and regulatory team. The MCT lawyers handle Internet, e-commerce and data protection issues, plus broadcasting, TV, film, publishing and advertising matters. The film lawyers advise on finance and production for a raft of clients from the big and small screens. As well as a good deal of *"small budget Bollywood stuff,"* the lawyers handle *"big movies rolling in from US studios."* Some of the major releases they have assisted with include *Casino Royale, The Da Vinci Code, The Chronicles* of Narnia, *The Queen* and *Miss Potter*. Speaking of the lawyers as much as the clients, one trainee stressed: *"You're working for top people who are recognised in the industry"* and, as such, the seat is much sought after. The *"cerebral and research-heavy"* EU/competition seat is popular. One recent competition law dispute involved BT and the company that operates the 118 118 service. Of the MCT experience one source said: *"In the main it was good, but I would have liked to do more drafting – a lot of the agreements are far too complicated for a trainee... they break new ground."* At least *"the business sectors are interesting, which makes the work you do more interesting."*

In Reading, Olswang shares a building next to the railway station with Osborne Clarke and Morgan Cole. Two trainees are recruited each year and can sit in property and IP. For their other seats – one of which must be corporate – they commute to London. Like their London contemporaries, they also have access to the single Brussels seat and various client secondments. And what of overseas opportunities? Although a strategic alliance with US firm Greenberg Traurig is spawning new business, as yet there are no signs of stateside seats.

bright ideas

Precisely describing the firm's character gave some trainees a problem. *"It's energetic and vibrant... oh, that makes it sound like a nightclub,"* worried one. *"It's more entrepreneurial, more passionate than other law firms,"* countered another, a third concluding: *"The Olswang way is getting results by coming up with creative and bright ways to achieve them."* Carrying this self-image makes Olswang picky when it comes to recruiting, so don't assume that just because the magic circle wants to see you, The Swang will too. Trainees here are confident individuals, not least because many already have experience of the working world. The batch we sampled from in 2007 included former record/TV

company employees, a former management consultant, a renowned DJ (*"he's going to Amsterdam on a corporate trip soon and I reckon he's going to be mobbed!"*) and an MC (signed, successful and still gigging internationally). In other words Olswang is far more interested in people with *"the ambition to be a good businessperson, who are astute and presentable"* than any Oxbridge trainee template. This ambition sits comfortably alongside an *"informal"* culture that *"astounds friends in the magic circle."* Said one proud source: *"We're not slopping around in jeans and trainers, but even trainees have their names and photos on the website alongside the partners."*

Olswang's High Holborn office was designed in the image of a sail and true to the 'green' implications of a subsidised staff restaurant named Ozone, recycling is currently a big thing. *"People are still adjusting to it,"* admitted one interviewee; *"at first it was a bit like the green police clamping down."* We suppose wind turbines on the roof are the next step! After hours, staff frequent The Enterprise and The Old Nick pubs, but every year the social highlights are departmental all-expenses-paid weekends away. The hottest destination right now is Budapest, and apparently the legendary ski weekends are back in some departments. No expense is spared for weekends away, nor for the Christmas party: *"This year's was brilliant. It was at the Titanic Bar and it had a Casino Royale theme."* Hardly evidence of the firm's supposed original thinking, but presumably the leftfield ideas are saved for clients' business problems.

and finally...

Make sure you've an accurate picture of what Olswang has to offer. If technology and media clients excite you, that's fine. Just remember that much of what you'll be doing will be property and corporate focused, and pretty much all of it will involve hard graft. In 2007, 14 of the 18 qualifiers stayed on with the firm.

Orrick, Herrington & Sutcliffe

the facts
Location: London
Number of UK partners/solicitors: 14/27
Total number of trainees: 16
Seats: 4x6 months
Alternative seats: Overseas seats

In early 2007, following months of negotiation regarding a prospective merger that could have created a top-ten global heavyweight, diplomatic relations between US powerhouses Orrick and Dewey Ballantine broke down. Orrick immediately vowed to redouble its offensive on the European market and its young training scheme is one of the weapons it is seeking to employ.

coudert d'etat
Born and raised in San Francisco in 1863, Orrick's ambitious growth has earned it a formidable reputation in the USA. More recently it has launched an aggressive programme of expansion in the European and Asian markets, creating an empire of over 900 lawyers throughout its 18 bases, of which around a quarter are now located outside the USA. Its foray into London began in 1998, but really gathered force in 2005 when it pounced on the vulnerable London arm of the now defunct Coudert Brothers. This was the crucial move for trainees, as not only did it see the London-presence of Orrick double to 50 lawyers, it marked the beginning of its formal training programme, carrying on where Coudert had begun and retaining nigh on all current and prospective trainees accepted by the firm. Having since failed to strike up a merger agreement with Dewey Ballantine, the firm has hatched a new expansion plan that places the London office on the front line of its European operations. Brimming with confidence after consecutive years of robust growth in numbers and turnover it is now working to double its ranks over the coming 18 months.

sky high
Orrick earned its spurs through work on the issuance of bonds for the construction of San Francisco's Golden Gate Bridge and has since then relied heavily on its strong name in finance, using it as a catalyst for expansion. In London the finance team is very much the engine room of the office, making it a must-do seat for trainees. In 2006 it made waves in the market with the lateral hire of ex-Cadwalader transatlantic securities expert James 'The Bond' Croke, and close collaboration with its overseas network provides access to major clients such as Goldman Sachs and JPMorgan. As a result, our parent publication *Chambers UK* has started to take note, earmarking it as *"one to watch in the collateralised debt obligation arena."* Unsurprisingly, this type of work is tricky to explain in layman's terms, but we'll have a go. In short, Orrick London is going great guns in relation to a type of structured finance product that securitises a diversified pool of debt assets. Moreover, we hear that the majority of the group's work is synthetic and that it acts for both issuers and managers. If all this jargon has you coming out in a cold sweat then maybe this is not the place for you. For those with a taste for all things financial, however, there is much on offer.

Described variously as *"intense"* and *"high-pressure,"* a seat in the finance division is not for the faint hearted, but those with strong tickers say it offers *"really interesting and stimulating work with some big clients."* One of the things that makes it interesting is the cross-border nature of the deals. *"I am working with a lot of lawyers in our overseas offices and also local counsel in other jurisdictions,"* said one source. The trainees work closely with partners and associates on large transactions and their role gives them a real range of experiences. *"One day you may be charged with commenting on, negotiating or drafting a transaction document, and then another you'll be given less exciting tasks like checking precedents, etc."* Experiences of client contact were similarly mixed, with some sources claiming near daily contact and others describing almost a backroom role. Through working so closely with partners, trainees always feel like *"part of the bigger picture."*

Structured finance is undoubtedly the department's main selling point; however, it can also offer trainees exposure to international acquisition and project finance work. In all areas of finance, the hours can be pretty tough, in part because the firm does not have paralegals to share the load with trainees. Said one trainee: *"All-nighters are not the norm, but on a big deal it is standard to work till the early hours."* At least these hours are spent in spectacular surroundings – Orrick's offices in Tower 42 give 360° views of the capital. One smug source spoke to us while *"looking out at the Gherkin, Canary Wharf and the Millennium Dome."* Add to this a healthy salary, (*"higher than most English firms"*) and the pace and demands of this flagship department are put in context.

well-troden path

Orrick London does not currently offer huge scope for seat choice so most trainees follow a similar path. In addition to a finance seat, they are likely to do a stint in the property department, which has a notable social housing practice and is largely domestic in focus. One of its largest transactions of late was for old client Notting Hill Housing Group, which acquired a major site for 174 private sale and social housing units at a consideration of £33m. *"If you show an interest, they are happy to throw you as much responsibility as you can handle"* ...within certain limits. *"It is a highly litigated area, so the firm supervises you heavily. This means you get a good training on the structuring and negotiation of deals."*

For their contentious seat trainees see both commercial litigation and international arbitration. The former is faster paced and *"alive;"* here

trainees draft witness statements and gather evidence, as well as making frequent visits to court. International arbitration on the other hand tends to involve large and complex disputes where *"organisational skills are essential"* to keep on top of vast quantities of paperwork. Overall, one trainee summed up the prevailing mood nicely: *"It's a good department, but it's small. You wouldn't come to this firm on the strength of its litigation team."* Similar things could be said of the office's corporate team. Here, the London office lags behind the rest of the firm, which has added significant firepower on the West Coast and in Paris in recent times. Had it proceeded, the merger with Dewey would certainly have been of great benefit to the corporate team. Nevertheless, trainees believed the disparity would not last, and that growth would be achieved in London in time. For now the compact corporate team offers trainees close contact with fee earners and good hands-on involvement in transactions. *"You are involved in a deal from beginning to end and informed throughout about how you are contributing."* Other seat options include competition and employment; however, the 2007 qualifiers found that everything boiled down to finance at the end of the day. Two of the four left due to a lack of non-finance vacancies; the other two snapped up finance positions.

united nations

Orrick's training scheme is only a nipper compared to some of those at the established City giants and as a result it is not as structured. What it can offer is *"on-the-job training"* and this received top marks from our interviewees. As the firm increases its intake to eight trainees a year, it recognises the need for the programme to evolve and has been consulting trainees on how to improve things, particularly in relation to formal training.

A *"work-hard, play-hard"* ethos means that there is plenty to get your teeth into outside of work. In this small office, few faces are unfamiliar and monthly drinks (at which a credit card is put behind the bar) are a good opportunity to get to know anyone guilty of hiding under their paperwork. We also caught a whiff of some ten-pin bowling-related fun and a client-schmoozing day at Windsor Races.

Trainees described themselves as *"an eclectic bunch"* and many commented on the *"strong characters on display that make it an interesting place to work."* This is undoubtedly aided by the incredibly diverse intake, with Sweden, France, Belgium, Iraq, Ireland and Kazakhstan all having representatives among the 2006/07 group. This international flavour has led to some interesting trainee nights out. *"So far this year we have had a Japanese night where we ate local food and ended up in Soho having a good old karaoke sing-song, and a Swedish-themed night where we had smörgåsbord."* At the time of our interviews our sources were busy locating suitably impressive sombreros for the forthcoming Mexican night. The firm is also doing its bit to drive home its international standing, recently setting up secondments to Orrick's Hong Kong and Paris offices... much to the delight of two lucky trainees!

and finally...

The words of one of Orrick's eclectic troupe summed up the scenario quite nicely: *"If you are interested in finance, property or international work then the firm has a lot to offer."* Anyone fitting the bill will have to start thinking about what they, in turn, can offer the firm. One look at the trainees reveals that language skills are looked upon favourably (although this is not a prerequisite to application) and *"most trainees have at least a year of prior professional experience either in law or elsewhere."*

Osborne Clarke

the facts

Location: Bristol, Reading, London
Number of UK partners/solicitors: 88/212
Total number of trainees: 42
Seats: 4x6 months
Alternative seats: Overseas seats, secondments

Osborne Clarke began life in 1748 in Bristol. More than 250 years on it has three UK offices (Bristol, Reading and London), three abroad (Cologne and Munich in Germany and Silicon Valley in California), plus affiliations with eight European firms which together make up the OC Alliance

we have the technology

OC grew rapidly around the turn of the millennium by focusing on technology-led clients. The downturn in technology work after the dotcom crash resulted in some reshuffling, partner losses and introspection on the part of the firm, leading eventually to a diversification of practice. At present there is a well-pronounced drive to improve the corporate department and secure more high-quality mid-market work. The plan looks to be paying off, with the firm now coming tenth in Hemscott's ranking of firms by the number of AIM clients they act for – OC represented 28 in 2006. Its general client list is looking rather healthy too: on the books are De Beers, M&S, Close Investments, Somerfield, Topland, Investec Investment Banking and the Insolvency Service of the Department for Business Enterprise and Regulatory Reform. It still has a raft of technology sector clients and these include big names such as Microsoft, Carphone Warehouse, Vodafone UK and Nintendo. In short, there has been a rapid rise in turnover and profits since those shaky, post-dotcommedy years.

Overseeing the return to form is Simon

Beswick, managing partner since 2003. Having just been re-appointed for another term of office, Beswick's current plan is nothing more dramatic than further consolidation across a range of departments, with corporate leading the way. Indeed, trainees sensed that the corporate lawyers were *"proud of the fact they are pushing the firm forward."* In the past couple of years it looked to us as if OC trainees were still hung up on the technology work that had been its trade mark and not keen enough on becoming corporate or other transactional lawyers. This year our sources thought the trainee group displayed *"a much broader range of interests."* Which is just as well, given the firm's more generalist plans. At least trainees are kept in the loop as to what's going on: *"The top bods come to each office and give a presentation on how the firm is doing and where they want it to be in a year's time."* They were left in no doubt after the last presentation that there needs to be a concerted effort to gain more top-quality work from large, prestigious companies.

one firm, three offices

The firm believes fervently in the idea of 'one firm, three UK offices', so trainees join OC the firm, not an individual office. The trainee seats are spread across all three offices, Bristol offering most, followed by London then Reading. The number of trainees in each office reflects this distribution. So does this make OC a Bristol-led firm? Well, it depends where your heart lies. A Bristol-minded trainee might well feel they worked at the heart of the firm and talk about how their employer differs from the other top player in the city – Burges Salmon. In doing so they would stress OC's international credentials. A London-centric trainee would see things entirely differently, viewing the office in the capital as the future of the firm. Indeed, one source joked: *"Bristol is where we chuck tax issues."* Over the two years trainees are likely to become familiar with all three offices, either by moving for seats or visiting on departmental training days. Sometimes training involves whole weekends away, with teams from across the network meeting to discuss their work, absorb a little law and then socialise.

Seats can be taken in the following practice areas: banking; commercial; corporate; employment, pensions and incentives; litigation; property; tax; and private client. Here's the rub: not all seats are available in all offices. Picking up on one of our London interviewee's comments, the tax department, for instance, is solely Bristol-based. Marking a shift from previous years, OC's website clearly warns potential applicants they should expect to do property and corporate seats. We got the impression that property is quite a *"deep-end"* seat, with trainees taking on their own caseload and working on files from beginning to end. Among the department's biggest deals have been npower renewables' bid to develop Forestry Commission land for wind farming and the financing of the residential element of the Broadmead extension in Bristol. Regular clients include Bristol Cathedral School, Bristol Zoo, Eurostar and QinetiQ plus a healthy list of property companies and house builders.

are ewe paying attention?

At present corporate tends to go to first-seaters, reflecting its nascent popularity (or lack of it depending on your perspective). The level of responsibility is somewhat stepped down in corporate and, given the size of deals and trainee tasks, they can often share work between themselves. Tasks are *"mostly administrative"* with only a few drafting opportunities, but given that organising documents gives a good overview of a corporate deal maybe this is what a trainee needs in their first seat. There can be high-pressure moments, like *"being in a completion meeting and everyone turning to you to find a certain document* in the folder... the expectation is that the trainee will know where everything is." Arguably, if corporate seats were occupied by more experienced trainees, tasks might be more demanding. Then again, we heard from one or two sources that if sufficient willingness and competence is shown, there is an opportunity to manage your own smaller deals a few months into the seat. The odd all-nighter is a possibility in all offices, and on occasion trainees may see recompense in the form of time off the following day. Talking of all-nighters, one trainee selected such an incident as the highlight of their training contract: "Once everyone has signed everything, people go from being awful and stressed to laughing and joking and enjoying the Champagne." In terms of training, at least in Reading, there are "sheep-dip sessions" at which groups of up to ten junior lawyers are guided through areas of corporate work by senior associates or partners. Finally with regard to corporate, we'd like to raise a mug of Darjeeling to the head of the corporate department in Bristol who "does a full tea round for the private equity team whenever he wants a cup himself."

Seats in the commercial and employment departments are immensely popular, which means they tend to go to fourth-seaters. The Bristol employment team can proudly boast relationships with major employers such as Motorola, Wincanton, Carnival, Eurostar and Western Power and the team frequently works with US corporations in relation to their European operations. The presence of pensions and employee incentives experts is also a boon for clients. Silicon Valley (for a TMT seat) is another really prized opportunity, but it is currently on hold as the office goes through a reshuffle. Secondments to the German office in Cologne – or to one of the Alliance firms – are always on the cards. Client secondments were described as "commercial awareness eye-openers," with those people who'd completed one emphasising how

things need to be done in "a practical, cost-effective way." These secondments are organised on an ad-hoc basis with e-mails sent out to gauge interest. Recently trainees have visited RAB Capital for six-month secondments.

In all seats there is a great deal of support available from the TKLs (training and know-how lawyers) and PAs (the OC name for secretaries), such that "it is definitely not the case that trainees are chained to photocopiers." In all three offices the hours hover around the 9am to 7pm mark, with corporate and banking usually the culprits for keeping people later.

lawyers in tights

The ad hoc social scene is more trainee or department-based in Bristol and London, whereas in Reading "it is more of a wider office thing because we're a smaller office." With only 58 staff in the Thames Valley, there is a lot more cross-departmental interaction – ideal for anyone who likes a close-knit atmosphere. Reading staff can often be found in Bar Four... when they're not indulging foodie passions at Italian restaurant Il Gusto (which, oddly, showcases belly dancers on the last Friday of the month). The London lawyers often head out on Thursday nights to the Lord Raglan pub, a very short walk from their office in a Norman Foster-designed building at One London Wall. Bristol – dubbed "chino-land" by one London trainee – has a lively Friday-night social scene centred on the redeveloped harbour. All three offices were described as quite swish. London, being a Foster, is "very glassy;" Bristol has its own building near Temple Meads train station; and the Thames Valley branch is growing to the extent that it extended its premises in 2006. It too is near the train station.

Logistically it would be very difficult to bring all three offices together for a party so at Christmas each one organises separate celebrations. We heard the most detail about the last London party. Along with a DJ, dancing and food, there was a huge vodka luge ice sculpture in the shape of the firm's cat/panther/mountain lion/ocelot (delete as desired) logo. Never one to shirk a challenge, OC does indeed throw a firm-wide party in the summer. The last one was held at Thornbury Castle in Gloucestershire and was well attended by staff from all the UK offices and the German offices. The medieval theme was a thinly veiled excuse for people to wear tights and settle old scores through jousting. In the words of one source, it was *"slightly scary that some people take fancy dress so seriously."* The OC UK and OC Germany football teams hold their own version of the World Cup each year. Despite the fact that *"there is a great deal of rivalry,"* we reckon it's probably safer than jousting. As a part of the firm's efforts to keep in touch with future joiners, they too are invited to the party. Tights are not mandatory. FYI: OC encourages people to study the LPC at UWE or the College of Law.

Overall we only noted one significant downside, which relates to some unresolved issues with seat allocation. Some of our sources thought HR were *"absolutely transparent"* about how people were selected for seats and offices; others felt they were *"cagey."* The firm assured us it is working on a new approach to seat allocation to improve the process, so watch this space. The impression we get is that there are just too many variables for anyone to arrive at the firm dead set on doing a seat in a particular department in a particular office... unless perhaps it's corporate or property. Of the 21 qualifiers in 2007, just 11 stayed on, several taking up corporate positions and the rest taking jobs across the firm's practice areas.

and finally...

If you are happy with the idea of a compulsory corporate and an all-but-compulsory property seat, this firm offers great-quality training and a selection of working environments. As in so many firms, trainees felt that completing a vac scheme with OC *"stands you in good stead for getting a training contract; in fact if you do one you are probably two thirds of the way there."*

Palmers

the facts

Location: Basildon, South Woodham Ferrers, Thurrock
Number of UK partners/solicitors: 10/18
Total number of trainees: 5
Seats: 4x6 months
Alternative seats: None

We know what you're thinking, because it was the first question we put to Palmers trainees too. Why Essex, when London is so close?

palmer reading

"I had no desire to be a part of the City, that's just not what I'm interested in," confided one source. Another agreed: *"I'd studied in London for several years and I knew I did not want to work there."* Okay, so you've crossed the capital off the list – that still leaves a lot of other options. Some Palmers trainees choose the county because of family links, it's true, but others have no connection whatsoever and came to the firm purely because of what it has to offer. But what is this exactly?

As one of south Essex's largest commercial/private client firms, Palmers is certainly well placed to offer a broad training contract. Founded in 1983, the firm now has a staff of over 120, which caters to a broad clientele. For private clients it offers residential conveyancing, family services, wills and probate advice, criminal representation and general litigation, debt and insolvency services. Business clients, meanwhile, consult the firm on issues relating to company and commercial law, company acquisitions and disposals, shareholder advice, partnerships, employment matters, IP and dispute resolution. The main office is situated in Town Square, Basildon, and there are two further offices in South Woodham Ferrers and Chafford Hundred, Thurrock. This last location in particular reflects the firm's push for growth, as the Thames Gateway regeneration will inevitably bring in new business and clients. *"Conveyancing, family and wills and probate work is a given – we're always going to have a reliable stream of instructions on that front because of our high street presence. But commercial is where the firm has the potential to grow,"* explained one source.

action packed

Right from the word go trainees can influence which seats they take: they make it *"abundantly clear"* at interview where they want to go and then get to state their preferences again at appraisal time. There are no compulsories and the choices are as follows: commercial litigation, commercial and residential property, IT, construction, corporate finance, corporate tax, crime, defamation, employment, family, insolvency, IP and private client. Most seats are taken in the Basildon HQ; the Chafford Hundred office (coco, IT, IP and family) and the South Woodham Ferrers office (private client, property) being visited much less frequently. Officially trainees take four six-month seats, but in reality the firm is prepared to extend seats for an extra couple of months, arrange split seats or allow trainees to return to a department for a second bite at the cherry, if they know that's where they want to qualify. The seating arrangements are correspondingly fluid: *"In my first seat I shared an office with another trainee; second seat I had my own office; and third seat I shared with my training principal."*

In the commercial litigation department trainees work on primarily contractual disputes, drafting witness statements or preparing cases for court. *"I was looking after disputes between £5,000 and £15,000,"* reported one. *"As well as the contract disputes, there were some debt-related disputes... non-payment of invoices."* The bigger litigation often stems from property or construction deals: *"We had a big property case while I was there,"* said a source who'd attended its mediation in London. *"It was great to see how it all worked, although it didn't half drag on – but that's all part of it I suppose."* In this seat there is plenty of scope for getting some court action yourself. *"If you show that you're capable of doing things, there's no limit – I attended court for enforcement hearings, summary judgment applications and directions hearings by myself. At the end of my seat I even did a small claims trial at the county court."*

Similar opportunities exist in the civil litigation and insolvency department. *"This group deals with agency matters, private client disputes, landlord and tenant work and bankruptcy cases."* Again there is enviable scope for major responsibility. *"About a month into the seat, I attended court with my principal and started advocating on possession hearings. The first couple of times your supervisor is there to make sure everything goes okay, but if you can handle it, the experience is yours from a very early stage."* In fact trainees cited this high level of autonomy as *"one of the best things about the department."* If it all sounds a bit scary, relax – *"if someone wasn't quite so confident then they'd cater for that as well."*

start with the corners

A commercial property seat develops drafting and negotiating skills. Said one source: *"I enjoyed the drafting, but I did not enjoy ploughing through all those commercial leases – some of them are monsters."* In previous years the seat has been split with coco. *"The two go hand in hand because if you're doing a business purchase, you have to do the due diligence and all the lease checks too."* Meanwhile, residential conveyancing sounds a bit like a jigsaw puzzle. "*My supervisor started me off with small bits of work on different parts of the process. To begin with I couldn't see the links, but suddenly everything slotted into place and before I knew it I was familiar with the whole process.*" As far as seats go, we're told this is fast-paced and stressful compared to others. "*You'll be working on one file and the phone will ring so you'll have to switch to another one just like that.*" Not that this is a bad thing. "*The work is interesting and you work hard for your clients, which is rewarding.*" Those of you who still aren't too keen should keep an open mind: "*I didn't enjoy it at all when I studied it, but coming here completely changed my mind.*"

A stint in the family department throws the trainee into divorces, childcare arrangements and injunctions in situations of domestic violence. "*I was in court a lot helping out... like a clerk... as well as drafting divorce petitions and preparing ancillary relief forms.*" The seat offers excellent client contact, and although at times it can be "*quite emotionally draining,*" there are definitely valuable skills to be gained. "*The first couple of times I was really nervous because you're afraid they're going to ask you difficult questions you don't know the answers to. But then you realise they know less than you do and you soon feel in control.*"

It's a sign of the firm's desire to meet its trainees' needs that a crime seat opened up last year. "*We only have one partner doing criminal law here and I don't think he's had a trainee for about seven years. So even though I expressed an interest in my application I didn't have high hopes. It was a fabulous surprise to be able to do the seat.*" As you'd expect, client contact and court time is plentiful, however, there's also a lot of legal aid paperwork to plough through. As for the subject matter, the partner takes on cases ranging from GBH, domestic violence and sexual assault right down to motoring offences.

macho macho man

As if all this variety of work weren't enough, trainees say Palmers has other strengths. Contracted hours are 9am to 5.30pm and there is "*no pressure whatsoever to work more than that unless it's a matter of emergency.*" Trainees also appreciated the partners' attitude: "*They're very positive and upbeat about the profession; they still clearly enjoy the job and I think that's very important. I wanted to be around like-minded people who were actually passionate about the law.*" There's a distinct lack of hierarchy at the firm: "*Everyone interacts with everyone and it's truly integrated.*" This integration extends between the offices. Thanks to a "*newfangled phone system and frequent e-mails,*" communication between the branches is good. "*If I need assistance on terms and conditions or some piece of non-contentious work, I'll ring up South Woodham because I know they have that specialism. Or if it's IP, the IP guy is in Thurrock.*" The partners also host quarterly fee earner lunches, which are "*a great chance to catch up on what people are doing.*"

The ability to gel easily was the one common trait trainees identified in their colleagues. "*We're all from different backgrounds, but if you want to get on in life, you have to get on with people. God that sounds awful – please don't put that in the book.*" Sadly, we're not as flexible with requests as Palmers is. Another thing worth noting is that "*the firm seems to be very open, especially when it comes to mature students – they like the fact that you've done something else before.*"

On the social side the Christmas party is the highlight of the year. At a hotel somewhere in the Essex countryside, all the offices combine forces for an evening of food, drinks and fun, sometimes in black tie, sometimes in fancy dress. Personally, we like the sound of fancy dress, as we're intrigued by the idea of "*partners dressed up as the Village People.*" On a more frequent basis, there are quiz nights, bowling evenings, summer barbecues and five-a-side football to keep everyone active after work.

and finally...

Even though Basildon is not the most happening part of the world, you have to be impressed at the way trainees describe their employer. *"This is an extremely good, professional firm which deals with everything from crime to coco,"* one summed up. Ultimately, Palmers caters well to different people's experience and confidence levels. *"If you're happy to have a go, then they're happy to let you."* Both of Palmers 2007 qualifiers stayed on, taking up jobs in residential conveyancing in Basildon and coco in Thurrock.

Pannone LLP

the facts

Location: Manchester, Hale
Number of UK partners/solicitors: 99/110
Total number of trainees: 35
Seats: 4x6 months
Alternative seats: Occasional secondmentss

Here are two facts for you to digest. Fact number one: Pannone announced a healthy turnover of £44m for the last financial year, which is an increase of 15% on the previous year. Fact number two: Pannone scooped an impressive third place in the *Sunday Times'* '100 Best Companies To Work For' survey, once again emerging as the highest ranked law firm in the poll.

a pat on the back

Is it really possible to balance the drive to be a thriving and profitable law firm while maintaining a reputation as *"a very friendly, down-to-earth and sociable"* workplace? Well, after chatting to some of Pannone's trainees we sense this firm has achieved the almost unachievable. *"Everyone tries to keep your motivation and morale up, you're constantly patted on the back,"* said one loved-up interviewee. It may

sound like a cliché, but the *"work hard, play hard"* attitude really seems to cut right through the firm with a precision not matched by many.

Life as a trainee is certainly no easy ride: *"You do have to graft and put the hours in."* It is made clear to trainees that they are expected to work an eight-hour day (excluding their lunch hour). As one positive source concluded: *"A lot of firms don't say what they expect you to work, so you might be stuck doing 12 hour days; here, as a general rule, you stop at eight hours,"* and while *"everyone has a strong work ethic, there is none of the pretentiousness of hanging around to be seen to be working."*

Pannone styles itself as *"the complete law firm,"* something emphasised by its near *"50-50 split"* between private client and commercial practice. Trainees cited this as one of its main attractions, one telling us: *"There are so many different areas of law covered, and a broad range is exactly what I wanted."* The training scheme offers the standard four six-month seats, and provided there is availability, recruits can decide which seats they'd like. *"They are very very accommodating and do their best to make sure you get the seat you want."* Although *"they might say, 'Have you thought about trying this seat,'"* they definitely will not *"push"* you into a department in which you've no interest. It is perfectly possible to stay on one or other side of the business, say trainees – *"Some of us take completely private client seats, some take completely commercial seats."*

All trainee seats are to be found in the main Manchester HQ as the small Hale office is merely an outreach branch for the benefit of private clients living on the south side of the city.

clinical finishing

We'll look first at the services for individuals. Pannone has exceptionally well-regarded clinical negligence and personal injury departments, each enjoying tier-one status in our parent publication *Chambers UK*. In the *"technically and medically complex"* clin neg department (which is purely claimant), regular tasks include drafting instructions to counsel, reviewing experts' reports and medical records, writing detailed letters to clients summarising the firm's advice and findings, and disclosure exercises. One lucky trainee told us: *"I can hand on my heart say I did very little in way of admin."* The quality of the cases that come to the department is described as *"brilliant"* due to a *"rigorous screening process,"* although there are also some *"lower value cases kicking about."* The team has handled numerous multimillion-pound claims for children suffering from cerebral palsy as a result of negligent midwifery and one case is now before the European Court of Human Rights. All those who experienced this seat found that, although it is a busy department, they had *"no qualms"* going to a supervisor and discussing things with them should their workload get too hectic.

During their seats in the renowned and ever-growing PI department trainees *"do everything,"* including drafting pleadings, visiting clients, taking statements and liaising with experts. Being given a lot of responsibility while you're learning the ropes is both invaluable and daunting at the same time. *"They don't just throw you in and say, 'Right go deal with this' – you get the experience* [by observing] *first and then test it out yourself."* Anyone eager for court time should make a beeline for this department as *"you get to go and watch a few hearings... and I have done a couple of things myself. It was slightly nerve-wracking, but you just need to bite the bullet and do it!"* There is also a chance you may get to see the work of the specialist travel litigation team when in this department. The lawyers here handle group actions, sometimes involving several hundred claimants in foreign jurisdictions. The firm has just secured Carole Nash Insurance as a lucrative client, and it is expected Pannone will be advising on upwards of 1,500 claims a year.

corporate exercise

If you get your kicks out of commercial law then rest assured there are plenty of seats where you could flex your corporate muscles. The coco team is continually expanding (for example, the number of assistant solicitors rose from nine to 16 in 2007), and its latest turnover figures are expected to be in excess of £5.6m. Within this department the firm offers specialist advice in IP, e-commerce and tax as well as mainstream corporate finance. An impressive client portfolio includes Texaco, Rentokil and Kellogg, and the firm has also secured a spot on the legal panel of Greater Manchester Passenger Transport Executive, which will see it advising on major transport projects such as the Manchester Metrolink £640m expansion. Should you choose a corporate seat, your to-do list will include drafting share purchase agreements and tonnes of research as well as a fair whack of basic admin and co-ordination.

If you like the sound of *"endless client meetings, conferences with counsel, attending trials, preparing trial bundles and doing case management conferences,"* then you might enjoy the commercial litigation department. In this *"fast-moving"* area of the firm, you are *"constantly busy as the work comes flooding in,"* but trainees still *"don't feel too pressured"* as supervisors *"always ask if your workload is manageable."* Spend time in commercial property and you'll be liaising with everyone from investors and developers to public sector organisations and leading financial institutions on the property lending side.

The employment seat offers contentious and non-contentious work, and you can be involved in one or other, or both, depending on *"what you express a preference in."* The department also has a *"good blend of clients,"* ranging from chief executives and directors to major employers like The Bank of England and Edexcel. The regulatory seat (formally known as 'business crime') sounds like an exciting one, and here trainees help the head of department with trading standards matters and fraud investigations, as well as liaising with the police and the Environment Agency.

a spoon full of sugar...

Pannone makes it very clear that it is proud to be a Manchester firm and gets straight to the point by insisting it is not interested in candidates who see the firm as a *"safety net"* application. Indeed Pannone goes a step further and actively states a preference for applicants with some kind of North West connection. If you're serious about wanting to work here, then a vacation scheme is highly recommended as the firm is aiming to recruit primarily via this route. Our sources spoke enthusiastically about it, saying it was a great way to see *"the type of people that work there."* As to who these people are, our sense is that the combination of increasing profits and turnover, together with the growing reputation as a much-loved employer, is making it ever easier for Pannone to recruit top-flight candidates.

Amusingly, the recruitment process involves a lunch with partners, each candidate being seated with a partner either side of them and the partners then moving round the table. *"It's a novel process,"* admitted one trainee, adding: *"I don't really have a problem speaking to complete strangers."* We rather like the idea, but then again we do wonder how easy it is to impress a managing partner while shovelling down forkfuls spaghetti or peas. Let's hope they choose the menu sympathetically.

We were constantly told about the friendly and approachable atmosphere at the firm, be it the *"welcome lunches"* whenever you join a new department or the *"Starbucks vouchers if you win an award."* Other perks include going home early on your birthday, Easter eggs and cakes. *"I have to mention the cakes,"* said one source; *"you get them all the time – birthdays, targets, year end..."* If all the sugar isn't enough to keep you on a high, then

maybe sweet words in appraisals will do the trick. These take the form of mid-seat reviews with the training partner, monthly or weekly (depending on department) meetings with supervisors and an end-of-seat appraisal. The meetings are great for requesting new experiences: *"If you want to try something else and your partner doesn't have anything, then they put the word round."*

decamp to the nou camp

Just because the firm, and indeed the trainee intake, has a higher female-to-male ratio, doesn't mean everything at Pannone is made of sugar and spice and all things nice. *"The amount of lunchtime training sessions is a downside,"* said one otherwise content source. *"Rarely a week goes by where you don't have one lunch interrupted."* Although after checking with the firm, it appears most of these are departmental, as there were only four lunchtime trainee sessions in the last year. Another contentious point is the (*"bloomin'"*) annual mooting competition, which is compulsory for second-years and sees Rodger Pannone make a guest appearance as one of the judges. *"Bizarre," "embarrassing"* and *"pointless"* were some of the words used to describe it, although a minority saw a point to the exercise.

Pannone's social calendar is bursting with good stuff. The trainees will often get together for lunch, birthdays and general nights out: *"We can quite often be found in Prohibition"* said one recruit. Bar 38 and Relish are also favourites. Among the many events organised by the firm, there are departmental meals and regular drinks set up by the social committee in a different venue each month. The firm has its own football and netball teams, and last year there was a football tour to Barcelona, where the team played against a member firm of the Pannone Law Group (a collection of independent European law firms that work in association with each other). This year the team went off to Milan, and most of the trainees tagged along for the ride. *"We go to support and have a few drinks and the firm subsidises the cost of the trip by £50."*

and finally...

Pannone is an expanding and successful firm, but it is also keen to stick to its Manchester roots and (Hale aside) remain a single-site operation. In this close-knit organisation, if you are *"keen and eager, then they are willing to help you progress."* Yes, this is a hard-working place, but be warned: *"If you're overly ambitious and the kind of person who will walk over other people to get to where you want, you won't fit in."* The qualifying trainees of 2007 obviously took to the firm's culture like ducks to water, because 14 out of 15 accepted jobs at the firm.

Paul, Hastings, Janofsky & Walker LLP

the facts

Location: London
Number of UK partners/solicitors: 8/27
Total number of trainees: 6
Seats: 4x6 months
Alternative seats: None
Extras: Pro bono – LawWorks

Conceived in Los Angeles 56 years ago, Paul Hastings has spread out across the globe, amassing 18 offices and over 1,000 lawyers along the way. A recent push in London has resulted in the adoption of a training scheme.

grow, grow, grow

Paul Hastings London marked its tenth birthday in the City by overseeing the first year of its trainee scheme. It is a symbolic move for a firm that has been slow in imposing itself on the UK legal profession. At the end of 2005, the softly

softly approach looked to be too frustrating for two of its top real estate partners, who left a sizeable hole when they departed for DLA Piper and Fried Frank. However, in the wake of this the firm has pursued a strategy of recruiting associates rather than partners and, as a result, its profits have rocketed and things are looking up. Over the course of 2006 the office's turnover leapt 84%, with the capital markets, real estate, tax and employment practices all key contributors to this impressive performance.

On the back of these strong financial results, the firm's worldwide managing partner Seth Zachary singled out London for growth. Indeed he intends to make the office the firm's second largest behind New York. This will require the firm to hike staff numbers from 40 lawyers to over 180, which is the number currently housed in its original home office in Los Angeles. In pursuit of this the firm has targeted a rise to 100 lawyers within two years and has moved into part of Allen & Overy's snazzy new building in the recently redeveloped Spitalfields area.

All of this will inevitably involve a return to lateral hires at partner level and it looks as if this process has already begun with the hire of US-qualified attorney Anthony Princi, who joins the London office from Orrick and brings with him a wealth of experience in creditor-side restructurings. The firm has also lured BLP's international projects head Jonathan Simpson, who comes with a roster of Eastern European government clients as well as leading financial institutions such as Citibank and RBS.

ready for takeoff

So what does the firm and its new training scheme look like at this stage? *"In London we have five main departments – real estate, employment, finance, corporate and tax. Trainees have to do the employment seat for their contentious requirement,* but otherwise it is essentially about choosing which one of the other four seats you don't want to do." Alternatively, there is the option of taking three different seats and returning to a favoured department for the fourth. In all seats, trainees share a room with an associate or partner and attend office-wide training and knowledge sessions.

Anyone who has previously heard of Paul Hastings will probably have come across it in relation to real estate, where it is one of the most dominant forces in the States. Although it has struggled to create the same spark in the UK, the 13-lawyer real estate team is an important part of its global practice and is frequently involved in UK aspects of massive international transactions. The lawyers represented Canadian developer Ivanhoe Cambridge on its $981m acquisition of three commercial shopping centres in Scotland, Canada and Spain. Only a few of the American firms in London have built significant real estate capability, and in this respect Paul Hastings really stands out. This is no small issue given the growing interest of North American investors in European real estate and the launch of US-style REITS (Real Estate Investment Trusts) in the UK. In London the firm is most prominent in hotel-sector deals, one highlight being advice to a consortium made up of Lehman Brothers Real Estate Partners, GIC (Government of Singapore) and Realstar on the acquisition of InterContinental Hotels' portfolio of 73 UK hotels for approximately £1bn.

So what does all this mean for trainees? "It is hammered into you on day one that we operate on a transactional basis on big multimillion-pound deals. It is not pure unadulterated real estate law." The responsibility-to-deal-value ratio is exceptionally good: "You work on massive deals where the magic circle would have 15 people on board, but we only have teams of four so you are treated almost like an associate." Almost is the operative word however, as "crap still falls down and there are also

plenty of grunt tasks to keep you busy." When not supporting the team on major transactions, client contact can be gained through running a few small lease and licence files under supervision.

Another of Paul Hastings' top practices to be imported from the USA to the London office is employment law. For trainees, time in the seat is split between advisory, transactional and contentious work. They can expect exposure to tribunals – and all the attendant bundling duties – plus "interviewing witnesses, assisting in the drafting of statements and loads of research." The transactional aspects of the seat mean due diligence exercises. The team's strength lies in employer representation and it was lately called in by an American client to defend it at an Employment Tribunal on a whistle blowing case.

In addition to these traditional strengths, corporate and finance are two areas the firm seeks to develop in London. The type of corporate work being done is typically cross-border (often on instruction from other Paul Hastings offices) and this inevitably leads to some testing hours. As one trainee saw it: "Everyone is going through the same and there is a very supportive atmosphere here." Among the typical tasks for a corporate trainee are "drafting corporate authorisations and confidentiality agreements, and reviewing parts of joint venture agreements." The finance department has a similar big-transaction focus, which unfortunately means next-to-no client contact for trainees. In particular, the team has thrown its weight behind asset finance in the aviation sector, an area in which one of its key clients is Engine Lease Finance, a company that has been financing transactions with a variety of lessees, including Air France/KLM, Virgin Atlantic, Gulf Air, GB Airways and Atlas Air.

mine's a half

When quizzed about the reality of training at an American firm in London, our sources agreed: "A *lot of the good things you hear about US firms ring true, but less so the negatives.*" First and foremost on the positive side are the salaries: these trainees bag £40,000 in their first year and £45,000 in their second. This rises to a whopping £90,000 should they stay with the firm on qualification. Then there is the advantage to be gained from "*working on small deal teams and getting a great level of responsibility,*" plus the attendant perks of cross-border work – namely opportunities to jet off around the globe. As yet there are no overseas seats for trainees, so they must get their travel fix on shorter business trips. Once qualified, however, an associate exchange programme allows lawyers to spend time working in another office.

Trainees were adamant that "*none of the nasty rumours in terms of being treated like shit are true.*" One added: "*I heard US firms were frightening, but here everyone is very approachable and willing to help. It makes a world of difference.*" However, there is no denying that the firm "*expects you to make yourself available at all times.*" Why else would they provide trainees with BlackBerrys to rest on their bedside tables at night? To add further context, we're told that the average billable hours in the London office are presently 5% higher than any other office at the firm.

So far no pattern has emerged in terms of the type of trainee who succeeds at Paul Hastings, but there is one simple message – academics really do count. Current trainees also believe it is important to "*demonstrate a high level of responsibility and a proactive nature, as you can't hide and you won't be spoon-fed here.*" Looking at the character of the office in general, one trainee had this to add: "*When they recruit people at any level, they are all from a particular mould – people who have a sense of humour and are friendly. There is no room for arrogant tossers.*" It was in relation to this that trainees displayed slight apprehension at the office's "*ambitious*" growth plans, fearing that the character of the office might change. At least the

training scheme isn't going to expand hugely in the near future. Four new joiners will arrive in 2008 and the firm would like to keep the intakes at that level for now.

Part of the office character involves "*treating trainees like adults,*" so a certain level of maturity is expected in return. Anyone applying straight from university would be advised to take note here, as this has led to a rather reserved social scene that is dominated by a "*one beer then home culture.*" However, we spoke to trainees just prior to a move to new premises and it was hoped that the new, buzzier location would "*spark something more on the social front.*" We also learned that quarterly associate events have been introduced and the new vacation scheme also has a social element to it.

and finally...
Paul Hastings London has the resources and power of an enormous global firm behind it and is embarking on one of the City's most ambitious growth strategies, making it one to watch.

Payne Hicks Beach

the facts
Location: London
Number of UK partners/solicitors: 28/24
Total number of trainees: 6
Seats: 4x6 months
Alternative seats: None

Payne Hicks Beach has existed since time immemorial, or at least since 1730 when the registration of solicitors began. Some of the firm's private clients may still have the dust of antiquity on their shoulders, but we think the commercial and property practices also merit a dignified tip of the hat. Given its Dickensian setting and well-established private client and family practices, training at PHB is about as far removed from the standard City package as Belgravia is from Bermondsey.

the woman in white (v white)

PHB's varied client list is a recipe for success: a large dose of the society pages with a dash of the *Sunday Times*' Rich List and a sprinkling of the business section for good measure. In addition to the old guard and the nouveau riche, PHB acts for charities like the London Oratory Society and the Royal College of Psychiatrists. PHB's family department has been instructed by the great and the good and it even got a piece of the action in the seminal case of White v White. Widely esteemed family partner and Lieutenant of the Royal Victorian Order, Fiona Shackleton has represented such A-listers as Prince Charles, Rick Stein, Professor Stephen Hawking and, most recently, Sir Paul McCartney. The family and private client practices are clearly central to the firm's success, a point that PHB recently emphasised by signing up to a new consortium of ten firms whose junior lawyers will receive specialised private client training at the College of Law.

The property department covers commercial, residential and agricultural property, as well as landed estates and property disputes. Clients include the Paper Company, the Salvation Army, Your-move, JPMorgan, Zurich and the Fiat Group. The department is also involved in the ongoing construction and disposal of the new village of Fairford Leys in Aylesbury. Within the dispute resolution department, PHB continues to work on some very interesting public and administrative law cases and is currently dealing with the Police Service of Northern Ireland's review of unresolved deaths. In the sports field, PHB acts for yachtswoman Dame Ellen MacArthur and 14 Olympic medallists, including gold winners Ben Ainslie MBE, Shirley Robertson OBE, Iain Percy and Sarah Ayton.

great expectations

PHB alternates between taking two and three trainees each year. Seat options include private client, family and property, plus dispute resolution and company/commercial (which itself includes employment). Trainees are always allocated their first two seats, with the firm usually happy to yield to the preferences of second-years. No seat is compulsory, but given their importance to the firm *"you're bound to do family or private client,"* if not both. Indeed, most trainees said they were initially attracted to PHB because of its *"terribly strong"* family and private client practices, so competition for seats in these departments is understandably fierce. The family seat is apparently *"a bit of a whirlwind."* The department *"has a younger vibe, and some of the partners and clients are quite glamorous."* The experience brings *"some really interesting work"* and *"quite a lot of responsibility,"* mainly drafting and research, attending court hearings and client meetings. There will inevitably be bundling duties, and if the outdoor clerk is off sick trainees can step in to *"do court runs and make applications."* Whereas family law has a huge *"people element,"* private client practice is by nature *"a cerebral and very complicated area"* and trainees here will encounter *"lots and lots of drafting."* Many clients have dual nationality or are UK residents domiciled elsewhere. Such a global spread of wealth necessitates *"mental gymnastics,"* especially when trainees need to get their heads round *"niche tax planning structures and multimillion-pound trusts."* Despite the mammoth size of some clients' wealth portfolios, trainees enjoy frequent contact with them and the occasional heritage chattel (family heirloom) visit thrown in.

By contrast, a seat in dispute resolution involves less responsibility. Aside from conducting research, it seems that trainees in dispute resolution are mostly consigned to *"bundling, lots of bundling"* and *"lots of photocopying."* It's not the most rewarding of options, even if the cases are frequently interesting. The property department, meanwhile, thrives on *"wheeling and dealing."* Our sources sensed it prefers visits from second-years because trainees are given *"total responsibility"* and run their own files. Trainees can also sink their polished teeth into *"conveyancing for landed estates, drafting residential and commercial leases and speaking to clients on the phone on a daily basis."* Although such a high level of responsibility is exhilarating, trainees admit: *"Sometimes you can't get people to answer your questions right away, so you can't afford to make mistakes."* Apart from the odd late night, office hours are reasonable across the firm, with a typical day ending at 6pm.

the old curiosity shop

Sitting amongst the Georgian splendour of New Square and Lincoln's Inn, surrounded by Romney portraiture and leather-bound books, PHB trainees proudly acknowledge the firm's *"traditional atmosphere."* The Lincoln's Inn location seems to transport them into a world of fog and gas lamps: *"You don't feel like you're in central London. It feels special,"* said one. This Dickensian atmosphere even extends to the office interior: instead of plasma screens, meeting rooms are chock full of *"antique furniture"* and *"in the property department, there's a working gas fire that you can warm your toes at when the partner's away."* Such old-school charm comes at a price, however: *"There is the odd mouse and the photocopier in No.3 jams so often that the engineer is like part of the furniture now."* As the firm has grown, its offices have had to branch out from the main 10 New Square building. For instance, the dispute resolution team is housed in No.3 and family sits in No.7. One trainee noted how this diffusion disrupts the PHB fraternity: *"No.10 is very separate from three and seven. You come across people all the time who you've never seen before."*

Despite the presence of self-confessed *"role model for people with Thirds"* Fiona Shackleton, nowadays PHB trainees tend to have very good degrees from Oxbridge or top redbricks, following on from stints in public/private schools. One trainee confessed: *"It's quite a middle-class, privately educated, good uni type of thing."* Freaks and geeks beware: *"It's not a firm for the way-out people or the geeky, boring types who stay for hours in the university library."* Instead, trainees are generally *"quite smart and quite traditional, although everyone's got a really good sense of humour."* Among a predominantly white, middle-class group of fee earners, some people have come from rather privileged backgrounds and we sense they fit in perfectly with PHB's distinctive culture. All three of the 2007 qualifiers stayed with the firm to take up jobs in the family and private client departments.

prince charming

The Lincoln's Inn area offers trainees a bar for every mood. There's the traditional Seven Stars with its house cat; the Law Society, which trainees see as *"the nice safe one down the road;"* the cheap and cheerful Penderel's Oak and, for those with a taste for Zubrowka vodka, Bar Polski. Sporting buffs can join the firm's tennis, cricket, hockey or netball teams, and the yearly Manches Cup sailing regatta is *"surprisingly, really good fun,"* although *"it's only trainees and young assistants – the partners never go."* Even those trainees who admit to being *"not terribly sporty"* are catered for by PHB's social calendar, which includes such gems as a flight on the London Eye and a yearly Trivial Pursuits play-off (20th anniversary edition, in case you were wondering). Every Thursday, in-house chef Fifi whips up a mouth-watering spread for fee earners to mingle over. One wise trainee warned: *"There's no rule that trainees can't drink at the staff lunch, but no one has ever dared to."* PHB hosts an annual summer garden party, although this year an unseasonable deluge forced the party inside, turning it into *"a rather rubbish drinks party in a room."* The Christmas party at Lincoln's Inn Hall tends to be well attended, perhaps because of the quality entertainment on offer. Every year the firm band performs, and it was most recently fronted by a trainee lead singer. Before you ask, one source insisted we point out that the band is not called The Payne Hicks Beach Boys. Shame. We wonder if the nimble-fingered partner who previously toured with the band Adam & The Ants ever indulges the PHB crowd with a nostalgic solo set? One can only dream...

and finally...

Fascinated by family or passionate about private client? If the answer is yes, and if you're more patrician than plebeian, we suggest you give PHB a ring.

Penningtons Solicitors LLP

the facts

Location: Basingstoke, Godalming, London, Newbury
Number of UK partners/solicitors: 65/85
Total number of trainees: 27
Seats: 4x6 months
Alternative seats: None

Penningtons will lose no time in telling you that it's over 200 hundred years old, and in that time it has developed into a firm with one of the most individual characters out there.

fortune's wheel

This is a firm that has experienced the slings and arrows of fortune. In the 1980s it was one of the best-known names in the profession. In the early 1990s disaster struck when an IRA bomb caused extensive damage to its London office at a time when most records were kept on paper. A part-

ner exodus exacerbated this calamity and it seemed for a while that the firm would have to arrange a merger to stay afloat. In the event it doggedly pursued an independent course and managed a reversal of fortune. These days the firm is certainly a force to be reckoned with in the South East.

Penningtons' recruitment literature implies a single, integrated organisation built of a larger London office and three smaller ones in the Home Counties. There is no switching offices during the training contract so, in practice, once you're settled in your nook contact with the wider Penningtons world is on nodding terms rather than kissing. When asked which office was the headquarters of the firm, after much head scratching one trainee replied: *"I don't know."* Their answer did not reflect uncertainty as to which office deserved the title, but more fundamentally whether the firm had a centre of gravity at all.

Lately there have been significant efforts to upgrade Penningtons' networking and strategic planning. When we rang trainees the Newbury office, for example, was due for a visit from the overall managing partner to outline her vision of the firm's future. There has also been a drive to step up referrals between offices and induce greater co-operation on projects, especially in relation to commercial preoperty. Other initiatives have included a rationalisation of its practice groups into three pan-office streams – business services, commercial property and private client.

basingfolk

It is important to remember when choosing an office for your training that there will be little chance to swap, so obviously the first step is to make sure the locale is somewhere that appeals. Godalming, for example, had the privilege of providing a film location for the Jude Law-

Cameron Diaz romcom *The Holiday*. It's not so easy to imagine this happening in Basingstoke, where the office is nice but looks out over an ugly morass of concrete architecture. Aesthetics aside, the 30-lawyer office provides a decent spread of seats to its four trainees. The popular employment law seat involves visits to various tribunals around the country – ideal if you suspect that a desk-bound existence will stifle your enthusiasm. The corporate finance department is making rapid strides and achieved a 31% increase in profits last year. Meanwhile, the real estate team has some tasty customers – locally headquartered Vodafone and the West Cornwall Pasty Co. to name just two.

"Basingstoke is not a hub of nocturnal activity," but to make up for this a busy round of events is organised by the office sports and social committee. There are theatre trips, ten pin bowling nights, quizzes and outings to comedy clubs. Staff even have their own line in amateur dramatics, with a periodic employment law play. The lawyers-cum-theatre impresarios hire a scriptwriter to pen a scenario that spotlights employment issues. Professional actors bring the situation to life, while an employment lawyer comments on the implications of the action. Whatever you might think of this approach to business development, the team has a stonkingly good clientele including such names as GMTV, Chubb Insurance, Fyffes Plc and the Courtauld Institute of Art. Not everyone chooses to live in the Basingstoke area, and with the fast train from Waterloo taking just 45 minutes, it's perfectly possible to commute from the capital (laughing smugly as everyone else files out of the cattle trucks going in the opposite direction). Penningtons is commonly criticised for its overly traditional approach, but this branch escapes the usual flak on account of an inflow of new blood arriving at partner level to quicken the pulse of the office.

village fate

Pretty as a postcard, Godalming offers *"good-quality commercial work"* and a rich pool of private clients. An ancient town dating back to the reign of Alfred the Great, its narrow streets are littered with historic monuments. You may come into professional contact with these buildings in the property department, where trainees are introduced to the delights of investigating title and producing complex reports for clients. The strong private client department brings contact with wealthy individuals seeking advice on wills and discretionary trusts. Personal injury and clinical negligence seats, meanwhile, see trainees drafting witness statements and representing the firm at inquests. This department deals with everything from slips and trips to catastrophic injuries caused by swimming pool accidents. On the clinical negligence side, the team fought and recently won a case for a mother whose baby suffered serious brain damage following mistreatment by an obstetrician.

Perhaps the village atmosphere makes the pace of life a little slower, and trainees hinted that at times they had to ask for additional work. Nevertheless, in spite of the *"quite traditional"* atmosphere and *"strict policy on personal Internet use,"* one source told us: *"I genuinely love it here."* The annual Godalming Christmas party was held in a medieval manor house last year and was a *"tame"* but really enjoyable affair with a live band and dancing. Throughout the year the sports and social committee masterminds events such as wine tastings. This office is home to nearly 40 lawyers and six trainees.

code of conduct

In lovely Newbury the three trainees per year tend to all have local connections. Certainly not keeping things local, the corporate finance team has been building a robust practice featuring clients with international interests, for example,

Williamson Tea Holdings and Abu Dhabi Commercial Bank. In saying this we mustn't overlook the traditional English establishments on its books – clients such as Basingstoke-based wine and spirit merchant Berry Bros & Rudd. Under close supervision, the dispute resolution seat gives trainees plenty of practice at bundling papers for court, answering routine correspondence and even *"a few bits of advocacy."* The employment team take a great deal of pleasure representing professional football teams across the South of England, and this is viewed as a fun and interesting seat, even if it can be susceptible to the occasional *"twiddling of thumbs."* For trainees, the standout department is family, which now has seven full-time lawyers and regularly comes up against leading firms in the field.

After work the most popular haunt is The King Charles Tavern, which achieves such ecstatic reviews it might be well worth visiting the town for just this one attraction. Last year we mentioned some unusual art in the office, namely a pastiche of Da Vinci's The Last Supper, with the faces of the partners superimposed on the 12 apostles. Well, the art historian in us feels bound to affix an interpretation. Choosing to depict themselves as the founding fathers of the church may reflect their status in the firm, a taste for patriarchal authority and a recherché sense of humour. At another important supper – the Christmas party, admittedly less sacerdotal – there was a mixed seating plan. No miracles were reported.

play to win

The rugby-playing predilections of some of the London trainees suggests that being a team player is an important asset. Most people tread traditional paths to the firm, one telling us they had chosen Penningtons because it was *"collegiate, like university."* Of course a strong sense of community may have been the result of working in an office that verges on *"overcrowded,"* so it's good news that by the time this book is published, the London staff will have moved into smart new digs near St Paul's.

Interviewees spoke highly of the property finance division that brought *"front-line experience"* acting for developers and banks. In coco, they are encouraged to sharpen their presentation skills through regular reports to the department on changes in the law. The decidedly sporty team in corporate advises Wycome Wanderers FC and also has a lot of experience working in the healthcare and care homes sectors. Another point worth making is that it has been developing its international business, not least in relation to India. The immigration option is a magnet for those who naturally shy away from seats like corporate. One source positively glowed with satisfaction when telling us about securing residency for clients in danger of being expelled from the country. *"It's great to see the impact when you phone the client up and tell them, 'You can get on with your life.'"* The only downside is that the likelihood of actually winning a job in the department on qualification is relatively slim.

For those who regret not spending a year abroad there is the travel department to remind them of the perils of holidaymaking. It recently brought a claim in Florida for a woman severely injured in a road traffic accident, which resulted in damages of £300,000. And the travel unit is not the only relatively unusual offering; there is also an electoral law unit, which has recently been helping the Conservative Party in litigation regarding allegations of postal vote fraud. In an incident straight out of the pages of a Tom Clancy novel, the dispute resolution department has been representing the State of Equatorial Guinea in the English courts in relation to claims against the conspirators responsible for the 2004 failed coup attempt.

va-va-voom

In light of chatter about making better use of resources, hitting targets and more co-operation between offices, one trainee told us Penningtons needed *"a bit more va-va voom at the higher levels."* In particular, management's failure to understand the latest trends in Feng Shui came under criticism: *"We've finally decided to modernise and move to open-plan offices at a time when most of the big-name firms are already reverting back to individual offices."* Where it does score highly is in the level of attention trainees receive from supervisors and other seniors. Everyone has a mentor in the year above, and for impartial advice, they are also assigned a principal. Regular three-monthly appraisals are for the most part taken very seriously. Trainees were especially upbeat about the pick-and-mix nature of the seat options, especially those who were uncertain which area of the law suited them. And because of the modest number of trainees, there are rarely problems in realising seat preferences, although it is well understood that NQ jobs in niche departments only arise as and when business needs dictate. In 2007, nine of the 13 qualifiers took up NQ positions.

Every month the trainees group gathers for a seminar on something like *"billing, business development or a legal topic."* Usually held in London, occasionally elsewhere, the sessions are followed by wind-down drinks. Even in the capital trainees spoke about a *"friendly hours culture"* and in the Home Counties many trainees regularly leave their office at 5pm. Out of the capital, the general tenor of the firm is geared towards a family life, so don't expect a raucous after-hours scene. What you can expect is for people to feel *"patriotic"* towards their office and for HR to be a welcome source of succour should you land yourself in tricky spot with your supervisor.

and finally...

This *"regional firm with an office in London"* has some extremely high-quality work and for this reason alone should appeal. If you want to work in London but aren't attracted by the big firms, or you have a reason to locate yourself in Surrey, Hampshire or Berkshire, Penningtons might well be your pick.

Pinsent Masons

the facts

Location: Birmingham, Bristol, Leeds, London, Manchester, Scotland
Number of UK partners/solicitors: 270/730
Total number of trainees: 125
Seats: 4x6 months
Alternative seats: Overseas seats, secondments
Extras: Pro bono – various legal advice schemes; language training

Pinsent Masons has its eye on the big time. Shaped by the 2004 union of pinstriped national firm Pinsents and construction leader Masons, the firm is now gearing up for a daring assault on Europe.

high hopes

The merger that created Pinsent Masons had three key purposes: to sell Pinsents' commercial and corporate expertise to Masons' long-standing construction, energy and technology clients; to build a more substantial London presence and compete with better-known City firms; and to develop further Masons' international network. The firm has made headway with the first goal: it advised Amey UK on its recent takeover of Owen Williams Group. There's still work to do to fully integrate the two legacy firms' clients, but, generally, Pinsent Masons' market presence has been enhanced by the merger – it performs

well in Chambers and Partners' survey of the law firms instructed by the FTSE 100, racking up a total of 14 such clients in the 2007 survey. With regard to the London plan, the firm's reputation for corporate deals has improved, particularly in relation to listings on AIM. And yet the firm hasn't managed to get itself into a single office in the capital. As for the third goal – Operation World Domination – things are looking pretty healthy. The firm recently joined the rush of major law firms to China, opening a Beijing office to compliment its existing Asian positions in Shanghai and Hong Kong. Its other outposts are in Dubai and Brussels, and it has just announced an alliance with several large independent European firms, the Pinsent Masons Luther Group. *"The strategy just seems to be one of ambition, basically,"* noted one trainee; *"we're seeking to expand in every practice area."*

The task back at home remains the same – continued integration of the two sides of the firm. A programme of refurbishment has left all UK offices similarly decorated and there's a general move towards open-plan working. Last year the firm launched its portentous-sounding 'Values Programme': *"It's about how we can work together, how we feel we should be acting towards each other,"* explained an on-message source. *"There are a lot of firms doing it right now."* Trainees are perhaps best placed to see Pinsent Masons as a single, unified entity. Their first few days of induction bring them all together in London for information talks about the firm, then after spreading out to their home offices for IT training, each new intake reconvenes in Bedfordshire for the PSC. *"It's a really nice way to get to know each other,"* they confirmed.

28 weeks later

We'll start in the old Pinsents heartland of the Midlands, where the general consensus was that refurbishment couldn't have come too soon to the Birmingham office: *"It was a bit retro before,"* one style-conscious trainee concluded, *"but now the open-plan makes it easier to get to know everybody."* As well as its corporate and finance departments, the office offers seats in planning and environment, construction and engineering, commercial litigation, employment, pensions, tax, insurance, property, projects and OTC. No, not the people who shoot guns and build woodland shelters at weekends – Pinsents' OTC is an outsourcing, technology and commercial team.

In banking and finance, even if it's your first seat, you'll experience an impressive range of activities. *"I enjoyed diving from one type of deal to another: one day a securitisation, one day MBO finance,"* recalled one trainee. *"We don't have out-and-out specialists, so it's a mixed bag in that seat."* One of the most notable instructions from the past year came from Barclays and RBS in relation to their funding of an investment in Midlands company Metal & Waste Recycling, a transaction which was one of the largest investments made in the local market in 2006. There is decent responsibility for trainees: *"I got into drafting relatively quickly, as well as dealing with clients and project management,"* said one. *"I was introduced to matters really well, given pointers and then allowed to get on with them."* This, it was agreed, is Pinsent Masons' approach to training: plenty of preparation and support followed by a decent go at things. Of course it does depend on the department. In OTC if you're involved in a major deal or case (there are both contentious and non-contentious seats) you could face *"a lot of proof-reading."* Still, it gives you a chance to get your head around *"all the techy three-letter acronyms."* Overall, *"there's a focus on pushing you and getting the best out of you,"* concluded one interviewee. *"I don't recall ever feeling bored or not challenged."*

If you do crave an extra challenge, you could join one of the office's many sports teams or throw yourself into Birmingham Trainee Solicitors' Society activities. *"It's really nice getting together with other trainees from the region and we always seem to do well in the sports competitions,"* said one sociable interviewee. There are also regular trainee drinks, lunches and outings: *"Pinsents seems to choose people who are likeminded so of course we gel well."* Each year there is a – now legendary – fancy dress Christmas party. *"Last time corporate came as zombies and performed Thriller. It was hilarious!"*

gunslingers

While banking, corporate, dispute resolution, employment, OTC, projects, construction and planning seats are on offer in Leeds, the weightiest department is property. A *"baptism of fire,"* the seat brings *"client contact from day one"* as you're handed several of your own files. *"It's great learning how to manage things and file documents on time and so on,"* said a former occupant of the seat. *"You develop organisational skills and confidence that stands you in good stead later on."* Once again, strong supervision and support balance out the responsibility: *"At first they check everything you touch, even a 'with compliments' slip,"* admitted one source. *"Then it all depends how much they trust you. If you do a small matter well, they'll try you on a larger one."* The lawyers have been advising Redhouse Projects on the development and sale of an ASDA distribution centre and helping Leeds City Council on the sale of part of Leeds' Harewood Quarter and accompanying agreements with developer Hammerson. Smaller than Birmingham, the Leeds office intake describes itself as *"close knit." "We're off to the greyhounds on Saturday, as it happens,"* one told us.

Back in 2004 the former Masons Manchester office absorbed the local branch of Pinsents. The view of one source was that *"the office is now in a nicer location overlooking the GMEX, not smack bang in the city where Pinsents was."* Manchester is a fiercely competitive legal market, and Pinsent Masons did initially go through some pain after merger. A slew of high-profile departures – ex-Pinsents partners – was followed by a period of calm, then the firm came out all guns blazing to rebuild through a series of daring raids on rivals Hammonds and Eversheds. The firm now swaggers confidently among the city's big guns. *"The newer partners only know the merged firm, so there's much more unity now,"* one second-year source confided.

Seats are offered in construction, corporate, banking, dispute resolution, employment, pensions, OTC, property and restructuring. A turn in the construction and engineering department is almost inevitable here. The work has a UK focus, with international matters primarily handled in London. The department offers contentious and non-contentious seats. Contentious work *"mostly means disputes between contractors and subcontractors over defective work or payments."* If you've been to Manchester recently you'll have noticed the army of cranes dominating the skyline. The city is undergoing a serious regeneration and trainees in the department will likely feel they are a part of it too. Sit in contentious 'C&E' and you'll *"get to hear the stories behind some of Manchester's biggest new buildings."* There is *"a lot of ADR and arbitration,"* but also a fair chance of seeing inside a courtroom.

As for the social scene, again the trainee group sticks together. *"We're all off to see Peter Kay in The Producers on Saturday,"* said a source. We're not sure if we caught Pinsent Masons before a particularly sociable weekend or if it's always like this... If you regard musicals with suspicion, rest assured there are regular football and cricket fixtures against the Leeds office and other local teams, plus a summer sports day. *"The social committee really does put a lot of work in."*

moving issues

Bristol is the firm's mini-est office. With just 20 lawyers it no longer has permanent trainees, instead offering the occasional seat for trainees from elsewhere in the network. Its two departments are construction and projects. Up in Scotland, the firm runs a full-blown Scottish training scheme in Glasgow and Edinburgh. In general, it is possible to take seats in other offices, especially if a department you're eager to work in isn't available in your home office.

London offers the fullest range of seats, from corporate and OTC to employment, property, litigation, projects and more. Working on projects can mean a one-way ticket to Adminville at times because the deals tend to be so massive. *"I was lucky to start towards the end of a big project,"* said one source. *"I had responsibility for technical schedules and getting them agreed. I often liaised with the client's technical people; they prepared the schedule and I did the legal elements to make it consistent with the overall agreement. I was on the phone to technical people daily."* A word to the wise: those trainees who time it right and work on a completion *"get to share in the excitement and Champagne."* Away from projects and PFI, trainees will encounter some of the firm's highest-value transactions when sitting in corporate. Last year lawyers advised major offshore drilling contractor Abbot Group plc on its £247m recommended cash offer for Norwegian drilling rig owner Songa Drilling, together with a $950m finance facility. Another client, brewer and pub owner Hardys & Hansons plc, sought the firm's advice on its £272m takeover by Greene King plc.

Until the firm manages to get all London staff in one location, most trainees will spend time in both the old Masons HQ in trendy Clerkenwell

and the more 'City' office near Moorgate. With its architect and design company neighbours, Aylesbury Street in Clerkenwell is the more *"relaxed"* of the two; CityPoint near Moorgate *"definitely feels like a big City firm with the big banks nearby and other law firms in the building."* It's a good 15-20 minute walk between the two buildings and so understandably the firm has expressed an intention to move to one location... eventually. Although we have to say, it doesn't seem to be in any hurry. *"Obviously one office would be the ideal,"* admitted one trainee, *"because you just don't see people in the other office that much, even though we try to take it in turns with holding meetings and so on."* Ad hoc socialising falls along office lines. The Priory is the destination for Aylesbury Streeters, while CityPointers make their way to the chain bars of Moorgate. *"Every month or so we make an effort to get all the trainees together,"* and there are London-wide Christmas and summer parties.

Across the offices, while supervisors offer trainees a fair degree of independence, this is a firm with a highly structured training experience. Monthly appraisals are scheduled and *"even in busy seats you'll always have three or four."* Trainees generally called them useful, noting: *"It's a chance to say if there's anything you'd like to do, as well as to receive feedback."* The NQ job allocation process is centralised, with an announcement made early in the fourth seat as to which departments have vacancies. All positions are subject to interview. Even the offices seem very managed environments: *"I wish there were kettles in the kitchens, not just vending machines,"* one Birmingham trainee sighed. *"We brought a kettle in but were told to remove it."* Overall, trainees feel their hours remain reasonable for the markets in which the firm operates, and the firm has been keeping a close eye on salary levels. The headline London rates are £36,000 for first-years and £39,000 for second-years. In the English regions the corresponding figures are £26,000 and £28,000. NQs earn £63,000 in London and £40,000 in the regions. In 2007, 36 of the 48 English qualifiers stayed on with the firm.

and finally...

This well-organised firm has a name that will take a young lawyer far, be it in the capital or in one of its other UK locations. The training scheme has plenty of scope for seat choice, reflecting the firm's good standing across the board. It also has a dominant name in relation to the construction and engineering sector, a factor which should attract any candidate with an interest in this area of the law.

Prettys

the facts
Location: Ipswich
Number of UK partners/solicitors: 13/32
Total number of trainees: 11
Seats: 4x6 months
Alternative seats: None
Extras: Pro bono – LawWorks

One hundred-year-old Suffolk firm Prettys made its century by doing what it originally set out to – providing legal services to a largely regional clientele from its base in Ipswich. Having ploughed a familiar field for such a long time, Ipswich's largest law firm is now *"going through a transitional phase."*

the bright lights of chelmsford

We were never entirely convinced that this was just another of those sleepy regional firms in a sleepy little town. Behind the grand Georgian frontage of its building on Elm Street was a bustling modern office with 135 staff catering to commercial clients as well as the great and the good of the county. Nevertheless, management

decided to expand Prettys' horizons beyond the big skies of Suffolk and opened up a new outpost in Chelmsford, Essex. *"We have large market share in Ipswich and it was never going to provide us with opportunity for the growth that we wanted,"* explained Keith Vincent, the new managing partner in Chelmsford. *"Norwich and Cambridge are over-lawyered and Colchester is a closed placed, so the natural place was Chelmsford."* As for the client base the firm hopes to tap into: *"We have strong shipping and transport practice and lots of those clients have places in Shell Haven and Tilsbury... Also, there are 13 banks in town, so lots of opportunity there. Chelmsford is nearer to Stanstead and the A12 corridor, also of course London and the Thames Gateway."* Keith stressed that London was not the big prize, but *"if the office drags some London work this way, then great."*

Some of the new lawyers have come from London; others have transferred from East of England firms (eg Eversheds, Birketts). The plan is to replicate the Ipswich office. Trainees sensed there had been changes since the creation of the Chelmsford branch. Not only has it meant new staff, but there's also a feeling that the whole firm is now *"becoming more commercial and stream-lined."* *"The new regime says we are going to push up commercial, property and corporate. There is still some private client in Ipswich, but every one thinks that if Chelmsford kicks off, the firm spirit will be a lot slicker and more commercial."*

For now all but one trainee seat is in Ipswich, although it is hoped there will be training opportunities in Chelmsford before long. None of the four seats are compulsory, leaving trainees free to request any of the departments. As in most firms, second-years have priority, so new arrivals shouldn't be too surprised if they don't get their first-choice seats. The variety on offer is pretty extensive: property, corporate, employment, commercial litigation, shipping, family, trusts and estates are all staples. Occasionally, more marginal options can be sampled – how about a seat working on bloodstock issues, French property or yachts?

start with the basics

Employment is as popular at Prettys as everywhere else in the country. *"It was everything I hoped for,"* reported one trainee. There is an array of work covering both contentious and non-contentious elements, and although *"the majority of time is probably taken up on research,"* trainees do get to draft letters of dismissal and employment contracts. The most fortunate also attend tribunals. The department provides *"phenomenal supervision"* in the form of *"constant constructive feedback – the partners really take the time to listen to you and give you praise when you have earned it,"* the net effect being that those who visit are *"sure to feel part of the team."* Though not everyone went as far as one trainee who suggested they were completely in awe of head of employment Matthew Cole, his qualities are well recognised within and beyond the firm and he has just been appointed as Prettys' Chief Operating Officer.

Property is a big department. Its clients include major names in the financial services sector, such as Citibank International, Nationwide and RBS, as well as more local entities such as the popular Suffolk tourist attraction Snape Maltings and Dance East. As a trainee in this busy department it is imperative that you find your feet quickly. On the basis that it improves their understanding of the basics of property practice, everyone gets a good grounding in residential property before being unleashed onto big-money commercial developments. Most of our interviewees acknowledged that being thrown in to this busy seat was *"a great way to learn"* although one did declare they were *"getting headaches on account of the amount of work."* Property litigation is also available as an option and this team works closely with its transactional counterpart.

sea battles

The commercial litigation seats provide *"masses of client contact,"* with trainees taking instructions direct from clients and partners *"happy for you to manage the case if you have proved yourself capable."* Cases touch on the full range of commercial activities from construction to insolvency and are played out in all arenas from High Court litigation to alternative dispute resolution. Undoubtedly it's a big endorsement that Prettys is the preferred adviser of various firms of solicitors (including Birkett Long in Colchester, Kennedys in Newmarket and Jackaman Smith & Mulley of Ipswich, Felixstowe and Diss), as well as local architects and NHS trusts. For those with a combative disposition, the *"aggressive litigation"* of the shipping department will be ideal. For some the work is *"a little dry... very much black letter law stuff,"* while others take to it immediately and relish drafting witness statements and pleadings. All agree it's a very pleasant team to work with. After a couple of months trainees are usually given a few of their own files, and there are always plenty of seminars to help increase their knowledge of the area. The clients include P&I clubs, underwriters, banks, shipyards and ship owners.

The corporate seat involves trainees in small and mid-sized acquisitions and disposals. Among the top deals from the past year are the £4m sale of medical diagnostics company Newmarket Laboratories to Cambridge-based Lab21, and the disposal of Covell Matthews Cambridge Architects to an AIM-listed company. The firm also acts for the likes of Goldstar Transport, Seven Asset Management, The Communications Practice, Care (UK) and Hanbury Davies. The fact that you may not have heard of these businesses should give you an idea of the geographical reach of the corporate practice... hence the opening of the Chelmsford office.

Prettys is still regarded as an excellent choice for private client and family services, despite its efforts to push commercial practice to the fore. As well as advising on wills, probate and general estate planning, the department offers a financial planning service that assists with personal injury settlements, post-death inheritance tax mitigation and trust administration, and personal investment/retirement planning. In the defendant insurance seat, our sources said they'd *"had a cracking time"* dealing with trench foot and frostbite cases for the MoD. Other clients include Lloyd's Syndicates, P&I Clubs, loss adjusters and public utilities. However, with the departure of the two main partners in this area, it rather looks like this work is *"no longer the focus it once was for the firm."*

far from alarming

Most trainees share offices with partners, though we also heard of some bunking in with NQs. Either way, they think that *"the training is excellent, and some of the partners are fantastic, a number of them having worked in the City."* Having told us that *"every floor has a slightly different atmosphere,"* sadly trainees were too coy to be specific. They say that as a whole *"Prettys is a friendly and outgoing firm"* and suggest that *"if you want to fit in here, you need to be confident"* and *"prepared to get stuck in."* Most partners make an effort to include trainees in marketing events, client lunches and the like, *"making a point of introducing you to clients from square one."*

The working day runs from 9am until 5pm, though most of our sources tended to stay an extra half hour or so to get through their work. On rare occasions they might end up staying after 7pm but *"you can't stay longer than 7.30pm unless you have a key to the office... and you'd have to set the alarm as well."* We can only agree with the trainee who suggested: *"We have it quite easy here; it's very relaxed compared to the City."*

You might assume that everyone who comes to Prettys is Suffolk born and bred. Not so. Whether they arrive from a big city or have always lived in the area, the important thing is to enjoy living and working in Ipswich. Some of our sources loved the place for its *"nice community atmosphere where you can bump into people you know from all over town while on the way to work."* Others found it *"far too quiet – everything closes at midnight... it's like the film Deliverance."* It makes sense that for those who dream of working on a multibillion-pound deal, clubbing until dawn and then heading back into the office for a client meeting, this is probably not the place. Despite a female-heavy trainee group, some sense the firm was still *"a bit of a boys' club"* at the top end because only one of the partners is female. Nonetheless, socially it is a very inclusive organisation and *"you always get asked if you want to go out for drinks."* We hear good things about Mannings and Morgans, and monthly office drinks have recently been *"initiated to get the whole firm together more regularly."* Departmental get-togethers have included such delights as girls' make-up parties. Sporting opportunities are open to both sexes; indeed, one female source told us: *"They are trying to get me to play cricket next week, but I think I'm going to get out of it."* If cricket or volleyball don't appeal, how about the annual hill walking weekend? Having exhausted the UK's paltry selection of mountains, the Pretty intrepid walkers went to France in 2007. Back in Ipswich, an active TSG arranges a ball, drinks evenings, curry nights pub, quizzes and the like.

In 2007, two of the six qualifiers took NQ jobs at the firm.

and finally...

If you remain in any doubt as to the commercial outlook of this firm, take a peek at its website. In relation to which, potential applicants should also note that as far as we're aware, the curious footwear you'll see (towering platform flip flops and shoe/in-line skate hybrids) are not compulsory office wear.

Reed Smith Richards Butler LLP

the facts

Location: London, Birmingham
Number of UK partners/solicitors: 108/158
Total number of trainees: 57
Seats: 4x6 months
Alternative seats: Overseas seats, secondments
Extras: Pro bono – Advocates for International Development, Liberty, Fairbridge Centre; language training

The transatlantic merger between the American Reed Smith and London-based Richards Butler in January 2007 looks set to be a fairytale marriage. The former brings corporate clout to the party, while the latter supplies an interesting guest list of domestic and international clients.

reed all about it

At first glance it's easy to imagine Reed Smith swallowing Richards Butler whole. Pre-merger, the firm had an army of 1,100 lawyers at its disposal; in comparison, Richards Butler was a relatively cosy 250-lawyer outfit. The clue as to why this isn't the case is in the title(s). Outside Europe, the firm goes by the name 'Reed Smith'; in the UK, however, it carries the legend of 'Reed Smith Richards Butler.' This equal partnership is typical of Reed Smith, which in its previous mergers has opted to leave native firms to their customary methods rather than sweeping in and changing everything in sight. It's also worth noting that although headquartered in Pittsburgh Reed Smith Richards Butler's largest office is in London.

Obviously, though, there will be a few differences going forward. Aside from the bonding of letterheads and computer systems, cross-selling will lead to more referrals between departments. The expanded workforce also means *"more hands can be brought to the pump when necessary."* The drive now is to emphasise the firm's global position and, with free Mandarin courses being offered to employees, there are strong signals that Asia is the next goal. Richards Butler, which derives 70% of its revenue from work with an overseas dimension and has offices throughout Europe and the Middle East, already has a presence in the region. Reed Smith's recent success in persuading RB's old Hong Kong office to form an alliance is a major coup and a big step in the right direction.

smokin' hot

We suspect the newly conjoined firm will continue to offer trainees arriving in a few years time a good mixture of sophisticated and diverse international work, without the overbearing finance or M&A focus characteristic of other big City firms with global clout. Seen as a *"pleasant alternative"* to the magic circle and other *"mega firms,"* the mood at Reed Smith Richards Butler is set by its dress code: smart-casual. None of our interviewees felt *"chewed up by the system;"* the culture is refreshingly free of airs and graces and the hours are relatively hospitable, with all-nighters a rare occurrence (in Birmingham, sources report, days usually end at 6pm). To top it all, the work is *"challenging and varied."*

Capability has been ratcheted up across the board as a result of the merger. The new firm exerts a strong pull in the financial services, media, shipping, energy, and trade and commodities sectors, and this broad range of expertise is reflected in the absence of any compulsory seats. One area in which the firm excels is advertising law, receiving instructions from Nike on the legitimacy of sales promotions or advising tobacco companies on the labelling of cigarette packets. Elsewhere, a highly capable media group (swelled by the addition of the entire Salans team) performs negotiations for a host of terrestrial TV channels. Life sciences is a particular strength of the US contingent, but the UK team

Well connected

At Reed Smith Richards Butler you'll feel part of the wider world.

That might be because our 21 offices, located over 3 continents, handle so much international work, or because our departments are structured across our offices so that you are regularly in touch with colleagues and clients in different countries. It could even be because all our trainee solicitors have the option to take international or client secondments.

But we think you'll feel connected mostly because we'll encourage you to get involved from the outset. You'll get access to real work, opportunities to take part in community projects or pro bono work and you'll still have a work/life balance that allows you to get out and do your own thing.

ReedSmith Richards Butler

The business of relationships.

www.reedsmith.com

NEW YORK
LONDON
CHICAGO
PARIS
LOS ANGELES
WASHINGTON, D.C.
SAN FRANCISCO
PHILADELPHIA
PITTSBURGH
OAKLAND
MUNICH
ABU DHABI
PRINCETON
N. VIRGINIA
WILMINGTON
DUBAI
BIRMINGHAM
CENTURY CITY
RICHMOND
GREECE

did its bit in 2006, advising on one of the largest M&A transactions of the year in the biotechnology sector.

the shipping news

Richards Butler has a deserved reputation for quality shipping work, but this department isn't actually the biggest source of revenue and doesn't seem to float everyone's boat. To some trainees it has an *"old-school"* air that doesn't provide *"the most dynamic environment."* Others, however, appreciate the responsibility granted by a department that focuses on a range of lower-value disputes rather than a limited number of large-scale matters. *"I was drafting submissions with a freedom I couldn't have had in a larger litigation seat,"* one trainee told us. *"I also got to deal with things like ships colliding and running aground, which I had no idea about at law school."* Those with a taste for contract law and extensive research also enjoyed their work. The group's star clients include Shell, which the firm recently assisted on the leasing of 25 vessels from Qatargas.

A coco seat will be heavy on drafting, which can *"wear a bit thin once you've drafted several resolutions."* However, trainees were mostly positive about the experience, relishing the kind of regular *"involvement in high-level stuff"* that *"really shows you how big deals work."* Of course, *"the hours aren't always so great."* But at least grunt work is kept to a minimum and, when it is meted out, *"it's usually necessary and about filling in gaps in knowledge."* Interviewees raved about a *"friendly team that involves you right from the start"* and enjoyed the buzz surrounding *"a lot of heavy-hitting clients"* listing on the LSE. For one recruit, the ultimate sweetener (quite literally) was receiving a *"box of chocolates with photos of all the lawyers in corporate on it."* The department is well known for its experience of AIM listings and is particularly strong in the pharmaceutical and life sciences sectors.

the real thing

The banking seat covers everything from small-scale advisory work to *"big, complicated transactions."* This year, the department handled more than 100 matters, worth a total of £2bn. It also acted for Bank of Ireland on the funding of the movie *Becoming Jane*, thanks to Richards Butler's solid name in the world of film finance. The highlight of one trainee's time here was involvement in financings in Eastern Europe: *"It was great to have the opportunity to work with emerging markets,"* they told us. Despite the departure of much of its insolvency team, the firm has pre-empted a downturn in the economy by working to preserve what was always a *"traditional strength"* of Richards Butler. A number of recent appointments suggest one trainee's impression that insolvency is *"on the rise again"* may not be far off the mark.

According to those who'd spent time there, the popular real estate department *"paces its work well. Even if you find yourself in the office 16 hours a day, you never feel too pressured."* This is largely due to a structure that leaves trainees *"to their own devices."* Said one: *"I got to run my own files, which really hit the spot!"* This brings with it an abundance of client contact and a constant stream of phone calls demanding *"off the cuff answers,"* which interviewees found challenging but rewarding. A raid on DLA Piper's real estate finance practice has upped the stakes for the group, which recently received a landmark mandate relating to the redevelopment of the iconic Battersea Power Station.

Reed Smith Richards Butler expects trainees to knock on doors for work rather than wait for it to be handed to them. The benefit of this is that new recruits have an opportunity to choose what most interests them; according to interviewees, this results in the freedom to develop your skills in particular areas. Another standout feature of the programme is the huge number of client secondments on offer. *"It really brought me out of myself and built up my confidence,"* said one interviewee about a situation in which trainees are frequently treated like qualified solicitors. The postings are often with fashionable or well-known brands like MTV, BBC and Rank. The firm also offers highly acclaimed overseas placements in locations such as Paris, Piraeus, Hong Kong, Abu Dhabi and Dubai.

birmingham begins

The Midlands branch is a reminder of Reed Smith's origins in the UK as a small firm called Warner Cranston. Since the Americans merged with that firm, life had carried on *"much as it did before"* and there seemed no reason to disrupt the pace of life north of London. The Richards Butler merger has given a boost to the small office, not least because of potential new work for legacy Richards Butler clients. The employment seat here brings trainees into contact with numerous examples of *"people behaving in stupid ways,"* ranging from allegations of misconduct and religious discrimination to unfair dismissal claims. Work in the litigation department includes IP disputes and offers an opportunity to test advocacy skills. In banking and finance, there are plenty of meaty deals to sink your teeth into, with some matters running into the tens of millions of pounds. These include assisting with the financing of Ricoh Arena, Coventry, and advising Lloyds TSB on its purchase of part of a French company. A substantial French clientele – owing to Reed Smith's office in Paris – means that knowledge of the language is a useful asset.

Decamping at the end of 2006 from Coventry to a *"new, glass building"* in Solihull, near Birmingham, has rejuvenated the Midlands team. With a gym on one side and wine bar nearby, this isn't surprising. While some claim to go swimming at lunchtime, we wonder if the ones who admit to spending their hour in the pub are being more honest... If the fact that Birmingham has more canals than Venice isn't enough to keep you here, there is the possibility of transferring to London. You'll spend a certain amount of time shuttling between the two cities anyway.

tale of two cities

So what do the Richards Butler legacy trainees think of joining an American firm? Interestingly, they don't feel like a cog in an American wheel, telling us that barring the odd video conference call, there are few signs of overseas influence. This is reflected in the fact that salaries are pegged with UK firms not US firms. For those concerned about separation anxiety, there is an annual retreat across the pond for everyone to get reacquainted. The merger itself has *"taken a remarkably short time"* to bed in and was celebrated with a lavish party in The Royal Courts of Justice that *"pulled out all the stops."* We suspect there were a few sore heads the following day... Since then, the two firms' London workforces have been mixed up with little or no *"personality clashes."* There have, of course, been a couple of hiccups along the way. Aside from IT glitches (now resolved), which had trainees hissing with frustration, splitting departments between offices has proven to be a headache – not least because the commute makes *"having a quick drink after work with friends in the other building a bit of a hassle."* Our interviewees were pretty confident that this is *"only a temporary situation,"* and expected the firm to move into digs big enough for everyone before too long. Until then, the Minerva House office gets the most praise for its open-plan layout and *"amazing location."* Offering a great view of the Thames, it is within walking distance of Borough Market. For night owls there are wine bars galore and a bevy of pubs on the waterfront. A shuttle bus connects staff to the Aldgate office on the eastern fringe of the City.

There is a *"nice, informal social network"* at Reed Smith Richards Butler. During the summer there are regular trips from Birmingham to London for nights out on the town. Recently, a women's initiative at the firm organised a well-received networking event at the Ralph Lauren store. *"We got to drink champagne, look at clothes, meet people and give to charity – it was a swanky affair."*

In 2007, 18 of the 22 qualifiers chose to stay with the firm.

and finally...

The merger producing Reed Smith Richards Butler was a meeting of equals that has broadened the repertoires of both firms. Here, trainees can sample a wide selection of work and top-quality instructions without the toil of a magic circle environment.

Reynolds Porter Chamberlain LLP

the facts

Location: London, Tiverton
Number of UK partners/solicitors: 66/170
Total number of trainees: 32
Seats: 4x6 months
Alternative seats: Secondments

Reynolds Porter Chamberlain has a funky new home, sleek fresh branding and a reinvigorated sense of purpose. Its traditionally superlative abilities across the full gamut of insurance work remain intact, but these days this City firm is also interested in beefing up its corporate and commercial side.

all change?

If not exactly a dozing giant, in recent years RPC has certainly been one of the sleepier top-50 outfits. It was known for its insurance and litigation expertise and a warm, familial atmosphere that to some read as distinctive and characterful, to others as conservative and overly comfortable. That's the past. Today trainees detect *"a definite drive to modernise,"* *"brush away the stuffy, old-school air"* and *"focus on the commercial side of the business."* Interestingly, they put the shift in emphasis down to last year's switch from multiple premises to a one-site, open-plan office at Tower Bridge. *"It all hinges on the move,"* we heard; *"the change of location has brought an obvious physical difference in the way we present ourselves, and there's now an element of expectation and excitement... a lot has changed and it's a much more modern place."*

The abolition of dress-down Fridays and a clean-desk policy are two superficial indications of a fresh outlook. Things go deeper, possibly to the extent that RPC's fundamental character may be changing. *"It's been great for the atmosphere and communication for us to start working open-plan,"* enthused trainees; *"now you don't have to have the whole worry about trundling down long corridors to see partners, you can see who's around and who's busy."* Such transparency *"brings all-round benefits"* and has also allowed trainees the perspective to observe *"what is going on in the move to balance the insurance and commercial work. Last year it was 70/30, now we're saying 60/40 and we want to get it to 50/50."* They also confirm that RPC is *"keener to get as much feedback as it can from clients, asking them about service and aiming to work to serve their needs in the way they want."* Some continued by telling us: *"People are waiting to see how far it all goes. There's a sense the firm is deciding what it does and doesn't want to be."* Summing up, one perceptive type opined: *"It's basically a case of still being under analysis rather than having a whole raft of measures ready to roll out. How things change will affect what RPC becomes in the market, the kind of chargeable hours we'll have to work and what kind of work-life balance we can expect. That's the long term, but everything happening now is incredibly positive."*

risky business

We couldn't have put it better ourselves, but one certainty going forward is that the insurance industry will continue to be central to RPC's activities. Flat turnover figures for 2006 reflect a tricky 12 months in core litigation and insurance markets and offer support for the decision to bulk up in corporate/commercial areas; however, RPC's insurance leanings are simply too strong for it to ignore or downplay. The recently reorganised insurance division offers trainees exposure to seats in each of its four arms (international risk & reinsurance, professional risk, construction & engineering and property & casualty risk) and some of the most complex matters handled by the firm. Time spent in insurance litigation means assisting with *"big claims passed on by insurers"* such as Allianz, Zurich and Lloyd's syndicates. The subject matter can be literally anything – product liability, property, financial, political risk or insurance coverage disputes. The latter type can be particularly engaging for a trainee since they often involve *"finding out if the claim is covered by a policy that is tailor made and open to interpretation."* A perfect example is advice given to the insurers of a Dutch bank on professional indemnity policy coverage issues following a consumer class action with a potential claim value of €500m arising out of the potential mis-selling of financial products. Cases such as this, which are *"huge and rumble on for years,"* tend to provide *"lots of research and document checking"* for trainees, although *"court visits, liaising with experts and witness statements"* help keep things interesting.

The large professional risk team defends accountants, lawyers, company directors and financial advisers, not to mention insurers like the AA, QBE and Atrium who are keen to minimise their professional policyholders' liability. Needless to say, trainees won't run cases like that for a London market underwriter concerning liability in the NatWest Three's alleged Enron fraud collusion case, but *"the experience of working on big cases is amazing."* By contrast there's a seat in the property & casualty risk team, where *"you get a lot of your own files"* defending workplace or public place injury cases. Despite the relatively small scale of the matters, *"high turnover means you have a lot of files on at once, so the workload can be intense and the work complex."* When it comes to the international risk & reinsurance team, that's when cases get really complex. Here, the lawyers are representing London and Bermudan reinsurers regarding a significant Chilean Copper Mine loss in excess of $300m. They are liaising with Chilean lawyers and adjusters as well as underwriting experts for mine risks, mine experts and forensic accounting experts. For trainees, *"being a smaller part of a big team"* in reinsurance is certainly a popular option, not least for the exposure it offers to product liability matters, *"the sort of claims where an insurer is dealing with a car manufacturer recalling 100,000 cars because a component in the brakes failed."* In fact while *"few if any people come to RPC specifically interested in insurance or having done it at law school,"* we heard nothing but unadulterated enthusiasm for this aspect of RPC's practice. The firm also dispenses non-contentious commercial and regulatory advice to the insurance companies.

media darlings

And speaking of such work, we should report on the firm's aim to target larger mid-market corporate transactions around the £50-250m mark. It's already having some success: it has lately had a hand in two cross-border deals worth €1.5bn and €500m, and recently advised Atlas Copco on the €75m acquisition of Anglo-American healthcare company Beacon Care Holdings. Meanwhile Associated Northcliffe Digital – the online division of long-term client the *Daily Mail* – used RPC lawyers for its £22m acquisition of Simply

Energy. Trainees relished their time in the corporate department, telling us about *"good deals, exposure to decent work and interesting clients, plus a bit of IP."* And all without *"any need to sign your life away... you might do the odd night until 10pm, but you're not stuck in the office all the time."* Much of the corporate work is generated by the strong relationships RPC's media team has built with a raft of clients including Condé Nast, The Guardian Group and Associated Newspapers.

Those media lawyers deserve some of the limelight themselves: they are renowned for their expertise in defamation cases and trainees love working with them. Said one source: *"I contested applications by myself, researched cases, located witnesses and spoke to them – it wasn't just bog-standard stuff."* Who wouldn't love to have helped out client Bloomsbury as it struggled to prevent illegal copying and early leaking of the latest Harry Potter release, not to mention the firm's advice to Associated Newspapers on the *London Lite* launch and *The New York Times* on contempt issues arising in connection with its coverage of UK terrorism trials. The popular new IT/IP team also benefits from the media relationships.

Other seat options include general commercial litigation, commercial property, 'regulatory and brokers' (*"a heavy FSA regulation slant"*) plus secondments to *"some pretty exciting media, sports and corporate clients"* such as IBML (Sports World's brand management company) and Carillion.

a clean sweep

RPC's four-seat training has historically *"not always been terribly transparent."* Few obtain first choices every time, and it's common to be thankful to get your first choice twice in the two years. Whether or not it is indeed so, the third seat is perceived as *"crucial"* to one's NQ prospects. The arrival of *"a new training partner who is very hands-on and is currently reassessing the way rotation works"* has perked everyone up no end, and the shift to open-plan working makes it possible to *"work for multiple partners."* Other TC spring cleaning involves dealing with *"the variable quality of feedback and formal appraisals"* and *"there's a new trainee committee and everything's been renamed. Instead of minder partners, you have your supervisor, a 'buddy' who was the last trainee in your seat, and a mentor at assistant level in the department you first start in."* Apparently this last innovation has proved especially popular.

In truth, our interviewees were largely more than happy with the quality of supervision and feedback they received, recognising that what gripes they had reflect a less proceduralised past. The same seems true of an NQ jobs process described as once *"having had a shroud of mystery around it,"* but which is now the subject of *"efforts by HR and the training partner to clarify it."* In 2007, nine of the ten qualifiers took up NQ jobs with the firm.

grazing at the stars

One of the many anxieties before the move to Tower Bridge was the fear that open-plan working would prove distracting. They needn't have worried, the only distractions are deliberate. *"There's a flock of sheep that moves around the building overnight as if by magic."* As yet, trainees haven't discerned a pattern to the flock's peregrinations, but they certainly have their theories. Our favourite is the one that has *"the big sheep ending up outside the department that's doing best,* [while] *getting the little black sheep is probably less complimentary."* The flock is one of several touches characteristic of the firm *"trying to be modern but with a sense of humour. Our office doesn't have the austerity of some other law firms' premises."*

Being different is an idea RPC is selling heavily in its current grad recruitment material. You may have seen its brochure featuring a real-life trainee in a series of comic-strip escapades. Our interviewees agreed that the way in which the campaign pushes quality of experience, quality of work and a personal touch is accurate. *"Nobody here is a hard-core maniac,"* said one; *"people like their work, want to do well and do so, but they also want to enjoy the other things life has to offer."* This attitude encourages trainee relations that are *"supportive, easy-going and very sociable."* The first-years are *"always out as a group"* and the café in the new building is a great meeting spot. Unfortunately, it also means that *"sometimes you don't leave the building for an entire day."* At least the mostly reasonable hours of *"9.30am to 6.30pm, sometimes as late as 9pm in corporate,"* means the days don't drag on quite as long as in certain other firms.

The Dickens Inn has de facto become the most regular watering hole, having been selected by the firm for various pre-move events, but trainees admitted: *"We haven't settled on a local yet, we're carefully judging the options."* Strict though the criteria may be, the fact a new bar is *"being added downstairs in the building"* probably means *"laziness will win the day."* In general there's a good after-work scene, with a social committee organising pub quizzes, drinks events for vac schemers and an annual summer party. When we called, said shindig was about to take place with a *"heroes and villains fancy dress theme."* It was described by one dry source as *"clever, because it means we can dress up as Spiderman or the like and partners can turn up as themselves."*

and finally...

Even though Reynolds Porter Chamberlain is going through a good deal of change, we doubt it will lose its characteristically supportive and distinctive identity. It's a sure bet for a contentious training contract and increasingly a good option for those wanting transactional experience without the big-firm lifestyle.

Rollits

the facts
Location: Hull, York
Number of UK partners/solicitors: 21/25
Total number of trainees: 6
Seats: 4x6 months
Alternative seats: None

Rollits is one of Hull's best-known firms, alongside Andrew M Jackson and Gosschalks. All three will be on the radar of any prospective trainee interested in mid-tier Yorkshire work. So where does Rollits fit in?

meally very good

Ask any well-read football fan about Hull and they will tell you of its not-so-proud record for being the largest city in England never to have had a top-flight football team. Relatively isolated geographically and playing third fiddle to Leeds and Sheffield, a similar thing could be said of its legal market. However, the firm is embedded in the premier league of Hull firms and therefore boasts a strong record at home and in mid-market work across the East Yorkshire region.

Rollits is at heart a commercial firm offering compact coco, commercial property and litigation teams that pack a punch. The firm showcased this recently by completing the substantial and extremely complex documentation surrounding the construction of the new Hull Truck Theatre in the Ferensway development that is transforming the city centre. Strong links to the local business community have also led to some international work, with the firm recently acting for packaging and design company McGurk Group in its sale to US-based SGS International. However, one area in which Rollits really distinguishes itself from local competitors is the food industry. Having built itself a name for representing the East Yorkshire food processors that grew up around the ports of Hull and Grimsby, the firm has recently been extending its reach in this sector. This was demonstrated by its work for Surrey-based Wellness Foods on the acquisition of Stream Foods, whose School Bars champion the idea of putting the fruit back in lunch boxes. This side of the business is led by partner Julian Wild, who brings 25 years prior experience of working for regional giant Northern Foods.

Another way in which the firm differentiates itself from those around it is through its reach. The unique formula of a Hull HQ and York outpost means that it can legitimately claim a home territory spanning East and North Yorkshire and North East Lincolnshire, drawing around 70% of its work from these hunting grounds. The remainder of the caseload is largely accounted for by the firm's specialisms in charities and education law, which bring in clients from all over the country.

sweet smell of success

The training model at Rollits is reasonably set, with a fairly strong expectation that everyone will do coco, commercial property and litigation. The fourth seat is an opportunity either to return to a favoured department or to sample the private client practice.

Commercial property is one of the firm's best-known fields and this department carries the Rollits flag throughout the region in a range of property development, social housing and planning work. It has recently been working with the Joseph Rowntree Foundation and Joseph Rowntree Housing Trust on the redevelopment of a 540-home model village on the outskirts of York. It is also a market leader in property security work, where it has secured places on the panels of Yorkshire Bank, HBOS and Svenska Handelsbanken. Trainees broke it down for us like this: "We work mainly for clients in Yorkshire, and Hull in particular, but we also have some national and City clients and a few in Lincolnshire and Leeds." They were particularly impressed by the variety of work on offer. "Its not an enormous firm so the department is not overly specialised," which means trainees get "bits and bobs from various people's files." Trainees are left to their own devices as much as possible to get on with "first registrations, completions and exchanges, amending and drafting leases" and, if they are lucky, honing client-handling skills.

The firm's coco group is similarly well regarded in Yorkshire and is a popular seat due to the relatively high level of contact with its "quality, local industrial clientele." However, its roster stretches much farther than Hull's industrial elite. Take DTR:UK for example, a leading architectural and design company with a presence across the North's commercial centres, which the firm advised in relation to its sale to SMC Group. The seat also incorporates employment work, where Rollets' reach extends to Newcastle and Sunderland-based employers. This aspect was the most popular with our sources, and they told us about "a lot of legal-expenses insurance work where you are involved in cases from the word go and get your own files." The seat comes with a fair share of admin tasks, but the quality work seems to more than make up for it. The same can be said for time spent in the firm's healthy dispute resolution practice. "The disputes that you see are very varied, as are your tasks as a trainee." This means: "preparing trial bundles, research, communication with clients and attending court." A highlight came when the Rollits litigators took a case to the Court of Appeal (J H Fenner & Co Ltd v Edlington Properties Ltd) concerning the equitable set-off of losses from tenant to landlord.

york around the clock

The chances are that each of these three seats will be taken in the Hull HQ, but anyone tempted by private client work may sample either the department's offerings at home or in York. At *"less than half the size of Hull,"* the second office is *"much quieter and more relaxed,"* although the beautiful surroundings of Roman and Medieval York put Hull to shame. The private capital department based there is small (two partners and two solicitors) but is nevertheless one of the best regarded in Yorkshire, with a remit covering estate planning, formation and management of trusts and Court of Protection work.

Drawing everything together for us, one helpful source surmised: *"You get a very hands-on training and a wide range of high-quality work."* Trainees said they felt like *"an important part of the team"* and on the whole were relaxed and comfortable in their working environment. *"It's not at all stuffy and everyone is willing to help when asked,"* confirmed one. Perhaps the most popular draw card for the firm is its interesting approach to hours: Rollits boots its trainees out of the office, even if they want to stay late. *"You are not encouraged to work all the hours that god sends, so the norm is probably to work 9am till 6pm. You can't stay later than 7pm anyway as security guards come round to lock up and we don't have keys or alarm codes as trainees."*

we still want ze money lebowski

There is no escaping the fact that Hull gets an extremely bad press and, as a result, the firm is keen to recruit trainees with a connection to the city and a good understanding of its attributes. However, in its bid to compete at a high level across the region, it seems happy to extend its search to those with a proven connection to the wider Yorkshire region. We should also say that it was clear from speaking with trainees that much of the media bashing is misplaced. While *"not the most cosmopolitan of cities,"* Hull is belatedly enjoying the sort of city-centre redevelopment that has transformed Leeds and Sheffield, and trainees with limited previous experience of it had found a happy home and were looking to qualify into the firm. In particular, praise centred on the low living costs, although a sarcastic snipe at the less-competitive salaries offered in Hull inevitably followed. In 2007, one of the two qualifiers stayed on at Rollits' Hull office, going into the dispute resolution team.

Other than a link to Yorkshire, the firm is seen as *"open-minded"* in its recruitment, seemingly appealing to trainees who are *"easy going but hard working."* After the security guards have thrown them out on a Friday, you can find them drinking with colleagues in either Revolution or Jaz. Mid-week fun is offered by Trainee Solicitor Group events, where trainees can exchange stories with friends at the city's other legal employers over drinks evenings, barbecues or even a spot of gambling. Rollits also encourages its trainees to get stuck into corporate events, the most popular recently being a number of pub sport competitions. One budding Lebowski explained this simple formula to us: *"You get put in teams, drink loads of beer and then go bowling."*

and finally...

For anyone with a more enlightened view of Hull than the national press, Rollits has a lot to offer. Said one satisfied trainee: *"You get something very different from the larger Yorkshire firms. There's a high standard of work for some large clients with a lot of involvement for trainees, but also a nice, relaxed attitude and environment where you don't feel like you're being monitored at every step."*

Russell-Cooke LLP

the facts

Location: London, Kingston-upon-Thames
Number of UK partners/solicitors: 44/86
Total number of trainees: 16
Seats: 4x6 months
Alternative seats: None

Russell-Cooke is an individual creature and has undergone significant expansion of late. The firm now houses 290 staff in various locations across the capital, handling upmarket private client and criminal work alongside a very respectable commercial practice.

emerging trend

An august firm of over 125 years' good standing, R-C commenced on something of a merger spree in 2003, gobbling up charity law specialist Sinclair Taylor & Martin, then niche PI outfit Evill & Coleman and then media/entertainment experts Harrison Curtis. Most recently it annexed Surrey-based Caporn Campbell, bringing additional capacity to the family and conveyancing departments as well as adding a private client team to its Kingston office. So are these mergers a good thing? Well, yes, according to trainees. In adding specialist steel in each new area, the series of unions has not diluted the firm's character. It is still a destination of choice for high-calibre candidates, *"the sort of people that had the grades to get into the bigger city firms but who had decided against that lifestyle."* Indeed, while there are fresh-faced young law graduates among trainees, others arrive via previous working experience that makes them *"a bit more choosy in terms of the environment they want to be in."* Nor have new abilities done anything but increase the breadth of choice for trainees: *"I was basically looking for somewhere that practised a wide range of areas under one roof,"* said one.

There's plethora of departments across offices. Conveyancing, crime, matrimonial and private client all feature in a Kingston office that specialises above all in childcare. In central London, Bedford Row has teams in commercial property, contentious property and professional regulation (which concentrates on cases for the Law Society). Meanwhile, the Putney base offers commercial and civil litigation, company/commercial, charities law, clinical negligence, judicial review, property, crime and matrimonial. It is worth bearing in mind that business needs sometimes take precedence over trainee choice when it comes to who gets what seat, and not all these departments will always offer a seat. In other words, setting your heart on a specific combo – crime in Kingston for example – might see you disappointed. Sage interviewees advise: *"It's a good idea to be quite open as to what you want to do so that you put your all into whatever department you get."*

property ladder

One 'choice' everyone must get used to is a compulsory commercial property seat in the Bedford Row office. The real estate team here lays claim to a glittering client list, including Allied Irish Bank, NatWest, Orient-Express Services, SMP Group and Advent International. It recently acted on a number of transactions for GLE Property Developments, including the purchase of the third phase of GLE's Riverwalk Business Park in Enfield from the London Development Agency. A typical trainee's day includes everything from completing land registry forms to drafting licences and leases. Although widely enjoyed, *"busy days and long hours,"* mean this is a full-on seat and one that can be daunting because *"on the first day you already have your own filing cabinet full of cases."* In time this translates into *"first-rate, hands-on experience."*

The contentious property department in Bedford Row received rave reviews, not least because of *"diligent and fastidious"* teaching. Deriving some of its work from the firm's real estate connections, the team also boasts an impressive independent client list that includes Tote Bookmakers and the Grainger Trust. Lawyers here were recently involved in a Court of Appeal case that examined statutory definitions in the Landlord and Tenant Act 1985. Commercial litigation in Putney is a popular choice for many trainees as the seat presents them with an opportunity to experience a range of different types of claim. Their responsibilities encompass drafting witness statements, sitting in on client interviews and *"some interesting research."* Among the firm's most newsworthy recent work is advice to both Chelsea FC and Jose Mourinho in FA Premier League Commission proceedings relating to the tapping up allegations surrounding Ashley Cole's transfer. Aside from such glamorous mandates, the team is busy with a diet of general commercial disputes, including disagreements between shareholders and problematic construction projects. Especially on larger cases, trainees can end up with mundane tasks, some also noticing an occasional *"lack of focus in the training."* The seat nevertheless retains its appeal.

halfway houses

R-C really does allow trainees to try out a broad spectrum of work from commercial and private client to a spot of legal aid, and despite the squeeze the Carter reforms have put on the legal aid market, the criminal law department is flourishing. Two new fee earners were recently added to a team that trainees are confident has a robust future. *"Whilst there isn't the profit in this kind of work that there used to be, the firm is certainly backing the criminal department to the hilt."* Recent cases includes R v Jado Pommell, an Operation Trident prosecution in which R-C's client was acquitted of charges of conspiracy to rob a Securicor van of £235,000, and a case undergoing

judicial review concerning the extradition of a client to the USA on a double homicide charge. Trainees described the seat as *"much more hands-on than other departments. You are mainly handling grass-roots legal aid work, given a fair degree of responsibility and a lot of client contact."* Work includes day-to-day contact with the CPS, drafting letters to clients, attending and proofing witness statements and making interim applications at court.

Trainees consider the environment at R-C to blend the best aspects of a City firm and a smaller suburban outfit. Although the hours tend to be heavier in the litigation and property seats, they are still *"quite civilised"* and *"there's certainly no culture of leaving your jacket on the back of your chair."* In fact reasonable days seem to the norm across departments and offices with the received wisdom being that *"there aren't a great deal of differences between any of the offices in terms of the everyday, working atmosphere."* Thus, small differences do catch the eye. Kingston is relatively unknown as the firm sends few trainees there. Bedford Row is *"more informal as the smaller size and single office creates more of a collegiate atmosphere."* The three offices in Putney have *"a bit of a feeling of the commuter belt about them, which dampens the social life a little."* Speaking of things social, Christmas and summer parties are prominent dates in the calendar, as is *"a very good executive conference at which all of the fee earners get together and talk about how we can improve the firm,"* and where *"everyone invariably gets very drunk afterwards."* Each of these events was lauded as *"a great opportunity to get to know everyone else at the firm."* With trainees spread across several locations, group drinks are *"difficult to co-ordinate"* and outlets for sporting urges are similarly sparser than some would like, although we can confirm that cricket and softball teams are happily playing away.

naturally nurturing?

Whilst the quality and breadth of work on offer at R-C is undeniably good, a number of sources commented on an approach to training that isn't entirely consistent. In essence, they suggested, *"the quality of training you receive is completely dependant upon the department you are in and how good a supervisor the partner is."* On the one hand this can result in *"more autonomy than I would have expected, and that helped me learn,"* and on the other *"sometimes it feels that learning is simply incidental to the work, the assumption being that you know what you are doing unless you wave your arms in the air."* In the hands of the right supervisor, life can be good: *"One of my seats was a perfect example of how training in any job should be – the partner was an excellent man-manager."* Our sources observed without rancour: *"We don't have any internal training seminars and these might be useful"* and also noted that *"of the two appraisals per seat, the half way through is often forgotten."* In summary, we'd say that trainees who flourish here are able to take the rough with the smooth. Similarly, while the salaries on offer are perfectly adequate, it's worth being aware that the firm's LPC assistance comes in the form of a loan that is repayable in the event that you do not accept an NQ job offer from the firm come qualification. That said, it was far more than financial prudence that saw four out of six qualifying trainees prove their attachment to R-C by accepting NQ jobs in 2007.

and finally...

Russell-Cooke's training contract is pitched somewhere between the experience of a City practice and that of a distinctly upmarket high-street operation, both in terms of practice coverage and day-to-day running. Don't mistake it for purely one or the other and you'll be ready to embrace the best aspects of a truly varied two years.

Salans

the facts

Location: London, Bromley
Number of UK partners/solicitors: 28/31
Total number of trainees: 8
Seats: 4x6 months
Alternative seats: Occasionally Moscow

Conceived in 1978 as a Franco-American venture, Salans is definitively not the average US firm. Its passport now boasts more stamps than a philately convention, and a canny ability to mine emerging markets for corporate, finance and banking work makes the firm a dark-horse choice for the transactionally minded trainee seeking an internationalist training.

god almaty! where?

Really, the only truly Yankee aspect of the firm is the wilfully pioneering spirit that has seen it successfully push into the most apparently inhospitable of legal markets, incidentally requiring the *Student Guide* team to make a swift grab for the nearest Atlas to keep up. Salans has planted its flag in far-flung Baku, Almaty and Kiev in building up a network of 18 offices stretching from the USA to China, with rapid growth continuing this year as it set up outposts in the Iberian Peninsula, Berlin, Shanghai and Hungary, adding 100 more lawyers so that fee-earners now number 550. Broadly speaking, the strategy has been to maximise the potential of emerging markets such as Russia, Eastern Europe, Central Asia and the Far East while benefiting from a presence in Western financial centres. In the past 12 months the firm swiped Pinsent Mason's Spanish alliance partner Masons Buxeda Menchén, acquired a five-partner, nine-lawyer Paris team fom Rambaud Martel, made a string of hires in Moscow, tied up a relationship agreement with Krupa Srokosz Patryas in southern Poland and garnered the Berlin and Shanghai offices of now-defunct Haarmann Hemmelrath.

Such speedy, organic expansion inevitably means Salans' operation is somewhat diffuse, with trainees uncertain *"exactly where the brains of the firm are,"* even if a healthy global revenue rise of 21% to $206m in 2006 indicates all is well. Some commentators have suggested Salans' status and competitiveness increases the further East one travels, and it's true that by striking into emerging markets early the firm has developed enviably capable operations in Moscow and Central Eastern Europe that are a cut above its mid-tier UK status. Certainly, the decision to move to billing in euros rather than dollars this year speaks volumes for the management's perception of the changing international focus of the firm, but don't imagine that the West is old news. Merger talks with US-centric giant Kirkpatrick & Lockhart may have collapsed this year, but the attempt clearly shows Salans is keen to bolster its London office and secure additional US capability.

not all quiet on the western front

When weighing up where the balance of power lies, trainees told us that London feels *"below Paris, New York and Moscow in the pecking order,"* but were unequivocal about the fact that the office's strongest relationship is with Russia. London is *"basically Moscow's bitch,"* joked one source. If that's not strictly true, it is the case that there is a healthy flow of work between the offices, particularly in the M&A, finance and energy sectors where a steady stream of cross-border transactions involving Russian oil and gas firms keeps things interesting. By way of illustration the corporate team advised Enel SpA (the Italian British Gas) on its $105m indirect acquisition of an interest in RusEnergoSbyt, a Russian limited liability company, a ground-breaking Russo-Western energy deal. However, London bods also held their own in advising international oil and gas producer Ascom Group on its $300m listing on the Luxembourg Stock Exchange and on the first Romanian IPO on the Main Market of the London Stock Exchange. In fact *"the majority of work in the UK is international or cross-border,"* which proves a *"major attraction"* for trainees in selecting the firm, even if travel opportunities mainly come in the form of *"short business trips"* rather than secondments. Highlighting the strength of London's ties with Moscow, the Russian office has recently begun to offer three-month seats to UK trainees, but this is currently the only such placement on offer. It's worth mentioning that although languages are looked upon favourably in recruitment and several of our sources possessed such skills, it seems they are rarely put to use at trainee level beyond a rare bit of translation.

Our interviewees had arrived at Salans eager for exactly the kind of mid-market international corporate, banking and finance, and capital markets work described above and it pays to be aware that Salans offers an emphatically non-magic circle training. As one of three or four trainees *"your face will become known,"* an intimacy relished by sources keen to avoid *"being in a herd of sheep."* By extension, though, *"this is not the place to just spend two years doing the photocopying and taking attendance notes,"* with *"enjoyable but sometimes overwhelming"* levels of responsibility often requiring robust independence of thought and action. Basically, *"the more confidence you have the more responsibility you get."* If there is a downside to the firm's size, rapid development and the ready exposure trainees get to decent work, it is that *"structures, formal training procedures and communication can leave something to be desired."* Sources reflected for example that *"there are some awfully demanding partners,"* adding that *"the quality of supervision varies"* and *"there's not a massive degree of dialogue over training."* However, everyone we interviewed was the kind of "*self-sufficient type*" to make the most of the opportunities on offer at a place that is "*moving surprisingly quickly; there's the magic circle on the other side on lots of work now.*" Indeed, looking further ahead, trainees suggest "*it's possible to make partner quite early.*"

salans selective

Rotation is a no-nonsense affair involving four seats with no compulsories, save that the first one or two are chosen for trainees. The simplicity of the system brooks few complaints. Given the firm's strengths, time in corporate and banking and finance are highly likely, but to be enjoyed rather than endured, because "*they are each as buzzing as the other.*" It's easy to see why. The elite asset finance team plays its cards close to its chest, but clients including Abbey National, Bank of Scotland, Barclays Bank, Citibank International and Lloyds TSB tell their own story. Time here means "*being an active member of the team on multimillion-pound loans,*" but a straight banking seat apparently offers "*by far the best experience; you're involved in all the big-ticket stuff; you help in negotiations, closing meetings and trying to win business.*" Big-ticket matters could be advising Chelsea Building Society on a £2bn financing package or assisting Deutsche Bank on the funding for the refurbishment of the Moskva Hotel in Moscow, with closures often marked by "*a swanky meal in a Michelin-starred restaurant.*" Elsewhere, the well-regarded consumer credit team recently secured the hire of consumer finance and technology expert Robert Courtneidge, while six months in the "*fantastic*" insolvency group brings "*lots of responsibility – I handled my own cases, drafted letters to clients and saw cases though.*" Readers may have noted that the firm possesses a Bromley office. This branch focuses on bulk debt recovery work and trainees don't usually spend time there.

you windsor some, you lose some

Corporate boasts a hefty caseload that sees lawyers advising on matters such as Russian finance outfit City Mortgage Bank's sale to Morgan Stanley. The scale of transactions can mean "*mundane work and writing minutes for companies*" but at its best "*the responsibility is almost unparalleled.*" One source had relished "*work for all nine partners, being involved in everything that was going, listening in on their ways of working,*" while another reflected "*I could have done more drafting, but in terms of understanding the transaction and the whole process it was definitely the best.*" Both banking and corporate organise retreats to give the international personnel a chance to meet in the flesh. Banking was the undoubted winner in the glamour stakes last year, holding its version in Krakow. The corporate team had to make do with the slightly less exotic surroundings of Windsor.

The litigation team handles "*matters major and minor,*" be they "*landlord and tenant disputes,*" work for the insolvency team or complex cases relating to partnerships and company law. The recent hire of a DWS arbitration lawyer to help bring a little of its Parisian arbitration expertise to the Big Smoke is potentially interesting for trainees, as is the arrival of an experienced practitioner into an employment team which has had "*quieter times recently.*"

Meanwhile, property is "*growing more and more,*" advising not long ago on the purchase of 67 properties of roadside chain Little Chef. Here trainees enjoy "*running 20-odd files yourself and a lot of responsibility from early on; I was dealing with clients all the time.*" A regular secondment to a large financial client was also praised, partly for the "*excellent experience*" on offer, but also for the regular hours. That said, the working day at the firm is really quite reasonable, with most escaping by 7pm. Even if the exigencies of the transactional world can sometimes demand later nights "*we're not talking Clifford Chance-style hours.*"

low lying, laid back

You won't find Salans advertising its wares at recruitment fairs and nor does the firm boast the highest profile within the profession, but trainees were keen to impress on graduates that they shouldn't discount the firm on that basis. Beyond the quality of work on offer, they praise the fact *"everybody knows your name and is willing to help out."* Without any bias towards particular a background, the firm seems to pick those who *"can get thrown into the deep end and swim"* and *"are not green when they walk through the door."* As a result it is not uncommon for trainees to have experience of a previous career. More generally recruits are *"outgoing and chatty"* with a *"down-to-earth and matter-of-fact"* approach reflecting Salans' drive. If you're considering an application, do be aware that there are currently no vacation schemes on offer.

Given its nature, socialising at the firm is relatively restrained and trainees admitted that a little more social cohesion and extra organised events would go down well. The occasional impromptu Friday drink does see trainees saunter down to the Heal and Tap a stone's throw away, while a canteen and cash machine in the building ensure that stomachs and wallets are well lined for nights out on the town. The offices, based by the wobbly Millennium Bridge, overlook the Thames, making them convenient for a summer night's stroll to Shakespeare's Globe Theatre.

and finally...

Relatively low profile but with plenty to offer, Salans training is a no-frills affair that's high on exposure to international and transactional work. In 2007, two of its four qualifier stayed with the firm, going into the property and banking departments.

Shadbolt & Co LLP

the facts

Location: London, Reigate
Number of UK partners/solicitors: 25/24
Total number of trainees: 8
Seats: 4x6 months
Alternative seats: Paris, secondments

Shadbolt's story is one of success based on excellence and experience. It's one of the finest construction and engineering sector practices around and is headquartered in Surrey. Er, hang on, Surrey?

shaddy dog story

Well, since you ask. In 1991 Dick Shadbolt, then construction law chief at what is now CMS Cameron McKenna, hung up his commuting spurs and quit the City. He held on to his best clients with the aim of working for them from his Surrey home. Before he knew it, he had rented office space in Reigate and set up a new specialist law firm that soon achieved substantial success. Fifteen years later Dick handed over the reins to fellow partner Liz Jenkins, who now presides over a staff of around 60 lawyers in two UK locations – the Reigate HQ and London – plus a small but growing Paris branch and associated offices in Greece and Dar es Saalam in Tanzania. Most clients come from the construction industry, many of them big-name contractors you might already recognise such as Amey, Costain, Carillion and Galliford Try. There is also another category of client – the companies or organisations for whom new buildings or projects are created. In this regard the firm acts for the BBC, Citibank and catering giant Sodexho as well as public sector bodies in health, education, housing and utilities.

draining work

A contentious construction seat in the Reigate office is the most likely of all seats. On smaller adjudication cases trainees can manage their own files. *"I did an adjudication on my own,"* recalled a source; *"I dealt with someone quite irate on the other end of the phone!"* Working on larger High Court actions inevitably involves *"the preparation of trial bundles and that kind of thing,"* but there's a good chance that you'll *"see both sides of it: the huge cases – we did two of the biggest High Court cases last year – and dealing with a small contractor who wants to pay the lawyer in cash."* These days the work is *"mainly adjudications and arbitration, especially in emerging markets such as Romania and Bulgaria."* However, it also looks as if the firm has a fascination for sewerage. Following its involvement in a sewerage plant dispute in 2004, which turned into the biggest ever case before the UK's Technology and Construction Court, Shadbolt has been instructed in two more major sewerage disputes in Northern Ireland and Scotland. In each instance, the firm's expertise was required to resolve problems arising out of ongoing Private Finance Initiative (PFI) projects. Construction cases can involve vast amounts of evidence and other information, some of it highly technical. Lawyers need to be detail-conscious, unafraid of large volumes of documentation and willing to roll their sleeves up for hard graft.

It's worth talking more about PFI as the area is a major source of growth for Shadbolt. The firm is involved in UK projects relating to, among other things, defence, healthcare and education. It advised the building contractor on the Bradford 'Building Schools for the Future' programme, which is delivering three new secondary schools to accommodate over 4,500 pupils in that city. In the social housing sphere lawyers have been assisting on a project relating to the £66m refurbishment of an estate in the London Borough of Camden, and in the health sector

the £1bn Barts Hospital PFI involving client Mowlem plc is occupying a variety of specialists at the firm. And we don't just mean construction specialists: the project has some complex HR issues, including the transfer of a workforce of almost 1,000 employees. On big projects the trainee will start off doing the smallest and simplest chores: *"Initially you look at the ancillary documents and deal with the warranties from subcontractors and the collateral warranties provided up the chain. By the end you might be dealing directly with the banks."* Our sources couldn't stress enough the importance of this aspect of the firm's business. *"Projects and PFI have really evolved in the last year, and the firm's interest seems to have shifted to the PFI and finance side,"* confirmed one. Furthermore, *"we've moved into representing the consortia* [taking on projects]. *Before, we were acting for our traditional clients, the building contractors and facilities management providers. The next step will be representing the banks."*

Shadbolt's expertise is by no means confined to the UK. The firm has been engaged by a large international contractor in a series of disputes with the government of an East African country, arising out of a multimillion-dollar contract for the rehabilitation of more than 100 km of road. It also worked on a submerged toll road tunnel at Thessaloníki in Greece and on the €700m Bucharest Bypass. The Paris office has recently doubled the number of partners it employs and offers seats to French-speaking trainees who want to sample disputes headed for the International Court of Arbitration.

constructive comments

Despite the emphasis on PFI practice, trainees admit that Shadbolt is still *"quite a specialist construction firm and the PFI focus could all shift if another huge case comes along for the contentious group."* Of course the firm does have lawyers working in other areas too – property, coco and employment for example – but as the Barts project shows, they spend much of their time supporting the construction and projects lawyers. The training contract reflects the balance of the firm's activities, with recruits spending at least one, and probably two, of their seats in construction and the remainder being chosen from projects, general commercial, property and employment. Client secondments are also available, presently to WS Atkins and Galliford Try. Most trainees do a secondment and, depending on which company they go to, might tackle property litigation, personal injury claims, general commercial or employment issues. Said one source: *"I was reviewing contracts and liaising with the company officers; I even negotiated an IP contract."*

Don't for one minute think you must arrive at Shadbolt a ready-prepared construction law specialist. *"I didn't have a clue about anything when I started,"* explained one trainee, telling us that because construction law is basically just contract and tort, *"you soon realise it's the same law you already know about, applied to particular situations... Through training sessions and seminars and day-to-day reading of cases you learn what you need."* Some trainees also take a night school course to acquire a formal qualification in construction law.

the surreyal life

Much as we'd like to paint a picture of Portakabins and muddy boots, the office environment is precisely what you'd expect of a law firm. Admittedly some of the clients would have to be described as a particular breed: *"Subcontractors don't generally care what the law says – they just want to get what they want and know what the cost will be,"* revealed one interviewee. With such a philosophy among clients, trainees learn to stand on their own two feet. *"Dealing with subcontractors on your own can be daunting, but if you have the right temperament you will thrive."* Partners

themselves inspire the confidence in trainees to *"change rapidly."* Said one, *"the empowerment you get from Liz Jenkins and Dick Shadbolt and the experience you gain at such an early stage in your career is invaluable."* With this in mind, trainees suggest *"you need to be a mature self-starter to come here."* They say this is a training scheme which *"doesn't baby you,"* largely because *"we've no massive support structure, no team of paralegals or ancillary staff doing copying."* The flip side is *"you are required to do proper work and are more rounded because of it."* The hours can go either way: *"You leave at 5.30 or 6pm when it is not busy. When it is you could do 12-hour days, seven days a week."*

town house, country house

There are stark differences between Shadbolt's two residences. The activities in Reigate are broader – *"much more general commercial"* – while the London office concentrates more on *"contentious construction and projects with smaller supporting commercial and property sections."* Quite naturally, *"people tend to gravitate to the office that suits them best."* Surrey affords *"picturesque surroundings, if you like that,"* and office hours hovering around 9.30am until 6pm. Londoners who quite like working there, but wouldn't want to live in a place where there isn't a decent pub and not much has happened since the Domesday can commute to Reigate in about 35 minutes from London Bridge, Victoria or Clapham Junction. Of course there are people who see the merits of the town – good restaurants, pleasant countryside and easy access to Gatwick, Brighton and Guildford, not to mention *"a homely office atmosphere that makes it a great place to do your first seat."* No doubt they dislike the *"City ethos"* of Shadbolt's office in the capital, which occupies a prime location next to St Paul's Cathedral and opposite the Millennium Bridge. *"You are near to good restaurants and the Tate*

SHEARMAN & STERLING LLP

Want to be a lawyer, not just a trainee?

At Shearman & Sterling LLP you will get hands on experience of high profile deals and be given responsibility and continued support to achieve your full potential.

Our reputation and worldwide experience means that you will work on major international transactions from day one. Because of our size you will be an integral and valued member of your team, working in the informal yet professional environment of our London office, which has now grown to over 300 people.

During your two-year training contract you will train in our core business practices, including project finance, banking and mergers and acquisitions and may have the opportunity to spend six months in our New York, Abu Dhabi or Singapore offices. We provide a maintenance grant and cover PgDL and LPC fees.

Modern and amazing sunsets down the Thames," trainees told us before also pointing out that working in London can lead to 10pm or 11pm finishes.

Whether rural or urban minded, *"a young group of people in both offices"* ensures a lively social scene. The qualification of one trainee just before our interviews propelled *"everyone out to celebrate, even partners from both offices."* And it doesn't take long for new recruits to get to know everyone: *"In my first week so many people offered to take me out to lunch,"* recalled a source fondly. Whether they stay beyond qualification largely depends on whether they become hooked by the firm's specialist practices and whether a job is available in their preferred location. In 2007, two of the four qualifiers stayed on, although interestingly neither went into construction teams.

and finally...

Shadbolt is at the top of its field and boasts three of the eight top lawyers in construction law, according to *Chambers UK*. Its compact size and clear focus ensure that trainees get to work right alongside these highly talented and successful individuals. What a start to a career...

Shearman & Sterling LLP

the facts

Location: London
Number of UK partners/solicitors: 24/97
Total number of trainees: 27
Seats: 4x6 months
Alternative seats: Overseas seats
Extras: Language training

American capitalism in the late 19th Century was an exciting business. As skyscrapers sprang up like trees and railroads spread across the map like roots across a garden, industrialists such as Jay Gould, Henry Ford and the Rockefellers became America's aristocracy. Standing alongside them in their domination was elite New York law firm Shearman & Sterling.

all around the world

This classic Manhattan firm now has offices stretching from San Francisco and São Paulo to Singapore and Shanghai – and that's just the S's. It was one of the earliest American firms to tackle Europe, opening up in Paris in 1963, Frankfurt and Dusseldorf in 1991 and Munich ten years later. As for the UK, it arrived in London in 1972, some 25 years ahead of the main pack, and is now one of the biggest imports into our legal profession.

The firm uses the classic four-seat training system, and though there are some decent advisory seats like antitrust and tax, the majority are transactional. Places in M&A are highly coveted and get trainees working on mind-bogglingly big deals such as last year's €13bn merger between parts of Nokia and Siemens. On such deals, there's *"a lot of paperwork to turn,"* but it is unlikely proof-reading and bibling will take all your time. More likely you'll be helping co-ordinate the work of other offices and associate firms around the globe, which does unfortunately mean *"lots of staying up waiting for Australia to call."* On the upside you'll normally be able to see deals reach their close, which provides the satisfaction and excitement that attracts people to M&A work in the first place. *"I had a couple of nights at the printers,"* admitted one trainee, *"but also a couple of thrilling all-night completions."* Another seemed enthralled by *"the buzz of seeing the deal signed, the pop of the Champagne corks, the long closing dinners."* Aside from mega-deals trainees are also likely to participate in smaller matters such as the sale of junk debts on which they can take more control. One trainee apparently closed such a sale for a mere pound.

The mammoth European finance division encompasses seats in financial institutions (banking), structured finance, capital markets, acquisition finance and leveraged finance, pretty much all of which vie for the title of most demanding, although banking is generally accepted to be *"the killer."* The project finance lawyers work open plan, giving the team *"a slightly more pally atmosphere"* than the others. Compared with sharing an office with your supervisor, it also means *"you're left to fend for yourself a little more"* and *"you work for more people. Someone will come by and see there's space on your desk and fill it with a file."* Typically the matters handled in the project finance division are huge and go on for months or even years, so you won't get the same satisfaction of tracking a deal from start to finish as you would in M&A. A common trainee task involves co-ordinating the completion of conditions precedent, which basically means *"every day you're chasing others to supply documents."* If that sounds dull, the thing to realise is *"you have to understand what every document does, which takes you to the very heart of the deal."* What's more, the task teaches valuable people skills. *"You're the annoying person chasing others – sometimes quite senior people – for documents,"* noted one interviewee, *"so you've got to learn diplomacy and how to handle different personalities."* Other finance seats could see you playing a more varied role on smaller matters – *"researching companies' structures and subsidiaries, going through constitutional documents, completing Companies House forms, board resolutions, etc."* In other words, *"proper brain work."*

brain ache

If you're looking for even brainier brainwork, ask for a turn in tax. As one source put it: *"It's an academic seat and you either like that sort of thing or you don't."* There is another attraction: *"To be honest, it's not the busiest seat. They don't like it if*

you try to stay late – they just say it can wait till tomorrow." Of course, this sudden change of pace feels a little odd. *"You have friends killing themselves staying late and you're there with hardly enough to do,"* one trainee recalled.

While discussing their LPC, one of our interviewees forgot the word 'advocacy'. If that seems hard to imagine, this is not necessarily your best option, as Shearman's London office is a very deal-focused place. The firm has abandoned the contentious seat requirement for the majority of trainees and instead sends everyone on a two-week course at the College of Law, supplemented by participation in a pro bono programme. *"We actually helped out real people... It's a change from just making money for big banks,"* one noted. For those who are determined to have a proper taste of litigation, there is a seat offering a decent introduction. *"I interviewed witnesses, drafted statements and went to court a lot,"* reported a former occupant. There is additionally a good chance of exposure to arbitration matters in the antitrust (competition) seat and a new slot with the employment law team.

International secondments are available to Singapore and Abu Dhabi, plus a relatively new option, New York. *"It's where the firm is based, it's where the global heads of most departments are and it's six months in New York – why wouldn't you want to go?"* chuckled one trainee. The Singapore gig involves *"an awesome flat in a complex with a swimming pool,"* and after a long week in the office *"it's pretty great flying out to Malaysia, Thailand or Hong Kong for the weekend."* With any secondment the workload depends on the department you join and your supervisor. We heard from trainees who'd complained of *"mountains of admin,"* while others suggested *"they basically treat you like a junior associate."* The main disadvantage seems to be that you have to come back. *"I got off the plane back to Britain in shorts and a t-shirt and it was snowing,"* remembered one glum source.

how to get ahead

So, how easy is it to get the seats you want? The simple answer is that *"business needs come first but generally they seem to accommodate people's wishes."* It's best to make your preferences known in person as well as through the formal channels. For example, officially the first seat is chosen by the firm, but *"as there's only a few of us you get to know HR before you start and can say what you're interested in."* When it comes to qualification jobs a quiet word is also worthwhile. *"No one needs to worry about not getting taken on, there's room for everybody,"* said one fourth-seater; *"it's just a question of which department."* In 2007 all seven qualifiers stayed, lending weight to this view. There's no formal announcement of vacancies, so *"you're encouraged to approach partners to find out if there's an opportunity for you. Or they might approach you and express an interest in you."* The firm has recently added more formality to the system to the extent that trainees indicate their four preferred qualification departments and *"the partners all get together and have a big talk about it."* It's an indication of the way Shearman's operates its scheme – it's formalised for the sake of fairness, but nevertheless initiative and networking are still rewarded. *"It's better to take control of your training contract,"* one source explained. *"You'll get better opportunities if you're clear about what you want."*

You'll be aware that American firms have a reputation for epic hours and on this point the trainees we spoke with seemed sanguine. *"It's a misconception that American firms slaughter their trainees,"* one assured us. *"I work no harder than my friends at magic circle firms."* In most departments *"you leave at 6pm if there's nothing pressing on your desk,"* because at busy times *"9am till 9pm is pretty common."* The worst-case scenario is probably to be in a finance department or M&A in the build up to closing a deal, when *"you could certainly have a week or two with very little sleep."*

Other departments have more regular hours of 9.30am to 7pm. *"Everyone gets sick of work sometimes, but what keeps me going is the people,"* one trainee told us. *"All the trainees have become friends,"* another added. The office is *"small enough that it's easy to arrange social events just by sending an e-mail round on Friday evening."* When it comes to venues, the office location near Liverpool Street station offers *"a weird choice"* between the ultra-City Exchange Square and the scruffy, trendy bars of nearby Shoreditch. If you're really beat from a long day, *"the Industry bar is at the back of the building and you can just fall into it."*

just say yes

So what sort of person is suited to the top-end deal making offered at Shearman? Not, it seems, the aggressive, competitive types you might expect. *"It's not dog eat dog at all,"* one source revealed, *"though you do need to be confident, as you get a lot of responsibility early on. You've got to be able to get on the phone to a client and not have a nervous breakdown."* Above all *"you need to be enthusiastic, not a 'no' person. Not a walkover, but a volunteer – someone who'll offer to stay late because they want to help not just because they're expected to."*

In the USA Shearman has long been associated with the elite Ivy League universities – Yale's law school, for example, is named after founding partner John Sterling. In the London office neither a law degree nor an Oxbridge education is de rigueur; in fact *"Shearmans felt more down-to-earth than some of the other big City firms I visited,"* one trainee told us. For all its elite background, Shearman's London office does seem more relaxed than you might think. *"Based on what friends at British City firms have told me, I'd say here it's much less hierarchical,"* one source concluded. Partners were described as mostly *"friendly and approachable"* and *"not old school."* Supervisors, usually senior associates, were generally considered *"friendly, approachable and*

supportive," and regular lunches between partners and new trainees while they are still at law
school help set the scene for future working relationships. *"I've never found anyone not willing to
answer a question,"* one source reported. And
despite all the hard work, *"it's not the kind of
place where you can't check your personal e-mail."*
The only fly in the ointment seems to be long-
term career progression in London: as with
some other US firms, few associates get made up
to partner. This issue came into the spotlight
earlier in 2007 following a flood of senior non-
partner departures.

and finally...

If you want the work and international opportunities of a large firm, while holding onto the
intimacy of a smaller office – and you're prepared
to put in the hours – this could be worth a look.
Remember that the firm regards itself as an international rather than American firm these days,
and also be aware that a good number of our
interviewees had participated in the firm's vacation scheme.

Sheridans

the facts

Location: London
Number of UK partners/solicitors: 20/16
Total number of trainees: 2
Seats: Notionally 4x6 months
Alternative seats: None
Extras: Pro bono – various projects, including music-
industry trusts

One of the first UK law firms to specialise in
media and entertainment matters, Sheridans has,
for over 50 years, advised some of the biggest
names in music, film, television and theatre. Over
time it has expanded into other practice areas,
including company commercial, litigation,
employment and property.

so much better...

Sheridans' client list reads like a *Who's Who* of the
entertainment industry. Already regarded as pre-
eminent, in 2006 the music practice was
propelled even higher with the addition of lawyer
James Sully from Harbottle & Lewis. The managers of bands including Franz Ferdinand and
Kaiser Chiefs were accordingly added to the firm's
existing client roster, which already included
artists such as, oh, for instance, Sir Paul McCartney. If we haven't already got you salivating then
try this on for size: the firm advised Kylie
Minogue on her Showgirl tour and Sharon, Ozzy,
Jack and Kelly Osbourne are regulars at its door.
Other artist clients include Pink Floyd, Kate Bush,
Jimmy Page and Phil Collins. The film and television team – a recent addition – has handled
projects for Andrew Lloyd Webber and regularly
acts for clients such as National Geographic TV
and Five. It also acts for Ash Atalla, producer of
The Office. Recent film work includes finance and
production work for *Amazing Grace*, and in the
world of theatre, the firm handles matters for The
Really Useful Group, including giving guidance
on the production of *The Sound of Music* and, for
Littlestar Services, on the *Mamma Mia*! shows
globally.

Assuming you've not been blinded by that
glittering roll call, you should read a little about
the training scheme. Trainees undertake at least
three, and possibly four, seats within the following departments: music, theatre and media; film
and television; property; company commercial;
employment and litigation. The structure is far
from rigid, so seats can last longer than six
months and trainees may be required to help out
in other areas if certain departments are franti-
cally busy. Split seats are possible, allowing
trainees to work for two departments at the same

time. In the past this has happened with property and litigation and the 'hybrid' option was well received by trainees. *"You learn how to deal with having a lot of things on your plate, how to manage your work and prioritise. It ingrains an organised approach in you, which makes you a better solicitor."* Working for two departments also ensures that *"rather than sitting twiddling your thumbs, you always have something to do."*

fight for your rights

If you're assigned to the music, theatre and media department (the aptly named 'entertainment seat'), chances are you'll find the work both interesting and challenging. *"The engine room of the firm,"* it offers intellectually stimulating work and excellent client contact. *"From the word go you get huge exposure to the top-notch work in which the firm is involved."* Trainees get their own small caseload and also assist partners on larger, more complex transactions by drafting, negotiating or perhaps conducting research. *"I suppose they all sound like typical trainee jobs, but in reality it's so much more than that,"* said one enthusiastic source. *"It's you speaking to the clients on the phone, you're the one drafting an agreement or conducting matters. I just don't think you get this degree of independence at every firm."* If that sounds scary rather than exciting, rest assured that a partner is on hand to oversee everything and guidance is plentiful. The department covers a broad spectrum of issues from band member agreements and copyright to royalty audits and distribution contracts, and the clientele is a mixture of individuals and companies. The scope of the film and television team is similarly expansive: it deals with writing agreements, format licences, cast and crew agreements and talent deals, as well as all aspects of film finance. *"They really let you get involved with interesting stuff across the board."*

Our overview of Sheridans' practice is by no means complete. The media departments undisputedly are the heart of the firm, but they sit alongside property, commercial, litigation and employment teams that have become strong in their own right. They are also integral to the formation of a rounded training contract. The firm handles both residential and commercial property, *"which is useful because you can follow what you learned at law school, starting off with easier files and progressing up the learning curve to the more complex commercial work."* A seat in the litigation department involves *"a lot of court visits – my advocacy skills have improved quite a bit,"* said one trainee. Many of the instructions stem from the entertainment sector – *"people arguing over rights that are attached to pieces of music, for example."* Management, publishing and recording disputes are all commonplace, as are IP matters, breach of confidence and defamation claims. This last area is particularly juicy *"because it often involves things that you've already read about in the papers."* There is a fair bit of commercial litigation (banking, insolvency, corporate) and some property lit too.

The coco seat means a steady stream of work. Said one trainee: *"In some firms you hear it's a bit feast and famine in the corporate department, but I've never had a day at Sheridans where I've had nothing to do."* That said, trainees are unlikely to find themselves stuck in the office at 2am: *"We're really not expected to work evenings and weekends. You have to muck in occasionally if there's a big deal on, but it's the exception, not the rule."* Trainees approve of the firm's attitude in this respect: *"You don't work exceedingly long hours, but you work hard while you're here, which is how I like it. You come in, get on with it and then have time to yourself at the end of the day."* Typical hours tend to be about 9am to 6.30pm.

shaken not stirred

There are several other aspects to the firm's attitude and approach that are worth a mention. First, the word 'friendly' was mentioned about a billion times in our interviews. Second, because of the firm's size and 'friendliness' it has so far avoided the need for formal appraisal processes and end-of-seat reviews. *"You're just given feedback on an ongoing basis. It works well; there's so much partner contact here that you always know how you're getting on and where there's room for improvement."* Third, this is a youthful and ambitious firm: *"It has a vibrant atmosphere, which helps with the push to make the firm better. We're always trying to improve and partners are always looking out for opportunities." "We're stepping up with the marketing and you can tell there's a real drive to make the firm stand out in its field. It's exciting and it's only going to get better."*

On the social side *"there's often lunch or drinks on. Someone sends an e-mail around periodically on a sunny Friday evening and we go to the pub."* For the annual summer party *"they always try to make it a bit different and last year was great fun. We had the afternoon off and went for tapas and cocktail-making lessons."* Themed Christmas parties are also de rigeur: *"Last year was 007, the year before that was Hollywood, with a casino and everything."* Not to mention a DJ and a *"Saturday Night Fever flashing dance floor."* Such events usually take place in what is rather mysteriously referred to as *"the space upstairs,"* a location variously described as *"a place for large meetings," "a gallery space"* and – somewhat less glamorous – *"a room where you can do due diligence."* It is also a frequent venue for client events, which in turn are *"great for putting names to faces."* Recently for example the firm held a '50-50' event in conjunction with Getty Images, which celebrated 50 years of famous directors and 50 years since Sheridans' establishment.

It's clear that Sheridan's goes for a certain sort of person: academically strong, practical and willing to work hard within a team. *"Be prepared to muck in – it's an all-hands-on-deck approach here,"* stressed one source. In return for your hard work, the firm will genuinely involve you in *"the marketing and the direction of the firm... It's a great place to start your legal career."* And to continue it, according to the single trainee who qualified in 2007 at stayed to work on music, theatre and media matters.

and finally...

A word to the wise: if you're applying to Sheridans simply because you practically live on Popbitch, you might be in for a shock. *"The firm looks for people who are interested in all of the work we do, not just the entertainment stuff."*

Sherrards Solicitors

the facts

Location: St Albans
Number of UK partners/solicitors: 13/14
Total number of trainees: 7
Seats: 3 or 4 seats of varying length
Alternative seats: None

Founded in 1880, this firm has grown from its high street roots to become a regional player in the northern Home Counties. Located not far from the railway station in St Albans, an ancient but small, upmarket commuter city just north of the capital, its suburban setting does not preclude it from taking on work from London businesses. Indeed, with the capital just 22 minutes away by train, its setting doesn't preclude it from taking on staff from there either.

pilgrims' choice

Sherrards offers clients advice on matters ranging from company/commercial, property and employment law to private client, franchising and social housing issues. It is particularly renowned in these last two areas, as reflected by rankings in *Chambers UK*. The social housing lawyers work with around 40 local authorities and housing associations and are specialists in housing litigation, particularly in the sphere of antisocial tenant disputes. With a client list including the likes of St Albans District Council, Riversmead Housing Association and Bedfordshire Pilgrims Housing Association, there are always cases centring on noise, environmental and racial issues, and the team is particularly skilled in the use of ASBOs, demotion orders and exclusion orders. As for the impressive franchising department, its tasty client list includes Domino's Pizza, Subway Developments, Bagel Factory and Esquires Coffee Houses, all of which give the firm plenty to sink their teeth into. The team assists businesses to franchise around the UK, as well as aiding clients with franchise development, franchise disputes and property-related issues.

Another department well worth mentioning is real estate, not least because of its size. This part of the practice was bolstered following a merger in 2000 with niche property boutique Peters & Co in nearby Little Chalfont. In more recent times it has worked on matters such as the acquisition of a development site in London, being turned into a 80-unit shopping centre. The biggest property clients come from the retail sector and include Budgens, Benjys and Ann Summers.

As a new addition to the True Picture this year, we were keen to learn where Sherrards sees itself going in the next few years. *"It's really expanding at the moment on a regional basis,"* said one source; *"we are having to look at where we are going to get more office space from, whether in the same building or elsewhere."* Another more reserved source added that *"it is looking to recruit, but not in any rush,"* telling us that *"organic growth"* is what the firm is concentrating on. We learned too that Sherrards has its eye on winning more referrals from US firms in London.

waving, not drowning

The official line on the seat system is a little unclear: *"It might be three seats of eight months, but they have yet to decide..."* We heard stories of people doing year-long stints in departments they enjoyed and people side-stepping areas of no interest to them. Said one trainee: *"Because it's a smaller firm, the system is not as defined and the flexibility in that respect is fantastic. It cuts out doing things you know you don't want to do, and the firm knows there is no point sticking you somewhere you don't want to be – it doesn't help your strengths and it doesn't help the firm. I like the way they have done things."* The downside is a degree of uncertainty: *"If you want to do a certain seat and you want to move departments to get it, you have to set it in motion yourself."* Whatever trainees think of the current system, it sounds as though there will be some changes. *"Recently there was a meeting between trainees, the training partner and the managing partner, so they could try and co-ordinate us moving round a bit better."*

Pretty much any area of the firm will host a trainee – commercial property, litigation, company/commercial, employment, property litigation, conveyancing and private client. The firm is *"weighted heavily in terms of commercial property"* and so most people tend to have a spell there *"unless they express a total dislike for it."* When we rang there was no seat in the social housing department; however, our sources reckoned that *"if a trainee expressed an interest the team would be very pleased to have them on board."*

The commercial property seat will bestow *"quite a lot of responsibility"* on you from the *"moment you start."* Generally trainees are viewed as *"a resource, there to be used"* by the whole department. At times it can feel like they had to *"churn,*

churn, churn out work and paper," but at least the range of tasks is good: assignment of leases, licences for alterations, lease renewals and lease surrenders. Trainees run their own files, and although they reported some "stomach-dropping moments," they felt comfortable because "you are sitting with your supervisor and you can shout and wave when you are feeling the pressure or not sure about something."

courtroom thrills

The litigation department handles commercial and insolvency disputes. Ideal for those who will enjoy the buzz of the courtroom, trainees get to do "a fair amount of advocacy." One source was a touch nervous about this: "I was terrified, but I really enjoyed it... they were so supportive and no one is pushed out of their depth." We also listened to stories of "all-night mediations" as well as the usuals of drafting particulars of claim and instructions to counsel. The employment department is "small but growing" and trainees say the work is "a lot more law based" than other practice areas, which gets them involved in plenty of research tasks. The team acts for employers and employees (more regularly the former) and the work is both contentious and non-contentious.

There is an end-of-seat appraisal, but trainees told us they wanted the system to be even more formalised. "We are meant to have one every three months, and they are very willing if you ask, but you have to be proactive and I think it would be good if it was set in stone," said one. A final point to note about the training: Sherrards is "trying to foster international links and build up alliances," so through AG Legal there have lately been some opportunities to do three-week exchanges with young Dutch lawyers and it is quite likely further visits will be made to other European firms.

open all hours?

So what makes trainees head to St Albans and join forces with Sherrards? "It stood out as being a regional firm. I wasn't fussed about going to the City and many of the partners have come from City firms anyway, so there is a high standard of work," said one recruit. Another put the firm's appeal down to the combination of "a relaxed attitude and really good work with London clients, but without the City lifestyle." Other popular reasons included the small trainee intake ("It's easier to be hands on, you're not another nameless or anonymous face"), the guidance available from supervisors ("because you sit with a partner, you can always ask or shout over the desk"), the type of work ("It's for big, West End clients who have almost become disillusioned with the service they get elsewhere") and the point at which the firm recruits it trainees ("I didn't want to wait two years").

To fit in at Sherrards you need to be "sociable, hard-working and willing to get involved." Trainees are often sent to "networking events, breakfast meetings and client soirées," which means it's important to have good people skills. Not all the trainees come fresh out of uni, and we were told the firm appreciates "a bit of experience." Links to St Albans aren't essential: "We have people who commute from London and Essex," explained one source. That said, Sherrards will be keen to find out how much you actually know about the area as it will want to be fairly certain its trainees are likely to stay on after qualification. In 2007, one of the two did so, going into litigation. The year before, three of the four qualifiers stayed on.

The offices are described as "lovely, and only ten minutes away from the town centre." There is free, onsite, secure parking and, if travelling by train, "you always get a seat because most people commute the other way into London." On the subject of working hours, we were told: "It's not a shop, you don't close at 5.30pm... I have been here till 8.30pm before, but that is nothing compared to the City." Socially, there are monthly "pizza and wine lunches in the boardroom" as well as "more informal gatherings to which the partners will come along too." We were impressed at what one trainee called the Friday Lunch Club – *"No one sees a problem with you disappearing for the odd hour and a half to the local Italian, or to go to the pub to have a beer, burger and chips."* The Christmas party is normally held at a local restaurant and comes complete with karaoke. Trainee nights out are typically *"pub crawls round St. Albans"* or a trip to a curry house. Interestingly, St Albans is one of several places around the UK which claims to have the most pubs per square mile. We're not suggesting that should influence your decision to apply, but we just thought you might like to know. Sports enthusiasts can get involved with cricket matches against local clients and Monday evening badminton.

and finally...

Sherrards is a tempting option for those keen to get involved with quality work in the Home Counties. It has the advantage of being far enough from the City to not feel the stress but near enough to commute to every day if you actually want to live in London.

Shoosmiths

the facts

Location: Birmingham, Basingstoke, Milton Keynes, Northampton, Nottingham, Reading, Solent
Number of UK partners/solicitors: 105/220
Total number of trainees: 36
Seats: 4x6 months
Alternative seats: Secondments

Quietly beavering away in its seven chosen locations, Shoosmiths has further growth on its mind.

shoosmiths redux

Once best known for bulk conveyancing and personal injury, since 2001 Shoosmiths has pursued *"a deliberate strategy to hold the volume business and boost the commercial division."* In the process it has undergone a transformation. The top-50 firm now employs around 1,400 people, work for commercial clients accounts for around 50% of its revenue, and each year revenues have jumped significantly. Clients include Lloyds TSB, Bank of Scotland, DaimlerChrysler, Volkswagen, Nissan, insurance company Zurich, IKEA and Toys 'R' Us, several of these using more than one branch of the firm, happy in the knowledge that they get what they want from the firm irrespective of where the work is done.

Seeing the firm as a single entity is perhaps easiest for new trainees, as they get to spend their first fortnight together on a combined induction/PSC event. Remembering the time away fondly, one source told us: *"You all live in a hotel, which is brilliant for a bit of gossip and drama, although the first things you say can haunt you for two years, so beware!"* After the two weeks holed up together in Northamptonshire, they scatter to Shoosmiths' seven offices to start the two-year journey to qualification. This means dedication to a single office, with the exception that the Northampton and Milton Keynes (MK) offices are conjoined for training purposes. *"You are not expected to go outside your home office,"* explained a source, *"and the intention is to allow you to do all four seats there."* Employment, property and coco departments are found in all offices bar Basingstoke, and then there are a few regional variations. Client secondments (eg to DaimlerChrysler) are open to all trainees, irrespective of office.

waine's world

The Northampton office can accommodate up to 500 staff in its open-plan building at The Lakes. The staple seat choices – commercial property, employment, litigation and coco – are supplemented by a few others, among them personal injury, private client and regulatory. This last seat offers a mixed bag of experiences, primarily health and safety, public liability issues (including food-related) and licensing. The lawyers here, for example, provide advice to the likes of Next and McDonald's. Another speciality of the office is finance litigation, a department headed by national training principal Waine Mannix. Dubbed Waine's World, the department is *"taking over most of the Northampton office and has got some of our biggest clients – banks, building societies and major car finance companies."* A large team assists these clients to recover debts owed through both secured and unsecured lending. There are car repossessions for motor finance companies and mortgage repossessions for building societies. *"You learn an awful lot really quickly and then after three months you think, 'Great but now I need something different.'"* The seat can be a *"perfect crash course in litigation, as you run a file from pre-litigation right up to charging orders,"* but not everyone loves it. For some the idea of *"taking away people's houses"* is unappealing or even *"morally objectionable."*

Northampton trainees have mixed views on the office's business-park location. Some felt it hampered the post-work social scene; others pointed out that *"there are villages nearby, we're a short drive out of town and there's a bus service to Northampton at lunchtime, so I don't buy the isolation argument."*

mk's the don

When it comes to commercial practice groups, MK looks to have overtaken Northampton in importance. *"The expansion of Waine's World and other departments"* led to overcrowding at The Lakes, so in the past year many staff have transferred to MK, notably the property team (minus the plot sales and bulk conveyancing teams) and most of the dispute resolution unit. They all joined the coco team in a large building that has room for further growth. *"When I first came there were about 40 people in this office, now we are 80 people and there's talk about taking over another part of another floor as we are already crammed to the rafters,"* said one source.

One of the things MK excels in is business process outsourcing. Its BPO lawyers recently acted for Silverstone Race Track catering managers Aspire Hospitality and also for Airport Logistics, which is now responsible for the staffing of Ocado's distribution fleet. Other big-name clients include British American Tobacco and Associated British Foods (producers of Twinings tea and Kingsmill loaves). MK and Reading are the only two offices offering IP seats, so presumably shoe-loving trainees scrambled, January sales-style, for the chance to assist Jimmy Choo in pursuing actions against New Look and Marks & Spencer recently. Lambretta, Nike and Thorntons also use the firm for their IP problems, as did the London office of hotshot US law firm Skadden, which subcontracted all the IP due diligence on the giant Caudwell-Phones4U corporate deal.

Working for big clients on increasingly valuable deals ramps up the pressure on lawyers and trainees alike. That said, even in busy corporate seats *"there is none of this macho City rubbish; they judge you purely on quality of work. I have worked late – one month in particular was hectic and I was in at the weekends as well – but they were almost apologetic about it."* So, with great work, decentish hours and a view that *"it's a lot more friendly than Northampton as everybody knows each other,"* is it any wonder that trainees are flocking to this fast-growing office over Northampton? The location, *"just five minutes walk from Centre MK,"* helps too.

a tale of two -inghams

It's much the same story of *"all-go"* growth and relocation in the Nottingham office, which offers commercial property, coco and employment plus property litigation. *"Our new office is in the plush*

Waterfront Plaza near to Jury's Inn. It's going to be much bigger and we'll have five floors." It sounds like trainees in the busy corporate and property seats get through a lot of work. *"I had so many files on the go in property,"* recalled one. *"It means you have to be so organised or things run away with you, but the support there is second to none."* In corporate, *"a few ex-City lawyers"* are bringing *"fantastic experience, drive and ambition to the office."* Nottingham hours are *"mostly fine and you can normally leave by 6.30pm. Then sometimes it might be 8pm, and I have done two 11pms."*

Staff socialising does leave some disappointed: *"We are good at arrivals and send-offs and there is a great office Christmas party, otherwise people generally go home to their families."* At least Nottingham has an active TSG, so *"the trainees in the city have a strong network and there are events every week."* Not to be outdone, the firm throws its own *"networking and marketing events for banks and surveyors... things like bowling or just drinks and nibbles."*

In early 2007 Shoosmiths' Birmingham office announced that it had hired its 100th employee. Having only opened in 2001, its development is impressive. Clients seem to think so too: last year the new Birmingham corporate team helped Midlands brewery Marston's PLC in its multimillion-pound acquisition of Sovereign Inns. As more seats became available in Birmingham, it acquired its own trainees rather than relying on transfers from elsewhere. However, if you're anywhere else in the network and you want an insolvency seat then Birmingham is the place to go. Here Shoosmiths acts for a number of national and local insolvency practitioners, including Baker Tilly and PwC. The assessment of one source was that, *"culture-wise, the Birmingham office is quite different to the rest. It is more like one of the other big regional firms, perhaps because most of the people working there are imports, not home grown."*

making waves

The choice of seats in the 100-strong Solent office is standard – commercial property, coco, litigation and employment – but the signature dishes are servings of marine law and landlord and tenant cases in the litigation seat. *"This office has come on in leaps and bounds,"* a southern trainee told us. *"We are starting to be a main player here..."* Sadly, Solent Shoosmiths is not situated on a megabucks super yacht, but instead on another business park *"sandwiched between Portsmouth and Southampton."* We're also advised that as *"its client base goes west not eastwards,"* *"a lot of the work is local,"* although lawyers *"work closely with the Reading office."* On the south coast, Shoosmiths is keen on local networking; indeed, we rather like the sound of *"Nachos Networking – held in a Mexican bar... trainees help out and are then let loose to join in."* Alas, Solent staff socialising has fewer whistles and tequila shots: *"It's a bit piecemeal to be honest... there is a pub on the business park, but it is not uppermost in everyone's thoughts – there's a mature atmosphere in this office."* Anyone looking for a scene should *"go to Southampton, mix with the professional groups and make some waves themselves."*

Reading continues the Shoosmiths' theme of *"going from strength to strength."* In the past year the office moved its 120-strong workforce to Apex Plaza, next to the train station. Here the standard trainee seat choices are supplemented with debt recovery and IP. Employment certainly gets good reviews: *"I had a lot of exposure to work permits for big clients, but most of my work was contentious and I got to represent a client at a case management hearing."* Nearby is the *"rather trendy"* Oakford Social Club and trainees have *"just set up a social committee."*

Last but not least, in Basingstoke Shoosmiths has a large 'legal expenses' division that acts for individuals referred by the AA and Capita. This part of the firm is in good health and grew its personal injury instructions from 25,000 in 2005/06 to 32,000 in 2006/07. A trainee confirmed: *"So many firms are moving away from that type of work and don't want to be seen to be doing it. We are proud of our bulk work; we do it well and we earn huge amounts off it."* The office also works on high-value clinical negligence claims, the most serious of which are usually birth injuries but can also be related to misdiagnoses of cancer or psychiatric claims. There is additionally an employment group. Basingstoke grows its own trainees through the internal promotion of case handlers. It's more of a nine to five-thirty kind of place and is situated about ten minutes' walk from the shops and bars in the centre of town.

shoo-shine

The topic of Shoosmiths' future certainly excited debate. *"As a brand we're gaining recognition,"* trainees told us, revelling in the *"ambition"* of a firm *"rapidly expanding in all offices."* However, it was *"talk of a London office"* that really got thoughts flying. *"There is a real split in the firm between those who want to keep growing bigger and better and go into the City, and those who want to stick to what we have got,"* said one interviewee. Another posed the key question: *"Can we be as big as we deserve without going to the City?"* Summing up the issue, a third trainee told us: *"The current locations are not always where people want us to be, so the whole debate is about whether we need a City office, and can we or can we not service London clients out of Reading."* Apparently *"time scales between six and 18 months are mentioned"* and, with *"younger equity partners very keen to invest,"* it seems a firm that has been a stalwart of the regions is now edging away from that particular strategy. If and when it does make

the leap trainees doubt it will significantly alter the fate and fortunes of the regional offices. As such, some nine of the 11 2007 qualifiers stayed with the firm.

Applicants who will fit in at Shoosmiths will be *"open-minded, not overblown"* and keen to have early exposure to clients. *"We're encouraged to get involved with marketing and know that our job is more than doing the work on our desks,"* stressed one source. While a 2:1 is the minimum requirement, Shoosmiths makes it clear that being 'book clever' isn't enough. It wants to recruit students who are *"capable of independent thought."* *"Grounded and clever"* is how one source described the trainee group, and we agree with them. Everyone we spoke to was knowledgeable about the firm and the market in which their office operated. For now, most (though not all) trainees share a preference for smaller towns over the capital. *"I like my green fields and fresh air and I'm not aspiring to corporate life in London,"* said one source who also valued Shoosmiths' *"caring, concerned attitude."* Another commented on how *"the guys at the top here believe it is in everyone's interests to know what the plan is... there is a culture of openness, honesty and sincerity."* Indeed, the *"hugely transparent management structure"* headed by chairman Andrew Tubbs and chief exec Paul Stothard was widely praised. *"These people know my name and I like knowing the people who dictate the firm's direction,"* one interviewee concluded.

and finally...

If Shoosmiths' current dynamism isn't appeal enough, consider quality of work as *"a massive selling point – as most of the departments are quite small, you are right in the firing line."* Even if you're not one to buy into promises of work-life balance, these claims alone should be persuasive.

Sidley Austin (UK) LLP

the facts

Location: London
Number of UK partners/solicitors: 37/78
(US+UK-qualified)
Total number of trainees: 17
Seats: 4x6 months
Alternative seats: None
Extras: Language training

To borrow the analysis of one of Sidley Austin's savvy trainees, this *"massive worldwide firm has been quite small and finance-centric in the UK."* Recently, however, it has turned its attention to *"growing its corporate team and building strength in various other areas."* That said, before you read any further, heed the warning of the interviewee who told us: *"If you think you won't like finance then you shouldn't do a training contract here."*

the f-word

Chicago-born Sidley Austin opened up in our capital in 1974 and immediately began to make a mark in structured finance deals. Having since expanded the office to more than 100 lawyers – around 80% of whom are UK-qualified – it is now routinely billed as the most successful US firm in the London securitisation market. One recent example of its talent includes close collaboration with the firm's lawyers in the USA in the representation of Washington Mutual Bank as it established the first covered bond programme under New York law. In another strand of high finance, this one resulting from Sidley Austin's merger in 2001 with New York firm Brown & Wood, the office has carved out a niche in advising issuers on international debt deals. In 2006 it advised on 253 such deals worth a total of £110bn. Behind these figures lie some of the world's most prestigious international banks – Credit Suisse, Deutsche Bank, Merrill Lynch, Barclays Capital, Bank of America, RBS, JPMorgan Securities and Lloyds TSB.

One of the things Sidley can offer these clients is a network of 16 offices, over 1,700 lawyers and a fancy website showing a satellite shot of Planet Earth for any doubters of its global credentials. With layer upon layer of worldwide talent, *"international finance is definitely Sidley's signature."* As a result, all trainees must take a seat in the flagship international finance group (IFG), where they can expect to encounter structured and financial instruments that they have never heard about before. *"There is no more than one sentence on securitisation in any book that I read during the LPC, so I wasn't at all prepared for it,"* admitted one interviewee. As well as a willingness to learn this stuff, the seat demands *"a high level of intelligence to get your head around new concepts and jargon."* Even with these boxes ticked, there is *"a very steep learning curve"* to overcome. Supervisors were widely praised for helping to keep trainees afloat, although some felt that the firm as a whole could do more to teach them to swim these unfamiliar waters. *"You go in completely blind and it would be nice to have formalised training at the start of the seat to help walk you through the basics."*

Despite the complexity of the subject matter, trainees were impressed at the faith the firm has in them. *"I was surprised at how much responsibility they gave me. There were plenty of boring tasks, but I was also drafting parts of the less complicated agreements, researching lots and acting as first point of contact for some clients."* All this leads to some exacting hours. *"I was lucky,"* said one trainee, *"I had a few midnight finishes but never an all-nighter. Some of my friends here got caught up in 36-hours-straight jobs."* The gratitude of this 'lucky' trainee sums up quite nicely the seat's infringement on one's personal time. Against this, the more committed are keen to counter claims of *"demoralising"* hours with tales of success and accompanying feelings of worth. *"The hours are not as bad as they sound as you feel like you are working towards something and there is such a good feeling when a deal closes."*

During their time in the group some trainees were focused on specific areas (eg securitisation, regulation and derivatives), while others were sat with supervisors who worked across the board. One area the firm has really blitzed is real estate finance, and its CMBS practice has gained worldwide repute. For the uninitiated – okay that's all of us – this stands for commercial mortgage-backed securities. A highlight here was the representation of Barclays as lead manager in the £918m commercial mortgage-backed security transaction of Gemini (ECLIPSE 2006-3) PLC, the seventh issuance in Barclays Capital's CMBS conduit programme. With so many different specialist areas on offer, those who get a taste for international financial markets usually take another six-month seat within the department.

all things asbestos
To fully please the firm, a good trainee will trot off from IFG to corporate. *"Bizarrely, this is a comparatively nice seat with pleasant hours."* Trainees put this down to the fact that their office is *"not doing as big M&A transactions as the major City firms."* That's not to say trainees couldn't see the strides the London arm was making in the area, for example, it recently acted for Merrill Lynch International on the joint venture acquisition of €5bn of non-performing real estate loans from Banca Intesa. The advances made by the corporate team are indicative of a trend in several corners of the office. A number of lateral hires have boosted the partnership and the trainee intake has also risen to ensure growth from the bottom up. As it grows, the firm is beginning to widen its practice offering in London. Most interesting here is its venture into litigation through the hire of ex-barrister Dorothy Cory-Wright,

who now heads up a four-lawyer insurance litigation team. The firm hopes to capitalise on her pedigree in representing insurance companies like Munich Re and Centre Re in asbestos liability disputes. The newly formed team is expected to take one trainee per seat, leaving the majority to complete a course at Kaplan, the London arm of Nottingham Law School, to satisfy the Law Society's requirements concerning exposure to contentious practice. The trainees we spoke to didn't seem to find this too onerous a burden, although most were in agreement that *"losing three or four Saturdays is a bit tedious."*

Other seat options include tax, employment, non-contentious insurance, capital markets, property, competition and regulatory. One of the more popular seats outside IFG is insolvency, where trainees can sit with a small team that works closely with the firm's global bankruptcy division. *"You work on big cross-border transactions, but as there are not that many lawyers in the group here you really feel part of the team."* Transatlantic phone calls and client contact are par for the course, as is exposure to some high-profile matters. One trainee was charged with a large due diligence exercise surrounding the restructuring of Federal Mogul, which originally hit the headlines in 2001 when it filed for bankruptcy in the USA amidst a plethora of asbestos claims against it. The seat is *"very academic"* and requires *"constant referral to the Insolvency Act and case law."*

we like you, we keep you
In an ideal world all trainees would like to see their working days cut down by an hour or two and a more formalised training scheme put in place to help them digest the complex ins and outs of finance law. Having said this, all were confident that the firm was listening to them and that advances could be made in the future, on the training at least. Consistently impressive NQ

retention rates suggest that overall the firm has got things right. At the heart of their satisfaction is the trade mark formula of the US firms in London – big international deals, top salaries and small domestic teams. And with so many years operating in the City, there are few firms better at maximising this lure. Another important fact behind the NQ retention rates is the *"laid-back qualification process." "You don't have to jump through hoops. It's simple – they find positions if they like you."* In 2007, four of the five qualifiers stayed with the firm, going into tax, insolvency, corporate and property.

But who does the firm like? Looking at our sample of interviewees, the first thing to note is that it has a taste for graduates of the best universities. Nevertheless, *"it is not looking for people who are head-down studious types."* It is more important, according to trainees, to have a sharp mind that is capable of grappling with the extremely complex concepts that will be thrown at you. *"They are looking for someone with intuition who will proactively look for responsibility and embrace it. They want someone who can take the lead."* With all these born leaders under one roof you might expect a conflict or two, yet by all accounts there is a warm vibe throughout the firm. Naturally, unpredictable working patterns make organised social events quite tricky, but trainees make sure they meet up every couple of months for a meal *"somewhere nice to relax."* Fair play to the firm, it picks up the bill. Talking of nice places, the firm's last summer party was held in Merchant Taylors Hall, while Christmas party venues have included The Four Seasons and Claridges in recent years.

and finally...

"Unless you go to the magic circle, this is the best place to do structured finance in the City," pronounced one source. For some applicants there will be no contest: in London, Sidley Austin is a fraction of the size of these firms and has scope for a more personalised training. *"You're not just part of the machine here; you really feel like you make a difference."* Do remember that there isn't the same broad spread of departments to choose between, so if you're invited to sign on the dotted line, be certain you are happy with the idea of working on mind-boggling high finance.

Simmons & Simmons

the facts
Location: London
Number of UK partners/solicitors: 113/226
Total number of trainees: 100
Seats: 4x6 months
Alternative seats: Overseas seats, secondments
Extras: Pro bono – Battersea Legal Advice Centre, language training

After a troubled 1990s when the firm was plundered by the aggressive poaching policies of a number of US firms that were looking to establish themselves on this side of the pond, Simmons & Simmons has steadied the ship and set forth on a course that relies heavily on its widely admired finance department. The firm now employs 2,000 people across 21 offices around the world.

doing deals
Simmons trainees are attracted to it because first and foremost they want to work in a big City firm and be involved on prestigious work. Then again, they want to do all this without suffering the stress, hours and anonymity that they fear will be the case at a mega-sized magic circle firm. As one trainee quipped: *"Simmons offers trainees an identity outside of trainee 44."* In terms of the quality of work on offer, the firm certainly keeps up its end of the bargain, especially in the current booming deal market. It has strong relationships

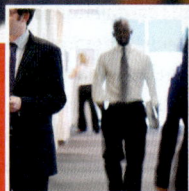

with a number of banking clients including Standard Bank, HSBC and BNP Paribas, and its position on Barclay's general advisory panel was recently reconfirmed. In the past couple of years, Simmons has snaffled a number of impressive mandates, including advising HSBC in relation to E.ON's €29.1bn all-cash offer for Endesa, and working for an international investment bank alongside Renaissance Capital on a number of emerging-markets corporate financings, including several in the Ukraine and the Russian Federation.

It's worth knowing that a large proportion of Simmons' lawyers work on finance and corporate transactions, and this impacts on the seat choices available to trainees. To explain, the departments and teams in which trainees can work are split into four categories: one for finance-orientated seats; another for corporate seats; a third for contentious seats; and then everything else is put into a miscellaneous fourth category. Trainees must take a seat in each of the first three categories and then one more from any category. In practice this might mean one seat drawn from all four categories or three seats taken in categories one and two plus one in category three.

With the finance department widely viewed as the driving force behind the firm's resurgence, it's an important stop-off point for trainees. The group has excellent relationships with its banking clients, and its repackaging service is held up for particular praise. As with many seats, six months in the capital markets department has its ups and downs. Trainees find there is typically *"a lot of proof-reading and adding amendments to documents, and although there is some drafting towards the end it is always quite straightforward."* However, *"because we have such good relationships with financial institutions, we are able to have daily contact with these clients and really build up the relationships with them. It is a good opportunity to get a feel of what it is like to be a qualified solicitor."*

One deal from 2006 earned the capital markets group a few awards. It was for Abu Dhabi National Energy (TAQA) in its debut international capital markets issue comprising $1bn bonds due 2016, $1.5bn bonds due 2036 and €750m bonds due 2013. Goldman Sachs acted as bookrunner and joint lead manager on the transaction, the largest international bond offering by a Middle Eastern company. The client relationships also provide a number of secondment opportunities for trainees and a majority of the potential secondments come in this sector. The corporate team, meanwhile, has been careful to utilise its network of international offices to create a buzz in the Middle East and Far East, as well as parts of Europe. The lawyers are no strangers to major deals with a Japanese element and last year advised Daiwa Securities on its financing of Nippon Sheet Glass's bid for Pilkington, valued at £2.2bn. Trainees find that in corporate seats the experience has both lows and highs. The lows are *"the days when you are photocopying and the nights when you find yourself in the office doing relatively mundane work."* They understood that *"this is the nature of the beast,"* and saw it as a compromise. *"You also get access to some good work, and you don't mind doing* [the mundane work] *so long as it is contrasted with tasks like attending client meetings and drafting."*

my word is my bond

Beyond corporate and finance there are other hot areas in energy and infrastructure, life sciences and TMT. In the past, many trainees have been drawn to the firm because it has such a good reputation in non-core areas of practice, especially IP and employment. Due to the fact that both of these seats are categorised as contentious, it is most unlikely that trainees would be able to complete both during the course of their training contract, and realistically they should not bank on getting either as demand has a nasty habit of outstripping supply. From those lucky enough to have experienced these seats, the feedback is overwhelmingly positive. *"I had always been interested in IP, it was one of the reasons I joined Simmons and the seat lived up to my expectations,"* said one interviewee. The typical work for a trainee in this department covers both trade mark and patent projects, as well as contentious and non-contentious issues. Over in the employment team the client list is mouthwatering. In the banking sector – Aon, ABN AMRO, Deutsche Bank, Morgan Stanley, Swiss Re, UBS and Visa. Beyond it – General Electric and NBC Universal.

The commercial litigation arm also achieved good press this year after it acted for the investment bank Bear Stearns in its dispute with an investment fund company regarding the price of some Parmalat-related notes and whether a deal had been concluded in a phone call. The High Court agreed that the bank had struck a deal, and it was later reported that this was one of the first cases to test in the English courts the city dictum 'my word is my bond'. A litigation seat may well expose a trainee to the delights of fraud and white collar crime. Sadly there is *"a fair amount of grunt work, such as putting together the bundles,"* but this is at least balanced by *"attending hearings and drafting particulars of claim and witness statements."*

the berries and the thorns

As well as a supervisor for each seat, trainees also get a mentor tasked with providing support, should they need it, throughout the duration of the contract. Assessments are centred on mid and end-of-seat appraisals with supervisors, the former being quite informal – *" more of a chat really, to see if you are on track."* The hours vary according to the department, with the usual suspects for long hours being corporate and banking. *"There was one occasion when I came in on Saturday and again on Sunday at 8am, and then I got home at 6am on Wednesday morning,"* recounted one sur-

prisingly upbeat source. IP and real estate are considered to be more sociable with a few 10 to 11pm finishes on record, although these were considered to be a rarity. One aspect of the hours that did rankle was their unpredictable nature: *"One week I can leave at 6pm every night and then the next week I am in from 6am until 4am. It makes it hard to plan a social life with friends from outside work."* In this respect we don't think a Simmons' trainee's life is so very different from those of their magic circle peers.

Despite the sometimes-gruelling nature of the hours, they were not the most consistent bugbear that cropped up during interviews. That honour goes to what some trainees suggest is an increasingly keen focus on the bottom line: *"You can really see the drive to make more profit,"* noted one, while another commented that *"it feels as if there has been a shift in the firm's attitude to its trainees and associates... we are left on the side a bit now."* How so? *"There is no opportunity to give feedback on supervisors or the support staff and so it is difficult to know how to address problems."* We also heard about a dearth of the kind of benefits that some other City trainees enjoy, eg unfettered gym subsidies and BlackBerrys. While we're on the subject of moans, traditionally we've heard a few gripes about Simmons' IT system. Although this has now been updated, it continues to raise eyebrows. Said one source: *"The new system, Vanilla, was meant to revolutionise things, which it hasn't."*

a world of choice

Returning to more positive topics, Simmons' international presence is undoubtedly a strong motivating factor for applicants, and many of the people we interviewed had jumped at the chance of a six-month stint abroad in such far-flung destinations as Abu Dhabi and Hong Kong, or closer to home in Paris or Frankfurt. *"It was fantastic working in a different part of the world and nice to have a good support network out there,"* reported one source. Trainees generally view the international seats as an excellent opportunity to learn and develop broader skills: *"Being in a smaller office with only a couple of English lawyers, I found I was being trusted to do more,"* said one. Indeed, according to our sources, the only downside is that *"if you can speak the language you may get stuck with a lot of translation work."*

In 2007, a new qualification system was put in place whereby the departments advise HR on what spaces they have for newly qualifieds and HR then meets with all fourth-seat trainees in order for them to list their preferred qualification departments. After this the departments then make a list of the trainees they would like to join them and the two lists are compared. *"If your first-choice department wants you, then you go there. If you are lower down* [their lists of preferences] *there is more jockeying between departments."* Initially there were *"a few teething problems for some people,"* but in the main trainees think it is *"a fair system."* It is worth stressing that it would be unwise to assume you can guarantee a position in one of the firm's smaller departments. As one trainee put it: *"Simmons is changing and becoming increasingly orientated towards finance. When I started I definitely thought it would be easier to qualify into a niche department than it is in reality."* This year 30 of the 45 qualifiers stayed on at the firm, the bulk of them going into financial and corporate teams. Naturally disappointed with the result, the firm told us: *"Most practice areas only have a certain number of positions available for trainees to qualify into, and once these positions are filled, we always try to accommodate people by offering them places in other areas with greater demand for newly qualified staff such as our financial markets and corporate practices. A number of trainees were happy to consider alternative practice groups, however a number of the trainees we could not retain were those who only wanted to take a position into a specific department and did not want to consider any other practice area and this has impacted upon our retention rates."*

green party

So what is this firm like as a place to work? *"In the past Simmons has been described as cuddly, and I think that is definitely taking it a bit too far,"* mused one trainee. *"It got that reputation because people said it was a nice place to work, which is true, but I think it is important to stress that it is a nice place to work hard."* The general consensus among our interviewees was that the firm *"could do a bit more for trainees' social lives."* They argued that *"the vast majority of events organised for trainees are during the vac scheme, and it would be nice to feel more valued in our own right for the hard work and hours we put in."* Clearly trainees are quite capable of making their own fun, and a posse of Simmons staff can usually be found in the local Corney & Barrow on a Friday night. As with most firms, the scene is a busy one at the start of the training contract and as the months go on it *"tails off as people go on secondment and get busier with work."* The biggest event is a biennial summer ball for the whole firm, to which staff can bring spouses and partners. More regularly there are league fixtures in hockey, cricket, rugby, football, softball and netball.

Our sources struggled to identify a Simmons type: *"There are a lot of different backgrounds in terms of education, a mix of law and non-law degrees and science and language backgrounds, and people from different cultures."* Having said that, *"the majority of trainees are in their twenties and have come to the firm straight from university and law school rather than having had previous careers."* We noted too that the majority come from top redbrick uni's and Oxbridge. One thing that connects many staff is a desire to help the firm go green. In 2007 Simmons announced its intention to invest £114,000 to become one of the country's first carbon-neutral law firms.

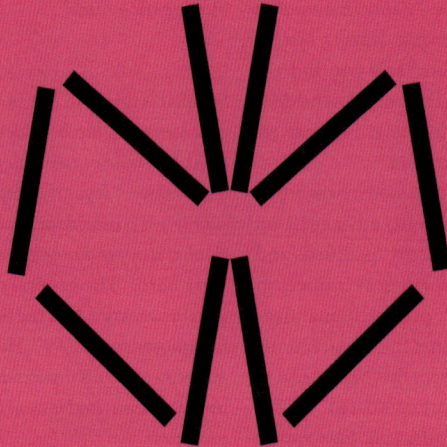

Unconventional

Move only three blocks so that the bat
will fly in a different direction.

Interested in a career in law?
For open days, summer vacation schemes
and training contracts please apply on-line at
www.sjberwin.com/gradrecruit

For enquiries contact:
E graduate.recruitment@sjberwin.com
T Graduate Recruitment Helpdesk 020 7111 2268

www.sjberwin.com

sj**berwin**

Berlin   Brussels   Frankfurt   London   Madrid   Milan   Munich   Paris   Turin

and finally...

Simmons is prospering in the current buoyant market. However, before they sit down to complete the application form, prospective applicants need to think hard about what they are looking for from a training contract and whether Simmons' finance-led future really appeals. Trainees warn that Simmons is *"not a soft option"* simply because it's smaller than the magic circle players.

SJ Berwin LLP

the facts

Location: London
Number of UK partners/solicitors: 108/259
Total number of trainees: 88
Seats: 4x6 months
Alternative seats: Overseas seats, secondments
Extras: Pro bono – Toynbee Hall Law Centre, death row appeals; language training

Just 25 years old, SJ Berwin is a young buck in the City. Its corporate focus, seemingly boundless energy and strong work ethic make it best suited to hungry, ambitious applicants.

berwinism

The firm's founder Stanley Berwin set up two firms in his lifetime. The first, Berwin & Co later became Berwin Leighton Paisner. After Berwin & Co, he worked for a stint in-house at Rothschild, which may be where he picked up his fine-tuned appreciation for clients' needs. After being prevented from once more taking the helm of Berwin & Co, Stanley launched his second new firm, SJ Berwin, based on the principles of giving the client what they need as quickly as they want it. And in doing so he wasn't afraid of putting a few noses out of joint. The firm went from strength to strength: it was a classic eighties boom success story, complete, we can only assume, with

lawyers charging around in Gordon Gekko-style pinstripes and red braces. People who worked with Stanley Berwin still describe him as *"a formidable figure,"* and trainees report that *"his influence pervades throughout the firm."* Said one: *"I doubt there would ever be a speech without Stanley Berwin being mentioned."*

Twenty-five years on, we're in the midst of another boom and SJB is performing better than ever. In 2006/07 revenue rose more than 20% to reach £189m, following two equally fantastic years. There has been a near doubling of turnover in the past three years. Bumper bonuses for all! Another major benefit for staff was a move to an amazing new building overlooking the Thames at Southwark Bridge. The firm spent a reported £28m in fitting-out costs so you can imagine how swish it is. When they moved, we could practically hear the Hurrahs! from our bunker – at last, the SJ Berwinites no longer need to grit their teeth each morning and trudge to work in shabby old buildings in the armpit of King's Cross. Hardly surprising then that our sources believe the firm is *"entering a new era"* and *"feels like a really buzzy place right now."*

into the dragon's den

SJB runs a traditional four-seat training scheme in which its corporate leanings are fully reflected. All recruits spend a year in the corporate department, which in turn is split into four teams, A to D. Team A handles general M&A in both the public and private spheres, including AIM work and IPOs. It is quite popular with trainees who *"take a very hands-on role within a small team"* and busy themselves by *"helping with bits of the prospectus and general deal coordination duties."* In 2007 the team scooped a huge mandate from hotel company Vector Hospitality on its £2.64bn float on the London Stock Exchange.

Teams B to D specialise in private equity and

venture capital, an area in which the firm is entirely established and rather impressive. The private equity practice is not simply a UK leader; SJB has a fine reputation across Europe and thriving practices in Berlin, Frankfurt, Madrid, Milan, Munich, Paris and Turin. The lawyers often work across the offices to pull together deals, among them Star Capital Partners' €330m sale of pan-European recycling business BUS Group. Here, in the beating heart of the firm, trainees are *"thrust in at the deep end"* to shoulder significant levels of responsibility. Said one source: *"I was in charge of a due diligence exercise, liaising with all of the client's offices and the client's lawyers in other countries, ensuring deadlines were met and information flowed from everywhere."* Recent deals have included Dutch investment fund Cyrte Investments' capital injection on the $50m leveraged buy-in of Hammer Film Productions; Lion Capital's £185m sale of shoe company Jimmy Choo and Duke Street Capital's £200m buyout of Burton's Foods (the makers of kiddie faves Jammie Dodgers and Wagon Wheels). It's all classic SJB stuff, so if you feel nervous about being thrust into a world of big and sometimes frantic deals, then don't apply here. With so many large deals being handled by a firm that has no desire to give ground to the others snapping at its heels, partners', associates' and trainees' hours are going to be long. While we cannot say the following experience is standard for all corporate trainees, one interviewee claimed not to have left the office before midnight for four months and found the seat *"really tough."* Remarkably, they then told us: *"I shocked myself in that I really missed the department when I left – I missed the team atmosphere."*

The jewel in SJB's private equity crown has to be Team C, its market-dominant fund formation practice which competes head-to-head with magic circle giant Clifford Chance. With so many valuable clients and so many of the UK's most experienced specialist lawyers to its name, it's lit-tle wonder the firm fell victim to an attack, and in the spring of 2007 three partners in the team were lured away to the ambitious London office of US firm Kirkland & Ellis. The market watches on with interest. Meanwhile, trainees report that life is *"very busy – the hours are consistently long, not like a transactional seat exactly, but you're working until 9pm most nights."*

tired and emotional

A stint in the finance team can count as a compulsory corporate seat, but the pace here is no easier. Our sources deemed their seats to be *"highly stressful"* and *"completely mental."* For one, at the peak of a transaction *"I was working until 10pm or 11pm for two or three weeks;"* another's worst hours were *"1am or 3am during the week plus some of weekend for about a week and a half."* Yet, again, the hard work appears to pay off: *"It really shows you what a team can achieve,"* reported an interviewee. All our sources agreed they had been *"given good responsibility – in fact they will give you as much as you can take."* Among the highlights from the banking team's year is a deal for RBS and various syndicate banks on a £230m debt facility for Care (UK). *"As a trainee, you are predominantly engaged in doing conditions precedent, checking documents, drafting board minutes, negotiating things."*

It doesn't take much research to learn that SJB's transactional arm has not been without its problems lately. Essentially it has found it difficult to recruit and retain enough associates to allow them the kind of balance between their personal and working lives that they crave. Being *"absolutely tired and emotionally drained"* after a deal is not unusual and not everyone wants to live like that long term. We did hear of some trainees being given monetary bonuses and/or time off in lieu of lost nights and weekends, and although *"it's not the firm's policy, it seems to be happening more often."* SJB is not alone in having this problem, but it is taking it very seriously and has started looking further afield to recruit lawyers. One recent campaign targeted lawyers in India.

a need to impress

Meanwhile, the real estate department beavers away in the background. Well, not the background exactly – the department accounts for around a fifth of SJB's revenue and it acts for some mammoth clients. It advised property developer Delancey on its agreement with HM Court Service regarding the UK's new Business Court in London's Fetter Lane; it assisted Hilton Group on the £417m sale and manage back of the London Metropole Hotel and the Birmingham Metropole Hotel (together, with 1,054 rooms, the largest hotel business in the UK); and it has a role in the £600m acquisition of the 13-acre Chelsea Barracks, being bought by a state-owned Qatar company in joint venture with Guernsey-based developer CPC Group. However the deal we most like is the one that has SJB property partners working alongside Berwin Leighton Paisner lawyers on the £650m joint property venture through which Tesco sold and then leased back 21 stores from SJB's client British Land. This is a perfect deal to tell you about because, like many major property deals, it was structured as a corporate deal.

Away from the mainstream corporate department things are quieter, but not that quiet. *"All departments at SJB are manic, so don't think just because you are going to a niche one you will get nine to five – SJB just does not do nine to five."* Niche seats are difficult to get and so *"you have to make it very clear you really want something right at the beginning."* Once in a sought-after seat, people then discover they need to work their behinds off to impress and stand a chance of being taken on after training. One such seat is in the media and communications team, which offers *"a good variety of work from film finance and production, to music, TV and broadcasting and advertising."* A much smaller group, it strikes trainees as *"very supportive with an open environment."* *"There is grunt work,"* but eventually trainees get to the stage where they are *"liaising directly with agents for producers of films."* Other seat options include commerce and technology; commercial litigation; construction; employment; EU and competition; financial services; intellectual property; planning and environment; reconstruction and insolvency and tax. Tax and financial services once came under the corporate umbrella, and the fact that this is no longer the case is indicative of a further push by the firm to get trainees into the mainstream transactional departments. Unsurprisingly, there are some trainees who don't want to do a contentious seat – or don't manage to get into one – so for them there is a short litigation course at the College of Law, supplemented with involvement in the firm's pro bono programme.

It is possible to take time away from London by getting yourself seconded to one of the European offices and anyone interested in politics (especially the Tory sort) may be interested in a placement in Westminster with corporate partner and Conservative MP Jonathan Djanogly. Client secondments are available to the likes of De Beers.

no spinning

At the last Christmas party, held at Billingsgate Fish Market, London staff were joined by their colleagues from the mainland Europe offices. The night began with a formal dinner and speeches celebrating the firm's 25th anniversary and later on things became more *"drunken."* The highlight was a fine performance by the Queen Street Players, an SJB band. Trainees have an annual budget of their own for two events. In summer 2007 half the money went on drinks in the office, followed by dinner at the Menier Chocolate Factory in Southwark. On a Friday night, lawyers can be found in nearby bar The Banker, and there is a monthly drinks event in Stanley's, the staff restaurant. Naming the works canteen after the founder is entirely appropriate – Stanley Berwin decreed that everyone should eat lunch together whenever possible. Even now, the firm offers staff a free meal every day. In the summer, lunch can be eaten on the vast roof terrace overlooking the river. Just inside, a table tennis game has been set up and there are fussball games in the banking and real estate departments. This may make SJB sound like a youth club, but trainees assure us this couldn't be further from the truth.

In 2007 SJB retained 29 of its 37 qualifying trainees. It is certainly worth mentioning that these individuals were given the option to take up to eight weeks off at any time in first six months after qualification, and they were also offered the chance to take one month's salary in advance.

and finally...

For the right type of person SJ Berwin is a great choice. If you think you have the *"entrepreneurial"* attitude and can hack the pace at this *"dynamic"* City upstart, then what are you waiting for?

Skadden, Arps, Slate, Meagher & Flom (UK) LLP

the facts

Location: London
Number of UK partners/solicitors: 23/120
Total number of trainees: 7
Seats: 4x6 months
Alternative seats: Overseas seats, secondments

New York giant Skadden, Arps, Slate, Meagher & Flom has almost as many names as it has worldwide offices, but when you're as successful as this international behemoth, you can call yourself anything you like.

google yankee doodler doing dandy

Apparently, legendary Joe Flom, the last surviving name partner at what for brevity's sake we'll call Skadden, doodles densely intricate designs of his own devising in the margins of his note books. At least, so sayeth the legal tome *Skadden: Power, Money, and the Rise of a Legal Empire*, which plots the firm's rise and rise on the back of groundbreaking M&A expertise as an object lesson in the corporatisation and evolution of post-war US law firms. Then there's the biography *The Law According to Joseph Flom*. If you're interested in the firm, perhaps you should read them. Obviously we haven't – after all, the whole point of the Internet is to offer a quick route to knowledge – but they do sound like page turners. If you're short of time, we'll save you even the hassle of a few web searches by telling you that in his many decades of practice the still-going-strong Mr Flom has been around to witness the rise of Skadden from small beginnings in 1940s New York to its current status as a global legal monster with over 2,000 lawyers ensconced in 22 worldwide offices.

Mr F is widely credited with instilling a hardnosed attitude that has taken the firm to the most rarefied heights of US and international practice. Competing equally with other American big-hitters, Skadden this year took a lead role for aluminium giant Alcoa on a $33bn bid for rival Alcan, and on News Corporation's $5bn unsolicited bid for Dow Jones. Over in the London branch, which opened as long ago as 1988, a flourishing corporate practice at the heart of a well-developed European network makes Skadden one of the most successful US firms in the UK. Up with the best of the magic circle on matters transactional, be these private equity, venture capital, M&A or capital markets, the London office is often to be found near the top of deal charts. This year it defended Arcelor from Mittal's £21.5bn takeover bid and assisted the private equity buyers in the £1.5bn sale of telecoms giant Cauldwell Group. The office's expansive outlook means *"little or no work is purely UK-based"* and close co-operation with non-UK colleagues is the norm. The London lawyers this year worked closely with their New York colleagues on Nasdaq's £4.2bn bid for the London Stock Exchange and took advantage of strong relations with Ford in the USA to advise the carmaker for the first time in Europe on the sale of Aston Martin to a UK-led consortium. Trainees say Skadden has *"a pretty seamless"* approach to such deals, and they should know – they are on the front line of this multi-jurisdictional, cross-office work. *"You're always on the phone to New York,"* said one. *"I also worked a lot with Moscow and Hong Kong; there's a real continuity across the network."*

class act

Skadden UK apparently shares the wider *"ambition and enthusiasm"* of the motherland, but assessing where the balance of power lies led our sources to pause for thought. *"I think we've now got more UK lawyers than US lawyers here in London; it feels like we're going that way,"* reflected one. Another told us: *"From my vantage point it's an office where people immediately look to the London management to set standards. To what extent they see their work and loyalty as being to the New York office is hard to say."* Whatever the exact position, the fact is Skadden is doing very well in London and trainees were proud to be part of a firm that isn't just *"always winning awards,"* but more importantly *"stays ahead of the game."* *"The office has been here for 20 years and yet it has continually adapted, looked at different opportunities and never stood still."* Proving their point, one result of a recent *"big report"* on the London operation has seen a class action litigation team established in light of an anticipated boom in such actions following Office of Fair Trading and EU rulings.

In fact trainees themselves are evidence of the firm's adaptability. Since the training scheme was first conceived in 2005, numbers of recruits have increased from just two to around four per year, with plans to take on seven new trainees in 2008 and ten in 2009. *"It sold itself as offering a very personal form of training, a bit more individual and focused,"* said one interviewee whose *"impression that I would have the opportunity to direct the training contract"* had proved accurate. The seats on offer include corporate, capital markets, private equity, energy, litigation, tax, banking, project finance and even the option to spend time in Skadden's Hong Kong office. *"Of course, your choices are subject to the firm's needs, but if you petitioned hard enough you could probably get a repeat corporate seat or maybe even another overseas option,"* thought one source. As 2006/07 was only the second year of Skadden's training contract, future joiners may find a more settled formula has been established and seat choice is less flexible. For now, the trainees feel rather like the pioneers of the scheme and also say they are *"consistently doing the level of work that our contemporaries on the other side of deals are not doing – associate's work."*

bob-a-job

Recent growth in the London office can *"almost entirely be accounted for by the hire of junior level associates, so it feels like a dynamic, energetic place, a place in which it's hard to sustain a culture of formality."* This verve – if we can call it that – together with the compact, collegial feel of the office led trainees to suggest *"you might not fit in here if you don't enjoy heavy responsibility and standing apart from the crowd in a way you wouldn't at a larger firm."* If there's pleasure taken in *"everyone knowing who you are,"* *"definitely getting autonomy and having work go out with your name on,"* remember the flip side is *"feeling exposed at times."* What it boils down to is that to flourish here you'll need to be *"a pretty determined, enthusiastic high-flier"* who is able *"to get on with your own work but wants something more and is willing to put in the extra effort to get a result."* The trainees we interviewed were *"pretty personable"* with *"oomph and ambition."* They reckon the perfect test for a wannabe Skaddenite is this: *"You look at a person and think, 'Can I work with them at 3am, still enjoy my job and pull together?'"*

And so we must deal with the subject of hours. Back in the 1960s, Skadden associates in the USA apparently awarded a monthly 'Beast of Burden' (BOB) award (supposedly named after a partner who had worked himself to an early death) to the lawyer who had suffered most punishment. While we're not suggesting anything like this goes on in London, a *"very hard-working culture"* is certainly prevalent. In part this reflects the requirements of heavy cross-office, cross-time-zone deals. *"Often you'll be in at 9am, do a heavy day's work, then mid-afternoon the States come online and you'll basically be expected to work to New York hours because most deals have a US component and New York people will want a conference call or work done during their working day."* Litigation *"is usually quieter in terms of hours,"* but when working on anything transactional, particularly in corporate seats, *"leaving at 9 or 10pm is fairly normal, and later is not unusual."* One source remembered *"working up to ten weekends in my corporate seat,"* with the consolation that *"only four were proper, solid, didn't-see-my-flat affairs, the rest were just a couple of hours or half a day."*

Given that it is early days for the Skadden training scheme, the firm is responsive to trainees' suggestions on how to improve it. Thus far the practice has been to place trainees with a mentor who provides work in the first month before they have the confidence to occupy their own offices and seek out matters for themselves. As a result of feedback, the firm has introduced the idea of trainees sitting with *"a mid-level asso-ciate supervisor."* Those of our sources who had experienced working in their own room and with a mid-level colleague told us: *"It's easier to learn by osmosis sitting with someone, and you do get extra feedback."* In terms of formal training sessions, the PSC is delivered externally and trainees are also welcome at junior and senior-level know-how sessions. They will also *"see the training partner every six weeks or so,"* so he can *"keep a bit of an eye on how you're doing."* Final appraisals (*"this is how you've done, do you have any problems?"*) are a good wrap up to each seat, and should there be any problems, be they with a supervisor or otherwise, the mentor is always there for guidance.

tell-tale crumbs

Here at the *Student Guide* we eschew gutter press kiss-and-tells for higher standards of journalism in the best traditions of George Orwell. However, we ain't afraid to break the lid off a good story when we get one, so hold on to your hats. Skadden's Canary Wharf premises are *"lovely – the best I've seen"* with – wait for it – *"a good support network, great secretaries and solid weekend resources."* What's more, trainees go wild for *"great biscuits in the conference rooms."* *"The white chocolate ones always seem to go first,"* said a source close to the firm. Thankfully, business casual Monday to Thursday and dress-down Fridays help keep dry cleaning bills to a minimum: getting white choc chips out of a Saville Row suit can be a nightmare.

The consequence of *"working long hours together means we tend to socialise together too."* Drinks on a Thursday or Friday at one of the Wharf's many watering holes are common, and people aren't averse to *"celebrating all the right occasions."* The most common reason for winding down is the completion of a deal, when *"meals, Champagne and generally being shown a welcome degree of appreciation"* are the order of the day.

From the sound of it, anyone who takes a seat in the Hong Kong office will have a blast socially, and as for letting your hair down elsewhere in the Skadden empire, just ask new trainees about their visit to New York for the annual new associates' retreat.

and finally...
In September 2007 Skadden's first ever trainees qualified and both accepted positions with the firm, having happily acted as guinea pigs. Remember, this firm doesn't offer a cast of thousands or a path to qualification carved on stone tablets. What you'll get is a flexible training on the front line of excellent transactional work and a sensational salary. The two years will be demanding in terms of hours and the spotlight will always shine on you, so make sure that's what you want.

Slaughter and May

the facts
Location: London
Number of UK partners/solicitors: 120/373
Total number of trainees: 168
Seats: 4x6 months
Alternative seats: Overseas seats
Extras: Pro bono – RCJ CAB, FRU, Islington and Battersea Law Centres, LawWorks; language training

Never one to follow the crowd, magic circle firm Slaughter and May does things its own way.

different thinking
Superficially, Slaughters has much in common with the other members of London's magic circle. Put simply: it's big and works on the largest corporate deals in the market. European steel giant Corus recently turned to the firm for advice on its £6.7bn sale to India's Tata; and lawyers advised the Department of Trade and Industry on the £2.34bn sale of its interest in British Energy Group and Thomson on the $8.8bn purchase of Reuters. Meanwhile, in the red-hot private equity sphere, the firm advised Alliance Boots on its $11.1bn management buyout backed by KKR. So, the firm is justifiably lauded for its spectacular M&A work, but other areas of practice are equally praiseworthy. BUPA, for example, brought in Slaughters' property experts for a £1.4bn sale of a portfolio of hospitals to Cinven; the tax department scored a notable victory in a long-running dispute over interest on rebates of wrongly paid corporate tax, and the competition team advised BA on a recent price-fixing investigation by the Office of Fair Trading. Across the board Slaughters excels – according to our parent publication *Chambers UK*, no firm works for more companies on the FTSE 100 list.

And yet there is much that differentiates Slaughters from its peers: while other firms divide departments into ever more specialised groupings, Slaughters flies the flag for the generalist. Unlike its magic circle rivals, Slaughters hasn't pursued a strategy of global expansion. Beyond small offices in Paris, Hong Kong and Brussels, its international strategy depends on a network of 'best friend' relationships with similarly elite firms across Europe and beyond. This distinctive strategy looks to have paid off – it's not always easy making an overseas network profitable and without one the firm has been able to keep its profits very high. Trainees don't seem concerned about the lack of an overseas network: *"Slaughters is an institution,"* they explained, *"because the corporate work is so exciting it will always attract a certain kind of person, and because it lives the philosophy of client service, it will always be busy."*

Corporate is Slaughters' core and all trainees will spend at least one six-month seat here, some as many as three. The firm's generalist approach means groups are based around senior partners

rather than particular types of work: thus, common trainee destinations include "NPB" – named after Nigel Boardman, the firm's biggest corporate superstar – or "GWJ" – led by corporate insurance guru Glen James. The epic size of the deals means trainees can't always plug straight into the nitty-gritty. "*In my first seat it was all process – setting up online data rooms, reviewing contracts, the inevitable bibling.*" A second stint in the department can bring improved responsibility though: "*I felt much more a part of the team,*" one second-year confirmed. "*I was put in charge of reviewing documents and went along to some negotiations. I wasn't any use, but my supervisor wanted me to see them.*" Trainees are encouraged to try smaller tasks and then build on them. The chance to work on some high-level sports transactions is another attraction, with the firm bridging an historic rivalry in representing both Tottenham Hotspur and Arsenal. "*I did transfer agreements for some well-known players,*" enthused one lucky so-and-so.

bestatheresta

Other seats include finance, financial regulation, environment, IP, TMT, competition, tax, real estate, pensions and employment, and dispute resolution. The first six of these are six-month seats, while tax lasts just three months and the others can be either three or six months long. Finance offers a steep learning curve: "*My supervisor was a partner specialising in derivatives, which for a second-seat trainee basically means confusion,*" admitted one source. Once up to speed though "*there's a lot of drafting work to be done in the lower levels of a deal, and quite a bit of in-depth research.*" For the academically minded seats such as tax and financial regulation are a great way of working with "*the brightest people in the firm*" in a "*rather library-like*" atmosphere. It may sound like the pressure's on, but actually "*it's really relaxed and pleasant because the deadlines*

don't come as thick and fast." Serious brainwork is required though: "*In a transactional department you'd have a day to research something, here you'll have a week, but because tax research is so notoriously difficult, you still might not find anything.*"

Slaughters isn't an automatic destination of choice for would-be property lawyers, but a real estate seat option is available and offers a decent level of work from day one. "*I was given more responsibility than I was expecting,*" said one veteran; "*there was corporate support work, but I also had small discrete projects to manage, from negotiating leases through to drafting and meeting with my own clients.*" Plus, "*you can often leave at 5.30pm.*"

And what about those of a litigious bent? Opportunities exist in the commercial dispute resolution department, as well as in the employment and pensions team. But beware – "*Employment and pensions was my contentious seat, officially,*" explained a source, "*but it was mostly corporate support – drafting compromise agreements, speaking to clients all the time. It was great responsibility, it just wasn't contentious.*" Those really focused on litigation need to push hard for a seat in the main dispute resolution department. The group is particularly adept at regulatory work, for example, advising life insurer Resolution on securing court approval for a major reorganisation and Bank of Ireland on a tax dispute. Here, too, trainee responsibility varies enormously, with the need for bundles meaning "*you can get very mundane work,*" but by contrast "*you'll also stand a good chance of taking witness statements, going to court or attending meetings.*"

such a thing as a free dinner

All the trainees we interviewed had enjoyed a healthy mix of lower-level and more challenging work, not least because of their willingness to push for things that stretched them. Allowing for the ebb and flow of the transactional world, hours generally take care of themselves too. *"It's certainly been up and down,"* one trainee recalled; *"in corporate I had a few 4am finishes,"* but *"they promised that there would be quiet times and there have been."* In finance seats, for example, an 8.30pm finish is common and *"there's definitely no face-time culture – if you've got plenty on, you stay till it's done. But if not, go home."* As an additional compensation *"the dinner in the canteen becomes free at 7pm."* We did hear of a couple of cases of trainees working rather torturous hours: *"I had one supervisor who was an absolute workaholic and expected me to be the same,"* confided one source.

Slaughters' svelte overseas office network doesn't preclude international secondments for trainees. There is a finance-focused seat in the Paris office (*"so small you can hear when the doorbell rings"*), EU/competition work in Brussels, a seat in Hong Kong and a string of overseas postings to best-friend firms in places such as Spain, New Zealand and New York. Most find *"it's no weirder to switch firms than switching offices... it's a new set of people, but they have close links to Slaughters and know the partners well."* Experiences obviously differ according to the firm in question, but all secondees we interviewed spoke glowingly of their experiences. Such seats offer the chance for a more intimate working environment, but also exposure to distinctive local working patterns. In France, *"the start of the week is quiet, but on a Friday afternoon clients suddenly send over lots of work to be done by Monday."* There is no guarantee of getting a seat abroad. The firm estimates that around 60% of those who would like to go are able to do so.

private on parade

To many, Slaughter's minimalist Bunhill Row headquarters sum up the firm's cold reputation, but trainees were bullish in rebutting such ideas. *"They are conservative and grey, but that just means there's no affectation,"* noted one. Another wondered: *"Where does the stern reputation comes from?"* *"It's not foreboding, it's just not all fluffy,"* we heard from people who relished the no-nonsense *"just get on with it"* approach to working life. *"It's certainly serious, but it should be, shouldn't it?"*

Consequently *"there is some truth to the reputation of partners not communicating with lesser mortals."* One perceptive source explained the balance as *"hierarchical in the way that the army is. You do know your place, and there is a distance between you and the partners. But I don't see anything wrong with that."* Amusingly, *"in a few cases intelligence has pushed out social ability – but that's a minority."* All this said, the atmosphere can be *"incredibly cordial,"* with transactional departments in particular featuring *"plenty of popping into each others' offices for coffee and a chat."* The TV screens in the canteen *"show football as well as Sky News,"* and there's even a jukebox, although opinion differs as to whether or not it has ever been played. *"Maybe someone got pissed and put a coin in once,"* a trainee hazarded. Overall, it is common purpose that bonds together a firm where genuine *"collegiality isn't necessarily equivalent to friendliness."* As an aside, despite a relatively high male-female ratio at the senior end, trainees of both genders agreed that the atmosphere feels *"the opposite of macho."*

How wonderful that *"you see some potential eccentrics among trainees."* Such ideas are amusing, of course, but it is the distinctive and often independent characters among of the firm's partners that make a difference to how the job feels day by day. One source wondered if a supervisor *"was crazy, she gave me so much responsibility,"* though relished the *"self-confidence"* such trust created. Another remembered that *"my corporate supervisor was a bit of a dragon: a combination of the shouter and the arch-critic. They'd tell me I didn't need to do something, then shout at me for not doing it. When I stood up for myself, they said in my* appraisal I couldn't take criticism." Others found it hard to build a rapport with some supervisors. These were the minority. With the majority, "if you've got a question and you've thought about it properly, they are happy to take the time to answer." And as at every firm, there's also the kind of partner who'll "bring you a cake back from their holidays."

rigged for silent running

As you might expect, Slaughters' trainees are mostly the type to grit their teeth and get on with it rather than agonising about their lot. Nonetheless, HR are generally considered "good listeners, very helpful" and "working well because you don't really notice them." Seat allocation brings the team to the fore and trainees seemed mostly happy with their efforts. Two visits to corporate is the only requirement, and even in this respect there seems to be some flexibility. With so many trainees to place, there will always be those left feeling unfulfilled. "I got one out of the three seats I asked for," recalled one trainee; "if you want to request changes they'll do what they can, but it's not always possible."

It is in the handling of overseas secondments and qualification job offers that trainees feel the firm should up its game. "They don't announce who's got what, so if you've missed out on a secondment, for example, you just hear on the grapevine that someone else has got it." Similarly, "there is no announcement about what jobs are available where," leaving trainees attempting to sound out their chosen departments to ensure there's a space. "It's definitely best to show your face so you're more than just a name on a piece of paper," one explained.

the same but different

"A wide practice, a high profile and prestige on your CV" aren't attributes unique to a Slaughters' training, but the trainees we spoke to had been most attracted by what is unusual about the firm's modus operandi. "I like their conservative approach," one admitted; "they don't patronise you." The "entirely-free-of-crap" training contract interview confirms this view. "There was no 'What animal would you most like to be' and no technical stuff. They were just interested in getting to know me." For others, the firm's work ethos is spot on: "I like their obsession with detail," a source confessed; "they'll process a document 30-40 times until it's right. I'm like that too." What's more, the firm's generalist approach means trainees "don't have to worry about being railroaded into a niche." So distinctively potent are these combined attributes that several of our interviewees had applied only to Slaughters among the magic circle: "I didn't like the way [other big firms] put themselves out, didn't appreciate slushy balls and free pens. It didn't seem like they were giving honest answers to questions, but Slaughters talked to me like an adult."

What does this specific ethos mean for recruitment? Well, the firm does have a reputation for being white, male and Oxbridge-heavy. On the first two points, the stats on the firm's own website beg to differ: As at May 2007, the trainee population was 47% female and 16% non-white. As for the Oxbridge domination, trainees freely acknowledged this idea has legs. Said one: "It's a bit ridiculous – in my intake of about 35 it was really Oxbridge heavy." Keen to dispel the idea that it's a closed shop, the firm advises us that it employs graduates of around 60 universities. As to whether there is a Slaughters' type, "you do get characters you wouldn't get elsewhere," a source observed; "lots of people have done something else before the law or have some bizarre hobby."

Traditionally Slaughters has excellent retention figures and, in 2007, 80 of the 87 qualifiers took up permanent positions with the firm. In some cases the appeal of the firm overrides problems getting the right department. Some 53

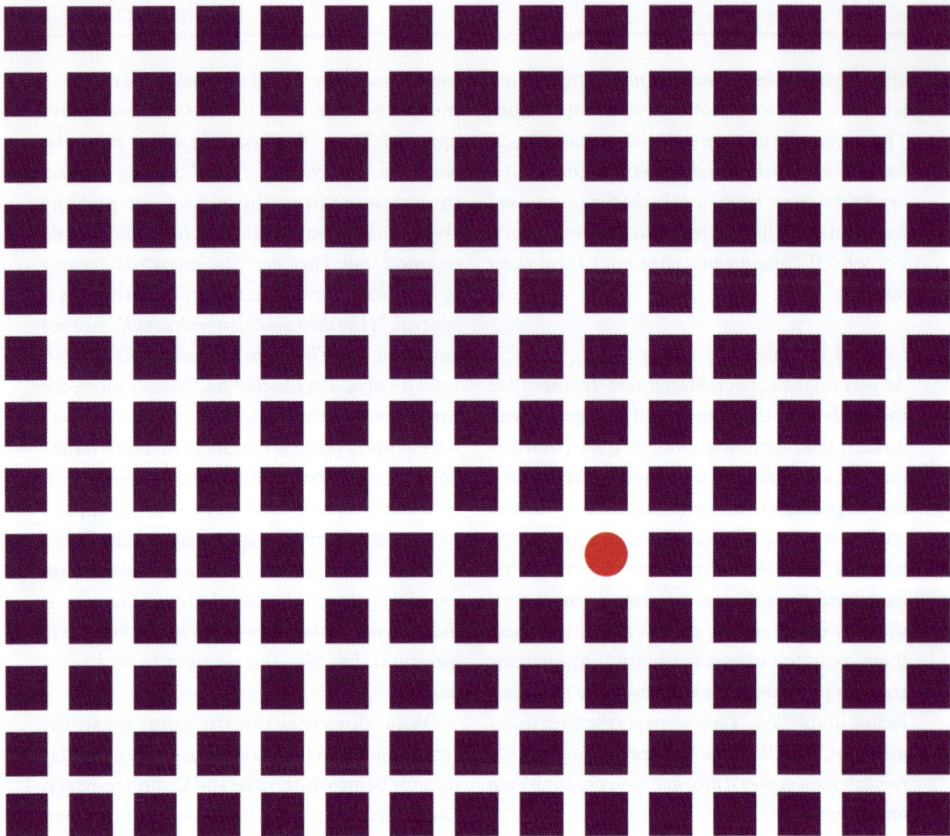

Got that Speechlys something?

Here at Speechly Bircham, we're as interested in your personal qualities as we are in your qualifications. We're looking for graduates who share our passion for the law and who relish the idea of building relationships with colleagues and clients alike. In return we're offering an environment where you'll be encouraged to make your own mark and you'll be rewarded for the difference you make.

**Think you've got that Speechlys something?
Find out more at speechlys.com/trainingcontracts**

Speechly Bircham

WINNER
AWARDS
2007
BEST TRAINER
MEDIUM CITY FIRM

Winner
'Best Trainer
Medium City
Firm' Award

qualifiers went into jobs in corporate/commercial and finance; another 26 distributed themselves around the other departments; one went to Hong Kong. More broadly, the generalist approach makes the department selection less complicated than in some other firms. *"It didn't feel like the biggest decision I'd ever make,"* explained one interviewee.

personal spacey

You should have gathered that Slaughter and May is not the kind of firm you join for endless parties; nonetheless, a trainee committee arranges events such as bowling, quizzes and a Christmas jolly. In addition, the whole firm manages to squeeze into the Grosvenor House Hotel for a black-tie ball every November, with hierarchy turned upside down as partners, assistants, trainees and secretaries mix together, even if *"the partners make polite conversation and then leave early."* Complete with *"crowd-pleasing indie-pop covers band,"* the ball seems like a genuine highlight.

It is hobbies rather than revelry that define Slaughters' social scene. The usual array of sports teams are represented and more cultured minds are served by a programme of talks ranging from *"those two young guys who climbed Everest, who showed us their feet"* to a history of Christianity in the British Isles. *"Normally they're not wildly oversubscribed,"* one trainee deadpanned, although Kevin Spacey's talk on running the Old Vic was an exception. One trainee reckoned you could *"live your entire life through the firm if you wanted to,"* but what is notably absent is *"a sense of enforced fun – I remember on my vac scheme at another firm I was asked why I didn't come to the softball. Here it's all on offer, but it's not noticed or judged if you're not interested."* What's more, unlike other big firms, Slaughters has no on-site gym, hairdresser, gift shop, swimming pool etc, so staff do have to venture into the outside world.

and finally...

In common with trainees at all the big firms, most Slaughters trainees don't see themselves as future partners, instead planning to stay for a few years before moving to a smaller firm or out of the law. You shouldn't mistake this for lack of respect, or even affection, for this deliberately different, sometimes prickly firm. *"For all its drawbacks, it's somewhere I will be very sad to leave. It's not just another faceless company... You find yourself developing a certain kind of loyalty, almost in spite of yourself."*

Speechly Bircham LLP

the facts

Location: London
Number of UK partners/solicitors: 61/101
Total number of trainees: 14
Seats: 4x6 months
Alternative seats: Secondments

A mid-sized commercial firm with a distinguished private client practice, Speechly Bircham has shown steady growth in the past few years. Trainees feel confident about the future and tell us the general credo that *"you get out what you put in"* rings particularly true. If you're looking for a no-nonsense training contract in a well-respected City firm, this might just be the place.

maintaining the status quo

Speechly has had a booming few years since setting itself a three-year target in 2004. In May 2007 it announced it had achieved its desired 50% increase in turnover and billed £40m in the 2006/07 financial year, when profits increased by a whopping 27%. The number of trainees recruited reflects this growth: five per year back in 2005, an expected ten for 2009. New partners have been gained across a range of practices, including three recent acquisitions into financial services and banking teams. Trainees commented on the *"huge growth"* within the firm, telling us it is *"actively looking for new premises."* It all makes Speechly *"an exciting place to be a trainee"* right now, yet our sources also commented on the firm's adherence to the traditional values of client satisfaction and professionalism. *"There's no mad rush to depart from what the firm has been successful at; it is very much keeping on in the same vein, just doing it on a larger scale."* So if *"the growth has definitely been visible but there's no question of the firm changing its ethos,"* what exactly is that ethos? *"Traditional but not stuffy,"* thought one source; from another: *"It's not a smoky atmosphere with wood panelled walls... but a client can ring up and expect to speak to a partner."*

where there's a will

In a straightforward four by six-month system, seat allocation was a bit of a hot topic for some of the trainees we interviewed. Nothing is compulsory, and there are a decent range of choices, but one or two people we spoke to had clearly *"given up"* on particular goals. The firm tries to give all trainees their first-choice seat and when this causes a problem asks them to sort it out among themselves. Although this has worked out satisfactorily in the past, we couldn't help wondering if it plays into the hands of the stronger characters in the group. In terms of demand, two of the most popular seats are private client and employment. The first, being in the firm's *"flagship department,"* attracts trainees for obvious reasons. The second is popular in almost every firm in the country. If you are dead-set on employment, be aware that Speechly only offers one seat per rotation. Private client, corporate, construction, property litigation, commerical dispute resolution and property offer slightly better odds with three places each.

In the past year there have been comings and goings in the corporate department, resulting in a net increase to 18 partners and the department now contributes approximately 30% of the firm's annual turnover. Concentrating on mid-market deals, Speechly represents a few companies you might be familiar with (Cable & Wireless, Ecclesiastical Insurance) and quite a few you won't. Trainees say there is a good balance of *"private and public company work"* and that transactions range from *"AIM deals that last three months"* to *"private equity funding that's over in ten days."* Corporate offers a combination of seats in financial services, corporate tax, pensions and banking and finance or public companies, private companies and IP. The longest hours are to be found in corporate. *"I had to do a couple of weekends but I didn't mind. I like the fact that you're part of a smaller team so there's more opportunity to contribute,"* said one source. Otherwise, the hours at Speechly are pretty good by City standards, with most trainees usually leaving between 6.30pm and 7pm. Another area where there have been notable hires at partner level is IP. Having taken the head of US law firm Faegre & Benson's London IP team in 2006, two other heads of IP came on board in early summer 2007. Those left smarting were London and Oxford firm Manches and the London office of national firm Hammonds.

In a private client seat trainees are quite often *"sent to see elderly people who can't make the trip into London."* Other tasks might include *"drawing out a family tree stretching back into the seventeenth century"* and managing as many as 20 small files. The department's clientele comprises *"high net worth individuals"* and *"not so wealthy but comfortably off people,"* with most of the work covering *"a mixture of tax issues and death."* Those looking for cases with an international angle will do well to pick this department. It has responded to the increasing internationalisation of the practice area by creating regional focus groups such as a recently launched Indian practice group. Other groups are targeted at business from the USA, France, Italy, Scandinavia and Latin America. So important is the firm's private client practice that it pursued a test case in the High Court concerning problems for the partners of limited liability partnership law firms when acting as executors of wills. Until the test case was decided, firms with private client practices were prevented from becoming LLPs unless they contacted thousands of clients offering to amend their wills for free. A successful outcome to the case in November 2006 not only earned Speechly the gratitude of the legal profession, but it also gave them a good excuse to rebrand the firm when it became an LLP. We'd say it was typical of Speechly that changes made to the website and letterhead were not especially dramatic. *"It just means the image the firm is projecting looks more contemporary,"* explained a trainee.

ahead of the game

In employment there is a certain amount of grunt work when trainees take charge of rooms full of documentation in preparation for trial. *"Those jobs can sound very dull and dreary, but it's actually a lot of responsibility. It's quite daunting having to phone up a QC and say your skeleton argument is wrong here, you've referred to the wrong document."* The department's employer clientele includes companies from the world of finance (Baring Asset Management, State Bank of India), recruitment and outsourcing (Drake International) and travel and leisure (Thomas Cook, Thai Airways and Trevor Sorbie International). It also acts for senior executives on contract negotiations, bonus payments and other incentive schemes, occupational stress, whistleblowing, unlawful discrimination and severance arrangements. Don't assume that you'll be skipping away carefree to the next seat – *"leaving those rooms full of documents is like leaving a child."* The workload

is brightened by regular attendance at court hearings and tribunals, and the same is true in commercial dispute resolution, which netted one lucky trainee a visit to Vienna to prepare a witness for providing testimony by video-link.

Trainees were very excited about Speechly's growing interest in sport and its *"integrated offering to the sports sector."* The head of the family team has acted for a number of high-profile clients over the years, including household names in media and sport. The 12-strong employment team also acts for a number of individuals within the sports sector and in the commercial dispute resolution team there's a partner who represents Formula One racing drivers. Another department worth mentioning is construction, which covers both contentious and non-contentious matters. The small, hardworking team acts for several large clients including Royal Bank of Scotland, P&O Estates, Greater London Authority and Visa. Enthusiasts stress that *"it's not about being interested in scaffolding and hard hats; it's more about seeing developments go up and taking notice of what's happening around you."* Other seat options include real estate and property litigation.

keep the faith

Regarding appraisals, we heard that *"the midseat reviews were scrapped this year...which wasn't very helpful as they provide feedback on things you can work on over the next three months."* The powers-that-be assured us that this was a one-off event owing to *"resource allocation issues."* Trainees were at least positive about supervisors' willingness to consult the whole department so *"you get feedback from all corners of the firm... you don't spend six months working for just one or two people."* Trainees were also happy with the individual guidance they received from supervisors, and although they admitted that trainee-specific know-how sessions were *"a little*

Look no further...

At Stephenson Harwood, we can offer you the chance to build a significant future in a rapidly developing, highly energetic and very friendly international commercial law firm.

We are a medium-sized firm with a distinguished reputation for quality, personalised training and award-winning work for top clients (Dispute Resolution Team of the Year). We currently have offices in five countries across Europe and Asia, including our principal office located just opposite St Paul's Cathedral.

Early responsibility means you'll see rapid personal development. We have 12 training contract vacancies for 2009.

www.shlegal.com

agr
The collective voice of graduate recruiters

**Voted 2006
'Best of the Best'
for graduate
recruitment practice**

At the Association of
Graduate Recruiter Awards

London - Guangzhou - Hong Kong - Paris - Piraeus - Shanghai - Singapore haphazard," the training delivered to the entire firm, or departments, was *"much better."* The breakfast time know-how sessions organised in private client certainly sort out the early risers from the sleepyheads.

Situated close to Chancery Lane and the Royal Courts of Justice, Speechly's office is well placed and the lack of an on-site canteen is compensated for by the proliferation of sandwich bars within easy reach. Trainees told us they were *"a really close-knit group"* and that they *"have lunch together about once a fortnight"* in Pizza Express or nearby Lincoln's Inn Fields. They also attend the monthly fee-earners' lunch at which the *"no-partners"* policy allows everyone to kick back and relax. Their favoured local pub is The Last in Shoe Lane. *"Anyone who fancies a beer knows there are likely to be people there on a Friday night."* Although the firm is moving to New Street Square in summer 2008, the new premises are only a few streets away, so The Last shouldn't lose its Speechly's clientele. Other calendar entries include quiz nights, barbecues, trips to the theatre, an annual trip to Ascot and the Christmas and summer parties. At these *"fairly formal"* events *"everyone makes a big effort and gets dressed up"* and *"you're invited to both of those from the time you're offered a training contract."* Regular football, netball and hockey matches provide an excellent opportunity to *"get to know people in other departments."*

As one trainee explained when we asked why they chose Speechly: *"I wasn't scared of working long hours...but I didn't want to be a small fish in a big pond, I wanted to be noticed for my contributions."* Several sources commented on the *"maturity"* of recruits, telling us: *"There's only one person who's come straight through from uni."* They say the ideal candidate is keen to take on new responsibilities and that *"trainees here need to have faith in their own ability."* We'd add that they generally come across as pragmatic, straight-

forward, sensible and intelligent. Not a bad combination from a client's perspective...

and finally...

Although Speechly Bircham accepts applications from students who have not taken part in its three-week summer vacation scheme, they form a significant part of the recruitment process and over half of the current trainees attended one. Previous participants describe the scheme as *"a very fair representation of life as a trainee."* Hardly surprising for a firm that does exactly what it says on the tin. In 2007, four out of five qualifiers accepted jobs.

Stephenson Harwood

the facts

Location: London
Number of UK partners/solicitors: 69/111
Total number of trainees: 34
Seats: 4x6 months
Alternative seats: Overseas seats
Extras: Pro bono – Hoxton and Camden law centres, language training

Established in 1875, Stephenson Harwood has grown to 83 partners and 219 associates in offices stretching from Europe to Asia. Truly global in outlook, a base in Guangzhou means the firm is one of only a handful of international outfits to claim a foothold in southern China. The hub, however, is London, accounting for 80% of revenue, 40% of which comes from those overseas clients.

AIMing for the top

Rewind just a few years and Stephenson Harwood was bobbing about in choppy waters, following its merger with shipping specialist Sinclair Roche & Temperley. A number of partners left (some voluntarily and some not so) and quite a few of the solicitors managed to find the exit too. Down in the lower ranks, NQ retention rates weren't much to write home about. Enter, stage left, Sunil Gadhia, the firm's new executive officer and all-round hero. Over the past three years he has steered the practice to greater success and introduced a *"new energy"* to the workplace. This recovery was accelerated by a raft of great lateral hires, each of whom brought some dishy clients to the party. Mary Bonar's appointment added the Go-Ahead Group, Transport for London and Siemens to the transport division's portfolio of big-name clients. Meanwhile, the Eastern markets practice in London was pepped up by the arrival of private equity specialist Vinay Ganga, who acts as counsel to investment consortium Origo Sino-India. Elsewhere, Stephenson Harwood continues to reap the rewards of its investment in Asia, witnessing a 14% rise in revenue from the region during 2006.

Although Stephenson Harwood is still a star performer in the shipping sector, it is no longer true to say that the whiff of sea air pervades every inch of the firm. Transportation (encompassing shipping and a strengthened aviation practice) is just one of three core client sectors – the others being financial services and real estate – and it has, for instance, emerged as a top specialist for AIM listings. The reality that *"there's a heck of a lot more going on here"* than just messing around with boats is reflected in the training contract, the only obligatory aspect of which is a single seat in either banking and asset finance (BAF) or shipping litigation. Trainees tell us no department *"lords it over another."*

firing on all cylinders

The real estate practice provides trainees with the most responsibility and is viewed as *"a nice group of people who do varied, interesting work."*

Choosing this seat will expose you to large property finance transactions and, under the tutelage of planning guru Michael Woods, might even enable you to expand your knowledge of environmental planning issues. The team's busy caseload has recently included advising on the sale of two dozen Macdonald Hotels to Moorfield Real Estate for the princely sum of £400m. It has also found time to add ABN AMRO and Deutsche Bank to its ever-growing client roster.

Commercial litigation is a formidable department and no stranger to disputes worth staggering amounts of money – four of its most recent instructions were in relation to disputes worth in the region of £2bn. If, at this point, you're resigning yourself to having to watch proceedings from the sidelines, think again. Here, you might get the chance to work alongside the senior partner on the juiciest matters. *"He's keen to get trainees into the department,"* reported one interviewee, *"so he makes sure everyone has a turn working with him and gives them a pretty long leash in terms of responsibility."* Those who plump for shipping litigation will also get to work on big cases, although one source found this group *"less friendly"* than others. It's arguable, however, that a hard-nosed approach is something of a necessity when handling claims such as those arising from the collision of a £13m super-yacht and a commercial ferry. You may have to *"sacrifice a few nights, but it's worth it for the confidence boost"* to be gained from the occasional appearance at a small appointment at the Royal Courts of Justice.

The finance department *"takes up a whole floor,"* reflecting its importance and the number of fee earners packed into it. Our interviewees agreed that of all the seats this one *"has some of the longest hours."* As compensation, the *"quality of work is fantastic."* Some found banking *"a tad repetitive,"* involving a little too much *"churning* out the same type of documents all the time." In contrast, aviation was characterised as "sexy and exciting," offering fast jets, a fast pace to the work and "interesting clients" – a bit like Top Gun, but with lawyers... The firm has triumphed in Chambers UK for its expertise in aviation-related asset finance, achieving ace status with a tier-one ranking. Its aviation clients include American Airlines and Delta Airlines.

stephenson bollywood

Stephenson Harwood is a lean organisation these days and the scale of its work means trainees can expect to graft, especially in corporate where hours can be demanding. This can equate to a good degree of responsibility and, for at least one trainee, "really feeling like a part of the team." To this end you should "expect to get your hands dirty," and it's not uncommon to find yourself knee-deep in documentation. Supervisors will keep a close eye on you, though, to make sure you're not just saddled with the routine stuff. You might even be whisked away by jet to get important documents signed, so keep your passport to hand. As well as acting on a Bollywood film company's ground-breaking listing on AIM, the firm zoomed into pole position when it advised Bayerische Landesbank on the sale of a majority stake in Formula One Management, the motor racing company.

life's a beach

Going abroad for a seat is incredibly popular and there are five offices in Europe and Asia, some of which welcome trainee secondees from London. Singapore sounds like the place to be: you get to exchange your typical London accommodation (lichen growing in the corners, windows tinted with grime) for a rent-free, three-bedroom apartment near the beach, complete with concierge service and one of the largest swimming pools in town. It's not hard to see why it's so popular.

Instead of popping down to the local Thai takeaway at the weekend, you can take advantage of the numerous budget airlines to explore South East Asia. We advise you to watch out for the local wildlife, though; apparently one trainee almost came a cropper after kicking a football into a giant, man-eating lizard. There's always a "bit of a bun fight" for these seats, but with eight trainees managing to secure stints overseas in 2007, chances of going away are far from slim. A tip from those in the know: put yourself forward as early as possible if you have your eye on the horizon.

Closer to home Stephenson Harwood's London office sits right opposite St Paul's. Unique features include a spine-tingling painting of what looks like dripping blood next to the library and a large roof terrace that provides breathtaking views of the Oxo Tower, Big Ben and the London Eye. It is often used for client entertainment. From the office windows you can admire the magnificent dome of Sir Christopher Wren's cathedral. Free staff passes mean you can get an even closer look and escape the hustle and bustle of City life at lunch times. A short hop away is the Millennium Bridge, which connects you with (among other places) the Tate Modern, if you're looking for a bit of culture. Our interviewees also spoke warmly of the charms of nearby pubs, The Rising Sun and Shaw's Booksellers.

sunil vision

Morale is high at the moment, following Stephenson Harwood's return to fighting form. Perhaps spurred on by this, the firm is running a feel-good campaign promoting healthy eating. It's ironic, then, that one of the few complaints levelled at it relates to the lack of a proper dining facilities. Nevertheless, there is no shortage of eateries within walking distance, ranging from upmarket sandwich shops to vegetarian soup outlets. If you want to do more than just eat well, there are plenty of sporting opportunities available – cricket, tennis, golf, football, netball, hockey and sailing. The football team is on champion form, having bested larger London rivals like Allen & Overy to twice win the legal league cup.

The firm prides itself on its friendliness and personal touch. One interviewee's recollection of being spoken to *"like an equal"* at a recruitment fair is true of the way in which trainees are treated once they start work. *"Everyone including the guy on reception"* will know your name and everyone from post boy to top brass gets invited to staff dinners and dances. Other signs of a genuinely warm working environment include careful scrutiny of trainees' hours just in case workloads need to be redistributed. Communication is definitely one trick this pony has got down pat. Management is even sent on courses to learn how to connect with junior staff. Thankfully this does not involve group-hugging sessions. All these initiatives are typical of Sunil Gadhia's style of leadership. He is *"far from your average manager,"* according to his loyal fan base. In turn, interviewees venture that a typical Stephenson Harwood lawyer is *"approachable, personable, switched-on and client focused."* The firm has a record of taking on applicants of all ages and backgrounds. According to our sources you should just be yourself at interview and if you're *"not bolshy or über-trendy,"* you'll probably do well.

and finally...

Stephenson Harwood has proved the dictum that what doesn't kill you makes you stronger. It looks to be steaming ahead with a renewed sense of purpose and confidence on a number of fronts and, as a further enticement for graduates, significantly boosted trainee salaries for next year. In 2007, eight of its 13 qualifiers stayed on with the firm.

Stevens & Bolton LLP

the facts

Location: Guildford
Number of UK partners/solicitors: 31/45
Total number of trainees: 7
Seats: 4x6 months
Alternative seats: None

If you are at the College of Law's Guildford branch, chances are you've already come across this successful South East law firm. Stevens & Bolton bills itself as offering a taste of City work in a Surrey town.

no smoke without fire

Given its Home Counties location, S&B manages to catch some impressive work and clients. Without doubt it is aided in this task by the presence of partners nabbed from City firms, notably Ken Woffenden from Simmons & Simmons, now head of corporate; Stephanie Dale from Denton Wilde Sapte, the employment partner who successfully represented British Airways in a conflict regarding retirement age; and more recently David Wilkinson from Bristows, who has helped the firm move into intellectual property practice. These lateral hires represent a shift in the make-up of the partnership, which had traditionally comprised local, home-grown lawyers. The last managing partner, his predecessor and his predecessor's father all trained with and spent their entire careers at S&B. The lateral hires have given the firm access to major clients – at present these include 11 FTSE 250 companies – that it would otherwise only have dreamed of. Client wins aside, trainees rather like working with *"a nice mixture of people,"* telling us: *"Having ex-City lawyers and more regional solicitors enables the firm to deal with people on different levels."*

The training contract is based on four six-month seats. Along with a compulsory coco seat, the contentious requirement can be satisfied by a stint in dispute resolution, family or employment and pensions. The remaining choices are real estate and tax and trusts.

The corporate and commercial department is very much at the heart of the firm. S&B is on the panel of multinational tobacco giant Gallaher and was involved in the £52m sale of the inspection and testing group of BSI, the UK's national standards body and owner of the Kitemark. If you are interested in reading about other recent S&B sales, acquisitions and MBOs, then take a look at the corporate tombstones on its website. Trainees told us: *"Our competition is not really in Guildford,"* naming City firms and national firms as competitors, although one did admit that *"the solicitors on the other side could be anything from a magic circle firm to a high street firm."* A seat in the department exposes trainees to a wide variety of work and supervisors seem happy to put them in the front-line, even on larger deals. Trainees are often trusted to be the *"main point of day-to-day contact for the client."* They praised the department for giving them *"a huge amount of support from junior fee earners and approachable partners,"* and cited this department as the most *"nurturing – people always take the time to explain things."* Tasks include drafting simple documents and organising data rooms (including visiting clients offices to sift through what is required for a deal).

rise and shine

The dispute resolution department has moved into *"really big, spacious"* new offices on the other side of the river from the main HQ. Staff may be distanced from the mothership but at least they have *"a great new litigation library"* and more breathing space. The department is described as exciting and busy, with trainees shadowing barristers when attending court. On smaller cases, trainees have the opportunity to meet clients, take witness statements and appear in the county court themselves to apply for orders from district judges. A decent number of support staff means there isn't an excessive amount of document bundling or pagination to do. Among the cases handled in the past year are a number of international matters – an international arbitration for Gibraltar Mines Limited, the owner of a large copper mine in British Columbia, against one of the world's largest commodity traders; acting for a finance company in litigation to recover a commercial airliner from an Afghan airline; acting for a FTSE 100 client in connection with the termination of an international distribution agreement; and acting for the Austrian subsidiary of another FTSE 100 client in connection with disputes against a Turkish distributor. Although one trainee mentioned international clients as something that had attracted them to the firm, when asked about the World Link for Law global network of which S&B is a member, the typical response from our interviewees was: *"You'll need to ask someone else about that."*

A seat in tax and trusts means delving into the private client world with its complex tax structures for the estates of wealthy folk, tax litigation and will drafting. Get your own probate file and *"you'll run the case on a day-to-day basis, which is good for building confidence."* The clients vary a great deal: from local people to superwealthy individuals with vast foreign assets. Real estate is another seat where there is the potential for trainees to take on their own smaller files. The supervisors are keen to hand over work and the workload is generally consistent. Some clients that you may have heard of are Adecco, Bank of Scotland, Lloyds TSB, Royal Free Hospital Trust and Sara Lee.

Trainees felt that the size of the firm allowed them a better overview of the work of the departments they visited than might be experienced by their peers at larger firms. Furthermore, they said that the pleasant and supportive environment means *"you actually like getting up in the morning."* Everyone in the firm *"including secretaries"* is invited to business planning meetings within each department. This adds to a sense of belonging as everyone can make a contribution and be consulted on the department's plans. The trainees we spoke to certainly felt they had received a good volume of work and were happy with the responsibility they were given. Some even thought that trainees are definitely *"tested"* and would *"come out a lot more confident than you might at other places."* However, there is still a dose of the *"standard work"* such as *"disclosure, bible making and indexing, etc."* With regard to research tasks, they commended the librarian for being very good at providing new slants on topics. In each seat there are two appraisals, designed to catch problems early and the small intake means trainees can liaise closely with the *"approachable"* HR personnel and training partner. Trainees virtually always sit with partners.

lily pads and taxi cabs

On the banks of the River Wey, near the train station, S&B's warehouse-style office provides a close-knit working environment in which *"the managing partner says 'Hello' and knows you personally."* The new office space is also well located (especially for *"nipping into town"*) but it was felt that to have everyone under one roof would bring the firm together more. The open-plan layout of the new office may be *"slightly different to what we're used to,"* however *"large dividers"* between the desks have meant people managed to maintain some private space. The prospect of bringing everyone together again looks less likely given plans to expand the firm further. It has already confirmed that it will be recruiting four trainees per year rather than three from now on, and by 2008 this should take the trainee population to a

lively eight. Awareness of S&B has already been boosted through sponsorship of three black cabs – sprayed green and parading the firm's branding – and a new recruitment campaign for qualified lawyers has been launched. If you want to see the firm's 'Wise Man Say...' campaign, look on its website. A sumo-sized Confucious-type character is depicted with the strapline: "Busy lawyer, like dragonfly, sometimes need rest on lily pad." Aside from the mild amusement this caused in our office, we were struck by the number of commercial lawyer vacancies posted on the page.

When they're not busy closing deals or lolling around on lily pads (maybe there's a flotilla of them anchored on the River Wey), staff like to socialise. Each of the departments has regular social gatherings and the firm as a whole has a few major events each year, including a Christmas quiz, Christmas ball and summer barbecue. In the last quiz there was an embarrassing picture round in which baby photos of lawyers needed to be identified. There are drinks on the last Thursday of every month, often humorously themed. *"A couple of trainees have dressed up in Hawaiian outfits and someone else once dressed up as James Bond."* Aside from these organised events, socialising can prove difficult as many staff drive to work or even reverse-commute from London. When we rang, for example, only two of the six trainees were living in Guildford and the remainder had elected to live in the capital. At least the office is just a 35-minute journey from Waterloo on a good day. Trainees spoke about a work/life balance considerably different to that experienced by their friends in the City. In general their hours are rarely longer than 8.45am to 6.30pm, although some had experienced *"more peaking than troughing"* in the corporate department.

The trainee group describes itself as *"good team workers and happy people."* But what else is typical? If you decide to apply to S&B, you might want to be aware that many of the current group have a connection to the area, some having family ties locally and virtually all having completed their LPC at the College of Law in Guildford. The firm gives presentations at the law school and this is where many of the trainees had their first contact with S&B. We also spotted that a majority of the trainees in recent years have had some kind of previous work history or a significant amount of prior legal experience before joining the firm. In 2007, only one of the three qualifying trainees stayed on with the firm, taking up a job in coco. This wasn't as good as the previous year, when two out of three stayed.

and finally...

Good quality training with experienced lawyers from diverse backgrounds, City-like transactional departments but with non-City lifestyle. Be absolutely certain Guildford is for you and you could go far with this firm.

Taylor Wessing LLP

the facts

Location: London, Cambridge
Number of UK partners/solicitors: 100/170
Total number of trainees: 48
Seats: 4x6 months
Alternative seats: Secondments
Extras: Pro bono – Blackfriars Settlement legal advice clinic, The Prince's Trust, St Mungo's homeless charity; language training

Expanding at home and abroad, Taylor Wessing was once known primarily as a major player in IP law. Increasingly this is viewed as just one facet of a firm with broad commercial strength and a secure position in the top 50. The last couple of years have been characterised by significant increases in revenue and profits, culminating in a 14% rise in UK turnover for 2006/07 to £91m.

This has allowed the firm to meet its four-year targets a year early.

taylor made

The modern day TW is a product of a five-year-old merger between London's Taylor Joynson Garrett and German firm Wessing. The trainees we interviewed had been drawn to it shortly after the merger by "the sense of a firm going places." But where exactly is it now going? Let's start with those impressive financial results. They've come on the back of "a strategy of offering a more rounded practice and building up the corporate side." Indeed, trainees have seen for themselves how "the emphasis has increasingly been concentrated on corporate, real estate and financial aspects." Flexing their muscles at the heart of the firm, corporate lawyers recently advised private equity partnership Rutland Partners on the £125m sale of Carron Energy, and pub group Avebury Holdings on its £219m sale to Punch Taverns. Finance lawyers advised client Lloyds TSB on a £100m Islamic finance deal involving a refinancing of Park Lane Properties.

The firm has continued to recruit at partner level – recent beneficiaries being the corporate, securities and real estate departments – to the extent that no one now questions the standalone capabilities of the main transactional areas or suggests they need to rely on work from IP clients. And yet, while sources say "we just don't feel IP led," it is also true that major pharmaceuticals companies are busy acquiring life sciences companies as a means of protecting long-term revenues as medical patent incomes dwindle. This reason alone means there is real logic to TW keeping up its reputation as the champion of companies with major IP assets. Which is why they must have been clapping their hands with glee when they heard about a schism in the IP department of prime competitor Bristows. The departure of five patent litigators from that firm, together with the recent capture of Linklaters' entire trade mark filing team, has left TW in an even more dominant position among the IP practices of Europe.

Our sources needed no prompting to pick out a *"defining feeling of dynamism"* in the air in London. This mood has also found expression in the firm's increasingly European outlook. Beyond the legacy of Wessing's German offices (Berlin, Dusseldorf, Frankfurt, Hamburg, Munich and Neuss), the firm has opened up in Paris, Alicante, Brussels and Shanghai, bringing its total number of offices to a healthy 12 worldwide. Cross referrals between the European offices have apparently increased by 45%. And there is now also the possibility of a merger with Dubai-based IT and construction law firm Key & Dixon. Certainly, trainees have *"really noticed an increase in European work"* and the simple act of *"calling on colleagues in other offices for advice"* is a regular reminder that *"the Wessing merger is seriously beginning to bear fruit."* From what we can tell, they relish *"working for clients across Europe and with people who speak different languages across all teams."*

centre of attention

London is the largest office in the network and operates as a separate profit pool, so notwithstanding the fact their Continental colleagues might not entirely agree, some sources were confident enough to suggest *"we feel like the centre of the firm here."* Adding to the sense of vibrancy in the London office, management has signed an agreement to move into a plush development on New Fetter Lane at the end of 2008. *"We've seen some early-stage drawings and they are pretty phenomenal,"* said one source; another added: *"It's a real statement of intent about improving and investing in the future."* The current Blackfriars abode is far from shoddy, but the move will undoubtedly allow further expansion.

One thing trainees hope won't change is *"our mid-sized status: the name may not have the cachet of a magic circle firm, but the low trainee numbers*

mean good responsibility, fantastic guidance and as a result being a good associate from the day you qualify." It's a winning combination for those determined to *"avoid the production line"* of larger City firms. The firm's size also allows a greater degree of flexibility in the training scheme than might be expected. The nature of TW's evolution means that corporate is now the only compulsory seat in the four-by-six month set-up. As well as mainstream deals, the work of the corporate group spans finance and projects, financial services, corporate tax and general commercial advice. Away from corporate, trainees can also visit IP, employment, real estate, private client, pensions, general commercial litigation, insolvency, construction and property litigation seats. First-hand commercial insights are afforded by regular client secondments to companies including British Airways.

you scratch my back…

Seat rotation has been a source of both pleasure and dissatisfaction in previous years, but this batch of TWers had good things to say about their allocations: *"Naturally the seats reflect the firm's strengths, so there are more in IP, corporate, finance and real estate than in niche areas like employment or private client."* Satisfaction clearly comes more easily when twinned with an awareness that *"there's no harm in strategic compromises now and again."* In the past we've found TW trainees to be frank in their interviews; for example, we learned that despite the firm's many positive attributes, a small minority of partners didn't provide the *"consistent support"* that is generally a feature of training. This year our sources were overall very happy with a system that *"doesn't put you under any more pressure than you put yourself."* *"The quality of work has been unexpectedly good,"* explained one; *"obviously there's a mixture of good and bad stuff and sometimes you're doing the mundane work, but more often it's like you're an* associate – there's no stiff hierarchy and you can talk to anyone." If a perceived "slight understaffing of paralegals" means grunt work is a fact of life, trainees still found that "supervisors actively encourage you to seek out responsibility."

Exactly what good stuff trainees can get their hands on depends on the seat. In finance and projects, trainees had come into contact with TW's "raft of outstanding banking clients" and been able to "draft loan agreements from scratch," "negotiate with the other side" and "get good hands-on experience." True, they'd also found themselves "regularly working until 11pm," but the crossover with "property finance in the banking arena" had offered some consolation with "lots of work with German counterparts on European transactions," not to mention the fact "I never worked a weekend." Real estate itself brings "responsibility from the word go," with the smaller scale of transactions allowing trainees to "see deals from start to finish." The nature of the department means "you enjoy a large role in project managing a transaction," whereas "in corporate you're more a small part of a large team and you often join halfway through a deal." Nevertheless, "people are keen for you to add value, so you're not just given discrete work without understanding the bigger picture." Long hours are a fact of life in corporate and unfortunately "ten to15 hours a day are to be expected as deals near completion."

patently good

And so to the IP practice for which TW is so well regarded. So-called 'hard IP' equals major pharma litigation, while 'soft IP' sees lawyers advising clients such as Bose, Kellogg, Associated Newspapers, Eidos, various music publishers and the estates of composers such as Rodgers and Hammerstein. Those deeply keen for non-contentious hard IP experience can head to TW's Cambridge office for a seat. Back in the capital there are great opportunities in patent litigation. Understand-

ably, "patent work is easier to grasp if you have a science background" and in every intake there are always three or four trainees with relevant qualifications. These are by no means prerequisite for a patent litigation and "any trainee can be part of a team working on something like a large anti-cancer drug case." The appeal of such big cases is obvious: "You might go to court for two weeks, do a lot of research, gather evidence, take witness statements and handle exhibits." Soft IP, with its trade marks, copyright, passing off and brand issues, may be highly popular, but our sources reckoned the issues are "grasped just as easily in hard IP when you do the right research." They advise that for both seats "it definitely helps to have done the commercial law elective on the LPC."

There is also a scattering of seats in smaller departments like employment, which represents clients like easyJet, Google and Specsavers, or pensions, where "you work almost academically and advise the trustees of big company pension schemes." Likewise, the "slightly leftfield" option of private client with its "client-facing matrimonial and probate work" provides a novel alternative to commercial disciplines. Those who enjoy nothing better than a good old scrap can seek satisfaction in general commercial litigation, insolvency, construction and property litigation. In these teams trainees particularly enjoy it when they "get to see cases from start to finish" – "maybe it'll be a dispute worth less than £100,000 and you'll handle the day-to-day correspondence, go in front of a master with requests, do relevant research and then work at putting it into a practical context." On bigger cases, while "you're obviously not taking the lead," trainees find it "fascinating to watch the process."

TW's forthcoming move isn't an enormous leap geographically (half a mile as the crow flies) and it seems unlikely to have an almighty impact on the identity of what is already a polished law firm on an even keel in the UK. "Everyone here is driven and determined but down to earth," trainees opined; *"among us there's a good mixture of law and non-law"* and a *"decent spread of people from well-regarded universities."* In fact, our sources were almost reluctant to differentiate TW from other mid-tier City firms: *"We're all pretty much the same,"* said one. A busy social committee pulls its weight, organising restaurant trips, book clubs and *"outings such as a trip to the dogs at Wimbledon."* The annual summer party (last year's was *"black tie at the Savoy, with a casino, a dance floor and plenty of champagne")* and departmental away days are also popular. For their part, trainees are often to be found drinking together in local hostelries in Blackfriars or *"participating fully"* in the firm's pro bono endeavours. Netball and football teams are there for the sport-inclined. Even if *"the pace does die down a bit over two years,"* the atmosphere remains easy, so that *"competition for NQ jobs does not turn into backstabbing."* In 2007, 16 of the 22 qualifiers stayed on at the firm, going into a broad spread of departments.

and finally...

Significant IP abilities may be at the heart of Taylor Wessing's past success, but they are merely one part of a broader commercial future.

Teacher Stern Selby

the facts

Location: London
Number of UK partners/solicitors: 21/24
Total number of trainees: 7
Seats: 4x6 months
Alternative seats: None
Extras: Pro Bono – Toynbee Hall Legal Advice Centre

Some 40 years on from Teacher Stern Selby's creation, Messrs Teacher and Stern are still around as consultants to the partnership but beyond that it's all eyes to the future.

k.i.s.s.i.n.g

When we rang them in early 2007, TSS was undergoing a review of its market positioning and branding with the help of a consultancy called Snog. *"The whole firm is getting a makeover!"* announced a trainee. *"Getting into The Lawyer's 'Rising 50' table gave us a lot of impetus and there's a sense that we have to keep that going. We're now at the stage when we're getting loads of quality work and it's spiralling."* When we went to press, Snog's big reveal was still awaited, but we can tell you that TSS is not typical of the residents of the ancient legal quarter of Bedford Row. *"The location says tradition, but the firm is modern. It's not even about the decor – it's about the approach the lawyers take."*

TSS' practice profile is heavily geared towards property law, with some exceptional hotspots in defamation/reputation management, sports law and education-related litigation. Every trainee visits the property, litigation and coco departments for seats that last between six and eight months, and the aim is to keep their experiences of each fairly broad. In 2006 TSS racked up £2bn worth of real estate deals, involving everything from leases of boozers in grim parts of the north of England to the £206m sale of one of the key financial exchanges in the City of London and the £430m acquisition of 180 Shell petrol stations. The City of London deal was for a Gibraltar-registered family trust, a not untypical organisation within a clientele of many overseas clients, a number of them wealthy individuals from Israel and other parts of the Middle East. In the petrol station deal, the assets were transferred by selling the company that owned the portfolio and not by transferring every single station individually. It was a classic example of how TSS's corporate lawyers work hand in hand with their property colleagues to structure deals. Trainees say property clients are *"the lifeblood of the firm"* and stress the importance of property in the training contract. *"I didn't think I would enjoy it,"* said one, *"but it was a good seat. I was running my own files and had a high level of autonomy working on leases and licences."* Even with deal negotiations, *"you have the freedom to have a good stab at them."*

As well as a seat working with a property litigation specialist, there are numerous other disputes to tackle in the litigation department. Trainees enjoyed litigation because of the endless supply of relatively straightforward but interesting tasks, such as drafting particulars of claim and statutory declarations for insolvency cases, and attending court to observe and take notes. Admittedly there is a spot of the old document jockeying, although *"it was only every once in a while I was drafted in to help on bundles,"* confirmed a relieved source. At each rotation someone is assigned to star player Jack Rabinowicz, who has developed an incredible reputation for medical and educational negligence cases. His work covers issues from special needs, bullying and school exclusions, to failure to secure a place at a school of choice. If you've a penchant for righting wrongs committed by the state this work should appeal. Bring your own superhero costume for your time with this *"mild-mannered, funny and warm"* partner.

a friend in need

Former KGB operative Alexander Litvinenko's poisoning caused a real hoo-hah, and for a while the owners of the Itsu Japanese restaurant chain were caught up in it. So what do you do when traces of polonium-210 send Geiger counters crazy in your restaurant? You call in gossipbuster extraordinaire Graham Shear. Admittedly this was (probably) the first time he'd contended with Russian spies and radioactivity, having previously been more used to tending to a clientele of lovely luvvies (Daniel Craig, Jude Law, Matthew Perry) and scandal-afflicted Premiership footballers. In 2006 Shear famously extracted an apology and settlement after the tabloids suggested Ashley

Cole had taken part in certain saucy activities. Taking a novel approach to the case, he gathered supporting evidence for Cole's libel claim via the Internet, a tactic that led one trainee to talk about the firm's work as *"cutting-edge and groundbreaking."* Also novel is Shear's attitude to developing new business: he is a founder of, and primary adviser to, the recently established Football Agents Association. Working alongside a lawyer to the stars, *"you're in the thick of things, although a lot of your experience is observational... you just help out as much as you can."* For this reason, *"a lot of Graham's trainees' day-to-day work comes from other lawyers. In fact he probably doesn't know what they do most of the time. It's a sporadic and exciting seat partly because he has a modern approach to law. He works preventatively and there's not too much on paper."*

Just as the *"very busy"* corporate department feeds off the property department, so it takes on work for sports clients. Last year there were deals concerning football clubs – advice to prospective purchasers of West Ham and the flotation of Watford AFC on AIM – and on deals like these it's sometimes impossible to go home at a sensible hour. All our sources had experienced their share of late nights in corporate: for one it was *"a lot of 8pm or 9pms and about four 3ams. For two months it was very busy like that, but there was quite a good atmosphere and there was always food and taxis home."* By all accounts, *"the majority of trainees place importance on work-life balance,"* but *"don't mind working late because there's no general requirement to put in face time."* A corporate trainee will always be *"at the bottom of the food chain"* but the challenges are there: *"You're not really one person's trainee so you get a great variety of things to do – some IP, some employment, corporate-structured property transactions... I drafted disclosure letters and board minutes and resolutions. I went to client meetings, and on big deals I'd sit in and make notes during phone negotiations. I also dealt with a lot of lawyers from other jurisdictions.*"

quality not quantity

Much as there is no guarantee of working for Rabinowicz or Shear, there are also no guaranteed jobs at the end of training; indeed, the retention rate has fluctuated between 16% and 100% in the past five years. "*It would be helpful, too, if there was someone with more HR experience to deal with the job situation,*" our sources concluded. "*That way we could have some consultation rather than simply being told – appraisals don't seem to be the time to raise the subject.*" This point was an issue for all those we spoke to, but at least "*problems over final seats and NQ jobs are the only negatives here. They are open about it – there's no closed doors – but they need to be more organised.*" The clear view was that "*the training is great but then you're forced to look elsewhere. Some sit tight and hope for the best but for the most part people will look around. It's an anxious time.*" Of the six 2007 qualifiers, three stayed on with the firm, each of them going into the property department.

In September 2007 only three new trainees joined the firm but, linked to this reduction, TSS is now providing funding for LPC fees. To get in here, "*academically you need to be at a certain level and you've got to be personable because there's a lot of client contact from day one. It's not for those who want to hide behind a computer screen.*" As one trainee put it: "*They want someone who is quite sparky. They're not aggressive but they challenge you a bit at interview. All the trainees here are quite confident.*" And from another: "*You have to show willing; if you sit and wait for things people will note that you are not proactive.*"

legal che guevaras

This is a firm with a strong Jewish heritage. Said one trainee: "*You know it is there but it is not by any means dominant.*" And they must be right because even a quick look at the firm's website will show you how multicultural TSS has become. Speaking about faith issues our sources were clear: "*Having the right connections helps much less than it might have done in the past. More emphasis is put on grades and good universities now.*" "*There's always talk of the firm becoming less religious,*" they continued; for example, the office used to close for both Easter and Christmas, and Rosh Hashanah and Yom Kippur. In 2007 the Jewish holidays were made normal working days that people could choose to take off by using days from their newly enhanced basic holiday allowance. All this said, faith issues still have a bearing on some aspects of the work: "*TSS understands that certain clients won't complete a deal on a High Holy Day. The interest could be banking up and the clients simply wouldn't do the deal,*" explained a trainee. Interestingly, even though "*a lot of business is effectively done in synagogues,*" some of the partners who are "*closest to the religious guys – the big Rich List clients worth billions of pounds – are not even Jewish themselves... they just understand those clients.*"

With around 100 staff and partners (40% of the partners are female) TSS still has a family feel; indeed, some trainees went so far as to call it "*homely.*" On the last Friday of every month there are drinks in the boardroom and at other times "*the usual suspects*" can be found in The Old Nick. The biggest social event is a firm-wide party in December. The last one was a masked ball and, as usual, every member of staff received a gift that had been carefully chosen for them. A new social committee has formed to enliven the remaining 11 months of the year. Perhaps they'll seek inspiration from the firm's victory for the Government of Cuba's music publishing arm after a six-year copyright claim. You may have seen a BBC TV show about Graham Shear's involvement in the case called *The Fight For Cuba's Music.*

and finally...

Given Teacher Stern Selby's determination to *"smarten up its image a bit,"* we could be hearing more noise than usual from Bedford Row. Be aware that the firm has a relatively new vac scheme, and try to get on it.

Thomson Snell & Passmore

the facts

Location: Tunbridge Wells, Thames Gateway
Number of UK partners/solicitors: 34/56
Total number of trainees: 9
Seats: 4x6 months
Alternative seats: None

Let's cast our minds back to the year 1570. It was the year of Guy Fawkes' birth. Shakespeare was learning his alphabet and Ivan the Terrible was busy rampaging across Russia. Meanwhile Nicholas Hooper, a curate at Tonbridge Parish Church, was setting himself up as a "scrivener and drafter of documents." Not every firm can trace its roots back over four centuries, but it was from these humble beginnings that Thomson Snell & Passmore evolved into the firm it is today. If you don't believe us, take a look in the *Guinness Book of Records*, where it is named as the "most durable firm."

past, present and future

More than 430 years on the firm has a staff of 220 working from offices in Tunbridge Wells and, more recently, Thames Gateway. Trainees describe a mixture of old and new that is helping to push the firm into the 21st century. *"It's proud of its traditional values and long-standing presence in the area,"* noted one, *"but it also realises it has to be progressive to move forward."* Nowhere is this more evident than in the corporate/commercial department. Historically known for its private client work, with clients returning *"year after*

year, generation after generation," the firm is now striving to develop its commercial side. *"There's a definite awareness that we need to be forward-thinking in this area, and the firm is making a big push to become better known for its commercial work."* With this aim in mind, the Thames Gateway satellite office was created. *"A lot of time and money have gone into that office. It hosts a lot of client events and seminars to keep potential clients and referrers updated, and it's attracting quite a lot of business."* Financially, progress is evident: the firm posted a year-end turnover growth of around 20% in 2006. Currently, the branch is home to three permanent staff, with others heading over there a couple of days each week. *"It's a networking base at the moment, but as investment and development in the region grows, it will do more fee earning."*

TS-P has eight departments: corporate and commercial; employment; commercial property; dispute resolution; private client; residential conveyancing; PI/clinical negligence and family. The departments are spread out over several buildings, although most are adjacent to each other, or at least on the same street. Trainees spend six months in any four of the departments, which can result in one extremely broad training contract. *"It provides an excellent all-round training. If you're not too sure where you want to specialise, this is a brilliant choice."* Trainees are allocated their four seats at the outset. *"A few months before you start, you fill out a form prioritising your top seats and they do their best to give you what you want."* In past years this system has worked well. *"I like knowing my whole schedule because you can plan it all out; it gives you peace of mind. Plus, if you do want a change there's scope to switch."*

the private life of clients

The *"absolutely huge"* private client department has four independent teams working on tax planning, probate, charity and court of protection matters. *"People always want to qualify here, so it's got a fresh and vibrant feel to it. It's so big it's almost like a firm within a firm."* Its popularity with trainees is perhaps due to the attractive combination of autonomy and variety of work. *"This seat arguably gives you the most responsibility, because it's easy to pick up small files and run them."* The firm advises high-flying and wealthy individuals on their personal estate planning, which leaves trainees very busy *"organising the sale of properties, getting advice from counsel, dealing with tax issues and speaking to potential beneficiaries. There's a huge amount of client contact to be gained."* Court of protection cases involve working alongside a partner who acts as a professional receiver for clients who are deemed incapable of dealing with their own affairs. *"I was co-ordinating care arrangements and that sort of thing,"* recalled one source. Be aware that there will be *"mountains of wills"* and because *"once you've drafted one will, you've basically drafted them all, they let you get on with it. I must have drafted 100."* True, it's not going to suit everybody (*"I found it depressing dealing with dead people all the time"*), but on the plus side *"the clients are all old ladies, so they're lovely. They bring you biscuits."*

The PI and clinical negligence departments are two of the largest in the region and *"deal with claims for the whole of the South. There's a real mixture, from the smaller £5-10,000 claims to £5m catastrophic injuries."* Recently the PI team represented a boy who suffered a serious head injury when struck by a car during his paper round. It also worked on the settlement of an employers' liability claim concerning a roadside patrolman who severely injured his arm when it became trapped under a vehicle. *"The seat allows you to get involved in both PI and clin neg, but if you're inclined towards one or the other you can say so,"* explained one trainee. *"I did a lot of clinical negligence work, myself. There are quite a few cerebral palsy cases, which can be harrowing but incredibly high-quality*

work. It's a very hands-on experience and towards the end of your seat you can run your own files."*

The family department offers a slightly different working environment. For a start, it's in a different building, on its own, above a dentist's office. *"It almost feels like you're in a high street firm when you do your seat here. I like it – it gives you more experience."* Trainees say the team may relocate as they think the building may be due for demolition. We certainly hope this is the case after one source casually informed us: *"There's Legionella in the water in that building, so there are no taps in the toilets. People bring in their own drinking water."* Water issues aside, trainees' experience in the family department varied wildly. *"It's a brilliant department,"* declared one; *"in terms of client contact and court time, it's quite remarkable."* Another, however, *"found it very quiet – I spend most of my time reading files, journals and text books."* While there may be peaks and troughs (*"people tend to have more marital breakdowns after Christmas, so perhaps it's a seasonal thing"*), it's clear that when there is work, it's pretty interesting. *"You get to see the ins and outs of people's relationships which can be quite shocking."*

A stint in the dispute resolution department begins quite gently. Thereafter you can expect to be drafting, taking witness statements, filling out claim forms and sitting behind counsel at court. We hear that one trainee even paid a visit to the Court of Appeal. Trainees also deal with cold calls from prospective clients, a task which *"keeps you on your toes, as you never know what's coming. You can soon weed out the ones which aren't going to go anywhere and refer the cases that seem to have some weight."* The department handles everything from professional negligence and health and safety issues, to general commercial and landlord and tenant disputes.

Those of you dreading commercial property can relax. *"I was not looking forward to it, but I surprised myself – I loved it."* The busy department has such a spread of work that trainees can pursue their individual interests. *"The general commercial team deals with commercial premises and investment properties, while the development team focuses on companies wanting to buy land and sell it as houses and flats."*

report card

Generally, the firm gets top marks for giving trainees the right amount of responsibility. The one department that lets the side down is corporate and commercial. *"I didn't get as much work as I would have liked,"* confided one trainee. *"The vast majority of my time there was spent photocopying. Elsewhere, the firm has support staff to do that, but in corporate they just seem a bit stuck in the past."*

Appraisals are scheduled every three months, and for the most part they tend to work well. *"Supervisors enjoy their jobs and you can tell that. They sit for hours in meetings talking about how they can improve our training experience."* Again, however, there is a bit of inconsistency: *"Some are a bit more hands-on than others,"* said one trainee. *"I didn't have my mid-seat appraisal in one of my seats,"* another piped up. *"I really could have used one because it would have given me the chance to say I wasn't getting enough work."* It's a shame because these niggles put a blip on an otherwise very positive report card.

chatterboxes

They're a right social bunch at TS-P, so if you're looking for a firm that will supply you with friends as well as training, we think it will suit. Most Fridays trainees can be found in a pub called The Barn. *"It's right next to us, I'm looking at it now out of my window,"* chirped one. When they do venture further, the choice is plentiful. *"Tunbridge Wells is a small place, but there are loads of bars."* Shops too – *"every lunch break you can head to a big shopping mall, which is brilliant... but not so good for the wallet."* The social committee organises drinks every month for everyone *"from office*

boys to senior partners – the stories are always great the day after." Then there are the theatre trips to London, bowling nights and sports (mostly football, cricket and pool). Each year a group of staff and partners make a day trip to France. *"They go off, have lunch, do a bit of shopping in the villages, pick up a bit of bread, or whatever else you do in France. They love it."* The annual Christmas party is held at the Spa Hotel in town. *"Last Christmas had a Montecarlo theme – we had a huge Scalectrix laid out. It was a bit odd, regressing to when I was eight years old, but it seemed to work."* Summer parties also carry a theme. *"The most recent was a funfair with rides and dodgems...frankly never a good thing after a few drinks."*

and finally...

This firm is very much tied to the area in which it has been ensconced for centuries. If you're a clubbing fanatic, then, perhaps look elsewhere; those with small-town tastes are quite likely to develop a real affection for the place and an appreciation for the quality of life that is possible. In 2007, all four qualifiers stayed on with the firm.

Thring Townsend Lee & Pembertons

the facts

Location: Bath, Bristol, Swindon, London
Number of UK partners/solicitors: 38/45
Total number of trainees: 14
Seats: 4x6 months
Alternative seats: Secondments

Fresh from a London merger with Lee & Pemberton, West Country firm Thring Townsend is making a big noise right now.

somethring up?

If you detect a rumbling in the West, it could well be the sound of Thring Townsend stretching out and establishing new territory. The story began some seven years ago, when Thrings & Long (Swindon) and Townsends (Bath), decided to pair up. The new firm's plans gained momentum in 2005 when Laytons' Bristol office was drawn into the fold, and things have recently been pushed to yet another level through a merger with 200-year-old Westminster private client specialist Lee & Pemberton. Gradual expansion in the West Country is one thing, but landing a London office is another, and it sounds as if everyone at the firm awaits the results with bated breath. *"It's all a bit wait-and-see,"* thought one source, adding: *"It is a pretty good match for us, so it shouldn't be too dramatic."* A shared, well-developed emphasis on agricultural and commercial work highlights similarities between the two firms that help explain why Thring sees L&P as a perfect mate. Time will tell, but for now we can say that Thring is among the best places in the country for agricultural law, and it has an array of other departments that could all benefit from a capital city presence, including company/commercial, commercial property, residential property, personal injury, family and tax and probate.

All those we interviewed either had links with the West Country or had in some manner familiarised themselves with that end of the M4 corridor before joining the firm. We suspect that the latest merger will only make the firm more attractive to good candidates from the region rather than change the nature or origin of those arriving at its door. Details are not yet finalised, but the firm tells us that L&P's small trainee population in London will likely be joined by one or two trainees from other offices. And just as the provincials can take seats in London, so the capitalists will be welcome out West. This will add extra scope to an already-flexible training contract: beyond an allocated first seat and a few considerations – for example, agriculture can't be done in Swindon or Bristol, residential property is only available in Bath – there are no compulsories. The appeal for any West Country graduate seeking a training contract that isn't purely commercial in focus is obvious.

hot bath

The layout of the Bath office is mostly open plan as a result of some extensive redesigning of its Georgian interior. The personal injury department has certainly embraced the conversion: *"It's a lot easier to bounce ideas off each other now and create a real team environment,"* we heard of a seat that offers trainees considerable variety, working for defendants and claimants. *"Major insurers one day and a small private claim the next."* On major cases trainees *"draft witness statements, meet with clients and generally make sure the case runs smoothly."* In a Swindon PI seat, sources had pored over pages and pages of doctors' notes while rooting out *"fraudulent claimants"* for insurers.

Company and commercial seats can be found in each of the offices, including Bristol, and involve *"assisting partners with sales and purchases, due diligence and lots of post-completion work, such as filings at Companies House and dealing with Stamp Duty Land Tax."* Trainees are able to get involved at every stage of a deal, seeing *"more responsibility than you might think."* Commercial property is a mainstay of the training scheme and is also available across offices. Trainees learn how to deal with simple landlord and tenant management issues: assigning leases, creating underlettings and granting licences to make alterations to premises. Much of the work is conducted for the likes of large pension funds, overseeing their investment portfolios in *"a fast-paced environment dealing with massive volumes of work."* While a residential property seat is only available in Bath, occasional pieces of private conveyancing are forthcoming in other offices. In commercial litigation, trainees can absorb the benefit of working on cases large and small. Some of our sources had been *"in court at least once every week;"* others suggested the real plus point of the seat is the *"focus on learning rather than earning."* Partners here make an especial effort to train their charges, with *"lots of research projects and presentations to the department"* particularly benefiting trainees.

swi are family

The largely open-plan Swindon office has a family department in which trainees could well be running their own cases *"within two months of being there."* Many matters handled are for Wiltshire County Council, which means ample opportunity to expand your knowledge of child and divorce law. In fact, even the most seasoned of practitioners were tested recently by instruction relating to a case of bigamy. Our interviewees assured us *"this was a far-from-frequent occurrence."*

If the allure of manure and tractors is impossible to resist then perhaps the agriculture department in Bath (*"it sees itself as King of the Jungle within the firm"*) will appeal. Enjoying a national reputation for its work in the sector, Thring represents the National Farmers Union and was called into action in 2007 to help manage the latest foot and mouth crisis in Surrey. Trainees frequently help out on contractual claims regarding farming machinery, *"basic Sale of Goods Act kind of stuff,"* and buying and selling land. The department has a unique atmosphere – *"a little more relaxed than the rest of the firm... more tweed on display than suits."* In keeping with the firm's broader expansion, *"agriculture grows almost day by day."*

bristol fashion

The Bristol office has a more traditional set-up, with lawyers in separate offices, *"though as the firm modernises, this may change."* It offers seats in coco, commercial property, commercial litigation and insolvency, and has just kick-started a construction practice having successfully poached two specialists from Burges Salmon. This is the smallest of the West Country offices, though it is also *"growing significantly."*

Relative freedom of movement between offices during training means you effectively sign up to the firm rather than one location. In fact, *"you are positively encouraged to experience life in at least two of locations and it is rare for a trainee to stay in one place for the whole two years."* Thankfully commuting between the locations isn't too taxing: Bristol to Bath takes about 20 minutes and it's half an hour from Swindon to Bath or Bristol. If you're seriously interested in the firm, chances are you know this already because most trainees arriving at Thring grew up in the region or came to it for study. Beyond the breadth of commercial, contentious and private practice experience the firm offers, it's probably fair to say that work-life balance is a major factor in choosing to train here, but given the firm's regional status and recent expansion, don't imagine that recruits have compromised on ambition. Trainees take pleasure from doing work *"similar to the stuff friends in London do"* but like *"to look at the countryside out of the office window."* This combination results in traditionally high NQ retention, and 2007 saw four out of six qualifiers accept NQ positions.

early birds

The culture at Thring sounds like its is based on inclusivity: *"The subsidised cafe downstairs is used by everyone from partners through to trainees, secretaries and the guys from accounts. No one is left out."* A predominantly young crowd meets up regularly for impromptu socialising, and there are drinks events once a month in Bath, once every two months in Swindon and four times a year in Bristol. Staff can be found in The Crown

in Swindon, The Green Park Tavern in Bath and The Three Sugar Loaves in Bristol. Quite where London fits into the social mix, we hope to be able to tell you next year.

Opportunities to test sporting prowess come via a football team that plays in a local league halfway between Swindon and Bath, as well as cricket matches, netball and even mixed tag-rugby, a sport that *"usually involves a drink or two afterwards."* There's plenty of time for such activities as trainees tend to leave the office somewhere between 5.30 and 6pm, the majority having started at about 9am. In Swindon, there's extra incentive for making an effort to get out of bed early: the on-site cafe offers a free breakfast.

and finally...

Mid-sized Thring Townsend attracts people looking for a broad training, decent work and a good social life all within a stone's throw of the countryside. This is no sleepy rural outfit; an expansive outlook and a foothold in London make this a very interesting proposition.

TLT LLP

the facts

Location: Bristol, London
Number of UK partners/solicitors: 73/94
Total number of trainees: 21
Seats: 4x6 months
Alternative seats: Secondments

This Bristol-headquartered outfit is in the ascendant. Big aspirations, high-calibre hires and impressive financial returns explain why *"this is an exciting time to be at the firm."*

carry on up the charts

TLT has pursued a place in the top 50 by carefully working its strengths. Our sources here have always felt *"closely involved in the firm and know where it is going,"* so we trusted them when they told us: *"Climbing the charts is still top of the firm's agenda."* But don't just take their word for it: the most recent years' financial results show turnover leaping and profits up.

Integral to TLT's rise has been an ability to mine seams of work across sectors such as leisure, retail, environment and technology. Several of the firm's commercial groups have received a significant push, not least the lawyers dealing with franchising law for a variety of businesses including Proton Cars. Licensing law is another of TLT's strengths and lawyers regularly act for Punch Taverns and Spirit Group. More broadly, the firm represents companies as diverse as First Choice holidays and the Energy Saving Trust. TLT has found itself closely involved in sustainable energy developments. In 2006 SLP Energy instructed the firm in connection with onshore wind farm projects, and lawyers also advised RidgeWind, another major producer of onshore wind energy, on several windfarm projects including a proposed ten-turbine development in Northumberland and a 15-turbine development in East Yorkshire. This experience was clearly helpful when advising construction group Alfred McAlpine on the £30m acquisition of environmental consultancy firm Enviros Group.

Despite all these national instructions, TLT has not forgotten its roots and maintains established relationships with regional businesses such as Wallace and Gromit's creators Aardman Animations. It came as no surprise to anyone that long-term client Avon Rubber chose TLT for its £63m sale of Avon Automotive to New York-based Petrol Automotive Holdings and, not so long ago, corporate lawyers were busy helping Bristol-based Somerfield's management on the company's £1.1bn private equity-funded buyout. That deal involved a swathe of real estate issues, and this was no problem for a firm with plenty of experience in that field. Just ask clients Imperial Tobacco, Renewable Energy Partnerships and Bank of East Asia, if in any doubt. Among the firm's top standalone property deals is Renew North Staffordshire/Stoke on Trent City Council's £3bn regeneration project. A major part of TLT's property business – volume conveyancing and mortgages – has been corralled into a separate venture called Ontrack, which is geared towards lenders such as Barclays Bank, Bristol & West, HBOS and RBS.

And speaking of the banking sector, the importance of these clients cannot be underestimated. Already known for its banking and financial services in Bristol, TLT gained further expertise when it merged in 2006 with compact London outfit Lawrence Jones, which had a £3m revenue stream plus clients like Allied Irish, Banco Espirito Santo and Caterpillar Financial Services. Subsequent partner hires have struck a similarly canny note: the arrival into the new London office of a finance and litigation expert from CMS Cameron McKenna was a big boost, as was swiping an insolvency specialist from Denton Wilde Sapte. Back in Bristol, new arrivals into the financial services team have reinforced TLT's ability to act for many retail banks, mortgage lenders and insurers on UK-wide issues.

wePod

Trainees are definitely plugged in to the buzz at TLT. *"There are firms bigger than us, with a higher turnover than us in the area, but they've already been at this stage. What's exciting is the prospect of being closely involved in the expansion."* It does sound like trainees currently enjoy a more or less perfect balance between the benefits of a smaller regional firm (*"an easy approach to people and an easy atmosphere"*) and the benefits of working for an ambitious employer on an upward trajectory. Whether or not this can be maintained remains to be seen, but for the time being at least *"you feel they*

want you to succeed with them." Our interviewees put this inclusive atmosphere down to a couple of factors: first, an attitude to training that means *"you're not just fodder for two years,"* and second, an egalitarian *"pod-based, open-plan seating arrangement that means everyone is friendly and accessible."* The pods are merely small groups of partners, assistants and trainees, but their impact is substantial: *"It gets rid of the bad sides of a chain of command; I felt from the start I could ask anyone anything,"* said one source. Close proximity to the whole team means *"you always get comments about whether your work was good or not."* It also makes a packed trainee workload easier to handle. Said one: *"Whenever I've been swamped I've just talked to my supervisor and sorted it out."* Formal appraisals come along every three months to put everything in perspective, and *"mid-seat reviews are the best as they give you stuff to focus on and improve."* For the most part our interviewees were just happy to be *"involved in quality work. Because the support staff are so good, you only have to do rubbish admin work when it's out of hours."*

For the record, there are no compulsory departments in the four-seat scheme although, *"being the core of the firm, commercial, corporate finance and real estate are the areas they push."* Seats available under the real estate banner include straight property, social housing, construction, and planning/development. Corporate or commercial seats offer everything from insolvency to banking/finance to environment and employment, and on the contentious side there are seats in family, commercial litigation and banking/finance litigation.

"In a property seat your work will actually count; you're treated like a fee earner in your own right," a source concluded, while another told us: *"I had my own retail leases and residential purchase files and also worked on multimillion-pound transactions."* Corporate finance seats bring involvement on *"large UK business acquisitions*

and sales, a lot of admin, drafting of disclosure documents and document organisation." At the same time "there is excitement – you're sometimes there until 11pm or midnight and you don't really know how it will pan out." In banking and financial services trainees have their own caseload of repossessions for major lenders as well as "dipping in and out of larger cases." Family is an especially popular contentious option, in part because of its file responsibility and client contact. Employment involves "research for fee earners, non-contentious advisory work generated by our advice line" and "court preparation," even if the nature of clients (eg major insurer Zurich) means "you don't get much chance to do advocacy because they can afford whichever barrister they want."

After "some past disappointments with seat assignment," the process of seat allocations and NQ job appointments have been revamped to prioritise third and fourth-seaters above first-years. There was a disappointing result in 2006, when only one of the four qualifiers took jobs with the firm, so we are pleased to report that all five of the 2007 qualifiers stayed on. Seat rotation is now also leaving most people "happy," although it has become "increasingly competitive" to secure a seat at TLT's small London office. Those two trainees who make the trip from Bristol every six months gain experience in areas as varied as "employment, shipping, commercial, property litigation, general commercial, aviation, banking and general corporate." They also get "the chance to become involved in business development." As if all that weren't enough, "beautiful serviced accommodation" and "travel back to Bristol every weekend" is all paid for by the firm. Other opportunities for flying the nest are client secondments to Orange and Somerfield.

weakest link

The hours in London are a shade longer than in Bristol, which for most of our sources had been "9am to 5.30pm on an average day and until 7pm regularly in corporate." A typical view was this: "I honestly can't complain, we're among the best-paid trainees in Bristol and we work hard, but I can mostly walk home in time for Hollyoaks." TLT sits on the upper storeys of one of the tallest buildings in the city, "five minutes from Temple Meads station and right by the floating harbour." Across the road Toto's is the perfect place for "a catch-up lunch, welcome meals and drinks for new trainees" – in fact any kind of celebration at all. A (hyper)active social committee organises endless events and trips "to Tamworth for indoor skiing, shopping at the Bullring," even "a trip to Disneyland." For those into sports there are hockey, softball, cricket and football matches on a regular basis.

The annual trainee-penned Christmas revue is one of the best ways for new arrivals to integrate. "We met over drinks from October to write it, then we performed it at the party. It was really good fun but incredibly nerve-wracking," reported a junior thesp. Considering their status in the firm, we're not talking biting Private Eye-style satire, it's more a case of "a few gentle punches, nothing offensive." Last year's production clearly had its finger on the contemporary mores of the firm: "It was a Weakest Link-themed piece... the Anne Robinson figure was played by someone being [managing partner] David Pester, aka Darth Pester. He'd expanded his evil empire so much that he had to knock some partners out... the contestants were trainees playing partners who'd be shuffled off stage when they lost." Um, isn't that how partner prospects are decided in every firm?

If you're considering applying to TLT, you'll want to know whether or not to develop a West Country accent in order to impress. Although "a connection to the area isn't vital," the majority of recruits do tend to have family ties or have studied around Bristol or the South West. When our sources characterised themselves as "quite bolshy

The adventure you're looking for, the guidance you need

It starts the moment you do – work of the highest quality with the support and guidance of some of the best people in the business. At Travers Smith, we are big enough to offer the most exciting opportunities but small enough for each individual to count. Choose a more inspiring path.

Please visit **www.traverssmith.com** or contact Germaine VanGeyzel, Graduate Recruitment Manager: **graduate.recruitment@traverssmith.com** 10 Snow Hill, London, EC1A 2AL, 020 7295 3000 *and outgoing,"* we kind of knew what they meant, even if we'd have phrased it so they sounded less shirty! *"There's quite a lot of variety here,"* added one source; *"some second-careers, others straight though, a variety of universities."* Everyone was keen to distinguish themselves from the trainees at regional rivals. *"We rank ourselves next to Osborne Clarke and Burges Salmon, but we reckon our hours are a lot better and our firm is more willing to accept people as they are,"* concluded one interviewee.

and finally...

Happily in and of its region, with ambitious yet sensible plans, TLT is a sound choice for Bristol-minded students. For all its achievements, it sounds to us as if the firm remains as down to earth as ever.

Travers Smith

the facts

Location: London
Number of UK partners/solicitors: 66/149
Total number of trainees: 36
Seats: 4x6 months
Alternative seats: Paris
Extras: Pro bono – ICSL and Paddington law centres, death row appeals; language training

Several centuries of advice for the City's financial institutions and corporates have made Travers Smith entirely comfortable in its skin. This top-notch, mid-tier firm does things its own way.

back to the future

If being a conservative firm means an aversion to sudden change or willy-nilly merger and acquisition then this is definitely a conservative place. When we asked trainees where they see the firm going, they looked back before looking to the future. In the words of one: *"Well, we just had a very good year financially and won lots of awards, so if we can repeat that success, I think that would be the aim."* Just elected for his third successive three-year term, managing partner Chris Carroll went on record as having observed much the same. "We see no pressing reason to change the way we do things, other than to try and do them better," he told *The Lawyer* magazine in December 2006. When you've an impressive reputation for quality service and your average annual profits top £800,000 per equity partner, it's not a bad philosophy. Sure, the firm had to close an under-performing Berlin office in 2006 to concentrate on a best-friend strategy in Germany, but at least it hadn't wasted millions on a string of other offices. Elsewhere, strong relationships with foreign firms has served Travers well, and it is a policy shortly to be rolled out in India, where Carroll has visited to generate referrals and hand pick new friends. Travers' Paris office is the exception to the rule, but it too is single-minded and only provides advice on English law.

In the UK what Travers excels at is transactional work. In the past year it advised ntl on aspects of its $6bn merger with Telewest, assisted the management on the £2.18bn sale of Coral Eurobet, helped Peel Ports on its £771m takeover of Mersey Docks and Harbour Company, and assisted luxury shoe business Jimmy Choo on its £185m sale to Towerbrook Capital Partners. As well as instructions from big companies, the firm enjoys strong relationships with private equity houses and banks, having recently advised Macquarie on a £1.8bn acquisition of Moto Service Stations, 3i on the €8.4bn recommended Osprey consortium takeover of Anglia Water and both successful bidding consortia regarding the takeovers of Aston Villa and West Ham United. There really seems no reason for Travers to plot a different course.

ménage a trois

The training scheme revolves around a four-seat system with mandatory periods in corporate, a contentious area (commercial litigation or employment), and real estate or banking. To complete the quartet, trainees select a 'wild card' seat somewhere in the commercial team (which includes IP/IT and EU/competition) or with the tax, pensions, corporate recovery or financial services departments. While the nature of each team's work means a variegated trainee experience, generally speaking there is *a distinct increase in responsibility in your third seat.*" Our sources found that *"ongoing feedback comes naturally with the room system, although* [mid and end-of-seat] *appraisals force people to sit down and think about what you need to do.*" Solid training sessions also get the nod of approval.

Throughout the firm, a room-sharing system sees trainees cohabit with a partner and an assistant. *"It's absolutely the best thing about training here,"* declared one source. *"Working so closely with massively intelligent people at different stages of their career, you see partners' and assistants' ways of dealing with matters from the initial call to the final moment.*" It means *"you can put to the assistant all the inevitable questions you don't want to ask the partner.*" Rough translation: *"Sometimes the partner gives you a task and they might as well be speaking another language. You nod and smile and then when they leave the room you ask the assistant what the hell you're supposed to do!*" It is frequently the case that a room of three people will handle the majority of a deal and this means *"learning comes organically because you're constantly observing and listening to what's going on.*" What this close proximity also creates is a sense of context – *"You see a deal played out in front of you the whole time and you never feel disconnected from the bigger picture.*" Of course,

"sometimes the discrete tasks or admin jobs can be painfully boring" for a trainee, but the continual contextual knowledge brings the consolation of *"always understanding what you're doing, why and how it fits in.*" While more administrative tasks are a reality of transactional departments, *"because you're right under people's noses they see you're capable and put better stuff your way so you get more responsibility quickly.*" The system creates *"a relaxed atmosphere,"* even if *"ultimately you still know who the partner is and who the trainee is.*"

corporate is king

The corporate practice *"feels like the centre of the firm,"* and although it is divided into private equity and corporate finance departments, *"they've become a lot more integrated over the last year.*" Trainees say that *"the nuts and bolts of the seats are similar,"* with an *"inevitable amount of the mundane due diligence"* in each. A source who'd sat in private equity had *"enjoyed great client contact, holding meetings with clients by myself or with an assistant.*" For another trainee, the *"public companies listing"* side of corporate finance meant *"getting to grips with regulatory issues, generating board minutes and company admin.*" While occasional client secondments are available across the firm, the corporate department offers the only overseas seat – a slot for a French-speaking trainee in Travers' Paris office. *"The reality of a banking seat is a lot of admin." "The seat involves a lot of working on conditions precedent and making sure everything is in place,"* explained one trainee, while another told us they had gained *"more responsibility as the seat progressed,"* concluding their time with *"the slightly terrifying task of running a whitewash meeting for a loan myself, but it was great to be entrusted with it.*" Pick the alternative choice of real estate and you'll get *"your own files and a lot of responsibil-*

ity." "*You figure a lot of things out yourself, even if little goes out without being checked.*"

Commercial litigation is "*a smaller, quieter team with better hours than most.*" Contentious requirements can also be met in the "*small, friendly*" employment team, which offers "*a mixture of corporate support and disputes work.*" Advocacy can be on the cards, but through somewhat gritted teeth our sources observed how "*all tribunals seem to settle before the day itself.*" Nothing a few well-timed prank calls wouldn't sort out... Those trainees wishing to gratify transactional lusts more fully can bypass the contentious realm altogether if they take a short course at the College of Law.

Over in the commercial practice group "*you help with corporate deals but you're also dealing with clients' trading matters, drafting and advising on commercial contracts, etc.*" Some trainees even found themselves "*the principal point of contact for clients... but I mean obviously I wasn't a one-stop shop.*" Finally, tax seats can be a pretty formidable experience at first as "*you're surrounded by really switched-on, intelligent people.*" However "*the massive effort they make to train you*" reduces the intimidation factor. One source told us how "*a partner went through a major transaction exhaustively to give me a complete basic breakdown.*"

ain't no mountain high enough

Over the years we've noticed the scales have tipped towards the guys within the trainee population. Further up the ladder men also dominate the ranks of qualified solicitors – of the 66 partners, seven are female but they all work in specialist departments (eg tax, employment, financial services) and there are none in the core corporate, banking, real estate and litigation departments. None of the partners made up in 2007 were women, which the firm says was "*merely an accident of history.*" Indeed, the firm

seems unabashed by its skewed gender statistics, with one partner citing practical reasons for the lack of high-ranking Travers women: "*Many more women leave the profession in their early 30s because they want more family time.*" Coupled with a majority of students arriving from Oxford, Cambridge, Bristol or Durham Universities, you can't help but wonder if these factors relate intrinsically to the firm's character. When we asked our trainee interviewees about this, both male and female alike agreed it wasn't something that they'd noticed. "*It doesn't feel like a male-dominated environment at all,*" they said, adding: "*Yes, there are old-school partners who are probably members of clubs, but there are also young partners who are nothing like that and some strong female partners.*" The firm introduced a new 'of counsel' career path in 2007 (partner-equivalent work responsibility without the full duties or benefits of partnership). At the same time a push for diversity has seen a panel established to monitor Travers' inclusivity, particularly focusing on recruitment and attracting students from a wider range of universities.

Travers trainees share the firm's calm assurance: they impress without bragging, betraying insecurities or trying too hard. "*Everyone's got a bit about them – pep and personality,*" observed one source. In a community that exhibits "*a genuine sense of pride, with everyone proud to say they work at the firm,*" people are "*bright but not cut-throat.*" In part this atmosphere results from the firm's size; we'd also suggest that the values of courtesy and loyalty persist because they're integral to the firm's distinctive and self-perpetuating personality.

Speaking of persistence, in transactional teams long hours mean "*you'll often stay until midnight,*" so it's a quality much valued. More regular days can be found in the smaller departments. As well as its main Snow Hill HQ close to

Smithfield Market, Travers recently took over a *"modern and snazzy"* building right next door to which the corporate teams have now moved. This has created more space in the old building and the neighbours are close enough not to cause any sense of isolation. The local pub, The Bishop's Finger, is the venue for anything from *"welcome drinks for new trainees,"* to end-of-seat drinks, to plain-old *"Friday drinks."* Departmental Christmas and Easter parties are supplemented with a firm-wide Christmas jolly, held last year at the Dorchester Hotel. *"It's safe to say that people let their hair down,"* said one tight-lipped source. On the sports front there's everything from rugby sevens and football to hockey and the Paris Half Marathon. A couple of lawyers put everyone in the shade in 2007 by scaling Everest for charity. Presumably they established a best-friend referral relationship with the Nepalese Sherpas at the same time. Putting a finger on what sums up Travers socially, one trainee described an *"ad hoc five-a-side tournament against partners, played in great spirit and everyone went for drinks afterwards,"* while another added: *"I've just been out at a lunch with the head of private equity – I'm sure that doesn't happen everywhere."* Such a working and social life encourages people to stay on with the firm when they qualify: in 2007 all but one of the 16 NQs took jobs in the firm's corporate, commercial, EU/competition, tax and real estate teams. One of the qualifiers in 2006 actually quit law but stayed on in a marketing role.

and finally...

Trainees come to Travers Smith for its *"fantastic reputation, quality of work, genuine responsibility and a sense of belonging."* Once there, few wish to leave.

Trethowans

the facts

Location: Southampton, Salisbury
Number of UK partners/solicitors: 24/18
Total number of trainees: 7
Seats: 4x6 months
Alternative seats: None

Hampshire and Wiltshire-based Trethowans is a solid mid-market player in both the commercial and private client spheres.

the land of nod

Once upon a time in 1866, George Nodder qualified as a solicitor and, ten years later, set up his own practice in the county town of Salisbury. The 20th century saw the firm move with the times, shortening its string of names to a comparatively brief Trethowans and in 1996 breaking into the Southampton market through a small merger. Today the firm is continuing apace by expanding its commercial capabilities to complement an established private client practice. Trethowans already covers a broad swathe of practice areas, but the firm is pushing for further growth in *"bespoke services for high net worth clients"* to insulate itself from the icy advances of Tesco Law. This, of course, is the colloquial name for the likely changes resulting from the Legal Services Bill, which is intended to open up the legal profession to businesses other than law firms.

Trainees reap the benefits of the firm's diverse practice and have the option of seats in corporate, commercial litigation, commercial and residential property, employment, licensing, personal injury and clinical negligence, family and private client.

On the commercial side Trethowans' excellent licensing practice is top ranked by *Chambers UK*. It acts for household names in the restaurant and gaming industries, among them Pizza Hut and

Ladbrokes. The firm has also recently expanded its commercial property practice through a combination of lateral hires and internal promotions. Trainees who want to experience property complete a residential property seat first to *"get to know how all the bits fit together,"* before tackling commercial property. Both residential and commercial seats offer *"a lot of client contact"* and *"quite challenging work,"* but beyond the supervised *"day-to-day running of files, searches and drafting letters,"* trainees find they generally have less responsibility than in other departments. A lucky few can also experience *"conveyancing with a difference"* in the small landed estates department which acts for landowners and tenants throughout the UK who collectively farm in excess of 35,000 acres.

fake or break?

Our sources claimed that training in the regions delivers a more comprehensive experience. Of their corporate and commercial seat, one enthused: *"I got to be involved in every part of the process of the transaction, from the contact stage through disclosure to the completion meeting with Champagne popped afterwards. In City firms you only work on one wedge of a big deal."* When supervised by partners, trainees can also get involved in business development. A seat in employment offers an interesting mix of contentious and non-contentious work, acting for both employers and employees. On the contentious side trainees prepare for employment tribunals, take witness statements and do *"quite a lot of research."* On the non-contentious side, they occupy themselves drafting employment contracts and attending client meetings. The team seems happy to be flexible and whenever possible defers to trainees' preferences about the balance of their workload. Supervisors also encouraged trainees to latch on to any interesting work available from other fee earners in order to experience their different styles of working.

The PI and clinical negligence department is going strong, with ongoing cases worth in excess of £50m in damages. Trainees swear a PI seat doesn't involve *"people making up accidents;"* instead they are *"pleasantly shocked"* by the interesting and *"exciting"* nature of claims. These run the gamut of seriousness from trips and slips through injury caused by defective products and catastrophic injuries. The department is particularly experienced in serious head and spinal problems, and trainees find that *"as well as being a lawyer you also have to know the relevant medical vocabulary."* Although the nature of the work means things can get *"pretty horrific,"* *"if you can cope it's really rewarding."*

The clients of the family and private client teams range from regular folk to high net worth individuals, most of whom live around the Salisbury area. Basic wills are the *"bread and butter"* of the private client department, where the majority of a trainee's work is probate and the administration of estates, with some trusts and tax work thrown in. A family seat provides greater client contact and a workload which one trainee estimated as a 70:30 split between cases involving divorce and cases involving children. Trainees can also practise their people skills via a scheme that offers free half-hour consultations to prospective clients of the family department.

where everybody knows your name

Generally, trainees must spend time in both the Southampton and Salisbury offices. This requirement didn't seem to bother the people we spoke to; one said they actually enjoyed the *"nomadic lifestyle."* People deal with the requirement either by commuting or renting a Southampton pied-à-terre. Given that office hours are a very reasonable 8.30 or 9am to 5pm, the commuting option doesn't look too awful. Trains between Southampton and Salisbury run regularly and take just over half an hour. Most of our sources drove, however.

The respective social lives of trainees in the Salisbury and Southampton offices are rooted in the distinct histories of the two cities. Historically, Southampton served as the trading port for the more refined Salisbury. A bit like the rowdy Southampton inhabitants of yore, trainees in the Southampton office regularly like to kick up the dust at Chambers pub, which offers a buy-one-get-one-free pizza deal. Salisbury trainees have noticeably quieter evenings: *"There is one pub nearby, but it's not very nice and most people have their own things to do at the weekend."* Recently the firm has livened up its official social calendar; on the last Friday of the month a couple of partners go to a bar and buy the first drinks of the night for whoever else wants to join them. This partner drinks scheme alternates between the Salisbury and Southampton offices, so perhaps there's hope yet for the Salisbury scene. Trethowans also hosts an annual Pimm's party, where clients are invited into the firm to join staff for drinks. Trainees told us they rather enjoyed their role serving refreshments: for novices at the business development game it's not a bad way of circulating and picking up tips.

Trethowans are a sporty bunch, which according to one trainee *"is representative of the firm's attitude"* towards the importance of competition and team morale. *"A lot of male partners are really into their sport and are keen to play against clients and other firms. Sometimes they take it a bit too seriously though!"* The sports available are netball, cricket, five-a-side football, touch rugby, charity swims and even a charity cycle race around the Isle of Wight. Though sporting activities seem to dominate, the Salisbury office also has an appreciation of culture befitting its location. Trethowans is a corporate patron of Salisbury Playhouse productions, the most recent being *Shadowlands*, about the life of CS Lewis. As with the rest of the firm, Trethowans' private client team doesn't miss an opportunity to advance itself and it has hosted a series of inheritance tax seminars in the Playhouse itself. In January 2007, the firm's website quoted head of private client Elizabeth Webbe: "We benefit by using the mediums [sic] of the theatre and storytelling to get across the sometimes complex issues involved in inheritance tax and estate planning." Indeed.

down and dirty

The Salisbury office is currently split between two sites and seems *"a bit of a rabbit warren,"* but will move to the new Salisbury Office Park in Easter 2008. These new digs include 21,000 square feet of state-of-the-art, open-plan floor space, which means *"a lot of people will have to change the way they work... for the better,"* particularly *"the more traditional people who are a bit stuck in their ways."* Everyone is keen to get a peek at the new *"decorative spiral staircase covered by a glass atrium,"* and trainees can already see the fringe benefits of the new location: *"It's opposite the gym so I won't have an excuse for not going."*

Regional firms usually like to look at candidates who have a connection to the area, and Trethowans is no exception. That connection can be demonstrated if *"you have family in the area, went to uni here or just want the lifestyle and can't stand the thought of commuting on the Tube."* In addition to a commitment to the South, Trethowans looks for *"reasonably outgoing"* trainees who possess both *"intellectual ability and a personality."* Lords and ladies of leisure need not apply: *"You have to be down-to-earth: Trethowans isn't looking for someone from a totally privileged background who has never got their hands dirty."* True enough, most of the people we spoke to had gained some full-time work experience before applying for their training contract. Clearly Trethowans appreciates maturity and hard graft more than an Oxbridge degree. And it seems to be a winning formula since three of the four 2007 qualifiers accepted jobs, going into PI and employment. The qualifier who left did so to relocate elsewhere in the UK.

and finally...

In the ever-crowded Southampton market, Trethowans is a familiar name; in Salisbury it is one of the biggest players in town. In either location it is a worthwhile choice for anyone seeking a mixed commercial-private client training. If you're happy with the idea of switching between its two locations then get that application started. And if you can confidently swing a cricket bat, so much the better.

Trowers & Hamlins

the facts

Location: London, Manchester, Exeter
Number of UK partners/solicitors: 88/146
Total number of trainees: 39
Seats: 4x6 months
Alternative seats: Overseas seats

Trowers & Hamlins twins expertise in two very distinct areas – the Middle East and social housing – and surrounds these hotspots with a growing general commercial practice. The majority of trainees and staff work in London and the firm has smaller UK branches in Manchester and Exeter, plus overseas bases in Abu Dhabi, Bahrain, Cairo, Dubai and Oman.

super, smashing, great

Things are going rather well for Trowers. In 2006/07 its revenue was up by 21% to £68.1m, having already soared the year before. Notable contributions were made by a newly invigorated corporate team, the public sector and banking groups and the commercial property team, each of which increased their revenues by around 40%. *"Targets are being smashed and it feels like the firm is growing in leaps and bounds,"* said one source, perhaps buoyed up by one of the bimonthly 'billing drive drinks' parties where people catch up on performance and cheer in the results from the past two months. Morale is running high, as exemplified by the fact that the firm came in at number 40 in the *Sunday Times*' most recent 'Best Companies To Work For' survey.

Trainees spend at least six months in a property seat, be this commercial property or social housing. In the former, they run their own smaller files and work with other team members on larger deals. There is *"a lot of overlap with the corporate department"* on transactions, and a great deal of direct client contact. The department recently advised on the £106.2m purchase of 111 Old Broad Street which, being directly opposite Tower 42, has been described as one of the best banking addresses in the heart of the City of London. Trowers also assisted client Abanar in its first venture into the student accommodation sector, through the purchase of buildings at the University of Huddersfield.

altogether now

It's much the same story for trainees in the social housing department, which has an absolutely peerless, 100%, top-of-the-tree reputation. In fact, the firm's name is synonymous with social housing law, in part because it advises central government, local government, regulatory bodies, plus a gazillion housing associations, including giants Peabody Trust and Metropolitan. For years its partners have helped to write the law in this area and drafted the standard contracts and leases used throughout the social housing sector. In our attempt to give the department due credit, we mustn't over-egg the pudding: this work may have dominated Trowers' business in the past, but this is no longer true today since the growth of other departments.

Before taking a seat in the department, one trainee thought social housing sounded like *"a cardigan-and-sandal-wearing thing."* In the sense that many of the people who work in social housing are passionate about what the movement ultimately stands for – providing affordable homes to those who need them – there is a whiff of *Guardian*-reader in firms dealing with this type of business and client. That said, trainees who visit the department soon learn that these same people have a very specific type of commercial viewpoint and deal with sometimes vast budgets. Trainees will get their own files relating to individual properties: they work on sales, purchases and *"mopping up problems"* so that whole estates can be grouped together and sold or financed. Running about 40-50 files of your own brings endless phone calls, bags of correspondence and ample opportunities to hone drafting skills. The department has worked on so many impressive schemes it is hard to select just one or two. This year we've chosen to mention Presentation Housing Association's purchase of the Paragon student accommodation block at Thames Valley University and the large-scale voluntary transfer of more than 11,000 homes from Sefton Metropolitan Borough Council to One Vision Housing.

A trainee in projects and construction will work on a great deal of development agreements and learn about project partnering contracts (PPCs), a concept in construction law pioneered by Trowers partner David Mosey. PPC was described as *"a kind of collegiate, consensus-based"* approach to getting projects done. On major matters *"there is a natural barrier to how much trainees can get involved on projects that go on for two or three years,"* so trainees must seek consolation that they are contributing in their own small way to some pretty important things. Mosey is presently leading a team advising on the $1.5bn Bahrain Bay development, which is the first use of project partnering in the Arabian Gulf. Another important Middle Eastern project is the $1bn expansion of the Mosque of the Prophet in the Holy City of Medina, Saudi Arabia, conducted by the Saudi Binladin Group.

hot, hot, hotter

Seats in the public sector commercial and the public sector housing departments entail *"a lot of legal research,"* if only to keep up to date with missives from the Department for Communities and Local Government. Much of the work relates to the Arms Length Management Organisations (ALMOs) that manage local authorities' housing stock. There are some coco-type activities, such as helping to set up Industrial and Provident Societies (IPSs – *"like charities but with slightly different governance"*), and a variety of tasks connected with Public Private Partnerships (PPPs). On these matters trainees *"organise documents, attend meetings and take minutes."* If you hadn't already noticed, you'll learn a lot of acronyms and abbreviations.

The corporate department is full of *"amiable types"* who are *"not as cut-throat"* as you might find in your typical City firm. UK deals they've picked up include a string of investments for private equity firm GI Partners in the leisure and healthcare sectors, including the acquisition of 290 pubs from Punch Taverns for £571m. The lawyers also work in tandem with the Gulf offices and have had involvement in a number of Middle Eastern telecommunications transactions with a combined value of over $900m. Although there are good experiences to be had in litigation – many of them property cases – trainees can opt to take a litigation course instead of a seat. About half the group does so. Other UK options include employment law, housing projects, banking and finance, tax, trusts and pensions, and London

International, plus a turn in Exeter, which offers free accommodation and a more laid-back environment with good opportunities for client contact. The Manchester office recruits two of its own trainees and offers seats in commercial property, housing, commercial litigation, and projects and construction.

Finally we must tell you about Trowers in the Middle East where, after more than 40 years, it is perfectly placed to handle the wave of projects emerging from the economic development of the region. A seat in the Gulf is virtually guaranteed to all who express an interest, not necessarily at the time they would like (it can reach a scalding 45°C in the summer) but, hey, there's always air con! It can be *"a culture shock"* and *"quite stressful"* when a trainee first arrives, but the expats have a knack of making them feel at home. The various perks include a car, apartment and extra pocket money for the duration. Trainees generally enjoy working closely with colleagues in a smaller office and they get fantastic levels of responsibility. Gulf secondees can expect ten-hour days and a week based on the Arabic lunar calendar rather than our regular Monday to Friday. English is the language of business, although we're sure a little Arabic helps with day-to-day living.

cold, cold, colder

Even if the weather isn't one of them, the larger London HQ has its benefits – more structured training and *"a good library, more HR and marketing people to help back you up."* And, bless them, the people in the central registry where clients' deeds are stored *"really stick their necks out for you."* The only question mark comes over whether secretarial support should be extended beyond 10pm, given the sort of matters now being handled. Trainee lunches every Monday include talks from senior lawyers or trainee presentations. Those working in other UK offices get involved through video link and recorded DVDs

are sent to trainees in the Middle East. Full marks to senior partner Jonathan Adlington who, as a big fan of *"personal interaction,"* has started inviting random groups of staff for lunch to discuss any concerns they might have. At appraisals trainees are given a grade just like at school. A for exceptional, B for good, etc. Some supervisors are totally candid about comments gleaned from around the department, others less so. After each appraisal trainees can have a chat with another partner, *"just to run through their experiences with someone independent."* In the lead up to qualification trainees go through the same rigmarole as external candidates: they must take psychometric and verbal reasoning tests and interview for their preferred job. In 2007, 15 of the 18 qualifiers stayed on at a time when there were double the number of jobs to qualifiers.

The firm's unusual, pink, triangular office building, Sceptre Court, basically forms *"one huge traffic island"* just by Tower Hill. It has an airy atrium and a swish sixth-floor client suite with distracting views. One small complaint concerns the air conditioning in the auditorium where lectures and seminars are held – (*"It's always too cold"*). At least the food in the canteen is hot... and between 8 and 9pm it is free. There is also a free breakfast for early birds. Aside from casual encounters in the canteen, the main opportunity to meet staff – including those from other offices – is at the annual summer party. There are Christmas celebrations too, with these parties organised by individual departments. Spur of the moment socialising takes place in The Minories or The Cheshire Cheese, which is quite a *"blokey"* pub with pool tables and football on the telly. Back in the office a recycling and environmental initiative is sweeping through the firm and plastic and glass rubbish are now split in each of the kitchens. With regard to charitable efforts there is much to say. A trainee sits on the CSR (Corporate Social Responsibility) committee and there are a variety of initiatives dealing with homeless organisation Broadway, advice to the local community through ProHelp and fun stuff such as a pancake race for a Tower Hill charity and dress-down days.

and finally…

The general appeal of Trowers & Hamlins' mid-sized firm culture has always made a stronger impact on students than the specific appeal of its market-leading practices. At a time when the housing and Middle Eastern practices are as healthy as ever, and the firm is thriving in the areas that now appear to connect the two, we sense a new mood of energy and optimism that is, frankly, very enticing.

Veale Wasbrough Lawyers

the facts

Location: Bristol
Number of UK partners/solicitors: 36/50
Total number of trainees: 12
Seats: 4x6 months
Alternative seats: None
Extras: Pro bono – Bristol Law Centre

Situated right in the heart of Bristol, Veale Wasbrough looks to be a perfect choice for those who want to experience quality public and private sector work while also leaving some quality time for themselves.

going public

In a bustling Bristol legal market, VW successfully distinguishes itself from regional competitors thanks to strong public law abilities and particular expertise in the area of education. *"The work that we do in the education field is of the same standard as the London firms, which is really exciting,"* trainees enthused. In fact, many had chosen VW over other Bristol firms precisely for its unique and *"inspiring"* blend of *"broad commercial experience and public sector matters."* The education team alone acts for over 700 independent schools, maintained schools, nurseries, academies, further education colleges and universities, including an Oxbridge college and six academies. Meanwhile, public law practitioners celebrated as the firm secured a coveted position on the 'full commercial' sub-panel of the government's new Catalist super-panel, qualifying it to handle anything from IT/telecoms and property and estates instructions to corporate and finance deals. Public sector clients also feature prominently in VW's real estate work, with recent appointments to act for local authorities on a number of town centre regeneration schemes, including one in High Wycombe. There has additionally been involvement on a multimillion-pound relocation and development project for the Department for Communities and Local Government.

Despite an impressive list of public sector clients, including the Highways Agency and MoD Estates, there is plenty to indicate that a trainee might choose the firm for its private sector commercial expertise. A cluster of big names turns to VW for advice, among them Pricewaterhouse-Coopers, Lloyds TSB, BAE Systems and Esso. Quintain Estates and Development, a FTSE 250-listed company, is currently instructing the firm in connection with the multimillion-pound acquisition and development of a number of student accommodation sites.

Meanwhile, the highly regarded litigation team has been kept busy with a diverse range of work. One ongoing contentious probate case involves a dispute over ownership of a showcase garden belonging to a famous, now-deceased garden designer and Chelsea Flower Show Gold Medallist. VW litigators have also been assisting the chief superintendent of Wiltshire Police on the high-profile Independent Police Complaints Commission's investigation into the death of

Rachael Whitear, the 21-year-old heroin addict whose photograph was used widely in an anti-drugs campaign. This has involved a successful application to overturn the Coroner's open verdict and to request a new inquest.

teacher's pets
Irrespective of the seats they completed, trainees raved about the balance the firm achieves between nurturing them and allowing enough responsibility. Said one: *"I am constantly surprised by how interesting the work is. I had pretty high expectations but I was still expecting to be given more photocopying... I have hardly had any."* Listening, we couldn't help but agree that VW seems to exhibit a good level of trust in its recruits. *"It was scary,"* admitted one source, recalling taking charge of an external presentation, *"but a great thing to do. I was well supported by my supervisor and everyone in my department. They even sat as a mini audience for me to practise on one afternoon."*

The first seat is chosen for trainees, but thereafter the firm does its best to accommodate their preferences and guarantees time in a favoured department at some point during the two years. In fact it seems willing to go out of its way to be accommodating: *"There was one trainee in my year who wanted to do tax, and even though the department doesn't normally take trainees it created a seat for him."* Appraisals take place every three months, at the middle and the end of each seat, and are attended by the head of HR as well as department supervisors. As they are relatively formal meetings, the focus on *"what you have achieved rather than on any negative aspects"* is roundly appreciated.

sitting comfortably
Personal injury is a popular choice for first-seat trainees. This claimant-focused department is located in a separate building close to VW's main premises and is recognised as being a good option for those wishing to gain more client contact. Said one trainee: *"I had more files to look after than in other seats, but I was overseen closely by my supervisor so I never felt unable to ask anything."* And you needn't worry about getting stuck with the least interesting cases: *"I always felt involved like a valued member of the team,"* commented a satisfied source, while another stated that: *"My supervisor was a partner and was working on a number of big-value claims, so I did a lot on those as well."*

Those assigned a seat in commercial property can look forward to a fair amount of responsibility. *"I think that I've been trusted from the beginning,"* said one of our sources; *"I have been helping out on some big deals, but I also have my own files dealing with small commercial leases. Being responsible for my own clients is great."* Ever popular, the employment seat is *"fantastic – I would love to be doing this every day of my career."* Typically the trainee's workload consists of a lot of contentious matters – visiting clients, drafting witness statements and pleadings, going to tribunals and preparing instructions for counsel. They will also get involved in advisory work, including preparing weekly newsletters for clients to update them on current employment law issues.

not wholly lowly
Veale Wasbrough has a reputation for being a very friendly firm, and rightly so according to current trainees. One told us: *"When I started, everyone – even the partners – went out of their way to say hello and to take a personal interest, even though I was only a lowly trainee."* Our interviewees also seemed to like the work ethic of a firm in which *"people are clearly happy and have the time to take pride in their work."*

If you are lucky enough to gain a place on the

VW vacation placement then make sure you smile at the current trainees as they are in the privileged position of being able to recommend particular students to HR. *"We can say who we think it might be worth interviewing after we have met them,"* explained one. Naturally we asked them what kind of candidates impress enough to make it all the way through the selection process? Their answer: *"Everyone seems bright, but the people who do really well are genuinely interested in the law and motivated in their own areas."* Sage sources also observed: *"There are quite a few who enjoy the academic side of the law but are not people's people; the firm doesn't tend to take over-confident or arrogant candidates either... it's a good balance."* The unifying characteristic is *"a down-to-earth feel"* and a good proportion of the trainees come from the South West or have studied for their degree locally. Trainees agree: *"It is fair to say that a connection with the area seems to help."* A word to the wise: many current trainees had attended the firm's vac scheme and considered it *"one of the best ways to demonstrate an interest in the firm."* Apart from anything else, spending time with VW will at the very least make you stand out from *"those candidates who have included the firm as one of 50 applications scattered about the country."*

soul food

Average hours run from 9am until 5.30/6pm and *"you are never forced to stay late – I know our salaries aren't as high as some of the bigger Bristol firms, but I also know that we have much nicer lives,"* commented one contented soul. This leaves plenty of time for socialising, something this lot aren't slow to exploit. A number of first-year trainees are on the Bristol TSG committee, and there is also a firm-wide social committee that organises bowling, cheese and wine tastings and that sort of thing. The committee is also responsible for the summer party, which was held this year at Bristol Zoo. The monkey house and aquariums were opened to staff and there was a disco. Presumably trainees enjoyed a moment of solidarity with the caged chimps. Friday drinks *"somewhere along the waterfront"* are always popular and *"normally elicit a fair crowd."* There are also sports teams to suit every interest and level of competency. These include cricket, netball for both boys and girls, rugby and touch rugby. Despite the terrible weather that dogged the summer of 2007, trainees were enthusiastic participants in a softball tournament. Neither was there any dampening of the spirits when it came to retention as all six 2007 qualifiers stayed on with firm.

and finally...

Veale Wasbrough offers a thorough and supportive training with the possibility of exploring both commercial and public law practice. If the prospect appeals, do what you can to secure a place on the vac scheme.

Vinson & Elkins RLLP

the facts

Location: London
Number of UK partners/solicitors: 8/16
Total number of trainees: 7
Seats: No formalised rotation
Alternative seats: None
Extras: Pro bono – various projects, incl. advice re London bombings

This world-beating international energy powerhouse is looking to match expansion through lateral hires with home-growing its own talent. Offering all the resources, cash and charm of a US firm, there is much to tempt prospective trainees to the V&E way.

power play

V&E was founded in Texas in 1917 to service the emerging oil industry, and the energy market has fuelled its growth ever since. These days it has 12 offices and over 700 lawyers worldwide. It was one of the first US firms to brave a move into London, when it opened an office in 1971, initially to capture work relating to the North Sea oil and gas industry. The London office has grown significantly since the 1970s and now plays an integral role in co-ordinating the firm's operations in Europe, Africa and the Middle East.

Having withstood some hard times following the collapse of its flagship client Enron, the London office has concentrated on building a much broader client base. It now offers wide-ranging corporate, projects and disputes advice to the likes of Shell, BP, Anadarko and BG Group, and a massive transaction for BG recently allowed the London office to showcase its ability. Working in conjunction with V&E's Houston and Washington offices, London lawyers secured a $1.2bn facility covering all aspects of the gas chain from exploration and production to sale in the USA, strengthening Trinidad & Tobago's position as the largest exporter of LNG to the country.

V&E's name carries enormous weight in relation to oil, gas, LNG and petrochemical projects, as well as conventional and renewable electricity projects. Its impressive industry knowledge has allowed it to extend its appeal beyond energy sector clients and led to some high-value corporate and M&A instructions from financial institutions. For example, it recently advised Credit Suisse First Boston and BNP Paribas in relation to a $375m financing for the public takeover of Norwegian company Exploration Resources by a French company.

Overall, the London lawyers are kept busy with project finance, M&A, securities and international dispute resolution/arbitration. In the last two years the office has really put its foot on the gas in all of these disciplines, *"hiring to its strengths"* in order to improve market share. Since 2005 this has meant poaching three partners from Shearman & Sterling to bolster its project finance and capital markets offerings, and hiring from Lovells and Denton Wilde Sapte to add to the M&A and energy teams. The relocation of the firm's global head of international dispute resolution, Jim Loftis, from Houston to London also underscores the strategic importance of London to the firm as a whole.

big bucks

V&E's growth at partner level is mirrored by an increased emphasis on its training scheme, which although still relatively new, has an expected intake of three people per year. Enthusiastic new training partners have implemented *"a more structured regime,"* albeit that this regime shuns the traditional seat system. Instead trainees are located in a two-person office with either a partner or associate (who acts as mentor) and receive work from any of the office's fee earners. Every six months they will switch to a different mentor, but continue working in the same departmentless fashion. This approach was extremely popular with the trainees we spoke to: *"There is variety on a day-to-day basis, so the work never gets dull."* Another benefit is that even on lengthy transactions they *"stay with the deal from birth to death."*

As the majority of transactions and cases have such high value, direct client contact can be limited. Nevertheless it does occur and there is a huge amount of other types of responsibility for those willing to step up to the plate. *"Working in such a small office, there really is no hiding. Everybody is aware of what you are capable of and you are given as much responsibility as you can and want to handle."* For one trainee this manifested itself in a trip to Madrid to represent the firm at a conference, while another was slightly less lucky in being left to co-ordinate London communications while the lead partner was handling a dispute from abroad. *"I was drafting letters, dealing with counsel, conducting interviews, taking witness statements and going to court to file proceedings,"* they told us.

"Pretty much all of the work is international. Even work for domestic clients usually has some cross-jurisdictional element to it." In particular trainees spoke of giving corporate advice to US companies in relation to European law and working in conjunction with V&E's Dubai office on a plethora of M&A and derivatives deals for Middle Eastern clients. International secondments have been mentioned as a possibility, although for now most trainees must make do with the odd business trip. Somewhat unreliable in their frequency and *"differing wildly on the glamour scale,"* these have seen trainees flown out to Paris, Brussels, Madrid, Hong Kong, Norway and Switzerland.

With all this responsibility and international exposure comes the cold hard reality of some pretty testing hours. *"During a bad month you can end up working evenings, nights and weekends,"* said one candid trainee. Another warned: *"You should not go into this with your eyes closed. I am busier than some of my friends at magic circle firms."* On the plus side there is no need to act big and tough about it all and *"provided you work hard when you need to, at quiet times you can even take a few hours off to catch a spot of tennis."* Hard work is also rewarded at the end of every month with a pay cheque fat and juicy enough to rival any of the big boys. First-years currently get £40,000 pa and second-years £42,000. In 2007 the single trainee who qualified chose to stay with the firm to work in corporate finance.

american pie

Having a *"young, down-to-earth"* partnership in London helps to foster a relaxed office environment in which trainees feel comfortable conversing with lawyers at all levels of seniority. This is aided by a smart-casual dress code and a level of familiarity that you just can't get in a big office. Drinks in the bars below the firm's CityPoint address attract all levels of staff, and team-building events such as a yacht race to the Isle of White also help keep a sense of togetherness.

Only four of the fee earners are originally from the USA, but the office still manages to have some American flavour, not least in its super-fancy 33rd floor offices (*"with amazing views over the city"*) and its 4th July lunch. Judging by the musings of one trainee on the customary cuisine of the day, there doesn't appear to be any desperate need to brush up on your knowledge of the American struggle for independence. *"I think we are going to eat some sort of pie or something,"* they told us. One thing that does appear to aid an application is the ability to speak a second (or third) language, or experience of working abroad. *"I think they look favourably on candidates who can offer something additional,"* concluded one source. Current trainees also believe that the energy focus naturally suits the *"scientifically-minded."* No one is going to expect a training contract applicant to be a guru on the energy industry, but think about it, you're going to need to mug up a bit if you want to make an impression here.

and finally...

V&E is a world-leading law firm in the energy sector and, as we all know, energy issues are centre stage these days. In short: big stuff, small office – not a bad combination at all.

Walker Morris

the facts
Location: Leeds
Number of UK partners/solicitors: 52/120
Total number of trainees: 34
Seats: 6x4 months
Alternative seats: Occasional secondments

This solid, independent Leeds outfit is proud of its Yorkshire roots and keen to remain there. Established as one of the big hitters in the region, it is going from strength to strength. Trainees can expect a well-balanced and structured training contract, and what's more they can also expect a job at the end of it.

one-stop shop
Leeds is now recognised as a thriving, vibrant and prosperous city, and this fact has not been ignored by the legal profession. The legal scene in the city is dominated by a set of firms commonly referred to as the Big Six (Walker Morris, Pinsent Masons, Eversheds, Addleshaw Goddard, Hammonds and DLA Piper), but while the other five are national firms with branches strategically placed around the UK, WM boldly remains the only independent outfit of the pack. It may be based in just one city, but it has a client base spanning the country. *"We have a very good reputation in the area, but the majority of the work is from outside,"* claimed one trainee. This assertion is backed up by the firm's many top-tier rankings in our parent publication *Chambers UK*.

The city of Leeds and WM's single-site policy were cited as the two main attractions for prospective trainees. Of the city they said: *"You get good-quality work without the drawbacks of London – there is no trade off."* Of the firm's Leeds-only policy, one said: *"Everyone knows everyone – that's useful for a trainee and good for career progression."* And another stated: *"It's a huge selling*

point; you can impress the people you want to impress."* The praise didn't stop there: *"It's enabled growth and a preferable working environment."* Or there. *"All the people who make the decisions are here; you don't feel like you are getting fobbed off with excuses."* When we questioned whether WM might follow in the footsteps of its rivals, trainees said: *"There is no danger the firm is going to open offices anywhere else, it prides itself on the fact it's one-site."*

If anything WM is looking to expand in Leeds and has resolutely started on this by welcoming six new lawyers into the partnership. This is the largest number of partner promotions it has ever made in one go. The firm is also proud of the fact that it achieved a 100% trainee retention rate in 2007, on which point trainees told us: *"It's brilliant, every single trainee stayed, and stayed in the department they wanted to qualify into."* The firm actually had over 20 positions available to the 15 qualifiers and recruited externally to fill the remaining slots.

talk amongst yourselves
The training scheme operates a six-by-four-month rotation and this is yet another enticement. *"I can't understand why you wouldn't have six seats, it works in favour of the trainees so much as it exposes you to a lot more and helps you progress."* If a trainee particularly likes a seat, they are welcome to return; some love a seat so much that they go back twice, giving them a full year in the department. The six-seat system definitely promotes the 'everybody knows everybody' attitude. As one source amusingly put it: *"You don't have to say, 'You know that guy with the moustache and the limp...'"* It also means *"people are more relaxed about seat choices"* because they know they have more chance of getting their preferences. The firm places everyone in their first three seats, which although it sounds restrictive *"still involves a certain element of listening to your*

views." The norm is *"to get you to experience litigation, property and some sort of corporate seat"* in the first year; second-years are then given their preferred options, as far as is possible. Unusually WM gets them to sort out among themselves who goes where, following a meeting with the grad recruitment partner. *"We try and be courteous to each other... it has worked out really well with no fighting,"* reported a source fresh from the process.

A property seat (which could either be commercial property or planning) sees trainees drafting, researching and answering client queries, as well as *"chasing people for documents."* The department is *"big with very much an atmosphere of people going in, getting their head down and working"* and trainees reported *"lots of responsibility, with a lot of files to run on your own."* Property is a good department to *"learn how to balance your time well."* The team has acted on some substantial deals, including Hull City Council's £235m project to improve local housing and Wakefield MBC's £200m development of the Wakefield Waterfront. Other clients include Netto, Bank of Ireland, Debenhams, Starbucks and Polo Ralph Lauren. Planning seats are *"good fun"* and involve *"a lot of running around and getting out and about."* Research, dealing with expert witnesses and taking notes at hearings with counsel are all typical tasks.

In the corporate seat trainees *"hit the ground running."* The department is *"going from strength to strength,"* which has only one downside – *"being very busy!"* Not that anyone minds *"getting exposure to multimillion-pound deals,"* such as Lancashire County Council's waste disposal PFI, which is the largest of its type in the UK and worth £2bn. One trainee was *"a little apprehensive that everyone would be stressed and unfriendly,"* only to find the team to be *"brilliant – really helpful and down-to-earth."* Trainees busy themselves with completing statutory

books, drafting board minutes and various other small documents, and preparing for completions. Breathe a sigh of relief because *"time spent at the photocopier is minimal."* The hours are naturally longer than in other departments and we did hear of *"a few 3ams."* It would be odd if this weren't the case.

The finance department offers two possible seats: banking and restructuring/insolvency. *"You choose your supervisor and that dictates which area you work in."* In this department trainees are *"the small cog in bigger deals,"* but generally feel comfortable there. *"Often I'd hear abbreviations I didn't have a clue about and I'd just ask,"* said one. As for what kind of tasks they carry out, it's mostly amending agreements, drafting ancillary documents and going to client meetings to take notes. Trainees enjoyed the networking opportunities available in this department, with one telling us that they had *"been along to the cricket, barbecues, theatre and various days in London."*

we come in peace

The sports team is incorporated into insolvency litigation department, which makes sense when you consider that Leeds United FC is a client. The firm has been involved in the restructuring of the club (*"we got to meet Ken Bates!"*) and also helped save Rotherham United from liquidation. If you're worried that having just two clubs on the WM client roster makes it a bit light, take comfort from the fact that the firm also represents Barnsley FC. Insolvency lit trainees are given bankruptcy files to run by themselves and it can be *"a real eye-opener seeing how businesses fail."* Some trainees even get to do their own advocacy. Construction litigation is a great seat for *"getting you used to talking to people."* We listened attentively as recruits told us how much they enjoyed the responsibility of being given some of their own files: *"I got good exposure, even though they keep you on a bit of a leash,"* said one obedient trainee. A spell in property litigation is another interesting way of building up your required contentious hours, and here recruits get to dabble in advocacy. *"You either love it or hate it,"* said one source. A trip down to the Royal Courts of Justice in the capital might even be on agenda. If the idea of spending four months loitering in the tax department sounds like your idea of hell then perhaps the enthusiasm of one of our sources might change your mind. *"It's a really good seat and a small department, which means the work you do is really valuable,"* they said. The work is clearly *"very technical,"* nonetheless, it doesn't take long to see why tax lawyers love their jobs: *"You get a nice sense of satisfaction if you save someone a few million pounds."*

Trainees were convinced that they were placed with supervisors *"with a similar personality"* and praised the training partner for his role in the matchmaking process. Most loved the fact that *"nine times out of ten"* you can expect to *"share an office with your supervisor,"* which means you are always *"in the thick of the action."* Supervisors can either be an associate or a partner, and this means *"partners aren't viewed as unapproachable. You don't think of them as alien beings, they are just the same..."* No comment. An informal approach extends to appraisals: *"You go out for lunch with your supervisor and chat about how the seat has gone... sometimes you just go out for lunch and don't even talk about your appraisal."* If you do something well – or not – then generally *"you'd know about it before the appraisal"* because supervisors *"try to maintain a running dialogue."*

band camp

The location of the offices is a real plus: *"It's so central, near the train station, near the city centre and we are conscious of being accessible to clients."* Due to a shortage of space, the firm now has satellite offices over the road to house the property, property litigation and construction teams. *"They don't want people to be squashed in and are keen to have no more than two people to an office,"* a source explained. Moving to another building has been discussed, but the firm doesn't want to compromise on location and is waiting for *"something to come up in a prime spot."*

"Down-to-earth, wants to be based in Leeds, likes a challenge, sociable and has a good sense of humour." That's the description of the ideal recruit. *"Arrogant, pompous and dull."* Those are the no-no's. Overall, trainees say the atmosphere is *"relaxed but ambitious,"* and while we were expecting to hear those infamous words *"work hard, play hard,"* we must admit we were actually convinced on the matter. *"People take their job seriously and want the firm to do well, but if everything is done at 6pm, you go home."* As for the play-hard bit, like a doting father WM rewards its kids when the hard work has paid off. There have been trips to Amsterdam and Prague (*"we got terribly, terribly drunk"*) and water skiing, Qasar, comedy clubs and summer parties (complete with a WM band doing *"covers of The Darkness as well as some classics"*). The firm provides *"a generous trainee budget"* which pays for various events. The highlight of the past year was a trip to a cottage in the Yorkshire Dales for the whole group. The firm puts on dinners to welcome future trainees, so that by the time they join they will have met each other a few times. Sports are also popular, especially netball, softball and football.

and finally...

"The future is bright," announced one buzzing trainee, and we understand why. The firm now takes on 20 trainees each year, and with healthy profits, a national client base, a full social life and, importantly, excellent retention rates, Walker Morris looks to us to be in riotously good form.

Ward Hadaway

the facts

Location: Newcastle-upon-Tyne
Number of UK partners/solicitors: 57/86
Total number of trainees: 21
Seats: 4x6 months
Alternative seats: None

This progressive young law firm has managed to maintain a buzz through consistent growth since its foundation in 1988. Having bagged a place at the forefront of the Newcastle commercial scene, it has its eye on a bigger slice of the pie.

if ward had its way

WH is rooted deeply in the North East market, where it now nurtures a plump client roster that includes global chemicals manufacturer Huntsman, industrial services contractor Pyeroy and business software supplier Sage (UK). Private sector clients have been the main catalyst for growth, but having raided Eversheds for its former managing partner, property lawyer Chris Hugill, and bagged a number of new NHS trust and local authority panel appointments, the public sector has really proved a lucrative source of business lately.

WH has been at the forefront of the regeneration wave sweeping down the Tyne and out across Newcastle. And it doesn't stop there: over the past year the firm has also received instructions from Durham County Council, Sunderland City Council and Doncaster Council on local regeneration schemes. The firm's rise in the North East has been so rapid that to maintain this momentum it has recognised the need to spill out into other markets. A move south into either Manchester or Leeds could be on the cards.

The WH ethos exudes ambition and confidence, both characteristics that were on clear display during our interviews with its enthusiastic trainees. These attributes aside, *"it is clear that they are not looking for clones. There is a good mix of ages and backgrounds among trainees."* One source added: *"They do not limit themselves to straight-A candidates and anything interesting on your CV can go a long way."* In this vein interviews were said to focus as much on personality as legal experience or academic achievement. It is the personal dimension that trainees believe sets the firm apart from its biggest rival – Dickinson Dees – which they regard as more formal and *"old school"* in its approach. The fact that WH sees itself as the natural rival of the region's long-established market leader is in itself symbolic of its progressive approach. Said one enthusiastic young pup: *"I would rather be number two trying to move up than number one looking down."* The firm will need to harness all of this energy if it is to further close the gap on its local counterpart and muscle in on other markets.

building for the future

The presumption in favour of retention of qualifying trainees is evident in WH's seat system. The fact that everyone is expected to use their fourth seat to return to their favoured department and therefore qualify with a year of relevant experience essentially means they have a choice of three seats, one in each of the firm's powerhouse areas of litigation, property and corporate/commercial. That said, we did hear about new initiatives to speak with trainees regarding their strengths and ambitions in order to *"place people where they want to be rather than where there is a chair that needs filling."*

While the firm's prowess in dispute resolution is second to none in the region, its breadth of practice also translates into a good choice of seats for trainees. One of the most popular is healthcare, an area in which the firm has powered ahead. At the heart of this success has been its reputation for NHS LIFT projects and a recent highlight was the firm's appointment to a four-firm panel to provide legal advice to a consortium of 19 NHS trusts across South Yorkshire. For trainees the workload in a healthcare seat includes plenty of contentious matters – *"preliminary analysis for our NHS trust clientele, frequent attendance at court for hearings and inquests, and visits to hospitals for meetings and interviews with doctors."*

Other areas of activity for WH's litigators include personal injury, professional negligence and employment, and the firm's real estate department also feeds a healthy property litigation department where trainees are exposed most often to lease renewal and adverse possession claims. However it is the transactional real estate group that has really cemented the firm's position in the local business community. It acts for practically all the region's major house builders and has worked on redevelopments such as the Haymarket Metro Station project. This, combined with its thriving public sector arm, has seen the real estate department's turnover almost double over the last four financial years. Trainees felt they had a lot to gain from working in such a climate, although the smaller transactions on which they could take a more prominent role were the most popular. *"From the start they give you a residential file to run yourself and so you are the first port of call for the client,"* said one source. This high level of responsibility is said to continue throughout the seat. *"I did my own exchanges and completions, which I didn't think I would ever do as a trainee."*

duncans and dragons

Across these seats trainees were in agreement on one point: *"They put pressure on you to work hard, but also expect you to do other things. On the whole it is a good work-life balance."* The corporate component of the training is perhaps the exception to this as it offers an inconsistent mix of thumb-twiddling and *"extreme hours."* It is these hours that have gained the department's Keel Row headquarters the affectionate nickname of *"the dark side"* among the *"warm and fuzzy"* property types across the road in the firm's other main office, Sandgate House. But it is not all dark on Keel Row and there was praise for the quality of work that passes through its door. Recent examples include a large transaction for *Dragon's Den* big-shot Duncan Bannatyne, when his health club chain acquired rival Living Well. Corporate seats offer some exciting client schmoozing prospects, with one trainee even trusted to hold his own at wine tasting. Rugby fans will also be glad to hear that the firm's sponsorship of Newcastle Falcons provides opportunities for a touch of corporate hospitality at Kingston Park.

WH is rightly proud of its position as a pillar of the local business community and, as such, is keen for prospective trainees to show some connections to the North East. While some of our sources were card-carrying Geordies, others had worked with more tenuous links to the area. Those less familiar with Newcastle's charms when they first started at the firm were struck by its *"great vibe,"* buzzing music scene, impressive cultural offering… and *"constantly crap weather."* Assuming there are a few dry days, it's easy to escape the buzz of the Quayside and *"within a few minutes' drive you can be out in the countryside, lunching by a lake or on a beach."*

Those who do pass muster at training contract interview are welcomed into a firm that is keen to grow from the bottom up as well as through lateral hires. Knowing that there is a good chance of a job on qualification (seven of the ten 2007 qualifiers stayed on) puts recruits at ease; furthermore, *"the firm encourages you to be yourself and bring your own ideas. Trainees are consulted on most things and you really feel like you have a voice."*

well and truly stuffed

Consecutive editions of the *Student Guide* have reported on the healthy appetites of WH's Quayside trainees. We're pleased to report that nothing's changed. *"Trainee lunches are still big news,"* a source assured us. How amusing then that that this year's firm-wide summer barbecue is so shrouded in controversy. Following a spiralling budget and a serious case of eyes bigger than bellies at last year's three-course silver-platter affair, we learned that the plans for the 2007 bash were far more modest. *"They have hired a chip van to wheel into a field somewhere,"* trainees told us. Classy.

At least the Christmas party is all about glamour. Future trainees are invited along as well, so it came as no surprise when one interviewee told us: *"I have been here nine months and have already been to three Christmas parties."* Mixed tables ensure that staff circulate properly, and the party is generally accepted to be a nice, relaxed affair. A popular addition to the social life of the firm is the programme of departmental day trips to reward hard-working employees. Destinations have included Glasgow, Edinburgh and Dublin, although the prize has to go to the healthcare department which set its sights on Amsterdam. Visiting Europe's naughtiest capital in the company of your boss might seem ill advised; however, reports were resoundingly positive. *"It was really nice to chat to everyone outside of the working environment,"* explained a source.

But for every feast there is a famine, and this year we are sad to have to advise readers that the casualty has been the firm's much celebrated football team. We first caught a sniff of this when one interviewee conceded that *"WH used to run the show, but now a lot of people have moved on from the team."* Extra digging revealed the full extent of the crisis: *"We have lost our first four games and even got hammered 8-0 by KPMG."* On a more positive note, the firm put together a strong contingent for the 3km Sunshine Run across the Quayside, raising money for Marie Curie. Other charitable events have included a series of pub quizzes. Shame about the footie though...

and finally....

If you are interested in a training contract in the North East then Ward Hadaway will undoubtedly be on your shortlist. If you are confident that you can display the necessary energy and enthusiasm, you'd be well advised to join this fast-moving enterprise as it follows through on its goal of geographical expansion.

Warner Goodman LLP

the facts

Location: Southampton, Fareham, Portsmouth
Number of UK partners/solicitors: 17/32
Total number of trainees: 7
Seats: Moving towards 4x6 months
Alternative seats: None

Warner Goodman LLP (Warner, Goodman & Streat as was) has undergone a rather dramatic transformation this year, rebranding itself to coincide with a commercially focused push. It has also improved its training programme to compete with the bigger fish in Hampshire's legal pond. However, the firm doesn't want to move forward at the expense of its 155-year history or its well-established general practice. With offices in Southampton, Fareham and Portsmouth, as well as two smaller outposts in Park Gate and Waterlooville, the firm seems to offer a buffet of choices for aspiring regional solicitors.

where the streats have no name

Warner Goodman has been around since 1852 and is one of the oldest practices on the South

Coast, although you might not guess it from their snazzy new image. In May 2007 the firm dropped the Streat from its name, converted to LLP status and launched a PR campaign to promote its new *"modern and friendly"* self. In one tasty tactic, the firm sent branded chocolates to key local clients in a bid to *"put Warner Goodman's name on their lips."* According to one trainee, the LLP conversion was prompted by the loss of several equity partners, and the partnership is now largely salaried. The newly slimmed-down Warner Goodman hopes its modernised image will help it compete with the likes of South Coast bigwigs Blake Lapthorn Tarlo Lyons and similarly made-over Coffin Mew LLP.

The firm is clearly making strategic efforts to distance itself from the high street in order to keep its collective head above the anticipated Tesco Law floodwaters. Warner Goodman is, of course, not alone in shoring up its practice; all firms with high street elements are wary of the impending onslaught of commoditised legal services. At the time of writing, Warner Goodman's new website was still in its infancy, and we sense that the firm's new strategy to develop its commercial muscle is at a similarly nascent stage. That said, given the confidence of the trainees we spoke to, we suspect Warner Goodman will have the strength to deal with the uncertainties facing the profession.

In relation to some of its more traditional practices – family, crime, residential conveyancing and personal injury – Warner Goodman remains a high street firm at heart. The clients of these departments often arrive off the street or via the *Yellow Pages*, and the firm still takes on some legal aid clients, specifically in family and crime. The private client practice has notably risen above the high street for cater to wealthy local individuals, including some big spenders with estates worth upwards of £2m.

Lest we deceive you into dismissing Warner Goodman Commercial, you should ask the firm about its commercial services, commercial property and employment practices. It didn't want us to mention any clients here, but according to commercial-hungry trainees, the firm wants to expand in specialised areas like IP/IT as well as *"generally try to grow commercially."*

times they are a-changin'

When we spoke with trainees, quite a few aspects of the training programme were altering, largely because of new training partner (and managing partner) Ian Curtis. For one thing, the formerly *"ad hoc"* appraisal system is now more organised and there are reviews every six months. Another major shift is that the old system of three eight-month seats is gradually changing in favour of four six-month seats. One of the benefits of training at a small firm can be the firm's ability to provide a more flexible seat allocation to accommodate trainees' interests, and our sources were quick to praise the firm in this respect. Since the appointment of the new training partner, *"you can request seats and it is more likely you'll be listened to."* Some of our interviewees were able to stay longer in the seats they'd most enjoyed and press the emergency eject button on those they found less appetising. This flexibility may not always be available; for example, *"the first-year trainees are all interested in commercial, so seat allocation could get interesting."* Whatever their duration, seats can be taken in commercial services, commercial property, conveyancing, civil litigation, crime, family, probate, employment and financial services. Commercial property and employment are especially coveted.

up pompey

The spread of Hampshire offices adds further variety to the training experience. Southampton is the hub of Warner Goodman Commercial and offers seats in commercial, family, employment,

PI, commercial property, residential conveyancing and commercial litigation. Portsmouth has seats in crime, conveyancing, family, commercial and commercial property. One enthusiastic trainee praised the Pompey commercial property scene, telling us: *"Portsmouth is an exciting place to be. There are a lot of new developments and regeneration projects, so much of our work deals with that."* Fareham is the administrative hub of the firm and takes one or two trainees for seats in conveyancing, probate, family, financial services and civil litigation for individuals. The satellite office in Park Gate is not long for this world and the conveyancing office in Waterlooville rarely take trainees.

Trainees are usually expected to work in more than one office, although those who can't bear to leave the environs of Southampton have previously succeeded in negotiating a Southampton-only training contract. For those who brave the commute between branches, road rage can rear its ugly head. One gracious yet clearly disgruntled trainee confided: *"The M27 can be a bit of a nightmare – it can take less time to get to Park Gate for 9am than central Southampton* [from the Southampton suburbs]."

As one contented trainee informed us, across the firm *"they give you the level of responsibility you are comfortable with."* So trainees can either *"deal with the incoming post"* or handle their own files, as they like. Without exception trainees seem very happy with their choice of firm, only really griping that the old building in which the Fareham office is housed *"is difficult to find your way around"* and *"our pay could be higher."* Nevertheless, trainees were quick to assure us that they were prepared to forgo a higher salary in favour of *"nice hours and a life outside the office."* All three qualifying trainees were satisfied enough to elect to stay on at the firm in 2007, taking jobs in civil litigation, commercial and family.

ladies who lunch

Southampton is the professional and social hub of the firm and trainees love the office's location. *"It's opposite the court and there are lots of restaurants and bars around for lunch and after work. It's also close enough that you can pop into town for a little shopping."* Even in busy Southampton, *"when you walk through the office at lunchtime, it's completely empty."* Office hours are typically 9am to 5pm, and one trainee classified a rare 5:30pm finish as *"the latest you'd ever stay."* Perhaps they'd not yet experienced a commercial seat as later nights occasionally feature in these departments.

The Southampton Trainee Solicitors Group is good at getting everyone together but, beyond the occasional drink at Bedford Place hotspots like Coco Rio, the social life of the Southampton office is dictated by and changes with each intake. In Portsmouth *"groups of trainees go out for curry nights every few months"* and *"there are lots of social e-mails flying around."* Given that there are only one or two trainees in the Fareham office, it is unsurprising that their social life is rather subdued. We were sad to hear that the previously stellar firm-wide Christmas party has been relegated to the history books. Now each office has its own smaller Christmas party, which seems to lack the pizzazz of a big shindig. At the time of our interviews, the summer party seemed to have been sorely neglected: *"We were meant to be having a summer party with a marquee, but nothing's happened so far. With the rebranding it's been overlooked."* Or maybe it was just the crap weather.

Warner Goodman wants to recruit trainees who want to become a permanent addition to the firm, rather like Ian Curtis, who appears from his bio on the firm's website to have taken devotion a little too far: *"If you snapped me in half you'd read Warner Goodman going through me like a stick of rock,"* he announces. We can happily confirm that prospective trainees need not go to such extremes. Recruits *"all tend to be local"* and apparently it helps if you are a University of Southampton (under)graduate. Trainees are *"outgoing and friendly,"* which they say *"helps us relate to clients."* They assure us they are *"all quite normal"* and claim that a *"down-to-earth"* demeanour will get you further than a flashy CV. In fact several of the latest intake used to work at the firm as paralegals and legal secretaries. We don't know if this is a feminist statement or a fluke, but all except one of the current trainees is female and the firm's website is thronged with female directors and associates. One trainee speculated: *"It's because girls work harder at school and perform better at interview."* They're probably right. In 2007 all four of the firm's qualifiers stayed on.

and finally...

Time will tell whether Warner Goodman can change its high street spots, but at the moment it looks like a solid choice for South Coasters who want a long-term career that affords an admirable mix of work with the chance to have a life outside the office.

Watson Burton LLP

the facts

Location: Leeds, London, Newcastle
Number of UK partners/solicitors: 42/147
Total number of trainees: 18
Seats: 4x6 months
Alternative seats: None

Venerable North East firm Watson Burton hasn't so much re-invigorated itself over the past ten years as injected a shot of adrenaline directly into its perfectly functional heart. Five consecutive years of 20%-plus growth in partner profits (culminating in a 38% improvement in 2006), turnover of £22m and new offices in Leeds and London equate to a hyperactive decade by any standards.

watson burton kinda papal

WB's Newcastle heritage is impeccable, having been founded way back in 1860 by local man Robert Spence Watson. A Quaker, a Liberal, a philanthropist and a lawyer, Watson pioneered the settlement of trade disputes by arbitration, founded what became Newcastle University and was instrumental in the creation of the city's public library. We mention this illustrious figure from times past because it was another strongly defined individual, ex-senior partner Andrew Hoyle, who steered the firm to its recent heady success. Under Hoyle's ambitious reign, WB expanded dramatically via PI work (much of it related to the compensation schemes for miners who had suffered industrial injury and illness), construction and engineering, corporate and private client matters, and the opening of new offices signalled its intention to compete at a national level.

One thing that didn't grow at the same rate was the seven-strong equity partnership group, whose compact size created eye-catching profit figures. Effectively, this meant Hoyle was a Pope-like figure in a select group of cardinals, acting with a single-minded authority and *"quite remote from the lower levels of the firm. We'd hear about him in the local press, but not see much of him at all,"* trainees explained. It also meant he was vulnerable to unrest, which in the best Machiavellian traditions of the Vatican eventually reared its head in mid-2006. Some commentators suggest a coup by the other six equity partners; the firm presents an amicable parting of ways. Either way, Hoyle very suddenly left the firm to be replaced by Rob Langley, the head of the construction group and a Watson Burtonite since 1981. The white smoke signalling Langley's succession was billowing out of the chimney practically before Hoyle had composed an on-message exit statement.

While the convocation was bricked up deciding the firm's fate, many staff and trainees were in the dark. *"At the time no one knew what was going on, there was an awful lot of tittle-tattle,"* they told us. Despite everything, no one had a bad word to say about Hoyle, while but praise for the new senior partner focused on *"moving positively ahead with a much greater focus on downwards communication."* *"Rob e-mails the entire firm,"* we heard, *"he's introduced monthly drinks for everyone."* If Hoyle represented an entrepreneurial authoritarian that took the firm to places it otherwise might not have reached, Langley is a *"dedicated Watson Burton man"* with *"consolidation"* on his mind. As one source observed: *"He's less concerned with being the fastest growing law firm or the profit and loss accounts. He seems to want to improve the stature of the firm, its status as a pillar of the community."* On record as planning to expand the equity partnership and *"let in the light and let talent through,"* Langley has given added incentive to trainees who see their long-term future with the firm.

solid foundations

"Consolidating the development and expansion that has occurred over recent years" is now the strategic aim of the firm. Construction and engineering is very much WB's beating heart, and with the new London office founded on these strengths it represents the firm's strongest national credentials. The team runs a helpline for the National Federation of Builders and four other major building associations. Other work includes substantial PFI, complex build and contractual work for major national developers. Lawyers have recently assisted Silverlink Property Developments on a £250m development in central Newcastle. Construction litigators are retained by multiple national clients and have significant clout in the North East. They acted recently for Scarborough Town Council on a £30m dispute concerning a DEFRA-funded coastal protection scheme. Professional indemnity is another area of

focus: the team has recently won a panel place with large insurer Zurich Professional. The real estate department won City of Sunderland Council and Keswick Pencil Factory as clients in 2006 and counts lenders (Bank of Scotland, Barclays Bank, Co-operative Bank and Lloyds TSB), occupiers (Laura Ashley, Northern Electric, Austin Reed and Country Casuals) and developers (Bellway, Darlington Homes and Northern Land Group) among regular customers.

The firm also enjoys a strong reputation for PI (primarily industrial disease, although it was drawn into the furore over miners' compensation scheme payments and criticised heavily for passing referral fees to claims farmers), private client and family law in Newcastle, while the coco, commercial litigation and insolvency teams are increasingly well regarded. It won one of only five places nationwide on The Co-operative Group and Co-operative Financial Services' commercial legal panel, advised the management team on the £940m Countrywide management buyout, and assisted Canadian surveillance company Extreme CCTV on the acquisition of a UK-based company. The two-year-old Leeds office is *"full service and a mirror image of Newcastle, but on a smaller scale."* Unfortunately it suffered from the departure of well-connected office founder Andrew Gosnay in 2006, but is performing relatively well in a highly competitive market.

In their own words, trainees are now at *"an open and expanding firm that is going places"* and benefit from *"all the advantages of a progressive, larger firm without the downsides of being swamped in a massive organisation."* There are no London seats or trainees, so the Newcastle-based majority either stay put or can opt to take a seat in Leeds if they wish. Seats in Tyneside are perfectly possible for the smaller intake of two in Leeds. In both locations, the firm has recently adopted a classic four by six-month rotation that will expose trainees to the WB holy trinity of *"corporate, com-*

mercial property and litigation," with the addition of the fourth seat being "a hopefully guaranteed free choice." Within each of the three main areas there are options: corporate can mean insolvency, corporate finance, commercial, employment, IP&IT or sports law; litigation comes in insurance, construction, commercial or PI flavours; and property can be either real estate or non-contentious construction. It's unusual but not impossible to take a seat in family or private client.

all trust up

Regarding a sharpened-up appraisal system, trainees said: "People are good at sitting you down day to day and letting you know how you're doing," and more formal end-of-seat appraisals are a welcome development. A new mentoring scheme means that in addition to their supervisors there is a partner in each department assigned to keep an eye on trainees. "The degree of application varies between departments, but they help check that you're going OK and have interesting work," confirmed a source. Generally speaking, trainees reported a good degree of responsibility in a training environment that "puts trust in you and that's great for your confidence." In construction this trust translated into "seeing a breadth of matters and drafting documentation" or "going to a mediation between architects and builders over whether a building had been correctly waterproofed." In corporate, managing "to be involved in all aspects of transactions, form pre-contractual negotiations and working out documents to closing," or even making it "to the RCJ in London on an insolvency case." Real estate offers "assignment to a small team," working on everything from "property aspects of major corporate transactions" and "leases for big companies" to "small-file work slanted towards commercial conveyancing for local businesses." Meanwhile, litigation might involve "some smaller files you run yourself and more mundane work on larger cases." On smaller matters trainees are "expected to draft

particulars of claim, liaise with the clients and the other side on a daily basis."

The seven-floor St James' Gate office is a "very comfortable, state-of-the-art place" replete with "flat screens everywhere, toned-down wood and 360° views of the city from the seventh-floor meeting rooms." Said one design-minded source: "They've struck a good balance between new and old: it's modern glass and chrome without it feeling like a wine bar or like it will date in a year's time." Close proximity to the train station and the centre of town also mean that commuting to work is as easy as "making it to the shops and back during your lunch break." Here, as in Leeds, working hours tend towards "9am to 5.30 or 6pm, but later if you're busy," with a "smart but not buttoned-up dress code if you're in the office." With solicitors "regularly whizzing" between Tyneside and the "fabulous" 1 City Square offices in central Leeds, there's a sense of equality between the two sites. Visitors and permanent resident alike confirmed that "Leeds is becoming more its own independent entity and everyone's working hard to create a sense of community." What's more, both have monumental items of décor: in Newcastle it's the "bizarre, outsized jungle plants in reception" while Leeds boasts a "several-storey high spiralling metal bird sculpture up the side of the building."

That said, Newcastle remains the cultural heart of the firm, if only on the basis of numbers and history. There, a "vibrant" social scene ranges from "lunch and a sly pint on a Friday" to "marketing events like a film screening with clients" to drinks at local bars – The Apartment, Coco's or the Jury's Inn – to an array of sporting activities. An "excellent" Christmas party was held last year at the Marriott Gosforth, which saw everyone (including those from Leeds) gather for "the usual kind of free-drinks, let-your-guard-down affair." Newcastle has a lot to offer residents, and professionally it has a well-developed legal landscape. Our sources were adamant that they had "a dis-

Broaden your horizons

Athens • Bangkok • Hamburg • London • New York • Paris • Rome • Singapore

Many City firms have a string of offices outside the UK. The chances are, as a trainee, you won't be the one to go and work there.

Here at Watson, Farley & Williams we believe in letting you find out how an international firm works by seeing for yourself.

This means that during your training period with us in London, you'll be offered a four month seat in one of our overseas offices.

We look for people who get a buzz out of being part of the commercial world and a valuable member of busy teams specialising in Corporate, Finance, Litigation and Tax.

For more information on vacation placements in 2008 and/or training contracts to commence in 2010, please visit our website at www.wfw.com or email us at graduates@wfw.com

Watson, Farley & Williams
www.wfw.com

tinctly different personality from trainees at the other firms in the city," telling us: *"We're independent and free-thinking,"* *"less aggressively competitive than elsewhere in the region."* We'd add that the majority tend to be either from the north of England, with the firm "[liking] *a local connection,"* be it to Yorkshire or Northumbria. On qualification, retention is generally good and in 2007 seven of the ten qualifiers took jobs with the firm.

and finally...
A Tyne thoroughbred, Watson Burton may have slowed its recent galloping pace, but we suspect it will offer trainees in Newcastle and Leeds an increasingly broad range of options and an increasingly national outlook over the next few years. Why not trot along for a look-see?

Watson, Farley & Williams

the facts
Location: London
Number of UK partners/solicitors: 37/70
Total number of trainees: 23
Seats: 4x6 months
Alternative seats: Overseas seats
Extras: Pro bono – Toynbee Hall Legal Advice Centre; language training

Asset finance, and in particular shipping finance, has always been a major forte at Watson, Farley & Williams. It was formed by ex-Norton Rose finance partners 25 years ago and took no time at all to establish itself as a leading operator in this field. And yet the firm is keen to get across the message that asset finance is *"not by any means the whole story."*

any way the wind blows
With clients such as Citibank, RBS, Bank of New York, ING, Royal Caribbean Cruise Lines and Credit Suisse on the roster, it's hard to ignore shipping finance. But it's also true that WFW is becoming a serious player in the renewable energy sector. *"It sounds good when you are telling your friends, and it's a growth sector so its pretty good they are focusing on it,"* said one trainee. Wind farms are the most common type, but there is also energy being produced through waste, biofuels and biomass. The firm's lawyers recently advised Dexia Bank and Dexia Credit Local on the financing of Belgium's offshore farm, and other projects have seen it working on matters in Italy, Germany, Greece and the UK.

Already a big noise in LNG storage and transportation, WFW is also keen to build up its natural resources practice by creating *"a specialist oil and gas team."* As one trainee put it (excuse the pun): *"It's an area they want to explore a bit further."* Just to emphasise the firm's commitment to this sector, WFW has been in talks with Chadbourne & Park regarding a possible merger between the two firms. If it proceeds it would bolster the firm's energy and projects practice enormously. *"There is an affinity in terms of everything,"* thought one trainee. *"It will complement what we do and it sounds like a perfect jigsaw fit."* Others were slightly more reserved, noting that it is *"quite exciting, but there is a worry that the cultures might clash."* Understandably some people were adopting a *"wait and see"* attitude, as the firm *"has been involved in merger talks several times"* without anything coming to fruition.

feel the spirit
WFW's adoption of a six-seat scheme makes it all the easier for trainees to tick off compulsory seats in the linchpin areas of finance (shipping or pure), corporate and litigation. There is also a guaranteed four-month seat abroad, *"which leaves you with two other choices"* to be taken in *"the more niche areas"* of tax, property, employment or com-

petition. We hear the firm is *"fairly receptive"* to trainees' views on where they want to go.

The work of the finance practice was described as *"the bread and butter of the firm."* Trainees must navigate their way through a seat in shipping finance or pure finance... or both. The asset finance lawyers handle notable deals, many of them financings of aircraft, ships, trains and facilities in the renewable energy sector. Recent deals have included assisting 21 clients in a €1.13bn wind farm portfolio refinancing and advising Air Mauritius on the sale and leaseback of aircraft. Trainees learn how to draft security documents, liaise with clients and insurers, do research and write advice memos. It's a fast-moving department and *"as soon as one transaction is finished you move onto the next."* Trainees didn't shy away from talking about the pressure they felt: *"Working 55-hour weeks, one thing after another, it was really stressful."* The *"remarkably complicated"* pure finance seat teaches trainees how to negotiate loan agreements and even gets them advising clients. In this seat, trainees say it is easy to *"feel the team spirit."*

The workload in the corporate seat is unpredictable: *"The hours started off fine, but for a period of two weeks they were hellish,"* recalled one veteran of the seat. Verification exercises in relation to AIM listings is *"a huge trainee task"* and this involves making sure *"every statement is true and accurate, and requesting all the third-party information."* The task involves *"looking on Google... but mainly checking with clients."* Trainees admitted that sometimes *"the time pressures can be crazy,"* nevertheless there were *"very few all-nighters for trainees"* – *"the firm doesn't put pressure on you to work past your bedtime on a daily basis."* By comparison, commercial litigation was said to be *"very quiet, but exciting and interesting."* If you're really lucky you might spend a few days in court *"watching the barristers go at it;"* more likely the seat will involve bundling, preparing written submissions and research. On the subject of legal research, one trainee was full of woe about being *"plunged into the minutiae trying to find a panacea"* on the basis that it can be *"slightly demoralising because you're never going to find it."*

a pitta the action

The guarantee of a seat abroad in one of WFW's international offices is one of the real attractions of this training contract. The choices are: Paris, Piraeus, Singapore and Bangkok, and at the start of the contract trainees are asked where and when they would like to go. Some will set off as early as their second seat. One trainee who went to Piraeus said it was *"brilliant;"* another *"had the time of* [their] *life."* The seat is *"hard work,"* but the firm *"does look after you"* and you get to stay in a flat that is *"five minutes from the marina."* The Greek office works predominantly on shipping finance, although it is looking to expand its corporate team. Before they go overseas the firm offers trainees Greek language lessons, so *"we could at least understand the alphabet."* French classes are available and we hear there are also Spanish classes, *"even though we don't have a Spanish office."*

Take a seat in Bangkok and you'll be *"treated as a real lawyer;" "the level of work is high and you have to get it right."* Perhaps the stay in a *"five-star hotel, living like a rock star literally two minutes from work,"* will compensate. The Singapore office is welcoming and the work is mainly corporate and finance. Trainees get their own flat and ready access to a *"boozy"* social life with *"about 20 other trainees from different law firms."* One of the benefits of going to an Asian office is the opportunity to do some sightseeing. The trainees we spoke to had between them visited Vietnam, Cambodia, Hong Kong, Australia, Thailand and Malaysia in their spare time. What's more, *"your money goes on forever so you have a fantastic lifestyle."* What with all the luxury living and travelling, it's a wonder anyone comes home.

bloggin' marvellous

Legal blogs are the latest fad and WFW thought it would set a trend and have its very own trainee blog, so first-years were asked to take it in turns to write a short account of their week at work. The blogging world, however, was not impressed and pointed out that WFW's product didn't follow standard blogging format and was merely an exercise in PR. It seems the trainees weren't overly keen on it either: *"We have been burdened with it this whole year – every eight weeks you have to write the same thing."* They could see some benefit to the process and believed *"it's done its job and given potential trainees quite a good idea of the things we do."* They refute claims that any of it was misleading, telling us: *"Where people had it really tough, they have been candid about it."*

Normally trainees are itching to tell us how non-hierarchal and friendly their law firms are, but one trainee – speaking about the solicitors' profession in general – obviously didn't feel this way. *"Don't do law if you want a consistent social life, as a trainee you are bottom-bottom and partners are way up in the clouds."* This doesn't mean that the culture at the firm isn't welcoming. In the past we have always been able to emphasise how contented trainees seem to be here. Almost all our WFW sources felt that way this year, stressing how *"everyone is approachable and you're not lost in this machine."* *"People know who you are,"* one continued; *"they smile at you in the corridors, they get to know you and you can build up relationships quite well."*

Trainees liked the fact that they always got to sit with their supervisor – sometimes a senior assistant, sometimes a partner, for one person the senior partner. If your supervisor is an assistant then quite often they *"claim you as their trainee;"* if it is a partner *"you get work from everyone in the team and, if they are busy it is up to you to go and find work."* Being busy is something trainees must prepare for: *"You do have to give up certain aspects of your life,"* said one rather frank trainee, adding that *"on certain days you won't be in control, but then there is also the adrenaline rush of seeing things happen, things that end up on the news and you think, 'I worked on that.'"*

When we asked what kind of person the firm is looking for, trainees mostly said: *"If you're down-to-earth, you'll get on."* One warned: *"Some supervisors have a rep, so you have to be able to take a bit of grief and not get too stressed and flustered."* On the subject of who wouldn't fit in, they were far more informative. Anyone too arrogant *"will have to adapt quickly or they will get cut down to size pretty sharpish."* And we were told in no uncertain terms: *"If you're rah-rah, cocky or you think you're the dog's danglies, then you will get some harsh lessons pretty quick."* Glad we're all clear on that.

whose round is it?

One thing trainees flagged up was the process of sorting out NQ jobs. We heard that the firm announced the number of jobs available, but then later increased this figure, leading to uncertain times in between: *"It's not been particularly smooth... most of our year were a little bit peeved,"* revealed one source. In the end, eight of the 12 2007 qualifiers stayed on.

A relatively small trainee intake of a dozen per year means the trainee group is pretty cohesive. On the subject of where to go for drinks after work, one cheeky source told us: *"It depends who is paying. If it's the firm or a partner then Corney & Barrow;"* otherwise *"it's the dodgy pub around the corner."* In-house chef Philippe is a much-loved figure at the firm. *"Everybody loves his food,"* although one calorie-conscious recruit warned: *"You'll get fat working here."* To help burn it off *"yachting and golfing days"* are very much on the agenda. Whether you have *"a good handicap or don't know what they are on about,"* people are always *"welcome to have a go."*

and finally…

Watson, Farley & Williams' size has always been one of its key advantages in terms of what it's like to work there. Were a merger to take place with Chadbourne & Park, this would not necessarily mean dramatic change as here in London C&P has only 40 or so lawyers. Given that this is already a very internationally focused training scheme and trainees sound like they are already working hard, one has to wonder how much change there would be at all.

Wedlake Bell

the facts

Location: London
Number of UK partners/solicitors: 41/55
Total number of trainees: 15
Seats: 4x6 seats
Alternative seats: None
Extras: Pro bono – Mary Ward Centre

Looking for somewhere that's not quite City but not exactly West End either? Somewhere to get rounded, commercial experience and private client work? Side by side with the barristers chambers in Georgian Bedford Row is Wedlake Bell, a long-established but decidedly 21st century firm.

right here, right now

It's a shame to ignore nearly 230 years of history, but with so much to say about WB's present success there's little point wasting time on the past. This is a firm with some excellent clients (eg DHL, Henderson Global Investors, Tesco, Victoria & Albert Museum) and some very good

lawyers. Trainees are exposed to both via a no-nonsense scheme in which the identity and order of their seats is made known at the start of the two years. They like the system because *"it allows you to look at your training as a whole, get complementary seats and see where your career is likely to go."* Admittedly there are downsides too: *"If you get all your choices then you are set for the whole two years. If not, you can end up with a year of stuff you aren't interested in."* And if new seats or secondments become available *"everything has to be shifted around and the right people won't always get the new opportunities."* At least it is sometimes possible to switch a seat with someone else should both parties be amenable.

As property and corporate are larger departments, trainees spend time in both. *"Commercial property is the powerhouse of the firm and all the other departments link into it,"* explained a source. Seats can be taken in straight commercial property, property finance, construction or property litigation, and all equate to a hectic six months. *"It's unique as a department in that you get your own matters and a lot of responsibility. You are a proper fee earner."* One trainee who had been slightly overwhelmed at times advised: *"You've got to be super-organised not to flip out because there's so much to do when you're working for people throughout the department."* Without doubt, the favourite client of certain members of the department is Surrey County Cricket Club; however, the importance of various real estate investors and retail sector clients should not be underestimated. Among the firm's hot deals of 2006 was a first-time instruction from property developer Quintain on its £14.3m purchase of a Nottingham student accommodation block, the £21m sale of a retail park in Hertfordshire for Henderson UK Property Fund and Ashtenne Industrial Fund's £41m acquisition of a portfolio of 11 industrial properties from Warner Estate.

does your garden grow?

Over in corporate things have been somewhat sticky. In 2007 WB became embroiled in a High Court gardening leave dispute after Cobbetts swiped two of its four corporate partners to set up a London office. Gardening leave, by the way, is when employees or partners are required to sit at home and wait out their full notice period before starting a new job. In WB's case the matter got more heated than usual. Now the pair have gone, the rest of the department continues to concentrate on its usual small-end mid-market M&A, AIM work and occasional plc clients. Corporate trainees generally work for several people, which means they get a good variety of tasks and witness several different working styles. In theory it's a good idea; in practice *"it can get a bit much"* as sometimes poor communication between lawyers means *"it's left to trainees to say, 'I have a lot on, I can't do this.' Effectively they rely on you to be a little bit assertive and ask for help when you need it."* As for the quality of tasks, one trainee told us: *"The best thing was completing on a transaction that I had seen from start to finish. I drafted all the ancillary documents and company filings and I went to all the meetings and saw how we whittled down an agreement into the final documents."* Concerns about trainees handling too many company secretarial duties have led to the firm *"try to recruit a paralegal to do it."* WB's membership of the Trans European Law Firms Alliance results in *"the occasional referral from abroad,"* but for the most part deals are domestic. Lawyers this year advised Eureka Mining on its £14.2m takeover by Celtic Resources Holdings, and the mining sector has been identified as a target for more clients and deals. Other important sectors are oil and gas, pharmaceuticals and healthcare, sports and gaming, and leisure and hotels.

WB also has a toehold in the world of hedge funds and offshore trusts. Indeed it is the only English law firm to operate from a Guernsey base, and this small office also handles property and private client instructions. Back in London trainees explained that the relatively large private client department undoubtedly helps define the firm: *"We're still known for private client work and the department is very busy at the moment. It acts for a lot of charities and some big, well-known traditional families."* Offshore matters and foreign clients sheltering assets mean trainees get to have a go at *"plenty of trusts work and a bit of probate and will drafting."* Far from private client work diminishing at the expense of commercial work, we heard *"the private client team has doubled since I applied here"* and WB recently joined with nine other firms in subscribing to a special training course in private client law at the College of Law.

shuttling along

Back in the world of commercial clients, contentious experience can be gained in seats including property litigation, business recovery and construction. Property lit is *"consistently busy"* and the construction seat carries the added bonus of becoming the National Specialist Contractors Council helpline for six months, essentially providing free legal advice to the council's members. All trainees in the litigation department take a turn doing 'court runs', ie filing, collecting and issuing papers, plus the odd minor application in front of a master or district judge. *"The firm makes sure every trainee does at least one piece of advocacy – I didn't sleep for a week beforehand,"* recalled one interviewee. Among the more unusual cases recently dealt with by the firm's litigators was the defence of the Badminton World Federation in a membership dispute with the Russian Badminton Federation at the Court of Arbitration for Sport in Lausanne.

Other seats include employment law, pensions (*"extremely technical, a lot of black letter law"*) and intellectual property and commercial (IPCOM). In the latter *"you get IP and IT matters* especially: there can be exciting brand work as well as more mundane things." The firm recently won a mandate to carry out brand protection work for BMW and it is a favourite of Tesco, for whom it won a High Court trade mark and passing-off case in 2006. In Tesco Stores Ltd v Elogicom Ltd & Ors, the defendants had registered 24 domain names incorporating the Tesco trade mark within them. This was not a typical 'cyber squatting' case where the names were being held with the aim of selling them to Tesco, nor were the domain names being used to nab customers for the defendants' own websites. What Elogicom did was to divert visitors to Tesco's own web site via a third party affiliate scheme and then take commission for the traffic it generated.

girls allowed, boy banned

Sources had been "surprised at how little crappy grunt work there is" in a training that is "pretty good because the firm isn't so big that you become lost at the bottom of a team of 50." And because the firm is partner-heavy, "it's fairly easy to see yourself working your way up the ladder." On the hours front, again it's good news. One trainee reported: "The worst I did was midnight, once, and the partner was so apologetic." "Of course it depends on the department," added a realist; "private client has the best work-life balance." Similarly, the social scene, depends on the department, with employment setting a pace that "can sometimes be hard to keep up with." Trainees make the effort to meet up for each other's birthdays and "the phrase 'girls' night out' bounces around on the e-mail all the time." Because there are so few male trainees, boys' nights out are open to "anyone under the age of 40." All staff are invited to quarterly drinks when the senior partner "rallies the troops with a fairly light speech." On occasion people have been known to let their hair down, switch on the telly and dance to MTV. There are quiz nights a couple of times a year and "a new lunchtime event to encourage cross-referring," which works rather like speed-dating. The Old Nick pub is the most common venue for post-work drinks, and in terms of sports the Wedlake Belles netball team has had another great year. We understand, too, that the property department's interest in cricket is as obsessive as ever.

new skool rules

With WB dating back to 1781, it's little wonder there are still a few traditional aspects to the organisation. However, "it is shedding that old-school stuff faster and faster," thought a source. The move from Covent Garden in 2004 and an influx of new people has "diluted" the influence of the "inner core of partners who have been here for god knows how long." There are remnants of "a real matey-ness among certain partners," but trainees freely admit "the amount of socialising has reduced – back in Covent Garden people would be in the pub at 5.30pm on the dot." A "more healthy" approach to socialising is seen as evidence that "we're a little bit more serious now, and that's no bad thing."

Most of our interviewees thought WB's marble-and-glass interior was a decent halfway house between "the scary corporate world" of the "hellish" big firms and the "shabby carpets" and "slightly grubby, nerdy feel of some mid-sized firms, with their shoddy-looking offices and terrible filing systems." The aversion many shared for "those driven, frightening people with streamlined hairstyles you meet at law school" means WB's preference for "people who are socially confident and can be trusted to socialise with the clients" goes down well. Of course, because the firm is "not a massive corporate monster," "you'll never have magic circle facilities" or "cabs home" or "massive deals you see in the FT." The payoff is "a different feeling," "good-quality work with people you know really well" and "a life! People think you're odd if you're still sitting at your desk at 7pm."

In September 2006 three of the six qualifiers stayed on with the firm, two going into private client and one into business recovery.

and finally...
Wedlake Bell's summer vac scheme looks like it is becoming an increasingly important part of the recruitment process. However, you should know that non-law grads must have started their GDL before applying for the scheme.

Weil, Gotshal & Manges LLP

the facts
Location: London
Number of UK partners/solicitors: 22/87
Total number of trainees: 21
Seats: 4x6 months
Alternative seats: None
Extras: Pro bono – various projects eg LawWorks, Battersea Law Centre

The London branch of US firm Weil, Gotshal & Manges (rhymes with the River Ganges) has developed over the last ten years to become the focal point of the firm's European operation and the second-largest office in its 19-office global network.

leader of the pack
Globally, WGM is the name on everyone's lips in restructuring, bankruptcy and insolvency circles. The firm has worked on some of the most infamous matters in recent times (think Enron, WorldCom and Parmalat). The London office, however, is slightly different as it has maintained a definite focus on corporate work, particularly private equity. In this sense, London is at the heart of the firm's plan to *"be the leader in private equity"* at least in Europe. The corporate and private equity lawyers handle big transactions, such as private equity house Terra Firma's £3.2bn bid for the EMI record label and Apax Partners' £130m disposal of The Stationery Office (publishers of The Highway Code and Hansard). WGM represents a number of private equity funds (3i, Lion Capital, Hg Capital, Advent International, AXA Private equity, Providence Equity Partners European Capital) and has also been instructed by the likes of GE, Premier Foods and Getty Images.

In a four-by-six month rotation, trainees must complete a stint in corporate and a contentious seat, although this latter requirement can be satisfied by going on a litigation course at BPP. Although there is *"plenty of opportunity to do other stuff,"* trainees say that in addition to corporate the main teams being pushed are securitisation and the *"young and ambitious"* capital markets team.

The corporate department has gone through a reshuffle in the past couple of years, but is going from strength to strength following the hire of Marco Compagnoni from Lovells in 2006. Corporate trainees get stuck into board minutes and due diligence, also assisting on joint venture agreements and co-ordinating all the local counsel involved on international transactions. Co-ordinating *"the mechanics of closing a deal"* can require them to jet off to different cities. Attending a meeting *"having slept for an hour and half, that's the sexy side to business travel,"* said one. The hours in this seat go up and down – regular midnight finishes when it is busy; out the door at 6.30pm when it's quiet. Most rookies were thrilled to be involved in the department's exciting deals, especially the part when they got to attend *"awesome completion dinners."* Most didn't have a clue about the private equity world when they began their training and often found it daunting to be thrown into unfamiliar territory. *"It all seemed very alien and I wondered how I would get used to it,"* admitted one. While this feeling does pass, trainees suggested that more training sessions on certain aspects of practice would be helpful. *"There is a culture of learning on the job here, but I would include more structured training, timed appropriately to whichever seat you are going into."*

The *"really complex"* securitisations seat offers *"loads of exposure to clients"* and a gazillion conference calls. Common tasks are proof-reading, filing and organising documents, bibling, drafting small documents and making amends to documents... in other words, lots of documents. When a deal nears completion, expect *"late nights and high-pressure days running around."* Although the seat is exhausting, it is *"satisfying to see how far you have come in six months."* The tax seat is quite a contrast as it is *"a mix of the commercial and academic"* and requires trainees to *"go back and find out what the law is."* They admitted it was *"impossible to pick up much"* in just six months, though still saw it as a good option. The other seats on offer include IP/IT, *"a small department where you get odd little bits and pieces;"* property, which is mainly *"corporate support;"* and the *"very international"* capital markets, where *"you are always sent to client meetings."* In a finance seat, you might get the responsibility of *"bringing a deal towards signing"* on your own, but it is also a seat which can leave you feeling *"pretty knackered."* Litigation is a *"fun department because they are all so young"* and it has a *"mixture of traditional High Court litigation and arbitration."* Trainees commented that they spent most of their time working on *"spin-off cases from those our New York Office is running."* The competition team acted for no-frills airline Ryanair in its bust-up with the French government recently. Other available seats are employment and restructuring and then there are the overseas seats – Silicon Valley in California (IP), New York (corporate) and, for French or German speakers, Paris or Frankfurt.

There was mixed feedback on seat allocation this year: some people were fine with everything; others commented on how it could be *"incredibly opaque and sometimes appears arbitrary and last-minute."* The implication was that trainees need to be *"aware of internal politics"* and prepared to *"play the game."*

weiling away the hours

If promises of headline-grabbing corporate deals already have you hooked, then it might be worth knowing WGM doesn't just let anyone in. *"They are quite picky in who they recruit; they don't interview or invite back as many people as larger firms,"* said one source. *"Most trainees here could have gone to several other firms,"* said one recruit, who then informed us that some people had five training contract offers on the table when they accepted WGM. The firm expects its trainees *"to take on responsibility early"* and is keen to recruit *"people who it can throw in at the deep end."* On the subject of responsibility, most trainees indicated they had lapped it up and were keen to prove themselves. *"It's what attracted me to the firm... if you don't like it, don't join, because you are expected to put yourself out there,"* warned one, adding: *"If you are doing well, they aren't going to make you do proof-reading, they will give you good tasks."* Sure, you'll be *"expected to ask questions... but people will want you to give it a go and see if you can do it, and have intuition as to what to do next rather than expect people to tell you how to take things further."* Trainees told us that if things do start to get too tough then they feel comfortable enough *"to say, 'Actually this has gone a bit too far for me.'"* Our sources had good things to say about the *"individual attention"* given to them by supervisors. Trainees always share an office with them and described this set-up as *"100% useful."*

With the hard work and responsibility come long hours. Not all year round; *"it depends what seat you are in,"* but if your team is on a deal then you're going to have to graft just as hard as they do. Trainees warned that it's not a case of *"do you want to stay?"* but rather *"you are expected to. They are grateful, but it's not something you can quibble over."* *"I didn't have any illusions about the hours,"* said one source; *"the hours are poor in any City firm that is doing transactional work. The hours are bad, but the lawyers on the other side are also doing the same hours."*

hide and seek

Recruits told us it was the allure of exciting deals and working opposite magic circle opponents, coupled with the modest trainee intake, which had attracted them to WGM. *"I really like the way there are only a few trainees and I was intrigued by the international aspects,"* explained one, while another noted: *"I wanted to work in a small office, but I wanted to be pushed to develop and to do top-end work."* Trainees felt that by being part of a small group *"you get to know people better, and if people know you and trust you then you're taken more seriously."* The flip side is that this is no place for people who want to hide away behind the photocopier, and if you're not quite up to the job – or you're just not into it – this becomes glaringly obvious. One honest source admitted: *"It's good for me because if I could hide, I would and it has forced me not to."*

It's also worth knowing that WGM places *"a massive emphasis"* on pro bono activities. *"In the litigation department we put together a last-minute injunction application on behalf of the NSPCC to stop a programme going out on ITV. A lot of the highs you get here are through the pro bono work we do."* If all this wasn't enough to tantalise potential applicants, WGM has increased its trainee salary and hiked NQ pay to a whopping £90,000. To put that into context, it is more than NQs earn in the firm's New York base, and significantly more than the magic circle pays in London. *"The increase went down pretty well, particularly because the firm has been doing an incredible amount of business."*

pimms o'clock

The firm looks for *"outgoing and sociable"* recruits who are *"down-to-earth, bright and driven."* Trainees say the informal mood among staff prevents *"the late nights and hectic completions from getting to you,"* adding that the dress code is *"business casual – hardly anyone wears ties."* Trainees appreciated this culture and the fact that *"everyone tends to know each other."* One source made a point of telling us they were perfectly comfortable strolling into the managing partner's office to ask questions. The office was described as *"quite smart, light and bright"* and foodies will be pleased to hear that it is located directly above a large M&S.

Our sources certainly seem to have enjoyed the firm's 'European Retreat', a *"big firm jolly"* which takes place every two years and is designed to *"strengthen links with the other offices"* and be *"good for morale."* Staff from all WGM's European offices attend, and in 2007 the event was held in Lisbon. *"We were in a giant hotel, there were talks on the history of the firm and a treasure hunt through the streets of the city with people in fancy dress giving you clues."* Other events of note in London are the annual black-tie Christmas party and a summer Pimm's and Champagne reception at which everyone *"lets their hair down and mingles."* Throughout the year trainees organise nights out at bars around Moorgate and there are regular events organised by the Women@Weil affinity group.

and finally...

Life at Weil, Gotshal & Manges is no easy ride, but if you are the kind of person who craves responsibility, enjoys the thrill of big corporate deals and is ready to work pretty damn hard, then this is definitely one to consider. Five of the nine 2007 qualifiers clearly thought they'd made the right choice and took up positions with the firm at the end of their contracts.

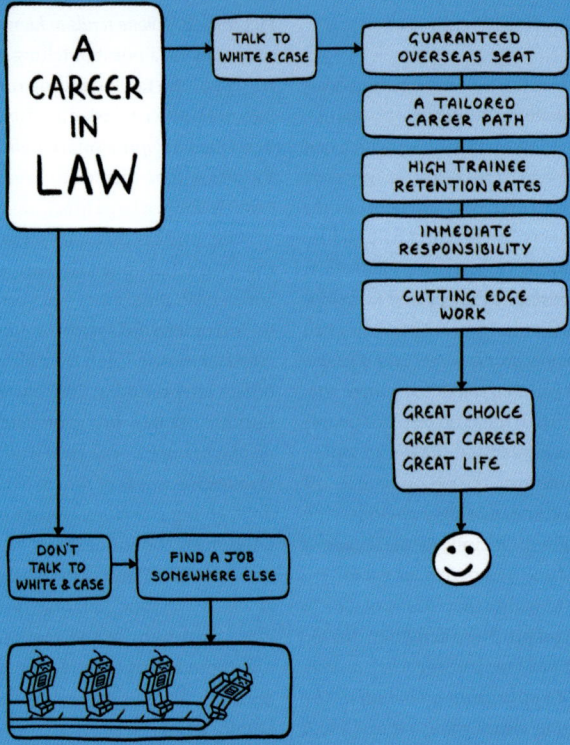

Make the right choice
www.whitecase.com/trainee

WHITE & CASE

White & Case LLP

the facts

Location: London
Number of UK partners/solicitors: 71/239
Total number of trainees: 54
Seats: 4x6 months
Alternative seats: Overseas seats
Extras: Pro bono – Mary Ward Law Centre, RCJ CAB, FRU, LawWorks; language training

In London for more than 35 years, global finance giant White & Case has undergone such rapid expansion that it is now a challenger to the UK's biggest firms.

world domination

Founded in 1901 in New York, White & Case started life as a banking and finance outfit, based on the friendship of one of the era's most influential men – JPMorgan financier Henry P 'Harry' Davison. During WWI, the British and French governments hired White & Case's main client, JPMorgan to purchase arms on their behalf from the United States. The firm acted on most of the armament contracts for the war, and in 1926, on the strength of the relationships it had built in Paris, it opened its first international office there. When the Berlin Wall fell in 1989, White & Case was quick to open offices in Eastern Europe, including Prague, Budapest, Warsaw and Moscow. Work for the Indonesian Republic during its debt crisis helped establish the firm's famous 'sovereign practice', which acts for heads of states and governments. White & Case has advised more countries in sovereign-related projects than any other law firm, particularly in (ex) communist and poorer countries.

Now in its 106th year, this colossus has more than 2,000 lawyers across North America, Europe, Asia and Latin America – there's even an outpost in Africa, which is probably the continent least visited by international law firms.

When the Roman Empire occupied a province, it did so with a canny combination of conquest and collaboration: making deals with local strongmen and adapting its systems – and even religion – to take in local customs. White & Case adopts a similar strategy. Its international offices are built primarily with local lawyers, and the firm is adept both at developing its own talent and poaching star names from other firms. In London White & Case has declared its determination to *"challenge the magic circle head on,"* prompting (yet another) aggressive expansion bid. The office scored eight of the 37 worldwide partner promotions last year and is continually raiding competitors. All told, the firm now has almost three times as many lawyers in London than in 2001 and is the biggest London office of a non-UK firm.

Also growing are the number and size of deals handled by the London lawyers. Fabulously named partner Francis Fitzherbert-Brockholes led the firm's work advising Indian real estate client DLF on its £1.2bn listing on the Indian National Stock Exchange, the biggest IPO ever for an Indian company. And proving it can do quick as well as big, the firm came to the rescue of long-standing client Deutsche Bank when, in just a month, it financed private equity house Novator Partners' £2.2bn buy-out of Icelandic drug company Actavis. The firm topped the tables for European collateralised loans in 2006, advising on more than half of all such deals carried out across the continent, according to Standard & Poor's. White & Case's UK turnover increased by an astonishing 38% in 2006.

As any teenager will tell you, growing up isn't easy. In the last few years White & Case has shaken up its London management several times, culminating in the firm's global chief operating officer, Jim Latchford, flying in during 2005 to head the office's executive committee. Then in January 2007 London COO Chris Schulten upped sticks to the relative calm of regional firm Bond Pearce. We'd like to say the merry-go-round has stopped turning, but given that the firm has just agreed a global governance overhaul and elected its first new global managing partner in eight years, we'll make no promises.

Through it all the focus has remained unchanged. In London the key strength is finance, and this in turn can be broken down into two major categories, the first of which is energy, infrastructure, projects and asset finance (EIPAS), where money is raised for tangible things like ships, LNG storage facilities and building mines. The other category is banking, structured finance and capital markets, where the subject matter is more esoteric. If all this sounds like a snooze then to be honest White & Case is not for you. However, *"if you are interested in finance, this is definitely the place to be."* Away from the finance seats, options include corporate, dispute resolution, employment, IP, tax, construction and real estate. While trainees do get to try out these areas, there's no question that finance is the main focus.

epic deals

EIPAS generates much of the firm's best work. Our parent publication *Chambers UK* ranks the firm in the top tier for energy projects, thanks to deals like the epic Qatargas project, which at $21.3bn is the largest ever energy project financing. The White & Case team has worked on this for several years. It has also advised the world's largest oil company, Saudi Aramco, on the $5.8bn financing of a massive refinery development on the Saudi West Coast. A trip to EIPAS is highly likely. Exactly which of the division's areas you see most of depends on which sub-department you go into and, luckily, most trainees get to state their preference. All the EIPAS seats involve their share

of standard trainee tasks, such as *"co-ordinating conditions precedent, filling in Companies House forms and proof-reading."* Asset finance, which revolves mostly around aeroplanes, includes repeat financings that allow trainees to play a bigger role. And even when there's grunt work to do, at least *"it's tangible – you know what the work's actually about, so it feels more worthwhile."* In projects, matters are so vast, and go on for so long, that responsibility tends to be minimal. *"NQs in projects do the kind of work trainees might do in banking,"* said one source. So what does that leave for trainees? *"I helped out on some documents, looked at some purchase agreements, did some proof-reading,"* said someone who'd visited in their first year. *"I wasn't massively involved."*

The banking and capital markets department has a *"younger, buzzier"* atmosphere, but also *"a scary reputation"* for complex work and long hours. *"I loved it, although it can be a bit daunting,"* admitted one source. *"You'll start off just proof-reading,"* then once you're settled in supervisors *"encourage trainees to carry out small matters independently."* In banking, for example, you could be responsible for *"documenting small Kazakh loan facilities."* Both banking and structured finance seats involve contact with major banks. *"You'll have e-mail and phone contact regularly, discussing their needs and making comments on documents,"* noted one veteran. *"It's nerve-wracking, but by the end you'll feel very confident."* Second-years reported being allowed to manage simple financings worth millions of dollars. Capital markets seats mean drafting aspects of prospectuses and *"a lot of liaising with the UK listing authority."* *"You're quite responsible,"* noted one trainee; *"there are a lot of hoops you've got to leap through for everything to go to plan."* The quality of work is helped by *"recently recruited paralegals who take care of the bibling, form-filling and so on."* As trainees were quick to point out, there are some serious hours to contend with and, for one, "*leaving between 9pm and 10pm was pretty much standard.*" Another said: "*I guess if you come in on Wednesday morning and finish at 10pm on Friday, you are working pretty hard.*" As a rule the longest hours arise towards the end of deals and when they do finally complete, there is "*a real sense of achievement that makes it all worthwhile.*"

growing pains

In the other departments the firm doesn't quite match up to the American-firm stereotype of long hours and no sleep. Most sources spoke of average hours of 9.30am to 8pm, although in a few cases we got the impression that trainees' schedules weren't monitored within their department as carefully as they might be. "*I got inundated until I asked my supervisor to manage my workload,*" said one. Another noted how "*when my billable hours topped 90 in a week, the training principal called up and got it stopped.*" So are supervisors too busy to look out for their trainees? "*Some take a real interest in you and some don't,*" one source said matter-of-factly. "*You know who you can go to for advice, and it isn't always your supervisor,*" said another. Trainees had no illusions as to their place in the firm's operations. "*If someone asks you to do something you can't say no – you're a trainee!*" "*In terms of what you do, it's about business needs more than the needs of your training.*" "*You take what you're given. They try to build up the responsibility, but it isn't always possible.*" Appraisals are often late, "*although the firm is tightening up on this.*" All in all we suspect the recent rapid growth of the training programme (16 trainees in 2001, 54 in 2007), and the fact that everyone at the firm is so busy, has caused a dip in the previously high levels of attention given to trainees by supervisors. At least there was praise for the system of weekly reports to tell partners about trainees' work mix. Also, our interviewees confirmed that when problems were raised they could expect them to be dealt with. "*HR is really helpful,*" one reported, although "*they seem swamped at times.*"

The firm has long expressed its commitment to learning on the job. This approach got a mixed reception from our interviewees: "*You do feel you're scrabbling in the dark at times,*" said one, "*but it means your confidence really builds.*" It is good news then that more formal training is being introduced, including induction sessions for all seats and many more invitations to training sessions targeted at associates.

living on a prayer

"*American firms have a reputation for being meritocratic and informal, and it's certainly the case here,*" said one source. "*It's not hierarchical – partners and secretaries will chat or have a drink at a social together.*" Another added that "*because it's grown fast, it's got the feel of a young office.*" The dress code is business casual, which means "*you're not really supposed to wear jeans, but if you do no one actually minds.*" A few sources suggested that the corporate department was "*a bit more formal,*" with "*a couple of bad apples who don't really acknowledge trainees,*" however these people are the exception. The social scene tends to be departmental rather than trainee-centred. Team ski trips are common in the winter and so, "*depending on the timing of your seats, you could even have two in one year.*" Banking seats have the added dimension of "*a lot of client socialising.*" Monthly office drinks and summer and winter parties bring the whole firm together, and there's a trainee Christmas party organised by HR.

In such a global firm it would be unusual to spend the whole of your training contract in London. Everyone takes a foreign seat, usually in the six months before qualification. Destinations range from Stockholm to Johannesburg and Asian seats tend to attract most competition. The small Tokyo office offers one of the newer secondments and it has something of a split culture: *"The Japanese lawyers work very, very hard,"* while the visiting trainees are *"less pressured than in London."* There's a mixture of work (*"banking one day and due diligence on a corporate matter the next"*) and after hours there are *"trainees from other UK firms to drink sake and sing karaoke with." "Bon Jovi is quite a common choice..."*

and finally...

White & Case offers the chance to work all over the world on some of the most complex finance work around. The price is long hours, some monotonous tasks for trainees and a fair amount of pressure after qualification. Compensation is to be found in a non-stuffy working environment where people are paid handsomely, and certainly above top UK-firm levels. In 2007, 12 of the 13 qualifiers stayed on, most going into finance jobs.

Wiggin LLP

the facts

Location: Cheltenham, London
Number of UK partners/solicitors: 14/23
Total number of trainees: 7
Seats: 4x6 months
Alternative seats: Secondments

Wiggin LLP is a market-leading *"purist media boutique"* offering a small handful of pretty unique training contracts each year. If you're feeling lucky, read on...

a timer to kill

Wiggin works in an industry where image is everything and it has certainly proved its ability to manage its own. You need look no further than its website to understand what we mean. The homepage instructs you to *"Think Media – Think Brighter – Think Wiggin"* as four timers mani-

cally count random sequences and distract you from images of a satellite, a sound mixer and a High Street Honey. Try clicking on the corporate movie for some tech-trance sounds and yet more manic timers. It is a gear crunching sports car of a website that makes quite a contrast to the understated cool of Wiggin's Cheltenham office. Cheltenham? It's fair enough that you're scratching your head – arguably there isn't a firm in the country better suited to a WC2 postcode. The fact that Wiggin has chosen to base itself in the Cotswolds says nothing at all about its work and everything about the partners and the personal lives they want to lead.

too rude

Little probing is needed to discover the firm's achievements. In June 2007 it scored brownie points with prized record industry client the British Phonographic Industry in winning it £41m damages from parallel importers CD WOW! The finding that the latter had breached UK copyright laws despite being based in Hong Kong has been hailed as a crucial victory for the British music industry. It has also been defending *Grazia* (through Emap) in proceedings brought by Kate Winslet. Anyone who keeps tabs on the weighty issue of celebrity dress sizes will know what we are talking about here, although for fear of having to call upon Wiggin's services ourselves, we'll hold back on the details. In another matter, the lawyers have been in the Court of Appeal for client Flextech, which owns the Living TV cable channel, to defend its decision to refuse to pay Universal for certain episodes of *The Jerry Springer Show* that it deems too indecent for television.

Such headline-hogging cases lead many hundreds of prospective trainees to fire off applications every year. Those lucky enough to be accepted are never disappointed at what lies behind the headlines: *"I have had exposure to* major record labels, terrestrial TV channels, publishing houses... You just wouldn't get that in any other place. When you read who we have on our books its incredible." Having contracted the infectious enthusiasm of the trainees, we resolved to do just this and came across Al Jazeera, BBC Films, BT, Channel 4, Condé Nast, EMI Records, Five, HBO, Hutchison 3G, ITV, Littlewoods, Manchester United, Miramax, Napster, Paramount Pictures, Playboy, Racing UK, Setanta, Time Warner Books, Twentieth Century Fox Film Corporation and Warner Bros. And, yes, we could go on...

porn, gambling and freebies

Trainees follow a standard four-seat rotation and get the chance to discuss their preferences with the training partner. "Media work is pervasive through every department, so where you sit doesn't really make a difference." The firm's 14 partners lead headline transactions and cases in every aspect of the media industry, and trainees are at their side every step of the way. Working for household-name clients provides "huge insight" into the industry. The hottest areas are online gaming and changes to digital transmission, although one trainee summed it up slightly differently: "Basically I've spent six months working on porn and gambling, which is quite... unique." The film team recently assisted on The Last King of Scotland, just one of many blockbusters it can claim to have had a hand in. On the cinematic adaptations of The History Boys and Venus, partners Charles Moore and Miles Ketley acted as lawyers and executive producers. They both have previous experience of working in Hollywood and have been instrumental in securing numerous transatlantic instructions for the firm.

Wiggin's contentious practice covers disputes in the publishing broadcasting and music industries. In publishing it has helped Orion to defend claims made by former Metropolitan Police Officer Michael Charman in the book Bent Coppers and undertaken pre-publication advice for a whole host of glossies and lads' mags. It has also been heavily involved in dispute avoidance in relation to phone competitions, following the large penalties imposed on the company behind Richard & Judy's premium-rate telephone quiz. "You are dealing with such big and demanding clients that they expect to be dealing with partners," explained a source. "You learn loads from sitting with them and watching, then speaking with them about how they handle things." For the musically minded, there is an opportunity to go on secondment at the BPI, where the lucky secondee will "work as a genuine in-house lawyer for record labels. It is the best exposure to the music industry you could possibly have." And it also comes with perks such as freebies to the Brit Awards. The arrival of lawyer Michael Brader from Olswang has also propelled the firm into the spotlight in sports law, where until now it has been best known for broadcasting-related issues for clients such as ntl/Virgin Media and Setanta.

Small property and corporate departments exist to service the needs of the media clientele, and they afford trainees a more front-line role. Recent corporate highlights include acting for Shine, the independent production company owned by Elisabeth Murdoch (daughter of Rupert), on its £35m acquisition of Kudos Film & Television. In this small firm trainees are an important resource on large transactions and so are given high levels of responsibility. One trainee recalled that "straight out of law school my first deal was a £170m sale of a client and we had one partner, one associate and me on the deal. The other side had 30-odd lawyers." There are minimal menial tasks to get through, as administrative chores such as bundling and photocopying are outsourced to a separate company "down in the dungeons of the building." The only drawback is that hours can be long by regional firm standards. Hardly surprising when you consider that Wiggin isn't doing regional work and doesn't offer a regional salary. *"We haven't got where we are without working hard,"* chirped a source.

swiggin'

"Slap-bang in the middle of town," the office is all Regency charm on the outside and modernity on the inside. A casual dress code allows staff a degree of self-expression, and one interviewee chose to exercise this with the slightly odd combo of flip-flops, shorts and a cheeky pair of under-the-desk slippers *"to slip on at any point I fancy."* When travelling to the capital lawyers are suited and booted as the London facility is the face of the firm. It has been decorated to exude a 'meeja' vibe, which unfortunately means *"a horrendous colour scheme"* guaranteed to exacerbate any hangover. The positives are 360°ʃ views of London, trendy Charlotte Street bars and restaurants for lunch, and a Nintendo Wii console *"just for messing around on."*

The firm draws trainees from far and wide (pretty much anywhere except Cheltenham we reckon). *"Some people have come from Oxbridge and posh private schools; others have grown up in rough areas and went to comprehensives,"* explained a source. They are *"thrown together in the first week by a common help-me, be-my-friend kind of desperation,"* which quickly gives way to genuine bonds as trainees find themselves *"living in each other's pockets."* They also soon develop a real love of the relaxed, five-minute-walk-home lifestyle of Cheltenham. *"It is a really good place to be based as it's small enough to get to know, but not so small that it has an isolated country feel."* Friends from elsewhere in the country are usually only too keen to spend their weekends catching up in the Cotswolds: *"My friends in London law firms beg me to put them up. I am pretty much booked for the whole year,"* chuckled a source.

There are ample opportunities to spend time in the capital as trainees make frequent trips to the firm's office facility in London. The 100-mile journey is *"dead easy"* if you can hitch a lift with one of the partners' fleet of dedicated drivers, although the train offers the opportunity to catch up on a bit of kip. Depending on the seat, *"at times you can be there for a whole week or more."* In such instances the chauffeurs are swapped for a five-star hotel and *"the opportunity to catch up with your friends mid-week."* Most trainees also use London trips to get their quota of buzzy nightlife as Cheltenham is not known for its trendy clubs and restaurants. *"If you are into clubbing this is not your place... unless you like cheesy clubs full of rugby players."* This doesn't stop trainees from making the best of what's around; indeed, the firm matches its strong work ethic with *"a reputation for partying hard."*

Friday evenings are the main showcase in this respect. A drinks trolley kicks off proceedings and *"this invariably leads to a decent crowd – already half cut – heading on to town."* *"There is a young partnership and lots of them act like trainees anyway so there is no problem sitting with them and catching some banter."* A successful night may end up in *"a dirty, dodgy little club"* called Subtone, which was loved and hated in equal amounts by our sources. A biannual solicitors' dinner is the peak of the social calendar for many: *"It's absolute carnage: last time we resorted to uni-style drinking games and there weren't too many pretty faces in the office the next day."* We hear these events have been so raucous that the firm has been banned from certain places in town. Trainees were hazy in their recollections of the summer and Christmas parties, but were confident that they had been a lot of fun. Unsurprisingly Wiggin isn't the most comfortable home for *"the meek and mild,"* but for any media-focused applicants willing to throw themselves into the mixer this is a brilliant option. *"The education you get as to the world of media law is second to none. I can't speak highly enough of it,"* concluded one trainee. It was a shame then that none of the three 2007 qualifiers ultimately stayed with the firm.

and finally...
Bringing the cool back into the law, Wiggin trainees get to spend the day working with an amazing media clientele then stroll home to a spacious Georgian house within minutes of the Cotswold countryside. Unfortunately this unique formula has mass appeal, so there is no chance of walking into a traineeship without a great CV and a high-quality application.

Wilsons

the facts
Location: Salisbury
Number of UK partners/solicitors: 30/80
Total number of trainees: 8
Seats: 4x6 months
Alternative seats: Secondments

Wilsons is a one-stop shop for private clients, trusts and charities. This Wiltshire gem is a top choice for anyone drawn to these types of client and hoping to live in the Southern Counties.

as old as the hills
One of the dangers of the Internet is that it's so easy to get sidetracked. When doing our homework on Wilsons we discovered a curious fact about the location of its offices: they are clustered over a ley line that connects Stonehenge, Old Sarum, Salisbury Cathedral and Clearbury Ring. Obviously we're sceptics, but this curious piece of information does lead rather neatly to the fact that Wilsons is a really ancient law firm. As its website proudly states: "We have been based in the cathedral city of Salisbury since our founda-

tion 275 years ago." If you think that's old then you should check out the vintage of some of the clients – some come from families that date back to the Domesday Book.

National renown is a relatively new phenomenon for Wilsons. It was only in the 1970s when a London lawyer called Anthony Edwards arrived from Farrer & Co that things started to hot up. Edwards stayed for 22 years, working his connections and developing a top-notch client base of wealthy individuals, trusts, landed estates and charities. Throughout the 1990s the firm went on to hire lawyers from crack London firms, most notably the private client team of McKenna & Co (now CMS Cameron McKenna) and a group from Fladgate Fielder. This was made possible because of the trend for big City firms to axe their private client departments on the basis that they made less money than commercial departments. The exodus of lawyers was matched by an exodus of clients and Wilsons grew fat and happy. The firm now also appeals to individuals who are creating wealth rather than just preserving it. A burgeoning overseas and offshore clientele (from over 45 jurisdictions worldwide) and a substantial stream of referrals from leading City law firms, banks and accountants has made the firm a national leader.

knowing me, knowing you
When we rang in early 2007 the firm had been able to indulge the seat requests of all six trainees. *"You have to do a contentious seat and they strongly recommend you to do a property option;"* beyond these it's a case of state your other two choices before starting.

In probate the focus is mainly on wealthier clients whose assets exceed the £300,000 taxable threshold. Trainees assist on files for really wealthy people and are also *"happy to draft wills for little old ladies"* with less money at stake. There's a certain knack to dealing with private clients: *"You need an extra level of knowledge in the sense that you have to get to know the individual well and learn about their family circumstances."* In a rash moment we asked one trainee if they'd come across clients like the F***ing Fulfords. *"No one's been that rude to me!"* they replied. Wilsons acts for countless farmers and over 65 landed estates across the UK – that's a lot of fields. In almost all cases *"the clients are interested in securing land and wealth for future generations,"* and for a trainee this often means sifting through boxes of dusty property deeds, *"piecing together title"* and making applications for first registration. Sometimes it's important to visit an estate because *"if you're buying house with land then you really need to walk the boundaries."* Keep wellies in the office.

cream of the crop

The upscale family department could keep Jilly Cooper in material for the rest of her career. On Wilsons' client roster are an international dressage champion, a Formula One driver, a judge and some QCs, an author, a boat builder, the owner of a game park in Africa, City directors and their wives, diplomats, and more retired generals and colonels than you can shake a swagger stick at. The small team has become so adept at dealing with divorce among wealthy farmers and landowners that they have been asked to appear on Radio 4's *Farming Today* programme. *"The clients can be bitter and advise you never to get married,"* warned one trainee. *"Their stories can be quite horrible and you sometimes deal with quite upsetting situations. You definitely have to be quite compassionate in the way you speak to clients."* As for needing an affinity for people of wealth and/or stature, *"it wasn't too bad stepping into that kind of world,"* a source confided. *"I didn't feel out of place and no one treated me like I was. Admittedly at times I thought, 'You have money to share, so why argue about something relatively small like school fees?'"* Interestingly, *"school fees were a big priority for most of the clients."*

The charities department is *"really expanding at the moment"* and was listed as the fourth biggest practice in the UK by the *RCM Top 3000 Charities* directory in 2006. It acts for independent schools as well as well-known organisations like the Royal National Lifeboat Institution, Age Concern, Barnardo's, Greenpeace and The National Trust. Charities law can be commercial, constitutional or contentious. *"Litigation in relation to will disputes involves some very interesting cases because charities are in an impossible situation. Legally they are obliged to realise a gift left to them in a will and yet there can be a difficulty in balancing bad publicity with gaining revenue."* Imagine a situation where someone has rewritten their will leaving everything to a charity just days before death. A relative who would otherwise have benefited is going to feel aggrieved and will sometimes sue.

get off one's land

The litigation seat *"covers quite a few things because you shadow your supervising partner and working for other people in the department."* Property and probate disputes are the most common. In one recent example the firm was victorious in the High Court for the claimants in a right of way dispute between neighbours. The court even took the unusual step of awarding aggravated damages. The luckiest trainees get to see the whole litigation process, including a trial. *"You see all the work you put in to preparing a case and then you see it presented by a barrister."* For the more mundane, administrative tasks there is *"an assistant who does a lot of the photocopying and puts bundles together."* As for advocacy, *"you might get to do something in family, but in this seat there aren't so many small applications."*

"The hours are really reasonable: 9am to 5.30pm, occasionally later and if you are in London you might be late back." *"I have never been so swamped that I've become stressed,"* confirmed

one, *"and if I've not had enough then I've just gone and asked."* Trainees are supervised by partners in all seats and report favourably on the nature of their work. One question to consider is whether you'll get exposure to commercial clients if you train at this firm. Clearly trusts, estates, charities and private clients far outnumber commercial clients, but there are some decent names kicking around, among them property agents Savills, academic bookshop Blackwell and a long-standing client called TurfTrax which provides real-time horseracing data on Channel 4 and the Internet.

breaking the law

Wilsons has four offices *"not quite in the centre of Salisbury,"* which itself is described as *"a pretty, Medieval market town"* with high house prices. A single building would be better, but viable options are almost non-existent. *"We were courted by a business park in Amesbury. They wanted us to move there and be the flagship tenant."* However, none of our interviewees had an appetite for out-of-town working, not least because they'd visited the Fareham office of Blake Lapthorne Tarlo Lyons, one of the Law South group firms with which they share training sessions. Trainees distinguished Blakes' and Wilsons' training schemes by telling us: *"Blakes has more specialised seats, they keep training broader here."* Trainees also liked the fact that *"everyone works in Salisbury and there are no branches. That means you know everyone and it's easy to talk to people in other departments."*

To keep people mixing, on the last Friday in every month there are happy hour drinks in the chill out area of one office building. Some people go on to the pub afterwards, usually The Boathouse. *"No expense is spared"* at the annual black-tie summer party and the year before last, after bankrupting themselves at the casino tables, partygoers danced to Wilsons' home-grown band, The Lawbreakers. At other times of the year trainees are taken to client events to *"be ambassadors for the firm."*

Of the firm's character one trainee said: *"I have never thought of it as a stuffy place, although I have heard people from outside say that. To me it feels modern in its approach to people and to employment issues such as flexible and part-time working and I think it is always looking at ways to become more modern."* Another source saw it slightly differently: *"It is still a traditional firm... but there is a new band of solicitors coming through."* Wilsons is deemed broadminded in its choice of trainees: *"Some are more outgoing, others are quieter, more technical, detailed people."* Either way, trainees believe that *"you don't have to force yourself to the front all the time. There's no competition between us."* NQ retention is usually high. In 2007 all three qualifiers stayed on, as did their predecessors the year before.

and finally...

The decision to pick Wilsons ought to be easy. Either you'll identify with the trainee who told us: *"I knew from an early stage that I wanted to focus on private clients and charities,"* or you'll have grown up in or around Salisbury. It won't suit those who want *"big-shot London deals,"* but no one can accuse the firm of overstating the calibre of work in its high-flying areas.

Withers LLP

the facts

Location: London
Number of UK partners/solicitors: 66/111
Total number of trainees: 32
Seats: 4x6 months
Alternative seats: Overseas seats, secondments
Extras: Language training

Whether it's high-profile divorces, retrieving a stolen painting while working in the art and cultural assets group or helping a new company list

Withers LLP (continued)

on AIM during a corporate seat, there's bound to be something that floats your boat at Withers.

abroad success

Since the firm was founded in London in 1890 there have been some big changes. Its merger in 2002 with US firm Bergman, Horowitz & Reynolds – similarly strong in private client matters – was both a turning point and a clear signal to anyone who still viewed Withers simply as a tweedy old firm servicing tweedy old clients. Offices in Milan, Geneva, New York, New Haven and Greenwich (Connecticut) make it an international player with a seriously sophisticated clientele. Yes, Withers became established primarily through its wealth planning and matrimonial advice, but these days its commercial teams are evolving to meet the needs of its fabulously wealthy clientele and a variety of companies, both quoted and unquoted. For example, lawyers recently advised on a cross-border tax structure for a £3bn US/UK hedge fund, and Premier League and First Division football clubs have sought advice on investments and the structuring of disposals involving the use of offshore trusts and loan notes. Well-known commercial clients include Ferrari, Virgin Mobile, Max Mara, Stella McCartney, Renault Formula 1 and Carphone Warehouse. *"John J Withers would in some ways be turning in his grave and in others he would be smiling – he would not recognise the place,"* pronounced a source.

Withers is definitely more dynamic than its heritage would imply. Behind the office's Georgian façade lies a sparkling glass atrium and a management that is fully aware of all the commercial imperatives. Even trainees were up to speed, saying: *"Law firms can't afford to be complacent and take their position for granted."* Withers has a lot to protect: it earns top rankings from *Chambers UK* in respect to trusts and personal tax, matrimonial finance and private children work, charities, and agriculture and rural affairs. *"For*

providing services for individuals from the moment they are born until the moment they expire we're the best firm in the City, if not the country, if not the world," bragged one proud trainee. Working with some of the best lawyers in these fields piles on the pressure for trainees. Said one: *"I felt like I was on a hot date with a beautiful woman and I didn't want to f**k it up."*

Seat allocation usually works out well. The wealth planning seat can occasionally be wriggled out of and, while family is always very popular, there's an acceptance that there is never likely to be more than one qualification job with the team each year. Seats are also available in real estate (which includes landlord and tenant, commercial and residential), litigation (including commercial, property, employment and contentious trusts options), corporate, IP, charities and something called 'estates, succession and trusts'.

that's my money!

The renowned private client department acts for trust companies, charities and private and investment banks such as Barclays Private Bank and HSBC Private Bank, in addition to jet-setting individuals with money to spend and taxes to avoid. Working with the largest private client team in the world will mean exposure to international tax planning and asset structuring for families across the globe. Clients range from sports and media personalities to major international figures. More than 15% of the *Sunday Times*' Rich List are represented, as are 10% of the 50 wealthiest families in Europe. Trainees described the work as *"quite mathematical, technical and particular – it's either your bag or it isn't."* Typically they draft wills, trusts and accompanying documents and carry out research into tax or other specific points of law, commonly gaining the most client involvement when working on probate and succession issues. For some the highlight was working with the *"incredibly dynamic and intelligent"* litigation team, speaking directly to clients and being given quality tasks from the outset. *"I felt as though they were my clients too,"* said one trainee. As well as providing inspiration for the rest of the team, the partners put in the longest hours: *"You could walk in at 7am and find Paul Hewitt working and you could leave at 1am and find Dawn Goodman working. You're never there alone."* The cases usually relate to disputed wills (testamentary capacity and claims of undue influence) after wealthy individuals have left money to charities rather than their dearly beloveds. When representing a charity most dealings are conducted via written correspondence to keep costs down and so trainees get plenty of drafting experience. Usually cases settle, but there is still *"a certain amount of paperwork and bundling"* which can be a drag unfortunately. Clients include major UK charities such as The British Red Cross, Cancer Research UK, Macmillan Cancer Relief and RSPB.

simply the best

Describing the family law team, one source declared: *"These people are the crème de la crème of the family law world."* Withers acts for *"some seriously rich people and some famous people too – the one defining factor they have in common is wealth."* The work is less harrowing than you might expect as, financially, *"you kind of feel there is enough to go round; no one is going to be left on the breadline."* With children caught up in many divorces, emotions can still run high. Typically trainees find it is harder to build a rapport with clients as *"situations are that much more stressful and people are not perhaps at their best."* Being non-judgemental is essential and *"you very quickly see that there is another side to every story."* Family is more pressured than other departments, and because divorces run to a strict timetable for court appearances there are plenty of deadlines to be met. As a result the hours are generally longer – you might leave at 8pm or 9pm on an average day – and there

is a a considerable volume of court bundling to be completed. *"We could probably do with another trainee,"* suggested one interviewee; *"there's certainly more than enough work to go round."* On the upside trainees frequently attend conferences with barristers, and court hearings crop up every week. And for some there's nothing better than being in the thick of a department where the law is actually being made. *"It's not just cases worth millions and millions of pounds, it's the cutting-edge cases. Miller and McFarlane, Charman, Sorrell – you name the top cases and they're all here."*

The family and property departments are closely connected as the transfer of matrimonial homes are a part of the residential team's workload. If you're thinking of becoming a family lawyer, property is a good place to gain extra experience. In the landed estates team trainees have the added bonus of visits to estates and meetings with clients. Back in the office their role sees them carrying out searches, investigating title and dealing with planning issues. One trainee had to *"tell a client that they couldn't buy their dream house because it didn't have necessary planning permission."*

corporate fashionistas

Working for commercial clients is an entirely different proposition at Withers compared with the big City firms. *"When you're dealing with smaller or medium-sized enterprises you're not just a cog in the wheel, you roll up your sleeves and you get stuck in,"* explained one source. In the coco seat there is always a lot of drafting (eg share sale agreements) and general due diligence duties, looking at IP issues, employee pensions, competition questions and company accounts, all of which is *"very time-consuming because of the breadth of material you're looking for."* While preparing the due diligence report for a large London fashion house, one trainee even had the chance to attend a few shows.

A secondment to Tate Britain and seats in the firm's two other European offices make a nice change. Anyone wanting to spend time in Milan working for clients in the luxury goods, manufacturing and banking sectors will need to be fluent in Italian. Interestingly, Withers claims to have more Italian-speaking lawyers than any other City firm; indeed our sources estimated that three or four of the trainees recruited each year have a connection with the country or the language. Most of a Milan trainee's work will be transactional. *"You're well looked after,"* remarked one past visitor. *"You can pick up the phone and speak to anyone in London without feeling you're intruding on their time."* There is no hard and fast rule concerning who gets to go to Geneva, although with 20% of the firm's fee-earning staff speaking two or more languages, there's never a shortage of candidates. The Geneva experience is a mix of commercial litigation, tax and estates work.

glamorous or bog standard?

Trainees range from PhD-wielding brainboxes to ex-sound engineers and in 2007 the age gap between oldest and youngest was ten years. *"You have to have a certain degree of self-confidence or you wouldn't be through the door,"* mused one interviewee. *"Enthusiasm"* is another hallmark. *"I've got a sense of humour of sorts and I've found at times that it's been appreciated,"* said one trainee. While people readily admitted that *"Withers doesn't have the most heady social life,"* there are regular departmental events and a core group of trainees goes out for drinks in the nearby Firefly and Puzzle pubs. After one year when the Christmas party was hosted in the office (*"if you get changed in the loos and go downstairs to a few meeting rooms you're not generally going to be in a very celebratory mood"*), Withers made a real effort last year and hired a swanky hotel. For the more adventurous there are non-compulsory subsidised ski trips organised by the corporate, litigation and wealth

planning departments. If group fun is not your thing, don't worry: *"People get on well but don't feel as though they are on the outside if they have to get back to Sevenoaks to see their children."*

As for who should pick this firm, one source summed things up well when they said: *"The whole thing with Withers being known for private client is in a sense a misnomer now. Whereas once a lot of the work would have come out of private client, increasingly the other departments are driving their own agendas, corporate being a good example."* And yet private client clearly remains a potent force at the firm since, in 2007, it opened its doors to five qualifying trainees. In total, nine of the 12 qualifiers stayed on that year, the others going into family, charities and litigation.

and finally...

Withers is an exceptional firm with an exceptional pedigree and some really high-flying partners. Their doors will be open to you – just don't expect them to spoonfeed you. Oh, and this could be the only firm with an office shaped like a pair of trousers. You'll see what we mean...

Wragge & Co LLP

the facts

Location: Birmingham, London
Number of UK partners/solicitors: 108/318
Total number of trainees: 61
Seats: 4x6 months
Alternative seats: Secondments
Extras: Pro bono – College of Law and other advice schemes; language training

When Midlands favourite Wragge & Co was a Birmingham-only operation it set the standard for staff satisfaction and an open style of management. Keen to be trained in its *"open, unstuffy and creative"* culture, students flocked to the firm.

Wragges expanded into the London market, where it now has a reasonably large office, and recently opened up in Hong Kong. It is even planning to launch in the virtual world of Second Life in a bid to source pro bono work from cyberspace. The question many people now ask is this: with the firm so much bigger, can it hold onto the things that made it such a great place to work?

sugar and spice

Many trainees are still drawn to Wragges for its *"fluffier side – the people culture and the opportunity to have a bit more of a work-life balance."* Rather tellingly, it is the only law firm to appear in both the *Sunday Times'* '100 Best Companies to Work For' and the *Financial Times'* '50 Best Workplaces in the UK' for five consecutive years. Don't be put off by the firm's recruitment website if it still has the cringe-worthy tagline "Go break the law!" We agree with trainees that this campaign is somewhat *"cheesy and patronising,"* but the aim is to show potential candidates that Wragges is *"bucking the trend"* in its approach to training contracts. "You can ask our senior partner for anything. Even for more sugar," claims the brochure as rosy-cheeked senior partner Quentin Poole does the tea-round. Some 30 trainees are represented by a double-page spread of gingerbread men and women, each one individually iced. And it's true, this firm is sweeter and spicier than your average; partners are *"remarkably friendly and respectful and it's absolutely non-hierarchical – you get to speak in meetings."* In both the London and Birmingham offices you *"can ask anyone to help you with the printer."*

Trainees tell us the firm is *"focused on enfranchising everyone"* and that it's clear that *"your opinion matters."* Quentin Poole and managing partner Ian Metcalfe host a monthly chatroom on the Intranet where *"the only question you can't ask is 'How much does so-and-so earn?' But salaries are transparent anyway."* The 'People First Committee' is a forum for everyone in the firm to voice their complaints or suggestions via a representative, and there is also a 'Bright Ideas Page' on the Intranet. People are currently being consulted on Wragges' *"inevitable move"* to a single site in Birmingham over the next few years. The firm is trying to get a feel for what people want to hold onto and where people want to move to, from whether they want a gym to the importance of an open-plan layout. Trainees were also the first to be told of the new designs in a minor re-branding exercise, an approach typical of Wragges and one that keeps them feeling involved and excited. *"It's nice to be consulted,"* said one, *"even though these pretty pictures probably won't change anything in terms of market perception."*

If being green is important to you then this is a firm that takes it seriously, with efforts such as donating unwanted stationery to local schools and, yes, another committee to monitor these issues. In fitting with its green credentials, 2007 saw Wragges win a lead role in BP's £199m green fuels investment programme in the north of England. There is also a partner dedicated to distributing pro bono work and trainees can do as much of this as they want. If you're still unconvinced that there's nothing special about the way Wragges runs its business then there's no hope for you. If you're sold on the idea of working at a feel-good firm, then you'll want to know what exactly it can offer you by way of training.

not forgetting the little people

Well, first it can offer exposure to some cracking clients. Marks & Spencer, HSBC, British Airways and GlaxoSmithKline are just a few examples of the many household names that instruct the firm. The majority of work comes from clients outside the Midlands, but Leicester City FC is a longstanding local client and the firm also acts for that global confectionary business whose origins stem back to a young Quaker called Cadbury and his one-man chocolate outfit in Birmingham's Bull

Street. Core areas of expertise include corporate finance, dispute resolution, finance and projects, employment and human resources, real estate and technology and commerce. Seats in property, litigation and corporate are compulsory for all trainees and then everyone has one option seat. That might sound a bit rigid, but in practice so many seats can count as a compulsory corporate seat that many trainees feel as if they have two option seats. Most say that in terms of seat selection it's *"pretty easy to get what you want."*

IP is seen as a *"sexy seat,"* while employment and pensions is as popular as ever and can be counted as either a compulsory corporate or compulsory litigation seat, depending on which supervisor you have and the balance of work undertaken. There are *"exciting times"* to be had in commercial litigation. Trainees are given their own small files to run, but also have *"a nice balance of dipping in and out of something really huge, being kept in the loop, feeling useful and making a valid contribution."* Trainees are typically given debt recovery files, where Wragge & Co is the client. Chasing former clients for unpaid bills is a *"good way to sharpen technique"* before being let loose on external clients. Attendance at mediations and assisting with arbitrations are also par for the course. Other litigation tasks involve *"advocacy for interim applications and small procedural claims,"* which can naturally be *"a bit daunting,"* but invariably turn out to be *"good experience."* In a real estate seat, trainees can find themselves acting for warehouse developers, on business park schemes or on regeneration projects. This large and busy department was described by some as *"a bit of a baptism of fire,"* not least because trainees have client contact in the first week and are running their own files by the end of the fortnight. It is *"a steep learning curve, but a great opening salvo."* In corporate/M&A the firm *"certainly tries to challenge you"* and the work is described as *"varied and interesting with more pace and pressure"* than most other departments. The people we spoke to

seemed appreciative of the *"time and effort put into the trainees."* One commented: *"Every single person coming out of M&A has raved about it"* and the firm even puts trainees' names on press releases concerning big transactions.

Naturally the tasks vary massively from department to department, as does the level of responsibility given to trainees. Our sources had experienced everything from *"nothing particularly taxing, long hours and boring work"* (eg hole-punching and filing) to being *"consistently busy but in quite a nice way – challenged but without being completely stressed out."* Even when given dull work one trainee was *"amazed that they apologised for it and I wasn't abandoned to it – I was involved in all the meetings and knew why it was important."* We're assured there is also *"no culture of getting extra respect for staying late – in fact it's frowned upon if you hang around when you have no work to do."* Naturally corporate and other transactional seats can demand longer hours; however, most trainees indicated the average day ran from 8.30am to 6.30pm.

The supervision can be quite hands-off, as this trainee explained: *"I had no one fussing over me or looking over my shoulder scrutinising me all the time."* If required, supervisors will *"sit with you for however long it takes"* to go through documents that you have put together, and you are *"always welcome to ask any questions."* It really *"boils down to how much you need."* There is no shortage of people to call upon: everyone is allocated a trainee buddy (*"good for asking stupid queries"*) and a principal (a partner who will take an interest in them for the duration of the contract). With inductions, introductions and lectures coming out of their ears, our sources confirmed an abundance of formal and informal training.

capital concerns

Competition for six months in the big smoke has been fierce over the past couple of years. If you were thinking of using the Birmingham office as a gateway into working in the City then it sounds like you're not the only person. Trainees tell us that the firm has recently found it *"a struggle to get people back"* after they do seats in the capital. Going forward, there is now separate recruitment for the London office, and the firm has yet to decide whether it will still have London seats for Birmingham trainees. If you're wondering whether London is likely to take over from Birmingham as the dominant office, trainees say not. In terms of expansion, Wragges *"has firmly got its foot in the door in London, but the mothership remains in Birmingham."*

Unlike many regional firms Wragges has not previously asked candidates to demonstrate ties to the West Midlands and, by our reckoning, most are drawn to the firm itself rather than Birmingham. Trainees from a diverse range of backgrounds told us: *"I wanted to join a firm that I could be proud of"* and *"to enjoy a greater quality of work by virtue of working in a more medium-sized firm outside London."* One trainee said: *"I probably decided on the firm despite Birmingham rather than because of it."*

The classic Wragges trainee is *"confident, open-minded and willing to work hard."* There is a heavy emphasis on teamwork and the *"single-team ethos"* had clearly been drummed into all those we spoke to. Trainees like to get *"stuck in and involved,"* including on the playing field. Formerly an avid rugby player, Ian Metcalfe is a real sports enthusiast and *"very keen that the firm is involved in all team sports in the region."* Activities include Thursday basketball practice and the *"alarmingly mixed"* tag-rugby, which actually turned out to be *"a great networking event."* Football, hockey, water polo and pub Olympics ("j*ust don't ask…"*) are also on the agenda through the lively Birmingham Trainee Solicitors' Society. Wragges' competitive streak meant it was *"a bitter blow"* to lose the BTSS inter-firm trophy to another of the 'big five' players last year.

house of fun

In the UK's second city, Wragges' office on Colmore Row is right in the legal heartland and *"surrounded by bars;"* indeed, Walkabout on Broad Street is described as *"a bit of a temple"* for trainees. Thursday nights are big and there is also a *"healthy budget for team drinks."* A recent away-day in the commercial litigation department involved a Medieval banquet at Coombe Abbey, complete with four-poster beds and a hung-over breakfast. Wragges' infamous themed Christmas parties are always held in January. In the fairground spectacular of recent times there were *"people hoiking up fabulous dresses and running to the merry-go-round as soon as it opened."* One trainee said of the Christmas bash: *"It's basically a free-for-all and an assault on the senses."*

Some trainees did wonder if the firm's *"current focus on profit and growth"* would *"undermine the friendliness"* of the firm. Among the doubters it was the expansion into the London market that is assumed to have had the greatest impact on the culture of the firm, some finding it had *"hardened off"* over the past couple of years. Echoing the sentiments of one of our sources two or three years ago, one lamented: *"It's not the legal Disneyland it's made out to be."* Fair enough, but who wants to work in a saccharine sweet environment anyway? Said another source decisively: *"They're not going to let the atmosphere slip away – they want to maintain the single-team culture, where everyone knows your name."* Happy to remain a part of it, 21 of the 25 trainees who qualified in 2007 stayed on with the firm.

and finally…

Wragge & Co has it all: top clients, great instructions, enthusiastic staff and trainees, and an inclusive working environment. When asked what they would change about the firm, the most common answer from our interviewees was along the lines of *"free Alkaselza and Mars Bar cake on Fridays."* Says it all really.

Weightmans

Weightmans is a top 75 law firm with a national presence offering real experience across 17 practice areas.

Our aim is to be both the law firm and employer of choice and as a result we are experiencing rapid growth.

With a reputation built on an open culture, solid values, trust and reliability, Weightmans recognises the importance of a happy and well motivated workforce.

Unlike many firms, we offer our trainees real legal experience during their training contract, including attendance at court and client meetings. Challenged from the outset, our trainees have the opportunity to demonstrate their talents across a range of seats following a focused training plan.

The quality of our training is an important commercial investment. Our retention rate is high and we want today's trainees to remain at Weightmans and be leaders in our future.

For further information, please visit www.weightmans.com or contact James See on 0151 242 7989

Deadline for applications is 31 July 2008

www.weightmans.com

Birmingham Leicester Liverpool London Manchester

Weightmans is an equal opportunities employer

a-z solicitors

Addleshaw Goddard

150 Aldersgate Street, London, EC1A 4EJ
Sovereign House, PO Box 8, Sovereign Street, Leeds LS1 1HQ
100 Barbirolli Square, Manchester, M2 3AB
Website: www.addleshawgoddard.com/graduates
Tel: (020) 7606 8855 / (0161) 934 6000 Fax: (020) 7606 4390 / (0161) 934 6060

firm profile

As a major force on the legal landscape, Addleshaw Goddard offers extensive and exciting opportunities to all its trainees across the entire spectrum of commercial law, from employment and banking to real estate, corporate finance, intellectual property, employment, PFI and litigation. Ranked 15th largest law firm in the UK with a fee income in 2006/7 of £176 million, Addleshaw Goddard was listed in both The Sunday Times and The Times as one of the 'Top 100 Best Companies to Work For' and 'Top 100 Graduate Employers' in 2007 and, as a trainee with this firm, you'll be a key member of the team from day one. Whether based in the London, Leeds or Manchester office (or out on secondment), you'll work closely with blue-chip clients within a supportive yet challenging environment, and be part of a structured training programme designed to ensure your success – now and in the future.

main areas of work

The firm has four main business divisions: finance and projects, contentious and comercial, corporate and real estate. Within these divisions as well as the main practice areas it also has specialist areas such as sport, intellectual property, employment and private client services such as family and trusts and tax.

trainee profile

Graduates who are capable of achieving a 2:1 and can demonstrate commercial awareness, motivation and enthusiasm. Applications from law and non-law graduates are welcomed, as are applications from students who may be considering a change of direction. We also have a diversity access programme for applicants on GDL or LPC with less conventional academic backgrounds. Further details can be found on our website.

training environment

During each six-month seat, there will be regular two-way performance reviews with the supervising partner or solicitor. Trainees have the opportunity to spend a seat in one of the firm's other offices and there are a number of secondments to clients available. Seated with a qualified solicitor or partner and working as part of a team, enables trainees to develop the professional skills necessary to deal with the demanding and challenging work the firm carries out for its clients. Practical training is complemented by high-quality training courses provided by both the in-house team and external training providers.

sponsorship & benefits

GDL and LPC fees are paid, plus a maintenance grant of £7,000 (London) or £4,500 (elsewhere in the UK). Benefits include corporate gym membership, season ticket loan, subsidised restaurant, pension and private healthcare.

vacation placements

Places for 2008 – 75; Duration – 1, 2 or 3 weeks (over Easter and the summer); location - all offices; Apply by 31 January 2008.

Partners	182
Associates	500+
Trainees	89

contact
The Graduate Recruitment Team
grad@addleshawgoddard.com

selection procedure
Interview, assessment centre

closing date for 2010
31 July 2008

application
Training contracts p.a. **45-50**
Applications p.a. **1,500**
% interviewed **10%**
Required degree grade **2:1**

training
Salary
1st year
London **£36,000**
Leeds/Manchester **£24,750**
2nd year
London **£39,500**
Leeds/Manchester **£27,600**
Holiday entitlement
25 days
% of trainees with
a non-law degree p.a. **45%**

post-qualification
Salary
London **£64,000**
Leeds/Manchester **£40,000**

% of trainees offered job
on qualification (2006) **80%**

other offices
London, Leeds, Manchester

Allen & Overy LLP

One Bishops Square, London E1 6AO
Tel: (020) 3088 0000 Fax: (020) 3088 0088
Email: graduate.recruitment@allenovery.com
Website: www.allenovery.com/careeruk

firm profile
Allen & Overy LLP is an international legal practice with 5,100 people working across 24 major centres worldwide. The practice's client list includes many of the world's top businesses, financial institutions, governments and private individuals.

main areas of work
Banking, corporate, international capital markets, dispute resolution, tax, employment and employee benefits, real estate and private client. Allen & Overy Partners frequently lead the field in their particular areas of law and the practice can claim both an enviable reputation amongst clients and unrivalled success in major deals.

trainee profile
You will need to demonstrate a genuine enthusiasm for a legal career and Allen & Overy. The practice looks for a strong, consistent academic performance; you should have achieved or be predicted at least a 2:1 (or equivalent). At Allen & Overy you will be working in a team where you will use your initiative and manage your own time and workload, so evidence of teamwork, leadership and problem solving skills are also looked for.

training environment

Allen & Overy offers a training contract characterised by flexibility and choice. The seat structure ensures that you get to see as many parts of the practice as possible and that your learning is hands-on, guided by an experienced associate or Partner. A series of evening presentations by departments facilitates your choice of a priority seat and other areas you may like to experience. Given the strength of the firm's International Finance Practice, trainees are required to spend a minimum of 12 months in at least two of the following departments: banking, corporate and international capital markets, with a contentious seat in either dispute resolution or employment. There are also opportunities for trainees to undertake an international or client secondment.

vacation placements
Allen & Overy offers approximately 120 vacation placement places across the year. For winter, you should apply from 1 October to the 31 October 2007. For spring and summer, apply from 1 October 2007 until 18 January 2008. The winter placement is for final year non-law students or graduates. Applications are welcomed from penultimate year law and non-law undergraduates for the spring and summer placements. Remuneration: £250.00 per week.

benefits
Private healthcare, private medical insurance, in-house medical facilities, interest-free season ticket loan, free in-house gym and subsidised staff restaurant.

sponsorship & awards
GDL and LPC course fees are paid along with contributions towards your maintenance costs. For the Allen & Overy LPC in London, a £7,000 maintenance grant is provided. For the GDL, £6,000 is provided in London and £5,000 elsewhere.

Partners 470*
Associates 1882*
London Trainees 240
*Denotes world-wide number

contact
Graduate Recruitment

method of application
Online application form

selection procedure
Interview

closing date for 2010
GDL candidates
18th Jan 2008
Law candidates 31st July 2008

application
Training contracts p.a. 120
Applications p.a. 2,500
% interviewed p.a. 15%
Required degree grade 2:1 (or equivalent)

training
Salary
1st year (2007) £36,200
2nd year (2007) £40,300
Holiday entitlement 25 days
% of trainees with a non-law degree p.a. 45%
% of trainees with a law degree p.a. 55%
No. of seats available in international offices
38 seats twice a year and 12 client secondments

post-qualification
Salary (2007) £65,000
% of trainees offered job on qualification 90%
% of partners who joined as trainees over 50%

international offices
Amsterdam, Antwerp, Bangkok, Beijing, Brussels, Bratislava, Budapest, Dubai, Frankfurt, Hamburg, Hong Kong, Luxembourg, Madrid, Milan, Moscow, New York, Paris, Prague, Rome, Shanghai, Singapore, Tokyo, Warsaw

asb *law*

Innovis House, 108 High Street, Crawley, West Sussex RH10 1AS
Tel: (01293) 861218 Fax: (01293) 861250
Email: donna.flack@asb-law.com   Website: www.asb-law.com

firm profile
A rising-50 firm, asb law has clear strategic plans and both the capacity and determination to earn the place as the leading full service firm in the South East. From offices in Brighton, Crawley, Croydon, Horsham and Maidstone the firm offers unrivalled coverage throughout Surrey, Sussex and Kent.
This is a vibrant partnership intent on capitalising on its position within two of the most dynamic development areas in the country, the Gatwick Diamond and Thames Gateway.
The firm's diverse client range includes businesses, financial institutions and public sector bodies of all shapes and sizes. The firm also has significant private client capability with full service offerings for mid- and high net worth individuals from the Family, Residential Property and Tax, Trusts and Probate Teams.
The firm's prestigious clients and the range of services it provides demonstrate effectively that it is more than possible to enjoy a challenging and rewarding career without the grind of a daily commute to the City.

main areas of work
Principal areas of work include corporate finance, commercial (contracts), employment, recovery and insolvency, commercial litigation, commercial property and defendant. The firm has clients across many industry sectors and has developed particular expertise in a number including banking, travel, aviation, technology and property litigation.
The Private Client Sector Teams are amongst the largest in the region and include members of STEP, Resolution and the Law Society Children Panel. The firm also has Partners qualified in collaborative law.

trainee profile
As you would expect, the firm is looking for strong intellectual ability. That ability must combine with drive, initiative, a clear client focus and a commercial approach. You should also be articulate and have demonstrable interpersonal skills. You should relish the prospect of early responsibility and contact with clients in a supportive environment.

training environment
The firm's two year programme divides into four six-month seats tailored to your strengths and particular interests. Training is structured to empower you to learn, take responsibility and interact with clients from an early stage. The seats can be in any of the firm's five offices, so a degree of flexibility is required. The firm is proud of its history of retaining its trainees on qualification, and on the number who go on to become associates and Partners themselves.

when and how to apply
Applications can be downloaded from www.asb-law.com and must be submitted online.

Sponsorship and benefits
An interest-free loan is available for the LPC which is repayable over the period of the training contract.

Partners	37
Vacancies	5
Total Trainees	10
Total Staff	260

contact
Donna Flack
Tel: (01293) 861218

method of application
Application form downloaded from firm's website

selection procedure
1 interview and an assessment centre

closing date for 2010
31 July 2008

application
Training contracts p.a. **5**
Applications p.a **500**
% interviewed **5%**
Required degree grade **2:1**

training salary
£19,000 (2007)

offices
Brighton, Crawley, Horsham, Croydon, Maidstone

Ashurst

Broadwalk House, 5 Appold St, London EC2A 2HA
Tel: (020) 7638 1111 Fax: (020) 7638 1112
Email: gradrec@ashurst.com
Website: www.ashurst.com

firm profile
Ashurst is a leading international law firm advising corporates and financial institutions, with core businesses in mergers and acquisitions, corporate and structured
finance. The firm's strong and growing presence around the world is built on extensive
experience in working with clients on the complex international legal and regulatory
issues relating to cross-border transactions.

main areas of work
Corporate; employment, incentives and pensions; energy, transport and infrastructure; EU and competition; international finance; litigation; real estate; tax; and
technology and commercial.

trainee profile
To become an Ashurst trainee you will need to show common sense and good judgement. The firm needs to know that you can handle responsibility because you will be
involved in some of the highest quality international work on offer anywhere. The
transactions and cases you will be involved in will be intellectually demanding, so
Ashurst looks for high academic achievers who are able to think laterally. But it's not
just academic results that matter. Ashurst wants people who have a range of interests
outside of their studies. And they want outgoing people with a sense of humour who
know how to laugh at themselves.

training environment
Your training contract will consist of four seats. For each, you will sit with a partner or
senior solicitor who will be the main source of your work and your principal supervisor
during that seat. Seats are generally for six months. Anything less than that will not give
you sufficient depth of experience for the responsibility Ashurst expects you to take on.
The firm asks trainees to spend a seat in the Corporate Department and one seat in the
International Finance Department. You are free to choose your remaining two seats, subject to availability.

benefits
Private health insurance, pension, life assurance, interest-free season ticket loan, gym
membership and 25 days holiday per year during training. Other benefits can be found
on the 'benefits and salaries' section of the firm's website.

vacation placements
Places for 2008: A two-week Easter placement scheme primarily aimed at final-year
non-law undergraduates and all graduates. Two three-week summer placement
schemes primarily aimed at penultimate-year law undergraduates. Remuneration
£275 p.w. Closing date 31 January 2008.

sponsorship & awards
GDL and LPC funding plus maintenance allowances of £7, 500 per annum. LPC distinction and first class degree awards of £500. Language tuition bursaries.

Partners	199
Assistant Solicitors	529
Total Trainees	96

contact
Stephen Trowbridge
Graduate Recruitment and
Development Manager

method of application
Online

selection procedure
Interview with Graduate
Recruitment and
Development Manager
followed by interview with
two Partners

closing date for 2010
31 July 2008

application
Training contracts p.a. **55**
Applications p.a. **2,500**
% interviewed p.a. **10%**
Required degree grade **2:1**

training
Salary (2007)
First year
£36,000
Second year
£40,000
Holiday entitlement **25 days**
% of trainees with a non-law
degree **58%**
Number of seats abroad
available p.a. **8**

post-qualification
Salary (2007) **£64,000**
% of trainees offered job
on qualification (2005) **90%**

overseas offices
Brussels, Dubai, Frankfurt,
Madrid, Milan, Munich,
New Delhi, New York,
Paris, Singapore,
Stockholm, Tokyo

Baker & McKenzie LLP

100 New Bridge Street, London EC4V 6JA
Tel: (020) 7919 1000 Fax: (020) 7919 1999
Email: london.graduate.recruit@bakernet.com
Website: www.ukgraduates.bakernet.com

firm profile

Baker & McKenzie LLP is a leading global law firm based in 70 locations across 38 countries. With a presence in virtually every important financial and commercial centre in the world, the firm's strategy is to provide the best combination of local legal and commercial knowledge, international expertise and resources.

main areas of work

Corporate; commercial; dispute resolution; banking; EU, competition and trade; employment; intellectual property; information technology; pensions; tax; projects; property; structured capital markets. In addition the firm has cross-departmental practice groups, such as media and communications, insurance and reinsurance, business recovery and environmental law.

trainee profile

The firm is looking for trainee solicitors who are stimulated by intellectual challenge and want to be 'the best' at what they do. Effective communication together with the ability to be creative and practical problem solvers, team players and a sense of humour are qualities which will help them stand out from the crowd.

training environment

Four six-month seats which include a corporate and a contentious seat, usually within the firm's highly regarded dispute resolution department. There is also the possibility of a secondment abroad or to a client. During each seat you will have a meeting to discuss individual seat preferences. In addition, you will receive formal and informal reviews to discuss your progress. Your training contract commences with a highly interactive and practical induction programme which focuses on key skills including practical problem solving, interviewing, presenting and the application of information technology. The firm's training programme includes important components on management and other business skills, as well as seminars and workshops on key legal topics for each practice area. There is a Trainee Solicitor Liaison Committee which acts as a forum for any new ideas or raises issues which may occur during your training contract. Trainees are actively encouraged to participate in a variety of pro bono issues and, outside office hours, there is a varied sporting and social life.

benefits

Permanent health insurance, life insurance, private medical insurance, group personal pension, subsidised gym membership, season ticket loan, subsidised staff restaurant.

vacation placements

London Summer Placement - Places for 2008: 30; Duration: 3 weeks; Remuneration (2007): £270 p.w.; Closing date: 31 January 2008.
International Summer Placement - Places for 2008: 3-5; Duration: 6-12 weeks divided between London and an overseas office; Remuneration (2008): £270 p.w.; Closing date: 31 January 2008.

Partners	88
Assistant Solicitors	191
Total Trainees	62

contact
Suzanne Dare

method of application
Online application form

selection procedure
Candidates to give a short oral presentation based on the facts of a typical client problem, interview with two partners, meeting with an associate

closing date for 2010
Non-law **18 Feb 2008**
Law **31 July 2008**

application
Training contracts p.a. **38**
Applications p.a. **2,000**
% interviewed p.a. **10%**
Required degree grade **2:1**

training
Salary
1st year (2007) **£36,500 +**
£3,000 'joining bonus'
2nd year (2007) **£39,000**
Holiday entitlement **25 days**
% of trainees with a non-law degree p.a.
Approx 50%
No. of seats available abroad p.a. **Variable**

post-qualification
Salary (2007) **£63,500**
% of trainees offered job on qualification (2007) **82%**

Baker & McKenzie LLP continued

sponsorship & awards
CPE/GDL funding: fees paid plus £6,000 maintenance.
LPC funding: fees paid plus £8,000.

additional information
As mentioned, trainees have the opportunity to spend three months working in one of the firm's overseas offices. Trainees have recently been seconded to its offices in Sydney, Hong Kong, Chicago, Washington DC, Brussels and Moscow. In addition, the firm also operates an Associate Training Programme which enables lawyers with 18-24 months pqe to spend between 6-24 months working in an overseas office.

trainee comments
"I spent my first three seats in Property, Corporate and EC, Competition and Trade. Each seat has given me the opportunity to become involved in quite different, yet equally interesting, and often extremely rewarding pieces of work. Each day is a learning experience, and thinking back to the beginning of my training contract, it is incredible how much I have grown, both professionally and personally. I am particularly excited at the prospect of spending the next three months on a secondment to one of our overseas offices. It would be difficult to pinpoint a single highlight of my time at Baker & McKenzie. That which stands out in my mind is the general satisfaction that I derive from my job, it's great to feel part of a team and to see the work you produce translate to valuable legal advice for a client. Moreover, the close friendships which I've forged with some of my colleagues have made my time here all the better."
(Francesco Savino - 4th seat trainee)

"I was initially attracted to Baker & McKenzie as the firm has top quality clients and takes part in major international transactions and yet it has a much smaller intake of trainees than magic circle firms. I did an International Vacation Scheme here which gave me the opportunity to spend three weeks in the London office followed by four weeks in the Sydney office. It was a really pleasant place to work owing to the friendly office environment and the fact that senior members of staff were very approachable.
I am currently based in the Firm's Structured Capital Markets group. My role involves a number of different activities including helping to draft securitization agreements, attending meetings with clients and attending departmental meetings and external conferences. I use what I have learnt through my degree, LPC and the Firm's internal training every day in all sorts of ways which I take for granted. For example, if I was asked to do a piece of research I immediately know how to go about it, how to get to grips with the issues quickly and how to communicate my responses concisely. Since joining Baker & McKenzie, I have found the work both interesting and challenging and I have been very pleased by the variety and level of work that trainees have the opportunity to get involved with."
(Laura Watson - 2nd seat trainee)

"The Firm's trainee training sessions are extremely useful and have been designed to complement both the LPC course and all that we learn in our seats from the experienced professionals around us. The Partners and associates that I have worked with have been really helpful and always take the time to explain the background and wider context of any transaction or case that we work on. The firm also operates an open door policy so you know that you can approach anyone with any queries or ideas that you may have."
(Jeremy Levy - 4th seat trainee)

overseas offices
Almaty, Amsterdam, Antwerp, Bahrain, Baku, Bangkok, Barcelona, Beijing, Berlin, Bogotá, Bologna, Brasilia, Brussels, Budapest, Buenos Aires, Cairo, Calgary, Cancun, Caracas, Chicago, Chihuahua, Dallas, Düsseldorf, Frankfurt, Geneva, Guadalarjara, Hanoi, Ho Chi Minh City, Hong Kong, Houston, Jakarta, Juarez, Kuala Lumpur, Kyiv, Madrid, Manila, Melbourne, Mexico City, Miami, Milan, Monterrey, Moscow, Munich, New York, Palo Alto, Paris, Porto Alegre, Prague, Rio de Janeiro, Riyadh, Rome, St Petersburg, San Diego, San Francisco, Santiago, São Paulo, Shanghai, Singapore, Stockholm, Sydney, Taipei, Tijuana, Tokyo, Toronto, Valencia, Vienna, Warsaw, Washington DC, Zürich

Barlow Lyde & Gilbert LLP

Beaufort House, 15 St Botolph Street, London EC3A 7NJ
Tel: (020) 7247 2277 Fax: (020) 7643 8500
Email: grad.recruit@blg.co.uk Website: www.blg.co.uk

firm profile

Barlow Lyde & Gilbert LLP is a leading international legal practice with more than 80 Partners and over 300 lawyers. The firm has offices in the City of London and Singapore, and affiliated undertakings in Hong Kong and Shanghai. The firm provides an extensive range of legal services to clients from many industries across the world, and are renowned for litigation and insurance expertise. The Dispute Resolution Practice is one of the UK's largest and highest rated. The firm's experience is wide-ranging, from complex boardroom or IT disputes to professional negligence actions and major reinsurance arbitrations. The firm scooped 'Litigation Team of the Year' at the Legal Week Awards in 2005, and again at both The Lawyer Awards and the Legal Business Awards in 2006. The firm's top ranked Insurance and Reinsurance Practice is one of the largest in the world, providing services of unparalleled breadth across the sector. The firm was ranked 'best in Europe' in the Reactions 2007 annual legal survey of over 100 in-house counsel, top executives and claim handlers at insurers, reinsurers and brokers. The firm's lawyers are also leaders in international transport and trade sectors. The firm has significant experience representing and advising some of the world's major players in the aerospace and marine, energy and trade fields, including airlines, ship owners, charterers, manufacturers, airports, insurers, regulatory agencies and international trade associations. The firm's Non-Contentious Department handles the full spectrum of corporate, financial, commercial and employment and pensions work for public and private companies from a wide range of sectors as well as financial institutions.

trainee profile

The firm recruits 18 to 20 trainees a year. The firm is looking for intelligent and motivated graduates with good academic qualifications and excellent communication skills. Trainees must be able to work independently or in a team, and are expected to display common sense and initiative. An appreciation of the client's commercial interests is essential.

training environment

During your training contract you will have six-month seats in four different practice areas. The firm always tries to accommodate a trainee's preference for a particular type of work. There may be opportunities to spend time in other offices, on secondment with clients or on exchange programmes with overseas law firms. A capable trainee will deal regularly with clients from an early stage in his or her training, subject to supervision. All trainees are expected to undertake and assist in practice development and client care. Successful candidates will enjoy a wide variety of social and sporting events at Barlow Lyde & Gilbert LLP, ensuring that trainees have the chance to meet and stay in contact with employees from across the firm.

work placement scheme

An increasing number of the firm's trainees come through the firm's work placement schemes. Whether you are a law or non-law student the firm will introduce you to life in a City law firm. You can even choose which department you want to spend time in. Please apply via the firm's website at www.blg.co.uk. The closing date for applications is 31 January 2008. The firm also runs open days and drop in days throughout the year.

sponsorship & awards

A maintenance grant is provided and fee are paid in full.

Partners	81
Assistant Solicitors	195
Total Trainees	39

contact
Caroline Walsh
Head of Graduate
Recruitment & Trainee
Development

method of application
Online application form

selection procedure
Interview day

closing date for 2010
31 July 2008

application
Training contracts p.a.
18-20
Applications p.a. **2,000**
% interviewed p.a. **10%**

training
Salary
1st year £32,000
2nd year £35,000
Holiday entitlement
5 weeks
post-qualification
Salary **£58,000**
Trainees offered job
on qualification (2007)
16 out of 17

other offices
Hong Kong, Shanghai,
Singapore

BARLOW LYDE & GILBERT

Bates Wells & Braithwaite London LLP

2-6 Cannon Street, London EC4M 6YH
Tel: (020) 7551 7777 Fax: (020) 7551 7800
Email: trainee@bwbllp.com
Website: www.bwbllp.com

firm profile

Bates Wells and Braithwaite is a commercial law firm servicing a wide range of commercial statutory, charity and social enterprises. The firm is expanding, progressive and is doing high quality work for clients and providing high quality training for those who work with the firm.

Whilst the firm is ranked joint first in three areas of law by the Legal 500 and ranked by them or Chambers in 15 other areas of law, the firm also believes in its staff enjoying a good work/life balance and living a life outside as well as inside the office.

main areas of work

The firm is well known for its work for a wide range and variety of clients given its size. This includes working with the charities and social enterprise sector, commercial organisations and individuals. The firm also has particular expertise in the arts and media, sports and immigration arenas together with strong departments dealing with employment, property and dispute resolution.

trainee profile

The firm is looking for trainees with not only a sound academic background and the ability to communicate clearly and effectively, but most importantly it is looking for trainees who positively want to join a firm such as Bates Wells & Braithwaite with its work mix approach, and with interests outside work which the firm would expect to be maintained, if not developed.

training environment

In the first year there are two six month seats, whilst in the second year there are three four month seats which, between them, cover a wide range of the work with which the firm is involved. From time to time the firm arranges secondments to clients on an ad hoc basis.

The firm runs a programme of internal seminars specifically addressed to trainees and operates a mentoring system, all designed to ensure that the trainees enjoy their time with the firm and to maximise the opportunities that are available for them during their training contract and beyond.

benefits

Interest-free loan for season ticket travel, subsidised use of gym and squash court, subsidised restaurant, one month's unpaid leave on qualification and the firm's pension scheme with match funding provided.

vacation placements

Places for 2008: 12 people for a duration of one week each. Closing date: 21st February 2008.

sponsorship & awards

LPC course fees paid and interest paid on student loans during LPC.

Partners	20
Assistant Solicitors	43
Trainees	10

graduate recruitment-contact
Peter Bennett (020) 7551 7777

method of application
Online via website

selection procedure
Interviews

closing date for 2010
24 July 2008

application
Training contracts per annum
5
Applications p.a. **600+**
% interviewed p.a. **5%**
Required degree **2:1**

training
Salary
1st year, £29,000
2nd year, £31,000
Holiday entitlement
5 weeks
post-qualification
Salary **£41,000**
% of trainees offered job on qualification (last 3 years)
100%

Beachcroft LLP

100 Fetter Lane, London EC4A 1BN
Tel: (020) 7242 1011 Fax: (020) 7831 6630
Email: trainee@beachcroft.co.uk
Website: www.bemore.beachcroft.co.uk

firm profile

Beachcroft LLP (formerly Beachcroft Wansbroughs) is one of the largest commercial law firms in the UK, with a turnover of over £111 million, a 12% increase on 2005/2006. An enviable client base and over 1,400 people working out of eight offices means they can provide truly exceptional career opportunities, whatever your aspirations.

Their national teams allow clients to benefit from some of the best specialists in the UK with expert local knowledge and a consistent commercial view wherever they are. For their fee earners and support staff it's a chance to work alongside nationally respected lawyers as part of progressive multi-disciplinary teams.

main areas of work

The firm operates through specialist practice area teams to deliver an integrated service to clients in six main industry groups: Financial Institutions (including the insurance industry), Health & Public Sector, Real Estate, Technology & Telecommunications, Industrial Manufacturing & Transportation and Consumer Goods & Services. Key clients include Guy's and St Thomas's NHS Foundation Trust, Balfour Beatty, Westfield Shoppingtowns, Zurich, Allianz Insurance, BAE Systems, L'Oreal, Unilever, Waitrose, Freescale Semiconductor and Getronics. The firm is helping them get more from their businesses, and they can help you get more from your career.

trainee profile

The firm looks for outgoing, commercially minded people preferably with a 2:1 honours degree in any subject. You will need to be an excellent team player and possess a mind capable of analysing, interpreting and applying complex points of law.

training environment

Training takes place over a two year period in London, Bristol, Manchester or Leeds, during which time you'll pursue a demanding study programme, whilst occupying four six-month seats in some of the key areas of commercial law. Responsibility will come early and the firm provides the supervision and support to enable you to develop and grow.

benefits

The firm operates a flexible benefits package where you can personalise your rewards – 'buying' or 'selling' options such as pension entitlement, private health care and holiday time. Additional benefits include well woman/man checks, free eye test, employment assistance programme, discounted insurance and many other fringe benefits.

vacation placements

Beachcroft runs a paid placement scheme for law and non-law students each summer. Please visit www.bemore.beachcroft.co.uk for further details.

sponsorship & awards

Beachcroft provides payment for GDL, LPC and £5,000 bursary.

Partners	147
Assistant Solicitors	297
Total Trainees	77

contact
Carrie Daniels
Graduate Recruitment Officer
Email: trainee@beachcroft.co.uk

method of application
Apply online at
www.bemore.beachcroft.co.uk

selection procedure
Assessment centre and panel interview

closing date
1 August each year

application
Training contracts per annum
30
Required degree
2:1 preferred

training
Salary
1st year, regions
£22,000 p.a.
2nd year, regions
£24,000 p.a.
1st year, London
£30,000 p.a.
2nd year, London
£33,000 p.a.

offices
Birmingham, Bristol, Brussels, Leeds, London, Manchester, Winchester

Berwin Leighton Paisner

Adelaide House, London Bridge, London EC4R 9HA
Tel: (020) 7760 1000 Fax: (020) 7760 1111
Email: traineerecruit@blplaw.com Website: www.blplaw.com

firm profile

Berwin Leighton Paisner LLP is a premier, full service City law firm, with particular strengths in real estate, corporate, finance and a strong litigation and dispute resolution capability. The firm has an open and friendly culture, combined with a strong commitment to career development and internal communication means that it has become a magnet for quality staff.

main areas of work

The full range of real estate work including investment, development, planning, construction, property finance, litigation and funds. Traditional corporate finance areas of M&A, equity capital markets and investment funds, as well as outsourcing, EU, competition, IT, telecoms and employment. An active Banking and Capital Markets Team with a growing securitisation capability, a Project Finance Team that is expanding internationally, and an Asset Finance Team. Strong and growing Corporate Tax Team, intellectual property, commercial litigation, and reinsurance and insurance. The firm is widely recognised for its expertise in a number of industry sectors, including real estate, hotels, leisure and gaming, defence, energy, utilities and retail.

lpc+

The firm runs the UK's first tailor-made LPC Course, called the LPC+. All trainees will study at the College of Law, where tutors are joined by BLP lawyers and trainers who help to deliver some of the sessions, using BLP precedents and documents, discussing how theory is applied to real cases and transactions.

trainee profile

The firm is looking for intelligent, energetic, positive and hard-working team players who have an interest in business and gain a sense of achievement from finding solutions.

training environment

BLP is an exciting, ambitious, dynamic and entrepreneurial firm. Yet when recruiting trainees, the focus is on quality rather than quantity. As a result, trainees are rewarded with a high degree of responsibility and involvement underpinned by an exceptional standard of training and support. BLP has always prided itself on providing the right environment for people to grow. Employees believe that BLP is a genuinely innovative and friendly firm with a refreshing lack of hierarchy, the open-door policy is something that trainees value tremendously. An induction covers the practical aspects of working in a law firm, from billing to client care. There are technical education programmes for each department, with weekly skills sessions and seminars for trainees as well as Professional Skills Courses.

vacation placements

Places for 2008: Assessment centres held during December, January and February at the firm's London office, applications accepted online before 31 January 2008 (at www.blplaw.com). Summer vacation scheme, two weeks, aimed at those in their penultimate year and above (law and non-law). Easter vacation scheme, one week, aimed at final year law students and those at a later stage of legal education/employment.

sponsorship

CPE/GDL and LPC+ fees paid and £7,200 maintenance p.a.

Partners 180
Assistant Solicitors 255
Total Trainees 80

contact
Jennie Bishop

method of application
Firm application form online

selection procedure
Assessment day & partner interview

closing date for 2010
31 July 2008

application
Training contracts p.a. **40**
Applications p.a. **1,500**
% interviewed p.a. **5%**
Required degree grade **2:1**

training
Salary
1st year (2006) **£33,000 +**
£2,500 golden hello
2nd year (2006) **£36,000**
Holiday entitlement **25 days**
% of trainees with a
non-law degree p.a. **46%**
No. of seats available
abroad p.a. **1**

post-qualification
Salary (2006) **£62,000**
% of trainees offered job
on qualification (2006) **96%**
% of assistants who joined
as trainees (2005) **47%**
% of partners who joined
as trainees (2005) **30%**

offices
London, Brussels, Paris,
Singapore, best friend
networks in 50 countries

Bevan Brittan

Kings Orchard, 1 Queen Street, Bristol, BS2 0HQ
Tel: (0870) 194 3050 Fax: (0870) 194 8954
Email: hr.training@bevanbrittan.com
Website: www.bevanbrittan.com

Partners	**62**
Total Trainees	**33**

contact
HR and Training
(0870) 194 3050

method of application
Online application

closing date for 2010
31 July 2008

post-qualification
% of trainees offered job
on qualification (2007) **88%**

other offices
Birmingham, Bristol,
London

firm profile
Bevan Brittan has firmly established itself as a truly national law firm and continues to attract high profile national and international clients and challenging, groundbreaking work. The firm is nationally recognised for its expertise in providing legal advice to clients in both the public and private sectors and is notable for being one of the very few practices whose work is equally strong in both sectors.

main areas of work
The firm is structured around four primary areas of the UK economy: built environment, health, government and education, and commerce, industry and services. The firm operates in cross departmental teams across these markets, harnessing the full range of skills and experience needed to provide top quality legal advice in the context of specialist knowledge of both the sector concerned and the client's business. Areas of work covered include banking, corporate, commercial, commercial litigation, projects, employment, medical law and personal injury, property, planning and construction.

trainee profile
Bevan Brittan recognises that the firm's success depends upon a team of lawyers dedicated to service excellence. Its success is maintained by attracting and keeping enthusiastic, bright people with sound common sense, plenty of energy and the ability to work and communicate well with others.

training environment
During each six-month seat, the core of your training will be practical work experience in conjunction with an extensive educational programme. Together the training is aimed at developing attitudes, skills and legal and commercial knowledge essential for your career success. You are encouraged to take on as much work and responsibility as you are able to handle, which will be reviewed on a regular basis with your supervising Partner. The firm is friendly and supportive with an open-door policy along with a range of social, sporting and cultural activities.

vacation placements
Places available for 2008: 50 across the three offices. Closing date: 31st March 2008.

sponsorship & awards
Bursary and funding for GDL and LPC.

Bingham McCutchen (London) LLP

41 Lothbury, London, EC2R 7HF
Tel: (020) 7661 5300 Fax: (020) 7661 5400
Email: graduaterecruitment@bingham.com Website: www.bingham.com

firm profile

With nearly 1,000 lawyers in 13 offices spanning the United States, the United Kingdom and Asia, Bingham focuses on serving clients in complex financial transactions, high-stakes litigation and a full range of sophisticated corporate and technology matters.
Bingham's London team of 40 high-flying finance, litigation and corporate lawyers is dedicated to providing a seamless and responsive service to the firm's international financial institution clients. The firm's London office capabilities have been carefully shaped to meet the complex needs of a demanding client segment. Through practical experience and in-depth study of the legal and business issues facing these clients, the firm's London lawyers provide counsel in an intelligent, savvy, forceful and focused way. The firm's London lawyers have represented institutions and funds in precedent-setting workouts and restructurings in the UK and across Europe, including Concordia Bus, Damovo Group, Focus DIY, Gate Gourmet, IWP International, Jarvis, J R Crompton, LeisureLink Holdings, Luxfer Holdings, Marconi, Parmalat, Queens Moat Houses, Schefenacker, Schieder Möbel, Sea Containers, TH Global and TMD Friction. The financial restructuring practice in London is closely integrated with the firm's restructuring and insolvency practice in the United States, Tokyo and Hong Kong, leading The International Who's Who of Business Lawyers in 2007 to name Bingham as 'Global Insolvency and Restructuring Law Firm of the Year' for the second consecutive year. Lawyers in the firm's London office also have extensive experience in the areas of finance, corporate, litigation and financial services regulatory.

main areas of work

Bingham's London office capabilities include financial restructuring, finance, corporate, litigation and financial services regulatory.

trainee profile

The firm is looking for top quality candidates who can demonstrate an exceptional academic record combined with evidence of extra-curricular achievement. Prospective trainees will show initiative, be solution driven and seek to be part of a challenging yet friendly environment.

training environment

The firm currently recruits two trainee solicitors a year. The training contract consists of four six-month seats, rotating between the office's primary practice areas: financial restructuring, finance, corporate, litigation and financial services regulatory. The intimate nature of the London office means that you will benefit from a bespoke training programme with a high level of Partner involvement. With the firm's small team approach, you will assume responsibilities from day one.

benefits

The firm offers an extensive compensation programme for trainees. As well as a highly competitive salary, the firm offers private health insurance, travel insurance, long term disability insurance, season ticket loan, life assurance and subsidised gym membership.

sponsorship & awards

LPC fees and maintenance grant of £8,000 per annum. PgDL fees and maintenance grant of £8,000 per annum.

Partners	**12**
Assistant solicitors	**25**
Total Trainees	**4**

contact
Lisa Poulley, Human Resources Manager or Vicky Anderson, Human Resources Officer.
(020) 7661 5300

method of application
Online application via firm website at www.bingham.com or via CV Mail

selection procedure
Currently face to face interviews

closing date for 2010
31 July 2008 (currently accepting applications for 2009)

application
Training contracts p.a.up to **2**
Required degree grade: **High 2:1 from a leading university and excellent A-levels**

training
Salary
1st year £40,000
2nd year £45,000
Holiday entitlement
25 days

post-qualification
Salary (2007) **£91,429**
% of trainees offered job on qualification (2006) **85%**

Overseas offices
Boston, Hartford, Hong Kong, Los Angeles, New York, Orange County, San Francisco, Santa Monica, Silicon Valley, Tokyo, Walnut Creek, Washington

Bircham Dyson Bell LLP

50 Broadway, London SW1H 0BL
Tel: (020) 7227 7000 Fax: (020) 7222 3480

firm profile

Bircham Dyson Bell is one of the top 10 fastest growing law firms in the UK. Employing 300 people, (with 52 partners), the firm has doubled its turnover within the last five years. In 2006 it was shortlisted for The Lawyer's 'Law Firm of the Year' award and in 2007 was shortlisted in both the Real Estate and Employment 'Department of the Year' categories. The firm acts for many high-profile clients from a wide-variety of sectors, including real estate, public and private companies, charities, private clients, and public sector organisations. The firm enjoys a market-wide reputation for the quality of its people, their knowledge, and their pro-active approach to clients.

main areas of work

Located in central London, Bircham Dyson Bell is recognised as having leading departments in the parliamentary, planning, public law, charity and private client fields. The firm also has strong corporate commercial, real estate and litigation teams.

trainee profile

Applications are welcome from both law and non-law students who can demonstrate a consistently high academic record. The firm is looking for creative thinkers with a confident and practical outlook who will thrive in a friendly, hard-working environment. Many of BDB's current trainees have diverse interests outside law.

training environment

The firm's training is designed to produce its future partners. To achieve this they aim to provide a balance of both formal and practical training and will give early responsibility to those who show promise. The two-year training contract consists of four six-month seats during which you will work alongside partners and other senior lawyers, some of whom are leaders in their field. As the firm practises in a wide variety of legal disciplines, trainees benefit from a diverse experience. Trainees undergo specific technical training in each seat in addition to the mandatory Professional Skills Course (PSC). Great emphasis is now placed on soft skills training and development. The firm prides itself in having introduced an innovative Careeer Development Framework which assists [qualified assistants] in following their careeer aspirations within the firm.

benefits

Group health care, life assurance, health insurance and pension schemes.

sponsorship & awards

Bircham Dyson Bell provides funding for GDL and LPC fees.

Partners	52
Fee Earners	127
Total Trainees	16

contact
David Mundy, Training Principal
(020) 7227 7000

method of application
Please visit the careers section of the firm's website,
www.bdb-law.co.uk and go to the graduate area

selection procedure
Two interviews with members of the Graduate Recruitment Team, comprising a number of partners, associates and HR

closing date for 2010
31 July 2008 for autumn 2010

application
Training contracts p.a. **8**
Applications p.a. **580**
% interviewed p.a. **9%**
Required degree grade:
2:1 degree preferred

training
Salary
1st year (1 October 2007) £30,000
2nd year (2007) £31,000
Holiday entitlement
25 days

post-qualification
Salary **£49,000**
% of trainees offered job on qualification (2006) **85%**

Bird & Bird

15 Fetter Lane, London EC4A 1JP
Tel: (020) 7415 6000 Fax: (020) 7415 6111
Website: www.twobirds.com

firm profile

Bird & Bird is a sector focused, full service international law firm. The firm has 148 Partners and over 900 staff across offices in Beijing, Brussels, Dusseldorf, Frankfurt, The Hague, Hong Kong, London, Lyon, Madrid, Milan, Munich, Paris, Rome and Stockholm. The firm is proud of its friendly, stimulating environment where individuals are able to develop first class legal, business and interpersonal skills. The firm's international reach and focus on sectors will enable you to work across borders and for a variety of companies, many of which operate at the cutting edge of the industries in which they operate. The firm has a leading reputation in many of the sectors on which it focuses: aviation and aerospace, banking and financial services, electronics, communications, information technology, life sciences, media and sport. From each of its offices, the firm provides a full range of legal services to these sectors.

main areas of work

Commercial, corporate, corporate restructuring and insolvency, dispute resolution, employment, EU and competition law, finance, intellectual property, outsourcing, public procurement, real estate, regulatory and administrative, tax.

trainee profile

The firm recruits strong graduates capable of developing expert legal skills and commercial acumen. A certain level of intelligence and common sense is a prerequisite (the firm looks for excellent A levels and a strong 2:1), but more importantly the firm is looking for well rounded individuals who will fit in well.

training environment

Following an introduction course, you will undertake four six-month seats. Some seats may be spent in the firm's international offices.

Trainees take on responsibility from day one and enjoy varied and challenging work for industry shaping clients. If you become a trainee with Bird & Bird, you will be given the chance to excel.

The firm runs a business skills development programme to provide you with the basic building blocks for your future development within the business of law. The firm is still personal enough for trainees to make their mark in the firm's friendly stimulating work place.

Trainees are encouraged to join the number of sports teams at the firm and to attend various social events.

benefits

BUPA, season ticket loan, subsidised sports club membership, life cover, PHI, pension, childcare and eyecare vouchers.

vacation placements

Places for 2008: 20; Duration: 2 x 3 weeks; Remuneration: £275 p.w; Closing Date: 31 January 2008.

sponsorship & awards

LPC and PgDL fees paid and a yearly maintenance grant of £5,500.

Partners 148*
Assistant Solicitors 430*
Total Trainees 31 in London
denotes worldwide figures

contact
Lynne Walters
lynne.walters@twobirds.com

method of application
Online application form via the firm website.

selection procedure
Insight and selection days in July and August

closing date for 2010
31 July 2008 for law and non-law students.

application
Training contracts p.a. **18**
Applications p.a. **900**
% interviewed p.a. **10 %**
Required degree grade **2:1**

training
Salary
1st year (2007) £31,000
2nd year (2007) £35,000
Holiday entitlement
25 days
% of trainees with a non-law degree p.a. **Varies**

post-qualification
Salary (2007) **£55,000**
% of trainees offered job on qualification (2006) **79%**

overseas offices
Beijing, Brussels, Dusseldorf, Frankfurt, The Hague, Hong Kong, London, Lyon, Madrid, Milan, Munich, Paris, Rome and Stockholm

Blake Lapthorn Tarlo Lyons

New Court, 1 Barnes Wallis Road, Segensworth, Fareham, Hampshire, PO15 5UA
Tel: (01489) 579990 Fax: (01489) 579126
Email: graduateinfo@bllaw.co.uk
Website: www.bllaw.co.uk

firm profile

Blake Lapthorn Tarlo Lyons is one of the largest regional law firms in the UK, with offices in London, Hampshire and Oxford. Their clients include a wide range of UK and multinational companies, from well-known retailers, banks, local authorities and property developers to major charities. They also act for private clients offering specialist services such as French property, tax planning and clinical negligence. Although a large practice they have retained a sense of community. The firm values diversity, which adds breadth to its expertise. Their professionals have very different backgrounds and skills, many having worked in city firms and in-house. Their advice is practical, providing clients with tailored solutions. They encourage innovation and imagination in order to enhance their client services.

main areas of work

The core practice areas are corporate and commercial, real estate, litigation and dispute resolution, and private client.

trainee profile

Fitting in at Blake Lapthorn Tarlo Lyons is about ability, enthusiasm and contribution. In order to maintain their standards of excellence, they need high-calibre people. To be successful you need to demonstrate significant personal achievement and strong interpersonal skills as well as an excellent academic record.

training environment

Training is carefully structured and designed to provide variety, responsibility and intellectual challenge. You will have a series of six-month placements in a range of departments. Working with a partner or senior solicitor, you will be exposed to a wide range of clients and work, in private and commercial practice areas. During each placement your supervisor will involve you directly in work so you learn from hands-on experience, as well as observation and instruction. The greater competence you demonstrate, the more responsibility you will be given.

benefits

Private healthcare, life assurance, contributory pension scheme, childcare vouchers and 'You at Work' flexible benefits.

sponsorship & awards

LPC fees and maintenance grant.

Partners	104
Assistant Solicitors	257
Total Trainees	27

contact
Mrs Lynn Ford

method of application
Online application form with link from website.

selection procedure
Interviews and Assessment Day

closing date for 2010
13 July 2008

application
Training contracts p.a. **17**
Applications p.a. **300**
% interviewed p.a. **25 %**
Required degree grade **2:1**

training
Salary
1st year (2007) £19,000
2nd year (2007) £20,500
Holiday entitlement
26 days

post-qualification
Salary (2007) **£33,500**
% of trainees offered job on qualification (2006) **86%**
% of trainees offered job on qualification (2005) **84%**

offices
Southampton, Portsmouth, Oxford, London, Fareham and Winchester

Boodle Hatfield

89 New Bond Street, London, W1S 1DA
Tel: (020) 7629 7411 Fax: (020) 7629 2621
Email: traineesolicitors@boodlehatfield.com
Website: www.boodlehatfield.com

Partners	**31**
Assistant Solicitors	**50**
Total Trainees	**10**

contact
Justine Fowler
(020) 7079 8200

method of application
Online application

selection procedure
Interviews with the Training Principal, a Partner and the HR Director plus an ability test in verbal reasoning

closing date for 2010
See website

application
Training contracts p.a. **6-8**
Required degree grade **2:1**

training
Salary
1st year £28,500
(Sept 2005)
2nd year £30,500
Holiday entitlement
25 days

post-qualification
Salary **£47,500**

regional offices
Oxford

firm profile
Boodle Hatfield is a highly successful medium-sized firm which has been providing bespoke legal services for more than 275 years. They still act for some of their very first clients and are proud to do so. The firm has grown into a substantial practice, serving the full spectrum of commercial and private clients, both domestically and internationally.

main areas of work
The ethos of facilitating private capital activity and private businesses underpins the work of the whole firm. The interplay of skills between four major areas – private client and tax, property, corporate and litigation – makes Boodle Hatfield particularly well placed to serve these individuals and businesses.

trainee profile
The qualities the firm looks for in its trainees are commitment, flexibility and the ability to work as part of a team. Students with 2.1 or above and high A levels should apply.

training environment
Trainees spend six months in up to four of the firm's main areas: Property, Corporate, Private Client & Tax, and Litigation. Boodle Hatfield is well known for the high quality of its training. All trainees are involved in client work from the start and are encouraged to handle their own files personally as soon as they are able to do so, with the appropriate supervision. The firm's trainees therefore have a greater degree of client contact than in many firms with the result that they should be able to take on more responsibility at an early stage. Trainees are given formal appraisals every three months which are designed as a two-way process and give trainees the chance to discuss their progress and to indicate where more can be done to help in their ongoing training and development.

benefits
Private healthcare, life assurance, season ticket loan, pension scheme, private health insurance, conveyancing grant, permanent health insurance.

vacation placements
Two week placement between June and September, for which 10 students are accepted each year. Applicants should apply via the application form on the website at www.boodlehatfield.com.

sponsorship & awards
LPC and GDL/CPE plus maintenance grant.

B P Collins

Collins House, 32-38 Station Road, Gerrards Cross SL9 8EL
Tel: (01753) 889995 Fax: (01753) 889851
Email: jacqui.symons@bpcollins.co.uk
Website: www.bpcollins.co.uk

firm profile
B P Collins was established in 1966, and has expanded significantly to become one of the largest and best known legal practices at the London end of the M4/M40 corridors. At its main office in Gerrards Cross, the emphasis is on commercial work, including corporate/commercial work of all types, commercial conveyancing and general commercial litigation. Alongside this there is a highly respected private client department specialising in tax planning, trusts, charities, wills and probates, and an equally successful family law team.

main areas of work
Corporate/commercial, employment, IT/IP, civil and commercial litigation, commercial conveyancing, property development, private client and family law.

trainee profile
Most of the partners and other fee-earners have worked in London at one time or another but, tired of commuting, have opted to work in more congenial surroundings and enjoy a higher quality lifestyle. Gerrards Cross is not only a very pleasant town with a large number of high net worth private clients but it is also a convenient location for serving the extremely active business community at the eastern end of the Thames Valley including West London, Heathrow, Uxbridge, Slough and Windsor. The firm therefore looks for trainees who are likely to respond to this challenging environment.

training environment
The firm aims to have six trainee solicitors at different stages of their training contracts at all times. Trainees serve five months in four separate departments of their choice. The final four months is spent in the department in which the trainee intends specialising. The firm has a training partner with overall responsibility for all trainees and each department has its own training principal who is responsible for day to day supervision. There are regular meetings between the training principal and the trainee to monitor progress and a review meeting with the training partner midway and at the end of each departmental seat. The firm also involves its trainees in social and marketing events including golf and cricket matches, and other sporting and non-sporting activities.

Partners	20
Assistant Solicitors	32
Total Trainees	6

contact
HR Manager Mrs Jacqui Symons

method of application
Handwritten covering letter & CV

selection procedure
Screening interview & selection day

closing date for 2008/9
31 May 2008

application
Required degree grade 2:1, A & B 'A' level grades.

training
Salary
1st year £20,000
2nd year £21,000

Brabners Chaffe Street LLP

Horton House, Exchange Flags, Liverpool L2 3YL
Tel: (0151) 600 3000 Fax: (0151) 227 3185
55 King Street, Manchester M2 4LQ
Tel: (0161) 236 5800 Fax: (0161) 228 6862
7-8 Chapel Street, Preston PR1 8AN
Tel: (01772) 823921 Fax: (01772) 201918
Email: trainees@brabnerscs.com
Website: www.brabnerschaffestreet.com

Partners	58
Associates	24
Assistant Solicitors	39
Fee Earners	28
Total Trainees	18

contact
Liverpool office:
Dr Tony Harvey
Director of Training and
Risk Management

method of application
Online

selection procedure
Interview & assessment day

closing date for 2010
Apply by 31 July 2008 for training contracts commencing in September 2010

application
Training contracts p.a. **10**
Required degree grade
2:1 or post-graduate degree

training
Salary
Not less than £20,000
Holiday entitlement **25 days**

offices
Liverpool, Manchester, Preston

firm profile
One of the top North West commercial firms, Brabners Chaffe Street LLP, in Liverpool, Manchester and Preston, has the experience, talent and prestige of a firm that has a 200-plus-year history. Brabners Chaffe Street LLP is a dynamic, client-led specialist in the provision of excellent legal services to clients ranging from large plcs to private individuals.

main areas of work
The LLP carries out a wide range of specialist legal services and Brabners Chaffe Street's client base includes plcs, public sector bodies, banks and other commercial, corporate and professional businesses. The LLP's client focused departments include banking, corporate, commercial (including sports law), employment, litigation (including media and sports law), property (including housing association and construction) and private client.

trainee profile
Graduates and those undertaking CPE or LPC, who can demonstrate intelligence, intuition, humour, approachability and commitment.

training environment
The LLP is one of the few law firms that holds Investor in People status and has a comprehensive training and development programme. It is listed in the *Sunday Times* Best 100 Employers to work for in both 2006 and 2007. Trainees are given a high degree of responsibility and are an integral part of the culture of the firm. Each trainee will have partner-level supervision. Personal development appraisals are conducted at six-monthly intervals to ensure that trainee progress is valuable and informed. The training programme is overseen by the firm's Director of Training and Development, Dr Tony Harvey, and each centre has a designated Trainee Partner. It is not all hard work and the firm has an excellent social programme.

sponsorship & awards
Assistance with LPC funding is available.

Bristows

3 Lincoln's Inn Fields, London WC2A 3AA
Tel: (020) 7400 8000 Fax: (020) 7400 8050
Email: info@bristows.com
Website: www.bristows.com

firm profile
Bristows specialises in providing legal services to businesses with interests in technology or intellectual property. The firm acts for some of the largest companies in the world and helps protect some of the most famous brands. Its work reaches beyond intellectual property law to corporate and commercial law, property, tax, employment law and litigation.

main areas of work
Intellectual property, IT, bio/pharma, corporate, competition, commercial litigation, mediation, ADR, publishing and media, employment, real estate and tax.

trainee profile
Bristows is looking for applicants with outstanding intellects, with strong analytical skills and engaging personalities. It is also looking for people who will contribute to the ethos of the firm. Bristows is a very friendly firm and believes that you get the best from people if they are in a happy and supportive working environment.

training environment
The firm's training programme gives you the knowledge and skills to build on the extensive hands-on experience you will gain in each of its main departments. You will be working closely with Partners, which will accelerate your training. Part of this training may also involve a secondment to one of a number of leading clients. With the international spread of its clients, the probability of overseas travel is high, especially upon qualification.

benefits
Excellent career prospects, a competitive package, firm pension scheme, life assurance and health insurance.

placement schemes
Schemes are run for one week during Easter break and two weeks during the Summer break. Remuneration: £200 p.w.; Closing Date: Easter/Summer – 28 February 2008.

sponsorship & awards
CPE/LPC fees plus £7,000 maintenance grant for each.

Partners	21
Assistant Solicitors	53
Total Trainees	14

contact
Trainee Recruitment & Training Officer

method of application
Application form

selection procedure
2 individual interviews

closing date for 2010
31 January 2008 for February interviews, 31 July 2008 for August interviews

application
Training contracts p.a.
Up to 10
Applications p.a. **3,500**
% interviewed p.a. **6%**
Required degree grade
2:1 (preferred)

training
Salary
1st year (2007) £33,000
2nd year (2007) £36,000
Holiday entitlement
4 weeks
% of trainees with a non-law degree p.a. **86%**

post-qualification
Salary (2007) **£50,000**
% of trainees offered job on qualification (2007) **80%**
% of assistants (as at 5/6/06) who joined as trainees **46%**
% of partners (as at 01/08/07) who joined as trainees **33%**

Browne Jacobson

Nottingham, Birmingham, London
Tel: (0115) 976 6000 Fax: (0115) 947 5246
Email: traineeapplications@brownejacobson.com
Website: www.brownejacobson.com/trainees

firm profile
Browne Jacobson is one of the largest and most successful law firms in the Midlands. The firm has more than tripled its turnover since 1996 and continues to drive double-digit annual growth.
The offices in Nottingham, Birmingham and London provide the flexibility to deal with national as well as regional clients, whilst also offering its people the opportunity to work in three vibrant city centres.
Browne Jacobson has a track record of attracting and retaining outstanding people, with an open, friendly and flexible culture that is valued by both its clients and its people. The firm has over 500 people, which means that it is large enough to attract some of the best talent in the country, but small enough to foster a supportive and flexible working environment.

main areas of work
Browne Jacobson is a full service law firm for commercial, insurance and public sector clients. The firm has a national reputation for its work in the health, retail and environmental sectors and is recognised as a regional heavyweight for corporate, property, public enquiry, litigation and professional risk work.

trainee profile
The firm is looking for talented law and non-law graduates who can bring with them enthusiasm, commitment, client focus and a flexible and friendly attitude. Browne Jacobson believes in being open, straightforward and easy to deal with, and is looking for individuals who will fit with this culture.

training environment
Trainees start with a comprehensive induction programme, a fast track professional skills course and then spend four periods of six months in some of the principal areas of the firm, gaining an overview of the practice.
Trainees get great training, a friendly and supportive working environment, and real career opportunities. Trainees are given quality work and exposure to clients from early on, but are supported in achieving results and recognised for their contribution.

sponsorship & awards
LPC/PGDL tuition fees paid, plus maintenance grant for LPC/PGDL of £5,000.

Partners	58
Associates	46
Assistant Solicitors	70
Fee Earners	258
Total Trainees	20
Total Staff	509

contact
Philippa Shorthouse

method of application
Apply online at www.brownejacobson.com /trainees.aspx or by CV and covering letter

selection procedure
Telephone interview, followed by an open day and/or assessment centre

closing date
31 July, two years before the training contract is due to commence

application
Training contracts p.a. **12**
Applications p.a. **700**
% interviewed p.a. **8%**
Required degree grade **2:1**

training
Salary
1st year £24,000
2nd year £26,500
Holiday entitlement **25 days**
% of trainees with a non-law degree p.a. **40%**

post-qualification
Salary **Market Rate**
Holiday entitlement **25 days**
% of trainees offered a job on qualification **80%**

brownejacobson

Burges Salmon

Narrow Quay House, Narrow Quay, Bristol BS1 4AH
Tel: (0117) 902 2766 Fax: (0117) 902 4400
Email: katy.edge@burges-salmon.com
Website: www.burges-salmon.com

firm profile
Burges Salmon is proof that law doesn't have to mean London.
Based in Bristol, the firm's turnover has more than tripled in recent years as it continues to win prestigious clients out of the hands of City rivals. Clients such as Orange, the Ministry of Defence and Mitsubishi Motors rely on its legal expertise and in doing so have helped cement the firm's reputation for creative, lateral thinking. Burges Salmon's primary asset is its people. Trainees benefit from supervision by lawyers who are leaders in their field with a formidable depth of experience. All this against the backdrop of Bristol: a city with a quality of life you would be hard pressed to find anywhere else in the UK.

main areas of work
Burges Salmon provides national and international clients such as The Crown Estate, Reuters and Chanel with a full commercial service through six main departments: corporate and financial institutions; commercial; property; tax and trusts; commercial disputes and construction; and agriculture, property litigation and environment.

trainee profile
Burges Salmon lawyers are hard working, motivated individuals with a strong academic background and enthusiasm for a career in law. Candidates must be commercially aware and possess excellent communication skills.

training environment
Trainees play a vital role in shaping the future of the firm and Burges Salmon invests a great deal of time and resource into training and development. Training is personalised to suit each individual, and the six seat structure allows the opportunity to experience a wider range of practice areas before making a decision on qualification. This dedication to trainees is demonstrated by a high retention rate, which is well above the industry average.

vacation placements
Burges Salmon runs two open days in February and offers 40 two-week vacation placements during the summer. Individuals visit two departments of their choice supervised by a Partner or senior solicitor, and attend court visits and client meetings. Current trainees run skills training sessions, sports and social events. Remuneration: £250 per week.

sponsorship and awards
The firm pays GDL and LPC fees at the institution of your choice. Maintenance grants of £6,000 are paid to LPC students, and £12,000 to students studying for both the GDL and LPC (£6,000 p.a.).

benefits
Annually reviewed competitive salary, 24 days paid annual leave, bonus scheme, pension scheme, private health care membership, life assurance, mobile phone, laptop, Christmas gift, corporate gym membership, sports and social club.

Partners 68
Assistant Solicitors 263
Total Trainees 42

contact
Katy Edge, Recruitment Manager

method of application
Employer's application form available on website

selection procedure
Penultimate year law students, final year non-law students, recent graduates and those considering a change of career are considered for open days, vacation placements and/or training contracts.

closing date for 2010
31 July 2008

application
Training contracts p.a. 20-25
Applications p.a. **1,500**
% interviewed p.a. **10%**
Required degree grade **2:1**

training
Salary
1st year (2007) **£28,000**
2nd year (2007) **£29,000**
Holiday entitlement **24 days**
% of trainees with a non-law degree p.a. **50%**

post-qualification
Salary (2007) **£41,000**
% of trainees offered job on qualification (2007) **94%**
% of assistants who joined as trainees (2007) **50%**
% of partners who joined as trainees (2007) **30%**

Capsticks

77-83 Upper Richmond Road, London SW15 2TT
Tel: (020) 8780 2211 Fax: (020) 8780 4811
Email: career@capsticks.co.uk
Website: www.capsticks.com

Partners	32
Assistant Solicitors	49
Total Trainees	10
Other Fee-earners	6

contact
HR department,
career@capsticks.co.uk

method of application
Application form, CV and
covering letter

selection procedure
Interview with Partner and
Director of HR

closing date for 2010
31 August 2008

application
Training contracts p.a. **4-5**
Applications p.a. **200**
% interviewed p.a. **7%**
Required degree grade
2:1 or above

training
Salary
1st year £28,000
2nd year £29,000
Holiday entitlement
25 days p.a.
% of trainees with a
non-law degree p.a. **50%**

post-qualification
Salary (2008)
£45,000
% of trainees offered job
on qualification (2007) **100%**

firm profile
Capsticks is widely regarded as the leading provider of legal services to the healthcare sector. The firm has grown substantially in the last few years and has ambitious plans for further expansion, both in its core market and by promoting its broader capability and expanding private sector client base.

main areas of work
The firm has over 90 fee earners working for over 200 NHS and other healthcare related and regulatory clients. The firm's client base is largely NHS, but with an increasing focus on healthcare regulatory bodies, private sector healthcare and PFI/PPP work. The firm's practice areas are split into five separate departments: clinical law, commercial, dispute resolution, employment and property.

trainee profile
The firm is diverse and encourages applications from all walks of life. The firm recruits four to five trainee solicitors each year and welcomes applications from candidates who are either on course for or have achieved at least a 2:1 (or equivalent) in their undergraduate degree. The firm expects candidates to be able to demonstrate they are committed to a career in healthcare law and are highly driven but well rounded team players, with good problem solving and communication skills.

training environment
Capsticks' broad range of practices and healthcare clients enables the firm to give its trainees an opportunity to experience a wide variety of legal work. Trainees are therefore able to acquire an in-depth knowledge of both healthcare law and the healthcare industry, in addition to developing the skills that any good lawyer needs. The training contract is designed to give trainees maximum exposure to the work of the firm and they undertake seats in all of the practice areas, namely clinical law, commercial, dispute resolution, employment and property.

benefits
Bonus scheme, 25 days holiday, pension contribution, permanent health insurance, private medical insurance, death in service benefit, childcare voucher scheme and season ticket loan.

vacation placements
The firm's vacation scheme runs from the end of June through to the middle of August and placements last for two weeks each. The firm encourages all prospective trainee solicitors to participate in the vacation scheme, as this is their primary means for selecting future trainee solicitors. The firm welcomes applications for a place on the 2008 vacation scheme between 19 November 2007 and 28 February 2008. Further details are available from the firm's website.

sponsorship & awards
The firm offers its future trainees financial support for both the Graduate Diploma in Law and the Legal Practice Course.

Charles Russell LLP

8–10 New Fetter Lane, London EC4A 1RS
Tel: (020) 7203 5000 Fax: (020) 7203 5307
Website: www.charlesrussell.co.uk

firm profile

Charles Russell LLP is a leading legal practice, providing a full range of services to UK and international businesses, governments, not-for-profit bodies, and individuals. It has eight offices: two in London, Cheltenham, Guildford, Cambridge, Oxford, Geneva and Bahrain. The practice is known for its client care, high quality, expertise and friendly approach. The strategy is simple – to help clients achieve their goals through excellent service. Many lawyers are ranked as leaders in their field. Experienced in carrying out cross-border corporate and commercial work, the practice also provides clients with access to 150 recommended law firms across the world as part of the two major legal networks, ALFA International and the Association of European Lawyers. The practice's lawyers and staff are highly motivated and talented people. The practice's commitment to training and development and strong team spirit is a key ingredient to being known as a friendly practice to work with and work at.

main areas of work

75% of the Practice's work is commercial. Principal areas of work include corporate finance and tax, commercial, insurance/reinsurance, EU & competition, litigation and dispute resolution, intellectual property, employment and pensions, real estate, technology, media and communications, charities, private client and family.

trainee profile

Trainees should be balanced, rounded achievers with an excellent academic background, and outside interests.

training environment

The practice recruits a small number of trainees for its size each year. This allows trainees to undergo the best possible training. Trainees usually spend six months in four of the following training seats – litigation and dispute resolution, corporate/commercial, real estate, private client, family and employment/pensions. Secondments to clients are also often available. Wherever possible the practice will accommodate individual preferences. You will be seated with a partner/senior solicitor. Regular appraisals are held to discuss progress and direction. Trainees are encouraged to attend extensive in-house training courses. The PSC is taught both internally and externally. Trainees are encouraged to take on as much responsibility as possible. A social committee organises a range of activities from quiz nights through to sporting events.

benefits

BUPA; PHI and Life Assurance: pension plan; season ticket loans; 25 days holiday plus additional day for house moves; dress-down Fridays; croissants, muffins and fruit are available between 8:00am and 9:00am each Friday in London.

sponsorship & awards

The practice pays for course fees whilst you are at law school and also offers a grant per academic year of £6,000 to London trainees, £4,500 to Guildford trainees and £3,500 to Cheltenham trainees.

Partners	93
Other fee-earners	240
Total trainees	31
Total staff	628

contact
graduaterecruitment@
charlesrussell.co.uk

method of application
Online application via the website

selection procedure
Assessment days to include an interview & other exercises designed to assess identified performance criteria

closing date for 2010
31st July 2008

application
Training contracts for 2008: **20**
Applications p.a.
Approx 1,500
% interviewed p.a. **7%**
Preferred degree grade **2:1**

training
Salary
1st year (2007) £31,000
2nd year (2007) £35,000
Holiday entitlement
25 days + additional day for house moves

post-qualification
Salary (2007) **£53,000**

regional offices
Also offers training contracts in its Cheltenham (2 places) & Guildford (4 places) offices.

Clarion Solicitors

Britannia Chambers, 4 Oxford Place, Leeds, LS1 3AX
Tel: (0113) 246 0622 Fax: (0113) 246 7488
Email: l.jackson@clarionsolicitors.com

firm profile

Clarion Solicitors is a major presence in Leeds, handling legal services for a growing number of leading businesses and individuals both locally and nationwide. The firm believes that legal services can and should offer genuine benefits and add real value to the lives of the businesses and individuals who use them. To accomplish that, it draws on all the intellectual capability and ability to innovate of all its people, as well as on their human values of humour, communication and engagement with the community. Clarion Solicitors' approach rests on an unwavering commitment to the traditions of integrity and professionalism, and also on a clear vision that more can be delivered to clients: greater clarity and innovation in thought and expression, more and better communication at all levels of the firm's activities, enhanced transparency in the processes through which the firm guides its clients, and a commitment and energy which focus clients' needs and intentions into a clear call to action.

main areas of work

Clarion Solicitors divides its people into six departments as follows: Corporate and Commercial, which incorporates employment and intellectual property teams alongside their corporate finance and commercial colleagues; Property, which includes both commercial and residential property teams; Dispute Resolution, which deals with the full range of disputes for businesses and individuals and includes specific expertise in mediation and alternative dispute resolution; Private Client, where teams handle both family law and a full range of estate planning and probate work; Corporate Recovery, which acts both for institutions and for companies in turnaround situations; and Business Crime and Regulatory, which handles advice on regulatory issues alongside one of the major criminal defence practices in the North of England.

trainee profile

The firm believes that to be involved in Clarion Solicitors is to be at the heart of one of the most exciting projects the legal profession can offer. The firm is looking for trainee solicitors who will share that belief and the values the firm stands for, and who will work with it over the long term to realise the immense potential of the firm.

training environment

At Clarion Solicitors trainees are considered to be part of the team from the very outset. Each of the firm's six departments offers the opportunity to the firm's trainees to spend one of their four six month seats as part of the department. The training given is hands-on, and driven by an ethos of openness, innovation, ambition and intellectual enquiry. The firm believes Clarion Solicitors offers a magnificent opportunity to trainee solicitors in a friendly, team-based environment. The firm is particularly proud that in 2006 the Lex 100 placed it as Lex 100 winner in no less than six categories.

vacation placements

The firm's summer placement scheme now plays an important role in selecting candidates for training contracts. In 2008 the firm will be offering a total of 30 one-week placements, with five candidates commencing on each of 23 June, 30 June, 7 July, 14 July or 21 July 2008. Applications must be received by 28 February 2008. All applications must take place via the firm's website at www.clarionsolicitors.com.

Partners	13
Assistant solicitors	34
Trainees	10

contact
Linda Jackson

method of application
Application form, available on website

closing date for 2010
28 February 2008

application
Training contracts p.a.: **4**
Applications p.a. **230**
% interviewed p.a. **25%**
Preferred degree grade **2:1**

training
Salary
Highly competitive

post-qualification
Salary (2007)
Highly competitive
trainees offered job on qualification (2007) **4 of 5**
% of Partners (as at 01/04/07) who joined as trainees **33%**

138 Edmund Street, Birmingham, BB 2E3
Tel: (0121) 234 9400 Fax: (0121) 234 9540
Email: careers@clarkewillmott.com
Website: www.futurepilots.co.uk

firm profile

Clarke Willmott is a UK law firm with a national reputation in key commercial and private client services. The firm's lawyers are, first and foremost, business advisers whose objectives are to help clients achieve their goals and to enhance the value of their opportunities. They take a straightforward, proactive approach, and have helped enterprises of all sizes and at all stages of the business lifecycle navigate a range of complex legal issues with positive results.

main areas of work

Services include corporate, commercial, real estate and construction, business recovery, dispute resolution, employment, health and safety, intellectual property, property and private capital as well as a range of services to private clients. The firm has specialist industry expertise in real estate (development, investment, residential and urban regeneration), banking & financial services, sport and food & drink.

trainee profile

The firm recruits commercially aware trainees who can demonstrate a clear commitment to a career in law. Clarke Willmott looks for trainees who have a confident, energetic approach and who have the ability to work and communicate well with others. Applications are welcomed from both and law and non-law graduates, with at least a 2:1 degree.

training environment

Trainees complete four six-month seats, providing a wide range of practical experience and skills in contentious and non-contentious work. Individual preference is sought and will be balanced with the firm's needs. Trainees work closely with partners and solicitors in a supportive team structure, and have regular reviews to ensure they are reaching their potential. Training in both legal and non-legal areas is provided to meet the needs of the individual trainee and the PSC is undertaken in-house.

sponsorship & benefits

Life assurance, group personal pension, gym membership, bonus based on the firm's financial performance, LPC fees paid, occupational sick pay, season ticket loans, eyecare vouchers, childcare vouchers.

Partners	84
Solicitors	127
Trainees	27

contact
Clare Gibson, Assistant HR Advisor, Bristol

method of application
Application form, available online

selection procedure
Interview

closing date for 2010
31 July 2008 (interviews September 2008)

application
Training contracts p.a.: **10**
Applications p.a. **c. 500**
% interviewed p.a. **15%**
Preferred degree grade **2:1**

training
Salary
1st year (2007) £22,500
2nd year (2007) £24,000
Holiday entitlement
22 days rising to 26 on qualification

post-qualification
Salary (2007) **£34,750-£36,000 (dependant on location)**
% of trainees offered job on qualification (2007) **c. 75%**

regional offices
Birmingham, Bristol, Southampton, Taunton

www.chambersstudent.co.uk

731

Cleary Gottlieb Steen & Hamilton LLP

City Place House, 55 Basinghall Street, London, EC2V 5EH
Tel: (020) 7614 2200 Fax: (020) 7600 1698
Email: longraduaterecruit@cgsh.com
Website: www.clearygottlieb.com

firm profile

Cleary Gottlieb is one of the leading international law firms, with 12 closely integrated offices located in major financial and political centres around the world. For more than 60 years, the firm has been pre-eminent in shaping the globalisation of the legal profession. Its worldwide practice has a proven track record for innovation and providing advice of the highest quality to meet the domestic and international needs of its clients.

main areas of work

Core practice groups in London are mergers and acquisitions, private equity, financing, and debt and equity capital markets (IPOs), plus additional self-standing practices in competition, tax, financial regulation, intellectual property and information technology.

trainee profile

Cleary seeks individuals, both law and non-law graduates, who are confident in their abilities, creative in their thinking, and who display a strong measure of common sense and commercial awareness. The firm expects candidates to attain at least a 2:1 degree from a leading university and AAB at A- Level or the equivalent. Alongside academic ability, the firm values evidence of extra-curricular achievement.

training environment

By limiting its graduate intake to ten trainees a year, Cleary is able to offer bespoke training that is individually tailored to the interests, experience and aptitudes of the individuals that join it. The firm does not believe that the transition from trainee solicitor to associate occurs overnight on qualification, but rather that the transition should be a smooth and gradual one. It therefore encourages its trainee solicitors to accept increased responsibility as soon as they are ready to do so. With appropriate levels of supervision, trainees operate as lawyers of the firm from the day that they join.

benefits

Virgin Active gym membership, BUPA private healthcare cover (personal and family), life insurance of twice annual salary, long-term disability insurance, childcare vouchers, employee assistance programme and subsidised staff restaurant.

vacation schemes

The London office offers 30 vacation places each year (10 at Easter and 10 in each of two summer schemes). Placements can also be accommodated over the Christmas period by individual arrangement. The firm actively encourages all candidates that are seriously considering applying for a trainee solicitor position with it to undertake a vacation placement. Applications for Easter and summer placements should be received by January 28 in the year of the scheme.

sponsorship & awards

Cleary funds the LPC for all future trainee solicitors. For non-law graduates, the firm also funds the CPE or the GDL. A maintenance grant of £8,000 is paid for each year of professional study.

Trainees	12
Partners	192
	(18 in London)
Total Staff	2384
	(189 in London)

contact
Shaun Goodman
Graduate Recruitment
Partner

method of application
Cover letter and CV

selection procedure
Future trainees are primarily selected from those having completed a vacation scheme with the firm

closing date for 2010
July 31 2008

application
Training contracts p.a. **10**
Required degree grade
High 2:1

training
Salary
1st year **£40,000**
2nd year **£45,000**

post-qualification
Salary **£92,000**

overseas offices
New York, Washington DC, Paris, Brussels, Moscow, Frankfurt, Cologne, Rome, Milan, Hong Kong and Beijing

CLEARY
GOTTLIEB

Clifford Chance

10 Upper Bank Street, Canary Wharf, London, E14 5JJ
Tel: (020) 7006 6006 Fax: (020) 7006 5555
Email: graduate.recruitment@cliffordchance.com
Website: www.cliffordchance.com/gradsuk

firm profile

Clifford Chance is an international law firm with offices in 20 countries across the world. As Global Law Firm of the Year*, it has built its reputation on exceeding clients' expectations whilst establishing an open, approachable and team-driven environment.

trainee profile

There's no typical Clifford Chance person, the firm recruits from a wide range of law and non-law backgrounds. As a trainee, you'll have the opportunity to gain a uniquely global perspective. So if you're interested in an international secondment, you could get the chance to spend six months abroad.

training environment

You will receive legal and business training that will provide you with the best foundation for your career. The firm is diverse and multicultural, and will help you to develop in a direction that reflects your individual talents and style.

benefits

As well as a competitive salary, you'll enjoy: a subsidised restaurant; free use of fitness centre, swimming pool, squash courts and wellness centre; the option of up to six weeks' leave on qualification and a pension.

vacation placements

The firm runs two-day winter workshops, based in the London office, and longer schemes during the spring and summer. A number of international placements will also be available during the summer. Selected candidates will have the opportunity to spend two weeks in London, followed by two weeks in one of the firm's European offices.

sponsorship & awards

Fees for GDL and LPC covered. Maintenance is also provided, please refer to website for details.

*Who's Who Legal Awards 2007.

London office
Partners 231
Lawyers 768
Trainees 250

contact
Contact HR (020) 7006 6006

method of application
Online at www.cliffordchance.com/gradsuk

selection procedure
Online verbal reasoning test followed by assessment day comprising an interview, a group exercise and a paper verbal reasoning test

application
Training contracts p.a. **130**
Applications p.a. **2,000**
% interviewed p.a. **25%**
Required degree grade **2:1**

training
Salary
1st year £37,500 (Aug 2007)
2nd year £40,300
Holiday entitlement **25 days**
% of trainees with a non-law degree p.a. **40%**
No. of seats available abroad p.a. **51**

post-qualification
Salary (Aug 2007) **£63,500**
% of trainees offered job on qualification (2006) **95%**

overseas offices
Amsterdam, Bangkok, Barcelona, Beijing, Brussels, Bucharest, Budapest, Dubai, Düsseldorf, Frankfurt, Hong Kong, Luxembourg, Madrid, Milan, Moscow, Munich, New York, Paris, Prague, Rome, São Paulo, Shanghai, Singapore, Tokyo, Warsaw, Washington DC

Clyde & Co

51 Eastcheap, London EC3M 1JP
Tel: (020) 7623 1244 Fax: (020) 7623 5427
Email: theanswers@clydeco.com   Website: www.clydeco.com/graduate

firm profile

With roots in international trade, Clyde & Co LLP's main objective is to help clients do business in over 120 countries around the globe. The firm values entrepreneurialism, commercial problem solving, excellence and the freedom to be an individual. Clients value the firm's hand on innovative approach. The firm's lawyers know the industries, the clients, and most importantly understand the commercial realities of business. Availability and responsiveness are key in the firm's core industries and these characteristics have become part of the mindset of a Clyde & Co lawyer.

The firm has expanded rapidly in recent years and is a dominant player in the insurance, reinsurance, international litigation, shipping, aviation, transport, international trade and energy, and commodities sectors. Clyde & Co has one of the largest Litigation Practices in the UK.

main areas of work

Aviation and Aerospace, Corporate/Commercial, Dispute Resolution, EC/Competition, Energy, Trade and Commodities, Insurance and Re-insurance, Real Estate Shipping, Transport and Logistics.

trainee profile

The firm is looking for graduates with excellent academic records, outgoing personalities and keen interests. Trainees need to have the social skills that will enable them to communicate effectively and build relationships with clients and colleagues. The ability to analyse problems, apply common sense and provide solutions to situations are all qualities the firm seeks. Ultimately Clyde & Co recruits to retain and they are seeking candidates who will remain with the firm beyond qualification.

training environment

You will gain early responsibility and be supported through close personal supervision and day-to-day coaching complemented by a wide range of training courses. You will undertake four six-month seats in London and Guildford, which will cover both transactional and contentious work. You may also choose to be seconded to one of the firm's overseas offices or have the opportunity for a client secondment.

benefits

An optional £1,000 interest free loan on joining, pension, life assurance, private medical insurance, subsidised gym membership, interest-free season ticket loan and coffee shop.

legal work experience

The firm runs two-week summer vacation schemes for 20 students. The dates for the 2008 schemes are 23 June to 4 July and 21 July to 1 August. Applications are made online and the closing date is 31 January 2008. For more details please visit the website at www.clydeco.com/graduate.

sponsorship & awards

GDL and LPC fees paid plus a maintenance grant of £7,000 in London/Guildford and £6,000 elsewhere.

Partners	140
Assistant Solicitors	270
Trainees	44

contact
Kate Wild
Trainee Solicitor
Recruitment Manager

method of application
Online via website
www.clydeco.com/graduate

selection procedure
Assessment session with Graduate Recruitment followed by interview with 2 partners

closing date for 2010
31 July 2008

application
Training contracts p.a. **24**
Applications p.a. **1,200 +**
% interviewed p.a. **10%**
Required degree grade **2:1**

training
Salary
1st year (2007) **£31,000**
2nd year (2007) **£34,000**
(Reviewed annually)
Holiday entitlement **25 days**
% of trainees with
a non-law degree p.a. **60%**

post-qualification
Salary (2007) **£55,000**

overseas offices
Abu Dhabi, Caracas, Doha, Dubai, Hong Kong, Los Angeles, Moscow, Nantes, New York, Paris, Piraeus, Rio de Janeiro, Shanghai, Singapore, and associate offices in Belgrade and St Petersburg

CMS Cameron McKenna LLP

Mitre House, 160 Aldersgate Street, London EC1A 4DD
Tel: (0845) 300 0491 Fax: (020) 7367 2000
Email: gradrec@cms.cmck.com Website: www.law-now.com

firm profile
CMS Cameron McKenna LLP is a leading international law firm and an integral part of CMS, the alliance of European Law firms. They've earned a reputation for outstanding client service, acute business awareness and for being passionate about client relationships. They work for some of the worlds leading companies, helping to solve their problems so they can run their businesses more efficiently. The firm believes that to give the best advice, lawyers must clearly understand the industry, marketplace and concerns of their clients. All lawyers have a specialist interest in at least one major industry sector and are committed to building long- term relationships with their clients.

main areas of work
The firm's clients benefit from an extensive range of tailored services, delivered through offices in the UK, Central Europe, North America and Asia. The firm's services include banking and international finance, corporate, real estate, commercial, energy projects and constructions, insurance and re-insurance.

trainee profile
The firm looks for high achieving team players with good communication, analytical and organisational skills. You will need to show initative and be able to accept personal responsibility, not only for your own work, but also for your career development. You will need to be resilient and focused on achieving results.

training environment
The firm is highly supportive and puts no limits on a trainee's progress. It offers four six-months seats over a period of two years. You will be awarded a priority seat when you start your training contract and will undertake a compulsory seat in these areas: corporate or banking, and a contentious seat. To develop you and your legal skills even further, you can expect to be seconded to a client or spend time in one of their international offices.
In each seat you will be allocated high quality work on substantial transactions for a range of government and blue-chip clients. The three compulsory modules of the Professional Skills Course will be completed on a fast track basis during the trainee induction. This enables trainees to be effective and participate on a practical level as soon as possible. The Professional Skills Course is complimented by a comprehensive in-house training programme that continues up to qualification and beyond.

vacation placements
Places for 2007/2008: 60: Easter, Christmas and summer. Duration: 2 weeks. Remuneration: £250pw. Closing date for Christmas scheme: 16 November 2007; Easter and summer: 28 February 2008.

benefits
Annual bonus, gym membership/subsidy, life assurance, pensions scheme with firm contributions, private healthcare, season ticket loan, confidential care line, subsidised restaurant and 25 days holiday with options to buy a further five days.

sponsorship & awards
GDL and LPC sponsorship is provided. From September 2007 you will be required to undertake your LPC at BPP Law School London where the firm will pay your fees and provide a maintenance grant of up to £7,500. Further details will be supplied on offer of a training contract.

C/M/S/ Cameron McKenna

Partners	131
Assistant Solicitors	603
Total Trainees	120

contact
Graduate Recruitment Team (0845) 300 0491

method of application
Online application form www.law-now.com/gradrec

selection procedure
2 stage selection procedure. Initial interview, group exercise and verbal reasoning test followed by an assessment centre

closing date
31 July 2008

application
Training contracts p.a. **60**
Applications p.a. **1,500**
% interviewed p.a. **35%**
Required degree grade **2:1**

training
Salary
1st year (2007) **£36,000**
2nd year (2007) **£40,000**
Holiday entitlement
25 days + option of flexible holidays
% of trainees with a non-law degree p.a. **50%**
No. of seats available abroad p.a. **Currently 12**

post-qualification
Salary (2007) **£64,000**
% of trainees offered job on qualification (2007) **96%**

Cobbetts LLP

58 Mosley Street, Manchester M2 3H2
Tel: (0845) 165 5045
Email: lawtraining@cobbetts.com
Website: www.cobbetts.com/graduate

firm profile

Cobbetts is one of the UK's leading law firms with offices in the four key commercial centres of Birmingham, Leeds, London and Manchester. With a consistent reputation for innovation, quality and job satisfaction, the firm continues its tremendous growth, with clients to match. The firm's client base of regional, national and international clients includes PLCs, mid-sized corporates, financial institutions and public sector / not for profit organisations, ensuring that trainees enjoy a breadth and depth of experience.

main areas of work

Cobbetts has developed true national practice areas – real estate, corporate, commercial, banking, employment, litigation services, social housing and private capital – and key specialist expertise in fields including media, the public sector, planning and public markets, in particular on to AIM.

trainee profile

Applications are encouraged from both law and non-law undergraduates who anticipate attaining a high class honours degree. Mature students and those wishing to change career are also encouraged to apply. Applicants must be personable with a determination to work hard and succeed.

training environment

Four six-month seats are available.
There is an opportunity for one trainee each year to spend three months in Brussels.

benefits

Opportunity to join BUPA scheme after four months, gym membership, social club, pension scheme, travel loan, death in service, counselling service.

sponsorship & awards

The firm offers financial assistance for the Graduate Diploma in Law and the LPC, will meet the cost of the Professional Skills Course and provides a maintenance grant which is currently £4,000.

Partners	110
Assistant Solicitors	117
Total Trainees	50

contact
Janet Toombs
(0845) 165 5045

method of application
Online

selection procedure
Assessment days plus vac

closing date for 2010
13 July 2008

application
Training contracts p.a.
Approx 25
Applications p.a.
approx.1,000
% interviewed p.a. **approx 10%**
Required degree grade
2:1

training
Salary for each year of training
1st year £21,000
2nd year £22,000
(both reviewed annually)
Holiday entitlement
Starting at 23 days

post-qualification
Salary NQ **£37,000**
Reviewed annually

% of trainees offered job on qualification **80%**

other offices
Birmingham, Leeds, London

Coffin Mew LLP

Fareham Point, Wickham Road, Fareham PO16 7AU
Tel: (01329) 825617 Fax: (01329) 825619
Email: sarajlloyd@coffinmew.co.uk
Website: www.coffinmew.co.uk

Partners	21
Associates	18
Assistant solicitors	30
Total trainees	13

firm profile

Coffin Mew LLP offers an exceptional training opportunity. The firm is rapidly expanding to become one of the larger southern regional firms with major offices located in the cities of Portsmouth and Southampton and just off the M27 Motorway at Fareham. The firm is in the enviable position of operating a balanced practice offering top quality commercial and private client services in approximately equal volume and is particularly noted for a number of niche practices with national reputations.

main areas of work

The firm is structured through nine core departments: Corporate & Corporate Finance, Commercial Services, Employment, Commercial Litigation, Property Litigation, Personal Injury, Property; Family & Childcare and Trust/Probate. Niche practices (in which training is available) include Intellectual Property; Insolvency; Finance and Business Regulation; Social Housing; and Medical Negligence.

trainee profile

The firm encourages applications from candidates with very good academic ability who seek a broad based training contract in a highly progressive and demanding but friendly and pleasant environment.

training environment

The training contract is divided into six seats of four months each which will include a property department, a litigation department and a commercial department. The remainder of the training contract will be allocated after discussion with the trainee concerned. The firm aims to ensure that the trainee spends the final four months of his or her training contract in the department in which he or she hopes to work after qualification.

sponsorship & awards

LPC funding available by discussion with candidates.

vacation placements

Open Week in July each year; applications for the 2008 Open Week may be made to the Practice Manager with accompanying c.v. between 1 November 2007 and 31 March 2008.

contact
Mrs Sara Lloyd
Practice Manager

method of application
Please see firm's website

selection procedure
Interview

closing date for July 2009/10
31 July 2008 (not before January 1 2008)

application
Training contracts p.a. **5/6**
Applications p.a. **400+**
% interviewed p.a. **5%**
Required degree grade **2:1 (save in exceptional circumstances)**

training
Salary
1st year
Competitive market rate
2nd year
Competitive market rate
Holiday entitlement **20 days**
% of trainees with a non-law degree p.a. **25%**

post-qualification
Salary (2007) **Competitive market rate**
% of trainees offered job on qualification (2006) **80%**
% of assistants who joined as trainees **30%**
% of partners who joined as trainees **40%**

coffin mew LLP

Collyer Bristow LLP

4 Bedford Row, London, WC1R 4DF
Tel: (020) 7242 7363 Fax: (020) 7405 0555
Email: terry.collins@collyerbristow.com
Website: www.collyerbristow.com

firm profile

London and Geneva based, the firm celebrates the breadth and diversity of its client base which includes multinationals, public and private companies, businesses and partnerships, public sector organisations and a substantial private client practice. Many of the firm's lawyers have trained and qualified with the firm and share their diverse experiences, outlooks and expertise with the firm's clients. The firm is famous for its ground-breaking in-house art gallery and is passionate in its support for the contemporary arts.

main areas of work

The firm advises a diverse range of businesses and individuals on challenges of all shapes, sizes and complexity and offers top quality legal advice in private client, family, property, company commercial and dispute resolution.

trainee profile

The firm is looking for self-starting graduates with a 2.1 degree. The firm also positively encourages those embarking on their second career. Common sense and an ability to understand the client's business are essential attributes.

training environment

You will spend six months in four of the firm's five key practice areas working with a range of people from senior Partners to more recently qualified solicitors. The firm has a mentoring, training and appraisal programme which nurtures the development of your technical expertise and client advisory skills. You will be encouraged at an early stage to take responsibility for your own files and to participate in managing the client's work.

benefits

25 days holiday, pension, private medical insurance, life assurance and season ticket loan.

sponsorship & awards

Full LPC funding and maintenance grant of £4,000.

Partners	30
Assistant solicitors	22
Total trainees	6

contact
Terry Collins
Graduate co-ordinator

method of application
Online application form

selection procedure
Interviews

closing date for July 2009/10
31 July 2008

training
Salary
1st year (2007) £25,500
2nd year (2007) £27,500
(Both reviewed annually)

Covington & Burling

265 Strand, London WC2R 1BH
Tel: (020) 7067 2000 Fax: (020) 7067 2222
Email: graduate@cov.com
Website: www.cov.com

firm profile
Covington & Burling LLP is a leading US law firm, founded in Washington, with offices in London, New York, San Francisco and Brussels. The London office was established in 1988 and has continued to grow progressively since then.

main areas of work
In London, the main areas of work are corporate & commercial, employment, insurance, tax, life sciences, dispute resolution, IP/IT, and competition. The firm is known worldwide for its remarkable understanding of regulatory issues as well as its depth and expertise in areas including IT, e-commerce and life sciences. In such work, the firm represents many blue-chip clients including Microsoft, Pfizer, Qualcomm, Bacardi, Krispy Kreme, Business Software Alliance and Armani.

trainee profile
The firm is looking for outstanding students who demonstrate genuine commitment to the legal profession and who have not only excellent academic ability, but also imagination, and the necessary practical and social skills required to respond to the evolving needs of its clients. In return, the firm can offer innovative and fascinating work in a stimulating and supportive environment.

training environment
The firm offers a unique and personal training programme to suit the individual needs of each trainee. Following a comprehensive introduction, trainees will spend six months in each of corporate and dispute resolution, and IP/IT departments. The third and fourth seats will be spent in two of the life sciences, employment, IP/IT or tax practice areas. The firm encourages trainees to take early responsibility in order to get the most out of their training period and trainees will receive regular feedback to enhance their development.

benefits
Pension, permanent health insurance, private health cover, life assurance and season ticket loan.

vacation placements
16 places during summer vacation. Closing date for applications 28 February 2008.

sponsorship & awards
GDL and LPC fees paid. Maintenance grant of £7,250 per annum.

Partners: 190
Associate Lawyers & Other Fee-earners: 460
Total Trainees London:
2008 8
2009 10
2010 12

contact
Graduate Recruitment Manager
(020) 7067 2098
graduate@cov.com

method of application
Online Application Form
See website www.cov.com

selection procedure
1st & 2nd interview

closing date for 2010
31 July 2008

application
Training contracts p.a. 6
Required degree grade 2:1

training
Salary:
1st year £36,500
2nd year £40,000
(subject to review)
Holiday entitlement 25 days

overseas offices
Brussels, New York, San Francisco, Washington

COVINGTON & BURLING LLP

Cripps Harries Hall LLP

Wallside House, 12 Mount Ephraim Road, Tunbridge Wells TN1 1EG
Tel: (01892) 506006 Fax: (01892) 506360
Email: graduates@crippslaw.com
Website: www.crippslaw.com

firm profile

A leading regional law firm and one of the largest in the South East, the firm is recognised as being amongst the most progressive and innovative regional practices.

The firm's organisation into client-focused, industry sector groups promotes a strong ethos of client service and ensures the firm's solicitors are not only excellent legal practitioners but also experts in specialist business sectors. The firm is regarded by many businesses, institutions and wealthy individuals as the natural first choice among regional law firms. Although long-established, the firm's profile is young, professional, forward-thinking, friendly and informal.

The firm achieved the Lexcel quality mark in January 1999, the first 'Top 100' firm to do so.

main areas of work

Commercial 17%, dispute resolution 18%, private client 26%, property 39%.

trainee profile

Individuals who are confident and capable, with lively but well organised minds and a genuine interest in delivering client solutions through effective and pragmatic use of the law; keen to make a meaningful contribution both during their contract and long term career with the firm.

training environment

The firm offers a comprehensive induction course, a well structured training programme, frequent one to one reviews, regular in-house courses and seminars, good levels of support and real responsibility.

The training programme is broader than most other firms and typically includes six seats in both commercial and private client areas. Trainees usually share a room with a partner or an associate and gain varied and challenging first hand experience.

sponsorship awards

Discretionary LPC funding: Fees – 50% interest free loan, 50% bursary.

Partners	41
Assistant Solicitors	50
Total Trainees	14

contact
Annabelle Lawrence
Head of Human Resources

method of application
Application form available
on website

selection process
One interview with Managing Partner and Head of
Human Resources

closing date for 2010
31 July 2008

application
Training contracts p.a. **8**
Applications p.a. **Up to 750**
% interviewed p.a. **6%**
Required degree grade **2:1**

training
Salary
1st year (2007) £20,000
2nd year (2007) £22,000
Holiday entitlement **25 days**
% of trainees with a non-law
degree p.a. **35%**

post-qualification
Salary (2007) **£33,000**
% of trainees offered job
on qualification (2007) **100%**
% of assistants/associates
(as at 1/5/07) who joined as
trainees **45%**
% of partners (as at 1/5/07)
who joined as trainees **22%**

CRIPPS HARRIES HALL LLP

Davenport Lyons

30 Old Burlington Street, London W1S 3NL
Tel: (020) 7468 2600 Fax: (020) 7437 8216
Email: dl@davenportlyons.com
Website: www.davenportlyons.com

firm profile

Davenport Lyons is a leading corporate and rights law firm offering a full service to clients in a range of market sectors including media, entertainment, property, retail, leisure, sport and banking. With a 38 Partner strong practice, over 60 fee earners and supporting operational function, they are a commercially focused law firm based in the luxurious surroundings of Mayfair. Coupled with the firm's desire to retain its warm and friendly environment, Davenport Lyons is the ideal place to start your career as a successful solicitor.

main areas of work

The firm provides a full range of services through its five departments: corporate, contentious rights and dispute resolution, property, employment and private client. Areas of expertise include: corporate, commercial, corporate tax, film and TV, music, defamation, contentious and non-contentious IP/IT, commercial dispute resolution, insolvency, liquor and entertainment licensing, property, property dispute resolution, tax and trusts, matrimonial and employment.

trainee profile

Davenport Lyons is looking for candidates with excellent academic qualifications (2:1 and above, good A level results) and interesting backgrounds, who are practical and can demonstrate good business acumen. Candidates should have a breadth of interests and foreign language skills are an advantage. In short, the firm is looking for well-rounded individuals.

training environment

The training programme consists of four six-month seats. During each seat trainees receive mid and end of seat reviews, and each seat has a dedicated trainee supervisor. Davenport Lyons has an on-going in-house training and lectures programme. They pride themselves on offering interesting, hands-on training with trainees being encouraged to develop their own client relationships and to handle their own files under appropriate supervision, therefore being treated as junior fee earners. The firm aims to make its training contracts informative, educational, practical, supportive and, let us not forget, as enjoyable as possible.

benefits

Season ticket loan; client introduction bonus; contribution to gym membership; discretionary bonus; 23 days holiday; life assurance; Employee Support Programme; pension scheme and private health.

vacation placements

A limited number of places are available on the Summer Vacation Scheme which runs during July and August. Remuneration is £200 per week. Closing date for applications 31 January 2008.

sponsorship & awards

The firm does not offer financial assistance.

Partners	38
Assistant Solicitors	36
Total Staff	203
Total Trainees	16

contact
Marcia Mardner
Head of HR
Michael Hatchwell
Training Partner

method of application
Online

selection procedure
Interviews

closing date for 2010
30 July 2008

application
Training contracts p.a. **8**
Applications p.a. **800**
% interviewed p.a. **8.6%**
Required degree grade **2:1**

training
Salary
1st Year trainee
£32,000 - £32,666
2nd Year trainee
£33,332 - £34,000
Holiday entitlement **23 days**
% of trainees with a
non-law degree p.a. **70%**

post-qualification
% of trainees offered job
on qualification (2006) **71%**

Davenport Lyons

Davies Arnold Cooper

6–8 Bouverie Street, London EC4Y 8DD
Tel: (020) 7936 2222 Fax: (020) 7936 2020
Email: daclon@dac.co.uk
Website: www.recruit.dac.co.uk

Partners	68
Total Fee-earners	167
Total Trainees	12
Total Staff	317

firm profile
Davies Arnold Cooper is an international law firm particularly known for its dispute resolution and real estate expertise. It advises in relation to specialist areas of law, including insurance, real estate, construction, employment and product liability, and has a leading Hispanic practice. The firm has offices in London, Manchester, Madrid and Mexico City.

main areas of work
Dispute resolution: 60%; real estate: 40%.

trainee profile
If you secure a training contract with Davies Arnold Cooper you will most probably have a 2:1 degree, either in law or in another academic subject, as well as good A level grades. You will definitely be a self-starter with plenty of energy and common sense. What you've done with your life so far counts for much more than where you went to school/university. The firm has a number of dual-qualified lawyers whose previous professions were medicine, accountancy, public service or the armed forces. They recognise that for you, a law career is a bigger decision than someone just leaving university, especially when it means giving up a decent salary.

training programme & environment
The firm encourages you to take on responsibility as soon as you join and will give you as much as you can handle, although you will always be supervised and never left alone to struggle. You will experience both contentious and non-contentious work and because the firm only takes on a handful of trainees every year, the chances are you will be able to select your preferred seats. There are five training contract positions available for September 2010. Applications should be made using the firm's application form which is available on request or from the website.

benefits
Current first year salary is £29,000. 25 days holiday, private medical insurance and season ticket loan.

sponsorship & awards
CPE and LPC fees paid plus maintenance grants.

Dechert LLP

160 Queen Victoria Street, London EC4V 4QQ
Tel: (020) 7184 7000 Fax: (020) 7184 7001
Email: application@dechert.com Website: www.dechert.com

firm profile
Dechert LLP is a dynamic international law firm, with 1,000 lawyers across the USA and Europe. Its largest offices are in Philadelphia, New York and London.

main areas of work – london
Dechert's largest practice areas in London are corporate and securities, hedge funds and other investment funds, and finance and real estate. The firm also has smaller teams advising in practice areas such as litigation, intellectual property, employment and tax.

trainee profile
Dechert looks for enthusiasm, intelligence, an ability to find practical solutions, and for powers of expression and persuasion. Graduates from any discipline are welcome to apply.

training environment
Your training contract will start with a visit to Philadelphia, to take part in the firm-wide induction. After that you will do six seats of four months. Every new seat is discussed with you, and will reflect your interests and ambitions. No two trainees have the same training contract. Your choice of seats and professional development is guided by both the Director of Training and your own Trainee Partner, who meet with you regularly.
For those who wish to travel, the firm offers secondments to its Brussels office, and sometimes to its offices in Munich and the USA.

vacation placements
Dechert runs schemes at Easter, and in the summer. The firm's vacation schemes are aimed at penultimate year law students. The closing date for applications is 29 February 2008.

sponsorship & awards
Dechert pays LPC fees plus £10,000 sponsorship.

trainee comments
'Dechert was definitely the right choice for me. Throughout my training contract, I have been treated as an individual and given the responsibility to develop and put into practice a wide range of legal skills. In particular, I really appreciated the helpful and constructive mentoring I have received at each stage, allowing me the freedom to pursue my own areas of interest, within a genuinely nurturing and friendly environment.' (Nia Godsmark, newly qualified into Tax, read Economics, Accountancy and Law at Bristol.)

'A number of factors have contributed to make my training contract an enjoyable experience. In each of my seats, I was encouraged from the beginning to take on as much responsibility as I felt comfortable with. Although initially a daunting prospect, I feel that, with the knowledge that I have the confidence of my colleagues, I have been able to perform to a higher standard. There has always been plenty of technical training available, and I have received individual training tailored to my personal professional development. Further, I feel that I have benefited from the friendly working environment and open door policy which exists in the office.' (Richard O'Brien, newly qualified into Corporate and Securities, read Law at Durham)

Partners 37*
Assistant Solicitors 81*
Total Trainees 25*
*denotes London figure

contact
Graduate Recruitment Manager

method of application
Online

selection procedure
Communication exercises & interviews with partners & assistant solicitors

closing date for 2010
31 July 2008

application
Training contracts p.a.
Up to 15
Applications p.a. **Approx 1,500**
% interviewed p.a. **Approx 9%**
Required degree grade **2:1**
(or capability of attaining a 2:1)

training
Salary
1st year £38,000
2nd year £43,000
Holiday entitlement **20 days**
% of trainees with a non-law degree p.a. **Varies**
No. of seats available abroad p.a. **3 or 4 (plus shorter secondments to US offices)**

post-qualification
Salary c.£63,000 to £72,500 (depending on practice area)
% of trainees offered job on qualification **80%**

overseas offices
Austin, Boston, Brussels, Charlotte, Hartford, Luxembourg, Munich, Newport Beach, New York, Palo Alto, Paris, Philadelphia, Princeton, San Francisco, Washington

Denton Wilde Sapte

One Fleet Place, London EC4M 7WS
Tel: (020) 7242 1212 Fax: (020) 7320 6555
Email: Laura.goode@dentonwildesapte.com
Website: www.dentonwildesapte.com

firm profile
Denton Wilde Sapte is an international law firm with a network of offices and associate offices spanning the UK, Europe, Middle East, CIS and Africa.

main areas of work
The firm provides a full range of commercial legal services to leading organisations across four core sectors: financial institutions; energy, transport and infrastructure; real estate and retail; and technology, media and telecoms.

trainee profile
The firm looks for candidates who are team players with a strong academic and extra curricular record of achievement.

training environment
As a trainee you will undertake four six-month seats. This will include a contentious seat, plus experience in the firm's transaction based departments such as banking, real estate, corporate etc. This may also include the opportunity to work in one of the firm's international offices or with one of the firm's clients.

You will be given as much responsibility as you can handle, and will be working with the law, with your team and with clients in real business situations.

The firm works hard to maintain a friendly and open environment where ideas are shaped and people work together to achieve goals.

Given the diversity of the firm's business, it looks for people with wide-ranging skills, aptitudes and personalities. You will need drive and ambition, with the potential to contribute to the growing success of the firm.

benefits
Flexible benefit scheme. Season ticket loan.

vacation placements
Open days during December 2007 and summer schemes during July 2008. Closing date for applications for open days is 23rd November 2007 and for summer schemes 8 February 2008.

sponsorship & awards
GDL and LPC tuition fees covered plus £6,000 maintenance grant for each year of study, £7,000 if studying in London.

Partners	165
Fee-earners	687
Total Trainees	72

contact
Laura Goode

method of application
Application form

selection procedure
First interview; selection test; second interviews and case study

closing date for 2010
31 July 2008

application
Training contracts p.a. **35**
Applications p.a. **1,500**
% interviewed p.a. **15%**
Required degree grade **2:1**

training
Salary
1st year £36,000
2nd year £40,000
Holiday entitlement **24 days**
% of trainees with a non-law degree p.a. **40%**
No. of seats available abroad p.a. **Currently 9**

post-qualification
Salary (2007) **£62,000**
% of trainees offered job on qualification (2006) **81%**

overseas offices
Abu Dhabi, Almaty, Cairo, Dubai, Dubai Internet City, Istanbul, Moscow, Muscat, Paris, Riyadh (Associate Office), Tashkent

Dickinson Dees LLP

St. Ann's Wharf, 112 Quayside, Newcastle upon Tyne NE99 1SB
Tel: (0191) 279 9046 Fax: (0191) 279 9716
Email: graduate.recruitment@dickinson-dees.com
Website: www.trainingcontract.com

firm profile
Dickinson Dees enjoys an excellent reputation as one of the country's leading commercial law firms. Based in Newcastle upon Tyne, Tees Valley and York the firm prides itself on the breadth of experience and expertise which enables it to offer services of the highest standards to clients. Whilst many of the firm's clients are based in the North, Dickinson Dees works on a national basis for national and internationally based businesses and organisations.

main areas of work
The firm has over 850 employees and is organised into four key departments (Company Commercial, Commercial Property, Litigation and Private Client) with 38 cross departmental units advising on specific areas. They also handle large volumes of high-quality work for a diverse client base.

trainee profile
The firm is looking for intellectually able, motivated and enthusiastic graduates from any discipline with good communication skills. Successful applicants will understand the need to provide practical, commercial advice to clients. They will share the firm's commitment to self-development and teamwork and its desire to provide clients with services which match their highest expectations.

training environment
Trainees are relatively few for the size of the practice and the environment is supportive and friendly. You are fully integrated into the firm and involved in all aspects of firm business. The training contract consists of four seats -one in each of the Commercial Property, Company Commercial and Litigation departments. You may be able to specialise for the fourth seat. Trainees sit with their supervisors and appraisals are carried out every three months. The firm has its own Training Department as well as a supportive Graduate Recruitment team. There are induction courses on each move of department with opportunities for trainees to get involved in the firm's training programme. The firm offers a tailored in-house Professional Skills Course which is run in conjunction with the College of Law.

work placements
Places for 2008: 40; Duration: 1 week; Remuneration: £200 p.w. The firm's work placement weeks are part of the recruitment process and all applicants should apply online at www.trainingcontract.com. Apply by 31 January 2008 for Easter and Summer placements.

sponsorship & awards
GDL/LPC fees paid and financial assistance offered.

Partners	78
Total Staff	850
Total Trainees	29

contact
Sally Brewis, Graduate
Recruitment Adviser

method of application
Apply online at
www.trainingcontract.com

selection procedure
Aptitude and ability tests,
negotiation exercise,
personality questionnaire,
interview

closing date for 2010
31 July 2008

application
Training contracts p.a.
up to **15 (Newcastle)**
up to **3 (Tees Valley)**
up to **3 (York)**
Applications p.a. **800**
% interviewed p.a. **10%**
Required degree grade **2:1**
in either law or non-law

training
Salary
1st year (2006) £19,000
2nd year (2006) £20,000
Holiday entitlement **25 days**
% of trainees with
a non-law degree p.a. **40%**
No. of seats available
abroad p.a. **2**
(3-month secondments)

post-qualification
Salary (2007) **£36,000**
% of trainees offered job
on qualification (2006) **90%**
% of partners (as at
01/08/07) who joined as
trainees **35%**

other offices
Tees Valley, York, London
Brussels (associated office)

DICKINSON DEES

DLA Piper UK LLP

Victoria Square House, Victoria Square, Birmingham B2 4DL
Tel: (020) 7796 6677 Fax: (0121) 262 5793
Email: recruitment.graduate@dlapiper.com Website: www.dlapiper.com

firm profile

DLA Piper is one of the world's largest full service commercial law firms with UK offices in Birmingham, Edinburgh, Glasgow, Leeds, Liverpool, London, Manchester and Sheffield.

The firm now has more than 7,000 employees working from over 60 offices across Europe, Asia and the US. The firm's current vision is to be the leading global business law firm and in 2006 The Lawyer awarded DLA Piper 'Global Law Firm of the Year' at their annual awards, proving that it is moving closer to that vision. Clients include some of the world's leading businesses, governments, banks and financial institutions and this impressive client base coupled with an emphasis on providing high quality service and teamwork, offers a challenging fast-paced working environment.

DLA Piper offers its trainees the opportunity to apply for international secondments to its Dubai, Hong Kong, Moscow and Singapore offices, as well as a number of client secondments.

DLA Piper holds the 'Investors in People' accreditation, demonstrating commitment to its employees and their ongoing development. As well as taking care of its own people, DLA Piper has extensive Corporate Social Responsibility/Pro Bono programmes in place. The firm feels that volunteering for these programmes helps to broaden the perspectives of the DLA Piper people that take part. For trainees, pro bono work (for companies like The Prince's Trust) means gaining valuable experience in running their own cases and experiencing a unique level of work and responsibility.

main areas of work

DLA Piper has the following main areas of work: corporate; employment, pensions and benefits; finance and projects; litigation and regulatory; real estate; and technology, media and commercial.

trainee profile

The firm is looking for individuals from either a law or non-law background who have a minimum of 3 Bs at A Level (or equivalent) and expect, or have achieved, a 2:1 degree classification - however, a strong academic background alone is no longer sufficient. DLA Piper looks for highly motivated and energetic team players with sound commercial awareness, outstanding communication and organisational skills. As well as this, in line with the firm's main focus of work, a keen interest in the corporate world is essential, as is an appetite for life!

As soon as future trainees are recruited DLA Piper does as much as possible to make them feel part of the firm, for example, writing to them regularly and organising social events where future trainees can meet one another as well as current members of staff.

Partners	1200
Other lawyers	1800
Total Trainees	184

contact
Sally Carthy, Head of Graduate Recruitment

method of application
Online application form

selection procedure
First interview, second interview, assessment afternoon

closing date for 2010
31 July 2008

application
Training contracts p.a. **95+**
Applications p.a. **2,200**
% interviewed p.a. **20%**
Required degree grade **2:1**

training
Salary (2007)
1st year (London) £36,000
2nd year (London) £39,000
1st year (English Regions) £25,000
2nd year (English Regions) £28,000
1st year (Scotland) £22,000
2nd year (Scotland) £25,000
% of trainees with a non-law degree p.a. **40%**

post-qualification
Salary (2007)
£63,000 (London)
£competitive market rate (regional offices and Scotland)

uk offices
Birmingham, Edinburgh, Glasgow, Leeds, Liverpool, London, Manchester, Sheffield

overseas offices
Austria, Belgium, Bosnia-Herzegovina, Bulgaria, China, Croatia, Czech Republic, France, Germany, Georgia, Hong Kong, Hungary, Italy, Japan, Netherlands, Norway, Poland, Russia, Slovakia, Spain, Thailand, Ukraine, UAE, USA.

DLA Piper UK LLP cont'd

training environment
From induction to qualification and beyond, DLA Piper ensures that its employees develop the necessary skills and knowledge to survive in a busy client-driven environment. Trainees complete four six-month seats during the course of their training contract. If you want responsibility, the firm will give you as much as you can handle and your progress will be monitored through regular reviews and feedback. The compulsory Professional Skills Course is run in-house and is tailored to meet the needs of the firm's trainees. This, combined with on-the-job experience, provides trainees with an excellent grounding on which to build their professional careers.

DLA Piper trainees are able to express a preference for their seats, and as much as possible is done to ensure that during the course of the training contract these preferences can be accommodated. In September 2007 nearly 90 percent of DLA Piper's qualifying trainees chose to stay with the firm.

summer placements
DLA Piper runs summer placement schemes across all of its UK offices. The scheme aims to give a thorough insight into life at the firm. Attendees shadow a fee-earner in two departments and are given a range of work to do, they are also allocated a trainee 'buddy' to help out with any queries. The scheme also includes presentations from departments and social events with the trainees.

Places for 2008: Approx 200; Duration: 2 weeks; Remuneration (2007 figures) £250 per week (London), £200 per week (regions and Scotland); Closing Date: 31 January 2008.

sponsorship & awards
Payment of LPC and GDL fees plus maintenance grant in both years of up to £7,000.

benefits
Trainees are entitled to join the firm's pension, private health cover, life assurance and permanent health insurance schemes. Holiday entitlement is 25 days per year.

overseas offices
Austria, Belgium, Bosnia-Herzegovina, Bulgaria, China, Croatia, Czech Republic, France, Georgia, Germany, Hong Kong, Hungary, Italy, Japan, Netherlands, Norway, Russia, Singapore, Slovak Republic, Spain, Thailand, Ukraine, UAE, USA.

trainee quotes
"I was really impressed by the way the graduate recruitment team kept in contact with me while I was still at university and law school. There's regular contact, support and you receive letters, the firm's magazine and press releases. You actually feel part of the team from the outset and reassured knowing that you can always pick up the phone if you have any queries. It's a great way to start."

DMH Stallard

100 Queens Road, Brighton BN1 3YB
Tel: (01273) 744270 Fax: (01273) 744290
Email: recruitment@dmhstalard.com
Website: www.dmhstallard.com

firm profile

DMH Stallard is an approachable and innovative firm with an open culture which encourages personal development and provides its personnel with a high level of support in order to achieve this. The firm offers expertise and service comparable to City firms to a range of commercial organisations, non-profit institutions and individual clients. By focusing on the client's needs DMH Stallard provides practical and creative solutions. DMH Stallard operates from offices in Brighton, Gatwick and London.

main areas of work

Corporate/commercial; commercial property; construction; planning and environmental; employment, intellectual property/IT; real estate asset management; dispute resolution; personal injury; private client; real estate dispute resolution.

trainee profile

The firm welcomes applications from motivated graduates from all backgrounds and age groups. Enthusiasm and commercial awareness are as prized as academic ability, and good communication skills are a must. Ideal applicants are those with the potential to become effective managers or strong marketeers.

training environment

Usually four six month seats taken from the following areas: employment, intellectual property/IT, corporate/commercial, planning and environmental, commercial property, dispute resolution, real estate dispute resolution, personal injury, real estate asset management, construction, technology and media, public law and private client. Trainees are closely supervised by the partner to whom they are attached but have every opportunity to work as part of a team and deal directly with clients.

vacation placements

Places for Summer 2008: Limited number of unpaid places; Duration: 1 week; Closing Date: 31 January 2008.

sponsorship & awards

50% loan and 50% funded, conditional on remaining with the firm. Bonus payments for those who have already paid for their LPC.

Partners	52
Assistant Solicitors	51
Total Trainees	19

contact
Jessica Leigh-Davis

method of application
Online application form

selection procedure
First and second stage assessment days including interviews

closing date for 2010
31 July 2008

application
Training contracts p.a. **10**
Applications p.a. **525**
% interviewed p.a. **7.6%**
Preferred degree grade **2:1**

training
Salary
1st year (2007)
£22,000 (Brighton & Gatwick)
£27,000 (London)
2nd year (2007)
£24,000 (Brighton & Gatwick)
£29,000 (London)
Holiday entitlement **23.5 days**

Dorsey & Whitney

21 Wilson Street, London EC2M 2TD
Tel: (020) 7588 0800 Fax: (020) 7588 0555
Website: www.dorsey.com

firm profile
Dorsey & Whitney is amongst the largest law firms in the world with more than 20 offices situated across three continents. The firm has over 650 lawyers worldwide. The London office of Dorsey & Whitney has over 50 fee earners. It continues to build on its traditional strengths in corporate law, litigation, real estate and intellectual property work through its wide range of practice groups.

main areas of work
The London office offers the full range of legal services including corporate finance, cross-border M&A, commercial litigation, tax, employment, real estate, intellectual property and private equity.

trainee profile
Dorsey & Whitney is looking for 'self-starters', capable of meeting the intellectual and business challenges of a successful multi-national practice. Candidates should be committed team players who enjoy rewarding client work. An honours degree at 2:1 level or above and some relevant work experience is also required.

training environment
The training contract is split into four individual 'seats' of six months each. Each trainee will be required to complete litigation and corporate seats. Secondments to major clients are available. All trainees are supplied with the encouragement and support necessary to maximise their potential. Through the mentoring, professional development and evaluation programmes, the firm strives to develop and retain the highest calibre lawyers.

benefits
Non-contributory pension schemes; health insurance and life insurance.

Partners	**16**
Total Fee Earners	**55**
Total Trainees	**7**

contact
Mitchell Moss, Partner
(020) 7588 0800

method of application
Application by letter with a current curriculum vitae addressed to Mitchell Moss.

closing date for 2010
31 July 2008

application
Training contracts p.a. **4** (currently under review)

training
Salary
1st year (2008) £35,000
2nd year (2008) £39,000
(plus £7,000 payment towards LPC cost)
Holiday entitlement **25 days plus public holidays**

post-qualification
Salary (2008) **£65,000 +** automatic bonus of up to **£30,000** depending on number of billable hours
Dorsey & Whitney aims to offer a qualified position to all candidates who have shown the appropriate level of performance during training, subject to the needs of the firm

Dundas & Wilson LLP

Northwest Wing, Bush House, Aldwych, London, WC2B 4EZ
Tel: (020) 7240 2401 Fax: (020) 7240 2448
Email: lorraine.bale@dundas-wilson.com

firm profile
Dundas & Wilson (D&W) is a leading UK commercial law firm with offices in London, Edinburgh and Glasgow. The firm services a wide range of prestigious clients, including major companies and public sector organisations, throughout the UK and abroad.

main areas of work
Lawyers are grouped into 14 specialist skill-based teams known as Market Areas: Banking, Construction and Engineering, Corporate, Corporate Recovery, Dispute Resolution, Environment, Employment, EU and Competition, IP / IT, Pensions, Planning and Transportation, Projects, Property and Tax.

trainee profile
D&W are looking for applicants with enthusiasm, commitment, adaptability, strong written and oral communication skills, excellent interpersonal skills, commercial awareness and an aptitude for problem solving and analysis.

training environment
The two year traineeship is split into four six-month seats. The firm aims to accommodate trainees' preferences when allocating seats as the firm wants to encourage trainees to take an active part in managing their career development.

During the traineeship trainees receive on-the-job training, two day seat training at the beginning of each seat, training in core skills such as drafting and effective legal writing and regular seminars. Trainees receive a formal performance review every three months and are allocated a mentor for each seat.

The firm's open plan environment means that trainees sit amongst assistants, associates, senior associates and Partners – this provides daily opportunities to observe how lawyers communicate both with clients and each other. This type of learning is invaluable and great preparation for life as a fully fledged lawyer.

benefits
Life assurance, permanent health insurance, group personal pension, season ticket loan, holiday purchase scheme.

vacation scheme
D&W offers four-week summer placements. To apply, please visit the website and complete the online application form. The closing date is 26 January 2008.

sponsorship & awards
GDL/CPE and LPC fees paid plus maintenance grant.

Partners	82
Lawyers	284
Trainees	50

contact
Lorraine Bale

method of application
Online application

selection procedure
Assessment day comprising interview, group exercise, occupational personality questionnaire and aptitude tests

closing date for 2010
31 July 2008

application
Training contracts p.a. **35 (12 in London)**
Applications p.a. **300**
% interviewed p.a. **15%**
Required degree grade **2:1 preferred**

training
Salary
**1st year (Scotland) £19,000 (England) £30,000
2nd year (Scotland) £22,000 (England) £33,500**
Holiday entitlement **25 days with ability to purchase an addtional 5 days**

offices
London, Edinburgh, Glasgow

DWF

Centurion House, 129 Deansgate, Manchester, M3 3AA
Tel: (0161) 603 5000   Fax: (0161) 603 5050
6 Winckley Square, Preston, PR1 3JJ
Tel: (01772) 556677   Fax (0870) 166 7161
West One, Wellington Street, Leeds, LS1 1BA
Email: trainees@dwf.co.uk   Website: www.dwf.co.uk

firm profile

DWF is a leading regional law firm with national and international reach. The firm provides a full range of legal services to businesses and individuals in the corporate market and the client base ranges from privately owned entrepreneurial companies to large multi-national organisations.

Following the firm's merger with Ricksons in January 2007, the firm employ around 800 people, including over 100 Partners across the North of England.

The firm is able to serve clients across the UK from offices in Leeds, Liverpool, Manchester and Preston and through the firm's network of relationships with law firms around the world, it is able to extend this service internationally. The business continues to expand, through a combination of organic growth, lateral hires and other consolidation activity.

main areas of work

DWF provide a full range of legal services: corporate, real estate, banking and finance, litigation, insurance, business recovery, people and private client. A full list of services available within these areas can be found on the firm's website at www.dwf.co.uk

DWF also provides legal services across a range of different industries and sectors, and has developed particular expertise in a number of specific areas. To enable clients to benefit from this expertise, the firm has developed a series of sector-focused teams: automotive, education, food and resourcing.

trainee profile

DWF's future depends on recruiting and retaining the right people. DWF only recruit people of the highest quality whether they be lawyers or non-lawyers. DWF is always on the look out for ambitious and driven professionals who are able to add value to their developing team. DWF wants its trainee solicitors to play a part in building on its success. The firm is looking for trainees who enjoy working as part of a busy team, respond positively to a challenge and have what it takes to deliver results for clients. The firm is looking for its partners of the future and in recent years virtually all of its qualifying trainees have been offered jobs. DWF is an equal opportunities employer and is committed to diversity in all aspects.

training environment

DWF provides a well structured training programme for all new trainee solicitors which combines the day to day practical experience of working with a Partner, associate or senior solicitor, backed by a comprehensive in-house lecture and workshop programme and the PSC course. You will very quickly become a vital member of the team, being delegated the appropriate level of responsibility from an early stage in your training.

Full supervision is provided and it is the firm's policy for each trainee to sit with a partner or associate, whilst working for a legal team as a whole. The two year training contract is divided into "seats". These will be spent in the firms main departments (corporate, insurance litigation, real estate, commercial litigation and people and private client) which gives opportunities to look at specialist areas of work within each department.

Partners	119
Assistant Solicitors	158
Total Trainees	30

contact
Vicky Macmillan
Professional Recruitment and
Trainee Specialist

method of application
Online application

selection procedure
2 stage interview/selection process

closing date for 2009/2010
31 July 2008

application
Training contracts p.a. **16**
Applications p.a. **c.800**
% interviewed p.a. **18%**
Required degree grade **2:1**
in any discipline

training
Salary
1st year (2007) £23,000
Holiday entitlement
**25 days p.a. minimum +
option to buy & sell holidays**

post-qualification
% of trainees offered job
on qualification (2007) **100%**

benefits
Flexible benefits scheme
including insurance, life
assurance, pension and
other benefits

vacation placements
30 places offered p.a.
Paid summer vacation
placements lasting 1 week

sponsorship & awards
LPC funding for tuition fees

Eversheds

Senator House, 85 Queen Victoria Street, London EC4V 4JL
Tel: (0845) 497 1067 Fax: (0845) 497 4919
Email: gradrec@eversheds.com
Website: www.eversheds.com Application Form Online at www.eversheds.com

firm profile
Eversheds LLP is one of the largest full service international law firms in the world with over 4,000 people and 32 offices in major cities across the UK, Europe and Asia. The firm works for some of the world's most prestigious organisations in both the public and private sector, offering them a compelling mixture of straightforward advice, clear direction, predictable costs and outstanding service.
It's a winning combination that has meant the firm is now expanding quicker than any of the firm's closest competitors. The firm acts for 111 Listed companies including 43 FTSE 250 companies, 30 of the 37 British based Fortune 500 companies and now has one of the fastest growing corporate teams in the City.
In 2006 the firm laid out a strategic plan that will see the firm build on these achievements and grow over the next few years into a major player on the legal stage around the world. The firm is looking for highly ambitious and focused trainees to help it achieve its goals.

main areas of work
Core work: corporate, commercial, litigation and dispute management, real estate, human resources (employment and pensions) and legal systems group.

trainee profile
Eversheds people are valued for their drive and legal expertise but also for their business advice too. The firm develops the same qualities in its trainees. As a trainee you'll be given as much responsibility as you can handle and will benefit from the firm's hands-on philosophy. The firm takes learning and development very seriously and will help you build the career you want.

training environment
The firm offers a full well-rounded training programme with the opportunity to focus your technical skills in each of the various practice groups as you rotate through four six-month seats. You will also take part in a full programme of personal and commercial development skills training, including finance and business, communication, presenting, business writing, client care, professional standards and advocacy.

vacation placements
Places for Summer 2008: 150. Duration: two weeks. Remuneration: London £240, regions £175. The following offices run a one-week Easter vacation scheme: Birmingham, Cambridge, Cardiff, Leeds, Manchester and Nottingham (London's Easter scheme is two weeks). Closing Date: 31 January 2008.

sponsorship & awards
GDL and LPC fees and maintenance grants in accordance with the terms of the firm's offer.

Partners 400+
Assistant Solicitors 2,000+
Total Trainees 180+

contact
gradrec@eversheds.com

method of application
Apply online at www.eversheds.com

selection procedure
Selection days include group and individual exercises, presentations and interview

closing date for 2010
31 July 2008

application
Training contracts p.a. **80**
Applications p.a. **4,000**
% interviewed p.a. **20%**
Required degree grade **2:1**

training
Salary
1st year London (2007) **£35,000**
2nd year London (2007) **£37,000**
Holiday entitlement **25 days**
% of trainees with a non-law degree p.a. **45%**
No. of seats available abroad p.a. **Up to 12**

post-qualification
Salary London (2007) **£62,000**
% of trainees offered job on qualification (2005) **82%**

offices
Barcelona*, Birmingham, Brussels, Budapest*, Cambridge, Cardiff, Copenhagen, Doha** Ipswich, Kuala Lumpur*, Leeds, London, Madrid*, Manchester, Milan*, Munich*, Newcastle, Norwich, Nottingham, Paris, Rome*, Shanghai*, Singapore*, Sofia*, Stockholm*, Valladolid*, Vienna*, Warsaw*, Wroclaw*
* Associated office
** In co-operation

Farrer & Co LLP

66 Lincoln's Inn Fields, London WC2A 3LH
Tel: (020) 7242 2022 Fax: (020) 7242 9899
Email: training@farrer.co.uk
Website: www.farrer.co.uk

firm profile

Farrer & Co is a mid-sized London law firm. The firm provides specialist advice to a large number of prominent private, institutional and commercial clients. Farrer & Co has built a successful law firm based on the goodwill of close client relationships, outstanding expertise in niche sectors and a careful attention to personal service and quality.

main areas of work

The firm's breadth of expertise is reflected by the fact that it has an outstanding reputation in fields as diverse as matrimonial law, offshore tax planning, employment, heritage work, charity law, defamation and sports law.

trainee profile

Trainees are expected to be highly motivated individuals with keen intellects and interesting and engaging personalities. Those applicants who appear to break the mould – as shown by their initiative for organisation, leadership, exploration, or enterprise – are far more likely to get an interview than the erudite, but otherwise unimpressive, student.

training environment

The training programme involves each trainee in the widest range of cases, clients and issues possible in a single law firm, taking full advantage of the wide range of practice areas at Farrer & Co by offering six seats, rather than the more usual four. This provides a broad foundation of knowledge and experience and the opportunity to make an informed choice about the area of law in which to specialise. A high degree of involvement is encouraged under the direct supervision of solicitors and partners. Trainees attend an induction programme and regular internal lectures. The training partner reviews trainees' progress at the end of each seat and extensive feedback is given. The firm has a very friendly atmosphere and regular sporting and social events.

benefits

Health and life insurance, subsidised gym membership, season ticket loan.

vacation placements

Places for 2008: 30; Duration: 2 weeks at Easter, two schemes for 2 weeks in summer; Remuneration: £250 p.w.; Closing Date: 31 January 2008.

sponsorship & awards

CPE Funding: Fees paid plus £5,000 maintenance. LPC Funding: Fees paid plus £5,000 maintenance.

Partners	**62**
Assistant Solicitors	**63**
Total Trainees	**18**

contact
Trainee Recruitment Manager

method of application
Online via the firm's website

selection procedure
Interviews with Trainee Recruitment Partner and partners

closing date for 2010
31 July 2008

application
Training contracts p.a.**10**
Applications p.a. **800**
% interviewed p.a. **5%**
Required degree grade **2:1**

training
Salary
1st year (sept 2007) £29,500
2nd year (sept 2007) £32,000
The firm operates a performance related bonus scheme based on both personal and firm performance
Holiday entitlement **25 days**
% of trainees with non-law degrees p.a. **40-60%**

post-qualification
Salary (2006) **£47,000**
trainees offered job on qualification (2006) **87%**
% of partners (as at July 05) who joined as trainees **66%**

Field Fisher Waterhouse LLP

35 Vine Street, London EC3N 2AA
Tel: (020) 7861 4000 Fax: (020) 7488 0084
Email: graduaterecruitment@ffw.com   Website: www.ffw.com/careers

firm profile
Field Fisher Waterhouse LLP (FFW) is a mid-sized City law firm that provides a broad range of legal services to an impressive list of clients that range from small unlisted UK companies to multinationals and foreign corporations. The firm prides itself on offering creative solutions and practical advice for clients in an ever-changing commercial world. Europe is its domestic market. It has offices in Brussels, Hamburg and London and an exclusive relationship with leading firms in Spain and Italy. The firm also has long standing affiliations with firms in France, the Czech Republic, Hungary and Poland.

main areas of work
Throughout their training contract trainees have the opportunity to work within IP & technology, corporate and commercial, banking and finance, regulatory and real estate. They also offer trainee seats in a wide range of other areas including public sector, litigation, employment, and travel and aviation.

trainee profile
The firm is looking to recruit trainees from both law and non-law backgrounds who have a strong academic background, excellent communication skills, enthusiasm and the ability to work as part of a team.

training environment
FFW offers a six seat training contract and their range of practice areas enable them to offer outstanding opportunities for training. Trainees are treated as a valued part of the team and are encouraged to assume early responsibility. Practical training is complemented by a comprehensive programme of in-house seminars, workshops and external courses, accompanied by regular feedback and a formal assessment at the end of each seat. The firm invests highly in the development and training of all its trainees and provides good quality work within a friendly, relaxed and supportive working environment. You will also have additional support from your fellow trainees, a buddy and a mentor who is a senior solicitor.

sponsorship & benefits
Sponsorship and a GDL (£5,500) and LPC (£6,000) maintenance grant is paid. Other benefits include: 25 days' holiday, life assurance, season ticket loan, medical insurance, GP service, and pension in addition to having two squash courts in the firm's offices.

vacation placements
Increasingly, trainees have come to the firm through the summer vacation scheme, which provides a useful way of getting an insider's view of FFW. The firm runs two two-week schemes during July where you have the opportunity to spend a week in two different departments and take part in a variety of work and social activities.
Please apply online for the Summer Vacation Scheme and Training Contracts, via the website at www.ffw.com/careers.
Deadline for 2008 Summer Vacation Scheme: 31 January 2008.
Deadline for 2010 Training Contracts: 31 July 2008.

Partners	100
Assistant Solicitors	175
Vacancies	20
Total Trainees	35

contact
Lucie Rees
Graduate Recruitment

method of application
Apply online via the firm website,
www.ffw.com/careers

selection procedure
Interviews and a written assessment

closing date for 2010
31 July 2008

application
Training contracts p.a. **20**
Applications p.a. **1,200**
Required degree grade **2:1**

training
Salary
1st year £33,000
2nd year £36,500
Holiday entitlement
25 days

post-qualification
Salary (2007) **£60,000**
% of trainees offered job on qualification (2007) **70%**

offices
London

Finers Stephens Innocent

179 Great Portland St, London W1W 5LS
Tel: (020) 7323 4000 Fax: (020) 7580 7069
Email: gradrecruitment@fsilaw.com
Website: www.fsilaw.com

firm profile

Finers Stephens Innocent is an expanding practice in Central London, providing a range of high quality legal services to corporate, commercial and private clients. The firm's philosophy includes close partner involvement and a cost-effective approach in all client matters. They have a working style which is unstuffy and informal, but still aspires to the highest quality of output, while offering a sensible work-life balance. The firm is a member of the Meritas international network of law firms.

main areas of work

Commercial property, company commercial, employment, private client, family, media, defamation. See the website for further details.

trainee profile

The firm requires academic excellence in all applicants. It also looks for maturity, personality, a broad range of interests, initiative, strong communication skills, and the ability to write clear English, and to think like a lawyer. The firm has for several years given equal consideration to applicants whether applying straight from university or having followed another career previously. Trainees get early responsibility, client contact and close involvement in transactions and litigation matters.

training environment

Between offering you a training contract and the time you start, the firm aims to keep regularly in touch with you, including offering you some work experience with them. When you start they provide a careful induction programme, after which you complete four six-month seats in different departments, sharing a room with either a Partner or Senior Assistant. The firm has three Training Partners who keep a close eye on the welfare and progress of trainees. There are regular group meetings with trainees, and an appraisal process which enables you to know how you are progressing, as well as giving you a chance to provide feedback on your training. The firm runs a variety of in-house training courses for trainees.

benefits

20 days holiday; pension; private medical insurance; life insurance; long-term disability insurance; season ticket loan.

sponsorship & awards

LPC and CPE course fees.

Partners	36
Assistant Solicitors	37
Total Trainees	11

contact
Personnel Department

method of application
CV & covering letter

selection procedure
2 interviews with the
Training Partners

closing date for 2010
30 June 2008

application
Training contracts p.a. **6**
Applications p.a. **800**
% interviewed p.a. **3%**
Required degree grade **2:1**

training
Salary
1st year £29,000
2nd year £31,000
Holiday entitlement **20 days**
% of trainees with a non-law
degree p.a. **0-50%**

post-qualification
Salary £47,000
% of trainees offered job
on qualification (2007) **80%**

Fladgate Fielder

25 North Row, London, W1K 6DJ
Tel: (020) 7462 2299 Fax: (020) 7629 4414
Email: trainees@fladgate.com Website: www.fladgate.com

firm profile
Fladgate Fielder is an innovative, progressive and thriving law firm based in the heart of London's West End which prides itself on its friendly and professional working environment.

main areas of work
The firm provides a wide range of legal services to a portfolio of prestigious clients in the UK and overseas, including multinationals, major institutions and listed companies, clearing banks, lenders and entrepreneurs. Fladgate Fielder's lawyers have experience in most major areas of practice and the firm combines an accessible and responsive style of service with first-class technical skills and in-depth expertise.

The firm has a strong international dimension based on multi-lingual and multi-qualified lawyers working in London and complemented by access to an extensive network of overseas lawyers. The firm operates specialist teams which serve continental Europe (with an emphasis on the Germanic countries), India, Israel, the US and the Middle East. The firm's three main departments comprise property (which includes separate planning, construction and property litigation teams), corporate (which includes tax, intellectual property and employment groups) and litigation. These are supported by a number of specialist cross-departmental teams that provide co-ordinated advice on a range of issues.

trainee profile
Fladgate Fielder seeks trainees with enthusiasm, leadership potential and excellent interpersonal skills. You must be able to work both independently and in a team, and will be expected to show common sense and initiative. Awareness of the commercial interests of clients is essential. You will have a minimum of a 2:1 degree, although not necessarily in law, together with three excellent A levels or equivalent. The firm is keen to attract candidates with language skills.

training environment
Typically, you will complete four six-month seats. Each seat will bring you into contact with new clients and colleagues, and you can expect to gain real hands-on experience of a variety of deals and projects, both large and small. In each seat you will work alongside senior lawyers who will supervise your development and ensure that you are involved in challenging and interesting work. In addition to on-the-job training, each department has a comprehensive training schedule of seminars and workshops covering a range of legal and skills training.

The firm has a modern culture and an open-door policy where trainees are given early responsibility and encouraged to achieve their full potential.

benefits
Pension, permanent health insurance, life assurance, season ticket loan, sports club loan, bonus scheme, private medical.

sponsorship & awards
The firm offers a £10,000 qualification bonus over two years to trainees retained upon qualification.

Partners	42
Assistant Solicitors	38
Total Trainees	8

contact
Mrs Annaleen Stephens, human resources manager

method of application
Please apply using the firm's application form. Further information and an application form are available at the firm's website www.fladgate.com

selection procedure
Assesment day and interview

closing date for 2009/2010
Apply by 31 July 2008

application
The firm operates a biennial recruitment programme and will be recruiting for the 2009 and 2010 intakes in Summer 2008.
Training contracts p.a. **4**
Required degree grade **2:1**

training
Salary
£27,500-£29,000
Holiday entitlement **22-25 days**

post-qualification
Salary **£55,000**
% of trainees offered job on qualification (2007) **100%**

Foot Anstey

21 Derry's Cross, Plymouth PL1 2SW
Tel: (01752) 675000 Fax: (01752) 675500
Email: training@foot-ansteys.co.uk Website: www.foot-ansteys.co.uk

firm profile

Based in the South West, Foot Anstey is committed to advising businesses, individuals and those requiring public funding. The firm is determined to provide a first class service to clients. Trainees are supervised by some of the best legal minds in the profession. The firm's retention rate for trainees upon qualification is excellent. Foot Anstey provides a progressive, supportive and determined working environment and is committed to developing its staff.

main areas of work

Main areas of work include: commercial property, property and construction litigation, company and commercial, dispute resolution, banking, employment, insolvency, clinical negligence, criminal advocates, family and childcare, private client and residential property. The firm has an extensive range of clients from commercial, public and private sectors (acting for numerous local, regional and national companies and high net worth individuals). Foot Anstey holds major contracts with the Legal Services Commission.

trainee profile

The firm welcomes applications from all law and non-law graduates who have a strong academic background, excellent communication skills and the ability to work as part of a team. Trainees are welcomed into a friendly and supportive environment where they will find the quality and variety of work both challenging and rewarding.

training environment

Foot Anstey's wide range of legal services enables it to offer trainees experience in a wide range of disciplines throughout its four offices. Trainees undertake four seats of six months. Whenever possible (with the exception of the first seat) trainees are able to select their seats. All trainees attend an induction course. Individual monthly meetings are held with supervisors. Appraisals are conducted halfway through each seat. Regular communication between the trainees and supervisors ensures an open and friendly environment. The Professional Skills Course is taught externally. The firm has Lexcel and Investors in People accreditations and an excellent training and development programme.

benefits

Include contributory pension, 25 days' holiday.

vacation placements

The deadline for the 2008 summer placement scheme is 31 March 2008.

sponsorship & awards

£9,600 grant towards LPC and living expenses.

Vacancies	10
Trainees	16
Partners	28
Total Staff	305

contact
Louise Widley
(01392) 685331

method of application
CV and covering letter to Richard Sutton at the Plymouth office address. Alternatively email it to: training@foot-ansteys.co.uk or apply online at www.foot-ansteys.co.uk

selection procedure
Assessment day

application
Training contracts p.a. **10**
Required degree grade
2:1 (preferred)

closing date for 2010
31 July 2008

training
Salary
1st year (2007) £19,500
2nd year (2007) £21,000
Holiday entitlement **25 days**

post-qualification
Salary (2007) **£31,500**
% of trainees offered job on qualification (2007) **100%**
% of assistant solicitors who joined as trainees (as at 30/04/07) **39%**
% of partners who joined as trainees (as at 30/04/07) **21.5%**

other offices
Plymouth, Exeter & Taunton

Forbes

73 Northgate, Blackburn BB2 1AA
Tel: (01254) 580000 Fax: (01254) 222216
Email: graduate.recruitment@forbessolicitors.co.uk

firm profile

Forbes is one of the largest practices in the north with 29 partners and over 350 members of staff based in nine offices across the north of England. The firm has a broad based practice dealing with both commercial and private client work and can therefore provide a varied and exciting training contract. The firm is however especially noted for excellence in its company/commercial; civil litigation; defendant insurer; crime; family and employment departments. It has a number of Higher Court Advocates and the firm holds many Legal Service Commission Franchises. Underlying the practice is a strong commitment to quality, training and career development – a commitment underlined by the fact that Forbes was one of the first firms to be recognised as an Investor in People and its ISO 9001 accreditation. For applicants looking for a 'city' practice without the associated hassles of working in a city then Forbes could be it. The firm can offer the best of both worlds – a large firm with extensive resources and support combined with a commitment to quality, people and the personal touch.

main areas of work

Company/commercial, civil litigation, defendant insurer, crime, family and employment services.

trainee profile

Forbes looks for high-calibre recruits with strong North West connections and good academic records, who are also keen team players. Candidates should have a total commitment to client service and identify with the firm's philosophy of providing practical straightforward legal advice.

training environment

A tailored training programme involves six months in four of the following: crime, civil litigation, defendant insurer in Leeds or Blackburn, matrimonial, and non-contentious/company commercial.

Partners	29
Assistant Solicitors	53
Total Trainees	15+

contact
Graduate Recruitment Manager

method of application
Handwritten letter and CV

selection procedure
Interview with partners

closing date for 2010
31 July 2008
If no invite to interview is received by 31/08/08 applicants to assume they have been unsuccesful.

application
Training contracts p.a. **4**
Applications p.a. **350 plus**
% interviewed p.a. **Varies**
Required degree grade **2:1**

training
Salary
1st year At least Law Society minimum
2nd year (2006) £18,322
Holiday entitlement
20 days p.a.

post-qualification
Salary
Highly competitive
% of trainees offered job on qualification (2006) **100%**

Ford & Warren

Westgate Point, Westgate, Leeds, LS1 2AX
Tel: (0113) 243 6601 Fax: (0113) 242 0905
Email: Debra.Hinde@forwarn.com
Website: www.forwarn.com

Partners	**21**
Assistant Solicitors	**70**
Total Trainees	**6**

firm profile

Ford & Warren is an independent, single office commercial law firm based in Leeds. Over the last 15 years the firm has sustained a rapid and generic growth without mergers or acquisitions so that it now occupies the whole of the prestigious Westgate Point office block in the heart of the commercial centre of Leeds. The firm has 21 partners, 70 solicitors and paralegals and a total staff of over 200. Ford & Warren has the following departments: Employment; Road and Rail; Transportation; Corporate; Commercial Litigation; Commercial Property; Insurance and PI; Tax and Inheritance; Matrimonial. The firm has a significant presence in the public sector particularly in health and education. The firm has areas of high specialisation where its lawyers have a national reputation and its client base includes the largest limited companies and PLCs. These areas include transportation and the licensed and leisure industries.

main areas of work

Employment and industrial relations; road and rail transportation; corporate; insurance and personal injury; commercial property/real estate; public sector; tax and inheritance; matrimonial. The Dispute Resolution/Commercial Litigation Department has five sections: commercial dispute resolution, property litigation, finance litigation, insolvency and debt recovery.

trainee profile

The firm is looking for hard working, self-reliant and enthusiastic individuals who will make a contribution to the firm from the outset. Applicants must have a strong academic background, a genuine enthusiasm for the law and the social abilities required to work effectively with colleagues and clients. The majority of lawyers practising at the firm joined as trainees.

training environment

The firm offers seats in employment, commercial litigtion, corporate, insurance and personal injury, commercial property and private client. Usually, trainees will undertake four seats of six months, although split seats may sometimes be available. The firm has a comprehensive in-house training programme for all lawyers and the PSC is also provided internally.

selection procedure

First interviews for 2010 will take place in late 2008 with a Partner and Associate of the firm. Successful candidates are invited to a second assessment interview involving at least one member of the managing board.

contact
Debra Hinde

method of application
Handwritten letter and CV or email

selection procedure
Interviews and exercise

closing date for 2010
31 July 2008

application
Training contracts p.a. **4**
Applications p.a. **500**
No required degree grade

Forsters LLP

31, Hill Street, London W1J 5LS
Tel: (020) 7863 8333 Fax: (020) 7863 8444
Email: acsweetland@forsters.co.uk
Website: www.forsters.co.uk

Partners	29
Assistant Solicitors	60
Total Trainees	10

contact
Amy Sweetland

method of application
Online application form

selection procedure
First interview with 2
Graduate Recruitment
Partners; second interview
with Managing Partner and
Graduate Recruitment
Partner

training
Salary
1st year (2007) £30,000
2nd year (2007) £32,000
Holiday entitlement **25 days**

post-qualification
Salary (2007) **£51,000**

firm profile

Forsters is a successful firm committed to being the best at what it does. Based in Mayfair in London's West End, Forsters was founded in 1998. Now with around 100 lawyers, it is recognised as being a progressive law firm which is highly regarded for its property and private client work as well as having thriving commercial, litigation and family law practices. The working atmosphere of the firm is friendly and informal, yet highly professional. A social committee organises a range of activities from quiz nights to sporting events.

main areas of work

The firm has a strong reputation for all aspects of commercial and residential property work. The groups handle investment funding; development; planning; construction; landlord and tenant; property taxation and residential investment and development. Forsters is also recognised as one of the leading proponents of private client work in London with a client base comprising a broad range of individuals and trusts in the UK and elsewhere. The firm's commercial practice specialises in acquisitions and financing for technology, communication and media companies whilst its litigation group conducts commercial litigation and arbitration and advises on a broad spectrum of matters.

trainee profile

Successful candidates will have a strong academic background and either have attained or be expected to achieve a good second class degree. The firm considers that factors alongside academic achievements are also important. The firm is looking for individuals who give a real indication of being interested in a career in law and who the firm feels would readily accept and work well in its team environment.

training environment

The first year of training is split into three seats of four months usually in three of the following departments: commercial property, private client, company commercial or litigation. In the second year the four month pattern still applies, but the firm discusses with you whether you have developed an area of particular interest and tries to accommodate this. Second year seats might include construction, employment, family or property litigation. The training is very 'hands on' as you share an office with a partner or assistant who will give you real responsibility alongside supervision. At the mid-term and end of each seat your progress and performance will be reviewed by way of an appraisal with a partner from the relevant department.

sponsorship & benefits

25 days holiday p.a., season ticket loan, permanent health insurance, life insurance, subsidised gym membership, contributory pension scheme, employee assistance programme, private healthcare (after six months), active social programme. Sponsorship post-offer: fees for CPE/GDL and LPC, plus a maintenance grant of £5,000 p.a.

vacation placements

Summer vacation scheme opportunities available. Places: 10. Remuneration: £250 pw. Deadline: 15 March 2008.

Freeth Cartwright LLP

Cumberland Court, 80 Mount Street, Nottingham NG1 6HH
Tel: (0115) 901 5504 Fax: (0115) 859 9603
Email: carole.wigley@freethcartwright.co.uk
Website: www.freethcartwright.co.uk

Members	63
Assistant Solicitors	67
Total Trainees	15

contact
Carole Wigley

method of application
Online application form

selection procedure
Interview & selection day

closing date for 2010
31 July 2008

training
Starting salary (2007)
£20,000

offices
Nottingham, Leicester,
Derby and Manchester

firm profile
Tracing its origins back to 1805, Freeth Cartwright LLP became Nottingham's largest firm in 1994 with successful offices now established in Derby, Leicester and Manchester. Whilst Freeth Cartwright LLP is a heavyweight commercial firm, serving a wide variety of corporate and institutional clients, there is also a commitment to a range of legal services, which includes a substantial private client element. This enables it to give a breadth of experience in training which is not always available in firms of a similar size.

main areas of work
Property and construction, commercial services, private client and personal litigation.

trainee profile
Freeth Cartwright LLP looks for people to bring their own perspective and individuality to the firm. The firm needs people who can cope with the intellectual demands of life as a lawyer and who possess the wider personal skills which are needed in its diverse practice.

training environment
Freeth Cartwright LLP is committed to providing comprehensive training for all its staff. The firm's training programme is based on in-house training covering technical matters and personal skills, supplemented with external courses where appropriate. The firm endeavours to give the best possible experience during the training period, as it believes that informal training on-the-job is the most effective means of encouraging the skills required in a qualified solicitor. One of the firm's senior partners takes responsibility for all its trainees and their personal development, overseeing their progress through the firm and discussing performance based on feedback. Normally, the training contract will consist of four six month seats in different departments, most of which are available in the firm's Nottingham offices, although it is possible for trainees to spend at least one seat in another location.

Freeth
Cartwright
LLP

Freshfields Bruckhaus Deringer

65 Fleet Street, London EC4Y 1HS
Tel: (020) 7936 4000 Fax: (020) 7832 7001
Email: uktrainees@freshfields.com
Website: www.freshfields.com/uktrainees

firm profile
Freshfields Bruckhaus Deringer is a leading international firm with a network of 27 offices in 16 countries. The firm provides first-rate legal services to corporations, financial institutions and governments around the world.

main areas of work
Corporate; mergers and acquisitions; banking; dispute resolution; joint ventures; employment, pensions and benefits; asset finance; real estate; tax; capital markets; intellectual property and information technology; project finance; private finance initiative; securities; antitrust, competition and trade; communications and media; construction and engineering; energy; environment, planning and regulatory; financial services; restructuring and insolvency; insurance; investment funds; public international law; arbitration.

trainee profile
The firm is looking for candidates with proven academic ability, an excellent command of spoken and written English, high levels of drive and determination, good team working skills and excellent organisational ability.

training environment
The firm's trainees receive a thorough professional training in a very broad range of practice areas, an excellent personal development programme and the chance to work in one of the firm's international offices or on secondment with a client. You'll be working with and learning from one of the most talented peer groups in the legal world, and will get the blend of support and freedom you need to evolve your career.

benefits
Life assurance; permanent health insurance; group personal pension; interest-free loan; interest-free loan for a season travel ticket; free membership of the firm's private medical insurance scheme; subsidised staff restaurant; gym.

vacation placements
Places for 2008: 100; Duration: 2 weeks; Remuneration: £550 (net); Closing Date: 18 January 2008 but apply as early as possible after 20 November 2007 as there may not be places left by the deadline.

sponsorship & awards
GDL and LPC fees paid plus maintenance grant of £7,250 for those studying the LPC and £6,250 for those studying the GDL.

Partners 474
Assistant Solicitors 1,718
Total Trainees 200
(London based)

contact
Deborah Dalgleish

method of application
Online application form

selection procedure
2 interviews and written test

closing date for 2010
31 July 2008

application
Training contracts p.a. **100**
Applications p.a. **c.2,000**
% interviewed p.a. **c.12%**
Required degree grade **2:1**

training
Salary
1st year £38,000
2nd year £43,000
Holiday entitlement **25 days**
% of trainees with a
non-law degree p.a. **c.45%**
No. of seats available
abroad p.a. **c.86**

post-qualification
Salary **£65,000**
% of trainees offered job
on qualification **c.95%**

overseas offices
Amsterdam, Barcelona, Beijing, Berlin, Bratislava, Brussels, Budapest, Cologne, Dubai, Düsseldorf, Frankfurt, Hamburg, Hanoi, Ho Chi Minh City, Hong Kong, Madrid, Milan, Moscow, Munich, New York, Paris, Rome, Shanghai, Tokyo, Vienna, Washington DC

Government Legal Service

GLS Recruitment Team, Chancery House, 53-64 Chancery Lane,
London WC2A 1QS
Tel: (020) 7649 6023
Email: glstrainees@tmpw.co.uk Website: www.gls.gov.uk

firm profile

The Government Legal Service (GLS) joins together around 1950 lawyers and trainees. They work in some 30 Government organisations, including major Departments of State and the regulatory bodies. A GLS lawyer's work is quite unique, and reflects the huge range of Government activities. GLS lawyers work in the public interest and have the rare opportunity to make a positive contribution to the well-being of the country. Many move around Government Departments as they progress, developing skills and acquiring knowledge of new areas of the law. Others choose to specialise in one area. Whatever route they take, they find the work hugely rewarding and stimulating.

main areas of work

GLS lawyers have just one client – the Government of the day – and that client requires advice and support on a host of domestic and international matters. As a GLS lawyer, you could deal with ground-breaking cases in the courts, advise Ministers, work on a public inquiry or become involved in the passage of legislation through Parliament.

trainee profile

As well as a good academic background, the GLS seeks strong analytical ability, excellent communication and interpersonal skills, and evidence of motivation for working in the public sector.

training environment

The GLS provides a unique and varied training environment for trainees and pupils. Generally, trainee solicitors work in four different areas of practice over a two-year period in the Government Department to which they are assigned. Pupil barristers divide their year's pupillage between their Department and chambers. The GLS prides itself on involving trainees and pupils in the full range of casework conducted by their Department. This frequently includes high profile matters and will be under the supervision of senior colleagues.

benefits

These include professional development opportunities, excellent pension scheme, civilised working hours, generous holiday entitlement and subsidised canteen facilities.

vacation placements

Summer 2008 vacation placement scheme; approx 60 places. Duration: 2-3 weeks. Closing date: 31 March 2008. Remuneration: £200-£250 pw.

sponsorship & awards

LPC and BVC fees as well as other compulsory Professional Skills Course fees. Funding may be available for the CPE. The GLS provides a grant of around £5-7,000 for the vocational year.

Total Trainees around 50

contact
glstrainees@tmpw.co.uk or visit www.gls.gov.uk

method of application
Online application form

selection procedure
Online verbal reasoning test followed by half day at assessment centre to undertake a group discussion exercise, a written exercise and an interview

closing date for 2010
31 July 2008

application
Training contracts p.a. **22-30**
Applications p.a. **800**
% interviewed p.a. **8%**
Required degree grade (need not be in law) **2:1**

training
Salary begins at over £21,300 in London and varies acording to Government Department. It is lower outside London.

Holiday entitlement **25 days on entry**

post-qualification
Salary varies according to Government Department; the vacancies section of the GLS website will give a flavour of what to expect.

% of trainees accepting job on qualification (2007) at least **98%**

Halliwells

3 Hardman Square, Spinningfields, Manchester, M3 3EB
Tel: (0870) 365 8918 Fax: (0870) 365 8919
Email: ekaterina.clarke@halliwells.com

firm profile
Halliwells is one of the largest independent commercial law firms in the North West and specialises in providing a full range of legal services to the business community. With clients on a local, national and international level, Halliwells has high aspirations far beyond its regional boundaries. Over the last few years the firm has increased substantially in both size and turnover and is widely acknowledged as one of the country's most successfully managed practices.

main areas of work
Corporate (Corporate, Banking and Tax), Corporate Recovery, Real Estate (Property, Planning and Licensing), Business Services (Employment and Intellectual Property), Dispute Resolution (Commercial Litigation, Insurance Liability, Regulatory and Construction), Private Client (Family and Trusts & Estates).

trainee profile
Candidates need to show a good academic ability but do not necessarily need to have studied law at university. They should demonstrate an ability to fit into a hardworking team. In particular, Halliwells is looking for candidates who will continue to develop with the firm after their initial training.

training environment
Each trainee will have five seats in at least three separate departments. These will usually include commercial litigation, corporate and commercial property. Individual requests from trainees for experience in a particular department will be accommodated wherever possible. Requests for inter-office secondments are also encouraged.
The trainee will work within one of the department's teams and be encouraged to assist other team members to help broaden their experience. Specific training appropriate to each department will be given and trainees are strongly encouraged to attend the firm's regular in-house seminars on legal and related topics.
A supervisor will be assigned to each trainee to support their development throughout the seat.

benefits
25 days annual leave, season ticket loan, subsidised gym membership, life assurance.

vacation placements
78 summer vacation placements places will be available during summer 2008. The firm operates three schemes at its Manchester, London and Liverpool offices, each lasts for two weeks. Schemes commence last week in June. Remuneration is £210 per week. Closing date for applications is 29 February 2008.

sponsorship & awards
The firm pays GDL fees and LPC fees plus a £6,500 maintenance grant for each course.

Partners 165
Assistant Solicitors 440
Total Trainees 76

contact
Ekaterina Clarke
(Graduate Recruitment Officer)
ekaterina.clarke@halliwells.com

method of application
Online application only

selection procedure
Group exercise, presentation and interview

closing date for 2010
31 July 2008

application
Training contracts p.a.
Manchester - 22
London - 8
Liverpool - 6
Sheffield - 4
Applications p.a. **1,500**
% interviewed p.a. **8%**
Required degree grade **2:1**

training
Salary
1st year (2007) £23,000
(London) £29,500
2nd year (2007) £24,000
(London) £30,500

post-qualification
Salary (2007) **£39,000**
(London) £62,000
% of trainees offered job on qualification (2007) **85%**

Hammonds

Rutland House, 148 Edmund Street, Birmingham B3 2JR
7 Devonshire Square, Cutlers Gardens, London EC2M 4YH
2 Park Lane, Leeds LS3 1ES
Trinity Court, 16 Dalton Street, Manchester M6O 8HS
Tel: (0800) 163 498 Fax: (0870) 839 3666
Email: graduaterecruitment@hammonds.com
Website: www.hammonds.com/trainees

firm profile
Hammonds is one of Europe's largest corporate law firms and a member of the Global 100. In the UK alone, the firm advises over 200 London Stock Exchange quoted companies and 30 FTSE 100 companies. The firm has offices in London, Birmingham, Leeds, Manchester, Brussels, Paris, Berlin, Munich, Rome, Milan, Madrid, Turin, Beijing and Hong Kong. The firm has 1,400 staff, including 189 Partners, 550 solicitors and 80 trainees. The firm is regarded as innovative, opportunistic and highly successful in the markets in which it operates.

main areas of work
Corporate; commercial dispute resolution; construction, engineering and projects; employment; EU and competition; finance law (including banking); intellectual property and commercial; media/IT; pensions; property; sports law; tax.

trainee profile
Hammonds seeks applications from all disciplines for vacation work and training contracts. Consideration given to four elements in trainee selection: strong academic performance (2:1 degree classification), evidence of work experience in the legal sector, excellent communication skills and significant achievement in non-academic pursuits.

training environment
40 trainee solicitors recruited each year. Trainees undertake six four-month seats during their training contract. Trainees have input in choice of seats and are encouraged to undertake a broad selection of seats to benefit their knowledge on qualification. Trainees benefit from two-tier supervision and challenging work. The firm provides a comprehensive induction programme including on-going departmental training, seminars and workshops throughout the training contract. Trainees undertake formal appraisal meetings with their supervisors during each seat. Hammonds' trainees benefit from exposure to clients, cross-border work and opportunity for seats on secondment. Trainees are involved in all aspects of professional life.

benefits
Pension, life assurance, subsidised gym membership, interest free season ticket loan and a flexible benefits package.

vacation placements
Places for 2008: 64 Summer Scheme; Duration: 2 weeks; Remuneration: £230 p.w. (London), £180 p.w. (Leeds, Manchester, Birmingham); Closing Date: 31 January 2008.

sponsorship & awards
PgDL and LPC fees paid and maintenance grant provided. Maintenance grant presently:
GDL: London, £6,000; Regional, £4,500.
LPC: London, £7,000; Regional, £5,000.

Partners	**189**
Assistant Solicitors	**550**
Total Trainees	**80**

contact
Graduate Recruitment Team

method of application
Online application form

selection procedure
Assessment and interview

closing date for 2010
31 July 2008

application
Training contracts p.a. **40**
Applications p.a. **1,300**
% interviewed p.a. **10%**
Required degree grade **2:1**

training
Salary
1st year (2007)
£25,000 regional
£35,000 London
2nd year (2007)
£27,000 regional
£38,000 London
Holiday entitlement **25 days**
% of trainees with a non-law degree p.a. **40%**
No. of seats available abroad p.a. **15**

post-qualification
Salary (2007)
London £60,000
Other £40,000
% of trainees accepting job on qualification (2006) **82%**

overseas offices
Brussels, Beijing, Paris, Berlin, Munich, Rome, Milan, Turin, Hong Kong, Madrid

Harbottle & Lewis LLP

Hanover House, 14 Hanover Square, London W1S 1HP
Tel: (020) 7667 5000 Fax: (020) 7667 5100
Email: kathy.beilby@harbottle.com
Website: www.harbottle.com

firm profile
Harbottle & Lewis LLP is a London based commercial law firm providing specialist advice primarily to the media, entertainment and communications industries.

main areas of work
Main areas of work encompasses all areas of media and entertainment including film, television, broadcasting, sport, music, publishing, computer games, advertising, fashion and theatre and the firm remains unique in having expertise right across these sectors. Much of the firm's work involves the technology, new media and telecoms industries and the firm has done ground-breaking work in connection with the digital exploitation of content and e-commerce generally. The firm's expertise in other areas such as aviation and charities is also widely recognised.

trainee profile
Trainees will have demonstrated the high academic abilities, commercial awareness, and initiative necessary to become part of a team advising clients in dynamic and demanding industries.

training environment
The two year training contract is divided into four six-month seats where trainees will be given experience in a variety of legal skills including company commercial, litigation, intellectual property and real property, working within teams focused on the firm's core industries. The firm has a policy of accepting a small number of trainees to ensure they are given relevant and challenging work and are exposed to and have responsibility for a full range of legal tasks. The firm has its own lecture and seminar programme in both legal topics and industry know-how. An open door policy and a pragmatic entrepreneurial approach to legal practice provides a stimulating working environment.

benefits
Lunch provided; season ticket loans.

sponsorship & awards
LPC fees paid and interest-free loans towards maintenance.

Partners	24
Assistant Solicitors	51
Total Trainees	10

contact
Kathy Beilby

method of application
CV & letter by post or email

selection procedure
Interview

closing date for 2010
31 July 2008

application
Training contracts p.a. **5**
Applications p.a. **800**
% interviewed p.a. **5%**
Required degree grade **2:1**

training
Salary
1st year £28,000 (2007)
2nd year £29,000 (2007)
Holiday entitlement
in the first year **23 days**
in the second year **26 days**
% of trainees with
a non-law degree p.a. **40%**

post-qualification
Salary (2007) **£47-50k**

HBJ Gateley Wareing LLP

One Eleven, Edmund Street, Birmingham B3 2HJ
Tel: (0121) 234 0069   Fax: (0121) 234 0079
Email: graduaterecruitment.england@hbj-gw.com
Website: www.hbjgateleywareing.com

firm profile
A 75 partner, UK commercial based practice with an excellent reputation for general commercial work and particular expertise in corporate, plc, commercial, employment, property, construction, insolvency, commercial dispute resolution, banking, tax and shipping.
The firm also offers individual clients a complete private client service including FSA-approved financial advice. The firm is expanding (488 employees) and offers a highly practical, commercial and fast-paced environment. HBJ Gateley Wareing has built an outstanding reputation across the UK for its practical approach, sound advice and professional commitment to its clients. The firm is a full range, multi-disciplinary legal business with expertise in many areas.
HBJ Gateley Wareing has an enviable reputation as a friendly and sociable place to work. The firm is committed to equality and diversity across the firm.

trainee profile
To apply for a placement in England: applications are invited from second year law students and final year non-law students and graduates. Applicants should have (or be heading for) a minimum 2.1 degree, and should have at least three Bs (or equivalent) at A-level. Individuals should be hardworking team players capable of using initiative and demonstrating commercial awareness.

training environment
Four six-month seats with ongoing supervision and appraisals every three months. PSC taken internally. In-house courses on skills such as time management, negotiation, IT, drafting, business skills, marketing, presenting and writing in plain English.

benefits
Current trainee offered as a 'buddy' – a point of contact within the firm, library available, invitation to summer party prior to joining.

vacation placements
Two-week placement over the summer. Deadline for next year's vacation placement scheme is 11 February 2008 and the closing date for 2010 training contracts is 31 July 2008. Apply online at www.hbjgateleywareing.com.

sponsorship & awards
CPE/LPC and a LPC maintenance grant of £4,500.

Partners	75(firmwide)
Vacancies	11(England)
Total Trainees	13(Midlands)
TotalStaff	488(firmwide)

contact
Sandra Deehan Graduate Recruitment

closing date for 2010
Training contracts:
31 July 2008
Vacation placements:
11 February 2008

training
Salary
1st year £24,000
2nd year £25,000

post-qualification
Salary £38,000

offices
Birmingham, Edinburgh, Glasgow, Leicester, London and Nottingham.

HBJ Gateley Wareing

Henmans LLP

5000 Oxford Business Park South, Oxford OX4 2BH
Tel: (01865) 780000   Fax: (01865) 778682
Email: welcome@henmansllp.co.uk
Website: www.henmansllp.co.uk

firm profile
Henmans LLP is the premier firm in Oxford, with more practice areas ranked in the top tier of the Chambers legal directory than any other Oxford firm. The firm has a national reputation in its specialist areas, handling commercial and personal matters for a wide range of clients both nationally and internationally. The firm also acts for a large number of charities and insurers. More than half of the firm's senior lawyers are acknowledged as experts within their fields, so clients are confident of receiving the most authoritative advice available. The firm's belief is that the best advisers are those who thoroughly understand your concerns, so the firm works hard to ensure that it has a detailed appreciation of your business or personal questions, and can offer the best possible advice.

main areas of work
The firm's core service of litigation is nationally recognized for its high quality. Henmans LLP also has an excellent reputation for its personal injury, clinical negligence, property, private client and charity work. The breakdown of work is as follows: Professional negligence and commercial litigation: 24%; personal injury: 27%; property: 17%; private client (including family)/charities/trusts: 25%; corporate/employment: 10%.

trainee profile

Commercial awareness, sound academic accomplishment, intellectual capability, IT literacy, able to work as part of a team, good communication skills.

training environment
Trainees are an important part of our future. Henmans LLP is committed to providing a high standard of training throughout the contract. Trainees are introduced to the firm with a detailed induction and overview of its client base. A trainee manual is provided in each seat to familiarise the trainee with the department's procedures. Experience is likely to be within the PI, property, family, professional negligence/commercial litigation and private client departments. The firm provides an ongoing programme of in-house education and regular appraisals within its supportive friendly environment. The firm values commitment and enthusiasm both professionally and socially as an integral part of its culture and trainees are encouraged to join in social activities and become involved with the life of the firm.

Partners	**23**
Other Solicitors & Fee-earners	**51**
Total Trainees	**6**

contact
Viv J Matthews (Mrs)
MA CH FCIPD
Head of HR

method of application
Application form on website

selection procedure
The interview process comprises an assessment day with Head of HR and partners, including an interview, presentation, verbal reasoning test, drafting and team exercise

closing date for 2010
31 July 2008

application
Training contracts p.a. **3**
Applications p.a. **300**

training
Salary
1st year (2007/8) £20,000
2nd year (2007/8) £22,000
Holiday entitlement **23 days + 2 firm days at Christmas. BUPA and pension also provided.**
% of trainees with a non-law degree p.a. **25%**

post-qualification
Salary (2004) **£32,000-33,000**
% of assistants who joined as trainees **25%**
% of partners who joined as trainees **20%**

Herbert Smith LLP

Exchange House, Primrose Street, London EC2A 2HS
Tel: (020) 7374 8000 Fax: (020) 7374 0888
Email: graduate.recruitment@herbertsmith.com Website: www.herbertsmith.com

firm profile
Herbert Smith is an international legal practice with over 1,100 lawyers and a network of offices in Europe and Asia. In addition, it works closely with two premier European firms with whom it has an alliance - the German firm Gleiss Lutz and the Dutch and Belgian firm Stibbe.
The firm has a diverse, blue-chip client base including FTSE 100 and Fortune 500 companies, major investment banks and governments. What makes Herbert Smith stand out is its culture: a collegial working environment, a pre-eminent market reputation in key practices and industry sectors and an ambition to be consistently recognised as one of the world's leading law firms.

main areas of work
Corporate (including international mergers and acquisitions); finance and banking (including capital markets); international litigation and arbitration; energy; projects and project finance; EU and competition; real estate; tax; employment and trusts; construction and engineering; insurance; investment funds; IP; US securities, IT & communications.

trainee profile
Trainees need a strong academic record, common sense, self-confidence and intelligence to make their own way in a large firm. They are typically high-achieving and creative thinking.

training environment
Structured training and supervision is designed to allow you to experience a unique range of contentious and non-contentious work. You will be encouraged to take on responsibilities as soon as you join the firm. You will work within Partner-led teams and have your own role. Individual strengths will be monitored, developed and utilised. As a trainee, you will rotate around four 'seats' of six months each, including one in litigation, one in corporate and a further non contentious seat in either finance or real estate. You can apply for a specialist seat such as IP, Tax, Trust, EU and Competition, Employment, Pensions and Incentives or our advocacy unit. Alternatively, you can apply to go on secondment to a client or to one or our international offices. Great emphasis is placed on professional and personal development and the firm runs its own legal development and mentoring programme.

sponsorship & benefits
CPE/GDL and LPC fees are paid plus up to £7,000 maintenance grant p.a. Benefits include profit related bonus scheme, permanent health insurance, private medical insurance, season ticket loan, life assurance, subsidised gym membership, group personal accident insurance, matched contributory pension scheme and interest free loan.

vacation placements
Places for 2007/08: 130. Winter 2007 (non-law students only), Spring and Summer 2008 (law and non-law students). Closing Dates: 12 November 2007 for Winter scheme; 31 January 2008 for Spring and Summer schemes. Opportunities in some of the firm's European offices.

Partners	234*
Fee-earners	741*
Total Trainees	178*

*denotes worldwide figures

contact
Graduate Recruitment Team

method of application
Online application form

selection procedure
Case study and interview

closing date for Sept 2010/Mar 2011
31 July 2008

application
Training contracts p.a. up to **100**
Applications p.a. **circa 2,000**
% interviewed p.a. **30%**
Required degree grade **2:1**

training
Salary
1st year £36,000
2nd year £40,000
Holiday entitlement
25 days, rising to 27 on qualification
ratio of law to non-law graduates is broadly equal

post-qualification
Salary (2006) **£64,000**
% of trainees offered job on qualification (Sept 2007)
100% (based on no. of jobs offered)

overseas offices
Bangkok, Beijing, Brussels, Dubai, Hong Kong, Moscow, Paris, Shanghai, Singapore, Tokyo

associated offices
Amsterdam, Berlin, Frankfurt, Jakarta, Munich, New York, Prague, Stuttgart, Warsaw

Hewitsons

42 Newmarket Road, Cambridge CB5 8EP
Tel: (01604) 233233 Fax: (01223) 316511
Email: mail@hewitsons.com (for all offices)
Website: www.hewitsons.com (for all offices)

firm profile

Established in 1865, the firm handles mostly company and commercial work, but has a growing body of public sector clients. The firm has three offices: Cambridge, Northampton and Saffron Walden.

main areas of work

Three sections: corporate technology, property and private client.

trainee profile

The firm is interested in applications from candidates who have achieved a high degree of success in academic studies and who are bright, personable and able to take the initiative.

training environment

The firm offers four six-month seats.

benefits

The PSC is provided during the first year of the training contract. This is coupled with an extensive programme of Trainee Solicitor Seminars provided by specialist in-house lawyers.

vacation placements

Places for 2008: A few placements are available, application is by way of letter and CV to Caroline Lewis; Duration: 1 week.

sponsorship & awards

Funding for the CPE and/or LPC is not provided.

Partners	**44**
Assistant Solicitors	**43**
Total Trainees	**15**

contact
Caroline Lewis
7 Spencer Parade
Northampton NN1 5AB

method of application
Firm's application form

selection procedure
Interview

closing date for 2010
End of August 2008

application
Training contracts p.a. **10**
Applications p.a. **850**
% interviewed p.a. **10%**
Required degree grade
2:1 min

training
Salary
1st year £23,500
2nd year £25,000
Holiday entitlement **22 days**
% of trainees with a
non-law degree p.a. **50%**

post-qualification
Salary **£35,000**
% of trainees offered job
on qualification (2005) **45%**
% of assistants (as at
1/9/05) who joined as
trainees **38%**
% of partners (as at 1/9/05)
who joined as trainees **32%**

Higgs & Sons

134 High Street, Brierley Hill DY5 3BG
Tel: (01384) 342100 Fax: (01384) 342000
Email: law@higgsandsons.co.uk
Website: www.higgsandsons.co.uk

firm profile
One of the leading law firms in the West Midlands, providing cutting-edge legal advice in a friendly and down-to-earth way to business and private paying clients across a wide variety of legal specialisations. Founded in 1875 the firm is committed to developing long term relationships with its clients. ISO9001 accredited.

main areas of work
For the business client: corporate and commercial, employment law, commercial litigation and commercial property work.
For the private client: wills, probate and trusts, employment law, personal injury, ULR and clinical negligence, conveyancing and civil litigation, negligence work, matrimonial/family and criminal.

trainee profile
Applications are welcome from law and non-law students who can demonstrate a consistently high academic record, a broad range of interpersonal skills and extra curricular activities and interests.

training environment
A first-class structured programme, fully supervised, based on experience in at least four major disciplines with regular assessments. An open-door policy. Preferences balanced with firm's needs.

benefits
Private Medical Insurance, Life Assurance, Stake Holder Pension.

Partners	26
Fee Earners	36
Total Trainees	7

contact
Margaret Dalton

method of application
Online application form or letter and CV

selection procedure
Interview with trainee committee

closing date for 2010
18th August 2008

application
Training contracts p.a. **4**
Applications p.a. **250 plus**
% interviewed p.a. **varies**
Required degree grade preferably **2:1**, will consider **2:2**

training
Salary **reviewed annually**
1st year £20,000
2nd year £22,000
Holiday entitlement
24 days p.a.

post-qualification
Salary **£30,000**
% of trainees offered job on qualification **100%**

Hill Dickinson

Pearl Assurance House, 2 Derby Square, Liverpool L2 9XL
Tel: (0151) 236 5400 Fax: (0151) 236 2175
Email: recruitment@hilldickinson.com
Website: www.hilldickinson.com

firm profile
Hill Dickinson LLP is one of the UK's leading independent law firms and is a national top 40 practice with offices in Liverpool, London, Manchester, Chester and Piraeus. Following the merger with Hill Taylor Dickinson in November 2006 and an aggressive programme of lateral hiring in the last year, the firm now has 152 Partners and a total staff complement of more than 1000.

main areas of work
Hill Dickinson is a major force in insurance and is well respected in the company and commercial arena. The firm's marine expertise is internationally renowned and is one of the largest marine practices in the UK following a merger with Hill Taylor Dickinson on 1st November 2006. The firm has a highly reputable Commercial Litigation Practice, an award winning Property Practice and is widely regarded as a leader in the fields of employment, intellectual property, NHS clinical/health related litigation and private client.

trainee profile
Commercial awareness and academic ability are the key factors, together with a desire to succeed. Trainees are viewed as the partners of the future and the firm is looking for personable individuals with whom it wants to work.

training environment
Trainees spend periods of six months in four different practice groups. Trainees are encouraged to accept responsibility and are expected to act with initiative. The firm has an active social committee and a larger than usual selection of competitive sporting teams.

vacation placements
Two week structured scheme with 12 places available for 2008. Apply online by 31 March 2008.

Partners	152
Assistant Solicitors	143
Associates	36
Total Trainees	32

contact
Victoria Wolff

method of application
Online application form

selection procedure
Assessment day

closing date for 2010
31st July 2008

training
Salary
1st year (2007) £22,000
2nd year (2007) £24,000
1st year (London) £30,000
2nd year (London) £32,000
Sponsorship: LPC
Holiday entitlement
25 days

post-qualification
% of trainees offered job
on qualification **90%**

offices
Liverpool, Manchester,
London, Chester, Greece

Hodge Jones & Allen

180 North Gower Street, London NW1 2NB
Tel: (020) 7388 0628 Fax: (020) 7874 8305
Email: hja@hodgejonesallen.co.uk
Website: www.hodgejonesallen.co.uk

Partners	18
Assistant Solicitors	44
Total Trainees	13

contact
HR Department

method of application
Application form (available online)

selection procedure
Interview with 2 Partners

closing date for 2010
24 August 2008 (apply one year in advance)

application
Training contracts p.a. **6-7**
Applications p.a. **500**
% interviewed p.a. **5%**
Preferred degree grade **2:1 min**

training
Salary: £20,000 year 1
£22,000 year 2
Holiday entitlement 20 days p.a.

post-qualification
Salary: £30,000
% of trainees offered job on qualification: **75%**

firm profile
Hodge Jones & Allen was founded in 1977 by three young radical lawyers, Henry Hodge, Peter Jones & Patrick Allen. They created a law firm that has developed a national reputation in its fields of expertise, and has grown to have 20 partners and 180 staff in total.
Henry Hodge retired from the firm in October 1999 to take up a full time judicial appointment and became only the third solicitor ever to be appointed to the High Court bench.
Peter Jones went on to become a Professor and Pro-Vice Chancellor at Nottingham Trent University.
Patrick Allen remains the Senior and Managing Partner of the firm
Although the firm is now the largest supplier of publicly funded legal services for the Legal Services Commission in London, the firm has increasingly developed private client work in addition. The split of private and publicly funded work is currently about even. The firm has been involved in a number of high profile cases including, the King's Cross fire, the Marchioness disaster, Broadwater Farm riots, Real IRA BBC-bombing trial, the second inquest into the New Cross fire, MMR vaccine litigation, the Organophosphate Litigation and Gulf War Syndrome litigation.
In April 2007, the firm relocated to its current premises, which have been fully modernised and refurbished. The premises are located a short walk away from Euston station, so the firm is now more centrally located in London and very accessible. The firm has good IT systems and comprehensive support departments.

main areas of work
Its main areas of work include human rights, civil liberties, miscarriage of justice, inquests, criminal law, personal injury, clinical negligence, multi party actions, civil litigation, professional negligence, property, probate, wills & trusts, housing and family law.

trainee profile
Trainees will have an excellent academic record, good communication skills, commitment, dynamism and ambition.

training environment
Trainees have a full induction on joining HJA covering the work of the firm's main departments, procedural matters and professional conduct. Training consists of four six-month seats and trainees normally share an office with a partner who assists them and formally reviews their progress at least once during each seat. The training is well structured and trainees have the benefit of a mentoring scheme. The firm provides good secretarial and clerking support so trainees can concentrate on legal work rather than administration. The degree of responsibility and client contact enjoyed by trainees at the firm is unrivalled, and the training is generally regarded as of an excellent standard.

benefits
Pension scheme, Life Assurance, disability insurance, quarterly drinks, summer outing and Christmas party.

Holman Fenwick & Willan

Marlow House, Lloyds Avenue, London EC3N 3AL
Tel: (020) 7488 2300 Fax: (020) 7481 0316
Email: grad.recruitment@hfw.co.uk

firm profile
Holman Fenwick & Willan is an international law firm and one of the world's leading specialists in maritime transportation, insurance, reinsurance, energy and trade. The firm is a leader in the field of commercial litigation and arbitration and also offers comprehensive commercial advice. Founded in 1883, the firm is one of the largest operating in its chosen fields with a team of over 200 lawyers worldwide, and a reputation for excellence and innovation.

main areas of work
The firm's range of services include marine, admiralty and crisis management, insurance and reinsurance, commercial litigation and arbitration, international trade and commodities, energy, corporate and financial.

trainee profile
Applications are invited from commercially minded undergraduates and graduates of all disciplines with good A levels and who have, or expect to receive, a 2:1 degree. Good foreign languages or a scientific or maritime background are an advantage.

training environment
During your training period the firm will ensure that you gain valuable experience in a wide range of areas. It also organises formal training supplemented by a programme of in-house seminars and ship visits in addition to the PSC. Your training development as an effective lawyer will be managed by the HR and Training Partner, Ottilie Sefton, who will ensure that your training is both successful and enjoyable.

benefits
Private medical insurance, permanent health and accident insurance, subsidised gym membership, season ticket loan.

vacation placements
Places for 2008: Dates: 23 June-4 July/14-25 July; Remuneration (2006): £250 p.w.; Closing Date: Applications accepted 1 Dec 2007-14 Feb 2008.

sponsorship & awards
GDL Funding: Fees paid plus £6,000 maintenance; LPC Funding: Fees paid plus £7,000 maintenance.

Partners	100+
Other Solicitors &	
Fee-earners	120+
Total Trainees	19

contact
Graduate Recruitment
Officer - Rachel Frowde

method of application
Online application form

selection procedure
2 interviews with partners
& written exercise

closing date for 2010
31 July 2008

application
Training contracts p.a. **8**
Applications p.a. **1,000**
% interviewed p.a. **5%**
Required degree grade **2:1**

training
Salary (Sept 2007)
1st year **£31,000**
2nd year **£33,000**
Holiday entitlement **22 days**
% of trainees with
a non-law degree p.a. **50%**

post-qualification
Salary **£55,000** (Sept 2007)
% of trainees offered job
on qualification
(Sept 2007) **100%**

overseas offices
Hong Kong, Paris, Piraeus,
Rouen, Shanghai,
Singapore, Dubai,
Melbourne

Howes Percival LLP

Oxford House, Cliftonville, Northampton NN1 5PN
Tel: (01604) 230400 Fax: (01604) 620956
Email: katy.pattle@howespercival.com
Website: www.howespercival.com

firm profile
Howes Percival LLP is a leading commercial law firm with offices in Leicester, Milton Keynes, Northampton and Norwich. This year the firm won the Leicestershire Law Society Firm of the year award and in 2006 the firm won the UK Regional Firm of the Year at the Legal Business Awards. The firm's working environment is progressive and highly professional and its corporate structure means that fee-earners are rewarded on merit and can progress to associate or partner status quickly. The type and high value of the work that the firm does places it in a position whereby it is recognised as being a regional firm by location only. The firm has the expertise, resources and Partner reputation that match a city firm.

main areas of work
The practice is departmentalised and the breakdown of its work is as follows: corporate 30%; commercial property 25%; commercial litigation 20%; insolvency 10%; employment 10%; private client 5%.

trainee profile
The firm is looking for ten well-educated, focused, enthusiastic, commercially aware graduates with a minimum 2:1 degree in any discipline. Howes Percival LLP welcomes confident communicators with strong interpersonal skills who share the firm's desire to be the best.

training environment
Trainees complete four six-month seats, each one in a different department. Trainees joining the Norwich office will remain at Norwich for the duration of their training contract. Within the East Midlands region, there is the opportunity to gain experience in each of the three East Midlands offices. Trainees report direct to a partner, and after three months and again towards the end of each seat they will be formally assessed by the partner training them. Trainees will be given every assistance by the fee-earners in their department to develop quickly and will be given responsibility as soon as they are ready.

benefits
Contributory pension scheme. Private health insurance. LPC/CPE funding, maintenance grant.

vacation placements
Vacation placements are available in June, July and August. Please apply in writing to Emma Kazmierczak, HR Assistant at the above address (enclosing your CV) indicating which location you would prefer. The closing date is 30 April 2008.

Partners	31
Solicitors	80
Total Trainees	18

contact
Miss Katy Pattle
HR Officer

method of application
Online application form

selection procedure
Assessment centres

closing date for 2010
31 July 2008

application
Training contracts p.a. **10**
Applications p.a. **300**
% interviewed p.a. **10%**
Required degree grade **2:1**

training
Salary
1st year **£23,500**
2nd year **£25,500**
Holiday entitlement
25 days p.a.

post-qualification
% of trainees offered job on qualification (2007) **57%**
% of assistants who joined as trainees **62%**
% of Partners who joined as trainees **19%**

Hugh James

Hodge House, 114-116 St Mary Street, Cardiff, CF10 1DY
Tel: (029) 2039 1009 Fax: (029) 20388 222
Email: diane.brooks@hughjames.com
Website: www.hughjames.com

firm profile
Hugh James is a dynamic, expanding leading regional practice. The Firm services clients both in the UK and internationally and, as a result, the firm is shortly opening an office in London. Hugh James prides itself on its friendly atmosphere, which extends to both the staff and clients, and the firm's professionalism. The firm aims to find the best and most practical solution to clients' legal matters.

main areas of work
The firm's three divisions: corporate and banking, property and Litigation, cover a diverse spectrum of legal work for a broad range of clients including major corporations, government bodies, charities and individuals.

trainee profile
The firm see its trainees as the future of the Firm and has a very high retention rate on qualification. Apart from an excellent academic record, the firm looks for highly motivated individuals with common sense, good communication and social skills, commercial awareness and a good sense of humour!

training environment
Trainees undertake four seats of six months each to ensure they get as broad a range of experiences of different aspects of the law as possible. The firm's trainees are treated as individuals. They form an integral part of whatever team they work in. They will have a great deal of responsibility and will be a useful and respected team member. They are not faceless photocopiers!

The training contract is very structured and Hugh James' trainees are given support and guidance throughout. Each trainee is allocated a supervisor in each seat. A formal appraisal is undertaken at the end of each six month period with a 'mid seat' appraisal every three months to make sure everything is running smoothly.

The first few weeks can be daunting and so we operate an induction programme. All new recruits are allocated a 'buddy' (one of the second year trainees), someone to call on for informal advice and support.

Ongoing education is provided through attendance at the Professional Skills Course and participation in the firm's in-house training programme.

benefits
Pension opportunities, 25 days holiday.

vacation placements
Places for summer 2008. Duration: two weeks; Closing Date:31st March 2008; Interviews April 2008.

sponsorship & awards
LPC course fees paid.

Partners	47
Assistant Solicitors	160
Total Trainees	17

contact
Diane Brooks
029 2039 1009

method of application
Online application form

selection procedure
interview and oral presentation

closing date for 2010
31 July 2008

application
Training contracts p.a. **7**
Applications p.a. **500**
% interviewed p.a. **10%**
Required degree grade **2:1**
(occasional exceptions)

training
Salary
1st year £17,999
2nd year £19,103
Holiday entitlement
25 days p.a.

post-qualification
% of trainees offered job on qualification (2007) **86%**
Salary **£33,990** (Sept 2007)

overseas offices
Cardiff, Methyr Tydfil, London

Hunton & Williams

30 St Mary Axe, London, EC3A 8EP
Tel: (020) 7220 5700 Fax: (020) 7220 5772
Email: LO_LegalRecruiting@hunton.com
Website: www.hunton.com

firm profile
Founded in 1901, Hunton & Williams is an international law firm with more than 1,000 lawyers serving clients from 18 offices around the world. The firm provides its clients with advice covering virtually every discipline of the law. The firm currently has 13 offices in the United States, two in Europe and three in Asia and can respond knowledgeably, effectively and quickly, whether the issue is international, national, regional or local.

The London office was established in 1999 and has recently moved to Lord Norman Foster's iconic landmark in the heart of the city. The office is expanding with plans to double in size.

main areas of work
In London the firm's major practice areas include: banking and finance; capital markets; corporate restructuring and insolvency; data protection; energy; employment; mergers and acquisitions; outsourcing; project finance; regulatory and technology. The office offers legal services under both English and US law and regularly advises on both UK and cross border transactions.

trainee profile
Both law and non-law graduates who achieve a minimum 2:1 degree result will be considered. Applicants must demonstrate business acumen and the desire to succeed in a fast pace commercial environment.

training environment
Relevant training is provided within the firm's main practice areas and regular appraisals are carried out during the course of each seat.

Trainees are highly integrated in office life and, in addition to transactional work, encouraged to be involved in business development and pro bono activities. Trainees are exposed to cutting edge legal work and given significant client contact and responsibility at an early stage.

vacation placements
A limited number of places are available for the summer vacation scheme.

benefits
Private Medical Insurance, Life Assurance, Permanent Health Insurance scheme, Pension and Occupational Health Service.

sponsorship & awards
LPC and GDL are funded.

Partners	9
Associates	18
Total Trainees	4

contact
Mrs Linda C. Felmington,
Director of Administration

method of application
Applications must include; a CV, hand written covering letter and the firm's application form, which should also be completed by hand. More information can be found on the website

selection procedure
Interviews and Assessment Days

closing date for 2010
31 July 2008

application
Training contracts p.a. **2**
Applications p.a. **300**
% interviewed p.a. **10%**
Required degree grade **2:1** **(minimum)**

training
Salary
1st year £33,000
2nd year £35,000
Holiday entitlement
25 days p.a.

post-qualification
under review

offices
Altanta, Bangkok, Beijing, Brussels, Charlotte, Dallas, Houston, Knoxville, London, Los Angeles, McLean, Miami, New York, Norfolk, Raleigh, Richmond, Singapore, Washington

IBB Solicitors

30 Capital Court, Windsor Street, Uxbridge, Middlesex, UB8 1AB
Tel: (08456) 381381 Fax: (01895) 381341
Email: Robert.Bushnell@ibblaw.co.uk
Website: www.ibblaw.co.uk

firm profile

IBB is a leading law firm located on the outskirts of West London, providing a full range of services to an extensive business, institutional and private client community. Due to its recent growth, IBB has expanded into larger premises in Uxbridge, taking on three floors of Capital Court, to accommodate its growing legal teams. It also continues to house legal teams at Lovell House, Uxbridge, Chesham and Ingatestone.

The firm has been rated as one of the top tier law firms in the region for its private client, commercial property and crime services by one of the UK's leading legal services directory, The Legal 500.

main areas of work

Charities, childcare, commercial litigation, commercial real estate, corporate, company and commercial, construction, corporate finance, crime, employment, family, insurance/reinsurance, intellectual property, personal injury, private client.

trainee profile

Success here means having the knowledge and the skills to apply that knowledge for clients. The firm recruits on the basis of potential. Selection is based on a number of criteria including academic ability (2:1 and good A levels), clear written and oral communication skills, the ability to assimilate information and gain the experience of working with others and the invaluable experience of researching and achieving tasks within the environment of a private practice .

training environment

Training contracts will begin in mid september and you will spend your first week on the firm's comprehensive induction programme. Your second week will be spent shadowing an existing trainee. You will complete four six-month seats, giving you the opportunity to gain experience of quite different areas of law. You will get hands-on experience and become an important part of the team.

benefits

25 days holiday, life assurance, stakeholder pension, private medical insurance.

Partners	32
Assistant Solicitors	41
Total Trainees	12

contact
Rob Bushnell
Robert.Bushnell@ibblaw.
co.uk
(01895) 207989

method of application
Online — www.ibblaw.co.uk

selection procedure
IBB creates a long list of applications and interview about 50 people; from those, they shortlist 12 people who are invited to a full day assessment centre.

closing date for 2010
31 July 2008

application
Training contracts p.a. **6**
Applications p.a. **400**
% interviewed p.a. **15%**
Required degree grade **2:1**

training
Salary for each year of training:
1st year £21,000
2nd year £23,000
Holiday entitlement: **25 days p.a.**

Ince & Co

International House, 1 St Katharine's Way, London E1W 1AY
Email: recruitment@incelaw.com

firm profile
From its origins in maritime law, the firm's practice today encompasses all aspects of the work areas listed below. Ince & Co is frequently at the forefront of developments in contract and tort law.

main areas of work
Aviation, business and finance, commercial disputes, energy, insurance and reinsurance, shipping and trade.

trainee profile
Hardworking, competitive individuals with initiative who relish challenge and responsibility within a team environment. Academic achievements, positions of responsibility, sport and travel are all taken into account.

training environment
Trainees sit with four different partners for six months at a time throughout their training. Under close supervision, they are encouraged from an early stage to meet and visit clients, interview witnesses, liaise with counsel, deal with technical experts and handle opposing lawyers. They will quickly build up a portfolio of cases from a number of partners involved in a cross-section of the firm's practice and will see their cases through from start to finish. They will also attend in-house and external lectures, conferences and seminars on practical and legal topics.

benefits
STL, corporate health cover, PHI, contributory pension scheme. Well Man/Well Woman health checks.

vacation placements
Places for 2008: 15; Duration: 2 weeks; Remuneration: £250 p.w.; Closing Date: 14 February 2008.

sponsorship & awards
LPC/CPE fees, £6,000 grant for study in London & Guildford, £5,500 grant for study elsewhere.

Partners	79*
Senior Associates	16*
Solicitors	72*
Total Trainees	29*

denotes worldwide figures

contact
Claire Kendall

method of application
online at www.incelaw.com

selection procedure
Interview with HR professional & interview with 2 partners from Recruitment Committee & a written test

closing date for 2010
31 July 2008

application
Training contracts p.a. **12**
Applications p.a. **1,000**
% interviewed p.a. **10%**
Required degree grade **2:1**

training
Salary
1st year £31,000
2nd year £34,000
Holiday entitlement **25 days**
% of trainees with a non-law degree p.a. **55%**

post-qualification
Salary **£59,000**
% of trainees offered job on qualification (2007)
100%. All accepted!
% of partners (as at 2005) who joined as trainees **Approx 70%**

overseas offices
Dubai, Hamburg, Hong Kong, Le Havre, Paris, Piraeus, Shanghai, Singapore

Irwin Mitchell

Riverside East, 2 Millsands, Sheffield S3 8DT
Tel: (0870) 1500 100 Fax: (0870) 197 3549
Email: graduaterecruitment@irwinmitchell.com
Website: www.irwinmitchell.com

firm profile

Irwin Mitchell was established over 90 years ago and is the fourth largest law firm, and the largest Personal Injury Practice, in the UK. The practice employs more than 2,300 employees. One of the unique features about the firm is the diversity of the areas of law in which the firm practice, from commercial law to insurance law, from business crime to major and multi-claimant personal injury litigation, not forgetting about the firm's expanding Private Client Department. The firm is different as it is the largest law firm in the UK which deals with such a range of clients.

main areas of work

Corporate services and private client 30%; insurance 39%; personal injury 31%.

trainee profile

The firm is looking for ambitious and well-motivated individuals who have a real commitment to the law and who can demonstrate a positive approach to work-life balance. Irwin Mitchell recruits law and non-law graduates and views social ability as important as academic achievement. Irwin Mitchell believes trainees are an investment for the future and endeavours to retain trainees upon qualification. In addition to the firm's training contract vacancies it also runs a work placement scheme giving potential training contract candidates a chance to experience what it is like to be a solicitor within the firm.

training environment

Irwin Mitchell offers a week long structured welcome programme to trainees joining the practice. In addition regular training events are held throughout the firm. The Professional Skills Course is financed by the firm and is run in-house, being tailored to meet the needs of the firm's trainees. During your training contract you will be given as much responsibility as you can handle, giving you a real opportunity to work with the law, your colleagues and to develop your client relationship skills. Your development will be encouraged through frequent reviews and feedback.

benefits

Healthcare scheme, contributory pension scheme, subsidised gym membership, away day and Christmas party.

sponsorship & awards

Payment of PGDL and LPC fees plus a £4,500 maintenance grant.

Partners	**96**
Assistant Solicitors	**210**
Total Trainees	**48**

contact
Alex Burgess,
Graduate Recruitment Assistant
graduaterecruitment@irwin mitchell.com

method of application
Please visit the firm's website www.irwinmitchell.com and complete the online application

selection procedure
Assessment centre & interview

closing date for 2010
31 July 2008

application
Training contracts p.a. **20-25**
Applications p.a. **1,500**
% interviewed p.a. **30%**
Required degree grade:
The firm does not require a specific degree grade

training
Salary
1st year £19,000
2nd year £21,100
(outside London)
reviewed annually in September
Holiday entitlement
24.5 days

post-qualification
% of trainees offered job on qualification **76%**

Overseas/Regional Offices
Birmingham, Leeds, London, Manchester, Newcastle, Sheffield, Marbella & Madrid, Glasgow

Jones Day

21 Tudor Street, London, EC4Y 0DJ
Tel: (020) 7039 5959 Fax: (020) 7039 5999
Email: recruit.london@jonesday.com
Website: www.jonesdaylondon.com/recruit

firm profile

Jones Day operates as one firm worldwide with 2,200 lawyers in 30 offices. Jones Day in London is a key part of this international partnership and has around 200 lawyers, including around 45 partners and 40 trainees. This means that the firm can offer its lawyers a perfect combination - the intimacy and atmosphere of a medium sized City firm with access to both UK and multinational clients.

main areas of work

Principal areas of practice at Jones Day include: corporate finance and M&A transactions; investment funds, private equity and corporate tax planning, banking, capital markets and structured finance, business restructuring, litigation, intellectual property tax and real estate. The London office also has teams of lawyers who are experienced in such areas as competition/antitrust, environmental and employment and pensions law.

trainee profile

The firm looks for candidates with either a law or non-law degree who have strong intellectual and analytical ability and good communication skills and who can demonstrate resourcefulness, drive, dedication and the ability to engage with clients and colleagues.

training environment

The firm operates a unique, non-rotational system of training and trainees receive work simultaneously from all departments in the firm. The training is designed to provide freedom, flexibility and responsibility from the start. Trainees are encouraged to assume their own workload, which allows early responsibility, a faster development of potential and the opportunity to compare and contrast the different disciplines alongside one another. Work will vary from small cases which the trainee may handle alone (under the supervision of a senior lawyer) to larger matters where they will assist a partner or an associate solicitor. The firm runs a structured training programme with a regular schedule of seminars to support the thorough practical training and regular feedback that trainees receive from the associates and partners they work with.

vacation placements

Places for 2007/08: Christmas (non-law): 20 places; 2 weeks; £400; closing date 31 October. Easter 2008 (non-law): 10 places; 2 weeks; £400; closing date 31 January. Summer 2008 (law): 40; 2 weeks; £400; closing date 31 January. Placements last for two weeks with an allowance of £400 per week. Students get to see how the firm's non-rotational training system works in practice by taking on real work from a variety of practice areas. They also get to meet a range of lawyers at various social events.

benefits

Private healthcare, season ticket loan, subsidised sports club membership, group life cover.

sponsorship & awards

CPE/PgDL and LPC fees paid and £8,000 maintenance p.a.

Partners	45
Assistant Solicitors	90
Total Trainees	40

contact
Jacqui Megson
Graduate Recruitment
Manager

method of application
CV and letter online at
www.jonesdaylondon.com/
recruit

selection procedure
2 interviews with partners

closing date for 2010
31 August 2008 - please
apply by end of July to ensure
an early interview slot

application
Training contracts p.a. **15-20**
Applications p.a. **1,500**
% interviewed p.a. **12%**
Required degree grade **2:1**

training
Salary
1st year (2007) **£39,000**
2nd year (2007) **£45,000**
Holiday entitlement
5 weeks

post-qualification
Salary (2007) **£70,000**
% of trainees offered job on
qualification (2007) **95%**

overseas offices
Continental Europe, Asia,
North America

Kendall Freeman

One Fetter Lane, London, EC4A 1JB
Tel: (020) 7583 4055 Fax: (020) 7353 7377
Email: traineerecruitment@kendallfreeman.com
Website: www.kendallfreeman.com

firm profile
Kendall Freeman handles high-value and complex matters for clients in the corporate and public sectors, banks and the insurance and reinsurance industry. The firm successfully competes and acts alongside the largest international and UK firms in the work that it does. Three of the firm's partners have been classed as 'World-Leading' litigation lawyers, acknowledging the extensive expertise the firm has in its core areas.

main areas of work
Commercial litigation, banking, corporate, employment, insolvency and restructuring, international law, insurance/reinsurance and energy and offshore engineering. Much of the work is international in context with many clients in the US, Europe and Bermuda.

trainee profile
The firm seeks engaging and motivated individuals from law or non-law backgrounds with initiative, good commercial sense and who want to make their mark. Trainees work hard and are rewarded with early responsibility and influence over the matters they work on. You'll be an integral part of the team and need to be the kind of person who wants to get involved and not be part of a crowd. Excellent people skills are vital as there will be lots of client contact. You should also have an excellent academic background.

training environment
The firm believes supervised experience to be the best training and because of its size it can offer excellent training with high-quality work in a more personal environment. Trainees spend six months in four of the firm's major practice areas and frequent workshops in each seat help develop skills in the different practice areas. Regular structured feedback and reviews enable you to fulfil your true potential. A multi-level support network of supervisors, Partner mentors and a buddy system, ensures you have the correct level of guidance and support is never overstretched. Any suggestions or concerns can be voiced at a trainee solicitors' committee, which meets quarterly. The firm was a winner in 9 out of 10 categories in the Lex 100 survey for 2006/7.

vacation placements
The firm offers a structured two-week placement for up to 10 students in July of each year.

benefits
Bupa, STL, subsidised gym membership, bonus scheme, pension scheme, life assurance.

sponsorship & awards
CPE/GDL and LPC funding, plus a maintenance grant of £6,500 (London)/£6,000 (outside London).

Partners	20
Assistant Solicitors	21
Total Trainees	15

contact
Sarah Warnes
(020) 7556 4414

method of application
Online application only
http://trainee.kendallfreeman.com

selection procedure
Assessment morning plus one interview with two partners

closing date for 2010
31 July 2008

application
Training contracts p.a. up to **8**
Minimum required degree grade **2:1**

training
Salary
1st year £34,000 (May 07)
2nd year £36,000 (May 07)

post-qualification
Salary £61,000 (May 07)

summer placements
Up to 10 p.a.
open days
3, accommodating up to 100 students
closing date for summer placements
28 February 2008
closing date for open days
16 May 2008

KENDALL FREEMAN

Kirkland & Ellis International LLP

30 St Mary Axe, London, EC3A 8AF
Tel: (020) 7469 2000 Fax: (020) 7469 2001
Website: www.kirkland.com

firm profile
Kirkland & Ellis International LLP is a leading international law firm with more than 1,300 lawyers representing global clients in complex corporate, restructuring, tax, litigation, dispute resolution and arbitration, and intellectual property and technology matters. The firm has offices in London, Chicago, Hong Kong, Los Angeles, Munich, New York, San Francisco and Washington, D.C.

main areas of work
For nearly 100 years, major national and international clients have called upon Kirkland & Ellis to handle complicated corporate, restructuring, tax, intellectual property, litigation and counseling matters. Today, more than 1,300 lawyers in eight international offices are dedicated to providing the highest quality service to clients around the world.

trainee profile
A strong academic profile is essential, along with a genuine interest and understanding of the firm's practice areas. The firm is looking for candidates who are bright, motivated and willing to work hard as part of a team in a professional, friendly and growing firm.

training environment
As one of a small number of trainees, you will be part of the firms growing expansion into Europe. A training contract at Kirkland & Ellis will allow you to very quickly become a valued member of a small team, who is given early responsibility to work on complex and often multi-jurisdictional matters.

The principal focus of your training will be on corporate law with a specialism in private equity. You will complete four six-month seats and obtain training in areas such as banking, arbitration, IP, restructuring and tax. In addition there will be an opportunity to undertake a secondment to one of the firm's other offices.

benefits
Private medical insurance, travel insurance, life insurance, pension, employee assistance plan, corporate gym membership

vacation placements
Places for 2008: up to 25. Duration: 2 weeks. Remuneration: £300 per week. Closing date for applications: 31/01/08

sponsorship & awards
GDL and LPC course fees and a maintenance grant of £7,500 p.a.

Partners 523*
Assistant solicitors 712*
*(firm-wide, as of May 31 2007)

contact
Kate Osborne

method of application
CV and covering letter

selection procedure
Interview

closing date for 2010
31 July 2008

training
Salary
1st year (2007) **£35,000**
2nd year (2007) **£40,000**
Holiday entitlement
25 days

post-qualification
(currently no data)

overseas/ regional offices
Chicago, Hong Kong, Los Angeles, Munich, New York, San Francisco, Washington D.C.

KIRKLAND & ELLIS
INTERNATIONAL LLP

Kirkpatrick & Lockhart Preston Gates Ellis LLP

110 Cannon Street, London, EC4N 6AR
Tel: (020) 7648 9000 Fax: (020) 7648 9001
Email: traineerecruitment@klgates.com
Website: www.klgates.com/europe_recruitment/graduate/

Partners	54
Trainees	21
Total Staff	301

firm profile
K&L Gates comprises 1,400 lawyers in 22 offices located in North America, Europe and Asia, and represents capitals markets participants, entrepreneurs, growth and middle market companies, leading FORTUNE 100 and FTSE 100 global corporations and public sector entities. Whilst the firm's international practice requires lawyers with diverse backgrounds and skills, the firm comes together in its shared values of investment and growth, both for the firm and the individual. The firm is committed to professional development and provides a cutting edge training programme.

main areas of work
K&L Gates is active in the areas of investment management and related funds work, mergers and acquisitions, private equity, real estate, intellectual property, music, digital media and sport, travel and leisure, construction, insurance litigation, securities enforcement, environmental matters, litigation and other forms of dispute resolution.

trainee profile
The firm welcomes applications from both law and non-law students. Law students should generally be in their penultimate year of study and non-law students should be in their final year of study. The firm also welcomes applications from relevant postgraduates or others who have satisfied the 'academic stage of training' as required by the Law Society. You should be highly motivated, intellectually curious, with an interest in commercial law and be looking for comprehensive training.

training environment
The firm ensures each trainee is given exceptional opportunities to learn, experience and develop so that they can achieve their maximum potential. Trainees spend six month seats in four of the following departments: corporate, dispute resolution and litigation, intellectual property, construction, tax and real estate. Each trainee sits with a supervisor and is allocated an individual mentor to ensure all round supervision and training. The firm has a thorough induction scheme which includes attendance at the firm's First Year Academy in Washington, and has won awards for its career development programme. High importance is placed on the acquisition of business and professional skills, with considerable emphasis on client contact and early responsibility. The training programme consists of weekly legal education seminars, workshops and a full programme of skills electives. Language training is also available.

benefits
25 days holiday per annum, subsidised gym membership, season ticket loan, private health insurance, bonus scheme, life assurance, medicentre membership and pension.

legal work placements
The firm's formal legal work placement scheme is open to penultimate year law students, final year non-law students, other relevant post graduates or others who have satisfied the 'academic stage of training' as required by the law society.

sponsorship
GDL funding: fees paid plus £5,000 maintenance grant. LPC funding: fees paid plus £7,000 maintenance grant.

contact
Hayley Atherton

method of application
Online at www.klgates.com/europe_recruitment/ or phone for a paper application on 0207 360 8305

selection procedure
Full assessment day

closing date for 2010
31 July 2008

application
Training contracts p.a. **up to 15**
Applications p.a. **1,000**
% interviewed p.a. **10%**
Required degree grade **2:1**

training
Salary
1st year (2007) **32,000**
2nd year (2007) **35,000**
% of trainees with a non-law degree p.a. **Varies**

post-qualification
Salary (2007) **£62,000**
% of trainees offered job on qualification (2007) **80%**

overseas offices
Anchorage, Beijing, Berlin, Boston, Coeur D'Alene, Dallas, Harrisburg, Hong Kong, London, Los Angeles, Miami, Newark, New York, Orange County, Palo Alto, Pittsburgh, Portland, San Fransisco, Seattle, Spokane, Taipei, Washington

Latham & Watkins

99 Bishopsgate, London, EC2M 3XF
Tel: (020) 7710 1000 Fax: (020) 7374 4460
Email: london.trainees@lw.com
Website: www.lw.com

firm profile
Latham & Watkins has more than 1,900 lawyers in 24 offices across Europe, America and Asia and the London office advises on some of the most significant and ground-breaking cross-border transactions in Europe. The firm believes that its non-hierarchical management style and 'one firm' culture makes Latham & Watkins unique.

main areas of work
Corporate, finance, litigation, employment and tax.

trainee profile
Candidates with a strong academic background, excellent communication skills and a consistent record of personal and/or professional achievement will be rewarded with first class training. The firm is dedicated to diversity and equal opportunity and values originality and creative thinking.

training environment
Latham & Watkins can provide a very different training experience to that offered by the rest of the elite law firms. Each trainee receives bespoke supervision and outstanding support while being encouraged to recognise that they have their own part to play in the growth and success of the firm. Each trainee also has meaningful responsibility from the outset and significant legal experience on qualification. Trainees may also be given the opportunity to spend one of their four six-month seats in one of the firm's overseas offices.

benefits
Healthcare and dental scheme, pension scheme and life assurance.

sponsorship & awards
All GDL and LPC costs are paid and trainees receive a maintenance grant of £8,000 per year whilst studying.

vacation placements
The firm has a one-week Easter vacation scheme and a two-week summer scheme. Students are paid £300 per week. The deadline for Easter scheme applications is 31st December and the deadline for Summer scheme applications is 31st January.

Partners	38
Assistant solicitors	115
Trainees	10

contact
Tracy Davidson

method of application
Online application form at www.lw.com

selection procedure
3 x 30 minute interviews with a partner and an associate

closing date for 2008
31 July 2008

application
Training contracts p.a. **10-15**
Required degree grade: **2:1**

training
Salary: **£37,500**. This increases by £500 every 6 months during the training contract.

post-qualification
Salary: **£96,000**

overseas/regional offices
Barcelona, Brussels, Chicago, Frankfurt, Hamburg, Hong Kong, London, Los Angeles, Madrid, Milan, Moscow, Munich, New Jersey, New York, Northern Virginia, Orange County, Paris, San Diego, San Francisco, Shanghai, Silicon Valley, Singapore, Tokyo, Washington DC.

Lawrence Graham LLP

4 More London Riverside, London, SE12 2AU
Tel: (020) 7379 0000 Fax: (020) 7379 6854
Email: graduate@lg-legal.com
Website: www.lg-legal.com

firm profile
LG is a London-based firm delivering a full range of commercial and legal solutions worldwide. Driven by its corporate and real estate practices, the key sectors in which the firm operates are financial services, real estate, insurance, hospitality & leisure, banking, IT, natural resources and the public sector. The firm has strong relationships with law firms around the world, particularly in the US and Asia, as well as a Monaco office.

main areas of work
The firm's four core departments are: business & finance (including corporate/M&A, banking & finance, IT & outsourcing, investment funds, employment, insurance, pensions, EU/competition, housing & local government); real estate (commercial property, planning, construction, environment & health & safety, real estate litigation and finance); dispute resolution (commercial litigation, corporate recovery, insurance & reinsurance disputes, shipping, contentious trusts & estates, corporate investigations); and tax & private capital. Work is often international in its scope.

trainee profile
The firm is looking for individuals from a variety of backgrounds with refined communication skills who can demonstrate a commitment to a career in the commercial application of law. A strong academic track record with a minimum 2:1 degree is a basic requirement. Also required is a good record of achievement in other areas - indicative of the ability to succeed in a demanding career - and evidence of team working skills and the ability to handle responsibility.

training environment
Under partner supervision trainees will be given early responsibility. Training is structured to facilitate the ability to manage one's own files and interact with clients. In addition to the Professional Skills Course, there are departmental training and induction sessions. Training consists of four six-month seats: a real estate, business & finance and a contentious seat are compulsory. The other seat can be either in tax & private capital or a second in business & finance or real estate.

benefits
Season ticket loan, life assurance.

vacation placements
Places for 2008: 32; Duration: 2 weeks during Easter break and 3 x 2 weeks between June and July; Remuneration: £250 p.w; Closing Date: 31 January 2008.

sponsorship & awards
GDL Funding: Course fees and maintenance grant. £4.5k outside London, £5k in London.
LPC Funding: Course fees and maintenance grant. £4.5k outside London, £5k in London.

Partners	85
Assistant Solicitors	117
Total Trainees	42

contact
Graduate Recruitment Officer

method of application
Firm's application form.
For law **After 2nd-year results**
For non-law **After final results**

selection procedure
Interview

closing date for 2010
31 July 2008

application
Training contracts **20-25**
Applications p.a. **800**
Required degree grade **2:1**

training
Salary
1st year (2007) £30,000
2nd year (2007) £34,000
% of trainees with a
non-law degree p.a. **40%**

post-qualification
Salary (2007) **£62,000**
% of trainees offered job
on qualification (2006) **75%**

Laytons

Carmelite, 50 Victoria Embankment, Blackfriars, London EC4Y 0LS
Tel: (020) 7842 8000 Fax: (020) 7842 8080
Email: london@laytons.com
Website: www.laytons.com

firm profile

Laytons is a commercial law firm whose primary focus is on developing dynamic business. The firm's offices in Guildford, London and Manchester provide excellent service to its commercial and private clients who are located throughout the UK. The firm's approach to legal issues is practical, creative and energetic. The firm believes in long-term relationships, they are 'client lawyers' rather than 'transaction lawyers'. The key to its client relations is having a thorough understanding of businesses, their needs and objectives. Working together as one team, the firm is supportive and plays to each others strengths.

main areas of work

Corporate and commercial, commercial property (including land development and construction), dispute resolution, debt recovery, insolvency, employment, intellectual property, technology and media, private client and trusts.

trainee profile

Successful candidates will be well-rounded individuals, commercially aware with sound academic background and enthusiastic and committed team members.

training environment

Trainees are placed in four six-month seats, providing them with an overview of the firm's business, and identifying their particular strengths. All trainees have contact with clients from an early stage, are given challenging work, working on a variety of matters with partners and assistant solicitors. Trainees will soon be responsible for their own files and are encouraged to participate in business development and marketing activities. The firm works in an informal but professional atmosphere and its philosophy is to invest in people who will develop and become part of its long-term success.

vacation placements

Places for summer 2008: 6. Duration: 1 week. Closing Date: 31 March 2008.

sponsorship & awards

LPC and CPE funding: consideration given.

Partners	33
Assistant Solicitors	39
Total Trainees	12

contact
Neale Andrews (Guildford)
Stephen Cates &
Lisa McLean (London)
Christine Barker (Manchester)

method of application
Application form (on website)

selection procedure
Usually 2 interviews

closing date for 2010
31 August 2008 (although posts are filled as soon as suitable candidates are identified)

application
Training contracts p.a. **8**
Applications p.a. **2,000**
% interviewed p.a. **5%**
Required degree grade
1 or 2:1 preferred

training
Salary
1st year (2007) Market rate
2nd year (2007) Market rate
Holiday entitlement
23 days per year

post-qualification
Salary (2007) **Market rate**
% of trainees offered job on qualification (2007) **83%**
% of assistants (as at 1/9/07) who joined as trainees **45%**
% of partners (as at 1/9/07) who joined as trainees **40%**

regional offices
Training contracts are offered in each of Laytons' offices. Apply directly to desired office. See website for further details: www.laytons.com

LeBoeuf, Lamb, Greene & MacRae

No. 1 Minster Court, Mincing Lane, London EC3R 7YL
Tel: (020) 7459 5000 Fax: (020) 7459 5099
Email: traineelondon@llgm.com   Website: www.llgm.com

firm profile
LeBoeuf, Lamb, Greene & MacRae is an international law firm with 750 lawyers world-wide in offices across Europe, the US, Africa, Middle East and Asia. The London office of LeBoeuf Lamb is the firm's largest international office, with 35 partners, and over 130 legal staff. The London office handles varied, interesting work and will suit people who want early responsibility. Culturally, the firm combines a dynamic and energetic atmosphere with a congenial, supportive environment.

main areas of work
General corporate, litigation and dispute resolution, energy, environment, corporate finance, project finance, capital markets, private equity, insurance, insolvency, real estate, tax, intellectual property and employment.

trainee profile
LeBoeuf, Lamb, Greene & MacRae is looking for outstanding people in the broadest possible sense. The firm welcomes applications from people with varied, non-traditional backgrounds. Interpersonal skills are very important: the firm likes bright, confident, engaging people. The London office is international in outlook and language skills are highly valued. The firm wants proactive people who will contribute from day one and who will thrive in a diverse and cosmopolitan environment.

training environment
Trainees spend six months in four seats. The firm encourages trainees to see and experience as much of the practice as possible. The firm's training programme is comprehensive and, in addition to the professional skills course, covers an induction programme, participation in internal seminars and training sessions, together with attendance at external courses. You will be encouraged to act on your own initiative from an early stage. Trainees sit with a partner or senior associate, who gives ongoing feedback; progress is formally reviewed every six months. There are opportunities for placements in Moscow and Paris.

benefits
Firm contributes to health, life and disability insurance, season ticket loan and discretionary performance-related bonus.

vacation placements
The firm runs two week summer schemes throughout June and July for penultimate year law undergraduates and graduates of all disciplines. Places for 2008: 15; Remuneration: £300 per week; Closing date: 31 January 2008. Please visit www.llgm.com for more details and an application form.

sponsorship & awards
Full payment of GDL/LPC fees and maintenance grant of £8,500 per annum.

stop press
On 27 August 2007 LeBoeuf Lamb and Dewey Ballantine announced that they have agreed to merge, subject to Partner approval, with effect from 1 October 2007. If approved, the combined firm, Dewey & LeBoeuf LLP, will have more than 1,300 lawyers in 26 offices around the globe and revenues approaching $1 billion. There will be more than 170 legal staff in the London office, making it the 5th largest US headquartered law firm in London.

Partners	35
Counsel	4
Associates	75
Total Trainees	17

contact
Gail Sorrell

method of application
Application form from
www.llgm.com

closing date for 2010
31 July 2008

application
Training contracts p.a. **20**
Applications p.a. **950**
% interviewed p.a. **6%**
Required degree grade 2:1,
A,A,B 'A'Level Equivalent

training
Salary
1st year £40,000
2nd year £45,000
Holiday entitlement **25 days**
% of trainees with a
non-law degree p.a. **45%**

post-qualification
Salary **(2007) £75,000 and
performance-related bonus**

overseas offices
Albany, Almaty, Beijing, Boston, Brussels, Chicago, Hartford, Houston, Jacksonville, Johannesburg, Los Angeles, Moscow, New York, Paris, Riyadh, San Francisco, Washington, D.C.

Lee & Priestley LLP

10-12 East Parade, Leeds, LS1 2AJ
Email: jackie.turner@leepriestley.com
Website: www.leepriestley.com

firm profile
Lee & Priestley LLP is a single site commercial practice based in Leeds, seeking to establish a national and international reputation in a number of specialist areas. The firm sees itself as an innovative and proactive advisor to fast growing, entrepreneurial and SME clients.

main areas of work
Corporate, property, insolvency, litigation, employment, private client, family.

trainee profile
The firm prides itself on the quality of its training experience, looking to produce lawyers who would be able and confident on qualification to make a significant contribution. Applicants must show that they are creative and confident and highly motivated.

training environment
The two year training contract typically comprises four six month seats or two six month and one twelve month seat in a combination designed to meet both the preferences of the trainees and the needs of the firm as a whole.

benefits
Pension schemes, flexible benefits, health scheme.

Partners	**15**
Lawyers	**35**
Total Trainees	**7**

contact
Jackie Turner

method of application
Online via website

selection procedure
Group presentation and individual interviews

closing date for 2009
31 December 2007
(interviews April 2008)

application
Training contracts p.a. **2-3**
Required degree grade **2:1**
(occasional exceptions)

training
Salary
above law society minimum
Holiday entitlement **25 days**

Lester Aldridge

Russell House, Oxford Road, Bournemouth BH8 8EX
Tel: (01202) 786161 Fax: (01202) 786110
Email: juliet.artal@LA-law.com
Website: www.lesteraldridge.com

firm profile
Lester Aldridge LLP is a dynamic business providing both commercial and private client services. The firm has highly successful niche markets, including asset finance, marine, retail and care sector.
A key regional player, the firm has an impressive client repertoire supported by the recruitment of outstanding staff.
Lester Aldridge's positioning on the South Coast offers a positive working environment and a great work life balance, whilst providing opportunities to work with first class lawyers, impressive clients, and opportunity for City experience via LA's London office.

main areas of work
Corporate, banking and finance 32%; litigation 30%; private client 21%; commercial property 12%; investments 5%.

trainee profile
Candidates should have a consistently strong academic record, be commercially aware and possess a broad range of interpersonal skills. Applicants should be highly motivated and have a desire to succeed working with teams to advise clients in dynamic and demanding industries.

training environment
Training contract consists of four six-month seats across the firm (preferences will be accommodated where possible). Direct client involvement is encouraged and each trainee is assigned a mentor to provide guiding and encouragement. Appraisals are carried out with team leaders at the end of each seat, as are three-monthly group meetings with the Managing Partner, to ensure that trainees gain a range of work and experience.

benefits
Life assurance, pension schemes, flexible benefits. Travel season ticket loan.

vacation placements
Places for 2008: 8; Duration: 2 weeks; Remuneration: £75 p.w.; Closing Date: 31 March 2008.

sponsorship & awards
LPC.

Partners	**31**
Total Trainees	**13**
Total Staff	**302**

contact
Juliet Artal

method of application
Letter, CV & completed application form

selection procedure
Interview by a panel of partners

closing date for 2010
31 July 2008

application
Training contracts p.a. **10**
Applications p.a. **300**
% interviewed p.a. **5%**
Required degree grade **2:1**

training
Salary
Starting: **£17,250 at present, increasing by £500 after each seat**
Holiday entitlement **22 days**
% of trainees with
a non-law degree p.a. **20%**

post-qualification
Salary (2004) **£31,000**
% of trainees offered job
on qualification (2005) **100%**
% of assistants (as at 1/9/05)
who joined as trainees **36%**
% of partners (as at 1/9/05)
who joined as trainees **10%**

offices
Bournemouth (2),
Southampton, Milton
Keynes & London

Lewis Silkin LLP

5 Chancery Lane, Clifford's Inn, London EC4A 1BL
Tel: (020) 7074 8000 Fax: (020) 7864 1200
Email: train@lewissilkin.com
Website: www.lewissilkin.com

Partners	45
Assistant Solicitors	75
Total Trainees	12

contact
Andrea Williams
HR Manager

method of application
Online application form

selection procedure
Assessment day, including
an interview with 2 partners,
an analytical exercise, and
psychometric test

closing date for 2010
31 July 2008

application
Training contracts p.a. **5**
Applications p.a. **500**
Required degree grade **2:1**

training
Salary
1st year **£31,000**
2nd year **£33,000**
Holiday entitlement **22 days**

post-qualification
Salary (2007) **£48,000**

firm profile
Lewis Silkin is a commercial firm with 45 partners. What distinguishes them is a matter of personality. For lawyers, they are notably informal, unstuffy…well, human really. They are 'people people'; as committed and professional as any good law firm, but perhaps more adept at the inter-personal skills that make relationships work and go on working. They place a high priority on the excellent technical ability and commercial thinking of their lawyers and also on their relationships with clients. Clients find them refreshingly easy to deal with. The firm has a friendly, lively style with a commitment to continuous improvement.

main areas of work
The firm has a wide range of corporate clients and provides services through five departments: corporate, employment & incentives, litigation, property, housing & construction, and media, brands & technology. The major work areas are commercial litigation and dispute resolution; corporate services, which includes company commercial and corporate finance; defamation; employment; marketing services, embracing advertising and marketing law; property, construction and project finance; technology and communications, including IT, media and telecommunications. They are UK leaders in employment law and have a strong reputation within social housing and the media and advertising sectors.

trainee profile
They are looking for trainees with keen minds and personalities, who will fit into a professional but informal team.

training environment
The firm provides a comprehensive induction and training programme, with practical hands-on experience from day one. You will sit with either a partner or senior associate giving you access to day-to-day supervision and guidance. The training contract consists of four six-month seats, working in four out of the firm's five departments.

benefits
These include individual and firm bonus schemes, life assurance, critical illness cover, health insurance, season ticket loan, group pension plan and subsidised gym membership.

vacation placements
There are three two week vacation scheme sessions which take place during June and July, giving 12 participants the opportunity to gain first hand experience of life at Lewis Silkin. Applications should be made via the firm's website between November 2007 and the end of January 2008.

open days
Three open days will be held during summer 2008 to give participants an overview of the firm, its main areas of work and a chance to meet fellow trainees and partners.
Applications should be made between November 2007 and the end of January 2008.

sponsorship & awards
Funding for LPC fees is provided plus £4,500 maintenance. Funding for GDL fees is provided.

Linklaters LLP

One Silk Street, London EC2Y 8HQ
Tel: (020) 7456 2000 Fax: (020) 7456 2222
Email: graduate.recruitment@linklaters.com
Website: www.linklaters.com/careers/ukgrads

firm profile
Linklaters LLP is the global law firm that advises the world's leading companies, financial institutions and governments on their most challenging transactions and assignments. This is an ambitious and innovative firm: the drive to create something new in professional services also shapes a very special offer to graduates.

main areas of work
While many law firms have strengths in particular areas, Linklaters is strong across the full range of commercial, corporate and financial law; this makes the firm an especially stimulating place to train as a business lawyer.

trainee profile
Linklaters people come from many different backgrounds and cultures; by working together to achieve great things for clients, they are encouraged to achieve their own ambitions and potential. Training with Linklaters means working alongside some of the world's best lawyers on some of the world's most challenging deals. The firm expects a lot of its trainees, but the rewards – personal and professional as well as financial – are very high indeed.

training environment
The firm recruits graduates from both law and non-law disciplines. Non-law graduates spend a conversion year at law school taking the Graduate Diploma in Law (GDL). All trainees have to complete the Legal Practice Course (LPC) before starting their training contracts. The firm meets the costs of both the GDL and LPC. The training contract is built around four six-month seats or placements in a range of practice areas. This develops well-rounded lawyers, but it also helps trainees plan their careers after qualifying.

sponsorship & benefits
GDL and LPC fees are paid in full, plus a maintenance grant. Life assurance, private medical insurance (PPP), permanent health insurance (PHI), pensions, corporate health club membership & in-house gym, in-house dental service, medical services (including flu jabs, eye & eyesight tests), wedding cheques, subsidised staff restaurant, maternity & paternity arrangements (enhanced), interest-free season ticket loan, adoptive leave, group personal accident & holiday travel insurance, performance-related bonus, profit-related bonus scheme, concierge service.

vacation placements
Linklaters offers a two-week Christmas Vacation Scheme for 30 final year non-law students, and three Summer Vacation Schemes (choice of either two or four weeks) for 80 penultimate year law students.

Partners 500+
Associates 1,500+
Trainees 250+*
*(London)

contact
Charlotte Hart

method of application
Application form (available online)

selection procedure
Critical reasoning test, 2 interviews plus commercial case study (same day).

application
Training contracts p.a. **130**
Applications p.a. **3,500**
Required degree grade **2:1**

training
Salary
1st year (2007) **£36,000**
Holiday entitlement **25 days**
% of trainees with a non-law degree p.a. **40%**

post-qualification
Salary **£64,000 +**
discretionary performance-related bonus

offices
Amsterdam, Antwerp, Bangkok, Beijing, Berlin, Bratislava, Brussels, Bucharest, Budapest, Cologne, Dubai, Frankfurt, Hong Kong, Lisbon, London, Luxembourg, Madrid, Milan, Moscow, Munich, New York, Paris, Prague, Rome, São Paulo, Shanghai, Singapore, Stockholm, Tokyo, Warsaw

Lovells

Lovells LLP, Atlantic House, Holborn Viaduct, London EC1A 2FG
Tel: (020) 7296 2000 Fax: (020) 7296 2001
Email: recruit@lovells.com
Website: www.lovells.com/graduates

firm profile
Lovells is an international legal practice comprising Lovells LLP and its affiliated businesses with offices in the major financial and commercial centres across Europe, Asia and the United States.

main areas of work
The practice's international strength across a wide range of areas gives it an exceptional reputation. The practice's core areas are corporate, dispute resolution, finance and commerce with specialist groups including real estate, intellectual property, employment, EU/Competition, insurance and tax.

trainee profile
The practice is looking for people whose combination of academic excellence and specialist knowledge will develop Lovells' business and take it forward. As well as demonstrating strong academic and intellectual ability, candidates should have strong communication and interpersonal skills, a professional, commercial attitude, and be happy working in a team yet capable of, and used to, independent action. Above all, candidates should have a single-minded ambition to succeed in a top legal practice.

training environment
Lovells treats continuous training and development as a priority for those undertaking the LPC, trainees and qualified lawyers. Clients expect informed, effective legal and business advice from all Lovells lawyers. As a trainee solicitor at Lovells you will participate in an extensive training programme, which covers legal, business and technology skills. The practice is committed to providing you with the highest possible standard of training, throughout your training contract and beyond, so you will develop into an accomplished legal and business adviser.

Trainees spend six months in four different areas of the practice to gain as much experience as possible. All trainees must spend six months in a corporate or finance group, and six months gaining contentious experience in the practice's dispute resolution group. In the second year of training, there is the option to spend a seat on secondment either to one of the practice's international offices or the in-house legal team of one of the firm's major clients.

Throughout your training contract, Lovells will work closely with you to advise and provide feedback on your progress. This involves formal and informal assessments as well as advice on practice areas, secondments and qualification. Trainees are offered as much responsibility as they can handle as well as regular reviews, six-monthly appraisals and support when they need it. Lovells' task is much more than merely recruiting – it means ensuring that your ambitions are met by the practice.

Partners 342
Assistant Solicitors 1609
Total Trainees 152

contact
recruit@lovells.com

method of application
Online application form

selection procedure
Assessment day: critical thinking test, group exercise, interview

closing date for 2010
31 July 2008

application
Training contracts p.a. **90**
Applications p.a. **2,500**
% interviewed p.a. **20%**
Required degree grade **2:1**

training
Salary
1st year (2007) £36,000
2nd year (2007) £40,000
Holiday entitlement **25 days**
% of trainees with a
non-law degree p.a. **40%**
No. of seats available
abroad p.a. **25**

post-qualification
Salary (2007) **£63,500**

international offices
Alicante, Amsterdam, Beijing, Brussels, Budapest, Chicago, Dubai, Düsseldorf, Frankfurt, Hamburg, Ho Chi Minh City, Hong Kong, London, Madrid, Milan, Moscow, Munich, New York, Paris, Prague, Rome, Singapore, Shanghai, Tokyo, Warsaw, Zagreb

Lovells continued

future trainee solicitor benefits

All trainees receive a £1,000 bonus and £1,000 advance in salary on joining the firm. The practice also offers £500 for a First Class degree result, £500 for getting the top overall marks within the Lovells LPC cohort, an interest-free season ticket loan (for London Underground and overground services) during the LPC year, Lovells discount card offering discounts at retailers local to the practice, and access to an extranet site specifically for future trainee solicitors .

trainee solicitor benefits

PPP medical insurance, life assurance, PHI, season ticket loan, in-house gym, subsidised staff restaurant, access to dentist, doctor and physiotherapist, discounts at local retailers.

vacation placements

The practice offers 90 vacation placements each year at Christmas, Easter and during the summer. Christmas 3-14th December 2007; Easter 17-28th March 2008; First Summer 16th June-4th July 2008; Second Summer 14th July-1st August 2008. Applications for all schemes open on 1st October 2008. The closing date for Christmas is 9th November 2008. For Easter and the summer programmes, please apply by 1st February 2008. Remuneration: £300 per week.

sponsorship & awards

GDL and LPC course fees are paid, and a maintenance grant is also provided of £8,000 for all students reading the LPC and GDL in London and £7,000 for students reading the GDL elsewhere.

additional information

All second year trainees have the opportunity to apply to spend six months abroad. This is not compulsory and if you want to remain in London you can do so. The practice currently sends trainees to Brussels, Frankfurt, Moscow, Hong Kong, Dubai, Paris, Singapore and Tokyo. Currently about 12 trainees will go to the international offices and about 12 will go on client secondments at each seat change.

future & current trainee comments

'When it came to choosing where to apply for a training contract, my first criterion was simple – I was only interested in applying to the very top firms. This goes well beyond the fact that Lovells is one of the largest firms in the city, though. What I was most interested in was that Lovells offers, first, an almost unrivalled breadth of practice, which means that during my first two years at the firm I will have ample opportunity to find the area into which I want to qualify. More important, though, is a client-list of the calibre that Lovells boasts which tells you that the quality of work here is amongst the highest in the city. You can't fail to be impressed – and tempted – by the prospect of working with high profile clients.' Nick Root [1st seat trainee]

'I chose Lovells for the reputation of the people as well as for the quality of work/client I knew I would experience. I have found partners to be approachable and helpful, and experienced a high level of client contact (I have enjoyed various client entertainment evenings) and a great team atmosphere. Adjusting to working life has been a bit of a challenge but I have made great new friends and am very happy with the level of training I have received. I have worked a lot of long hours but the support of the team has made it a lot easier. My knowledge and confidence has increased way beyond expectation in a very short time.' Una Ferris [4th seat trainee]

Lupton Fawcett LLP

Yorkshire House, East Parade, Leeds LS1 5BD
Tel: (0113) 280 2000 Fax: (0113) 245 6782
Email: hr@luptonfawcett.com
Website: www.luptonfawcett.com

firm profile
Lupton Fawcett is a well-established yet dynamic and integrated practice. The firm offers a full range of legal services to both commercial and private clients alike on a quality-driven and client-led basis with the emphasis on providing first-class cost effective and practical solutions which exceed the clients' expectations. The firm was one of the first in Leeds to hold both Investors in People and the Law Society's Lexcel quality standard.

Lupton Fawcett is the trading name of Lupton Fawcett LLP, a limited liability partnership, registered in England and Wales, with partnership number OC316270. The registered office is at the above address, where a list of Members' names is open to inspection. Regulated by the Law Society. Authorised and Regulated by the Financial Services Authority.

main areas of work
The commercial division offers the chance to gain experience in corporate, commercial property, employment, intellectual property, insolvency and commercial and chancery litigation. On the private client side, opportunities are available in financial services, trusts and probate, family and residential conveyancing. Further specialist areas of the firm include employment, licensing and advocacy, IT and e-commerce, sports law, debt recovery, insurance litigation and specialist personal injury.

trainee profile
Although strong academic achievements are required, the firm places a high value on previous experience and interests which have developed commercial awareness, maturity and character. Trainees will also be able to demonstrate enthusiasm, confidence, good interpersonal and team skills, humour, initiative, commitment and common sense.

training environment
Training at Lupton Fawcett is normally split into four six-month seats. Trainees office share with the director or associate with whom they are working and are an integral part of the team, assuming a high degree of responsibility. Appraisals following each seat take place to ensure that progress is monitored effectively. A full in-house training programme enables continual development as well as from training gained from excellent hands-on experience. Trainees will have the chance to meet clients and be responsible for their own work, as well as being involved in and actively encouraged to join in marketing and practice development initiatives. There is a full social programme in which the trainees are encouraged to participate as well as sporting events organised by the office and an excellent informal social culture.

benefits
Health insurance, season ticket loans. All trainees are eligible to recieve a payment of £10,000 towards costs of CPE/GAL/LPC with the remainder to be used as a living allowance. Terms and Conditions apply.

Directors	28
Assistant Solicitors	17
Associate Solicitors	15
Total Trainees	4

contact
HR Department
(0113) 280 2251

method of application
Online at
www.luptonfawcett.com

selection procedure
Interviews & assessment days

closing date for 2010
31 July 2008

application
Training contracts p.a. **2-3**
Applications p.a. **300**
% interviewed p.a. **10**
Required degree grade **2:1** preferred

training
Salary
Competitive with similar size/type firms
Holiday entitlement
23 days

post-qualification
Salary
Competitive with similar size/type firms
% of trainees offered job on qualification (2005-06) **99%**

Mace & Jones

19 Water Street, Liverpool L2 0RP
Tel: (0151) 236 8989 Fax: (0151) 227 5010
Email: duncan.mcallister@maceandjones.co.uk
Pall Mall Court, 61-67 King Street, Manchester, M2 4PD
Tel: (0161) 214 0500 Fax: (0161) 832 8610
Website: www.maceandjones.co.uk

firm profile

Mace & Jones is a leading regional practice in the North West with a national as well as a regional reputation for its commercial expertise, especially in employment, dispute resolution/insolvency, corporate and real estate. It also has one of the best Private Client Teams in the region. The firm's clients range from national and multinational companies and public sector bodies to owner managed businesses and private individuals, reflecting the broad nature of the work undertaken. Sound practical advice is given always on a value-for-money basis.

main areas of work

Dispute resolution/insolvency 15 percent; real estate 25 percent; corporate 15 percent; employment 20 percent; personal injury/private client/family 25 percent.

trainee profile

Ability, motivation and the determination to succeed are prerequisites. The trainee profile demonstrates the firm's commitment to appointing trainees from a wide range of backgrounds and experiences.

training environment

Trainees complete an induction course to familiarise themselves with the work carried out by the firm's main departments, administration and professional conduct. Training consists of four six-month seats in the following departments: corporate, employment, dispute resolution/construction, real estate, family law and private client law. Strenuous efforts are made to ensure that trainees are able to select a training seat of their choice. Trainees are actively encouraged to participate in every aspect of the firm's activities and regularly act as mentors for undergraduates. The PSC is taught externally.

Partners	36
Assistant Solicitors	42
Total Trainees	11

contact
Duncan McAllister
Liverpool Office

method of application
Online

selection procedure
Interview with partners and HR

closing date for 2009
31 July 2008

application
Training contracts p.a. **5/6**
Applications p.a. **250**
% interviewed p.a. **10%**
Required degree grade **2:1**

training
Salary
1st year (2007) £17,000
2nd year (2007) £17,500
Holiday entitlement **20 days**
% of trainees with a
non-law degree p.a. **40%**

post-qualification
Salary **Negotiable**
% of trainees offered job
on qualification (2007) **100%**
% of assistants (as at 1/7/07)
who joined as trainees **25%**
% of partners (as at 1/9/07)
who joined as trainees **20%**

MACE&JONES

insider
Property Awards
NORTH WEST 2007
PROPERTY LAW FIRM OF THE YEAR

Macfarlanes

10 Norwich Street, London EC4A 1BD
Tel: (020) 7831 9222 Fax: (020) 7831 9607
Email: gradrec@macfarlanes.com
Website: www.macfarlanes.com

firm profile
Macfarlanes is a leading law firm in the City of London with a strong international outlook. The firm's success is founded on first-class lawyers, hard work and excellent training at all levels. Much of their work is international, acting in complex cross-border transactions and international disputes. This work is driven by the firm's excellent relationships with leading independent law firms outside the UK.

main areas of work
The firm has a large corporate, property and litigation department and, unusually for a City firm, a significant private client department. They serve a broad range of clients in the UK and overseas, from multinationals, quoted companies and banks to private individuals.

trainee profile
Trainees need to be highly motivated, high-achieving graduates from any discipline with (or expecting) a strong 2:1 degree or higher, who are looking for top quality work and training in a cohesive firm where everyone's contribution counts and can be seen to count. Macfarlanes needs people who can rise to a challenge and who will relish the opportunities and responsibilities that will be given to them.

training environment
Anyone joining Macfarlanes cannot expect to lose themselves in the crowd. Because they recruit fewer trainees, each individual is expected to play their part. There are other benefits attached to working in a firm of this size: it helps retain an informal working atmosphere – people quickly get to know one another and are on first name terms across the board. There is the sense of community that comes from working closely together in smaller teams. Everyone at Macfarlanes has a vested interest in getting the best out of each other, including their trainees.

benefits
A comprehensive benefits package is provided.

vacation placements
Places for 2008: 66; Duration: 2 weeks; Remuneration: £250 p.w.; Closing Date: 29 February 2008.

sponsorship & awards
CPE/GDL and LPC fees paid in full and a £7,000 maintenance allowance. Prizes for those gaining distinction or commendation on the LPC.

Partners 72
Assistant Solicitors 153
Total Trainees 50

contact
Vicki Dimmick

method of application
Online via website

selection procedure
Assessment day

closing date for 2010
31 July 2008

application
Training contracts p.a. **30**
Applications p.a. **900**
% interviewed p.a. **20%**
Required degree grade **2:1**

training
Salary
1st year £36,000
2nd year £40,000
Holiday entitlement **25 days,
rising to 26 on qualification**
% of trainees with a
non-law degree p.a. **50%**

post-qualification
Salary (2007) **£64,000**
% of trainees offered job
on qualification (2007) **100%**
% of partners (as at 1/9/07)
who joined as trainees **58%**

www.chambersstudent.co.uk

797

Maclay Murray & Spens LLP

151 St Vincent Street, Glasgow G2 5NJ
Tel: (0141) 248 5011
Website: www.mms.co.uk

Partners	72
Assistant Solicitors	171
Total Trainees	55

firm profile

Maclay Murray & Spens is a full service, independent, commercial legal firm offering legal solutions and advice to clients throughout the UK and beyond. The firm has offices in Aberdeen, Glasgow, Edinburgh, London and Brussels and the firm's objective is to provide a consistently excellent quality of service across the firm's entire service range and from every UK office.

main areas of work

Banking and finance, capital projects, commercial litigation and advocacy, construction and engineering, corporate, employment pensions and benefits, EU, competition and regulatory , IP and technology, oil and gas, planning and environmental, private client, property, public sector and tax.

trainee profile

Applicants should have a strong academic background (minimum 2:1 degree) as well as demonstrate a number of key skills including an inquiring mind and a keenness to learn, commitment, professionalism, determination to see a job through, first class communication skills, the ability to get on with colleagues and clients at all levels, an ability to operate under pressure in a team environment, as well as a sense of humour. The firm welcomes non-law graduates.

training environment

MMS will provide you with a very broad range of practice experience, including legal writing, drafting, research work, and an element of client contact. This is one of the firm's strengths as a business and a long standing attraction for candidates.

By working as a team member on more complex transactions, you are given the opportunity to gain experience over a broad range of work. You will also be encouraged to meet and work alongside clients from different backgrounds and diverse areas of industry and commerce.

benefits

At MMS trainees are paid competitive salaries as well as provided with an attractive benefits package. All of the firm's employees receive a combination of fixed and variable holidays totalling 34 days each year. The firm also offers a contributory pension scheme, death in service benefit worth four times your annual salary, support with conveyancing fees, enhanced maternity and paternity pay, income protection insurance and discounted access to medical and dental plans.

MMS also believes that the benefits provided should be more than just monetary. As such, the firm encourages departments, teams and offices to meet on an informal basis.

sponsorship & awards

From 2009, successful trainees will be supported with the cost of their Diploma of Legal Practice in Scotland and their Legal Practice Certificate in London.

In Scotland, trainees that do not receive a funded place on the Diploma will be able to apply for up to £3,000 towards the cost of the course. In London, MMS will contribute up to £10,000 towards the cost of the Legal Practice Certificate. These payments will be made when you start your training contract with the firm.

contact
trainee.recruitment@mms.co.uk

method of application
Application forms only, accessed at www.mms.co.uk/traineeship

selection procedure
Following an initial interview a number of candidates will be invited to attend a second interview with 2 Partners, where they will also complete a roleplay and research exercise. Offers will be made to the successful candidates very soon after the second interview

closing date for 2010
London traineeship August 2008
Scottish traineeship October 2008

application
Training contracts p.a. **30**
Applications p.a.
Scotland 300
London 150
Required degree grade **2:1**

training
Salary (2007)
(Scotland) 1st year £17,000
(London) 1st year £30,000
Holiday entitlement **All of our employees receive a combination of fixed and variable holidays totalling 34 days per year.**

post-qualification
Salary (2007)
(Scotland) £33,000
(London) £54,000

overseas/regional offices
Aberdeen, Edinburgh, Glasgow, London and Brussels

Manches

Aldwych House, 81 Aldwych, London WC2B 4RP
Tel: (020) 7404 4433 Fax: (020) 7430 1133
Email: sheona.boldero@manches.com
Website: www.manches.com

firm profile
Manches is a full-service commercial firm based in London and the Thames Valley with strengths across a range of services and industry sectors. Their current strategy has seen a greater concentration and focus on the firm's core industry sectors of technology & media, property, retail and construction, while continuing to be market leaders in family law. The firm offers 10 trainee places each September.

main areas of work
Industry Sectors: Technology & media, property, retail and construction.
Legal Groups: Commercial property, commercial litigation, corporate finance, construction, family, trusts & estates, employment, intellectual property, information technology, biotechnology (Oxford office only), and environment & planning (Oxford office only).

trainee profile
Manches aims to recruit a broad cross-section of candidates with different ranges of experiences and backgrounds. However, all candidates should demonstrate consistently good academic records, together with cheerful enthusiasm, high levels of commitment, an appreciation of commercial issues, the ability to think for themselves and have warm and approachable social skills.

training environment
The firm gives high-quality individual training. Trainees generally sit in four different seats for six months at a time. The firm's comprehensive induction week, followed by its practically based "learning by doing" training programme enables them to take responsibility from an early stage, ensuring that they become confident and competent solicitors at the point of qualification. Trainees have the opportunity to actively participate in departmental meetings, presentations, client seminars and briefings and they receive regular appraisals on their progress.

benefits
Season ticket loan, BUPA after six months, permanent health insurance, life insurance, pension after six months.

vacation placements
Places for 2008: 24 approx.; Duration: 1 week; Closing Date: 31 January 2008; Remuneration: under review.

sponsorship & awards
GDL and LPC fees are paid in full together with an annual maintenance allowance (currently £5,000 p.a.).

Partners 59
Assistant Solicitors 65
Total Trainees 20

contact
Sheona Boldero
sheona.boldero@manches.com

method of application
Online application form

selection procedure
1st interview with HR, 2nd Interview with 2 partners.

closing date for 2010
31 July 2008

application
Training contracts p.a. **10**
Applications p.a. **900**
% interviewed p.a. **5%**
Required degree grade **2:1 min**

training
Salary
1st year (2008)
London £28,000
2nd year (2008)
London £31,000
Holiday entitlement **24 days**

post-qualification
Salary
London £50,000
% of trainees offered job on qualification (2007) **80%**

Martineau Johnson

No 1 Colmore Square, Birmingham B4 6AA
35 New Bridge Street, London, EC4V 6BW
Tel: (0870) 763 2000 Fax: (0870) 763 2001
Email: jennifer.seymour@martjohn.co.uk
Website: www.graduates4law.co.uk and www.martineau-johnson.co.uk

firm profile

Martineau Johnson is a dynamic and passionate law firm that combines a commercial and vibrant atmosphere with a personal and caring attitude.

Providing national and international advice to its clients, the firm is recognised as market leader in many of its areas of practice and is well known for providing high level expertise.

Martineau Johnson look for enthusiastic and committed graduates with good degrees, not necessarily in law, to contribute to its successful practice.

State of the art premises in the heart of Birmingham city centre, coupled with its expanding London office, provide trainees with an ideal base to gain experience in a variety of core and niche practice areas.

As a founder member of Multilaw, an international network of law firms, opportunities also stretch far beyond the UK.

The firm's commitment to client care and quality is endorsed by the ISO 9001 standard.

main areas of work

Commercial 26%; corporate services 23%; commercial disputes management 21%; property 18%; private client 12%.

trainee profile

Trainees are vital to Martineau Johnson's future and no effort is spared to give the best possible experience and support to them, whilst treating them as individuals. There is a very high retention rate at the end of training contracts, when trainees are generally offered roles in their preferred departments and specialisms.

training environment

Martineau Johnson's aim is to work in partnership with trainees, providing them with mentoring, supervision, support and an exposure to the key areas of the firm's practice. Trainees are actively encouraged to be an integral part of the team delivering legal solutions to its clients whilst benefiting from quality work, flexible seat rotation in a small and friendly team environment. Trainees gain experience in three main areas, corporate commercial disputes, commercial property and they are then given the opportunity to experience work in areas of their chosen specialism. There are opportunities for Birmingham-based trainees to be exposed to the London scene.

Trainees benefit from a bespoke career development and training programme which is tailored to their personal needs; it covers not only legal technical matters, but also a business and commercial approach which has never been more central to successful professional careers.

In giving training and offering experience that matches the best city firms Martineau Johnson offers a rare opportunity for trainees to lay great foundations for their legal career in a fast moving, ever changing but caring environment.

Partners	**46**
Assistant Solicitors	**100**
Total Trainees	**21**

contact
Jennifer Seymour

method of application
Online application form
www.graduates4law.co.uk

selection procedure
Assessment centre - half day

closing date for 2010
31 July 2008

application
Training contracts p.a. **10-12**
Applications p.a. **500**
% interviewed p.a. **10%**
Required degree grade **2:1**

training
Salary
1st year (2006) c. £21,000
2nd year (2006) c. £22,500
Holiday entitlement **25 days**
% of trainees with a
non-law degree (2005) **40%**

post-qualification
Salary (2007) **£38,000**
% of trainees offered job
on qualification (2007) **88%**
% of assistants (as at 1/9/06)
who joined as trainees **49%**
% of partners (as at 1/9/06)
who joined as trainees **42%**

MARTINEAU JOHNSON

Maxwell Winward LLP

100 Ludgate Hill, London EC4M 7RE
Tel: (020) 7651 0000   Fax: (020) 7651 4800
Email: recruitment@maxwellwinward.com
Website: www.maxwellwinward.com

Partners	**21**
Assistant Solicitors	**35**
Total Trainees	**8**

firm profile

Maxwell Winward, created when leading property firm Maxwell Batley and built environment specialist Winward Fearon merged on 1 April 2007, specialises in a number of key areas which have been strengthened considerably by the merger. The firm is experiencing a period of unprecedented dynamism and growth, whilst remaining a compelling alternative to larger firms in its specialist fields of practice. The firm has a modern focus and a friendly, unstuffy ethos where trainees are treated as future solicitors of the business. Trainees are encouraged to interact with everyone in the firm as one of the team to develop the abilities they will need on qualification and into the future.

main areas of work

The firm specialises in Real Estate, Construction (both contentious and non-contentious), Corporate, Company/Commercial, Projects and Dispute Resolution. As well as acting for several high-profile blue-chip clients, the firm also acts for a number of smaller commercial clients and some high net worth individuals.

trainee profile

Successful candidates will have at least a 2:1 in any discipline. It is important that candidates are willing to learn and have enthusiasm, common sense and commercial awareness as well as a genuine interest in the firm's specialist areas.

training environment

The varied nature of the firm's work means that trainees are given a range of experience from all of the different practice areas. The training contract is split into four six-month seats in each of the different practice areas. Whilst trainees are closely supervised, the firm is keen to ensure that they are given valuable practical experience, as much client contact as possible and the responsibility to gradually gain the confidence to tackle matters with little supervision.

The firm arranges internal seminars for trainees in order to give them formal training to complement the day to day experience that comes with assisting on 'real-life' matters.

benefits

20 days holiday, Season ticket loan, Private health insurance.

sponsorship & awards

Contribution towards fees and maintenance for GDL and LPC.

contact
The Practice Manager

method of application
CV and covering letter

selection procedure
Two interviews

closing date for 2009 and 2010
27 July 2008

application
Training contracts p.a. **4**
Applications p.a. **250**
% interviewed p.a. **20%**
Required degree grade **2:1**

training
Salary
1st year (2007) £29,000
2nd year (2007) £31,500
Holiday entitlement **20 days**

post-qualification
Salary (2007) **£48,000**
% of trainees offered job
on qualification (2007) **100%**

Mayer Brown[1]

11 Pilgrim Street, London EC4V 6RW
Tel: (020) 7248 4282 Fax: (020) 7782 8790
Email: graduaterecruitment@mayerbrown.com
Website: www.mayerbrown.com/london/careers/gradrecruit

firm profile
Mayer Brown is among the largest law practices in the world with over 500 Partners and more than 1,400 lawyers worldwide. It has offices in Berlin, Brussels, Charlotte, Chicago, Cologne, Frankfurt, Houston, Los Angeles, New York, Palo Alto, Paris and Washington DC. The firm also has an alliance with leading Italian law firm Studio Legale Tonucci, an association with the Mexican firm Jauregui, Navarette y Nader and trade consulting offices in Shanghai and Beijing in China.

main areas of work
The firm advises leading financial and commercial companies around the world. Its client base includes many of the FTSE 100 and Fortune 500 companies together with other global leaders in target industries. The major emphasis in Europe is across industry sectors including chemicals, construction and engineering, energy, insurance and reinsurance, mining, pensions, pharmaceuticals and biotechnology, real estate, TMT and securitisation. Working within this framework core practice lines include corporate and securities (including M&A and corporate finance), litigation and dispute resolution, finance and banking, financial restructuring and insolvency, tax, environment, employment, pensions, intellectual property, outsourcing, advertising, music and publishing, antitrust and international trade.

trainee profile
The practice is interested in motivated students with a good academic record and a strong commitment to law. Commercial awareness gained through legal or business work experience is an advantage. Applications are welcomed from both law and non-law students.

training environment
Students looking for a leading international law practice that offers exposure to a multitude of blue-chip companies and a wide range of international work, combined with the confidence of knowing they have a place in its future, should contact Mayer Brown. Trainees will participate in a lively, energetic and positive business culture, spending time in four six-month seats including the Corporate and Litigation Departments. The practice's culture of getting immersed in a client's business means that there are excellent secondment opportunities. In addition to the Professional Skills Course, the practice offers an individual professional development and training programme. Three-monthly appraisals assist trainees in reaching their true potential.

benefits
Benefits include 25 days holiday per annum, interest free season ticket loan, subsidised sports club membership and private health scheme.

vacation placements
Places for 2008: 32; Duration: 3 weeks during Easter and Summer vacations. Experience in two of the principle work groups plus a programme of seminars, visits and social events.

sponsorship & awards
The firm will cover the cost of the GDL and LPC fees, and provide a maintenance grant of £6,500 (£7,000 for London and Guildford).

[1] Mayer Brown is a combination of two limited liability partnerships: one named Mayer Brown International LLP, incorporate in England; and one named Mayer Brown LLP, established in Illinois, USA.

Partners	106
Assistant Solicitors	176
Total Trainees	60

contact
Maxine Goodlet, Graduate Recruitment Manager

method of application
Online application form

selection procedure
Two stage assessment process including an interview, a business analysis exercise, a group online verbal reasoning test

closing date for Sept 2010/March 2011
31 July 2008

application
Training contracts p.a.
Approx 25-30
Applications p.a. 1,000+
% interviewed p.a. 10-15%
Required degree grade 2:1

training
1st year £36,000
2nd year £40,000
Holiday entitlement 25 days
% of trainees with a non-law degree p.a. 41%
No. of seats available abroad p.a. 3

post-qualification
Salary (2007) £64,000
% of trainees offered job on qualification (2007) 75%
% of partners who joined as trainees 35%

overseas offices
Berlin, Brussels, Charlotte, Chicago, Cologne, Frankfurt, Houston, London, Los Angeles, New York, Palo Alto, Paris, Washington DC, Hong Kong

McDermott Will & Emery UK LLP

7 Bishopsgate, London EC2N 3AR
Tel: (020) 7577 6900 Fax: (020) 7577 6950
Website: www.mwe.com/london
Email: graduate.recruitment@europe.mwe.com

firm profile

McDermott Will & Emery UK LLP is a leading international law firm with offices in Boston, Brussels, Chicago, Düsseldorf, London, Los Angeles, Miami, Munich, New York, Orange County, Rome, San Diego, Silicon Valley and Washington DC. The firm's client base includes some of the world's leading financial institutions, largest corporations, mid-cap businesses, and individuals. The firm represents more than 75 of the companies in the Fortune 100 in addition to clients in the FTSE 100 and FTSE 250. Rated as one of the leading firms in The American Lawyer's Top 100, by a number of indicators, including gross revenues and profits per Partner.

London Office: The London office was founded in 1998. It is already recognised as being in the top 10 of the 100 US law firms operating in London by the legal media. The firm has 80 lawyers at present in London, almost all of whom are English-qualified. The firm provides business oriented legal advice to multinational and national corporates, financial institutions, investment banks and private clients. Most of the firm's partners were head of practice at their former firms and are recognised as leaders in their respective fields by the most respected professional directories and market commentators.

main areas of work

Banking and finance; securitisation and structured finance, corporate, including international corporate finance and M&A; private equity, EU competition; employment, IP, IT and e-business; litigation and arbitration; pensions and incentives; taxation; telecoms and US securities. London is the hub for the firm's European expansions.

trainee profile

The firm is looking for the brightest, best and most entrepreneurial trainees. You will need to convince the firm that you have made a deliberate choice.

training environment

The primary focus is to provide a practical foundation for your career with the firm. You will experience between four and six seats over the two-year period and the deliberately small number of trainees means that the firm is able to provide a degree of flexibility in tailoring seats to the individual. Trainees get regular support and feedback.

benefits

Private medical and dental insurance, life assurance, permanent health insurance, season ticket loan, subsidised gym membership, employee assistance programme, 25 days holiday.

sponsorship & awards

GDL and LPC funding and maintenance grant.

Partners	605*
	29 (London)
Associate Lawyers & Other Fee-earners	504*
	51 (London)
Total Trainees	3 in 2006
	4 in 2007

denotes worldwide figures

contact
Aine Wood

method of application
CV & covering letter. See website for selection criteria

selection procedure
Application form, written test and one interview with Partners

closing date for 2010
31 July 2008

training
Salary
1st year (2007) £39,000
2nd year (2007) £43,000

post-qualification
Salary (2007) £75,000

McDermott
Will & Emery

McGrigors LLP

5 Old Bailey, London, EC4M 7BA
Tel: (020) 7054 2500
Email: graduate.recruitment@mcgrigors.com
Website: www.mcgrigors.com

firm profile
McGrigors is a law firm based across the UK with 78 partners and 366 lawyers in total. As the only law firm in the UK that practices in all three jurisdictions, McGrigors has the strength and depth to commit to multiple, large, complex and high-value transactions simultaneously, and has earned an enviable reputation for providing excellent technical legal services, whilst at the same time being small enough to retain a friendly feel. The firm has a blue-chip client list which includes KPMG, Ministry of Defence, Royal Bank of Scotland, Fairview New Homes Ltd and BP.

main areas of work
Practice areas include banking and finance, commercial litigation, competition, construction procurement, contentious construction, corporate, dispute resolution, employment, energy, health & safety, human rights, intellectual property & commercial, planning & environment, projects/PPP, project finance, public law, public policy, real estate, tax litigation, and telecoms. McGrigors has a particular focus on a number of key industry sectors including energy & utilities, house builders, regeneration, financial services, infrastructure & public sector.

trainee profile
The firm takes on people, regardless of background, who have drive, ability, and confidence. Trainees need to prove that they are interested in business, not simply black letter law, as the firm prides itself on providing commercial solutions to clients. In addition, its trainees are highly visible in the firm and are expected to get actively involved, whether in business or social events.

training environment
The firm's training is based upon a standard rotation of six-month seats in four main practice areas. To widen trainees' experience and enable them to see a broader range of legal work, the firm encourages trainees to spend a seat in one of the other offices, and there are also opportunities for a secondment to a client. The firm was recently nominated as Best Trainer amongst Large City Firms in the lawcareers.net awards and their last Law Society Monitoring Visit concluded that training of trainee solicitors at McGrigors was 'excellent and of a very high standard'.

benefits
The firm offers private medical cover, income protection, life assurance, pension, a daily lunch allowance, 35 days holidays including bank holidays, season ticket loan, and plenty of social events throughout the year.

sponsorship & awards
CPE and LPC fees are paid plus maintenance of £6,000 for each year in England.

Partners	78*
Assistant Solicitors	154*
Total Trainees	67*

*denotes firm wide

contact
Georgina Bond – London
Margaret-Ann Roy –
Scotland/Belfast

method of application
Online application

selection procedure
Half day assessment including interview, presentation and aptitude tests

closing date
31 Jan 2008 for summer scheme
31 July 2008 for 2010 training contracts

application
No. of training contracts p.a.
12-15 in London
15-20 in Scotland
1 in Belfast
% interviewed - **15%**
Required degree grade realistic estimate of **2.1** or higher

training
Salary
London **1st year £32,000**
2nd year £37,000
Scotland **1st year £18,000**
2nd year £21,000
Holiday **35 days including bank holidays**

post-qualification
Salary
London **£62,000**
Scotland **£35,000**
% offered job **85%**

overseas/regional offices
London, Edinburgh, Glasgow, Aberdeen, Belfast (Baku, Azerbaijan and a satellite office in the Falkland Islands)

Memery Crystal LLP

44 Southampton Buildings, London, WC2A 1AP
Tel: (020) 7242 5905 Fax: (020) 7242 2058
Email: recruitment@memerycrystal.com Web: www.memerycrystal.com

firm profile
Memery Crystal LLP is a medium sized law firm that has grown from strength to strength and is now one of the UK's leading law firms in its specialist areas. The firm's ethos is that people come first, whether they are clients, members of the firm or fellow advisers. This philosophy has enabled the firm to bring out the best in the lawyers who work here and those to whom the firm provides a service have recognised Memery Crystal through numerous awards.

main areas of work
The firm's main practice areas are company/commercial, dispute resolution and real estate. Within these areas, specialist groups deal with corporate finance, employment, property litigation, tax, insolvency, construction, insurance, corporate crime, regulatory law, digital technology and e-commerce.

trainee profile
The firm is looking for candidates who have achieved a high standard of education; show a willingness to take on responsibility; are commercially aware; respond to challenges; have the drive and ambition to succeed; and are seeking fulfilment and recognition in their chosen profession.

training environment
During your training you will have a balance of formal and practical training. Your development will be closely monitored with appraisals carried out every 3 months. You will sit either with a Partner, associate or senior assistant who will monitor your progress on a regular basis. During the course of your training contract, there will be a regular rotation of seats within the firm.

benefits
The firm provides a bonus scheme, life assurance, health cover, travel insurance, season ticket loan, group pension plan and subsidised gym membership.

vacation placements
There are four two-week vacation places which take place at Easter and in June. Applications should be made via the website.

sponsorship & awards
Funding for LPC and GDL fees is provided.

Partners	21
Assistant Solicitors	44
Total Trainees	10

contact
Helen Cowen

method of application
Online application form

selection procedure
First interview followed by assessment centre

closing date for 2010
31 July 2008 for training

application
Training contracts p.a.**5/6**
Applications p.a. **150**
Required degree grade **2:1**

training
Salary
1st year (2007) £27,500
2nd year (2007)£29,500
Holiday entitlement
22 days p.a.
% of trainees with a non-law degree **40%**

post-qualification
Salary (2007) **£54,000**

Michelmores LLP

Woodwater House, Pynes Hill, Exeter, EX2 5WR
Tel: (01392) 688 688 Fax: (01392) 360 563 Email: enquiries@michelmores.com
Clarges House, 6-12 Clarges Street, London, W1J 8DH
Tel: (020) 7242 5905 Fax: (020) 7242 2058

Partners	32
Total Staff (inc. Partners) 286	
Assistant solicitors	56

firm profile

Michelmores is a dynamic Exeter and London based full service law firm providing first class service to a wide range of local, national and international clients including several central government departments. The firm has an established track record of attracting quality recruits at every level and the firm's trainee solicitor retention rate is excellent. Combining state of the art technology in a new purpose built building with a management style which promotes the highest professional standards and an informal atmosphere, the firm has created a great place to work capable of attracting the very best lawyers. The partnership has retained a collegiate style which helps to foster a happy law firm renowned for the enthusiasm of its lawyers from Senior Partner down to first year trainee. The firm has just been included in the lawyer 'Rising 50' list of law firms nationally seen as rising stars.

contact
Tim Richards
(tcr@michelmores.com)

method of application
Online application form

selection procedure
interview and written assessment

closing date for 2010
1 July 2008

main areas of work

The firm enjoys a high reputation for its work in the fields of company commercial, dispute resolution and commercial property while the firm's Private Client Department (including the firm's Family Team) continues to thrive. The firm also has specialist teams in areas such as Projects/PFI, Technology and Intellectual Property, Construction and Medical Negligence.

application
Training contracts p.a. **10**
Applications p.a. **200**
% interviewed - **25%**
Required degree grade **2:1**
(occasional exceptions)

trainee profile

The firm welcomes applications from both law and non-law graduates. The firm is looking for trainees with a strong academic background who are team players who genuinely want to share in the firm's success and help it to continue to grow and improve. Common sense and strong inter personal skills are prerequisites.

training
Salary
1st year (2007) £19,500
2nd year (2007)£20,500
Holiday entitlement
28 days p.a.
% of trainees with a non-law degree **10%**
number of seats available abroad **0 (although occasional foreign secondments available)**

training environment

As a Michelmores' trainee you will usually spend 6 months in each of the firm's main departments (company commercial, litigation, commercial property and private client). You will work closely with a particular Partner in each department and will be pleasantly surprised at the level of client exposure, responsibility and involvement that is afforded to you. The firm's trainees are given both the opportunity to handle work themselves while under supervision and to work as part of a team. The quality of the firm's training is high. You will be expected to attend relevant training sessions within the firm on areas such as marketing and IT skills and time management and will also be encouraged to attend conferences, seminars and marketing events. The firm offers the opportunity of spending part of your training contract in the London office.

post-qualification
Salary (2007) **£31,500**
% offered job **100%**

sponsorship & benefits

Optional private healthcare, permanent health insurance, payment of LPC fees, subsidised staff restaurant, subsidised gym with fitness assessments and personal training, free parking. Prize for first class degrees and distinction in LPC.

vacation placements

The firm runs an annual vacation scheme in the early part of July for one week. Application forms are available on the website. Completed forms should arrive by 28 February 2008.

Mills & Reeve

112 Hills Road, Cambridge CB2 1PH
Tel: (01223) 222336 Fax: (01223) 355848
Email: graduate.recruitment@mills-reeve.com Web: www.mills-reeve.com/graduates

Partners	79
Assistant Solicitors	330
Total Trainees	45

firm profile
Mills & Reeve act for commercial organisations; ranging from PLCs to multinationals to start-ups, as well as more than 70 universities and colleges, more than 100 healthcare trusts and NHS bodies, and over 65 local government institutions. The firm also has a national centre of excellence in private client services.

Mills & Reeve has offices in Birmingham, Cambridge, London and Norwich.

For the fourth year running Mills & Reeve has been listed in the Sunday Times Top 100 Best Companies to Work For, which recognises that the firm puts people at the centre of its business.

main areas of work
A full-service law firm. Core sectors are: corporate and commercial, banking and finance, technology, insurance, real estate, healthcare, education and private client.

trainee profile
The firm welcomes applications from both law and non-law disciplines. Candidates should already have or expect a 2.1 degree or equivalent. Trainee solicitors should display energy, maturity, initiative, enthusiasm for their career, a professional approach to work and be ready to accept early responsibility.

training environment
Trainees complete six four-month seats and are recruited to the Birmingham, Cambridge and Norwich offices. Trainees can temporarily move to another office, including London, to complete a seat not practised in their base office. The firm will support the move with an accommodation allowance.

Trainees work alongside a partner or senior solicitor. Regular feedback is given to aid development. Performance is assessed by a formal review at the end of each seat.

The firm encourages early responsibility. Training is supported by a full induction, in-house training programme developed by the firm's team of professional support lawyers and the professional skills course (PSC).

Job opportunities on qualification are good and a high proportion of trainees remain with the firm.

benefits
Life assurance, a contributory pension scheme, 25 days holiday, bonus scheme, sports and social club, subsidised staff restaurants and catering facilities, season ticket loan, discounted rate for private medical insurance, corporate gym membership. The firm runs a flexible benefits scheme.

vacation placements
Applications for two week placements during the summer must be received by 31 January 2008.

sponsorship & awards
The firm pays the full costs of the CPE/GDL and LPC fees and a maintenance grant during the GDL and LPC.

contact
Fiona Medlock

method of application
Online

selection procedure
Normally one day assessment centre

closing date for 2010
31 July 2008 for training contracts
31st January 2008 for work placements

application
Training contracts p.a.**22**
Applications p.a. **Approx 650**
% interviewed p.a. **10%**
Required degree grade **2:1**

training
Salary
1st year £23,000
2nd year £24,000
Holiday entitlement
25 days p.a.
% of trainees with a non-law degree **40%**

post-qualification
% of trainees offered job on qualification (2007) 82%

Mishcon de Reya

Summit House, 12 Red Lion Square, London WC1R 4QD
Tel: (020) 7440 7000 Fax: (020) 7430 0691
Email: graduate.recruitment@mishcon.com
Website: www.mishcon.com

Partners	54
Assistant Solicitors	92
Total Trainees	17

firm profile

Mishcon de Reya is a mid-sized central London law firm offering a diverse range of legal services for businesses and individuals. The firm's foundation is a dynamic range of corporate clients that seek effective advice through close collaboration. Through expertise and entrepreneurial spirit the firm delivers legal and commercial solutions to businesses of all sizes.

main areas of work

Mishcon de Reya's expertise falls into four main areas: corporate, litigation, real estate and family. The firm also has a number of specialist groups including banking & debt finance, betting & gaming, IP, insolvency, fraud, corporate tax, employment, financial services, immigration, IT, media & public advocacy and personal tax, trusts and probate.

trainee profile

Applications are welcome from penultimate-year law students, final year non-law students and other graduates wishing to commence a training contract in two years' time. The firm wants people who can meet the highest intellectual and business standards, while maintaining outside interests. Candidates should therefore be enterprising, enthusiastic and committed, and see themselves as future Partners.

training environment

Trainees have the opportunity to experience four different seats of six months each. All trainees get exposure to at least three of the four core departments and are also able to gain experience in specialist groups during their time with the firm. Trainees share a room with a Partner or assistant solicitor. Because of the relatively few training contracts offered, trainees can expect to be exposed to high quality work with early responsibility. In order to support this, the firm has a wide-ranging training programme and provides extensive internal training in addition to the Professional Skills Course. Quarterly appraisals and monitoring in each seat ensures trainees gain a range of work and experience.

benefits

Medical and travel insurance, EAP, subsidised gym membership, season ticket loan, group income protection, life assurance and pension, in-house doctor.

vacation placements

Places for 2008: 15; Duration: 2 weeks; Expenses: £250 p.w.; Closing Date: 31st March 2008.

sponsorship & awards

CPE and LPC funding with annual allowance.

contact
Human Resources Department

method of application
Online application form

closing date for 2010
31 July 2008

application
Training contracts p.a. **10-12**
Applications p.a. **1,000+**
% interviewed p.a. **5%**
Required degree grade **2:1**

training
Salary
1st year £30,000
2nd year £32,000
Holiday entitlement
25 days p.a.
Occasional secondments available

post-qualification
% of trainees retained (2006) **86%**
% of assistants who joined as trainees **39%**
% of Partners who joined as trainees **22%**

Morgan Cole

Bradley Court, Park Place, Cardiff, CF10 3DP
Tel: (029) 20385385 Fax: (029) 20385300
Email: recruitment@morgan-cole.com   Website: www.morgan-cole.com

Partners	47
Lawyers	179
Total Trainees	24

firm profile
Morgan Cole is one of the leading regional commercial law practices in the country, providing a comprehensive service to both individual and corporate clients in both the public and private sectors. The firm has a reputation for excellence and therefore attracts the highest quality of staff from all fields. The firm is a founder member of the Association of European Lawyers, one of five leading UK law firms responsible for establishing a network of English speaking lawyers throughout Europe. The firm's areas of work consists of seven practice areas: insurance, health and regulatory; dispute management; commercial; corporate; private client; employment and banking. Within these practice areas the firm's work includes: acquisitions and disposals; technology; insolvency; intellectual property; joint ventures; management buy-outs and buy-ins; partnerships; PFI; commercial property; construction; personal injury; professional indemnity; commercial litigation and alternative dispute resolution.

trainee profile
Successful candidates should be commercially aware, self motivated individuals with drive and initiative who are able to apply a logical and common-sense approach to solving client problems. The firm is seeking applications from graduates/undergraduates in both law and non-law subjects, preferably with at least a 2:1 degree.

training environment
Trainees spend six months in four different practice areas, and since each practice area handles a wide variety of work within its constituent teams, there is no danger of over specialisation.

Vacation scheme
A vacation scheme is held in the Oxford, Reading, Cardiff and Swansea offices between June and July. The application deadline date is 30 April 2008.

sponsorship & awards
The firm offers full funding of fees for attendance on the CPE/PgDL and LPC as well as making a contribution towards maintenance.

Trainee Places for 2008:

Cardiff/Swansea	6
Oxford/Reading	6
Total	12

contact
Christine Henderson

method of application
Apply online at
www.morgan-cole.com/careers

selection procedure
Assessment Centre

closing date for 2010
31 July 2008

application
Required degree grade
Preferably 2:1

training
Salary
1st & 2nd year
The firm pays competitive salaries which are reviewed annually in line with market trends

other offices
Cardiff, Croydon, Bristol, Oxford, Reading, Swansea

Morrison & Foerster

CityPoint, One Ropemaker Street, London, EC2Y 9AW
Tel: (020) 7920 4000 Fax: (020) 7496 8500
Email: LNAttyRecruit@mofo.com Website: www.mofo.com

firm profile
Morrison & Foerster is an international firm with over 1,000 lawyers across offices in
the U.S., Europe and Asia. Founded in 1883, the firm remains dedicated to providing
clients, which include some of the largest financial institutions, Fortune 100 companies, and technology and life science companies, with legendary service. The firm's
attorneys share high standards, a commitment to excellence and a passion for helping
clients succeed. The firm is also recognised for its longstanding commitment to pro
bono work.

main areas of work
Antitrust, bankruptcy and restructuring, capital markets, communications and media,
corporate, energy, entertainment, environmental, financial services, financial transactions, government contracts, intellectual property, investment management, land use
and natural resources, life sciences, litigation, outsourcing, privacy, project finance and
development, real estate, tax and technology transactions.

trainee profile
Morrison & Foerster takes pride in promoting a diverse workplace. The firm is looking
for individuals with academic and other achievements that evidence their talent, motivation, energy and creativity. As a trainee, you will receive work assignments suitable
for a first or second year associate, and the support and training to excel in your work.
The firm welcomes applications from all degree backgrounds.

training environment
The training contract comprises four six-month seats. All trainees take seats in Technology Transactions and Corporate, plus a contentious seat in either litigation or
employment law. The fourth seat is either Tax, Capital Markets or Financial Transactions. While the firm believes that direct participation and hands-on training provide
the most rewarding opportunity, practical experience will be supported by both a mentor and a comprehensive training programme throughout your training contract. You
will work directly with associates and Partners; playing an active part in each matter to
which you are assigned.

benefits
Life assurance; health, dental and long-term disability insurance; group personal pension; season ticket loans.

vacation placements
Places for Summer 2008-09; Duration: 2 weeks; Remuneration: Travel and subsistence
allowance.

sponsorship & awards
100% CPE, GDL & LPC paid plus £8,000 maintenance p.a.

Partners	16
Associates	26
Total Trainees	3

contact
Margaret Mannell (020)
7920 4000

method of application
Please see our website
http://www.mofo.com/care
er/index.html

selection procedure
Interviews

closing date for 2010
Suitable applicants are
considered throughout the
year

application
Training contracts p.a. **3**
Applications p.a. **500**
% interviewed p.a. **10%**
Required degree grade **2:1**

training
Salary
1st year £32,500
2nd year £36,000
Holiday entitlement
25 days p.a.

post-qualification
Salary
£68,000 (2007)
% of trainees offered job on
qualification **100%**

overseas offices
Beijing, Brussels, Denver,
Hong Kong, Los Angeles,
New York, Northern
Virginia, Orange County,
Palo Alto, Sacramento, San
Diego, San Francisco,
Shanghai, Singapore,
Tokyo, Walnut Creek,
Washington D.C.

Nabarro

Lacon House, Theobald's Road, London WC1X 8RW
Tel: (020) 7524 6000 Fax: (020) 7524 6524
Email: graduateinfo@nabarro.com
Website: www.nabarro.com

Partners	125
Assistant Solicitors	248
Total Trainees	60

firm profile
One of the UK's leading commercial law firms with offices in London and Sheffield. The firm is known for having an open but highly professional culture and expects its lawyers to have a life outside work.

contact
Jane Drew

method of application
Online only

main areas of work
Corporate and commercial law; real estate; TMT (Technology, media and telecommunications); projects; PPP; PFI; pensions and employment; commercial litigation; construction and engineering; IP/IT; planning and environmental law.

selection procedure
Assessment Day (including interview)

closing date for 2010
31 July 2008

trainee profile
Nabarro welcomes applications from undergraduates and graduates with law or non-law backgrounds. Candidates must be able to demonstrate strong intellectual ability through the achievement of at least an upper second at degree level or equivalent relevant experience. Applicants also need exceptional qualities including: enthusiasm, drive and initiative, common sense, strong interpersonal skills and team working skills.

application
Training contracts p.a. **35**
Applications p.a. **1,500**
Required degree grade **2:1**

training environment
Trainees undertake six four-month seats which ensures maximum exposure to the firm's core practice areas (company commercial, real estate and litigation).
In addition to the core seats, trainees have the opportunity to gain further experience by spending time in specialist areas (eg pensions, IP/IT, tax, employment), possibly in Brussels, or completing a further seat in a core area. In most cases trainees will return to the seat they wish to qualify into for the remaining four months of their training contract. This ensures a smooth transition from trainee to qualified solicitor. The firm aims to retain all trainees on qualification.

training
Salary
1st year (2007)
London £36,000
Sheffield £25,000
2nd year (2007)
London £40,000
Sheffield £28,000
Holiday entitlement **26 days**

post-qualification
Salary (2007)
London £62,500
Sheffield £38,000
(reviewed annually)

benefits
Trainees are given private medical insurance, pension, 26 days holiday entitlement per annum, a season ticket loan, access to a subsidised restaurant and subsidised corporate gym membership. Trainee salaries are reviewed annually.

overseas offices
Brussels

vacation placements
Places for 2007: 60; Duration: 3 weeks between mid-June and end of August; Closing Date: 8 February 2008.

sponsorship & awards
Full fees paid for GDL and LPC and a maintenance grant (London and Guildford: LPC £7,000, GDL £6,000; elsewhere: LPC £6,000, GDL £5,000).

N A B A R R O

Norton Rose

3 More London Riverside, London, SE1 2AQ
Tel: (020) 7283 6000 Fax: (020) 7283 6500
Email: grad.recruitment@nortonrose.comWebsite: www.nortonrose.com/graduate

firm profile
Norton Rose LLP is a constituent part of Norton Rose Group, a leading international legal practice offering a full business law services from offices across Europe, the Middle East and Asia. Knowing how Clients' businesses work and understanding what drives their industries is fundamental to the firm. Norton Rose lawyers share industry knowledge and sector expertise across borders, enabling the firm to support clients anywhere in the world. The firm is strong in corporate finance, financial institutions, energy and infrastructure, transport and technology. Norton Rose Group comprises Norton Rose LLP and its affiliates and has over 1000 lawyers operating from offices in Amsterdam, Athens, Bahrain, Bangkok, Beijing, Brussels, Dubai, Frankfurt, Hong Kong, Jakarta*, London, Milan, Moscow, Munich, Paris, Piraeus, Prague, Rome, Shanghai, Singapore and Warsaw.

main areas of work
Corporate finance; banking; dispute resolution; property, planning and environmental; taxation; competition and regulatory; employment, pensions and incentives; intellectual property and technology.

trainee profile
Successful candidates will be commercially aware, focused, ambitious and team-orientated. High intellect and international awareness are a priority, and language skills are appreciated.

training environment
Norton Rose LLP operates an innovative six-seat system. The first four seats (16 months) include one seat in each of the practice's core departments – corporate finance, banking and dispute resolution – plus an optional seat in one of the firm's other, non-core departments – employment, pensions and incentives, tax, competition and EC, intellectual property and technology, or property, planning and environmental. The remaining eight months can be spent in the department in which you wish to qualify, or you can visit a different practice area for four months to help you to decide, and spend the last four months in your qualification seat. Alternatively, from your third seat onwards, you can elect to spend four months in one of the practice's international offices or apply for a client secondment. The practice's flexible seat system makes the transition from trainee to qualified solicitor as smooth as possible. The system has won the practice's trainees' approval, and from their point of view, develops associates with the adaptability and expertise the firm needs for its future.

benefits
Life assurance (21+), private health insurance (optional), season ticket loan, subsidised gym membership.

placement programmes
Places for 2007: 15 winter. Places for 2008: 30 summer and 15 winter; Duration: summer: Four weeks, winter: Two weeks; Remuneration: £250 p.w.; Closing Date: 31 October 2007 for Christmas 2007, 31 January 2008 for summer and 31 October 2008 for Christmas 2008. Approximately six open days per year are also held.

Partners	248*
Assistant Solicitors	689*
Total Trainees	102

*denotes worldwide figures

contact
Karen Potts

method of application
Online only

selection procedure
Interview and group exercise

closing date for 2010
31 July 2008

application
Training contracts p.a. 55
Applications p.a. 2,500+
% interviewed p.a. 9%
Required degree grade 2:1

training
Salary
1st year £35,700
2nd year £40,200
Holiday entitlement 25days
% of trainees with a non-law degree p.a. 40%
No. of seats available abroad p.a. 22 (per seat move)

overseas offices
Amsterdam, Athens, Bahrain, Bangkok, Beijing, Brussels, Dubai, Frankfurt, Greece, Hong Kong, Jakarta,* London, Milan, Moscow, Munich, Paris, Piraeus, Prague, Rome, Shanghai, Singapore, Warsaw
*Associated office

Olswang

90 High Holborn, London WC1V 6XX
Tel: (020) 7067 3000 Fax: (020) 7067 3999
Email: traineesolicitor@olswang.com
Website: www.olswang.com

firm profile

Olswang is a leading law firm renowned for its ground-breaking work in the technology, media, communications and real estate industries. Founded in 1981, the firm has grown to a staff of nearly 600, including over 80 partners and four European offices. In 2007 the firm extended its international capability by opening an office in Berlin that focuses on the real estate and finance industries. Olswang also has an established alliance with US law firm Greenberg Traurig LLP, as well as providing its services in over 80 countries through a network of like-minded leading law firms. For the past three years Olswang has been ranked among the top 100 UK employers in The Sunday Times' 100 Best Companies to Work For.

main areas of work

Advertising; banking; bio-sciences; commercial litigation; corporate and commercial; media litigation; e-commerce; employment; EU and competition; film finance and production; information technology; insolvency; intellectual property; music; private equity; real estate; sponsorship; sport; tax; telecommunications; TV/broadcasting.

trainee profile

Being a trainee at Olswang is both demanding and rewarding. The firm is interested in hearing from individuals with a 2:1 degree and above or equivalent, exceptional drive and relevant commercial experience. In addition, it is absolutely critical that trainees fit well into the Olswang environment which is challenging, busy, individualistic, meritocratic and fun.

training environment

Olswang wants to help trainees match their expectations and needs with those of the firm. Training consists of four six-month seats in the corporate, media, communications and technology, litigation, finance or real estate groups. You will be assigned a mentor, usually a partner, to assist and advise you throughout your training contract. In-house lectures supplement general training and three-monthly appraisals assess development.

benefits

Immediately: life cover, medical cover, dental scheme, subsidised gym membership, subsidised staff restaurant, season ticket loan. After six months: pension contributions. After 12 months: PHI.

vacation placements

Places for 2008: June & July; Duration: 2 weeks; Remuneration: £275 p.w.; 17 students per scheme; Closing Date: 31 January 2008.

sponsorship & awards

LPC and GDL fees paid in full. Maintenance grant of £7,000 (inside London), £6,500 (outside).

Partners	83
Assistant Solicitors	190
Total Trainees	44

contact
Victoria Edwards
Recruitment Manager

method of application
Online

selection procedure
Business case scenario, interview, psychometric test and written exercises

closing date for 2010
31 July 2008

application
Training contracts p.a. **24**
Applications p.a. **2,000**
% interviewed p.a. **4%**
Required degree grade **2:1**

training
Salary
1st year (2007) £35,000
2nd year (2007) £39,000
Holiday entitlement **24 days**
% of trainees with a non-law degree p.a. **50%**

post-qualification
Salary (2007) £62,000

overseas offices
Brussels, Berlin

O'Melveny & Myers LLP

Warwick Court, 5 Paternoster Square, London, EC4M 7DX
Tel: (020) 7088 0000 Fax: (020) 7088 0001
Email: graduate-recruitment@omm.com Website: www.omm.com

firm profile

A top 20 global law firm staffed by over 1000 lawyers in 13 offices, O'Melveny's clients include many of the world's largest financial institutions, leading private equity houses, investment banks and corporates. The London office is known for its entrepreneurial leadership and its commitment to excellence which underpin its approach to recruitment. It has sought to hire the best lawyers recognised for their skills and creative approach in their respective fields to service and grow the firm's workflow. The expertise of the team is enhanced by being able to draw on the extensive reservoir of know-how and experience from the firm's offices around the world, allowing it to provide its clients with the best local and international advice. The success achieved by the London office in a relatively short time has been recognized in the form of various industry accolades and also in the deals upon which it has been instructed. For example, it acted for GIC (Government of Singapore Investment Corporation Pte Ltd) on two of the largest M&A deals in Europe in 2006, being the successful consortium bids for BAA Plc (£10.3 billion) and AB Ports Plc (£2.8 billion).

trainee profile

The London office is seeking to recruit at least 4-6 high calibre graduates for training contracts each year. It has committed to a trainee programme relatively early in its stage of development because the partners firmly believe in investing in people who will be the future qualified lawyers of the firm. As such, successful candidates must be ambitious, have proven academic ability, high levels of drive and determination, good team working skills and be able to demonstrate sound commercial awareness. The office has a strong entrepreneurial and collegiate style and candidates should be able to demonstrate their ability to contribute to that.

training environment

Because of the relatively small size of the annual intake, the firm is able to take into account individual preferences when tailoring the training programme subject to the trainee completing the core competencies. As such, trainees will usually complete seats with Partners or senior lawyers in each of the firm's Corporate, Funds Formation and Finance Practices and now in its Litigation/International Arbitration Practice (launched in 2007). There may also be opportunity to gain experience in the firm's Competition/Anti-Trust Practice (based partly in London and partly in the Brussels office), and to work with the firm's tax, real estate and IP practitioners. The firm encourages trainees to be proactive and take responsibility at an early stage. As a firm, O'Melveny & Myers places great importance on training for its lawyers at all levels which it views as key to the firm's ability to offer high quality legal services to its clients and so trainees will participate alongside qualified lawyers in the legal and non-legal skills training programme established by the London office.

Each trainee will be provided with the support and encouragement necessary to maximise their potential. Progress is monitored with mid and end of seat reviews and feedback is given throughout each seat. The compulsory Professional Skills Course is run by an external provider.

vacation schemes

The office runs a series of summer vacation schemes. These will be for two weeks at a time between June and September. For applications for 2008 Summer vacation schemes, please apply via www.cvmailuk.com

Partners	9
Other fee-earners	40+
Trainees	8

contact
Jan Birtwell, Graduate Recruitment Partner

method of application
Application can be made via www.cvmailuk.com

selection procedure
Interview process

closing date for 2010
31 July 2008

training
Salary
1st year (2007): £37,500
2nd year (2007): £41,500
These are current rates which are reviewed annually

post-qualification
Market rate

overseas offices/ regional offices
Beijing, Brussels, Century City, Hong Kong, Los Angeles, Newport Beach, New York, San Francisco, Shanghai, Silicon Valley, Tokyo and Washington D.C.

Orrick, Herrington & Sutcliffe

Tower 42, Level 35, 25 Old Broad Street, London EC2N 1HQ
Tel: (020) 7562 5000 Fax: (020) 7628 0078
Email: recruitlondon@orrick.com
Website: www.orrick.com

firm profile

Orrick was founded in 1863 in San Francisco, California, and is now one of the world's leading international law firms with more than 980 lawyers worldwide. Orrick is known for its market-leading finance practices, as well as its corporate, restructuring, intellectual property and litigation practices.

Orrick's London core practices are acquisition finance, arbitration and litigation, banking, capital markets, trade and asset finance, competition and European Union law, corporate and corporate finance, employment, energy and project finance, global bankruptcy and debt restructuring, international dispute resolution, private investment funds, real estate, structured finance and securitisation and tax. Much of Orrick's client work involves cross-border transactions which have increased substantially in recent years with the development of the firm's European network consisting of offices in London, Paris, Milan, Rome and Moscow.

trainee profile

If you set your standards high, have a strong work ethic and are a bright, talented graduate of any discipline, early responsibility and broad-based experience are guaranteed. Applicants should have at least three A-level passes at grades A and B and a 2:1 degree.

training environment

Orrick is not a firm for every graduate: They value team players and reward collaboration over competition. They give individuals the opportunity to flourish in a lively work environment and encourage interaction among lawyers across international offices at every level of experience within the firm. They support learning through a steadfast focus on training and a mentoring programme that will provide you with the right foundation for building your legal career and for working with clients. There are regular appraisals throughout the two year training contract. Trainees work closely with fee earners and gain practical experience in research, drafting, procedural and client-related skills. The firm offers the benefits of a major international law firm providing leading practices in a variety of sectors with the opportunity for interaction in an informal office environment, and an opportunity to sit a six month seat in either our Paris or Hong Kong offices.

benefits

Pension, health insurance, subsidised gym membership, season ticket loan, private medical insurance, dental care and childcare voucher scheme.

sponsorship & awards

PgDl: Funding: Fees paid.
LPC: Funding: Fees paid plus maintenance (discretionary).

Partners 14 (London)
Of Counsel 4 (London)
Assistants 23 (London)
Total Trainees 16 maximum

contact
Simon Cockshutt

method of application
On line at
www.orrick.com/london/gradrecruitment

selection procedure
2 interviews with partners

closing date for 2010
31 July 2008

application
Training contracts p.a. up to **8**
Required degree grade **2:1**

training
Salary
1st year (2007): £32,000
2nd year (2007): £36,000
Holiday entitlement 25 days

Overseas offices
Beijing, Hong Kong, London, Los Angeles, Milan, Moscow, New York, Orange County, Pacific Northwest, Paris, Rome, Sacramento, San Francisco, Shanghai, Silicon Valley, Taipei, Tokyo and Washington DC.

Osborne Clarke

2 Temple Back East, Temple Quay, Bristol BS1 6EG   Tel: (0117) 917 3178
Email: graduate.recruitment@osborneclarke.com
Website:www.osborneclarke.com

Partners	108
Lawyers	263
Trainees	42

firm profile

Osborne Clarke is one of Europe's most respected and dynamic law firms. The firm's success is the result of delivering excellent business-focused legal advice in an energetic, straightforward and efficient way.

Osborne Clarke advises market leading and high performing organisations on their UK and international legal needs from its City, national and European offices and the Osborne Clarke Alliance.

The firm's main areas of expertise include corporate, finance and property transactions and the full spectrum of business law services, including commercial contracts, employment, pensions, outsourcing and dispute resolution.

main areas of work

Banking, corporate, employment, pension & incentives, litigation/dispute resolution, property, commercial and tax.

trainee profile

If you are a highly driven individual with good analytical, communication and organisational skills the firm would like to hear from you. Commercial acumen and the ability to build relationships with clients and colleagues are essential and foreign language skills are an advantage. Ideally, candidates should have grades A - B at A Level or equivalent, as well as a minimum 2:1 degree grade in any discipline. Applications are welcomed from candidates seeking a career change who can demonstrate strong commercial skills.

training environment

The focus at Osborne Clarke is on developing a high performance culture and the firm's aim is to develop trainees into legal business advisers. The Osborne Clarke trainee development programme offers legal, management and business skills training to develop the professional skills needed to progress as a lawyer in the firm.

The training contract is made up of four seats, each lasting six months in four different practice areas. Three of these seats are usually corporate, property and litigation. Trainees work closely with their training supervisors and fee earners in the department and can expect a high level of responsibility and client contact at an early stage in their training contract. Regular reviews and coaching sessions are held to ensure that trainees are reaching their potential. There are also opportunities for trainees to spend a seat in one of the firm's other offices including Germany or on a client secondment.

benefits

25 days holiday entitlement, life assurance, private medical insurance, permanent health insurance, employer's pension contributions, profit share scheme, interest free season ticket loan, gym discount.

vacation schemes

Places for 2008 – 20 placements in Bristol, London and Reading during April, June and July.

sponsorship & awards

The firm provides full funding for GDL and LPC tuition fees plus a maintenance grant for sponsored candidates.

contact
Heather Stallabrass,
Graduate Recruitment
Officer

method of application
Online application form

selection procedure
Assessment centre comprises of group exercises, psychometric test, partner interview

closing date for 2010
31 July 2008

application
Training contracts p.a. **20**
Applications p.a. **1,000**
% interviewed p.a. **12%**
Required degree grade: **2:1,**
any discipline

training
1st year £30,000-£34,000
2nd year £31,000-£35,000
Holiday entitlement **25 days**
% of trainees with a non-law degree p.a. **40%**

post-qualification
£41,000-£63,000

offices
Bristol, Cologne, London, Munich, Silicon Valley, Thames Valley

Pannone LLP

123 Deansgate, Manchester M3 2BU
Tel: (0161) 909 3000 Fax: (0161) 909 4444
Email: julia.jessop@pannone.co.uk
Website: www.pannone.com

firm profile
A high-profile Manchester firm continuing to undergo rapid growth. The firm prides itself on offering a full range of legal services to a diverse client base which is split almost equally between personal and commercial clients. The firm was the first to be awarded the quality standard ISO 9001 and is a founder member of Pannone Law Group – Europe's first integrated international law group. Pannone was again voted 3rd in the 'Sunday Times' 100 Best Companies to Work For in 2007 and is the highest placed law firm in the survey.

main areas of work
Commercial litigation 16%; personal injury 25%; corporate 13%; commercial property 8%; family 8%; clinical negligence 6%; private client 5%; employment 5%; construction 3%; regulatory 6%; residential property 5%.

trainee profile
Selection criteria include a high level of academic achievement, teamwork, organisation and communication skills, a wide range of interests and a connection with the North West.

training environment
An induction course helps trainees adjust to working life, and covers the firm's quality procedures and good practice. Regular trainee seminars cover the work of other departments within the firm, legal developments and practice. Additional departmental training sessions focus in more detail on legal and procedural matters in that department. Four seats of six months are spent in various departments and trainees' progress is monitored regularly. Trainees have easy access to support and guidance on any matters of concern. Work is tackled with gusto here, but so are the many social gatherings that take place.

vacation placements
Places for 2008: 120; Duration: 1 week; Remuneration: None; Closing Date: Easter 25 January 2008, Summer 13 July 2008. Recruitment for training contracts is primarily through vacation placements.

sponsorship & awards
Full grant for LPC fees.

Partners 99
Assistant Solicitors 110
Total Trainees 35

contact
Julia Jessop

method of application
Online only

selection procedure
Individual interview, second interview comprises a tour of the firm & informal lunch

closing date for 2010
13 July 2008

application
Training contracts p.a. **14**
Applications p.a. **1,000**
% interviewed p.a. **14%**
Required degree grade **2:1**

training
Salary
1st year (2007) £22,000
2nd year (2007) £24,000
Holiday entitlement **23 days**
% of trainees with a non-law degree p.a. **30%**

post-qualification
Salary (2007) **£33,000**
% of trainees offered job on qualification (2006) **100%**
% of assistants who joined as trainees **27%**
% of partners who joined as trainees **21%**

Paul, Hastings, Janofsky & Walker (Europe) LLP

10 Bishops Square, 8th Floor, London, E1 6EG
Tel: (020) 3023 5100 Fax: (020) 3023 5109
Email: melaniedamecourt@paulhastings.com
Website: www.paulhastings.com

firm profile

With 1,200 attorneys serving clients from 18 worldwide offices, Paul Hastings provides a full range of services to clients around the globe. The firm has established long standing partnerships with many of the world's top financial institutions, Fortune 500 companies and other leading corporations. The firm helps clients anticipate market evolutions in order to create market advantage. Paul Hastings represents and advises clients across a full range of practices, industries and regions.

main areas of work

Paul Hastings' principle practice areas in London are corporate, finance, employment, litigation, real estate and tax.

trainee profile

The firm seeks individuals with a wide variety of skills who combine intellectual ability with enthusiasm, creativity and a demonstrable ability to thrive in a challenging environment. The firm expects candidates to have a high level of achievement both at A level (or equivalent) and degree level. This would typically mean an upper second or first class degree and a majority of A grades at A level. The firm recruits both law and non-law graduates.

training environment

Paul Hastings will provide you with a first class training and development programme, combining on-the-job training and professional courses. The firm will monitor your progress on a formal and informal basis to ensure you receive ongoing training and have the opportunity to give feedback on the programme itself and on those areas that are most important to you.

benefits

Private healthcare, life assurance, pension scheme, season ticket loan.

sponsorship & awards

Paul Hastings offers sponsorship and maintenance grants.

Partners	9
Assistant Solicitors	24
Total Trainees	6

contact
Melanie d'Amecourt

method of application
online application form available on website

selection procedure
Interview

closing date for 2010
31 July 2008

application
Training contracts p.a. **3-4**
Required degree grade **2:1**

training
Salary
1st year (2007) £40,000
2nd year (2007) £45,000
Holiday entitlement
25 days

post-qualification
Salary (2007) **£90,000**

overseas/regional offices
Atlanta, Beijing, Brussels, Chicago, Hong Kong, London, Los Angeles, Milan, New York, Orange County, Palo Alto, Paris, San Diego, San Francisco, Shanghai, Stamford, Tokyo, Washington DC

Paul *Hastings*

Payne Hicks Beach

10 New Square, Lincoln's Inn, London WC2A 3QG
Tel: (020) 7465 4300 Fax: (020) 7465 4400
Email: lstoten@phb.co.uk
Website: www.phb.co.uk

firm profile
Payne Hicks Beach is a medium-sized firm based in Lincoln's Inn. The firm acts for both private clients and businesses. It is highly rated for private client and matrimonial advice and also specialises in commercial litigation, property and corporate and commercial work.

main areas of work
Private client 41%; matrimonial 22%; property 17%; commercial litigation 13%; corporate and commercial 7%.

trainee profile
The firm looks for law and non-law graduates with a good academic record, an ability to solve practical problems, enthusiasm and an ability to work hard and deal appropriately with their colleagues and the firm's clients.

training environment
Following an initial induction course, trainees usually spend six months in four of the firm's departments. Working with a partner, they are involved in the day to day activities of the department, including attending conferences with clients, counsel and other professional advisers. Assessment is continuous and trainees will be given responsibility as they demonstrate ability and aptitude. To complement the PSC, the firm runs a formal training system for trainees and requires them to attend lectures and seminars on various topics.

benefits
Season travel ticket loan, life assurance 4 x salary, permanent health insurance, contribution to personal pension plan.

sponsorship & awards
Fees for the CPE and LPC are paid.

Partners	28
Assistant Solicitors	24
Total Trainees	5

contact
Miss Louise Stoten

method of application
Letter & CV

selection procedure
Interview

closing date for 2010
1 August 2008

application
Training contracts p.a. **3**
Applications p.a. **1,000**
% interviewed p.a. **3%**
Required degree grade **2:1**

training
Salary
1st year (2007) £28,500
2nd year (2007) £30,500
Holiday entitlement
4 weeks
% of trainees with a
non-law degree p.a. **50%**

Penningtons Solicitors LLP

Bucklersbury House, 83 Cannon Street, London EC4N 8PE
Tel: (020) 7457 3000 Fax: (020) 7457 3240
Website: www.penningtons.co.uk

firm profile
Penningtons Solicitors LLP is a thriving, modern law firm with a 200-year history and a deep commitment to top quality, partner-led services. Today, the firm is based in London and the South East with offices in London, Basingstoke, Godalming and Newbury.

main areas of work
In the business sphere, Penningtons advise on matters relating to all aspects of commercial property, intellectual property, management buy-outs and buy-ins, mergers, acquisitions and joint ventures, as well as dispute resolution. Advice is also given on information technology, business recovery, commercial contracts, agricultural and environmental law, and company secretarial services are offered. The firm also helps families and individuals with advice on property, tax and estate planning, family law, general financial management, the administration of wills and trusts, charities, personal injury, clinical negligence and immigration. Clients often ask Penningtons to advise on both their private and commercial affairs.

trainee profile
Penningtons seeks high calibre candidates with enthusiasm and resilience. A high standard of academic achievement is expected: three or more good A level passes and preferably a 2:1 or better at degree level, whether you are reading law or another discipline.

training environment
You will be given a thorough grounding in the law, spending time in three or four of the firm's departments – corporate and commercial, litigation, dispute resolution, property and private client. The firm ensures a varied training is given, avoiding too specialised an approach before qualification. Nonetheless, the experience gained in each department gives you a solid foundation, equipping you to embark on your chosen specialisation at the end of your training contract with the firm. Penningtons knows its trainee solicitors are happiest and most successful when busy with good quality work. The firm believes in introducing trainees to challenging cases. The value of giving its trainees responsibility, and allowing direct contact with clients is recognised. However, experienced solicitors are always ready to give support when needed.

benefits
Life assurance, critical illness cover, pension, private medical insurance, 23 days holiday, interest free season ticket loan, sports and social events.

vacation placements
The firm offers both summer vacation placements and information days. Applications are accepted from 1 December 2007 to 31 March 2008.

sponsorship & awards
Full fees and maintenance for the LPC plus a maintenance grant of £4,000.

Partners 71*
Assistant Solicitors 130*
Total Trainees 27
* denotes worldwide figures

contact
Tamsin Kennie

method of application
Online via firm's website

closing date for 2010
31 July 2008

application
Training contracts p.a. **14**
Applications p.a. **1,000**
% interviewed p.a. **5%**
Required degree grade **2:1**

training
Salary
1st year (2007)
£28,000 (London)
2nd year (2007)
£30,000 (London)
Holiday entitlement **23 days**

Pinsent Masons

CityPoint, One Ropemaker Street, London, EC2Y 9AH
Email: gradrecruiting@pinsentmasons.com
Website: www.pinsentmasons.com/graduate

firm profile
Pinsent Masons is a top 15 UK law firm that is committed to sector-focused growth through its core sectors approach. This approach aligns the firm to specific business sectors to achieve market-leading positions. As a result, the firm has developed a successful and innovative approach to building strong, broad and deep corporate relationships. Client service is at the core of the firm and it works with a substantial range of FTSE 100 and FTSE 250, Fortune 500 and AIM quoted organisations as well as a variety of public sector clients.

main areas of work
Banking & finance, corporate, dispute resolution & litigation, employment, insurance & reinsurance, international construction & energy, outsourcing, technology and commercial, pensions, projects, property, tax and UK construction & engineering.

trainee profile
The firm welcomes applications from both law and non-law graduates with a good honours degree. In addition to a strong academic background, the firm is looking for people who can combine a sharp mind with commercial acumen and strong people skills to work in partnership with its clients' businesses.

training environment
Trainees sit in four seats of six months across the practices, and are supervised by partners or associates. There are also opportunities for trainees to be seconded to clients. The firm offers a supportive team culture with early responsibility and contact with clients is encouraged.
In addition to the training required by the Law Societies, the firm offers a broad-ranging and custom-made training programme designed to deliver superb technical and management skills that link with the needs of the business. This is the first stage in the firm's focused development programme that supports individuals on the route to partnership.
The firm has an open-door policy and informal atmosphere with a positive focus on work-life balance.

summer vacation placements
Places for 2008: 150; Duration: 2 weeks; Closing Date: 31 January 2008.

sponsorship & awards
In England, a full sponsorship is offered for the CPE and LPC fees, as well as a maintenance grant. In Scotland, financial assistance is offered for Diploma fees, together with a maintenance grant.

Partners	270+
Lawyers	1,000
Total Trainees	125

contact
Spencer Hibbert
Recruitment Hotline:
(0845) 300 3232

method of application
Online application form

selection procedure
Assessment day including interview

closing date for 2010
31 July 2008 (English offices) and 21 October 2008 (Scottish offices)

application
Training contracts p.a. **55**
Applications p.a. **2,000+**
Required degree grade **2:1**

training
Salary
1st year (2007)
£36,000 (London)
2nd year (2007
£39,000 (London)
Holiday entitlement **25 days**

post-qualification
Salary (2007) **£63,000**
(London)

UK offices
London, Birmingham, Bristol, Edinburgh, Glasgow, Leeds, Manchester

Pinsent Masons

Prettys

Elm House, 25 Elm Street, Ipswich IP1 2AD
Tel: (01473) 232121 Fax: (01473) 230002
Email: agage@prettys.co.uk
Website: www.prettys.co.uk

firm profile

Prettys is one of the largest and most successful legal practices in East Anglia. The firm is at the heart of the East Anglian business community, with the expanding hi-tech corridor between Ipswich and Cambridge to the west, Felixstowe to the east and the City of London 60 minutes away to the south. The firm also has offices in Chelmsford and is currently moving to larger premises in Chelmsford as it continues to expand. It provides an even closer link to London. The firm's lawyers are approachable and pragmatic. It provides expert advice to national and regional businesses.

main areas of work

Prettys' broad-based practice allows it to offer a full-service to all its clients. Business law services: company, commercial, shipping, transport, construction, intellectual property, information technology, property, property litigation, employment, commercial litigation, insurance, professional indemnity, health and safety and executive immigration. Personal law services: French property, personal injury, clinical negligence, financial services, estates, agriculture, conveyancing and family.

trainee profile

Prettys' trainees are the future of the firm. Applicants should be able to demonstrate a desire to pursue a career in East Anglia. Trainees are given considerable responsibility early on and the firm is therefore looking for candidates who are well motivated, enthusiastic and have a good common sense approach. Good IT skills are essential.

training environment

A two-week induction programme will introduce you to the firm. You will receive continuous supervision and three-monthly reviews. Training is in four six-month seats. Trainees work closely with a partner, meeting clients and becoming involved in all aspects of the department's work. Frequent training seminars are provided in-house. The Law Society's Monitoring of Training Officer recently visited the firm and concluded "Prettys offers a very strong commitment to training within a supportive environment."

additional information

One day placements are available (apply to Angela Gage).

Directors	2
Partners	14
Total Trainees	12

contact
Angela Gage
Human Resources Manager

method of application
Application letter & CV

closing date for 2010
July 31 2008

application
Training contracts p.a. **5**
Required degree grade
**2:1 preferred in law or other relevant subject.
Good A Levels**

training
Salary
Above Law Society guidelines

Holiday entitlement **25 days**

post-qualification
% of trainees offered job
on qualification (2007) **85%**

PricewaterhouseCoopers Legal LLP

1 Embankment Place, London, WC2N 6DX
Tel: (020) 7212 1616 Fax: (020) 7212 1570
Website: www.pwclegal.co.uk

firm profile

PricewaterhouseCoopers Legal LLP (formerly Landwell) is a member of the PricewaterhouseCoopers international network of firms. It is a niche law firm with close working relationships with the business specialisms of PricewaterhouseCoopers LLP ('PwC') as well as network firms across the world, giving the firm access to over 2,000 legal professionals in 40 countries.

The firm delivers services through key divisions including areas of specialisation such as corporate restructuring, M&A and private equity work, intellectual property, IT, employment, immigration, pensions, financial services, banking, commercial contracts, real estate and litigation (commercial and Tax). Depending on the transaction type, the firm's lawyers work either on a domestic standalone basis or as part of a wider team of company lawyers from the international network. Its strong working relationship with PwC also enables its lawyers additionally to work in multi-competency teams of business advisers delivering complete solutions to a variety of complex business problems.

Clients include local, national and multinational companies; partnerships and LLPs; governments; and financial institutions. The firm recognises that today's lawyers must adapt to the changing needs of clients and must offer more than just legal services. By adopting a multi-disciplinary approach working alongside experts within PwC, solutions are not pigeon-holed under the disciplines of accountancy, tax and law, and PricewaterhouseCoopers Legal LLP (through its relationship with PwC) provides its clients with a single seamless offering of legal, tax and consultancy expertise. A diverse workforce enhances creativity and PricewaterhouseCoopers Legal LLP strives to achieve and maintain diversity throughout the firm.

trainee profile

The firm wants to see applicants with a genuine interest in business law and the ambition to be part of a new model of legal practice. In return, it offers you something unique. The firm's relationship with PwC means you will work alongside experts in PwC as part of a multi-disciplinary team which differentiates PricewaterhouseCoopers Legal LLP from the majority of existing law firms. While the quality of the work and the excellence of the training can match those of any traditional law firm, the lawyers at PricewaterhouseCoopers Legal LLP spend a significant part of their time working alongside clients and other professionals as part of a unique approach to the provision of integrated business services.

training environment

A formal induction programme will introduce you to the firm. You will receive continuous supervision and three-monthly reviews. Training is in four six-month seats.

vacation schemes

The firm runs a summer vacation programme for two weeks in June and July, for which they welcome quality applications.

sponsorship & awards

Trainee lawyers joining the firm are eligible to apply for a scholarship award to assist with the costs of the PgDiploma in Law Course and the Legal Practice Course. If successful, you will receive the total cost of the tuition and examination fees (from the date of signing your contract) and also a significant contribution towards your living expenses. More details can be found on the firm's website.

Vacancies	9
Trainees	12
Partners	13
Total staff	135

method of application
Complete the online application form from the website www.pwclegal.co.uk

closing date for 2010
Trainees: July 31 2008
Summer vacation programme 2008: March 31 2008

application
Required academic grade
**280 UCAS points or equivalent
2:1 degree or equivalent**

training
Salary
London
1st year (2007) £30,000
2nd year (2007) £35,000

PRICEWATERHOUSE COPERS 🖎 LEGAL

Pritchard Englefield

14 New St, London EC2M 4HE
Tel: (020) 7972 9720 Fax: (020) 7972 9722
Email: po@pe-legal.com
Website: www.pe-legal.com

firm profile
A niche City firm practising a mix of general commercial and non-commercial law with many German and French clients. Despite its strong commercial departments, the firm still undertakes family and private client work and is renowned for its ever-present international flavour.

main areas of work
All main areas of commercial practice including litigation, commercial/corporate/banking (UK, German and French), IP/IT, property and employment, also estate and trusts (UK and off-shore), pensions, charities, personal injury and family.

trainee profile
High academic achievers with fluent German and/or French.

training environment
An induction course acquaints trainees with the computer network, online library and finance & administrative procedures and there is a formal in-house training programme during the first week. Four six-month seats make up most of your training. You can usually choose some departments, and you could spend two six-month periods in the same seat. Over two years, you learn advocacy, negotiating, drafting and interviewing, attend court, use your language skills every day and meet clients from day one. Occasional talks and seminars explain the work of the firm, and you can air concerns over bi-monthly lunches with the partners comprising the Trainee Panel. PSC is taken externally over two years. The Social Committee of the firm organises regular drinks parties, French film evenings, quiz nights and of course a Christmas party.

benefits
Some subsidised training, monthly luncheon vouchers, and eligibility for membership of the firm's private medical insurance scheme as well as an interest free loan for an annual season ticket.

sponsorship & awards
Full funding for LPC fees.

Partners	21
Assistant Solicitors	13
Other Fee Earners	7
Total Trainees	6

contact
Graduate Recruitment

method of application
Standard application form available from Graduate Recruitment or online

selection procedure
1 interview only in September

closing date for 2010
31 July 2008

application
Training contracts p.a. **3**
Applications p.a. **300–400**
% interviewed p.a. **10%**
Required degree grade **Generally 2:1**

training
Salary
1st year (2007) £22,250
Subject to 6 month review
Holiday entitlement **25 days**
% of trainees with a non-law degree p.a. **Approx 50%**

post-qualification
Salary (2007)
Approx £42,000
% of trainees offered job on qualification (2002) **75%**
% of assistants (as at 1/9/03) who joined as trainees **50%**
% of Partners (as at 1/9/03) who joined as trainees **40%**

Reed Smith Richards Butler LLP

Beaufort House, 15 St. Botolph Street, London, EC3A 7EE
Tel: (020) 7247 6555 Fax: (020) 7247 5091
Email: graduate.recruitment@reedsmith.com
Website: www.reedsmith.com

Partners	108*
Fee-earners	158*
Total Trainees	57

denotes UK figures

contact
Mark Matthews

method of application
Online application form

selection procedure
Selection exercise,
interview, verbal reasoning
assessment

closing date for 2010/11
31 July 2008

application
Training contracts p.a. **32**
Applications p.a. **1500**
% interviewed p.a. **7%**
Required degree grade **2:1**

training
Salary
1st year (2007) **£30,000**
2nd year (2007) **£33,000**
Holiday entitlement **25 days**
% of trainees with a
non-law degree p.a. **35%**
No. of seats available
abroad p.a. **10**

post-qualification
Salary (2007)
£63,000 plus bonus
% of assistants who
joined as trainees **59%**
% of partners who
joined as trainees **45%**

overseas offices
New York, Paris, Los
Angeles, Chicago,
Washington DC, San
Francisco, Philadelphia,
Pittsburgh, Northern VA,
Wilmington, Richmond,
Munich, Dubai, Abu Dhabi,
Piraeus.

firm profile
Key to Reed Smith Richards Butler's success is its ability to build lasting relationships: with clients and with each other. United through a culture defined by commitment to professional development, team-work, diversity, pro bono and community support, the firm has grown to become one of the 15 largest law firms in the world. Its 21 offices span three continents and include almost 700 people in London and Birmingham (that's around 20% of its global presence). While the offices benefit from an international framework, but each one retains key elements of the local business culture.

main areas of work
The firm is particularly well known for its work advising leading companies in the areas of financial services, life sciences, shipping, energy, trade and commodities, advertising, technology and media. It provides a wide range of commercial legal services for all these clients, including a full spectrum of corporate, commercial and financial services, dispute resolution, real estate and employment. Much of the work is multi-jurisdictional.

trainee profile
The firm is looking for individuals with the drive and potential to become world-class business lawyers. They want 'players' rather than 'onlookers' with strong intellect, initiative, the ability to thrive in a challenging profession and the personal qualities to build strong relationships with colleagues and clients.

training environment
On offer is a four-seat programme in which trainees are able to exercise much influence over the choice and timings of seats. There are many opportunities for secondments to clients and the firm's overseas offices. Trainees also benefit from being able to take a wide range of courses in its award-winning corporate university, developed in partnership with the highly rated Wharton School of the University of Pennsylvania. There are 30 vacancies for training contracts commencing in August 2010 and February 2011.

benefits
Performance related bonus, pension, life insurance, private health insurance, interest-free season ticket loan, subsidised staff restaurant, staff conveyancing allowance.

vacation placements
The firm offers up to 40 places each year to applicants who will, on arrival, have completed at least two years of undergraduate study. Placements are available in both the London and Birmingham offices.

sponsorship & awards
GDL Funding: Fees paid plus £6,000 maintenance. LPC Funding: Fees paid plus £7,000 maintenance

Reynolds Porter Chamberlain LLP

Tower Bridge House, St Katharine's Way, London, E1W 1AA
Tel: (020) 3060 6000 Fax: (020) 3070 7000
Email: training@rpc.co.uk
Website: www.rpc.co.uk/training

firm profile
Reynolds Porter Chamberlain LLP is a forward thinking London based law firm with a wide-ranging practice and some great clients. It is best known as one of the UK's leading insurance and litigation practices but it also has a highly rated and fast growing Corporate and Commercial Practice, as well as property, construction, employment and intellectual property expertise. Another key area for the firm is media; the firm has handled some of the most sensitive and high-profile defamation actions in recent years. Based in brand new offices in the city, the firm works in an open, collaborative environment designed to bring out the best in its people and to ensure that the service the firm offers to clients is second to none.

main areas of work
Litigation 60%; corporate 15%; commercial property 10%; construction 10%; media 10%.

trainee profile
The firm appoints 15 trainees each year from law and non-law backgrounds. Although proven academic ability is important (the firm requires a 2:1 or above), it also looks for natural communicators with energy, enthusiasm, and an awareness of the commercial world.

training environment
As a trainee you will receive first rate training in a supportive working environment. You will work closely with a partner and be given real responsibility as soon as you are ready to handle it. At least six months will be spent in each of the main areas of the practice and the firm encourages trainees to express a preference for their seats. This provides a thorough grounding and the chance to develop confidence as you see matters through to their conclusion. In addition to the internally provided Professional Skills Course, the firm provides a complementary programme of in-house training.

benefits
Four weeks holiday, bonus schemes, private medical insurance, income protection and death-in-service benefits, pension, season ticket loan, subsidised gym membership, subsidised dental insurance, Ride2Work scheme, active social calendar.

vacation placements
Places for Summer 2008: 24; Duration: 2 weeks; Remuneration: £275 p.w.; Closing Date: 29 February 2008.

sponsorship & awards
GDL Funding: Fees paid plus £6,500 maintenance.
LPC Funding: Fees paid plus £6,500 maintenance.

Partners	65
Assistant Solicitors	250
Total Trainees	30

contact
Kate Gregg
Legal Resourcing Manager

method of application
Online application system

selection procedure
Assessment days held in September

closing date for 2010
08 August 2008

application
Training contracts p.a. **15**
Applications p.a. **900**
% interviewed p.a. **6%**
Required degree grade **2:1**

training
Salary
1st year (2007) **£31,000**
2nd year (2007) **£35,000**
Holiday entitlement **20 days**
% of trainees with a non-law degree p.a. **Approx 25%**

post-qualification
Salary (2007) **£54,000**
% of trainees offered job on qualification (2007) **90%**
% of assistants (as at 1/9/06) who joined as trainees **20%**
% of partners (as at 1/9/06) who joined as trainees **30%**

Salans

Millennium Bridge House, 2 Lambeth Hill, London EC4V 4AJ
Tel: (020) 7429 6000 Fax: (020) 7429 6001
Email: london@salans.com

firm profile

Salans has an open and friendly culture with an informal, but hardworking environment. It is a multinational law firm with full-service offices in the City of London, Paris and New York, together with further offices in Almaty, Baku, Berlin*, Bratislava, Bucharest, Budapest, Istanbul, Kyiv, Moscow, Prague, Shanghai, St Petersburg and Warsaw. The firm currently has over 600 fee-earners, including 154 Partners worldwide, with 30 partners residing in the London office. Its lawyers strongly believe in assisting individuals and groups unable to access legal services, through a positive commitment to pro bono work. Salans was named the Eastern Europe Law Firm of the Year at the Chambers Awards 2004, and were runners-up in the Employment Team of the Year Award at The Lawyer Awards. In 2007 Salans were finalists at the Lawyer Awards for 'International Law Firm of the Year'.

main areas of work

London Office: Banking and finance; corporate and commercial litigation; employment; real estate; insolvency and corporate recovery; information technology and communications; betting and gaming; shipping and arbitration.

trainee profile

You will have high academic qualifications, including good A-Level (or equivalent) results, and the ability to approach complex problems in a practical and commercial way. The firm is looking for highly motivated, creative and enthusiastic team players. It looks to recruit trainees who make a difference, want early responsibility and live life in the fast lane of the ever-changing legal world. Relevant work experience demonstrating a desire to pursue a career in law will be viewed positively, and language and computer skills are also valued.

benefits

Private healthcare, pension, life assurance, critical illness cover, season ticket loan.

sponsorship & awards

LPC tuition fees paid.

Partners (Worldwide)	**154**
Assistant Solicitors (Worldwide)	**400+**
Total Trainees (London)	**7**

contact
Angela Butler
HR Manager

method of application
Letter & CV

selection procedure
Interview programme and selection workshop

closing date for 2010
31 July 2008

application
Training contracts p.a. **3-4**
Applications p.a. **300-400**
% interviewed p.a. **6%**
Required degree grade **2:1**

training
Salary
1st year (2007) £30,000
2nd year (2007) £32,500
Holiday entitlement **25 days**
% of trainees with a
non-law degree p.a. **Variable**
No. of seats available
abroad p.a. **One**
(occasional)

post-qualification
Salary (2007) **TBA**
% of trainees offered job
on qualification (2007) **50%**

overseas offices
Almaty, Baku, Berlin*,
Bratislava, Bucharest,
Budapest, Istanbul, Kyiv,
Moscow, New York, Paris,
Prague, Shanghai, St
Petersburg and Warsaw

*Salans LLP

Shadbolt & Co LLP

Chatham Court, Lesbourne Road, Reigate RH2 7LD
Tel: (01737) 226277 Fax: (01737) 226165
Email: recruitment@shadboltlaw.com
Website: www.shadboltlaw.com

firm profile

Shadbolt & Co LLP is an award-winning, dynamic, progressive firm committed to high quality work and excellence both in the UK and internationally. The atmosphere at the firm is friendly, relaxed and informal and there are various social and sporting activities for staff. The firm comprises a lively and enterprising team with a fresh and open approach to work. The firm's qualified staff have a high level of experience and industry knowledge and some are widely regarded as leading practitioners in their field.

main areas of work

The firm is well known for its strengths in major projects, construction and engineering and dispute resolution and litigation with established expansion into corporate and commercial, employment, commercial property and IT and e-commerce. The firm provides prompt personal service and its client list includes some of the world's best known names in the construction and engineering industries.

trainee profile

Applicants must demonstrate that they are self-starters with a strong academic background and outside interests. Leadership, ambition, initiative, enthusiasm and good interpersonal skills are essential, as is the ability to play an active role in the future of the firm. Linguists are particularly welcome, as are those with supporting professional qualifications. The firm welcomes non-law graduates.

training

Four six month seats from construction and commercial litigation, arbitration and dispute resolution, major projects and construction, employment, corporate and commercial and commercial property. Where possible individual preference is noted. Work has an international bias. There are opportunities for secondment to major clients and work in the overseas offices. Trainees are treated as valued members of the firm, expected to take early responsibility and encouraged to participate in all the firm's activities, including practice development. The firm is accredited by the law society as a provider of training and runs frequent in-house lectures. The PSC is taught externally.

sponsorship & benefits

Optional private healthcare, permanent health insurance, group life assurance, paid study leave, season ticket loan, discretionary annual bonus of up to 5% of salary, paid professional memberships and subscriptions, full refund of LPC upon commencement of training contract.

vacation placements

Places for 2008: 6; Duration: 2 weeks; Remuneration: £200 p.w.; Closing Date: 28 February 2008; Interviews: March 2008. Please submit the online form no earlier than January 2008.

Partners	25
Snr Assoc/Assoc	24
Total Trainees	8
Total Staff	104

contact
Andrea Pickett

method of application
Online application form

selection procedure
Interview (1) written assessment & group exercise

closing date for 2010
31 July 2008 (interviews September 2008)

application
Training contracts p.a. **4**
Applications p.a. **100**
% interviewed p.a. **20%**
Required degree grade **2:1**
(occasional exceptions)

training
Salary
1st year (2007) £29,000
2nd year (2007) £33,000
Holiday entitlement
20 days rising to 25 on qualification, with opportunity to 'buy' an additional 5 days holiday p.a.
% of trainees with a non-law degree p.a. **50%**
No. of seats available abroad p.a. **1**

post-qualification
Salary (2007) **£52,000**
% of trainees offered job on qualification (2007) **100%**
% of assistants (2007) who joined as trainees **45%**
% of partners (2007) who joined as trainees **0%**

other offices
Reigate, City of London, Paris,
associated offices:
Bucharest, Dar es Salaam

Shadbolt & Co LLP
Solicitors

Shearman & Sterling LLP

Broadgate West, 9 Appold Street, London EC2A 2AP
Tel: (020) 7655 5000 Fax: (020) 7655 5500

firm profile
Shearman & Sterling LLP is one of New York's oldest legal partnerships, which has transformed from a New York-based firm focused on banking into a diversified global institution. Recognised throughout the world, the firm's reputation, skills and expertise are second to none in its field. The London office, established in 1972, has become a leading practice covering all aspects of English and European corporate and finance law. The firm employs over 200 English and US trained legal staff in London and has more than 1,000 lawyers in 20 offices worldwide.

main areas of work
Banking, leveraged finance and structured finance. Project finance. M&A. Global capital markets. International arbitration and litigation. Tax. EU and competition. Financial institutions advisory & asset management (legal and regulatory advice to financial instititions and infrastructure providers, both in a retail and wholesale context, and both online and off-line). Executive compensation & employee benefits (sophisticated advice on the design and implementation of compensation and benefits arrangements). Intellectual property. Real estate.

trainee profile
The firm's successful future development calls for people who will relish the hard work and intellectual challenge of today's commercial world. You will be a self-starter, keen to assume professional responsibility early in your career and determined to become a first-class lawyer in a first-class firm. The firm's two year training programme will equip you with all the skills needed to become a successful commercial lawyer. You will spend six months in each of four practice areas, with an opportunity to spend six months in Abu Dhabi, New York or Singapore. You will be treated as an integral part of the London team from the outset. The firm will expect you to contribute creatively to all the transactions you are involved in. The firm has an informal yet professional atmosphere. Your enthusiasm, intellect and energy will be more important than what you wear to work. The firm will provide you with a mentor, arrange personal and professional development courses and give you early responsibility.

sponsorship & awards
Sponsorship for the CPE/PgDL and LPC courses, together with a maintenance grant of £7,000.

Partners 29
Assistant Solicitors 115
Total Trainees 27

contact
Kirsten Davies
Tel: (020) 7655 5082

method of application
Online at
www.shearman.com

selection procedure
Interviews

closing date for 2010
31 July 2008

application
Training contracts p.a. **15**
Required degree grade **2:1**

training
Salary
1st year (2007) £36,500
2nd year (2007) £39,500
Holiday entitlement
24 days p.a.
% of trainees with non-law degree p.a. **40%**
No of seats available abroad **3**

post-qualification
Salary (2007) **£75,000**
% of trainees offered job on qualification (2007) **100%**

overseas offices
Abu Dhabi, Bejing, Brussels, Düsseldorf, Frankfurt, Hong Kong, Mannheim, Menlo Park, Munich, New York, Paris, Rome, San Francisco, Sao Paulo, Shanghai, Singapore, Tokyo, Toronto, Washington DC

Shoosmiths

The Lakes, Northampton NN4 7SH
Tel: (0870) 086 3223 Fax: (0870) 086 3001
Email: join.us@shoosmiths.co.uk
Website: www.shoosmiths.co.uk

firm profile
Growing steadily with seven offices across the midlands and south of England, Shoosmiths is one of the big players outside London. The firm is run like a business. Shoosmiths is a progressive, forward thinking law firm with a real spirit of enterprise. The firm really values its people by giving them the freedom, recognition and support to succeed, and its clients find the firm open, accessible and easy to work with.

main areas of work
The firm has a large variety of practice areas including commercial property, dispute resolution, corporate and commercial, employment, intellectual property, banking, planning, private client and personal injury.

trainee profile
You'll be open-minded and flexible and will care about your own personal development. One of your aims will be to become a rounded professional, as well as a successful solicitor, and you'll look to balance your career with a life outside of the office. Work wise, you'll care about the quality of service you give to clients (internal and external), and you'll want to make a real and direct contribution to the firm's commercial success.

training environment
With the 2007 LawCareers.net Best Trainer award under its belt, the firm offers a training contract which revolves around real work. The firm only places one or two trainees in each department which means that you'll be listened to and valued, and will get much greater personal access to and attention from your Partner and colleagues.
The firm also wants you to use the two year training contract as a time to try out new things, both at your desk and away from it. The firm's thinking is that if it allows you the freedom to innovate and experiment, you will develop really useful skills for your future career.

benefits
Flexible holidays, pension (after 3 months service), life assurance, various staff discounts, Christmas bonus.

vacation placements
The firm offers placements of up to two weeks during June, July and August. Please apply online via the website. The closing date for summer placement applications is 28 February each year.

sponsorship & awards
GDL & LPC funding; the firm pays fees plus a maintenance grant.

Partners	105
Total staff	1450
Total Trainees	36

contact
Sally Stagles

method of application
Online application form

selection procedure
Full day assessment centre

closing date for 2010
31 July 2007

application
Training contracts p.a. **17**
Applications p.a. **1,000**
% interviewed p.a. **10%**
Required degree grade **2:1**

training
Salary
from £21,000
Holiday entitlement
23 days + option to flex

post-qualification
Salary **£36,000**

offices
Northampton, Nottingham, Solent, Thames Valley, Milton Keynes, Basingstoke, Birmingham

Sidley Austin LLP

Woolgate Exchange, 25 Basinghall Street, London EC2V 5HA
Tel: (020) 7360 3600 Fax: (020) 7626 7937
Email: ukrecruitment@sidley.com
Website: www.sidley.com

firm profile
Sidley Austin LLP is one of the world's largest full-service law firms. With more than 1,700 lawyers practising on four continents (North America, Europe, Australasia and Asia), the firm provides a broad range of integrated services to meet the needs of its clients across a multitude of industries.

main areas of work
Corporate & securities; debt & equity capital markets, corporate reorganisation and bankruptcy, employment, financial services regulation, insurance, IP/IT, real estate and real estate finance, securitisation and structured finance and tax.

trainee profile
Sidley Austin LLP look for focused, intelligent and enthusiastic individuals with personality and humour who have a real interest in practising law in the commercial world. Trainees should have a consistently strong academic record and a 2:1 degree (not necessarily in law).

training environment
The firm is not a typical City firm and it is not a 'legal factory' so there is no risk of being just a number. Everyone is encouraged to be proactive and to create their own niche when they are ready to do so. Trainees spend time in the firm's main groups. In each group trainees will sit with a partner or senior associate to ensure individual training based on 'hands on' experience. You will be encouraged to take responsibility where appropriate. Regular meetings with your supervisor ensure both the quality and quantity of your experience. In addition, there is a structured timetable of training on a cross-section of subjects and an annual training weekend.

benefits
Private health insurance, life assurance, contribution to gym membership, interest-free season ticket loan, income protection scheme, pension and subsidised restaurant.

sponsorship & awards
Tuition fees for the GDL/CPE and the LPC Maintenance grant of £7,000 p.a.

Partners	41
Assistant Solicitors	78
Total Trainees	14

contact
Lucy Slater,
HR Administrator

method of application
Application form

selection procedure
Interview(s)

closing date for 2010
28 July 2008

application
Training contracts p.a. **15**
Applications p.a. **500**
% interviewed p.a. **15**
Required degree grade **2:1**

training
Salary
1st year (2007) **£38,000**
2nd year (2007) **£42,000**
Holiday entitlement **25 days**
% of trainees with a
non-law degree p.a. **50%**

overseas offices
Beijing, Brussels, Chicago, Dallas, Frankfurt, Geneva, Hong Kong, London, Los Angeles, New York, San Francisco, Shanghai, Singapore, Sydney, Tokyo, Washington DC

Simmons & Simmons

CityPoint, One Ropemaker Street, London EC2Y 9SS
Tel: (020) 7628 2020 Fax: (020) 7628 2070
Email: recruitment@simmons-simmons.com
Website: www.simmons-simmons.com/traineelawyers

firm profile
Dynamic and innovative, Simmons & Simmons has a reputation for offering a superior legal service, wherever and whenever it is required. The firm's high quality advice and the positive working atmosphere in its 21 international offices has won admiration and praise from both the legal community and business clients.

main areas of work
Simmons & Simmons offers its clients a full range of legal services across numerous industry sectors. The firm has a particular focus on the world's fastest growing sectors, that is: Energy and infrastructure; financial institutions; life sciences; and technology. Simmons & Simmons provides a wide choice of service areas in which its lawyers can specialise. These include corporate and commercial; communications, outsourcing and technology; dispute resolution; employment and benefits; EU and competition; financial markets; IP; projects; real estate; taxation and pensions.

trainee profile
Simmons & Simmons is interested to find out about your academic successes but will also explore your ability to form excellent interpersonal relations and work within a team environment, as well as your levels of motivation, drive and ambition.
Show evidence of a rich 'life experience' as well as examples of your intellectual capabilities and you will be provided with everything you need to become a successful member of the firm.

training environment
The training programme at Simmons & Simmons is constantly evolving to build the skills you will need to be successful in the fast moving world of international business. The firm provides experience in a range of areas of law and a balanced approach to gaining the knowledge, expertise and abilities you will need to qualify in the practice area of your choice.

vacation placements
The firm's summer internship scheme is one of its primary means of selecting candidates for a career at Simmons & Simmons. Your placement will enable you to gain first-hand experience of a busy and dynamic international law firm as well as gain exposure to everything from the firm's service areas to the kinds of deals and transactions the firm works on.
Undergraduates usually apply for internships in their penultimate year. However, the firm is also happy to offer internships to final year students, graduates, mature and international students and those changing career.

sponsorship & awards
The firm will cover your full tuition fees at law school and offer a maintenance allowance of up to £7,500.

Partners	234
Assistant Solicitors	568
Total Trainees	144

contact
Anna King Graduate Recruitment Officer

method of application
Online application, at www.simmons-simmons.com/traineelawyers Applications should be made from 01 November, 2007

selection procedure
Assessment day

closing date for 2010
31 July 2008

application
Training contracts p.a. **50**
Applications p.a. **2,000**
% interviewed p.a. **15%**
Required degree grade **2:1**

training
Salary
£36,000, 1st and 2nd seat
£40,000, 3rd and 4th seat
Holiday entitlement **25 days**
% of trainees with a non-law degree p.a. **50%**
No. of seats available abroad p.a. **varies**

post-qualification
Salary (2007) **£63,500**
% of trainees offered job on qualification (2006) **84%**

overseas offices
Abu Dhabi, Amsterdam, Brussels, Dubai, Düsseldorf, Frankfurt, Hong Kong, Lisbon, London, Madeira, Madrid, Milan, New York, Oporto, Padua, Paris, Qatar, Rome, Rotterdam, Shanghai, Tokyo.

SJ Berwin LLP

10 Queen Street Place, London, EC4R 1BE
Tel: (020) 7111 2268   Fax: (020) 7111 2000
Email: graduate.recruitment@sjberwin.com
Website: www.sjberwin.com/gradrecruit

firm profile

SJ Berwin LLP is a pan-European firm and celebrates its 25th anniversary this year. The firm was founded with the objective of providing outstanding legal advice in a dynamic and different environment. The firm's growth has been fast and furious and in less than 20 years we achieved Top 20 City Firm status. Much of the firm's work is international and clients range from major multinational business corporations and financial institutions to high net-worth individuals. As a result the firm has established a strong reputation in corporate finance.

main areas of work

SJ Berwin's clients are sophisticated buyers of legal services, principally entrepreneurial companies and financial institutions, whom the firm advises on a range of services including corporate finance, commercial, employment and pensions, EU and competition, finance, financial services, intellectual property, litigation, media, real estate, reconstruction and insolvency and tax. For more information about the firm's service groups please go to www.sjberwin.com.

trainee profile

The firm wants ambitious, commercially minded individuals who seek a high level of involvement from day one. Candidates must have a strong academic record, be on track for, or have achieved, a 2:1 or equivalent in their undergraduate degree, and have demonstrated strong team and leadership potential.

training environment

The two-year training contract is divided into four six-month seats. As over 50 per cent of the firm's fee-earners work is in the corporate finance department, trainees can expect to spend at least half of their training contract there. Trainees may also choose to take a corporate or EU seat in one of the firm's European offices.

how to apply

The firm welcomes applications from all disciplines and all universities. Applications must be made using the firm's online form available at www.sjberwin.com/gradrecruit. The same form can be used to indicate your interest in an open day, a vacation scheme and/or a training contract.

benefits

25 days holiday, private healthcare, gym membership/subsidy, life assurance, pension scheme, season ticket loan, free lunch.

Partners	170
Assistant Solicitors	500
Total Trainees	87

contact
Graduate Recruitment Team

method of application
Online application form

selection procedure
2 interviews (early September)

closing date for 2010
31 July 2008
Summer vacation scheme
31 January 2008

application
Training contracts p.a. **50**
Applications p.a. **2,000**
10% interviewed p.a.
Required degree grade **2:1**

training
Salary
£36,000, 1st year
£40,000, 2nd year
Holiday entitlement **25 days**
% of trainees with a
non-law degree p.a. **40%**

post-qualification
Salary (2008) **£64,000**
% of trainees offered job
on qualification (2007) **84%**

overseas offices
Brussels, Frankfurt, Madrid, Berlin, Paris, Munich, Milan, Turin.

Skadden Arps, Slate, Meagher & Flom (UK) LLP

40 Bank Street, Canary Wharf, London E14 5DS
Tel: (020) 7519 7000 Fax: (020) 7519 7070
Email: graduate@skadden.com   Website: www.skadden.com

Partners	23*
Assistant Solicitors	120*
Trainees	7*
*London office	

firm profile

Skadden is one of the leading law firms in the world with approximately 2,000 lawyers in 22 offices across the globe. Clients include corporate, industrial, financial institutions and government entities. The London office is the gateway to the firm's European practice where they have some 250 lawyers dedicated to top-end, cross-border corporate transactions and international arbitration and litigation. The firm has handled matters in nearly every country in the greater European region, and in Africa and the Middle East. The firm is consistently ranked as a leader in all disciplines and amongst a whole host of accolades, the firm was recently voted 'Global Corporate Law Firm of the Year' (*Chambers and Partners*), 'Best US Law Firm in London' (*Legal Business*) and 'Best Trainer' in the US law firm in London category (*Law Careers. Net Training and Recruitment Awards*).

contact
Kate Harman
Graduate Recruitment
Assistant

method of application
Online application

selection procedure
A selection event
comprising of an interview
and a short exercise

closing date for 2010
31 July 2008

main areas of work

Lawyers across the European network focus primarily on corporate transactions, including domestic and cross-border mergers and acquisitions, private equity, capital markets, leveraged finance and banking, tax, corporate restructuring and energy and projects. The firm also advise in international arbitration and litigation and regulatory matters.

application
Training contracts p.a. **10**
Applications p.a. **700**
% interviewed p.a. **8%**
Required degree grade **2:1**

trainee profile

The firm seeks to recruit a small number of high-calibre graduates from any discipline to join their highly successful London office as trainee solicitors. The firm is looking for candidates who combine intellectual ability with enthusiasm, creativity and a demonstrable ability to rise to a challenge and to work with others towards a common goal.

training
Salary
1st year £40,000
2nd year £43,000
Holiday entitlement **25 days**
% of trainees with a
non-law degree p.a. **50%**

training environment

The firm can offer you the chance to develop your career in a uniquely rewarding and professional environment. You will join a close-knit but diverse team in which you will be given ample opportunity to work on complex matters, almost all with an international aspect, whilst benefiting from highly personalised training and supervision in an informal and friendly environment. The first year of your training contract will be divided into two six month seats where you will gain experience in corporate transactions and international litigation and arbitration. In the second year of your training contract, you will have the opportunity to discuss with the firm your preferences for your remaining two seats. The firm also offers the opportunity for second year trainees to be seconded to our Hong Kong office for a six month seat.

overseas offices
Beijing, Boston, Brussels,
Chicago, Frankfurt, Hong
Kong, Houston, London,
Los Angeles, Moscow,
Munich, New York, Palo
Alto, Paris, San Francisco,
Singapore, Sydney, Tokyo,
Toronto, Vienna,
Washington DC,
Wilmington.

benefits

Life insurance, private health insurance, private medical insurance, travel insurance, joining fee paid at Canary Wharf gym, subsidised restaurant, employee assistance programme and technology allowance.

vacation placements

Skadden offers the opportunity for penultimate year law and non-law students to experience the culture and working environment of the firm through two week vacation placements. Vacation placements are paid and take place during Easter and over the course of the summer. The deadline for applications is 04 January 2008 for placements in 2008.

sponsorship & awards

The firm pays for GDL and LPC course fees and provides a £8,000 grant for each year of these courses.

Skadden

Slaughter and May

One Bunhill Row, London EC1Y 8YY
Tel: (020) 7600 1200 Fax: (020) 7090 5000
Email: trainee.recruit@slaughterandmay.com (enquiries only)
Website: www.slaughterandmay.com

Partners	133
Associates	421
Total Trainees	181

contact
Charlotte Houghton

method of application
Online (via website)
preferred or by posting to
the firm a CV and covering
letter

selection procedure
Interview

application
Training contracts p.a.
Approx 85-95
Applications p.a. **2,000+**
% interviewed p.a. **25%**
Required degree grade
Good 2:1 ability

training
Salary (May 2007)
1st year £36,000
2nd year £40,000
Holiday entitlement
25 days p.a.
% of trainees with a
non-law degree **Approx 50%**
No. of seats available
abroad p.a. **Approx 30-40**

post-qualification
Salary (May 2007) **£63,500**
% of trainees offered job
on qualification (2007) **93%**

overseas offices
Paris, Brussels and Hong
Kong, plus "Best Friend"
firms in all the major
jurisdictions.

firm profile
One of the leading law firms in the world, Slaughter and May enjoys a reputation for quality and expertise. The corporate, commercial and financing practice is particularly strong and lawyers are known for their business acumen and technical excellence. As well as its London office, in order that the firm provides the best advice and service across the world, it nurtures long-standing relationships with the leading independent law firms in other jurisdictions.

main areas of work
Corporate, commercial and financing; tax; competition; financial regulation; dispute resolution; technology, media and telecommunications; intellectual property; commercial real estate; environment; pensions and employment.

trainee profile
The work is demanding and the firm looks for intellectual agility and the ability to work with people from different countries and walks of life. Common sense, the ability to communicate clearly and the willingness to accept responsibility are all essential. The firm expects to provide training in everything except the fundamental principles of law, so does not expect applicants to know much of commercial life. Trainees are expected to remain with the firm on qualification.

training environment
Four or five seats of three or six months duration. Two seats will be in the field of corporate, commercial and financing law with an option to choose a posting overseas (either to one of the firm's offices or to a "best friend" firm), or competition or financial regulation. One seat in either dispute resolution, intellectual property, tax or pensions and employment is part of the programme and a commercial real estate seat is also possible. In each seat a partner is responsible for monitoring your progress and reviewing your work. There is an extensive training programme which includes the PSC. There are also discussion groups covering general and specialised legal topics.

benefits
BUPA, STL, pension scheme, subsidised membership of health club, 24 hour accident cover.

work experience – summer 2008
Places: 60; Duration: 2 weeks; Remuneration: £275 p.w.; Closing Date: 25 January 2008 for penultimate year (of first degree) students only.

sponsorship & awards
CPE and LPC fees and maintenance grants are paid.

Speechly Bircham LLP

6 St Andrew Street, London EC4A 3LX
Tel: (020) 7427 6400 Fax: (020) 7353 4368
Email: trainingcontracts@speechlys.com
Website: www.speechlys.com

firm profile

Speechly Bircham is a City law firm that provides a distinctive blend of advisory, transactional and disputes services in its five core areas of practice: corporate, private client, employment, property and construction. With over 180 lawyers, the firm acts for UK and international listed companies, banks and financial institutions, privately owned companies as well as high net worth individuals, families and trusts.

The firm's several discrete practice groups have an acknowledged reputation and performance which are competitive with those of larger firms. The structure of the firm and its ability to provide Partner time and attention make it a good alternative to large City firms for many clients. The legal affairs of each client are managed by a single Partner, responsible for ensuring that the service is delivered quickly and cost effectively.

Much of the firm's work has an international dimension, whether for UK clients doing business overseas, supervising and co-ordinating the work of foreign law firms, or advising overseas clients with business and financial interests in the UK.

The firm was also delighted to have been awarded 'Best Trainer - Medium City Firm' at the Law Careers.Net Training and Recruitment Awards 2007.

main areas of work

Speechly Bircham's principal practice areas are: banking and finance, commercial litigation, construction and engineering, corporate, corporate tax, employment, family, financial services, IP, technology and commercial, pensions, private client, private equity, property and property litigation.

trainee profile

Both law and non-law graduates who are capable of achieving a 2:1. The firm seeks intellectual individuals who enjoy a collaborative working environment where they can make an impact.

training environment

Speechly Bircham divides the training contract into four six-month seats. Emphasis is given to early responsibility and supervised client contact providing trainees with a practical learning environment.

benefits

Season ticket loan; private medical insurance; life assurance; stakeholder pension scheme, 23 days holiday rising to 25 days on qualification.

vacation placements

Places for 2008: 20. The firm's summer placement scheme for students gives them the chance to experience a City legal practice. In a three-week placement, students will be asked to research and present on a current topical issue at the end of their placement; Duration: 3 weeks; Remuneration: £250 p.w; Closing Date: 15 February 2008.

sponsorship & awards

GDL and LPC fees paid in full together with a maintenance grant.

Partners	62
Assistant Solicitors	111
Total Trainees	20

contact
Nicola Swann
Director of Human Resources

method of application
Application form (available online)

selection procedure
Interview

closing date for 2010
31 July 2008

application
Training contracts p.a. **10**
Applications p.a. **588**
% interviewed p.a. **22%**
Required degree grade **2:1**

training
Salary
1st year
£31,000-32,000
2nd year
£33,000-£34,000
Holiday entitlement **25 days**
% of trainees with a
non-law degree p.a. **50%**

post-qualification
Salary (2007) **£56,000**

SpeechlyBircham

Stephenson Harwood

One St Paul's Churchyard, London EC4M 8SH
Tel: (020) 7809 2812 Fax: (020) 7003 8263
Email: graduate.recruitment@shlegal.com
Website: www.shlegal.com/graduate

firm profile
Established in the City of London in 1828, Stephenson Harwood was the overall winner at the 2006 Association of Graduate Recruiters Awards, an independent national voice for all employers involved in graduate recruitment. The firm was praised for its entire campaign as well as being singled out for the prize for best literature. Stephenson Harwood has developed into a large international practice, with a commercial focus and a wide client base.

main areas of work
Corporate (including corporate finance, funds, corporate tax, business technology); employment, pensions and benefits; banking and asset finance; dry and wet shipping litigation; commercial litigation; and real estate.

trainee profile
The firm looks for high calibre graduates with excellent academic records, business awareness and excellent communication skills.

training environment
As the graduate intake is relatively small, the firm gives trainees individual attention, coaching and monitoring. Your structured and challenging programme involves four six month seats in areas of the firm covering contentious and non-contentious areas, across any department within the firm's practice groups. These seats include 'on the job' training and you will share an office with a partner or senior associate. In-house lectures complement your training and there is continuous review of your career development. You will have the opportunity to spend six months abroad and have free language tuition where appropriate. You will be given your own caseload and as much responsibility as you can shoulder. The firm plays a range of team sports, offers subsidised membership of a City health club (or a health club of your choice) and has privileged seats for concerts at the Royal Albert Hall and access to private views at the Tate Gallery.

benefits
Subsidised membership of health clubs, private health insurance, BUPA membership, season ticket loan and 25 days paid holiday per year.

vacation placements
Places for 2008: 18; Duration: 2 weeks; Remuneration: £260 p.w.; Closing Date: 17 February 2008.

sponsorship & awards
Fees paid for CPE and LPC and maintenance awards.

Partners	83*
Assistant Solicitors	219*
Total Trainees	34
*denotes world-wide figures	

contact
Romina Chambers (Graduate Recruitment)

method of application
Online application form only

selection procedure
assessment centre

closing date for Sept/March 2009/2010
31 July 2008/2009

application
Training contracts p.a. **12**
% interviewed p.a. **10%**
Required degree grade **2:1**

training
Salary
1st year (2007) **£35,000**
2nd year (2007) **£40,000**
Holiday entitlement **25 days**
% of trainees with a non-law degree p.a. **50%**
No. of seats available abroad p.a. **8**

post-qualification
Salary (2007) **£62,000**
% of trainees offered job on qualification (2006) **100%**
% of assistants (as at 1/9/06) who joined as trainees **38%**
% of partners (as at 1/9/06) who joined as trainees **43%**

overseas offices
Paris, Piraeus, Singapore, Guangzhou, Hong Kong, Shanghai

associated offices
Greece, South Africa, Kuwait, Croatia, France, Bucharest

Stevens & Bolton LLP

The Billings, Guildford, Surrey GU4 1YD
Tel: (01483) 302264 Fax: (01483) 302254
Email: gradrec@stevens-bolton.co.uk
Website: www.stevens-bolton.co.uk

firm profile

Stevens & Bolton LLP is among a small batch of firms offering lawyers and clients a real alternative to London from a south east base. The firm's client base is located all over the country, as well as overseas and the firm believes it would be the envy of some larger firms. To support the firm's aim to become a nationally recognised firm, the firm sponsors the BlackRock Masters Tennis event at the Albert Hall. The event is broadcast on BBC TV and last year over 20 firms paid to take a corporate box.

The business is both successful and profitable. The firm's work is 80% commercial, the remainder being private client work advising medium and high net-worth individuals. Clients includer FTSE 100 businesses, subsidaries of major international groups and growing, owner managed companies. The firm receives instructions from household names such as Rentokil Initial plc, Hays plc, The BOC Group and Morse plc to name a few in the last financial year revenue was a shade over £14 million and profit on equity partner stood at £305,000. To sum up, Legal Business described the firm as '...a City firm without the EC postcode.'

main areas of work

Corporate and commercial, real estate, dispute resolution, employment and pensions, tax & trust, private client and family.

trainee profile

The firm requires a good academic record and individuals with interests such as music, sport, travel and who have a genuine enthusiasm to work in the law.

training environment

Usually you will sit with a Partner who will act as your supervisor and you will get real responsibility early on. You will see first hand that the quality of the service the firm provides is on a par with national and City firms. Your training with the firm will see you working for six months at a time in four different areas of the firm. One seat will be corporate and commercial plus three others from real estate, dispute resolution, employment, tax and trust and family. The majority of the firm's trainees go on and qualify into their chosen areas of work in the firm.

benefits

Private medical insurance, life assurance, pension, rail or car park season ticket loan, permanent health insurance and 25 days holiday.

sponsorship & awards

Providing no local authority grant is available, full fees for the GDL and LPC plus a £4,000 maintenance grant for each course.

vacation placements

The firm will be running a placement scheme in the summer of 2008. Please see our website for further details.

Partners	31
Associates	45
Total Trainees	6

contact
Julie Bounden
(01483) 302264

method of application
Online application form available from website

selection procedure
Two interviews & other processes

closing date for 2010
30 September 2008

application
Training contracts p.a. **4**
Applications p.a. **200**
% interviewed **13%**
Required degree grade **2:1**

training
Salary
1st year (2007) **£24,500**
2nd year (2007) **£26,500**
Holiday entitlement **25 days**

post-qualification
Salary (2007) **£42,500**

overseas/regional offices
Guildford only

S&B Stevens & Bolton LLP

Taylor Walton

28-44 Alma Street, Luton LU1 2PL
Tel: (01582) 731161 Fax: (01582) 457900
Email: luton@taylorwalton.co.uk
Website: www.taylorwalton.co.uk

Partners	23
Assistant Solicitors	32
Total Trainees	7

contact
Jim Wrigglesworth

method of application
CV with covering letter

selection procedure
First & second interview
with opportunity to meet
other partners

closing date for 2010
30 July 2008

application
Required degree grade
2:1 or above

firm profile
Strategically located in Luton, Harpenden and St Albans, Taylor Walton is a major regional law practice advising both businesses and private clients. Its strengths are in commercial property, corporate work and commercial litigation, whilst maintaining a strong private client side to the practice. It has a progressive outlook both in its partners and staff and in its systems, training and IT.

main areas of work
Company/commercial 15%; commercial property 20%; commercial litigation 15%; employment 10%; family 5%; private client 10%; residential property 25%.

trainee profile
Candidates need to show excellent intellectual capabilities, coupled with an engaging personality so as to show that they can engage and interact with the firm's clients as the practice of law involves the practice of the art of communication. Taylor Walton sees its partners and staff as business advisers involved in clients' businesses, not merely stand-alone legal advisers.

training environment
The training consists of four six-month seats. The trainee partner oversees the structural training alongside a supervisor who will be a partner or senior solicitor in each department. The firm does try to take trainees' own wishes in relation to seats into account. In a regional law practice like Taylor Walton you will find client contact and responsibility coupled with supervision, management and training. There is an in-house training programme for all fee-earning members of staff. Trainees are given the opportunity to discuss their progress with their supervisor at a monthly appraisal meeting. In addition, at the end of each seat there is a post seat appraisal conducted by the trainee partner. The PSC is taught externally. The firm is friendly with an open door policy and there are various sporting and social events.

vacation placements
Places for 2008: 8; Duration: Up to 3 weeks; Remuneration: £195 per week; Closing Date: 30 March 2008.

sponsorship & awards
Full LPC sponsorship.

Taylor Wessing LLP

Carmelite, 50 Victoria Embankment, Blackfriars
London EC4Y 0DX
Tel: (020) 7300 7000 Fax: (020) 7300 7100Website: www.taylorwessing.com

Partners	264
Fee-earners	643
Trainees	48 (UK)

firm profile
Taylor Wessing offers a full service to its clients providing a powerful source of legal support for commercial organisations doing business in Europe. The firm advises major corporations, medium-sized companies, financial and public institutions as well as growing enterprises. Taylor Wessing offers industry-focused advice by grouping together lawyers from different legal areas, but with in-depth sector experience. With the firm's renowned expertise in intellectual property, it is particularly strong in knowledge-based industries, such as IT and telecommunications, life sciences and healthcare, media and entertainment, leisure, fashion and travel. Other core industries include construction and engineering, infrastructure projects and the banking and finance sectors.

main areas of work
The firm offers specialist services in all aspects of national and international commercial law, in particular, corporate/M&A, tax, finance and projects, construction and real estate, intellectual property, EC law/antitrust, employment and pensions, dispute resolution and private client.

trainee profile
High intellectual ability is paramount and the firm seeks a minimum of ABB grades at A Level and at least a 2.1 degree in any discipline. The firm looks for team players who have excellent communication skills, energy, ambition, an open mind and a willingness to learn. You will also need to demonstrate a commitment to a career in law and a genuine interest in business.

training environment
As part of your training, you will spend six months in four different departments, including a seat in the corporate department. There is also the possibility of a secondment to another office or a client. Trainees work closely with a number of partners and associates in the departments – so are directly involved in high-quality work from the start. At the beginning of the training and throughout you have ongoing discussions about your interests and how they fit in with the growth and needs of the departments. There is support every step of the way, with regular feedback and appraisals in the middle and at the end of each seat. Not forgetting the Professional Skills Course, which is run in-house, along with other training courses as necessary during the two years.

benefits
Private medical care, permanent health insurance, season ticket loan, subsidised staff restaurant, non-contributory pension scheme.

vacation placements
Places for 2008: 38 Duration: 2 weeks; Remuneration: £250 per week; Closing date: 31 January 2008.

sponsorship & awards
GDL and LPC fees paid in full. Maintenance grant £7,000 per annum.

contact
Graduate Recruitment Department

method of application
Online application form

selection procedure
Assessment Centre to include interview, group exercise and psychometric test

closing date for 2010
31 July 2008

application
Training contracts p.a. **24**
Applications p.a. **1,195**
% interviewed p.a. **8%**
Required degree grade **2:1**

training
Salary
1st year **£35,000**
2nd year **£39,000**
Holiday entitlement **25 days**
% of trainees with a non-law degree p.a. **40%**

post-qualification
Salary **£62,500**
% of trainees offered job on qualification (2003-04) **82%**

overseas offices
Berlin, Brussels, Cologne Dusseldorf, Frankfurt, Hamburg, Munich, Paris and representative offices in Alicante and Shanghai. Associated office in Dubai.

Teacher Stern Selby

37-41 Bedford Row, London WC1R 4JH
Tel: (020) 7242 3191 Fax: (020) 7242 1156
Email: r.raphael@tsslaw.com
Website: www.tsslaw.com

firm profile
A central London-based general commercial firm, with clientele and caseload normally attributable to larger firms. It has a wide range of contacts overseas.

main areas of work
Commercial litigation 24%; commercial property 41%; company and commercial 22%; secured lending 9%; private client 2%; clinical negligence/education/judicial review 2%.

trainee profile
Emphasis falls equally on academic excellence and personality. The firm looks for flexible and motivated individuals, who have outside interests and who have demonstrated responsibility in the past.

training environment
Eight months in three departments (company commercial, litigation and property). Most trainees are assigned to actively assist a partner who monitors and supports them. Trainees are fully involved in departmental work and encouraged to take early responsibility. Trainees are expected to attend in-house seminars and lectures for continuing education. The atmosphere is relaxed and informal.

vacation placements
Places for 2008: Approximately 25 places to those that have applied for training contracts.

sponsorship & awards
Considered.

Partners 21
Assistant Solicitors 28
Total Trainees 7

contact
Russell Raphael

method of application
Online application

selection procedure
2 interviews

closing date for 2010
31 July 2008

application
Training contracts p.a. **3-4**
Applications p.a. **500**
% interviewed p.a. **5%**
Required degree grade
2:1 (not absolute)

training
Salary
1st year (2010) £31,000
Holiday entitlement
25 days
% of trainees with a
non-law degree p.a. **50%**

post-qualification
Salary (2007) **£45,000**
% of trainees offered job
on qualification (2007) **50%**
% of assistants (who joined
as trainees **32%**
% of partners who joined
as trainees **50%**

tsslaw

Thomas Eggar

The Corn Exchange, Baffins Lane, Chichester PO19 1GE
Tel: (01243) 813129
Email: mick.cassell@thomaseggar.com
Website: www.thomaseggar.com

firm profile

Thomas Eggar is one of the top 100 law firms in the UK. Based in the South East, it is one of the country's leading regional law firms with a staff of over 420. The firm offers both private client and commercial services to a diverse range of clients, locally, nationally and internationally. It also offers financial services through Thesis, the firm's investment management arm, which is the largest solicitor-based investment unit in the UK.

main areas of work

Apart from its strength in the private client sector, the firm handles property, commercial and litigation matters; among its major clients are banks, building societies and other financial institutions, railway and track operators and construction companies.

trainee profile

The firm seeks very able trainees who exhibit good business acumen, with a 2.1 degree in any discipline. Applications can be made up to 1 August 2008 for training contracts to commence in March/September 2010 and March 2011. Applications should be in the form of a CV and covering letter. You should give details of your attachment to the South East region in your covering letter. During 2008 the application process will also adopt an on-line facility.

training environment

Trainees would normally have four seats covering commercial property, commercial, litigation and private client. In order to give good exposure to various specialisations, some of the seats are likely to be in different offices.

vacation placements

There is a limited summer placement scheme in July and August each year: this runs for five days and can be within any one of our locations. Applications should be made with CV and covering letter to Mick Cassell by 31 March 2008. Please give details of your accommodation plans in your covering letter. Travel expenses are paid.

sponsorship & awards

LPC 50% grant, 50% loan.

Vacancies	6
Partners	60
Trainees	12
Total Staff	438

contact
Mick Cassell

method of application
Letter & CV during 2007 and on-line during 2008

selection procedure
CV, assessment centre and interview

closing date for 2010
1 August 2008

training
The firm aims to pay the going rate for a South Eastern regional firm. A London weighting is paid to those who undertake seats in the London office. The firm also pays a taxable travel allowance to all its trainees.
Required degree grade
2:1 (any discipline)

other offices
Chichester, Gatwick, London, Worthing

Thomson Snell & Passmore

3 Lonsdale Gardens, Tunbridge Wells, Kent TN1 1NX
Tel: (01892) 510000 Fax: (01892) 549884
Email: solicitors@ts-p.co.uk
Website: www.ts-p.co.uk

Partners	**34**
Assistant Solicitors	**46**
Total Trainees	**9**

firm profile

Thomson Snell & Passmore continues to be regarded as one of the premier law firms in the South East. The firm has a reputation for quality and a commitment to deliver precise and clear advice which is recognised and respected both by its clients and professional contacts. It has held the Lexcel quality mark since January 1999. The firm is vibrant and progressive and enjoys an extremely friendly atmosphere. Its offices are located in the centre of Tunbridge Wells and attract clients locally, nationally and internationally.

main areas of work

Commercial litigation 14%; corporate and employment 14%; commercial property 14%; private client 24%; personal injury/clinical negligence 12%; residential property 15%; family 7%.

trainee profile

Thomson Snell & Passmore regards its trainees from the outset as future assistants, associates and partners. The firm is looking for people not only with strong intellectual ability, but enthusiasm, drive, initiative, strong interpersonal and team-working skills.

training environment

The firm's induction course will help you to adjust to working life. As a founder member of Law South your training is provided in-house with trainees from other Law South member firms. Your two-year training contract is divided into four periods of six months each. You will receive a thorough grounding and responsibility with early client exposure. You will be monitored regularly, receive advice and assistance throughout and appraisals every three months. The Training Partner will co-ordinate your continuing education in the law, procedure, commerce, marketing, IT and presentation skills. Trainees enjoy an active social life which is encouraged and supported.

sponsorship & awards

Grant and interest free loan available for LPC.

contact
Human Resources
Manager
Tel: (01892) 510000

method of application
On-line application form
available from website

selection procedure
Assessment interview

closing date for 2010
31 July 2008

application
Training contracts p.a. **5**
Applications p.a.
Approximately 500
% interviewed p.a. **5%**
Required degree grade
2:1 (any discipline)

training
Salary for each year of
training
**Competitive regional
salary**
Holiday entitlement **25 days**

post-qualification
% of trainees offered job
on qualification **75%**

overseas/regional offices
Network of independent
law firms throughout
Europe and founding
member of Law South

Thring Townsend Lee & Pembertons Solicitors

6 Drakes Meadow, Penny Lane, Swindon, SN3 3LL
Tel: (01793) 410 800 Fax: (01793) 539 040
Email: solicitors@ttuk.com   Website: www.ttuk.com

firm profile

Employing over 300 staff in Bath, Bristol, London and Swindon, the firm provides a balanced portfolio of commercial, agricultural and private client services with an impressive national and international client base.

The firm has an open and friendly culture with a vibrant work ethic.

main areas of work

Agriculture: Believed to be the largest stand-alone, specialist Agriculture Team in the country. Commercial property: An excellent reputation for specialist skills in strategic land, options and pension funds. Corporate and Commercial: Acting for national and international household names. Litigation: A substantial practice with specialists in commercial litigation and claimant professional negligence work. Personal Injury: A niche practice specialising in catastrophic brain and spinal injuries and industrial disease claims. Family: Leading the way in the Southwest for Collaborative Family Law. Wills and Probate, Tax and Trusts: Advising private family trusts, substantial tax planning advice and estate administration. Private Property: Advising individuals and companies, investment landlords and clients resident abroad.

trainee profile

The firm wants confident, well-rounded individuals who are pro-active, dedicated and commercially aware. The firm looks for a minimum 2:1 degree and strong A-levels but is open to applicants with a 2:2 degree who perhaps have something else to offer.

training environment

A dynamic learning environment with an equal mix of structure and flexibility to cater for individual needs and career goals.

A structured two-year training contract split into four six-month seats. Trainees gain experience within at least three different practice areas including contentious and non-contentious.

In addition, the firm offers dedicated Partner supervisor; mid-seat and end-seat appraisal feedback; client management skills development; training courses; social events and competitive salary and benefits package.

benefits

Three extra concessionary days holiday. Private medical insurance. Private healthcare. Subsidised restaurants. Life Assurance. Paid professional memberships and subscriptions.

sponsorship & awards

Not currently offered.

Partners	46
Assistant Solicitors	46
Total Trainees	14

contact
Pat Mapstone (01793) 412 502

method of application
application form and CV

selection procedure
1st and 2nd stage interviews, 2nd comprising an interview with Partner and senior solicitor

closing date for 2010
31 July 2008

application
Training contracts p.a. **9**
Applications p.a. **300+**
% interviewed p.a. **10%**
Required degree grade
2:1 prefered

training
Salary: **£17,750 (1st year)**
        £19,250 (2nd year)
Holiday entitlement
20 days (1st year)
25 days (2nd year)

post-qualification
Salary (2007) **£34,000**
% of trainees offered job
on qualification **70%**

overseas/regional offices
Bath, Bristol, London, Swindon

TLT Solicitors

One Redcliff St, Bristol BS1 6TP
Tel: (0117) 917 7777 Fax: (0117) 917 7778
Email: fallan@TLTsolicitors.com Website: www.TLTsolicitors.com

Partners	**75**
Assistant Solicitors	**300**
Total Trainees	**17**

firm profile

TLT is built around the needs of its clients and is described by industry commentators as 'the firm to watch'. TLT remains one of the fastest-growing law firms in the UK and on 1 June 2007 London-based commercial law firm Constant & Constant joined TLT, representing the latest move in the firm's 12-month investment strategy. Turnover has risen threefold since 2002. Headcount has more than tripled to nearly 700. Growth for the firm provides the resources to be able to support its clients.

A high percentage of the firm's lawyers are identified as true experts in their respective fields and behind their legal advice is an insight and understanding of the commercial challenges clients face. The firm encourages and supports involvement in the wider community, which includes 'pro bono' legal advice to a variety of charities and TLT staff volunteering.

main areas of work

TLT is a full-service UK law firm. It concentrates on providing industry focused multi-discipline integrated solutions. The firm's leading strengths are in the financial services and leisure sectors. Other chosen markets include retail, the built environment and technology and media. Constant & Constant is the maritime division of TLT. TLT's core legal specialisms are real estate, banking and finance, commercial, corporate, employment, dispute resolution and litigation. Client services are provided through dedicated, cross-firm specialist teams including banking and asset finance, construction, debt recovery (on behalf of lenders), environmental, insolvency and turnaround, IT and IP, total reward, property development, leisure, licensing, regulatory, retail, maritime and international trade, social housing and tax.

trainee profile

Strong academic background together with commitment and drive to succeed.

training environment

TLT's commitment to excellence will ensure that trainees benefit from a well developed and challenging training programme. Training is delivered through four seats of six months duration, chosen in consultation with the trainee. In each seat the trainee will sit with a lawyer although their work will be drawn from all members of the team in order to gain the widest possible experience. Regular monitoring and development planning ensures that trainees get the most out of their training and helps them to identify their long term career path from the varied specialisms on offer.

benefits

Pension, private medical insurance, life assurance and subsidised sports/health club membership, 25 days holiday entitlement.

vacation placements

36 paid placements available, each lasting 1 week. Apply online by 31 January 2008.

sponsorship & awards

CPE and LPC fees plus maintenance payment

contact
Human Resources

method of application
Firm's application form online

selection procedure
Assessment Centre

closing date for 2010
31 July 2008

application
Training contracts p.a. **10**
Applications p.a. **500+**
% interviewed p.a. **10%**
Required degree grade **2:1 prefered**
non-law degree p.a. **17%**

training
Salary: **£24,000 (1st year)**
£25,000 (2nd year)
Holiday entitlement **25 days**

post-qualification
Market rate

offices
Bristol, London, Piraeus

Travers Smith

10 Snow Hill, London EC1A 2AL
Tel: (020) 7295 3000 Fax: (020) 7295 3500
Email: graduate.recruitment@traverssmith.com
Website: www.traverssmith.com

firm profile
A leading City firm with a major Corporate and Commercial Practice. Although less than a quarter of the size of the dozen largest firms, they handle the highest quality work, much of which has an international dimension.

main areas of work
Corporate law (including takeovers and mergers, financial services and regulatory laws), commercial law (which includes commercial contracts, IT and intellectual property), dispute resolution, competition law, corporate recovery/insolvency, tax, employment, pensions, banking and real estate. The firm also offers a range of pro bono opportunities within individual departments and on a firm wide basis. Solicitors from the firm were recently awarded two separate national awards in recognition of their outstanding contributions to pro bono work.

trainee profile
The firm looks for people who combine academic excellence with common sense; who are articulate, who think on their feet, who are determined and self motivated and who take their work but not themselves seriously. Applications are welcome from law and non-law graduates.

training environment
Travers Smith has earned a phenomenal reputation in relation to its size. The work they undertake is exciting, intellectually demanding and top quality involving blue-chip clients and big numbers. This means that their trainees gain great experience right from the outset.

The firm has a comprehensive training programme which ensures that trainees experience a broad range of work. All trainee solicitors sit in rooms with partners and assistants, receive an individual and extensive training from experienced lawyers and enjoy client contact and the responsibility that goes with it from the beginning of their training contract.

benefits
Private health insurance, permanent health insurance, life assurance, corporate health club membership, subsidised bistro, season ticket loan.

vacation placements
Summer 2008: 3 schemes with 15 places on each; Duration: two weeks; Remuneration: £250; Closing Date: 31 January 2008. The firm also offers a two week Christmas scheme for 15 students.

sponsorship & awards
GDL and LPC paid in full plus maintenance of £7,000 per annum to those in London and £6,500 per annum to those outside of London.

Partners	**66**
Assistant Solicitors	**149**
Total Trainees	**36**

contact
Germaine VanGeyzel

method of application
CV and covering letter online or by post

selection procedure
Interviews (2 stage process)

closing date for 2010
31 July 2008

application
Training contracts p.a. **25**
Applications p.a. **2,000**
% interviewed p.a. **15%**
Required degree grade **2:1**

training
Salary
1st year (2007) £36,000
2nd year (2007) £40,000
Holiday entitlement **25 days**

post-qualification
Salary (2007) **£64,000**
% of trainees offered job on qualification (2006) **94%**

Trethowans

The Director General's House, Rockstone Place, Southampton, SO15 2EP
Tel: 023 8032 1000   Fax: 023 8032 1001
Email: kate.lemont@trethowans.com   Web: www.trethowans.com

firm profile

A leading regional practice in the South of England, with two offices across Wiltshire and Hampshire, offering a comprehensive range of services (except criminal) for businesses and individuals throughout the UK. Commercial clients range from start-ups to larger corporates, with a particular emphasis on owner managed businesses. Southampton remains the focus for the majority of the firm's corporate and commercial services. The commercial services offered are comparable to those of a London practice, but a competitive price structure and direct Partner involvement are key bases for differentiation. Partners and fee-earners offer genuine expertise in their respective fields, and acknowledged reputations include property, employment, commercial/corporate work and licensing for national brand names. Private client work is undertaken across all sites with the Salisbury office at its core. Specialist areas include personal injury (head and catastrophic injuries), clinical negligence, family, residential property, trusts and tax, wills, probate, landed estates and agriculture.

main areas of work

The breadth of the firm's practice areas provides a broad experience for trainees across a comprehensive range of areas: corporate, commercial, commercial property, commercial litigation, employment, personal injury, residential property, family, landed estates and private client work.

trainee profile

Trainees should possess sound academic abilities and be able to demonstrate commercial acumen. Flexibility, ambition and enthusiasm are valued. Candidates should be good communicators and adopt a problem solving approach to client work.

training environment

Trainee solicitors normally undertake four separate specialist seats, each lasting six months. The firm offers a flexible approach in deciding trainees' seats to suit individual needs, while providing a broad training programme in accordance with the Law Society's guidelines. Trainees have their own desks and work closely with the supervising fee-earner/Partner to whom they are responsible. They are considered an integral part of each team and become closely involved in the department's work to obtain first-hand legal experience. Each trainee is appraised every six months by their supervisor and the Training Partner. This enables the trainee scheme to be continually evaluated and also ensures that the highest possible standards are maintained. Prospects for trainees are excellent, most trainees are offered a post as an assistant solicitor at the end of their training contract.

benefits

Incremental holiday entitlement up to 28 days, contributory pension scheme, death in service benefit, PHI scheme, performance-related bonus scheme, car parking, new staff recruitment bonus, childcare voucher scheme.

sponsorship and awards

Course fees paid for LPC

Partners	**24**
Assistant Solicitors	**21**
Total Trainees	**7**

contact
Kate Lemont
023 8082 0503

method of application
Applications by application form (available online) and covering letter

selection procedure
Two stage process; interview and assessment day

closing date for 2010
25 July 2008

application
Training contracts p.a. **3-4**
Applications p.a. **100+**
% interviewed p.a. **15%**
Required degree grade
2:1

training
Salary: in excess of Law Society minimum
Holiday entitlement **23 days**

post-qualification
Market rate
% of trainees offered position on qualification
85%

Regional offices
Salisbury, Southampton

TRETHOWANS

Trowers & Hamlins

Sceptre Court, 40 Tower Hill, London EC3N 4DX
Tel: (020) 7423 8000 Fax: (020) 7423 8001
Email: hking@trowers.com Website: www.trowers.com

Partners	**106**
Assistant Solicitors	**179**
Total Trainees	**39**

firm profile

Awarded law firm of the year at the Lawyer Awards 2007 and being ranked 40th, one of only seven law firms who were listed in the 2007 'Sunday Times Best Companies to Work for' are two reasons why Trowers & Hamlins is a desirable law firm to train with. Based in the City, they are a medium sized international firm with offices in the UK and the Middle East with specialisms ranging from Housing and Urban Regeneration to Litigation, Islamic Finance and international infrastructure projects. Their training contracts offer the prospects of work in their London, regional or Middle Eastern offices, and have a maximum of six trainees abroad every six months. As well as excellent client focused opportunities, they also offer the chance to get involved with community projects and pro bono work. Sound good? Then read on...

main areas of work

Being the number one firm for social housing projects, it's obvious that they cover a variety of property work (housing, public sector & commercial). But that's not all they do. They also have award winning projects and construction and structured finance teams and Chambers & Partners consistently confirm their status as one of the No 1 firms in the Middle East. Their other major practice areas include corporate, banking and finance, employment, litigation, private client and commercial property.

trainee profile

Excellent academics are, of course, essential. However, the firm believes in the merits of having a diverse workforce. Their commitment to this is demonstrated by their 5th position in 'The Lawyer's' Ethnicity League Table (for the Commission for Racial Equality/Black Solicitors Network)in 2006. They encourage applications from all backgrounds and disciplines. They look for candidates who combine a passion for the law with commercial awareness but who are real individuals. If you possess excellent communication and analytical skills, are a strong and effective team player who wants to work in a fast paced, challenging but fulfilling environment then they want to hear from you.

training environment

The firm prides itself on the quality of training that they offer. You will typically rotate around four departments sitting with either a Partner or a Senior Solicitor. Client contact is something they encourage from an early stage and you will find that you are quickly given real responsibility. Their dedication to your training is further demonstrated through their bespoke trainee development programme.

benefits

25 days holiday, bonus schemes, pension and health care (after 6 months), life assurance, interest free season ticket loan, subsidised staff restaurant and wide choice of social events.

vacation placements

Places for 2008: 25-30; Duration: 2 weeks; Remuneration: £225 p.w. (London); Location: London and Manchester; Closing Date: 1 March 2008; Open Day: June 2008.

sponsorship & awards

GDL and LPC fees paid together with a maintenance grant of £5,500 (£6,000 for London) p.a..

contact
Hannah King, Graduate Recruitment Officer

method of application
Online application form

selection procedure
Interviews, psychometric tests & practical test

closing date for 2010
1 August 2008

application
Training contracts p.a. **22**
Applications p.a. **1,600**
% interviewed p.a. **4%**
Required degree grade **2:1 or higher**

training
Salary (subject to review)
1st year £29,000
2nd year £31,000
Holiday entitlement **25 days**
% of trainees with a non-law degree p.a. **40%**
No. of seats available abroad p.a. **12**

post-qualification
Salary (2007) **£57,500**
% of trainees offered job on qualification (2007) **80%**

offices
London, Exeter, Manchester, Abu Dhabi, Dubai, Oman, Bahrain and Cairo

th trowers & hamlins

Walker Morris

Kings Court, 12 King Street, Leeds LS1 2HL
Tel: (0113) 283 2500 Fax: (0113) 245 9412
Email: hellograduates@walkermorris.co.uk
Website: www.walkermorris.co.uk

firm profile
Based in Leeds, Walker Morris is one of the largest commercial law firms in the North, with over 580 people, providing a full range of legal services to commercial and private clients both nationally and internationally.

main areas of work
Litigation 40%; property 27%; company and commercial 26%; private clients 2%; tax 2%; other 3%.

trainee profile
Bright, articulate, highly motivated individuals who will thrive on early responsibility in a demanding yet friendly environment.

training environment
Trainees commence with an induction programme, before spending four months in each main department (commercial property, corporate and commercial litigation). Trainees can choose in which departments they wish to spend their second year. Formal training will include lectures, interactive workshops, seminars, interactive video and e-learning. The PSC covers the compulsory elements and the electives consist of a variety of specially tailored skills programmes. Individual IT training is provided. Opportunities can also arise for secondments to some of the firm's major clients. Emphasis is placed on teamwork, inside and outside the office. The firm's social and sporting activities are an important part of its culture and are organised by a committee drawn from all levels of the firm. A trainee solicitors' committee represents the trainees in the firm but also organises events and liaises with the Leeds Trainee Solicitors Group.

vacation placements
Places for 2008: 48 over 3 weeks; Duration: 1 week; Remuneration: £200 p.w.; Closing Date: 31 January 2008.

sponsorship & awards
LPC & PGDL fees plus maintenance of £5,000.

Partners	**52**
Assistant Solicitors	**120**
Total Trainees	**35**

contact
Tom Peel

method of application
Online application form

selection procedure
Telephone & face-to-face interviews

closing date for 2010
31 July 2008

application
Training contracts p.a. **20**
Applications p.a.
Approx. 800
% interviewed p.a.
Telephone **16%**
Face to face **8%**
Required degree grade **2:1**

training
Salary
1st year (2007) £22,000
2nd year (2007) £24,000
Holiday entitlement **24 days**
% of trainees with a
non-law degree p.a.
30% on average

post-qualification
Salary (2007) **£38,000**
% of trainees offered job
on qualification (2007) **100%**
% of assistants (as at 1/7/07)
who joined as trainees **60%**
% of partners (as at 1/7/07)
who joined as trainees **50%**

Ward Hadaway

Sandgate House, 102 Quayside, Newcastle upon Tyne NE1 3DX
Tel: (0191) 204 4000 Fax: (0191) 204 4098
Email: recruitment@wardhadaway.com
Website: www.wardhadaway.com

firm profile
Ward Hadaway is one of the most progressive law firms in the North East and is firmly established as one of the region's heavyweights. The firm attracts some of the most ambitious businesses in the region and its client base includes a large number of plcs, new start-ups and well established private companies.
As a business founded and located in the North East, the firm has grown rapidly, investing heavily in developing its existing people, and recruiting further outstanding individuals from inside and outside of the region. The firm is listed in the top 100 UK law firms.

main areas of work
The firm is divided into five main departments; litigation, property, corporate, commercial and private client, with a number of cross departmental teams. The firm is commercially based, satisfying the needs of the business community in both business and private life. Clients vary from international plc's to local, private clients. The firm is on a number of panels including; the Arts Council, NHS (four panels), English Heritage, Department of Education and the General Teaching Council.

trainee profile
The usual academic and professional qualifications are sought. Sound commercial and business awareness are essential as is the need to demonstrate strong communication skills, enthusiasm and flexibility. Candidates will be able to demonstrate excellent interpersonal and analytical skills.

training environment
The training contract is structured around four seats, each of six months duration. At regular intervals, and each time you are due to change seat, you will have the opportunity to discuss the experience you would like to gain during your training contract. The firm will give high priority to your preferences. You will sit with a Partner or Associate which will enable you to learn how to deal with different situations. Your practical experience will also be complemented by an extensive programme of seminars and lectures. All trainees are allocated a 'buddy', usually a second year trainee or newly qualified solicitor, who can provide as much practical advice and guidance as possible during your training. The firm has an active social committee and offers a full range of sporting and social events.

benefits
23 days holiday (26 after five years service), death in service insurance, contributory pension, flexible holiday scheme.

vacation placements
Vacation placements run spring/summer between April and July and are of 1 week's duration. Applications should be received by 28 February 2008.

sponsorship & awards
CPE & LPC fees paid and maintenance grants in accordance with the terms of the firm's offer.

Partners	57
Total Trainees	21

contact
Tracy McCluskey, HR Executive

method of application
firm's application form

selection procedure
Assessment Centre and interview

closing date for 2010
31 July 2008

application
Training contracts p.a. **12**
Applications p.a. **400+**
% interviewed p.a. **10%**
Required degree grade **2:1**

training
Salary
1st year (2006) **£19,500**
2nd year (2006) **£21,000**
Holiday entitlement **23 days**
% of trainees with a non-law degree p.a. **Varies**

post-qualification
Salary (2006)
£35,000

Warner Goodman LLP

Portland Place, 66 West Street, Fareham, Hampshire, PO16 0JR
Tel: (01329) 222 038 Fax: (01329) 822 714
8/9 College Place, London Road, Southampton, SO15 2FF
Coleman House, 2-4 Landport Terrace, Portsmouth, PO1 2RG
11St George Walk, Waterlooville, Hampshire, PO7 7TU
Email: enquiries@warnergoodman.co.uk
Website: www.warnergoodman.co.uk

firm profile

Warner Goodman LLP is highly regarded in Hampshire as one of the county's most forward thinking and dynamic firms. The firm values its people highly and invests a lot of time in developing and nurturing their many talents. Work-life balance is respected and a flexible approach for those with caring responsibilities helps the firm retain many high performing fee earners. The firm takes particular pride in delivering professional client friendly services across its 8 legal disciplines. Advances in e-conveyancing, HIPs and paperless transactions are all exemplified at Warner Goodman.

main areas of work

Conveyancing, Private Client, Personal Injury, Clinical Negligence, Family and Crime. WG Commercial handles all aspects of Employment, Company Commercial, Commercial Litigation, Commercial Property, Landlord and Tenant and Licensing.

trainee profile

The firm seeks to recruit talented and bright law graduates with a flair for communication and a common sense approach to business. They value an approachable, down to earth attitude. This way they can continue their track record in first-rate client service and can continue to put their clients first. Although law graduates are preferred, the firm's primary focus is on character and intellectual strength, and outstanding graduates of other disciplines are always considered.

sponsorship & awards

Please see our website.

Partners	17
Assistant Solicitors	32
Total Trainees	3 per year

contact
Pamela Praine

method of application
online

selection procedure
Interview

closing date for 2010
31 July each year

application
Online application form.

training
Training is provided across the firms three main offices, and covers each of the practice groups. Input from trainees is sought as to their preferred choice of seat

post-qualification
Continuing Professional Development is promoted throughout the firm. Departmental meetings are regularly held where team members provide updates on their specialist practice areas

regional offices
Southampton, Portsmouth, Waterlooville

Watson Burton LLP

1 St James' Gate, Newcastle upon Tyne NE99 1YQ
Tel: (0191) 244 4444 Fax: (0191) 244 4500
Email: enquiries@watsonburton.com
Website: www.watsonburton.com

firm profile
Watson Burton LLP is one of the top law firms in the North of England with almost 200 years' experience and a well earned reputation for helping its clients succeed. Over the last few years, the firm has grown rapidly, opening an office in Leeds in 2005 and in London in 2006.

During the last 12 months Watson Burton LLP's higher national profile has facilitated the strategic recruitment of new Partners and associates, bringing greater depth to key areas of the firm and attracting major new clients including several plcs.

For the firm's trainees, this represents an exciting time to join the firm, providing you with an opportunity to work across the full range of legal services for a leading law firm that is going places and also has a strong commitment to corporate social responsibility.

main areas of work
Watson Burton LLP's business is mainly commercial and they have particular strengths in business advice, property services, construction, employment, dispute resolution, debt recovery, professions and insurance, technology, IP and media, corporate finance, education and wealth protection.

trainee profile
The firm seeks to recruit talented and bright law graduates with a flair for communication and a common sense approach to business. They value an approachable, down to earth attitude. This way they can continue their track record in first-rate client service and can continue to put their clients first. Although law graduates are preferred, the firm's primary focus is on character and intellectual strength, and outstanding graduates of other disciplines are always considered. They have positions in both the Newcastle and Leeds offices and recruit separately to appoint trainees into these positions.

training environment
The firm provides top-class training from modern office environments in both Leeds and Newcastle. They have the best technology and the right resources to provide a thorough and comprehensive introduction to the law. And they have a vast team of experienced lawyers who you can call on for assistance and guidance where needed. Watson Burton LLP's training programme includes both in-house and external seminars. Trainees are encouraged to assist in the firm's marketing from day one. Alongside careful and regular supervision, they offer trainees a high level of responsibility at an early stage.

sponsorship & benefits
The firm provides ample study leave, offers paid professional memberships and subscriptions, and give full payment for LPC fees.

Partners	39
Assistant Solicitors	68
Total Trainees	23

contact
Margaret Cay
(0191) 244 4301
margaret.cay@watsonburton.com

method of application
Download & complete the application form on the website, return along with a covering letter, to Margaret Cay, stating which office you wish to be considered for.

closing date for 2010
31 July 2008

application
Training contracts p.a. **6**
Applications p.a.
around **1,000**
% interviewed p.a. **2%**
Required degree grade **2:1**

training
Salary
£18,000 rising by £1,500 over the two year training period.

post-qualification
Salary
Not less than £35,000
% of trainees offered job on qualification (2006)
100%

regional offices
Newcastle, Leeds and London

Watson, Farley & Williams LLP

15 Appold Street, London EC2A 2HB
Tel: (020) 7814 8000 Fax: (020) 7814 8017
Email: graduates@wfw.com
Website: www.wfw.com

firm profile
Established in 1982, Watson, Farley & Williams has its strengths in corporate, banking and asset finance, particularly ship and aircraft finance. The firm aims to provide a superior service in specialist areas and to build long-lasting relationships with its clients.

main areas of work
Shipping; ship finance; aviation; banking; asset finance; corporate; litigation; e-commerce; intellectual property; EU/Competition; taxation; property; insolvency; telecoms; project finance.

trainee profile
Outgoing graduates who exhibit enthusiasm, ambition, self-assurance, initiative and intellectual flair.

training environment
Trainees are introduced to the firm with a comprehensive induction course covering legal topics and practical instruction. Seats are available in at least four of the firm's main areas, aiming to provide trainees with a solid commercial grounding. There is also the opportunity to spend time abroad, working on cross-border transactions. Operating in an informal and friendly atmosphere, trainees will receive support whenever necessary. You will be encouraged to take on early responsibility and play an active role alongside a partner at each stage of your training. The practice encourages continuous learning for all employees and works closely with a number of law lecturers, producing a widely-read 'digest' of legal developments, to which trainees are encouraged to contribute. All modules of the PSC are held in-house. The firm has its own sports teams and organises a variety of social functions.

benefits
Life assurance, PHI, BUPA, STL, pension, subsidised gym membership.

vacation placements
Places for 2008: 30; Duration: 2 weeks; Remuneration: £250 p.w.; Closing Date: 24th February 2008.

sponsorship & awards
CPE and LPC fees paid and £6,500 maintenance p.a. (£5,500 outside London).

Partners 68
Assistant Solicitors 150
Total Trainees 23

contact
Graduate Recruitment Manager

method of application
Online application

selection procedure
Assessment centre & Interview

closing date for 2010
31 July 2008

application
Training contracts p.a. **12**
Applications p.a. **1,000**
% interviewed p.a. **20-30%**
Required degree grade **Minimum 2:1 & 24 UCAS points or above**

training
Salary
1st year (2007) £34,000
2nd year (2007) £38,000
Holiday entitlement **22 days**
% of trainees with a non-law degree p.a. **50%**
No. of seats available abroad p.a. **12**

post-qualification
Salary (2007)
Not less than £62,500 at the time of writing
% of trainees offered job on qualification (2007) **80%**
% of assistants (as at 1/9/04) who joined as trainees **60%**
% of partners (as at 1/9/04) who joined as trainees **4%**

overseas offices
New York, Paris, Piraeus, Singapore, Bangkok, Rome, Hamburg

Wedlake Bell

52 Bedford Row, London, WC1R 4LR
Tel: (020) 7395 3000 Fax: (020) 7395 3100
Email: recruitment@wedlakebell.com
Website: www.wedlakebell.com

firm profile
Wedlake Bell is a medium-sized law firm providing legal advice to businesses and high net worth individuals from around the world. The firm's services are based on a high degree of partner involvement, extensive business and commercial experience and strong technical expertise. The firm has over 90 lawyers in central London and Guernsey, and affiliations with law firms throughout Europe and in the United States.

main areas of work
For the firm's business clients: Banking & asset finance; corporate; corporate tax; business recoveries; commercial; intellectual property; information technology; media; commercial property; construction; residential property.
For private individuals: Tax, trusts and wealth protection; offshore services; residential property.

trainee profile
In addition to academic excellence, Wedlake Bell looks for commercial aptitude, flexibility, enthusiasm, a personable nature, confidence, mental agility and computer literacy in its candidates. Languages are not crucial.

training environment
Trainees have four seats of six months across the following areas: corporate, corporate tax, business recoveries, banking, construction, media and IP/IT, employment, pensions, litigation, property and private client. As a trainee the firm encourages you to have direct contact and involvement with clients from an early stage. Trainees will work within highly specialised teams and have a high degree of responsibility. Trainees will be closely supervised by a partner or senior solicitor and become involved in high quality and varied work. The firm is committed to the training and career development of its lawyers and many of its trainees continue their careers with the firm often through to partnership. Wedlake Bell has an informal, creative and co-operative culture with a balanced approach to life.

sponsorship & benefits
LPC fees paid and £4,000 maintenance grant where local authority grant not available. During training contract: pension, travel loans, subsidised gym membership, health insurance and life assurance.

vacation placements
Places for 2008: 8; Duration: 3 weeks in July; Remuneration: £200 p.w.; Closing Date: End of February, 2008.

Partners	41
Assistant Solicitors	52
Total Trainees	14

contact
Natalie King

method of application
Application form

selection procedure
Two interviews

closing date for 2010
End of July 2008

application
Training contracts p.a. **7**
Required degree grade **2:1**
training
Salary
1st year (2007) £28,000
2nd year (2007) £30,000
Holiday entitlement
1st year **23 days**
2nd year **24 days**
% of trainees with a
non-law degree p.a. **50%**

overseas offices
Guernsey

Weightmans LLP

India Buildings, Water Street, Liverpool L2 0GA
Tel: (0151) 227 2601 Fax: (0151) 227 3223
Email: hr@weightmans.com
Website: www.weightmans.com

Partners	(over) 90
Trainees p.a.	up to 14
Total staff	(over) 750

method of application
online:
www.weightmans.com

closing date for 2010
31 July 2008

other offices
Birmingham, Leicester,
London, Manchester

firm profile

Weightmans is a top 75 national law firm with offices in Birmingham, Leicester, Liverpool, London and Manchester. With over 750 people in dedicated teams, including over 90 Partners, the firm's aim is to be both the law firm and employer of choice. The firm offers a comprehensive range of legal services to commercial, insurance and public sector clients, including insurance litigation, healthcare, professional indemnity, commercial property, commercial litigation and employment.

trainee profile

Weightmans looks to recruit up to 14 trainee solicitors each year. When considering training contract applications, the firm looks for applicants from diverse backgrounds who can demonstrate an ability to achieve results. Above all, the firm values well motivated candidates with a practical and pragmatic approach who can make a positive impact on a team.

training environment

Weightmans offers trainees real legal experience during the training contract, including attendance at court and client meetings. Challenged from the outset, trainees have the opportunity to demonstrate their talents across a range of seats. They follow a focused training plan which will enable them to develop business as well as legal skills. The quality of Weightmans' training is an important commercial investment. The firm's retention rate is high and they want today's trainees to remain at Weightmans and be leaders in the future.

application details

Apply before 31 July 2008. Their application form is available online at www.weightmans.com.

benefits

Weightmans pay a starting salary well above the minimum recommended by the Law Society, and this is reviewed every year to ensure that it is competitive. The firm also offers an excellent benefits package, which includes flexi-time, a pension, health cover, life assurance and 25 days holiday. From the moment you accept a training contract with Weightmans, the firm pledge support to you, paying all course fees for LPC and GDL.

Weightmans

www.chambersstudent.co.uk

855

Weil, Gotshal & Manges

One South Place, London EC2M 2WG
Tel: (020) 7903 1074 Fax: (020) 7903 0990
Email: graduate.recruitment@weil.com
Website: www.weil.com

firm profile
Weil Gotshal & Manges is a leader in the marketplace for sophisticated, international legal services. With more than 1,100 lawyers across the US, Europe and Asia, the firm serves many of the most successful companies in the world in their high-stakes matters and transactions.

main areas of work
Established in 1996, the London office now has over 110 lawyers. It has grown rapidly to become the second largest of the firm's 18 offices – it is the hub of the firm's European practice. Key areas are private equity, M&A, business finance and restructuring, capital markets, securitisation, banking and finance, dispute resolution and tax. The firm's expertise covers most industries including real estate, manufacturing, financial services, energy, telecommunications, pharmaceuticals, retailing and technology. Due to the international nature of the business, the firm's lawyers are experienced in working closely with their colleagues from other offices – this ensures a co-ordinated approach to providing effective legal solutions efficiently.

vacation placements
Places for 2008 Easter & Summer: 20 places. Closing date for applications by online application form: 14 February 2008.
New for 2008: 5 vacation students will have the opportunity of spending 3 weeks in the firm's New York office.

Partners	21
Assistant Solicitors	65
Total Trainees	21

contact
Jillian Singh

method of application
online application form

closing date for 2010
31 July 2008

application
Training contracts p.a. **12**
Required degree grade **2:1**

training
Salary
1st year (2007) £41,000
Holiday entitlement **23 days**

overseas offices
Austin, Boston, Budapest, Dallas, Frankfurt, Houston, Miami, Munich, New York, Paris, Prague, Providence, Silicon Valley, Singapore, Shanghai, Warsaw, Washington DC, Wilmington

White & Case LLP

5 Old Broad Street, London EC2N 1DW
Tel: (020) 7532 1000 Fax: (020) 7532 1001
Email: trainee@whitecase.com
Website: www.whitecase.com/trainee

firm profile
White & Case LLP is a global law firm with more than 2,000 lawyers worldwide. The firm has a network of 35 offices, providing the full range of legal services of the highest quality in virtually every major commercial centre and emerging market. They work with international businesses, financial institutions and governments worldwide on corporate and financial transactions and dispute resolution proceedings. Their clients range from some of the world's longest established and most respected names to many start-up visionaries. The firm's lawyers work on a variety of sophisticated, high-value transactions, many of which feature in the legal press worldwide as the firm's clients achieve firsts in privatisation, cross-border business deals, or major development projects.

main areas of work
Banking and capital markets; construction and engineering; corporate (including M&A and private equity); dispute resolution (including arbitration & mediation); employment & benefits; energy, infrastructure, project & asset finance; IP, PPP/PFI; real estate; tax; and telecommunications.

trainee profile
Trainees should be ambitious, creative and work well in teams. They should have an understanding of international commercial issues and have a desire to be involved in high profile, cross-border legal matters.

training environment
Trainees undertake four seats, each of six months in duration. The firm guarantees that one of these seats can be spent in Asia, Europe or Africa. Regardless of where they work, trainees get a high level of partner and senior associate contact from day one, ensuring they receive high quality, stimulating and rewarding work. Trainees are encouraged to take early responsibility and there is a strong emphasis on practical hands-on training, together with plenty of support and feedback. The firm recruits and develops trainee solicitors with the aim of retaining them on qualification.

benefits
The firm operates a flexible benefits scheme, through which you can select the benefits you wish to receive. Currently, the benefits include private medial insurance, dental insurance, life assurance, pension, critical illness insurance, travel insurance, retail vouchers, gym membership, season ticket loan and green bikes.

vacation placements
Places for 2008: 20-25 one-week Easter placements and 40-50 two-week Summer placements available. Remuneration: £350 per week; Closing Date: 31 January 2008.

sponsorship & awards
GDL and LPC fees paid and £7,500 maintenance p.a. Prizes for commendation and distinction for LPC.

Partners 68
Assistant Solicitors 213
Total Trainees 55

contact
Ms Emma Fernandes

method of application
Online application via firm website

selection procedure
Interview

closing date for 2010
31 July 2008

application
Training contracts p.a.**30-35**
Applications p.a. **1,600**
Required degree grade **2:1**

training
Salary
£41,000, rising by £1,000 every 6 months
Holiday entitlement **25 days**

All trainees are guaranteed to spend a seat overseas

post-qualification
Salary (2006) **£76,000**

overseas offices
Almaty, Ankara, Bangkok, Beijing, Berlin, Bratislava, Brussels, Budapest, Dresden, Düsseldorf, Frankfurt, Hamburg, Helsinki, Hong Kong, Istanbul, Johannesburg, London, Los Angeles, Mexico City, Miami, Milan, Moscow, Munich, New York, Palo Alto, Paris, Prague, Riyadh, São Paulo, Singapore, Shanghai, Stockholm, Tokyo, Warsaw, Washington DC

Wiggin LLP

10th Floor, The Met Building, 22 Percy Street, London, W1T 2BU
Tel: (020) 7612 9612   Fax (012) 4222 422395
The Promenade, Cheltenham GL50 1WG
Tel: (01242) 224114 Fax: (01242) 224223

Email: law@wiggin.co.uk Website: www.wiggin.co.uk

firm profile

Wiggin are experts in the constantly evolving field of media law. They focus exclusively on media with particular emphasis on film, music, sport, gaming, technology, broadcast and publishing. They are recognised for the uncompromising excellence of their work and an unrelenting determination to deliver the best possible results for their media clients. In over 10 years they have earned an international reputation for their innovative approach, fresh thinking and cutting edge experience in media law; a sector that is changing with mesmerizing speed. The firm offers a highly personalised relationship, working in partnership with its clients to address the complex legal challenges that the fast evolving media industry presents. They have the knowledge and experience, as well as the commitment and confidence, to deliver straightforward and genuine advice motivated only by the need to achieve the best possible outcome for clients. Based primarily out of their Cheltenham office, and also in London, and with blue-chip clients based all over the World (primarily London and the west coast of America) the firm goes to where clients need them to be.

main areas of work

Commercial 42%, Corporate 12%, Litigation 42%, Property 4%.

trainee profile

If you want to experience high profile media issues in a forward thinking environment then contact Wiggin. They're looking for you if you can demonstrate a passion for media and the law, strong academic ability and a commitment to success... One word of warning though, their seats are not for the faint hearted! They need trainees that relish hard work and a challenge. They'll be at the law fairs so come and see what they are all about.

training environment

Training is split into four seats and these will be allocated from company/commercial, commercial media (2 seats), media litigation, employment, film and property. Although based at the Cheltenham office, you will be meeting clients in London and could end up on a six-month secondment there with the British Phonographic Industry (the record industries trade association).

They don't want you to do the photocopying. Their trainees are encouraged to take an active role in transactions, assume responsibility and deal directly with clients. In-house seminars are held regularly and training reviews are held every three months. You'll get an experience just like your friends in the City but within the exciting and niche area of media law and within a firm small enough to recognise the importance of a personal approach.

benefits

Life assurance, private health cover, pension scheme, permanent health insurance, gym membership at corporate rates.

sponsorship & awards

PgDL and LPC fees and £3,500 maintenance p.a.

Partners	14
Assistant Solicitors	22
Total Trainees	8

contact
Office Manager

method of application
Online application only –
www.wiggin.co.uk

selection procedure
Two-day selection

closing date for 2010
31 July 2008

application
Training contracts p.a. **4**
Applications p.a. **500**
% interviewed p.a. **8%**
Required degree grade **2:1**

training
Salary
1st year (2007) **£26,500**
2nd year (2007) **£31,500**
Holiday entitlement **20 days**
+ one day per annum up
to max 25 days
% of trainees with a
non-law degree p.a. **50%**

post-qualification
Salary (2007) **£45,500**
% of trainees offered job
on qualification (2007) **0%**
% of assistants (as at 2007)
who joined as trainees **40%**
% of partners (as at 2007)
who joined as trainees **30%**

Wilsons Solicitors LLP

Steynings House, Summerlock Approach, Salisbury, Wiltshire, SP2 7RJ
Tel: (01722) 412 412 Fax: (01722) 427 610
Email: jo.ratcliffe@wilsonslaw.com
Website: www.wilsonslaw.com

Partners	30
Trainees	8
Total Staff	152

contact
Mrs J Ratcliffe
jo.ratcliffe@wilsonslaw.com

method of application
Application via website or CV

selection procedure
interview and assessment day

closing dates for 2008 training scheme:
31 July 2008 for training contract to commence in September 2010

application
Training contracts p.a. **4**
Required degree grade **2:1**

Salary
market rate
Holiday entitlement **22 days**

office
Salisbury

firm profile

Wilsons is ranked as one of the leading private client law firms in the country and now has the largest team of private client lawyers outside London, eleven of whom are considered to be 'leaders in their fields'.

Clients include wealthy individuals, entrepreneurs, companies, landed estates, trust companies and charities and many have an international dimension to their interests. The work the firm does for clients is best described as 'quirky' because of the particular issues they face.

main areas of work

Private client business is the firm's largest single area of work and it permeates the other areas of the firm, which include Charity, Family, Tax and Trusts, Probate, Agriculture, Property, Company Commercial, Employment and Litigation Teams.

trainee profile

Clients expect quality in the advice given and the service received and that is why the firm aims to employ the highest quality people. The firm places considerable emphasis on teamwork. An open approach to management means information is available across the firm and a flat structure means plenty of potential for positions of responsibility.

training environment

Despite the firm's national and international client base it is situated 90 miles outside London in Salisbury. Many of the firm's lawyers come from London firms and many of the clients continue to be London-based. This ensures an exceptional quality of work within a beautiful location. If quality of life is crucial to you, the firm would like to meet you.

A two-year training contract enables trainees to sample four disciplines in six-month seats from different areas.

benefits

Pension (2% in first year, 3% in second year), life assurance (2 x salary), choice of optional benefits and private medical insurance.

work experience placements

1 week available in July at the firms offices in Salisbury.

sponsorship & awards

On joining the firm as a trainee the firm can offer you an interest free loan of up to £4,500 for the Legal Practice Course. The firm is committed to your training contract and would hope to retain you once you qualify. If you stay with Wilsons for two years after qualifying the loan will be written off.

Withers LLP

16 Old Bailey, London EC4M 7EG
Tel: (020) 7597 6000 Fax: (020) 7329 2534
Email: emma.macdonald@withersworldwide.com
Website: www.withersrecruitment.com

firm profile
Withers LLP is the first international law firm dedicated to the business and personal interests of successful people, their families, their businesses and their advisers.

main areas of work
The wealth of today's private client has increased in multiples and many are institutions in their own right. With its merger in 2002 the firm has been able to respond to these changing legal needs and offer integrated solutions to the international legal and tax needs of its clients. With 100 Partners and 600 people the firm has unparalleled expertise in commercial and tax law, trusts, estate planning, litigation, charities, employment, family law and other legal issues facing high net worth individuals.

Withers' reputation in commercial law along with its status as the largest Private Client Team in Europe and leading Family Team sets it apart from other City firms.

International exposure at Withers does not mean working in one of the firm's foreign offices, although trainees can do seats abroad if they wish. A lot of the work done in London crosses numerous jurisdictions. The firm's international client base includes more than 15% of Britain's wealthiest citizens (based on the Sunday Times Rich List), at least 10% of the 50 wealthiest families based in Europe with US connections and a significant number of the Forbes 400 list of Richest Americans.

trainee profile
Each year the firm looks for a diverse mix of trainees who are excited by the prospect of working with leaders in their field who are often in the public eye as spokespersons for the profession. Trainees should have a high degree of determination, ambition and be able to demonstrate business acumen and entrepreneurial flair.

training environment
Trainees spend six months in four different departments. Teams are small (files are typically handled by one senior fee earner and a trainee) so the client will know your name and will expect you to engage with him on anything ranging from their property in Kensington to a revolutionary product they have invented. The firm also seconds trainees to the client. Buddy and mentor systems as well as on the job training ensure trainees are fully supported from the outset.

application
Apply online by July 31 2008 to begin training in August 2010. Interviews usually take place between April and September.

vacation scheme
The firm's work experience scheme was nominated for 'Best Vacation Scheme' in 2006. The firm runs placements at Easter and over the summer in London. Apply online by 31 January 2008 for places in 2008.

sponsorship
Fees plus £5 000 maintenance for both the GDL and LPC are paid.

Partners	100
Total Staff	600
Trainees	32

contact
Emma MacDonald
Senior Recruitment Officer

method of application
Application form (available online)

selection procedure
2 interviews incl. written exercise and presentation

closing dates for 2010
training scheme:
31 July 2008
2008 work experience:
31 January 2008

application
Training contracts p.a. **18**
Applications p.a. **700**
% interviewed p.a. **10%**
Required degree grade **2:1**, **ABB at A-Level**

training
Salary
1st year (2007) £31,000
2nd year (2007) £33,000
Holiday entitlement 23 days
% of trainees with a
non-law degree p.a. 50%

post-qualification
Salary (2007) £55,000

offices
London, Milan, Geneva, New York, New Haven, (Connecticut), Greenwich (USA)

withers LLP

Wollastons

Brierly Place, New London Road, Chelmsford, Essex CM2 0AP
Tel: (01245) 211211 Fax: (01245) 354764
Email: graduate.recruitment@wollastons.co.uk
Website: www.wollastons.co.uk

firm profile

Wollastons is a dynamic, regional law firm, widely recognised as the leading, commercial practice in Essex. Wollastons has a strong reputation as a forward-thinking and energetic organisation, offering high levels of service to both businesses and private clients. The firm's first-class resources, including sophisticated IT, and the lively atmosphere attracts high calibre lawyers, keen to work in a modern, professional environment. The Investors in People accreditation demonstrates a strong commitment to staff development and training at all levels.

main areas of work

Main practice areas include corporate and commercial; commercial property; commercial disputes; employment; planning and property disputes; private client and family.

trainee profile

Applications are welcomed from able and ambitious graduates with 300 UCAS points (gained in 3 subjects, excluding general studies) and a 2:1 degree. Candidates should have a commercial outlook, be confident, outgoing and able to demonstrate a wide range of interests. A link with the Essex area would be desirable.

training environment

Trainees have four six-month seats. These will normally include: company and commercial; commercial disputes; commercial property and employment. Trainees sit with a partner or a senior solicitor and form an integral part of the team. Trainees are fully involved in a wide range of interesting work and, although work is closely checked, trainees are encouraged to take responsibility from an early stage. The firm is very friendly and informal and trainees receive a great deal of individual attention and support. Progress is kept under constant review with mid-seat and end of seat appraisals.

sponsorship & awards

LPC fees paid.

Partners	12
Fee-earners	43
Total Trainees	4 (2 p.a.)

contact
Jo Goode, Graduate
Recruitment Manager
(01245) 211253

method of application
CV and online application
form, see website for
details

selection procedure
3 stage interview process

application
Training contracts p.a. **2**
Applications p.a. **Approx 500**
Interviewed p.a. **Approx 50**
Required degree grade
2:1

training
Salary
1st year £24,000
2nd year £25,000

Wollastons
solicitors

INVESTOR IN PEOPLE

Wragge & Co LLP

55 Colmore Row, Birmingham B3 2AS
Tel: Freephone (0800) 096 9610
Email: gradmail@wragge.com
Website: www.wragge.com/graduate

Partners	110
Assistant Solicitors	419
Total Trainees	60

firm profile

Wragge & Co is a major UK law firm providing a full service to some of the world's largest and most successful organisations, including 35 FTSE 100 and 50 FTSE 250 companies. It is the only law firm in both the Financial Times 50 Best Workplaces in the UK and the Sunday Times 100 Best Companies to Work For. Working from London or Birmingham on high profile national and international instructions, you will be part of a team passionate about providing the very best client service.

Wragge & Co is a relationship firm, taking time to form lasting relationships with clients to ensure understanding of what makes their businesses tick. Relationships and excellent client service are two of the firms driving forces. To make sure it gets both right, you may find yourself on secondment, experiencing life and work as a client. Relationships within the firm are just as important. The firm is a single team, working together to support colleagues and clients alike. The firm values minimum hierarchy so it is open plan. Everyone has the same space. In fact, being open and honest is one of the firm's most precious values.

main areas of work

The firm has nationally recognised teams in specialist areas including employment, banking, antitrust, outsourcing, PFI and regeneration. This year Wragge & Co was named pensions law provider of the year at the FT Business Pensions and Investment Provider Awards. The firm is also Managing Intellectual Property's UK law firm of the year.

The firm's core areas of legal advice include corporate finance, dispute resolution, finance and projects, human resources, real estate and technology and commerce. The quality of work is reflected in the firm's client list which includes British Airways, Cadbury Schweppes, Capgemini UK, H J Heinz, HSBC, Marks & Spencer, McDonalds and Birds Eye.

trainee profile

The firm is looking for graduates of 2:1 standard at degree level, with some legal or commercial work experience gained either via a holiday job or a previous career. You should be practical, with a common sense and problem solving approach to work, and be able to show adaptability, enthusiasm and ambition.

vacation placements

Easter and summer vacation placements are run at Wragge & Co. As part of our scheme you will get the opportunity to experience different areas of the firm, attend client meetings and get involved in real files. You can apply online at www.wragge.com/graduate.

training contracts

The firm is currently recruiting for 30 training contracts to commence in September 2010/March 2011. You can apply online at www.wragge.com/graduate. The closing date is 31 July 2008. If you are a non-law student, please return your form as soon as possible, as the firm will be running assessment days over the forthcoming year.

contact
Joanne Dowsett,
Graduate Recruitment Advisor

method of application
Applications are made online at
www.wragge.com/graduate

selection procedure
Telephone discussion & assessment day

closing date
Sept 2010/March 2011: 31 July 2008. If you are a non-law student, please complete your application form as soon as possible, as the firm will be running assessment days over the forthcoming year

application
Training contracts p.a. **30**
Applications p.a. **1,000**
% interviewed p.a. **25%**
Required degree grade **2:1**

training
Salary Birmingham (Sept 2007)
1st year £25,000
2nd year £28,000
Holiday entitlement **25 days**
% of trainees with a non-law degree p.a. **Varies**

post-qualification
Salary (2007)
Birmingham £40,000
London £62,000
% of trainees offered job on qualification
(Sept 2006) **100%**

Wragge&Co

Wragge & co LLP is a Limited Liability Partnership

barristers

barristers timetable

law students • penultimate undergraduate year	non-law students • final year
Throughout the year	Start thinking about getting some relevant work experience. Do plenty of research into chambers/mini-pupillages
By the end of January 2008	Apply for the GDL
By the end of April	Apply for a pupillage under the year early scheme on OLPAS
May	Apply for a GDL scholarship from an Inn of Court. If successful, join that Inn
June to September	Do pre-GDL mini-pupillages
September/October 2008	Start final year of degree	Start GDL
November	By November apply through BVC Online for the BVC. Apply to an Inn of Court for a scholarship
During final year/GDL	Apply for pupillage to non-OLPAS sets. Do mini-pupillages
April/May	Before 1st May apply for pupillage through OLPAS
June	Apply for Inn membership
September 2009	Start the BVC. Apply by September 28th the September tranche of OLPAS; make further pupillage applications to non-OLPAS sets
April/May	If unsuccessful last year, apply for pupillage before 1st May
June	Finish BVC
September	Apply for pupillage before 28th September through OLPAS if you have yet to be successful
October 2010	Start pupillage
Summer	Be offered tenancy at your pupillage chambers or apply for tenancy or a 3rd six elsewhere
October 2011	Start tenancy
2041	Be appointed to the High Court Bench
2051	Get slapped on the wrist by Ministry of Justice for falling asleep in court

barcode

Don't let the often curious terms used at the Bar confuse or intimidate you!

barrister – a member of the Bar of England and Wales.

bench – the judiciary.

bencher – a senior member of an Inn of Court. Usually silks and judges, known as masters of the bench.

brief – the documents setting out case instructions.

bvc – the Bar Vocational Course. Currently, its successful completion entitles you to call yourself a barrister in non-legal situations (ie dinner parties), but does not of itself give you rights of audience. Moves are afoot to require part of pupillage to have been completed before the title is conferred.

bvc online – the application system through which applications to Bar school must be made.

cab-rank rule – self-employed barristers cannot refuse instructions if they have the time and experience to undertake the case. You cannot refuse to represent someone because you find their opinions or actions objectionable.

call – the ceremony whereby you become a barrister

chambers – a group of barristers in independent practice who have joined together to share the costs of practising. Chambers is also the name used for a judge's private office.

circuit – The courts of England and Wales are divided into six circuits: North Eastern, Northern, Midland & Oxford, South Eastern, Western, and Wales & Chester circuits.

clerk – administrator/manager in chambers who organises work for barristers and payment of fees, etc

counsel – a barrister.

cracked-trial – a case that is concluded without a trial. This will be because the defendant offers an acceptable plea or the prosecution offers no evidence. Cracked and ineffective trials (where there is a lack of court time or the defendant or a witness does not attend) frustrate the bench and are considered a waste of money.

devilling – (paid) work done by a junior member of chambers for a more senior member.

employed bar – some barristers do not engage in private practice at chambers, but are employed full-time by a company or public body.

first and second six – pupillages are divided into two six-month periods. Most chambers now only offer 12-month pupillages, however it is still possible to undertake the two sixes at different sets.

inns of court – ancient institutions that alone have the power to 'make' barristers. There was a time when there was a proliferation of them but now there are only four: Gray's Inn, Inner Temple, Lincoln's Inn and Middle Temple.

junior – a barrister not yet appointed silk. Note: older juniors are known as senior juniors.

junior brief – a case on which a junior is led by a senior. Such cases are too much work for one barrister alone and may involve a lot of research or run for a long time. Ordinarily, junior counsel will not conduct advocacy.

keeping term – eating the dinners in hall required to be eligible for call to the Bar.

mini-pupillage – a short period of work experience spent in chambers.

olpas – the Online Pupillage Application System.

pupillage – the year of training undertaken after Bar school and before tenancy.

pupilmaster – a senior barrister with whom a pupil sits and who teaches the pupil. The Bar Council is encouraging the term pupil supervisor.

QC – one of Her Majesty's Counsel, formerly appointed by the Lord Chancellor. The system fell into abeyance in 2004 and has now been revived with a new, more open appointments system.

set – as in a 'set of chambers'.

silk – a QC, so named because of their silk robes.

supervisor – the new name for a pupilmaster.

tenant/tenancy – permission from chambers to join their set and work with them. A 'squatter' is someone who is permitted to use chambers' premises, but is not actually a member of the set. A 'door tenant' is someone who is affiliated with the set, but does not conduct business from chambers' premises.

a shot at the bar

will you make it?

As jobs go, being a barrister is hard to beat for excitement, truly extraordinary experiences, a sense of personal fulfilment and kudos. At the same time the Bar is a highly competitive world in which the hours can be punishing and the work arduous. Equally arduous for many is the process of getting a foot in the door so prepare yourself for the most challenging game of musical chairs you've ever played. Roughly one in three people who enrol on the BVC end up with a pupillage, and one in five from the original number end up with tenancy in chambers. Look at the table below if you think this is an exaggeration.

What you really want to know is will you be one of the lucky ones? This is a hard question to answer, especially for yourself. Meet enough pupils and barristers and you can see what makes someone successful. Ask a chambers recruiter to define the qualities they look for and they will speak in fairly general terms (academic credentials, people skills, analytical skills, commitment, passion, an ability to express ideas) and then round off with a statement to the effect that 'you know a good one when you see one'. If only there was something like a height chart that you could measure your suitability against.

Just because you're really gobby/argumentative/confident and your nan/your boyfriend/the barman at your local says you'd make a great barrister doesn't mean you will. Equally, just because you got 17 A*s in your A-levels and can complete The Times crossword in three minutes doesn't mean

you will either. Those people who make it at the Bar are the ones who offer the right traits for their chosen area of practice. Crime: it's all about guts, personality and a readiness for any challenge. You need an affinity with ordinary people and the way you communicate should draw others in. You need to be to-the-point and down-to-earth more than you need to be a genius. You should be able to assimilate and recall facts easily. Commercial practice is a far more sophisticated game. This part of the Bar is stuffed with brain boxes – especially in Chancery work – and those who love nothing more than to create a masterpiece of written advice. Advocacy is certainly an important element, though it is unlike that displayed at the criminal Bar. Persuading a judge is a different proposition to persuading a jury; someone who can deliver a clever legal argument succinctly will do far better than a charming raconteur.

By reading the **Chambers Reports** and **Barristers Practice Areas** you will understand more about the skills needed in different parts of the Bar.

is the cost of training prohibitive?

Deciding to embark on a career as a barrister could be one of the most expensive life choices you make. The GDL conversion course is quite expensive, the BVC is painfully expensive, and during a poorly funded pupillage year your circumstances are likely to remain impecunious. The Bar Council requires all pupillages to be funded by chambers at a minimum level of £833.33 per month, and many criminal and

	99-00	00-01	01-02	02-03	03-04	04-05	05-06	06-07
BVC applicants	2,370	2,252	2,119	2,067	2,570	2,883	n/a	2,917
BVC enrolments	1,490	1,407	1,386	1,332	1,406	1,697	1,745	1,932
Students passing the BVC	1,201	1,110	1,182	1,121	1,251	n/a	1,515	n/a
First six pupils	681	695	812	586	518	571	351[1]	n/a
Second six pupils	704	700	724	702	557	598	127[1]	n/a
Pupils awarded tenancy	511	535	541	698	601	544	278[2]	n/a

Certain figures were unavailable from the Bar Council at the time of going to press. Please check our website.
[1] *Figure for period 1st October 2005-16th March 2006*
[2] *Figure for period 1st October 2005-15th December 2005*

mixed sets think that figure is just fine. It's a completely different story for pupils at commercial sets as the awards they receive are more akin to those of trainee solicitors at commercial firms, and funds can be advanced for law school. Read the Funding section on page 72 for more ideas on how to pay for law school. Of all the potential sponsors out there, the four Inns of Court have the deepest pockets.

If you thought the Bar would allow you to serve your community and earn a pile of cash, take note. The remuneration for publicly funded work has always been pretty bad and it all came to a head in autumn 2005 when talks between leaders of the Bar and the Lord Chancellor about proposed cuts collapsed. Some criminal barristers started refusing work. Promises of a complete review into the provision of advocacy services calmed passions. Then in July 2006 Lord Carter of Coles published a set of proposals as part of his overarching review/shake-up of the provision of publicly funded legal services. Civil, family and criminal services are all subject to a range of new changes, not least affecting the way they are funded. These changes are being implemented throughout late 2007 and early 2008. See **Get Carter** on page 18 for more details.

If you thought training as a barrister was a good way to become a highly paid business adviser, don't let us stop you – around 20 barristers in London are thought to be earning £2 million or more per year. For the pupils who make it to tenancy in good-quality sets, the future looks very good indeed and within just a couple of years they can expect to overtake their solicitor colleagues in the money stakes.

Do remember, though, that the Bar is like football in the sense that within any area of practice there are a few Premier League sets and many others in lower divisions. The difference in earnings at the top and the bottom is substantial.

i want to get started

If you're still at university there's plenty you can do to prepare yourself for a shot at the Bar. If there is anything a little outré about your CV – you're mature or you have poor A-levels, for instance – getting a First is a really good idea. 2:1s are two a penny and as for 2:2s, well, if you end up with one of these you'll have to be pretty remarkable in some other respect to persuade a recruiter to give you a try. In general, chambers are much more interested in your undergraduate performance than what you can muster up at Bar School, and for the record we have it on excellent authority that good pupillages can be secured with the scantiest of passes on the GDL. That said, 'Very Competent' grades proliferate on the BVC, so why be awkward and get a 'Competent'?

mini adventures

Let's look a little closer at your commitment to the Bar. The best way to demonstrate that you possess any is to carry out some mini-pupillages, which is just high-falutin' barristerspeak for work experience. They come in two flavours: assessed and unassessed. During an unassessed mini you will observe a barrister in his or her chambers and probably also in court. How much you will be involved in proceedings varies hugely. In the course of a good mini you will sit in on a pre-trial conference (with the client's permission) and will be included in discussions about the law. One person we spoke to was invited to spend nearly every moment from fry-up to nightcap with their supervising barrister, though we suspect this is not the norm. Another reported turning up at chambers on the appointed day only to be told by a clerk to go to a particular court; after finding the court and sitting in the public gallery for a while, they eventually tracked down their putative supervisor in the robing room where they were greeted with something between bemusement and indifference. It is not unheard of for mini-pupils at commercial sets to go days at a time without seeing the inside of a court. Don't become fixed on the idea of spending a whole week with chambers as you may find it easier (and more beneficial) to get a couple of days here and there. Arguably the benefits are the same and you'll be able to compare your experiences.

Some sets will only recruit those who have undertaken an assessed mini-pupillage. These minis are more formal and will keep you on your toes. The most likely scenario is that you'll be given a set of papers to analyse and then be asked to produce a piece of written work. Take notes throughout and don't be afraid to ask your supervisor questions at appropriate moments. Afterwards, write notes on what you saw and learned about the place and the work you did. Think about the quality of any advocacy you observed and what you thought about the lifestyle in general. This will be helpful when completing pupillage application forms and chatting with recruiters at interviews. In fact, approach all relevant 'experience' from now on mindfully and with a pen.

how do i get one?

Not all sets offer mini-pupillages, so start off by checking their websites and making a list of those to which you're going to apply. A set's website will tell you the format your application should take and the person to whom it should be addressed. In general, chambers will want a CV and covering letter.

As with everything else in this game, demand for mini-pupillages is high so apply as you would Calamine lotion on a rash – liberally and at the first sign of an itch for the Bar. This is when personal contacts really come in to their own. People get pupillage by means of whom they know less than some people would have you believe, but getting a mini is different. Speak to any barristers you know and make your intentions clear. If Uncle Eddie dated some woman at 17 Ramshackle Row back in the 80s, get him to contact

her again. She'll either report him to the police as a stalker or you'll get a contact. Most barristers are flattered by the idea of some youngster wanting to follow in their footsteps and are genuinely willing to help. If your little black book isn't overflowing then create your own contacts. Apply to an Inn of Court to be assigned a sponsor, and if you've started dining at your Inn then for goodness sake stop hiding in the corner and schmooze.

Do enough mini-pupillages to give you a good sense of what areas of practice interest you, but if you are close to needing your toes to count them you are in danger of looking like you've nothing else going on in your life.

prizes mean points

The Bar Council prescribes that BVC students undertake a certain amount of pro-bono work. To ensure that you do land on something that interests you and has real weight on a pupillage application form it is a good idea to start researching as soon as possible. There are plenty of ways to get involved in pro bono work and page 33 lists a non-exhaustive selection.

What else should you do? *"Everything you can,"* advises one QC. Get involved with every debating and mooting opportunity that crops up. At law school you'll have the chance to enter mock trial competitions and you might also want to keep an eye out for essay competitions. The scholarships offered by the Inns are not just a way of funding your education – don't underestimate the capacity of a prize or award to mark you out from other well-qualified candidates.

olpas: getting a foot in the door

The Online Pupillage Application System has operated since 2001. It is not compulsory for chambers to participate, but every pupillage provider is required by the Bar Council to advertise its vacancies on the OLPAS website, **www.pupillages.com**. The info is also produced in the *Pupillages and Awards Handbook*, published to coincide with the opening of the online system and the National Pupillage Fair held in March in London. OLPAS has two 'seasons': summer and autumn. The closing date for summer season applications is 1 May, allowing three months for interviews with offers made after 31 July. The autumn season opens at the end of August and closes on 28 September, with just a month for interviews and offers being made after 31 October. A set of chambers may participate in one or other season. It need not participate in either.

Students may apply through OLPAS during as many seasons as they like, but are limited to 12 sets in each. Most LLB candidates make applications during their final year at uni, although some of the top commercial sets encourage students to apply in their penultimate year in an attempt to snap up the best candidates. Twelve-month pupillages are the most convenient option, although it is not unusual for pupils to end up doing a 'first six' in one set and a 'second six' in another.

The beauty of OLPAS is that all correspondence regarding interviews, offers and rejections is sent via e-mail. This is actually likely to lead to RSI as you spend whole days impatiently pressing the 'refresh' button in the hope that a message has landed in your inbox. Some sets show a healthy disdain for the whole shebang and choose to call on that old-fashioned contraption, the mobile telephone.

perfect pitch

Think carefully when choosing where to apply. If you know you're top dollar and that's what you're after then off you go. If you're not sure of your calibre then take a look at the CVs of a chambers' latest recruits. This will give you some indication of the kind of person the set wants. If you didn't go to one of 'those two' universities, why apply exclusively to sets whose members are all dyed-in-the-wool Oxbridge types. Also, you must appear consistent. Chambers won't see which other sets you are applying to, but because of the way the OLPAS form is designed they will see the list of your preferred practice areas.

an exercise in form filling?

Here are our top five tips:

- **Keep it personal:** Include nothing that you cannot talk about eloquently, evenly passionately. A good example of this is FRU. Who isn't commencing/about to complete their FRU training? If you haven't actually signed out a case, mentioning FRU will look desperate. Anchor your spiel in your own experiences and your application will be more persuasive.

- **Keep it pithy:** As Shakespeare once said, brevity is the soul of wit. It should also be the spirit of an OLPAS form. For each section you can write no more than 150 words. Keep it concise and this will be plenty. Long sentences can be tedious and your chances are greatly improved if the recruiter stays conscious.

- **Avoid being trite:** You will be asked to explain why you want to be a barrister and why you are interested in your chosen practice areas. That a career at the Bar offers an attractive combination of academia and practicality is a given. This is the section where you run most danger of getting lost in the crowd so think what the obvious answer is and then write something more meaningful.

- **Write proper:** 'Practice' is the noun; 'practise' is the verb. If you haven't learnt this already, now is the time. As one senior QC put it: *"Given that this is a job in which a strong command of the English language is paramount, we are often amazed at some of the fundamental errors that crop up in the OLPAS applications."*

- **Don't make silly mistakes:** Your mantra should go something like this: *"Save, print, check. Save, print, check."* With some sets getting 500 applications, they are itching for a reason to put yours in the bin. Don't give them this one.

olpas is not the only fruit

A good number of sets recruit pupils outside the OLPAS machinery because they don't like its format or timetable. A set's decision not to be part of the online scheme says nothing about its quality: it's more a reflection of their view that their interests will be better served by other means. For example, some chambers choose not to participate because their special interest in aspects of an applicant's background cannot be adequately satisfied by reading a completed OLPAS form.

The application method at each non-OLPAS set will be different; however, all must still advertise vacancies on www.pupillages.com. Research things well in advance to make sure you don't miss any deadlines. As one successful applicant counselled: *"Applying to non-OLPAS sets requires a great deal of motivation. There are a lot of them out there and many of them are very good. They should be taken very seriously."* Some sets choose to mirror the OLPAS timetable in their own application procedures, but many don't and this can bring its own problems. One pupil cautioned: *"The exploding offer phenomenon is a real difficulty. Shortly before my first OLPAS interview I was made a very attractive offer from a non-OLPAS set that I just couldn't pass up. While they were a great set, it did stop me from trying my hand elsewhere."*

expect the spanish inquisition

So you've got an interview – well done. Our first piece of advice: dress like you're going to court not the set of *Ally McBeal*. Opt for neat and discreet with hair tidy, teeth flossed, tie sober, jacket done up. Most first interviews are reasonably painless. The panel will want you to stand out and they will want to like you. Most chambers will be grading you on standard criteria that include everything from intellect to personality. Check their website to see if they publish any guidelines.

As a rough guide, you can expect your first interview to involve a discussion of the hottest topics in your prospective practice area and some gentle investigation into you and your application form. Of course, we need not tell you to read *The Times* every Tuesday, keep your subscription to *Counsel* up to date or suggest you set the Bar Council website as your homepage. Yet, preparation for your interviews should consist of more than boning-up on the law; it is important to be clued-up on current affairs too. And when we say clued-up what we really mean is develop an opinion. "Oh yes, terrorism, isn't it awful" is never going to cut it. Finally, think about what isn't on your CV and how you can account for anything that is missing or disappointing grades. It is probably best to approach these things with honesty rather than creativity but, whichever you go for, prepare your answer well.

For second interviews expect a larger panel made up of a broader cross-section of people from chambers. While the format of the interviews may vary between sets, the panel will always want to assess the depth of your legal knowledge, your advocacy potential and your mettle. Weaknesses on you CV will be sniffed out and pursued with tenacity. Don't let them push you around, if you can support your position then stick to it. Resolve is just as necessary for a career at the Bar as receptivity; they want to know that you can fight your corner.

Criminal and mixed sets will commonly give you an advocacy exercise, such as a bail application or a plea in mitigation (their basic structures will fit on a post-it, so why not note them down and keep with you at all times). Most, if not all, sets will pose a legal problem of some sort, with the amount of preparation time you are given ranging from ten minutes to a week. If you know that this is going to happen then do take an appropriate practitioner's text unless you know that one will be made available to you. That said, chambers generally aren't looking for faultless knowledge of substantive law, but are trying to get an insight into how your mind works. As one seasoned interviewer explained: *"We are more interested in seeing how a candidate approaches a problem than whether or not they get the right answer."*

A second interview is often the time when an ethics question may raise its head. You can prepare by reading the Bar's Code of Conduct, which is available on the Bar Council's website. It's a real page turner.

Of course, to all rules there are exceptions. Some sets only conduct one round of interviews. If you are invited somewhere like this expect the interview to be reasonably long and rigorous. Other chambers don't have a second round but instead host a drinks evening to which all successful first-round interviewees are invited. Sounds like the easy option, but approach with caution and don't get pissed and indiscrete.

pupillage: don't forget your flashes

If you find yourself among the one in three or so who end up with pupillage, you can expect the trials to begin again. How the year is divided varies from set to set. Yet no matter how many pupil supervisors you have, the broad division is between the first, non-practising six months and the 'second six' when pupils are permitted to be on their feet in court. During the first six, pupils are fairly tethered to their supervisor, shadowing them at court, conferences and in chambers. The days of being strategically placed next to a window to protect your master from the offensive glare of the sun are gone. That said, you can't rule out all errand running.

It goes without saying that you must understand the nature of any given task before you embark on it. One beleaguered pupil told us of the day they were loitering in the corridors of the RCJ when a sizable member of chambers asked them to perform an errand. *"He said, 'Dash back to chambers and pick up my court stuff, and don't forget my flashes.' So, off I go, confident that I am the only person this side of The Strand who doesn't* know what flashes are. More fool me. No one in chambers has the foggiest, so I grab what I understand to be court dress. As it turned out flashes – which are just bands – were the least of my problems. Unfortunately for me, the man in question shares a room with a petite lady barrister. I am saved from taking him her lacy collar but not her gown. The effect could be likened to covering a giraffe with a pony blanket."

A second six at a Chancery set is likely to be little different from the first six. Even if entitled to accept a brief to appear in court, because of the nature of the work you will probably still be far too inexperienced to take it. A second six at a busy criminal set, however, could mean court every day. *"I really didn't have a clue the first time I had to get robed up,"* said one young barrister. *"Before leaving chambers I had to get my supervisor to do my collar for me and in the robing room someone kindly told me that my bands were the wrong way round. It should have come as no surprise to me that when I tried to go to the loo my boxers were on wrong too."*

crunch time

Gaining pupillage is not the end of it; gaining tenancy is the real prize. Effectively, an offer of tenancy is an invitation from a set to take space in their chambers and share the services of the clerking and administrative team. It's not exactly a job offer as you will be self-employed, but it can feel rather like one. How many tenants a set takes on post-pupillage is usually as dependent on the amount of space and work available in chambers as on the quality of the candidates. If you are curious about a set's growth you can check to see how many new tenants have joined in recent years by checking the list of members on its website. You can then compare the number of recent additions to the number of pupillages offered in recent years.

Usually tenancies are awarded after a vote of all members of chambers after taking advice from a committee, clerks and possibly also instructing solicitors. Decisions are commonly made in the July of the pupillage year, allowing unsuccessful pupils time to cast around for other tenancy offers or a 'third six' elsewhere. There is evidence to suggest that civil and commercial sets have higher pupil-to-tenant conversion rates than criminal sets. Certainly, it is quite usual for a 12-month criminal pupillage to be followed by a third or subsequent six somewhere other than a pupil's first set. If you mentally prepare yourself for being passed around the houses, you'll be pleasantly surprised if things go more smoothly.

dust yourself off and try again

What if you still don't have pupillage by the time you have finished the BVC? Rather than seeing an enforced year out as a grim prospect, view it as a time to improve your CV and become more marketable. If you are interested in a specialist area of practice consider a master's degree. If the thought of another year in education brings you out in a cold sweat then seek out some useful practical experience. The most obvious answer is to apply

for paralegaling and outdoor clerking jobs at law firms. The work you do as a paralegal may give you an enviable understanding of how a case actually works and how solicitors – your future clients – work. As an outdoor clerk you will be in court all the time taking notes. This will give you insight into the procedures and politics of trials. The year might also be spent with an organisation that works in an area related to your legal interest. We have interviewed several lawyers who secured pupillages following a period with a charity or not-for-profit organisation.

and finally…

If we're honest, we don't expect too many readers to have changed their minds about a career at the Bar after reading this section. The one thing that wannabe-barristers have in common is a belief that if anybody is going to succeed then why not them. That's fair enough because self-belief is what will sustain them through the darkest days. Those who do succeed are in for what one sage member of the profession describes as *"quite simply, the best job in the world."*

lincoln's inn

www.lincolnsinn.org.uk

The biggest of the four, beautiful Lincoln's Inn is the setting for the opening scenes in Dickens' Bleak House. Its large membership boasts some A-list celebrities, including Cherie and Tony, and the Inn is favoured by overseas barristers. Students recommended its "free-flowing wine and the great atmosphere." Its library is described as "impossibly grand with stained-glass windows, thick carpets and bad lighting," but also as "the best in the Inns". Apparently "the librarians are incredibly helpful." As well as the usual activities, the Inn organises an annual trip to visit the ECJ, the ECHR and the Hague Tribunal.

inner temple

www.innertemple.org.uk

From Chaucer to Charlie Falconer, this Inn has more history than we've had hot dinners. It is a place for firsts: the first female barrister was a member, as was Dame Elizabeth Butler-Sloss, who became the first female High Court judge and then the first female Lord Justice of the Court of Appeal. It gives some generous scholarships and runs an "excellent advocacy course with feedback from judges and silks." Its wood-panelled library has a good collection. The Students' Association's social diary is busy and the mooting society is a regular contender in international competitions.

The four ancient Inns of Court bear a striking resemblance to Oxbridge colleges (chapel, hall, library, etc) and were originally places of residence and learning for young barristers. The Inns still perform some important functions: they alone have the power to 'call' a person to the Bar and before you can be called you must 'keep term' by attending 'dinners' or other 'qualifying sessions' organised by the Inns.

Students must join one of the Inns by the June before they start their BVC, but our advice is to investigate what they have to offer much earlier than this as the Inns have millions of pounds to award in annual scholarships to GDL and BVC students as well as to pupils. Take care not to miss the deadlines for applying as these fall earlier than you'd imagine: commonly in the calendar year before the start of the course to which the award relates. You don't have to be a member of an Inn to apply for one; the trick is to make applications and then join the Inn where you've been successful. You must join an Inn if you're going to take its money and having picked one of the four, that's it – you can't then switch. There's a competitive selection process for scholarships, so expect an interview. The panel will look at the usual criteria: academics, commitment to a career at the Bar, etc. With some awards, but certainly not all, the Inn will consider your financial circumstances.

The Inns reserve funds to help students from the regional BVC institutions meet their costs when visiting the Inn, and for students of any BVC provider to help pay for qualifying sessions. There are additional funds for certain international internships. For specific details of the amounts on offer, start by checking the Inns' websites and ask them if they publish any other related material.

The Inns can be a great source of general help and advice to a prospective barrister. If you want to go and visit them just ring to arrange a tour. All have mentoring schemes that will match student members with a practitioner in their chosen field, and they also run marshalling schemes so students can spend a week sitting alongside a judge, observing court proceedings and discussing the case at the end of the day. For pupils there are advocacy workshops and seminars at Cumberland Lodge in the heart of Great Windsor Park. All four Inns offer mooting, whether it be at internal, inter-Inn or national competition level, and the Inns' various students' associations all have active social calendars.

middle temple
www.middletemple.org.uk

As former member Charles Dickens put it, the Middle Temple has "something of a clerkly monkish atmosphere which public offices of law have not disturbed and even legal firms have failed to scare away." All applicants are interviewed and we heard "the scholarship policy is good; the money goes where it's needed." Debating is a particular forte and the 'Christmas Revels' are notorious. Students recommend lecture nights for "copious amounts of food and wine and excellent guest speakers."

gray's inn
www.graysinn.org.uk

Here, at the smallest and most traditional Inn, toasting is the order of the day during dinners, particularly on Grand Day when a communal chalice of wine is passed down the table in "pious memory of Good Queen Bess." Students enjoy the communial atmosphere: "You get to know other students and Benchers really quickly and there are always familiar faces at dinner." Gray's Inn library is described as "quite plain, but good, with the most helpful librarians of the four Inns."

the chancery bar

You'll see from the diagram on page 163 that the High Court has three divisions: Family, Queen's Bench (QBD) and Chancery. Cases are allocated to and heard by the most appropriate division based on their subject matter, but what makes a case suitable for the Chancery Division? Historically it has been the venue for cases with an emphasis on legal principles, foremost among them the concept of equity. Put another way, Chancery work epitomises legal reasoning.

Cases are often categorised as either 'traditional' (trusts, probate, real property, charities and mortgages) or 'commercial' (company law, shareholder cases, partnership, banking, pensions, financial services, insolvency, professional negligence, tax, media and IP). Most Chancery sets will undertake both types of work, albeit with varying emphases.

To muddy the waters, however, the distinction between Chancery practice and commercial practice (historically the latter is dealt with in the QBD) is less apparent than it once was. Barristers at commercial sets can frequently be found on Chancery cases and vice versa, though some areas, such as tax and IP, beg specialisation.

the realities of the job

- This is an area for those who love the law and love to grapple with its most complex aspects. It's all about the application of long-standing legal principles to modern-day situations.
- Boffins beware: you need to be a master of communication and very practical in the legal solutions you offer to clients. Solicitors will come to you with complex and puzzling cases. After unravelling them you must explain legal arguments and principles in such a way that the solicitor and lay client both understand. At the same time, you also need to be able to present your argument to a judge in a persuasive and sophisticated manner.
- While advocacy will be a core element of your work, you will spend most of your time in chambers, perusing papers, considering arguments, drafting pleadings, skeletons and advices, or conducting settlement negotiations.
- Some instructions fly into chambers, need immediate attention and then disappear just as quickly. Others can rumble on for years – although not quite as long as Dickens' Jarndyce v Jarndyce.
- There's plenty of variety in Chancery practice. The traditional side appeals to those more inclined towards human interest – little old lady who signed her house over to the window cleaner, the bonkers billionaire who disinherited his children, or the errant tenants who haven't paid rent for years. Commercial Chancery practitioners get to deal with the blood-on-the-boardroom-table disputes, the Equitable Lifes and the bust-ups between co-writers of million-selling songs.
- Your schedule won't be set by last-minute briefs for next-day court appearances. Instead, you'll need self-discipline and an instinctive sense of exactly how much time and energy you need to devote to each of the instructions on your desk.
- As in any area of practice, at first you'll be instructed on low-value cases – straightforward possession proceedings in the county court, winding-up applications in the Companies Court, appearances before the bankruptcy registrars. In the more prominent sets, you'll be brought in as second or third junior on larger, more complex cases.

some tips

- An excellent academic record is essential. Most pupils in leading sets have a First-class degree, although a surprising number are non-law grads. Whatever you study at university, you should enjoy the analytical process involved in constructing arguments and evaluating the answers to problems. If you're not a natural essay writer, you're unlikely to be a natural-born Chancery practitioner.

- Don't wander into this area by accident. Are you actually interested in equity, trusts, company law, insolvency, IP or tax? If the grit and excitement of crime sounds more appealing then follow your instincts.
- Show an aptitude for public speaking. If you're studying law, get involved in mooting.
- Complete at least a couple of mini-pupillages with – or including – Chancery sets.
- Though not necessarily an accurate portrayal of modern practice, Dickens' novel Bleak House is the ultimate Chancery saga. Give it a whirl, or rent the DVD.

current issues

- The scope of the Chancery Division means that practitioners get involved in the most enormous commercial and public law matters. Chancery barristers were all over the BCCI cases in 2005, as well as Equitable Life and Spectrum. Another Chancery victory was the shaming of Stephen Byers in the Railtrack litigation (Weir & Ors v Secretary of State for Transport/Department of Transport). The Apple v Apple row involved The Beatles' former record company Apple Corps taking the US computer giant to task in relation to trade mark rights in the name Apple. After a high court judgment for the computer company, the two parties settled their differences.
- The amount of international work carried out in the Chancery Division shows no signs of falling off. Russian and Eastern European business affairs are taking up a sizeable amount of court time in the commercial arena, and massive off-shore business and private client trusts in the Cayman Islands, the British Virgin Islands, Bermuda and the Channel Islands means that more barristers than ever are clipping through airport terminals. But no one knows what they're up to and they can't say: multimillion-pound advisory work is as ever kept very quiet.
- The Chancery Bar seems immune to the shrinking work and tumbling brief fees found elsewhere in practice. At this, the Rolls-Royce end of the Bar, practitioners continue to attract not only plenty of high-value, complex domestic cases, but also an increasing number of offshore and cross-border instructions.

the commercial bar

The Commercial Bar handles a variety of business disputes. In its purest definition, a commercial case is heard by the Commercial Court or one of the county court business courts. A broader and more realistic definition includes matters dealt with by both the Queen's Bench and Chancery Divisions of the High Court, and the Technology and Construction Court (TCC). The Commercial Bar deals with disputes in all manner of industries from construction, shipping and insurance to banking, entertainment and manufacturing.

Almost all disputes are contract and/or tort claims, and the Commercial Bar remains rooted in common law. That said, domestic and European legislation is increasingly important and commercial barristers' incomes now reflect the popularity of the English courts with overseas litigants. Cross-border issues including competition law, international public and trade law and conflicts of law are all growing in prominence.

Alternative methods of dispute resolution – usually arbitration or mediation – are also popular because there is some prospect of preserving commercial relationships that would otherwise be destroyed by the litigation process.

the realities of the job

- The barrister's job is to steer the solicitor and lay client through the litigation process, selecting the most appropriate manoeuvres to put them in a better position with their opponent. Clients position themselves through witness statements, pleadings and pre-trial 'interlocutory' skirmishes. The role blends advice and paper advocacy with courtroom advocacy, and much of the barrister's time is spent in chambers, assessing the likelihood of winning, and then probably doing a deal.

- Advocacy is certainly at the centre of the job. Even so, most of it is paper-based, which means that written skills are just as important as oral skills, possibly more so. The good barrister will spot the argument that most others won't see and identify the one that is most likely to be persuasive.

- To build confidence and allow you to get used to the sound of your own voice in court, you will handle your own small cases as a new junior barrister. These will include common law matters such as personal injury, employment cases, possession proceedings and winding-up or bankruptcy applications.

- New juniors become exposed to larger commercial cases by assisting more-senior colleagues. As a 'second junior' you will carry out research and prepare first drafts of documents to assist the 'first junior' and the QC leading the case. Just as importantly, you will observe them in action in court, learning how to cross-examine witnesses and how best to present arguments.

- In time, your own cases will increase in value and complexity: claims relating to shipping, insurance and reinsurance, commodities, banking, and general contractual matters are all standard fare. Most commercial barristers specialise by building up expertise on cases within a particular industry sector – eg shipping, insurance, entertainment or banking. It gives them the added value that solicitors look for when deciding who to instruct. This added value is usually a product of a barrister's commercial acumen. You have to develop this and be able to understand the client's business objectives. Clearly you should bear a set's specialities in mind when deciding where to accept pupillage.

- Bear in mind also that commercial cases can be very fact-heavy. The evidence for a winning argument can be buried in a room full of papers. The barrister will need to work closely with the instructing solicitor to manage the documentation.

- Are you willing to fully commit yourself to developing your practice? You'll have to work long hours, often under pressure. Furthermore, to survive, your service standards must be impeccable and your style user-friendly. A solicitor could send you something that's urgent or poorly organised, but you can't complain. Even if they ring you late in the day, you need to be obliging. Get into a good set, though, and you can make an exceedingly good living.

some tips

- Competition for pupillage at the commercial Bar is fierce. A first-class degree is commonplace, and you'll need impressive references.

- You also need to be able to show evidence of mooting and debating at university and/or law school.

- Complete at least a couple of mini-pupillages at commercial and common law sets.

- Don't underestimate the value of non-legal work experience; commercial exposure of any kind is going to help you understand the client's perspective and motivations.

current issues

- The trend for huge litigation with multiple interests was nowhere more evident than last year, with massive cases like the BCCI fallout, in which the liquidators of the bank brought a case against the Bank of England (as well as the Bank of India and others in separate cases), which was eventually dropped by Deloitte & Touche, BCCI's liquidators in November 2005, bringing an end to 14-year proceedings. Another massive case was the Equitable Life drama – a £2.6 billion negligence case against former auditor Ernst & Young – that was eventually settled. Spectrum Plus was a third monster: the House of Lords overturned a 2004 decision by the Court of Appeal to clarify the order in which creditors of insolvent companies are paid. Take a look at Taylor Thomson v Christie's (a dispute about £2 million fake Louis XV urns) and HSH Nordbank v Barclays Capital as well.
- In what is seen by some to be enduring faith in the uprightness of British law, a lot of Eastern European and Russian concerns are now brought before the courts here, coinciding with a decline in similar domestic litigation.
- Solicitor-advocates are on the march, although the increase in alternative dispute resolution (ADR) or in-house involvement means that smaller cases are unlikely to demand representation.
- Shrinking small-end work has impacted on the livelihood of junior barristers in common law sets; however the commercial Bar is faring well.

the common law bar

English common law derives from the precedents set by judicial decisions rather than from the contents of statutes. Most common law cases turn on principles of tort and contract and are dealt with in the Queen's Bench Division (QBD) of the High Court and the county courts. At the edges, common law practice blurs into both Chancery and commercial practice. Yet the work undertaken in common law sets is broader still, and one of the most appealing things about working at one of these sets is the variety of work available.

Employment and personal injury are bread and butter for juniors. They also deal with licensing matters, clinical negligence, landlord and tenant, winding-up and bankruptcy applications, and small commercial and contractual disputes. At some sets you'll even get inquests and criminal cases. Common law barristers tend to carry on practising on a full range of cases throughout their careers, but there is an opportunity to begin to specialise between five and ten years' call.

the realities of the job

- Will there be much advocacy? Yes, lots. On average you could expect to be in court three days per week. Even second-six pupils can have their own cases. Small beginnings such as 'noting briefs' (where you attend court simply in order to report back on the proceedings) and masters' and district judges' appointments lead to lower-value 'fast-track' personal injury trials then longer, higher-value, 'multi-track' trials and employment tribunals.
- In addition to minor instructions which they can run solo, newer barristers assist as a junior on more complex cases, conducting research, drafting documents and observing more-senior lawyers in court to learn how to present arguments and cross-examine.
- Interpersonal skills are important. A client

who has never been to court before will be very nervous, and it's your responsibility to put them at ease. This is especially important if they are a witness. They may be expecting someone older than you, but somehow you have to win their trust and confidence.

- In order to deal with the volume and variety of cases that will come your way you will need a good grasp of the law and the procedural rules of the court, and must be adept at assimilating the facts of each case.
- At the junior end, work comes in at short notice, so the night before going to court you may have to digest a file of documents. Planning ahead can be difficult; your friends may have to get used to you letting them down at short notice.
- But it's not all about advocacy. When you're not in court you'll be in chambers, researching, assessing the merits of cases and meeting with solicitors and lay clients. There will also be plenty of statements of claim, defences and opinions to draft.

some tips

- Though there are a lot of common law sets, pupillages and tenancies don't grow on trees. You'll have to impress to get a foot in the door and then make your mark to secure your next set of instructions.
- If you want to specialise, thoroughly research the sets you apply to.
- As ever, mini-pupillages are a good way to show your commitment, and you'll also want to show that you've taken part in mooting and debating.

current issues

- The trend for mediation and arbitration of disputes has reduced the number of cases going to court, and this has resulted in less small-end work for juniors. The position is

also exacerbated by a trend for solicitors to undertake more advocacy themselves, although while solicitor-advocates frequently take on directions hearings, they are still rarely seen at trial.

- Legal aid cutbacks and conditional fee agreements – especially for PI claims – have definitely affected remuneration. The government is also planning further changes to the public funding of legal services: read **Get Carter** on page 18.

the criminal bar

Horace Rumpole, Henry Farmer in The Brief, Kavanagh QC... most people know more about the criminal Bar than any other part of the legal profession. Are the lives of these courtroom heroes anything like reality? Arguably criminal barristers do need an appreciation for theatre and an innate sense of dramatic timing. But good oratory will only take you so far. A keen tactical sense, an agile understanding of the law and good-time management will also prove invaluable.

Barristers are instructed by solicitors to represent defendants in cases brought before the UK's criminal courts. Lesser offences are increasingly dealt with by solicitors in the magistrates' courts; more serious charges go to the Crown Courts, which are essentially still the domain of barristers. Most defendants prefer this.

The job includes everything from theft, fraud, drugs and driving offences to assaults of varying degrees of severity and murder. Second six pupils cut their teeth on motoring offences, committals and directions hearings in the magistrates' courts, and by the end of their pupillage should expect to be instructed in their own right and not infrequently make it into the Crown Court. Within two or three years junior tenants will probably have seen it all. Their trial work will start small – smaller offences such as common assault – and then move onto ABH, robbery and possession of drugs with intent to supply. Perform well and impress the instructing solicitor and this could lead to a role as a junior on a major Crown Court trial.

A summary of the expanding opportunities at the Crown Prosecution Service is given on page 20.

the realities of the job

- Pupils and juniors rely on the relationships that their seniors and managers have built with instructing solicitors. Although it is important to market yourself in the early years, be relatively subtle. Denigrate others or acquire a reputation as a 'diary watcher' and this will come back and bite you.
- Defendants can be tricky creatures and at times you'll need the patience of a saint. You have to listen to what they have to say, and give them a realistic assessment of their case and the likely ramifications of their stance; you certainly won't be thanked for your cheery optimism when they get sent down.
- A jury is a captive audience, and the impact of a closing speech can swing the result either way. If you can't learn how to give a charismatic performance your appeal to solicitors will be as limited as your income stream.
- Criminal barristers are connecting with and persuading people at all times, whether they are defendants, witnesses, victims, judges, members of a jury or even their own clerks in chambers. Interpersonal skills are hugely important in almost all aspects of the job, not just while advocating. It goes without saying that at times you'll meet some unpleasant or scary characters. Others will have pretty unfortunate lives, some will be addicted to alcohol or drugs, have poor home lives and little education.

- Even the most skilful advocate knows that success rests on effective case preparation, and never forgets that the law and sentencing policies evolve constantly.
- Stamina and adaptability are both vital. You'll have to manage several cases on any one day, some of them poorly prepared. If you're lucky they'll all be at the same court; otherwise you'll be haring between venues. You'll have to take additional cases without prior warning and cope with missing defendants and witnesses on a regular basis. Soon enough you'll believe you can cope with anything. Chances are you can.

some tips

- It goes without saying that both mini-pupillage experience and plenty of mooting and debating is required before you can look like a serious applicant.
- The criminal Bar tends to provide more pupillages than other areas, but these don't necessarily translate into tenancies because the market is so competitive. Third and fourth sixes are not uncommon at the criminal Bar these days so be prepared for this possibility.
- There are many ways of getting exposure to the criminal justice system and plenty of your contemporaries will be on the case. See page 31 for tips on useful voluntary activities.

current issues

- Thus far getting on 'the CPS list' has allowed barristers to prosecute as well as defend. Recent figures reveal the CPS' annual bill for external advocates prosecuting cases of between one and ten days in length is around £81 million. It has decided to bring all advocacy in-house, a move which will save an estimated £34 million by March 2008. Whereas CPS instructions gave young barristers useful trial experience on both sides of the fence, the new system will leave advocates firmly on one side or other. CPS defence jobs will provide financial certainty and job security for those who take them but the change will hit the pockets of juniors in private practice. As if all this weren't bad enough, legal aid cutbacks will make the life of junior tenants even more demanding than ever. The government is on the brink of overhauling the system of public funding for criminal cases, and we'd recommend you get up to speed on the likely changes. Our feature **Get Carter** on page 18 is a good place to start. The rise of solicitor-advocates has also impacted on the amount of work available. If you're willing to accept the likelihood of more limited financial rewards, the criminal Bar should still prove irresistible...

the employment bar

It's hardly surprising that employment lawyers are busy: the general public is more aware of employment rights than ever before and cases are widely reported in mainstream newspapers. You'll recall stories about Prince Harry's former art teacher at Eton and various banking executives in the City, some of whom have claimed millions of pounds in compensation for breach of contract, harassment or discrimination.

Accessibility is a key aim of the employment tribunal system. Legal representation is not required and only rarely will there be a costs penalty for the unsuccessful party. Such is the emphasis on user-friendliness that employment claims can even be issued online. Nonetheless, many cases are so complex, or worth so much money, that specialist legal representation is sought from solicitors and barristers.

Tribunals deal with claims relating to redundancy; unfair dismissal; discrimination on the grounds of gender, sexual orientation, race, reli-

gion or age; workplace harassment; contract claims and whistle-blowing. The people who make the claims are called 'applicants'; the employers who defend them are called 'respondents'. High-value claims and applications for injunctions to prevent the breach of restrictive covenants or use of trade secrets are usually dealt with in the county courts or the High Court.

the realities of the job

- Most advocacy takes place in employment tribunals or the Employment Appeals Tribunal, as opposed to the courts. The atmosphere and proceedings in each are deliberately less formal so, for example, hearings are conducted with everyone sitting down and barristers do not wear their wigs.
- Tribunals follow the basic pattern of examination in chief, cross-examination and closing submissions; however barristers have to modify their style, especially when appearing against someone who is unrepresented.
- A corporate respondent might consider a QC well worth the money, while the applicant's pocket may only stretch to a junior. But what a fantastic opportunity for a junior to advocate against a silk. The other type of opponent frequently encountered is the solicitor-advocate – this area of practice is full of them.
- Employment specialists tend to be good with people. Clients frequently become emotional or stressed, and it's part of the barrister's job to ensure that this doesn't prevent the satisfactory resolution of the case. If you think about it, employees can spend more time in the workplace with colleagues than with their families, and so there are an endless number of situations and conflicts that can arise.
- Few juniors limit themselves solely to employment practice; most also undertake civil or commercial cases, some criminal matters. Similarly, few juniors act only for applicants or

only for respondents. At senior level this changes because respondents can generally afford to pay the higher legal fees of seniors.

- UK Employment legislation mirrors EU law and changes with great rapidity, and you'll be forever having cases stayed while others with similar points are being heard on appeal. Keeping abreast of developments in the law is crucial because you won't always have much time to prepare for trial.

some tips

- Find out about how to get involved with the work of the Free Representation Unit (see page 34). It has much to offer students and pupils by way of exposure to employment law, and realistically no application for pupillage will look complete without some involvement of this kind.
- Mini-pupillages and mooting or public speaking are as important for budding employment barristers as any other kind.
- Practically any kind of temporary or part-time job will give you first-hand experience of being an employee. Not to be underestimated, especially when you consider that as a barrister you will be self-employed.

current issues

- High-value claims by employees in the banking sector continue to make headlines. Witness Helen Green's £800,000 award in her bullying case against Deutche Bank.
- The Bar continues to feel the impact of equal pay cases, which as they largely bypass City firms are tying up a large proportion of silks and juniors. Degnan and others v Redcar and Cleveland Borough Council went to the Court of Appeal and cases spread from the North East across the country. Barristers settled Wilson v North Cumbria Acute Hospitals NHS Trust, a case involving 1,500 women employed by Cumberland Infirmary and West Cumbria Hospital that lasted eight years. Each woman is likely to receive between £35,000 and £200,000, leaving the NHS with a massive bill.

- The Work and Families Bill covers new rights to maternity and paternity leave for parents, and the relationship between employer and parent during a period of childcare leave. The Bill includes a new right to request flexible working.
- Age discrimination cases are coming to the fore and various aspects of the law will be tested in the near future.

the family bar

A lot of marriages break down in the UK and divorce can be a messy business, especially when it involves children. According to the government's number-crunchers, 53% of the couples divorcing in 2004 had at least one child aged under 16, and together their divorces affected nearly 150,000 children, some 64% of them under the age of 11. The law can never fix the problems caused by marital breakdown and other family situations, but it is one of the few tools people have at their disposal. Consequently, a huge amount of court time is allotted to divorce, separation, adoption, child residence and contact orders, financial provision and domestic violence.

This is an emotionally charged and demanding practice area for a barrister, who is likely to be involved only in the most complex or combative cases. Juniors learn the ropes on simple county court matters, progressing to complex matters in the Family Division of the High Court. In the early years there will be a lot of private law children work (disputes between parents), small financial cases and injunctions in situations of domestic violence.

the realities of the job

Financial cases and public and private law children's work each offer their own unique challenges and intellectual demands.

- A certain degree of emotional resilience is required, but you also need a capacity for empathy as the work involves asking clients for intimate details of their private life and breaking devastating news to the emotionally fragile. Private law children's cases can sometimes involve serious allegations between parents and require the input of child psychologists. The public law counterpart (care proceedings between local authorities and parents) invariably includes detailed and often harrowing medical evidence.

- For most people, getting involved with the courts is just as much a once-in-a-lifetime experience as the divorce itself. They will rely on you to guide them through this unfamiliar terrain.

- The end result of a case will have a significant impact on the lives touched by it, so it is crucial to find the most appropriate course of action for each client. The best advocates are those who can differentiate between a case and client requiring a bullish approach and those crying out for settlement and concessions to be made. The job calls for communication, tact and maturity.

- Where possible, mediation is used to resolve disputes in a more efficient and less unsettling fashion. This requires a different approach to litigation.

- Teamwork is crucial. As the link between the client, the opposing barrister, the judge, solicitors and social workers, it is important that you win the trust and confidence of everyone.

- The legislation affecting this area is comprehensive, and there's a large body of case law. You must keep abreast of all new decisions because, while no two families are identical,

the basics remain the same in relation to the problems they experience. The job is, therefore, more about negotiating general principles than adhering strictly to precedents.

- Finance-oriented barristers need an understanding of pensions and shares and a good grounding in the basics of trusts and property.

some tips

- The family Bar is quite small and competition for pupillage is intense. Think about how you can evidence your interest in family law. Our **Pro Bono and Volunteering** section on page 33 should give you some tips.

- Younger pupils might find it daunting to advise on mortgages, marriages and children when they've never experienced any of these things personally. Arguably those embarking on a second career, or who have delayed a year or two and acquired other life experiences, may have an advantage.

- Check the work orientation of a set before applying for pupillage, particularly if you don't want to narrow your options too early.

- Mini-pupillages will give you that all-important taste of life as a family barrister.

current issues

- A few years ago barristers believed that mediation and an increase in solicitor-advocates threatened a downturn in work for juniors. Yet, with the exception of children's cases in which solicitors have always been encouraged to do their own advocacy, the volume of instructions appear to have continued largely unabated… as has the incidence of divorce in the UK.

- London is becoming the divorce capital of Europe. In such cases the wealth and assets involved far outstrip the reasonable needs of the parties, and lawyers are looking for precedents. The House of Lords recently obliged with decisions in two hot cases – Miller, where the issue is how to deal with a short marriage, and McFarlane, where the wife had given up a career to raise a family. Neither could have foretold the size of the £48 million payout ordered in August 2006 to the ex-wife of insurance magnate John Charman. The court of Appeal upheld the decision in 2007.

- Lawyers are interested to see how the courts will handle the division of assets following the breakdown of a civil partnership.
- The government's latest review of public funding for legal services will affect family cases and presumably the pockets of family barristers. Read **Get Carter** on page 18 for more information.

public law and the bar

Public bodies must operate within statutory constraints and their decisions may be challenged on procedural grounds. Perhaps they haven't considered the relevant facts in reaching a decision; perhaps the body or officer didn't have the authority to make the decision at all; perhaps they won't reveal how and why they made a decision; perhaps it is deemed to undermine a person's rights, as embodied in the European Convention on Human Rights.

Centred on the Administrative Court, public law cases range from pro bono or legal aid matters for individuals to commercial judicial review for magic circle firms and government instructions. In particular, a barrister with a local authority clientele will have a very wide range of work, much of it relating to planning, housing or environmental matters, education, health and children. Cases concerning community care issues and the provision of social services by local authorities are especially hot at the moment, and judicial reviews of immigration decisions still make up a significant chunk of the Administrative Court's case list. At the other end of the spectrum sit some high-profile and contentious matters, such as the case of Ann Marie Rogers who went to court after she was denied the breast cancer drug Herceptin by Swindon NHS. In Ms Rogers' case the judge ruled that the trust had not been acting unlawfully when it denied her the treatment, but she was given leave to appeal against the decision. Similarly the Administrative Court was recently asked to consider the case of baby 'MB' when his parents and doctors failed to agree on whether he should be kept alive.

Where an event is deemed to be of great public importance, inquiries are commissioned by the government and then operate independently. The Bloody Sunday Inquiry, the Victoria Climbie Inquiry and the Hutton Inquiry into the death of Dr David Kelly illustrate well the different types of issue that come under scrutiny. Another type of inquiry is the planning inquiry, which usually arises because of a conflict between the interests of a local community and the proposed developer – the much-publicised Terminal 5 Inquiry into the extension of Heathrow Airport is a good example. In all these inquiries, barristers will speak on behalf of the many interested parties.

Most public law barristers also work in other areas: some are crime specialists; others have commercial caseloads. For example, criminal barristers will often handle issues relating to prisoners or breaches of procedure by police, and commercial barristers might handle judicial reviews of DTI decisions. In reality, even those who do not profess a specialism in public law may also undertake judicial review work.

the realities of the job

- The barrister will only spend a part of their time in court, with the rest spent in chambers drafting skeleton arguments and opinions. If representing public bodies, they will need to advise on the implications of their decisions and whether their structures comply with public law principles.

- Junior barristers do get to hone their advocacy skills early on. The preliminary 'permissions' stage of judicial review proceedings provides excellent opportunities in the form of short 30-minute hearings. However, in this area of law there are usually just the barristers and the judge: no jury, no witnesses or cross-examinations.
- The Administrative Court is one of the most inundated branches of the High Court, so you'll need to develop an efficient style of advocacy. Long and dramatic performances are rarely well received; you must learn how to cut to the chase and deliver the pertinent information, draw on the relevant case law or statutory regulations and present your arguments promptly.
- You'll need a genuine interest in the fundamental laws by which we live and the legislative process. If administrative and constitutional law subjects were not your favourites you might want to rethink your decision.
- Public law is a discursive area of practice where you are more likely to find interesting arguments than you are a precise answer.
- Providing real remedies for real people demands a practicality, common sense and a willingness to stand back and look at the broader implications of what you are saying. Individual applicants and public bodies both have an equally valid interest in proper decision-making processes and you have to be able to see both sides of the coin.
- Barristers who work on planning inquiries may have to spend periods of time away from home.

some tips

- Sets usually go for people with excellent academic credentials, often those with masters' degrees. Certainly you'll need to show a keen intellect. Sets with local or central government clientele are also attracted to those with prior experience of the public sector, eg a role within local government or time spent as an MP's researcher.
- Get a few mini-pupillages under your belt, do as much mooting as possible and read quality newspapers to familiarise yourself with the public law issues raised in them.
- The Human Rights Act has undoubtedly affected public law, although it is still early days in relation to various areas, for example, the issue of privacy.
- Public international law appeals to many students but there are few openings at the pupillage stage. Traditionally, PIL has been the preserve of academics – the leading names are predominantly sitting or ex-professors at top universities and Foreign Office veterans, with the occasional pure but very experienced barrister thrown in. Governments want tried-and-tested counsel and will expect those they instruct to be recognised, published authors. This is not an area of work you'll fall into by accident, nor is it one you're likely to get into until much more experienced. If the academic route is not for you, good luck in your search for pupillage at a leading public law set.
- Interesting opportunities are available within the Government Legal Service. See pages 400 and 938.

current issues

- The number of people looking for pupillage in the field far exceeds the number of available positions, so you must evidence your commitment. A CV referencing voluntary work at a law centre or specialist voluntary organisation (eg the Howard League for Penal Reform), or membership of Liberty or Justice will help, as will a healthy interest in current affairs and the latest cases in the news.

- In immigration law there have been many modifications of late, among them changes affecting people applying for leave to remain or settle in the UK. Another example is the rule that migrant applications now need to be submitted to and dealt with at diplomatic posts overseas. This is causing concern amongst lawyers who feel that a move away from a centralised system will lead to loss of efficiency and poorer supervision. There is also much criticism of the abolition of various appeal rights and the substitution of an administrative review procedure.

- It looks as if there is more change to come. In March 2006 the Home Office published a paper on proposals for the UK immigration system called 'Controlling our Borders: Making Migration Work for Britain – Five Year Strategy for Asylum and Immigration'.

- The Government's latest review of public funding for legal services will affect public law cases and, as a result, the livelihoods of barristers acting for legally aided clients. See **Get Carter** on page 18.

- Anti-terror laws have been a hot topic. In the past year the House of Lords has ruled against the Government in cases examining the legality of the detention of foreign nationals without trial and the admissibility in UK courts of evidence obtained by torture.

- In 2005 the Court of Appeal looked at whether the Human Rights Act applies to British forces in post-war Iraq, and whether it was violated.

- Clinical advances have also led to important decisions: in the so-called 'designer-baby case' the House of Lords allowed a couple to have fertility treatment to select an embryo whose umbilical cord could be used to save the life of an existing child.

shipping, international trade and the bar

Essentially, shipping and international trade concerns the carriage of goods or people by sea, air and land, plus all aspects of the financing, construction, use, insurance and decommissioning of the vessels, planes, trains and other vehicles that carry them. A large proportion of the world's trade goods are transported by sea, and consequently a large number of the cases dealt with by barristers concern ships – what happens when they are arrested, sunk or salvaged, and what happens when there is a problem concerning the condition or ownership of their cargo.

Shipping and trade cases mostly turn on contract and tort; indeed English case law is awash with examples from the world of shipping – everything from rotten grain cargos to a criminal case about some sailors who ate a cabin boy. Shipping cases can be complicated because of the number of parties involved or the nature of the events leading to the dispute. Imagine a Greek-owned, Pakistani-crewed, Russian-captained ship, last serviced in Singapore, carrying forestry products from Indonesia to Denmark. It might be insured in London and chartered by a French company. There might be a collision with a Liberian-registered vessel somewhere off the west coast of Africa; the salvors who deal with the stricken vessels could be Dutch. Luckily for the Bar, the English courts are very often the preferred forum for the resolution of such complex matters. Indeed, London has a very prominent position in the world of shipping and international trade, not least because of the involvement of its insurance market.

You'll encounter the terms 'wet' and 'dry' shipping. These refer to the location of the dispute, so for example: wet cases include difficulties at sea; dry cases relate to disputes in port or concerns over the manufacture and financing of vessels.

The Bar also has a number of aviation specialists and those with experience dealing with road haulage and other modes of transportation. The sets that dominate all these areas will also be able to offer experts in the realm of commodities trading. Trade disputes are often resolved through arbitration conducted in various parts of the world, Paris and London being among the most important.

the realities of the job

- Cases are fact-heavy and paper-heavy. To develop the best arguments for a case you need an organised mind and a willingness to immerse yourself in the documentary evidence. This can be time-consuming and exhausting.
- There are opportunities for international travel.
- Cases can run on for years and involve large teams of lawyers, both solicitors and barristers. The young barrister will work their way up from second or third junior to leader over a number of years.
- New juniors do get to run their own smaller cases, eg charter party and bills of lading disputes.
- It's inevitable that at first the world of shipping and trade will seem very alien. Before long you'll pick up the language and customs.
- Your solicitor clients will usually work at one of the established shipping firms. Your lay clients, however, are going to be a real mixed bag of financiers, ship owners, operators, traders and charterers, P&I clubs, salvors and underwriters.

some tips

- The leading sets are easy to identify. A mini-pupillage with one or more of them will greatly enhance your understanding of the work involved.
- Despite the prominence of English law, the work calls for an international perspective and an appreciation of international laws. This can be developed within a first or masters' degree and on the BVC.
- Advocacy, both written and oral, is at the heart of the work. Show recruiters your flair for it by getting involved in mooting.
- What the heck is commodities trading? Step one: watch the Eddie Murphy/Dan Aykroyd movie *Trading Places*.

current issues

- There is a general downturn in cargo claims due to the increased safety of ships and the success of various conventions such as the International Safety Management Code.
- An upturn in the commodities market and the international sale of goods – not least because of economic growth in China – has caused freight and hire rates to spike.
- P&I clubs in particular continue to be increasingly watchful of costs. This has sparked the recent development of instructing barristers directly, cutting out the solicitor middleman.
- Clients are further trying to save money by embracing mediation.

chambers UK bar practice areas tables 2008

Administrative & Public Law
London
Band 1
Blackstone Chambers *London*

Band 2
11KBW *London*
39 Essex Street *London*
Brick Court Chambers *London*
Doughty Street Chambers *London*
Landmark Chambers *London*
Matrix Chambers *London*

Band 3
1 Crown Office Row *London*
1 Temple Gardens *London*
3 Hare Court *London*
4-5 Gray's Inn Square *London*
Garden Court Chambers *London*

Banking & Finance
London
Band 1
3 Verulam Buildings *London*
Fountain Court Chambers *London*

Band 2
Brick Court Chambers *London*
One Essex Court *London*

Band 3
3-4 South Square *London*
Essex Court Chambers *London*

Band 4
20 Essex Street *London*
Serle Court *London*

Banking & Finance
Western
Band 1
Guildhall Chambers *Bristol*

Chancery: Commercial
London
Band 1
Maitland Chambers *London*

Band 2
4 Stone Buildings *London*
Serle Court *London*

Band 3
3-4 South Square *London*
Wilberforce Chambers *London*

Band 4
3 Stone Buildings *London*
Enterprise Chambers *London*
New Square Chambers *London*
XXIV Old Buildings *London*

Chancery: Traditional
London
Band 1
Wilberforce Chambers *London*

Band 2
5 Stone Buildings *London*
Maitland Chambers *London*
Radcliffe Chambers *London*

Band 3
New Square Chambers *London*
Serle Court *London*
Ten Old Square *London*
XXIV Old Buildings *London*

Band 4
9 Stone Buildings *London*

Civil Liberties
London
Band 1
Blackstone Chambers *London*
Doughty Street Chambers *London*
Matrix Chambers *London*

Band 2
11KBW *London*
39 Essex Street *London*
Brick Court Chambers *London*
Garden Court Chambers *London*

Band 3
1 Crown Office Row *London*
Landmark Chambers *London*
Tooks Chambers *London*

Civil Liberties
Northern
Band 1
Garden Court North *Manchester*

Clinical Negligence
London
Band 1
1 Crown Office Row *London*
3 Serjeants' Inn *London*

Band 2
Doughty Street Chambers *London*
Hailsham Chambers *London*
Outer Temple Chambers *London*

Band 3
1 Chancery Lane *London*
2 Temple Gardens *London*
Cloisters *London*
Crown Office Chambers *London*
Seven Bedford Row *London*

Band 4
39 Essex Street *London*
42 Bedford Row *London*

practice areas at the bar (continued)

Commercial Dispute Resolution
London
Band 1
Brick Court Chambers *London*
Essex Court Chambers *London*
Fountain Court Chambers *London*
One Essex Court *London*

Band 2
20 Essex Street *London*
3 Verulam Buildings *London*
Blackstone Chambers *London*

Band 3
7 King's Bench Walk *London*
Serle Court *London*

Band 4
Erskine Chambers *London*
Maitland Chambers *London*
XXIV Old Buildings *London*

Commercial Dispute Resolution
Northern
Band 1
Exchange Chambers *Liverpool*
Kings Chambers *Manchester*

Commercial Dispute Resolution
North Eastern
Band 1
Enterprise Chambers *Leeds*
Kings Chambers *Leeds*

Band 2
Chancery House Chambers *Leeds*

Competition/European Law
London
Band 1
Brick Court Chambers *London*
Monckton Chambers *London*

Band 2
11KBW *London*
20 Essex Street *London*
Blackstone Chambers *London*
Matrix Chambers *London*

Construction
London
Band 1
Atkin Chambers *London*
Keating Chambers *London*

Band 2
4 Pump Court *London*

Band 3
39 Essex Street *London*
Crown Office Chambers *London*
Four New Square *London*

Company
London
Band 1
Erskine Chambers *London*

Band 2
4 Stone Buildings *London*

Band 3
3-4 South Square *London*
Maitland Chambers *London*
Serle Court *London*

Band 4
Enterprise Chambers *London*
New Square Chambers *London*
One Essex Court *London*
XXIV Old Buildings *London*

Crime
London
Band 1
2 Bedford Row *London*
3 Raymond Buildings *London*
6 King's Bench Walk *London*
Cloth Fair Chambers *London*
QEB Hollis Whiteman *London*

Band 2
2 Hare Court *London*
Doughty Street Chambers *London*

Band 3
18 Red Lion Court *London*
25 Bedford Row *London*
9-12 Bell Yard *London*
Carmelite Chambers *London*
Garden Court Chambers *London*
Matrix Chambers *London*
Seven Bedford Row *London*

Band 4
187 Fleet Street *London*
23 Essex Street *London*
5 Paper Buildings *London*
9 Bedford Row *London*
Atkinson Bevan Chambers, 2 Harcourt Buildings *London*
Charter Chambers *London*
Furnival Chambers *London*

Band 5
15 New Bridge Street *London*
2 Dyers Buildings *London*
Nine Lincoln's Inn Fields *London*
Tooks Chambers *London*

Employment
London
Band 1
11KBW *London*
Blackstone Chambers *London*
Littleton Chambers *London*

Band 2
Cloisters *London*
Devereux Chambers *London*
Matrix Chambers *London*
Old Square Chambers *London*

Band 3
12 King's Bench Walk *London*
Essex Court Chambers *London*
Outer Temple Chambers *London*

Employment
Western
Band 1
Old Square Chambers *Bristol*
Queen Square Chambers *Bristol*

Band 2
Albion Chambers *Bristol*

Employment
Midlands
Band 1
No5 Chambers *Birmingham*
St Philips Chambers *Birmingham*

Employment
Northern
Band 1
9 St John Street *Manchester*

Band 2
Atlantic Chambers (formerly 14 Castle St) *Liverpool*

Band 3
8 King Street *Manchester*
St Johns Buildings *Manchester*

Environment
London
Band 1
39 Essex Street *London*
Francis Taylor Building *London*
Old Square Chambers *London*

Band 2
4-5 Gray's Inn Square *London*
Landmark Chambers *London*
Matrix Chambers *London*

Band 3
1 Crown Office Row *London*
6 Pump Court *London*
Blackstone Chambers *London*
Brick Court Chambers *London*

Environment
Midlands
Band 1
No5 Chambers *Birmingham*

Environment
Northern
Band 1
Kings Chambers *Manchester*

Family/Matrimonial
London
Band 1
1 Hare Court *London*
1 King's Bench Walk *London*
Queen Elizabeth Building (QEB) *London*

Band 2
1 Garden Court Family Law *London*
29 Bedford Row Chambers *London*
4 Paper Buildings *London*

Band 3
1 Crown Office Row *London*
14 Gray's Inn Square *London*
42 Bedford Row *London*
Coram Chambers *London*
Renaissance Chambers *London*

Fraud: Criminal
London
Band 1
2 Bedford Row *London*
3 Raymond Buildings *London*
Cloth Fair Chambers *London*
QEB Hollis Whiteman *London*

Band 2
18 Red Lion Court *London*
9-12 Bell Yard *London*
Seven Bedford Row *London*

Band 3
23 Essex Street *London*
6 King's Bench Walk *London*
Furnival Chambers *London*

Band 4
187 Fleet Street *London*
2 Hare Court *London*
25 Bedford Row *London*
5 Paper Buildings *London*

Band 4
Carmelite Chambers *London*

Band 4
Charter Chambers *London*
Doughty Street Chambers *London*
Matrix Chambers *London*

Fraud: Civil
London
Band 1
3 Verulam Buildings *London*
Fountain Court Chambers *London*
One Essex Court *London*
Serle Court *London*

Band 2
4 Stone Buildings *London*
Blackstone Chambers *London*
Brick Court Chambers *London*
Essex Court Chambers *London*

Band 3
11 Stone Buildings *London*
Maitland Chambers *London*
New Square Chambers *London*

practice areas at the bar (continued)

Immigration
London
Band 1
Garden Court Chambers *London*

Band 2
Doughty Street Chambers *London*
Matrix Chambers *London*
Tooks Chambers *London*

Band 3
1 Pump Court *London*
39 Essex Street *London*
6 King's Bench Walk *London*
Blackstone Chambers *London*
Mitre House Chambers *London*
Renaissance Chambers *London*

Immigration
Midlands
Band 1
Number 8 Chambers *Birmingham*

Immigration
Northern
Band 1
Garden Court North *Manchester*

Information Technology
London
Band 1
11 South Square *London*
4 Pump Court *London*
8 New Square *London*

Band 2
3 Verulam Buildings *London*
Atkin Chambers *London*
Henderson Chambers *London*
Hogarth Chambers *London*
Three New Square *London*

Insolvency/Corporate Recovery
London
Band 1
3-4 South Square *London*

Band 2
11 Stone Buildings *London*
4 Stone Buildings *London*
Erskine Chambers *London*
Maitland Chambers *London*

Band 3
Enterprise Chambers *London*
Serle Court *London*
XXIV Old Buildings *London*

Insurance
London
Band 1
7 King's Bench Walk *London*
Brick Court Chambers *London*

Band 2
Essex Court Chambers *London*
Fountain Court Chambers *London*

Band 3
20 Essex Street *London*
3 Verulam Buildings *London*
4 Pump Court *London*
Devereux Chambers *London*

Band 4
3 Stone Buildings *London*
Blackstone Chambers *London*
One Essex Court *London*

Intellectual Property
London
Band 1
11 South Square *London*
8 New Square *London*
Three New Square *London*

Band 2
Hogarth Chambers *London*

Band 3
One Essex Court *London*
Wilberforce Chambers *London*

International Arbitration: General
Commercial & Insurance
London
Band 1
Essex Court Chambers *London*

Band 2
20 Essex Street *London*

Band 3
7 King's Bench Walk *London*
One Essex Court *London*

Band 4
Brick Court Chambers *London*
Fountain Court Chambers *London*
Quadrant Chambers *London*

International Arbitration: Construction/Engineering
London
Band 1
Atkin Chambers *London*
Keating Chambers *London*

Media & Entertainment
London
Band 1
Blackstone Chambers *London*

Band 2
8 New Square *London*

Band 3
11 South Square *London*
5RB *London*
Essex Court Chambers *London*
Hogarth Chambers *London*

Personal Injury
London
Band 1
12 King's Bench Walk *London*
39 Essex Street *London*

Band 2
9 Gough Square *London*
Crown Office Chambers *London*
Farrar's Building *London*
Outer Temple Chambers *London*

Band 3
1 Temple Gardens *London*
2 Temple Gardens *London*
Devereux Chambers *London*
Old Square Chambers *London*

Band 4
1 Chancery Lane *London*
1 Crown Office Row *London*
Doughty Street Chambers *London*

Personal Injury
Western
Band 1
Guildhall Chambers *Bristol*
Old Square Chambers *Bristol*
St John's Chambers *Bristol*

Personal Injury
Wales & Chester
Band 1
30 Park Place *Cardiff*
33 Park Place *Cardiff*
9 Park Place *Cardiff*

Personal Injury
Midlands
Band 1
No5 Chambers *Birmingham*
Ropewalk Chambers *Nottingham*

Personal Injury
Northern
Band 1
9 St John Street *Manchester*
Byrom Street Chambers *Manchester*
Deans Court Chambers *Manchester*

Band 2
18 St John Street *Manchester*
Exchange Chambers *Liverpool*
St Johns Buildings *Manchester*

Personal Injury
North Eastern
Band 1
Park Lane Plowden *Leeds*

Planning
London
Band 1
Landmark Chambers *London*

Band 2
Francis Taylor Building *London*

Band 3
2-3 Gray's Inn Square *London*
4-5 Gray's Inn Square *London*

Band 4
39 Essex Street *London*
6 Pump Court *London*

Planning
Midlands
Band 1
No5 Chambers *Birmingham*

Planning
Northern
Band 1
Kings Chambers *Manchester*

Police Law: Mainly Defendant
All Circuits
Band 1
5 Essex Court *London*

Band 2
3 Serjeants' Inn *London*

Band 3
1 Chancery Lane *London*
9 Gough Square *London*
Ely Place Chambers *London*

Police Law: Mainly Claimant
All Circuits
Band 1
Doughty Street Chambers *London*

Band 2
Garden Court Chambers *London*

Band 3
Matrix Chambers *London*
Tooks Chambers *London*

practice areas at the bar (continued)

Real Estate Litigation	Shipping & Commodities	Tax: Private Client
London	**London**	**London**

Real Estate Litigation

London

Band 1
Falcon Chambers *London*

Band 2
Maitland Chambers *London*

Band 3
Landmark Chambers *London*
Wilberforce Chambers *London*

Band 4
Enterprise Chambers *London*
Henderson Chambers *London*
Selborne Chambers *London*
Serle Court *London*
Tanfield Chambers *London*

Band 5
New Square Chambers *London*
Radcliffe Chambers *London*

Shipping & Commodities

London

Band 1
20 Essex Street *London*
7 King's Bench Walk *London*
Quadrant Chambers *London*

Band 2
Essex Court Chambers *London*
Stone Chambers *London*

Tax

London

Band 1
Gray's Inn Tax Chambers *London*
Pump Court Tax Chambers *London*

Band 2
11 New Square *London*

Band 3
One Essex Court *London*
Tax Chambers 15 Old Square *London*
Temple Tax Chambers *London*

Tax: Private Client

London

Band 1
5 Stone Buildings *London*
Gray's Inn Tax Chambers *London*
Pump Court Tax Chambers *London*

Tax: Indirect Tax

London

Band 1
Gray's Inn Tax Chambers *London*
Monckton Chambers *London*
Pump Court Tax Chambers *London*

Band 2
Essex Court Chambers *London*
Tax Chambers 15 Old Square *London*

chambers reports

Making an informed choice about where to apply for pupillage is no easy task. Getting as far as working out the practice area in which you want to specialise is just the start; you then need to select your dozen OLPAS sets and consider how many other non-OLPAS choices to make. How do you know where you'll fit in and whether a set will be interested in you?

Chambers' websites are by and large pretty good at delivering pertinent information concerning size, nature of work, location, etc, but Internet surfing will only take you so far. The best course of action is to go and see inside a set for yourself on a mini-pupillage. There's still that same problem – which do you approach? Because it is impossible to do minis at every set that takes your fancy, the Student Guide has done some of the hard work for you. Since the summer of 2003 we have been calling in on an ever-increasing number of chambers, taking time to speak with pupils, juniors, QCs, clerks and chief execs.

The task is a big one so we took the decision to visit around half the sets each year. This year's roll call of 56 sets includes 25 new features – 29 features from our 2007 edition and two from our 2006 edition. Each year our collection of reports grows larger.

We have tried to visit as many different types of set as possible to give a good flavour for the range of potential areas of practice out there. Our tour took us from the grandeur of the Chancery Bar to the more modest surroundings of sets conducting mainly publicly funded work. There should be something to suit all tastes, be they commercial, common law, criminal, family, IP, tax, regional or otherwise. Given that most sets (and pupillages) are based in London, the majority of those covered are in the capital, but last year we went up to Manchester to see three sets and called in on the two giant-sized chambers in Birmingham. We have also reprinted our 2006 edition feature on Exchange Chambers in Liverpool and added a new feature on Bristol set St John's Chambers.

The wild card in the pack is the Government Legal Service which, although not a set operating out of chambers, still offers what we regard as a cracking pupillage.

What we have deliberately avoided is poor-quality sets. We make no excuses for our decision to choose only top sets. Bear in mind, however, that our selected sets are not the only ones in the Premier League in each practice area. Given the time we would visit many others.

Whichever chambers you do choose, be reassured that the prime aim of recruiters is to find talented applicants and then to persuade them to accept an offer. They do not expect ready-formed barristers to turn up at their door for interview, and gladly make allowances for candidates' lack of knowledge or experience on specific subjects. Much has been said and written about how awful pupillage interviews can be, and how pupillage itself amounts to little more than a year of pain and humiliation. From what we can tell this is not the norm. Sure, interviews can be challenging, but they are for the most part designed to get the best out of candidates. As for pupillage, it is in the best interests of any set that it should provide a useful and rewarding experience for pupils.

The itinerary for our visits included conversations with members of the pupillage committee, pupilmasters or supervisors, the senior clerk, junior tenants and, most crucially, current pupils. The aim was not merely to get the low-down on pupillage at each set but also to learn something about each chambers' life and to pick up tips for applicants. To this end we drank endless cups of tea, munched our way through five kilos of biscuits and took numerous guided tours, checking out artwork and libraries along the way. If we've communicated the qualities that make each set unique then we've done our job and it's over to you to make your choices.

Top Tips For Internet Research

- Check the pupillage page on a set's site to look for: info on mini-pupillages and how to apply for them; how to apply for a pupillage; application forms for non-OLPAS sets; confirmation of the OLPAS season in which a set participates; numbers of places; funding details; the structure of pupillage; the set's policy document on pupillage and the selection of pupils.

- Look at the list of members and in particular the biographies of the set's cadre of junior tenants. This can reveal much about what appeals to chambers' recruiters, particularly in relation to academic and other achievements. You will also be able to see the areas in which baby juniors gain experience.

- Gongs and rankings! Various organisations give out awards, and Chambers and Partners is no exception. Ours are handed over at an annual Bar Awards ceremony in October. The sets' websites frequently publicise the findings and editorial comment of the annually published legal directories, not least our own – *Chambers UK*. The entire contents of our directory can be read online for free.

- Knowing which recent cases a set is most proud of will help you at interview.

- If you get wind of who will be on the interview panel do your homework on them before you submit yourself to a grilling from them.

- Take note of the identity of any clients that are mentioned on a set's website.

- The weekly mainstream legal press, *The Lawyer* and *Legal Week*, are both available online and, although coverage of the Bar is sparse in comparison to the solicitors firms, big stories will usually be covered and there will be the occasional interesting article about key barristers and sets.

- Keep an eye on the Bar Council's own website www.barcouncil.org.uk.and the magazine *Counsel*.

the chambers reports sets

No	set	Location	Head of Chambers	(QCs/Juniors)
1.	Atkin Chambers	London	Nicholas Dennys	14/20
2.	2 Bedford Row*	London	William Clegg	16/47
3.	Blackstone Chambers	London	Mill/Beazley	30/41
4.	Brick Court Chambers	London	Sumption/Hirst	26/41
5.	Cloisters	London	Robin Allen	4/42
6.	Crown Office Chambers	London	Antony Edwards-Stuart	14/71
7.	Devereux Chambers	London	Colin Edelman	9/34
8.	Doughty Street Chambers	London	Robertson/Thornton	17/73
9.	Erskine Chambers	London	John Cone	7/18
10.	Essex Court Chambers	London	Gordon Pollock	33/42
11.	One Essex Court	London	Anthony Grabiner	20/43
12.	20 Essex Street	London	Iain Milligan	16/30
13.	39 Essex Street*	London	Davies/Wilmot-Smith	23/54
14.	Falcon Chambers	London	Gaunt/Fetherstanhaugh	10/26
15.	Fountain Court	London	Michael Brindle	22/39
16.	Garden Court Chambers	London	Davies/Griffiths	15/91
17.	One Garden Court*	London	Ball/Cobb	7/45
18.	Government Legal Service*	London	n/a	n/a
19.	2-3 Gray's Inn Square*	London	Mark Lowe	9/43
20.	4-5 Gray's Inn Square*	London	Appleby/Straker	12/36
21.	1 Hare Court*	London	Philip Moor	8/28
22.	2 Hare Court*	London	David Waters	13/40
23.	Henderson Chambers*	London	Roger Henderson	7/32
24.	Hogarth Chambers**	London	Wilson/Wyand	4/22
25.	Keating Chambers*	London	John Marrin	17/32
26.	7 King's Bench Walk*	London	Gavin Kealey	16/27
27.	11 King's Bench Walk	London	Tabachnik/Goudie	13/38
28.	Landmark Chambers*	London	Christopher Katkowski	18/45

the chambers reports sets *continued*

No	set	Location	Head of Chambers	(QCs/Juniors)
29.	Maitland Chambers	London	Lyndon-Stanford/Aldous/Driscoll	15/49
30.	Matrix	London	n/a	16/42
31.	Monckton Chambers*	London	Paul Lasok	11/35
32.	Four New Square*	London	Roger Stewart	12/49
33.	Old Square Chambers*	London	John Hendy	11/53
34.	XXIV Old Buildings*	London	Steinfeld/Mann	6/27
35.	Outer Temple*	London	Philip Mott	14/51
36.	Pump Court Tax Chambers*	London	Andrew Thornhill	10/16
37.	4 Pump Court*	London	Friedman/Moger	14/36
38.	Quadrant Chambers*	London	Persey/Rainey	9/30
39.	QEB Hollis Whitman	London	Vivian Robinson	14/39
40.	Queen Elizabeth Building	London	Lucy Stone	2/29
41.	3 Raymond Buildings*	London	Clive Nicholls	15/32
42.	5RB*	London	Browne/Page	6/23
43.	3 Serjeants' Inn*	London	Francis/Grace	8/33
44.	Serle Court	London	Lord Neill of Bladen	13/37
45.	3/4 South Square	London	Michael Crystal	18/25
46.	4 Stone Buildings	London	George Bompass	6/21
47.	2 Temple Gardens*	London	Benjamin Browne	8/42
48.	3 Verulam Buildings	London	Symons/Jarvis	18/40
49.	Wilberforce Chambers	London	Jules Sher	18/29
50.	No5 Chambers*	Birmingham/London/Bristol	Gareth Evans	20/176
51.	St Philips Chambers*	Birmingham	William Davis	10/138
52.	Exchange Chambers**	Liverpool/Manchester	Turner/Braithwaite	13/85
53.	Deans Court Chambers*	Manchester/Preston	Mark Turner	10/65
54.	Kings Chambers*	Manchester/Leeds	Frances Patterson	8/64
55.	St Johns Buildings*	Manchester	Michael Redfern	10/106
56.	St John's Chambers	Bristol	Christopher Sharp	6/70

* 2006 visits. ** 2005 visits. All others visited in 2007

chambers reports

Atkin Chambers

Chambers UK rankings: Construction, energy & natural resources, information technology, international arbitration: construction/engineering, professional negligence: technology & construction

Situated between the Inns of Court School of Law and BPP and backing on to Gray's Inn Gardens, Atkin Chambers is a stalwart of the construction Bar. It's also home to a good proportion of the best practitioners in the field. But things weren't always so: *"Chambers grew out of an administrative law set. In 1959 Ian Duncan Wallis helped edit Hudson's* [a leading text on building contracts], *and he and his generation of members turned chambers into a well-known set for construction."* These days, all 34 members (an impressive 14 of them silks) take instructions from, or relating to, the construction or engineering sector. A few have other related specialisms, for example in the areas of IT and energy. Over the years Atkin barristers have played their part in many of the big clashes in the Technology and Construction court (TCC). As for the current legal shenanigans over Wembley Stadium, *"most people here have involvement in those cases... along with everyone else at the construction Bar."* When it comes to international practice, some members have deliberately edged into overseas cases, notably in Asia and the Middle East.

If you think direct experience of the construction industry or specialist academic knowledge is a prerequisite for an Atkin pupillage then you're much mistaken. Of the 33 full members of chambers, only two have scientific degrees and four others non-law degrees. Our sources revealed that it is Atkin's quality reputation and high earning potential that attracts pupils, rather than a burning passion for construction cases. As one pupil explained: *"On a day-long visit here they gave me a set of papers, and after speaking to people*

it became clear that the work is simply contract and tort in a construction context."

Atkin is definitely in the premier league of chambers, so unsurprisingly it receives many applications. Some 200 Olpas hopefuls are whittled down to 15 candidates for a single *"not unfriendly"* interview with a panel of six barristers. A legal question is posed ten minutes before interview and there's also a discussion on a topic with a moral or ethical angle (in recent years Naomi Campbell's privacy claim). The panel appreciates that *"no one has studied construction law,"* so what they want to see is a good grasp of the essentials of contract and tort that form the basis of practice. Successful applicants do not all have Firsts – although many will – but being *"articulate and sensible"* is a must.

In pupillage, two seats of three months are followed by a single six-month seat, and each of the three pupils sits with the same three pupilmasters. The latter *"take training very seriously,"* and we hear *"there's no intellectual let-up."* The first three months are spent shadowing the PM as they write opinions, draft pleadings and represent clients in trials and interlocutory applications, arbitrations, mediations and adjudications, all the while observing how they negotiate with other counsel and deal with questions of ethics. In the second three months there's more emphasis on pupils producing work, either for the PM or other members of chambers. A mixture of *"current work and papers from the previous year"* make for *"a good learning process."*

The subject matter is *"not all bricks and mortar, sewers and drains;"* the pupils we spoke to had experienced *"a worldwide Moreva injunction to freeze bond monies on a project in India,"* a claim *"concerning a flooding in a hotel at Heathrow"* and *"Tube safety questions,"* not to mention issues affecting *"rail networks and power stations..."* The technical aspects of claims should never be underestimated. Whether it's understanding the explanations of technical experts and *"using them to your advantage"* or talking to a PM and trawling the Internet to buttress a *"no-knowledge standpoint,"* pupils must be constantly prepared to display *"logical, reasoned analysis."* The scale of many cases makes for large teams of barristers, solicitors and technical experts/quantity surveyors working together and there will often be mind-boggling quantities of documentary evidence. With all this, there is some risk of pupils becoming *"document fags,"* and for those in the earlier part of their careers it means taking a junior or second junior role on large cases for some while. That said, *"the clerks ensure juniors have experience of small trials and hearings too."*

In the second three months pupils must start to show what they have learned, and after taking written soundings on a pupil's progress the pupillage committee offers a six-month review. Assuming the six-month break opportunity is not exercised (it almost never is), pupils are permitted to begin earning during their second six. It is unclear how much small-end work the recently re-jigged clerking team will feed pupils, but it seems as if the second six is still more of a chambers-based experience than in many sets.

The second six is all about judging suitability for tenancy. Or is it 'The Tenancy'? Over five weeks, pupils must complete set pieces for each of five members on 'The List'. Then there's 'The Test', which is based around a fictional set of papers and culminates in advocacy. The other element of assessment comes via three formal advocacy exercises over the year, and even if *"the feedback is good"* it can be *"difficult to shake the sense of being assessed."* This sense is heightened during the *"stressful period"* of The List; pupils continue to handle their regular workload as well, meaning weekend graft is practically essential. At the end of the five weeks *"everyone writes a report on you,"* but despite the stresses, pupils wouldn't have it otherwise. *"It relieves a lot of pressure and politics,"* they commented.

Outside The List weeks, there is no real reason for pupils to stay late. It's a different story after pupillage though: chambers' reputation ensures a steady flow of great work. While this means barristers *"never have to worry about where the next case is coming from,"* it also requires them to work *"very, very hard."* To demonstrate your suitability for tenancy, sources suggest pupils *"work their socks off."* The all-member tenancy decision is made in July, following a report from the six-strong pupillage committee. Usually a single pupil is taken on, though chambers insists there is scope for taking on everyone who meets the required standard.

The thorough and *"meritocratic"* assessment regime means meeting members at afternoon tea need not be too trying. *"Actually it can be fun if you get some of the characters down for tea. It's not often that people talk about work."* More broadly speaking, the junior end is reasonably heavily Oxbridge-dominated and around 40% are female, with gender a non-issue. *"It's more a case of you being young than being female."* A *"very professional"* and *"reasonably quiet, pretty relaxed"* place, Atkin takes its work *"seriously."* *"Every member has their own room"* and in terms of management, *"everyone has a vote"* but the majority seem to be *"busy concentrating on their practices."* So who really runs chambers? The answer: *"Augusto, our housekeeper. He's been here a year now and we could no longer function without him."*

Atkin's great rival is Keating Chambers, so we were keen to discover what differentiates the two. *"We are more homogeneous, smaller. We have not gone down the expansionist route through external recruitment. That's been a conscious decision,"* members explained. A *"more collegiate, less corporate"* place, no one we spoke to at Atkin was sure there's truth to the perception that their chambers is more academic and reserved than Keating. However, one concrete difference they mentioned is that Atkin's clients are more often the employer in a building dispute, while Keating frequently represents the contractors. Dealing with a director of a large multinational plc can require a different style than when the client is a director of a building company, they explained.

Baby juniors will be in court *"at least every month,"* which may not sound like much, but when construction claims go all the way to court they can be there for a while. Moreover, more than in almost any other sector, construction cases often settle by way of an alternative to court litigation. So *"right from the junior end you will be exposed to arbitrations, mediations and adjudication."* Then there's the personal relationships inherent to a construction project; as well as what went wrong, you need to see *"who cocked up, whose board is going to fire them, when there were changes in management during the project... it's all part of the story."*

If you're licking your lips at the prospects we've described, time spent on one of Atkin's newly revamped mini-pupillages would be no bad thing. Remember above all that unfamiliarity with construction law shouldn't put you off: generations of pupils have chosen this chambers for its premier status, not its specialisation. As one canny pupil put it: *"The work is as lucrative as at the top general commercial sets and similarly international."*

2 Bedford Row

Chambers UK rankings: Crime, fraud: criminal, health & safety

In business since 1983, 2 Bedford Row sits just behind High Holborn on the edge of Gray's Inn. Attached to the set and its most well-known members is a certain gravitas in the world of

criminal law that most others can only dream of. Serious and high-profile crime is the name of the game and a dizzying array of headline-grabbing cases has seen members defending the likes of the Soho nail bomber David Copeland, Michael Stone (the Chillingden murders) and Tony Martin (who shot a burglar in his own home). Renowned founder and head of chambers William Clegg QC has certainly racked up his fair share of major national and international cases, including successfully defending a British paratrooper accused of murdering an Iraqi teenager. In the past year, members have also appeared for the defence in the Jubilee Line fraud and the QPR blackmail trial; several others appeared at the Old Bailey defending those accused of the Kent Securitas robbery, in which £53m in cash was stolen. Peruse the pages of your first-year criminal law textbooks and you'll see several more cases bearing a 2 Bedford Row stamp: R v Brown (yes, that one) and the Herald of Free Enterprise prosecution to name but two.

In addition to defence matters, chambers takes on prosecution work and public inquiries – think Harold Shipman, Victoria Climbie and Stephen Lawrence. Unusually for a criminal outfit, the set has also carved out a niche in a number of areas of regulatory law. Many tenants now undertake work on behalf of HM Revenue and Customs, the Health and Safety Executive, the General Medical Council and various sports regulatory bodies, as well as defending across the regulatory sector.

While pupillage may offer exposure to these more specialised areas of law, a pupil's experience is likely to focus on gaining a thorough grounding in general crime. To this end, the set has developed a system whereby pupils are allocated two supervisors for each six, rather than just one. As well as bringing them into contact with more members of chambers, this approach means *"if one supervisor is caught up in a long case the pupil* can go with the other." It gains full marks from pupils who point out that it is handy to switch onto smaller cases if, for example, you end up with the prospect of sitting behind counsel on a six-month fraud trial. In-house advocacy training sessions are also offered during the second six, with feedback provided to pupils. Sources suggested these are "an opportunity to show what you can do," and though not officially assessed, pupils told us they felt sure "they must be gauging what you're like."

The first six will inevitably involve plenty of shadowing, either at "three to four-day Crown Court trials" or longer stretches where serious crimes are at issue. One pupil recounted his experience of a particularly gruesome murder trial in which, after conviction, the defence QC "went back over my notes to analyse all the legal arguments and to draw up grounds for appeal – it was great that he used my work." As the second six approaches, pupils are advised to "get down to the mags" to pick up a few tips before boarding the advocacy rollercoaster. Watching third-sixers on their feet in the magistrates' court is a great way to see how advocacy is done in that setting and gives an opportunity "to ask silly questions without worrying." Once the second six starts the pupil's schedule is hectic, and we heard from one in July who told us he had been on his feet "every day, bar one, since March." All pupils defend a trial during the first week of the second six to ensure they are ready for the onslaught of trials over the months that follow. All the experience will "stand you in good stead elsewhere if you're not taken on here." As well as dashing from court to court, pupils need to put themselves about in chambers doing work for as many members as they can. That said, supervisors "don't want to overburden pupils," so the schedule should never get too out of hand.

And what of the atmosphere in chambers? "It's not a case of don't speak until you're spoken to,"

insisted one source; "members are always supportive and approachable" and it's not uncommon for seniors to stop by the basement library where pupils tend to congregate. There's also "a bit of banter at the end of the day" with the clerks. Even the dress code is fairly informal: "I know pupils elsewhere who are always required to wear a three-piece suit, but I can't imagine that here."

Tenancy decisions are made in September by a committee of senior and junior members. Rather than just relying on the opinions of those in chambers, the set encourages pupils to obtain references from instructing solicitors who "have a much better idea of whether a pupil has shone in a particular case." The clerks will also have a good idea as to how the pupils are performing, and of their strengths and weaknesses. In their second six, all pupils work closely with the clerk who deals with magistrates' court work. If they get hold of something in the Crown Court then they'll deal with any number of other clerks. "But the junior clerks are overseen, so the senior clerk knows what's going on...They know which pupils will rush back after court," and, by implication, which pupils won't.

As at many criminal chambers, making the tenancy grade is tough. Chambers' official line is that it always has room for outstanding applicants and is always looking to recruit. However, most years one person is taken on – sometimes more – and it must be remembered that there are often third-sixers in the equation as well. In September 2007, two of the four pupils (one had moved on and one had time to make up), a third-sixer and a squatter were all vying for tenancy. In other words, outstanding means pretty darn hot. Knowing that those not taken on "all go to good sets" and "aren't booted out but allowed to stay and sort something out" does at least take the edge off the nervous wait for the decision. If you do need a drink to calm your nerves or to wind down after a harrowing day in court there's no need to stray far. The Old Nick pub across the road from chambers tends to have one or two members propping up the bar, so *"familiar faces are almost guaranteed."* It's almost as common to *"see senior members buying a round."*

Competition for pupillage at 2 Bedford Row is about as fierce as it comes. A successful first-round interview (*"large volume* [around 450 candidates], *short meet-and-greet with one or two legal questions gently thrown in"*) is followed by a more involved second-round grilling including a plea in mitigation. Take time to form a few opinions about current legal issues (eg whether it is right for a sex offender to have their sentence increased) as you'll need to *"show you are serious about crime"* to stand a chance. We hardly need to say that you must display the usual *"great academic results, motivation and judgement,"* but what really counts is *"evidence of a strong human touch"* because chambers wants people whose demeanour will convince any lay or professional client that they really care about what they are doing. Given that many people only acquire this with age or life experience, it's not surprising that 2 Bedford Row often takes on pupils with some kind of career history. One we spoke to had been an actor and then worked in publishing for several years. A quick glance at the biogs of the juniors in chambers reveals a genuine diversity in recruitment and absence of Oxbridge dominance.

2 Bedford Row is one of a handful of top-notch criminal sets with the *"real stars"* who are instructed on the country's leading cases. *"There can be no better place to learn,"* one pupil insisted. We'd find it hard to disagree.

Blackstone Chambers

Chambers UK rankings: Admin & public law, civil liberties, commercial dispute resolution, competition/European law, employment, environment, financial services regulation, fraud: civil, immigration, insurance, media & entertainment, professional discipline, public international law, sport, telecommunications

Many sets claim to be forward-thinking but Blackstone Chambers is the original Bar innovator. Turbocharged by its 1998 move from 2 Hare Court, its trés chic premises at Blackstone House are just the outer trappings of a genuinely steely drive to be a modern organisation in a sometimes archaic profession; there's a great deal of substance to its style. Enjoying an enviable, top-drawer reputation for public law, employment and civil liberties issues, as well as being highly respected for its commercial law capabilities, the 71 barristers (including 30 silks) who now call chambers home have worked on some of the highest-profile and precedent-setting cases of recent years. Members have successfully represented a Guantànamo Bay detainee in the judicial review of the refusal of British identity, assisted a cancer patient in obtaining the drug Herceptin from the NHS and appeared in the House of Lords to establish that state immunity protects Saudi officials from prosecution when facing allegations of torture.

As such, there seems little reason to deviate from a *"programme of building slowly but surely, only looking for real stars when we recruit."* Nevertheless, the breadth of members' expertise and chambers' status has brought about an expansion in focus. EU/competition and regulatory advice is *"very much a growth area for the future of the commercial Bar"* and the presence of five Blackstone barristers in the Optigen v HMCE case (a major carousel fraud case ruled on at the ECJ with EU-wide ramifications) highlights the set's ability to move with the times and find synergies between its varied competition, public and regulatory strengths. Chambers is also keen to expand the amount of public international work it handles, with its long-running involvement for Serbia & Montenegro against Bosnia & Herzegovina in the case at the ICJ as the perfect calling card. What's more, strength in the media, sports and environmental arenas continues to develop, with recent instructions including representing Ashley Cole's agent in disciplinary proceedings brought against him by the FA for arranging that meeting with the Special One and advising the adjudicator appointed by the ICC in relation to Pakistan captain Inzamam-ul-Haq's charges of ball tampering.

Chambers and Partners
Human Rights & Public Law
Set of the Year 2007

You won't be surprised to hear that securing an interview, let alone a pupillage, is tough work. The set consults applications for *"an ability to write in an elegant and concise way"* and looks for *"some first-class marks in a 2:1 if not a First"* and *"clear enthusiasm for the Bar via mini pupillages or similar."* That said, recruiters *"aim to keep in mind that two potentially great pupils may be utterly different in terms of personality and strengths."* The first opportunity to show off your abilities is a *"very thorough"* first-round interview where candidates undergo a light grilling on a subject they have selected from a topical list, hopefully demonstrating *"an ability to assimilate information and put together an argument."* Successful negotiation of this stage leads to a week-long (potentially part-funded) mini pupillage in chambers. *"Shadowing a barrister and completing a set piece of written work"* are the main features, all of which give chambers a better idea of candidates' *"real potential and skills."* The second interview in July, attended by the 15 or so who have made it through, is as much about assessing *"their fit with Blackstone"* as anything else. Candidates will probably be asked to talk about their time in chambers and any cases in which they have been involved.

Chambers stresses that it is *"not looking for a finished product at this stage – what we want to see is potential."* The four (occasionally five) pupils who arrive each autumn quickly get used to a pupillage *"characterised by a focus on learning."* After a week of induction, there is a three-month *"settling-in period"* during which pupils *"acclimatise to the practice of law"* and work on *"the basics of producing pleadings and structuring arguments."* One of the aims at this point is to ensure pupils are *"happy in chambers and working in a pleasant environment."* Life isn't always easy, however; in addition to working on a supervisor's caseload and attending court, the end of each month sees all pupils spend two days on a blind-marked written assessment. In total, seven assessments are completed which, together with copies of the *"full formal feedback in written form"* issued to pupils at the end of each three-month seat plus pupil supervisor reports, are integral to the July tenancy decision. One pupil observed: *"The feedback varies according to the style of the supervisor, but it's always with the tone 'you deserve to be here, but here are areas you've fallen below the highest standards'."*

To ensure a *"degree of normalisation in assessment,"* pupils rotate between the same four pupil supervisors, each of whom makes significant efforts to include their charges in their work. *"The best pupils are helpful and you'll incorporate some of their thoughts, which makes for a collaborative process,"* reflected one. For their part, pupils tell us: *"What's amazing about barristers here is their ability to deal with cases of*

20 files yet summarise the essence incredibly succinctly." Even if the "usual batch of skeletons, research pleadings and drafting first advices" figures prominently, a commercially focused supervisor might mean sports and media cases such as "helping a sports personality appeal a ban." Sitting with another supervisor, meanwhile, could mean "helping to sue a Russian oligarch by proving he's domiciled in England." Time with a public law practitioner can entail "lots of immigration," while employment brings "plenty of discrimination cases and tribunals." Daily life can be "all front-page work, glamorous and important," but pupils must be prepared to accept they will "not always agree morally" with the side they're working for.

This pattern continues into the second six when there is "a conscious decision not to send pupils out to court alone." They continue to work for their supervisors and beat their advocacy skills into shape via seven in-house sessions, two of which are videoed. Being taped as you cross-examine "ham-acting witnesses from chambers" sounds dreadful to us, but chambers pays for drinks after each outing and, apparently, "it's useful to see how you appear and what your faults might be." Said one source about the process in general: "There's such a steep learning curve that within weeks you're aware that what you did a fortnight ago could be much better, not least because people are prepared to spend time with you going through your work." When it comes to deciding tenancy in July, it's "the overall story" that counts. Blackstone keeps in mind "the fact that some people will become great advocates, others will become creative lawyers shaping the law, while others will excel at processing information and presenting a case – there's no chambers type." For those who gain tenancy (two out of five in 2007) the supportive Blackstone values continue to be in evidence. As well as an interest-free loan

of up to £30,000 for the first 15 months, a three-month training period of "shadowing junior tenants at county courts and tribunals" facilitates a relatively seamless transition into practice. Chambers feels this is necessary because "tenants come out of the traps rapidly in terms of volume of instructions" and, with such a range of work, it tends to be "two years before you sit down with the clerks and decide where you want to specialise."

Sitting down with the clerks also means taking a good look at the vast fish tank occupying much of their room. It is one of the more obvious manifestations of Blackstone's "gregarious and fun" atmosphere. Across chambers an effort is made to "create a relatively relaxed environment during what is a naturally stressful period." Although a dress-down code does not apply to pupils because "they have to be in meetings at a moment's notice," hours "between 8.30ish and 6.30ish" are reasonable compensation. Invitations to the Christmas party and other social events are extended to pupils, while drinks parties on the famous Blackstone roof terrace and Friday night outings take place regularly. "Champagne... there seems to be a lot of drinking champagne," mused one pupil.

We'd say the common thread connecting recruits is "academic rigour" tempered by "commercial orientation," while "the cross-section of work on offer lends itself to diversity. The set is as good as its word in being open-minded as regards to who and what you are, and where you come from." While this idea is very laudable, do be aware that only a few members of Blackstone Chambers have a CV that mentions neither Oxford nor Cambridge University. Wherever you're applying from, you'll do well to remember that for Blackstone the overriding criterion is excellence, so prepare your application accordingly.

Brick Court Chambers

Chambers UK rankings: Admin & public law, aviation, banking & finance, civil liberties, commercial dispute resolution, competition/European law, environment, fraud: civil, insurance, international arbitration: general commercial & insurance, professional negligence, public procurement, sport, telecommunications

Among the commercial Bar's front runners, Brick Court is best known for significant achievements in its *"three prongs"* of expertise – EU/competition, commercial law and public law. For pupils and members desiring *"the unique opportunity to spread their practice across disciplines, even at a senior level,"* Brick Court is the Holy Grail. It's a classic case of success breeding success: *"Our position means we receive a steady stream of cutting-edge and, well, sexy work,"* observed one of the senior clerks. This makes the job of upholding the set's reputation easy. *"It may sound like I'm exaggerating, but sometimes we're the ones who have to put the brakes on."* A cursory glance at Brick Court's list of members and their recent cases makes it clear that Brick Court more than warrants its status. Chambers' 26 silks include Jonathan Sumption and Sir Sydney Kentridge, whose recent respective exploits include representing the government in the claim brought by Railtrack shareholders and involvement in the case challenging the hunting ban. Right down to the baby junior who ran an Information Tribunal case concerning whether details of former prime minister Tony Blair's meetings with Rupert Murdoch should be made public, everyone pulls their weight. EU specialists regularly appear at the Competition Appeal Tribunal, the Court of Justice and the Court of First Instance in Luxembourg. Recent highlights include advising O_2 and various other mobile phone operators in connection with roaming charges throughout the

EU and successfully defending Goldman Sachs against allegations of misrepresentation and negligence brought by investment fund IFE. The set has also been representing Virgin Media in its dispute with BSkyB.

Although some pupils may arrive at Brick Court fixed upon a certain area of work, others *"mix their practice – 50% competition and 50% commercial, for example."* Strategy-wise this balance ensures that *"one aspect isn't emphasised over another,"* and goes some way to explaining the set's *"achievement in juggling the priorities of three such defined areas of expertise. You might expect factional disagreements, but it's all very grown up and apolitical."* Sheer breadth of practice is the reason why many pupils choose Brick Court over public law rivals Blackstone or Doughty Street, commercial competitors Fountain Court, Essex Court or One Essex Court, and EU adversaries Monckton Chambers. *"Predominantly, I was interested in European law,"* said one source, *"but I wanted broader commercial experience."* Another had been able to explore the various flavours of competition law through exposure to supervisors with mixed competition, commercial and public practices.

Chambers and Partners Competition/EU Set of the Year 2007

The set is *"keen to expose pupils to all of its strengths"* without recourse to a fixed rotation through each area of expertise. During the year, pupils move between three or four supervisors, who they assist on cases of varying sizes. Recent examples of the type of work undertaken are *"drafting a skeleton argument for a private action involving company law,"* *"considering the social security aspects of the EU Convention on Human Rights"* and *"being asked to provide advice relating to a well-advanced tax case as if I was the silk in* charge." Each completed piece of work, whether for a supervisor or another member of chambers, will be followed by formal feedback, *"even if it's just a few lines,"* that contributes to the material reviewed by the tenancy committee. *"Supervisors are extremely supportive in these instances,"* pupils report. There are also monthly, assessed advocacy sessions in which pupils compete against each other before a panel of QCs. *"Finding yourself on your feet being probed by some of the top practitioners in their fields is incredibly daunting to begin with,"* said one source. Supervisors and members of the pupillage committee admit to *"trying to come up with impossible questions,"* but add that the real pleasure *"comes from watching the pupils develop and be able to field what we fire at them."* This, in conjunction with feedback on written work, *"is most telling in the final decision,"* which is made in July.

In March and late June, all pupils undertake standardised written assessments, the first of which contributes to an Easter feedback session that *"gives you a sense of whether you're likely to be kept on."* Whatever the outcome, most tend to stay for the second six because of the cachet of the Brick Court name on their CV. Those that do have to look elsewhere come July can expect support from the set. Before then, real-world advocacy experience can be gained via employment tribunals and social security and possession hearings, but *"it's recognised as important to keep working extensively for your pupil supervisors."* The tenancy committee's ultimate recommendations are rarely countermanded; both pupils and the set are in agreement that *"the choice is on merit and if you make the grade you will stay on."* In recent years the numbers offered tenancy have fluctuated from none to three. A generous pupillage allowance means *"earning your keep isn't an issue"* and *"enough space, work and the fair prospect of jobs"* go some way to alleviating stress.

Equitable co-existence seems to be the order of the day at Brick Court, where members display a *"confidence and happiness born of success."* On the basis of the utterly frank and warm welcome we received on visiting, we side with our interviewees in finding it difficult to explain the set's reputation for austere reserve. *"That's about ten to 15 years out of date,"* said one senior junior who had come to Brick Court from elsewhere. *"It's slickly run and there's an emphasis on professionalism in management, on doing things properly, but it's as down-to-earth and diverse as any other modern chambers,"* added another. *"Obviously you're not going to call Sir Sidney Kentridge 'Sid' on the first day, but the atmosphere is relatively relaxed."* While tenants may not be *"in each other's houses every weekend,"* there's a *"sense of collegiality"* and a well-developed social scene. A recent innovation at the set's Essex Street premises sees members gather *"every second Thursday for drinks"* – possibly, if the weather is good, on the rather delightful fifth-floor roof garden. Less formally, juniors have been known to celebrate a successful case by *"getting thoroughly lashed together."* They have also enjoyed the more cerebral and cultural delights of a *"conference in Rome"* and undertaken a *"100km walk together in aid of Oxfam."* Pupils are *"welcomed at most social events"* and more than one source spoke of *"true and genuine friendships"* forged during this time.

So, we'll leave it to the roughly 10% of applicants who make it past the 30-minute, first-round interview to judge whether or not the set deserves its 'reserved' tag. Those who do will be required to take a mini pupillage. A *"real effort has been made to revamp"* these five day sessions, with sandwiches, feedback sessions and close attention now being lavished on participants *"because we're proud of our members, what we do and how we work."* However, a piece of assessed work and a supervisor writing a report on your performance means that the week is not entirely consequence-free. The mini pupillage obviously provides chambers with *"a much better take on individuals than the snapshot of an interview alone."* The selection process rounds off with an *"intense"* final interview, including a presentation and cross-examination on a pre-supplied case. A word of advice: because Brick Court operates both outside and inside OLPAS there can be a June-July rush on mini pupillages once the OLPAS applications are in. With this in mind, a sensible person might get their CV to the set earlier in the year.

Work is *"cerebral"* and *"highly demanding"* at Brick Court and chambers attracts the highest quality candidates. With former academics and an economist among recent pupils, intellectual ability is clearly rated highly at interview. Nevertheless, recruits enjoy *"the lack of a 'does your face fit' culture"* at chambers. There is also a significant tradition of non-law graduates arriving at the set, reflecting efforts to make the *"interview process accessible to all."* Most value is placed on *"the demonstration of good advocacy and interpersonal skills in a commercial environment."* For those who make the grade (two out of three in 2007) the rewards are substantial: *"We aim to get juniors financially sorted ASAP,"* clerks told us, *"so they can concentrate on good-quality work, excelling in their field and impressing their peers and their seniors."*

Cloisters

Chambers UK Rankings: Clinical negligence, employment

Despite its 54 years of age, Cloisters is a modern, innovative set that, like Madonna, has remained up to date by constant reinvention. Situated close to Temple Church and Inner Temple Hall, it was originally a criminal set that practised a little bit of civil law. The civil side developed until eventually there was an even split between the two types of practice. To avoid a tug of war, members decided to part company, and the criminal practitioners departed for other sets, most going to Charter and Tooks Chambers. What remained was the complex but cohesive unit we now recognise as Cloisters, a 46-strong set specialising in professional negligence, personal injury and employment law.

Chambers' work is often precedent setting. In the past year alone, members appeared in three of the four employment cases to reach the House of Lords, including Lawson v Serco (determining the jurisdiction of the employment tribunal) and the age discrimination case Rutherford v Secretary of State. Members have appeared in numerous other big discrimination cases such as Serco v Redfearn (race), Hendricks v Commissioner of Police (race and sex) and Wilson v South Cumbria Acute NHS Trust (the biggest ever equal pay case). Cloisters' personal injury practitioners are known for their expertise in occupational stress and bullying at work cases, and frequent crossover between discrimination and stress claims means that counsel often take cases through both the employment tribunal and the civil courts. As such, they need to be able to appeal to different types of audience – standing before a High Court judge has quite a different feel to addressing an employment tribunal. *"In tribunals you dress less formally, you express yourself and put your questions differently, you don't stand up... and you frequently find yourself dealing with litigants in person."* Such variety keeps advocates on their toes.

Two good illustrations of Cloisters' work in the PI field are a claim against the MoD relating to injuries sustained on a training exercise and a claim made by an employee who was attacked by an inmate at a young offenders' institution. In the latter case, the claimant won £1.5m. Clinical negligence claims, commonly against the NHS, can be heart wrenching and extremely difficult. Members have handled cases involving catastrophic brain injuries worth over £5m, and a pupil we interviewed had recently assisted his supervisor on *"a very complex quantum case... involving figures of seven to eight million,"* following the negligent deprivation of oxygen to a baby during birth. As these examples demonstrate, Cloisters' work comprises *"a massive amount of human interest"* on *"cutting-edge legal issues."* Members are also instructed by public authorities in a small number of public law cases, touching on education, immigration, social security and mental health, and advises the three former equality commissions that now make up the Commission for Equality and Human Rights. The set conducts a healthy mix of claimant and defendant work: *"It would be naïve to take the view that it's always the employee being treated terribly."*

Despite its overwhelming pragmatism, Cloisters has its roots in the radical left. It was set up by a group of conscientious objectors (several of them members of the Communist Party) back in the 1950s, and there is still *"a liberal ethos"* in chambers. While the ideal of *"championing the rights of the individual against the evil, all-pervasive State"* has, *"in reality, gone,"* chambers clings to its egalitarian ideals, treating pupils like *"any other member of chambers"* for the duration of their stay. Champagne socialists they definitely are not; indeed, senior clerk Glenn Hudson spoke disparagingly of the hypocrisy of certain sets that, having *"cornered an area of the market where they make money out of the least fortunate in life,"* are still *"evangelical"* about doing it. At Cloisters each barrister takes on at least five days of pro bono work per year, either at legal advice centres or for clients who *"just miss out on legal aid."* *"Clerk with a heart"* Hudson is *"a sucker for a hard-luck story"* – a truth he was forced to accept when one sob-story client turned up wearing a mink coat, accompanied by her chauffeur.

Over 400 applicants will compete for a place in the first round of interviews. A word of advice: the paper filter is *"the hardest stage,"* so improve your chances by being succinct, avoiding *"unnecessary verbiage"* and, if you have under-achieved in any particular area, explaining the reasons why. Get to a second interview and you'll be faced with a tort or contract-based legal problem, which you will have had a week to prepare. As well as displaying academic excellence, prospective pupils must show that they *"have the wherewithal to do the job,"* and that means exceptional advocacy skills, the ability to deal with difficult clients and sufficient relevant experience to show well-founded reasons for wanting to do the job. The perfect way to show this is through FRU, as *"it a) gets your CV looking good and b) gives you experience you won't get any other way."* A turn-off would be *"people who know all the answers, but deliver them in a dull way."* Unless they're in court, the barristers go about their day-to-day business in casual dress, so don't turn up for interview expecting everybody to be in a flash Saville Row suit – *"if you've done your research, you'll know that,"* said one source.

Pupils sit with two supervisors for three months each during a first six that can feel much like *"drowning under paper,"* as the work entails hours reading through complex medical reports. Court attendances range in location from *"employment tribunals up and down the country"* to the Court of Appeal, and in subject matter, from straightforward road traffic accidents to multimillion-pound birth injury and misdiagnosis cases. It's *"an intense period"* and you'll spend a lot of time *"working at a desk in the library under a lot of time pressure."* Nevertheless, the work is varied and stimulating: while one supervisor's practice could be 80% PI and clin neg, another's might focus on international employment law. One pupil recently assisted on a case involving *"a contract given to someone in London who lives in Italy, but mostly* works in Africa." As well as raising jurisdictional questions, this could mean working unusual hours and taking part in teleconferences. First-six pupils learn how to draft grounds and notices of appeal, skeleton arguments for employment tribunals and EAT hearings, and help to produce presentations for clients on things such as recent changes to employment law. They are also likely to see some general commercial cases, drafting particulars of claim, attending conferences and taking part in mediations. *"You have to understand that you're much more of an observer than an active participant... the client has come to get advice from a barrister – and that's not you!"* At least there's the satisfaction of knowing that *"if your paperwork is good enough, it will be adopted."*

Second-six pupils are given a much freer rein. They take on their own caseload and carry out advocacy in the county courts and employment tribunals. *"The transition is very swift; you'll just get a call from the clerks on your first day saying, 'There's a hearing in the High Court, can you go?'"* It goes without saying that the answer is 'yes'. Pupils also continue to work for their supervisor during the second six, and as if that weren't enough, they are additionally expected to juggle work for other members of chambers and complete a series of rigorous, formal assessments. These consist of a drafting exercise, a research exercise, an advocacy assessment and a formal interview. The assessments count a great deal in the September tenancy decision – up to 95% – and some of our sources felt somewhat disappointed that after a full 12 months working with supervisors, their feedback forms only counted as 5% of the assessment. In theory, as many pupils as reach the required standard will be offered tenancy; in recent years, one per year has been the norm.

Despite having a lot on their plates during the second six, pupils still find this period *"liberating."* Said one: *"If you don't find the first six a bit frustrating, you shouldn't have come to the Bar."* There's a real drive and enthusiasm about Cloisters' pupils; they share a genuine interest in their work and, despite toiling hard, seem to benefit from endless reserves of energy. Equally thriving is the social life outside chambers – there are always lunches and impromptu parties to attend. *"You'll see us in Gaucho's a lot... every time someone joins, leaves, has a baby or gets pregnant – it's a great excuse to crack open the champagne."*

All in all, Cloisters is a set with a lot going on, both inside and outside its doors. *"Friendly, fun and adolescent"* were just some of the adjectives used to describe the place, and maybe you'll pick up on this feeling when you visit. Amusingly, we noticed that some of the art hanging in the conference rooms was titled 'Inner Turmoil' and 'Mixed Emotions' – hardly reflective of the set, we think...

Crown Office Chambers

Chambers UK rankings: Clinical negligence, construction, health & safety, personal injury, product liability, professional negligence, professional negligence: technology & construction

Created by the merger of two top-drawer insurance sets back in 2000, Crown Office Chambers is by some margin the largest common law set in the capital and has a strong backbone of insurance-based litigation expertise that crosses several practice areas. The set's 85 practitioners continue to operate out of premises in One Paper Buildings and 2 Crown Office Row, but the intervening years since our last visit have seen *"the merger really bed down – we've ironed out any cultural differences. There are no 'back in the day' issues."* This has been bolstered by a very modern approach to practice, which sees one of the two senior clerks focus exclusively on marketing the set's considerable abilities. Already benefiting from close relationships with solicitors such as Halliwells, CMS Cameron McKenna, Pinsent Masons, Lovells and Beachcroft, this willingness to spread the COC word has *"helped secure a strong foothold in the provinces, Newcastle being a good example."*

Given that COC has just enjoyed its *"best-ever year in terms of billing"* there seems little reason to deviate from the strategy of *"consolidating and developing core strengths."* This isn't to say the set is averse to change. While construction, insurance, product liability, professional negligence and personal injury are at its heart, it continues to make strides in the education arena. Chambers has also raised its profile in the health and safety area; *"aiming for the defence of regulatory prosecutions market."* Elsewhere, the overall balance between defendant and claimant insurance instructions – traditionally weighted towards the former – has edged to *"roughly 60/40"* of late. Representing the human guinea pigs in the disastrous Northwick Park Hospital Parexel TGN 1412 drug trial is a case in point. Having said that, the defence of major class action litigation continues apace, with members of chambers involved in the 2007 Pleural Plaques case – one of *"the biggest disease suits of the last ten years"* – and advising Merck on litigation relating to its withdrawn drug Vioxx. The set has also been involved *"in all the Ladbroke Grove train crash claims for AIG and Thames Trains."*

Unsurprisingly, gaining one of the four or five pupillages offered each year is fairly tricky. The first hurdle to be cleared is the set's substantial, non-OLPAS application form. You'll find a copy online and chambers takes its contents *"very seriously. It's hard to demonstrate good interpersonal skills on a written form, but it's very easy to show yourself badly."* Of the approximately 126 applications received for 2007, 23 made it to the first-stage interview and a mere 11 to the second.

The nature of both these rounds is similar, with candidates facing *"ethics questions"* and off-the-wall posers to get them thinking on their feet. One of our favourites is: *"Explain an iPod to a Martian."* According to recruiters, the point is *"not to catch people out,"* but to assess *"applicants' oral skills and ability to present and analyse facts in different ways. We're looking for potential that we can exploit during pupillage."* Pupils agree that COC is *"as interested in your personality as your academic ability"* – you might, for instance, be asked *"to justify why one charitable project should receive a grant over another, then have to argue the opposing case."* Privileging a balance of the oral and the academic is important here because *"the early years are centred around advocacy – in common law you have to think on your feet and have the adaptability to make persuasive arguments for positions that may not be particularly attractive."* We'd advise brushing up on these skills if offered an interview.

One of the set's main aims is *"to ensure that pupillage is a training period, not a year-long, nightmarish interview."* Listening to pupil supervisors talk about *"the satisfaction of charting improvement"* and their attempts *"to make pupils feel like part of the team,"* it seems that reality matches the pitch. For their part, recruits were enthusiastic about the process, telling us: *"You always know what's expected of you."* Each will sit with the same four supervisors throughout the year (the posting follows the July tenancy decision), with the aim of maximising exposure to different areas of work and facilitating a consistent and fair assessment.

This year's supervisors offered pupils the experience of practice in *"clinical negligence, construction, PI/commercial and straight PI,"* and no matter where you begin *"there tends to be a complete amnesty on mistakes for the first few weeks."* Pupils might get to grips with common law practice by *"working on smaller defendant PI or clin neg cases for* a local authority or hospital trust" or handling *"discrete points of research relating to specialist construction proceedings."* In the second six *"a little more is expected of you,"* but the pattern of life continues in a similar fashion, with the working day lasting from *"around 8.30am to 6-6.30pm"* and including weekly court visits with your supervisor. In each seat, pupils must complete *"two fixed, written tasks that are set and marked by a specialist in the practice area."* Together with the supervisor's report, these form the basis of an *"end-of-seat letter, which outlines points for you to consider."* They also contribute to the material considered when deciding on tenancy. After Christmas, a *"half-time chat"* with the head of the pupillage committee, Matthew Boyle, is also intended to keep pupils on track. At more or less the same time the *"serious advocacy course"* begins, which involves training and *"four different exercises in front of a panel of 'judges' played by members of chambers."* Supervisors emphasise that they are *"looking for a general upward trajectory during the year rather than landmarks in development. You know, people often do badly in their first advocacy test, or maybe they mess up a written assessment – our system is designed to not give mistakes such as these disproportionate weight."* This is noted by pupils, who appreciate chambers' clear assessments and open lines of communication.

The early years of common law practice here involve a broad spread of work: *"It's five to seven years before you begin to specialise,"* not least because *"you think you know what area you're interested in but then opportunity takes you somewhere else entirely."* The second six is just the beginning of this process; there's *"an enormous amount of work for pupils"* and little reason or opportunity to specialise. As well as working for their supervisors, pupils will be in court two or three times a week making small applications, appearing at CMCs or in small claims arbitrations, each of which is like a *"microcosm of the kind of six-week trial you might handle ten years after being called."* Although most proceedings are located within reach of the M25, travel much further beyond is not unheard of. Certainly juniors can expect to clock up the miles on countrywide expeditions.

The July tenancy decision is *"taken very seriously"* and the process is under constant review. Essentially it sees the pupillage committee considering written and advocacy assessments, formal pupil-supervisor reports and comments from other members of chambers. Signs of consistent development are an integral part of the committee's eventual decision, which is (almost invariably) accepted by chambers. The system wins the support of pupils, who are confident that they are *"judged on merit, not what some crusty old member thinks of the one piece of work you did for him."* In 2007, three of the four pupils were offered tenancy.

"Whatever happens come July, I'll be happy to have been a pupil here," said one source, reflecting the views of others and endorsing the set's attempts to create a welcoming and learning-focused atmosphere. Pupils are assigned *"aunts and uncles"* (disinterested juniors) of whom they may ask *"the stupid questions you don't want to put to anyone else."* Their other job is to take pupils out for drinks. Continuing with the social theme, there are weekly gatherings in chambers, which *"everyone attends."* As well as using these as an opportunity to get used to the recent introduction of the use of first names *"for everyone from clerks to senior members"* pupils can sample *"a bottle or two opened by a wine-mad QC."* An annual Christmas party – at Pangaea's of Mayfair last year – is also on the cards, as are other regular drinks and events with clients. Importantly, *"the fair structure of assessment means that all of us pupils get on with each other – we go for lunch, dinner and drinks together."* Recent intakes have been Oxbridge-heavy, but *"it doesn't feel like there's a set type of candidate or fixed criteria for entrance."*

Devereux Chambers

Chambers UK rankings: Employment, insurance, personal injury, telecommunications

Behind the hustle and bustle of the Strand is Devereux Court and the quiet, fountained gardens of the Temple's northern fringes. Devereux Chambers is a characterful and purposeful common law set with a genial touch. Known these days for its three-pronged employment, personal injury and commercial law focus, chambers has arrived at its current state via *"20 years of gradual evolution, rather than a series of conscious decisions."* Back in the 1970s the set existed on a balanced diet of crime and PI; in the 1980s, the development of trade union ties saw PI emerge pre-eminent. More recently, it has strengthened its relationships with solicitors practising in the no-win, no-fee PI arena and now handles a raft of substantial defendant and claimant matters. These include precedent-setting stress-related claims against major banks. For example, members successfully represented Deutsche Bank employee Helen Green in a case regarding workplace bullying. Despite PI's early rise to prominence, chambers is nevertheless dedicated to treating *"each practice area as an equal partner."* Having fully exploited the employment law opportunities created by its union connections, the set is regularly involved in high-value discrimination claims, which often have *"widespread procedural and legislative consequences."* One such matter was BUPA v Cann, a test case concerning the interplay of the statutory grievance procedures and discrimination time limits. Devereux barristers represented the Disability Rights Commission in this case. Elsewhere, current head of chambers Colin Edelman QC's commercial abilities have contributed to Devereux's move towards the upper echelons of the commercial Bar. Particularly well known in insurance and reinsurance circles, members of chambers have litigated a claim connected with the World Trade Center and 9/11, been involved in the fallout from the Parmalat Group's collapse and defended the Willis Group against a suit brought by Cable & Wireless relating to the administration of the latter's captive insurer. As befits a story of continual development, Devereux is now expanding its High Court employment litigation practice, making gains on the non-insurance side of commercial matters and developing its expertise in group claims and those arising from brain, spinal and catastrophic injuries.

One consequence of organic growth is *"a mixture of characters* [within chambers], *a lack of hierarchy between groups"* and an *"informal atmosphere."* Put simply by one source: *"No one's stuck up."* Judging by the bright and breezy nature of the barristers and pupils we met, we'd have to agree. You'll experience it for yourself if you're one of the 30-40 applicants selected from around 300 to attend a first-round interview that is described by chambers' recruiters as *"a brief conversation to determine characters and abilities."* Pupils confirm this is a *"light-hearted"* session, and for the 15 or so who make the grade, a drinks party in chambers ahead of the second interview provides another chance to take the set's temperature and (possibly) *"relax."* It does then get more serious: second-round interviewees choose a subject from *"an array of legal problems"* on which they must answer some probing questions following as little as 30 minutes' preparation time. Members of the interview panel emphasise that *"we're not looking for the correct answer per se, it's more about clarity of thought and expression,"* adding *"law can be learnt – we're interested in an interviewee's way of thinking."* One tenant recalls choosing this set because it *"challenged me the most at interview."*

Pupils move between three supervisors for two successive three-month periods and one six-month period, with tenancy decided in July.

Pupillage is intended to *"expose everyone to the breadth of common law practice"* and involves the two pupils admitted every year sitting in turn with specialists in each of the set's core areas. In the two first-six seats, for instance, you might find yourself *"writing skeleton arguments for a Court of Appeal commercial case," "attending conferences on serious brain injury or cerebral palsy matters"* or *"working on discrete points for a five-day race discrimination tribunal."* It is common for pupils *"to be sent to do county court fast-track stuff because it's likely this is where they'll start."* Pupillage can sometimes feel like a thankless period; however, our sources said that they had managed to build genuinely reciprocal relationships with their supervisors and *"if your work is up to standard, it will be recognised and you'll see elements of it in the final product."* One interviewee spoke of his surprised pleasure at *"meeting some other members of chambers and being told that my supervisor had really been talking up my involvement on a case."*

Devereux took on one of its two pupils this year, and there was a consensus among our interviewees that *"gaining pupillage in the first place is the hardest step."* This isn't to say the standards aren't exacting (in fact it has a lot to do with the high level of ability among pupils); instead, the sense is that *"chambers will work with you and pick you up when you fall. And you aren't going to get unceremoniously dumped halfway through the year."* An assessment process that *"looks at overall development, not specific mistakes"* matches this impression. Supervisors fill in report sheets and pupils compete *"one or two written assessments per practice group."* Together, these count towards the final tenancy decision. Said one pupil: *"I did the first written exercise badly, but was able to redo it and show improvement on my errors."*

Although pupils will conduct the odd piece of work for other members of chambers, generally speaking the aim is *"to keep assessment within the parameters of set work and reports so as to avoid a* situation where one unfortunate assignment has a greater impact on the decision-making process than any other."* Advocacy is *"very important to the set"* and throughout the year regular assessed exercises serve to train pupils up. Luckily for some, only the second-six sessions (*"when pupils should be more proficient because of time spent in court"*) are assessed for purposes of the tenancy decision. Here, the set bears in mind that *"everyone has different, often equally effective, styles and approaches when advocating."*

Some years ago, limited space in Devereux's main premises led to the annexation of rooms in Queen Elizabeth Building, where around half of chambers now resides. Beautiful views of the Thames and Middle Temple Gardens compensate for being a little further away from the RCJ and, in truth, the short walk through Fountain Court is a pleasant one. This geographical separation doesn't seem to have an appreciable effect when it comes to the social lives of the *"practical and outgoing"* types who populate chambers. There are regular pub visits – especially to watch sporting fixtures on TV – informal monthly sandwich lunches *"which you go to if you're free,"* and the opportunity to *"chat with silks at the Christmas party in Middle Temple Hall."* The annual staff v members football match and not infrequent games of cricket add to the general merriment, but there's no three-line whip on attendance. Pupils emphasise *"you can do what you want to do and be what you want to be here."* Broadly speaking, people seem to possess either a 2:1 or First-class degree (and additionally some have prior commercial experience), strongly defined interests beyond the law and *"pretty good travel stories."* Cumulatively, the result is an affable atmosphere that speaks of a set at ease with itself. As ever, we see Devereux as chipper, inclusive, supportive and an all-round excellent choice.

Doughty Street Chambers

Chambers UK rankings: Admin & public law, civil liberties, clinical negligence, crime, defamation/privacy, fraud: criminal, immigration, personal injury, police law: mainly claimant, product liability, social housing

Should we really practise what we preach? Sure, the rank hypocrisy of an existence lived totally at odds with the principles you espouse would be damning, but after all, we're pragmatic beings in an imperfect world. However, several hours in the company of pupils and members of leading public law set Doughty Street convinced us they're all about living what they think and believing in what they do. *"I see the law as a tool for social justice and change,"* explained one, while another talked eloquently of the satisfaction of *"dealing every day with issues that go to the heart of what our country is and what it stands for."* But don't mistake Doughty Streeters for doe-eyed idealists: *"Human rights isn't a shrine to worship; it's about the practical application of the law in the real world."* The majority of pupils arrive at chambers via some related aspect of civil liberties or public law, be it academia, hands-on charity work or journalism. We point this out because it's distinctive. In our peregrinations around the intellectual and commercial miscellany that is the Bar we rarely come across lawyers so passionately and personally engaged with their profession. If you're one of the many entirely respectable people for whom this sort of passion is alien, you probably don't belong at Doughty. Observed one recruiter: *"At law fairs people sometimes ask us, 'How do I show an interest in human rights law?' This is the wrong way round. The people we take are already interested, they don't need to ask."*

The fact that the 90 members who make up chambers are able to pursue their passions so effectively is in no small part due to Doughty practising what it preaches. Founded in 1990, the 17 years of its existence have centred on *"a commitment to... defending freedom and citizens' rights"* and the values of *"equality, respect and diversity."* Recruitment, training and assessment are characterised as *"relentlessly fair,"* while the development of new premises just across the road from Doughty's Georgian home is bringing *"better facilities, more space"* and – just as importantly – *"better disabled access. We've only got one disabled toilet at the moment."* Maintaining such values at home sounds moderately exhausting, but then Doughty's calibre of work means it has much to live up to.

Recognised by *Chambers UK* across a broad spectrum of 'worthy' areas of practice, from administrative & public law, social housing and prisoners' rights to immigration, media and defamation, the set is at the cutting edge of civil liberties disputes. If you can think of a recent high-profile matter concerning terrorism, immigration or human rights, Doughty is likely to have been involved. Members worked on R v Hamza, the Court of Appeal case concerning the solicitation to murder of individuals outside the UK, and an ongoing House of Lords appeal pivoting on the interpretation of the Prevention of Terrorism Act 2005. On the immigration side, the set has provided counsel in proceedings relating to asylum claims under the Refugee Convention. Of the criminal matters comprising half of Doughty's workload, highlights include advising on an ECHR legal challenge over whether or not fingerprints and DNA samples taken from people acquitted of crimes can be kept by the police. A key role in Saramati v France, Germany & Norway, which relates to NATO responsibility for uncleared cluster bombs in Kosovo and state obligations to protect life, further illustrates the set's capabilities.

Given that this representative smattering is only the tip of the iceberg, it isn't surprising that arriving pupils eager to put their beliefs into practice *"feel like kids in a sweet shop."* Don't imagine you're in for an easy ride, though; beyond the relative freedom of being able to choose your preferred supervisor/practice area for the first six, life as one of the four or five pupils at Doughty is tough. It's *"like a fancy version of The Apprentice, but with odds so daunting there's no time for competition. You just get on with it and hope you'll be the person to make the grade."* Whether spent with a civil or criminal (or mixed) practitioner, the first six is busy because supervisors *"try to involve pupils in cases as much as possible, getting them to do research but also to develop their practical skills."*

Consequently, pupils might find themselves attending conferences with clients, going to court (*"often the very highest"*), working on *"a skeleton argument regarding the inadmissibility of evidence in a terrorism case,"* handling the *"particulars of a civil claim against the police"* or *"assisting on public inquiry or corporate social responsibility matters."* Once into the second six, everyone is sent out into the world to learn on their feet by hearing criminal, immigration and asylum cases and *"by being kicked around by a variety of magistrates."* Bail applications and the like are *"great for cementing your advocacy skills,"* but despite a generally criminal bent to this period, *"the clerks are good at keeping an eye out for suitable civil matters if that's what you're interested in."* Civil work tends to involve more research and prep for written advices and pleadings than the heavily advocacy-based criminal matters. Hopping around the capital does incur some cost, but Zone 1-2 travel expenses are covered by chambers and second-six pupils can claim some additional travel expenses.

Usually only one pupil per year is accepted as a tenant, and chambers is serious about ensuring *"equality and fairness"* when making its selection. To begin with, there are *"appraisal sessions between supervisors and pupils every six weeks"* before the October tenancy decision. Formal written feedback for *"every piece of work you do"* and an end-of-first-six report are also part of the mass of material collated by the pupillage committee for review at the decision-making chambers meeting. The results of three written assessments are also important, and there's an assessed advocacy exercise, *"either a civil matter or a criminal bail application."* These sessions *"can be brutal,"* said one pupil, but according to a senior junior they are crucial: *"It's damaging to send pupils out in the second six without confidence or an understanding of how they could improve."* All in all, *"there's no point brown-nosing"* – if you're chosen, it will be on merit alone. This entails working hard throughout the year, but no one seems to mind. Given that one interviewee found the time to write an academic book during pupillage, the odd late night or few hours put in at the weekend probably don't even register on the radar of your average Doughty pupil...

And that's one of the few times the words 'average' and 'Doughty pupil' will figure in the same sentence – recent pupils have included ex-charity workers, legal academics and journalists and overseas correspondents. It's not that the set won't consider fresh-faced youngsters, but you can see how first-hand experience of the genocide in Rwanda might prove an advantage at interview. The set receives 500-650 applications a year through OLPAS, each of which will be pored over by at least two members of chambers. *"Brilliance"* in any sense helps differentiate candidates, as does *"a demonstrable commitment to working for other people"* that goes beyond a placement or two. Scrupulous equality means that a degree attained through extreme difficulties may be treated as being as significant as an achievement as an Oxbridge First; either way, those who make it to the first-round interview (around 50) are a high-quality selection. This is *"a tough 20 minutes"* in which candidates must discuss a question provided ten minutes before. *"In my year it was: 'Is a war just if it's legal?'"* recalled one source. As in the second interview, the set looks for *"the ability to* strip an idea down like a mechanic and identify the core problem." The 20 or so people invited back are given a problem to research and prepare 48 hours before presenting and discussing it in front of a panel of three. This sounds daunting, especially when you might be *"given the UN draft definition of terrorism and asked to define it in your own terms."* Successful applicants remembered the experience as *"energising – it's a discussion rather than being put before a firing squad."*

We were thoroughly inspired by our brief visit to Doughty Street. Its inhabitants are objective, highly intellectual, witty and personable to boot. Said one interviewee: *"We take pride in pushing the interpretation of the law"* and *"there's a wealth of other people's experiences to draw upon here."* A strong *"family feel"* sees *"no distinction between pupils, tenants, QCs and staff,"* many of whom gather for regular Friday evening drinks in the garden. This casual atmosphere is reflected in the informal dress sported by members when not in court.

If what we say about the passion and dedication of Doughty Street barristers resonates with your beliefs and ambitions, then you shouldn't spare an ounce of effort on your application.

Erskine Chambers

Chambers Rankings: Commercial dispute resolution, company, insolvency/corporate recovery

Erskine Chambers was formed 40-odd years ago with the aim of creating a first-class specialist company law set. Having achieved exactly that, its members draw in top-level instructions from multinational companies around the world. Says one satisfied client: *"They are like Brighton rock – quality from one end to the other."* The things that keep Erskine barristers busy are shareholder dis-putes, hostile takeovers, major mergers, problems concerning directors' duties and a whole raft of technical questions relating to businesses that are either on the up or plummeting into insolvency. We rather like the sound of poison pills, which turn out to be shareholder rights plans designed to avoid hostile takeovers. You may have read about some of the matters Erskine barristers have worked on. In the field of company law there's been Philip Green's aggressive bid for M&S, the Equitable Life disaster, the Patak's Pickle inter-family spice wars and the Dubai Ports World takeover of P&O. No other set comes close for company law. Erskine is also very well regarded in relation to insolvency, with major cases including the Eurotunnel restructuring and the restructur-ing of Federal-Mogul, one of the largest and longest running cross-border restructurings in history.

If you think about what defines big business these days, it's globalisation. Erskine's work is no less international than its clients' activities and so members have become used to working as experts or advocates in other jurisdictions, such as the USA, Hong Kong, Bermuda, the Cayman Islands, Malaysia, Singapore, the Bahamas and the British Virgin Islands. The set also has a strong South Africa connection through its member Leon Kuschke, who is a South African silk.

Originally known as 24 Old Buildings, chambers adopted the Erskine name in 1989 in an effort to develop a more corporate persona. A recent move to refurbished accommodation at 33 Chancery Lane has kept everyone happy: plush conference rooms and a spacious reception area help to project a more modern image to clients, the barristers have more floor space (many seem to prefer using it for filing over the ample shelf-space) and the more traditional among them are happy to remain within Lincoln's Inn. As clerk Mark Swal-low explained: *"The new building is in keeping with our reputation for delivering a professional service."*

Professional is certainly a word we'd use to describe this diligent set. *"We get along well,"* said one source, *"but people tend to get in, get behind their desks and just work."* So how do they explain this eagerness for hard graft? According to one senior member: *"If you mention company law to a commercial barrister, their eyes will glaze over because they don't appreciate the refinement of the things we do. But once you're doing it, the excitement is unbounded."* It is suggested that if tax law has any appeal, you might also be suited to company law. Requiring an agile brain, a capacity to be *"precise, self-assured and principled,"* and a respect for the rules, it's a discipline that attracts serious intellects. Our Erskine contacts spoke admiringly of *"all those artificial rules that have been set up, with which companies have to comply,"* and explained how *"we pride ourselves on knowing them inside out."* In order to *"appreciate the subtleties"* of these rules, *"you have to maintain a consciousness that a company only exists because of the statute that created it – it's an artificial construct."* While the client may view corporate responsibility as *"a nicety,"* wanting the most commercially viable solution available, the company law barrister is tasked with *"finding a way of getting from A to B without trampling all over the flower-bed... you have to get there in an intellectually pure way."* One source likened it to *"a game of chess or bridge."*

Alongside the core areas of company and insolvency law, members also take on some commercial and banking matters; nevertheless, this is not a place to come for pupillage if you're sitting on the fence about what you want to do. If you're still keen, here are our tips on how to get your foot in Erskine's door. First, show interest in company law. Really you should be studying, or have studied, this; you might even be able to show that you've some sort of history in the commercial world. *"If somebody is going to join us, we've got to know that they're going to be comfortable doing it*

for the rest of their lives," enforced a member of the pupillage committee, hastily adding: *"...their working lives, that is."* Second, do a week's unassessed mini pupillage. This is probably the best way of finding out if company law really is for you. Technically, a mini is not a formal requirement for applicants, but in practice it could well be the *"stepping stone"* they need. Erskine has opted out of OLPAS and also offers deferred pupillages. An extremely good pupillage award of £40,000 is there to tempt quality applicants.

The set usually recruits one or two pupils, who sit with four supervisors for three months each. Throughout the year they will also carry out work for most other members of chambers. *"People genuinely take an interest,"* confirmed one pupil, *"because if you are kept on, they're going to be working with you regularly."* The latter is certainly true: members continually find themselves opposite each other on cases – yet another reason why *"it's vital to maintain a sense of professionalism. You need to be able to fight hard and yet still come back to chambers and not continue the battle."* With cases lasting for long periods of time at the senior end, this can be quite a challenge.

Pupils get the chance to see work at all levels of seniority, from attending hearings in the Court of Appeal and assisting on deals such as the Equitable Life/Canada Life business transfer scheme to observing baby juniors carrying out the kind of work they'll be doing themselves after pupillage. A baby junior's caseload is largely composed of company law and insolvency instructions, often from smaller clients or even companies listed on AIM, as well as a broad mixture of more general commercial matters such as applying for freezing and interim injunctions, resolving contractual disputes and civil fraud issues. *"It's definitely not shipping or aviation type stuff,"* said one source; *"our commercial work often has a strong company or insolvency law flavour."*

Just before Christmas there is an informal review of a pupil's first three months; another is scheduled for the six-month stage. There are no *"artificial exercises or grading systems"* and pupils *"essentially do real work all the time."* This breaks down as follows: approximately 60% drafting (sometimes having a *"first go"* and then comparing notes with your pupilmaster), 25% attending conferences and court, and 15% *"nose-in-book type stuff"* (carrying out research for yourself or others, which you could then be asked to comment on in a client conference). If you're considering pupillage here you need to ask yourself if you are willing to forego advocacy and your own cases for the first year or so of your career. In this part of the Bar, the stakes are high and *"in pupillage you never get on your feet and you never do your own work."* It's fair to say that advocacy skills are *"not something factored into the tenancy decision at all."* Baby juniors rely on skills picked up from watching senior barristers and, although there is gentle encouragement to take on FRU work, it's generally assumed that *"when the time comes, you'll just pull your finger out."*

Overall, *"flamboyance doesn't tend to be a hallmark here;"* even so, it's important to project a confident image to clients and to be calm and self-assured. To enhance their interpersonal skills, pupils who are lucky enough to be offered tenancy will generally finish their year away from chambers. To compensate for the lack of advocacy experience they complete a stint of two to three months at One Essex Court, where they are *"thrown into £1,000 small debt claims"* and exposed to *"some messier bits of litigation."* The triumphant return to chambers at the end of the official pupillage period is immediately followed by a three-month secondment to a City law firm (eg Slaughter and May, where new tenants are entrusted to the care of corporate finance legend Nigel Boardman). An invaluable insight into how things work on the solicitors' side of the fence, this is also a time to learn about the practicalities that often evade the eye of the specialist company law barrister, such as Listing Rules (regulations for publicly listed companies administered by the FSA). A stint at Slaughter and May could then be followed by a further three months at a firm such as Skadden Arps or Herbert Smith, meaning it could be six months before new tenants return to full-time practice in chambers.

With only 18 juniors and seven silks, this is a relatively small set and so people have to trust and like each other. And yet there is also a great need to build and maintain Chinese Walls between colleagues working on opposite sides of a case. Erskine is not for the abrasive egoist or the attention-seeker: a tenancy here means knuckling down to hard work and maintaining respect for the team. One thing's for sure: whether the economy is booming or it has taken a downturn, the net result for Erskine barristers is always positive. In good times and bad, the phones never stop ringing.

Essex Court Chambers

Chambers UK rankings: Banking & finance, commercial dispute resolution, employment, energy & natural resources, fraud: civil, insurance, international arbitration: general commercial & insurance, media & entertainment, public international law, shipping & commodities, tax: indirect tax

A child of the sixties, Essex Court Chambers is no rambling hippy. In its ultra-smooth yet understated premises in Lincoln's Inn Fields, moody black and white photos of St Paul's, Lloyds of London and Nelson's Column line the walls. Glass security doors slide shut with quiet efficiency. Branded pens, paper and sweets tempt the empty hand. It all adds up to an unmistakable air of purpose and activity. This is no more than you'd expect of a chambers firmly established as one of the commercial Bar's magic circle.

Known in the first instance for expertise in shipping and insurance matters, latterly members of chambers have brought their considerable abilities to bear in the fields of employment, banking and finance, tax, and media and entertainment, developing widely respected practices along the way. By way of illustration, our colleagues at *Chambers UK* recognise Roderick Cordara QC in the top band for tax, Sir Christopher Greenwood as number one in public international law, Andrew Hochhauser QC as a leader in employment, and head of chambers Gordon Pollock QC as a top dog when it comes to almost any type of major litigation. Clearly when this set does something, it likes to do it well, and with 33 silks among its 75 practitioners the chances are it will do it excellently. Major instructions include acting for US pharmaceutical giant Merck in connection with a series of multibillion-dollar insurance claims related to the drug Vioxx and assisting a sizeable US ship owner with a disputed partnership termination concerning a fleet of 11 vessels. The set also grabbed its fair share of headlines while representing The Beatles in a royalty dispute with EMI and successfully defending HSBC in one of the first sexual orientation discrimination cases. Away from High Court litigation, between them VV Veeder QC and Toby Landau have done wonders for Essex Court's standing in the field of international arbitration.

When it comes to securing a pupillage offer, any application has to be similarly stellar. Although recruiters told us "*a First is helpful but isn't essential,*" we couldn't help noticing how the CVs of juniors and pupils list scholarships, national or international mooting prizes and Firsts by the armful. Basically, you'll need to show "*something out of the ordinary.*" A good master's degree, experience in a commercial environment

or a bit of pizzazz in your personality and interview technique can all assist in catching the recruiter's eye. Chambers has settled upon a new approach to interviewing, having decided its single-stage approach wasn't ideal. Now, around 35 of the 200-odd applicants are invited to two rounds of interviews with panels of "*silks and senior barristers*" aiming to assess their "*suitability, commitment and personality.*" Ten or so are then invited to a one-day in-house selection process that is somewhat akin to a mini pupillage, but focused on assessing advocacy skills and "*how they'd cope within a barrister's environment.*" Generally speaking, three or four will return to take their first hesitant pupil-steps come the autumn. They can't however, afford to be too tentative. The pupillage, although "*it is on offer for the full 12 months and we would honour the offer,*" involves a tenancy decision only six months in, just after Easter. Those who aren't accepted tend to take the opportunity to steal the march on contemporaries in second sixes and secure a second-six elsewhere rather than complete the year. Nevertheless, none of those we interviewed had anything bad to say about the process, which "*gives you a fair, clear way of getting your chance to impress.*"

The first three months involves pupils sitting

Chambers and Partners International Arbitration Set of the Year 2007

with one supervisor "*handling the same work they do.*" This might mean "*drafting pleadings for a fraud trial,*" "*preparing a cross-examination in an arbitration*" or "*drafting an argument for a case in the Court of Appeal.*" Supervisors complete progress reports at the end of this period and can generally be relied upon to provide feedback, but this period isn't "*truly assessed*" and is more about learning. There is, however, a *"half-time appraisal meeting"* and a specially devised, post-Christmas *"assessed conference-skills test."* In this, pupils conduct a meeting in which members of chambers pose as client and instructing solicitor and, clearly, work out their issues by *"being difficult and asking if you're willing to do something* [professionally] *improper."*

Thereafter, the real business of an Essex Court pupillage – *"The Rota"* – begins. Pupils spend five successive two-to-three week periods carrying out work on behalf of the five different senior practitioners (be they silks or senior juniors) who comprise the committee responsible for deciding tenancy. The breadth of members' expertise means this period can involve any and every sort of commercial work (this year's supervisors specialised in employment, reinsurance shipping and general commercial litigation). While some, in an effort to assess fairly, reserve the same piece of test work for each pupil, others will give them what they are doing at the time. What they all have in common is *"a reputation for being supportive."* The fact that The Rota's structure is so clearly laid out *"removes the sense of the unexpected; it turns a year-long interview into a focused 12-week interview."*

Although this period is undoubtedly *"brief and stressful,"* it does mean *"you don't spend all year trying to engineer a situation in which you meet the QC who might have some sway"* over tenancy. Those who do make the grade (three in 2007) find they *"immediately relax and gain the confidence to focus on training as a learning process"* instead. Weekly tuition from silks and the opportunity to go on secondment to law firms, attend lectures or visit international courts with top members of chambers are just some of the ways second-sixers diversify their experiences. Advocacy, however, isn't on the cards until tenancy proper (*"unless you do FRU work"*). At Essex Court the pupillage year is about having *"space to breathe and develop your interests in the broad field of commercial law,"* even if conferring with clerks allows you *"a limited bias towards a certain area."* One consequence of the unusually even ratio of silks and other barristers is that work tends towards the complex from the start. One junior observed: *"The first few months after being taken on were difficult, there weren't really the run-of-the-mill, smaller claims that you maybe get elsewhere."* Starting off as a junior on others' cases is normal – we chatted to one recently-called member who is *"in court about 25% of the time"* and has *"handled disputes to do with IP ownership of a TV show, unpaid share options and a Russian power station contract."* This backs up claims made by clerks that *"there are interlocutory hearings and small cases to be dealt with – not everything here is vast."* As a set that prides itself on the quality of its oral advocacy (in fact, sponsoring a student mooting competition) watching closely for tips is helpful from the moment you arrive.

Despite the near 50-50 QC/barrister balance, there is no caste system. Members speak proudly of a *"strong culture of discussion without any stuffy formality,"* which equates to a welcoming atmosphere for pupils evident in even the smallest details. *"On the first day,"* recounted one, *"we were given sheets with everyone's name and photo"* – highly useful in a chambers so large that *"realistically, you'll never know everyone."* A relatively casual dress code and an *"accessible social scene"* all contribute to making pupils feel as at home as possible. Weekly Friday lunches, trips to the Seven Stars pub and chambers' summer and Christmas parties (to which pupils can expect invitations) all offer the opportunity to meet new colleagues or encounter familiar faces.

While there isn't a chambers type per se, extreme intelligence and an absence of introversion is the common theme. Certainly, a holistic focus on *"human, factual and legal interest"* is one factor that keeps Essex Court safely out of an academic or legal ivory tower. If this combination appeals, you enjoy complex legal scenarios and you think you might make the grade, chances are you'll be considering all of the big commercial chambers. What we'd say is that Essex Court provides a distinctively structured pupillage, and one which should give you all the support you need to become a top-drawer commercial barrister.

One Essex Court

Chambers UK rankings: Banking & finance, commercial dispute resolution, company, energy & natural resources, fraud: civil, insurance, intellectual property, international arbitration: general commercial & insurance, professional negligence, tax

Of the top sets at the commercial Bar, One Essex Court prides itself on having the most generalist practitioners. As a result, its specialism could be described as *"providing high-quality advice on highly complex problems at the highest level."* In the course of a week, one member's highly busy schedule included working on a commercial property case in Derbyshire, an aluminium fraud in Tajikistan, a contractual dispute involving gas pipelines between Singapore and Indonesia, advising the government of a country we are unable to name on arms procurement and acting for Ferrero in a case about Turkish hazelnuts. It's little wonder pupils spoke enthusiastically about witnessing *"all sorts of crazy stuff all over the world"* – and out in space, too, as the case involving *"a freezing injunction in relation to a satellite"* demonstrates.

OEC also claims to be *"the most relaxed and informal"* of the magic circle commercial sets *"by a considerable margin,"* attributing this to its unique history. It was founded in 1966 by four barristers, along with legendary *"fifth man"* and senior clerk, Reg Murrell. The five broke away

from a set in Mitre Court where, as the story goes, the dictatorial head of chambers (a relative of Leo Tolstoy) was making life extremely difficult. OEC is still viewed by some members of the Establishment as something of a Johnny-come-lately at the commercial Bar, but its members are proud of the set's history and keen to continue its ethos of open access. *"We're about as meritocratic as you can be,"* said one. *"We're not a set that's been providing judges to the Chancery Division for the last hundred years, and we're not the slightest bit concerned who your parents are or where you went to school."* The set is open and inclusive in its style of management – every committee has clerks on it, and while pupils spoke of hearing *"appalling stories about pupillage in other sets"* where there might be *"an officer and NCO sort of relationship between pupils and supervisors,"* here it was stressed that barristers, pupils and clerks are all on first-name terms.

**Chambers and Partners
Overall Set of the Year 2007**

**Banking & Finance
Set of the Year 2007**

**Commercial Litigation
Set of the Year 2007**

Committees there may be, but there is also strong leadership from head of chambers Lord Grabiner QC and senior clerk Paul Shrubsall. Grabiner is described as *"a committed and powerful figurehead who believes in his clients' cases,"* but also *"not a snob – he doesn't use long, Latinate terms."* This emphasis on keeping things down to earth runs throughout chambers: *"You're providing a solution that is practical and user-friendly, not writing a legal essay,"* explained one barrister. Another commented: *"I run my* meetings as conferences in the true sense. I don't sit there and pontificate from on high... we operate very much as a team." The dress code is also relaxed: "I would generally wear jeans and a T-shirt to work," said one barrister – although for pupils, this would be a mistake. "There is an idea that there is an elderly member of chambers who would be offended to see a pupil not dressed in a suit... but we haven't identified who that is yet!" Pupils work from around 9am until 7pm and we get the impression that the pace is demanding. One candid source said: "You do put pressure on yourself... you don't want to disappoint your supervisor." Working times and practices vary greatly throughout the rest of chambers: some people practise almost entirely from home and – catching up with the rest of the world – about 20 of the 63 members now have BlackBerrys.

A pie chart of chambers' work would have to be cut differently from year to year. As a commercial barrister you need to be ready to turn your hand to insolvency at one moment, mergers and acquisitions the next and a contractual bust-up after that – everything depends on the state of the economy. You'll also need intellectual curiosity to take enjoyment in solving complex legal problems and, at the least, "not be repelled by the commercial world." OEC has learned over the years that there's no blueprint for a successful barrister. "Some pupils come out of the egg with the confidence of Muhammad Ali;" others are "very diffident." Recruiters are therefore careful to ask themselves "what value can chambers add?" and "what latent potential is there for us to build on?" While many successful applicants have come to the set with stunning legal academic backgrounds, they're definitely not dry, technical boffins. Being a "practical thinker" is just as important and the challenge for the recruiters is to spot who has it all. One told us: "Once they get to interview, it's astonishing the number of people with the most glittering academic records who just

bomb – and those without who absolutely cane it." Nevertheless, if you don't have a superb academic background, you're going to have to make one hell of a case. One member explained: "If you've got a First from any university, we'll interview you, but if you haven't, there has to be another string to your bow – and having won a gold medal at the Chelsea Flower Show won't help you." As an example, one successful applicant who had a 2:1 had been a former president of the Oxford Union. Finally, chambers looks for "people we can enjoy spending time with... if there's a spark about them that's a great asset to the set."

Pupillage is described as "an amazing learning curve – you start off as a very naïve BVC student who's done a few pleadings and suddenly you're into incredibly exhilarating, complex stuff, assisting on huge, sprawling cases." One pupil attended a full three-day trial in her first three months. The preparation took several weeks, but then watching Ian Glick QC and Laurie Rabinowitz QC argue it out in the House of Lords, with five law lords questioning them, was described as "the best tutorial ever." There will be a great deal of interpretation of contracts (eg a Bulgarian bank's shareholders' agreement, a contract for supply of gas or a telecommunications company in Nigeria) and the rest of time will be spent researching legal points, drafting advices and skeleton arguments and occasionally pleadings. On most written work, pupils have a go and then compare notes with their supervisor. In some cases, a pupil's work will be used. "They always say thank you so much, but it actually feels like an amazing privilege to have made a contribution, even in some small way." Advocacy is an important part of pupillage here: seven or eight court visits in the first six are followed by the chance to get up on your feet in the second. A second-sixer's caseload will consist of small claims in the county courts (mainly possession hearings and road traffic accidents) and while "you might have a hearing only once a week, you'll spend hours and hours preparing for it." OEC believes that advocacy on your own cases is definitely the best way of preparing for tenancy, when life will constantly throw curve balls such as witnesses not turning up. The set believes it's important to learn how to deal with these things from the off.

Supervisors *"very much take into account that people are still developing in the first three months of pupillage,"* so it's generally the second and third seats that are *"taken more seriously."* Written reports are completed for every piece of work a pupil produces for other members of chambers, and after three months each supervisor produces a written report. At the six-month stage there is a formal review with Laurence Rabinowitz QC and Paul Shrubsall, who will inevitably have to deliver bad news to some. *"If at six months someone clearly isn't going to get tenancy, it's only fair to let them know,"* said a source.

Pupils are included in much of chambers' life: *"You get invited to all the social events and your name goes on the website. You even have a little CV on there – it really feels as though they're holding you out as one of their people."* Small things like this make a big difference. And when pupillage finally finishes, *"it's more than relief – it's euphoria."* This is unsurprising given that tenancy is effectively a job for life. As one person commented: *"One of the reasons pupillage gets such a bad press is that what comes after it is so amazing."* The tenancy decision is made at a meeting of all members. Those who do not make the cut are helped in their search for a third six. Paul Shrubsall has *"an unrivalled network of contacts... he will spend weeks ringing round and arranging interviews."* However, this year all four pupils were sufficiently impressive to be taken on.

One Essex Court is more than just one of the best commercial sets at the Bar – it is a thriving and supportive place to complete pupillage. As one pupil told us: *"I just look around me at the*

barristers here and think, 'I'd love to be like you.' Working with people like them is such a buzz."* The set has come a long way since those early days when it occupied just four rooms and a hall in the space that now forms the reception area. It now fills Nos One to Four Essex Court, plus most of Devereux Court and 12 rooms in 4 Brick Court. Paul Shrubsall smiles as he remarks that his *"game of Monopoly just keeps getting bigger and bigger."*

20 Essex Street

Chambers UK rankings: Banking & finance, commercial dispute resolution, competition/European law, insurance, international arbitration: general commercial and insurance, public international law, shipping & commodities

20 Essex Street comes from a background of shipping and international law. An old set – it dates back at least as far as 1926 – it is still conscious of this shipping heritage, but it's no longer the whole story. *"Chambers recognised over the last 15 years that it needs to have a wider profile than just pre-eminence in shipping practice."* That said, *"even though we are now well known in other areas, why would you leave your core?"* Why indeed? The international focus is still there too, and in 2006 the set won a Queen's Award for Enterprise, reflecting sustained growth in its export of legal services. So these days chambers' business is focused around four main themes – commercial, EU, public international law and domestic public law – and within these broad descriptions there are subspecialisms. Shipping, commodities and international trade, insurance, banking and finance, competition law, sports and human rights all figure, among other things. What's more, the set estimates that almost half of its work comes from overseas law firms and in

around 80% of instructions the client is overseas. Nor do 20 Essex Street barristers handle litigation alone: a panel of 18 arbitrators is made up of veteran QCs, former judges and a former partner from law firm Herbert Smith, so that around 60% of the cases are dealt with by way of arbitration rather than High Court litigation.

Head of chambers Iain Milligan was one of the key players in the sprawling Equitable Life litigation, and among the scores of noteworthy cases handled by members the EC competition dispute over replica football kit pricing also stands out. Stephen Morris QC represented the Office of Fair Trading in the Court of Appeal when it upheld the Competition Appeals Tribunal ruling (and a whopping £6.3m fine) that JJB Sports had conspired with Umbro, Manchester United and other retailers to fix prices for England and Man U shirts. Making it the target for many applicants interested in the field, 20 Essex is also home to public international law experts and barristers developing specialist human rights practices. The latter have recently been instructed on issues such as detention in Guantánamo Bay, control orders here in the UK and the rights of British pensioners living abroad. If you are such an applicant, be aware that PIL is rarely accessible to anyone who hasn't already made a name for themselves in the field, usually as an academic. A wiser approach is to choose the set for its mainstream combination of commercial law and domestic public law activities, treating any encounter with PIL or human rights issues as a bonus.

Pupils sit with four supervisors for three months each, most of the time working on 'live' instructions for either their supervisor or another member of chambers. *"It would be wrong to think they will hold your hand... you are not being tutored here."* But, having been given a piece of work to complete, the pupil will always get adequate feedback on their efforts. *"I put my work back to back*

with theirs to see what they have done differently and why they have done it." Each supervisor is likely to have broad practice reflecting the spread of chambers work. Consequently, pupils are often faced with areas of law about which they know very little, in which case the supervisor will give guidance and assistance. They also make every effort to ensure the pupil works for as many members of chambers as possible before the tenancy decision. As pressured as things can get, the risk of burnout is minimised by a policy discouraging pupils from working after 6pm or at weekends. In any event, pupils do not have a key to chambers.

The pupillage year does not incorporate advocacy other than through set-piece exercises taken after Christmas, which pit pupil against pupil in real case scenarios. *"There are very limited opportunities to get out,"* explained a pupil; *"although I have seen a few arbitrations and a very interesting hearing in the Court of Appeal."* Did they feel at a disadvantage as a result? Not really. *"Chambers is right to not get you in court in the first nine months of pupillage; instead they put the emphasis on what you will be doing in real life as a tenant here."*

At the six-month stage pupils' progress is reviewed and anyone deemed unlikely to be offered tenancy is recommended to seek a second six elsewhere. For others the journey continues until the July tenancy decision, which is made by all members. Usually, one or two of the four pupils taken on each year are granted tenancy and those who are successful are then given the opportunity to augment their advocacy experience by carrying out road traffic cases in the final weeks of pupillage. Once installed as fully-fledged tenants, newbies work closely with other junior members to ease them in and are also given the chance to go on secondment to a law firm. Such placements are usually overseas and recent destinations have included Hong Kong, Shanghai and Norway.

Knowing that it is vital for pupils to work for as many people as possible, we wondered if it was equally important to invest time in trying to forge relationships so as to maximise their chances of gaining tenancy. In other words, should prospective pupils polish up their schmoozing skills? Sources (pupil and tenant alike) emphasised the only interaction that counts is work-related; nevertheless, chambers tea is a good chance to meet people and it isn't unknown for some members to host informal drinks in their rooms. Otherwise, this isn't a set that hangs out together in the pub 24/7. Instead, socialising is limited to a few set events per year, including a garden party for clients and a Christmas party, not forgetting football and cricket matches and a golf day.

If you like the sound of the set so far, be advised: pupillage applicants need to be pretty impressive to get a look in. One of the recruiters told us: *"A master's is not essential if you have an outstanding academic record, including a First from an academically rigorous institution."* Of course, if you do take a further degree the pressure is then on to get top grades. And just in case you were wondering, *"a First is becoming regarded as the norm"* for pupillage here and in other top sets. So if *"in a sea of applicants, more than enough have great academic records,"* how does this set distinguish them? The answer is simple – interests other than study. Mooting and debating are a must and the recruiters also like to see people with hobbies and passions. At the interview stage – and there is just one interview – they look for candidates who can give structure to their answers and deliver them without the sort of awkward nerves that will prevent them from engaging with a court or tribunal. The interview itself lasts 30 minutes and also requires the candidate to analyse a problem question given 15 minutes beforehand. It is true that chambers receives fewer applications than the big names such as Brick Court or Fountain Court, but it is nevertheless chasing the same

people. The most junior of our interviewees indicated they had received pupillage offers from the same group of sets and their reasons for picking 20 Essex from the pack were similar. A mini pupillage is apparently the perfect way to pick out those key characteristics that distinguish it from rivals: international leanings and a slightly calmer, more understated feel compared to some of the other top commercial players.

Major cases, big names, a stack of mediators with hundreds of years of practice between them – we wondered what it must feel like to start out as a pupil among such luminaries. *"It's slightly surreal being surrounded by so many members whose careers are at the polar opposite of where yours is. Overall I'd say it's very interesting to be in the same set as legendary figures..."* However, given that *"Sir Christopher* [Staughton] *made the tea and wheeled it in not so long ago,"* we detected no great need to be overly deferential to these lofty figures. In fact, all round this seems to be a set lacking in pretension and possessed of significant integrity. Said one of our sources proudly: *"Nobody would say about us that you need to be careful with X or Y. We are decent people to be against and to work with but we're not pushovers; we maintain a decency about the way we do a job... it needn't be a war."*

39 Essex Street

Chambers UK rankings: Admin & public law, civil liberties, clinical negligence, construction, costs litigation, environment, immigration, local government, personal injury, planning, product liability, professional discipline, professional negligence: technology & construction

Until 1990, our subject set was a small common and public law outfit known as 2 Garden Court. In the 17 years since moving to Essex Street it has grown substantially, developing a commercial and construction law wing in the process. An environmental and planning team from Eldon Chambers joined in 2002 and the set now has 76 barristers, making it one of the more substantial in London. Although its main thrust is now commercial and common law practice, chambers still wins accolades for human rights, immigration, administrative law, local government instructions and costs litigation. Indeed, the range of work covered is quite staggering: barristers represented the Daily Mirror in its House of Lords spat with Naomi Campbell over privacy and then legal costs, but they are also lauded for giving pro bono advice. Close ties to the Environmental Law Foundation, Free Representation Unit and Liberty (director Shami Chakrabarti was a pupil here) see silks and pupils offering free advice and representation on everything from housing clearance orders in Lancashire to challenging overseas communication interceptions before the European Court of Human Rights. Chambers additionally has a high proportion of members with qualifications beyond the law, and counts former solicitors, doctors and engineers among its ranks. We reckon it's not hard to sell the services of a fully qualified mechanical engineer in a messy construction dispute or a barrister with NHS consultant experience in the defence of clinical negligence.

Pupils rotate between four supervisors every three months, typically dividing their time between chambers' cornerstones of practice in public and private law. Although the pupillage committee is adamant that their training is as wide as possible, a pupil's individual experience will be taken into account. So, for example, one pupil with a background in medical and bioethics spent an extra month with a clinical negligence practitioner. For the most part pupils follow a carefully prescribed pupillage, as detailed on the schedule presented to them on the first day. "*It's clear from the very beginning that they've really*

thought it through," said one. "*They're very focused on providing a good legal education.*" Pupils are "*forcibly evicted*" from the building at 6pm each day and are not expected to work at weekends. As one supervisor put it: "*We absolutely do not want them to be burning the midnight oil, and we are ruthless if anyone breaks the code.*" Pupils typically work only for their supervisor, and even in the second six, when they take on work of their own, assignments continue to be filtered through and monitored by one person. "*It works well because you're never overloaded or committed to four people at once,*" explained a current pupil. "*We have one piece of work at a time, and in the later seats you're even encouraged to prioritise your own work over other commitments.*" This doesn't mean other members of chambers have no involvement: a shadow pupillage committee sets four formal written assessments to be completed in the second six and contributes to the tenancy recommendation of the official pupillage committee in July. These assessments are useful for exposing pupils to areas of law that might not be covered in their four seats. Informally, members are likely to throw their doors and most interesting cases open to the pupils, and one had actually witnessed a tussle between a senior silk and her pupil supervisor over who had the more interesting case for her to shadow that week. Supervisors also enlist baby juniors to introduce pupils to things like small claims appearances because "*they usually haven't done a small claim themselves for years.*" Additionally juniors will assist supervisors in delivering a general introduction-to-court pep talk plus a fat folder of costs information, standard RTA preparation documents and other useful goodies. Getting pupils involved in seminars is yet another way of introducing them to chambers' business: one had delivered an advice session on mental health law to social workers with her supervisor. "*So many people here are genuinely interested and want you to do well. If you've sought advice on an RTA, and you meet that person after court, they will always stop and ask how it went – and they get so excited if you win."* To cap it all there is confidential mentoring available from a volunteer agony aunt or uncle, who takes no part in the tenancy decision and can answer embarrassingly basic questions like how to address a judge outside court.

Chambers and Partners Environment/Planning Set of the Year 2007

Chambers is adamant that pupils are properly guided through pleadings and skeleton arguments, rather than running around researching minor points for the supervisor's own cases. One pupil explained: *"We're encouraged to do complete pieces of work – a pleading or decision. The point is to let you try and create something on your own, which is far more rewarding."* Deadlines are deemed to be realistic and feedback is provided on every piece of work. A formal report summarises the pupil's progress at the end of each seat, although there's a clear sense that later reports carry more weight. As one supervisor put it: *"The first seat or two is the time for all of the pain and agony and making a twit of oneself."* A new advocacy assessment was introduced for the first time in 2005 and takes place in the summer, distracting pupils nicely during the run-up to the tenancy decision. *"I now feel pretty savvy about intricate procedures, costs, expert witnesses and that kind of thing,"* said one pupil before summing up her experience in the immortal sound bite: *"You learn stuff here."*

Although not mandatory for pupillage applicants, the best way to test suitability for 39 Essex Street is a mini pupillage. As well as shadowing barristers in and out of court, students complete a written assessment that will then accompany any subsequent application to chambers. Aspiring pupils need to display impressive CV feathers – academic excellence, mooting, outside interests, volunteer or pro bono work, etc. *"We want people with a spark; people who are high academic achievers yet capable of empathy with clients from all walks of life,"* confirmed a supervisor. *"By the end of pupillage, we hope pupils will have developed their textbook skills, honed their common sense and be capable of doing things like calming an anxious client before an infant approval hearing."* In recent years the set has given tenancy to around two-thirds of its pupils, and it has a good track record of finding third-six placements for the rest. There was good news regarding tenancy for all three pupils in 2006 and in 2007 two of the three gained a permanent place in chambers. Those who stay can initially expect a broad practice with secondment opportunities at the FSA, various local authorities and health sector organisations.

Intensive legal training demands brain food, and this set has no shortage of ideas for nourishment. Everyone knows exactly where the Fox's biscuit tins are stored (in the basement) and the third floor of chambers is notorious for its cake runs. Pupils are welcomed on their first day with a four-hour lunch and can look forward to a Friday lunch once a fortnight, with drinks every other Thursday evening. There is strict adherence to the rule that forbids pupils from buying lunch in the company of more senior barristers and each spring the clerks host a pupil-clerk dinner, an event that also attracts a healthy number of baby juniors.

Chambers believes that pupils and members should maintain their work/life balance; in fact supervisors must devote a paragraph of each seat report to how pupils have managed to continue their extra-curricular activities. We doubt it counted as an extra-curricular activity but we rather liked the story of how one pupil was taken whale-watching in the middle of the day by a silk. Of course, this was more to do with a London-wide obsession with a stranded creature in the Thames rather than a passion for cetology on either's part. At Christmas, rather than the more traditional booze-fest on offer at many sets, chambers holds a children's party complete with Father Christmas and elves. Pupils can expect to participate fully in this and all other social events, although any elf duties are subject to the costume fitting.

Falcon Chambers

Chambers UK Rankings: Agriculture & rural affairs, real estate litigation

Its rooms flanking an ancient courtyard on the south side of Fleet Street, Falcon Chambers is one of those old-fashioned gems of the Bar – a small, specialist set providing expertise in one area of law. With the Temple Church as its backdrop, and Inner Temple Hall just a stone's throw away, it's strange that Falcon is not actually part of the Inn, belonging instead to one of the City's ancient guilds. Yet from a burgeoning property practitioner's point of view, it has everything to offer. The intellectual capital in chambers is undeniably strong. Of the 34 members, 20 make it into the top ranks (band two or above) of our parent publication *Chambers UK*. When it comes to land law, these barristers really know their stuff. Said a junior member: *"If you have a question on the 1954 Landlord & Tenant Act, you go to Kirk Reynolds QC; if you want to know about easements, Jonathon Gaunt QC edits the leading text book..."* It was reassuring to hear our interviewees wax lyrical about the delights of real property and describe the joy of driving around London, saying to family and friends: *"See that fish and chip shop? I did the rent review on that."* Of course, *"it bores them stupid,"* but nevertheless the barristers love it!

"I like it more and more," said one source, perhaps referring to the intellectual curiosity of *"trying to puzzle out what somebody meant by a sentence, a paragraph... even a word."* There have been several important cases lately that turn on the interpretation of the word 'house' in the Leasehold Reform Act 1967. Following the removal of the residence qualification in amendments made to the law in 2002, many leasehold enfranchisement cases (in which tenants can claim the right to acquire the freehold to a property) revolve around this question. Then there are site visits, colour-coded maps and large helpings of English social history, be this 18th Century canals, the development of the railways or who owns the foreshore of the tidal Thames. *"Sometimes I sit in my room and think, I'm getting paid for this!"* laughed one source.

> ### Chambers and Partners
> ### Real Estate Set of the Year 2007

When we visited Falcon in July 2007, there were no pupils. This was not for want of searching. With their impeccable standards, it could be that Falcon's interview process asked a little too much of prospective pupils or even (whisper it) made practice sound too much like hard work. Either way, when faced with this *"hiatus,"* the recruitment committee decided it was time to revamp the interview process. As a result, chambers director Edith Robertson had spent the previous few days *"inhaling Tipp-Ex,"* blanking out applicants' schools, universities and degree classes from their application forms before passing them onto the interview panel. The aim of this was to *"remove any unconscious prejudice,"* especially favouritism towards people with Firsts. Edith also sat in on the last round of interviews, in a bizarre role reversal, in order to *"assess the interview panel,"* each member of which was given feedback. At the second interview, the legal problem given to candidates has been made more accessible, so that the overall style of the interview is now described as *"chatty but focused."* With two pupils starting in October 2007, efforts to improve things look to have paid dividends. In total, about 60 people apply for pupillage, 18 of whom are interviewed and five or six of whom make it back to a second interview. *"We're looking for the right people, long term... but if we had an embarrassment of riches, we'd take them all."* Chambers has recently pulled out of OLPAS, describing the decision to recruit by its own methods as *"giving it a whirl."*

If you regard completing pupillage at a specialist set as limiting your options, you'd be wrong. Yes, you need to have a genuine interest in contract and property law, but *"the Chancery sets up in Lincoln's Inn will always place a premium on the expertise gained at a niche set."* Especially if, like Falcon, it's the number-one player in its field. As you probably already know, land law can seem tedious and dry at university, but there's actually a great deal of variety and interest to be found in practice. Acting for big property companies such as British Land on multimillion-pound transactions, or acting in small possession hearings, this is a litigation-heavy part of the Bar. With real estate a limited resource, increasingly people will be *"squabbling over little bits of it."* This is not an area in which advocacy relies on *"grand flourishes...and tripping up witnesses to prove they're lying;"* instead, cases tend to be short and snappy. *"My last one took three hours to argue and get judgment on,"* reported one barrister. Property cases commonly involve a lot of facts and require evidence from a variety of experts, including surveyors, valuers and *"the occasional oddball local historian."* For example, one junior worked on a case where a moss expert was brought in to ascertain whether a stone wall had been moved by a local farmer.

Baby juniors tend to concentrate on *"the paperwork side of things,"* but by two or three years into practice things even out. Typical advocacy at this level includes county court possession hearings, business tenancy renewals and service charge disputes between landlords and their tenants. For real court ding-dongs there are plenty of *"nuisance neighbour"* disputes, where you'll encounter people who *"really hate each other quite an extraordinary amount."* Equally, you could be representing *"a big supermarket chain that owns a shop with a flat upstairs."* As this demonstrates, the range of work at the junior end is enormous and there is no correlation between complexity and value.

When it comes to pupillage, Falcon's USP is its weeklong induction course, taught by the highly regarded Dr Martin Dixon of Cambridge and City Universities. Held in late September, this week is a chance for Falcon pupils to *"get their heads round landlord and tenant law"* and meet other members of chambers in El Vino's, the wine bar immortalised by Rumpole of the Bailey. Pupillage is broken into four three-month seats, each with a different supervisor, through whom a steady flow of work comes in from *"the afternoon of your first day."* Pupils tell us that chambers *"prefers that you do things well than to a deadline"* and, in time, their work will be sent out to clients if it's of a sufficiently high standard. As well as gaining feedback and guidance from supervisors, pupils attend an advocacy training course that runs from February to the end of April. Run by junior practitioners, it gives basic tips on things like *"how to ensure your case gets put higher up the list,"* *"what to do if a witness doesn't turn up"* and *"how to deal with a ratty judge."* The course culminates in a mock application judged by a member of the recruitment committee. If you do well, it will stand you in good stead come tenancy decision time.

Something described as *"a real bummer"* is the fact that, if pupils aren't putting in an outstanding performance, the recruitment committee may decide to open the tenancy decision to outsiders. Justifying this approach, one member explained that they will by then have gathered feedback from *"two and a half supervisors"* in the form of written reports. And what if there is no external competition? Does this mean it's a shoo-in for one or more pupils? Not always... however, *"if someone is very very good, they'll probably be tipped the wink."* While nail biting their way through the second six, pupils are allowed to take on paid work so that, by the end of pupillage, they *"already have the seeds of a practice."* Feedback from instructing solicitors is provided on how they do in court (where they'll be once or twice a week), and though the work is pretty standard – stuff that *"an experienced practitioner could prepare in 12 minutes"* – there's no stigma attached to taking two days to prepare thoroughly. Before the tenancy decision is made, a final written assessment requires both pupils to draft the same piece of work.

Various members described the set as *"the most cohesive I've been in"* and *"unbelievably incestuous."* Being a part of a specialist set undoubtedly leads to a strong sense of collegiality, yet despite the odd bit of *"public school tomfoolery,"* it's a welcoming place where doors are open and people feel comfortable *"shouting questions"* across the corridor. Tea and toast is served each afternoon in the library (along with genuine Scottish shortbread, sent down to London by the chambers director's mother) and on Fridays, Inner Temple Hall does the catering for lunch. Unlike the rest of chambers, which has a trendy modern design featuring blue lights, a curved, glass brick wall and even a glass lift, the library is all traditional leather and hardwood – is this more reflective of Falcon's true spirit, we wonder?

While attempts to revive the cricket team are waning, what was described to us as *"a bit of a sailing thing"* has recently resulted in a few members setting off on *"a big jolly"* to Grand Cayman. Back in Ol' Blighty, there are occasional parties and outings to Ye Olde Cock Tavern. Summer entertainment takes place in the charming courtyard which separates chambers from the hustle and bustle of Fleet Street. It is the subject of a centuries-old dispute between the Cordwainers, the ancient guild that owns the buildings, and the City of London. While a City-employed street sweeper comes in each morning to mark his territory, chambers assures us: *"We see it as our own."*

If all this appeals, be sure to carry your enthusiasm through to interview. Recruiters are looking for *"fizziness... a raw energy we can channel and train"* and *"somebody whom a judge is going to be compelled to listen to."* As one source confided: *"There are already enough bright but dull barristers turning good cases into bad ones."* A mini pupillage is advisable, and three days should provide ample opportunity to meet members of chambers and attend lectures on how to make a good application. Finally, lest you need further convincing, here's a junior member's personal assurance of the healthy work ethic in chambers: *"If you come into chambers at the weekend, expect to have to turn the alarm off."*

Fountain Court Chambers

Chambers UK rankings: Aviation, banking & finance, commercial dispute resolution, fraud: civil, insurance, international arbitration: general commercial & insurance, product liability, professional negligence

Working in a broad range of disciplines and industry sectors, this magic circle set is recognised as a market leader in commercial law. Take a looks at the top commercial trials of the last few years and you'll see how frequently Fountain

Court barristers crop up. In mammoth cases such as Three Rivers, Equitable Life and BCCI, they were at the forefront of proceedings. Nicholas Stadlen QC (The Bank of England's lead counsel in BCCI) has recently been in court again in Rabobank v NatWest, a case expected to be worth hundreds of millions of pounds. For those with an interest in fraud, chambers has broad experience of conspiracy and deceit at the highest level, with freezing injunctions, forensic accountancy, tracing claims and foreign law all playing a part in such cases. The £80m multiparty claim made in 2005 by Cable & Wireless and its insurer Pender is just one example of the set's work in this area. In the field of aviation, members are regularly involved in disputes about the purchase, lease and maintenance of aircraft, including private jets, with additional work arising from the implications of deep vein thrombosis sustained during air travel. Heavyweight clients in the pharmaceuticals, telecommunications, energy, oil and gas industries supply much of the work at the senior end of chambers; notable public sector clients include the Post Office, the NHS, the British Transport Police and the UK and other governments. Cases cross jurisdictions, meaning that the barristers have ample opportunities to get out and about; Christopher Bathurst QC specialises in arbitration in Singapore and Anthony Boswood QC recently acted in an ICC arbitration in Johannesburg where the sum at issue was in excess of $900m.

Fountain Court is a set that's proud of the achievements of past members. It has produced a former Attorney General (Peter Goldsmith), a Lord Chancellor (Charlie Falconer) and a Lord Chief Justice (Thomas Bingham) and the President of the Family Division (Sir Mark Potter). There's something smooth and refined about Fountain Court; its practitioners seem to have it all – brains, money, reputation. These days, it's Bankim Thanki QC who is said to epitomise the set. Described by colleagues as *"intellectually outstanding, but also a human being – charming and witty,"* we were assured that, if we met him, we'd *"understand instantly."* We have and we did.

Pupils sit with one pupilmaster in their first three months, returning to them for their final three. In the intervening six months there is plenty of variety: as well as working for two new pupilmasters, one pupil carried out work for 20 members of chambers in less than five months. The PMs monitor each piece of work a pupil completes, filling out a short report on anything that takes more than a day or two. The aim is to ensure that *"nothing slips through the net"* and pupils have one piece of work to complete at a time. In practice, pupils can have two or three things on the go, but their schedules should never become too stretched. The general consensus is that *"pupillage is always a stressful time, but having a clear structure helps reduce that."* Certainly, according to our sources, *"no one gets picked on to do extra work while they're in the library,"* and having a number of supervisors avoids *"old-school horror stories of personality clashes."* Naturally the first few weeks can be a shock to the system: *"It's a big step up from Bar school, just in terms of tiredness. After the first week I was wiped out,"* said one pupil. More than long working hours, they attributed this to *"the consciousness of being in a room with someone else and the intellectual challenges."*

Typically, the first three months involve *"looking up various points of law,"* for example, *"researching the fiduciary duties owed by an agent, or a causation issue."* Pupils also sit in on teleconferences, client meetings and the odd High Court hearing. One lucky pupil saw part of the Rabobank trial unfolding. There is no formal assessment in the first three months and small mistakes won't be held against you, but that's no reason to get cocky – *"correcting your pupilmaster is a big no no."* After Christmas, pupils find themselves drafting *"particulars of claim in contractual* disputes" or "witness statements for freezing injunctions," "reading through papers, looking at the various merits of a claim" and sometimes, on big cases, finding out the position of the law on a specific issue. "It can be very complex," explained a pupil; "often the law is unclear, the facts are complicated and it's part of a much bigger picture." Even for straightforward contractual points, pupils concurred that they'd "always look in Chitty to be sure." A six-month review makes it fairly clear whether a pupil is heading in the right direction. "It's not a case of 'Well done, you're in,' but you do get a steer," explained a member of the pupillage committee. Assessment is ongoing and supervisors prepare reports for both the six-month review and the tenancy meeting in June or July.

Advocacy during pupillage is very rare, and there is no formal advocacy training, so when going to court with your supervisor it's doubly important to pay attention and make detailed notes. It has to be stressed that this is a paper-heavy pupillage: if you want to be on your feet from the second six, you're looking in the wrong place. Nervous outings to court must wait until the early phase of tenancy, when baby juniors are likely to be sent to glamorous locations such as Staines. Chambers stresses that it is "not too grand and expensive for small claims," an approach that ensures regular instructions for Fountain's least experienced members. "It's absolutely vital that new tenants hit the ground running and spend time in court... if possible, from day one," explained a clerk.

The commercial Bar may attract more bookish types than, say, the criminal Bar, but that's no reason to set up home in the library. "Gone are the ivory towers, and thank god!" declared one source. Having got rid of these, one wonders if chambers will next look at the dreaming spires. These absolutely dominate the CVs of Fountain Court barristers. So how much do academics count? The short answer is a great deal. Insiders admit

that it's "hard to refuse someone who's won international mooting competitions, has a starred First and a BCL" in favour of someone with "a high 2:1 and some debating experience." However, don't assume that this alone will guarantee you a place: successful candidates will show not only intellectual ability, but also "personality, charm and wit."

Of 200 pupillage applicants, 50 will generally have Firsts, and as only about 25 will make it through to interview, "it's basically a one in, one out." "My massive bugbear is people who start bullshitting," said one member of the pupillage committee. "For me, quoting case law is just disastrous. People who complete these forms in an erudite bubble forget that someone is actually going to read them." Make it to a first-round interview and you'll find it to be a fairly "relaxed and friendly chat." The second interview is entirely different. Faced with a panel of eight people, candidates must tackle a legal problem and a question about a current topic – "usually something one of the panel has come across in the paper that morning." Carrying out a mini pupillage presents no clear advantage, as chambers takes the view that applicants "have enough to think about without us making this a requirement." That said, doing a mini, somewhere, in a relevant area of practice is still a good idea because "we want to see that you've looked closely at a chambers similar to ours and have something interesting to say about it."

Fountain Court chambers prides itself on being a "collegiate" set which is "closely attuned to commercial reality." It is a democratic place rather than being clerk or committee-driven, and it is relatively unusual in that it has two joint heads of chambers. The "one member, one vote" policy means that "you could take on Michael Brindle if you wanted" and, when it comes to tenancy decision, the open meeting can go on for hours.

Despite a colour scheme that's reminiscent of the Barbie mansion, complete with mock marble columns, lemon yellow corridors and liver pink conference rooms, Fountain Court is a hub of blokey banter. We're not talking lads-down-the-pub-type banter, more common-room camaraderie among people who know they have made it to an elite institution. Much of the chat takes place over lunch in the spacious kitchen of the annex at 14 Essex Street, an event that is fast overtaking afternoon tea as the most sociable part of the day. As they say in the Temple: *"Lunch is the new tea."* People from all levels of seniority show up (Anthony Boswood QC is a regular), though pupils are less involved. Said one: *"You can see it and observe it, but you can't really fully experience it until you're on the other side."* The talk is generally unrelated to work – perhaps football (Fountain Court has a five-a-side team and a full eleven) or cricket (one member recalled bowling a spinner straight into Michael Lerego's arm during his pupillage) or maybe even a subject of broad interest to the profession, such as Lord Irvine's wallpaper. Even though there are successful women here, we sensed a predominantly male atmosphere in chambers, and this was conjured up well by one person's comment about the ideal candidate being *"academically stratospheric... but a good bloke."*

Many feel that *"the future of the set is secured"* by its strong bank of juniors and that its *"more of the same"* strategy means its direction will not change. Representing commercial clients with money to spend, Fountain doesn't need to worry about funding cutbacks, nor is it hostage to the fortunes of any single industry sector. While the set has some room for growth in its current location in the Temple, an ongoing conversation about the merits of moving out of the Inn could signal at least one major transformation in years to come – Fountain Court could find itself without a fountain.

Garden Court Chambers

Chambers UK Rankings: Admin & public law, civil liberties, crime, immigration, police law: mainly claimant, social housing

Francis Bacon's 1625 essay, 'Of Gardens', paints an idealistic picture of cultivated beauty and natural wildness living alongside one another, where "the breath of flowers is far sweeter in the air...than in the hand." Visitors to Garden Court Chambers are greeted on their arrival by the heady aroma of arum lilies, an abundance of which fill an ornate reception area with a stunning Georgian fireplace and coat of arms. The set resembles Bacon's garden in another way too. His essay represents a Utopian vision of peace and harmony, where a thousand flowers of all colours are allowed to bloom. Garden Court Chambers shares the aim of promoting such a Utopian society, bringing justice and equality to all.

A trip through cyberspace will show you that the set's major practice areas include immigration, crime, employment & discrimination, family, mental health, social housing and prison law. While these may give the impression that chambers, with its 110 or so members, is in reality made up of several smaller outfits, most practitioners are in fact members of several practice teams, with each area cross-fertilising the others. For example, immigration draws on human rights, European Community law, international law and constitutional law. Indeed, the established text on the subject, *Macdonald's Immigration Law and Practice*, is written by Garden Court's Ian MacDonald QC. Within this field, members appear in multiple jurisdictions for clients ranging from prisoners on death row, the Ilois community in exile on Mauritius and various sports teams and personalities, to a wide variety of companies and corporate bosses, and the odd Russian oligarch.

The majority of all the set's work is *"unashamedly from a claimant's perspective,"* so if it's a discrimination case, Garden Court will be representing the employee; if it's a landlord and tenant issue, Garden Court will act for the tenant, and if it's a problem involving benefits... well, you get the picture. This is the main differential between other sets involved in human rights law (notably Doughty Street and Matrix), who also act for public authorities and the government. Arguably, Garden Court is the most prominent of the politically driven and campaigning sets at the English Bar.

Our interviewees told us that they were attracted to Garden Court because they wanted to *"encourage social justice and help tackle society's inequalities."* Many applicants for pupillage have a background in the voluntary or public sectors, for example, acting as the manager of a Citizen's Advice Bureau or running a disabled person's advice centre. With close on 800 applicants competing for 30 places at interview, and only six taken on for pupillage (of whom only one will be offered tenancy), it's no wonder the people who make it through have the kind of CVs that inspire feelings of inadequacy. Said one source, who'd spent his gap year in Jamaica assisting on capital appeals for prisoners on death row, before helping an NGO take human rights cases to Washington: *"What I've done is relatively tame, really."* It turns out, he wasn't just being modest: another pupil acted as a human shield in Iraq before touring the country with a troop of clowns, providing diversion for hundreds of children numbed by the brutality of war. Her story provides the subject for a play, *Fallujah*, which was performed in Brick Lane in 2007. And this is not the only theatrical production inspired by members of Garden Court. Dexter Dias's scathing indictment of the failures in the prison service, following the racist murder of Zahid Mubarek at the Feltham Young Offenders Institu-

tion in 2000, led to the play *Gladiator Games*, which completed a successful run at the Theatre Royal Stratford East.

The inquiry brought about by the Mubarek case, comparable in its importance to the Stephen Lawrence Inquiry for the changes it helped bring about, exemplifies the ideological thrust of chambers' work to make society safer, more tolerant and humane, and to *"ensure that the voices of the weak are heard."* On a par is members' work on the review of control orders under the Prevention of Terrorism Act, representation of claimants in police-related offences including false imprisonment, malicious prosecution and trespass to property/person, and the case in the US Supreme Court of Hamdan v Rumsfeld, which upheld the habeas corpus and fair trial rights of Guantanomo detainees, declaring proposed military tribunals unlawful. Mark Muller QC's commitment to fighting the excesses of the war on terror was recognised when he and Dexter Dias were nominated for Liberty's Human Rights Lawyer of the Year 2006 award, and Dexter was briefed to represent the principal defendant in the first prosecution under the Terrorism Act 2006. Garden Court's work was no less in the public eye before the recent spate of terrorism cases took over our court system: members were involved in the Pinochet extradition cases, the Omagh bombing case and the overturning of miscarriages of justice relating to the Birmingham Six and the case of Derek Bentley.

While it might sound intimidating to be surrounded by such inspirational people, pupils insisted that the atmosphere in chambers is *"friendly and inclusive,"* possibly because up to ten pupils and third-sixers share a room together, which gives the place *"a common room kind of feel"* and allows them to *"ask silly questions."* Pupils see three distinct areas of chambers' practice during their first six, immigration and crime generally being two of these. A single pupil supervisor takes the reins for the first six months, meaning *"their work influences you a lot."* At the same time, it is possible to carry out work for other members of chambers in order to see a better mix. To make the most of pupillage, *"it's best if you turn up knowing where you want to go,"* but with administrative and public law, social housing, police and prison work, employment, family, human rights and civil law all being practised alongside the core areas of immigration and crime, there's *"a lot to choose from."* Pupils are given training in substantive areas of law as well as advocacy classes on a regular basis, and every month there is a meeting with two members of the pupillage and tenancy committee to *"nip any problems in the bud."*

In the second six, pupils are on their feet from day one – a cue to ditch the stilettos and invest in some comfortable footwear. They pick up briefs from other members of chambers for interlocutory hearings and carry out magistrates' court advocacy on a more or less daily basis, meaning *"you quickly get used to the courts."* Even if you have an aversion to crime, it's a common belief that *"you can see the difference in a barrister's witness handling skills if they have a criminal background,"* so it's deemed valuable experience. If you have a burning desire to do more civil work, which tends to be paper-heavy, it's *"up to you"* to ask the clerks to book you a couple of days back in chambers. The high volume of court work continues for baby juniors so, *"you've clearly got to have an aptitude for advocacy"* and, as the work can be mentally taxing and physically tiring, *"if you're not passionate about battling for an individual's rights, you should look somewhere else."* When it comes to the tenancy decision, pupils are all up against each other, so even success could be accompanied by a bitter taste – *"you know that if you get it, they won't."* The decision is made as late as September, after two written assessments (one

civil and one criminal), an oral interview and an advocacy exercise. How much your performance up until that point counts is unclear.

If you think it's worth a shot, applications to chambers are made through OLPAS, with pupils selected after two rounds of interviews. The first lasts only ten minutes and requires applicants to talk about a topical issue, usually political or legal in nature. The second involves a *"fairly straightforward"* criminal advocacy exercise, for which candidates are given 30 minutes to prepare. A series of questions will also test the individual's commitment to chambers' work. Said one tenant, looking back fondly: *"I really enjoyed the interview… I could have waxed lyrical for hours."* Garden Court certainly isn't the place for cynics: people are genuinely convinced of the value of what they do. Said one: *"I'd rather leave the Bar than work somewhere else."* A final tip: *"Polished, public school, debating society types are a real turn off. It's all surface, and that's what we're trying to get behind."*

After a tour of the building (which cost the set £9m when it moved in 2005), we were allowed a brief glance into the rooms of joint heads of chambers, Owen Davies QC and Courtenay Griffiths QC. Here we found a perfect dichotomy of anarchy and order worthy of Bacon himself. While Griffiths' room has row upon row of neatly maintained files, Davies' room is an hallucination of ostrich feathers, pink candelabras and antique rugs. A sign reading *"Kill All The Lawyers"* hangs above a gold shop mannequin wearing the holy trinity of wig, aviation goggles and pirate hat; a cuckoo clock announces the time to an eerie goblin mask that emerges from a Harley-Davidson helmet; and a stack of Cambridge Audio equipment plugged into a pair of commanding floorstanders provides an eclectic soundtrack of indie, folk, jazz and fugue. Yin and yang they may be, but in their leadership these men appear to achieve an effect as harmonious – and delicate –

as the tuning on Davies' state-of-the-art amp. With fees about to be slashed, the court system in chaos and an increasing number of solicitor advocates soaking up junior work, there's no doubt that the future for legal aid sets is uncertain. However, the attitude in Garden Court is very much: *"We will survive"* and *"at times like this, we're good at getting stuck in."* Their enthusiasm is catching; a day after our visit, we took up their invitation to join members and staff on a sponsored run.

We can't over emphasise the importance of *"evidencing the claims"* you make when applying to a set like this. And it's clear that Garden Court leads by example, not only talking the talk, but walking the walk – and, in some cases, sprinting.

1 Garden Court

Chambers UK rankings: Family

1 Garden Court lies deep in the heart of the Inns, Fountain Court to its left, Middle Temple hall dead ahead with its gardens to the right stretching all the way to the Thames Embankment. On the day of our visit, sunlight streamed through the windows of chambers' newly decorated waiting area. The set had had a real makeover since our previous visit two years before, the most notable change being the acquisition of three floors in neighbouring premises, effectively doubling the space available to members. This physical expansion was a significant step for the set. Members no longer shoehorn themselves into cramped corners and are, instead, eager to fill the extra space by lengthening the list of members. They plan to do this through lateral 'hires' and the recruitment of tenants from among their own pupils. In 2006 three pupils took tenancy in a year when two senior barristers took silk, bringing the total QC tally in chambers to seven.

The set has been in its current incarnation since 1989, when it was formed after a group of barristers from Lamb Building – a set that had been around since the 1950s – decided to set up a specialised family law outfit. It proved to be a smart decision as, at around 53 members strong, 1GC is now the largest specialist family set in the country, offering a complete service to both privately and publicly funded clients. Its members cover ancillary relief, care and adoption, international and private child law, local authority child law, mediation, and human rights. The importance of child and care cases should not be underestimated.

During their year in chambers pupils undertake three seats of four months in an attempt to experience the spread of work undertaken at the set. The first, non-practising six is a time for attending court with their supervisors, creating first drafts of advices and opinions and preparing case chronologies, etc. *"My supervisors were very supportive,"* confirmed a source. *"They were all very busy but insisted that I left by 6pm."* Naturally there will be times in the second six when the briefs and instructions pile up and longer hours are necessary: *"You just have to play it by ear – if there was work to be done then you would just have to do it. I did very few weekends though."*

Once regularly on their feet in the second six, pupils start to get a sense of which areas of family work they prefer. Chambers doesn't rush them, however, believing that it is best for them to grow slowly into their practices. As one source said: *"When you are first in court you are just happy to be taking on cases and getting paid; being out and about everyday is great."* Second-six pupils' instructions include Family Law Act applications and injunctions, directions hearings in public law cases and writing advices on jurisdiction questions. During this time they can expect to be in court almost every day of the week and see relatively little of supervisors. That's not to say they won't be around to give guidance; pupils know that members are happy to take panicked phone calls, even late at night. Additionally, a junior tenant acts as a formal pupil liaison.

When there is something particularly unusual going on in chambers, pupils will be allowed to participate; one of our sources had been allowed to assist a silk for the duration of a major matter and *"this provided an opportunity to see a more complex case than a pupil normally would."* Getting a *"sense of what a seven-week hearing is actually like and seeing what the job is like at the top end of the profession"* is undoubtedly a fantastic experience for pupils, but it also allows *"silks to meet the pupils and make a more informed decision at tenancy time."* One other bonus is that it may enable pupils to *"earn a bit of extra dosh."* Incidentally, for a family set with a good chunk of publicly funded work, the size of the pupillage award is not bad.

Chambers prides itself on being a democratic place, operating a one-member one-vote policy for the tenancy decision. Prior to this, pupils undergo a series of interviews and exercises, including answering ethics questions, making a presentation on a case and undertaking written work on a particular aspect of family law. The tenancy committee also seeks recommendations from the senior clerk and instructing solicitors before it meets to prepare its report to the rest of the membership. Any opinions at variance with the majority are put into a minority report that is also presented to the members. At the most recent tenancy vote, the pupils were judged to be equally talented and so all three were made offers.

Chambers has opted out of the OLPAS system to discourage applications from those without a genuine focus on family practice. *"It's an absolute requisite that an application discloses an interest in or a commitment to family law. Perhaps a candidate has taken a module in it, or at least states that they have interest in it – you would be surprised to*
learn how many people don't appear to even know what we do." Is there a type of character that would best fit in? Initially, our sources claimed not. After pushing them a little, we learned chambers is *"not good with very stuffy sorts – other sets have hunters and shooters who went to this or that school and university, but we don't want anybody frightfully uptight."* A five-member panel spends an evening turning a mound of over 200 applications into a shortlist list of 20. These candidates are invited to a single-stage interview on a Saturday early in July. The questioning is thorough. *"When candidates arrive they are given a test question to look over. We start the interview with a general chat about their CV to settle them down. We then move on to more specific questions such as, 'Why the Bar?' and then, most importantly, 'Why family?'"* The test question is used to establish candidates' ability to reason and justify and (whether or not candidates have law degrees) it is *"a great sifter."* Chambers recruiters told us: *"You can immediately tell if a candidate is analytical and has the right kind of approach for us,"* before adding that *"we will often throw candidates a bit of a googly at the end of the interview to see if they can hit it back."* Here's one tip: make sure you've got a few genuine questions to ask at the end of the interview because *"we are not at all impressed with candidates who ask us a question already covered in interview. What we do like is a candidate who has done their homework: someone who has researched chambers' recent work or recent developments in the field and comes up with an interesting question is really going to pique our curiosity."*

1GC is conscious of its place in the family law community, staging around 30 seminars a year in London and the regions to keep solicitors abreast of developments in the field. Pupils are encouraged to attend these whenever possible, both for their own edification and to meet the solicitors who will be their future clients. The informal social scene at chambers tends to be *"based more on where you are physically in the building than on seniority."* Several members regularly go for drinks on a Friday evening.

We'll finish with a quote from the junior who told us: *"1 Garden Court is the whole package. Not only does it have an excellent reputation at the family law Bar, but the variety of work you can do here is second to none."*

Government Legal Service (GLS)

Long ago the phrase *"employed barrister"* was a legal oxymoron, but just because life as a GLS lawyer doesn't involve clerks, silks, afternoon tea and your own self-regulated pay cheque doesn't mean it isn't worth serious thought. The small matter of a regular salary, and even – whisper it incredulously – a pension, may convince you to read on.

In essence the GLS is a legal service provider with *"one client – the Government."* Its CEO, we suppose, would technically be the Queen. Some 30 departments and over 600 barristers fall under its capacious administrative umbrella, but of the 25 training places offered each year few are for pupils. Needless to say, getting in is tough, so be clear about what motivates you. Most likely it will be an ardent interest in public and administrative law, as well as policy and legislation. As GLS sources put it: *"We don't just advise on what the law is, we advise on what the law should be."* Just to whet your appetite, here are some matters which can fall within the GLS remit: currency and coinage issues; litigation concerning night noise at Heathrow airport; prison inquests; advice on law regarding smacking children; fraudulent trading and insider dealing; implementation of the Aarhus Convention on environmental information; judicial reviews; advising ministers; and preparing drafts of bills (eg new gambling legislation). Confines of space mean we can't do justice

to the full variety of work available, but even a glance at the GLS website (www.gls.gov.uk) will give a fuller flavour of just how extraordinary the work can be for GLS barristers.

Actually, we shouldn't use that word. The GLS speaks of 'lawyers' rather than solicitors or barristers, even though training for both follows the norms of private practice with the pupils defined as such for one year and trainees for two. There are significant similarities in the advisory work opportunities available to trainees and pupils, and the GLS values *"the skills of individuals as lawyers, whatever their preferred branch of the profession."* This being so, we refer you to page 346 for a full picture of what's on offer for trainees. Whether trainee or pupil, paperwork is the order of the day. All pupils must complete an advisory seat and, in contrast to private practice, will interact directly with policymakers ('clients' in GLS jargon). Although most of the pupils we spoke to stressed the fundamentally advisory nature of the practice (*"If you want to stand up and talk, go to a criminal set instead"*), any hard-won mooting experience will be put to good use in other ways. Said one pupil: *"Advocacy here isn't just about the courtroom – it is required in conference and negotiation and on paper."* In other words, persuading those policymakers and government ministers requires impressive intellectual agility. In addition, *"it's quite easy to move to a department like the Treasury Solicitors, where opportunities for advocacy might be available. You just have to take the initiative."*

Movement around the GLS is encouraged from the top down and qualified lawyers move throughout their careers. This promotes broad experience and expertise, but does mean it is harder to specialise in the first few years post-pupillage than in private practice. The general pattern is for pupils to spend four months in three departments or up to six months in a set of chambers. Those who had taken this latter route suggested it is better to start off with a few weeks in a GLS department before moving to a chambers, telling us: *"It would have been much more difficult to understand what it means to be a government lawyer if I'd headed straight into private practice."* Once in chambers, however, pupils enjoy the benefits of private practice without the drawbacks: *"I was treated just the same as the other pupils but had none of the stress,"* enthused one source. Another added: *"I didn't have to do as much work for other members of chambers, so I could focus on subjects most important to my development."* Alternatives to six months in a chambers can include a secondment to the CPS, where one pupil was up on their feet prosecuting in magistrates' courts: *"Managing my own cases and handling such varied and stimulating work was really exciting."*

Helping knit the year together, each pupil is assigned a general pupil supervisor who meets regularly with their charge to set objectives and suggest seats. While there are additional seat-specific pupil supervisors, pupils will also answer to their line manager in each department. Encouraged to work autonomously, pupils are *"pretty much thrown in at the deep end"* and seem to operate more independently of pupil supervisors than their peers in private practice. In fact, work is allocated to pupils in the same way as it is to qualified lawyers, with pupil supervisors and line managers basically there to offer feedback. *"You're not left entirely to your own devices; it's about being supervised rather than observing,"* explained one pupil, another adding: *"It's just as easy to ask others on the team if I have a question – someone's always assigned to look over your work, particularly in the first month of a new seat."*

In terms of work, advice and drafting looms large. A recent crop of pupils had assisted policymakers during the bird flu crisis, drafted for the Special Immigration Appeals Commission, attended the floor of the (Parliamentary) House of Lords to advise on live debates and prepped policymakers en route to the European courts. One pupil had even worked directly for the Lord Chancellor. A specific thrill of GLS pupillage is involvement in the *"exciting"* world of lawmaking and several sources had advised on *"very high-profile bills – you'd go home in the evening and see it on the news..."*

With pupils and trainees dispersed across many departments, they need an effective unifying tool. The Legal Trainee Network is behind many of the social events and there are additionally various department events, although *"it's not as if we have senior silks to buy everyone drinks with their gold credit cards."* Money is, of course, a consideration for those weighing up work as a government lawyer and on this subject all our sources were pretty much in agreement that their remuneration was *"not as much as a commercial pupillage award, but not dreadful... and you'll never have to work an 80-hour week."* Indeed, their civil-service hours are 10am to 6pm and it's *"almost unheard of"* to work at the weekends. Flexible working is encouraged, even for pupils.

Standard hours, regular wages and life as a barrister? If the formula appeals, get in line. Application is centralised via the GLS, but you will be admitted to the supervision of a preferred 'home' department. Decide which department(s) interest(s) you most and research thoroughly, not least to discover whether they take pupils. Our sources agreed that *"applying is more difficult for pupils. Some departments haven't taken pupils before and there are generally fewer places."* Vacation placements offer the perfect chance to suss out a department and are encouraged throughout the GLS. Applications to become a trainee or pupil are made two years in advance, beginning with a paper application and online verbal reasoning test. Successful applicants are then called for an assessment day in September. Negotiate this hurdle and you're in, and eligible to have the

GLS pay your BVC fees and a maintenance grant. One final boon is that the GLS hires pupils on the assumption that they will be suitable GLS lawyers within the year. *"It's not a guarantee, but unless something goes very wrong you will be offered a position."*

All in all, it is the opportunity to experience a variety of law far beyond the scope of usual private practice that defines the GLS, and we can only conclude that this is one of the most rewarding pupillages to be found at the Bar. Our interviewees had nothing but encouragement for those considering a life less set-based. Said one: *"I think that people do get tunnel vision about chambers, but they should look at the options – I'm so glad I came here."*

2-3 Gray's Inn Square

Chambers UK rankings: Consumer law, licensing, local government, planning, social housing

The cosy waiting area of 2-3 Gray's Inn Square features an enormous fishbowl crammed with candyrock that tingled our sweet tooth upon arrival. Equally chock-full of eminent advocates and groundbreaking legal proceedings, the illustrious history of 2-3 Gray's Inn could fill a book. In fact, it has. Penned by Malcolm Spence QC, the elegantly attired, venerable planning silk (who lives in a flat next to chambers), it charts the set's rise throughout the 20th century. If you peruse it, you'll discover that criminal proceedings were among the set's highest profile cases of the last 30 years, with stars like Anthony Scrivener QC defending Private Lee Clegg before the House of Lords and representing Sion Jenkins in his recent murder retrial following the death of his foster daughter.

It may therefore come as a surprise to find that, today, planning and public law are the set's bread and butter and private sector developers, local government and social housing organisations dominate the clientele. Immigration and asylum matters are also handled, as are employment, community care issues and health and safety controls. The set has been clever at future-proofing itself at a time when funding issues have dented many in the profession. The recent transfer of licensing from magistrates to local government has seen it become a go-to dock for licensing work, and it looks set to provide the same niche in gambling law over the next few years. For pupils, this range means it's possible to follow a common, public or administrative bent and enjoy a great variety of work. At this set, pupils' interests can take unpredicted turns.

The set typically offers two twelve-month pupillages each year and pupils rotate between three pupil supervisors for four months at a time. The first six sees pupils getting to grips with sets of papers, skeleton arguments and opinion writing, but the style of each seat depends very much on the pupil supervisor and the work to hand. While it is common for pupils to work through a historic case as an academic exercise and then discuss it with their pupil supervisor, they are encouraged to assist on significant live cases. In such circumstances *"it's a really rewarding thing to have put a point forward to your pupil supervisor and to then hear it presented to the bench."* Other members are allowed to give work to pupils, but pupil supervisors do not hesitate to impose limits if they perceive their charges are overburdened. Towards the end of the first six, pupils are encouraged to shadow junior counsel for a more accurate taste of the court-heavy second six and are also sent out to observe the different advocacy styles of more-senior barristers. Recently, pupils gazed on admiringly at the House of Lords as Anthony Scrivener QC handled an enormous civil action centring on 'economy class symptoms' (aka DVT) suffered by airline passengers.

Testament to the frequency with which they're on their feet in the second six, not one pupil was in chambers on the morning we visited and only perseverance ensured we gained interviews. From day one of the second six they begin to take on their own work, securing a healthy diet of two to three court appearances a week. Appearances in Greater London tend to be the norm and, although the first time is *"just as daunting as it sounds,"* all the pupils agreed that they felt well supported by chambers. A sit-down chat with chief clerk Martin Hale before the second six begins also ensures they know exactly what chambers requires of them. One challenge faced by pupils at 2-3 Gray's Inn is the likelihood, particularly when representing a local authority, of facing a litigant in person rather than another barrister. *"There are far more personal-conduct issues in this kind of court work,"* explained one pupil. *"You learn how to handle situations that just don't arise elsewhere."* When their diaries allow, pupils continue to devil for other members of chambers and work for their pupil supervisor. Inevitably, the hours do lengthen beyond an eight-hour day in the second six, although working at the weekends tends to be for pupils' own clients rather than anyone else.

While there can be no disputing the set's commitment to pupils, this wasn't the most rigidly assessed pupillage we've encountered. Other than one advocacy exercise at the end of the first six (simulating a typical second-six case), they are not required to complete any other assessments before the tenancy decision is made in July. It is the case that pupil supervisors complete formal reports and any member of chambers who has experienced a pupil's work (whether paper-based or advocacy) will fill in a feedback form, but this isn't the sort of bells-and-whistles structured assessment some sets adopt. Pupils were quick to point out that an overly systematic approach wouldn't be representative of the set's culture. As

one said: *"This was very much the friendliest set I'd encountered at interview and that hasn't changed throughout my time here. The culture is one of education and discussion, and open doors – I have never once felt that I was interrupting anyone or asking a stupid question. Everyone wants you to do well."* Indeed they do. Victory in the courtroom was a personal highlight for many of our sources: *"It's so rewarding doing your own work and taking that responsibility, but even more enjoyable when you manage to persuade the judge and win the case."* On returning to base, pupils find that everyone else is quick to shower praise, not least because a tradition decrees that a pupil's first victory be celebrated with cakes for the clerks' room. Not just any old Victoria sponge: Konditor & Cook is still the patisserie of choice for these clerks, who were treated twice in one week by this year's pupils.

We don't think there's better proof that a good atmosphere and pastoral care permeates this set. Proud to be traditional, yet relaxed and friendly, despite numbering 52 barristers, 2-3 Gray's Inn retains a small-chambers feel. *"Although quite a few people do a lot of work from home, or are often away at planning inquiries, there is always a core group around chambers."* The dynamism of the juniors is especially striking, with younger members at the forefront of a recent surge in immigration and housing instructions. *"There's a lot of initiative and creativity here,"* said one pupil; *"the junior end is just phenomenal."*

Pupils are always invited to seminars and client events and can expect to be networking with solicitors and silks from the outset. Within chambers, they are welcomed with drinks on their first day and are always invited to chambers' parties. The set also indulges in sporadic Saturday cricket matches, though participation in these is absolutely voluntary.

The crucial July tenancy decision is made following assessment including reports from pupil supervisors, input from the clerks and feedback from members. Even then outright rejection to a pupil who shows great promise but has not quite proved themselves is not the only outcome. Chambers is prepared to consider, somewhat unusually, an invitation to pupils who might be borderline or otherwise not quite ready to stay on as a pupil for another 6 months. Happily, this deferment has confirmed the set's instinct on a number of occasions with the pupil being offered a tenancy. As the senior clerk said: *"We take the time to see if people turn out well."* In 2006 chambers gave tenancy to two of its three pupils. In 2007 it offered both its pupils a third six. Nor does chambers like to see visitors leave empty-handed: we left, pockets stuffed, with the set's own-brand chocolates and some of that candyrock.

4-5 Gray's Inn Square

Chambers UK rankings: Admin & public law, education, environment, local government, planning, professional discipline

Back in the 1950s this set was a small but bustling common law outfit. It became one of the first to move out of the precincts of the Temple to Gray's Inn in 1965. Come the 1980s, the set had developed an impressive commercial and banking practice, showing a flair for international work. Then, in 2000, seven members left for Matrix Chambers and a further eight public law practitioners shipped out following abandoned merger talks with Monckton Chambers. Instead of folding, the remaining 30-odd barristers rallied and the set has since grown to almost 50 members who between them cover a staggering number of local government, commercial and planning law instructions.

Acclaimed above all else for their planning expertise, over half the members are happily occupied with public law and planning inquiries and High Court applications for judicial review, as well as complex planning and environmental advice to developers, local authorities and objectors. Two members, for example, have been representing the Greater London Authority at a major public inquiry into Thames Water's proposals for a desalination plant on the Thames at Beckton. This specialist practice dovetails nicely with the set's public law work, an area in which barristers represent clients on almost anything concerning public bodies – judicial reviews (including impressive human rights work), employment tribunals, European law and much more. Over 300 local authorities across the country regularly seek advice from the set, such that its *"local government work covers everything, alphabetically, from abattoirs to zoos."* In one particularly interesting case, members represented the returning officer for the 2006 local elections in the St Katherine and Wapping ward of Tower Hamlets. In this case (eventually decided by the Court of Appeal) three prospective Respect party candidates, whose nomination papers were invalid, failed to secure judicial intervention in the electoral proceedings.

Other strains of work include sports and media law, professional negligence and defamation. In a recent action, 4-5 Gray's Inn QC Richard Spearman helped Lance Armstrong secure a libel victory against the *Sunday Times* following their publication of an article that implied he had used performance-enhancing drugs. Despite the high profile of such cases, it is chambers' growing commercial wing that increasingly catches the eye. Commercial judicial reviews, multi-jurisdictional banking cases, international trading and insurance work are bringing in a growing proportion of chambers' revenue and occupying the time of up to 20 members.

Clearly happy to embrace change, 4-5 Gray's Inn overhauled its pupillage programme some years ago, cutting the number of pupils from six to a maximum of three and establishing a tenancy selection committee. Pupils are now allocated four seats of three months each, with either three or four different pupilmasters to ensure breadth of experience in time for the third-seat tenancy decision. As one pupil supervisor explained: *"Pupils have nine months to prove themselves. We make a report on every piece of their work, whether from the pupil supervisor or other member of chambers, and it's all filed and taken into account before we make a recommendation to our management committee. We then have a full meeting of chambers where any objections and impressions are discussed, before the vote."* Nine months may not leave long to make a good impression, but at least the carefully structured system leaves no one in the dark about how they're doing.

The recruits we interviewed were impressed by the commitment shown to pupillage, demonstrated as early as the first interview when, as one told us, *"I felt that they genuinely wanted to know about me."* An initial grilling sees applicants face five or six members, including the head of chambers, and those who make it through to round two face a whole-day assessment. At this stage a legal problem must be worked into a skeleton argument for presentation before another panel. *"It was incredibly daunting,"* remembered one pupil, *"but also very reassuring. They didn't press me for legal knowledge, but really tested my analytical skills with some very searching questions."*

Once installed as a pupil, similar advocacy tests are an integral part of the ongoing assessment. After any assessment, a written report is submitted to the record and pupils get feedback, courtroom tips and a chance to *"appreciate the wider legal context"* through informal discussion with the panel. Such master classes in advocacy are important because pupils' court experience is limited throughout their training, unless they take on pro bono matters. Said one recent tenant:

"I didn't appear in court at all during my pupillage, and although at the time I did want to get on my feet, I'm now pleased that I didn't. The pupillage focused on preparation and paperwork, which is 99% of good court work anyway. Now I have that confidence of preparation." Other sage words came from a source who pointed out that *"too many court appearances wouldn't reflect the practice of the set – about half of the work here is advisory."*

Rest assured that time spent at your desk in chambers doesn't equate to tedium. Pupils are given a good level of work from the off, shadowing supervisors through conferences and becoming increasingly active in devilling for other members of the set. They encounter *"a huge range of drafting – everything from small bits of larger proceedings to whole opinions, pleadings and skeleton arguments."* Throughout, feedback is constant, with supervisors correcting and advising on each piece of work produced. Pupils are tested for flexibility, commitment and *"ruthless"* diary management. In addition, the set encourages pupils to take a short secondment outside chambers, and one of those we spoke to had spent time with a London-based American law firm. For all of the activity, the consensus was that this is a *"civilised"* rather than manic training and that, *"despite high expectations, chambers feels your life shouldn't be taken over by pupillage. It adopts a nurturing attitude that goes from senior members right down to the clerks."*

We sense that 4-5 Gray's Inn has achieved a pleasing equilibrium between the seriousness of a heavy workload and a light modus operandi. New pupils are greeted with open doors, first names and a welcome party where even senior members trot out to meet them. *"Approachable"* is very much the colour of the wallpaper here and baby juniors can be relied upon to take pupils under their wing. The set holds a formal May dinner in addition to its annual Christmas party, and also upholds a time-honoured tradition of providing a picnic lunch spread in the gardens of Gray's Inn every Monday throughout the summer.

At least one pupil secures tenancy each year and they find that the pastoral touch characterising pupillage continues. Two clerks are assigned to each team of barristers, according to call and, as they take their first steps, baby juniors benefit from the clerks' efforts to *"persuade leaders to take them on, push them forward for jobs and generally get them known."* A decision to expand into numbers 6 and 3 Grays Inn Square has ensured enough space for everyone to have their own room, and only the newest of tenants share space.

So what is this set looking for in pupillage applicants? First, it wants people with exceptional analytical and advocacy skills, so work on your mooting form. Second, it wants to see potential with regard to the ability to relate to lay clients as well as professionals. If you're serious about this set, we recommend participation in its biannual mini-pupillage scheme, which enables four would-be-applicants at a time to sample its wares. Apply early if you want to get onto a session and look lively once you're in situ. As far as 4-5 Gray's Inn is concerned, they'll start getting to know you then and there.

1 Hare Court

Chambers UK rankings: Family/matrimonial

On the day we visited 1 Hare Court an electrical explosion on Fleet Street had left much of the Inns without power. However, the chaos we noted on our arrival in chambers proved to be but a temporary loss of composure from a set that contemplates the legal market with perfect equanimity. Long respected for its excellent family and matrimonial law abilities, divorce continues to be the stock in trade at a set *"historically seen as more commercial than QEB,"* but vying with that set for top billing in the field.

Consequently, while children's law (child abduction, residence or contact applications), inheritance, trusts of land and even medical ethics cases do feature, 1 Hare Court is increasingly concentrating on the most rarefied ancillary relief cases, in which it is not unusual for members to act on both sides of the case. In fact, ancillary relief now constitutes over 90% of chambers' caseload, with barristers continually involved in high-profile separations that lead to ground-breaking decisions.

Chambers and Partners Family Set of the Year 2007

Divorce is, of course, an issue *"affecting the whole of society from the richest to the poorest, from the famous or infamous to the completely unknown."* Precedent-setting decisions tend to emerge from the divorces of the fabulously wealthy and, here, members of chambers have worked on the divorce of former Arsenal footballer Ray Parlour, the Miller divorce involving a disputed £30 million fortune, and the MacFarlane case, which dealt with the financial implications of divorce for a wife who had given up her career for marriage. More recently, barristers (including family bar prima barristerina Nicholas Mostyn) have been engrossed in assisting Sir Paul McCartney on his divorce from Heather Mills (who is also represented by a member of chambers) and Mrs Charman in her divorce of the insurance multi-millionaire John Charman, one of the richest men in the City with assets said to be approaching £150 million.

The story of how 1 Hare Court came into being is a relatively simple one. In the 1970s a merger of two sets – one expert in family cases, the other in pure divorce matters – led to the creation of 1 Mitre Court Buildings, which grew organically until the early 21st century when two events turbocharged its development. When the set lured five senior barristers from rival 29 Bedford Row shockwaves went through the matrimonial Bar and the set's reputation went from very good to stellar. Not long after this, it moved into premises at 1 Hare Court (*"newly refitted, all mod cons and technology"*), finally uniting all its members under one roof for the first time. The benefits of *"appearing cohesive and modern"* are obvious and *"the move has also given a real energy boost"* to the set. Extra space has allowed it to recruit well at the junior end. Its success has not gone unrecognised: a Chambers and Partners 'Family Set of the Year' award sits proudly in the reception and members proudly told us that one of the clerking team had recently scooped the Bar Council's award for 'Junior Clerk of the Year'.

Three pupils join chambers each year and the set requires them to switch pupil supervisor every four months. First and foremost this gives them the opportunity to observe *"three different styles of approach to essentially similar work."* As one pupil commented: *"There are some aggressive courtroom performers, but you need to develop your own style for the family court and for me that's a more conversational, less formal approach... one that is attuned to the emotions in the room."* Unless they have *"a pretty convincing reason otherwise"* members become pupil supervisors as soon as they are eligible as the set is concerned to see *"a ten to 15-year age gap, not a 25-year one"* between pupil and supervisor. The result for pupils is *"good relationships"* with supervisors *"who are always there to listen"* and *"take the default position that your work is good and point out where it isn't."*

Attendance at court and tribunals *"three to four times a week"* with a supervisor is backed up by the basic tasks of *"going through five or six lever-arch files,"* *"making disclosures of assets,"* *"research,"* *"filleting bank, mortagage or tax and trusts data into spreadsheets"* and *"taking notes at conference."* Because assets are often held overseas, complex jurisdictional conflict issues arise. As well as shadowing their supervisors, pupils are encouraged to *"spend time with more junior members to experience domestic violence cases or children's cases."* The overall result is that *"as a pupil you will get a taste of all aspects of family law."*

In the first four months of pupillage supervisors give *"a lot of leeway, because no one studies ancillary relief before arriving and you still need to get a grounding."* Subsequently, pupils find a *"marked raising of expectations in the second four months, when you're expected to put the learning into practice."* Because this second period bridges the traditional transition into the practising six, it also sees pupils acquire rights of audience. It is a time to start handling their own smaller family and matrimonial finance instructions. In the third and final four-month period, pupils are acutely aware of the required *"high standards in terms of the documents you produce and your focus on the important issues in a case."* The tenancy decision is taken towards the end of July by the six-strong Tenancy and Pupillage Committee and is based on the collated written reports of each supervisor and *"feedback from anyone who you've worked for"* plus an interview. Normally only one pupil is taken on, but all those we spoke to were confident that *"you're being judged fairly on your own abilities and merit, so you can't complain."* Proving as much, in 2007 two of the three pupils gained tenancy.

Those who do stay on find that *"developing a flexible arsenal of different techniques"* is the way forward. They benefit from *"a great team of clerks"* (who may or may not call them Mr or Miss, depending on how closely they follow the plan to use first names only). Pupils and junior tenants are on occasion to be found drinking together in some local pub, although *"few people's social lives* revolve around chambers." The sense overall is that "taking pride in work" and "a strong work ethic, but with a light touch" is the common theme for members in a set that "rightly thinks highly of itself and is confident in continuing to do well."

Let's assume you have this set on your shortlist; what should you know about its approach to recruitment? What is clear is that chambers is taking an "increasingly structured" approach, reflecting the need to "follow the spirit as well as the letter of our equal opportunities policy." The recruiters tell us they are determined to privilege excellent candidates of whatever background and are willing to look further than the most traditional universities, placing importance instead on "something exceptional in extra-curricular terms" and "something that indicates a particular interest in family law." Needless to say, sound academic achievement remains as important as ever and a dissertation on a family law topic would be a plus. It is also worth pointing out that as first-hand experience of marital finance or the divorce courts is unlikely unless you shadow a barrister, a family law mini-pupillage is highly recommended and chambers offers its own week-long version.

A first-round interview is "relatively informal and relaxed," but the second features a panel of six people who will ask "a sequence of questions that test a candidate's ability to think and justify themselves." As to reasons why you want to be a divorce lawyer, think carefully. As one sage source observed: "It would be a bit worrying if you said you'd wanted to divorce people since the age of 13." What is more likely to sway the panel is "an understanding or interest in human nature and personality" because "even though the case might be a long time after an actual split, divorce still has the capacity to be a very emotional experience on many levels." Along with a head for figures, this need to "enjoy working with real people, real problems and real emotions rather than faceless corporations" is paramount. Whether it's a phe-

nomenally rich banker with assets stashed in complex trusts, "a husband who's run up tens of thousands on hookers," a "standard middle-class divorce" or the occasional legal aid matter, few cases are the same.

2 Hare Court

Chambers UK rankings: Crime, fraud: criminal

Who says crime doesn't pay? After 50 years as one of the Bar's leading criminal sets – handling everything from murder and terrorism to the kidnapping of pop stars, and people and drug trafficking – 2 Hare Court has made it do just that. It is one of the few sets that both prosecutes and defends in equal measure and shows no sign of abandoning its tradition of sending senior members to the bench. Taking the idea of comprehensive coverage to its logical conclusion, members recently acted on both sides of R v Milroy Sloane (a perversion-of-the-course-of-justice case brought against the woman who accused the Hamiltons of rape), while barristers have also figured prominently in the Bloody Sunday Inquiry, the Barry George trial (murder of Jill Dando), the Lee Bowyer public order charge and the Victoria Beckham kidnap plot. Strong relationships with government departments such as Defra, HSE and the Environment Agency ensure a steady stream of high-profile instructions. The set's impressive credentials also mean routine involvement on the part of the Serious Fraud Office and HM Revenue & Customs in some of the most complex and newsworthy fraud cases. Recent highlights include the R v Alibhai appeal (largest anti-piracy case in English legal history, concerning Microsoft software products). Another string to chambers' bow is a well-defined licensing and gaming practice.

The pupillage committee works hard to ensure that pupils are exposed to a wide variety of work during their 12 months. *"We don't see the point in pupils spending all their time with people who prosecute, or just those who do fraud, so we mix it up."* Pupils added: *"It seems they try and vary the personality types too, so some supervisors are more rigorous and some more relaxed."* The first six is spent predominantly in the company of a designated supervisor, learning the ins and outs of court procedures and the skills needed to handle clients. Where possible, the pupil will also work with other members. The emphasis is upon *"pupils being treated as members of chambers; we're proud of them and want to include them in every aspect of chambers' life from trial to lunch."* When things get busy, late nights and weekends are not uncommon. Pupils were sanguine on this point: *"When you come to a set as good as this and have faced such fierce competition for the place, the expectations are high and you don't want to disappoint. It comes down to this: are you committed to this job or not?"*

As the start of second-six looms, life becomes all about advocacy. *"The last month of first-six is mainly spent following other members around and getting as much exposure to the magistrates' court as possible."* This period is also an opportunity to engage in a mopping-up exercise and, together with their supervisors, pupils *"consider what you haven't seen yet and go see it."* Duly armed with broad experience and a helpful information pack *"that could be considered an idiot's guide to anything you would normally do during your second six,"* pupils get up on their feet. And, once up, they rarely sit down. Chambers' lofty position in the overall hierarchy of criminal sets is reflected in the quality of work second-six pupils and new tenants enjoy, but our sources had nevertheless travelled far with their early briefs. At least the set pays travel expenses. Towards the end of pupillage, things start to change: *"You spend the majority of your time in the Crown Court conducting mentions, plea and directions hearings, sentences, applications to dismiss and legal arguments."* There is even *"the possibility of a first Crown Court trial, depending on the individual and the relationships they have built with solicitors."* And if that isn't enough to fill their time, there's also the opportunity to take a two-week secondment at the CPS.

Advocacy is at the heart of a 2HC pupillage and, with in-house *"advocacy exercises for pupils every two weeks in chambers,"* you wouldn't think there'd be much call for further support. How wrong. Our sources detailed a new scheme: *"We have three resident judges at the Old Bailey and we do evening mock trials. This year we have had two."* Even though it must be every aspiring criminal barrister's dream to appear in the Old Bailey, it's fair to say that doing so – even in a mock trial – is daunting. *"I was absolutely nerve-wracked, especially looking around the courtroom at everybody's faces,"* admitted one pupil, *"but once I got going I no longer felt intimidated and at the end I got some brilliant feedback."* As in a number of other criminal sets *"it is unusual for pupils to be taken on after 12 months because it is unlikely that we would learn enough about them within the second six."* Any likely candidates for tenancy stay on at 2HC for a third six, after which a tenancy decision is reached. A committee considers feedback from instructing solicitors and judges and assesses their performance in court and written work. Pupillage is undoubtedly a long haul and current pupils advised *"pacing yourself appropriately."* On the plus side, *"we have no minimum or maximum number of tenants each year,"* confirmed a source; *"if a candidate demonstrates star quality and excellence and it is felt that they will have a flourishing career here, then they will be taken on."*

Life at 2HC is described as *"friendly but very tough."* *"You have to be an extrovert to come here,"* some sources thought, adding that *"shrinking vio-*

lets might struggle." Crime sets are sometimes characterised as dangerously social places and here, true to form, members *"socialise with each other at the pub regularly."* They also make an effort outside the Temple: *"Quite a few of us recently went to the christening of a member's child in Cyprus and we all went to the wedding of another."* They take *"pride in being a friendly set,"* and pupils confirmed that they had been included in the social side of chambers. *"When we're in the pub with members of the pupillage committee after advocacy exercises, they really try to make us feel like we can talk to them."*

For students looking for pupillage, 2HC is one of the most popular on the criminal circuit. It gets hundreds of applications and, on average, invites 50 candidates for a 15-minute first interview. Analysing the quality of applicant, one member of the committee told us: *"Everyone has marshalled or done numerous mini-pupillages,"* so the selection process aims to detect evidence of *"application, intellect and aptitude"* through a consideration of candidates' broader experiences. *"Whether you play a musical instrument or climbed Everest, for instance, can be more telling,"* one recruiter told us. *"Although academic success is important, it's not the sole criteria; we have interviewed those with a 2:2."* A dozen candidates make it through to the second-round interviews, when the questioning tends to focus more on criminal matters, normally including a practical exercise such as a plea in mitigation. Undoubtedly a tough process, the interviewers are aware that some candidates may not previously have undertaken such tasks. *"We are not looking for a polished performance but for advocacy potential."* There are 40 mini-pupillages per year at this set so if you're serious about applying for pupillage perhaps you should also be serious about getting a mini here.

Henderson Chambers

Chambers UK rankings: Health & safety, information technology, product liability, professional discipline, public procurement, real estate litigation

A set that definitely doesn't like to be pinned down by narrow legal categories or outside preconceptions, Henderson defines itself both by the scope of its practice and a working culture characterised by *"strength derived from unity."* Perhaps this latter trait reflects the long history of a set that has consistently evolved at its own pace over the last 60 years. To illustrate: way, way back, what was then 2 Harcourt Buildings enjoyed a reputation as a preeminent divorce set. Come the 1950s, criminal and civil practitioners co-existed at the set. Fast forward to the 1970s and crime was phased out, thus allowing civil matters to take centre stage. An already *"strong pedigree in tort"* made the development of product liability and health and safety practices all the easier. Other successful practices have been built in relation to IT, local government and public law, European law and real estate. As one no-nonsense source observed: *"you get* [incorrectly] *pigeon-holed for your abilities – I mean, we have been involved in some of the largest sports PI cases, advise Formula One and the greyhound racing regulatory body, but we don't market ourselves as a sports law set, so we're not seen as such even though the work is there."*

Although resistant to easy categorisation, the set fully deserves its reputation for excellence in certain areas. Members have advised on some of the largest-ever group actions involving products such as MMR/MR vaccine and tobacco, plus litigation over Sudan Red 1, benzene contamination and Lloyds Names. The set's H&S abilities see barristers involved with everything from industrial disease litigation and public inquiries to defending HSE or local authority prosecutions.

Furthermore, strong relationships with the railway industry and rail regulators mean that Henderson has participated in some of the most significant rail disaster inquiries and corporate manslaughter cases of recent times. Even though members are well known for defending big pharmaceutical and tobacco companies, an increasing number of claimant insurance matters are also taken on. One current instruction relates to a group action by miners against solicitors firms and a trade union concerning their handling of industrial disease compensation claims.

Having briefly experimented with a modern practice manager, Henderson quickly returned to the more traditional steerage of head of chambers and senior clerk. An internal structure centred on 'business groups' is complemented by the *"fantastic entrepreneurial abilities"* of senior clerk John White. Any notion of merger has been eschewed in favour of *"organic and gradual expansion"* and growth in recent years means that the set is on the verge of taking on another floor of the Harcourt buildings. A slinky reception and waiting area suggest you're very much in the 21st century with Elizabeth Blackadder prints and a plasma screen TV booming out BBC News 24 updates. Once on the upper floors there are roaring fires, abundant artwork and views of Temple Gardens.

How do pupils, juniors and even more senior members fit into this matrix of work and styles? There is no straightforward answer; indeed many settled on Henderson because of the *"broad experience on offer in the early years."* Said one source: *"You don't need to profess undying commitment to product liability to get in; everyone is free to develop their own interests and specialisms alongside chambers' traditional fortes."* Provided with a laptop and two supervisors (*"about eight to 15 years' call to ensure a broader range of work"*) over the course of the year, pupils initially work solely for their supervisor before being farmed out to other members. The work undertaken in the first six will initially be characterised by the work of the pupilmaster, but will become more varied with time. Throughout, a pupil is likely to encounter product liability claims, Health & Safety prosecutions, employment and property litigation as well as large property damage and insurance coverage disputes. On the day we visited, one pupil was rushing off to the V&A museum *"to research a contractual point in a potential copyright dispute."* Uniquely, all pupils spend four weeks in Brussels working with the set's long-time associated members who are now part of the law firm McDermott Will & Emery/Stanbrook LLP. Although their accommodation over there is pot luck (*"sometimes amazing, sometimes not"*), the quality of work and experience is uniformly *"fantastic, with close-quarters exposure to EU law."*

The second six is all about *"being on your feet in court or at tribunal anything up to three times a week."* Pupils cut their teeth on *"property and housing, PI and small employment matters,"* but also get to *"junior on larger cases; for example, public procurement."* The clerks keep a watchful eye on a pupil's progress to ensure as broad an experience as possible. Breadth of experience is also likely for juniors up to five or six years' call. One young junior who had just been instructed on their first judicial review (*"a disgruntled applicant for a local authority business grant"*) reflected that *"what's exciting is continually picking up something entirely new and getting to the heart of the matter. You have to be able to expand the boundaries of your knowledge and process information quickly but, more importantly, you have to have the confidence to act on it in court."*

The feedback system at Henderson is one of the most impressive we've come across on our chambers visits. Every piece of work in pupillage is submitted together with a feedback form to be filled out by the relevant member of chambers. *"Everything is very constructively framed,"* commented sources, *"but you're told about your mistakes. You will be picked up if your legal reasoning was insufficient or just plain poor."* This constant commentary *"takes the horror out of the process"* because *"you always know what you have to work on."* It also makes the three-monthly appraisals and the tenancy decision a more transparent process. Early in the summer, a pupil's feedback forms are collated, together with an overview written by each supervisor and feedback via clerks from solicitors. Once this material has been submitted to the tenancy committee *"you wait for a call from the head of chambers."* With one new tenant per year being the norm, someone is usually left disappointed, but it is not absolutely unheard of for several pupils to be successful. In 2006 two pupils accepted tenancy, one of them a third-sixer and in 2007 one of the pair did the same.

Those who take tenancy tend to be *"open people with a relaxed manner socially and a willingness to learn the hard way."* This set prides itself on *"a mutually supportive atmosphere"* with a *"cohesive, congenial"* ethos. One of the more characterful members garages a large remote-controlled battle tank in his room – *"it will sometimes trundle past your door and down the corridor if he's a bit restless."* Outside the confines of the building, pupils join junior tenants for drinks, and the fact that two juniors recently married each other gave cause for more celebrations than usual this year. Add in events like a *"Champagne-powered Christmas party at the Bucks Club"* and set-promoting moments like a recent product liability seminar that had *"solicitors queuing up to get in,"* and there are many occasions to rally round the Henderson flag.

If this set gets onto your shortlist you'll need to know what to expect from its recruiters. The *"intentionally relaxed and informal yet exacting"* interview process currently bucks the trend of setting a written problem for discussion. *"This approach winds candidates up; we prefer people to be fresh, calm and very much themselves."* Of greatest importance to the interview panel is *"roundness of personality, an interest in broad, common law work and a commitment to exploring diversity of practice."* In short, you're *"not expected to have fixated on one area of practice before you arrive"* because chambers believes strongly that *"even though increasing specialisation is a watchword at Bar, there's still a call for broadly experienced barristers with varied ability."*

Hogarth Chambers

Chambers UK rankings: Information technology, intellectual property, media & entertainment

As all you legal historians will be aware, celebrated 18th century painter and satirist William Hogarth caused considerable upheaval when he had the nerve to suggest that artists' work should be protected from other people passing it off as their own. He felt so strongly about this that he successfully petitioned Parliament to introduce a copyright bill. And so the foundations for successive generations of intellectual property lawyers were laid down...

When One Raymond Buildings and 5 New Square merged in 2001, Hogarth was deemed an apt figurehead for their alliance. A further merger with 19 Old Buildings in 2004 brought more IP practitioners on board. High-profile cases such as Arsenal v Reed (where a man selling Arsenal merchandise outside the stadium was prosecuted for breach of copyright) and Douglas v Hello! (where a man and a woman got upset at a magazine taking pictures of them eating cake) have cemented the set's strong reputation in IP and related fields. Nonetheless, there are still enough pure Chancery practitioners knocking around in Hogarth Chambers to ensure pupils are exposed to a variety of work, if they wish.

The fact that the set takes only one pupil per year enables it to tailor the whole experience according to the pupil's needs and practice preferences. In theory, the pupillage is split into four three-month periods spent with different pupil supervisors; in practice this can vary depending on whether a pupil has particular strength in a given area such as patents or media and entertainment. It's certainly not uncommon for a pupil to be away from their supervisor for a number of weeks to assist another member on a case in an area in which they have expressed interest. The idea is that *"the pupil has the opportunity to excel."* Recent recruits were quick to salute the efficacy of the system, saying: *"It stops you feeling like a spare part when you're able to contribute in an area that you actually know something about."* It is possible to have a pure IP pupillage, which will encompass the full range of both 'hard' and 'soft' work. The reason for offering it is simple – chambers wants to ensure that those fully intent on specialising in IP from the outset are not put off by the thought of months spent on Chancery matters. Pupils will find themselves jetting off (at chambers' expense) to Luxembourg or Munich with their pupil supervisors to sit in on European trade mark or patent cases.

A pupillage at Hogarth won't give you much advocacy experience. The majority of a pupil's time is spent in chambers researching and then producing written work, ie opinions and pleadings. Although some of the subject matter can be a little dry (corkscrew patents, anyone?), there is ample glamorous 'soft' IP work on offer. *"The sort of person who thrives here has the ability to analyse material in considerable depth and then explain it clearly and concisely."* With a varied client list that includes drugs companies, manufacturers and elements of the artistic community, it is vitally important to be able to maintain a real handle on the facts to ensure that your advice is accessible yet comprehensive.

So how do you become the intellectual property of Hogarth, for a year at least? Chambers expects a hand-written covering letter with typed CV. It's hard to tell whether this is an attempt to thwart the copy-and-paste approach to covering letters or if they just want to see how close you sat to the front in calligraphy class; either way it undoubtedly gives candidates the chance to *"make their case for interview clearly."* What the recruiters look for above all is *"strong academic credentials,"* and whilst the briefest glance at the CVs of junior tenants might indicate that the best place to establish these credentials is Oxbridge, it is worth noting that the two most recent pupils (and most recent tenant) studied elsewhere. *"We're after people who aren't afraid to engage with a complex subject in real depth,"* noted one member, and the more a candidate can demonstrate this the better their chance of being invited to a first interview. An assessed mini-pupillage is *"a good foot in the door."* Do well and you've probably just doubled your chance of a pupillage interview. The set also values good interpersonal skills as *"when you're dealing with a wide-ranging client base including blue-chip companies such as Nike and Microsoft you need people who are able to press the flesh and inspire clients with confidence."*

At interview the emphasis is on a candidate's ability to think quickly and *"fight their corner well."* With the interview panel attempting to pick holes in your argument, *"your back is against the wall and it's very much a case of sink or swim."* If you stay afloat through to the second round, expect more of the same, but also be on the look out for increasingly bizarre questions. One of our sources was asked to describe a spiral staircase without using the words 'spiral' or 'staircase'...

At 5 New Square the fourth floor is home to many junior tenants and is the driving force behind chambers' social life. Friday evenings might see people amble down to the Seven Stars or go for drinks at someone's home. A not-to-be-missed event – especially if you see yourself as a bit of a Freddie Flintoff – is the annual cricket match against patent and trade mark attorneys Marks & Clerk which *"always leads to quality banter."* Indeed, getting known by solicitors, patent attorneys and trade mark agents is essential in the early years; to this end junior practitioners are encouraged to get involved with seminars and write articles on new developments.

The daily ritual of chambers tea does not seem to be too much of an ordeal for pupils. Admittedly no one portayed it as the most fun you can have without laughing, but it is *"a good opportunity to get everyone on side."* Attendance at tea is not compulsory but pupils tend to *"go with the flow of their pupil supervisor"* so removing the anxiety of the decision about whether to pop in for a cheeky digestive. Speaking of decisions, when the tenancy decisions were made in 2006 and 2007, the set chose not to award tenancy to the year's pupil.

We're not sure if we quite agree with the person who described the set as having *"a magical vibe to it"* as the dominant characteristics of those we spoke to were more connected to intelligence, hard work and ambition than hocus-pocus and abracadabra. More Hogarth than Hogwarts then, and we think that's just the way they like it.

Keating Chambers

Chambers UK rankings: Construction, energy & natural resources, international arbitration: construction/engineering, professional negligence: technology & construction

If you've browsed the shelves of your university law library you may be familiar with one of this set's proudest offerings – *Keating on Building Contracts*. The so-called building contracts bible was last updated by chambers' luminaries Stephen Furst QC and the Hon Mr Justice Ramsey. Only recently appointed a judge, the latter is continuing the set's proud history of sending members to the bench, but don't imagine Keating to be hidebound by tradition...

Purchased by its members three years ago, chambers' expansive, bright and disarmingly calm premises at 15 Essex Street are two minutes from The Royal Courts of Justice and the TCC, housing some 48 barristers. Keating's transformation into a leading construction set started in the early 1980s and today all members are specialists in construction cases. Frequently instructed on different sides of the same case, they handle big-money matters from around the world, with ongoing instructions including myriad disputes relating to the new Wembley Stadium, power stations in several South American countries, Russia's mining industry consolidation and transport projects including the Taiwan high-speed rail link.

Chambers and Partners Construction Set of the Year 2007

Admitting that their work is less attractive to students than the cases offered in more general commercial sets, Keating barristers were keen to advertise its appeal. *"Construction has been at the forefront of jurisprudence for the last 20 years. It's a very dynamic area. What we do is contract and tort,"* explained one. Many of the recent leading cases in the law of negligence have been construction-related and this *"exploration of negligence"* is inevitable when you consider that construction projects are essentially *"a contractual matrix of employers, contractors, subcontractors and subsubcontractors, coupled with the likelihood that one or more will go bust."*

If the academic nature of the work doesn't grab you, the lure of advocacy might. *"You may need to roll your sleeves up and cross-examine a site* foreman, contractor or employer. They could give conflicting factual accounts as to what they did or didn't agree on." It's this human dimension to work that prevents cases from being purely fact-based or technical. As one barrister explained: "*Factual witnesses may also be protecting their own position, and you have to be sensitive to the reality of the politics within companies.*" Fortunately, "*as a pupil you pick it up because your pupilmasters chat through these dynamics with you.*"

However, you should never underestimate the technical and factual aspects. Sometimes cases rest on rooms full of supporting documents, although as one old hand revealed: "*With most there's just a handful of really important documents that could fit into one lever-arch file... you do have to identify those documents and to do so you have to be able to grasp and manage the rest.*" As for the technical side, "*first you learn the basics, then more sophisticated concepts of engineering, sometimes chemistry, sometimes physics...*" True, at least half a dozen members are technically qualified, but amazingly we met barristers at Keating who'd studied only arts subjects and law after the age of 16.

A Keating pupillage involves four spells of three months with different supervisors to ensure broad experience. Pupils also undertake work for other members of chambers, although "*pupilmasters are active in making sure people are not overloaded.*" The view of one PM was that pupils "*should be able to manage workload without being here seven days a week.*" Nonetheless, working evenings and weekends is normal, so unless you're prepared to place your career centre-stage consider your application carefully – "*£35,000 is a big investment in someone and you have to remind yourself of that.*" The set thrives by "*not being stuck in an ivory tower; clients come here because we understand their business...*" and pupils' lives reflect that commerciality. "*It's about rolling up your sleeves and realising you are part of a team with solicitors, experts and clients.*"

Pupils spend most of their time learning how to draft statements of case, particulars of claim, defences and replies. Opinion-writing practice might focus on the liability of an architect for incorrectly estimating future project costs, for example. Additionally, there are opportunities to see PMs and other barristers in action, be it in court or arbitration proceedings or in conference with solicitors and lay clients. Compared to ten years ago there is now significantly greater flexibility of approach in resolving construction disputes and this means a broader range of skills to acquire. "*Pupils help to prepare cases day in day out, they research cross-examination ideas and witness statements; draft mediation position papers, learning that they have to have a different tone to a set of submissions to a judge.*" While there are no set written assessments, "*effectively everything we do is assessed.*" By contrast, there are four formal advocacy exercises in the year and these take place in one of chambers' many arbitration rooms, with a member taking the role of the judge.

In the second six and the early months of tenancy, pupils cut their teeth on small applications and RTA trials, progressing at an early stage to second-junior work on bigger cases. Specifically an advantage of being at a specialist set, juniors can "*get a lot of cross-referrals from other people's practices,*" meaning higher-quality work. Within two to three years after pupillage, young barristers can earn as much as in the major commercial and Chancery sets.

The all-members tenancy decision is made in July after considering a report from the eight-strong tenancy committee comprising the head of chambers, two silks and a spread of juniors. They consider reports from each PM (and any other barrister familiar with the pupil's work) as well as feedback from instructing solicitors and general comments from senior clerks on pupils' conduct and demeanour. "*We try to strip politics out of the decision, but personality does count,*" acknowledged one committee member. In the last five years pupillage hasn't always produced an abundance of new tenants, yet there is an appetite for growth at Keating and in 2006 three of the four pupils gained tenancy, although neither of the two 2007 pupils did. Every member has their own room, and even baby juniors enjoy plenty of space.

As to what leads to success, one PM told us: *"We're looking for a real star; someone who surprises you with their ability at that age."* Taking this idea a step further, it's about *"demonstrating that very serious thought has gone into your work, coming up with good points after a couple of hours."* The tip from one PM was to *"try and put on a few years and act as old as you can sensibly get away with."*

Unlike many of the top Chancery and commercial sets, Keating isn't a pure Oxbridge environment. And just in case you were thinking that this is a male-dominated part of the Bar, half the members under ten years' call are women. One young junior admitted that, even today, a few clients are initially doubtful about instructing a female barrister but can be won over quickly.

Male or female, the barrister's best ally is the Keating brand, and don't members know it – *"rarely do people think they are better than the brand."* By all accounts, *"everyone has time for each other"* in an atmosphere that is *"wonderfully, blissfully apolitical; probably because everyone is happy with their practice and can't work the steam up to get bothered by things."* Thursday is a day for lunching together, although pupils aren't invited. Instead, when time allows they are taken to the pub after work, usually The Edgar Wallace or Daly's Wine Bar. The legendary annual garden party is a time for people to let their hair down, and every now and then it's a time for romance. *"It's led to three weddings,"* revealed a source. Other social distractions include cricket and football, parties at members' houses and occasional point-to-point days with *"champagne and sarnies out of the back of cars."*

As with any kind of specialist practice, a mini-pupillage is a must if you're serious about an application. Keating offers ten week-long, funded and assessed opportunities plus up to 25 that are unfunded and unassessed. Attendance should equip you with a sense of the set's work so you don't look stupid at a pupillage interview. Familiarising yourself with the basic concepts of ADR will also help, but no one expects a fully prepped construction expert at interview. That can come later.

7 King's Bench Walk

Chambers UK rankings: Commercial dispute resolution, insurance, international arbitration: general commercial & insurance, professional negligence, shipping and commodities

Described by one observer as a "smooth classic", 7KBW is the matinee idol of a world slowly disappearing from view. Our initial impressions did little to dispel the sense that this is the Bar of which films – and dreams, perhaps – were made. Sleek but compact rooms with working fireplaces and pink tape scattered about; on one wall a portrait of an 18th century judge observing proceedings with an amused but detached air – this is genuinely the stuff of legal legend. Yet in the last ten years 7KBW has aimed to distance itself from its deeply traditional past by promoting a more user-friendly environment. Although pupils are intently aware of what they are in a position to inherit, they find that the emphasis is less about bowing to one's seniors than maintaining exacting standards. The recollection of being admonished by a senior barrister for referring to a senior barrister as *"Mr"* prompted one former pupil to point out that everyone under 15 years call is close-knit and wont to share a drink rather than *"standing to attention."* Another important shift has seen a growing number of women members – if the current headcount of seven sounds scarce, bear in mind that for many years it was just one. So, no elaborate image makeovers or drastic restructuring, but a gradual evolution befitting a set with a long history to live up to. The contribution made to chambers history in 2006 was the appointment of six new silks, the highest number for any set in this year.

Chambers and Partners Insurance Set of the Year 2007

Although chambers' main home is still no 7, KBW barristers also reside in Nos 4, 8, 9, and part of 10, making it the biggest set still based in the Inns of Court. Over the centuries 7KBW has produced some of the most prominent figures at the Bar: in 1820 Serjeant Wilde defended and saved Queen Caroline's life and honour in the face of an accusation of adultery, and in the 1850s Lord Halsbury occupied rooms here with renowned prosecutor Sir Harry Bodkin Poland. Together they defended a former Governor of Jamaica on a murder charge. The modern-day set was born in 1967 following the merger of 7KBW with 3 Pump Court (another commercial set of antiquity) and over the following four decades chambers has become synonymous with breeding masterful judges. Lords Denning, Brandon, Goff, Hobhouse and Mance as well as Lord Justice Longmore and Messrs Justice Tomlinson, Cooke and Flaux are all former members. Work-wise, shipping was the traditional mainstay until the 1990s, when the set's prominence in the massive Lloyd's insurance litigation highlighted its insurance and reinsurance groups as among the foremost in the country. Insurance now accounts for almost 70% of all work, with members taking central roles in enormous, high profile cases. The

Barings litigation was a recent highlight, as were the cases covering insurance liabilities for breast implants and asbestos-related illnesses plus some interesting marine insurance matters. General commercial cases make up the remainder of the workload with banking, professional negligence and international arbitration featuring regularly.

Instructions pour in to 7KBW from *"just about everyone;"* not for nothing is the set known as the place to come for rigorous, technical and often dazzling application of the law. One pupil enthused: *"There are some absolute geniuses here. They're very understated – people don't boast, probably because they don't have to – but there are just so many clever, clever barristers."* You may be thrilled to hear that court work is just as important as drafting here, with another pupil describing the sight of two senior 7KBW silks against each other in court as *"extraordinary – the most brilliant advocacy I've seen."* Breeding such stellar performers often results in departures to the Bench (*"often too early, I think,"* moaned the senior clerk), which is why pupillage aims to train hopefuls in the same mould. So, if you don't fancy being groomed as an insurance and reinsurance expert look elsewhere, but if policies and finances are your thing expect a dazzling range of experience.

Pupils each sit with four pupil supervisors, the first for three months, then for progressively shorter periods of time with each subsequent PS. Unusually, in only the first three months is the emphasis on learning the ropes and taking work exclusively from the PS; pupils are expected to be *"almost fully fledged"* by the time they move on to their second assignment. By the third switch *"the pressure can get fairly intense and I would say that the learning curve is absolutely vertical,"* reported a source. After the initial three months, pupils can expect to work for any member of chambers, all of whom will make a concerted effort to try out each of them ahead of voting in the final tenancy decision. It means pupils do *"anything and every-*

thing, from drafting pleadings for a QC with huge amounts of paperwork to following up a small research point. It's a good mix of live cases, some of which have been ongoing for one or two years, and previous judgments, where we're encouraged to give something a go ourselves." Current pupils had covered a massive employment class action in the USA and worked on a previous judgment for a £170 million oil drilling platform. They were quick to praise their overseers as "very pleasant and down-to-earth, with absolutely no airs and graces," with one former pupil telling us: "I'm still always popping my head around the door to ask my old pupilmaster's advice."

The pace and pressure of pupillage is undoubtedly strenuous with very high expectations, although the end-of-first-six review and advocacy assessment is only rarely the prompt for a departure. For the most part pupils feel "the confidence in us is very reassuring;" "we're treated very humanely, often sent home at 6 or 7pm, and there's a general sense of goodwill towards pupils." Fulsome feedback and "careful allocation of work and assessments" means "we're always given a reasonable amount of time to do our very best and we know how we're doing." One pupil had recently spent a week on circuit with a High Court Judge, but when it comes to advocacy they are not that lucky – second-six pupils do not appear in court alone themselves. Is this a hindrance? Apparently not: "Too many court appearances wouldn't gel with the work that chambers does. Also, there's just so much to learn – we can't waste time with bail applications."

Two senior clerks are the "driving force" of chambers' social life; they even arrange a night out for pupils and juniors in December. Pupils are also invited along to formal chambers events, as well as the newly initiated monthly buffet lunch. Afternoon tea, however, remains off limits for pupils, the rationale being "we don't want pupils to feel uncomfortable nor do we want to create a

desperate-to-impress situation." Not that they'd have to try that hard to impress. Although the Oxbridge quotient is high, chambers says it wants "the best, irrespective of university." Backing up this claim, recent pupils have come from South Africa, Australia, New Zealand and France. Getting through the single-stage pupillage interview is no cakewalk and includes tough questioning from a five-person panel on a skeleton argument – unsurprisingly, something like an application for leave to appeal to the House of Lords. "We look for analytical and intellectual rigour, and we do take our pupils to task," confirmed a source; "we treat them as if they know what they're doing." Pupils are explicitly told not to compete with one another, though we can't help thinking that it must be hard not to.

New tenants can expect secondments to City law firms and some of the best work around. One junior cited a solo appearance before the Court of Appeal and a turn in the House of Lords with a leader in his first two years. We were suitably impressed. We'll leave the last word to one of the pupils though: "This isn't for the faint-hearted and I feel very lucky indeed to be here."

11KBW

Chambers UK Rankings: Admin & public law, civil liberties, competition/European law, education, employment, local government, public procurement

Set up by Lord Irvine in 1981, 11KBW has just celebrated its 25th birthday. The set has gained a strong reputation over the years, building significant expertise in employment and public law. In the latter, its areas of focus include education, human rights, information law and judicial review. General commercial work is also practised by most members. Lord Irvine left chambers in 1997, at the dawn of the New Labour era, to become Lord Chancellor under his former pupil, Tony Blair. Blair's days as prime minister are now over, but 11KBW's star is still very much in the ascendant. Boasting an array of eminent silks including Eldred Tabachnik, Nigel Giffin and John Cavanagh QC (not the one off the telly), the set has had members involved in many of the big cases over the years. It also looks pretty good at the lower end, with plenty of up-and-coming juniors expected to make QC in the future. For junior tenants, the set offers the ideal mix of trial advocacy, written work, working alone and being led, while pupils enjoy the glamour of working for pre-eminent individuals in their field. With the set's rigorous approach to assessment and feedback, carrying out a pupillage at 11KBW is in some ways like attending a very good school – which is perhaps appropriate for a set specialising in education law.

Chambers and Partners
Employment Set of the Year 2007

11KBW's practice has developed with the world around it. Education law wasn't there from the start but now it's huge, and in the future it is envisaged that there will be more instructions in relation to information law. *"We're ahead of the field in getting that work,"* explained a clerk; *"the Information Commissioner is a regular client and a lot of public authorities also instruct."* Employment and public law are still the core disciplines, bringing in issues such as housing, welfare benefits and detention, removal and extradition. There are also nine members of chambers who act on government panels. Philip Sales QC is the First Treasury Junior (Common Law), and regularly appears before the European Court of Human Rights in Strasbourg on behalf of the Government. In January 2007 Jonathan Swift (not the one from Lilliput) was appointed to the Treasury as First Junior (Chancery). *"It's quite a compliment to us,"* remarked senior clerk Lucy Pilbro – especially as this is the first time that both Treasury Devils (as the role is known) have belonged to the same set.

While employment law is an area that has relevance and interest for almost everyone, public law regularly gives rise to topical debates such as the RemedyUK-initiated judicial review of the Government's training mechanism for junior doctors. Members acted for the Department for Health and the British Medical Association in this case. Other examples include the case surrounding Shambo, the sacred Hindu bullock which tested positive for tuberculosis. Clive Lewis, who acts as First Junior Counsel to the National Assembly for Wales, took on this case. Another you may have read about is the test case raised by Christian magistrate Andrew McClintock regarding adoption by same sex couples, in which a discrimination claim was made against the Department for Constitutional Affairs. And finally, there have been cases relating to prisoners detained in Guantanamo Bay. Philip Sales QC and Ben Hooper acted on the Al-Rawi case, in which the Foreign Secretary was challenged on his decision not to request the release and return of three detainees. Mr Al-Rawi has now been returned to the UK and the case awaits a further appeal in the House of Lords.

As these examples demonstrate, 11 KBW works in areas of law that have *"a tangible effect on the lives of the people involved."* As such, its barristers need to be good at reading people. In employment cases, for example, *"you're often looking at a breakdown of relationships between people in the workplace"* or, in cases involving discrimination, *"trying to perceive people's motives."* One member described the work as being like *"Heat magazine for nerds."* Employment and public law are still quite technical areas, requiring intellectual rigour and analysis, but you'll also need to be able to adjust to dealing with *"the bloke off the street, a local authority or a major corporation."*

Of course, you also need to be able to appeal to a judge. Advocacy forms a fundamental part of chambers work and, as well as a formal advocacy test, pupils are expected to carry out at least one FRU case during the year. Junior barristers will typically appear in court at least once a week, with employment tribunals providing *"fantastic"* experience, as *"you get to take part in lots of full trials, from cross-examining witnesses to opening and closing submissions."* For every day spent in court there will generally be two days preparing, and the experience as a whole is described as *"very satisfying – there's a lot of personal interaction with the client, especially as cases can last four or five days."* Two thirds of a baby barrister's work will come from employment tribunals, the remainder being made up of commercial and public law cases, often led by a QC. This is a great way of experiencing high-level work – drafting the skeleton argument for a case in the Court of Appeal, reading through a dozen lever-arch files of documents and generally attaining *"a detailed familiarity with the case"* that your leader may not have. *"You can do an infinite amount of work in the preparation for a trial,"* explained a junior, but everyone finds their optimum level. *"We've all met those people at university who can work 18 hours solidly in the run up to exams... but I'm definitely not one of those."*

As well as gaining exposure to *"exceptional quality work,"* there are other benefits to starting your career at 11KBW. *"You get opponents as a junior practitioner who try and throw their weight around and intimidate you,"* explained one baby junior, *"but as soon as they see where you're from, they stop."* If you're getting harangued about a topic you don't know much about, you can also *"phone a friend"* back in chambers. *"Everyone gets on and is supportive of each other,"* explained a source, and with wide participation in events such as the 25th birthday bash at Tate Modern – which attracted over 300 clients – there's also *"a ready-made forum for new tenants and pupils to go and network."* Another thing no one has to worry about is a lack of work: *"We've just had to buy two new trolleys,"* explained a clerk, *"because people are in court so much nowadays!"*

The set takes up to four pupils a year, the exact number being entirely dependent on the calibre of applicants. On several occasions in recent years it has taken only one pupil. Getting an interview for pupillage can be tough. It's also an unofficial requirement that you do an assessed mini-pupillage, so make sure you apply for one of these well in advance. If you get to interview, you'll find yourself opposite a panel of five or six barristers for a full 40 minutes, discussing a House of Lords case sent in the post a week before. You'll need to show confidence, lateral thinking, a good legal brain and an ability to think on your feet, especially as a certain amount of devil's advocacy is played at this stage. A member of the pupillage committee advises candidates to *"see the question as a challenge, and take it."*

Pupillage is divided into two three-month periods and one six-month period, each with a different supervisor. It's not an interview so much as *"a probationary period"* as there's no cap on the number of tenants taken on – another benefit of having plenty of work to go round. Across chambers there are some early-risers who come in at the crack of dawn and a flock of night birds who prefer to work by lamplight. Pupils, however, generally arrive at about 8.30am and are encouraged to leave by 6.30pm. Assessment follows a rigorous system of marking and double-marking almost every piece of work a pupil completes. As a result, by the end of ten months, most of the senior members will either have seen the pupil's written work or worked with them directly. More junior tenants will have got to know them informally as their role is generally limited to *"chatting and taking them out for lunch."* Reports on assessed pieces of work are put into a file – a bit like coursework – and handed to the pupillage committee, which makes its recommendation to members in July. Once the dust has settled, the last few months are a chance to *"recuperate and prepare for tenancy."* At this stage a successful pupil will spend time shadowing juniors in order to make the adjustment from *"highfalutin' High Court stuff"* to *"a trip to Reading on a Monday morning."* In 2007, all three pupils were lucky enough to be offered tenancy.

In a set that has found the formula for success, no big changes are afoot. Following the 25th birthday celebrations, 11KBW engaged in some stylish rebranding, described as *"giving ourselves a face-lift."* Its premises are next in line for a makeover, and there are plans to connect number eleven with some of the rooms in numbers nine and ten, as well as improving the reception area and refurbishing conference rooms.

Despite the requirement for bookish behaviour, *"we don't have the attitude of being locked away in our ivory towers,"* explained one member. Another agreed, stressing that the set had no *"air of superiority,"* nor did it nurture *"the great divide"* between clerks and barristers. Said one source: *"Without exception, people here are accessible and approachable."* This may be so, but accessing pupillage at this popular set will be no easy task.

Landmark Chambers

Chambers UK rankings: Admin & public law, agriculture & rural affairs, civil liberties, environment, local government, planning, real estate litigation

Landmark's brand new premises on the corner of Fleet Street and Fetter Lane have a certain air of Bond-villain hideout about them. A silent lift transports you to the reception where you are greeted by an impeccably polite host who was once former head receptionist at the New Zealand Parliament building. You glance around: an army of clerks goes about its business behind plate glass windows; the conference rooms boast all manner of Q-inspired gadgetry; giant plasma screens hang from several walls; the door to the post room bears the ominous legend 'No Entrance to Barristers'. Is there a pool filled with carnivorous fish? Are the chief exec and head of chambers hatching plots in their corner offices with views across the City? Well, no. In truth, the slick detail of the new premises reveals little more about Landmark than its confidence as a business and a defining aura of professionalism. While other chambers take baby steps away from the Inns, Landmark has powered into its second external home, confidently signing a 15-year lease of 180 Fleet Street. It has reason to be optimistic: the set's combined turnover grew by 10% to £15.9 million in 2006.

Formed just four years ago from a merger of leading planning and public law chambers 4 Bream Buildings and planning set Eldon Chambers, Landmark is widely acknowledged to be the Bar's pre-eminent planning law chambers. Its capacity for other types of public law and a burgeoning environmental law practice are also well known. Landmark planning barristers have worked on multiple aspects of the site proposals and associated regeneration schemes for the 2012 Olympics, as well as on inquiries into the Shard of Glass (aka London Bridge Tower) and Arsenal's new Emirates Stadium. The set's public law practitioners were involved in The Hutton Inquiry and aspects of the London Eye's landlord's attempts to either recover possession of the site or increase its rent. Their environmental law colleagues have featured on The Shell Haven Inquiry into the new Thames Gateway port and matters pertaining to the Crossrail Bill. Among chambers' best known figures is new head

Christopher Katkowski QC, commonly referred to as Kit Kat.

Chambers is *"working hard to stay at number one"* and is doing so in a number of ways. Working on the basic premise that *"specialisation is the way forward: it's what clients want,"* there is a mandate to engage more directly with specific sectors; for example, *"the water industry, which is facing massive reservoir and water shortage issues."* At the same time, in the area of public law, recruitment at senior level is helping the set towards its target of *"being on a par with Blackstone."* In property law, the aim is to *"add quality people"* and *"develop the areas of overlap, say, between property and human rights."* This desire for increased specialisation does not narrow a pupil or junior tenant's prospects; indeed those we interviewed saw Landmark as offering both *"an enormous amount of varied, junior-level work"* and *"a real opportunity to shape your own career."*

Pupils sit with a total of four supervisors, the first three covering the set's main practice areas in no particular order. Being exposed to the full extent of chambers' work helps develop *"an understanding of the complex intersection between disciplines; for example, focusing on right-to-property matters crosses over public and property law."* Within the 'seat' structure there is some room for manoeuvre. One pupil had *"secured more time for public law-oriented work in my three months in property because it was my forte."* The exact nature of work does vary between disciplines; for example, property law is *"more chambers-based drafting and research"* than public law, which can involve more *"site visits, conferences and heavy opinion writing."* Whatever the practice area, supervisors *"give virtually constant feedback, both positive and negative,"* on the pupils' attempts at skeleton arguments, research notes and draft pleadings. As well as occasional work for other members, each three-month period involves a short time shadowing a QC (*"so that you see high-profile cases and the top-end stuff"*). It doesn't sound as if pupils are stretched to breaking point at this stage. One told us: *"You're sometimes almost physically thrown out of the office if you're still there after 6pm."* Chambers' recruiters were clear in their views on pupillage, telling us of their *"determination that it should not be a horrible experience"* and their belief that *"pupillage is a coaching and mentoring exercise to help pupils achieve their potential."* Whatever happened to having a rugby ball thrown at you at interview or a year of character-building slavery for a lunatic pupilmaster?

In the second six, being on your feet in court once or twice a week is *"an essential part of the process."* At this stage pupils are still carefully protected by their supervisors and the clerks, and none of them go out without completing an advocacy exercise. *"To be honest it was more scary getting up in front of senior people in chambers to practise than on the first day in court,"* one source confessed. After their practice run, Leasehold Valuation Tribunals and small possession hearings await the second sixer.

Landmark pupils were relatively sanguine about the tenancy decision, confident that *"if there is the capacity for three pupils to stay, and three are good enough, three will be kept on."* Such composure is perhaps a product of an assessment system that sees pupils complete the same three QC-set written tasks (one per practice area). Each assessment is *"contemporary and based on what the QC is working on."* Pupils told us that their most recent assessment had been *"to write a speech for the European Court of Human Rights."* These tests – together with supervisor reports and external feedback – influence the tenancy decision. In both 2006 and 2007 two of the three pupils were offered tenancy. Those who aren't offered tenancy are helped with their search for a third six elsewhere; those who are enter *"a bubble* of constant work" where regular "practice meetings with clerks" enable them to "define and develop [a] career depending on interest and ambition." Based on our interviews this is no hollow claim: describing their caseloads, young juniors listed educational tribunal work, public inquiries and claimant immigration cases plus work on planning matters for housing associations and local authorities. They had also had involvement with environmental cases, freedom of information matters and judicial reviews.

At Landmark, the social life is "balanced and not all-encompassing." A group of junior tenants meets for drinks at the Wine Cellar "just downstairs" or, "now we're a little better off, cocktails at One Aldwych." This group forms a welcoming committee for incoming pupils, organising "dinners and drinks" as well as providing "heads around the door and advice on where to turn if you need help with work." Supervisors are said to make time to get to know their charges, and one pupil told us they had come to enjoy "daily tea, cake and chat breaks at 4.30pm with my supervisor."

We observed a high calibre of pupil at Landmark. While there were no common denominators in terms of university background, degree subject or personality, all possessed postgraduate qualifications and had practical experience in a field related to the set's interests. Whether it was working for immigration and housing charities, being an election observer in Eastern Europe or taking a post at the EU or UN, these pupils were able to demonstrate close involvement with public, environment and/or planning law. Perhaps in an attempt not to scare off applicants, one chambers recruiter explained that "any evidence of interest in the set's work is enough; perhaps there was a local planning case that caught the candidate's eye and they went to the inquiry." The interview process was undergoing review when we visited and the plan was to add a second stage or some form of assessment exercise. Suffice to say that if you are one of the 150 who apply, or one of the roughly 20 who are called to interview, you can expect "straightforward questions that aren't intimidating but focus on competencies" and "give you the chance to shine." Landmark has just added to its calendar a pupillage open day complete with Q&A session because "student feedback told us they weren't involved enough." It sounds like the perfect precursor to a mini-pupillage.

Maitland Chambers

Chambers UK Rankings: Agriculture and rural affairs, Chancery: commercial, Chancery: traditional, charities, commercial dispute resolution, company, fraud: civil, insolvency/corporate recovery, partnership, professional negligence, real estate litigation

Maitland's website uses a quote from our parent publication, Chambers UK: "Maitland has become synonymous with 'great brains', as evinced by the now familiar term of disparagement employed when describing another set: 'They're good but not a Maitland.'" It's fair to say that this set has brains and a head big enough to hold them, but if Maitland has a big ego, it is at least justified. Chambers UK puts it in its top band for commercial Chancery, a position it has become well used to since its formation in 2001 through a merger of 13 Old Square and 7 Stone Buildings. Not that this was the end of its merger phase – in 2004 Maitland was joined by the members of 9 Old Square.

Combining a healthy mix of specialists and generalists, the set has 64 members, 15 of them silks, and is frequently compared to a solicitors firm for its staffing and size. As well as commercial Chancery, the set is proficient in areas as diverse as IP, company law, agriculture, property and entertainment law. Its instructions come from around the world, and there are particularly strong links with the offshore tax havens in the Caribbean, the Cayman Islands, the Channel Islands and the Isle of Man. More general commercial work has its base in Hong Kong, whilst many US entities are represented in broad commercial litigation, *"not on US soil, but up in the multi-jurisdictional ether."* Recent case highlights include Donegal International Ltd v Zambia & Anor, a much-publicised case involving a US vulture fund which bought cheap distressed debt in Zambia and forced a claim for more than ten times the purchase price through the UK courts. Although the vulture fund achieved a favourable monetary judgment, Maitland was said to have won a *"moral victory"* for its Zambian client. Other examples include a multi-party dispute about online music downloads involving iTunes, Yahoo!, AOL and the British Phonographic Industry; the insolvency case surrounding the collapse of MG Rover (Guy Newey QC acted as a DTI inspector in the accompanying investigation); property litigation involving the land surrounding Wembley Stadium; a House of Lords case regarding the leases and types of trading allowed by the Covent Garden Market Authority; and a commercial contract dispute involving Universal Studios in the Court of Appeal. The nature of much of the set's offshore work means that members are also regularly instructed to attend the Privy Council.

A 12-month pupillage at Maitland is a serious affair. Supervisors take a *"regulatory role"* to protect charges from being ambushed by multiple members of chambers, also ensuring they receive a broad mix of high-quality work. *"I'm quite strict: if* [other members] *want something done, they come through me,"* said a supervisor. Pupillage is actually a relatively short time (the tenancy decision is made in mid-June), so it's important for pupils to spend their time on *"appropriate tasks"* which will help *"tool them up for practice."* The first three months are spent *"getting embarrassing mistakes out of the way,"* and then, after Christmas, a pupil's performance really starts to count. The first supervisor takes a less influential role in the tenancy decision, while supervisors from January to June have to ensure that everything on the pupillage checklist gets ticked off. One remarked that their job was akin to *"bird spotting."* In May or June written reports are gathered by the pupillage committee (Pupco) from each of these supervisors and a recommendation is then made to the entire membership.

Pupils described the year as *"fair"* and said they were *"treated with respect and professionalism."* *"It's not a culture of aggressive assessment,"* said one, *"but you're told when you get it wrong."* The set is too big for pupils to be given an individual introduction to every member of chambers, but after Christmas they meet a fair few people because they change supervisors roughly every six weeks. This suits them fine because *"having to meet everyone and remember their names in the first week would be horrific!"* They described chambers' work as *"crunchy,"* a term translated as meaning *"mentally demanding"* and *"involving a lot of mulling things over."* Given the crunchiness of it all, even with the civilised hours of 9am to 6pm during pupillage, it was understandable that pupils spoke of getting that Friday feeling as the week drew to a close.

Maitland isn't known for attracting the most colourful characters: having a top-notch brain and common sense are far more important. So if the name Pupco makes you think of bounding, yapping puppies, think again. Close rival Wilberforce Chambers has a few members who bring their dogs into work, but at Maitland we could more easily see them owning perfectly groomed cats. Our overriding impression was that, if you're anything less than a perfectionist, you'd be happier elsewhere.

Going to court is an important part of pupillage at Maitland, and supervisors insist that pupils take an active role. One source explained the drill: *"They read through all the papers beforehand, decide what they would do if they were the advocate and then have a lengthy discussion with their supervisor beforehand."* With all the extra time this takes, *"it can be quite onerous being a supervisor"* and we got the impression that not everyone who qualified was chomping at the bit to become one. There are five advocacy training exercises during pupillage, the principal purpose of which is to *"get a feel for doing your own submissions before you have to do it for a paying client."* Said a source: *"You need to know what those nerves are going to feel like... and you need to experience what it feels like to have some cranky judge turn your skeleton argument upside down."* Pupils divide the rest of their time between drafting, reading through paperwork and carrying out complex legal research. There is no prospect of getting on your feet in court as a pupil. At least the range of legal disciplines covered is wide – company law, insolvency, civil fraud, personal bankruptcy, partnership, professional negligence, property, probate, landlord and tenant and general commercial cases will all come across pupils' desks. Said a source: *"One of the most difficult tasks is learning what all the books and authorities are."* Thankfully there's not much photocopying or making tea and *"your work is always taken seriously as a valid educational exercise, even if it isn't being used."* Nevertheless, *"until chambers has given you the nod, they don't want you representing a client or writing opinions with Maitland's name on it."*

Maitland is big enough that members can opt in and opt out of social activities as they please. Many choose to drop in for afternoon tea on their way back from court; others prefer the weekly pub trips organised by the social committee (Pubco), which are far more relaxed affairs. The social side of pupillage is important, as it provides *"a less artificial experience...you get the chance to see people as they really are."* For the rest of the time, as one member recalled: *"It can feel a bit like being at the bottom of a pond looking up at the world above the surface...it's all a blur."*

If this is the case, being taken on feels like *"breaking through the surface and seeing things clearly."* The advantage of commercial Chancery, as opposed to straight commercial practice, said a recently qualified junior, is that *"you get a lot of your own cases and trials."* A baby junior's practice is generally split 50/50 between their own cases and being led, with the former providing a vital opportunity to *"cut your teeth."* *"A full three-day trial over who owns some parking spaces may not be glamorous, but it is incredibly useful experience when you're the one heading up the litigation team."* Work varies between *"contractual spats over the delivery of widgets"* and application-based insolvency work to cases where *"the precedents are fairly balanced and it hasn't yet been canvassed in the courts... so you know the decision is likely to end up in a textbook."* In these cases, juniors will *"turn up at small application hearings,"* while a QC will be called in to do the cross-examination, a fine art where *"asking the wrong question could get you in a lot of trouble."* As complexity and value bear no direct relation to one another, *"sometimes a thin set of papers with only five sheets will turn into a legal nightmare with some incredibly tricky arguments and questions over the choice of law."* What this means is that even work at the junior end can throw up some meaty issues. However, it is worth bearing in mind that the time you dedicate to a problem is ultimately *"a question of costs"* – something ardent perfectionists could find frustrating.

Maitland is a set where excellence is expected and pupils are pushed hard. It's not about the speed with which you work but the quality of the final product. As a pupil put it, the culture is *"a thinking one... as opposed to the hours culture down in the Temple."* Now surely Maitland wouldn't dream of looking down its nose at pure commercial sets... would it?

Matrix Chambers

Chambers UK Rankings: Administrative and public law, civil liberties, competition/European law, crime, defamation/privacy, education, employment, environment, fraud: criminal, immigration, police law: mainly claimant, public international law

With a name that provokes images of Keanu Reeves bending round bullets in a long leather coat, and offices with Cage & Fish-style unisex toilets that are more reminiscent of a solicitors firm, it's easy to understand why Matrix is the household name of barristers' chambers. Across the country, people know of the set, whether it's via the tabloid press – courtesy of founding member, Cherie Booth QC – or the law reports. But don't let the glitz and the glamour distract you. Ultimately, Matrix is a serious-minded set, where important, precedent-setting work is carried out on a daily basis. Ben Emmerson QC, Philippe Sands QC and Raza Husain represented seven of the appellants in the 2004 House of Lords case which decided that indefinite detention without trial of foreign terrorist suspects was incompatible with the European Convention on Human Rights. Rabinder Singh QC and Alex Bailin were also instructed by Liberty in this case, in which the Anti-Terrorism, Crime and Security Act introduced after 9/11 was described as something out of the Stalinist era and *"the stuff of nightmares."* In the world of commerce and industry, Philippe Sands QC has been instructed in an international arbitration of a dispute involving the Hashemite Kingdom of Jordan and the construction of a dam, while Clare Montgomery QC appeared in the FSA's challenge to the flotation of an $84bn Russian oil group on the London Stock Exchange. Her case incorporated elements of public law, commercial law and criminal law. In short, open any paper, on any day, and senior practice manager Amanda Illing is confident that you'll find a piece relating to chambers' work.

Stop! We need to backtrack a moment because the word chambers is officially termed *"the c-word"* here at Matrix. Other banned words include pupil, pupillage, pupilmaster, tenant and clerk. Matrix offers traineeships, and if you are invited to interview for one you'll need to attend its offices to meet some of the barristers. Semantics aside, the traineeship is not drastically different from pupillage anywhere else: applicants still go through OLPAS, trainees sit with four supervisors for periods of three months each, and in early July, following two written and advocacy assessments, a decision is made about whether the trainee is invited to stay on permanently. Needless to say, by the end of 12 months, trainees are *"stunningly fluent in Matrix-speak."*

The main difference is the level of involvement trainees have in selecting their supervisors (in effect, Matrix will *"design a package around their interests")* and the number and variety of disciplines covered. Given the trend towards specialisation at the Bar, this is decidedly unusual. *"We like to think we're bucking that trend, demonstrating the positive aspects of cross-fertilisation between different areas,"* said a source. The set is divided into three teams: crime and public international law; employment, discrimination and media; and public law (which takes in commercial and competition law, legal aid and judicial review). Trainees sit with at least two teams during the year.

Don't worry too much about deciding which areas you'd like to specialise in beforehand: *"I'm rather in favour of students having an open mind,"* said one recruiter; *"having fixed ideas too early can be a bad thing."* In fact, *"the biggest message"* delivered at a law careers day jointly held by Matrix and magic circle law firm Clifford Chance for school age students in Camden and Tower Hamlets is *"take the degree in the subject you're interested in... you can always convert to law afterwards."* This might sound surprising from a set with such a strong academic focus and several legal scholars, but it's true enough. Just in case you were wondering, Philippe Sands QC is Professor of Law at UCL and James Crawford SC is Professor of International Law at Cambridge.

Unlike some of the evangelical human rights sets, Matrix has no policy regarding who it will represent: barristers act for the government and other public authorities as well as claimants. While people are passionate about their work – one member literally jumped up and down with excitement on receipt of a recent brief – it's not so much about fighting for a cause or capturing the moral high ground as exploring and establishing legal principles.

Unsurprisingly, your average Matrix barrister has a sparkling academic record. However, they tend to have also excelled in a number of other things before arriving at the Bar. Whether it's working in a Citizen's Advice Bureau or volunteering for an NGO, the message is clear: if you're fresh out of university, *"go away and do something useful, then come back in five years."* Perhaps this shouldn't always be taken literally; the recruiters at Matrix would be the first to admit that *"not everyone can afford to take a year out to volunteer for Liberty."* Equally, you could be so brilliant that you don't need an internship at the Legal Aid Department of Malawi or to win the World Debating Championships. Yet experience suggests these types of experience do help, and with somewhere in the region of 400 applicants vying for just two places, it's understandable that successful candidates *"tend to be a little bit older."*

Until recently, Matrix was verging on becoming a little superannuated itself. Founded by a group of established practitioners in 2000, they have inevitably matured somewhat and this has necessitated an injection of new blood at the junior end. Several younger barristers have joined the set, and recruiting new trainees also features heavily in the plan for growth. If they meet the (albeit high) quality threshold, trainees stand every chance of being taken on. As one put it: *"You're only in competition with yourself."*

Ironically, although a commitment to offering training opportunities is one of the set's core values, its top-heaviness was at risk of jeopardising the quality of the training on offer. Until recently, trainees and baby juniors lacked low-level work. For example, both the trainees we spoke to shared an interest in crime, yet although Matrix boasted countless *"very successful practitioners who are in the Old Bailey all the time,"* small-end magistrates' court work was thin on the ground. The practice managers duly set about looking for work for them and – from the tired looks on their faces – we'd say that ever since they barely had time between cases to pause for breath.

Uniquely, going out looking for interesting new cases is something Matrix barristers and their instructing solicitors do together. In some cases, the search is even driven by *"political"* motives, as trainee supervisor David Wolfe's interest in academy schools and developments in the provision of healthcare demonstrates. Whoever supervises, you can guarantee that the work will be *"top-drawer."* A certain amount depends on the personality of the barrister you're working with (*"they have their quirks,"* chuckled a trainee); one interviewee even *"did some devilling for Cherie,"* describing her as *"really encouraging and easy to work with."* Drafting opportunities are in plentiful supply and you basically do *"everything your supervisor does."* Importantly, trainees learn about differences in tactical approach and style because, with each supervisor, they are *"copied into every e-mail and conference-called into every phone call."* One very important lesson is how to make the right choice of font. While one supervisor was *"a Times New Roman kind of guy,"* another *"dabbled in Verdana."* Contractual hours are 9am to 6pm, but trainees confessed to *"working at home to catch up,"* agreeing unanimously that the experience is *"quite intense."*

At the end of six months, trainees receive feedback from their first two supervisors via a formal review. Supervisors also submit reports to the traineeship committee, and these are eventually used at the general meeting to help decide whether trainees should be invited to join Matrix permanently. At that meeting, a two-thirds majority is needed to reach a decision.

In their second six, trainees generally take on some of their own cases, although *"Matrix isn't known for its baby barrister work."* Case management discussions at employment tribunals, a county court trial over *"a bizarre contract point"* and taking notes in a long murder trial at the Old Bailey are all recent examples of second-six work. Certainly, the prospect of representing people and fighting for their interests is *"a rush,"* but *"it's like someone said in ER, 'You need to be scared of making mistakes or patients could die.'"* To make sure they're up to the challenge, an advocacy assessment in May gives trainees *"a very rough ride,"* with paragraph-by-paragraph feedback provided afterwards. Advocacy training sessions from juniors give useful pointers for appearances in employment tribunals and bail applications in the mags' court. In addition, trainees can be sent out on secondment in their second six. Whether it's a week with the Disability Rights Commission, a stint in the BBC's litigation department or a five-day jaunt with *The Times'* litigation team, being treated as in-house counsel is *"an ego boost"* and, who knows, *"perhaps one day they'll instruct you..."*

If you see yourself working in a set boasting its own chill-out zone, conference rooms complete with mini-bars and a Thursday lunch-club where you could end up *"sitting next to Rabinder Singh chatting about Big Brother,"* Matrix could be your ticket to living the dream. It's a topsy-turvy world that will test and challenge you every step of the way, and – as you'd expect of a set located in an ex-police station – breaking in is no easy feat.

Monckton Chambers

Chambers UK rankings: Competition/European law, public procurement, tax: indirect tax, telecommunications

As everyone knows, exteriors can be misleading. The sunny gardens of Gray's Inn look like a welcoming oasis in the heart of Holborn, but the weary public can only rest there for two hours in the middle of the day. Similarly, if you walk into the gardens from Theobald's Road and cast your eye to the right you'll see an immaculate 17th century brick terrace with period sash windows. But if you were to press your nose to the glass of Monckton Chambers you'd find much more than aged wigs and dusty legal tomes. Ten years ago the set *"took the view that for everyone to work to their fullest capacity we needed a full-time marketing and administration team."* It adopted a sleek *"corporate"* face to go with the administrative changes, and a slick refurbishment of its premises – including the addition of Nos 1 and 2 Raymond Buildings – shows the set has the steel to follow through on what it starts.

The history of this set goes right back to the 1930s when renowned constitutional lawyer Walter Monckton was head of chambers. Following a distinguished career as a barrister Monckton twice became a cabinet minister, then chairman of Midland Bank and eventually earned the title of viscount. A trusted adviser to Edward VIII, he is widely credited as the author of the King's 1936 abdication speech.

After moving to Gray's Inn in the 1960s the set began to develop its competition law practice, gaining a stranglehold on work before the Monopolies and Mergers Commission (now the Competition Commission), initially for the regulators then increasingly for private sector clients. In recent times members have represented adidas, the OFT in the MasterCard litigation in the Competition Appeals Tribunal (CAT), several parties in the replica football kits case, and the British Horseracing Board in its private competition litigation with At The Races in the Court of Appeal. A number of members of chambers are especially well regarded for their expertise at the intersection of competition, state aid and procurement advice. Competition and EU law now amounts to roughly a third of chambers' workload, with tax and VAT cases making up another significant tranche. In tax matters, Monckton barristers have taken key roles in Marks & Spencer v HMRC and Hutchison 3G and Others v CCE, which is potentially the biggest VAT case ever in terms of the amount of money at stake. The third of Monckton's main areas is public law, where it handles commercial and regulatory judicial reviews as well as human rights matters. Aside from the three core strands there is plenty of other expertise within chambers; for example, our colleagues at *Chambers UK* regard the set highly for public procurement and telecommunications work, while environmental, construction and general commercial cases are all handled with aplomb.

Another important influence on Monckton came in the 1980s when good relations were cemented with various government departments. All Monckton juniors now aim to get on at least one list of government-approved counsel and this source of work is important to the set. In the simplest terms, Monckton is one of the premier sets for European, competition and tax law, rivalled by only a small handful of other elite outfits.

With numbers capped to two per intake and every single pupil in the last four years offered tenancy, there's a real sense that if you can make it through the pupillage recruitment stage, there's an excellent chance your name will be added to the roll call of Monckton barristers within a year. First-round interviewees are invited for a getting-to-know-you chat with five panellists and are sometimes asked to endure, sorry enjoy, a mini-pupillage before the second interview some weeks later. At this stage applicants receive a mock brief and, just 30 short minutes later, are grilled by the rigorous pupillage committee which *"tests for outstanding analytical skill and for sharp, intellectual prowess."*

Of course, winning tenancy should never be taken for granted. Pupils sit with four supervisors for three months each, with the all-important decision coming in July at the end of the third stint. They become very familiar with the individual practices of their supervisors, so if the person you sit with has a very niche practice, then chances are you'll *"know more of the area by the end of your seat than all but about six or seven practitioners at the entire Bar."* One pupil explained: *"Some of the work is extremely specialist... I had done no public procurement work, and for a few weeks I was flying by the seat of my pants."* But pupils aren't just restricted to such specialist work; for example, they could also discover the delights of VAT law or indulge a long-held passion for EU law.

The first three months is all about getting to grips with life as a Monckton barrister and pupils will work almost exclusively for their supervisor. In a reflection of the nature of practice in chambers, pupils will spend a considerable amount of time researching points of law and having a go at writing opinions. There's more of the same in the second three months, by which time they'll have visited court a few times to see how their supervisor handles advocacy. At this stage other members of chambers are also encouraged to find work for the pupils to ensure that they are exposed to a range of legal issues. In the final three-month period before the tenancy decision the pace quickens – one pupil had recently assisted on an *"extremely high-profile case, which was quite something to see on the Ten O'Clock News when I got home."* Another had used fluent German to translate a piece of legislation for a matter being heard by the European Court of Human Rights. Our sources agreed that pupillage is *"intellectual and challenging." "There's a lot of background research on very intricate points of law, or bespoke drafting for the area's experts."* And they have to be able to adapt to different styles of working as *"some of the pupil supervisors are very collaborative and others are more inclined to let you get on with it. Either way, the expectations are very high."*

Compared to most other sets, this is not a court-heavy environment. Chambers will pay for additional advocacy courses, but within pupillage itself there is little formal advocacy assessment. Our sources were sanguine on this point, one recognising that *"if I'd gone elsewhere after pupillage the advocacy might have been more of an issue, but the amount I'd done as a pupil – and beforehand – was appropriate for my practice at Monckton."* In some sets, second-six pupils are prevented from taking their own paid work but here at Monckton, if the clerks can find something, they are free to take it. Usually it will be something like a small VAT tribunal application; nothing too demanding. With tenancy decided in July after nine months in chambers, it's not uncommon for successful pupils to take on a fair bit of their own work before tenancy begins. Fondly reflecting on the closing stages of the year, a new tenant remarked: *"I found that there really isn't much that separates the pupils from the baby*

juniors – apart from managing your own practice, of course." Clerks and more senior colleagues will do their utmost to put baby juniors forward for work: *"I've been busy since the first week and have no worries about where the work is coming from,"* confirmed one. What they can expect is a string of VAT tribunals, various smaller government instructions and roles as second or third junior on cases at the Competition Appeal Tribunal.

Monckton Chambers may portray a slick, almost corporate, image to the outside world but within chambers there is a good-natured, informal atmosphere. On the day we visited, this mood was summed up by a group of senior and junior barristers dressed in jeans and bright shirts sitting having coffee in a bright, glass-panelled conference room. New faces are warmly welcomed by chambers and from the outset pupils can participate in all social events, perhaps even taking a position in the newly formed football team. If our visits to Monckton are anything to go by we reckon a new recruit could feel comfortable here pretty quickly.

Four New Square

Chambers UK rankings: Construction, financial services regulation, product liability, professional negligence, professional negligence: technology & construction

Elegant, sleek and industrious, Four New Square in Lincoln's Inn bears worthy comparison with the racehorse that runs in its colours. But while chambers' current nag, Burnham Hill, is proving rather more successful than its predecessor, Wasted Costs, this set has long been known as a true professional liability law thoroughbred. All members of chambers practise in this field, with instructions galloping in from almost every major (and minor) litigation firm or insurer in the country. Recent cases have included Cable & Wireless' claim against law firm Collyer-Bristow and others, and the Football League's claim against law firm Hammonds. Additionally, chambers' business extends to construction (members are involved in Wembley Stadium claims), insurance and reinsurance, product liability and other group actions (eg vCJD and tobacco), financial matters and general commercial litigation, with a recent and developing line in commercial Chancery work. Given the set's reputation for hard graft, don't be surprised to see it moving up the field in many of these practice areas.

Chambers and Partners Professional Negligence Set of the Year 2007

Proving it's not averse to change, Four New Square's interview process involves a standard first-round interview (albeit with no less than ten members of chambers) and advocacy exercise, followed by a less conventional few days spent in chambers, when would-be pupils shadow members and submit a piece of written work. The prize at stake is pupillage for up to four people who are happy with the idea of getting up to their eyeballs in professional indemnity, building disputes and contract claims. Taking part in one of the set's three four-day mini-pupillages could help get a sense for such work, but does not replace these assessed days spent in chambers.

With confidence being bolstered by the set's ambitious outlook and the space available in its main building and two Chancery Lane annexes, pupils told us: *"It is made clear from the start that we're not pitted against each other... if we were all to meet the objective criteria, we'd all get tenancy."* In 2005, none of their own pupils were taken on –

chambers instead recruited from its third six intake. In 2006 all three accepted tenancy offers, while at time of going to print in 2007 the two pupils were awaiting a decision. Objective assessment is aided by the fact that pupils rotate around the same four supervisors for three seats each. The first two seats last three months, the third stretches from the start of the second six until after the tenancy decision at the end of June. Pupil supervisors are selected with the aim of offering pupils the broadest experience within professional indemnity. Their charges start off by shadowing them and learning how to get to grips with paperwork. Court attendances naturally afford greater thrills, even if you are only observing. *"It can be really exciting and you do very much feel like one of the team,"* confirmed one pupil.

Our sources observed continuity of experience across the opening six months: *"The first seat is of course about learning the ropes and then building on that, but otherwise there wasn't much difference between my first and second seats,"* said one, with another noting that *"I was writing skeleton arguments and cross-examinations right from the start – the type of work itself doesn't really change."* Though ideally the pupil's performance does. In addition to regular informal feedback, chats with pupillage head Ben Hubble at the end of each seat give the pupil a more formal report on their progress. At the beginning of the second six everyone gets five written tasks (usually advice or a skeleton argument) set by a five-member panel. Feedback on these help ensure *"you always know where you're going and what you need to work on."*

In the first six months pupils only work for their supervisor, but the main feature of the second six is time in court. *"We believe that barristers should be advocates and we place a huge amount of emphasis on this throughout the pupillage,"* said one supervisor. First-six outings accompanying baby juniors to a variety of hearings will have given them an idea of what they'll face, but no amount of preparation can disguise the *"significant"* change of pace when pupils finally go it alone. *"It's challenging but good to be more independent. Your Pupil Supervisor will set you slightly less work throughout the second six, just to make sure that you have adequate time to prepare. And they'll always go through your court work and cross-examination questions with you."* Second-sixers are instructed on everything from small commercial debt claims and possession hearings to RTAs, simple fast-track trials and employment tribunals. *"Very supportive"* clerks carefully cultivate relationships with solicitors to ensure a steady supply of such work. Add in ready support from baby juniors and more senior members and it's no wonder *"you really start to feel as if you're finally able to do what you set out to do in law school."*

But there's more... Pupils must also square up to each other before an audience from chambers for three moots, the first of which takes place before Christmas. The largest audience is to be found at the final engagement, which usually takes place in an RCJ courtroom before Mr Justice Rupert Jackson, a former silk at the set. According to one sanguine source: *"The first moot is the most nerve-wracking but after that you get into the swing of it and it's very enjoyable."* Even performing in front of a High Court judge isn't as scary as you might expect; three of the pupils of 2006 had spent a week marshalling for Justice Jackson. Apparently *"you can hold forth in front of any district judge after that moot."*

Not to mince words, there's lot of work to get through in this pupillage and expectations are high. Chambers doesn't actively encourage pupils to slave until midnight but should occasion and your supervisor's workload demand, you will be expected to get stuck in. Right from the early years of tenancy barristers put a lot into their careers and must be prepared to devote whatever time is necessary to get the job done. Our impression is of a set committed to recruiting at junior level and prepared to reward those who work hard. *"The culture is very much a meritocracy... If you're good enough you will go through. We have a lot of work at the junior end and we're prepared to take four out of four if they make the grade."* If they don't, pupils know about it come the end of June, leaving plenty of time to look elsewhere. Those who do stay on start tenancy under the watchful and supportive eye of their former pupil supervisor, as well as being allocated a clerk who will help establish and develop practice preferences. *"It's a bespoke clerking system,"* concluded one new junior, *"your interests are taken into account and members as well as clerks will recommend you for work."* Like pupils, juniors are brought into the *"big, ritzy cases"* so they can gain vital experience as a second or third junior while also managing their own caseload of smaller matters.

Socially, there's perhaps nothing better than the communal thrill of Burnham Hill's race day performances. When they aren't watching the wonder horse in action there's always the odd Saturday playing cricket. *"We're a sporty team,"* said one member (although they didn't suggest that having a good square cut would assist a bid for tenancy). Indeed pupils praised an *"inclusive and relaxed atmosphere"* which allowed them to participate in other non-legal pursuits with members. Monthly drinks in chambers, the Christmas party, a summer party attended by members' children; it all sounded rather pleasant. Almost as fresh-faced as the teeny tots, the recent appointment of (young silk) Roger Stewart as head of chambers is a good indicator of where this relatively young, focused and modern set at.

Old Square Chambers

Chambers UK rankings: Employment, environment, health & safety, personal injury

Numbering over 60 barristers, Old Square is first and foremost an employment and PI specialist set with environmental, clinical negligence, product liability and health and safety law making up most of the remainder of its work. The nature of the employment practice has changed from the applicant-heavy days of the 1970s such that chambers now offers a *"good balance between claimant and respondent work."* Beyond advice to a wide range of employers, the set has formidable trade union links – head of chambers John Hendy QC is standing counsel to no less than nine unions – and regularly advises on high-profile problems like the 2006 Gate Gourmet/TGWU stand-off at Heathrow, and the thousands of equal pay disputes in the health sector and beyond. Public inquiries figure prominently, with barristers having recently represented the Prison Officers Association in the Zahid Mubarek Inquiry, and involvement in almost all the major rail crash inquiries of the last few years. John Hendy QC was instructed on behalf of a number of those bereaved in the Potters Bar rail crash and sought a judicial review of the Secretary of State for Transport's refusal to hold a public inquiry into the tragedy. While the application did not succeed, the matter has not been put to bed. The High Court judge who presided over the inquest has asked the government to reconsider its refusal to hold a public inquiry. Their response is currently awaited. Several seniors have forged a name for themselves in the area of major environmental litigation and the instructions they receive can be a boon for the set's juniors. Some of them have been led in the House of Lords on cases such as Sutradhar v Natural Environment Research Council (the Bangladesh water poisoning litiga-

tion). The set has had a hand in a number of well-known product liability litigations of recent times, among them the multiparty action over the drug Larium. Other work has dealt with the safety of consumer goods including cars, cosmetics and toys.

Old Square Chambers-branded pens and conference notepads in the meeting rooms are not quite what you'd expect of a set where barristers maintain *"we're a collective of very different individuals rather than a team."* Laughing off the idea of a *"house style,"* one source said: *"We don't even have a dress code."* In a sense there is a house style: Old Square has clear ideas about what barristers should not be. It is proud to have been one of the first places to relax conventional clerk/barrister formalities – *"We broke the mould there and it's very much first-name terms for everyone now."* Old Square says it continues to *"try to do away with redundant traditions."* While we certainly detected an easy atmosphere at the place there's no doubting the hard graft expected from barristers. Briefly donning his Sgt Major cap, the senior clerk barked: *"It's not a holiday camp here, but everyone is in it together."* Another source concurred: *"People work very hard but aren't competitive; we take pride in others' successes."*

Pupils sit with four supervisors over the course of 12 months, although the tenancy decision is made in the last week of June before the fourth changeover. The pupils we interviewed were most interested in the set's employment and PI specialisms, but it is possible for recruits to request particular supervisors or to ask to work in particular areas. *"Chambers are always aware of what you're interested in even if they try to expose you to all areas of practice."* A review at the end of each seat gives pupils the opportunity to assess personal strengths and weaknesses with their supervisor, so that *"although it can sometimes be a bit of a guessing game during the seat, when the review comes around you get a very thorough idea* of where you are and what they think of you." There are currently no formal written assessment exercises for pupils to undertake, except for the purpose of tenancy interview, and they seemed quite happy about this. *"We'd have been really overworked if they'd been added in; formalising things like that would have added to the stress."*

The work given to pupils and the expectations of them varies from supervisor to supervisor, but all the pupils we spoke to had enjoyed *"a good mix of court and paperwork, with plenty of exposure to supervisors of different styles and years of call."* In addition to research assignments and notes for clients or conferences, skeleton arguments and other drafting tasks are standard from day one. When not assisting their supervisor, first-six pupils devil for other members of chambers who are supposed to approach them via the supervisor. In practice our sources had been perfectly comfortable sourcing devilling work themselves. By the second six this is construed as *"a good sign that pupils are getting much better at managing their own workload."*

The nature of chambers' work means that pupils are in court for themselves throughout the second six. They are assigned a particular clerk and limited to three days of court appearances per week until the tenancy decision. *"The second six really marks this pupillage out from the others,"* commented one new tenant. *"The work is really good quality, but it is managed very well. Being limited to three days in court allows more time to give the cases the preparation they need."* Everyone seems to understand that being *"brand new on your feet makes everything scary and you take twice as long as you should to prepare."* The clerks are careful about where they send pupils; *"you're covering your own expenses so they try to keep the instructions close to London."* The furthest our pupil sources had been was Birmingham and Bournemouth, although one supervisor felt that *"it's not a bad idea to get used to travelling for six*

hours to attend a ten-minute hearing. It's the reality of practice."* Pupils' solo appearances are primarily RTA and infant approval hearings, with smaller employment matters featuring increasingly. One pupil told us how they had assisted on a five-day High Court stress-at-work trial with another member of chambers. *"In the first six, it was rare to be in chambers after 6.30pm,"* said one pupil, *"but as you start juggling your own work you will work long hours."* From an early stage, new tenants notice a drop-off in smaller instructions and their diaries begin to fill up with fast-track PI trials and employment tribunals. One baby junior told us he had already been led three times by the head of chambers.

Chambers has a 14-member strong – and growing – Bristol base to which all pupils are despatched for at least a week, the main purpose being to allow them to meet all members of chambers. There is an option for pupils to undertake the whole or a larger part of their pupillage in Bristol and, in some years one of the pupillage vacancies will be in Bristol.

Chambers' single-interview recruitment process was praised by our junior sources. One declared it to be *"by far my friendliest pupillage interview; my most enjoyable even."* Perhaps less enjoyable for pupils, the tenancy decision is reached after a formal interview, and pupils are asked to clear a week in their diaries at the end of June to undertake a written assessment and prepare for an oral argument to be made to a panel. By all accounts, *"you're given plenty of opportunities to fight your corner and there's no regimental-style questioning."* Having enlisted most of the two to three pupils each year, there's weight to the claim that *"you're made to feel like a member of the set right from the start of your pupillage."* Furthermore, pupils are involved in the social scene including the recently instigated monthly drinks. *"Everyone here had become so busy so we thought it a good idea to try and organise some social events. This week we have a Champagne-tasting session,"* a baby junior explained.

We got a strong sense that the pupils feel supported here at Old Square Chambers. The senior source who told us: *"We want to see excellent barristers at the end of pupillage and we will go very far to help someone develop those skills"* didn't need to try hard to convince us of this fact. In September 2006, Old Square Chambers moved to new premises on Bedford Row. We're looking forward to our invitation to visit members and pupils in their new home.

XXIV Old Buildings

Chambers UK rankings: Aviation, Chancery: commercial, Chancery: traditional, commercial dispute resolution, company, insolvency/corporate recovery, partnership, pensions, professional negligence

Some 30 years ago a well-established traditional Chancery set and a newish civil set merged to create XXIV Old Buildings, tucked away in a quiet corner of Lincoln's Inn. This brief thumbnail sketch is all you need to know of what has passed because you get the sense history isn't weighing heavily on this *"genuinely unpretentious"* set. Chambers is performing excellently; in 2007 turnover was £11.15m.

Handling a broad mixture of traditional and commercial Chancery work, insolvency matters, commercial litigation and pensions, not to forget expertise in partnerships and professional negligence, XXIV Old Buildings is in part defined by the multidisciplinary abilities of its barristers. *"Most people have specialist experience in anything up to five areas of practice,"* we were told, a statement backed up by our colleagues at *Chambers UK*, who rank joint head of chambers Alan Steinfield in a

whopping eight fields. Carefully planned strategic development has produced a relatively compact 32-strong membership, with recent recruitment designed to *"strengthen core areas"* and develop the set's ability to *"support a wider commercial business approach."* Recent arrivals have brought aviation and travel expertise plus offshore trusts know-how and commercial experience.

XXIV can offer clients a broad service, but perhaps the most distinctive and attractive feature of chambers is its overseas capabilities. Here, it has a unique calling card in the guise of a Geneva annexe. International and offshore instructions, whether in traditional Chancery, tax and trusts or large-scale commercial litigation, account for more than a third of chambers' business. Consequently, silks, juniors and sometimes even pupils are just as likely to be working in BVI or the Cayman Islands as in London. They must be equally at home offering advice to the president of an African republic after an attempted coup d'etat as assisting a moneyed UK national on a landlord and tenant dispute. Recent cases have included a multi-jurisdictional matter that is taking place in BVI, Switzerland, Sweden, Russia, the Netherlands, the Bahamas and London. This highly complex dispute concerns the ownership of a very valuable shareholding in a Russian mobile telecommunications company. In another case a £120 million UK claim was brought by AWG (Anglia Water Group) over fraudulent misrepresentation in the run up to its purchase of water services construction company Morrison in 2000. Away from commercial matters, the much-publicised case of Sherrington v Sherrington centred on a £10 million disputed will, and members are also involved in a large number of *"arts"* related litigations, for example, Republic of Iran v The Barakat Gallery. In this case the Iranian government are seeking recovery of certain artefacts said to have been plundered from a site in Iran.

A multidisciplinary approach and strong international caseload mean XXIV Old Buildings is well placed to ride out any potential decline in domestic claims. It also demands that pupils possess and develop a varied skill set. Current pupils told us, first and foremost, that *"if you're not interested in Chancery then you'd be a fool to apply here,"* but also highlighted the very specific capabilities required to flourish here. *"It's academically very challenging because there's a lot of highly technical black letter law; more so than in commercial work,"* stated one source. Chambers' recruiters confirmed that they look for *"commercial awareness, intelligence and imagination; if you don't understand the business scenario you don't understand the problem so you can't apply the law. And yet if you don't understand the law you can't help the business client by proposing a solution."*

In short, you have to ask yourself whether you could be comfortable engrossing yourself in seriously detailed research one minute, then applying the results of your research *"often in entirely new ways or transplanted to a parallel jurisdiction"* the next. Moreover, you have to be able to explain both the legal research and the subsequent ideas to clients and solicitors in plain English. Despite the fact that it isn't a prerequisite for a successful application, we observed that many current pupils and juniors had previous experience in industry or commercial law. Chambers' recruiters additionally observed: *"Barristers in this field deal with sophisticated, high-achieving and demanding clients in fluid commercial situations, so a degree of maturity of personality is an important attribute."*

Full details of what you might expect at a pupillage interview appear on the 'Recruitment and Pupillage' page of the XXIV Old Buildings website. In itself this is reflective of the set's commitment to transparency and good practice. In brief, the first round involves a 30-minute panel interview during which you'll discuss a pre-set legal problem. Successful candidates move onto a longer, second-round interview when there will be another legal problem, set the day before the interview. Don't expect to get too far unless you can display *"articulacy, flexibility, good reasoning skills and the ability to respond to another line of argument."*

Roughly 40 candidates attend the first interview and two at most are rewarded with pupillage. Once in situ, pupils benefit from a highly structured year that places the emphasis firmly on learning. They switch pupilmaster four times *"to ensure exposure to all our main areas of work."* Pupils spend their time on *"first drafts of pleadings, witness statements and research,"* not forgetting *"going along to court and conferences"* and even *"being a sounding board and sometimes coming up with an idea that gets used."* By all accounts, it's impossible to forget that *"you're under constant scrutiny,"* even if *"it is all done with a light touch."* Our sources had received a healthy level of informal feedback, coupled with the opportunity to repeat similar tasks *"so you can work on your faults."*

It's important to be on the ball from day one because, at the end of the first six, a pupil who is judged not to have a serious chance of gaining tenancy may be asked to move on. Assuming they are still there for the second six, life continues in much the same vein, with pupils only likely to be up on their feet in court once the tenancy decision has been made. In common with many Chancery sets, the view is that pupillage is for learning not earning, but the size of XXIV Old Buildings' pupillage award compensates for this. If chambers decides to recruit from current pupils, it is common for two contenders to be looking at a single place, although *"if you're good enough, and there's capacity, the set may keep on two."* Again the policy document on the website contains full details but, to summarise, they face a written test and an advocacy exercise. One thing we'll add is that overly competitive behaviour between pupils is not recommended as *"it's quietly known that stupidity like that doesn't do you any favours."* In 2006 one of the two pupils gained tenancy, but in 2007 both did.

Overall, chambers benefits from an *"informal"* and (that word again) *"unpretentious"* atmosphere and a *"cohesive identity and feel."* As one pupil pointed out: *"It's not like the stereotype of the solitary criminal barrister – you're often working on larger cases with a QC and several juniors."* Again, in contrast to criminal practice, *"we're not in court five days a week and we're rarely in front of a jury."* The out-of-hours social scene is pleasant rather than riotous and pupils tell us that *"a group of juniors looks after you especially well when you start."* A recent dinner and theatre trip to see 'A Man for All Seasons' offered more of a busman's holiday than a break. *"It starred Martin Shaw, so in effect we spent our evening off watching Judge John Deed."*

Outer Temple Chambers

Chambers UK rankings: Clinical negligence, employment, health & safety, pensions, personal injury, professional discipline

In a neat metaphor for the way Outer Temple Chambers straddles the different elements of the Bar, its building can be accessed via both the hustle and bustle of the Strand and the hallowed environs of the Temple. Back in 2001, the 32 former incumbents of 35 Essex Street held a strategy meeting at which, rumour has it, a phenomenal quantity of beer was downed. Even so, they hatched a five-year plan to buy a new building and a strategy to create standalone work groups in each of the set's key practice areas. Six years on, how's it all going?

The move to 222 Strand has united all members under one roof and the work group template has paid dividends. The set has swelled in size, in breadth of coverage and in reputation. Today some 63 barristers call Outer Temple Chambers home, a majority practising across PI, clinical negligence and healthcare, crime with a regulatory bent, and employment and pensions. Others handle public and family law, professional negligence and commercial cases, and disciplinary and regulatory matters. Diversification has not come at the cost of excellence; our colleagues on *Chambers UK* rank chambers highly in several areas.

Growth has been facilitated through judicious lateral recruitment, the most recent addition being a group of five PI barristers from 199 Strand. *"We took the view that we needed to augment our groups to make them viable. A barrister can't be an expert in five or more areas of law, so we went hunting and got some very good people in,"* explained a source. Members old and new have acted in prominent cases, one of these being a recent landmark High Court victory for the parents of a severely disabled child who were resisting efforts to have his ventilator turned off. In PI, members secured a settlement of £6.8m for a client who was severely brain damaged in a road traffic accident. Turning to crime, the set takes on both prosecution and defence instructions and has a nice line in fraud. Recently, barristers successfully persuaded the Court of Appeal to uphold the conviction of an employee involved in a £12m password fraud at HSBC bank. As well as regular instructions from the Serious Fraud Office, there have been numerous manslaughter instructions from the CPS following major rail crashes (Hatfield, Potters Bar, Ladbroke Grove) and work-related and other deaths caused by negligence. Following the manslaughter conviction of two brothers in the Damilola Taylor case, senior silk Alan Rawley QC has been appointed to the panel carrying out the independent review of the forensic work conducted during the police investigation. In truth there's so much interesting, high-value work that we simply can't summarise it here.

Step into chambers and you are immediately struck by a sense of diverse and abundant activity. With three floors and multiple staircases, it's quite possible that a pupil could spend an entire year here and never meet everyone. Our sources admitted, *"the size of chambers is good or bad depending on your view of what you want from chambers life. If you want to know and be friends with all members then the recent expansion means it can't provide that."* However, if a pupil does happen upon an unknown pocket, chances are they'll be warmly received because the set prides itself on *"not being stuffy"* and claims that *"none of us take ourselves too seriously – we're sharp and quick-witted but very relaxed."*

Chambers does not recruit through OLPAS, preferring instead to see 14 or so applicants sometime around Easter for a 30-45 minute first-round interview. It sounds fairly gruelling: *"In addition to a general chat and maybe a hypothetical legal question, we ask interviewees to prepare a five-minute talk from a list of ten topics that we give them 15 minutes before the interview. People should also expect some surprises..."* The seven best candidates are invited back for a second time the following day to endure *"a legal question, an ethical question and a more in-depth talk about their application form."* We say endure, but chambers assures us that *"we just want candidates to flourish when faced with fairly demanding questions."* Chambers offers a generous pupillage award (£35,000 at the time of going to press) and has considered the sum carefully. *"We want to pitch one peg below the big commercial sets. We want to attract the very best candidates, but we don't want people coming here because we are giving loads of money."*

Pupillage is divided into four sets of three months and the average pupil will sit with pupilmasters whose specialisms ensure broad coverage of chambers' work. By way of example, one source told us they had spent three months with an employment barrister, three with one specialising in PI and clin neg and three with one of chambers' more commercially oriented members. Life for pupils sounds reasonably straightforward. Said one: *"On my first day I was told quite explicitly that – barring exceptional circumstances – I was only expected to be here from 9am till 6pm and that I would never be judged on the amount of time my jacket spent on the back of my chair."* All written work is commented upon and, at the end of each quarter, pupils sit down with their PM and the head of the pupillage committee to discuss a formal, written report on their progress.

In the second six, pupils are on their feet pretty swiftly. They undertake a wide range of work including infant settlement approval hearings, employment tribunals, winding-up petitions and possession hearings. There's also criminal work to be sampled. *"It came as a bit of a surprise to find myself in a magistrates' court doing everything you could think of other than full-blown trials,"* confessed one source, quickly adding: *"I'm very pleased to have done it as the experience was great."* The pace undoubtedly changes in the practising six and pupils reflected on the fact that *"the most immediate difference is the hours; you go from knowing you're not expected to stay late to suddenly finding yourself working until 3am and getting up at 6am to go to a tribunal."* The fact that second-sixers are also encouraged to do work for other people requires them to acquire the all-important skills of prioritisation and time management.

All pupils are formally assessed through four pieces of written work and, until recently, four advocacy assessments, the last two of which are open to all members of chambers. The pupillage committee has now decided that the first two advocacy exercises will be more about education and less about assessment, on the basis that they can then be more effective at helping pupils get on their feet in court. After the assessments are completed the committee discusses the pupils' quarterly reviews, their assessment results and any other general feedback before making a recommendation which is put to the chambers vote. *"Seventy-five percent is the magic number that gets you tenancy."* A good record in awarding tenancy explained why our pupil sources were sanguine about this process. *"The sense that if you do well you will get taken on has meant that there's never been any sense of competition between us. We're told we'll all be taken on if we meet the standard."* The absence of any third-sixers also helps.

Outer Temple Chambers has a *"warm"* atmosphere. Afternoon tea is a feature of daily life, but our sources assured us that *"it is quite typical of chambers that tea is a wholly informal affair conducted in a pokey kitchen. It was initiated by a junior tenant to instil a community feeling in chambers after the recent expansion."* A pupil told us: *"I am as free to speak at afternoon tea as I am in any other part of my life."* The overall picture is of an appealing set with an appealing pupillage scheme. But with another of those famous strategy weekends taking place in autumn 2007, we can only guess at how we might describe chambers in five years time...

Pump Court Tax Chambers

Chambers UK Rankings: Tax, tax: indirect tax, tax: private client

Taxes are a fact of life for us all but they are more a way of life for the members of Pump Court Tax Chambers. This is a QC-heavy, tight-knit community of 26 barristers, all dedicated wholeheartedly to tax law. It is also a self-declared traditional set that doesn't come with the marketing and sharp-edged interiors that now characterise many commercial chambers.

In the last 50 years Pump Court has evolved into one of the leading specialist sets in the field and there isn't a facet of tax law that at least one member can't tackle. It competes with mainstream Chancery sets in the trusts realm and has a couple of rivals on the VAT front, but when it comes to pure tax there's no substitute for dedicated expertise: *"Commercial sets would like to see tax as a bolt-on* [to their main business] *but it's impossible just to dabble."*

Chambers and Partners
Tax Set of the Year 2007

It's a source of frustration for chambers that students think tax law is about *"crunching numbers and wading through accounts."* The sheer range of issues and activities that fall under the tax umbrella may come as a pleasant surprise to some – personal tax planning for individuals, trusts or estates; employee remuneration cases on share options or pension schemes; the UK and international tax aspects of corporate M&A, demergers, transfer pricing and structured finance. In the realm of indirect taxes there is VAT, Landfill Tax and stamp taxes relating to property transactions. And then to round off the list there's a raft of professional negligence cases involving tax advice. As our sources stressed the subject is *"not at all narrow;"* in fact *"much of it borders on public and European law with human rights points and proportionality issues often arising."* Those looking to get right to the top of this field should note that *"there is a disproportionate number of tax cases in the House of Lords; tax always passes the public interest test."* The intersection of tax law with several other legal disciplines leads to *"considerable interaction with other sets,"* and there is *"a good referral system when there are non-tax elements to instructions such as insolvency, company-commer-*

cial or insurance." Pump Court "drafts in juniors" to work on non-tax points, with such collaboration resulting in "plenty of teamwork."

Instructions are equally as likely to come from accountants as from solicitors, and the UK and foreign governments also send a steady stream of work. "I expect our client list is the wish list of most chambers," one source postulated, and considering "most City firms and the Big Four accountants" use the set, this is quite likely. It was also pointed out that direct relationships with accountants allow "more commercial, less formal relationships than when there is an instructing solicitor" as an intermediary. The other really important point to make here is that such clients are tax experts themselves and so they expect their barristers to have an exceptionally high level of knowledge and expertise.

Tax cases are normally "light on facts, heavy on law," making this type of practice a "very pure, intellectual and conceptual" area where barristers concentrate on "solving knotty legal problems," not unravelling what happened when, where and with whom. Instructions are sometimes so "short and pithy" that they fit onto one sheet of paper. The relevance of this for a pupil is that they do not encounter the fact-heavy cases that can lead to "sitting in a dark room sifting through 40 boxes of files from Freshfields, hoping to find the crucial contract." It follows that the set looks for "rigorous analytical skills" in its potential pupils. "Being prepared to read legislation carefully and take analysis through to its conclusion" is key. "But we're not looking for geeky people who want to bury their heads in paperwork," a source added hastily; "we want all-rounders who enjoy the academic side of the law." Reassuringly, chambers' recruiters "don't expect any tax knowledge" from pupillage applicants: "We just want to see how you think."

With there being so many misconceptions about tax law, Pump Court Tax has had to find ways to reach out and convert students. As well as unassessed mini-pupillages, assessed (and paid) minis have been introduced to give would-be applicants insight into life at the tax Bar. Student visitors are shown a range of work and are asked to write an opinion. The week is intended to be mutually beneficial and "the aim is that by the end we have a good idea whether or not someone is pupillage material." An assessed mini is not a prerequisite to making an application and if you do decide to throw your hat into the ring, do remember that this set has now opted out of OLPAS after finding the shackles of the online system too "restrictive."

Pump Court Tax is "not wedded to any particular type of pupillage." First sixes, second sixes but more usually 12-month stints are offered, depending on the applicant. A first six may be extendable to a year and those doing a second six usually have a Chancery or commercial first six behind them. Even pupils in chambers for only six months can expect to sit with "four or five pupilmasters all doing completely different areas of practice." Pupils have their own room but sometimes sit with their PM to "hear how to interact with accountants and solicitors." Chambers likes to "start pupils off with a relatively young pupilmaster... rather than chucking them in with a senior." Despite the brevity of the programme pupils see "a fair amount of litigation" and get "a good grounding in private client, corporate work and VAT." There may even be exposure to high-level work; the current pupil told us about finishing off "written observations for the European Court of Justice."

As pupilmasters are "realistic about the fact tax is difficult, a couple of glaring mistakes won't be held against you." The baby junior we spoke to told us he "didn't feel the pressure of being examined or assessed until the very end." Potential tenants complete one or two assessments, which are then copied to every member of chambers and have an influence on the tenancy decision.

Those who are awarded tenancy must learn the virtue of patience. Such is the complexity and value of cases that *"the bulk of work comes from devilling for the first couple of years."* As a more senior source stressed: *"We can't let them loose on* [their own] *client work right away."* In 2006 one of the two pupils was awarded tenancy and another pupil was awarded tenancy in March 2007, while the following September a further one of two was taken on.

Though the barristers spend less time in front of judges than those at crime, common law or commercial sets, there are advocacy opportunities before the General and Special Commissioners and the High Court in London, plus at VAT tribunals across the country. Those with established VAT practices can be in court *"non stop,"* and the growing European dimension of tax law means that members are appearing with increasing regularity at the ECJ in Luxembourg. For pupils and baby juniors a *"cautious"* approach means that advocacy will be thin on the ground; with a foot in the door you *"might get very small cases at the General Commissioners or VAT tribunal"* but there will be no advocacy as a pupil.

When the clock strikes eleven each morning chambers' business halts for coffee, a ritual that is *"like the afternoon tea you have in Chancery sets but more worthwhile."* This is no social gathering; the main idea is to talk about the law and current cases. The prospect of sitting with your cup of Kenco while silks argue complex points is *"quite daunting at first though soon enough you begin to understand what they're talking about."* The trick is to listen and not contribute, not only to *"hear the rhythm of arguments"* but to enjoy the *"stimulating sensation that you are close to the action."* The morning coffee tradition endures for the simple reason that *"large sums of money are at stake and clients like to know they are getting broad input on their problem."* After all, 26 heads are better than one.

Of all the misconceptions around, the one about *"the tax Bar being full of old men in the library"* is perhaps the most inaccurate. *"This set is a great advert for the Bar,"* we were told. Indeed there is a growing female contingent moving up the ranks to redress the male dominance at the top end. Chambers regards itself as *"genuinely friendly"* without the *"them-and-us mentality of some chambers."* Invitations to formal drinks and dinners are always extended to pupils, the recent Revenue Bar annual dinner being *"a surprisingly enjoyable evening,"* apparently. What's important is that pupils *"don't feel like second-class citizens"* in this particular tax haven.

You may have never studied tax and you may not think it's sexy, but don't knock it if you haven't tried it. Those at Pump Court Tax Chambers certainly know they're onto something, so if you're a real brain box we'd recommend a mini-pupillage if you're curious to find out what that something is.

4 Pump Court

Chambers UK rankings: Construction, information technology, insurance, professional negligence, professional negligence: technology & construction

Although elegant courtyards with graceful doorways are hardly a rarity around the Inns, we think Pump Court, situated between the Temple Church and the thoroughfare of Middle Temple Lane, is one of the loveliest. Tucked into the corner of this enclosure is number 4, which for all of the detached period charm of its architecture is decidedly *"not an ivory tower set."* An early history of criminal and family practice (still principal areas of activity as recently as 15 years ago) may explain the *"unpretentious"* and *"non-traditional"* atmosphere at a chambers which these days focuses on construction, insurance, technology and professional negligence. The set enjoys a significant presence in the Technology and Construction Court, where a number of members sit on the bench in some capacity.

Chambers and Partners Information Technology Set of the Year 2007

While a healthy number of pupils arrive at the set with a keen interest in construction or IT law, most undertake a general training in which they gain exposure to all four of the set's key areas. Normally three pupils rotate around the same three supervisors in three-month stints, although chambers discourages members who are working on long-running or especially large cases from taking pupils. With the tenancy decision made in June, they have just nine months in which to prove themselves – not long, even if *"ample space and plenty of work at the junior end"* mean all three pupils have a good chance of being taken on if they make the grade.

Chambers doesn't believe in throwing pupils in at the deep end. *"We don't have huge first-seat expectations,"* said one pupilmaster. *"We expect people to pick things up quickly and be effective legal researchers from day one, but if things go wrong, they go wrong – we're very forgiving."* Early on, pupils are presented with a folder of *"the basics"* and encouraged to interact with clerks by signing in each morning. Shadowing barristers at court appearances, fulfilling discrete research points and first attempts at drafting and advisory work are all on the cards. Clearly careful of their charges, supervisors were at pains to stress that pupils finish at 6pm each day and never work weekends. *"We're not slave drivers,"* declared one. As they enter their second seat, just after Christmas, pupils start to take on work for other members of chambers, albeit that this is strictly

filtered through senior clerk Carolyn McCombe. Feedback is collected on each piece of work undertaken and a vigilant pupillage committee keeps an eye on pupils' breadth of exposure to ensure there are no practice area *"black holes."* Whatever the subject matter (whether honing an eye for legal detail on the diagrams and expert reports of construction cases or getting to grips with the make-up and traditions of the insurance world) the first six is emphatically about learning the all-important skills of drafting.

In addition to their work for supervisors and other members, pupils also complete two written and two advocacy-based assessment exercises during the first six. The written assessments are submitted anonymously, while the advocacy exercise usually pits pupils against each other. We're told that any sense of inter-pupil competition is contained within the exercise as *"assessment here is so transparent that there really isn't any one-upmanship among pupils."* A mid-December informal chat with the pupillage director and a formal end-of-first-six review help keep pupils apprised of their progress.

Having shadowed juniors in court during the last few weeks of the first six, second sixers head out under their own steam to cover smaller hearings. *"Although there's definitely a lot more work to handle in the second six, I did feel prepared,"* confirmed one source. Although their hours lengthen, an average week with three court appearances means *"you're never too overloaded."* That said, grace under pressure is definitely required as pupils juggle work for supervisors, other members of chambers and their own clients... all while contending with heightened levels of expectation. *"We usually see a steep improvement in the last seat in terms of thorough and rigorous analytical skills. We try to make it as pleasant as possible, but there's no escaping the very high standards that are required in order to be kept on,"* commented one supervisor.

"Everyone here makes the time to help; I was never made to feel gormless for asking," breathed one pupil with audible relief. The paperwork involved in construction cases can be challenging as it takes a little time to pick up the terminology of, say, gravel laying; the intricacies of insurance policies are also mind-boggling at times. Yet members assured us that *"no one should be put off by these specialisms"* and *"all of these areas of law have a lot more in common with each other than not."* We have it on good authority that *"you can learn a lot in a few days with a dictionary of mechanical terms."*

Not all of a second-six pupil's work will be particularly technical in its subject matter. Many of their instructions related to RTAs, infant settlements and small insurance claims. Those we spoke to were excited by their new independence, one telling us: *"The first case is a real highlight. Not only do you have sole responsibility, but you're putting everything you've observed into practice and it all starts coming together."* Cross-examining elderly drivers, for example, teaches *"a lot about posing questions and when to bite your lip."*

As the tenancy decision looms, a committee considers the pupils' performance in the written and oral assessments, together with supervisors' reports and feedback from other members. The committee's recommendations are generally accepted by the rest of the membership. Successful pupils are likely to display *"common sense and good judgement"* as well as a demonstrably *"sustained and a steady improvement in oral advocacy and confidence."* In 2006 all three pupils gained tenancy, but come 2007 none of the three did so.

Once pupils are newly minted as 4 Pump Court tenants, it's a little easier for them to enjoy the camaraderie of the set. Inhabited mainly by practitioners under seven years' call, the top floor of the building is a hive of activity as members drop into each others' rooms with queries or coffee. Weekly drinks and regular buffet lunches are open to all and the juniors get together for pub and curry trips. These occasions are not closed to pupils, but our sources confessed that, *"while you can drop your guard a little, you're always aware of the assessment process simmering away in the background."* Lest this sound too ominous, our sources were quick to praise *"a really well-regulated pupillage with fantastic pastoral support."*

This set interviews a year earlier than most, so apply in good time. Candidates are grilled in a single interview that incorporates a legal problem and some ethical or moral questions on topical subjects. Evidence of sound advocacy skills are likely to hold more sway than a dubious profession of a lifelong love of construction law, but do think carefully about the set's strengths in its chosen areas of practice. A short mini-pupillage – these are offered throughout the year – would be highly beneficial to your understanding of 4 Pump Court's work.

Quadrant Chambers

Chambers UK rankings: Aviation, international arbitration: general commercial & insurance, shipping & commodities, travel

When we last visited Quadrant, the dust had barely settled on the magnificent Fleet Street conversion housing the chambers formerly known as 4 Essex Court. Three and a half years later and we remain impressed by the set's accommodation: a large glass atrium links four grade II-listed buildings, which in their time housed a branch of Lloyds Bank and the renowned 17th-century Rainbow coffee house. With just under 50 barristers currently in chambers, the set has ample space for modern facilities – in a neat combination of modern commercial savvy and decorous tradition, a former ladies' dining room now features cutting-edge video conferencing equipment as well as a delicately decorated ceiling. A suite of meeting rooms for mediations and a location just a few steps away from the Royal Courts of Justice allow Quadrant to offer a perfect base for foot-weary, out-of-town solicitors.

Much used by ancient mariners, the humble quadrant, which lends the set its title, is an apt namesake. Shipping work has steered the set ever since founder Barry Sheen QC developed a wet shipping practice after quitting the navy post-WWII. Appointed as judge in the Admiralty Court in 1978, Cap'n Sheen started a tradition of senior Quadrant QCs being appointed to the Admiralty Bench. Those following in his wake included Sir Anthony Clarke QC (now Master of the Rolls) and Sir David Steel QC, who helped chambers break into the insurance world via Lloyd's of London. Latterly, ex-head of chambers Nigel Teare QC followed them to the High Court, but demonstrating the set's broad commercial abilities was appointed to the QBD. Then, in the late 90s, the acquisition of new members from niche aviation law set 5 Bell Yard added an airborne twist. Traditionally known for its work on liability arising from air crashes or phenomena such as Deep Vein Thrombosis, the aviation specialists also do well on general carriage issues and tour operator disputes. In addition to hulls, wings, international trade and goods carriage, chambers also enjoys a wide range of general commercial instructions, including some sports and media matters. The other key thing to know about Quadrant's work is the amount of disputes, particularly international, that are resolved through arbitration. Chambers has long been top of the tree in shipping-related arbitration, but more recently members have popped up in a string of important insurance, reinsurance and aviation arbitrations.

The existence of the core specialisms shouldn't put off pupils hoping to gain broad commercial experience. Once in situ they can expect a general commercial training that allows exposure to each of the four main areas of practice. To reiterate, that's: commercial litigation, shipping, aviation plus insurance and reinsurance. *"You can't be too picky at this stage,"* explained a source, *"it's about learning how to think like a commercial barrister and taking it from there."*

Pupils sit with four pupilmasters for three months each, being assigned a shadow supervisor who *"keeps an eye on you and does things like involve you in his workload when your main pupilmaster is busy."* Both mentors complete a written report on the pupil, which is discussed in an end-of-three-month review. A wide pool of pupilmasters ensures exposure to different types of practice, and the first period especially is a whirl of *"whatever the individual supervisor is doing at the time."* Paperwork fills a pupil's day, whether it be finding your feet with research points or progressing onto full sets of papers with a view to presenting advice or drafting claims or defences. *"The idea is to get the pupils thinking commercially,"* said one pupilmaster who shared the set's tolerant perspective on early-day errors: *"We all make mistakes."*

"There's a huge emphasis on developing pupils here," sources told us. Whether it's *"getting a second set of papers sent through from solicitors"* so pupils can have their own copies to work on or *"encouraging us to work for other members of chambers,"* everyone agreed that *"we're pushed to succeed."* Devilling opportunities (effectively having a member of chambers subcontract work to you) are plentiful and could see the pupil contributing to a merchant shipping case in the Court of Appeal, for example. One pupil who had *"seen some wigs in my time here..."* had devilled for his shadow pupilmaster in a three-week High Court trial as well as assisting a silk in preparation for the House of Lords. Definitely *"not an everyday experi-*

ence." Yet pupils stressed it is the range of work not just the high-profile nature of cases that characterises their training. As the year progresses an increasing number of members will enlist their services, although pupilmasters carefully regulate such additional work. *"They don't let you get swamped and they're always aware of what you're doing."*

Pupils do not undertake paid work before the tenancy decision in July, which means that getting on their feet is an exercise restricted to chambers – albeit one attended by most of the Pupillage Committee. There are usually two or three of these advocacy exercises throughout the first nine months and chambers seeks to make them as realistic as possible, with senior silks sitting on the 'bench' to watch pupils battle it out. *"After months of paperwork it's quite exciting to prepare a mock brief for a Court of Appeal appearance or a three-day trial,"* confirmed one pupil. Ample support and *"plenty of time to prepare"* mean the experience is not too traumatic. Following the tenancy decision, tenants-to-be can expect to be in court for smaller carriage of goods matters and debt recovery hearings for banks, as well as advising on small contractual or banking disputes. There can also be some surprises: one pupil had assisted a silk in a case lost at the first instance but referred for appeal. Following the pupil's successful tenancy bid, *"the same silk called me back as a junior in the Court of Appeal."* For those who do not make the grade in July, chambers has been known to suggest a deferral of the decision until October in some cases. In 2006 the set's sole pupil took tenancy and in 2007 two of the three did so.

All new tenants are allowed to select a 'godfather' to act as a long-term mentor and additionally share a room with another more senior member who casts a friendly eye over their work. The net result is that there is never any risk of isolation in the crucial early years of tenancy. Even those working at far-flung ends of the vast building are quite likely to encounter one another in Daly's Wine Bar just down the street. *"We have no time for institutionalised jollity,"* said one member, *"but that doesn't mean that people here don't get along and socialise outside working hours."*

Commercial and straightforward are the watchwords here and applicants should be prepared to display these traits in the rigorous interview process. Those selected at the paper stage are sent a written assessment to be completed and returned. Around 20 of those who impress are then called for interview, where they will be grilled on their assessment in what one member unashamedly referred to as *"an intense, tough interview."* Incidentally, *"it's also when we find out if someone's tutor wrote the test brief..."* (Surely not.) Although non-law graduates are handed the same brief as those with an LLB, the focus is not so much on legal knowledge as on analysis and argument, and we were assured that the top candidates *"distinguish themselves irrespective of the conditions."* Quadrant pupils reflected on the *"gruelling but fair interview,"* telling us: *"They don't ask silly questions."*

The clean, modern lines of Quadrant's converted historic home leave no doubt that this is a pragmatic commercial operation that takes only what it needs from tradition. *"We're straightforward,"* opined one member; *"all about being decent and upfront."* Eager pupillage applicants are advised to demonstrate a commercial bent as the set seeks *"sensible, coherent and confident future tenants who are focused on the commercial Bar."* If you are detail-oriented and contract law is one of your favourite areas, these are good signs that Quadrant's work will suit you.

QEB Hollis Whiteman

Chambers UK Rankings: Crime, fraud: criminal, professional discipline

Established after WWII, things really got going for Hollis Whiteman around 25 years ago when, in 1982, the criminal set at 3 King's Bench Walk merged with the set at Queen Elizabeth Buildings. In 2006 things became uncomfortable when three leading QCs and two senior juniors (who were about to take silk) left the set accompanied by senior clerk Michael Greenaway and first junior clerk Nick Newman. They went off to form a new crime set called Cloth Fair Chambers. There's no doubt it was a blow but, arguably, the sudden departure of some of its most senior members and its senior clerks gave the set a much-needed wake-up call. *"It forced us to get away from that apathy that can exist at a set that's been successful for a very long time,"* confided one source. While *"the backbone of chambers is still here,"* we were left with the impression that the loss of Michael Greenaway hurt the most.

Now with 14 silks and 39 juniors, QEB Hollis Whiteman has done a good job of picking itself up. Head of chambers Vivian Robinson QC announced a strategic review of management that would lead to the appointment of the set's first chambers' director, Vicky Thompson, and a new senior clerk, Bill Conner. Together, they have modernised chambers, seeing it through an image spruce up and website revamp. Even more important to this focused crime set are the changes being made in response to the Carter reforms of legal aid. As one junior member said: *"There are turbulent times ahead and bold, brave moves will be needed."* Happy to prosecute or defend, QEB Hollis Whiteman is a crime set through and through. However, it is developing new strands of work – health and safety litigation, trading standards, licensing and food law, plus representation at regulatory and disciplinary tribunals. *"We are not moving away from pure criminal work, rather we are looking at it from all possible angles,"* explained a source.

Chambers has always attracted cases and inquiries of a high-profile nature, and among the leading cases of past years are the prosecutions arising out of Operation Tulip (the biggest cocaine smuggling operation in the UK), the murder trials of Roy Whiting (Sarah Payne's murderer), Harold Shipman and Grant Harris (the Queen's gynaecologist, who killed his wife). Hollis Whiteman barristers were involved in the perjury trial of Jeffrey Archer, the Bloody Sunday and Victoria Climbie Inquiries and the Dome Robbery trial. On the fraud side, cases include the Versailles fraud, BCCI and Maxwell (in which Robert Maxwell stole over £400m from company pensions). One of the most recent cases to hit the headlines was the July 2007 trial of a pensioner accused of bludgeoning his wife to death after 50 years of marriage. Peter Clarke QC was prosecutor in this case, the details of which may well become eclipsed by the fact that during the proceedings, while the defendant was giving evidence, a young juror was discovered listening to an MP3 player under her hijab. She herself was then charged with contempt of court.

What lies ahead for the criminal Bar is yet to become clear. Portents of gloom are cast about on a regular basis, but here at QEB Hollis Whiteman you sense they are preparing for battle. The stereotype of the criminal Bar (staying up drinking till the wee small hours and striding around being self-congratulatory) is not entirely unfounded, but as one member confided, it is the *"bad criminal sets"* that are *"folding left, right and centre... there'll be no room for that soon."* Over in QEB Hollis Whiteman, there is *"a bit more impetus about the future."*

Head of the pupillage committee, Peter Clarke QC, is a stalwart of the set, and of the criminal Bar in general. His grandfather defended Oscar Wilde and the room in which we interviewed him is kitted out with fine *"family furniture"* – one benefit of a set that has *"remained in touch with tradition."* If you're picturing leather upholstered, horse hair-stuffed chairs and elegant bronze statues, you're spot on. There's something very solid and unreconstructed about chambers – one of our sources happily confirmed: *"We're not up our own arses like the right-on sets."* In prospective pupils, recruiters seek *"a ground-level commitment, ideally demonstrated by something you've gone out and done."* When filling out the application form, you should aim for originality and *"a lightness of touch... something that will at least half raise the corners of my mouth in a smile."* Avoid clichés such as *"the mini pupillage gave me an insight into the life of a barrister,"* try putting in an anecdote instead. Maybe fill out the form after a few drinks and then see what you think of your efforts in the cold light of sobriety.

Applications, which go through OLPAS, are assessed by an entirely transparent and objective marking system. Marks are picked up or lost in categories including general legal experience, presentation and sense of humour, and 21 out of 30 will get you to a first interview. Of around 250 applicants, 80 or so make it this far, taking part in a 25-minute interview with a panel of three barristers. Some 40 candidates will make it to a second interview, which generally sees four or five people receiving offers of pupillage. The interviews are described as jovial, relaxed and *"a thousand times nicer than anywhere else."* One junior remembered being offered a glass of wine when they arrived, which made some serious debate about *"obvious topics"* such as torture and ethics all the easier to get into. Advocacy exercises are not favoured by the set as a means of assessment as *"it's not a level playing field for those who haven't done the BVC."* Nor are they looking for after-dinner speakers: *"Public speaking and advocacy are quite different things."*

The first six months of pupillage are standard enough. Almost all time is spent with the pupilmaster, who remains with the pupil until March. Later on, if pupils have any worries about clients' behaviour or being alone in the cells, it is this PM who will be their first port of call for advice. PM's are generally of at least ten years' call, so forgive them if they *"look blank"* when you ask them a question about the magistrates' courts. On her first day, one pupil was given a full set of murder papers to read, along with forensic evidence including post mortem photographs of the victim. It goes without saying you develop a strong stomach pretty sharpish. Written work takes up much of a pupil's time; for example, drafting schedules of evidence, skeleton arguments, case summaries and advices on unduly lenient sentences, evidence or appeals. As a pupil earns more trust, work comes in thick and fast from both their PM and other members of chambers.

The second six is unusual – and downright oxymoronic – in that it actually lasts for nine months. It culminates in a late tenancy decision in January, a date chosen to give chambers extra time to make the right decision and give pupils a greater range of advocacy experiences. The set does not take on third-sixers, so no rivals from other sets will join halfway through. Some years no pupils are offered tenancy, others some or all might be. Come September, the second-sixers act as unofficial mentors to the new intake of first-sixers. *"It's fun and it feels a bit like a sixth form,"* chuckled one pupil. On the downside, 18 months is a long time to wait for the tenancy decision and *"you start to think, 'I just want to know.'"* At least the second six features plenty of advocacy in both the magistrates' and the Crown Court. Pupils can expect to see theft, burglary and robbery, ABH and traffic offences. Among the highlights for our sources were *"a speeding policeman"* and a breach of a probation order, heard in the Crown Court. The Youth Court is useful for experiencing *"more* serious stuff... which still won't go to the Crown Court." To some extent, a pupil's fate is in the hands of the solicitors who instruct them. While one pupil we met had only ventured into the Crown Court a handful of times in five months, another had spent about a quarter of his time there. Assisting other members of chambers is not uncommon and there is a "trickle-down effect... to keep work in chambers."

Going to court four or five days a week, pupils have to put in a lot of time in order to keep on top of things. "When you know someone is sitting in prison, relying on you, you can't go to bed without making sure you've read the brief," explained a pupil, who had on one occasion worked until 2am and been up again at 5am. A more normal day might be 8.30am until 6.30pm, and during the first six it's not unusual to leave even earlier. The main method of assessment during the second six is whether solicitors choose to reinstruct you; they certainly provide important feedback to the clerks. To get pupils ready for the hectic second six, an intensive advocacy training programme runs throughout the first six months. "I got nervous about it every week," said one source. Pupils have the first month to settle in before the fun truly starts, and then they are taken through each part of a full trial, bit by bit, on a weekly basis, from the bail application right up until the closing submissions. Feedback is provided from members of chambers at all levels of seniority (hence the nerves) and the programme culminates in a full mock trial in the Old Bailey. For this, pupils are required to don wigs and gowns for the first time, an experience that "makes you feel like a right wally." Coughing up £700 in exchange for these items apparently "feels like the most unsatisfactory purchasing experience ever."

Pupillage at QEB Hollis Whiteman is a serious undertaking, as is any attempt to forge a career at the criminal Bar. A junior member warned, "it's massively hard work and you've got to be dedi-

cated." On the plus side, "even the poxiest health and safety prosecution is exciting" and adrenalin runs high. "It's an incredible feeling when you've just saved someone from an awful fate." With the set still standing firm in the wake of the Carter reforms, members find "all the more reason to feel fortunate to be in chambers like these."

Queen Elizabeth Building

Chambers UK rankings: Family/matrimonial

Queen Elizabeth Building is a family set dealing mainly in ancillary relief (to the lay person this means the financial side to divorce), although at the junior end there is a concerted effort being made to expand into broader areas of family law. The set is at the top of its field, and has been called in to represent parties in some of the biggest divorces in history. We need only mention Diana and Charles and you get the picture. Other landmark cases include Charman v Charman, in which the ex-wife of John Charman, head of Axa Insurance Group, was awarded £48m of her former husband's £131m fortune, Harb v King Fahd bin Abdul Aziz (a case with a human rights element, which involved an intervention from the Secretary of State for Constitutional Affairs) and Miller v Miller, in which Melissa Miller won a £5m settlement after a 33-month marriage. At this, the pointy end of family law, our sources stressed the importance of "keeping your nose in the law reports and seeing what's happening."

QEB is also known for sending a string of senior members to the bench. Previous head of chambers Andrew Moylan QC has only just been elevated to the High Court, joining the nine that have become members of the judiciary before him. Losing people from the top shouldn't be too much of a problem for QEB, however, as it has a raft of respected juniors back in chambers, a number of whom will likely take silk. Moylan was replaced as head of chambers in 2007 by the *"acerbically witty"* Lucy Stone QC, and the general feeling is that she *"will keep chambers going in the right direction."* Stone isn't the first female head of chambers but, with a young son, she is the first working mum to lead the set.

The set takes a fresh approach to recruitment. It's not just about having an Oxbridge background – *"I come from a background where I don't have any other lawyers in my family and I was the first person to go to university,"* explained one pupil. *"Others come from the more standard white, upper-middle-class background, but we are all very different."* What is important is having a head for numbers and *"an understanding of business and finance,"* both of which are a far cry from the cuddly, sympathetic image you might have of a family law barristers. It is, of course, important to seem empathetic towards clients, but the trick is not to get emotionally involved. *"You have to apply a level and cool head to every problem,"* stressed a source.

Pupil supervisors have devised *"a bare-essentials list of things pupils have to see, so they're up and running by their second six."* These include basic drafting, a knowledge of court procedure and observing a good mixture of junior and senior work. Each pupil shadows a junior in order to witness what the early stages of tenancy might be like, while simultaneously being exposed to the more complex work of their supervisors. Day-to-day tasks include bits of discrete legal research, writing the odd opinion on a point of law, and some quite complex donkey work, for example tracking transactions between different bank accounts and drafting schedules. *"There's always admin-type things like photocopying, but other than that nothing which I'd say is boring or mundane,"* commented one pupil. Members often work opposite each other on cases and represent a broad range of clients from celebrities and public figures to *"the ordinary bloke off the street."* Naturally in the early years there are more of the latter than the former, and *"you'll trawl the county courts going up and down the country to places such as Milton Keynes, Slough and Lincoln."* Being entrusted to carry out tasks for your pupil supervisor after the first few months makes you feel valued but terrified – *"you'll find yourself sitting in court with a schedule you've prepared thinking, oh my god, something's going to be wrong."* However, supervisors will *"always take the blame"* for your mistakes in court, and if you're praised, they'll *"make sure you get the credit for it."*

Pupils get to go to court three or four times a week, and they tell us *"it's fun and interesting"* to see how people deal with each other, especially when they're great friends in chambers. *"They don't take any prisoners; there's no letting anyone have an easy time,"* noted one source. Things can get hectic for pupils, so the clerks make sure they aren't overburdened with work. Senior clerk Ivor Treherne has been with the set since the 1970s. *"Ivor's a legend,"* said one pupil, while another told us: *"Ivor and Steve [Morley] are like rocks."* Indeed, the barristers have great respect for the clerks and we learned that *"there's a real reticence to tell them to do things. When you start here, there's a habit of saying, 'I'm going to be leaving a bit early today, is that okay?' But to their credit, they'll sit you down and tell you that you're the boss, there's no need to ask."* Clerks still address pupils and barristers as Sir or Ma'am. *"The other thing is referring to people by their initials or surname. When you first start it kind of feels slightly odd, but the clerks are happy and that's really the main thing."*

The general consensus is that *"you fit in with your supervisor's hours."* Lunch is *"sometimes with the laptop,"* but *"we're not a chambers that encourages hour-counting, we like to kick them out the door at 6.15pm and encourage them not to start before 8.45pm."* Pupils sit with four supervisors for four months and one for six weeks, during which time they gain common law experience. This is described as *"really useful… it broadens you."* At the junior end of chambers, there is actually a surprisingly broad mix of family work, including a fair amount of *"non-money stuff"* such as child abduction cases and non-molestation orders. The common law cases seen by pupils include possession actions and bankruptcy proceedings, all of which is *"excellent for pupils as it gets them court time, which is what they want."*

Reports filled out at the end of each seat are circulated around chambers and there is additionally a gruelling advocacy test. This is a nerve-wracking experience in front of the head of chambers, another QC and a senior junior. Making it so challenging is *"slightly deliberate – if they can do it, they can deal with any judge."* With the ordeal safely behind them, one pupil told us: *"As soon as you get in there, you realise it's nothing to be afraid of. Ivor is sitting in the corner, which is a real help… it's comforting to have him there."*

The July tenancy decision is made by all members; even those who can't attend the meeting send something in writing. *"We are deciding people's futures here, so we take it very seriously."* The set is proud of its record of finding third sixes and tenancies for those who don't get offered a home at QEB. This is a largely committee-driven set, albeit that an agenda is sent out to everyone before most committee meetings. *"It's not a one-member-one-vote system, but you are very much involved,"* explained one junior tenant. The set has a traditional feel to it and *"takes pride in its sense of history."* Surrounded by Middle Temple Gardens, its building might be post-war, but the staircases are literally encased in wood panelling. Emphasising the somewhat staid décor is a rogues' gallery of oil paintings featuring past senior members who have gone to the bench.

The pupils' view of the culture in chambers reflects its mix of old and new. *"There's a balance of the old-school, traditional type of barristers and people who run their practice in a far more modern, innovative way, focusing on care for the solicitor and the lay client."* QEB has a strong *"family feel"* to it. *"Some sets treat chambers as a building where administrative acts take place,"* explained one tenant; *"but here it's more a case of keeping office hours. People will work 10- 20% of the time from home and the rest here, as opposed to doing it the other way around."* Getting together over afternoon tea is an important tradition, and one that was defended by pupils. *"When I tell my contemporaries from Bar school about it, they raise their eyebrows, but as a first-six pupil I found it to be a really positive experience. It's a chance to chill out, talk about the football and meet members of chambers who you wouldn't otherwise be exposed to."* Tea usually lasts for half an hour, but it can go on: *"Think of the staffroom in a school – it can get excitable at times!"*

There is a welcome party held for pupils in the first week – *"so they get to meet us all informally over a glass of fizz"* – and with an open-door policy, pupils quickly get to know who everyone is, as well as hearing discussions about where the law is going and how judges are responding to different issues. *"As a pupil I was touched by how many people who were working on multimillion-pound cases stopped to help me with my tiny little case worth a few hundred quid,"* said one source. One pupil admitted: *"You start off feeling like you're in the Big Brother house – you're constantly making sure your tie's straight and your shoes are polished."* As the tenancy decision approaches, this inevitably starts up again, *"but in the interim you just get on with it all."* In fact, the time until Christmas is considered a *"bedding-in period"* and, *"although pupils never believe this,"* before December it's *"really too early to be thinking about tenancy."*

Pupillage interviews are carried out by a panel of three, which normally includes the head of chambers. The set takes a wholly objective approach to interviewing, planning everything well in advance. Before going in, interviewees are given 20 minutes to prepare an answer to a legal problem in the area of tort or contract law. Reassuringly, it's about seeing how your mind works rather than getting the right answer. The panel also considers self-presentation, motivation and time management, particularly the ability to stay calm under pressure. Of the 20 interviewees, up to three receive offers.

QEB tells us it is *"about the right size now; we always saw 30 as the optimum number."* Its belief that *"small is beautiful"* leads us to conclude that the set we see today is likely to be the set we will see in five or ten years' time.

3 Raymond Buildings

Chambers UK rankings: Crime, fraud: criminal, licensing, professional discipline

Blue blooded, patrician, living in an ivory tower – these are all accusations that have been levelled at 3 Raymond Buildings. As one member readily admitted when we visited them, *"there is no doubt that we are different. We have a character and reputation that marks us out from the general criminal fold."* So what's the truth about this, one of the country's finest criminal sets?

Even a cursory glance at the long list of top cases in which members have been involved will convince you of its credentials. Of late, they have secured the first two dismissals in the Hatfield rail crash prosecutions, prosecuted Siôn Jenkins and the defendants in the Chohan family murders, and secured the conviction of Afghan warlord Zardad. As the leading set for extradition cases, chambers has members working on the matters that make the biggest headlines – cases such as the NatWest Three (one member represented the directors facing extradition to America, another represented the US Government and a third acted for the

Attorney General) and Muslim cleric Abu Hamza (where two members are representing the US Government). As one member explained: *"In extradition work there is no trial; there are no witnesses to handle – it is pure law. You are at Bow Street Magistrates' Court and the High Court very quickly. The first line of appeal without leave is at the High Court and this exposure forces you to be disciplined about time limits, etc. You need a much sharper appreciation of the law because Lord Justice So-and-So will eat you for breakfast if you don't."* Our source went on to say that experience on extradition cases means that *"when you are conducting a regular criminal trial, you are so much fitter."*

The expression 'regular criminal trials' sounds like something of an understatement when you consider some of the complex and academic matters that are sent to the set. Take, for example, the question of whether undertaking an act in order to prevent the commission of war crimes can be used as a defence to criminal charges, or whether the customary international law 'crime of aggression' is in fact a crime under English law. Both of these issues have taken the set's barristers to the House of Lords in the past year. Chambers is known for its academic approach to practice. *"We are a three-dimensional set,"* said one source. *"It is no longer enough to have your standard crime approach when you are undertaking international work, fraud and so on. What we try to do is always look at the potential civil aspects of a criminal case and the other way round."* Continuing this theme, we were told: *"We are better at the law and we aren't scared of delving into the more esoteric aspects of the law. We think this makes us much better criminal practitioners than your usual."*

Already, you'll have a fair idea about the calibre of pupil the set wants to recruit. Chambers offers three pupillages per year and last year received over 400 applications through OLPAS. How many applicants are invited to a first interview depends entirely on the quality that year. *"If* we got 400 brilliant applications then we would interview all of them. This year we interviewed between 70 and 80; last year it was 100." That's a remarkable number. "Part of the criteria is obviously good academics – it is impossible to ignore that." The recruiters were clear in telling us that "an Oxbridge degree is not a prerequisite here" and indeed the further down the member board you go, the less Oxbridge-dominated it is.

All first-round interviewees must tackle a structured problem on a recent legal issue or improvised scenario. "We give them this to see their reaction. It is not about whether someone is right or wrong – let's face it, they are invariably wrong – it is more to see their judgement, how they handle it and what that says about their intellectual ability. Their knowledge base is somewhat taken as read."

Again, the number of candidates who come back for a second interview depends on the quality that year. More than 20 were invited back in 2006. The second interview is very much like the first, just longer and more detailed with an advocacy exercise. "We are really trying to see the person... this means we have to take a lot of different factors into consideration. For instance, the people we interview can differ quite widely in terms of age: we have to allow for lack of confidence when interviewing somebody very young compared to somebody who is older; someone who may have already had a career." As to whether there's a personality type, again, we're told not. "No matter what people think, we are not just workaholic spods," said a source. "Of course the people here work hard and are academic... but we are still rounded people."

Make it through to pupillage and you'll experience a year that is divided into four-month blocks, each spent with a different supervisor. Chambers tries to consider pupils' preferences when assigning their second and third supervisors. "I told them that I wanted to do extradition work and was given James Hines and Hugo Keith." A pupil's request might have more to do with getting their face better known around chambers: "If you say you don't know people on other floors, then they'll put you there."

One pupil spoke particularly positively about the fact that they'd witnessed a good many of chambers' top cases from the past year. "I have had such wonderful exposure from the mags to the High Court, to the Court of Appeal, to the Lords. I have worked on skeleton arguments for headline cases. I have been able to go to the Bailey and watch things like the latest Siôn Jenkins trial. There are such massive resources to tap into here." In terms of what second-six pupils can expect by way of their own instructions, it's very much what you would expect from a regular criminal set – mags, mags and more mags. "I went to the Crown Court once during pupillage and my client pleaded," revealed a baby junior. Another hot area for chambers following recent regulatory changes is liquor licensing, so pupils and baby juniors can expect a fair amount of work in this field.

Pupils undergo no formal assessments until just before the tenancy decision. Pupils submit two pieces of their work and are interviewed by a panel that also asks them to conduct a piece of advocacy. Their pupil supervisors are asked to supply a letter of reference and further feedback is sought from other members of chambers plus judges and solicitors. One junior tenant suggested that "if you have done very well over the course of the year but let yourself down in interview, you can still get an offer. It works the other way round too; tenancy can be won during interview."

More pupils are recruited than could possibly be taken on but the beauty of a pupillage here is that not being offered tenancy isn't going to mean the death of your career. "We've a great track record of ensuring that those who don't get taken on aren't booted out straight away; they will be found a place at another chambers. We have excellent contacts and really want our ex-pupils to end up at the right place for them."

5RB

Chambers UK rankings: Defamation/privacy, media & entertainment

Residing in freshly outfitted rooms at 5 Raymond Buildings, next to the expansive flower beds and shady paths of Gray's Inn Gardens, you'd never suspect that 5RB has been closely involved with matters of intrigue and outraged decency since the year dot. Founded by the legendary Sir Valentine Holmes, who enjoyed successes in a plethora of famous libel cases in the 1940s and 50s, the set continues to be at the very forefront of pioneering defamation and privacy work for the rich, famous and infamous. Basically if you're loaded and have tangled with the media, be it newspapers, magazines, book publishers or TV channels, chances are you'll turn to 5RB to clear your name. Kate Moss did just that when Channel Five broadcast a programme that claimed she'd consumed so much cocaine that she'd entered a coma. A certain Wayne Rooney was helped to an out-of-court settlement with *The Sun* and *News of the World* publishers News Group over allegations that he slapped fiancée Coleen in a nightclub. Strong relationships with newspaper groups also see 5RB represent publishers – Associated Newspapers, for example, when HRH Prince Charles brought a claim following *The Mail on Sunday*'s publication of extracts from his diary. Such is the set's renown that its barristers frequently represent both sides in the same case. Good examples are the Douglas/Hello! privacy scrap following publication of photos from the Hollywood couple's wedding, and the dispute between the Beckhams and News Group over the *News of the World*'s allegations that the Beckhams' marriage was a sham.

On merit and specialised excellence, this purposeful chambers certainly deserves its orbit in the rarefied atmosphere of movers and shakers, so it is no surprise that, *"going forward, we're stay-ing focused on our core areas."* Admittedly, there has been an element of diversification: 5RB is developing an IP capacity and a number of sports personality defamation/privacy cases and strong relationships with The Jockey Club have seen the set decide to *"market our sports law abilities hard."*

The process of evolution has instead found an outlet in marketing, the most visible tools of which are an über-cool, monochrome website and the set's trendy name. *"You have no idea how long it took to come up with it, considering all the alternatives and getting approval from everyone,"* revealed a source. 'Raymonds', 'Arbies', maybe even 'High Five' – the possibilities must have been endless...

If you're struck by how attractive chambers' work appears, you're not alone. As one pupil commented: *"When you say you're in media law everyone is immediately interested, even other barristers and solicitors."* So, be under no illusions that the competitive process of gaining a pupillage has an extra edge at 5RB. Becoming one of the lucky few (up to two per year) means negotiating a *"relaxed, three-person panel interview"* in which *"the last thing we want to do is inhibit or intimidate people"* as well as a written test *"on a hypothetical question centred around some area of media law."* You'll also need to demonstrate *"genuine interest in our specialist areas,"* whether through a media law dissertation, *"being familiar with prominent current cases,"* a media mini-pupillage or wider experience in-house at newspapers, broadcasters or publishers. Going a step further to show *"a real thirst for and interest in news and the media, and also an understanding of the media, its economics and priorities"* is undoubtedly an advantage that *"gives the interviewers a sense of who is really committed to the area, rather than simply thinking it sounds interesting."* Be aware that while the set has recruited for 2007 and 2008, it currently does not plan to do so for 2009, so you may not find it in Olpas.

Looking further down the line, the *"ever-*

developing nature of the area" requires a skill set incorporating "interest in tactical lawyering and nuanced technicalities," as well as "an ability to adapt arguments innovatively and flexibly." Because the career path at 5RB leads "towards a great deal of high-profile, High Court jury advocacy," the potential to become an impressive advocate matters too.

Pupils divide their year equally between four different pupil supervisors, of which one will likely be an IP specialist and the remaining three defamation specialists. Don't worry, three of the same doesn't equate to dull times because "within privacy/media/defamation law there is a phenomenal amount of procedure to learn and variety to experience." It might be "claimant Jockey Club tribunals or sports law defamation" with one pupil supervisor, "big, defendant newspaper cases" with another and "high-profile defamation for big names" with a third. However, just because you're representing celebs doesn't actually mean you'll be dropping into A-list parties yourself. "I did meet Carole Caplin once, but that was it," confessed a pupil. The work does mean regularly interacting with "heads of legal at news companies, and as a young lawyer in media work that's actually pretty exciting."

In both the first and second six, a pupil's work comes direct from pupil supervisors, either in the form of "academic tasks – basically 'dead issues' where you complete them and then go through them together" or "simultaneously doing a pupil supervisor's work and maybe even supplying the first draft if it's good enough." While the former method ensures "great feedback," the latter offers "a more interesting experience" and "the occasional thrill of working on household-name cases." Unless they bring their own laptop to chambers, pupils share a PC for frequent "research and opinion-writing tasks." They can expect written appraisals of their performance on tasks during each three-month stint, all of which are collated after six

months. "If you're not flourishing, people will explain why," we were told.

Because there is "next to no pupil-level advocacy beyond the very rare application for an extension of time," the second six involves almost no court time. For this reason, pupils are encouraged (if they haven't being doing it already) to sign up with FRU or the Islington Legal Advice Centre. Although they admitted to envying contemporaries elsewhere when they headed off to court alone, few felt that the short-term loss was significant. "All the time you're watching, talking with and listening to colleagues, observing courtroom style, picking up tips from silks and gaining experience." In fact, this pattern continues post-pupillage because "there is just not a lot of entry-level civil work."

Most pupils spend a short time on secondment to one of the media organisations with links to 5RB – eg The Times or Channel Four – and there is an opportunity to earn much-needed ready cash through "pre-publication advisory work" or "taking witness statements on larger cases for your pupil supervisors." This advisory work or 'night lawyering' for newspaper publishers is a key component of a junior's working life and is described as "vital to learning about practice in this area of law." It may not sound much, but sitting in the newspaper's offices scanning copy for potentially contentious or libellous material is a perfect introduction to the pitfalls and scrapes of the publishing world. In the meantime, you could do far worse than read Piers Morgan's diaries, The Insider, for an in-depth exposé of the national media.

In between pupillage and junior tenancy is of course the small matter of the tenancy decision. This process involves the pupillage committee considering feedback from each pupil supervisor and any other member for whom the pupil has worked. It is not unheard of for two pupils to be kept on in the same year. This was the case in 2006, although in 2007 neither pupil gained tenancy. Those who are less fortunate can rely on *"a full explanation and help to achieve tenancy or a third six elsewhere."*

5RB tells us it is a *"liberal set"* and, *"unlike many chambers, not factional at all."* It sounds like it is similarly cohesive in social situations, as *"you could find the head of chambers at a pub quiz with the junior tenants."* Normally there are drinks in the clerks' room at the end of the week, to which *"pupils are invited, but there's no sense that you have to schmooze everyone."* Pupils also appreciate *"being invited along when your supervisor goes out with clients – you're not made to feel invisible."* Perhaps best of all, aspiring 5RB tenants told us they felt privileged to have *"got the Holy Grail of pupillages."*

3 Serjeants' Inn

Chambers UK rankings: Clinical negligence, police law: mainly defendant, professional discipline

Situated in an old bank on Fleet Street, flanking the Temple, No. 3 Serjeants' Inn is somewhere between a boutique hotel and a movie set. Yet the grandeur of the premises belies the set's history, ethos and personality. Established as recently as 1974, this is a young set with a somewhat pioneering spirit. Chambers is best known for its medical law practice, an area where it has a wealth of quality advocates covering both claimant and defendant work, the latter for NHS trusts, private hospitals and their insurers, as well as medical defence bodies. Members have been instructed in almost every headline-grabbing case of recent times: Bland (the separation of conjoined twins), Sidaway (extent of a doctor's duty to inform patients prior to gaining consent) as well as the public inquiries into Harold Shipman and the Bristol Royal Infirmary.

Despite the obvious *"dedication and passion"* barristers have for their work, we reckon 3SI has an opportunistic streak. Its dominance of the medical field was borne out of a determination to exploit the emerging clinical negligence market in the 1980s. The work has unsurprisingly broadened in scope and now incorporates all manner of advice on clinical issues and the healthcare

> **Chambers and Partners**
> **Professional Discipline**
> **Set of the Year 2007**

profession generally. Disciplinary proceedings brought by the General Medical Council (GMC) and other professional bodies are a key source of work. For example, one of the set's QCs recently helped Professor Sir Roy Meadow successfully appeal a GMC ruling that he should be struck off the medical register. You may recall that Meadow's evidence was instrumental in the wrongful murder conviction of three innocent mothers, including solicitor Sally Clarke who served three years of a life sentence.

According to one junior source: *"It takes a while to get going on medical stuff and it's likely you'll get experience in other things first, such as PI, which is related in terms of the damages."* This hadn't alarmed our source: *"Chambers know what they're doing; the clerks have lots of experience in nurturing people's practices. I have had a gradual introduction but I am entirely happy with the way things are developing."*

At the moment we would suggest paying serious attention to chambers' police law group, which is one of the best around. Acting mainly for police authorities, barristers defend civil actions brought against the police, work on judicial reviews and disciplinary proceedings, and assist the police in obtaining ASBOs or orders for the closure of crack dens. The headcount of experts in this area continues to grow and it is now a major source of revenue. 2006 has also been a good year for the set's employment practitioners with the establishment of a formal practice group. The other string to chambers' bow is construction law.

It is almost an understatement to say that pupillage is taken seriously here. The year is divided into three periods of four months so that pupils can try their hand at each of the main practice areas. Particular interests can be accommodated and there is dialogue between pupils and the pupillage committee before a new supervisor is chosen. The sales pitch is that chambers offers *"a combination of interesting, paper-based work that can be technically challenging, balanced with a good amount of court work. This place is perfect for anybody who wants to work with human clients but doesn't want to dirty their fingers with crime."*

Drafting skills are a cornerstone of civil practice and a great deal of attention is paid to developing the quality and style of pupils' opinion writing and pleadings. All paperwork undertaken during pupillage is assessed in the sense that *"everything is formally written down and fed back to the pupils. It is also used to help make the final tenancy decision."* Pupils are additionally reminded that being self-critical will better prepare them for when they are out on their own. *"You are encouraged to think about better, more efficient ways of working,"* perhaps utilising chronologies and spreadsheets more or *"being more creative in how you approach things."* A formal in-house programme of advocacy assessment has been running for the past two years and is split into two parts. *"For each session we have three members of chambers including a junior and a senior who are involved and give us feedback."* A typical assessment might involve a basic trip-and-slip case.

Long hours are discouraged in the early stages by applying a strict 9am to 6pm policy. As soon as pupils get on their feet in the second six this changes and 12-hour days and weekend work are not unusual. As you may be aware, it is increasingly difficult for civil pupils to gain good advocacy experience due to a diminution in the amount of small-end work available. To remedy this, chambers ensures that pupils undertake a good amount of magistrates' court appearances. This work is available because of the special efforts made by senior clerk Nick Salt, who maintains contact with criminal sets willing to pass on small instructions. Recalling the start of the second six, one source told us: *"It really is a baptism of fire but once over the initial shock it is fantastic training; it really toughens you up."* As may the travel – don't always expect to be able to work in or near the capital.

This is a straightforward kind of set with a commitment to keeping pupils apprised of their performance every step of the way. Younger tenants assured us that, as a result, when the tenancy decision is made there are no real surprises. Supporting the idea that the pupillage year is taken seriously, tenancy decisions are left until the autumn. On the one hand this gives pupils the maximum amount of time in which to flourish and prove their credentials; on the other, those pupils who do not get taken on will miss the start of the cycle for applying for third sixes elsewhere. We're led to believe this is less of a problem than you might think, as chambers is large and busy enough that neither a paucity of work nor space need have an adverse effect on decisions. Those who simply don't make the grade are usually allowed to squat until they can find another home. In 2006, both pupils were offered tenancy; chambers had not made its 2007 decision by the time we went to press.

Chambers was remarkably candid in telling us that the calibre of the pupils and tenants on paper has improved greatly since the set was first

chambers reports

established. *"It is possible that our current silks wouldn't make it to the first round,"* they half-joked. Certainly all the junior members have impressive CVs, many of them educated at Oxbridge, LSE, UCL and the like. Academics alone will not impress the pupillage committee, and candidates must display other desirable qualities to succeed. Members see themselves as having a down-to-earth style that comes from both academic strength and practical minded-ness. In truth there are no hard-and-fast rules as to what makes a candidate ideal for this set, so the only advice we can offer is that it is pointless trying to appear a certain way at interview. What you can work on is how you demonstrate your interest in their specific areas of expertise. Unsurprisingly, undertaking a 3SI mini-pupillage is a good idea. Though not formally assessed, a mini pupil's performance will be taken into account in their application for full pupillage. It may have been a coincidence but all of those we interviewed in chambers had done minis with the set.

They say the chambers that drinks together, stays together (or something along those lines). Pupils appreciate members' efforts to include them socially, whenever possible, and also appreciate being allocated an 'aunt' or 'uncle' to act as informal mentor. *"It's nice to have someone you can chat to; they have a different perspective on things. Having someone to turn to who has been through pupillage relatively recently is just another part of the jigsaw."* It is clear that in the junior ranks people genuinely do get on famously and enjoy spending time together outside the work environment. There's even a group ski trip each winter. The knock-on effect is a self-sustaining support network within chambers for those just starting out on their careers. They way we see it, as good as things are here, all the policies and proce-dures in the world are no substitute for healthy work relationships.

Serle Court

Chambers UK Rankings: Banking & finance, Chancery: commercial, Chancery: traditional, commercial dispute resolution, company, financial services regulation, fraud: civil, insolvency/corporate recovery, partnership, professional negligence, real estate litigation, telecommunications

Situated in the heart of Lincoln's Inn, Serle Court formed through the merger of the Chancery set at 13 Old Square and the commercial set at 1 Hare Court. Since its inception in 2000, it has gone from strength to strength in well over a dozen practice areas ranging from the main-stream (shipping, insurance and reinsurance, property, probate and partnership law) to the specialist (sports law, charities, Arabic laws). For-get the fusty, ivory towers image traditionally associated with Chancery practice: Serle Court manages to make its business modern and inno-vative. High-profile cases such as NatWest v Rabobank and the BCCI litigation illustrate how well it is regarded in the finance sector; in trusts matters members are regularly instructed in off-shore jurisdictions such as the Cayman Islands; and in partnership law, members played a notable role in developing the use of LLPs by professional services firms and other businesses. Commercial litigation and mediation continue to be growing areas, and in the area of entertain-ment law, members successfully defended the Marley family against a claim by the former bassist of The Wailers, as well as acting in a claim regarding the copyright of songs subsequently licensed to Madonna.

With magic circle firms regularly instructing these barristers on behalf of blue-chip compa-nies, it's no surprise that the list of Serle Court members, past and present, is pretty impressive. Sir Michael Briggs, recently appointed as a High

Court judge, is just one of many senior members who have gone to the bench, so it's a good job chambers has a healthy roster of juniors. The set is administered by chief executive Nicola Sawford and senior clerk Steve Whitaker, who insist that having a loyal and committed staff has cemented the set's success. Four clerks have been at the set (and its two legacy components) for a combined total of more than 120 years, and when we visited, a big party was being planned for the impending retirement of one of them. As one source stressed: *"After a merger you need people to buy in 100%, and that's exactly what happened here."*

Commercial chancery is an intellectually demanding area of the Bar, and one that is hard to rival for factual complexity. Nevertheless, pupils described Serle Court as a set that *"allows you to be you,"* and insisted: *"As long as you have the base ability, they appreciate that it manifests itself in different ways, allowing you to develop into the barrister you're meant to be."* While personalities vary, a stunning academic record is the norm, as is a long attention span, an excellent eye for detail and a capacity for hard graft. The biggest part of the job is providing written advice and drafting services; the advocacy that does exist is the type where *"you have ample preparation and know the facts backwards."* Furthermore, you need to be comfortable with lots of paperwork, *"pragmatic... and able to get on well with business clients."*

Serle Court does not recruit through OLPAS, instead preferring to get its own system started several months earlier. Importantly, the application form is a chance to show off your written advocacy skills – and your capacity to be succinct. Of the 120 or so applicants each year, 30 make it to first interview. The best advice we can pass on is this: *"Get a good night's sleep before"* and *"don't lapse into debate mode... someone who declaims as if to a huge imaginary audience is a real turn off."* The interview is structured such that a CPE/GDL student will be at no disadvantage, and the panel looks for people who *"take a healthy interest in legal issues in the world around them."*

Those who are offered pupillage will sit with four different supervisors for three months each. They become exposed to high and low-value work for clients ranging from banks, trust funds and companies to private individuals. The areas of law they encounter include both commercial and traditional Chancery, property and IP, but as one pupil's first piece of work on minority shareholders shows, there's no guarantee of encountering topics familiar from law school. The pupil in question took two extra days to complete the work because he had to give himself *"a crash course in company and insolvency law."* This wasn't such a disaster as supervisors show a flexible attitude to timing, giving their charges *"as long as they want"* to carry out each assignment. Besides, pupils rarely carry out live work, so there are no external pressures. Indeed, for some, this could be a potential pitfall: before tenancy is offered pupils do *"very little that is used... and if it is, it's carefully checked."*

The general ethos seems to be that *"you don't get the best out of people if they constantly feel under the cosh."* Accordingly, the day usually begins around 8.30am and ends around 6.30pm. In terms of breaks, there is morning coffee in the St. George's Café and afternoon tea in chambers' library. Both are well attended and pupils are encouraged to join in the chat. Mini pupils, however, should refrain from spying on these hallowed intervals. Pupils are welcome to join members for drinks at the Gaucho Grill or The Seven Stars, as well as for cricket, football and (coming soon) softball matches. Pupils share rooms with their supervisors, who monitor their work to ensure they gain a breadth of drafting experience. They also get farmed out to other members to watch interesting cases, see a variety of practice areas and perhaps *"observe an expert cross-examination."* One pupil even carried out some work on a criminal case at another set, assisting on the complicated trusts point it involved.

Assessment is ongoing, although the first three months are *"quite heavily discounted."* Supervisors fill out appraisal forms at the end of each seat and these are submitted to the tenancy committee. There is at least one assessed advocacy exercise in which pupils *"play the same role,"* so their performances can be measured against each other. In April, supervisors and members of the tenancy committee meet to discuss the first six, following which feedback is given. This can lead to an early decision; in 2007, a sufficiently strong consensus was reached for the committee to reconvene and offer both pupils tenancy in May. The decision is usually made in June or early July. Serle Court has a healthy flow of work and further room for expansion, so if a pupil meets the mark he or she will be offered tenancy, regardless of whether the other pupil is being taken on.

During their final three months, pupils who have been offered tenancy shadow junior practitioners in the county courts, where *"everything is less smart and more chaotic"* and it's *"common for the judge not to have had the papers in advance."* District Judges are not specialised, often doing *"family one minute, commercial the next,"* so paradoxically, *"although they need more time, they get less."* It can be *"hard to anticipate what point they're going to seize on,"* so the experience is an invaluable one for anyone on the verge of starting their own practice. At the same time pupils also get the chance to assist on some big cases (*"feeling very much like the junior on the team"*) as well as devilling for senior members of chambers. Juniors might be in court five times a month, though this doesn't have an adverse impact on their earnings: in the first two years of tenancy at least £100K is *"guaranteed... and often bettered."* One thing you might not expect is a six-month secondment to the Cayman Islands just after taking tenancy. Sun, sea, sand and a constant flow of instructions after

returning home – it's not such a bad idea.

There's a real sense of cohesion at Serle Court: *"At a full chambers meeting of 50-odd lawyers, there are going to be disagreements, but they'll still walk out that door and whatever decision has been made, they're behind it, with no griping in rooms afterwards and no bitter taste in the mouth."* The support network for juniors is excellent: *"Everyone is conscious of having been there before and we regularly trot into each others' rooms saying, oh my goodness, what do I do with this?"* And when, at 6pm, members say they're *"popping out for a con, we know where they're going!"* chuckled a clerk.

3/4 South Square

Chambers UK Rankings: Banking & finance, Chancery: commercial, company, insolvency/corporate recovery

The set is best known for its vast insolvency and corporate recovery practice; indeed its name is so synonymous with this area that solicitors suggest it is *"the IBM choice – why would you go anywhere else?"* Over the years members of 3/4 South Square have left their mark on all the big corporate collapses and restructurings – BCCI, Maxwell, Lloyd's syndicates, Barings, Enron, Marconi, Parmelat, MyTravel, the list goes on and on. It also has experts in fraud, banking and finance, commercial litigation, company law, insurance and reinsurance and arbitration. There's a rough 60/40 split between insolvency and broader commercial matters. While it's probably true that the Insolvency Act is the *"life blood"* of the set, other important disciplines are interpretation of contract, property law, trusts, tort and EU law. *"If you can't handle EU law, don't come here,"* advised one interviewee. One of the more *"sexy"* areas is fraud, not least because fraudsters range from the perplexingly normal to "colourful, famous crooks." Pupils agreed that when working in this area, "it can be a bit like being in a Bond film."

As almost all of the work has a commercial edge, it's important to keep clients' business interests in mind at all times. Commercial awareness is a term you've undoubtedly heard many times, but it can be devilishly hard to define, not least when you're trying to show you have it. Sometimes the easiest way is to get a job in a commercial enterprise and observe how and why management make decisions. For a barrister, it's about looking at cases from a fresh perspective and maintaining an awareness of the commercial context. "In every case you study at law school, and every textbook example, that context will be there, but it can be easily overlooked," explained a pupil. Insolvency barristers receive instructions from specialist insolvency practitioners as well as solicitors, and at times they come into contact with some "very aggressive and difficult" individuals at personal bankruptcy hearings. Having a real-world view on things is imperative. Equally as important, however, is a healthy interest in raw legal principles, and as one pupil pointed out: "The Insolvency Act is the second longest statute on the books after the Company Act 2006, which is the other one we specialise in." There's no getting around it; if you want pupillage at 3/4 South Square, you're going to have to cover all the bases.

Chambers offers up to four pupillages each year, each person sitting with around half a dozen supervisors of up to 15 years' call for periods of six weeks. Supervision is described as a "collaborative process" in which pupils are asked to identify the gaps in their knowledge, so that supervisors can provide them with experiences to fill them.

It's an intense year and "you really do hit the ground running." "Difficult stuff is thrown at you from an early stage" and "people aren't going to hold your hand – you either sink or swim." Pupils complete the same set pieces of work for supervisors, and doing them at different times avoids scrapping for books in the library. Our interviewees spoke warmly of their treatment during pupillage: "Chambers really wants you to find out how to work, so pupillage is very much geared towards letting you make your own decisions." Time management, for example, is largely left to the pupil. Supervisors will ensure they have access to interesting work, but it's up to them to decide whether they can take it on and, more importantly, ask when it needs to be completed. Pupillage is not going to be a totally smooth learning curve – "everyone makes mistakes" – but be reassured there are people to ask for advice and support, and "pupils are never faced with someone being difficult for the sake of it." In the first three months, their performance is less crucial, and it is the supervisors they sit with after Christmas who take the most active role in the tenancy decision.

"This isn't the place to come if you want to be on your feet in the second six," we learned. Indeed, advocacy skills aren't even formally assessed during pupillage (although it is important to give "intelligent, lucid responses" when receiving feedback from supervisors). Adequate advocacy opportunities come in time, and until about eight years' call juniors spend roughly equal amounts of time representing clients alone and being led by seniors. After this time, their role becomes more advisory. Another key thing to mention is that the set has a strong international practice, with associate members in Germany, Hong Kong, Singapore, the USA, Australia, South Africa, Scotland and Trinidad and Tobago. One pupil described the "magical mystery island tour" his work had led him on, taking in "the British Virgin Islands, Mauritius, the Cayman Islands, the Seychelles, South Korea, the Isle of Man, Jersey and Guernsey." Needless to say, many cases have a trusts element.

Members' hours fluctuate dramatically –

some arrive in the wee small hours to catch the Hong Kong traffic, while others work late to fit in with New York. Even for pupils 12-hour days are not unheard of, although usually their average is 9am until 7pm. *"You'll write lots of long opinions and research notes and go through different drafts of one piece of work, but there's also a lot of time thinking about what you've read and staring into space."* It's important to be able to *"think creatively and logically in order to combat the complexity of the work."*

After the first six months, *"no-hopers are told where they stand and given a choice about staying on or looking for a second six elsewhere."* The final tenancy decision is made in July at a meeting of all members; typically two make the cut each year. Technically, pupils don't need to compete for tenancy, but we sensed there was a *"combative"* element to the process. While we interviewed them, the pupils engaged in a game of one-upmanship: one had been in court 11 times since Christmas, visiting the Chancery division, the Companies Court and the Privy Council. Another, who had been in court only twice, was quick to point out that he had written a chapter for a book and several articles for various pupil supervisors during the same period. *"If you really like writing and academic publications, there's a lot going on,"* they told us.

Despite the picture we've so far painted, 3/4 South Square is by no means a macho set. The junior end boasts a healthy number of female practitioners, and from what we saw, wrap-around cardigans have more currency than sharp suits and shoulder-pads. The dress code is informal (although pupils still wear suits) and there's a professional, business-like atmosphere. At the hub of chambers is a strong administration team run by charismatic senior practice manager Paul Cooklin (the set has done away with the term clerk). *"If you have a technical problem, you go to Yvonne. If you have a pupillage query, you go to Ali-son. For broader chambers issues, there's Vicky... if you need something typed, you go to Jenny and Julie,"* pupils willingly explained. In this set *"everybody knows your name"* and junior tenants go for regular drinks at the Cittie of Yorke and the Adjournment Bar. *"People are very hard-working, but they still know when to take time off."*

You're advised to take the company law elective on the BVC and, if you're considering postgraduate study, the corporate insolvency paper on the BCL. Another new and developing area to consider is restitution law. The pupillage committee takes into account that not everyone will have studied that much law by the time they reach interview. *"We don't find setting legal problems very helpful; we prefer to start everyone with an ethics question, for which no prior knowledge is required."* Interestingly, one of the recruiters told us: *"Their ethical approach matters quite a lot to us."* Anyone who impresses in an assessed mini-pupillage (for which chambers pays £500) is fast-tracked to a second-round interview. Most candidates go through two rounds, although a third interview is used in cases where the panel can't quite decide on someone, perhaps because they've underperformed due to nerves. Successful candidates are then invited to attend a drinks party in chambers to meet more of the members.

Insolvency law is a fast-paced and challenging discipline, and with companies going bust and individuals teetering on the brink of bankruptcy, you need to be *"thick-skinned and resilient,"* especially in situations that can be *"panicky and stressful for the client."* After meeting with pupils at 3/4 South Square, we were left thinking they were tough cookies. All up, we'd describe 3/4 South Square as a slick and ballsy set, where pupils learn their trade in a challenging and stimulating environment. If you're driven, focused and open-minded, there is every chance to shine; just be prepared for some firm handshakes at interview.

4 Stone Buildings

Chambers UK Rankings: Chancery: commercial, company, financial services regulation, fraud: civil, insolvency/corporate recovery

Nestling in the north-east corner of Lincoln's Inn is 4 Stone Buildings, a small but self-assured set with a reputation for *"fighting with the heavy-weights."* Members regularly appear in large commercial disputes, particularly those involving company law, and pride themselves on their *"business acumen, work ethic and amiability."* While company law has a reputation for being *"quite dry at times,"* members appreciate that *"there's more to life"* and their practices extend to *"more fun stuff"* in the form of general commercial cases, fraud, asset tracing and insolvency. Cases range from the monumental (Equitable Life, Three Rivers) to *"short and snappy personal insolvency cases."* The Maxwell affair, in which media mogul Robert Maxwell took over £400m from his employees' pension funds to boost the company's share price, kept one member in court for 150 days. In the case of BCCI, the volume of paperwork gave one barrister an excuse to move into one of the largest rooms in chambers.

While advisory work is a staple for some members, for most litigation is the *"bread and butter."* As one member put it: *"I didn't come to the Bar to do the job of a solicitor."* It's worth pointing out that not all litigation involves newspaper barons or other interesting characters. As an eminent judge once said: *"A company is a persona ficta... it does not have a soul to be damned or a body to be kicked."* Yet dealing with the inhabitants of Companies House need not be without its human drama and personal relationships with clients. The barristers deal with real people (liquidators, administrators, bankers, company directors, accountants), all of them busy professionals who *"want to know the answer and don't*

have time for flannel." For them, litigation is *"an inherently financial thing,"* an exercise in risk management, so your legal advice must be tempered by commercial considerations. The closest you'll come to Joe Public is in shareholder disputes involving Section 459, Companies Act petitions and even then, *"it's likely to be a man who manages his own company, maybe turning over £50,000, maybe £20m."*

The commercial demands at 4 Stone Buildings require pupils to *"make the transition from academic life – where they will have excelled – to practical, real life."* The client will want to know, *"should he sell his business today or wait until tomorrow?"* and a good barrister will need to be able to convince him of the right answer, *"even if it means going against his gut instinct."* An approach which merely considers all of the relevant legal

---

Chambers and Partners
Insolvency/Corporate Restructuring
Set of the Year 2007

---

principles is unlikely to work as *"getting the legal answer right is only half the battle."* If you're lucky enough to get a pupillage interview, bear this in mind when tackling the legal problem. *"We're looking for someone who can make the switch,"* said one of the recruiters. This also means showing you have the *"raw materials"* to argue a case in court. *"Making a nervous candidate more nervous doesn't serve much point,"* so the panel won't pressurise candidates for the sake of it. *"If we're giving you a hard time, you're probably getting it right,"* confided a source. Mental agility, fluency and practical business sense are all sought: *"We're not expecting someone aged 21 or 22 to wow us with their total knowledge of the law... in fact, the question is designed to be arguable either way."*

Chambers is home to some top QCs, among

them Robert Hildyard, Robert Miles and head of chambers George Bompas. Jonathon Crow, who recently took silk, was previously the First Treasury Devil, while several juniors currently act as Treasury Counsel. We won't attempt to name every respected barrister here; it's enough to say that in a *Chambers UK* table measuring the ratio of individual rankings to size of set, 4 Stone Buildings took second place. So what's it like stepping into such a high-flying environment?

First, you need to know that pupillage is about *"being taught, not tested."* Supervisors are paternalistic towards their charges and there's a sense of pupils being nurtured and coaxed into practice. As one pupil told us: *"There has definitely been an implicit understanding of how I work as an individual, and an effort to accommodate that."* Pupils sit with four supervisors for three months each to experience a range of work. One supervisor's practice might be *"very company law focused,"* requiring the pupil to *"grapple with accounts;"* another's might be *"centred around smaller contractual disputes;"* and a third could be *"incredibly blue-chip, with the barrister instructed consistently by magic circle firms."* Assessment is *"informal and definitely not in your face,"* but *"you get used to the feeling that your work is being looked at very carefully."* There are no *"artificially contrived"* advocacy exercises or tests and all the work pupils do is real. Pupils' carry out research and draft documents for their supervisors, often saving them time. In return, they give a lot back. For example, one supervisor told us: *"Before a conference, I get the pupil to sit down with me and pretend to be me, while I pretend to be the client."* The pupil will be given all the papers to read before accompanying a barrister to court and might also have a go at drafting the skeleton argument. After each visit to court, both pupil and supervisor sit down for post-match analysis.

Room sharing with supervisors works well. *"If I have a particularly poor conference, it's useful*

for the pupil to see how not to do it," chuckled a source. Pupil advocacy is rare, although in the months just after taking tenancy, *"you will pick up some of your own cases."* The pupils' work is *"very paper heavy: you have to do a lot of fact handling and reading company accounts... so forensic skills are incredibly important."* Being farmed out to other members of chambers to *"see an interesting House of Lords case"* or *"be exposed to a silk who needs some help,"* is important as this allows pupils to meet every member of chambers at least once by mid-July, when the tenancy decision is made. Another opportunity for pupils to *"throw themselves around"* and get their faces known is at daily tea. Responsibility for the tenancy decision *"rests primarily on the supervisors' shoulders,"* but all members of chambers attend the meeting and take a lively interest in the result. Usually one tenancy is awarded each year; occasionally it is two.

A pupil's day generally runs from 9am to 6.30pm, although by January the workload keeps them busy. At that stage, *"I began to really enjoy the work and wanted to put in the hours,"* one source explained. If things become too much to handle, *"help is always there and you're not censured for availing yourself of it."* Clearly everyone works hard here, but they also know when to stop. Fell running, skiing, sailing and flying are just some of the members' hobbies. George Bompas is a pilot and after the BCCI case settled, one barrister upped sticks to South America for five months. Family life is clearly important, and many members have three or four children; each year the head of chambers likes to *"get the families together for a picnic in Lincoln's Inn Fields."* Senior Clerk David Goddard – aka *"God"* – is undoubtedly a father figure, having been with the set since 1983, before many of you were born. Suggestions that he has *"royal inroads"* (members act as Attorney Generals to the Duchy of Lancaster and Prince Charles) only add to the aura of mystery surrounding him. Assurances to the contrary left us wondering who else could be responsible. The member whose wife was one of Princess Di's bridesmaids, perhaps?

With a rock-solid core and *"consistency of quality throughout,"* to some people this set is *"a small SAS-type unit."* To us, 4 Stone Buildings combines a reputation for feisty court performances and very civilised behaviour back in chambers. It's one of those places where women are described as *"ladies"* and a faint smell of cigar smoke pervades the air. As one source said: *"It feels like being a member of a rather select club."*

2 Temple Gardens

Chambers UK rankings: Clinical negligence, personal injury, professional discipline, professional negligence

One of the stalwarts of Inner Temple, 2tg's small doorway opens onto a warren of rooms with – we were assured – the very best views of Inner Temple gardens and the Thames. Founded by Walter Frampton (who acted on the divorce of that Mrs Simpson) and BLA Malley after WWII, the set has occupied the same premises ever since. Initially a criminal and civil set with a strong insurance bent, in 1960 barristers elected to focus solely on civil instructions, gradually building up a highly regarded personal injury, clinical negligence, employment and general commercial practice. The membership has swelled, such that now over 50 barristers practise across an extraordinary palate of areas. True, personal injury remains the bedrock of the set, but public law, media and entertainment and property practices have also been putting up shoots of late. As the senior clerk puts it: *"We're a multi-specialist rather than a generalist set – our practice groups are very close-knit and work to help each other out."*

Pupillage here is similarly varied but, with pupils encouraged to nominate supervisors, it does consider personal tastes. Saying this, chambers is keen that pupils *"turn their hand to everything – we want to see pupils manage situations irrespective of practice area."* To that end, recruits divide their time between three pupil supervisors, two in the first six months and then a third from Easter through the tenancy decision to the end of pupillage in October. The first three months are a settling-in period: *"I assume that pupils know nothing to begin with,"* said one supervisor, *"but try to develop their factual analysis and paperwork ability, building up to more complex instructions."* Thus, our sources had experienced *"research points or being asked to complete a set of papers for later comparison and review."* At this stage, the set is also careful *"not to place pupils under huge time pressure that can really destroy confidence."*

In general, first-six pupils also accompany supervisors in conferences and attend many of the five to ten seminars held per year by each of the eight practice groups. Offering wine and nibbles may give pupils the appearance of being unpaid waiters, but in fact it helps networking: *"It's much easier to approach a group of solicitors if you have a full bottle of wine in your hand..."* At the other end of the scale, members of chambers are happy to whisk pupils off to court to observe particularly interesting cases, and one of this year's pupils had even donned a wig and robe for a Court of Appeal matter.

During the second three months, other barristers can approach pupils with work, and *"working for a lot of people"* is common. This ensures that, by the end of pupillage, plenty of people can provide a view on the performance and potential of each pupil. This is particularly crucial given the absence of other written assessments. A review at the end of each 'seat' incorporates these reports as well as comments from the supervisor (and clerks where relevant). *"We're kept informed,"* pupils told us; *"feedback is continuous."* Chambers also puts pupils through two advocacy exercises, one in the first six and the second two weeks before the tenancy decision. Sources stressed the *"educational rather than assessment nature of the exercise – the point is to make an impression rather than gain a grade."* The second exercise is the more spectacular, with pupils pitted against one another in a full-blown mock trial, usually presided over by either a silk or a former member of chambers on the bench. This year's full personal injury trial, complete with staff 'witnesses', lasted *"about three hours but was good fun."* Having already experienced real-world advocacy in the second six, pupils say you are *"not likely to make a fool of yourself."*

Chambers has pupils out on their feet from day one of the second six. Indeed, it is *"so committed to advocacy that we will guarantee pupils' earnings in the second six. They will do everything from small claims and fast-track cases to interlocutory hearings."* RTAs and defective property claims are common and trips to courts as far away as Cardiff are not unusual. Clerks try to limit court appearances to three a week at this stage. The change of pace is *"a real baptism of fire,"* but pupils emphasised that their workload is managed carefully to ensure *"you never get snowed under."* Pupils are also encouraged not to *"spend hours suffering in silence."*

The tenancy decision is made by the end of June and, having taken on 93% of pupils as tenants over the preceding five years, chambers has an impressive record. Those not approved for tenancy in June benefit from a second-chance policy and will be reviewed throughout a third six, with the possibility of tenancy the following year. In 2007 one out of two was invited to stay on. All new tenants appoint a mentor who offers an ear and friendly advice throughout the first year. The set also tries to prevent a *"juniors'*

ghetto" from developing, so it's not uncommon for new juniors to share corridors, or even rooms, with silks.

If you're already planning an application, you might want to sample the set's short mini-pupillage, which is universally praised as *"a perfect indicator of what to expect."* Certainly, chambers seems to put as much thought into the three-day scheme as it does pupillage proper. Recent attendees had watched court appearances (including one in the House of Lords), been invited to the weekly Friday drinks and undertaken a short assessment that *"makes a good impression if you then apply for pupillage."* Chambers receives a lot of applications and it sounds as if the initial cut at the paper stage is a deep one. With current tenants having worked at the European Court of Human Rights, as management consultants and even as a keyboard player for Morcheeba, we'd suggest that a mixed diet of extra-curricular activities would be the best complement to excellent academics. Once at interview, demonstrating the qualities of *"clear thinking, self-reliance, resilience and individuality"* becomes important. It would be a lot to fit into a short interview, so the set hosts a day-long assessment for around 40 first-round applicants. The assessment day includes group exercises such as mini-debates and quick-fire conferring tasks, while members of chambers drop in to give short talks on their practices and the practicalities of life at the Bar. Between ten and 15 candidates progress to a full-blown interview. We were interested to note that the vast majority of recent recruits had non-law degrees, with more than a few of them being second-careerers.

With our sources in agreement that *"it is to everyone's advantage to promote the 2tg name,"* the senior clerk felt that solicitors and insurance companies were instructing the set rather than individuals. Chambers is *"not characterised by political games,"* one member told us, with others mentioning *"a strong team ethos."* The pupils we met defined the set by its convivial atmosphere, saying: *"It's easy to approach people, whether with a coffee in your hand or about a point of law."* The weekly Friday drinks event is a good time for *"off-duty interaction and the chance to be human."* The big date in the social calendar is chambers' Christmas party, the last of these having taken place aboard a Thames riverboat.

The highest praise from pupils came in relation to their assessment of chambers' *"terribly straightforward"* character. *"You can take people at their word,"* said one; *"if they give a compliment it's because they do mean it."* Combine this with breadth of practice, an advocacy-heavy year and a good pupil-to-tenant conversion rate, and 2tg looks like a good bet.

3 Verulam Buildings

Chambers UK Rankings: Banking & finance, commercial dispute resolution, financial services regulation, fraud: civil, information technology, insurance, professional negligence, telecommunications

3 Verulam Buildings is an ambitious commercial set, motivated by the shared vision of a future in the magic circle. Its core work in banking and financial services law has expanded over the years to include insurance, fraud and insolvency plus an interesting line in media and entertainment law and a strong arbitration practice. Barristers from the set frequently appear opposite the members of other prestigious sets such as One Essex Court and Fountain Court, and it is *"in the same mould"* as these giants that 3VB sees itself developing. Incremental changes to the set's profile, the calibre of instructions received and the size of its premises have gradually made 3VB a force to be reckoned

with. We heard its name mentioned again and again during our tour of the inns, and with silks from other chambers praising the quality of 3VB juniors after leading them on big cases, the coming years are sure to bring further success.

The number of 3VB juniors ranked in our parent publication, *Chambers UK*, is exceptional. A dozen are ranked for commercial litigation alone, and there are ten ranked for banking and finance, with *"superstars"* Sonia Tolaney and Adrian Beltrani making it into the top tier. Among the silks, Ali Malek QC stands out together with former General Counsel to the FSA Michael Blair and popular head of chambers Christopher Symons. For recent major cases, look no further than the mammoth arbitration over Lloyd's New Central Fund (a case involving insurance brokers) or the $600m JPMorgan v Springwell litigation (relating to alleged mis-selling of Russian and other emerging market investments). Members have been involved in most major civil fraud cases over recent years (Maxwell, BCCI, Polly Peck), as well as a number of large insurance/reinsurance disputes rising out of 9/11, Equitable Life and the current *"spiral of personal injury claims."* In the world of big business, you may find that not every case leaves a sweet taste in the mouth. In early 2007, William Blair QC (brother of Tony) was instructed on the Zambia vulture fund case, in which British Virgin Islands-based company Donegal International sued the African nation for £42m in repayment of a debt it had taken out years before from Romania. Donegal had bought the debt from Romania in 1999 for less than $4m.

With extensive building work going on to connect numbers 1 to 5 Verulam Buildings, a stunning new admin area, conference rooms, seminar facilities and a waiting room that is now certainly not (as we once said) the smallest at the Bar, it's clear to see why *"there's a real buzz* about the place" and "a feeling of going somewhere." As senior practice manager Nick Hill proclaimed: "Others inherit their name; we're out there earning ours."

There is one very good reason why students might know 3VB's name – it offers the biggest pupillage award out there. A huge amount of effort, as well as money, goes into making pupillage an attractive and viable entry point into the profession, "especially for people who don't form part of the conveyor belt of white, Oxbridge-educated males on their way to the Bar." Chambers says its aims are twofold: to find future tenants and (failing that) to make sure pupils are well placed at the end of the year so as to gain tenancy elsewhere. Some 11 out of 15 pupils have taken tenancy at 3VB over the past five years – in 2007 it was two out of three – and those who were unsuccessful have found homes in very good sets.

Pupils are taken on for 12 months and change supervisors four times. They also have a more junior 'shadow pupil supervisor' who ensures they also see simpler work. This blend of "big, exciting cases" and "small cases you can get to grips with and follow from start to finish" is one of the best things about pupillage here. Work coming from other members of chambers is permitted but "rigidly controlled" by the supervisor, and pupils are given regular feedback. Said one: "I always know where my work stands in terms of the required standard, and I also know what I need to do to get it to the required standard." Supervisors take their role seriously. As one told us: "You can achieve so much more if you don't follow the traditional paradigm of sitting back, letting the pupil do the work and then pointing out their mistakes afterwards." Pupils and supervisors engage in regular dialogue, with pieces of work (research, drafting opinions, skeleton arguments, particulars of claim, defences and replies) the springboard for further discussion. Supervisors also go out of their way to elucidate

"areas of the Bar that can otherwise remain a mystery for years" and genuinely seem to enjoy sharing their rooms. "Pupils are good company... it can be quite a lonely profession."

Pupils are assessed via written reports throughout the year and a handful of advocacy exercises are "designed to remove any complacency and make pupils prepare carefully." Said one: "They give you a rough ride... but you also get very, very thorough feedback." On the insistence of Andrew Onslow QC (pupillage committee head for the past five years), a moderator is also present to "make sure no confidence shattering goes on." In the second six, pupils are permitted to take their own cases, although this "depends very much on circumstances at the time." Court appearances are not regular and pupils are never sent out to take notes on long trials as, "frankly, the way a pupil impresses his or her supervisor is by the quality of their written work and the way they interact in discussions – and those things happen in chambers." When pupils do run their own small cases, these will be simple things like winding-up petitions and straightforward directions hearings. The set's banking practice generates plenty of low-value instructions for baby juniors; think mortgage matters and (very topically) "endless cases over bank charges." Remember, chambers represents one type of client in all of these cases, and it isn't the man on the street.

3VB offers un-assessed mini-pupillages. We say un-assessed, but actually everyone is expected to produce a piece of written work at the end of the week, on which a report is written and kept on file. A mini-pupillage is not compulsory for pupillage applicants, though we reckon it's advisable. Each year there are three or four pupillages and the set receives more than 200 applicants. Said one recruiter: "The hardest part is getting it down to the 40 we see at first interview." Be aware that if you have no debating or mooting experience, the recruiters will be asking: "Why on earth are you thinking about the Bar?" To stand a chance you'll need to convince them you have energy, brains and practical common sense. Advocacy skills are important, but intelligence is even more so.

The expansion into extra space at Verulam Buildings means the set is not constrained in how it grows. This is great for pupils as *"it's not like you're down in a pit with knives and a loin cloth, and one will survive."* The July tenancy decision can result in any number of pupils offered tenancy – if they meet the standard, *"we jolly well give them the chance."* Baby juniors have *"the best of both worlds,"* working alone on cases to build up a following and being led on big cases, which helps *"buy that nice house in Islington."* Many new juniors complete a three or six-month secondment to the FSA and shorter visits of two or three weeks to firms of solicitors. The clerks take care that no one ever gets into the position where they *"emerge blinking into the sunlight after two years as fourth junior in the basement of a solicitors' office"* (as is rumoured to happen at some well-known sets), and a mentor helps relieve the inevitable pressure of *"spending the first two years of practice in a constant state of panic."* In short, in no time at all you're a seasoned practitioner, taking on *"anything non-criminal with a lot of money involved."* *"Call me a knockabout commercial litigator,"* chuckled one junior tenant.

Members enjoy *"some of the nicest surroundings of the Inns."* There are glorious views of Gray's Inn Walks (laid out in 1606 by Francis Bacon) and the atmosphere is cordial and light. *"There's no 80s-macho, up-there-with-the-big-boys culture,"* said one source. On a reasonably regular basis a group of barristers will have informal drinks at the nearby Cittie of Yorke or trendy gastropub The Yorkshire Grey. There's also a tradition of pupils going for *"great fish and chips"* available in Lincoln's Inn on a Friday lunchtime. Afternoon tea isn't quite 3VB's style, but members *"pop in and out of each other's rooms"* frequently. Other things to mention are an annual dinner, a summer party at Christopher Symons' house and the occasional cricket match. When it comes to decision-making, tenants at all levels can participate through rolling membership of the management and practice development committees. *"We don't live by committee, but the ones we have work hard to make sure things happen,"* said one member.

There's no other way of saying it: this is a very nice set. It is sometimes more modest about its achievements than it need be, but maybe that's part of its charm...

Wilberforce Chambers

Chambers UK rankings: Chancery: commercial, Chancery: traditional, charities, intellectual property, pensions, professional negligence, real estate litigation

Lincoln's Inn-based Chancery giant Wilberforce Chambers turned 48 in 2007, yet the set shows no sign of a mid-life crisis. In summer 2006, new head of chambers Jules Sher QC took over from Edward Nugee QC who had held the position for 30 years. *"He obviously has his own ideas,"* revealed one source, implying that we could see some changes. Not that Wilberforce has been standing still: back in the 1980s it was one of the first sets to recognise the importance of establishing itself as a brand rather than just an address.

Today, the Wilberforce name is synonymous with excellent legal advice and top-class litigation. Among its best-known cases are Grupo Torras, Equitable Life, Charman v Charman (there was a heavy trusts element to this divorce) and the collapses of BCCI, the Mirror Group and Baring's Bank. Pensions are Wilberforce's playground. In 2005, after a revolt was threatened by High Court judges over changes to their pensions, Wilberforce's experts represented the judges threatening legal action against the Department of Constitutional Affairs. Little over a month later, a ministerial statement announced that judges would be released from the controversial tax on pension pots of over £1.5m.

While most members concentrate on Chancery Division cases, they also advise on or appear in commercial cases heard in the Queen's Bench Division. Members have very specialised

practices; for example, former partner at magic circle law firm Linklaters, Anna Carboni, is an IP expert. Wilberforce is doing rather well in IP, having been instructed on behalf of Simon Fuller in the dispute over the format of *X Factor*, and by Mars in its tussle with Nestlé, when it wanted to launch a competing chocolate bar called Have a Break. Wilberforce also receives a healthy number of international instructions from the likes of Hong Kong and Singapore as well as tax havens such as Bermuda, Jersey and the Cayman Islands.

Pupils seem in awe of the barristers here and are keenly aware of the standards required of them. *"It is an incredibly able set,"* remarked one, *"and some of the best people in the area are here."* Wilberforce has gone from strength to strength over the past decade and has continually outgrown the various buildings and annexes it occupies. With 29 juniors, 18 QCs and 21 administrative staff, including eight clerks, two housekeepers and a librarian, it's quite a family. Indeed, the set has grown so much that it is now rethinking its strategy. Having identified an opti-

mum number of about 50 members a decade ago, chambers is now considering whether bigger might be better. At the same time it also wants the entire set to be under one roof. Senior clerk Dannie Smilie doesn't rule out the idea of leaving the Inn altogether – *"why not?"* he asks, pointing out that even the Business Court of the RCJ is moving into a new building in Rolls Passage.

To do well here you need to be commercially minded and have a good head for figures, particularly if you're thinking about messing around with tax cases. Commercial Chancery involves all the types of work that might be described as 'business law' but fall within the remit of the Chancery Division. Chancery practice is a technical, rigorous, intellectually challenging discipline that requires barristers to unravel complex problems in such a way as to make them crystal clear for a judge. Logic and precision are key, so don't expect to be able to ad lib or sweep the court along with rhetoric. As one source put it, it is "[law] *for the anally retentive."* Having *"a good, clear written style is imperative as paper advocacy is just as important as standing up in court."* The majority of time is spent in chambers, although when cases do reach court, trials tend to run on.

Unashamed intellectual prowess is what pupils need. It's not just a case of being brainy, but knowing how to work your brain like it's on a catwalk. As one of the recruiters phrased it, it's about having *"inquisitiveness, sharpness and subtlety of mind."* Chambers tells us that having the required intelligence doesn't necessarily mean having a First, and it's fair to say that not everyone at Wilberforce does... although those people are definitely in the minority.

The quality of a candidate's thinking is really tested during the second interview, when they must talk their way through a legal problem. Just like they always told you at GCSE maths, you need to show how you worked out your answer – even if you get the wrong answer. *"The worst mis-*

take is an un-thought-out mistake," revealed a recruiter. A good rehearsal is to practise "seeing both sides of an argument very quickly and outlining the key points." Take the jury system, for example, and give yourself 15 minutes to pick it apart and build it up again. One thing worth taking into account is that "it's absolutely not about cases; it's a knowledge and understanding of basic legal principles and common sense that we're looking for." What this means in practice is that "people who've just started studying law can do just as well, if not better, than those with law degrees."

The initial, long-list interview will have been "more general, just a discussion about a topic of legal interest that's in the public eye and a more old-fashioned getting-to-know-you series of questions." Smart candidates will also have got themselves on a mini pupillage. Until now these have lasted for a week and been assessed, but after feedback the set has now reduced the experience to three days and there is no formal assessment.

Pupils sit with three supervisors in their first six and two in the second. They are exposed to "property, company insolvency, probate, trusts... pretty much anything that comes the set's way." All of the magic circle firms instruct, and lay clients range from multinationals to "one-man bands." Pupils will always encounter private client matters, which lead them to examine some of the complicated issues that trusts throw up and see a fair amount of real estate problems. Over the year pupils see different areas of practice and learn what the work is like at different levels of seniority. Younger members of chambers "remember the pitfalls" and happily offer advice. Advocacy for pupils is thin on the ground: "I had a quiet time," recalled one source; "I wasn't in court amazingly frequently." Throughout pupillage there is informal assessment. "In some chambers they mark specific pieces of work; here they want to gain an overall impression of you, so every individual piece of work counts." In some ways, this makes it more

pressurised, "but if you do let something slip, it's not game over." Pupils recommended taking the time to get things right rather than rushing to complete as much as possible: "There's always time to get faster in this profession." Hours "depend totally on your pupil supervisor as you tend to mimic them," though 9am-6pm might be average for a pupil. "Almost all levels of seniority will work one day at the weekend," commented a clerk, whose job it is to find a happy medium for barristers who "moan when they're busy and moan when things are quiet."

The tenancy decision is made after nine months, although "you'll still be given a good strong steer at six months as to whether you're on course." The final decision is made at an open meeting to which all members are invited and "probably about a quarter of chambers come along, certainly less than half." In 2007, both pupils were offered tenancy.

Does personality count in the decision? Undoubtedly, yes. "We do not want people who are too abrasive, even though they may well make extremely good barristers," said one source. And from another: "We work as a group and a sort of team. A lot of us are very successful, hard-working and ambitious, but we're also fairly laid back – we aim for a certain lightness of touch, while still doing the weighty work." Said head of the pupillage committee, John Furber QC: "There are a lot of people like me who aren't home-grown, but the question is always asked, 'Will they fit in with the culture?'" A senior clerk commented: "I certainly feel it's a tighter, happier ship than one or two of our competitors, who've found it difficult to break down some of the individual groups from the various banners they came under."

We asked a pupil to describe the Wilberforce culture and he immediately came up with the following: "Professional, inclusive, friendly, approachable." The clerks are "mostly on first-name terms" with barristers and there are no sirs or ma'ams here. On the social side, *"it's not the criminal Bar where everyone's getting plastered every night,"* but there are drinks and a monthly meal for all members (sadly, not pupils). Barristers regularly lunch together in Lincoln's Inn and there are also impromptu nights out for those at the junior end.

Undoubtedly you need to be a braniac to make an impression here; however, people skills are just as essential for inspiring confidence in wealthy clients or company directors who are used to getting their own way. This is one of those sets where the barristers need to have it all...

No5 Chambers, Birmingham, London, Bristol

Chambers UK rankings: Chancery, clinical negligence, commercial dispute resolution, crime, employment, energy & natural resources, environment, family/matrimonial, health & safety, personal injury, planning

For the best part of a century, the beating heart of the Birmingham Bar was brick-built Fountain Court, home to some nine sets. Now there are just two. One of these is the largest set in the country with seven practice groups, two further offices in London and Bristol and a self-confessed *"Fantasy Football League"* approach to choosing *"the very best barristers around the country. We don't merge – we select."* Rather than leave its Midlands home in search of bigger and better work, it has created a national hub from Steelhouse Lane, Birmingham, complete with Japanese-style decor and bright modern art. Welcome to No5.

The rate of expansion at the chambers has been remarkable. Only 30 barristers strong in the early 1980s, an ambitious but measured 'hiring' strategy of *"quality rather than quantity"* has seen that figure rise to approaching 200 today. PI is a strength in chambers, with clinical negligence

and criminal practice occupying many other members. A planning team is going great guns. Three other practice groups focus on family, employment and Chancery/commercial, and there is a growing profile in white-collar crime and regulatory and business law. Chambers director Tony McDaid describes the melange as *"groups of specialists under one umbrella."* Each practice group has its own head, deputy head, marketing initiatives as well as a dedicated group of clerks. As the chambers has developed, it has embraced new areas of law which has seen the recent addition of the agriculture group.

A membership measured in triple digits doesn't equate to tens of pupils. In fact, the average intake each year is just two, and they are restricted to the set's Birmingham HQ. *"We make a market-driven decision on pupils,"* said recruiters. *"We're very aware of things like decreasing criminal work at the junior end; we want to continue to promise quality work."* No5 aims *"to look beyond academic qualifications to find the raw talent. If we insist on only the most prestigious academic candidates, we might well miss out on a better barrister."* The main challenge for a pupillage candidate is to *"catch the selection committee's eye,"* but with past pupils including a former paediatric neurosurgeon and an archaeology graduate, there's clearly no hard-and-fast rule for achieving that. Applicants who make it to the first-round interview face a series of general and legal questions from a small panel of three, with a second *"more-gruelling"* interview awaiting those who impress. The second stage involves squaring up to six members. Chambers does not set a problem but expects candidates to *"think on your feet about any number of issues."* Those who had successfully negotiated the process advise pupillage hopefuls to *"rise to the challenge... if they play devil's advocate, don't be afraid to stand up for yourself."*

All recruits must commit to as broad a

pupillage as possible. Assigned one pupilmaster in an *"appropriate practice group"* for the duration of the year, the first three months see them *"gaining a grounding in that practice area and the profession."* In other words, drafting, pleading and shadowing at court. Thereafter, they take one-month stints in three other practice areas. To illustrate, one source had started out in the PI group and then hopped to the family and criminal groups. The latter was *"with a grade-four prosecutor, largely busy with CPS instructions, but also defence work."* Throughout these short periods, pupils keep in close contact with their original supervisor. *"Mine liked to see me every day, at the very least once or twice a week,"* confirmed a source. *"You can tailor your pupillage here,"* a current pupil told us; *"they do listen to what you'd like to do".* Indeed, a review at the end of the first three months – usually with the head of the pupillage committee – is an opportunity to voice preferred interests as much as it is an appraisal of work. Whilst pupils will shadow or assist other members of chambers on *"particularly interesting cases,"* devilling is kept to a minimum. There will however be an advocacy exercise at the six month review.

Pupils spend the final month of the first six acquiring a taste for *"grubbier junior work"* before getting on their feet in the second six. By trailing junior barristers it offers the chance *"to see the kind of work you'll soon be doing yourself – pupilmasters here are much more senior juniors, and their caseloads are high-level."* The second six begins a tornado of *"just about anything and everything."* One source got off to a flying start with *"a coroner's inquest in which I was for the driver of the car... that was quite a plunge."* Meanwhile, a breathless list from another included *"interim applications on larger cases, Chancery injunctions, breach-of-contract trials for smaller companies, employment discrimination cases, pre-*

hearing work..." Close communication between the clerking teams is vital to ensure a full and varied diary. By this time they operate out of the communal areas scattered throughout chambers and are in court at least four or five times a week, *"often in two different courtrooms on the same day."* Extensive travel is a fact of life for a No5 pupil: *"Four days a week I will be anywhere between Birmingham, Coventry, Wolverhampton and Stafford, and at least once a week in Manchester or even Cardiff."* In the second six, the three-monthly reviews continue and are sometimes scheduled more often. Everyone we interviewed felt *"very well supported,"* taking comfort in the possession of *"plenty of mobile phone numbers, all ready to be dialled when I'm in a panic at 9pm the night before a hearing."*

The tenancy decision is officially taken by the management board towards the end of the second six, following a recommendation made by the head of the pupillage committee. It considers pupilmasters' reports plus feedback from clerks and other members. Chambers are keen to keep pupils informed and it isn't unheard of for them to be given a sense of their chances as early as six months in. The pupillage committee is adamant that *"we're not taking on pupils for the sake of pupillage"* and a 100% recruitment record in the last eight years supports this claim. The early phase of tenancy is *"not that much different"* to the second six, as movement across practice groups is encouraged. Even a committed clin neg junior was aware that *"I'll have to do the smaller stuff in a number of areas before grappling with complex clinical negligence cases."*

This breadth of practice at No5 is a big draw for new tenants and pupils. They seem to find the prospect of being just one of a large number of tenants relatively unconcerning. *"It doesn't feel as if there are more than 60 people here,"* opined one source. Pupils added that they felt there was *"a real sense of community – you'll know everyone on your floor and, because there's a large junior-junior population, you get to know people right across all seven practice areas."* Accordingly, social interaction at the set is well developed, but not overtly institutional. *"We don't have weekly drinks, but there are football teams, a cricket team and a fairly big group of people who'll go for a drink together,"* explained one new junior. Another told us: *"I've felt nothing but welcome here; there's a fantastic atmosphere with lots of small, tight-knit groups."* Brum's renaissance means there are plenty of bars and restaurants for socialising, but it also helps explain why none of the people we spoke to had any regrets about their choice of city. *"I live ten minutes from chambers,"* announced one. *"I'm not sitting in a tube for 40 minutes and I have the most fantastic workload."* An application could be in order if this equation appeals.

St Philips Chambers, Birmingham

Chambers UK rankings: Chancery, commercial dispute resolution, consumer law, crime, employment, family, insolvency/corporate recovery

The Birmingham skyline looks rather jazzy these days. From the Smartie-covered cloud of Selfridges to The Rotunda and the Holloway Circus Tower, this is a city with some serious crane action and some bizarre architecture. A little closer to the ground on Temple Row, facing the cathedral for which it is named, is St Philips, a seriously merged and remarketed superset that is just as big and shiny as the Bull Ring itself.

Born six years ago following the mergers of Nos 1, 2 and 7 Fountain Court, the set chose to embrace a bold new future by incorporating itself. A chief executive and extensive administrative team joined the ranks of barristers and clerks in an arrangement that chambers readily admits has a lot in common with a law firm. They enjoy

impressive facilities in Temple Row with a newly completed refurbishment with state of the art facilities. Barristers choose between occupying a shared room, a desk in an open-plan office or using a hot-desking facility in an annexe.

Crisp direct management and marketing drives have replaced tradition and ceremony, and this is obvious from the moment you step into the minimalist, state-of-the-art reception area and gleaming conference suite. Putting the seal on the impression, chief executive Jonathan Fox told us: *"We're a business and we operate like a law firm, with my role here being that of an on-site management consultant. The barristers here are self-employed but they are now free to get on with the law rather than administration and accounts – we hire others to provide that kind of support. We offer the ultimate self-employed environment."*

One consequence of relinquishing management to experts is that barristers *"have to be ambitious and focused; they can't just put their feet up."* By signing a service-level agreement all barristers are committed to certain performance requirements, and they are kept apprised of St Philips' growing turnover by monthly bulletins. But for all of its corporate trappings, this is still a set of barristers of chambers... just. The perks of self-employment (like the flexibility to work a three-day week or take sabbaticals) are all readily available, albeit with the added proviso that *"barristers must appreciate that they're working within a larger entity."*

Larger is certainly the word. *"There are no London sets like this,"* said one pupil. *"It's not only the strongest commercial set in Birmingham but also absolutely prepared for the future of the Bar."* A current headcount reveals 171 barristers working across the main practice areas – commercial, civil, crime and family. There are plans afoot to beef up the employment and PI groups. Commercial Chancery, banking and professional negligence cases are also handled, as well as niche areas like courts martial and tax law. Neither is there any prospect of publicly funded work being dropped. In short, there's little that this multidisciplinary set can't or won't do. In their own words: *"We cover almost every other area of practice apart from very specialised work like human rights law that demand a presence in London."* Instructions arrive primarily from the Midlands and Black Country, but chambers' management is also chipping away at the traditional exodus of local work to London.

The set takes a maximum of four pupils per year, each of whom are assigned a principal pupil supervisor in the practice area which most interests them. *"It's a generalist pupillage but weighted to your preference,"* explained one; *"chambers are always aware of where you'd like to be."* The first four months are spent with the main supervisor, then pupils take a month in each of two other areas of law to ensure breadth of exposure. This period is all about *"living and breathing your pupil supervisor's workload,"* drafting defences or counter claims for court appearances and eventually devilling for other members of chambers. *"I was never left standing by the photocopier or, alternatively, dogsbodied out to other barristers,"* assured a source, adding that fairly civil hours, *"continuous feedback"* and quarterly performance reviews ahead of the October tenancy decision amount to good treatment. As a nice touch, new recruits are now each given a clerking contact *"so that they have someone to smile at and a place to go if they lose papers or can't remember where files go."*

Come the second six, surprises arrive thick and fast in the form of court instructions. Some of our sources were in court up to twice a day on everything from criminal proceedings in the magistrates' courts and small interim applications on personal injury claims to family court directions hearings. One pupil had appeared in an extended employment tribunal while another was still relishing the commendation received from a judge in a criminal case that *"made all the nights of preparation worthwhile."* Indeed, so busy are second-sixers that chambers enforces a one-day-per-week reprieve when they meet their supervisor *"to check in and stay connected."* It's nice to hear that supervisors go to observe pupils in court on occasion, but even if they're not there, the chances are another member of chambers will be in the robing room at least. Far from checking up on pupils they are great for answering any *"last-minute concerns about cases."*

Amusingly, any pupil making an appearance in Walsall County Court will be under instruction from the clerks to visit a famous local sweet shop. Which got us wondering: can you share even a bottomless bag of sweets with so many barristers? In theory, the fact that there is overlap between the different practice areas means everyone knows everyone else. The reality is not far off: *"Although things like dinners and nights out tend to be organised by practice groups, there are still all kinds of cross-chambers events."* Group activities include a regular billiards play-off in chambers' bright social area, which is also the converging point for monthly drinks. Cricket is another favourite, with the set recently trouncing old rivals No.5 Chambers and local solicitors Wragge & Co. Pupils are included in everything. *"Everyone is just so friendly – if I ever had the slightest concern on my face someone would stop and ask me if I was alright,"* said one pupil. Another agreed: *"I don't have one negative memory of my pupillage. I'd be delighted to work here."*

Ah yes, tenancy. The decision in October is reached following careful consideration of the feedback from supervisors, members and clerks. Chambers is looking for *"moral principles, flexibility, analytical ability, advocacy skills and the potential to be high-achieving barristers."* The senior clerk estimates that in his 25 years at the set just one pupil has been turned away. This is fairly typical of pupillages outside London where, once you're in, you tend to stay. In 2006 both pupils were offered tenancy and as we went to print in 2007 the four pupils were still awaiting a decision. Recruitment is an intense one-day affair, with first interviews taking place in the morning and only ten applicants staying on for lunch and a go at a legal problem. Daunting stuff but if you do make it to that stage current pupils will be on hand to give a tour of the building and soothe frayed nerves. As for whether you should make an application, St Philips isn't in London, but it does offer a London-sized pupillage award and the scope to suit every taste for practice.

Exchange Chambers, Liverpool, Manchester

Chambers UK rankings: Chancery, commercial dispute resolution, crime, insolvency/corporate recovery, local government, partnership, personal injury, police law, social housing

With a ticket to ride in one pocket and a host of outdated stereotypes in the other we boarded the 9.18 from Euston to Liverpool's Lime Street and wondered what to expect from our visit to Exchange Chambers. What we found was a regional superset with a wide practice and some high-profile cases.

Exchange takes its name from its previous location at Exchange Flags outside Liverpool Town Hall. The set moved to Derby Square about 14 years ago and is now right on the doorstep of Liverpool Crown Court. There are a whopping 98 members, the majority in Liverpool and 34 in Manchester, where Exchange set up an annexe a few years back. Among the members are 13 silks, an impressive tally for a set outside London.

It is probably overstating things to describe the happenings of the past few years as a revolution, but there's little doubt that the make-up of the set's practice has changed considerably. It was once the case that criminal work dominated.

Although there is a small family team, these days work is roughly split into three different areas: criminal, personal injury and commercial/Chancery. It is this last area that has grown the most of late, with the set now taking instructions on matters that might previously have been sent down to one of the London sets. Recent high-profile instruction has come from football agent Paul Stretford in fighting Football Association charges concerning his acquisition of the right to represent Wayne Rooney, a case that went to the High Court. In the last year, barristers were also involved in prosecuting a Lancashire electoral roll fraud case.

The criminal team hosts big name players such as Tim Holroyde QC and David Turner QC, the latter heavily involved in defending one of the

Chambers and Partners Regional Set of the Year 2007

directors of the company that employed the Chinese cockle pickers who died in the Morecambe Bay tragedy. In the personal injury group at Exchange, the presence of spinal injury specialist Bill Braithwaite QC is enough to ensure a valuable and varied caseload, including the House of Lords case of Horton v Sadler, which had a significant impact on time limits for appealing in PI cases. As one would expect of a set with a long list of specialist barristers, the list of instructing solicitors is equally long – Exchange barristers work for Addleshaw Goddard, Halliwells, Burton Copeland and Pannone & Partners to name but a few. The set is also active prosecuting cases for HM Revenue & Customs, the Health and Safety Executive and the DTI.

Our magical mystery tour of chambers enabled us to cover every inch of the large single floor that accommodates the set's Liverpool-based practitioners. Step through from the hotel-like exterior and you're in the hub of chambers – in the main reception area with its potted plants and photos of members of the judiciary adorning the walls, barristers, clerks and admin staff bustle around. Separate waiting rooms prevent *"that embarrassing situation where company directors and alleged child molesters are sat next to each other; each thinking that the other is in the same situation."* Along the striking red corridors, barristers occupy rooms painted in various bold shades. Whether it's because of space limitations or simply that they're a sociable bunch, each room is shared by as many as six of them, often from differing practice groups.

The long and winding road to pupillage at Exchange Chambers starts with the set's own branded application (it isn't in Olpas), and with nearly 600 applications to consider each year, it's no surprise chambers has outsourced the job. A strong academic record will be the first consideration for the recruiter. Next, the question is whether the applicant has clearly researched the set or not. *"We want people who know what we're all about, a generic reason for choosing us will not impress."* It's a two-stage interview process here: showing that you possess *"leadership, presence and poise"* in the first 30-minute interview will improve your chances of being invited back to the second test of endurance. This lasts for two days and provides the opportunity to meet most members of chambers whilst also undertaking a series of different advocacy exercises. At the end of day one, you get the chance to 'unwind' by going out for a meal with some members. Go easy on the wine though, your social skills are being assessed.

A day in the life of an Exchange pupil is undoubtedly a demanding one. *"Beneath all of the banter and all the fun, we work really hard and expect the same from our pupils,"* confided one source. Whilst you're not quite working eight days a week, you evidently have to be prepared to adopt the *"ferocious work ethic"* shared by members if you want to be a success. A common law pupil has one pupil supervisor and two deputies who specialise in differing practice areas. The pupil drafts claims and writes opinions for his or her supervisor and is expected to be up to scratch within about six months. During this period, work will also be undertaken for other members of chambers in order to ensure every section on the Bar Council checklist is ticked off. In the second six, pupils can take on their own work and end up travelling a fair amount. By all accounts it is *"a terrifyingly pure adrenaline rush"* when you're on your feet for the first time. Let's hope it's addictive because you'll be doing a lot of it as the years go by. On the criminal side, work tends to be a mixture of bail applications, mentions and summary trials. There is also the chance to practise pure commercial law if that's the route that appeals to you. This route requires a six-month stay in Manchester as this is where a number of the commercial practitioners are based. If you want to go down this route, you should flag it up in your application form.

Regular review meetings are held with the pupil's supervisor and the chambers director and this is the opportunity to *"highlight any problems and underline all the positives."* At Exchange, it seems nobody is afraid to ask for a little help from their friends when the need arises. *"We're always sharing problems with each other."* Nonetheless, the ability to think for yourself is highly prized: *"If a pupil shows initiative, then we're very happy."* Tenancy prospects are remarkably healthy for pupils at this set. To not get taken on *"you're going to have to do something pretty awful"* and this might well explain the degree of rigour when recruiting pupils. The supervisor we spoke to summed it up as *"equality of effort,"* saying: *"We've obviously seen some potential in the pupil and we feel that we've failed if we don't allow it to be fulfilled."*

It seems that the legendary Scouse wit is alive

and well at Exchange Chambers. Members of all levels of seniority eat lunch together in one of the larger rooms, and joint head of chambers David Turner QC, who has a reputation for being *"a bit of a wag,"* is especially adept at bringing pupils out of their shells with his *"wicked sense of humour."* Friday night drinks at a local bar are always *"a bit of a laugh"* and have been known to end up as *"a bit of a session."* Chambers' Christmas party involves a group lunch and then *"it descends from there."* Speaking of descents, it has been known for a group of members to jump on an Easyjet flight for a weekend of Alpine skiing.

Everyone we spoke to loved Liverpool and its way of life. Exchange Chambers is very much the big noise in town right now and it has ambitions to be the set in the North West. In order to thrive here, your commitment to the city and to the work must go further than being able to whistle *A Hard Day's Night.*

Deans Court Chambers

Chambers UK rankings: Clinical negligence, crime, family/matrimonial, health & safety, personal injury

A hundred years and more on the Northern Circuit has left Deans Court Chambers with a darned fine reputation for high-quality work and admirable service standards. In recent criminal matters members have prosecuted Harold Shipman and defended clients as diverse as footballers Roy Keane and Jonathan Woodgate, and Lin Liang Ren, the Chinese gangmaster found guilty of the manslaughter of 21 cockle pickers at Morecambe Bay. In the field of personal injury members have worked on such issues as Gulf War Syndrome, while family lawyers have been responsible for the welfare of countless children in the region and protected the financial interests of those going through divorce. In health and safety matters one member is making a name for himself in relation to local authorities' liability for outbreaks of legionnaires' disease. There is even a growing commercial and Chancery practice. Put together, it adds up to excellent-quality work across several disciplines.

Located on St John Street – legal enclave and Manchester's version of Harley Street – Deans Court's premises exhibit the locale's usual Georgian trappings. Downstairs, a large and airy reception lies just beyond a broad sweep of stairs. Above, the barristers' accommodation points to industry and legal brainstorming. Of particular note is the 'rogues gallery' of past and current members who have ascended to the bench. Deans Court is certainly proud of its reputation as a silk-heavy Manchester set with a history of judicial appointments, and the senior clerk is not above standing new pupils in front of the portraits to impress on them the need to work hard and dream big. Already 75 members strong including 10 silks, chambers has an appetite for further growth, both via pupils and more-senior lateral hires.

Deans Court is structured into a series of practice groups: civil litigation (where personal injury is dominant), family, crime, health and safety and regulatory, and now also professional and business risks. The pupillage committee encourages the busiest of these groups to screen some 417 OLPAS applications, with a view to members of these groups conducting first interviews with some 30 candidates. Those candidates who impress move to a second interview with the pupillage committee, when they must tackle a legal problem requiring them to use first principles to analyse a scenario. *"They wanted to see if you could take on board a different viewpoint,"* recalled one junior tenant, *"and if you knew when to defend your point and when to concede to a better point."*

Having been recruited with a specific practice group in mind, new pupils are allocated a supervisor from within that group. After two months they sit with two more supervisors for a month each to gain exposure to other types of practice. The family pupil we spoke to had also spent time with a criminal practitioner and a civil practitioner specialising in personal injury. One recent pupil had chosen to focus on two areas – crime and Chancery. An unusual combination, but one that was accommodated nonetheless.

In their sixth month, pupils work with younger tenants to pick up tips for the second, very busy, practising half of the year. A source took us through her recent weeks' work: "*A family injunction, a criminal pre-trial review in the magistrates' court, a plea in mitigation, a pre-hearing review in a public law family case, an ancillary relief final hearing... quite a lot of contact disputes and injunctions, small claims trials – either RTAs or contract disputes – pleas in mitigation... I've had to hit the ground running and I see now that the first six was designed to build me up and support me.*" For any reader who hasn't yet got the message, for talented and committed young barristers there's more than enough work at the Manchester Bar to keep a new barrister fully employed. And, whilst the market is becoming increasingly competitive, there's no need to jostle with peers to get it, nor any need to take on cases where the train fare costs more than the brief fee.

Ample support is available in the second six and beyond. "*The barristers have all said to me 'just ring at any time of day or night',*" our pupil source confirmed. A new junior concurred, speaking of "*a pupil supervisor who made it clear the relationship was one for life,*" but also warned that the early years are demanding. "*The ethos here is extremely hard working and the clerks are always looking for a lot of work to be covered... At the junior end you continue to turn your hand to all sorts, although you do have some ability to direct things.*" New juniors can be in court daily and although telephone CMCs and such appointments have reduced some of the work available to junior members, the strength of chambers in the market place still dictates that there is work available to junior members who have the dedication and belief to pursue a career at the Bar. However, a new pilot scheme could change all that. Ten minutes after meeting us, one of the juniors was due to speak in a case management conference miles away in Bedford – via the telephone.

Chambers is busy and needs to recruit new tenants every year. "*This means you have a far greater sense of security,*" a source told us. "*I know the performance of the other pupils is not impacting on me; if I mess it up then it's entirely down to me.*" However, the standards required of those hoping to be called to the Bar are constantly rising and pupils should be aware that academic and advocacy skills need to be coupled with a desire for hard work.

A key challenge for any pupil is to develop relationships with instructing solicitors (insurance companies and local authorities too, if working in personal injury). Deans Court holds seminars and social events to keep its members at the forefront of clients' minds, and the barristers on the Northern Circuit certainly don't ignore social engagements. There's a strong sense of belonging on the Northern Circuit, and there are "*lots of well-attended messes – dinners at the Midland and Lowry Hotels, informal drinks at Heathcotes on Deansgate.*" These events attract not only pupils but also more senior barristers and even the odd judge. "*Up here you get to know all your contemporaries; in fact it's difficult to walk more than a hundred yards without seeing someone you know.*"

The appeal of life in Manchester as a barrister is easy to see – lower house prices, an easier commute to work, a vibrant, characterful city, a strong sense of belonging and plenty of decent work.

The majority of Deans Court members have some kind of pre-existing connection to the region, and you should bear this in mind if considering applying here. Illustrative of a genuinely broad-minded approach to recruitment, a recent tenant achieved a First from a lesser-known university through real dedication at a time in her life when she had other significant demands placed upon her. She impressed the recruiters in a way that someone who sailed through A-levels and Oxbridge never could. Amusingly, we found out what irks the pupillage committee – people they refer to as *"BarStars."* Essentially, these are legal equivalents of those delusional contestants on the X-Factor who spout platitudes about how they were destined for a singing career. You've been warned: don't plan to describe how you've dreamed of being a barrister since the age of seven; do think carefully about how to prove your commitment to a legal career.

Even if your academic credentials are impressive, you'll still need to clock up some mini-pupillage time (naturally Deans Court offers minis) and you'll need to shine at interview. In short, it is no easier to win a pupillage at Deans Court than it is at any leading London set. Two pupils gained tenancy in 2006 and in 2007 three of the four pupils gratefully accepted the same offer.

Kings Chambers, Manchester, Leeds

Chambers UK rankings: Chancery, clinical negligence, commercial dispute resolution, costs litigation, dispute resolution: mediators, employment, environment, insolvency/corporate recovery, local government partnership, personal injury, planning, social housing

If you think Manchester is a dour, rain-sodden, independent state about three and a half weeks by stopping train from Chancery Lane, then think again. A mere two hours after hopping on a Pendolino at Euston, we were hopping off at a sun-kissed Manchester Piccadilly station and seeking out the 60-year-old set that is the Northern challenger to London's commercial and planning giants.

Back in 1946, businessman-turned-barrister Charles Norman Glidewell saw the opportunity to capitalise on the arrival of town and country planning legislation by creating a specialist planning operation. You've got to hand it to him; half a century on and the chambers he founded is one of the UK's leading sets for all aspects of town planning and highway regulation. In the intervening period the practice has expanded to include environmental and public law (think pollution assessments and diverse local government instructions), which now accounts for a third of the set's workload. The housing boom in the 1970s added a new string to the bow and in 1980 Peter Smith (later Justice Smith of *The Da Vinci Code* judgment fame) established the set's Chancery and commercial team, which generates some 40% of revenue. The third major practice team deals with common law and has, for a decade, focused exclusively on clinical negligence, personal injury law, employment, costs and litigation funding, licensing and disciplinary law. All publicly funded work (essentially family and criminal law) was cut in the 1990s to *"give credibility to our increasing commercial profile."*

In autumn 2006, Kings Chambers relocated to Spinningfields – Manchester's Canary Wharf – where *"glass and space"* replaced the set's former *"rabbit warren"* accommodation in King Street. The new Manchester premises features state-of-the-art IT and Hot Desk facilities. Across the Pennines, Kings Chambers' Leeds base is also poised for expansion. Currently home to 13 of the set's 70-odd barristers, this is no mere Manchester annexe. All the Leeds barristers are members of both the Northern and North Eastern Circuits and can call upon full clerking and admin facilities in each city.

While tenants can move between cities easily and explore the set's breadth of practice, exclusively Manchester-based pupils must select a pupillage within one of the three main practice areas. "Chambers is very clear about the specialisation," one pupil told us, adding that "there is considerable flexibility within each team." Depending on the potential for – but not the guarantee of – tenancy following training, pupillages are offered according to the needs of each practice group. That said, no one has been refused tenancy in the last eight years and chambers is proud to "train people entirely with an eye to their remaining at the set." When we visited, the two Chancery and commercial pupils reflected on a set-up that minimises inter-pupil conflict. "It's not at all a dog-eat-dog situation and you are well supported by your peers," said one. Pupils are invited to various client networking and social events from day one. "You're introduced to solicitors and strongly encouraged to develop relationships both in and outside of the set – the entire set treats pupils as potential tenants." Never underestimate the importance of networking and filling up your little black book, as our sources said: "It's often the smaller, less obvious firms that will give you really good-quality experience."

Pupils are assigned two pupilmasters, each for a six-month stint. In the first six, pupils shadow their PM in court and at conferences, gaining exposure to a variety of work. Our sources agreed the first six was a "very well-managed and civilised introduction," with one admitting that "it was hard work, but not as intense as I thought it would be. Typical hours for me were about 9am to 6pm." In addition to working with their own PMs, towards the end of the first six, pupils accompany junior barristers to court in order to see what lies ahead in the second, practising six. Assessment is continuous, with three-monthly informal reviews, as well as a "good chat" with the senior clerk before the start of the second six to assess pupil's strengths and preferences. Said the man himself: "We're involved from the very start. When they get into their second six we're very good at picking out appropriate cases, giving people a little push when needed... as well as sneaking into courtrooms to watch them in action."

It's not unusual for a pupil to appear in court four or five times a week in their second six, working 12-hour days and often preparing for court the night before. Although still supervised and supported during this time, pupils are expected to become increasingly self-sufficient but can expect any problems to be addressed long before the tenancy interview in September. Instructions do come primarily from Manchester, Liverpool, Leeds and throughout the North and North East, but it is not unusual for pupils to handle cases in London and further afield, nor to be dealing with solicitors from national firms throughout the country. If we tell you that one source had visited Stoke-on-Trent, Gateshead and Leeds in one week you'll see why we were told that "you'll need a car."

Socially the achievements of the Christmas and summer party committees deserve special mention. Younger tenants do find time to enjoy "some Friday boozing," but generally speaking it's true to say that Kings' barristers are busy people. Other sets regard them as a breed apart, given their high-end commercial focus. We doubt our sources would have agreed that this makes them less sociable or pleasant to work alongside, but don't expect them to be the ringleaders of robing-room hi-jinks.

Many members congregate in the large lunch room at midday. Pupils are "strongly encouraged" to be present to make tea for all and can expect "to stick to first names" in conversation.

Once fully-fledged tenants, they will participate thoroughly in chambers' life, whether representing junior members on the executive committee, investing in the building or signing up to the five-a-side football team and debating club. Much to our disappointment, the usual mettle required for the set's Christmas lunch – when pupils are left to man the phones for an afternoon as members eat, drink, and make merry with prank phone calls back to chambers – went untested this year. Pupils waited in vain for suspicious phone calls requesting 'urgent' injunctions or similar emergencies, in what was an uncharacteristically muted show of festive devilment. We wouldn't be surprised if the powers that be weren't hatching a darker plan for next year's shindig.

Of course, you'll need to secure a place before you can appreciate the social scenery, and attending the annual mini-pupillage fair is the best first step. This three-day event includes advocacy workshops, court visits and guest speakers from the Northern Circuit. A *"fantastic"* taste of what to expect, it is testament to the set's interest in new pupils that most members schedule time to participate. If you manage to make a good first impression here, the *"mild grilling"* of the pupillage interview proper (CV-probing plus questions geared towards an area of interest) should seem less formidable. Bear in mind that you'll be asked which specialisation you are interested in, so turn up with reasonably firm ideas rather than just a general desire for *"something businessy."* Despite chambers' self-professedly *"bookish"* reputation, fitting the egghead mould isn't anywhere near as important as demonstrating *"backbone and a real passion for the law."*

St Johns Buildings, Manchester

Chambers UK rankings: Clinical negligence, crime, employment, family/matrimonial, personal injury

Early in 2006 the BBC launched *New Street Law*, a legal drama following the fortunes of two opposing common law sets at the Manchester Bar. It was the classic formula of impassioned courtroom scenes, secret crushes on opposing counsel, and wigs and robes galore. Many of the external shots were filmed in St John's Street, which you'd assume would add authenticity, but for those we spoke to at St John's Buildings this is the point at which art and reality parted. Said one junior tenant: *"The flamboyant courtroom scenes are fairly unrealistic, but the thing that cracks me up is how they've tried to make St John's Street look like a bustling thoroughfare – it emphatically is not."*

Quiet as the street may appear in reality, it is home to no less than four sets of barristers, of which our subject set, with over 100 common law practitioners, is by far the largest. It was founded in the 1940s when a small group of Jewish barristers came together at number 28 St John Street. Over the next 40 years chambers acquired a reputation for diversity and a sense of inclusion that was unprecedented for the era. At the same time its profile increased steadily, and it was to send the first female High Court judge, Dame Joyanne Bracewell, to the bench. In 2002 the set merged with its next-door neighbour at 24a, a crime-focused heavyweight around since the 1970s. Just two years later the combined set, by now renamed St John's Buildings, was further bolstered by the addition of the members of Merchant Chambers, whose commercial law expertise plugged an acknowledged gap in St John's service. Finally, in 2005, ten more practitioners joined from Queens Chambers, a smaller common law and commercial outfit. This brings the current head-count to 105 barristers, right up there as one of the largest sets in the UK. St John's critics predicted the mergers wouldn't work, and yet it has continued to be financially successful while retaining the essentials of its tight-knit culture. Said one source: *"It really doesn't feel as if over a hundred people work here."*

St John's barristers belong to one or more of the five practice groups – personal injury, crime, commercial, employment and family law – and a full administrative team is assigned to each group. The largest are crime, personal injury and family, with around 30 barristers each; a further 20 members of chambers divide themselves between the commercial and employment groups. Although interdisciplinary working is typical, barristers are encouraged to develop specialisms. At the helm of the set, alongside head of chambers, Michael Redfern, is chief clerk Chris Ronan, for whom the phrase 'running a tight ship' is a mild understatement. Applicants be warned: this same meticulous approach is applied to pupils, whose progress is monitored closely from day one.

A pupil's first six is spent shadowing a supervisor. The pupil can choose to specialise in a practice area from the outset or, alternatively, try to get as much experience as possible in a number of areas. *"I wouldn't recommend ruling anything out,"* said one pupil; *"sometimes a particular area of law doesn't sound all that interesting, but you won't know until you've tried it."* Day-to-day experiences include court attendance with the supervisor, preliminary research and drafting plus assistance on case preparation. Whichever direction their pupillage takes, all first sixers also complete a two-week stint in a different practice group to make sure they haven't pigeon-holed themselves too early. The consensus is that the first six provides *"a good grounding and paves the way for what's ahead."*

There is a shift of emphasis in the second six when pupils take on paid work. *"No matter how much preparation you have, it's still daunting, but you never feel as if you're standing by yourself in the courtroom. Everyone makes themselves available to the pupils, and it's not at all uncommon to ring other members of chambers at rather anti-social hours in a panic about a point to be delivered in the morning."* The pupil learns to be flexible and available at all times. *"Your diary will be completely unpredictable; you must expect it to change from day to day and at the last minute. I find I have to move very quickly from one thing to the next without getting a chance to really think about it until the end of the week... only to start all over again on Monday."* The second-six pupil's work is monitored by their original supervisor and chief clerk Ronan, who meets with them once a month for what he describes as *"a progress review – we look at reports and billing, and discuss any difficulties."* Towards the end of the year the pupil spends time shadowing baby juniors to gain a clearer understanding of what the immediate future will hold for them. Overall, chambers' approach is simple: *"We expect people to learn from experience"* and *"we want them to get used to working hard from the beginning of the second six."* By the end of pupillage the idea is to have produced *"analytical, competent practitioners who know the law and who can present a succinct and coherent case. They won't be the finished article but they'll hopefully be well on their way."*

The claim that pupillage is only offered with a view to a tenancy at the end is supported by the fact that no pupil has been disappointed in the last few years. Former pupils told us that *"chambers make a big investment in your legal training and don't keep you hanging on for a decision."* The tenancy decision is made by the widest possible panel, usually including the head of chambers, the head of the pupillage committee, the supervisors and members of the clerking team.

The Northern circuit has plenty of work for young barristers – the consensus from the clerks' room at St John's is that *"no one under five years' call is looking for work"* – but what of its quality? Again, they tell us that unless you're looking to develop a specialist practice in, say, tax or media law the circuit can more than sustain an ambitious advocate. The circuit, and the wider professional community in Manchester, is also said to have a sense of community unmatched by London. The strong social aspect to membership of the circuit ensures that pupils at different sets have forged relationships before they ever face each other in court. And from an early stage they become acquainted with *"pretty much everyone in the robing room – as well as the judges."* On the idea of training in London, one baby junior told us: *"I imagine you'd be a very small fish in that pond, and it's just not the case in Manchester. There's such good camaraderie and support for young barristers here."* Another member of chambers agreed: *"It's large enough not to be cliquey but small enough to have permanent contact and communication."* In late 2006 the set opened up an annexe in Preston, but at this stage it does not feature in the pupillage scheme.

St John's has its own lively social scene. Book club meetings, for example, throw up very divergent opinions, and at the time of our visit no less than 50 tenants were flushed with their success in the Great Manchester Run, which apparently provoked some healthy competition for both training times and the race proper. But at the heart of everything, however, is a lunchroom, deep in the bowels of the building. Rather like a revolving door, this room, with its large red table, caters for over 100 barristers by never emptying completely. A new tenant explained the drill: *"People drop in on their way to and from court for a cup of tea before rushing off... there's always a good exchange of stories from court, which is all the more interesting when it's something outside your own practice area.*

I was welcomed there on the first day of my mini-pupillage and now I'm sitting across the table from prospective pupils, asking them about their interests and career plans..." The two pupils who accepted tenancy in 2007 are now able to do the same.

If you've a mind to sit at that red table yourself, here are some tips from the inside. Be adaptable, flexible and prepared for anything. Make yourself available to members and solicitors, and make a point of getting to know your clerks. Don't plan too far in advance. On a more practical note, make sure that your mobile phone is always charged and try to get some driving lessons in before your second six. Oh, and enjoy yourself! As this year's latest baby junior put it: *"This can be such a satisfying and enjoyable job, and your pupillage is only the beginning."*

St John's Chambers, Bristol

Chambers UK Rankings: Agriculture & rural affairs, Chancery, commercial dispute resolution, crime, family/matrimonial, licensing, partnership, personal injury

Bristol's St John's Chambers has two homes, each of which could not be more different. Its criminal site in St Bartholomew's Square resembles a traditional London barristers chambers, situated around a quiet courtyard and approached via an ancient archway. Gone are the copies of *Country Living* in the waiting room; instead, well-thumbed editions of *FHM*, *Heat* and *GQ* sit in unpretentious piles in a bustling reception area where the phones are constantly ringing. To the south east of the city, the new civil site is slick, angular and dominated by a disconcerting hush. The only sound to break the silence is the tap-tap of computer keys and the opening and closing of the automatic lift doors, as they announce their passenger's arrival on the fifth floor. Breaking all barristerial traditions, the office follows an open plan design, complete with sofas and a lounge area. Although they still use it, the term 'chambers' sounds anachronistic here. Chambers' website describes St John's as *"taking an innovative approach."* After our visit, we don't doubt it.

St John's covers a wealth of legal disciplines and over the years has handled cases that have been both precedent setting and high profile – proof, were it needed, that the best work isn't always in London. A landmark decision was procured by a member of the set in the case of Welsh v Stokes, which involved a horse rearing and falling backwards onto its 17-year-old rider, causing a serious head injury that left her with no memory of the accident. The case raised the question as to whether a claim could be based on the evidence of hearsay alone, as the only witness to the accident had spoken to another motorist, then left the scene never to be traced. In a case generating masses of media interest, Kambiz Moradifar represented the defendant in a claim relating to the use of frozen embryos created with his ex-partner, Natallie Evans, who was later left infertile by cancer therapy. In April 2007, the European Court of Human Rights in Strasbourg passed judgment supporting the decision that, without permission from both parties, the embryos couldn't be used. On the criminal side, Kerry Barker was prosecutor in the case of Eunice Spry, the foster mother found guilty of routinely beating, abusing and starving the three children in her care over a 19-year period. Eunice Spry was convicted of 26 counts of sadistic cruelty.

To better manage and promote itself, St John's has divided its members into departments, which in a way makes it sound like a solicitors' firm. The range of areas covered is vast – traditional Chancery (tax, property and agricultural affairs), mainstream commercial disputes, personal injury, family, crime, and public and administrative law. There's also a small employment team and numerous smaller groups dedicated to niche areas like licensing, construction and holiday litigation. As a complement to the variety of work on offer, pupils are allowed to structure their time to suit their own interests. You don't have to know exactly where your interests lie in advance ("there's nothing wrong with turning up with an open mind"), but as times goes on, it's imperative that pupils get their face known in the areas in which they'd like to practise. This is because, when it comes to deciding who should be offered tenancy, you're effectively trying to win over just one department – *"what the department says goes."* Thankfully, chambers never appoints a pupil whom it *"can't easily see being taken on"* and there is *"none of the cannon fodder approach"* that is common *"uptown"* in London.

Gaining a pupillage in the first place is no easy feat: last year more than 500 applications were received and only 25 people made it to the first round of interviews. If you're bright and show potential on your OLPAS form, chambers will make every effort to ensure you're given a fair chance, with every application looked at by at least two people. If they disagree on a particular candidate, a further two people are brought in. This year, eight candidates made it through to second interview, where they performed an advocacy exercise and were grilled on their views on a House of Lords case (both of which were sent to them in advance). Choosing pupils is *"an art rather than a science... there's something of a feel to it,"* but it's definitely important for applicants to show a commitment to the Bristol Bar. *"We're suspicious of training someone up who's planning on moving straight back to London."* Chambers aims to recruit two pupils a year, and unless you do something drastically wrong, past evidence shows that both tend to be taken on as tenants.

Most pupils begin their first six in the civil department, where they are allocated their first supervisor and start with some drafting *"to give them a good grounding and get them settled in."* They sit at hot desks (as opposed to the partitioned pods most members occupy. Glass offices are used by just a handful of senior members. Other hot-deskers are required to clear their files into a locker at the end of each day, but pupils are allowed to remain at one desk and keep their paraphernalia scattered around. Having someone who's in the same boat beside you during the first few weeks is *"reassuring,"* and a strong pupil network in Bristol provides further support. On the whole, there's a notable absence of hierarchy: *"You see people asking each other's opinions all the time... they'd be happy to ask mine."*

As the months pass, it's up to you to consider where you'd like to go next and speaking to members at chambers tea is a great way of figuring out your next move. One source recommended being quite proactive because *"if you don't like where you are and you don't say anything, you'll probably find you're still there in six months."* As pupils move into new departments, their supervisors change. There's no set rule, but this generally happens after three months. Everyone is encouraged to spend a couple of weeks *"down in criminal"* to get a taste for the work and they all see at least two different civil departments. For those who are serious about crime, it's possible to *"move in"* with the department from Christmas onwards. A two-week stint with the Crown Prosecution Service gives another viewpoint.

The second six is where pupils *"come into their own"* and take on a caseload. They can expect to be on their feet *"at least three days a week"* and this *"can sometimes feel like too much."* One source admitted that *"with hindsight, it would have been useful to spend more time with junior practitioners"* during the first six. *"It's quite common to get the papers the night before"* and *"they don't make many time allowances for you being a pupil."* Court locations include Bristol and Bath, Swansea, Hereford, Trowbridge and Gloucester. One pupil

even had a case taken to the Court of Appeal. As a result of all the to-ing and fro-ing, pupils *"don't see much of each other"* during the second six and the time spent on preparation can really bank up. Eight o'clock isn't an unreasonable time to arrive in the morning, but then again, it's not unheard of to be out by 5pm on a good day. *"It's certainly not about visibly clocking up the hours,"* explained a source, *"just doing what is needed."*

Baby juniors carry out a variety of advocacy ranging from small claims, road traffic and other personal injury claims to company winding-up orders, mortgage repossessions and personal bankruptcy petitions. In an area such as family, it's common for team members to be all out at court at once, whereas members of the commercial Chancery team are more frequently to be found at their desks. For an intellectual challenge, Chancery is the right area: *"I don't know where else you have to look at cases going back to 1700,"* enthused a pupil in the middle of some interesting research. In PI, on the other hand, a new tenant told us: *"I'm sure that somewhere in my psyche I'm a failed doctor!"* For fledgling criminal practitioners, the *"depleted diet"* of magistrates' court work is a real concern, due to increasing numbers of solicitor-advocates. *"One pupil's first piece of advocacy was a plea in mitigation in the Crown Court,"* explained a supervisor; *"it's testing stuff."* Fortunately, two intensive weekends organised by the Western Circuit at a hotel in Winchester provide expert advocacy training from judges and practitioners, and there's a bit of drinking involved too.

The open-plan arrangement means pupils learn a lot by osmosis, but it also means that one-to-one supervision requires a little ingenuity. *"My supervisor takes phone conferences into a break-out room and puts them on the loud speaker for me,"* explained a pupil. *"With pieces of drafting, he'll e-mail me his version and we'll talk about it over lunch."* Formal reviews with supervisors and members of the pupillage committee take place every three months.

Socially, the Bristol Bar is tight knit, particularly at the junior end. Many people studied together at Bristol University or the UWE, and the courts are small enough for you to keep bumping into the same people. Not everyone has a local connection and in recent years St John's has lessened the extent to which it makes this factor part of the recruitment criteria. However, there's no doubt that the geographical location is important for many. Members frequently prop up the bar in The Hole in The Wall, which contains an ancient chink reputedly used by press gangs keen to spy fresh victims. According to legend, it was also frequented by Long John Silver. A village outside Bristol plays host to the annual summer party, at which there's a marquee and *"a bouncy castle for the kids."* This idyllic snapshot of provincial professional life is made complete by cricket matches on long summer evenings. All things considered, it's easy to see why St John's is so popular with applicants and easy to see why an impressive OLPAS form is so essential.

a-z barristers

Blackstone Chambers (I Mill QC and T Beazley QC)

Blackstone House, Temple, London EC4Y 9BW   DX: 281
Tel: (020) 7583 1770 Fax: (020) 7822 7350
Email: pupillage@blackstonechambers.com
Website: www.blackstonechambers.com

No of Silks	30
No of Juniors	41
No of Pupils	4 (current)

contact
Miss Julia Hornor
Practice Manager

method of application
OLPAS

pupillages (p.a.)
12 months **4-5**
Required degree grade
Minimum 2:1
(law or non-law)

income
Award **£38,000**
Earnings not included

tenancies
Junior tenancies offered
in last 3 years **46%**
No of tenants of 5 years
call or under **7**

chambers profile
Blackstone Chambers occupies modern, fully networked premises in the Temple.

type of work undertaken
Chambers' formidable strengths lie in its principal areas of practice: commercial, employment and EU, public law, human rights and public international law. Commercial law includes financial/business law, international trade, conflicts, sport, media and entertainment, intellectual property and professional negligence. All aspects of employment law, including discrimination, are covered by Chambers' extensive employment law practice. Public law incorporates judicial review, acting both for and against central and local government agencies and other regulatory authorities, all areas affected by the impact of human rights and other aspects of administrative law. EU permeates practices across the board. Chambers recognises the increasingly important role which mediation has to play in dispute resolution. Seven members are CEDR accredited mediators.

pupil profile
Chambers looks for articulate and intelligent applicants who are able to work well under pressure and demonstrate high intellectual ability. Successful candidates usually have at least a 2:1 honours degree, although not necessarily in law.

pupillage
Chambers offers four (or exceptionally five) 12 month pupillages to those wishing to practise full-time at the Bar, normally commencing in October each year. Pupillage is divided into four sections and every effort is made to ensure that pupils receive a broad training. The environment is a friendly one; pupils attend an induction week introducing them to the Chambers working environment. Chambers prefers to recruit new tenants from pupils wherever possible. Chambers subscribes to OLPAS; applications should be made for the summer season.

mini pupillages
Assessed mini pupillages are available and are an important part of the application procedure. Applications for mini pupillages must be made by 30 April; earlier applications are strongly advised and are preferred in the year before pupillage commences.

funding
Awards of £38,000 per annum are available. The pupillage committee has a discretion to consider applications for up to £10,000 of the pupillage award to be advanced during the BVC year. Since Chambers insists on an accessed mini pupillage as part of the overall application procedure, financial assistance is offered either in respect of out of pocket travelling or accommodation expenses incurred in attending the mini pupillage, up to a maximum of £200 per pupil.

Cloisters

Cloisters, 1 Pump Court, Temple, London, EC4Y 7AA
Tel: (020) 7827 4000 Fax: (020) 7827 4100
Email: clerks@cloisters.com
Website: www.cloisters.com

No of Silks	3
No of Juniors	43
No of Pupils	2

contact
pupillage@cloisters.com

method of application
via OLPAS

pupillages (p.a.)
2 for 12 months

chambers profile
Cloisters is a leading set with particular expertise in employment, equality, discrimination and human rights, personal injury and clinical negligence, media and sport, and public and regulatory law. Cloisters is known for its legal excellence, approachability, superb customer service and cost-effectiveness. It recruits only barristers who can offer these qualities.

type of work undertaken
Cloisters acts for both applicants and respondents in all its specialist areas. Members of Chambers regularly appear in ground breaking and high profile cases. In 2006, Cloisters appear in 66% of all House of Lords employment cases. The Cloisters Personal Injury Team had a very strong 2006, appearing in many landmark cases. One of their specialisms is in cases involving occupational stress or bullying at work, which contains elements of both personal injury and employment law. Members of the clinical negligence team secured more than £60m for claimants last year. They handle a full range of cases, including cases worth more than £5m. The Cloisters sport practitioners handle disciplinary regulations, consultative work, litigation, non-professional sporting activity cases and matters arising from sports cases such as employment or contractual issues.

pupil profile
Chambers welcomes applications from outstanding candidates from all backgrounds and academic disciplines, including lawyers coming late to the bar.

pupillage
Chambers offers two twelve month pupillages to those wishing to practise full-time at the bar, normally commencing in October each year. Each pupil is supervised and the supervisor changes every three months to show the pupil different areas of practice. Second six pupils will be allocated work by clerks subject to availability of work and pupil ability.

mini-pupillage
Applications should be made in writing to Rachel Chambers with accompanying CV.

funding
Cloisters offers two funded pupillages each year. Each pupil will receive an award (currently £30,000 per year). Pupils can also ask for an advance.

2 Hare Court

2 Hare Court, Temple, London EC4Y 7BH
Tel: (020) 7353 5324 Fax: (020) 7353 0667
Email: clerks@2harecourt.com
Website: www.2harecourt.com

No of Silks	13
No of Juniors	40
No of Pupils	2

contact
Orlando Pownall QC

method of application
OLPAS (summer)

pupillages (p.a.)
Up to 3 12 month
pupillages
Minimum degree **2:1**

tenancies
According to ability

annexes
None

chambers profile

2 Hare Court has long been recognised as one of the UK's leading chambers specialising in criminal law and other related fields. It is described by Chambers and Partners Guide as being in "the top band for crime on the back of widespread approval for the way in which its practitioners conduct themselves in the big trials" and by the Legal 500 as "a set of choice for many solicitors for a range of general as well as high profile and complex crime". Its first rate reputation is based on a proven track record of high quality client care together with excellence in advocacy and trial management.

type of work undertaken

The strength and depth of experience amongst its members enables this chambers to undertake all types of criminal work, particularly the more serious and complex matters such as murder, terrorism, serious fraud, corporate and financial crime, international drug trafficking, corruption and organised crime. The cases in which members of chambers have appeared read like a who's who of recent criminal litigation. Members are also regularly instructed in other related areas particularly in regulatory work before bodies as diverse as the General Medical Council and the Football Association, licensing and gaming, health and safety, environmental health, food and drugs and public inquiries.

pupil profile

Chambers select as pupils articulate and well motivated individuals of high intellectual ability who can demonstrate sound judgement and a practical approach to problem solving. Candidates should have at least a 2.1 honours degree.

pupillage

Chambers offers up to three 12 month pupillages starting in September. The year is divided into two six month periods although pupils are assigned to a different pupil master for each of the four months to ensure experience in different areas of crime. Chambers pays for the "Advice to Counsel" course and runs their own in-house advocacy training.

mini pupillages

The programme runs throughout the year with one mini pupil taken each week and two each week in the summer except between mid-December and mid-January and throughout August. Applicants must be at least 18 years old and either be studying for a higher education qualification or on or about to start either the CPE or BVC course. Please see the website for further details of the scheme, the application process and to download an application form.

funding

12 month pupils will be sponsored through a combination of an award scheme, guaranteed earnings and additional earnings. No clerks' fees or deductions are taken from earnings.

2 HARE
COURT

Community
Legal Service

Quality Mark - Legal Services
Accredited Chambers

Maitland Chambers

7 Stone Buildings, Lincoln's Inn, London WC2A 3SZ
Tel: (020) 7406 1200 Fax: (020) 7406 1300
Email: clerks@maitlandchambers.com
Website: www.maitlandchambers.com

chambers profile
Chambers UK has rated Maitland as the pre-eminent commercial Chancery litigation set every year since 2001.

type of work undertaken
Chambers is instructed on a very wide range of cases – from major international litigation to county court disputes. Much of the work is done in London, though the set frequently advises and appears for clients in other parts of the United Kingdom and abroad. Members are recommended as leaders in their field in commercial Chancery, company, charities, insolvency, media and entertainment, traditional Chancery, property litigation, partnership, pensions, banking, energy, tax, agriculture and professional negligence.

pupil profile
Academically, Maitland Chambers looks for a first or upper second. Pupils must have a sense of commercial practicality, be stimulated by the challenge of advocacy and have an aptitude for and general enjoyment of complex legal argument.

pupillage
Pupils sit with at least three different barristers but spend their first few months with one supervisor in order that the pupil can find his or her feet and establish a point of contact which will endure throughout the pupil's time in chambers. Pupils also undertake a structured advocacy training course which consists of advocacy exercises conducted in front of other members of chambers.

mini pupillages
Applications are considered twice a year with a deadline of 30 April for the period June to November, and 31 October for December to May. Applications should be made with a covering letter and cv (listing university grades) to the Pupillage Secretary.

funding
Chambers offers up to three, 12-month pupillages, all of which are funded (£40,000 for pupils starting in October 2007). Up to £10,000 of the award may be drawn down in advance during BVC year.

No of Silks	15
No of Juniors	49
No of Pupils	up to 3

contact
Valerie Piper
(Pupillage Secretary)
pupillage
@maitlandchambers.com

method of application
See Chambers website
from January 2008.
Application deadline for
pupillage in 2009-10 is 4
February 2008

pupillages (p.a.)
Up to 3 funded

income
£40,000 p.a.

tenancies
5 in last 3 years

maitland
CHAMBERS

Quadrant Chambers (Nigel Teare QC)

Quadrant House, 10 Fleet Street, London EC4Y 1AU
Tel: (020) 7583 4444 Fax: (020) 7583 4455
Email: pupillage@quadrantchambers.com
Website: www.quadrantchambers.com

chambers profile

Quadrant Chambers is one of the leading commercial chambers. Chambers offers a wide range of services to its clients within the commercial sphere specialising particularly in maritime and aviation law. Quadrant Chambers is placed in the first rank in both specialisms by Chambers Guide to the Legal Profession. In shipping law, seven silks and nine juniors were selected by Chambers, and Chambers concluded that 'these highly commercial barristers are at the forefront of the aviation field. In both these areas the set had more 'leaders in their field' selected than any other set of chambers. Quadrant Chambers advises on domestic and international commercial litigation and acts as advocates in court, arbitration and inquiries in England and abroad.

type of work undertaken

The challenging and rewarding work of chambers encompasses the broad range of commercial disputes embracing arbitration, aviation, banking, shipping, international trade, insurance and reinsurance, professional negligence, entertainment and media, environmental and construction law. Over 70% of chambers work involves international clients.

pupil profile

Quadrant Chambers seeks high calibre pupils with good academic qualifications (at least a 2.1 degree) who exhibit good written and oral skills.

pupillage

Chambers offer a maximum of four funded pupillages of 12 months duration (reviewable at six months). Pupils are moved amongst several members of Chambers and will experience a wide range of high quality commercial work. Outstanding pupils are likely to be offered a tenancy at the end of their pupillage. Further information can be found on the website.

mini pupillages

Mini pupillages are encouraged in order that potential pupils may experience the work of Chambers before committing themselves to an application for full pupillage.

funding

Awards of £37,500 p.a. are available for each funded pupillage – part of which may be forwarded during the BVC, at the Pupillage Committee's discretion.

No of Silks	9
No of Juniors	32

contact
Secretary to Pupillage Committee

method of application
Chambers' application form

pupillages (p.a.)
1st 6 months **4**
2nd 6 months **4**
12 months
(Reviewed at 6 months)
Required degree
Good 2:1+

income
1st 6 months
£18,750
2nd 6 months
£18,750
Earnings not included

tenancies
Current tenants who served pupillage in Chambers **19**
Junior tenancies offered in last 3 years **6**
No of tenants of 5 years call or under **7**
Income (1st year)
c. £50,000

Serle Court

Serle Court, 6 New Square, Lincoln's Inn, London WC2A 3QS
Tel: (020) 7242 6105 Fax: (020) 7405 4004
Email: pupillage@serlecourt.co.uk
Website: www.serlecourt.co.uk

chambers profile
'Commercial powerhouse of the Chancery Bar...' Chambers & Partners Guide to the
UK Legal Profession 2006. Serle Court is one of the leading commercial chancery sets
with 48 barristers including 13 silks. Widely recognised as a leading set, Chambers is
recommended in 20 different areas of practice by the legal directories. Chambers has a
stimulating and inclusive work environment and a forward looking approach.

type of work undertaken
Litigation, arbitration, mediation and advisory services across the full range of
chancery and commercial practice areas including: administrative and public law,
banking, civil fraud, commercial litigation, company, financial services, human rights,
insolvency, insurance and reinsurance, partnership, professional negligence, property,
regulatory and disciplinary, trusts and probate.

pupil profile
Candidates are well-rounded people, from any background. Chambers looks for
highly motivated individuals with first class intellectual ability, combined with a practical approach, sound sensibility and the potential to become excellent advocates. Serle
Court has a reputation for 'consistent high quality' and for having 'responsive and able
team members' and seeks the same qualities in pupils.

pupillage
Pupils sit with different pupil supervisors in order to experience a broad a range of
work. Two pupils are recruited each year and Chambers offers: an excellent preparation for successful practice; a genuinely friendly and supportive environment; the
opportunity to learn from some of the leading barristers in their field; a real prospect
of tenancy.

mini-pupillages
About 30 available each year. Apply online at www.serlecourt.co.uk.

funding
Serle Court offers awards of £40,000 for 12 months, of which up to £12,500 can be
drawn down during the BVC year. It also provides an income guarantee worth up to
£100,000 over the first two years of practice.

No of Silks	13
No of Juniors	35
No of Pupils	2

contact
Kathryn Barry
Tel (020) 7242 6105

method of application
Chambers application form,
available from website or
Chambers. Not a member
of OLPAS

pupillages
Two 12 month pupillages

tenancies
Up to 2 per annum

serle court

3-4 South Square

3-4 South Square, Gray's Inn, London WC1R 5HP
Tel: (020) 7696 9900   Fax: (020) 7696 9911
Email: pupillage@southsquare.com
Website: www.southsquare.com

No of Silks	18
No of Juniors	26
No of Pupils	3

contact
Pupillage Secretary
Tel (020) 7696 9900

method of application
CV with covering letter

pupillages (p.a.)
Up to four, 12 month
pupillages offered each
year

chambers profile
Chambers is an established successful commercial set, involved in high-profile international and domestic commercial litigation and advice. Members of Chambers have been centrally involved in some of the most important commercial cases of the last decade including Barings, BCCI, Lloyds, Maxwell, Railtrack, TXU, Enron, Marconi, NTL and Global Crossing.

type of work undertaken
3-4 South Square has a pre-eminent reputation in insolvency and restructuring law and specialist expertise in banking, financial services, company law, professional negligence, domestic and international arbitration, mediation, European Union Law, insurance/reinsurance law and general commercial litigation.

pupil profile
Chambers seek to recruit the highest calibre of candidates who must be prepared to commit themselves to establishing a successful practice and maintaining Chambers' position at the forefront of the modern Commercial Bar. The minimum academic qualification is a 2:1 degree.

pupillage
Pupils are welcomed into all areas of Chambers' life and are provided with an organised programme designed to train and equip them for practice in a dynamic and challenging environment. Pupils sit with a number of pupil supervisors for periods of six to eight weeks and the set looks to recruit at least one tenant every year from its pupils.

mini pupillages
Chambers also offers funded and unfunded mini-pupillages – please see the set's website for further details.

sponsorship & awards
Currently £40,000 per annum (reviewable annually).

4 Stone Buildings

4 Stone Buildings, Lincoln's Inn, London WC2A 3XT
Tel: (020) 7242 5524 Fax: (020) 7831 7907
Email: d.goddard@4stonebuildings.com

No of Silks	6
No of Juniors	21
No of Pupils	2

contact
David Goddard
(020) 7242 5524

method of application
On Chambers own
application form

pupillages (p.a.)
2 x 12 months

tenancies
On average 1 per year

annexes
None

chambers profile
An established friendly company/commercial set involved in high profile litigation and advice.

type of work undertaken
4 Stone Buildings specialise in the fields of company law, commercial law, financial services and regulation and corporate insolvency.

pupil profile
Candidates are expected to have first class, or good second class degrees. But mere intellectual ability is only part of it: a successful candidate must have the confidence and ambition to succeed, the common sense to recognise the practical advice a client really needs, and an ability to get on well with clients, solicitors and other members of Chambers - and the clerks.

pupillage
The set aim to give all pupils the knowledge, skills and practical experience they need for a successful career at the Bar. They believe that it is important for all pupils to see as much as possible of the different kinds of work in Chambers. This enables pupils to judge whether their work suits them, and enables different members of Chambers to assess the pupils. Each pupil therefore normally spends time with two or more pupil-masters within any six month period. If other members of Chambers have particularly interesting cases in Court, pupils will be encouraged to work and attend Court with them. All pupils work in their pupil masters' rooms, read their papers, attend their conferences, draft pleadings and documents, write draft opinions and accompany their pupil supervisors to Court. Pupils are treated as part of Chambers, and are fully involved in the activities of Chambers while they are with 4 Stone Buildings.

mini pupillages
Up to 20 mini-pupillages offered per year of up to a weeks duration. Application by letter and CV.

sponsorship & awards
£39,000 per 12 months.

funding
As above.

3 Verulam Buildings (Christopher Symons QC/John Jarvis QC)

3 Verulam Buildings, Gray's Inn, London WC1R 5NT DX: LDE 331
Tel: (020) 7831 8441 Fax: (020) 7831 8479
Email: chambers@3vb.com
Website: www.3vb.com

chambers profile
3 Verulam Buildings is a large commercial set with a history of expansion by recruitment of tenants from amongst pupils. Over the past 10 years, on average, two of its pupils have become tenants every year. Chambers occupies recently refurbished, spacious offices overlooking Gray's Inn Walks with all modern IT and library facilities. Chambers prides itself on a pleasant, friendly and relaxed atmosphere.

type of work undertaken
A wide range of commercial work, in particular banking and financial services, insurance and reinsurance, commercial fraud, professional negligence, company law, entertainment, arbitration/ADR, insolvency, IT and telecoms as well as other general commercial work. Members of Chambers regularly appear in high profile cases and a substantial amount of Chambers' work is international.

pupil profile
Chambers looks for intelligent and ambitious candidates with strong powers of analysis and reasoning, who are self confident and get on well with others. Candidates must have at least a 2:1 grade in an honours subject which need not be law.

pupillage
Chambers seeks to recruit three or four funded 12 months pupils every year through OLPAS. Each pupil spends three months with four different members of Chambers to gain experience of different types of work. Chambers also offers unfunded pupillages to pupils who do not intend to practise at the Bar of England and Wales.

mini pupillages
Mini pupillages are available for university, CPE or Bar students who are interested in finding out more about Chambers' work. Chambers considers mini pupillage to be an important part of its recruitment process. Candidates should have, or expect to obtain, the minimum requirements for a funded 12 month pupillage. Applications are accepted throughout the year and should be addressed to James MacDonald.

funding
In the year 2008-09 the annual award will be at least £42,000, up to £15,000 of which may be drawn during the BVC year.

No of Silks	19
No of Juniors	40
No of Pupils	4

contact
Mr George McPherson (Pupillage)
Mr Christopher Harris (Mini Pupillage)

method of application
OLPAS & mini pupillage CV & covering letter stating dates of availability

pupillages (p.a.)
12 months **4**
Required degree grade **2:1**

income
In excess of **£42,000** (which was the award for 2007-08)
Earnings not included

tenancies
Current tenants who served pupillage in Chambers **Approx 41**
Junior tenancies offered in last 3 years **8**
No of tenants of 5 years call or under **9**

Wilberforce Chambers

8 New Square, Lincoln's Inn, London WC2A 3QP
Tel: (020) 7306 0102   Fax: (020) 7306 0095
Email: pupillage@wilberforce.co.uk   Website: www.wilberforce.co.uk

No of Silks	**18**
No of Juniors	**29**

method of application
Online via website

pupillages (p.a.)
2 x 12 months

mini-pupillages
Total of 21 places

income
£40,000 (2009/2010)

minimum qualification
2:1 degree

tenancies in last 3 years
3

chambers profile
Wilberforce Chambers is a leading Commercial Chancery set of Chambers and is involved in some of the most commercially important and cutting edge litigation and advisory work undertaken by the Bar today. Members are recognised by the key legal directories as leaders in their fields. Instructions come from top UK and International law firms, providing a complex and rewarding range of work for international companies, financial institutions, well-known names, sports and media organisations, pension funds, commercial landlords and tenants, and private individuals. Clients demand high intellectual performance and client-care standards but in return the reward is a successful and fulfilling career at the Bar. Chambers has grown in size in recent years but retains a united and friendly 'family' atmosphere.

type of work undertaken
Practice areas include property, pensions, private client, trust and taxation, professional negligence, general commercial litigation, banking, company, financial services, intellectual property and information technology, sports and media and charities.

pupil profile
Chambers look to offer two 12 month pupillages. You should possess high intellectual ability, excellent communication skills and a strong motivation to do Commercial Chancery work. You need to be mature and confident, have the ability to work with others and analyse legal problems clearly, demonstrating commercial and practical good sense. Chambers look for people who have real potential to join Chambers as tenants at the end of their pupillage. Chambers takes great care in its selection process and puts effort into providing an excellent pupillage. Chambers has a minimum requirement of a 2:1 degree in law or another subject, and has a track record of taking on CPE students.

pupillage
Chambers operates a well-structured pupillage programme aimed at providing you with a broad experience of Commercial Chancery Practice under several pupil supervisors with whom you will be able to develop your skills. Chambers aims to reach a decision about tenancy after approximately 9-10 months, but all pupils are expected to stay for the remainder of their pupillage on a full pupillage award.

mini-pupillages
Chambers encourages potential candidates for pupillage to undertake a mini-pupillage in order to learn how Wilberforce Chambers operates, to meet members of Chambers and to see the type of work that it does, but a mini-pupillage is not a prerequisite for pupillage. Chambers runs three separate mini-pupillage weeks (two in December and one in July). Please visit the website for an application form and for further information.

funding
Chambers offers a generous and competitive pupillage award which is reviewed annually with the intention that it should be in line with the highest awards available. The award is currently £40,000 for 12 months and is paid in monthly instalments. A proportion of the award (up to £13,500) can be drawn down during the BVC year.

WILBERFORCE CHAMBERS W

notes

notes

notes

notes